INSTRUCTORS...

Would you like your **students** to show up for class **more prepared**?
(Let's face it, class is much more fun if everyone is engaged and prepared...)

Want an **easy way to assign** homework online and track student **progress**?
(Less time grading means more time teaching...)

Want an **instant view** of student or class performance relative to learning objectives? *(No more wondering if students understand...)*

Need to **collect data and generate reports** required for administration or accreditation? *(Say goodbye to manually tracking student learning outcomes...)*

Want to **record and post your lectures** for students to view online?

 With **McGraw-Hill's *Connect*™ *Plus Accounting*,**

INSTRUCTORS GET:

- Simple **assignment management**, allowing you to spend more time teaching.
- **Auto-graded** assignments, quizzes, and tests.
- **Detailed Visual Reporting** where student and section results can be viewed and analyzed.
- Sophisticated **online testing** capability.
- A **filtering and reporting** function that allows you to easily assign and report on materials that are correlated to accreditation standards, learning outcomes, and Bloom's taxonomy.
- An easy-to-use **lecture capture** tool.
- The option to **upload course documents** for student access.

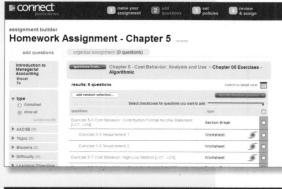

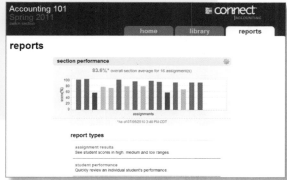

Want an online, **searchable version** of your textbook?

Wish your textbook could be **available online** while you're doing your assignments?

 ### *Connect™ Plus Accounting* eBook

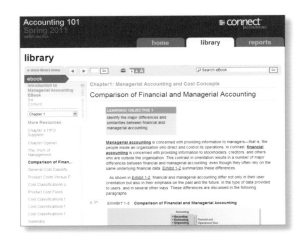

If you choose to use *Connect™ Plus Accounting*, you have an affordable and searchable online version of your book integrated with your other online tools.

Connect™ Plus Accounting eBook offers features like:

- Topic search
- Direct links from assignments
- Adjustable text size
- Jump to page number
- Print by section

 Want to get more **value** from your textbook purchase?

Think learning accounting should be a bit more **interesting**?

 ### Check out the STUDENT RESOURCES section under the *Connect™* Library tab.

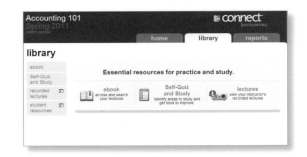

Here you'll find a wealth of resources designed to help you achieve your goals in the course. You'll find things like **quizzes, PowerPoints, and Internet activities** to help you study. Every student has different needs, so explore the STUDENT RESOURCES to find the materials best suited to you.

Third Edition

Survey of Accounting

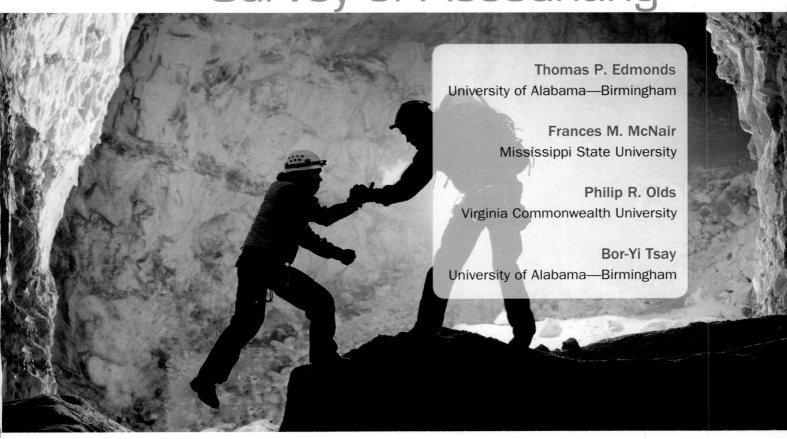

Thomas P. Edmonds
University of Alabama—Birmingham

Frances M. McNair
Mississippi State University

Philip R. Olds
Virginia Commonwealth University

Bor-Yi Tsay
University of Alabama—Birmingham

McGraw-Hill
Irwin

McGraw-Hill
Irwin

SURVEY OF ACCOUNTING

Published by McGraw-Hill/Irwin, a business unit of The McGraw-Hill Companies, Inc., 1221 Avenue of the Americas, New York, NY 10020. Copyright © 2012, 2010, 2007 by The McGraw-Hill Companies, Inc. All rights reserved. No part of this publication may be reproduced or distributed in any form or by any means, or stored in a database or retrieval system, without the prior written consent of The McGraw-Hill Companies, Inc., including, but not limited to, in any network or other electronic storage or transmission, or broadcast for distance learning.

Some ancillaries, including electronic and print components, may not be available to customers outside the United States.

This book is printed on acid-free paper.

3 4 5 6 7 8 9 0 CTP/CTP 1 0 9 8 7 6 5 4 3 2 1

ISBN   978-0-07-811085-6
MHID   0-07-811085-8

Vice president and editor-in-chief: *Brent Gordon*
Editorial director: *Stewart Mattson*
Publisher: *Tim Vertovec*
Executive editor: *Steve Schuetz*
Executive director of development: *Ann Torbert*
Development editor II: *Katie Jones*
Vice president and director of marketing: *Robin J. Zwettler*
Marketing director: *Brad Parkins*
Marketing manager: *Michelle Heaster*
Vice president of editing, design, and production: *Sesha Bolisetty*
Lead project manager: *Pat Frederickson*
Senior buyer: *Michael R. McCormick*
Designer: *Matt Diamond*
Senior photo research coordinator: *Jeremy Cheshareck*
Lead media project manager: *Brian Nacik*
Media project manager: *Joyce J. Chappetto*
Typeface: *10/12 Times LT Standard*
Compositor: *Aptara®, Inc.*
Printer: China Translation & Printing Services Ltd.

Library of Congress Cataloging-in-Publication Data

Survey of accounting / Thomas P. Edmonds . . . [et al.]. — 3rd ed.
　　p. cm.
　　Includes index.
　　ISBN-13: 978-0-07-811085-6 (alk. paper)
　　ISBN-10: 0-07-811085-8 (alk. paper)
　　1. Accounting. I. Edmonds, Thomas P.
HF5636.S97 2012
657—dc22

　　　　　　　　　　　　　　　　　　　2010050238

This book is dedicated to our students, whose questions have so frequently caused us to reevaluate our method of presentation that they have, in fact, become major contributors to the development of this text.

• SUCCESS HAPPENS FOR A REASON

This textbook emerged as a market leader within a short time frame because it provides a more effective teaching methodology. Here is what sets us apart from our competitors.

• LINKING INDIVIDUAL ACCOUNTING EVENTS WITH FINANCIAL STATEMENTS

A horizontal financial statements model replaces the accounting equation as the predominant teaching platform in this text. The model arranges the balance sheet, income statement and statement of cash flows horizontally across a single line of text as shown below. The linkage between business events and financial statements is developed by having students record the effects of transaction data directly into the model. The acquisition of cash from the issue of stock is shown as an example in the following model (N/A indicates not affected; FA abbreviates financing activities):

Assets = Liabilities + Stockholders' Equity			Revenue − Expense = Net Inc.			Cash Flow
+	N/A	+	N/A	N/A	N/A	+ FA

The statements model enables students to more clearly see how accounting relates to real-world decision making. Under the traditional approach, students learn to journalize a series of events and to present summarized information in financial statements. They never see how individual transactions affect financial statements. When students record transactions into a statements model, they see a direct link between business events and financial statements. Most business people think, "if I take this particular action, how will it affect my financials," not "if I do these fifteen things how will they be journalized." Accordingly, the statements model approach provides a learning experience that is more intuitive and relevant than the one provided by traditional teaching methodology.

• BROAD BASED USER FOCUS

Individual event analysis also *broadens the user focus to include internal as well as external users.* Typically, a user oriented approach focuses on external users such as investors and creditors. Certainly, investors and creditors need to understand how events affect financial statements. Anticipating future business events and their impact on financial performance is a major factor in evaluating investment opportunities and credit worthiness. Since business executives (internal users) are dependent on investors and creditors to provide funding for their operations, they too are interested in how events affect financial statements. Indeed, executives make few decisions without considering how those decisions affect "bottom line" financial performance measures. Accordingly, focusing on how individual transactions affect financial statements encourages students to develop an internal as well as external user focus.

• A UNIQUE APPROACH TO THE STATEMENT OF CASH FLOWS

We provide comprehensive coverage of the statement of cash flows. *Cash flow coverage starts in Chapter 1 and continues in every chapter throughout the text.* With respect to scope of coverage, this text places the statement of cash flows on parity with the income statement and balance sheet. While the statement of cash flows is critically important in the real world, coverage of the statement is often slighted and usually relegated to the last chapter in the text. The primary reason for this treatment is that teaching students to convert accrual accounting data into cash flow is complicated. We remove this complexity by introducing the statement through a highly simplified teaching approach. We begin by teaching students to classify individual cash transactions as financing, investing, or operating activity. Students then compile the classified transactions into a formal statement of cash flows. Preparing the statement under this direct, transaction by transaction, approach reduces the learning task to a simple classification scheme.

● THINNING THE TREES TO EXPOSE THE FOREST

We have made a concerted effort to reduced complexity in the early chapters to promote the development of a strong conceptual foundation. Specifically, *we delay coverage of depreciation, interest computations, and gains and losses.* For example, the introduction to depreciation is presented in Chapter 6 thereby allowing students to develop an understanding of accounting for deferrals without the unnecessary complication of contra accounts. Likewise, we delay the introduction of gains and losses so that students can develop an understanding of cash flow from operating activities in a simplified learning environment. These subjects are not omitted, but rather their introduction is delayed.

● IFRS AND OTHER INTERNATIONAL ACCOUNTING ISSUES

We not only provide comprehensive coverage of Generally Accepted Accounting Principles (GAAP) but also expose students to International Financial Reporting Standards (IFRS). Clearly, GAAP is the predominant practice in the United States. However, ever *increasing globalization requires awareness of international standards* as well. The book contains textboxes titled "Focus on International Issues". These boxes include content regarding IFRS and other interesting international topics. Exercises allow the instructor to reinforce the international content through homework assignments. The textbox approach allows flexibility in the level of emphasis instructors choose to place on this subject.

● SERVICE COMPANIES EMPHASIZED

We place greater emphasis on service companies. For example, our budgeting chapter uses a merchandising business while most traditional texts use a manufacturing company. *Using a service company is not only more relevant but also simplifies the learning environment* thereby making it easier for students to focus on budgeting concepts rather than procedural details. This is only one example of our efforts to place greater emphasis on service companies.

● AN ETHICS FRAMEWORK

We provide extensive coverage of ethics. The accounting scandals of Enron, MCI WorldCom, HealthSouth and others led to the enactment the Sarbanes-Oxley Act (SOX). SOX places significant pressure on accountants to identify and eliminate fraudulent reporting. This text not only provides coverage of appropriate content but also *provides a framework for emphasizing ethics throughout the text.* This framework is used to solve an ethics case that is included in the Analyze, Think, and Communicate (ATC) section of end-of-chapter materials for every chapter in the text. Specifically, look at ATC Problem 5 in each chapter. These cases relate the ethics framework to the specific subjects covered in the each chapter.

Thomas P. Edmonds

Thomas P. Edmonds, Ph.D., is the Friends and Alumni Professor of Accounting at the University of Alabama at Birmingham (UAB). Dr. Edmonds has taught in the introductory area throughout his career. He has coordinated the accounting principles courses at the University of Houston and UAB. He currently teaches introductory accounting in mass sections and in UAB's distance learning program. He is actively involved in the accounting education change movement. He has conducted more than 50 workshops related to teaching introductory accounting during the last decade. Dr. Edmonds has received numerous prestigious teaching awards including the Alabama Society of CPAs Outstanding Educator Award and the UAB President's Excellence in Teaching Award. Dr. Edmonds's current research is education based. He has written articles that have appeared in many publications including the *Accounting Review, Issues in Accounting Education, Journal of Accounting Education,* and *Advances in Accounting Education.* Dr. Edmonds has been a successful entrepreneur. He has worked as a management accountant for a transportation company and as a commercial lending officer for the Federal Home Loan Bank. Dr. Edmonds began his academic training at Young Harris Community College. His Ph.D. degree was awarded by Georgia State University. Dr. Edmonds's work experience and academic training have enabled him to bring a unique perspective to the classroom.

Philip R. Olds

Professor Olds is Associate Professor of Accounting at Virginia Commonwealth University (VCU). He serves as the coordinator of the introduction to accounting courses at VCU. Professor Olds received his A.S. degree from Brunswick Junior College in Brunswick, Georgia (now Costal Georgia Community College). He received a B.B.A. in accounting from Georgia Southern College (now Georgia Southern University) and his M.P.A. and Ph.D. degrees are from Georgia State University. After graduating from Georgia Southern, he worked as an auditor with the U.S. Department of Labor in Atlanta, Georgia. A former CPA in Virginia, Professor Olds has published articles in various professional journals and presented papers at national and regional conferences. He also served as the faculty adviser to the VCU chapter of Beta Alpha Psi for five years. In 1989, he was recognized with an Outstanding Faculty Vice-President Award by the national Beta Alpha Psi organization. Professor Olds has received both the Distinguished Teaching Award and the Distinguished Service Award from the VCU School of Business.

Frances M. McNair

Frances M. McNair holds the KPMG Peat Marwick Professorship in Accounting at Mississippi State University (MSU). She has been involved in teaching principles of accounting for the past 12 years and currently serves as the coordinator for the principles of accounting courses at MSU. She joined the MSU faculty in 1987 after receiving her Ph.D. from the University of Mississippi. The author of various articles that have appeared in the *Journal of Accountancy, Management Accounting, Business and Professional Ethics Journal, The Practical Accountant, Taxes,* and other publications, she also coauthored the book *The Tax Practitioner* with Dr. Denzil Causey. Dr. McNair is currently serving on committees of the American Taxation Association, the American Accounting Association, and the Institute of Management Accountants as well as numerous School of Accountancy and MSU committees.

Bor-Yi Tsay

Bor-Yi Tsay, Ph.D., CPA is Professor of Accounting at the University of Alabama at Birmingham (UAB) where he has taught since 1986. He has taught principles of accounting courses at the University of Houston and UAB. Currently, he teaches an undergraduate cost accounting course and an MBA strategic cost management course. Dr. Tsay received the 1996 Loudell Ellis Robinson Excellence in Teaching Award. He has also received numerous awards for his writing and publications including the John L. Rhoads Manuscripts Award, John Pugsley Manuscripts Award, Van Pelt Manuscripts Award, and three certificates of merits from the Institute of Management Accountants. His articles have appeared in *Journal of Accounting Education, Management Accounting, Journal of Managerial Issues, CPA Journal, CMA Magazine, Journal of Systems Management,* and *Journal of Medical Systems.* He currently serves as a member of the board of the Birmingham Chapter, Institute of Management Accountants. He is also a member of the American Institute of Certified Public Accountants and Alabama Society of Certified Public Accountants. Dr. Tsay received a B.S. in agricultural economics from National Taiwan University, an M.B.A. with a concentration in accounting from Eastern Washington University, and a Ph.D. in accounting from the University of Houston.

Real-World Examples

The text provides a variety of thought-provoking, real-world examples of financial and managerial accounting as an essential part of the management process. There are descriptions of accounting practices from Zales. These companies are highlighted in blue in the text.

The Curious Accountant

Suppose the U.S. government purchases $10 million of fuel from **ExxonMobil**. Assume the government offers to pay for the fuel on the day it receives it from Exxon (a cash purchase) or 30 days later (a purchase on account).

Assume that Exxon is absolutely sure the government will pay its account when due. Do you think Exxon should care whether the government pays for the goods upon delivery or 30 days later? Why? (Answers on page 159.)

The Curious Accountant

Each chapter opens with a short vignette that sets the stage and helps pique student interest. These pose a question about a real-world accounting issue related to the topic of the chapter. The answer to the question appears in a separate sidebar a few pages further into the chapter.

Answers to The Curious Accountant

Exxon would definitely prefer to make the sale to the government in cash rather than on account. Even though it may be certain to collect its accounts receivable, the sooner Exxon gets its cash, the sooner the cash can be reinvested.

The interest cost related to a small account receivable of $50 that takes 30 days to collect may seem immaterial; at 4 percent, the lost interest amounts to less than $.20. However, when one considers that Exxon had approximately $27.6 billion of accounts receivable, the cost of financing receivables for a real-world company becomes apparent. At 4 percent, the cost of waiting 30 days to collect $27.6 billion of cash is $90.7 million ($27.6 billion × .04 × [30 ÷ 365]). For one full year, the cost to Exxon would be more than $1.1 billion ($27.6 billion × 0.04). In 2009, it took Exxon approximately 32 days to collect its accounts receivable, and the weighted-average interest rate on its debt was approximately 4 percent.

Focus on International Issues

These boxed inserts expose students to international issues in accounting.

FOCUS ON INTERNATIONAL ISSUES

RESEARCH *AND* DEVELOPMENT VS. RESEARCH *OR* DEVELOPMENT

For many years some thought the companies that followed U.S. GAAP were at a disadvantage when it came to research and development (R&D) costs, because these companies had to immediately expense such cost, while the accounting rules of some other countries allowed R&D cost to be capitalized. Remember, recording costs as an asset—capitalizing it—means that net income is not immediately reduced. The global movement toward using IFRS is reducing, but not eliminating, the different accounting treatments for R&D.

Like U.S. GAAP, IFRS require *research* costs to be expensed, but they allow *development* costs to be capitalized. This IFRS rule itself can present challenges, because sometimes it is not clear where research ends and development begins. Basically, once research has produced a product, patent, and so forth, that the company believes will result in a revenue generating outcome, any additional costs to get it ready for market are development costs.

"The Curious Accountant and Real-World Examples, all make the text better and would make it a pleasure to teach from."

VIVIAN WINSTON,
INDIANA UNIVERSITY

MOTIVATE STUDENTS? •

✓ **CHECK YOURSELF 2.1**

During 2012, Anwar Company earned $345,000 of revenue on account and collected $320,000 cash from accounts receivable. Anwar paid cash expenses of $300,000 and cash dividends of $12,000. Determine the amount of net income Anwar should report on the 2012 income statement and the amount of cash flow from operating activities Anwar should report on the 2012 statement of cash flows.

Answer   Net income is $45,000 ($345,000 revenue − $300,000 expenses). The cash flow from operating activities is $20,000, the amount of revenue collected in cash from customers (accounts receivable) minus the cash paid for expenses ($320,000 − $300,000). Dividend payments are classified as financing activities and do not affect the determination of either net income or cash flow from operating activities.

Check Yourself
These short question/answer features occur at the end of each main topic and ask students to stop and think about the material just covered. The answer follows to provide immediate feedback before students go on to a new topic.

REALITY BYTES

"Closed for Inventory Count" is a sign you frequently see on retail stores sometime during the month of January. Even if companies use a perpetual inventory system, the amount of inventory on hand may be unknown because of lost, damaged, or stolen goods. The only way to determine the amount of inventory on hand is to count it. Why count it in January? Christmas shoppers and many after-Christmas sales shoppers are satiated by mid-January, leaving the stores low on both merchandise and customers. Accordingly, stores have less merchandise to count and "lost sales" are minimized during January. Companies that do not depend on seasonal sales (e.g., a plumbing supplies wholesale business) may choose to count inventory at some other time during the year. Counting inventory is not a revenue-generating activity; it is a necessary evil that should be conducted when it least disrupts operations.

Reality Bytes
This feature provides examples or expansions of the topics presented by highlighting companies and showing how they use the accounting concepts discussed in the chapter to make business decisions.

A Look Back

We first introduced accounting for receivables in Chapter 2. This chapter presented additional complexities related to accounts receivable, such as the *allowance method of accounting for uncollectible accounts.* The allowance method improves matching of expenses with revenues. It also provides a more accurate measure of the value of accounts receivable on the

A Look Forward

Chapters 1 and 2 focused on businesses that generate revenue by providing services to their customers. Examples of these types of businesses include consulting, real estate sales, medical services, and legal services. The next chapter introduces accounting practices for businesses that generate revenue by selling goods. Examples of these companies include **Wal-Mart**, **Circuit City**, **Office Depot**, and **Lowes**.

A Look Back/A Look Forward
Students need a roadmap to make sense of where the chapter topics fit into the whole picture. A Look Back reviews the chapter material and a Look Forward introduces new material to come in the next chapter.

"The Reality Bytes and Check Yourself sections in the chapters enhance the presentation."
ROBERT PATTERSON,
PENN STATE-ERIE

"I like the Check yourself examples."
BRUCE DARLING,
UNIVERSITY OF OREGON

Regardless of the instructional approach, there is no shortcut to learning accounting. Students must practice to master basic accounting concepts. The text includes a prodigious supply of practice materials and exercises and problems.

Self-Study Review Problem

These sections offer problems and solutions of major chapter concepts.

A step-by-step audio-narrated series of slides is provided on the text website at www.mhhe.com/edmondssurvey3e

SELF-STUDY REVIEW PROBLEM

Gifford Company experienced the following accounting events during 2012.

1. Started operations on January 1 when it acquired $20,000 cash by issuing common stock.
2. Earned $18,000 of revenue on account.
3. On March 1 collected $36,000 cash as an advance for services to be performed in the future.
4. Paid cash operating expenses of $17,000.
5. Paid a $2,700 cash dividend to stockholders.
6. On December 31, 2012, adjusted the books to recognize the revenue earned by providing services related to the advance described in Event 3. The contract required Gifford to provide services for a one-year period starting March 1.
7. Collected $15,000 cash from accounts receivable.

Exercise and Problem Sets

• Check figures
The figures provide a quick reference for students to check on their progress in solving the problem.

• Excel
Many exercises and problems can be solved using the Excel™ spreadsheet templates contained on the text's Online Learning Center. A logo appears in the margins next to these exercises and problems for easy identification.

Event No.	Assets			=	Liabilities		+	Stockholders' Equity			Rev.	−	Exp.	=	Net Inc.	Cash Flows
	Cash +	Accts. Rec. +	Supp.	=	Accts. Pay. +	Unearn. Rev.	+	Com. Stk. +	Ret. Earn.							
1	25,000 +	NA +	NA	=	NA +	NA	+	25,000 +	NA		NA	−	NA	=	NA	25,000 FA

Problem 2-28   *Effect of deferrals on financial statements: three separate single-cycle examples*

eXcel

Required

a. On February 1, 2012, Heider, Inc., was formed when it received $80,000 cash from the issue of common stock. On May 1, 2012, the company paid $60,000 cash in advance to rent office space for the coming year. The office space was used as a place to consult with clients. The consulting activity generated $120,000 of cash revenue during 2012. Based on this information alone, record the events and related adjusting entry in the general ledger accounts under the accounting equation. Determine the amount of net income and cash flows from operating activities for 2012.

b. On January 1, 2012, the accounting firm of Bonds & Associates was formed. On August 1, 2012, the company received a retainer fee (was paid in advance) of $30,000 for services to be performed monthly during the next 12 months. Assuming that this was the only transaction completed in 2012, prepare an income statement, statement of changes in stockholders' equity, balance sheet, and statement of cash flows for 2012.

c. Edge Company had $2,200 of supplies on hand on January 1, 2012. Edge purchased $7,200 of supplies on account during 2012. A physical count of supplies revealed that $900 of supplies was on hand as of December 31, 2012. Determine the amount of supplies expense that should be recognized in the December 31, 2012 adjusting entry. Use a financial statements model to show how the adjusting entry would affect the balance sheet, income statement, and statement of cash flows.

CHECK FIGURES
a. Net Income: $80,000
b. Net Income: $12,500

Problem 2-29   *Effect of adjusting entries on the accounting equation*

LO 2

Required

Each of the following independent events requires a year-end adjusting entry. Show how each event and its related adjusting entry affect the accounting equation. Assume a December 31 closing date. The first event is recorded as an example.

CHECK FIGURE
b. adjustment amount: $1,250

CONCEPTS REINFORCED? •

Analyze, Think, Communicate (ATC)

Each chapter includes an innovative section entitled Analyze, Think, Communicate (ATC). This section contains:

- Business application cases related to the annual report for Target Company

- **Writing Assignments**

- **Group Exercises**

- **Ethics Cases**

- **Internet Assignments**

- **Excel Spreadsheet Applications** e**X**cel

- **Real Company Examples**

Target Corporation

ANALYZE, THINK, COMMUNICATE

ATC 6-1 Business Applications Case *Understanding real-world annual reports*

Required

Use the Target Corporation's annual report in Appendix B to answer the following questions.

a. What method of depreciation does Target use?
b. What types of intangible assets does Target have?
c. What are the estimated lives that Target uses for the various types of long-term assets?
d. As of January 30, 2010, what is the original cost of Target's: Land; Buildings and improvements; and Fixtures and equipment (see the footnotes)?
e. What was Target's depreciation expense and amortization expense for 2009 (see the footnotes)?

ATC 6-2 Group Assignment *Different depreciation methods*

Sweet's Bakery makes cakes, pies, and other pastries that it sells to local grocery stores. The company experienced the following transactions during 2012.

1. Started business by acquiring $60,000 cash from the issue of common stock.
2. Purchased bakery equipment for $46,000 with a four year life and a $6,000 salvage value.
3. Had cash sales in 2012 amounting to $42,000.
4. Paid $8,200 of cash for supplies which were all used during the year to make baked goods.
5. Paid other operating expenses of $12,000 for 2012.

Required

a. Organize the class into two sections and divide each section into groups of three to five students. Assign each section a depreciation method: straight-line or double-declining-balance.

Group Task

Prepare an income statement and a balance sheet using the preceding information and the depreciation method assigned to your group.

Class Discussion

b. Have a representative of each section put its income statement on the board. Are there differences in net income? How will these differences in the amount of depreciation expense change over the life of the equipment?

ATC 6-3 Research Assignment *Comparing Microsoft's and Intel's operational assets*

Companies in different industries often use different proportions of current versus long-term assets to accomplish their business objective. The technology revolution resulting from the silicon microchip has often been led by two well-known companies: Microsoft and Intel. Although often thought of together, these companies are really very different. Using either the most current Forms 10-K or annual reports for Microsoft Corporation and Intel Corporation, complete the requirements below. To obtain the Forms 10-K, use either the EDGAR system following the instructions in Appendix A or the company's website. Microsoft's annual report is available on its website; Intel's annual report is its Form 10-K.

"I like the real life examples; I like the Analyze, Think and Communicate."

DEBBIE GAHR, WAUKESHA COUNTY TECHNICAL COLLEGE

• WHAT WE DID

We have reorganized the content to more closely follow a traditional balance sheet sequencing approach. Specifically, the first three chapters introduce the accounting cycle for service and merchandising businesses. Thereafter, topics are presented in the order they normally appear in a balance sheet with accounting for assets being discussed first, followed by accounting for liabilities, and finally accounting for equity. We moved topics associated with corporate governance from Chapter 2 into Chapter 4. Chapter 4 now includes coverage of Accounting for Cash, Internal Controls, and Ethics. Accounting for Inventory Cost Flow was moved from Chapter 4 into Chapter 5. Chapter 5 now includes Accounting for Receivables and Inventory Cost Flow. A comparative table of contents is shown below:

To reduce duplication we consolidated coverage of financial ratios into Chapter 9 Financial Statement Analysis. While we continue to cover statement interpretation issues in each chapter, financial ratios are presented in Chapter 9. Removing coverage of financial ratios from each chapter provided additional space that has allowed us to add coverage of topics. For example, we added basic coverage of auditing practices in Chapter 4. In addition, we added coverage of bond discounts and premiums in Chapter 7. The straight-line method of amortizing discounts and premiums is covered in the main body of the text and the effective interest rate method is covered in the chapter appendix. Also, we added coverage of manufacturing costs flow through raw materials, work-in-process, and finished goods inventory in Chapter 10. Finally, we revised the ATC end of chapter materials to contain a consistent set of cases and exercises. Specifically, the ATC section now includes a business application case, a group assignment, a research assignment, a writing assignment, and an ethics case in each chapter.

TO MAKE IT BETTER!

SPECIFIC CHAPTER CHANGES

Chapter 1 An Introduction to Accounting

- Added a discussion of the role of accounting in society.
- More clearly described the relationship between assets and expenses.
- Updated **Curious Accountant** with new scenario including high-profile companies and products.
- Updated **Focus on International Issues** textbox.
- Revised **Reality Bytes** with new content about a new high-profile company and products.
- Updated **Check Yourself** text box content to reflect current dates and relevant scenarios.
- Updated exercises, problems, and cases.

Chapter 2 Understanding the Accounting Cycle

- Reorganized Exhibit 2.1 and 2.7 to include transaction data.
- Updated **Curious Accountant** with current data from real-world companies.
- Removed content related to corporate governance and ethics. This content now appears in Chapter 4 with related issues such as internal control.
- Updated **Check Yourself** text box content to reflect current dates and relevant scenarios.
- Updated exercises, problems, and cases.

Chapter 3 Accounting for Merchandising Businesses

- Updated **Curious Accountant** with current data from real-world companies.
- Revised **Reality Bytes** with new content about a new scenario, company and products.
- Updated **Check Yourself** text box content to reflect current dates and relevant scenarios.
- Updated exercises, problems, and cases.

Chapter 4 Accounting for Internal Controls, Accounting for Cash, and Ethics

- Accounting for **inventory cost flow** has been moved from this chapter and placed in what is now Chapter 5 of the revised third edition text. Cooperate governance and ethics content have been moved into Chapter 4. These changes are in keeping with a balance sheet sequence of content presentation. Specifically, we cover internal control, ethics, and accounting for cash in Chapter 4. Coverage of accounts receivable and a discussion of inventory cost flow now appear in Chapter 5. Thereafter, we continue to discuss topics in the order they would appear in a customary top down reading of a balance sheet.
- Added coverage of The Committee of Sponsoring Organizations of the Treadway Commission (COSO) framework for internal controls.
- Added coverage of the external audit function and the types of audit opinions.
- Replaced **Curious Accountant** content with new scenario including high-profile companies and characters.
- Added a new **Reality Bytes** textbox.
- Updated **Check Yourself** text box content to reflect current dates and relevant scenarios.
- Updated exercises, problems, and cases.

Chapter 5 Accounting for Receivables and Inventory Cost Flow

- Added a discussion of inventory cost flow. This content was discussed in Chapter 4 of the previous edition of the text. The move was made to promote a consistent pattern of presenting information in the sequence it normally is covered in a formal balance sheet. Coverage of accounting for cash which was previously included in Chapter 5 has been moved forward to Chapter 4.
- Updated *Curious Accountant* with current data from real-world companies.
- Added a new *Focus on International Issues* textbox.
- Revised *Reality Bytes* with new content about a new high-profile company and products.
- Updated *Check Yourself* text box content to reflect current dates and relevant scenarios.
- Updated exercises, problems, and cases.

Chapter 6 Accounting for Long-Term Operational Assets

- Updated *Curious Accountant* with current data from real-world companies.
- Replaced *Focus on International Issues* with new scenario related to international financial reporting standards (IFRS).
- Revised *Reality Bytes* with new content about a new high-profile company and products.
- Updated *Check Yourself* text box content to reflect current dates and relevant scenarios.
- Updated exercises, problems, and cases.

Chapter 7 Accounting for Liabilities

- Added coverage of straight-ling amortization of discounts and premiums.
- Added a chapter appendix covering the effective interest rate method of amortization of discounts and premiums.
- Replaced *Curious Accountant* content with new scenario including high-profile companies and products.
- Replaced *Focus on International Issues* with new scenario related to international financial reporting standards (IFRS).
- Revised *Reality Bytes* with new content about a new high-profile company and products.
- Updated *Check Yourself* text box content to reflect current dates and relevant scenarios.
- Updated exercises, problems, and cases.

Chapter 8 Proprietorships, Partnerships, and Corporations

- Updated *Curious Accountant* with current data from real-world companies.
- Replaced *Focus on International Issues* with new scenario related to international financial reporting standards (IFRS).
- Revised *Reality Bytes* with new content about a new high-profile company and products.
- Updated *Check Yourself* text box content to reflect current dates and relevant scenarios.
- Updated exercises, problems, and cases.

Chapter 9 Financial Statement Analysis

- Replaced *Curious Accountant* content with new scenario including high-profile companies and products.
- Revised *Reality Bytes* with new content about a new high-profile company and products.
- Updated *Check Yourself* text box content to reflect current dates and relevant scenarios.
- Updated exercises, problems, and cases.

Chapter 10 An Introduction to Managerial Accounting

- Added coverage of manufacturing cost flow including raw materials inventory, work-in-process inventory and finished goods inventory. Coverage includes preparation of the schedule of cost of goods manufactured and sold.
- Updated *Curious Accountant* with new scenario including high-profile companies and products.
- Updated *Focus on International Issues* textbox.
- Revised *Reality Bytes* with new content about a new high-profile company and products.
- Updated *Check Yourself* text box content to reflect current dates and relevant scenarios.
- Updated exercises, problems, and cases. Added exercises and problems associated with the schedule of cost of goods manufactured and sold.

Chapter 11 Cost Behavior, Operating Leverage, and Profitability Analysis

- Replaced *Curious Accountant* content with new scenario including high-profile companies and products.
- Replaced *Focus on International Issues* content with new subject matter.
- Replaced *Reality Bytes* with new content about a new high-profile companies and products.
- Updated *Check Yourself* text box content to reflect current dates and relevant scenarios.
- Updated exercises, problems, and cases.

Chapter 12 Cost Accumulation, Tracing, and Allocation

- Replaced *Focus on International Issues* content with new subject matter.
- Updated *Reality Bytes.*
- Updated *Check Yourself* text box content to reflect current dates and relevant scenarios.
- Updated exercises, problems, and cases.

Chapter 13 Relevant Information for Special Decisions

- Updated *Curious Accountant.*
- Updated *Focus on International Issues.*
- Updated *Check Yourself* text box content to reflect current dates and relevant scenarios.
- Updated exercises, problems, and cases.

Chapter 14 Planning for Profit and Cost Control

- Updated *Curious Accountant.*
- Updated *Reality Bytes.*
- Updated *Check Yourself* text box content to reflect current dates and relevant scenarios.
- Updated exercises, problems, and cases.

Chapter 15 Performance Evaluation

- Replaced *Curious Accountant* content with new scenario including high-profile companies and products.
- Updated *Check Yourself* text box content to reflect current dates and relevant scenarios.
- Updated exercises, problems, and cases.

Chapter 16 Planning for Capital Investments

- Updated *Curious Accountant.*
- Updated *Focus on International Issues.*
- Updated *Reality Bytes.*
- Updated *Check Yourself* text box content to reflect current dates and relevant scenarios.
- Updated exercises, problems, and cases.

HOW CAN TECHNOLOGY

McGRAW-HILL's *CONNECT*™ *ACCOUNTING*

 **Less Managing. More Teaching. Greater Learning.**

McGraw-Hill's *Connect*™ *Accounting* is an online assignment and assessment solution that connects students with the tools and resources they'll need to achieve success.

McGraw-Hill's *Connect Accounting* helps prepare students for their future by enabling faster learning, more efficient studying, and higher retention of knowledge.

Connect Accounting offers a number of powerful tools and features to make managing assignments easier, so instructors can spend more time teaching. With *Connect Accounting*, students can engage with their coursework anytime and anywhere, making the learning process more accessible and efficient. *Connect Accounting* offers you the features described below.

Simple Assignment Management

With *Connect Accounting*, creating assignments is easier than ever, so you can spend more time teaching and less time managing. The assignment management function enables you to:

- Create and deliver assignments easily with selectable end-of-chapter questions and test bank items.
- Streamline lesson planning, student progress reporting, and assignment grading to make classroom management more efficient than ever.
- Go paperless with the eBook and online submission and grading of student assignments.

Smart Grading

When it comes to studying, time is precious. *Connect Accounting* helps students learn more efficiently by providing feedback and practice material when they need it, where they need it. When it comes to teaching, your time also is precious. The grading function enables you to:

- Have assignments scored automatically, giving students immediate feedback on their work and side-by-side comparisons with correct answers.

- Access and review each response; manually change grades or leave comments for students to review.

Instructor Library

The *Connect Accounting* Instructor Library is your repository for additional resources to improve student engagement in and out of class. You can select and use any asset that enhances your lecture. The *Connect Accounting* Instructor Library for Edmonds 3e includes:

- *eBook*
- *PowerPoint files*
- *Instructor's and Solutions Manuals*
- *Test Bank*
- *Excel Spreadsheet Solutions*

Student Library

The *Connect Accounting* Student Library is the place for students to access additional resources. The Student Library provides:

- Quick access to lectures, practice materials, eBook, and more.
- Instant practice material and study questions, easily accessible on the go.

Student Progress Tracking

Connect Accounting keeps instructors informed about how each student, section, and class is performing, allowing for more productive use of lecture and office hours. The progress-tracking function enables you to:

- View scored work immediately and track individual or group performance with assignment and grade reports.
- Access an instant view of student or class performance relative to learning objectives.
- Collect data and generate reports required by many accreditation organizations, such as AACSB and AICPA.

Tegrity

Increase the attention paid to lecture discussion by decreasing the attention paid to note taking. For a minimal charge Tegrity offers new ways for students to focus on the in-class discussion, knowing they can revisit important topics later. Tegrity enables you to:

- Record and distribute your lecture with a click of a button.
- Record and index PowerPoint presentations and anything shown on your computer so it is easily searchable, frame by frame.
- Offer access to lectures anytime and anywhere by computer, iPod, or mobile device.
- Increase intent listening and class participation by easing students' concerns about note-taking. Tegrity will make it more likely you will see students' faces, not the tops of their heads.

McGraw-Hill's *Connect™ Plus Accounting*

McGraw-Hill's reinvents the textbook learning experience for the modern student with *Connect™ Plus Accounting*. A seamless integration of an eBook and *Connect Accounting*, *Connect Plus Accounting* provides all of the *Connect Accounting* features plus the following:

- An integrated eBook, allowing for anytime, anywhere access to the textbook.
- Dynamic links between the problems or questions you assign to your students and the location in the eBook where that problem or question is covered.
- A powerful search function to pinpoint and connect key concepts in a snap.

In short, *Connect Accounting* offers you and your students powerful tools and features that optimize your time and energies, enabling you to focus on course content, teaching, and student learning. *Connect Accounting* also offers a wealth of content resources for both instructors and students. This state-of-the-art, thoroughly tested system supports you in preparing students for the world that awaits. For more information about *Connect Accounting*, go to **www.mcgrawhillconnect.com,** or contact your local McGraw-Hill representative.

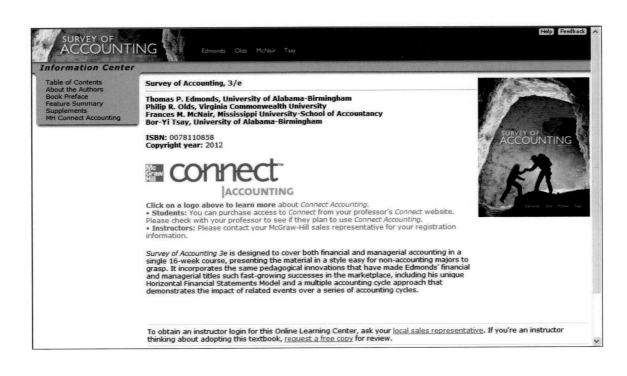

Online Learning Center (OLC)
www.mhhe.com/edmondssurvey3e

More and more students are studying online. That's why we offer an Online Learning Center (OLC) that follows **Survey of Accounting 3e** chapter by chapter. The OLC includes the following:

- Excel Spreadsheets
- Interactive Quizzes
- PowerPoint Slides

CourseSmart.com

CourseSmart is a new way to find and buy eTextbooks. At Course-

Smart you can save up to 45 percent off the cost of a printed textbook, reduce your impact on the environment, and gain access to powerful web tools for learning. CourseSmart has the largest selection of eTextbooks available anywhere, offering thousands of the most commonly adopted textbooks from a wide variety of higher education publishers. Coursemart eTextbooks are available in one standard online reader with full text search, notes and highlighting, and email tools for sharing notes between classmates.

TEGRITY CAMPUS: LECTURES 24/7

Tegrity Campus is a service that makes class

time available 24/7 by automatically capturing every lecture in a searchable format for students to review when they study and complete assignments. With a simple one-click start-and-stop process, you capture all computer screens and corresponding audio. Students can replay any part of any class with easy-to-use browser-based viewing on a PC or Mac. Educators know that the more students can see, hear, and experience class resources, the better they learn. In fact, studies prove it. With Tegrity Campus, students quickly recall key moments by using Tegrity Campus's unique search feature. This search helps students efficiently find what they need, when they need it, across an entire semester of class recordings. Help turn all your students' study time into learning moments immediately supported by your lecture.

To learn more about Tegrity watch a 2-minute Flash demo at **http://tegritycampus.mhhe.com.**

ASSURANCE OF LEARNING READY

Many educational institutions today are focused on the notion of *assurance of learning,* an important element of some accreditation standards. **Edmonds Survey of Accounting 3e** is designed specifically to support your assurance of learning initiatives with a simple, yet powerful solution. Each test bank question for **Survey of Accounting** maps to a specific chapter learning outcome/objective listed in the text. You can use our test bank software, EZ Test and EZ Test Online, or in *Connect Accounting* to easily query for learning outcomes/objectives that directly relate to those objectives for your course. You can then use the reporting features of EZ Test an*d Connect Accounting* to aggregate student results in similar fashion, making the collection and presentation of assurance of learning data simple and easy.

ONLINE COURSE MANAGEMENT

No matter what online course management system you use (WebCT, Black-Board, or eCollege), we have a course content ePack available for your course. Our new ePacks are specifically designed to make it easy for students to navigate and access content online. They are easier than ever to install on the latest version of the course management system available today. Don't forget that you can count on the highest level of service from McGraw-Hill. Our online Digital Learning Consultants are ready to assist you with your online course needs. They provide training and will answer any questions you have throughout the life of your adoption.

McGraw-Hill Higher Education and Blackboard have teamed up. What does this mean for you?

1. **Your life, simplified.** Now you and your students can access McGraw-Hill's *Connect* and Create™ right from within your Blackboard course—all with one single sign-on. Say goodbye to the days of logging in to multiple applications.

2. **Deep integration of content and tools.** Not only do you get single sign-on with *Connect* and Create,

you also get deep integration of McGraw-Hill content and content engines right in Blackboard. Whether you're choosing a book for your course or building *Connect* assignments, all the tools you need are right where you want them—inside of Blackboard.

3. **Seamless Gradebooks.** Are you tired of keeping multiple gradebooks and manually synchronizing grades into Blackboard? We thought so. When a student completes an integrated *Connect* assignment, the grade for that assignment automatically (and instantly) feeds your Blackboard grade center.

4. **A solution for everyone.** Whether your institution is already using Blackboard or you just want to try Blackboard on your own, we have a solution for you. McGraw-Hill and Blackboard can now offer you easy access to industry leading technology and content, whether your campus hosts it, or we do. Be sure to ask your local McGraw-Hill representative for details.

SUPPLEMENTS FOR INSTRUCTORS

Instructor's Resource CD

ISBN-13: 9780077317690 **(ISBN-10: 0077317696)**
This CD includes electronic versions of the Instructor's Manual, Solutions Manual, Test Bank, and computerized Test Bank, as well as PowerPoint slides, all exhibits in the text, and spreadsheet templates with solutions. This CD-ROM makes it easy for instructors to create multimedia presentations.

Instructor's Manual

This comprehensive manual includes step-by-step, explicit instructions on how the text can be used to implement alternative teaching methods. It also provides guidance for instructors who use the traditional lecture method. The guide includes lesson plans and demonstration problems with student work papers, as well as solutions. It was prepared by Tom Edmonds.

Solutions Manual

Prepared by the authors, the manual contains complete solutions to all the text's end-of-chapter exercises, problems, and cases.

Test Bank

This test bank in Word format contains multiple-choice questions, essay questions, and short problems. Each test item is coded for level of difficulty and learning objective. In addition to an expansive array of traditional test questions, the test bank includes new types of questions that focus exclusively on how business events affect financial statements.

PowerPoint Presentation

These slides can serve as interactive class discussions.

AACSB STATEMENT

The McGraw-Hill Companies is a proud corporate member of AACSB International. Understanding the importance and value of AACSB accreditation, **Edmonds *Survey of Accounting 3e*** recognizes the curricula guidelines detailed in the AACSB standards for business accreditation by connecting selected questions in the test bank to the six general knowledge and skill guidelines in the AACSB standards.

The statements contained in ***Survey of Accounting 3e*** are provided only as a guide for the users of this textbook. The AACSB leaves content coverage and assessment within the purview of individual schools, the mission of the school, and the faculty. While ***Survey of Accounting 3e*** and the teaching package make no claim of any specific AACSB qualification or evaluation, we have within ***Survey of Accounting 3e*** labeled selected questions according to the six general knowledge and skills areas.

McGRAW-HILL CUSTOMER CARE CONTACT INFORMATION

At McGraw-Hill, we understand that getting the most from new technology can be challenging. That's why our services don't stop after you purchase our products. You can contact our Product Specialists 24 hours a day to get product-training online. Or you can search our knowledge bank of Frequently Asked Questions on our support website. For Customer Support, visit **www.mhhe.com/support.** One of our Technical Support Analysts will be able to assist you in a timely fashion.

SUPPLEMENTS FOR STUDENTS

McGraw-Hill's *Connect™ Plus Accounting*

This integrates all of the text's multimedia resources. Students can obtain state-of-the-art study aids, including McGraw-Hill's *Connect™ Accounting* and online access to an eBook.

McGraw-Hill's *Connect™ Accounting*

McGraw-Hill's *Connect Accounting* is a web-based assignment and assessment platform that gives students the means to better connect with their coursework, with their instructors, and with the important concepts that they will need to know for success now and in the future. Students can practice important skills at their own pace and on their own schedule. All applicable Exercises and Problems are available with McGraw-Hill's *Connect*.

Online Learning Center (OLC)

www.mhhe.com/edmondssurvey3e
See page xviii for details.

Excel Templates **eXcel**

These templates allow students to develop spreadsheet skills to solve selected assignments identified by an icon in the end-of-chapter material.

We would like to express our appreciation to the people who have provided assistance in the development of this textbook.

We recognize the following instructors for their invaluable feedback and involvement in the development of *Survey of Accounting,* Third Edition. We are thankful for their feedback and suggestions.

Reviewers

Mollie Adams, *Virginia Polytechnic Institute*
David Bukovinsky, *Wright State University*
Susan Cain, *Southern Oregon University*
Thomas Casey, *DeVry University—Tinley Park*
Suzanne Cercone, *Keystone College*
Bruce Darling, *University of Oregon*
Harry Davis, *Baruch College*
Harry Davis, *Bernard M. Baruch College*
Julie Dilling, *Fox Valley Technical College*
Edwin Doty, *East Carolina University*
Barbara Fox, *Northern Illinois University*
Debbie Gahr, *Waukesha County Technical College*
Dana Garner, *Virginia Polytechnic Institute*

Gladys Gomez, *University of Mary Washington*
Harry Hughes, *University of Tennessee, Knoxville*
Kim Hurt, *Central Community College*
Melanie Middlemist, *Colorado State University*
Gay Mills, *Amarillo College*
Sandra Owen, *Indiana University Bloomington*
Robert Patterson, *Penn State-Erie, the Behrend College*
Vanda Pauwels, *Texas Tech University*
Daniel Ricigliano, *Buffalo State College*
Shiv Sharma, *Robert Morris University*
Jim Shelton, *Harding University*
George Smith, *Newman University*
Vivian Winston, *Indiana University Bloomington*

Special thanks to the talented people who prepared the supplements. These take a great deal of time and effort to write and we appreciate their efforts. Rebecca Toledo of Alverno College prepared the Test bank and Quizzes. Sally Gilfillan of Longwood University prepared the PowerPoints and accuracy checked the Test Bank. LuAnn Bean of Florida Institute of Technology prepared the Instructor's Manual and accuracy checked the PowerPoints and Quizzes; and Jack Terry prepared the Excel Templates. We also thank our accuracy checker Beth Woods for her work. A special thanks to Linda Bell of William Jewell College for her contribution to the Financial Statement Analysis material that appears in the Instructor Manual and text Web site.

In addition to the helpful and generous colleagues listed above, we thank the entire McGraw-Hill/Irwin *Survey of Accounting 3e* team, including Stewart Mattson, Tim Vertovec, Steve Schuetz, Katie Jones, Pat Frederickson, Michelle Heaster, Michael McCormick, Matt Diamond, Jeremy Cheshareck, Joyce Chappetto, and Brian Nacik. We deeply appreciate the long hours that you committed to the formation of a high-quality text.

Thomas P. Edmonds • Philip R. Olds • Frances M. McNair • Bor-Yi Tsay

Brief Contents

Contents

Chapter 1   An Introduction to Accounting   2

Chapter 2   Understanding the Accounting Cycle   44

Chapter 3   Accounting for Merchandising Businesses   86

Chapter 6   Accounting for Long-Term Operational Assets   200

xxviii

Chapter 7 Accounting for Liabilities 240

Chapter 8 Proprietorships, Partnerships, and Corporations 286

Chapter 9   Financial Statement Analysis   318

Chapter 10   An Introduction to Managerial Accounting   358

Chapter 11   Cost Behavior, Operating Leverage, and Profitability Analysis   396

Chapter 14 Planning for Profit and Cost Control 498

Chapter Opening 498

The Planning Process 500

Three Levels of Planning for Business Activity 500

Advantages of Budgeting 501

   Planning 501

   Coordination 501

   Performance Measurement 501

   Corrective Action 501

Budgeting and Human Behavior 501

The Master Budget 502

Hampton Hams Budgeting Illustration 503

   Sales Budget 503

   Inventory Purchases Budget 505

   Selling and Administrative Expense Budget 507

Cash Budget 508

Pro Forma Income Statement 511

Pro Forma Balance Sheet 512

Pro Forma Statement of Cash Flows 512

A Look Back 513

A Look Forward 514

Self-Study Review Problem 514

Key Terms 516

Questions 516

Multiple-choice Questions 517

Exercises 517

Problems 522

Analyze, Think, Communicate 526

Chapter 15 Performance Evaluation 530

Chapter Opening 530

Decentralization Concept 532

   Responsibility Centers 532

   Controllability Concept 532

Preparing Flexible Budgets 533

Determining Variances for Performance Evaluation 535

Sales and Variable Cost Volume Variances 535

   Interpreting the Sales and Variable Cost Volume Variances 535

   Fixed Cost Considerations 536

Flexible Budget Variances 537

   Calculating the Sales Price Variance 538

   The Human Element Associated with Flexible Budget Variances 539

   Need for Standards 540

Managerial Performance Measurement 540

Return on Investment 540

   Qualitative Considerations 541

Factors Affecting Return on Investment 542

Residual Income 543

   Calculating Multiple ROIs and/or RIs for the Same Company 545

   Responsibility Accounting and the Balanced Scorecard 545

A Look Back 546

A Look Forward 546

Self-Study Review Problem 1 546

Self-Study Review Problem 2 548

Key Terms 549

Questions 550

Multiple-choice Questions 550

Exercises 550

Problems 555

Analyze, Think, Communicate 558

Chapter 16   Planning for Capital Investments   562

CHAPTER 1

An Introduction to Accounting

LEARNING OBJECTIVES

After you have mastered the material in this chapter, you will be able to:

1 Explain the role of accounting in society.

2 Construct an accounting equation using elements of financial statements terminology.

3 Record business events in general ledger accounts organized under an accounting equation.

4 Classify business events as asset source, use, or exchange transactions.

5 Use general ledger account information to prepare four financial statements.

6 Record business events using a horizontal financial statements model.

CHAPTER OPENING

Why should you study accounting? You should study accounting because it can help you succeed in business. Businesses use accounting to keep score. Imagine trying to play football without knowing how many points a touchdown is worth. Like sports, business is competitive. If you do not know how to keep score, you are not likely to succeed.

Accounting is an information system that reports on the economic activities and financial condition of a business or other organization. Do not underestimate the importance of accounting information. If you had information that enabled you to predict business success, you could become a very wealthy Wall Street investor. Communicating economic information is so important that accounting is frequently called the *language of business*.

The Curious Accountant

Who owns **Starbucks**? Who owns the **American Cancer Society** (ACS)? Many people and organizations other than owners are interested in the operations of Starbucks and the ACS. These parties are called *stakeholders*. Among others, they include lenders, employees, suppliers, customers, benefactors, research institutions, local governments, cancer patients, lawyers, bankers, financial analysts, and government agencies such as the Internal Revenue Service and the Securities and Exchange Commission. Organizations communicate information to stakeholders through *financial reports*.

How do you think the financial reports of Starbucks differ from those of the ACS? (Answer on page 11.)

ROLE OF ACCOUNTING IN SOCIETY

Explain the role of accounting in society.

How should society allocate its resources? Should we spend more to harvest food or cure disease? Should we build computers or cars? Should we invest money in IBM or General Motors? Accounting provides information that helps answer such questions.

Using Free Markets to Set Resource Priorities

Suppose you want to start a business. You may have heard "you have to have money to make money." In fact, you will need more than just money to start and operate a business. You will likely need such resources as equipment, land, materials, and employees. If you do not have these resources, how can you get them? In the United States, you compete for resources in open markets.

A **market** is a group of people or entities organized to exchange items of value. The market for business resources involves three distinct participants: consumers, conversion agents, and resource owners. *Consumers* use resources. Resources are frequently not in a form consumers want. For example, nature provides trees but consumers want furniture. *Conversion agents* (businesses) transform resources such as trees into desirable products such as furniture. *Resource owners* control the distribution of resources to conversion agents. Thus resource owners provide resources (inputs) to conversion agents who provide goods and services (outputs) to consumers.

For example, a home builder (conversion agent) transforms labor and materials (inputs) into houses (output) that consumers use. The transformation adds value to the inputs, creating outputs worth more than the sum of the inputs. A house that required

$220,000 of materials and labor to build could have a market value of $250,000.

Common terms for the added value created in the transformation process include **profit, income,** or **earnings.** Accountants measure the added value as the difference between the cost of a product or service and the selling price of that product or service. The profit on the house described above is $30,000, the difference between its $220,000 cost and $250,000 market value.

Conversion agents who successfully and efficiently (at low cost) satisfy consumer preferences are rewarded with high earnings. These earnings are shared with resource owners, so conversion agents who exhibit high earnings potential are more likely to compete successfully for resources.

Return to the original question. How can you get the resources you need to start a business? You must go to open markets and convince resource owners that you can produce profits. Exhibit 1.1 illustrates the market trilogy involved in resource allocation.

The specific resources businesses commonly use to satisfy consumer demand are financial resources, physical resources, and labor resources.

Financial Resources

Businesses (conversion agents) need **financial resources** (money) to get started and to operate. *Investors* and *creditors* provide financial resources.

■ **Investors** provide financial resources in exchange for ownership interests in businesses. Owners expect businesses to return to them a share of the business income earned.

■ **Creditors** lend financial resources to businesses. Instead of a share of business income, creditors expect businesses to repay borrowed resources at a future date.

The resources controlled by a business are called **assets.** If a business ceases to operate, its remaining assets are sold and the sale proceeds are returned to the investors and creditors through a process called business **liquidation.** Creditors have a priority claim on assets in business liquidations. After creditor claims are satisfied, any remaining assets are distributed to investors (owners).

EXHIBIT 1.1

Market Trilogy in Resource Allocation

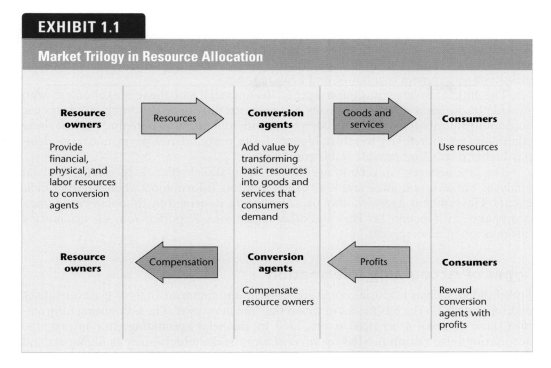

To illustrate, suppose a business acquired $100 cash from investors and $200 cash from creditors. Assume the business lost $75 and returned the remaining $225 ($300 − $75) to the resource providers. The creditors would receive $200; the owners would receive only $25. If the business lost $120, the creditors would receive only $180 ($300 − $120); the investors would receive nothing.

As this illustration suggests, both creditors and investors can lose resources when businesses fail. Creditors, however, are in a more secure position because of their priority claim on resources. In exchange for their more secure position, creditors normally do not share business profits. Instead, they receive a fixed amount of money called **interest.**

Investors and creditors prefer to provide financial resources to businesses with high earnings potential because such companies are better able to share profits and make interest payments. Profitable businesses are also less likely to experience bankruptcy and liquidation.

Physical Resources

In their most primitive form, **physical resources** are natural resources. Physical resources often move through numerous stages of transformation. For example, standing timber may be successively transformed into harvested logs, raw lumber, and finished furniture. Owners of physical resources seek to sell those resources to businesses with high earnings potential because profitable businesses are able to pay higher prices and make repeat purchases.

Labor Resources

Labor resources include both intellectual and physical labor. Like other resource providers, workers prefer businesses that have high income potential because these businesses are able to pay higher wages and offer continued employment.

Accounting Provides Information

How do providers of financial, physical, and labor resources identify conversion agents (businesses) with high profit potential? Investors, creditors, and workers rely heavily on accounting information to evaluate which businesses are worthy of receiving resources. In addition, other people and organizations have an interest in accounting information about businesses. The many **users** of accounting information are commonly called **stakeholders.** Stakeholders include resource providers, financial analysts, brokers, attorneys, government regulators, and news reporters.

The link between conversion agents (businesses) and those stakeholders who provide resources is direct: businesses pay resource providers. Resource providers use accounting information to identify companies with high earnings potential because those companies are more likely to return higher profits, make interest payments, repay debt, pay higher prices, and provide stable employment.

The link between conversion agents and other stakeholders is indirect. Financial analysts, brokers, and attorneys may use accounting information when advising their clients. Government agencies may use accounting information to assess companies' compliance with income tax laws and other regulations. Reporters may use accounting information in news reports.

Types of Accounting Information

Stakeholders such as investors, creditors, lawyers, and financial analysts exist outside of and separate from the businesses in which they are interested. The accounting information these *external users* need is provided by **financial accounting.** In contrast, the accounting information needed by *internal users,* stakeholders such as managers and employees who work within a business, is provided by **managerial accounting.**

The information needs of external and internal users frequently overlap. For example, external and internal users are both interested in the amount of income a business earns. Managerial accounting information, however, is usually more detailed than financial accounting reports. Investors are concerned about the overall profitability of Wendy's versus Burger King; a Wendy's regional manager is interested in the profits of individual Wendy's restaurants. In fact, a regional manager is also interested in nonfinancial measures, such as the number of employees needed to operate a restaurant, the times at which customer demand is high versus low, and measures of cleanliness and customer satisfaction.

Nonbusiness Resource Usage

The U.S. economy is not *purely* market based. Factors other than profitability often influence resource allocation priorities. For example, governments allocate resources to national defense, to redistribute wealth, or to protect the environment. Foundations, religious groups, the Peace Corps, and other benevolent organizations prioritize resource usage based on humanitarian concerns.

Like profit-oriented businesses, civic or humanitarian organizations add value through resource transformation. For example, a soup kitchen adds value to uncooked meats and vegetables by converting them into prepared meals. The individuals who consume the meals, however, are unable to pay for the kitchen's operating costs, much less for the added value. The soup kitchen's motivation is to meet humanitarian needs, not to earn profits. Organizations that are not motivated by profit are called **not-for-profit entities** (also called *nonprofit* or *nonbusiness organizations*).

Stakeholders interested in nonprofit organizations also need accounting information. Accounting systems measure the cost of the goods and services not-for-profit organizations provide, the efficiency and effectiveness of the organizations' operations, and the ability of the organizations to continue to provide goods and services. This information serves a host of stakeholders, including taxpayers, contributors, lenders, suppliers, employees, managers, financial analysts, attorneys, and beneficiaries.

The focus of accounting, therefore, is to provide information useful to making decisions for a variety of business and nonbusiness user groups. The different types of accounting information and the stakeholders that commonly use the information are summarized in Exhibit 1.2.

EXHIBIT 1.2

Accounting as Information Provider

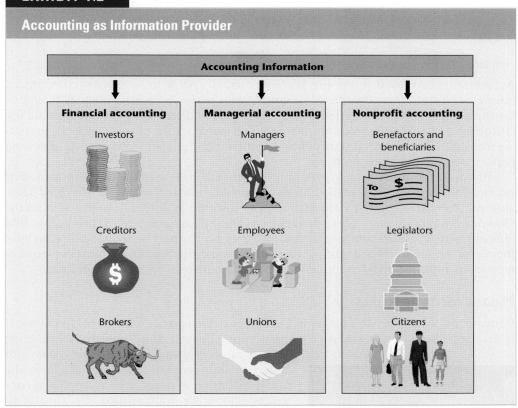

Careers in Accounting

An accounting career can take you to the top of the business world. *BusinessWeek* studied the backgrounds of the chief executive officers (CEOs) of the 1,000 largest public corporations. More CEOs had backgrounds in finance and accounting than any other field. Exhibit 1.3 provides additional detail regarding the career paths followed by these executives.

What do accountants do? Accountants identify, record, analyze, and communicate information about the economic events that affect organizations. They may work in either public accounting or private accounting.

Public Accounting

You are probably familiar with the acronym CPA. CPA stands for certified *public* accountant. Public accountants provide services to various clients. They are usually paid a fee that varies depending on the service provided. Services typically offered by public accountants include (1) audit services, (2) tax services, and (3) consulting services.

- *Audit services* involve examining a company's accounting records in order to issue an opinion about whether the company's financial statements conform to generally accepted accounting principles. The auditor's opinion adds credibility to the statements, which are prepared by the company's management.

- *Tax services* include both determining the amount of tax due and tax planning to help companies minimize tax expense.

- *Consulting services* cover a wide range of activities that includes everything from installing sophisticated computerized accounting systems to providing personal financial advice.

EXHIBIT 1.3

Career Paths of Chief Executive Officers

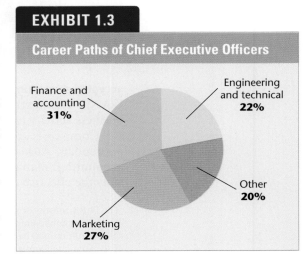

Finance and accounting **31%**

Engineering and technical **22%**

Other **20%**

Marketing **27%**

All public accountants are not certified. Each state government establishes certification requirements applicable in that state. Although the requirements vary from state to state, CPA candidates normally must have a college education, pass a demanding technical examination, and obtain work experience relevant to practicing public accounting.

Private Accounting

Accountants employed in the private sector usually work for a specific company or nonprofit organization. Private sector accountants perform a wide variety of functions for their employers. Their duties include classifying and recording transactions, billing customers and collecting amounts due, ordering merchandise, paying suppliers, preparing and analyzing financial statements, developing budgets, measuring costs, assessing performance, and making decisions.

Private accountants may earn any of several professional certifications. For example, the Institute of Certified Management Accountants issues the *Certified Management Accounting (CMA)* designation. The Institute of Internal Auditors issues the *Certified Internal Auditor (CIA)* designation. These designations are widely recognized indicators of technical competence and integrity on the part of individuals who hold them. All professional accounting certifications call for meeting education requirements, passing a technical examination, and obtaining relevant work experience.

Measurement Rules

Suppose a store sells a MP3 player in December to a customer who agrees to pay for it in January. Should the business *recognize* (report) the sale as a December transaction

or as a January transaction? It really does not matter as long as the storeowner discloses the rule the decision is based on and applies it consistently to other transactions. Because businesses may use different reporting rules, however, clear communication also requires full and fair disclosure of the accounting rules chosen.

Communicating business results would be simpler if each type of business activity were reported using only one measurement method. World economies and financial reporting practices, however, have not evolved uniformly. Even in highly sophisticated countries such as the United States, companies exhibit significant diversity in reporting methods. Providers of accounting reports assume that users are educated about accounting practices.

The **Financial Accounting Standards Board (FASB)**[1] is a privately funded organization with the primary authority for establishing accounting standards in the United States. The measurement rules established by the FASB are called **generally accepted accounting principles (GAAP).** Financial reports issued to the public must follow GAAP. This textbook introduces these principles so you will be able to understand business activity reported by companies in the USA.

Companies are not required to follow GAAP when preparing *management accounting* reports. Although there is considerable overlap between financial and managerial accounting, managers are free to construct internal reports in whatever fashion best suits the effective operation of their companies.

[1]The FASB consists of seven full-time members appointed by the supporting organization, the Financial Accounting Foundation (FAF). The FAF membership is intended to represent the broad spectrum of individuals and institutions that have an interest in accounting and financial reporting. FAF members include representatives of the accounting profession, industry, financial institutions, the government, and the investing public.

FOCUS ON INTERNATIONAL ISSUES

IS THERE GLOBAL GAAP?

As explained in this chapter, accounting is a measurement and communication discipline based on rules referred to as *generally accepted accounting principles (GAAP)*. The rules described in this text are based on GAAP used in the United States, but what rules do the rest of the world use? Is there a global GAAP, or does each country establish its own unique GAAP?

Not long ago each country developed its own unique GAAP. Global companies were required to prepare multiple sets of financial statements to satisfy each country's GAAP. The use of multiple accounting standards across the globe made comparing company performance difficult and expensive. To address the need for a common set of financial standards, the International Accounting Standards Committee was formed in 1973. The committee was reorganized as the **International Accounting Standards Board (IASB)** in 2001. The IASB issues **International Financial Reporting Standards (IFRS),** which are rapidly gaining support worldwide. In 2005, companies in the countries who were members of the European Union were required to use the IFRS as established by the IASB, which is headquartered in London. Today, over 100 countries require or permit companies to prepare their financial statements using IFRS.

As of 2009 most of the major economic countries had either switched from their local GAAP to IFRS, or had rules in place to make the switch by 2012. One notable exception is the United States, but even here, the Securities and Exchange Commission announced in 2008 that it was seriously considering adopting rules that would allow U.S. companies to use either GAAP or IFRS. Although not finalized when this book was being prepared, many accountants in the United States believe this will occur. Additionally, there is an active process in place to reduce the differences between IFRS and U.S. GAAP.

There are many similarities between the IASB and the FASB. Both the FASB and the IASB are required to include members with a variety of backgrounds, including auditors, users of financial information, academics, and so forth. Also, both groups primarily require that their members work full-time for their respective boards; they cannot serve on the board while being compensated by another organization. (The IASB does allow up to three of its members to be part-time.) Members of each board serve five-year terms, and can be reappointed once. The funds to support both boards, and the large organizations that support them are obtained from a variety of sources, including selling publications and private contributions. To help maintain independence of the boards' members, fundraising is performed by separate sets of trustees.

There are significant differences between the IASB and the FASB, and one of these relates to size and geographic diversity. The FASB has only seven members, all from the United States. The IASB has fourteen members, and these must include at least four from Asia, four from Europe, four from North America, one from Africa, and one from South America.

Not only is the structure of the standards-setting boards different but the standards and principles they establish may also differ significantly. In this chapter, you will learn that GAAP employs the *historical cost concept.* This means that the assets of most U.S. companies are shown on the balance sheet at the amount for which they were purchased. For example, land owned by U.S. Steel, Inc., that has a market value of millions of dollars may be shown on US Steel's financial statements with a value of only a few hundred thousand dollars. This occurs because GAAP requires US Steel to show the land at its cost rather than its market value. In contrast, IFRS permits companies to show market values on their financial statements. This means that the exact same assets may show radically different values if the statements are prepared under IFRS rather than GAAP.

Throughout this text, where appropriate, we will note the differences between U.S. GAAP and IFRS. However, by the time you graduate, it is likely that among the major industrialized nations, there will be a global GAAP.

Reporting Entities

Think of accountants as you would of news reporters. A news reporter gathers and discloses information about some person, place, or thing. Likewise, an accountant gathers and discloses financial information about specific people or businesses. The people or businesses accountants report on are called **reporting entities.** When studying accounting you should think of yourself as an accountant. Your first step is to identify the person or business on which you are reporting. This is not always as easy as it may seem. To illustrate, consider the following scenario.

Jason Winston recently started a business. During the first few days of operation, Mr. Winston transferred cash from his personal account into a business account for a company he named Winston Enterprises. Mr. Winston's brother, George, invested cash in Winston Enterprises for which he received an ownership interest in the company. Winston Enterprises borrowed cash from First Federal Bank. Winston Enterprises paid cash to purchase a building from Commercial Properties, Inc. Winston Enterprises earned cash revenues from its customers and paid its employees cash for salaries expense.

How many reporting entities are described in this scenario? Assuming all of the customers are counted as a single entity and all of the employees are counted as a single entity, there are a total of seven entities named in the scenario. These entities include: (1) Jason Winston, (2) Winston Enterprises (3) George Winston, (4) First Federal Bank, (5) Commercial Properties, Inc., (6) the customers, and (7) the employees. A separate set of accounting records would be maintained for each entity.

Your ability to learn accounting will be greatly influenced by how you approach the entity concept. Based on your everyday experiences you likely think from the perspective of a customer. In contrast, this text is written from the perspective of a business entity. These opposing perspectives dramatically affect how you view business events. For example, as a customer you consider a sales discount a great bargain. The view is different from the perspective of the business granting the discount. A sales discount means an item did not sell at the expected price. To move the item, the business had to accept less money than it originally planned to receive. From this perspective, a sales discount is not a good thing. To understand accounting, train yourself to interpret transactions from the perspective of a business rather than a consumer. Each time you encounter an accounting event ask yourself, how does this affect the business?

✓ CHECK YOURSELF 1.1

In a recent business transaction, land was exchanged for cash. Did the amount of cash increase or decrease?

Answer   The answer depends on the reporting entity to which the question pertains. One entity sold land. The other entity bought land. For the entity that sold land, cash increased. For the entity that bought land, cash decreased.

ELEMENTS OF FINANCIAL STATEMENTS

LO 2

Construct an accounting equation using elements of financial statements terminology.

The individuals and organizations that need information about a business are called *stakeholders.* Stakeholders include owners, lenders, government agencies, employees, news reporters, and others. Businesses communicate information to stakeholders through four financial statements:[2] (1) an income statement, (2) a statement of changes in equity, (3) a balance sheet, and (4) a statement of cash flows.

The information reported in **financial statements** is organized into ten categories known as **elements.** Eight financial statement elements are discussed in this chapter: assets, liabilities, equity, contributed capital, revenue, expenses, distributions, and net income. The other two elements, gains and losses, are discussed in a later chapter. In practice, the business world uses various titles to identify several of the financial statement elements. For example, business people use net income, net *earnings,* and net *profit* interchangeably to describe the same element. Contributed capital may be called *common stock* and equity

[2]In practice these statements have alternate names. For example, the income statement may be called *results of operations* or *statement of earnings.* The balance sheet is sometimes called the *statement of financial position.* The statement of changes in equity might be called *statement of capital* or *statement of stockholders' equity.* Since the Financial Accounting Standards Board (FASB) called for the title *statement of cash flows,* companies do not use alternate names for that statement.

Answers to The Curious Accountant

Anyone who owns stock in Starbucks owns a part of the company. Starbucks has many owners. In contrast, nobody actually owns the American Cancer Society (ACS). The ACS has a board of directors that is responsible for overseeing its operations, but the board is not its owner.

Ultimately, the purpose of a business entity is to increase the wealth of its owners. To this end, it "spends money to make money." The expense that Starbucks incurs for advertising is a cost incurred in the hope that it will generate revenues when it sells coffee. The financial statements of a business show, among other things, whether and how the company made a profit during the current year. For example, Starbucks' income statements show how much revenue was generated from "company-owned retail" operations versus from "licensing operations."

The ACS is a not-for-profit entity. It operates to provide services to society at large, not to make a profit. It cannot increase the wealth of its owners, because it has no owners. When the ACS spends money to assist cancer patients, it does not spend this money in the expectation that it will generate revenues. The revenues of the ACS come from contributors who wish to support efforts related to fighting cancer. Because the ACS does not spend money to make money, it has no reason to prepare an *income statement* like that of Starbucks. The ACS's statement of activities shows how much revenue was received from "contributions" versus from "special events."

Not-for-profit entities do prepare financial statements that are similar in appearance to those of commercial enterprises. The financial statements of not-for-profit entities are called the *statement of financial position*, the *statement of activities*, and the *cash flow statement*.

may be called *stockholders' equity, owner's capital,* and *partners' equity.* Furthermore, the transfer of assets from a business to its owners may be called *distributions, withdrawals,* or *dividends.* Think of accounting as a language. Different terms can describe the same business event. Detailed definitions of the elements and their placement on financial statements will be discussed in the following sections of the chapter.

Using Accounts to Gather Information

Detailed information about the elements is maintained in records commonly called **accounts.** For example, information regarding the element *assets* may be organized in separate accounts for cash, equipment, buildings, land, and so forth. The types and number of accounts used by a business depends on the information needs of its stakeholders. Some businesses provide very detailed information; others report highly summarized information. The more detail desired, the greater number of accounts needed. Think of accounts like the notebooks students keep for their classes. Some students keep detailed notes about every class they take in a separate notebook. Other students keep only the key points for all of their classes in a single notebook. Similarly, some businesses use more accounts than other businesses.

Diversity also exists regarding the names used for various accounts. For example, employee pay may be called salaries, wages, commissions, and so forth. Do not become frustrated with the diversity of terms used in accounting. Remember, accounting is a language. The same word can have different meanings. Similarly, different words can be used to describe the same phenomenon. The more you study and use accounting, the more familiar it will become to you.

Accounting Equation

The resources that a business uses to produce earnings are called *assets.* Examples of assets include land, buildings, equipment, materials, and supplies. Assets result from historical events. For example, if a business owns a truck that it purchased in a past transaction, the truck is an asset of the business. A truck that a business *plans* to purchase in the future, however, is not an asset of that business, no matter how certain the future purchase might be.

The resource providers (creditors and investors) have potential **claims**[3] on the assets owned by a business. The relationship between the assets and the providers' claims is described by the **accounting equation:**

$$\text{Assets} = \text{Claims}$$

Creditor claims are called **liabilities** and investor claims are called **equity.** Substituting these terms into the accounting equation produces the following expanded form:

$$\overbrace{\text{Assets} = \text{Liabilities} + \text{Equity}}^{\text{Claims}}$$

Liabilities can also be viewed as future *obligations of the enterprise.* To settle the obligations, the business will probably either relinquish some of its assets (e.g., pay off its debts with cash), provide services to its creditors (e.g., work off its debts), or accept other obligations (e.g., trade short-term debt for long-term debt).

As indicated by the accounting equation, the amount of total assets is equal to the total of the liabilities plus the equity. To illustrate, assume that Hagan Company has assets of $500, liabilities of $200, and equity of $300. These amounts appear in the accounting equation as follows:

$$\overbrace{\text{Assets} = \text{Liabilities} + \text{Equity}}^{\text{Claims}}$$
$$\$500 = \$200 + \$300$$

The claims side of the accounting equation (liabilities plus equity) may also be viewed as listing the sources of the assets. For example, when a bank loans assets (money) to a business, it establishes a claim to have those assets returned at some future date. Liabilities can therefore be viewed as sources of assets.

Equity can also be viewed as a source of assets. In fact, equity represents two distinct sources of assets. First, businesses typically acquire assets from their owners (investors). Many businesses issue **common stock**[4] certificates as receipts to acknowledge assets received from owners. The owners of such businesses are often called **stockholders,** and the ownership interest in the business is called **stockholders' equity.**

Second, businesses usually obtain assets through their earnings activities (the business acquires assets by working for them). Assets a business has earned can either be distributed to the owners or kept in the business. The portion of assets that has been provided by earnings activities and not returned as dividends is called **retained earnings.** Since stockholders own the business, they are entitled to assets acquired through its earnings activities. Retained earnings is therefore a component of stockholders' equity. Further

---

[3]A claim is a legal action to obtain money, property, or the enforcement of a right against another party.

[4]This presentation assumes the business is organized as a corporation. Other forms of business organization include proprietorships and partnerships. The treatment of equity for these types of businesses is slightly different from that of corporations. A detailed discussion of the differences is included in a later chapter of the text.

expansion of the accounting equation can show the three sources of assets (liabilities, common stock, and retained earnings):

$$\underbrace{\text{Stockholders' equity}}$$

Assets = Liabilities + Common stock + Retained earnings

✓ CHECK YOURSELF 1.2

Gupta Company has $250,000 of assets, $60,000 of liabilities, and $90,000 of common stock. What percentage of the assets was provided by retained earnings?

Answer   First, using algebra, determine the dollar amount of retained earnings:

Assets = Liabilities + Common stock + Retained earnings
Retained earnings = Assets − Liabilities − Common stock
Retained earnings = $250,000 − $60,000 − $90,000
Retained earnings = $100,000

Second, determine the percentage:

Percentage of assets provided by retained earnings = Retained earnings/Total assets
Percentage of assets provided by retained earnings = $100,000/$250,000 = 40%

RECORDING BUSINESS EVENTS UNDER THE ACCOUNTING EQUATION

An **accounting event** is an economic occurrence that changes an enterprise's assets, liabilities, or stockholders' equity. A **transaction** is a particular kind of event that involves transferring something of value between two entities. Examples of transactions include acquiring assets from owners, borrowing money from creditors, and purchasing or selling goods and services. The following section of the text explains how several different types of accounting events affect a company's accounting equation.

Record business events in general ledger accounts organized under an accounting equation.

Asset Source Transactions

As previously mentioned, businesses obtain assets (resources) from three sources. They acquire assets from owners (stockholders); they borrow assets from creditors; and they earn assets through profitable operations. Asset source transactions increase total assets and total claims. A more detailed discussion of the effects of asset source transactions is provided below:

EVENT 1   Rustic Camp Sites (RCS) was formed on January 1, 2012, when it acquired $120,000 cash from issuing common stock.

When RCS issued stock, it received cash and gave each investor (owner) a stock certificate as a receipt. Since this transaction provided $120,000 of assets (cash) to the business, it is an **asset source transaction.** It increases the business's assets (cash) and its stockholders' equity (common stock).

	Assets			=	Liab.	+	Stockholders' Equity		
	Cash	+	Land	=	N. Pay.	+	Com. Stk.	+	Ret. Earn.
Acquired cash through stock issue	120,000	+	NA	=	NA	+	120,000	+	NA

Notice the elements have been divided into accounts. For example, the element *assets* is divided into a Cash account and a Land account. Do not be concerned if some of these account titles are unfamiliar. They will be explained as new transactions are presented. Recall that the number of accounts a company uses depends on the nature of its business and the level of detail management needs to operate the business. For example, Sears would have an account called Cost of Goods Sold although GEICO Insurance would not. Why? Because Sears sells goods (merchandise) but GEICO does not.

Also, notice that a stock issue transaction affects the accounting equation in two places, both under an asset (cash) and also under the source of that asset (common stock). All transactions affect the accounting equation in at least two places. It is from this practice that the **double-entry bookkeeping** system derives its name.

EVENT 2   RCS acquired an additional $400,000 of cash by borrowing from a creditor.

This transaction is also an asset source transaction. It increases assets (cash) and liability claims (notes payable). The account title Notes Payable is used because the borrower (RCS) is required to issue a promissory note to the creditor (a bank). A promissory note describes, among other things, the amount of interest RCS will pay and for how long it will borrow the money.[5] The effect of the borrowing transaction on the accounting equation is indicated below.

	Assets			=	Liab.	+	Stockholders' Equity		
	Cash	+	Land	=	N. Pay.	+	Com. Stk.	+	Ret. Earn.
Beginning balances	120,000	+	NA	=	NA	+	120,000	+	NA
Acquired cash by issuing note	400,000	+	NA	=	400,000	+	NA	+	NA
Ending balances	520,000	+	NA	=	400,000	+	120,000	+	NA

The beginning balances above came from the ending balances produced by the prior transaction. This practice is followed throughout the illustration.

Asset Exchange Transactions

Businesses frequently trade one asset for another asset. In such cases, the amount of one asset decreases and the amount of the other asset increases. Total assets are unaffected by asset exchange transactions. Event 3 is an asset exchange transaction.

EVENT 3   RCS paid $500,000 cash to purchase land.

This asset exchange transaction reduces the asset account Cash and increases the asset account Land. The amount of total assets is not affected. An **asset exchange transaction** simply reflects changes in the composition of assets. In this case, the company traded cash for land. The amount of cash decreased by $500,000 and the amount of land increased by the same amount.

	Assets			=	Liab.	+	Stockholders' Equity		
	Cash	+	Land	=	N. Pay.	+	Com. Stk.	+	Ret. Earn.
Beginning balances	520,000	+	NA	=	400,000	+	120,000	+	NA
Paid cash to buy land	(500,000)	+	500,000	=	NA	+	NA	+	NA
Ending balances	20,000	+	500,000	=	400,000	+	120,000	+	NA

---

[5]For simplicity, the effects of interest are ignored in this chapter. We discuss accounting for interest in future chapters.

Another Asset Source Transaction

EVENT 4   RCS obtained $85,000 cash by leasing camp sites to customers.

Revenue represents an economic benefit a company obtains by providing customers with goods and services. In this example the economic benefit is an increase in the asset cash. Revenue transactions can therefore be viewed as *asset source transactions*. The asset increase is balanced by an increase in the retained earnings section of stockholders' equity because producing revenue increases the amount of earnings that can be retained in the business.

	Assets			=	Liab.	+		Stockholders' Equity			
	Cash	+	Land	=	N. Pay.	+	Com. Stk.	+	Ret. Earn.	Acct. Title
Beginning balances	20,000	+	500,000	=	400,000	+	120,000	+	NA	
Acquired cash by earning revenue	85,000	+	NA	=	NA	+	NA	+	85,000	Revenue
Ending balances	105,000	+	500,000	=	400,000	+	120,000	+	85,000	

Note carefully that the $85,000 ending balance in the retained earnings column is *not* in the Retained Earnings account. It is in the Revenue account. It will be transferred to the Retained Earnings account at the end of the accounting period. Transferring the Revenue account balance to the Retained Earnings account is part of a process called *closing the accounts.*

Asset Use Transactions

Businesses use assets for a variety of purposes. For example, assets may be used to pay off liabilities or they may be transferred to owners. Assets may also be used in the process of generating earnings. All **asset use transactions** decrease the total amount of assets and the total amount of claims on assets (liabilities or stockholders' equity).

EVENT 5   RCS paid $50,000 cash for operating expenses such as salaries, rent, and interest. (RCS could establish a separate account for each type of expense. However, the management team does not currently desire this level of detail. Remember, the number of accounts a business uses depends on the level of information managers need to make decisions.)

In the normal course of generating revenue, a business consumes various assets and services. The assets and services consumed to generate revenue are called **expenses.** Revenue results from providing goods and services to customers. In exchange, the business acquires assets from its customers. Since the owners bear the ultimate risk and reap the rewards of operating the business, revenues increase stockholders' equity (retained earnings), and expenses decrease retained earnings. In this case, the asset account, Cash, decreased. This decrease is balanced by a decrease in the retained earnings section of stockholders' equity because expenses decrease the amount of earnings retained in the business.

	Assets			=	Liab.	+		Stockholders' Equity			
	Cash	+	Land	=	N. Pay.	+	Com. Stk.	+	Ret. Earn.	Acct. Title
Beginning balances	105,000	+	500,000	=	400,000	+	120,000	+	85,000	
Used cash to pay expenses	(50,000)	+	NA	=	NA	+	NA	+	(50,000)	Expense
Ending balances	55,000	+	500,000	=	400,000	+	120,000	+	35,000	

Like revenues, expenses are not recorded directly into the Retained Earnings account. The $50,000 of expense is recorded in the Expense account. It will be transferred to the Retained Earnings account at the end of the accounting period as part of the closing process. The $35,000 ending balance in the retained earnings column shows what would be in the Retained Earnings account after the balances in the Revenue and Expense accounts have been closed. The current balance in the Retained Earnings account is zero.

EVENT 6   RCS paid $4,000 in cash dividends to its owners.

To this point the enterprise's total assets and equity have increased by $35,000 ($85,000 of revenue − $50,000 of expense) as a result of its earnings activities. RCS can keep the additional assets in the business or transfer them to the owners. If a business transfers some or all of its earned assets to owners, the transfer is frequently called a **dividend.** Since assets distributed to stockholders are not used for the purpose of generating revenue, *dividends are not expenses.* Furthermore, dividends are a transfer of *earnings,* not a return of the assets acquired from the issue of common stock.

	Assets			=	Liab.	+	Stockholders' Equity			
	Cash	+	Land	=	N. Pay.	+	Com. Stk.	+	Ret. Earn.	Acct. Title
Beginning balances	55,000	+	500,000	=	400,000	+	120,000	+	35,000	
Used cash to pay dividends	(4,000)	+	NA	=	NA	+	NA	+	(4,000)	Dividends
Ending balances	51,000	+	500,000	=	400,000	+	120,000	+	31,000	

Like revenues and expenses, dividends are not recorded directly into the Retained Earnings account. The $4,000 dividend is recorded in the Dividends account. It will be transferred to retained earnings at the end of the accounting period as part of the closing process. The $31,000 ending balance in the retained earnings column shows what would be in the Retained Earnings account after the balances in the Revenue, Expense, and Dividend accounts have been closed. The current balance in the Retained Earnings account is zero.

EVENT 7   The land that RCS paid $500,000 to purchase had an appraised market value of $525,000 on December 31, 2012.

Although the appraised value of the land is higher than the original cost, RCS will not increase the amount recorded in its accounting records above the land's $500,000 historical cost. In general, accountants do not recognize changes in market value. The **historical cost concept** requires that most assets be reported at the amount paid for them (their historical cost) regardless of increases in market value.

Surely investors would rather know what an asset is worth instead of how much it originally cost. So why do accountants maintain records and report financial information based on historical cost? Accountants rely heavily on the **reliability concept.** Information is reliable if it can be independently verified. For example, two people looking at the legal documents associated with RCS's land purchase will both conclude that RCS paid $500,000 for the land. That historical cost is a verifiable fact. The appraised value, in contrast, is an opinion. Even two persons who are experienced appraisers are not likely to come up with the same amount for the land's market value. Accountants do not report market values in financial statements because such values are not reliable.

Accountants recognize the conflict between *relevance* and *reliability.* As a result, there are exceptions to the application of the historical cost rule. When market value can be clearly established, GAAP not only permits but requires its use. For example, securities that are traded on the New York Stock Exchange must be shown at market value rather than historical cost. We will discuss other notable exceptions to the historical cost principle later in the text. However, as a general rule you should assume that assets shown in a company's financial statements are valued at historical cost.

EXHIBIT 1.4

Accounting Events

1.	RCS issued common stock, acquiring $120,000 cash from its owners.
2.	RCS borrowed $400,000 cash.
3.	RCS paid $500,000 cash to purchase land.
4.	RCS received $85,000 cash from earning revenue.
5.	RCS paid $50,000 cash for expenses.
6.	RCS paid dividends of $4,000 cash to the owners.
7.	The land that RCS paid $500,000 to purchase had an appraised market value of $525,000 on December 31, 2012.

General Ledger Accounts Organized Under the Accounting Equation

Event No.	Assets			=	Liabilities	+	Stockholders' Equity			Other Account Titles
	Cash	+	Land	=	Not es Payable	+	Common Stock	+	Retained Earnings	
Beg. bal.	0		0		0		0		0	
1.	120,000						120,000			
2.	400,000				400,000					
3.	(500,000)		500,000							
4.	85,000								85,000	Revenue
5.	(50,000)								(50,000)	Expense
6.	(4,000)								(4,000)	Dividend
7.	NA		NA		NA		NA		NA	
	51,000	+	500,000	=	400,000	+	120,000	+	31,000	

Summary of Transactions

The complete collection of a company's accounts is called the **general ledger.** A summary of the accounting events and the general ledger account information for RCS's 2012 accounting period is shown in Exhibit 1.4. The revenue, expense, and dividend account data appear in the retained earnings column. These account titles are shown immediately to the right of the dollar amounts listed in the retained earnings column.

RECAP: TYPES OF TRANSACTIONS

The transactions described above have each been classified into one of three categories: (1) asset source transactions; (2) asset exchange transactions; and (3) asset use transactions. A fourth category, claims exchange transactions, is introduced in a later chapter. In summary

LO 4

Classify business events as asset source, use, or exchange transactions.

- *Asset source transactions* increase the total amount of assets and increase the total amount of claims. In its first year of operation, RCS acquired assets from three sources: first, from owners (Event 1); next, by borrowing (Event 2); and finally, through earnings activities (Event 4).

- *Asset exchange transactions* decrease one asset and increase another asset. The total amount of assets is unchanged by asset exchange transactions. RCS experienced one asset exchange transaction; it used cash to purchase land (Event 3).

- *Asset use transactions* decrease the total amount of assets and the total amount of claims. RCS used assets to pay expenses (Event 5) and to pay dividends (Event 6).

As you proceed through this text, practice classifying transactions into one of the four categories. Businesses engage in thousands of transactions every day. It is far more effective to learn how to classify the transactions into meaningful categories than to attempt to memorize the effects of thousands of transactions.

PREPARING FINANCIAL STATEMENTS

LO 5

Use general ledger account information to prepare four financial statements.

As indicated earlier, accounting information is normally presented to external users in four general-purpose financial statements. The information in the ledger accounts is used to prepare these financial statements. The data in the ledger accounts in Exhibit 1.4 are color coded to help you understand the source of information in the financial statements. The numbers in *green* are used in the *statement of cash flows.* The numbers in *red* are used to prepare the *balance sheet.* Finally, the numbers in *blue* are used to prepare the *income statement.* The numbers reported in the statement of changes in stockholders' equity have not been color coded because they appear in more than one statement. The next section explains how the information in the accounts is presented in financial statements.

The financial statements for RCS are shown in Exhibit 1.5. The information used to prepare these statements was drawn from the ledger accounts. Information in one statement may relate to information in another statement. For example, the amount of net income reported on the income statement also appears on the statement of changes in stockholders' equity. Accountants use the term **articulation** to describe the interrelationships among the various elements of the financial statements. The key articulated relationships in RCS's financial statements are highlighted with arrows (Exhibit 1.5). A description of each statement follows.

Income Statement and the Matching Concept

A business must make sacrifices in order to obtain benefits. For example, RCS must sacrifice cash to pay for employee salaries, rent, and interest. In turn, RCS receives a benefit when it collects cash from its customers. As this example implies, sacrifices are defined as decreases in assets; and benefits are increases in assets. In accounting terms sacrifices are called expenses; and benefits are called revenues. *Therefore, expenses are decreases in assets; and revenues are increases in assets.*[6]

The **income statement** matches the expenses with the revenues that occur when operating a business. If revenues exceed expenses, the difference is called **net income.** If expenses are greater than revenues, the difference is called **net loss.** The practice of pairing revenues with expenses on the income statement is called the **matching concept.**

The income statement in Exhibit 1.5 indicates that RCS has earned more assets than it has used. The statement shows that RCS has increased its assets by $35,000 (net income) as a result of operating its business. Observe the phrase *For the Year Ended December 31, 2012,* in the heading of the income statement. Income is measured for a span of time called the **accounting period.** While accounting periods of one year are normal for external financial reporting, income can be measured weekly, monthly, quarterly, semiannually, or over any other desired time period. Notice that the cash RCS paid to its stockholders (dividends) is not reported as expense. The decrease in assets for dividend payments is not incurred for the purpose of generating revenue. Instead, dividends are transfers of wealth to the owners of the business. Dividend payments are not reported on the income statement.

[6]The definitions for revenue and expense is expanded in subsequent chapters as additional relationships among the elements of financial statements are introduced.

EXHIBIT 1.5   Financial Statements

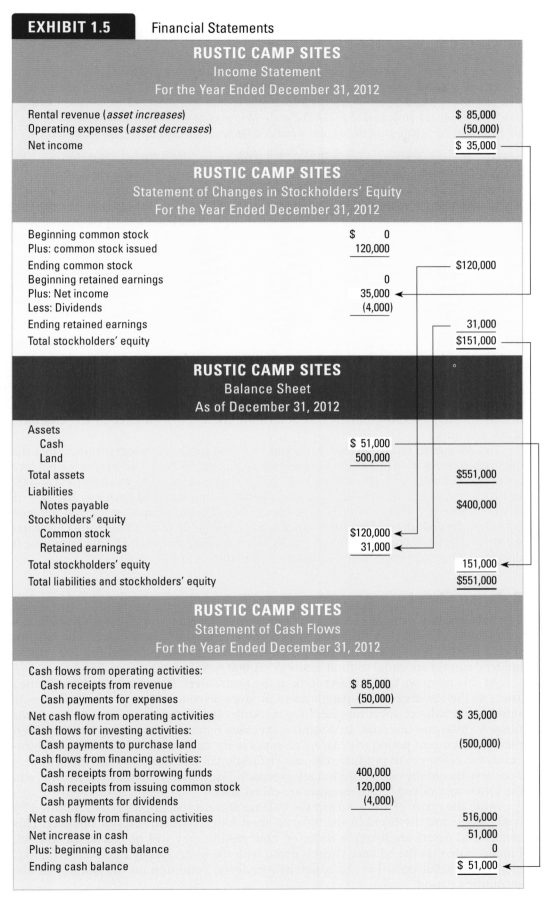

RUSTIC CAMP SITES
Income Statement
For the Year Ended December 31, 2012

Rental revenue (*asset increases*)	$ 85,000
Operating expenses (*asset decreases*)	(50,000)
Net income	$ 35,000

RUSTIC CAMP SITES
Statement of Changes in Stockholders' Equity
For the Year Ended December 31, 2012

Beginning common stock	$ 0	
Plus: common stock issued	120,000	
Ending common stock		$120,000
Beginning retained earnings	0	
Plus: Net income	35,000	
Less: Dividends	(4,000)	
Ending retained earnings		31,000
Total stockholders' equity		$151,000

RUSTIC CAMP SITES
Balance Sheet
As of December 31, 2012

Assets		
Cash	$ 51,000	
Land	500,000	
Total assets		$551,000
Liabilities		
Notes payable		$400,000
Stockholders' equity		
Common stock	$120,000	
Retained earnings	31,000	
Total stockholders' equity		151,000
Total liabilities and stockholders' equity		$551,000

RUSTIC CAMP SITES
Statement of Cash Flows
For the Year Ended December 31, 2012

Cash flows from operating activities:		
Cash receipts from revenue	$ 85,000	
Cash payments for expenses	(50,000)	
Net cash flow from operating activities		$ 35,000
Cash flows for investing activities:		
Cash payments to purchase land		(500,000)
Cash flows from financing activities:		
Cash receipts from borrowing funds	400,000	
Cash receipts from issuing common stock	120,000	
Cash payments for dividends	(4,000)	
Net cash flow from financing activities		516,000
Net increase in cash		51,000
Plus: beginning cash balance		0
Ending cash balance		$ 51,000

✓ CHECK YOURSELF 1.3

Mahoney, Inc., was started when it issued common stock to its owners for $300,000. During its first year of operation Mahoney received $523,000 cash for services provided to customers. Mahoney paid employees $233,000 cash. Advertising costs paid in cash amounted to $102,000. Other cash operating expenses amounted to $124,000. Finally, Mahoney paid a $25,000 cash dividend to its stockholders. What amount of net income would Mahoney's report on its earnings statement?

Answer   The amount of net income is $64,000 ($523,000 Revenue − $233,000 Salary Expense − $102,000 Advertising Expense − $124,000 Other Operating Expenses). The cash received from issuing stock is not revenue because it was not acquired from earnings activities. In other words, Mahoney did not work (perform services) for this money; it was contributed by owners of the business. The dividends are not expenses because the decrease in cash was not incurred for the purpose of generating revenue. Instead, the dividends represent a transfer of wealth to the owners.

Statement of Changes in Stockholders' Equity

The **statement of changes in stockholders' equity** explains the effects of transactions on stockholders' equity during the accounting period. It starts with the beginning balance in the common stock account. In the case of RCS, the beginning balance in the common stock account is zero because the company did not exist before the 2012 accounting period. The $120,000 of stock issued during the accounting period is added to the beginning balance to determine the ending balance in the common stock account.

In addition to reporting the changes in common stock, the statement describes the changes in retained earnings for the accounting period. RCS had no beginning balance in retained earnings. During the period, the company earned $35,000 and paid $4,000 in dividends to the stockholders, producing an ending retained earnings balance of $31,000 ($0 + $35,000 − $4,000). Since equity consists of common stock and retained earnings, the ending total equity balance is $151,000 ($120,000 + $31,000). This statement is also dated with the phrase *For the Year Ended December 31, 2012,* because it describes what happened to stockholders' equity during 2012.

Balance Sheet

The **balance sheet** draws its name from the accounting equation. Total assets balances with (equals) claims (liabilities and stockholders' equity) on those assets. The balance sheet for RCS is shown in Exhibit 1.5. Note that total claims (liabilities plus stockholders' equity) are equal to total assets ($551,000 = $551,000).

At this point we take a closer look at the term *assets*. Previously, we have defined assets as the resources a company uses to produce revenues. More precisely, the assets shown on a balance sheet represent the resources that a company plans to use *in the future* to generate revenues. In contrast, expenses represent the assets that have been used in the current period to generate revenues in the current period. In summary, businesses use resources to produce revenue. The resources that *have been sacrificed* to produce revenues in the current period are expenses. The resources that *will be sacrificed* in the future to produce future revenues are called assets.

Note the order of the assets in the balance sheet. Cash appears first, followed by land. Assets are displayed in the balance sheet based on their level of **liquidity.** This means that assets are listed in order of how rapidly they will be converted to cash. Finally, note that the balance sheet is dated with the phrase *As of December 31, 2012,* indicating that it describes the company's financial condition on the last day of the accounting period.

✓ **CHECK YOURSELF 1.4**

To gain a clear understanding of the balance sheet, try to create one that describes your personal financial condition. First list your assets, then your liabilities. Determine the amount of your equity by subtracting your liabilities from your assets.

Answer   Answers for this exercise will vary depending on the particular assets and liabilities each student identifies. Common student assets include automobiles, computers, stereos, TVs, phones, MP3 players, clothes, and textbooks. Common student liabilities include car loans, mortgages, student loans, and credit card debt. The difference between the assets and the liabilities is the equity.

Statement of Cash Flows

The **statement of cash flows** explains how a company obtained and used *cash* during the accounting period. Receipts of cash are called *cash inflows,* and payments are *cash outflows.* The statement classifies cash receipts (inflows) and payments (outflows) into three categories: financing activities, investing activities, and operating activities.

Businesses normally start with an idea. Implementing the idea usually requires cash. For example, suppose you decide to start an apartment rental business. First, you would need cash to buy the apartments. Acquiring cash to start a business is a financing activity. **Financing activities** include obtaining cash (inflow) from owners or paying cash (outflow) to owners (dividends). Financing activities also include borrowing cash (inflow) from creditors and repaying the principal (outflow) to creditors. Because interest on borrowed money is an expense, however, cash paid to creditors for interest is reported in the operating activities section of the statement of cash flows.

After obtaining cash from financing activities, you would invest the money by building or buying apartments. **Investing activities** involve paying cash (outflow) to purchase long-term assets or receiving cash (inflow) from selling long-term assets. Long-term assets are normally used for more than one year. Cash outflows to purchase land or cash inflows from selling a building are examples of investing activities.

After investing in the productive assets (apartments), you would engage in operating activities. **Operating activities** involve receiving cash (inflow) from revenue and paying cash (outflow) for expenses. Note that cash spent to purchase short-term assets such as office supplies is reported in the operating activities section because the office supplies would likely be used (expensed) within a single accounting period.

The primary cash inflows and outflows related to the types of business activity introduced in this chapter are summarized in Exhibit 1.6. The exhibit will be expanded as additional types of events are introduced in subsequent chapters.

The statement of cash flows for Rustic Camp Sites in Exhibit 1.5 shows that the amount of cash increased by $51,000 during the year. The beginning balance in the Cash account was zero; adding the $51,000 increase to the beginning balance results in a $51,000 ending balance. Notice that the $51,000 ending cash balance on the statement of cash flows is the same as the amount of cash reported in the asset section on the December 31 year-end balance sheet. Also, note that the statement of cash flows is dated with the phrase *For the Year Ended December 31, 2012,* because it describes what happened to cash over the span of the year.

EXHIBIT 1.6

Classification Scheme for Statement of Cash Flows

Cash flows from operating activities:
   Cash receipts (inflows) from customers
   Cash payments (outflows) to suppliers

Cash flows from investing activities:
   Cash receipts (inflows) from the sale of long-term assets
   Cash payments (outflows) for the purchase of long-term assets

Cash flows from financing activities:
   Cash receipts (inflows) from borrowing funds
   Cash receipts (inflows) from issuing common stock
   Cash payments (outflows) to repay borrowed funds
   Cash payments (outflows) for dividends

✓ **CHECK YOURSELF 1.5**

Classify each of the following cash flows as an operating activity, investing activity, or financing activity.

1. Acquired cash from owners.

2. Borrowed cash from creditors.

3. Paid cash to purchase land.

4. Earned cash revenue.

5. Paid cash for salary expenses.

6. Paid cash dividend.

7. Paid cash for interest.

Answer   (1) financing activity; (2) financing activity; (3) investing activity; (4) operating activity; (5) operating activity; (6) financing activity; (7) operating activity.

The Closing Process

As previously indicated transaction data are recorded in the Revenue, Expense, and Dividend accounts during the accounting period. At the end of the accounting period the data in theses accounts is transferred to the Retained Earnings account. The process of transferring the balances is called **closing.** Since the Revenue, Expense, and Dividend accounts are closed each period, they are called **temporary accounts.** At the beginning of each new accounting period, the temporary accounts have zero balances. The Retained Earnings account carries forward from one accounting period to the next. Since this account is not closed, it is called a **permanent account.**

Since RCS started operations on January 1, 2012, the beginning Retained Earnings account balance was zero. In other words, there were no previous earnings available to be retained by the business. During 2012, amounts were recorded in the Revenue, Expense, and Dividend accounts. Since the Retained Earnings account is separate from the Revenue, Expense, and Dividend accounts, the entries in these temporary accounts did not affect the Retained Earnings balance. Specifically, the *before closing* balance in the Retained Earnings account on December 31, 2012, is still zero. In contrast, the Revenue account has a balance of $85,000; the Expense account has a balance of $50,000; and the Dividends account has a balance of $4,000. The closing process transfers the balances in the Revenue, Expense, and Dividend accounts to the Retained Earnings account. Therefore, *after closing* the balance in the Retained Earnings account is $31,000 ($85,000 − $50,000 − $4,000) and the Revenue, Expense, and Dividend accounts have zero balances.

Since the asset, liability, common stock, and retained earnings accounts are permanent accounts, they are not closed at the end of the accounting period. After the closing account process, RCS's general ledger will contain the following account balances as of December 31, 2012.

Cash	+	Land	=	Notes Payable	+	Common Stock	+	Retained Earnings
51,000	+	500,000	=	400,000	+	120,000	+	31,000

Take note that the December 31, 2012, ending account balances become the January 1, 2013, beginning account balances. So, RCS will start the 2013 accounting period with these same accounts balances. In other words, the current period's after closing ending balances become the next period's beginning balances.

✓ CHECK YOURSELF 1.6

After closing on December 31, 2012, Walston Company had $4,600 of assets, $2,000 of liabilities, and $700 of common stock. During January of 2013, Walston earned $750 of revenue and incurred $300 of expense. Walston closes it books each year on December 31.

1. Determine the balance in the Retained Earnings account as of December 31, 2012.
2. Determine the balance in the Retained Earnings account as of January 1, 2013.
3. Determine the balance in the Retained Earnings account as of January 31, 2013.

Answer

1. Assets = Liabilities + Common Stock + Retained Earnings

   $4,600 = $2,000 + $700 + Retained Earnings

   Retained Earnings = $1,900

2. The balance in the Retained Earnings account on January 1, 2013, is the same as it was on December 31, 2012. This year's ending balance becomes next year's beginning balance. Therefore, the balance in the Retained Earnings account on January 1, 2013, is $1,900.

3. The balance in the Retained Earnings account on January 31, 2013, is still $1,900. The revenue earned and expenses incurred during January are not recorded in the Retained Earnings account. Revenue is recorded in a Revenue account and expenses are recorded in an Expense account during the accounting period. The balances in the Revenue and Expense accounts are transferred to the Retained Earnings account during the closing process at the end of the accounting period (December 31, 2013).

THE HORIZONTAL FINANCIAL STATEMENTS MODEL

Financial statements are the scorecard for business activity. If you want to succeed in business, you must know how your business decisions affect your company's financial statements. This text uses a **horizontal statements model** to help you understand how business events affect financial statements. This model shows a set of financial statements horizontally across a single page of paper. The balance sheet is displayed first, adjacent to the income statement, and then the statement of cash flows. Because the effects of equity transactions can be analyzed by referring to certain balance sheet columns, and because of limited space, the statement of changes in stockholders' equity is not shown in the horizontal statements model.

> **LO 6**
>
> Record business events using a horizontal financial statements model.

The model frequently uses abbreviations. For example, activity classifications in the statement of cash flows are identified using OA for operating activities, IA for investing activities, and FA for financing activities. NC designates the net change in cash. The statements model uses "NA" when an account is not affected by an event. The background of the *balance sheet* is red, the *income statement* is blue, and the *statement of cash flows* is green. To demonstrate the usefulness of the horizontal statements model, we use it to display the seven accounting events that RCS experienced during its first year of operation (2012).

1. RCS acquired $120,000 cash from the issuance of common stock.
2. RCS borrowed $400,000 cash.
3. RCS paid $500,000 cash to purchase land.
4. RCS received $85,000 cash from earning revenue.
5. RCS paid $50,000 cash for expenses.
6. RCS paid $4,000 of cash dividends to the owners.
7. The market value of the land owned by RCS was appraised at $525,000 on December 31, 2012.

Event No.	Balance Sheet											Income Statement						Statement of Cash Flows	
	Assets			=	Liab.	+	Stockholders' Equity												
	Cash	+	Land	=	N. Pay.	+	Com. Stk.	+	Ret. Earn.			Rev.	−	Exp.	=	Net Inc.			
Beg. bal.	0	+	0	=	0	+	0	+	0			0	−	0	=	0		NA	
1.	120,000	+	NA	=	NA	+	120,000	+	NA			NA	−	NA	=	NA		120,000	FA
2.	400,000	+	NA	=	400,000	+	NA	+	NA			NA	−	NA	=	NA		400,000	FA
3.	(500,000)	+	500,000	=	NA	+	NA	+	NA			NA	−	NA	=	NA		(500,000)	IA
4.	85,000	+	NA	=	NA	+	NA	+	85,000			85,000	−	NA	=	85,000		85,000	OA
5.	(50,000)	+	NA	=	NA	+	NA	+	(50,000)			NA	−	50,000	=	(50,000)		(50,000)	OA
6.	(4,000)	+	NA	=	NA	+	NA	+	(4,000)			NA	−	NA	=	NA		(4,000)	FA
7.	NA	+	NA	=	NA	+	NA	+	NA			NA	−	NA	=	NA		NA	
Totals	51,000	+	500,000	=	400,000	+	120,000	+	31,000			85,000	−	50,000	=	35,000		51,000	NC

Recognize that statements models are learning tools. Because they are helpful in understanding how accounting events affect financial statements, they are used extensively in this book. However, the models omit many of the details used in published financial statements. For example, the horizontal model shows only a partial set of statements. Also, since the statements are presented in aggregate, the description of dates (i.e., "as of" versus "for the period ended") does not distinguish periodic from cumulative data.

REAL-WORLD FINANCIAL REPORTS

As previously indicated, organizations exist in many different forms, including *business* entities and *not-for-profit* entities. Business entities are typically service, merchandising, or manufacturing companies. **Service businesses,** which include doctors, attorneys, accountants, dry cleaners, and maids, provide services to their customers. **Merchandising businesses,** sometimes called *retail* or *wholesale companies,* sell goods to customers that other entities make. **Manufacturing businesses** make the goods that they sell to their customers.

Some business operations include combinations of these three categories. For example, an automotive repair shop might change oil (service function), sell parts such as oil filters (retail function), and rebuild engines (manufacturing function). The nature of the reporting entity affects the form and content of the information reported in an entity's financial statements. For example, governmental entities provide statements of revenues, expenditures, and changes in fund equity while business entities provide income statements. Similarly, income statements of retail companies show an expense

Service

Merchandising

Manufacturing

REALITY BYTES

On April 19, 2010, the stock of BP, Plc. (formally known as British Petroleum) was trading at $59.48 per share. On that same day, the stock of Chevron Corp. was trading at $81.32 and the stock of Exxon Mobil Corp. was trading at $68.23. About six weeks later, on June 4, 2010, these companies' stocks had fallen to $37.16, $71.28, and $59.53 per share, respectively. Why did this happen? Did the companies report a large drop in their net earnings during these six weeks? No. What happened was that on April 20, 2010, the Deepwater Horizon oil well, owned by BP, failed and began discharging 60,000 barrels of oil daily into the Gulf of Mexico.

While it is easy to see why this event could cause BP's stock to lose 38 percent of its value, why would this cause Chevron's stock to fall 12 percent and Exxon's stock to fall 13 percent? These two companies did not have any oil spills during this time. One reason that the stock price of most oil companies declined significantly after BP's problems was that investors were concerned the failure would result in tighter regulation of all oil companies. Additionally, there was the concern that the government would ban, or seriously reduce, all future deepwater drilling. More regulations, and certainly a ban on future drilling, could drastically reduce the future earnings potential of all oil companies, not just BP.

As this situation illustrates, investors frequently use information not yet reported in a company's annual report. The annual report focuses on historical data, but investors are more concerned about the future. The historical information contained in the annual report is important because the past is frequently a strong predictor of the future. However, current negative news, such as an oil spill, may give investors more information about a company's future than last year's annual report. For example, while the oil spill was bad news for the oil companies, it was, in financial terms, good news for companies that manufacture the oil-booms used to prevent oil from reaching the beaches. Similarly, a new company, that has never earned a profit, may have an idea that is so innovative investors rush to buy it stock, even though they expect it to be a few years to have positive earnings. Also, investors and creditors may be motivated by nonfinancial considerations such as social consciousness, humanitarian concerns, or personal preferences. While accounting information is critically important, it is only one dimension of the information pool that investors and creditors use to make decisions.

---

item called *cost of goods sold,* but service companies that do not sell goods have no such item in their income statements. You should expect some diversity when reviewing real-world financial statements.

Annual Report for Target Corporation

Organizations normally provide information, including financial statements, to *stake-holders* yearly in a document known as an **annual report.** The annual report for Target Corporation is reproduced in Appendix B of this text. This report includes the company's financial statements. Immediately following the statements are footnotes that provide additional details about the items described in the statements. The annual report contains commentary describing management's assessment of significant events that affected the company during the reporting period. This commentary is called *management's discussion and analysis* (MD&A).

The U.S. Securities and Exchange Commission (SEC) requires public companies to file an annual report in a document known as a 10-K. Even though the annual report is usually flashier (contains more color and pictures) than the 10-K, the 10-K is normally more comprehensive with respect to content. As a result, the 10-K report frequently substitutes for the annual report, but the annual report cannot substitute for the 10-K. In an effort to reduce costs, many companies now use the 10-K report as their annual report.

Special Terms in Real-World Reports

The financial statements of real-world companies include numerous items relating to advanced topics that are not covered in survey accounting textbooks, especially the first chapter of a survey accounting textbook. Do not, however, be discouraged from browsing through real-world annual reports. You will significantly enhance your learning if you look at many annual reports and attempt to identify as many items as you can. As your accounting knowledge grows, you will likely experience increased interest in real-world financial reports and the businesses they describe.

We encourage you to look for annual reports in the library or ask your employer for a copy of your company's report. The Internet is another excellent source for obtaining annual reports. Most companies provide links to their annual reports on their home pages. Look for links labeled "about the company" or "investor relations" or other phrases that logically lead to the company's financial reports. The best way to learn accounting is to use it. Accounting is the language of business. Learning the language will serve you well in almost any area of business that you pursue.

 ## A Look Back

This chapter introduced the role of accounting in society and business: to provide information helpful in operating and evaluating the performance of organizations. Accounting is a measurement discipline. To communicate effectively, users of accounting must agree on the rules of measurement. *Generally accepted accounting principles (GAAP)* constitute the rules used by the accounting profession in the United States to govern financial reporting. GAAP is a work in progress that continues to evolve.

This chapter has discussed eight elements of financial statements: *assets, liabilities, equity, common stock (contributed capital), revenue, expenses, dividends (distributions),* and *net income.* The elements represent broad classifications reported on financial statements. Four basic financial statements appear in the reports of public companies: the *balance sheet,* the *income statement,* the *statement of changes in stockholders' equity,* and the *statement of cash flows.* The chapter discussed the form and content of each statement as well as the interrelationships among the statements.

This chapter introduced a *horizontal financial statements model* as a tool to help you understand how business events affect a set of financial statements. This model is used throughout the text. You should carefully study this model before proceeding to Chapter 2.

 ## A Look Forward

To keep matters as simple as possible and to focus on the interrelationships among financial statements, this chapter considered only cash events. Obviously, many real-world events do not involve an immediate exchange of cash. For example, customers use telephone service throughout the month without paying for it until the next month. Such phone usage represents an expense in one month with a cash exchange in the following month. Events such as this are called *accruals.* Understanding the effects that accrual events have on the financial statements is included in Chapter 2.

 A step-by-step audio-narrated series of slides is provided on the text website at www.mhhe.com/edmondssurvey3e.

 ## SELF-STUDY REVIEW PROBLEM

During 2013 Rustic Camp Sites experienced the following transactions.

1. RCS acquired $32,000 cash by issuing common stock.
2. RCS received $116,000 cash for providing services to customers (leasing camp sites).
3. RCS paid $13,000 cash for salaries expense.
4. RCS paid a $9,000 cash dividend to the owners.

5. RCS sold land that had cost $100,000 for $100,000 cash.
6. RCS paid $47,000 cash for other operating expenses.

Required

a. Record the transaction data in a horizontal financial statements model like the following one. In the Cash Flow column, classify the cash flows as operating activities (OA), investing activities (IA), or financing activities (FA). The beginning balances have been recorded as an example. They are the ending balances shown on RCS's December 31, 2012, financial statements illustrated in the chapter. Note that the revenue and expense accounts have a zero beginning balance. Amounts in these accounts apply only to a single accounting period. Revenue and expense account balances are not carried forward from one accounting period to the next.

Event No.		Balance Sheet										Income Statement					Statement of Cash Flows
		Assets			=	Liab.	+	Stockholders' Equity				Rev.	−	Exp.	=	Net Inc.	
	Cash	+	Land	=	N. Pay.	+	Com. Stk.	+	Ret. Earn.								
Beg. bal.	51,000	+	500,000	=	400,000	+	120,000	+	31,000			NA	−	NA	=	NA	NA

b. Explain why there are no beginning balances in the Income Statement columns.
c. What amount of net income will RCS report on the 2013 income statement?
d. What amount of total assets will RCS report on the December 31, 2013, balance sheet?
e. What amount of retained earnings will RCS report on the December 31, 2013, balance sheet?
f. What amount of net cash flow from operating activities will RCS report on the 2013 statement of cash flows?

Solution

a.

Event No.		Balance Sheet										Income Statement					Statement of Cash Flows	
		Assets			=	Liab.	+	Stockholders' Equity				Rev.	−	Exp.	=	Net Inc.		
	Cash	+	Land	=	N. Pay.	+	Com. Stk.	+	Ret. Earn.									
Beg. bal.	51,000	+	500,000	=	400,000	+	120,000	+	31,000		NA	−	NA	=	NA	NA	
1.	32,000	+	NA	=	NA	+	32,000	+	NA		NA	−	NA	=	NA	32,000	FA
2.	116,000	+	NA	=	NA	+	NA	+	116,000		116,000	−	NA	=	116,000	116,000	OA
3.	(13,000)	+	NA	=	NA	+	NA	+	(13,000)		NA	−	13,000	=	(13,000)	(13,000)	OA
4.	(9,000)	+	NA	=	NA	+	NA	+	(9,000)		NA	−	NA	=	NA	(9,000)	FA
5.	100,000	+	(100,000)	=	NA	+	NA	+	NA		NA	−	NA	=	NA	100,000	IA
6.	(47,000)	+	NA	=	NA	+	NA	+	(47,000)		NA	−	47,000	=	(47,000)	(47,000)	OA
Totals	230,000	+	400,000	=	400,000	+	152,000	+	78,000		116,000	−	60,000	=	56,000	179,000	NC*

*The letters NC on the last line of the column designate the net change in cash.

b. The revenue and expense accounts are temporary accounts used to capture data for a single accounting period. They are closed (amounts removed from the accounts) to retained earnings at the end of the accounting period and therefore always have zero balances at the beginning of the accounting cycle.

c. RCS will report net income of $56,000 on the 2013 income statement. Compute this amount by subtracting the expenses from the revenue ($116,000 Revenue − $13,000 Salaries expense − $47,000 Other operating expense).

d. RCS will report total assets of $630,000 on the December 31, 2013, balance sheet. Compute total assets by adding the cash amount to the land amount ($230,000 Cash + $400,000 Land).

e. RCS will report retained earnings of $78,000 on the December 31, 2013, balance sheet. Compute this amount using the following formula: Beginning retained earnings + Net income − Dividends = Ending retained earnings. In this case, $31,000 + $56,000 − $9,000 = $78,000.

f. Net cash flow from operating activities is the difference between the amount of cash collected from revenue and the amount of cash spent for expenses. In this case, $116,000 cash inflow from revenue − $13,000 cash outflow for salaries expense − $47,000 cash outflow for other operating expenses = $56,000 net cash inflow from operating activities.

KEY TERMS

accounting 2
accounting equation 12
accounting event 13
accounting period 15
accounts 11
annual report 25
articulation 18
asset exchange transaction 14
asset source transaction 13
asset use transaction 15
assets 4
balance sheet 9
claims 4
closing 22
common stock 12
creditors 4
dividend 16
double-entry bookkeeping 14
earnings 4
elements 10
equity 12
expenses 15
financial accounting 6
Financial Accounting Standards
    Board (FASB) 8

financial resources 4
financial statements 10
financing activities 21
general ledger 17
generally accepted accounting
    principles (GAAP) 8
historical cost concept 16
horizontal statements
    model 23
income 4
income statement 18
International Accounting
    Standards Board (IASB) 9
International Financial
    Reporting Standards
    (IFRS) 9
interest 5
investing activities 21
investors 4
labor resources 4
liabilities 10
liquidation 4
liquidity 20
managerial accounting 6
manufacturing businesses 24

market 4
matching concept 18
merchandising
    businesses 24
net income 18
net loss 18
not-for-profit entities 6
operating activities 21
permanent accounts 22
physical resources 5
profit 4
reliability concept 16
reporting entities 9
retained earnings 12
revenue 10
service businesses 24
stakeholders 6
statement of cash flows 10
statement of changes in
    stockholders' equity 10
stockholders 12
stockholders' equity 12
temporary accounts 22
transaction 12
users 6

QUESTIONS

1. Explain the term *stakeholder*. Distinguish between stakeholders with a direct versus an indirect interest in the companies that issue accounting reports.
2. Why is accounting called the *language of business?*
3. What is the primary mechanism used to allocate resources in the United States?
4. In a business context, what does the term *market* mean?
5. What market trilogy components are involved in the process of transforming resources into finished products?
6. Give an example of a financial resource, a physical resource, and a labor resource.
7. What type of return does an investor expect to receive in exchange for providing financial resources to a business? What type of return does a creditor expect from

providing financial resources to an organization or business?
8. How do financial and managerial accounting differ?
9. Describe a not-for-profit or nonprofit enterprise. What is the motivation for this type of entity?
10. What are the U.S. rules of accounting information measurement called?
11. Explain how a career in public accounting differs from a career in private accounting.
12. Distinguish between elements of financial statements and accounts.
13. What role do assets play in business profitability?
14. To whom do the assets of a business belong?
15. What is the nature of creditors' claims on assets?

16. What term describes creditors' claims on the assets of a business?

17. What is the accounting equation? Describe each of its three components.

18. Who ultimately bears the risk and collects the rewards associated with operating a business?

19. What does a *double-entry bookkeeping system* mean?

20. How does acquiring capital from owners affect the accounting equation?

21. What is the difference between assets that are acquired by issuing common stock and those that are acquired using retained earnings?

22. How does earning revenue affect the accounting equation?

23. What are the three primary sources of assets?

24. What is the source of retained earnings?

25. How does distributing assets (paying dividends) to owners affect the accounting equation?

26. What are the similarities and differences between dividends and expenses?

27. What four general-purpose financial statements do business enterprises use?

28. Which of the general-purpose financial statements provides information about the enterprise at a specific designated date?

29. What causes a net loss?

30. What three categories of cash receipts and cash payments do businesses report on the statement of cash flows? Explain the types of cash flows reported in each category.

31. How are asset accounts usually arranged in the balance sheet?

32. Discuss the term *articulation* as it relates to financial statements.

33. How do temporary accounts differ from permanent accounts? Name three temporary accounts. Is retained earnings a temporary or a permanent account?

34. What is the historical cost concept and how does it relate to the reliability concept?

35. Identify the three types of accounting transactions discussed in this chapter. Provide an example of each type of transaction, and explain how it affects the accounting equation.

36. What type of information does a business typically include in its annual report?

37. What is U.S. GAAP? What is IFRS?

MULTIPLE-CHOICE QUESTIONS

Multiple-choice questions are provided on the text website at www.mhhe.com/edmondssurvey3e.

EXERCISES

All applicable Exercises are available with McGraw-Hill's *Connect Accounting.*

Exercise 1-1   *The role of accounting in society*   **LO 1**

Free economies use open markets to allocate resources.

Required

Identify the three participants in a free business market. Write a brief memo explaining how these participants interact to ensure that goods and services are distributed in a manner that satisfies consumers. Your memo should include answers to the following questions: If you work as a public accountant, what role would you play in the allocation of resources? Which professional certification would be most appropriate to your career?

Exercise 1-2   *Distributions in a business liquidation*   **LO 1**

Assume that Kennedy Company acquires $1,600 cash from creditors and $1,800 cash from investors.

Required

a. Explain the primary differences between investors and creditors.
b. If Kennedy has a net loss of $1,600 cash and then liquidates, what amount of cash will the creditors receive? What amount of cash will the investors receive?
c. If Kennedy has net income of $1,600 and then liquidates, what amount of cash will the creditors receive? What amount of cash will the investors receive?

LO 1

Exercise 1-3   *Careers in accounting*

Accounting is commonly divided into two sectors. One sector is called public accounting. The other sector is called private accounting.

Required

a. Identify three areas of service provided by public accountants.
b. Describe the common duties performed by private accountants.

LO 1

Exercise 1-4   *Identifying the reporting entities*

Kenneth Chang recently started a business. During the first few days of operation, Mr. Chang transferred $30,000 from his personal account into a business account for a company he named Chang Enterprises. Chang Enterprises borrowed $40,000 from First Bank. Mr. Chang's father-in-law, Jim Harwood, invested $64,000 into the business for which he received a 25 percent ownership interest. Chang Enterprises purchased a building from Morton Realty Company. The building cost $120,000 cash. Chang Enterprises earned $28,000 in revenue from the company's customers and paid its employees $25,000 for salaries expense.

Required

Identify the entities that were mentioned in the scenario and explain what happened to the cash accounts of each entity that you identify.

LO 2

Exercise 1-5   *Titles and accounts appearing on financial statements*

Annual reports normally include an income statement, a statement of changes in stockholders' equity, a balance sheet, and a statement of cash flows.

Required

Identify the financial statements on which each of the following titles or accounts would appear. If a title or an account appears on more than one statement, list all statements that would include it.

a. Common Stock
b. Land
c. Ending Cash Balance
d. Beginning Cash Balance
e. Notes Payable
f. Retained Earnings
g. Revenue
h. Cash Dividends
i. Financing Activities
j. Salaries Expense

LO 2

Exercise 1-6   *Components of the accounting equation*

Required

The following three requirements are independent of each other.

a. Craig's Cars has assets of $4,550 and stockholders' equity of $3,200. What is the amount of liabilities? What is the amount of claims?
b. Heavenly Bakery has liabilities of $4,800 and stockholders' equity of $5,400. What is the amount of assets?
c. Bell's Candy Co. has assets of $49,200 and liabilities of $28,200. What is the amount of stockholders' equity?

LO 2

Exercise 1-7   *Missing information in the accounting equation*

Required

Calculate the missing amounts in the following table.

Company	Assets	=	Liabilities	+	Common Stock	+	Retained Earnings
					Stockholders' Equity		
A	$?		$25,000		$48,000		$50,000
B	40,000		?		7,000		30,000
C	75,000		15,000		?		42,000
D	125,000		45,000		60,000		?

Exercise 1-8   *Missing information in the accounting equation*

LO 2

As of December 31, 2012, Eber Company had total assets of $156,000, total liabilities of $85,600, and common stock of $52,400. During 2013 Eber earned $36,000 of cash revenue, paid $20,000 for cash expenses, and paid a $2,000 cash dividend to the stockholders.

Required

a. Determine the amount of retained earnings as of December 31, 2012, after closing.
b. Determine the amount of net income earned in 2013.
c. Determine the amount of retained earnings as of December 31, 2013, after closing.
d. Determine the amount of cash that is in the retained earnings account as of December 31, 2013.

Exercise 1-9   *Missing information for determining net income*

LO 2

The December 31, 2012, balance sheet for Classic Company showed total stockholders' equity of $82,500. Total stockholders' equity increased by $53,400 between December 31, 2012, and December 31, 2013. During 2013 Classic Company acquired $13,000 cash from the issue of common stock. Classic Company paid an $8,000 cash dividend to the stockholders during 2013.

Required

Determine the amount of net income or loss Classic reported on its 2013 income statement. (*Hint:* Remember that stock issues, net income, and dividends all change total stockholders' equity.)

Exercise 1-10   *Effect of events on the accounting equation*

LO 2, 3

Olive Enterprises experienced the following events during 2012.

1. Acquired cash from the issue of common stock.
2. Paid cash to reduce the principal on a bank note.
3. Sold land for cash at an amount equal to its cost.
4. Provided services to clients for cash.
5. Paid utilities expenses with cash.
6. Paid a cash dividend to the stockholders.

Required

Explain how each of the events would affect the accounting equation by writing the letter I for increase, the letter D for decrease, and NA for does not affect under each of the components of the accounting equation. The first event is shown as an example.

Event Number	Assets	= Liabilities	+	Common Stock	+	Retained Earnings
				Stockholders' Equity		
1	I	NA		I		NA

LO 2, 3

Exercise 1-11 *Effects of issuing stock*

Shiloh Company was started in 2012 when it acquired $15,000 cash by issuing common stock. The cash acquisition was the only event that affected the business in 2012.

Required

Write an accounting equation, and record the effects of the stock issue under the appropriate general ledger account headings.

LO 2, 3

Exercise 1-12 *Effects of borrowing*

Marcum Company was started in 2012 when it issued a note to borrow $6,200 cash.

Required

Write an accounting equation, and record the effects of the borrowing transaction under the appropriate general ledger account headings.

LO 2, 3

Exercise 1-13 *Effects of revenue, expense, dividend, and the closing process*

Rhodes Company was started on January 1, 2011. During 2012, the company experienced the following three accounting events: (1) earned cash revenues of $13,500, (2) paid cash expenses of $9,200, and (3) paid a $500 cash dividend to its stockholders. These were the only events that affected the company during 2012.

Required

a. Write an accounting equation, and record the effects of each accounting event under the appropriate general ledger account headings.
b. Prepare an income statement for the 2012 accounting period and a balance sheet at the end of 2012 for Rhodes Company.
c. What is the balance in the Retained Earnings account immediately after the cash revenue is recognized?
d. What is the balance in the Retained Earnings account after the closing process is complete?

LO 2, 3

Exercise 1-14 *Effect of transactions on general ledger accounts*

At the beginning of 2012, J & J Corp.'s accounting records had the following general ledger accounts and balances.

J & J CORP. Accounting Equation							
Event	Assets		=	Liabilities	+	Stockholders' Equity	Acct. Titles for RE
	Cash	Land		Notes Payable		Common Stock / Retained Earnings	
Balance 1/1/2012	10,000	20,000		12,000		7,000 / 11,000	

J & J Corp. completed the following transactions during 2012.

1. Purchased land for $5,000 cash.
2. Acquired $25,000 cash from the issue of common stock.
3. Received $75,000 cash for providing services to customers.
4. Paid cash operating expenses of $42,000.
5. Borrowed $10,000 cash from the bank.
6. Paid a $5,000 cash dividend to the stockholders.
7. Determined that the market value of the land is $35,000.

Required

a. Record the transactions in the appropriate general ledger accounts. Record the amounts of revenue, expense, and dividends in the Retained Earnings column. Provide the appropriate titles for these accounts in the last column of the table.

b. Determine the net cash flow from financing activities.

c. What is the balance in the Retained Earnings account as of January 1, 2013?

Exercise 1-15 *Classifying events as asset source, use, or exchange*   LO 4

BJ's Business Services experienced the following events during its first year of operations.

1. Acquired $10,000 cash from the issue of common stock.
2. Borrowed $8,000 cash from First Bank.
3. Paid $4,000 cash to purchase land.
4. Received $5,000 cash for providing boarding services.
5. Acquired an additional $2,000 cash from the issue of common stock.
6. Purchased additional land for $3,500 cash.
7. Paid $2,500 cash for salary expense.
8. Signed a contract to provide additional services in the future.
9. Paid $1,000 cash for rent expense.
10. Paid a $1,000 cash dividend to the stockholders.
11. Determined the market value of the land to be $8,000 at the end of the accounting period.

Required

Classify each event as an asset source, use, or exchange transaction or as not applicable (NA).

Exercise 1-16 *Classifying items for the statement of cash flows*   LO 5

Required

Indicate how each of the following would be classified on the statement of cash flows as operating activities (OA), investing activities (IA), financing activities (FA), or not applicable (NA).

a. Paid $4,000 cash for salary expense.
b. Borrowed $8,000 cash from State Bank.
c. Received $30,000 cash from the issue of common stock.
d. Purchased land for $8,000 cash.
e. Performed services for $14,000 cash.
f. Paid $4,200 cash for utilities expense.
g. Sold land for $7,000 cash.
h. Paid a cash dividend of $1,000 to the stockholders.
i. Hired an accountant to keep the books.
j. Paid $3,000 cash on the loan from State Bank.

Exercise 1-17 *Preparing financial statements*   LO 2, 3, 5

Montana Company experienced the following events during 2012.

1. Acquired $30,000 cash from the issue of common stock.
2. Paid $12,000 cash to purchase land.
3. Borrowed $10,000 cash.
4. Provided services for $20,000 cash.
5. Paid $1,000 cash for rent expense.
6. Paid $15,000 cash for other operating expenses.
7. Paid a $2,000 cash dividend to the stockholders.
8. Determined that the market value of the land purchased in Event 2 is now $12,700.

Required

a. The January 1, 2012, general ledger account balances are shown in the following accounting equation. Record the eight events in the appropriate general ledger accounts. Record the amounts of revenue, expense, and dividends in the Retained Earnings column. Provide the appropriate titles for these accounts in the last column of the table. The first event is shown as an example.

MONTANA COMPANY								
Accounting Equation								
Event	Assets		=	Liabilities	+	Stockholders' Equity		Acct. Titles for RE
	Cash	Land		Notes Payable		Common Stock	Retained Earnings	
Balance 1/1/2012	2,000	12,000		0		6,000	8,000	
1.	30,000					30,000		

b. Prepare an income statement, statement of changes in equity, year-end balance sheet, and statement of cash flows for the 2012 accounting period.

c. Determine the percentage of assets that were provided by retained earnings. How much cash is in the retained earnings account?

LO 5

Exercise 1-18   *Retained earnings and the closing process*

Davis Company was started on January 1, 2012. During the month of January, Davis earned $4,600 of revenue and incurred $3,000 of expense. Davis closes its books on December 31 of each year.

Required

a. Determine the balance in the Retained Earnings account as of January 31, 2012.

b. Comment on whether retained earnings is an element of financial statements or an account.

c. What happens to the Retained Earnings account at the time expenses are recognized?

LO 5

Exercise 1-19   *Relationship between assets and retained earnings*

Washington Company was organized when it acquired $2,000 cash from the issue of common stock. During its first accounting period the company earned $800 of cash revenue and incurred $500 of cash expenses. Also, during the accounting period the company paid its owners a $200 cash dividend.

Required

a. Determine the balance in the Retained Earnings account before and after the temporary accounts are closed.

b. As of the end of the accounting period, determine what percentage of total assets were provided by retained earnings.

LO 5

Exercise 1-20   *Historical cost versus market value*

Hilltop, Inc., purchased land in January 2009 at a cost of $270,000. The estimated market value of the land is $350,000 as of December 31, 2012.

Required

a. Name the December 31, 2012, financial statement(s) on which the land will be shown.

b. At what dollar amount will the land be shown in the financial statement(s)?

c. Name the key concept that will be used in determining the dollar amount that will be reported for land that is shown in the financial statement(s).

Exercise 1-21　*Relating accounting events to entities*

Wright Company was started in 2012 when it acquired $25,000 cash by issuing common stock to Cal Wright.

Required

a. Was this event an asset source, use, or exchange transaction for Wright Company?

b. Was this event an asset source, use, or exchange transaction for Cal Wright?

c. Was the cash flow an operating, investing, or a financing activity on Wright Company's 2012 statement of cash flows?

d. Was the cash flow an operating, investing, or a financing activity on Cal Wright's 2012 statement of cash flows?

Exercise 1-22　*Effect of events on a horizontal financial statements model*

City Consulting Services experienced the following events during 2012.

1. Acquired cash by issuing common stock.
2. Collected cash for providing tutoring services to clients.
3. Borrowed cash from a local government small business foundation.
4. Purchased land for cash.
5. Paid cash for operating expenses.
6. Paid a cash dividend to the stockholders.
7. Determined that the market value of the land is higher than its historical cost.

Required

Use a horizontal statements model to show how each event affects the balance sheet, income statement, and statement of cash flows. Indicate whether the event increases (I), decreases (D), or does not affect (NA) each element of the financial statements. Also, in the Cash Flows column, classify the cash flows as operating activities (OA), investing activities (IA), or financing activities (FA). The first transaction is shown as an example.

Event No.	Cash	+	Land	=	N. Pay	+	C. Stock.	+	Ret. Ear.	Rev.	−	Exp.	=	Net Inc.	Statement of Cash Flows
			Balance Sheet									Income Statement			
1.	I	+	NA	=	NA	+	I	+	NA	NA	−	NA	=	NA	I　FA

Exercise 1-23　*Record events in the horizontal statements model*

Expo Co. was started in 2012. During 2012, the company (1) acquired $11,000 cash from the issue of common stock, (2) earned cash revenue of $18,000, (3) paid cash expenses of $10,500, and (4) paid a $1,000 cash dividend to the stockholders.

Required

a. Record these four events in a horizontal statements model. Also, in the Cash Flows column, classify the cash flows as operating activities (OA), investing activities (IA), or financing activities (FA). The first event is shown as an example.

Event No.	Cash	=	N. Pay	+	C. Stock.	+	Ret. Ear.	Rev.	−	Exp.	=	Net Inc.	Statement of Cash Flows
			Balance Sheet							Income Statement			
1.	11,000	=	NA	+	11,000	+	NA	NA	−	NA	=	NA	11,000　FA

b. What does the income statement tell you about the assets of this business?

LO 6

Exercise 1-24 *Effect of events on a horizontal statements model*

Solito, Inc., was started on January 1, 2012. The company experienced the following events during its first year of operation.

1. Acquired $50,000 cash from the issue of common stock.
2. Paid $12,000 cash to purchase land.
3. Received $50,000 cash for providing tax services to customers.
4. Paid $9,500 cash for salary expense.
5. Acquired $5,000 cash from the issue of additional common stock.
6. Borrowed $10,000 cash from the bank.
7. Purchased additional land for $10,000 cash.
8. Paid $8,000 cash for other operating expenses.
9. Paid a $2,800 cash dividend to the stockholders.
10. Determined that the market value of the land is $25,000.

Required

a. Record these events in a horizontal statements model. Also, in the Cash Flows column, classify the cash flows as operating activities (OA), investing activities (IA), or financing activities (FA). The first event is shown as an example.

Event No.	Balance Sheet										Income Statement						Statement of Cash Flows
	Cash	+	Land	=	N. Pay	+	C. Stock.	+	Ret. Ear.		Rev.	−	Exp.	=	Net Inc.		
1.	50,000	+	NA	=	NA	+	50,000	+	NA		NA	−	NA	=	NA		50,000 FA

b. What is the net income earned in 2012?
c. What is the amount of total assets at the end of 2012?
d. What is the net cash flow from operating activities for 2012?
e. What is the net cash flow from investing activities for 2012?
f. What is the net cash flow from financing activities for 2012?
g. What is the cash balance at the end of 2012?
h. As of the end of the year 2012, what percentage of total assets were provided by creditors, investors, and retained earnings?
i. What is the balance in the Retained Earnings account immediately after Event 4 is recorded?

LO 4, 6

Exercise 1-25 *Types of transactions and the horizontal statements model*

Partner's Pet Store experienced the following events during its first year of operations, 2012.

1. Acquired cash by issuing common stock.
2. Purchased land with cash.
3. Borrowed cash from a bank.
4. Signed a contract to provide services in the future.
5. Paid a cash dividend to the stockholders.
6. Paid cash for operating expenses.
7. Determined that the market value of the land is higher than the historical cost.

Required

a. Indicate whether each event is an asset source, use, or exchange transaction.
b. Use a horizontal statements model to show how each event affects the balance sheet, income statement, and statement of cash flows. Indicate whether the event increases (I), decreases (D), or does not affect (NA) each element of the financial statements. Also, in the Cash

Flows column, classify the cash flows as operating activities (OA), investing activities (IA), or financing activities (FA). The first transaction is shown as an example.

Event No.	Balance Sheet									Income Statement					Statement of Cash Flows
	Cash	+	Land	=	N. Pay	+	C. Stock.	+	Ret. Ear.	Rev.	−	Exp.	=	Net Inc.	
1.	I	+	NA	=	NA	+	I	+	NA	NA	−	NA	=	NA	I FA

Exercise 1-26 *International Financial Reporting Standards*

IFRS

Seacrest Company is a U.S.–based company that develops its financial statements under GAAP. The total amount of the company's assets shown on its December 31, 2012, balance sheet was approximately $225 million. The president of Seacrest is considering the possibility of relocating the company to a country that practices accounting under IFRS. The president has hired an international accounting firm to determine what the company's statements would look like if they were prepared under IFRS. One striking difference is that under IFRS the assets shown on the balance sheet would be valued at approximately $275 million.

Required

a. Would Seacrest's assets really be worth $50 million more if it moves its headquarters?

b. Discuss the underlying conceptual differences between U.S. GAAP and IFRS that cause the difference in the reported asset values.

PROBLEMS

All applicable Problems are available with McGraw-Hill's *Connect Accounting*.

Problem 1-27 *Accounting's role in not-for-profits*

LO 1

Teresa Hill is struggling to pass her introductory accounting course. Teresa is intelligent but she likes to party. Studying is a low priority for Teresa. When one of her friends tells her that she is going to have trouble in business if she doesn't learn accounting, Teresa responds that she doesn't plan to go into business. She says that she is arts oriented and plans someday to be a director of a museum. She is in the school of business to develop her social skills, not her quantitative skills. Teresa says she won't have to worry about accounting, since museums are not intended to make a profit.

Required

a. Write a brief memo explaining whether you agree or disagree with Teresa's position regarding accounting and not-for-profit organizations.

b. Distinguish between financial accounting and managerial accounting.

c. Identify some of the stakeholders of not-for-profit institutions that would expect to receive financial accounting reports.

d. Identify some of the stakeholders of not-for-profit institutions that would expect to receive managerial accounting reports.

Problem 1-28 *Accounting entities*

LO 1

The following business scenarios are independent from one another.

1. Beth Mays purchased an automobile from Mills Bros. Auto Sales for $9,000.

2. Bill Becham loaned $15,000 to the business in which he is a stockholder.

3. First State Bank paid interest to Levi Co. on a certificate of deposit that Levi Co. has invested at First State Bank.

4. Southside Restaurant paid the current utility bill of $128 to Midwest Utilities.

5. Filmore, Inc., borrowed $50,000 from City National Bank and used the funds to purchase land from Tuchols Realty.

CHECK FIGURE

1. Entities mentioned: Beth Mays and Mills Bros. Auto Sales

6. Jing Chu purchased $10,000 of common stock of International Sales Corporation from the corporation.

7. Bill Mann loaned $4,000 cash to his daughter.

8. Research Service Co. earned $5,000 in cash revenue.

9. Yang Imports paid $1,500 for salaries to each of its four employees.

10. Meyers Inc. paid a cash dividend of $3,000 to its sole shareholder, Mark Meyers.

Required

a. For each scenario, create a list of all of the entities that are mentioned in the description.

b. Describe what happens to the cash account of each entity that you identified in Requirement *a*.

LO 2, 5

Problem 1-29   *Relating titles and accounts to financial statements*

Required

Identify the financial statements on which each of the following items (titles, date descriptions, and accounts) appears by placing a check mark in the appropriate column. If an item appears on more than one statement, place a check mark in every applicable column.

Item	Income Statement	Statement of Changes in Stockholders' Equity	Balance Sheet	Statement of Cash Flows
Notes payable				
Beginning common stock				
Service revenue				
Utility expense				
Cash from stock issue				
Operating activities				
For the period ended (date)				
Net income				
Investing activities				
Net loss				
Ending cash balance				
Salary expense				
Consulting revenue				
Dividends				
Financing activities				
Ending common stock				
Interest expense				
As of (date)				
Land				
Beginning cash balance				

LO 2, 3, 5, 6

e**X**cel

Problem 1-30   *Preparing financial statements for two complete accounting cycles*

Webster Consulting experienced the following transactions for 2012, its first year of operations, and 2013. *Assume that all transactions involve the receipt or payment of cash.*

Transactions for 2012

1. Acquired $20,000 by issuing common stock.
2. Received $35,000 cash for providing services to customers.
3. Borrowed $25,000 cash from creditors.
4. Paid expenses amounting to $22,000.
5. Purchased land for $30,000 cash.

Transactions for 2013

Beginning account balances for 2013 are:

Cash	$28,000
Land	30,000
Notes payable	25,000
Common stock	20,000
Retained earnings	13,000

CHECK FIGURES
b. Net Income 2012: $13,000
b. Retained Earnings 2013: $33,500

1. Acquired an additional $24,000 from the issue of common stock.
2. Received $95,000 for providing services.
3. Paid $15,000 to creditors to reduce loan.
4. Paid expenses amounting to $71,500.
5. Paid a $3,000 dividend to the stockholders.
6. Determined that the market value of the land is $47,000.

Required

a. Write an accounting equation, and record the effects of each accounting event under the appropriate headings for each year. Record the amounts of revenue, expense, and dividends in the Retained Earnings column. Provide appropriate titles for these accounts in the last column of the table.
b. Prepare an income statement, statement of changes in stockholders' equity, year-end balance sheet, and statement of cash flows for each year.
c. Determine the amount of cash that is in the retained earnings account at the end of 2012 and 2013.
d. Examine the balance sheets for the two years. How did assets change from 2012 to 2013?
e. Determine the balance in the Retained Earnings account immediately after Event 2 in 2012 and in 2013 are recorded.

Problem 1-31 *Interrelationships among financial statements*

Gofish Enterprises started the 2012 accounting period with $50,000 of assets (all cash), $18,000 of liabilities, and $4,000 of common stock. During the year, Gofish earned cash revenues of $38,000, paid cash expenses of $32,000, and paid a cash dividend to stockholders of $2,000. Gofish also acquired $15,000 of additional cash from the sale of common stock and paid $10,000 cash to reduce the liability owed to a bank.

LO 2, 3, 5, 6
CHECK FIGURE
a. Net Income: $6,000
Total Assets: $59,000

Required

a. Prepare an income statement, statement of changes in stockholders' equity, period-end balance sheet, and statement of cash flows for the 2012 accounting period. (*Hint:* Determine the amount of beginning retained earnings before considering the effects of the current period events. It also might help to record all events under an accounting equation before preparing the statements.)
b. Determine the percentage of total assets that were provided by creditors, investors, and retained earnings.

LO 4

Problem 1-32 *Classifying events as asset source, use, or exchange*

The following unrelated events are typical of those experienced by business entities.

1. Acquire cash by issuing common stock.
2. Purchase land with cash.
3. Purchase equipment with cash.
4. Pay monthly rent on an office building.
5. Hire a new office manager.
6. Borrow cash from a bank.
7. Pay a cash dividend to stockholders.
8. Pay cash for operating expenses.
9. Pay an office manager's salary with cash.
10. Receive cash for services that have been performed.
11. Pay cash for utilities expense.
12. Acquire land by accepting a liability (financing the purchase).
13. Pay cash to purchase a new office building.
14. Discuss plans for a new office building with an architect.
15. Repay part of a bank loan.

Required

Identify each of the events as an asset source, use, or exchange transaction. If an event would not be recorded under generally accepted accounting principles, identify it as not applicable (NA). Also indicate for each event whether total assets would increase, decrease, or remain unchanged. Organize your answer according to the following table. The first event is shown in the table as an example.

Event No.	Type of Event	Effect on Total Assets
1	Asset source	Increase

LO 6

Problem 1-33 *Recording the effect of events in a horizontal statements model*

Texas Corporation experienced the following transactions during 2012.

1. Paid a cash dividend to the stockholders.
2. Acquired cash by issuing additional common stock.
3. Signed a contract to perform services in the future.
4. Performed services for cash.
5. Paid cash expenses.
6. Sold land for cash at an amount equal to its cost.
7. Borrowed cash from a bank.
8. Determined that the market value of the land is higher than its historical cost.

Required

Use a horizontal statements model to show how each event affects the balance sheet, income statement, and statement of cash flows. Indicate whether the event increases (I), decreases (D), or does not affect (NA) each element of the financial statements. Also, in the Cash Flows column, classify the cash flows as operating activities (OA), investing activities (IA), or financing activities (FA). The first transaction is shown as an example.

Event No.	Cash	+	Land	=	N. Pay	+	C. Stock.	+	Ret. Ear.	Rev.	−	Exp.	=	Net Inc.	Statement of Cash Flows
					Balance Sheet							**Income Statement**			
1.	D	+	NA	=	NA	+	NA	+	D	NA	−	NA	=	NA	D FA

Problem 1-34 *Recording events in a horizontal statements model*

Cooley Company was started on January 1, 2012, and experienced the following events during its first year of operation.

1. Acquired $30,000 cash from the issue of common stock.
2. Borrowed $40,000 cash from National Bank.
3. Earned cash revenues of $48,000 for performing services.
4. Paid cash expenses of $45,000.
5. Paid a $1,000 cash dividend to the stockholders.
6. Acquired an additional $20,000 cash from the issue of common stock.
7. Paid $10,000 cash to reduce the principal balance of the bank note.
8. Paid $53,000 cash to purchase land.
9. Determined that the market value of the land is $75,000.

CHECK FIGURES
a. Net Income: $3,000
e. Net Cash Flow from
   Operating Activities: $3,000

Required

a. Record the preceding transactions in the horizontal statements model. Also, in the Cash Flows column, classify the cash flows as operating activities (OA), investing activities (IA), or financing activities (FA). The first event is shown as an example.

Event No.	Balance Sheet											Income Statement						Statement of Cash Flows
	Cash	+	Land	=	N. Pay	+	C. Stock.	+	Ret. Ear.			Rev.	−	Exp.	=	Net Inc.		
1.	30,000	+	NA	=	NA	+	30,000	+	NA			NA	−	NA	=	NA		30,000 FA

b. Determine the amount of total assets that Cooley would report on the December 31, 2012, balance sheet.
c. Identify the asset source transactions and related amounts for 2012.
d. Determine the net income that Cooley would report on the 2012 income statement. Explain why dividends do not appear on the income statement.
e. Determine the net cash flows from operating activities, financing activities, and investing activities that Cooley would report on the 2012 statement of cash flows.
f. Determine the percentage of assets that were provided by investors, creditors, and retained earnings.
g. What is the balance in the Retained Earnings account immediately after Event 3 is recorded?

ANALYZE, THINK, COMMUNICATE

ATC 1-1 Business Applications Case *Understanding real-world annual reports*

Required

Use the Target Corporation's annual report in Appendix B to answer the following questions. Note that net income and net earnings are synonymous terms.

Target Corporation

a. What was Target's net income for 2009?
b. Did Target's net income increase or decrease from 2008 to 2009, and by how much?
c. What was Target's accounting equation for 2009?
d. Which of the following had the largest percentage change from 2008 to 2009: net sales, cost of sales, or selling, general, and administrative expenses? Show all computations.

ATC 1-2   Group Assignment   *Missing information*

The following selected financial information is available for HAS, Inc. Amounts are in millions of dollars.

Income Statements	2014	2013	2012	2011
Revenue	$ 860	$1,520	$ (a)	$1,200
Cost and expenses	(a)	(a)	(2,400)	(860)
Income from continuing operations	(b)	450	320	(a)
Unusual items	-0-	175	(b)	(b)
Net income	$ 20	$ (b)	$ 175	$ 300
Balance Sheets				
Assets				
Cash and marketable securities	$ 350	$1,720	$ (c)	$ 940
Other assets	1,900	(c)	2,500	(c)
Total assets	2,250	$2,900	$ (d)	$3,500
Liabilities	$ (c)	$ (d)	$1,001	$ (d)
Stockholders' equity				
Common stock	880	720	(e)	800
Retained earnings	(d)	(e)	800	(e)
Total stockholders' equity	1,520	1,345	(f)	2,200
Total liabilities and stockholders' equity	$2,250	$ (f)	$3,250	$3,500

Required

a. Divide the class into groups of four or five students each. Organize the groups into four sections. Assign Task 1 to the first section of groups, Task 2 to the second section, Task 3 to the third section, and Task 4 to the fourth section.

Group Tasks

    (1) Fill in the missing information for 2011.
    (2) Fill in the missing information for 2012.
    (3) Fill in the missing information for 2013.
    (4) Fill in the missing information for 2014.

b. Each section should select two representatives. One representative is to put the financial statements assigned to that section on the board, underlining the missing amounts. The second representative is to explain to the class how the missing amounts were determined.

c. Each section should list events that could have caused the unusual items category on the income statement.

ATC 1-3   Research Assignment   *Finding real-world accounting information*

This chapter introduced the basic four financial statements companies use annually to keep their stakeholders informed of their accomplishments and financial situation. Complete the requirements below using the most recent (20xx) financial statements available on the McDonald Corporation's website. Obtain the statements on the Internet by following the steps below. (The formatting of the company's website may have changed since these instructions were written.)

1. Go to www.mcdonalds.com.
2. Click on the "Corporate" link at the bottom of the page. (Most companies have a link titled "investors relations" that leads to their financial statements; McDonald's uses "corporate" instead.)
3. Click on the "INVESTORS" link at the top of the page.

4. Click on *"McDonald's 20xx Annual Report"* and then on *"20xx Financial Report."*
5. Go to the company's financial statements that begin on page 45 of the annual report.

Required

a. What was the company's net income in each of the last 3 years?
b. What amount of total assets did the company have at the end of the most recent year?
c. How much retained earnings did the company have at the end of the most recent year?
d. For the most recent year, what was the company's cash flow from operating activities, cash flow from investing activities, and cash flow from financing activities?

ATC 1-4   Writing Assignment   *Elements of financial statements defined*

Sam and his sister Blair both attend the state university. As a reward for their successful completion of the past year (Sam had a 3.2 GPA in business, and Blair had a 3.7 GPA in art), their father gave each of them 100 shares of The Walt Disney Company stock. They have just received their first annual report. Blair does not understand what the information means and has asked Sam to explain it to her. Sam is currently taking an accounting course, and she knows he will understand the financial statements.

Required

Assume that you are Sam. Write Blair a memo explaining the following financial statement items to her. In your explanation, describe each of the two financial statements and explain the financial information each contains. Also define each of the elements listed for each financial statement and explain what it means.

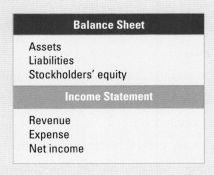

Balance Sheet
Assets
Liabilities
Stockholders' equity
Income Statement
Revenue
Expense
Net income

CHAPTER 2

Understanding the Accounting Cycle

LEARNING OBJECTIVES

After you have mastered the material in this chapter, you will be able to:

1 Record basic accrual and deferral events in a horizontal financial statements model.

2 Organize general ledger accounts under an accounting equation.

3 Prepare financial statements based on accrual accounting.

4 Describe the closing process, the accounting cycle, and the matching concept.

5 Explain how business events affect financial statements over multiple accounting cycles.

6 Classify accounting events into one of four categories:

 a. asset source transactions.

 b. asset use transactions.

 c. asset exchange transactions.

 d. claims exchange transactions.

CHAPTER OPENING

Users of financial statements must distinguish between the terms *recognition* and *realization*. **Recognition** means formally *reporting* an economic item or event in the financial statements. **Realization** refers to collecting money, generally from the sale of products or services. Companies may recognize (report) revenue in the income statement in a different accounting period from the period in which they collect the cash related to the revenue. Furthermore, companies frequently make cash payments for expenses in accounting periods other than the periods in which the expenses are recognized in the income statement.

To illustrate assume Johnson Company provides services to customers in 2012 but collects cash for those services in 2013. In this case, realization occurs in 2013. When should Johnson recognize the services revenue?

Users of *cash basis* accounting recognize (report) revenues and expenses in the period in which cash is collected or paid. Under cash basis accounting Johnson would recognize the revenue in 2013. When it collects the cash. In contrast, users of **accrual accounting** recognize revenues and expenses in the period in which they occur, regardless of when cash is collected or paid. Under accrual accounting Johnson would recognize the revenue in 2012 (the period in which it performed the services) even though it does not collect (realize) the cash until 2013.

Accrual accounting is required by generally accepted accounting principles. Virtually all major companies operating in the United States use it. Its two distinguishing features are called *accruals* and *deferrals*

- The term **accrual** describes a revenue or an expense event that is recognized ***before*** cash is exchanged. Johnson's recognition of revenue in 2012 related to cash realized in 2013 is an example of an accrual.
- The term **deferral** describes a revenue or an expense event that is recognized ***after*** cash has been exchanged. Suppose Johnson pays cash in 2012 to purchase office supplies it uses in 2013. In this case the cash payment occurs in 2012 although supplies expense is recognized in 2013. This example is a deferral.

The Curious Accountant

Suppose Arno Forst wishes to purchase a subscription to *Fitness magazine* for his sister for her birthday. He pays $12 for a one-year subscription to the Meredith Corporation, the company that publishes *Fitness, American Baby, Better Homes and Gardens, The Ladies Home Journal,* and several other magazines. It also owns 12 television stations. His sister will receive her first issue of the magazine in October.

How should Meredith Corporation account for the receipt of this cash? How would this event be reported on its December 31, 2012, financial statements? (Answer on page 60.)

ACCRUAL ACCOUNTING

Record basic accrual and deferral events in a horizontal financial statements model.

The next section of the text describes seven events experienced by Cato Consultants, a training services company that uses accrual accounting.

EVENT 1   Cato Consultants was started on January 1, 2012, when it acquired $5,000 cash by issuing common stock.

The issue of stock for cash is an **asset source transaction.** It increases the company's assets (cash) and its equity (common stock). The transaction does not affect the income statement. The cash inflow is classified as a financing activity (acquisition from owners). These effects are shown in the following financial statements model:

Assets	=	Liab.	+	Stockholders' Equity							
Cash	=			Com. Stk.	+	Ret. Earn.	Rev.	−	Exp.	=	Net Inc.	Cash Flow
5,000	=	NA	+	5,000	+	NA	NA	−	NA	=	NA	5,000 FA

Accounting for Accounts Receivable

EVENT 2   During 2012 Cato Consultants provided $84,000 of consulting services to its clients. The business has completed the work and sent bills to the clients, but not yet collected any cash. This type of transaction is frequently described as providing services *on account.*

Accrual accounting requires companies to recognize revenue in the period in which the work is done regardless of when cash is collected. In this case, revenue is recognized in 2012 even though cash has not been realized (collected). Recall that revenue represents the economic benefit that results in an increase in assets from providing goods and services to customers. The specific asset that increases is called **Accounts Receivable.** The balance in Accounts Receivable represents the amount of cash the company expects to collect in the future. Since the revenue recognition causes assets (accounts receivable) to increase, it is classified as an asset source transaction. Its effect on the financial statements follows.

Assets			=	Liab.	+	Stockholders' Equity							
Cash	+	Accts. Rec.	=			Com. Stk.	+	Ret. Earn.	Rev.	−	Exp.	=	Net Inc.	Cash Flow
NA	+	84,000	=	NA	+	NA	+	84,000	84,000	−	NA	=	84,000	NA

Notice that the event affects the income statement but not the statement of cash flows. The statement of cash flows will be affected in the future when cash is collected.

EVENT 3   Cato collected $60,000 cash from customers in partial settlement of its accounts receivable.

The collection of an account receivable is an **asset exchange transaction.** One asset account (Cash) increases and another asset account (Accounts Receivable) decreases. The amount of total assets is unchanged. The effect of the $60,000 collection of receivables on the financial statements is as follows.

Assets			=	Liab.	+	Stockholders' Equity							
Cash	+	Accts. Rec.	=			Com. Stk.	+	Ret. Earn.	Rev.	−	Exp.	=	Net Inc.	Cash Flow
60,000	+	(60,000)	=	NA	+	NA	+	NA	NA	−	NA	=	NA	60,000 OA

Notice that collecting the cash did not affect the income statement. The revenue was recognized when the work was done (see Event 2). Revenue would be double counted if it were recognized again when the cash is collected. The statement of cash flows reflects a cash inflow from operating activities.

Other Events

EVENT 4   Cato paid the instructor $10,000 for teaching training courses (salary expense).

Cash payment for salary expense is an **asset use transaction.** Both the asset account Cash and the equity account Retained Earnings decrease by $10,000. Recognizing the expense decreases net income on the income statement. Since Cato paid cash for the expense, the statement of cash flows reflects a cash outflow from operating activities. These effects on the financial statements follow.

Assets			=	Liab.	+	Stockholders' Equity								
Cash	+	Accts. Rec.	=			Com. Stk.	+	Ret. Earn.	Rev.	−	Exp.	=	Net Inc.	Cash Flow
(10,000)	+	NA	=	NA	+	NA	+	(10,000)	NA	−	10,000	=	(10,000)	(10,000) OA

EVENT 5   Cato paid $2,000 cash for advertising costs. The advertisements appeared in 2012.

Cash payments for advertising expenses are asset use transactions. Both the asset account Cash and the equity account Retained Earnings decrease by $2,000. Recognizing the expense decreases net income on the income statement. Since the expense was paid with cash, the statement of cash flows reflects a cash outflow from operating activities. These effects on the financial statements follow.

Assets			=	Liab.	+	Stockholders' Equity								
Cash	+	Accts. Rec.	=			Com. Stk.	+	Ret. Earn.	Rev.	−	Exp.	=	Net Inc.	Cash Flow
(2,000)	+	NA	=	NA	+	NA	+	(2,000)	NA	−	2,000	=	(2,000)	(2,000) OA

EVENT 6   Cato signed contracts for $42,000 of consulting services to be performed in 2013.

The $42,000 for consulting services to be performed in 2013 is not recognized in the 2012 financial statements. Revenue is recognized for work actually completed, *not* work expected to be completed. This event does not affect any of the financial statements.

Assets			=	Liab.	+	Stockholders' Equity								
Cash	+	Accts. Rec.	=			Com. Stk.	+	Ret. Earn.	Rev.	−	Exp.	=	Net Inc.	Cash Flow
NA	+	NA	=	NA	+	NA	+	NA	NA	−	NA	=	NA	NA

Accounting for Accrued Salary Expense (Adjusting Entry)

It is impractical to record many business events as they occur. For example, Cato incurs salary expense continually as the instructor teaches courses. Imagine the impossibility of trying to record salary expense second by second! Companies normally record transactions when it is most convenient. The most convenient time to record many expenses is when they are paid. Often, however, a single business transaction pertains to more than one accounting period. To provide accurate financial reports in such cases, companies may need to recognize some expenses before paying cash for them. Expenses that are recognized before cash is paid are called **accrued expenses.** The accounting for Event 7 illustrates the effect of recognizing accrued salary expense.

EVENT 7   At the end of 2012. Cato recorded accrued salary expense of $6,000 (the salary expense is for courses the instructor taught in 2012 that Cato will pay cash for in 2013).

Accrual accounting requires that companies recognize expenses in the period in which they are incurred regardless of when cash is paid. Cato must recognize all salary expense in the period in which the instructor worked (2012) even though Cato will not pay the instructor again until 2013. Cato must also recognize the obligation (liability) it has to pay the instructor. To accurately report all 2012 salary expense and year-end obligations, Cato must record the unpaid salary expense and salary liability before preparing its financial statements. The entry to recognize the accrued salary expense is called an **adjusting entry.** Like all adjusting entries, it is only to update the accounting records; it does not affect cash.

This adjusting entry decreases stockholders' equity (retained earnings) and increases a liability account called **Salaries Payable.** The balance in the Salaries Payable account represents the amount of cash the company is obligated to pay the instructor in the future. The effect of the expense recognition on the financial statements follows.

Assets			=	Liab.	+	Stockholders' Equity								
Cash	+	Accts. Rec.	=	Sal. Pay.	+	Com. Stk.	+	Ret. Earn.	Rev.	−	Exp.	=	Net Inc.	Cash Flow
NA	+	NA	=	6,000	+	NA	+	(6,000)	NA	−	6,000	=	(6,000)	NA

This event is a **claims exchange transaction.** The claims of creditors (liabilities) increase and the claims of stockholders (retained earnings) decrease. Total claims remain unchanged. The salary expense is reported on the income statement. The statement of cash flows is not affected.

Be careful not to confuse liabilities with expenses. Although liabilities may increase when a company recognizes expenses, liabilities are not expenses. Liabilities are obligations. They can arise from acquiring assets as well as recognizing expenses. For example, when a business borrows money from a bank, it recognizes an increase in assets (cash) and liabilities (notes payable). The borrowing transaction does not affect expenses.

✓ CHECK YOURSELF 2.1

During 2012, Anwar Company earned $345,000 of revenue on account and collected $320,000 cash from accounts receivable. Anwar paid cash expenses of $300,000 and cash dividends of $12,000. Determine the amount of net income Anwar should report on the 2012 income statement and the amount of cash flow from operating activities Anwar should report on the 2012 statement of cash flows.

Answer   Net income is $45,000 ($345,000 revenue − $300,000 expenses). The cash flow from operating activities is $20,000, the amount of revenue collected in cash from customers (accounts receivable) minus the cash paid for expenses ($320,000 − $300,000). Dividend payments are classified as financing activities and do not affect the determination of either net income or cash flow from operating activities.

EXHIBIT 2.1

Transaction Data for 2012 Recorded in General Ledger Accounts

1	Cato Consultants acquired $5,000 cash by issuing common stock.
2	Cato provided $84,000 of consulting services on account.
3	Cato collected $60,000 cash from customers in partial settlement of its accounts receivable.
4	Cato paid $10,000 cash for salary expense.
5	Cato paid $2,000 cash for 2012 advertising costs.
6	Cato signed contracts for $42,000 of consulting services to be performed in 2013.
7	Cato recognized $6,000 of accrued salary expense.

	Assets			=	Liabilities	+	Stockholders' Equity			
Event No.	Cash	+	Accounts Receivable	=	Salaries Payable	+	Common Stock	+	Retained Earnings	Other Account Titles
Beg. bal.	0		0		0		0		0	
1	5,000						5,000			
2			84,000						84,000	Consulting revenue
3	60,000		(60,000)							
4	(10,000)								(10,000)	Salary expense
5	(2,000)								(2,000)	Advertising expense
6										
7					6,000				(6,000)	Salary Expense
End bal.	53,000	+	24,000	=	6,000	+	5,000	+	66,000	

Summary of Events and General Ledger

The previous section of this chapter described seven events Cato Consultants experienced during the 2012 accounting period. These events are summarized in Exhibit 2.1. The associated general ledger accounts are also shown in the exhibit. The information in these accounts is used to prepare the financial statements. The revenue and expense items appear in the Retained Earnings column with their account titles immediately to the right of the dollar amounts. The amounts are color coded to help you trace the data to the financial statements. Data in red appear on the balance sheet, data in blue on the income statement, and data in green on the statement of cash flows.

Organize general ledger accounts under an accounting equation.

Vertical Statements Model

The financial statements for Cato Consultants' 2012 accounting period are represented in a vertical statements model in Exhibit 2.2. A vertical statements model arranges a set of financial statement information vertically on a single page. Like horizontal statements models, vertical statements models are learning tools. They illustrate interrelationships among financial statements. The models do not, however, portray the full, formal presentation formats companies use in published financial statements. For example, statements models may use summarized formats with abbreviated titles and dates. As you read the following explanations of each financial statement, trace the color coded financial data from Exhibit 2.1 to Exhibit 2.2.

Prepare financial statements based on accrual accounting.

Prepare a vertical financial
statements model.

EXHIBIT 2.2   Vertical Statements Model

CATO CONSULTANTS
Financial Statements*
Income Statement
For the Year Ended December 31, 2012

Consulting revenue	$84,000
Salary expense	(16,000)
Advertising expense	(2,000)
Net income	$66,000

Statement of Changes in Stockholders' Equity
For the Year Ended December 31, 2012

Beginning common stock	$ 0	
Plus: Common stock issued	5,000	
Ending common stock		$ 5,000
Beginning retained earnings	0	
Plus: Net income	66,000	
Less: Dividends	0	
Ending retained earnings		66,000
Total stockholders' equity		$71,000

Balance Sheet
As of December 31, 2012

Assets		
Cash	$53,000	
Accounts receivable	24,000	
Total assets		$77,000
Liabilities		
Salaries payable		$ 6,000
Stockholders' equity		
Common stock	$ 5,000	
Retained earnings	66,000	
Total stockholders' equity		71,000
Total liabilities and stockholders' equity		$77,000

Statement of Cash Flows
For the Year Ended December 31, 2012

Cash flows from operating activities		
Cash receipts from customers	$60,000	
Cash payments for salary expense	(10,000)	
Cash payments for advertising expenses	(2,000)	
Net cash flow from operating activities		$48,000
Cash flow from investing activities		0
Cash flows from financing activities		
Cash receipt from issuing common stock	5,000	
Net cash flow from financing activities		5,000
Net change in cash		53,000
Plus: Beginning cash balance		0
Ending cash balance		$53,000

*In real-world annual reports, financial statements are normally presented separately with appropriate descriptions of the date to indicate whether the statement applies to the entire accounting period or a specific point in time.

Income Statement

The income statement reflects accrual accounting. Consulting revenue represents the price Cato charged for all the services it performed in 2012, even though Cato had not by the end of the year received cash for some of the services performed. Expenses include all costs incurred to produce revenue, whether paid for by year-end or not. We can now expand the definition of expenses introduced in Chapter 1. Expenses were previously defined as assets consumed in the process of generating revenue. Cato's adjusting entry to recognize accrued salaries expense did not reflect consuming assets. Instead of a decrease in assets, Cato recorded an increase in liabilities (salaries payable). An **expense** can therefore be more precisely defined as *a decrease in assets or an increase in liabilities resulting from operating activities undertaken to generate revenue.*

Statement of Changes in Stockholders' Equity

The statement of changes in stockholders' equity reports the effects on equity of issuing common stock, earning net income, and paying dividends to stockholders. It identifies how an entity's equity increased and decreased during the period as a result of transactions with stockholders and operating the business. In the Cato case, the statement shows that equity increased when the business acquired $5,000 cash by issuing common stock. The statement also reports that equity increased by $66,000 from earning income and that none of the $66,000 of net earnings was distributed to owners (no dividends were paid). Equity at the end of the year is $71,000 ($5,000 + $66,000).

Balance Sheet

The balance sheet discloses an entity's assets, liabilities, and stockholders' equity at a particular point in time. Cato Consultants had two assets at the end of the 2012 accounting period: cash of $53,000 and accounts receivable of $24,000. These assets are listed on the balance sheet in order of liquidity. Of the $77,000 in total assets, creditors have a $6,000 claim, leaving stockholders with a $71,000 claim.

Statement of Cash Flows

The statement of cash flows explains the change in cash from the beginning to the end of the accounting period. It can be prepared by analyzing the Cash account. Since Cato Consultants was established in 2012, its beginning cash balance was zero. By the end of the year, the cash balance was $53,000. The statement of cash flows explains this increase. The Cash account increased because Cato collected $60,000 from customers and decreased because Cato paid $12,000 for expenses. As a result, Cato's net cash inflow from operating activities was $48,000. Also, the business acquired $5,000 cash through the financing activity of issuing common stock, for a cumulative cash increase of $53,000 ($48,000 + $5,000) during 2012.

Comparing Cash Flow from Operating Activities with Net Income

The amount of net income measured using accrual accounting differs from the amount of cash flow from operating activities. For Cato Consulting in 2012, the differences are summarized below.

	Accrual Accounting	Cash Flow
Consulting revenue	$84,000	$60,000
Salary expense	(16,000)	(10,000)
Advertising expense	(2,000)	(2,000)
Net income	$66,000	$48,000

Many students begin their first accounting class with the misconception that revenue and expense items are cash equivalents. The Cato illustration demonstrates that a company may recognize a revenue or expense without a corresponding cash collection or payment in the same accounting period.

The Closing Process

LO 4

Describe the closing process, the accounting cycle, and the matching concept.

Recall that the temporary accounts (revenue, expense, and dividend) are closed prior to the start of the next accounting cycle. The closing process transfers the amount in each of these accounts to the Retained Earnings account, leaving each temporary account with a zero balance.

Exhibit 2.3 shows the general ledger accounts for Cato Consultants after the revenue and expense accounts have been closed to retained earnings. The closing entry labeled Cl.1 transfers the balance in the Consulting Revenue account to the Retained Earnings account. Closing entries Cl.2 and Cl.3 transfer the balances in the expense accounts to retained earnings.

EXHIBIT 2.3

General Ledger Accounts for Cato Consultants

Assets		=	Liabilities		+	Stockholders' Equity	
Cash			**Salaries Payable**			**Common Stock**	
(1)	5,000		(7)	6,000		(1)	5,000
(3)	60,000		Bal.	6,000			
(4)	(10,000)					**Retained Earnings**	
(5)	(2,000)					Cl.1	84,000
Bal.	53,000					Cl.2	(16,000)
						Cl.3	(2,000)
Accounts Receivable						Bal.	66,000
(2)	84,000						
(3)	(60,000)					**Consulting Revenue**	
Bal.	24,000					(2)	84,000
						Cl.1	(84,000)
						Bal.	0
						Salary Expense	
						(4)	(10,000)
						(7)	(6,000)
						Cl.2	16,000
						Bal.	0
						Advertising Expense	
						(5)	(2,000)
						Cl.3	2,000
						Bal.	0

Steps in an Accounting Cycle

An accounting cycle, which is represented graphically in Exhibit 2.4, involves several steps. The four steps identified to this point are (1) recording transactions; (2) adjusting the accounts; (3) preparing financial statements; and (4) closing the temporary accounts. The first step occurs continually throughout the accounting period. Steps 2, 3, and 4 normally occur at the end of the accounting period.

The Matching Concept

Cash basis accounting can distort reported net income because it sometimes fails to match expenses with the revenues they produce. To illustrate, consider the $6,000 of accrued salary expense that Cato Consultants recognized at the end of 2012. The instructor's teaching produced revenue in 2012. If Cato waited until 2013 (when it paid the instructor) to recognize $6,000 of the total $16,000 salary expense, then $6,000 of the expense would not be matched with the revenue it generated. By using accrual accounting, Cato recognized all the salary expense in the same accounting period in which the consulting revenue was recognized. A primary goal of accrual accounting is to appropriately match expenses with revenues, the **matching concept.**

Appropriately matching expenses with revenues can be difficult even when using accrual accounting. For example, consider Cato's advertising expense. Money spent on advertising may generate revenue in future accounting periods as well as in the current period. A prospective customer could save an advertising brochure for several years before calling Cato for training services. It is difficult to know when and to what extent advertising produces revenue. When the connection between an expense and the corresponding revenue is vague, accountants commonly match the expense with the period in which it is incurred. Cato matched (recognized) the entire $2,000 of advertising cost with the 2012 accounting period even though some of that cost might generate revenue in future accounting periods. Expenses that are matched with the period in which they are incurred are frequently called **period costs.**

Matching is not perfect. Although it would be more accurate to match expenses with revenues than with periods, there is sometimes no obvious direct connection between expenses and revenue. Accountants must exercise judgment to select the accounting period in which to recognize revenues and expenses. The concept of conservatism influences such judgment calls.

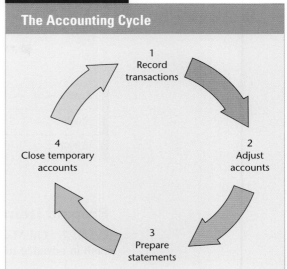

EXHIBIT 2.4

The Accounting Cycle

1 Record transactions
2 Adjust accounts
3 Prepare statements
4 Close temporary accounts

The Conservatism Principle

When faced with a recognition dilemma, **conservatism** guides accountants to select the alternative that produces the lowest amount of net income. In uncertain circumstances, accountants tend to delay revenue recognition and accelerate expense recognition. The conservatism principle holds that it is better to understate net income than to overstate it. If subsequent developments suggest that net income should have been higher, investors will respond more favorably than if they learn it was really lower. This practice explains why Cato recognized all of the advertising cost as expense in 2012 even though some of that cost may generate revenue in future accounting periods.

SECOND ACCOUNTING CYCLE

The effects of Cato Consultants' 2013 events are as follows:

EVENT 1   Cato paid $6,000 to the intructor to settle the salaries payable obligation.

Cash payments to creditors are *asset use transactions.* When Cato pays the instructor, both the asset account Cash and the liability account Salaries Payable decrease. The

LO 5

Explain how business events affect financial statements over multiple accounting cycles.

cash payment does not affect the income statement. The salary expense was recognized in 2012 when the instructor taught the classes. The statement of cash flows reflects a cash outflow from operating activities. The effects of this transaction on the financial statements are shown here.

Assets	=	Liab.	+	Stk. Equity		Rev.	−	Exp.	=	Net Inc.	Cash Flow
Cash	=	Sal. Pay.				Rev.	−	Exp.	=	Net Inc.	Cash Flow
(6,000)	=	(6,000)	+	NA		NA	−	NA	=	NA	(6,000) OA

Prepaid Items (Cost versus Expense)

EVENT 2   On March 1, 2013, Cato signed a one-year lease agreement and paid $12,000 cash in advance to rent office space. The one-year lease term began on March 1.

Accrual accounting draws a distinction between the terms *cost* and *expense*. A **cost** *might be either an asset or an expense.* If a company has already consumed a purchased resource in the process of earning revenue, the cost of the resource is an *expense.* For example, companies normally pay for electricity the month after using it. The cost of electric utilities is therefore usually recorded as an expense. In contrast, if a company purchases a resource it will use in the future to generate revenue, the cost of the resource represents an *asset.* Accountants record such a cost in an asset account and **defer** recognizing an expense until the resource is used to produce revenue. Deferring the expense recognition provides more accurate **matching** of revenues and expenses.

The cost of the office space Cato leased in Event 2 is an asset. It is recorded in the asset account *Prepaid Rent.* Cato expects to benefit from incurring this cost for the next twelve months. Expense recognition is deferred until Cato uses the office space to help generate revenue. Other common deferred expenses include *prepaid insurance* and *prepaid taxes.* As these titles imply, deferred expenses are frequently called **prepaid items.** Exhibit 2.5 illustrates the relationship between costs, assets, and expenses.

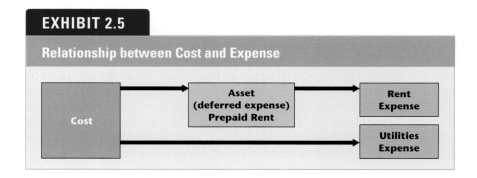

EXHIBIT 2.5

Relationship between Cost and Expense

Cost → Asset (deferred expense) Prepaid Rent → Rent Expense

Cost → Utilities Expense

Purchasing prepaid rent is an asset exchange transaction. The asset account Cash decreases and the asset account Prepaid Rent increases. The amount of total assets is unaffected. The income statement is unaffected. Expense recognition is deferred until the office space is used. The statement of cash flows reflects a cash outflow from operating activities. The effects of this transaction on the financial statements are shown here.

Assets		= Liab. + Stk. Equity						
Cash	+ Prep. Rent			Rev.	− Exp.	= Net Inc.	Cash Flow	
(12,000)	+ 12,000	= NA +	NA	NA	− NA	= NA	(12,000)	OA

Accounting for Receipt of Unearned Revenue

EVENT 3   Cato received $18,000 cash in advance from Westberry Company for consulting services Cato agreed to perform over a one-year period beginning June 1, 2013.

Cato must defer (delay) recognizing any revenue until it performs (does the work) the consulting services for Westberry. From Cato's point of view, the deferred revenue is a liability because Cato is obligated to perform services in the future. The liability is called **unearned revenue.** The cash receipt is an ***asset source transaction.*** The asset account Cash and the liability account Unearned Revenue both increase. Collecting the cash has no effect on the income statement. The revenue will be reported on the income statement after Cato performs the services. The statement of cash flows reflects a cash inflow from operating activities. The effects of this transaction on the financial statements are shown here.

Assets =	Liab.	+ Stk. Equity					
Cash =	Unearn. Rev.			Rev.	− Exp.	= Net Inc.	Cash Flow
18,000 =	18,000	+	NA	NA	− NA	= NA	18,000 OA

Accounting for Supplies Purchase

EVENT 4   Cato purchased $800 of supplies on account.

The purchase of supplies on account is an ***asset source transaction.*** The asset account Supplies and the liability account Accounts Payable increase. The income statement is unaffected. Expense recognition is deferred until the supplies are used. The statement of cash flows is not affected. The effects of this transaction on the financial statements are shown here.

Assets =	Liab.	+ Stk. Equity					
Supplies =	Accts. Pay.			Rev.	− Exp.	= Net Inc.	Cash Flow
800 =	800	+	NA	NA	− NA	= NA	NA

Other 2013 Events

EVENT 5   Cato provided $96,400 of consulting services on account.

Providing services on account is an ***asset source transaction.*** The asset account Accounts Receivable and the stockholders' equity account Retained Earnings increase.

Revenue and net income increase. The statement of cash flows is not affected. The effects of this transaction on the financial statements are shown here.

Assets	=	Liab.	+	Stk. Equity						
Accts. Rec.	=			Ret. Earn.	Rev.	−	Exp.	=	Net Inc.	Cash Flow
96,400	=	NA	+	96,400	96,400	−	NA	=	96,400	NA

EVENT 6   Cato collected $105,000 cash from customers as partial settlement of accounts receivable.

Collecting money from customers who are paying accounts receivable is an *asset exchange transaction.* One asset account (Cash) increases and another asset account (Accounts Receivable) decreases. The amount of total assets is unchanged. The income statement is not affected. The statement of cash flows reports a cash inflow from operating activities. The effects of this transaction on the financial statements are shown here.

Assets			=	Liab.	+	Stk. Equity						
Cash	+	Accts. Rec.					Rev.	−	Exp.	=	Net Inc.	Cash Flow
105,000	+	(105,000)	=	NA	+	NA	NA	−	NA	=	NA	105,000 OA

EVENT 7   Cato paid $32,000 cash for salary expense.

Cash payments for salary expense are *asset use transactions.* Both the asset account Cash and the equity account Retained Earnings decrease by $32,000. Recognizing the expense decreases net income on the income statement. The statement of cash flows reflects a cash outflow from operating activities. The effects of this transaction on the financial statements are shown here.

Assets	=	Liab.	+	Stk. Equity						
Cash	=			Ret. Earn.	Rev.	−	Exp.	=	Net Inc.	Cash Flow
(32,000)	=	NA	+	(32,000)	NA	−	32,000	=	(32,000)	(32,000) OA

EVENT 8   Cato incurred $21,000 of other operating expenses on account.

Recognizing expenses incurred on account are *claims exchange transactions.* One claims account (Accounts Payable) increases and another claims account (Retained Earnings) decreases. The amount of total claims is not affected. Recognizing the expenses decreases net income. The statement of cash flows is not affected. The effects of this transaction on the financial statements are shown here.

Assets	=	Liab.	+	Stk. Equity						
		Accts. Pay.	+	Ret. Earn.	Rev.	−	Exp.	=	Net Inc.	Cash Flow
NA	=	21,000	+	(21,000)	NA	−	21,000	=	(21,000)	NA

EVENT 9   Cato paid $18,200 in partial settlement of accounts payable.

Paying accounts payable is an *asset use transaction.* The asset account Cash and the liability account Accounts Payable decrease. The statement of cash flows reports a cash outflow for operating activities. The income statement is not affected. The effects of this transaction on the financial statements are shown here.

Assets	=	Liab.	+	Stk. Equity		Rev.	−	Exp.	=	Net Inc.	Cash Flow
Cash	=	Accts. Pay.				Rev.	−	Exp.	=	Net Inc.	Cash Flow
(18,200)	=	(18,200)	+	NA		NA	−	NA	=	NA	(18,200) OA

EVENT 10   Cato paid $79,500 to purchase land it planned to use in the future as a building site for its home office.

Purchasing land with cash is an *asset exchange transaction.* One asset account, Cash, decreases and another asset account, Land, increases. The amount of total assets is unchanged. The income statement is not affected. The statement of cash flows reports a cash outflow for investing activities. The effects of this transaction on the financial statements are shown here.

Assets			=	Liab.	+	Stk. Equity		Rev.	−	Exp.	=	Net Inc.	Cash Flow
Cash	+	Land						Rev.	−	Exp.	=	Net Inc.	Cash Flow
(79,500)	+	79,500	=	NA	+	NA		NA	−	NA	=	NA	(79,500) IA

EVENT 11   Cato paid $21,000 in cash dividends to its stockholders.

Cash payments for dividends are *asset use transactions.* Both the asset account Cash and the equity account Retained Earnings decrease. Recall that dividends are wealth transfers from the business to the stockholders, not expenses. They are not incurred in the process of generating revenue. They do not affect the income statement. The statement of cash flows reflects a cash outflow from financing activities. The effects of this transaction on the financial statements are shown here.

Assets	=	Liab.	+	Stk. Equity		Rev.	−	Exp.	=	Net Inc.	Cash Flow
Cash	=			Ret. Earn.		Rev.	−	Exp.	=	Net Inc.	Cash Flow
(21,000)	=	NA	+	(21,000)		NA	−	NA	=	NA	(21,000) FA

EVENT 12   Cato acquired $2,000 cash from issuing additional shares of common stock.

Issuing common stock is an *asset source transaction.* The asset account Cash and the stockholders' equity account Common Stock increase. The income statement is unaffected. The statement of cash flows reports a cash inflow from financing activities. The effects of this transaction on the financial statements are shown here.

Assets	=	Liab.	+	Stk. Equity		Rev.	−	Exp.	=	Net Inc.	Cash Flow
Cash	=			Com. Stk.		Rev.	−	Exp.	=	Net Inc.	Cash Flow
2,000	=	NA	+	2,000		NA	−	NA	=	NA	2,000 FA

Adjusting Entries

Recall that companies make adjusting entries at the end of an accounting period to update the account balances before preparing the financial statements. Adjusting entries ensure that companies report revenues and expenses in the appropriate accounting period; adjusting entries never affect the Cash account.

Accounting for Supplies (Adjusting Entry)

EVENT 13   After determining through a physical count that it had $150 of unused supplies on hand as of December 31, Cato recognized supplies expense.

Companies would find the cost of recording supplies expense each time a pencil, piece of paper, envelope, or other supply item is used to far outweigh the benefit derived from such tedious recordkeeping. Instead, accountants transfer to expense the total cost of all supplies used during the entire accounting period in a single year-end adjusting entry. The cost of supplies used is determined as follows.

Beginning supplies balance + Supplies purchased = Supplies available for use

Supplies available for use − Ending supplies balance = Supplies used

Companies determine the ending supplies balance by physically counting the supplies on hand at the end of the period. Cato used $650 of supplies during the year (zero beginning balance + $800 supplies purchase = $800 available for use; $800 available for use − $150 ending balance = $650). Recognizing Cato's supplies expense is an *asset use transaction.* The asset account Supplies and the stockholders' equity account Retained Earnings decrease. Recognizing supplies expense reduces net income. The statement of cash flows is not affected. The effects of this transaction on the financial statements are shown here.

Assets	=	Liab.	+	Stk. Equity					
Supplies	=			Ret. Earn.	Rev.	−	Exp.	=	Net Inc.	Cash Flow
(650)	=	NA	+	(650)	NA	−	650	=	(650)	NA

Accounting for Prepaid Rent (Adjusting Entry)

EVENT 14   Cato recognized rent expense for the office space used during the accounting period.

Recall that Cato paid $12,000 on March 1, 2013, to rent office space for one year (see Event 2). The portion of the lease cost that represents using office space from March 1 through December 31 is computed as follows.

$12,000 Cost of annual lease ÷ 12 Months = $1,000 Cost per month

$1,000 Cost per month × 10 Months used = $10,000 Rent expense

Recognizing the rent expense decreases the asset account Prepaid Rent and the stockholders' equity account Retained Earnings. Recognizing rent expense reduces net income. The statement of cash flows is not affected. The cash flow effect was recorded in the March 1 event. These effects on the financial statements follow.

Assets	=	Liab.	+	Stk. Equity					
Prep. Rent	=			Ret. Earn.	Rev.	−	Exp.	=	Net Inc.	Cash Flow
(10,000)	=	NA	+	(10,000)	NA	−	10,000	=	(10,000)	NA

✓ CHECK YOURSELF 2.2

Rujoub Inc. paid $18,000 cash for one year of insurance coverage that began on November 1, 2012. Based on this information alone, determine the cash flow from operating activities that Rujoub would report on the 2012 and 2013 statements of cash flows. Also, determine the amount of insurance expense Rujoub would report on the 2012 income statement and the amount of prepaid insurance (an asset) that Rujoub would report on the December 31, 2012, balance sheet.

Answer Since Rujoub paid all of the cash in 2012, the 2012 statement of cash flows would report an $18,000 cash outflow from operating activities. The 2013 statement of cash flows would report zero cash flow from operating activities. The expense would be recognized in the periods in which the insurance is used. In this case, insurance expense is recognized at the rate of $1,500 per month ($18,000 ÷ 12 months). Rujoub used two months of insurance coverage in 2012 and therefore would report $3,000 (2 months × $1,500) of insurance expense on the 2012 income statement. Rujoub would report a $15,000 (10 months × $1,500) asset, prepaid insurance, on the December 31, 2012, balance sheet. The $15,000 of prepaid insurance would be recognized as insurance expese in 2013 when the insurance coverage is used.

Accounting for Unearned Revenue (Adjusting Entry)

EVENT 15 **Cato recognized the portion of the unearned revenue it earned during the accounting period.**

Recall that Cato received an $18,000 cash advance from Westberry Company to provide consulting services from June 1, 2013, to May 31, 2014 (see Event 3). By December 31, Cato had earned 7 months (June 1 through December 31) of the revenue related to this contract. Rather than recording the revenue continuously as it performed the consulting services, Cato can simply recognize the amount earned in a single adjustment to the accounting records at the end of the accounting period. The amount of the adjustment is computed as follows.

$$\$18,000 \div 12 \text{ months} = \$1,500 \text{ revenue earned per month}$$

$$\$1,500 \times 7 \text{ months} = \$10,500 \text{ revenue to be recognized in 2013}$$

The adjusting entry moves $10,500 from the Unearned Revenue account to the Consulting Revenue account. This entry is a *claims exchange transaction.* The liability account Unearned Revenue decreases and the equity account Retained Earnings increases. The effects of this transaction on the financial statements are shown here.

Assets	=	Liab.	+	Stk. Equity						
		Unearn. Rev.	+	Ret. Earn.	Rev.	−	Exp.	=	Net Inc.	Cash Flow
NA	=	(10,500)	+	10,500	10,500	−	NA	=	10,500	NA

Recall that revenue was previously defined as an economic benefit a company obtains by providing customers with goods and services. In this case the economic benefit is a decrease in the liability account Unearned Revenue. **Revenue** can therefore be more precisely defined as *an increase in assets or a decrease in liabilities that a company obtains by providing customers with goods or services.*

✓ CHECK YOURSELF 2.3

Sanderson & Associates received a $24,000 cash advance as a retainer to provide legal services to a client. The contract called for Sanderson to render services during a one-year period beginning October 1, 2012. Based on this information alone, determine the cash flow from operating activities Sanderson would report on the 2012 and 2013 statements of cash flows. Also determine the amount of revenue Sanderson would report on the 2012 and 2013 income statements.

Answer   Since Sanderson collected all of the cash in 2012, the 2012 statement of cash flows would report a $24,000 cash inflow from operating activities. The 2013 statement of cash flows would report zero cash flow from operating activities. Revenue is recognized in the period in which it is earned. In this case revenue is earned at the rate of $2,000 per month ($24,000 ÷ 12 months = $2,000 per month). Sanderson rendered services for three months in 2012 and nine months in 2013. Sanderson would report $6,000 (3 months × $2,000) of revenue on the 2012 income statement and $18,000 (9 months × $2,000) of revenue on the 2013 income statement.

Answers to The Curious Accountant

Because the Meredith Corporation receives cash from customers before actually providing any magazines to them, the company has not earned any revenue when it receives the cash. Thus, Meredith has a liability called *unearned revenue.* If it closed its books on December 31, then $3 of Arno's subscription would be recognized as revenue in 2012. The remaining $9 would appear on the balance sheet as a liability.

Meredith Corporation actually ends its accounting year on June 30 each year. A copy of the 2009 balance sheet for the company is presented in Exhibit 2.6. The liability for unearned subscription revenue was $319.1 ($170.7 + $148.4) million—which represented about 30.1 percent of Meredith's total liabilities!

Will Meredith need cash to pay these subscription liabilities? Not exactly. The liabilities will not be paid directly with cash. Instead, they will be satisfied by providing magazines to the subscribers. However, Meredith will need cash to pay for producing and distributing the magazines supplied to the customers. Even so, the amount of cash required to provide magazines will probably differ significantly from the amount of unearned revenues. In most cases, subscription fees do not cover the cost of producing and distributing magazines. By collecting significant amounts of advertising revenue, publishers can provide magazines to customers at prices well below the cost of publication. The amount of unearned revenue is not likely to coincide with the amount of cash needed to cover the cost of satisfying the company's obligation to produce and distribute magazines. Even though the association between unearned revenues and the cost of providing magazines to customers is not direct, a knowledgeable financial analyst can use the information to make estimates of future cash flows and revenue recognition.

| **EXHIBIT 2.6** | Balance Sheet for Meredith Corporation |

CONSOLIDATED BALANCE SHEETS
Meredith Corporation and Subsidiaries
As of June 30 (amounts in thousands)

	2009	2008
Assets		
Current assets		
Cash and cash equivalents	$ 27,910	$ 37,644
Accounts receivable		
(net of allowances of $13,810 in 2009 and $23,944 in 2008)	192,367	230,978
Inventories	28,151	44,085
Current portion of subscription acquisition costs	60,017	59,939
Current portion of broadcast rights	8,297	10,779
Deferred income taxes	—	2,118
Other current assets	23,398	17,547
Total current assets	340,140	403,090
Property, plant, and equipment		
Land	19,500	20,027
Buildings and improvements	125,779	122,977
Machinery and equipment	276,376	273,633
Leasehold improvements	14,208	12,840
Construction in progress	9,041	17,458
Total property, plant, and equipment	444,904	446,935
Less accumulated depreciation	(253,597)	(247,147)
Net property, plant, and equipment	191,307	199,788
Subscription acquisition costs	63,444	60,958
Broadcast rights	4,545	7,826
Other assets	45,907	74,472
Intangible assets, net	561,581	781,154
Goodwill	462,379	532,332
Total assets	$1,669,303	$2,059,620
Liabilities and Shareholders' Equity		
Current liabilities		
Current portion of long-term debt	$ —	$ 75,000
Current portion of long-term broadcast rights payable	10,560	11,141
Accounts payable	86,381	79,028
Accrued expenses		
Compensation and benefits	42,667	40,894
Distribution expenses	12,224	13,890
Other taxes and expenses	26,653	47,923
Total accrued expenses	81,544	102,707
Current portion of unearned subscription revenues	170,731	175,261
Total current liabilities	349,216	443,137
Long-term debt	380,000	410,000
Long-term broadcast rights payable	11,851	17,186
Unearned subscription revenues	148,393	157,872
Deferred income taxes	64,322	139,598
Other noncurrent liabilities	106,138	103,972
Total liabilities	1,059,920	1,271,765
Shareholders' equity		
Series preferred stock, par value $1 per share	—	—
Common stock, par value $1 per share	35,934	36,295
Class B stock, par value $1 per share, convertible to common stock	9,133	9,181
Additional paid-in capital	53,938	52,693
Retained earnings	542,006	701,205
Accumulated other comprehensive income (loss)	(31,628)	(11,519)
Total shareholders' equity	609,383	787,855
Total liabilities and shareholder' equity	$1,669,303	$2,059,620

Accounting for Accrued Salary Expense (Adjusting Entry)

EVENT 16   Cato recognized $4,000 of accrued salary expense.

The adjusting entry to recognize the accrued salary expense is a ***claims exchange transaction.*** One claims account, Retained Earnings, decreases and another claims account, Salaries Payable, increases. The expense recognition reduces net income. The statement of cash flows is not affected. The effects of this transaction on the financial statements are shown here.

Assets	=	Liab.	+	Stk. Equity						
		Sal. Pay.	+	Ret. Earn.	Rev.	−	Exp.	=	Net Inc.	Cash Flow
NA	=	4,000	+	(4,000)	NA	−	4,000	=	(4,000)	NA

Summary of Events and General Ledger

The previous section of this chapter described sixteen events Cato Consultants experienced the during the 2013 accounting period. These events are summarized in Exhibit 2.7 on page 63. The associated general ledger accounts are also shown in the exhibit. The account balances at the end of 2012; shown in Exhibit 2.3, become the beginning balances for the 2013 accounting period. The 2013 transaction data are referenced to the accounting events with numbers in parentheses. The information in the ledger accounts is the basis for the financial statements in Exhibit 2.8 on pages 64 and 65. Before reading further, trace each event in the summary of events into Exhibit 2.7.

Vertical Statements Model

Financial statement users obtain helpful insights by analyzing company trends over multiple accounting cycles. Exhibit 2.8 presents for Cato Consultants a multicycle **vertical statements model** of 2012 and 2013 accounting data. To conserve space, we have combined all the expenses for each year into single amounts labeled "Operating Expenses," determined as follows.

	2012	2013
Other operating expenses	$ 0	$21,000
Salary expense	16,000	36,000
Rent expense	0	10,000
Advertising expense	2,000	0
Supplies expense	0	650
Total operating expenses	$18,000	$67,650

Similarly, we combined the cash payments for operating expenses on the statement of cash flows as follows.

	2012	2013
Supplies and other operating expenses	$ 0	$18,200*
Salary expense	10,000	38,000
Rent expense	0	12,000
Advertising expense	2,000	0
Total cash payments for operating expenses	$12,000	$68,200

*Amount paid in partial settlement of accounts payable

EXHIBIT 2.7

Ledger Accounts with 2013 Trnsaction Data

1. Cato paid $6,000 to the instructor to settle the salaries payable obligation.
2. On March 1, Cato paid $12,000 cash to lease office space for one year.
3. Cato received $18,000 cash in advance from Westberry Company for consulting services to be performed for one year beginning June 1.
4. Cato purchased $800 of supplies on account.
5. Cato provided $96,400 of consulting services on account.
6. Cato collected $105,000 cash from customers as partial settlement of accounts receivable.
7. Cato paid $32,000 cash for salary expense.
8. Cato incurred $21,000 of other operating expenses on account.
9. Cato paid $18,200 in partial settlement of accounts payable.
10. Cato paid $79,500 to purchase land it planned to use in the future as a building site for its home office.
11. Cato paid $21,000 in cash dividends to its stockholders.
12. Cato acquired $2,000 cash from issuing additional shares of common stock.

The year-end adjustments are:

13. After determining through a physical count that it had $150 of unused supplies on hand as of December 31, Cato recognized supplies expense.
14. Cato recognized rent expense for the office space used during the accounting period.
15. Cato recognized the portion of the unearned revenue it earned during the accounting period.
16. Cato recognized $4,000 of accrued salary expense.

Assets		=	Liabilities	+	Stockholders' Equity

Cash

Bal.	53,000
(1)	(6,000)
(2)	(12,000)
(3)	18,000
(6)	105,000
(7)	(32,000)
(9)	(18,200)
(10)	(79,500)
(11)	(21,000)
(12)	2,000
Bal.	9,300

Accounts Receivable

Bal.	24,000
(5)	96,400
(6)	(105,000)
Bal.	15,400

Supplies

Bal.	0
(4)	800
(13)	(650)
Bal.	150

Prepaid Rent

Bal.	0
(2)	12,000
(14)	(10,000)
Bal.	2,000

Land

Bal.	0
(10)	79,500
Bal.	79,500

Accounts Payable

Bal.	0
(4)	800
(8)	21,000
(9)	(18,200)
Bal.	3,600

Unearned Revenue

Bal.	0
(3)	18,000
(15)	(10,500)
Bal.	7,500

Salaries Payable

Bal.	6,000
(1)	(6,000)
(16)	4,000
Bal.	4,000

Common Stock

Bal.	5,000
(12)	2,000
Bal.	7,000

Retained Earnings

Bal.	66,000

Dividends

Bal.	0
(11)	(21,000)
Bal.	(21,000)

Consulting Revenue

Bal.	0
(5)	96,400
(15)	10,500
Bal.	106,900

Other Operating Expenses

Bal.	0
(8)	(21,000)
Bal.	(21,000)

Salary Expense

Bal.	0
(7)	(32,000)
(16)	(4,000)
Bal.	(36,000)

Rent Expense

Bal.	0
(14)	(10,000)
Bal.	(10,000)

Supplies Expense

Bal.	0
(13)	(650)
Bal.	(650)

| **EXHIBIT 2.8** | Vertical Statements Model |

CATO CONSULTANTS
Financial Statements
Income Statements
For the Years Ended December 31

	2012	2013
Consulting revenue	$84,000	$106,900
Operating expenses	(18,000)	(67,650)
Net income	$66,000	$ 39,250

Statements of Changes in Stockholders' Equity
For the Years Ended December 31

	2012	2013
Beginning common stock	$ 0	$ 5,000
Plus: Common stock issued	5,000	2,000
Ending common stock	5,000	7,000
Beginning retained earnings	0	66,000
Plus: Net income	66,000	39,250
Less: Dividends	0	(21,000)
Ending retained earnings	66,000	84,250
Total stockholders' equity	$71,000	$ 91,250

Balance Sheets
As of December 31

	2012	2013
Assets		
Cash	$53,000	$ 9,300
Accounts receivable	24,000	15,400
Supplies	0	150
Prepaid rent	0	2,000
Land	0	79,500
Total assets	$77,000	$106,350
Liabilities		
Accounts payable	$ 0	$ 3,600
Unearned revenue	0	7,500
Salaries payable	6,000	4,000
Total liabilities	6,000	15,100
Stockholders' equity		
Common stock	5,000	7,000
Retained earnings	66,000	84,250
Total stockholders' equity	71,000	91,250
Total liabilities and stockholders' equity	$77,000	$106,350

continued

EXHIBIT 2.8	*Concluded*

Statements of Cash Flows
For the Years Ended December 31

	2012	2013
Cash Flows from Operating Activities		
Cash receipts from customers	$60,000	$123,000
Cash payments for operating expenses	(12,000)	(68,200)
Net cash flow from operating activities	48,000	54,800
Cash Flows from Investing Activities		
Cash payment to purchase land	0	(79,500)
Cash Flows from Financing Activities		
Cash receipts from issuing common stock	5,000	2,000
Cash payments for dividends	0	(21,000)
Net cash flow from financing activities	5,000	(19,000)
Net change in cash	53,000	(43,700)
Plus: Beginning cash balance	0	53,000
Ending cash balance	$53,000	$ 9,300

Recall that the level of detail reported in financial statements depends on user information needs. Most real-world companies combine many account balances together to report highly summarized totals under each financial statement caption. Before reading further, trace the remaining financial statement items from the ledger accounts in Exhibit 2.7 to where they are reported in Exhibit 2.8.

The vertical statements model in Exhibit 2.8 shows significant interrelationships among the financial statements. For each year, trace the amount of net income from the income statement to the statement of changes in stockholders' equity. Next, trace the ending balances of common stock and retained earnings reported on the statement of changes in stockholders' equity to the stockholders' equity section of the balance sheet. Also, confirm that the amount of cash reported on the balance sheet equals the ending cash balance on the statement of cash flows.

Other relationships connect the two accounting periods. For example, trace the ending retained earnings balance from the 2012 statement of stockholders' equity to the beginning retained earnings balance on the 2013 statement of stockholders' equity. Also, trace the ending cash balance on the 2012 statement of cash flows to the beginning cash balance on the 2013 statement of cash flows. Finally, confirm that the change in cash between the 2012 and 2013 balance sheets ($53,000 − $9,300 = $43,700 decrease) agrees with the net change in cash reported on the 2013 statement of cash flows.

✓ CHECK YOURSELF 2.4

Treadmore Company started the 2012 accounting period with $580 of supplies on hand. During 2012 the company paid cash to purchase $2,200 of supplies. A physical count of supplies indicated that there was $420 of supplies on hand at the end of 2012. Treadmore pays cash for supplies at the time they are purchased. Based on this information alone, determine the amount of supplies expense to be recognized on the income statement and the amount of cash flow to be shown in the operating activities section of the statement of cash flows.

> **Answer**   The amount of supplies expense recognized on the income statement is the amount of supplies that were used during the accounting period. This amount is computed below.
>
> **$580 Beginning balance + $2,200 Supplies purchases = $2,780 Supplies available for use**
>
> **$2,780 Supplies available for use − $420 Ending supplies balance = $2,360 supplies used**
>
> The cash flow from operating activities is the amount of cash paid for supplies during the accounting period. In this case, Treadmore paid $2,200 cash to purchase supplies. This amount would be shown as a cash outflow.

TRANSACTION CLASSIFICATION

Classify accounting events into one of four categories:

a. asset source transactions.
b. asset use transactions.
c. asset exchange transactions.
d. claims exchange transactions.

Chapters 1 and 2 introduced four types of transactions. Although businesses engage in an infinite number of different transactions, all transactions fall into one of four types. By learning to identify transactions by type, you can understand how unfamiliar events affect financial statements. The four types of transactions are

1. *Asset source transactions:* An asset account increases, and a corresponding claims account increases.

2. *Asset use transactions:* An asset account decreases, and a corresponding claims account decreases.

3. *Asset exchange transactions:* One asset account increases, and another asset account decreases.

4. *Claims exchange transactions:* One claims account increases, and another claims account decreases.

Also, the definitions of revenue and expense have been expanded. The complete definitions of these two elements are as follows.

1. **Revenue:** Revenue is the *economic benefit* derived from operating the business. Its recognition is accompanied by an increase in assets or a decrease in liabilities resulting from providing products or services to customers.

2. **Expense:** An expense is an *economic sacrifice* incurred in the process of generating revenue. Its recognition is accompanied by a decrease in assets or an increase in liabilities resulting from consuming assets and services in an effort to produce revenue.

<< A Look Back

This chapter introduced accrual accounting. Accrual accounting distinguishes between *recognition* and *realization.* Recognition means reporting an economic item or event in the financial statements. In contrast, realization refers to collecting cash from the sale of assets or services. Recognition and realization can occur in different accounting periods. In addition, cash payments for expenses often occur in different accounting periods from when a company recognizes the expenses. Accrual accounting uses both *accruals* and *deferrals.*

■ The term *accrual* applies to a revenue or an expense event that are recognized before cash is exchanged. Recognizing revenue on account or accrued salaries expense are examples of accruals.

■ The term *deferral* applies to a revenue or an expense event that are recognized after cash has been exchanged. Supplies, prepaid items, and unearned revenue are examples of deferrals.

Virtually all major companies operating in the United States use accrual accounting.

A Look Forward

Chapters 1 and 2 focused on businesses that generate revenue by providing services to their customers. Examples of these types of businesses include consulting, real estate sales, medical services, and legal services. The next chapter introduces accounting practices for businesses that generate revenue by selling goods. Examples of these companies include Wal-Mart, Circuit City, Office Depot, and Lowes.

A step-by-step audio-narrated series of slides is provided on the text website at www.mhhe.com/edmondssurvey3e

SELF-STUDY REVIEW PROBLEM

Gifford Company experienced the following accounting events during 2012.

1. Started operations on January 1 when it acquired $20,000 cash by issuing common stock.
2. Earned $18,000 of revenue on account.
3. On March 1 collected $36,000 cash as an advance for services to be performed in the future.
4. Paid cash operating expenses of $17,000.
5. Paid a $2,700 cash dividend to stockholders.
6. On December 31, 2012, adjusted the books to recognize the revenue earned by providing services related to the advance described in Event 3. The contract required Gifford to provide services for a one-year period starting March 1.
7. Collected $15,000 cash from accounts receivable.

Gifford Company experienced the following accounting events during 2013.

1. Earned $38,000 of cash revenue.
2. On April 1 paid $12,000 cash for an insurance policy that provides coverage for one year beginning immediately.
3. Collected $2,000 cash from accounts receivable.
4. Paid cash operating expenses of $21,000.
5. Paid a $5,000 cash dividend to stockholders.
6. On December 31, 2013, adjusted the books to recognize the remaining revenue earned by providing services related to the advance described in Event 3 of 2012.
7. On December 31, 2013, Gifford adjusted the books to recognize the amount of the insurance policy used during 2013.

Required

a. Record the events in a financial statements model like the following one. The first event is recorded as an example.

Event No.	Assets			=	Liab.	+	Stockholders' Equity							Cash Flow
	Cash +	Accts. Rec. −	Prep. Ins. =		Unearn. Rev. +		Com. Stk. +	Ret. Earn.		Rev. −	Exp. =	Net Inc.		
1	20,000 +	NA −	NA =		NA +		20,000 +	NA		NA −	NA =	NA		20,000 FA

b. What amount of revenue would Gifford report on the 2012 income statement?
c. What amount of cash flow from customers would Gifford report on the 2012 statement of cash flows?
d. What amount of unearned revenue would Gifford report on the 2012 and 2013 year-end balance sheets?
e. What are the 2013 opening balances for the revenue and expense accounts?

f. What amount of total assets would Gifford report on the December 31, 2012, balance sheet?

g. What claims on assets would Gifford report on the December 31, 2013, balance sheet?

Solution to Requirement a

The financial statements model follows.

Event No.	Cash	+	Accts. Rec.	+	Prep. Ins.	=	Unearn. Rev.	+	Com. Stk.	+	Ret. Earn.		Rev.	−	Exp.	=	Net Inc.		Cash Flow	
										Assets = Liab. + Stockholders' Equity										
2012																				
1	20,000	+	NA	+	NA	=	NA	+	20,000	+	NA		NA	−	NA	=	NA		20,000	FA
2	NA	+	18,000	+	NA	=	NA	+	NA	+	18,000		18,000	−	NA	=	18,000		NA	
3	36,000	+	NA	+	NA	=	36,000	+	NA	+	NA		NA	−	NA	=	NA		36,000	OA
4	(17,000)	+	NA	+	NA	=	NA	+	NA	+	(17,000)		NA	−	17,000	=	(17,000)		(17,000)	OA
5	(2,700)	+	NA	+	NA	=	NA	+	NA	+	(2,700)		NA	−	NA	=	NA		(2,700)	FA
6*	NA	+	NA	+	NA	=	(30,000)	+	NA	+	30,000		30,000	−	NA	=	30,000		NA	
7	15,000	+	(15,000)	+	NA	=	NA	+	NA	+	NA		NA	−	NA	=	NA		15,000	OA
Bal.	51,300	+	3,000	+	NA	=	6,000	+	20,000	+	28,300		48,000	−	17,000	=	31,000		51,300	NC
	Asset, liability, and equity account balances carry forward												Rev. & exp. accts. are closed							
2013																				
Bal.	51,300	+	3,000	+	NA	=	6,000	+	20,000	+	28,300		NA	−	NA	=	NA		NA	
1	38,000	+	NA	+	NA	=	NA	+	NA	+	38,000		38,000	−	NA	=	38,000		38,000	OA
2	(12,000)	+	NA	+	12,000	=	NA	+	NA	+	NA		NA	−	NA	=	NA		(12,000)	OA
3	2,000	+	(2,000)	+	NA	=	NA	+	NA	+	NA		NA	−	NA	=	NA		2,000	OA
4	(21,000)	+	NA	+	NA	=	NA	+	NA	+	(21,000)		NA	−	21,000	=	(21,000)		(21,000)	OA
5	(5,000)	+	NA	+	NA	=	NA	+	NA	+	(5,000)		NA	−	NA	=	NA		(5,000)	FA
6*	NA	+	NA	+	NA	=	(6,000)	+	NA	+	6,000		6,000	−	NA	=	6,000		NA	
7†	NA	+	NA	+	(9,000)	=	NA	+	NA	+	(9,000)		NA	−	9,000	=	(9,000)		NA	
Bal.	53,300	+	1,000	+	3,000	=	0	+	20,000	+	37,300		44,000	−	30,000	=	14,000		2,000	NC

*Revenue is earned at the rate of $3,000 ($36,000 ÷ 12 months) per month. Revenue recognized in 2012 is $30,000 ($3,000 × 10 months). Revenue recognized in 2013 is $6,000 ($3,000 × 2 months).

†Insurance expense is incurred at the rate of $1,000 ($12,000 ÷ 12 months) per month. Insurance expense recognized in 2013 is $9,000 ($1,000 × 9 months).

Solutions to Requirements b–g

b. Gifford would report $48,000 of revenue in 2012 ($18,000 revenue on account plus $30,000 of the $36,000 of unearned revenue).

c. The cash inflow from customers is $51,000 ($36,000 when the unearned revenue was received plus $15,000 collection of accounts receivable).

d. The December 31, 2012, balance sheet will report $6,000 of unearned revenue, which is the amount of the cash advance less the amount of revenue recognized in 2012 ($36,000 − $30,000). The December 31, 2013, unearned revenue balance is zero.

e. Since revenue and expense accounts are closed at the end of each accounting period, the beginning balances in these accounts are always zero.

f. Assets on the December 31, 2012, balance sheet are $54,300 [Gifford's cash at year end plus the balance in accounts receivable ($51,300 + $3,000)].

g. Since all unearned revenue would be recognized before the financial statements were prepared at the end of 2013, there would be no liabilities on the 2013 balance sheet. Common stock and retained earnings would be the only claims as of December 31, 2013, for a claims total of $57,300 ($20,000 + $37,300).

KEY TERMS

Accounts Receivable 46	Accrued expenses 48	Asset source
Accrual 45	Adjusting entry 48	transaction 46
Accrual accounting 45	Asset exchange transaction 46	Asset use transaction 47

QUESTIONS

1. What does accrual accounting attempt to accomplish?

2. Define *recognition*. How is it independent of collecting or paying cash?

3. What does the term *deferral* mean?

4. If cash is collected in advance of performing services, when is the associated revenue recognized?

5. What does the term *asset source transaction* mean?

6. What effect does the issue of common stock have on the accounting equation?

7. How does the recognition of revenue on account (accounts receivable) affect the income statement compared to its effect on the statement of cash flows?

8. Give an example of an asset source transaction. What is the effect of this transaction on the accounting equation?

9. When is revenue recognized under accrual accounting?

10. Give an example of an asset exchange transaction. What is the effect of this transaction on the accounting equation?

11. What is the effect on the claims side of the accounting equation when cash is collected in advance of performing services?

12. What does the term *unearned revenue* mean?

13. What effect does expense recognition have on the accounting equation?

14. What does the term *claims exchange transaction* mean?

15. What type of transaction is a cash payment to creditors? How does this type of transaction affect the accounting equation?

16. When are expenses recognized under accrual accounting?

17. Why may net cash flow from operating activities on the cash flow statement be different from the amount of net income reported on the income statement?

18. What is the relationship between the income statement and changes in assets and liabilities?

19. How does net income affect the stockholders' claims on the business's assets?

20. What is the difference between a cost and an expense?

21. When does a cost become an expense? Do all costs become expenses?

22. How and when is the cost of the *supplies used* recognized in an accounting period?

23. What does the term *expense* mean?

24. What does the term *revenue* mean?

25. What is the purpose of the statement of changes in stockholders' equity?

26. What is the main purpose of the balance sheet?

27. Why is the balance sheet dated *as of* a specific date when the income statement, statement of changes in stockholders' equity, and statement of cash flows are dated with the phrase *for the period ended?*

28. In what order are assets listed on the balance sheet?

29. What does the statement of cash flows explain?

30. What does the term *adjusting entry* mean? Give an example.

31. What types of accounts are closed at the end of the accounting period? Why is it necessary to close these accounts?

32. Give several examples of period costs.

33. Give an example of a cost that can be directly matched with the revenue produced by an accounting firm from preparing a tax return.

34. List and describe the four stages of the accounting cycle discussed in Chapter 2.

MULTIPLE-CHOICE QUESTIONS

Multiple-choice questions are provided on the text website at www.mhhe.com/edmondssurvey3e.

EXERCISES

All applicable Exercises are available with McGraw-Hill's
Connect Accounting.

Where applicable in all exercises, round computations to the nearest dollar.

LO 2, 3

Exercise 2-1   *Effect of accruals on the financial statements*

Valmont, Inc., experienced the following events in 2012, in its first year of operation.

1. Received $20,000 cash from the issue of common stock.
2. Performed services on account for $50,000.
3. Paid the utility expense of $12,500.
4. Collected $39,000 of the accounts receivable.
5. Recorded $9,000 of accrued salaries at the end of the year.
6. Paid a $5,000 cash dividend to the shareholders.

Required

a. Record the events in general ledger accounts under an accounting equation. In the last column of the table, provide appropriate account titles for the Retained Earnings amounts. The first transaction has been recorded as an example.

VALMONT, INC.							
General Ledger Accounts							
Event	Assets		=	Liabilities	+	Stockholders' Equity	Acct. Titles for RE
	Cash	Accounts Receivable		Salaries Payable		Common Stock	Retained Earnings	
1.	20,000					20,000		

b. Prepare the income statement, statement of changes in stockholders' equity, balance sheet, and statement of cash flows for the 2012 accounting period.
c. Why is the amount of net income different from the amount of net cash flow from operating activities?

LO 2, 3

Exercise 2-2   *Effect of collecting accounts receivable on the accounting equation and financial statements*

Schroder Company earned $14,000 of service revenue on account during 2012. The company collected $11,500 cash from accounts receivable during 2012.

Required

Based on this information alone, determine the following. (*Hint:* Record the events in general ledger accounts under an accounting equation before satisfying the requirements.)

a. The balance of the accounts receivable that Schroder would report on the December 31, 2012, balance sheet.
b. The amount of net income that Schroder would report on the 2012 income statement.
c. The amount of net cash flow from operating activities that Schroder would report on the 2012 statement of cash flows.
d. The amount of retained earnings that Schroder would report on the 2012 balance sheet.
e. Why are the answers to Requirements *b* and *c* different?

LO 2, 3

Exercise 2-3   *Effect of prepaid rent on the accounting equation and financial statements*

The following events apply to 2012, the first year of operations of Sentry Services.

1. Acquired $45,000 cash from the issue of common stock.
2. Paid $18,000 cash in advance for one-year rental contract for office space.

3. Provided services for $36,000 cash.
4. Adjusted the records to recognize the use of the office space. The one-year contract started on May 1, 2012. The adjustment was made as of December 31, 2012.

Required

a. Write an accounting equation and record the effects of each accounting event under the appropriate general ledger account headings.
b. Prepare an income statement and statement of cash flows for the 2012 accounting period.
c. Explain the difference between the amount of net income and amount of net cash flow from operating activities.

Exercise 2-4   *Effect of supplies on the financial statements*

LO 1, 3

Green Copy Service, Inc., started the 2012 accounting period with $16,000 cash, $10,000 of common stock, and $6,000 of retained earnings. Green Copy Service was affected by the following accounting events during 2012.

1. Purchased $9,600 of paper and other supplies on account.
2. Earned and collected $39,000 of cash revenue.
3. Paid $7,000 cash on accounts payable.
4. Adjusted the records to reflect the use of supplies. A physical count indicated that $2,200 of supplies was still on hand on December 31, 2012.

Required

a. Show the effects of the events on the financial statements using a horizontal statements model like the following one. In the Cash Flows column, use OA to designate operating activity, IA for investing activity, FA for financing activity, and NC for net change in cash. Use NA to indicate accounts not affected by the event. The beginning balances are entered in the following example.

Event No.	Assets			=	Liab.	+	Stockholders' Equity			Rev.	–	Exp.	=	Net Inc.	Cash Flows
	Cash	+	Supplies	=	Accts. Pay	+	C. Stock	+	Ret. Earn.						
Beg. Bal.	16,000	+	0	=	0	+	10,000	+	6,000	0	–	0	=	0	0

b. Explain the difference between the amount of net income and amount of net cash flow from operating activities.

Exercise 2-5   *Effect of unearned revenue on financial statements*

LO 1, 3, 5

Michael Stone started a personal financial planning business when he accepted $120,000 cash as advance payment for managing the financial assets of a large estate. Stone agreed to manage the estate for a one-year period, beginning April 1, 2012.

Required

a. Show the effects of the advance payment and revenue recognition on the 2012 financial statements using a horizontal statements model like the following one. In the Cash Flows column, use OA to designate operating activity, IA for investing activity, FA for financing activity, and NC for net change in cash. Use NA if the account is not affected.

Event No.	Assets	=	Liab.	+	Stockholders' Equity	Rev.	–	Exp.	=	Net Inc.	Cash Flows
	Cash	=	Unearn. Rev.	+	Ret. Earn.						

b. How much revenue would Stone recognize on the 2013 income statement?
c. What is the amount of cash flow from operating activities in 2013?

Exercise 2-6   *Unearned revenue defined as a liability*

LO 3

Harry Baldwin received $500 in advance for tutoring fees when he agreed to help Joseph Jones with his introductory accounting course. Upon receiving the cash, Harry mentioned that he would have to record the transaction as a liability on his books. Jones asked, "Why a liability? You don't owe me any money, do you?"

Required

Respond to Jones' question regarding Baldwin's liability.

LO 3

Exercise 2-7 *Distinguishing between an expense and a cost*

Eddie Kirn tells you that the accountants where he works are real hair splitters. For example, they make a big issue over the difference between a cost and an expense. He says the two terms mean the same thing to him.

Required

a. Explain to Eddie the difference between a cost and an expense from an accountant's perspective.
b. Indicate whether each of the following events produces an asset or an expense.
   (1) Recognized accrued salaries.
   (2) Paid in advance for insurance on the building.
   (3) Used supplies on hand to produce revenue.
   (4) Purchased supplies on account.
   (5) Purchased a building for cash.

LO 3

Exercise 2-8 *Revenue and expense recognition*

Required

a. Describe an expense recognition event that results in a decrease in assets.
b. Describe an expense recognition event that results in an increase in liabilities.
c. Describe a revenue recognition event that results in an increase in assets.
d. Describe a revenue recognition event that results in a decrease in liabilities.

LO 3

Exercise 2-9 *Transactions that affect the elements of financial statements*

Required

Give an example of a transaction that will

a. Increase a liability and decrease equity (claims exchange event).
b. Increase an asset and increase equity (asset source event).
c. Decrease a liability and increase equity (claims exchange event).
d. Increase an asset and decrease another asset (asset exchange event).
e. Increase an asset and increase a liability (asset source event).
f. Decrease an asset and decrease a liability (asset use event).
g. Decrease an asset and decrease equity (asset use event).

LO 3

Exercise 2-10 *Identifying deferral and accrual events*

Required

Identify each of the following events as an accrual, deferral, or neither.

a. Provided services on account.
b. Collected accounts receivable.
c. Paid one year's rent in advance.
d. Paid cash for utilities expense.
e. Collected $2,400 in advance for services to be performed over the next 12 months.
f. Incurred other operating expenses on account.
g. Recorded expense for salaries owed to employees at the end of the accounting period.
h. Paid a cash dividend to the stockholders.
i. Paid cash to purchase supplies to be used over the next several months.
j. Purchased land with cash.

Exercise 2-11 *Prepaid and unearned rent*   **LO 2**

On August 1, 2012, Woodworks paid Warehouse Rentals $54,000 for a 12-month lease on warehouse space.

Required

a. Record the deferral and the related December 31, 2012, adjustment for Woodworks in the accounting equation.

b. Record the deferral and the related December 31, 2012, adjustment for Warehouse Rentals in the accounting equation.

Exercise 2-12 *Classifying events on the statement of cash flows*   **LO 3**

The following transactions pertain to the operations of Fleming Company for 2012.

1. Acquired $40,000 cash from the issue of common stock.
2. Performed services for $12,000 cash.
3. Provided $55,000 of services on account.
4. Received $36,000 cash in advance for services to be performed over the next two years.
5. Incurred $30,000 of other operating expenses on account.
6. Collected $45,000 cash from accounts receivable.
7. Paid $4,000 cash for rent expense.
8. Paid $12,000 for one year's prepaid insurance.
9. Paid a $5,000 cash dividend to the stockholders.
10. Paid $22,000 cash on accounts payable.

Required

a. Classify the cash flows from these transactions as operating activities (OA), investing activities (IA), or financing activities (FA). Use NA for transactions that do not affect the statement of cash flows.

b. Prepare a statement of cash flows. (There is no beginning cash balance.)

Exercise 2-13 *Effect of accounting events on the income statement and statement*   **LO 3**
of cash flows

Required

Explain how each of the following events and the related adjusting entry will affect the amount of *net income* and the amount of *cash flow from operating activities* reported on the year-end financial statements. Identify the direction of change (increase, decrease, or NA) and the amount of the change. Organize your answers according to the following table. The first event is recorded as an example. If an event does not have a related adjusting entry, record only the effects of the event. All adjustments are made on December 31.

	Net Income		Cash Flows from Operating Activities	
Event No.	Direction of Change	Amount of Change	Direction of Change	Amount of Change
a	NA	NA	NA	NA

a. Acquired $50,000 cash from the issue of common stock.
b. Paid $4,800 cash on October 1 to purchase a one-year insurance policy.
c. Collected $18,000 in advance for services to be performed in the future. The contract called for services to start on September 1 and to continue for one year.
d. Earned $22,000 of revenue on account. Collected $18,000 cash from accounts receivable.
e. Sold land that had cost $10,000 for $10,000.
f. Accrued salaries amounting to $8,000.

g. Provided services for $12,000 cash.

h. Paid cash for other operating expenses of $3,500.

i. Purchased $1,800 of supplies on account. Paid $1,500 cash on accounts payable. The ending balance in the Supplies account, after adjustment, was $600.

LO 1, 6

Exercise 2-14   *Identifying transaction type and effect on the financial statements*

Required

Identify whether each of the following transactions is an asset source (AS), asset use (AU), asset exchange (AE), or claims exchange (CE). Also show the effects of the events on the financial statements using the horizontal statements model. Indicate whether the event increases (I), decreases (D), or does not affect (NA) each element of the financial statements. In the Cash Flows column, designate the cash flows as operating activities (OA), investing activities (IA), or financing activities (FA). The first two transactions have been recorded as examples.

Event No.	Type of Event	Assets	=	Liabilities	+	Stockholders' Equity Common Stock	+	Stockholders' Equity Retained Earnings	Rev.	−	Exp.	=	Net Inc.	Cash Flows	
a	AS	I		NA		I		NA	NA		NA		NA	I	FA
b	AE	I/D		NA		NA		NA	NA		NA		NA	D	IA

a. Acquired cash from the issue of common stock.

b. Purchased land for cash.

c. Paid cash advance for rent on office space.

d. Collected cash from accounts receivable.

e. Performed services for cash.

f. Purchased a building with part cash *and* issued a note payable for the balance.

g. Paid cash for operating expenses.

h. Paid cash for supplies.

i. Paid a cash dividend to the stockholders.

j. Incurred operating expenses on account.

k. Paid cash on accounts payable.

l. Received cash advance for services to be provided in the future.

m. Recorded accrued salaries.

n. Performed services on account.

o. Adjusted books to reflect the amount of prepaid rent expired during the period.

p. Paid cash for salaries accrued at the end of a prior period.

LO 1

Exercise 2-15   *Effect of accruals and deferrals on financial statements: the horizontal statements model*

K. Little, Attorney at Law, experienced the following transactions in 2012, the first year of operations.

1. Purchased $2,800 of office supplies on account.

2. Accepted $30,000 on February 1, 2012, as a retainer for services to be performed evenly over the next 12 months.

3. Performed legal services for cash of $87,000.

4. Paid cash for salaries expense of $38,500.

5. Paid a cash dividend of $10,000 to the stockholders.

6. Paid $1,800 of the amount due on accounts payable.

7. Determined that at the end of the accounting period, $300 of office supplies remained on hand.

8. On December 31, 2012, recognized the revenue that had been earned for services performed in accordance with Transaction 2.

Required

Show the effects of the events on the financial statements using a horizontal statements model like the following one. In the Cash Flow column, use the initials OA to designate operating activity, IA for investing activity, FA for financing activity, and NC for net change in cash. Use NA to indicate accounts not affected by the event. The first event has been recorded as an example.

Event No.	Assets		=	Liabilities			+	Stk. Equity	Rev.	−	Exp.	=	Net Inc.	Cash Flow
	Cash	+ Supp.	=	Accts. Pay.	+	Unearn. Rev.	+	Ret. Earn.						
1	NA	+ 2,800	=	2,800	+	NA	+	NA	NA	−	NA	=	NA	NA

Exercise 2-16 *Effect of an error on financial statements*   LO 2, 3

On May 1, 2012, Virginia Corporation paid $18,000 cash in advance for a one-year lease on an office building. Assume that Virginia records the prepaid rent and that the books are closed on December 31.

Required

a. Show the payment for the one-year lease and the related adjusting entry to rent expense in the accounting equation.

b. Assume that Virginia Corporation failed to record the adjusting entry to reflect using the office building. How would the error affect the company's 2012 income statement and balance sheet?

Exercise 2-17 *Net income versus changes in cash*   LO 2, 3

In 2012, Cherry Design billed its customers $58,000 for services performed. The company collected $46,000 of the amount billed. Cherry Design incurred $41,000 of other operating expenses on acount. Cherry Design paid $30,000 of the accounts payable. Cherry Design acquired $40,000 cash from the issue of common stock. The company invested $20,000 cash in the purchase of land.

Required

Use the preceding information to answer the following questions. (*Hint:* Identify the six events described in the paragraph and record them in general ledger accounts under an accounting equation before attempting to answer the questions.)

a. What amount of revenue will Cherry Design report on the 2012 income statement?

b. What amount of cash flow from revenue will Cherry Design report on the statement of cash flows?

c. What is the net income for the period?

d. What is the net cash flow from operating activities for the period?

e. Why is the amount of net income different from the net cash flow from operating activities for the period?

f. What is the amount of net cash flow from investing activities?

g. What is the amount of net cash flow from financing activities?

h. What amounts of total assets, liabilities, and equity will Cherry Design report on the year-end balance sheet?

LO 3

Exercise 2-18 *Adjusting the accounts*

Keystore Systems experienced the following accounting events during its 2012 accounting period.

1. Paid cash to purchase land.
2. Recognized revenue on account.
3. Issued common stock.
4. Paid cash to purchase supplies.
5. Collected a cash advance for services that will be provided during the coming year.
6. Paid a cash dividend to the stockholders.
7. Paid cash for an insurance policy that provides coverage during the next year.
8. Collected cash from accounts receivable.
9. Paid cash for operating expenses.
10. Paid cash to settle an account payable.

Required

a. Identify the events that would require a year-end adjusting entry.
b. Explain why adjusting entries are made at the end of the accounting period.

LO 4, 5

Exercise 2-19 *Closing the accounts*

The following information was drawn from the accounting records of Kwon Company as of December 31, 2012, before the temporary accounts had been closed. The Cash balance was $4,000, and Notes Payable amounted to $2,000. The company had revenues of $6,000 and expenses of $3,500. The company's Land account had a $9,000 balance. Dividends amounted to $500. There was $6,000 of common stock issued.

Required

a. Identify which accounts would be classified as permanent and which accounts would be classified as temporary.
b. Assuming that Kwon's beginning balance (as of January 1, 2012) in the Retained Earnings account was $2,600, determine its balance after the nominal accounts were closed at the end of 2012.
c. What amount of net income would Kwon Company report on its 2012 income statement?
d. Explain why the amount of net income differs from the amount of the ending Retained Earnings balance.
e. What are the balances in the revenue, expense, and dividend accounts on January 1, 2013?

LO 4

Exercise 2-20 *Closing accounts and the accounting cycle*

Required

a. Identify which of the following accounts are temporary (will be closed to Retained Earnings at the end of the year) and which are permanent.
   (1) Land
   (2) Salaries Expense
   (3) Retained Earnings
   (4) Prepaid Rent
   (5) Supplies Expense
   (6) Common Stock
   (7) Notes Payable
   (8) Cash
   (9) Service Revenue
   (10) Dividends
b. List and explain the four stages of the accounting cycle. Which stage must be first? Which stage is last?

Exercise 2-21   *Closing entries*

Required

Which of the following accounts are closed at the end of the accounting period?

a. Accounts Payable
b. Unearned Revenue
c. Prepaid Rent
d. Rent Expense
e. Service Revenue
f. Advertising Expense
g. Dividends
h. Retained Earnings
i. Utilities Expense
j. Salaries Payable
k. Salaries Expense
l. Operating Expenses

Exercise 2-22   *Matching concept*

Companies make sacrifices known as *expenses* to obtain benefits called *revenues*. The accurate measurement of net income requires that expenses be matched with revenues. In some circumstances matching a particular expense directly with revenue is difficult or impossible. In these circumstances, the expense is matched with the period in which it is incurred.

Required

Distinguish the following items that could be matched directly with revenues from the items that would be classified as period expenses.

a. Sales commissions paid to employees.
b. Utilities expense.
c. Rent expense.
d. The cost of land that has been sold.

Exercise 2-23   *Identifying source, use, and exchange transactions*

Required

Indicate whether each of the following transactions is an asset source (AS), asset use (AU), asset exchange (AE), or claims exchange (CE) transaction.

a. Acquired cash from the issue of stock.
b. Paid a cash dividend to the stockholders.
c. Paid cash on accounts payable.
d. Incurred other operating expenses on account.
e. Paid cash for rent expense.
f. Performed services for cash.
g. Performed services for clients on account.
h. Collected cash from accounts receivable.
i. Invested cash in a certificate of deposit.
j. Purchased land with cash.

Exercise 2-24   *Identifying asset source, use, and exchange transactions*

Required

a. Name an asset exchange transaction that will *not* affect the statement of cash flows.
b. Name an asset exchange transaction that will affect the statement of cash flows.
c. Name an asset source transaction that will *not* affect the income statement.
d. Name an asset use transaction that will affect the income statement.
e. Name an asset use transaction that will *not* affect the income statement.

LO 3

Exercise 2-25   *Relation of elements to financial statements*

Required

Identify whether each of the following items would appear on the income statement (IS), statement of changes in stockholders' equity (SE), balance sheet (BS), or statement of cash flows (CF). Some items may appear on more than one statement; if so, identify all applicable statements. If an item would not appear on any financial statement, label it NA.

a. Prepaid rent
b. Net income
c. Utilities expense
d. Supplies
e. Cash flow from operating activities
f. Service revenue
g. Auditor's opinion
h. Accounts receivable
i. Accounts payable
j. Unearned revenue
k. Dividends
l. Beginning cash balance
m. Ending retained earnings
n. Rent expense
o. Ending cash balance

Exercise 2-26   *Analyzing the cash flow effects of different types of expenses*

The following income statements are available for Hopi, Inc., and Zuni, Inc., for 2012.

	Hopi, Inc.	Zuni, Inc.
Revenue	$100,000	$100,000
Wages expense	70,000	55,000
Depreciation expense	10,000	25,000
Net earnings	$ 20,000	$ 20,000

Required

Assume that neither company had beginning or ending balances in its Accounts Receivable or wages Payable accounts. Explain which company would have the lowest *net cash flows from operating activities* for 2012.

PROBLEMS

All applicable Problems are available with McGraw-Hill's
Connect Accounting.

LO 1

Problem 2-27   *Recording events in a horizontal statements model*

The following events pertain to King Company.

1. Acquired $25,000 cash from the issue of common stock.
2. Provided services for $5,000
3. Provided $18,000 of services on account.
4. Collected $11,000 cash from the account receivable created in Event 3.
5. Paid $1,400 cash to purchase supplies.
6. Had $300 of supplies on hand at the end of the accounting period.
7. Received $3,600 cash in advance for services to be performed in the future.

8. Performed one-half of the services agreed to in Event 7.

9. Paid $6,000 for salaries expense.

10. Incurred $2,400 of other operating expenses on account.

11. Paid $2,000 cash on the account payable created in Event 10.

12. Paid a $2,000 cash dividend to the stockholders.

Required

Show the effects of the events on the financial statements using a horizontal statements model like the following one. In the Cash Flows column, use the letters OA to designate operating activity, IA for investing activity, FA for financing activity, and NC for net change in cash. Use NA to indicate accounts not affected by the event. The first event is recorded as an example.

	Assets			=	Liabilities			+	Stockholders' Equity			Rev.	−	Exp.	=	Net Inc.	Cash Flows
Event No.	Cash	+ Accts. Rec.	+ Supp.	=	Accts. Pay.	+ Unearn. Rev.	+ Com. Stk.	+	Ret. Earn.									
1	25,000	+ NA	+ NA	=	NA	+ NA	+ 25,000	+	NA		NA	−	NA	=	NA	25,000 FA

Problem 2-28 *Effect of deferrals on financial statements: three separate single-cycle examples*   e**X**cel

Required

a. On February 1, 2012, Heider, Inc., was formed when it received $80,000 cash from the issue of common stock. On May 1, 2012, the company paid $60,000 cash in advance to rent office space for the coming year. The office space was used as a place to consult with clients. The consulting activity generated $120,000 of cash revenue during 2012. Based on this information alone, record the events and related adjusting entry in the general ledger accounts under the accounting equation. Determine the amount of net income and cash flows from operating activities for 2012.

b. On January 1, 2012, the accounting firm of Bonds & Associates was formed. On August 1, 2012, the company received a retainer fee (was paid in advance) of $30,000 for services to be performed monthly during the next 12 months. Assuming that this was the only transaction completed in 2012, prepare an income statement, statement of changes in stockholders' equity, balance sheet, and statement of cash flows for 2012.

c. Edge Company had $2,200 of supplies on hand on January 1, 2012. Edge purchased $7,200 of supplies on account during 2012. A physical count of supplies revealed that $900 of supplies was on hand as of December 31, 2012. Determine the amount of supplies expense that should be recognized in the December 31, 2012 adjusting entry. Use a financial statements model to show how the adjusting entry would affect the balance sheet, income statement, and statement of cash flows.

Problem 2-29 *Effect of adjusting entries on the accounting equation*   LO 2

Required

Each of the following independent events requires a year-end adjusting entry. Show how each event and its related adjusting entry affect the accounting equation. Assume a December 31 closing date. The first event is recorded as an example.

Event/ Adjustment	Total Assets			=	Liabilities	+	Stockholders' Equity		
	Cash	+	Other Assets	=	Liabilities	+	Common Stock	+	Retained Earnings
a	−7,200	+	+7,200	=	NA	+	NA	+	NA
Adj.	NA		−5,400	=	NA	+	NA	+	−5,400

a. Paid $7,200 cash in advance on April 1 for a one-year insurance policy.
b. Purchased $1,400 of supplies on account. At year's end, $150 of supplies remained on hand.
c. Paid $8,400 cash in advance on March 1 for a one-year lease on office space.
d. Received a $18,000 cash advance for a contract to provide services in the future. The contract required a one-year commitment starting September 1 to be provided evenly over the year.
e. Paid $24,000 cash in advance on October 1 for a one-year lease on office space.

LO 3, 5, 6

CHECK FIGURES
b. Net Income, 2012: $19,300
b. Net Income, 2013: $84,650

Problem 2-30   *Events for two complete accounting cycles*

Energy Consulting Company was formed on Junuary 1, 2012.

Events Affecting the 2012 Accounting Period

1. Acquired cash of $80,000 from the issue of common stock.
2. Purchased $4,200 of suplies on account.
3. Purchased land that cost $30,000 cash.
4. Paid $4,200 cash to settle accounts payable created in Event 2.
5. Recognized revenue on account of $75,000.
6. Paid $46,000 cash for other operating expenses.
7. Collected $68,000 cash from accounts receivable.

Information for 2012 Adjusting Entries

8. Recognized accrued salaries of $5,800 on December 31, 2012.
9. Had $300 of supplies on hand at the end of the accounting period.

Events Affecting the 2013 Accounting Period

1. Acquired an additional $10,000 cash from the issue of common stock.
2. Paid $5,800 cash to settle the salaries payable obligation.
3. Paid $6,000 cash in advance for a lease on office facilities.
4. Sold land that had cost $25,000 for $25,000 cash.
5. Received $8,400 cash in advance for services to be performed in the future.
6. Purchased $1,800 of supplies on account during the year.
7. Provided services on account of $90,000.
8. Collected $92,000 cash from accounts receivable.
9. Paid a cash dividend of $10,000 to the stockholders.

Information for 2013 Adjusting Entries

10. The advance payment for rental of the office facilities (see Event 3) was made on September 1 for a one-year lease term.
11. The cash advance for services to be provided in the future was collected on June 1 (see Event 5). The one-year contract started June 1.
12. Had $350 of supplies on hand at the end of the period.
13. Recognized accrued salaries of $6,500 at the end of the accounting period.

Required

a. Identify each event affecting the 2012 and 2013 accounting periods as asset source (AS), asset use (AU), asset exchange (AE), or claims exchange (CE). Record the effects of each event under the appropriate general ledger account headings of the accounting equation.
b. Prepare an income statement, statement of changes in stockholders' equity, balance sheet, and statement of cash flows for 2012 and 2013, using the vertical statements model.

LO 2, 3

CHECK FIGURES
b. $33,000
h. ($3,000)

Problem 2-31   *Effect of events on financial statements*

Reed Company had the following balances in its accounting records as of December 31, 2012.

Assets		Claims	
Cash	$ 75,000	Accounts Payable	$ 32,000
Accounts Receivable	45,000	Common Stock	90,000
Land	30,000	Retained Earnings	28,000
Totals	$150,000		$150,000

The following accounting events apply to Reed's 2012 fiscal year:

Jan.   1   Acquired an additional $50,000 cash from the issue of common stock.
April   1   Paid $8,400 cash in advance for a one-year lease for office space.
June   1   Paid a $4,000 cash dividend to the stockholders.
July   1   Purchased additional land that cost $15,000 cash.
Aug.   1   Made a cash payment on accounts payable of $28,000.
Sept.   1   Received $9,600 cash in advance as a retainer for services to be performed monthly
            during the next eight months.
Sept. 30   Sold land for $12,000 cash that had originally cost $12,000.
Oct.   1   Purchased $1,500 of supplies on account.
Dec.   31   Earned $75,000 of service revenue on account during the year.
       31   Received $70,000 cash collections from accounts receivable.
       31   Incurred $24,000 other operating expenses on account during the year.
       31   Recognized accrued salaries expense of $8,000.
       31   Had $400 of supplies on hand at the end of the period.
       31   The land purchased on July 1 had a market value of $21,000.

Required

Based on the preceding information, answer the following questions. All questions pertain to the 2012 financial statements. (*Hint:* Record the events in general ledger accounts under an accounting equation before answering the questions.)

a.   What two transactions need additional adjusting entries at the end of the year?
b.   What amount would be reported for land on the balance sheet?
c.   What amount of net cash flow from operating activities would Reed report on the statement of cash flows?
d.   What amount of rent expense would be reported in the income statement?
e.   What amount of total liabilities would be reported on the balance sheet?
f.   What amount of supplies expense would be reported on the income statement?
g.   What amount of unearned revenue would be reported on the balance sheet?
h.   What amount of net cash flow from investing activities would be reported on the statement of cash flows?
i.   What amount of total expenses would be reported on the income statement?
j.   What total amount of service revenues would be reported on the income statement?
k.   What amount of cash flows from financing activities would be reported on the statement of cash flows?
l.   What amount of net income would be reported on the income statement?
m.   What amount of retained earnings would be reported on the balance sheet?

Problem 2-32   *Identifying and arranging elements on financial statements*

The following information was drawn from the records of Paso & Associates at December 31, 2012.

Supplies	$ 2,500	Unearned revenue	$ 5,400
Consulting revenue	120,000	Notes payable	40,000
Land	70,000	Salaries payable	9,000
Dividends	10,000	Salary expense	58,000
Cash flow from fin. activities	30,000	Common stock issued	30,000
Interest revenue	6,000	Beginning common stock	40,000
Ending retained earnings	50,100	Accounts receivable	32,000
Cash	66,000	Cash flow from inv. activities	(21,000)
Interest payable	4,000	Cash flow from oper. activities	18,000
Interest expense	9,000	Prepaid rent	8,000

LO 3

CHECK FIGURES
2012 Net Income: $59,000
2012 Total Assets: $178,500

Required

Use the preceding information to construct an income statement, statement of changes in stockholders' equity, balance sheet, and statement of cash flows. (Show only totals for each activity on the statement of cash flows.)

LO 3

Problem 2-33   *Relationship of accounts to financial statements*

Required

CHECK FIGURES
a. BS
z. BS

Identify whether each of the following items would appear on the income statement (IS), statement of changes in stockholders' equity (SE), balance sheet (BS), or statement of cash flows (CF). Some items may appear on more than one statement; if so, identify all applicable statements. If an item would not appear on any financial statement, label it NA.

a. Accumulated depreciation
b. Salary expense
c. Prepaid insurance
d. Beginning common stock
e. Beginning retained earnings
f. Supplies expense
g. Operating expenses
h. Cash flow from operating activities
i. Debt to assets ratio
j. Total liabilities
k. Ending common stock
l. Interest expense
m. Consulting revenue
n. Cash flow from investing activities
o. Service revenue
p. Unearned revenue
q. Certificate of deposit
r. Interest receivable
s. Depreciation expense

t. Accounts receivable
u. Notes payable
v. Insurance expense
w. Salaries payable
x. Total assets
y. Accounts payable
z. Notes receivable
aa. Cash
bb. Supplies
cc. Cash flow from financing activities
dd. Interest revenue
ee. Ending retained earnings
ff. Net income
gg. Dividends
hh. Office equipment
ii. Debt to equity ratio
jj. Land
kk. Interest payable
ll. Rent expense

LO 3, 5

Problem 2-34   *Missing information in financial statements*

Required

CHECK FIGURES
n. $8,000
t. $5,000

Fill in the blank (as indicated by the alphabetic letters in parentheses) in the following financial statements. Assume the company started operations January 1, 2010, and that all transactions involve cash.

	For the Years		
	2010	**2011**	**2012**
Income Statements			
Revenue	$ 700	$ 1,300	$ 2,000
Expense	(a)	(700)	(1,300)
Net income	$ 200	$ (m)	$ 700
Statement of Changes in Stockholders' Equity			
Beginning common stock	$ 0	$ (n)	$ 6,000
Plus: Common stock issued	5,000	1,000	2,000
Ending common stock	5,000	6,000	(t)
Beginning retained earnings	0	100	200
Plus: Net income	(b)	(o)	700
Less: Dividends	(c)	(500)	(300)
Ending retained earnings	100	(p)	600
Total stockholders' equity	$ (d)	$ 6,200	$ 8,600

continued

Balance Sheets

Assets			
Cash	$ (e)	$ (q)	$ (u)
Land	0	(r)	8,000
Total assets	$ (f)	$11,200	$10,600
Liabilities	$ (g)	$ 5,000	$ 2,000
Stockholders' equity			
Common stock	(h)	(s)	8,000
Retained earnings	(i)	200	600
Total stockholders' equity	(j)	6,200	8,600
Total liabilities and stockholders' equity	$8,100	$11,200	$10,600

Statements of Cash Flows

Cash flows from operating activities			
Cash receipts from revenue	$ (k)	$ 1,300	$ (v)
Cash payments for expenses	(l)	(700)	(w)
Net cash flows from operating activities	200	600	700
Cash flows from investing activities			
Cash payments for land	0	(8,000)	0
Cash flows from financing activities			
Cash receipts from loan	3,000	3,000	0
Cash payments to reduce debt	0	(1,000)	(x)
Cash receipts from stock issue	5,000	1,000	(y)
Cash payments for dividends	(100)	(500)	(z)
Net cash flows from financing activities	7,900	2,500	(1,300)
Net change in cash	8,100	(4,900)	(600)
Plus: Beginning cash balance	0	8,100	3,200
Ending cash balance	$8,100	$ 3,200	$ 2,600

ANALYZE, THINK, COMMUNICATE

ATC 2-1 Business Applications Case *Understanding real-world annual reports*

Required

Use the Target Corporation's annual report in Appendix B to answer the following questions. Note that net income and net earnings are synonymous terms.

a. Which accounts on Target's balance sheet are accural type accounts?

b. Which accounts on Target's balance sheet are deferral type accounts?

c. Compare Target's 2009 *net earnings* to its 2009 *cash provided by operating activities.* Which is larger?

d. First, compare Target's 2008 net earnings to its 2009 net earnings. Next, compare Target's 2008 cash provided by operating activities to its 2009 cash provided by operating activities. Which changed the most from 2008 to 2009, net earnings or cash provided by operating activities?

Target Corporation

ATC 2-2 Group Assignment *Financial reporting and market valuation*

The following financial highlights were drawn from the 2009 annual reports of Microsoft Corporation and Apple Inc.

	Microsoft	Apple
Revenue	$58.4 Billion	$42.9 Billion
Net income	$14.6 Billion	$ 5.7 Billion
Cash and short-term investments	$39.7 Billion	$23.1 Billion

Even so, as of May 26, 2010, Wall Street valued Microsoft at $219.19 billion and Apple at $222.12.

Divide the class into groups of four or five students.

Required

Have the members of each group reach a consensus response for each of the following tasks. Each group should elect a spokes person to represent the group.

Group Tasks

(1) Determine the amount of expenses incurred by each company.

(2) Comment on how the concept of conservatism applies to the financial information presented in this case.

(3) Speculate as to why investors would be willing to pay more for Apple than Microsoft.

Class Discussion

Randomly call on the spokes persons to compare their responses for each of the group tasks.

ATC 2-3 Research Assignment *Investigating nonfinancial information in Nike's annual report*

Although most of this course is concerned with the financial statements themselves, all sections of a company's annual report are important. A company must file various reports with the SEC, and one of these, Form 10-K, is essentially the company's annual report. The requirements below ask you to investigate sections of Nike's annual report that explain various nonfinancial aspects of its business operations.

To obtain the Form 10-K you can use either the EDGAR system following the instructions in Appendix A or the company's website.

Required

a. In what year did Nike begin operations?

b. Other than athletic shoes, what products does Nike sell?

c. Does Nike operate businesses under names other than Nike? If so, what are they?

d. How many employees does Nike have?

e. In how many countries other than the United States does Nike sell its products?

ATC 2-4 Writing Assignment *Conservatism and Matching*

Glenn's Cleaning Services Company is experiencing cash flow problems and needs a loan. Glenn has a friend who is willing to lend him the money he needs provided she can be convinced that he will be able to repay the debt. Glenn has assured his friend that his business is viable, but his friend has asked to see the company's financial statements. Glenn's accountant produced the following financial statements.

Income Statement		Balance Sheet	
Service Revenue	$ 38,000	Assets	$85,000
Operating Expenses	(70,000)	Liabilities	$35,000
Net Loss	$(32,000)	Stockholders' Equity	
		Common Stock	82,000
		Retained Earnings	(32,000)
		Total Liabilities and	
		Stockholders' Equity	$85,000

Glenn made the following adjustments to these statements before showing them to his friend. He recorded $82,000 of revenue on account from Barrymore Manufacturing Company for a contract to clean its headquarters office building that was still being negotiated for the next month. Barrymore had scheduled a meeting to sign a contract the following week, so Glenn was sure that he would get the job. Barrymore was a reputable company, and Glenn was confident that he could ultimately collect the $82,000. Also, he subtracted $30,000 of accrued salaries expense and the corresponding liability. He reasoned that since he had not paid the employees, he had not incurred any expense.

Required

a. Reconstruct the income statement and balance sheet as they would appear after Glenn's adjustments.

b. Write a brief memo explaining how Glenn's treatment of the expected revenue from Barrymore violated the conservatism concept.

c. Write a brief memo explaining how Glenn's treatment of the accrued salaries expense violates the matching concept.

CHAPTER 3

Accounting for Merchandising Businesses

LEARNING OBJECTIVES

After you have mastered the material in this chapter, you will be able to:

1 Identify and explain the primary features of the perpetual inventory system.

2 Show the effects of inventory transactions on financial statements.

3 Explain the meaning of terms used to describe transportation costs, cash discounts, returns or allowances, and financing costs.

4 Explain how gains and losses differ from revenues and expenses.

5 Compare and contrast single and multistep income statements.

6 Show the effect of lost, damaged, or stolen inventory on financial statements.

7 Use common size financial statements to evaluate managerial performance.

8 Identify the primary features of the periodic inventory system. (Appendix)

CHAPTER OPENING

Previous chapters have discussed accounting for service businesses. These businesses obtain revenue by providing some kind of service such as medical or legal advice to their customers. Other examples of service companies include dry cleaning companies, maid service companies, and car washes. This chapter introduces accounting practices for merchandising businesses. **Merchandising businesses** generate revenue by selling goods. They buy the merchandise they sell from companies called suppliers. The goods purchased for resale are called **merchandise inventory.** Merchandising businesses include **retail companies** (companies that sell goods to the final consumer) and **wholesale companies** (companies that sell to other businesses). **Sears, JCPenney, Target**, and **Sam's Club** are real-world merchandising businesses.

The Curious Accountant

Janice recently purchased a gold necklace for $250 from her local **Zales** jewelry store. The next day she learned that Zoe bought the same necklace on-line from **Blue Nile** for only $200. Janice questioned how Blue Nile could sell the necklace for so much less than Zales. Zoe suggested that even though both jewelry sellers purchase their products from the same producers at about the same price, Blue Nile can charge lower prices because it does not have to operate expensive bricks-and-mortar stores, and thus has lower operating costs. Janice disagrees. She thinks the cost of operating large distribution centers and Internet server centers will offset any cost savings Blue Nile enjoys from not owning retail jewelry stores.

Exhibit 3.1 presents the income statements for Zales and Blue Nile. Based on these income statements, do you think Janice or Zoe is correct? (Answer on page 104.)

EXHIBIT 3.1   Comparative Income Statements

BLUE NILE, INC.
Consolidated Statements of Operations
(in thousands, except per share data)

	Year Ended	
	January 3, 2010	January 4, 2009
Net sales	$302,134	$295,329
Cost of sales	236,790	235,333
Gross profit	65,344	59,996
Selling, general and administrative expenses	45,997	44,005
Operating income	19,347	15,991
Other income, net:		
Interest income, net	122	1,420
Other income, net	209	445
Total other income, net	331	1,865
Income before income taxes	19,678	17,856
Income tax expense	6,878	6,226
Net income	$ 12,800	$ 11,630

ZALE CORPORATION AND SUBSIDIARIES
Consolidated Statements of Operations
(in thousands, except per share amounts)

	Year Ended July 31,	
	2009	2008 As Restated
Revenues	$1,779,744	$2,138,041
Cost and expenses:		
Cost of sales	948,572	1,089,553
Selling, general and administrative	927,249	985,028
Cost of insurance operations	7,000	6,744
Depreciation and amortization	58,947	60,244
Other charges and gains	70,095	(10,700)
Operating (loss) earnings	(232,119)	7,172
Interest expense	10,399	12,364
Other income	—	(3,500)
Loss before income taxes	(242,518)	(1,692)
Income tax (benefit) expense	(53,015)	4,761
Loss from continuing operations	(189,503)	(6,453)
Earnings from discontinued operations, net of taxes	—	7,084
Net (loss) earnings	$ (189,503)	$ 631

PRODUCT COSTS VERSUS SELLING AND ADMINISTRATIVE COSTS

Identify and explain the primary features of the perpetual inventory system.

Companies report inventory costs on the balance sheet in the asset account Merchandise Inventory. All costs incurred to acquire merchandise and ready it for sale are included in the inventory account. Examples of inventory costs include the price of goods purchased, shipping and handling costs, transit insurance, and storage costs.

Since inventory items are referred to as products, inventory costs are frequently called **product costs.**

Costs that are not included in inventory are usually called **selling and administrative costs.** Examples of selling and administrative costs include advertising, administrative salaries, sales commissions, insurance, and interest. Since selling and administrative costs are usually recognized as expenses *in the period* in which they are incurred, they are sometimes called **period costs.** In contrast, product costs are expensed when inventory is sold regardless of when it was purchased. In other words, product costs are matched directly with sales revenue, while selling and administrative costs are matched with the period in which they are incurred.

ALLOCATING INVENTORY COST BETWEEN ASSET AND EXPENSE ACCOUNTS

The cost of inventory that is available for sale during a specific accounting period is determined as follows.

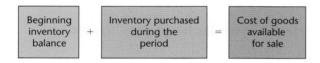

The **cost of goods available for sale** is allocated between the asset account Merchandise Inventory and an expense account called **Cost of Goods Sold.** The cost of inventory items that have not been sold (Merchandise Inventory) is reported as an asset on the balance sheet, and the cost of the items sold (Cost of Goods Sold) is expensed on the income statement. This allocation is depicted graphically as follows.

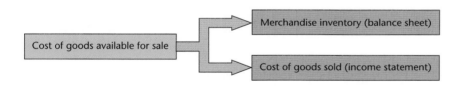

The difference between the sales revenue and the cost of goods sold is called **gross margin** or **gross profit.** The selling and administrative expenses (period costs) are subtracted from gross margin to obtain the net income.

Exhibit 3.1 displays income statements from the annual reports of **Blue Nile** and **Zales.** For each company, review the most current income statement and determine the amount of gross margin. You should find a gross profit of $65,344 for Blue Nile and a gross margin of $831,172 ($1,779,744 − $948,572) for Zales.

PERPETUAL INVENTORY SYSTEM

Most modern companies maintain their inventory records using the **perpetual inventory system,** so-called because the inventory account is adjusted perpetually (continually) throughout the accounting period. Each time merchandise is purchased, the inventory account is increased; each time it is sold, the inventory account is decreased. The following illustration demonstrates the basic features of the perpetual inventory system.

LO 2

Show the effects of inventory transactions on financial statements.

June Gardener loved plants and grew them with such remarkable success that she decided to open a small retail plant store. She started June's Plant Shop (JPS) on January 1, 2012. The following discussion explains and illustrates the effects of the five events the company experienced during its first year of operation.

Effects of 2012 Events on Financial Statements

EVENT 1   JPS acquired $15,000 cash by issuing common stock.

This event is an asset source transaction. It increases both assets (cash) and stockholders' equity (common stock). The income statement is not affected. The statement of cash flows reflects an inflow from financing activities. These effects are shown here.

Assets				Liab.		Stockholders' Equity							
Cash	+	Inventory	+	Land	=	Accts. Pay.	+	Com. Stk.	+	Ret. Earn.	Rev.	−	Exp.	=	Net Inc.	Cash Flow
15,000	+	NA	+	NA	=	NA	+	15,000	+	NA	NA	−	NA	=	NA	15,000 FA

EVENT 2   JPS purchased merchandise inventory for $14,000 cash.

This event is an asset exchange transaction. One asset, cash, decreases and another asset, merchandise inventory, increases; total assets remain unchanged. Because product costs are expensed when inventory is sold, not when it is purchased, the event does not affect the income statement. The cash outflow, however, is reported in the operating activities section of the statement of cash flows. These effects are illustrated below.

Assets				Liab.		Stockholders' Equity							
Cash	+	Inventory	+	Land	=	Accts. Pay.	+	Com. Stk.	+	Ret. Earn.	Rev.	−	Exp.	=	Net Inc.	Cash Flow
(14,000)	+	14,000	+	NA	=	NA	+	NA	+	NA	NA	−	NA	=	NA	(14,000) OA

EVENT 3A   JPS recognized sales revenue from selling inventory for $12,000 cash.

The revenue recognition is the first part of a two-part transaction. The *sales part* represents a source of assets (cash increases from earning sales revenue). Both assets (cash) and stockholders' equity (retained earnings) increase. Sales revenue on the income statement increases. The $12,000 cash inflow is reported in the operating activities section of the statement of cash flows. These effects are shown in the following financial statements model.

Assets				Liab.		Stockholders' Equity							
Cash	+	Inventory	+	Land	=	Accts. Pay.	+	Com. Stk.	+	Ret. Earn.	Rev.	−	Exp.	=	Net Inc.	Cash Flow
12,000	+	NA	+	NA	=	NA	+	NA	+	12,000	12,000	−	NA	=	12,000	12,000 OA

EVENT 3B   JPS recognized $8,000 of cost of goods sold.

The expense recognition is the second part of the two-part transaction. The *expense part* represents a use of assets. Both assets (merchandise inventory) and stockholders' equity (retained earnings) decrease. An expense account, Cost of Goods Sold, is reported on the income statement. This part of the transaction does not affect the statement of cash flows. A cash outflow occurred when the goods were bought, not when they were sold. These effects are shown here.

Assets			=	Liab.	+	Stockholders' Equity							
Cash	+ Inventory	+ Land	=	Accts. Pay.	+	Com. Stk.	+ Ret. Earn.	Rev.	−	Exp.	=	Net Inc.	Cash Flow
NA	+ (8,000)	+ NA	=	NA	+	NA	+ (8,000)	NA	−	8,000	=	(8,000)	NA

EVENT 4 JPS paid $1,000 cash for selling and administrative expenses.

This event is an asset use transaction. The payment decreases both assets (cash) and stockholders' equity (retained earnings). The increase in selling and administrative expenses decreases net income. The $1,000 cash payment is reported in the operating activities section of the statement of cash flows. These effects are illustrated below.

Assets			=	Liab.	+	Stockholders' Equity							
Cash	+ Inventory	+ Land	=	Accts. Pay.	+	Com. Stk.	+ Ret. Earn.	Rev.	−	Exp.	=	Net Inc.	Cash Flow
(1,000)	+ NA	+ NA	=	NA	+	NA	+ (1,000)	NA	−	1,000	=	(1,000)	(1,000) OA

EVENT 5 JPS paid $5,500 cash to purchase land for a place to locate a future store.

Buying the land increases the Land account and decreases the Cash account on the balance sheet. The income statement is not affected. The statement of cash flow shows a cash outflow to purchase land in the investing activities section of the statement of cash flows. These effects are shown below.

Assets			=	Liab.	+	Stockholders' Equity							
Cash	+ Inventory	+ Land	=	Accts. Pay.	+	Com. Stk.	+ Ret. Earn.	Rev.	−	Exp.	=	Net Inc.	Cash Flow
(5,500)	+ NA	+ 5,500	=	NA	+	NA	+ NA	NA	−	NA	=	NA	(5,500) IA

Financial Statements for 2012

JPS's financial statements for 2012 are shown in Exhibit 3.2. JPS had no beginning inventory in its first year, so the cost of merchandise inventory available for sale was $14,000 (the amount of inventory purchased during the period). Recall that JPS must allocate the *Cost of Goods (Inventory) Available for Sale* between the *Cost of Goods Sold* ($8,000) and the ending balance ($6,000) in the *Merchandise Inventory* account. The cost of goods sold is reported as an expense on the income statement and the ending balance of merchandise inventory is reported as an asset on the balance sheet. The difference between the sales revenue ($12,000) and the cost of goods sold ($8,000) is labeled *gross margin* ($4,000) on the income statement.

EXHIBIT 3.2

Financial Statements

2012 Income Statement		12/31/12 Balance Sheet		2012 Statement of Cash Flows	
Sales revenue	$12,000	Assets		Operating activities	
Cost of goods sold	(8,000)	Cash	$ 6,500	Inflow from customers	$12,000
Gross margin	4,000	Merchandise inventory	6,000	Outflow for inventory	(14,000)
Less: Operating exp.		Land	5,500	Outflow for selling	
Selling and		Total assets	$18,000	& admin. exp.	(1,000)
admin. exp.	(1,000)	Liabilities	$ 0	Net cash outflow for	
Net income	$ 3,000	Stockholders' equity		operating activities	$ (3,000)
		Common stock	$15,000	Investing activities	
		Retained earnings	3,000	Outflow to purchase land	(5,500)
		Total stockholders' equity	18,000	Financing activities	
		Total liab. and stk. equity	$18,000	Inflow from stock issue	15,000
				Net change in cash	6,500
				Plus: Beginning cash balance	0
				Ending cash balance	$ 6,500

✓ CHECK YOURSELF 3.1

Phambroom Company began 2012 with $35,600 in its Inventory account. During the year, it purchased inventory costing $356,800 and sold inventory that had cost $360,000 for $520,000. Based on this information alone, determine (1) the inventory balance as of December 31, 2012, and (2) the amount of gross margin Phambroom would report on its 2012 income statement.

Answer

1. $35,600 Beginning inventory + $356,800 Purchases = $392,400 Goods available for sale
   $392,400 Goods available for sale − $360,000 Cost of goods sold = $32,400 Ending inventory

2. Sales revenue − Cost of goods sold = Gross margin
   $520,000 − $360,000 = $160,000

Transportation Cost, Purchase Returns and Allowances, and Cash Discounts Related to Inventory Purchases

LO 3

Explain the meaning of terms used to describe transportation costs, cash discounts, returns or allowances, and financing costs.

Purchasing inventory often involves: (1) incurring transportation costs, (2) returning inventory or receiving purchase allowances (cost reductions), and (3) taking cash discounts (also cost reductions). During its second accounting cycle, JPS encountered these kinds of events. The final account balances at the end of the 2012 fiscal year become the beginning balances for 2013: Cash, $6,500; Merchandise Inventory, $6,000; Land, 5,500; Common Stock, $15,000; and Retained Earnings, $3,000.

Effects of 2013 Events on Financial Statements

JPS experienced the following events during its 2013 accounting period. The effects of each of these events are explained and illustrated in the following discussion.

EVENT 1   **JPS borrowed $4,000 cash by issuing a note payable.**

JPS borrowed the money to enable it to purchase a plot of land for a site for a store it planned to build in the near future. Borrowing the money increases the Cash account and the Note Payable account on the balance sheet. The income statement is not affected. The statement of cash flow shows a cash flow from financing activities. These effects are shown below.

Assets				=	Liabilities		+	Stockholders' Equity						
Cash +	Accts. Rec. +	Inventory +	Land =		Accts. Pay. +	Notes Pay. +		Com. Stk. +	Ret. Earn.		Rev. −	Exp. =	Net Inc.	Cash Flow
4,000 +	NA +	NA +	NA =		NA +	4,000 +		NA +	NA		NA −	NA =	NA	4,000 FA

EVENT 2   **JPS purchased on account merchandise inventory with a list price of $11,000.**

The inventory purchase increases both assets (merchandise inventory) and liabilities (accounts payable) on the balance sheet. The income statement is not affected until later, when inventory is sold. Since the inventory was purchased on account, there was no cash outflow. These effects are shown here.

Assets				=	Liab.		+	Stockholders' Equity						
Cash +	Accts. Rec. +	Inventory +	Land =		Accts. Pay. +	Notes Pay. +		Com. Stk. +	Ret. Earn.		Rev. −	Exp. =	Net Inc.	Cash Flow
NA +	NA +	11,000 +	NA =		11,000 +	NA +		NA +	NA		NA −	NA =	NA	NA

Accounting for Purchase Returns and Allowances

EVENT 3   **JPS returned some of the inventory purchased in Event 2. The list price of the returned merchandise was $1,000.**

To promote customer satisfaction, many businesses allow customers to return goods for reasons such as wrong size, wrong color, wrong design, or even simply because the purchaser changed his mind. The effect of a purchase return is the *opposite* of the original purchase. For JPS the **purchase return** decreases both assets (merchandise inventory) and liabilities (accounts payable). There is no effect on either the income statement or the statement of cash flows. These effects are shown below.

Assets				=	Liab.		+	Stockholders' Equity						
Cash +	Accts. Rec. +	Inventory +	Land =		Accts. Pay. +	Notes Pay. +		Com. Stk. +	Ret. Earn.		Rev. −	Exp. =	Net Inc.	Cash Flow
NA +	NA +	(1,000) +	NA =		(1,000) +	NA +		NA +	NA		NA −	NA =	NA	NA

Sometimes dissatisfied buyers will agree to keep goods instead of returning them if the seller offers to reduce the price. Such reductions are called allowances. **Purchase allowances** affect the financial statements the same way purchase returns do.

Purchase Discounts

EVENT 4   JPS received a cash discount on goods purchased in Event 2. The credit terms were 2/10, n/30.

To encourage buyers to pay promptly, sellers sometimes offer **cash discounts.** To illustrate, assume JPS purchased the inventory in Event 2 under terms **2/10, n/30** (two-ten, net thirty). These terms mean the seller will allow a 2 percent cash discount if the purchaser pays cash within 10 days from the date of purchase. The amount not paid within the first 10 days is due at the end of 30 days from date of purchase. Recall that JPS returned $1,000 of the inventory purchased in Event 1 leaving a $10,000 balance ($11,000 list price − $1,000 purchase return). If JPS pays for the inventory within 10 days, the amount of the discount is $200 ($10,000 × .02).

When cash discounts are applied to purchases they are called **purchases discounts.** When they are applied to sales, they are called sales discounts. Sales discounts will be discussed later in the chapter. A *purchase discount* reduces the cost of the inventory and the associated account payable on the balance sheet. A purchase discount does not directly affect the income statement or the statement of cash flow. These effects are shown here.

	Assets				=	Liab.		+	Stockholders' Equity						
Cash +	Accts. Rec. +	Inventory +	Land =			Accts. Pay. +	Notes Pay. +		Com. Stk. +	Ret. Earn.		Rev. −	Exp. =	Net Inc.	Cash Flow
NA +	NA +	(200) +	NA =			(200) +	NA +		NA +	NA		NA −	NA =	NA	NA

If JPS paid the account payable after 10 days, there would be no purchase discount. In this case the balances in the Inventory and Account Payable accounts would remain at $10,000.

EVENT 5   JPS paid the $9,800 balance due on the account payable.

The remaining balance in the accounts payable is $9,800 ($10,000 list price − $200 purchase discount). Paying cash to settle the liability reduces cash and accounts payable on the balance sheet. The income statement is not affected. The cash outflow is shown in the operating section of the statement of cash flows. These effects are shown below.

	Assets				=	Liab.		+	Stockholders' Equity						
Cash +	Accts. Rec. +	Inventory +	Land =			Accts. Pay. +	Notes Pay. +		Com. Stk. +	Ret. Earn.		Rev. −	Exp. =	Net Inc.	Cash Flow
(9,800) +	NA +	NA +	NA =			(9,800) +	NA +		NA +	NA		NA −	NA =	NA	(9,800) OA

The Cost of Financing Inventory

Suppose you buy inventory this month and sell it next month. Where do you get the money to pay for the inventory at the time you buy it? One way to finance the purchase is to buy it on account and withhold payment until the last day of the term for the account payable. For example, suppose you buy inventory under terms 2/10, net/30. Under these circumstances you could delay payment for 30 days after the day of purchase. This way you may be able to collect enough money from the inventory you sell

REALITY BYTES

Many real-world companies have found it more effective to impose a penalty for late payment than to use a cash discount to encourage early payment. The invoice from Arley Water Works is an example of the penalty strategy. Notice that the amount due, if paid by the due date, is $18.14. A $1.88 late charge is imposed if the bill is paid after the due date. The $1.88 late charge is in fact interest. If Arley Water Works collects the payment after the due date, the utility will receive cash of $20.02. The collection will increase cash ($20.02), reduce accounts receivable ($18.14), and increase interest revenue ($1.88).

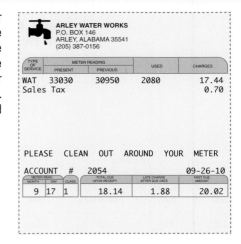

to pay for the inventory you purchased. Refusing the discount allows you the time needed to generate the cash necessary to pay off the liability (account payable). Unfortunately, this is usually a very expensive way to finance the purchase of inventory.

While the amount of a cash discount may appear small, the discount period is short. Consider the terms 2/10, net/30. Since you can pay on the tenth day and still receive the discount, you obtain financing for only 20 days (30-day full credit term − 10-day discount term). In other words, you must forgo a 2 percent discount to obtain a loan with a 20-day term. What is the size of the discount in annual terms? The answer is determined by the following formula.

Annual rate = Discount rate × (365 days ÷ term of the loan)

Annual rate = 2% × (365 ÷ 20)

Annual rate = 36.5%

This means that a 2 percent discount rate for 20 days is equivalent to a 36.5 percent annual rate of interest. So, if you do not have the money to pay the account payable, but can borrow money from a bank at less than 36.5 percent annual interest, you should borrow the money and pay off the account payable within the discount period.

Accounting for Transportation Costs

EVENT 6   The shipping terms for the inventory purchased in Event 2 were FOB shipping point. JPS paid the freight company $300 cash for delivering the merchandise.

The terms **FOB shipping point** and **FOB destination** identify whether the buyer or the seller is responsible for transportation costs. If goods are delivered FOB shipping point, the buyer is responsible for the freight cost. If goods are delivered FOB destination, the seller is responsible. When the buyer is responsible, the freight cost is called **transportation-in.** When the seller is responsible, the cost is called **transportation-out.** The following table summarizes freight cost terms.

Responsible Party	Buyer	Seller
Freight terms	FOB shipping point	FOB destination
Account title	Merchandise inventory	Transportation-out

Event 6 indicates the inventory was delivered FOB shipping point, so JPS (the buyer) is responsible for the $300 freight cost. Since incurring transportation-in costs is necessary to obtain inventory, these costs are added to the inventory account. The freight cost increases one asset account (Merchandise Inventory) and decreases another asset account (Cash). The income statement is not affected by this transaction because transportation-in costs are not expensed when they are incurred. Instead they are expensed as part of *cost of goods sold* when the inventory is sold. However, the cash paid for transportation-in costs is reported as an outflow in the operating activities section of the statement of cash flows. The effects of *transportation-in costs* are shown here.

		Assets			=	Liab.			+	Stockholders' Equity						
Cash	+	Accts. Rec.	+ Inventory	+ Land	=	Accts. Pay.	+ Notes Pay.	+	Com. Stk.	+ Ret. Earn.		Rev.	− Exp.	= Net Inc.		Cash Flow
(300)	+	NA	+ 300	+ NA	=	NA	+ NA	+	NA	+ NA		NA	− NA	= NA		(300) OA

EVENT 7A   **JPS recognized $24,750 of revenue on the cash sale of merchandise that cost $11,500.**

The sale increases assets (cash) and stockholders' equity (retained earnings). The revenue recognition increases net income. The $24,750 cash inflow from the sale is reported in the operating activities section of the statement of cash flows. These effects are shown below.

		Assets			=	Liab.			+	Stockholders' Equity						
Cash	+	Accts. Rec.	+ Inventory	+ Land	=	Accts. Pay.	+ Notes Pay.	+	Com. Stk.	+ Ret. Earn.		Rev.	− Exp.	= Net Inc.		Cash Flow
24,750	+	NA	+ NA	+ NA	=	NA	+ NA	+	NA	+ 24,750		24,750	− NA	= 24,750		24,750 OA

EVENT 7B   **JPS recognized $11,500 of cost of goods sold.**

When goods are sold, the product cost—*including a proportionate share of transportation-in and adjustments for purchase returns and allowances*—is transferred from the Merchandise Inventory account to the expense account, Cost of Goods Sold. Recognizing cost of goods sold decreases both assets (merchandise inventory) and stockholders' equity (retained earnings). The expense recognition for cost of goods sold decreases net income. Cash flow is not affected. These effects are shown here.

		Assets			=	Liab.			+	Stockholders' Equity						
Cash	+	Accts. Rec.	+ Inventory	+ Land	=	Accts. Pay.	+ Notes Pay.	+	Com. Stk.	+ Ret. Earn.		Rev.	− Exp.	= Net Inc.		Cash Flow
NA	+	NA	+ (11,500)	+ NA	=	NA	+ NA	+	NA	+ (11,500)		NA	− 11,500	= (11,500)		NA

EVENT 8   JPS paid $450 cash for freight costs on inventory delivered to customers.

Assume the merchandise sold in Event 7A was shipped FOB destination. Also assume JPS paid the freight cost in cash. FOB destination means the seller is responsible for the freight cost, which is called transportation-out. Transportation-out is reported on the income statement as an operating expense in the section below gross margin. The cost of freight on goods shipped to customers is incurred *after* the goods are sold. It is not part of the costs to obtain goods or ready them for sale. Recognizing the expense of transportation-out reduces assets (cash) and stockholders' equity (retained earnings). Operating expenses increase and net income decreases. The cash outflow is reported in the operating activities section of the statement of cash flows. These effects are shown below.

	Assets			=	Liab.		+	Stockholders' Equity						
Cash +	Accts. Rec. +	Inventory +	Land =		Accts. Pay. +	Notes Pay. +		Com. Stk. +	Ret. Earn.		Rev. −	Exp. =	Net Inc.	Cash Flow
(450) +	NA +	NA +	NA =		NA +	NA +		NA +	(450)		NA −	450 =	(450)	(450) OA

If the terms had been FOB shipping point, the customer would have been responsible for the transportation cost and JPS would not have recorded an expense.

EVENT 9   JPS paid $5,000 cash for selling and administrative expenses.

The effect on the balance sheet is to decrease both assets (cash) and stockholders' equity (retained earnings). Recognizing the selling and administrative expenses decreases net income. The $5,000 cash outflow is reported in the operating activities section of the statement of cash flows. These effects are shown below.

	Assets			=	Liab.		+	Stockholders' Equity						
Cash +	Accts. Rec. +	Inventory +	Land =		Accts. Pay. +	Notes Pay. +		Com. Stk. +	Ret. Earn.		Rev. −	Exp. =	Net Inc.	Cash Flow
(5,000) +	NA +	NA +	NA =		NA +	NA +		NA +	(5,000)		NA −	5,000 =	(5,000)	(5,000) OA

EVENT 10   JPS paid $360 cash for interest expense on the note described in Event 1.

The effect on the balance sheet is to decrease both assets (cash) and stockholders' equity (retained earnings). Recognizing the interest expense decreases net income. The $360 cash outflow is reported in the operating activities section of the statement of cash flows. These effects are shown below.

	Assets			=	Liab.		+	Stockholders' Equity						
Cash +	Accts. Rec. +	Inventory +	Land =		Accts. Pay. +	Notes Pay. +		Com. Stk. +	Ret. Earn.		Rev. −	Exp. =	Net Inc.	Cash Flow
(360) +	NA +	NA +	NA =		NA +	NA +		NA +	(360)		NA −	360 =	(360)	(360) OA

RECOGNIZING GAINS AND LOSSES

EVENT 11   JPS sold the land that had cost $5,500 for $6,200 cash.

When JPS sells merchandise inventory for more than it cost, the difference between the sales revenue and the cost of the goods sold is called the *gross margin.* In contrast, when JPS sells land for more than it cost, the difference between the sales price and the cost of the land is called a **gain.** Why is one called *gross margin* and the other a *gain?* The terms are used to alert financial statement users to the fact that the nature of the underlying transactions is different.

JPS' primary business is selling inventory, not land. The term *gain* indicates profit resulting from transactions that are not likely to regularly recur. Similarly, had the land sold for less than cost the difference would have been labeled **loss** rather than expense. This term also indicates the underlying transaction is not from normal, recurring operating activities. Gains and losses are shown separately on the income statement to communicate the expectation that they are nonrecurring.

The presentation of gains and losses in the income statement is discussed in more detail in a later section of the chapter. At this point note that the sale increases cash, decreases land, and increases retained earnings on the balance sheet. The income statement shows a gain on the sale of land and net income increases. The $6,200 cash inflow is shown as an investing activity on the statement of cash flows. These effects are shown below:

Assets				=	Liab.			+	Stockholders' Equity						
Cash	+ Accts. Rec.	+ Inventory	+ Land	=	Accts. Pay.	+ Notes Pay.	+ Com. Stk.	+ Ret. Earn.		Gain	− Exp.	= Net Inc.		Cash Flow	
6,200	+ NA	+ NA	+ (5,500)	=	NA	+ NA	+ NA	+ 700		700	− NA	= 700		6,200	IA

✓ CHECK YOURSELF 3.2

Tsang Company purchased $32,000 of inventory on account with payment terms of 2/10, n/30 and freight terms FOB shipping point. Freight costs were $1,100. Tsang obtained a $2,000 purchase allowance because the inventory was damaged upon arrival. Tsang paid for the inventory within the discount period. Based on this information alone, determine the balance in the inventory account.

Answer

List price of inventory	$32,000
Plus: Transportation-in costs	1,100
Less: Purchase returns and allowances	(2,000)
Less: Purchase discount [($32,000 − $2,000) × .02]	(600)
Balance in inventory account	$30,500

MULTISTEP INCOME STATEMENT

JPS' 2013 income statement is shown in Exhibit 3.3. Observe the form of this statement carefully. It is more informative than one which simply subtracts expenses from revenues. First, it compares sales revenue with the cost of the goods that were sold to produce that revenue. The difference between the sales revenue and the cost of goods sold is called *gross margin.* Next, the operating expenses are subtracted from the gross margin to determine the *operating income.* **Operating income** is the amount of income that is generated from the normal recurring operations of a business. Items that are not expected to recur on a regular basis are subtracted from the operating income to determine the amount of *net income.*[1]

EXHIBIT 3.3

JUNE'S PLANT SHOP
Income Statement
For the Period Ended December 31, 2013

Sales revenue	$ 24,750
Cost of goods sold	(11,500)
Gross margin	13,250
Less: Operating expenses	
Selling and administrative expense	(5,000)
Transportation-out	(450)
Operating income	7,800
Nonoperating items	
Interest expense	(360)
Gain on the sale of land	700
Net income	$ 8,140

EXHIBIT 3.4

Income Statement Format Used by U.S. Companies

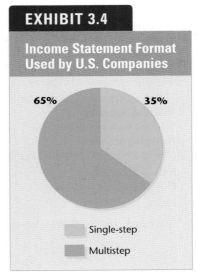

65%　　　35%

Single-step
Multistep

Data Source: AICPA, *Accounting Trends and Techniques.*

EXHIBIT 3.5

JUNE'S PLANT SHOP
Balance Sheet
As of December 31, 2013

Assets		
Cash	$25,540	
Merchandise inventory	4,600	
Total assets		$30,140
Liabilities		
Notes payable		$ 4,000
Stockholders' equity		
Common stock	$15,000	
Retained earnings	11,140	
Total stockholders' equity		26,140
Total liabilities and stockholders' equity		$30,140

　　Income statements that show these additional relationships are called **multistep income statements.** Income statements that display a single comparison of all revenues minus all expenses are called **single-step income statements.** To this point in the text we have shown only single-step income statements to promote simplicity. However, the multistep form is used more frequently in practice. Exhibit 3.4 shows the percentage of companies that use the multistep versus the single-step format. Go to Exhibit 3.1 and identify the company that presents its income statement in the multistep format. You should have identified Blue Nile as the company using the multistep format. Zale's statement is shown in the single-step format.

[1]Revenue and expense items with special characteristics may be classified as discontinued or extraordinary items. These items are shown separately just above net income regardless of whether a company uses a single-step or multistep format. Further discussion of these items is beyond the scope of this text.

EXHIBIT 3.6

JUNE'S PLANT SHOP
Statement of Cash Flows
For the Period Ended December 31, 2013

Operating activities		
Inflow from customers	$ 24,750	
Outflow for inventory*	(10,100)	
Outflow for transportation-out	(450)	
Outflow for selling and administrative expense	(5,000)	
Outflow for interest expense	(360)	
Net cash outflow for operating activities		$ 8,840
Investing activities		
Inflow from sale of land		6,200
Financing activities		
Inflow from issue of note payable		4,000
Net change in cash		19,040
Plus beginning cash balance		6,500
Ending cash balance		$25,540

*Net cost on inventory $9,800 + transportation-in $300 = $10,100

Note that interest is reported as a *nonoperating* item on the income statement in Exhibit 3.3. In contrast, it is shown in the *operating* activities section of the statement of cash flows in Exhibit 3.6. When the FASB issued Statement of Financial Accounting Standard (SFAS) 95, it required interest to be reported in the operating activities section of the statement of cash flows. There was no corresponding requirement for the treatment of interest on the income statement. Prior to SFAS 95, interest was considered to be a nonoperating item. Most companies continued to report interest as a nonoperating item on their income statements even though they were required to change how it was reported on the statement of cash flows. As a result, there is frequent inconsistency in the way interest is reported on the two financial statements.

Also note that while the gain on the sale of land is shown on the income statement, it is not included in the operating activities section of the statement of cash flows. Since the gain is a nonoperating item, it is included in the cash inflow from the sale of land shown in the investing activities section. In this case the full cash inflow from the sale of land ($6,200) is shown in the investing activities section of the statement of cash flows in Exhibit 3.6.

LOST, DAMAGED, OR STOLEN INVENTORY

LO 6

Show the effect of lost, damaged, or stolen inventory on financial statements.

Most merchandising companies experience some level of inventory **shrinkage,** a term that reflects decreases in inventory for reasons other than sales to customers. Inventory may be stolen by shoplifters, damaged by customers or employees, or even simply lost or misplaced. Since the *perpetual* inventory system is designed to record purchases and sales of inventory as they occur, the balance in the merchandise inventory account represents the amount of inventory that *should* be on hand at any given time. By taking a physical count of the merchandise inventory at the end of the accounting period and comparing that amount with the book balance in the Merchandise Inventory account, managers can determine the amount of any inventory shrinkage. If goods have been lost, damaged, or stolen, the book balance will be higher than the actual amount of inventory on hand and an adjusting entry is required to reduce assets and equity. The Merchandise Inventory account is reduced, and an expense for the amount of the lost, damaged, or stolen inventory is recognized.

REALITY BYTES

"Closed for Inventory Count" is a sign you frequently see on retail stores sometime during the month of January. Even if companies use a perpetual inventory system, the amount of inventory on hand may be unknown because of lost, damaged, or stolen goods. The only way to determine the amount of inventory on hand is to count it. Why count it in January? Christmas shoppers and many after-Christmas sales shoppers are satiated by mid-January, leaving the stores low on both merchandise and customers. Accordingly, stores have less merchandise to count and "lost sales" are minimized during January. Companies that do not depend on seasonal sales (e.g., a plumbing supplies wholesale business) may choose to count inventory at some other time during the year. Counting inventory is not a revenue-generating activity; it is a necessary evil that should be conducted when it least disrupts operations.

Adjustment for Lost, Damaged, or Stolen Inventory

To illustrate, assume that Midwest Merchandising Company maintains perpetual inventory records. Midwest determined, through a physical count, that it had $23,500 of merchandise inventory on hand at the end of the accounting period. The balance in the Inventory account was $24,000. Midwest must make an adjusting entry to write down the Inventory account so the amount reported on the financial statements agrees with the amount actually on hand at the end of the period. The write-down decreases both assets (inventory) and stockholders' equity (retained earnings). The write-down increases expenses and decreases net income. Cash flow is not affected. The effects on the statements are as follows.

Assets	=	Liab.	+	Equity	Rev.	−	Exp.	=	Net Inc.	Cash Flow
(500)	=	NA	+	(500)	NA	−	500	=	(500)	NA

Theoretically, inventory losses are operating expenses. However, because such losses are normally immaterial in amount, they are usually added to cost of goods sold for external reporting purposes.

EVENTS AFFECTING SALES

To this point we assumed JPS did not offer cash discounts to its customers. However, sales, as well as purchases of inventory, can be affected by returns, allowances, and discounts. **Sales discounts** are price reductions offered by sellers to encourage buyers to pay promptly. To illustrate, assume JPS engaged in the following selected events during January 2014.

EVENT 1A   JPS sold on account merchandise with a list price of $8,500. Payment terms were 1/10, n/30. The merchandise had cost JPS $4,000.

The sale increases both assets (accounts receivable) and shareholders' equity (retained earnings). Recognizing revenue increases net income. The statement of cash flows is not affected. The effects on the financial statements follow.

	Assets				=	Liab.	+	Stockholders' Equity			Rev.	−	Exp.	=	Net Inc.	Cash Flow
Cash	+	Accts. Rec.	+	Inventory	=	Note Pay.	+	Com. Stk.	+	Retained Earnings						
NA	+	8,500	+	NA	=	NA	+	NA	+	8,500	8,500	−	NA	=	8,500	NA

EVENT 1B   JPS recognized $4,000 of cost of goods sold.

Recognizing the expense decreases assets (merchandise inventory) and stockholders' equity (retained earnings). Cost of goods sold increases and net income decreases. Cash flow is not affected. The effects on the financial statements follow.

Assets			=	Liab.	+	Stockholders' Equity			Rev.	−	Exp.	=	Net Inc.	Cash Flow
Cash	+	Accts. Rec.	+	Inventory	=	Note Pay.	+	Com. Stk.	+	Retained Earnings				
NA	+	NA	+	(4,000)	=	NA	+	NA	+	(4,000)	NA	−	4,000	=	(4,000)	NA

Accounting for Sales Returns and Allowances

EVENT 2A   A customer from Event 1A returned inventory with a $1,000 list price. The merchandise had cost JPS $450.

The sales return decreases both assets (accounts receivable) and stockholders' equity (retained earnings) on the balance sheet. Sales and net income decrease. Cash flow is not affected. The effects on the financial statements follow.

Assets			=	Liab.	+	Stockholders' Equity			Rev.	−	Exp.	=	Net Inc.	Cash Flow
Cash	+	Accts. Rec.	+	Inventory	=	Note Pay.	+	Com. Stk.	+	Retained Earnings				
NA	+	(1,000)	+	NA	=	NA	+	NA	+	(1,000)	(1,000)	−	NA	=	(1,000)	NA

EVENT 2B   The cost of the goods ($450) is returned to the inventory account.

Since JPS got the inventory back, the sales return increases both assets (merchandise inventory) and stockholders' equity (retained earnings). The expense (cost of goods sold) decreases and net income increases. Cash flow is not affected. The effects on the financial statements follow.

Assets			=	Liab.	+	Stockholders' Equity			Rev.	−	Exp.	=	Net Inc.	Cash Flow
Cash	+	Accts. Rec.	+	Inventory	=	Note Pay.	+	Com. Stk.	+	Retained Earnings				
NA	+	NA	+	450	=	NA	+	NA	+	450	NA	−	(450)	=	450	NA

Accounting for Sales Discounts

EVENT 3   JPS collected the balance of the accounts receivable generated in Event 1A. Recall the goods were sold under terms 1/10, net/30.

ALTERNATIVE 1   The collection occurs before the discount period has expired (within 10 days from the date of the sale).

JPS would give the buyer a 1 percent discount. Given the original sales amount of $8,500 and a sales return of $1,000, the amount of the discount is $75 [($8,500 − $1,000) × .01]. The sales discount reduces the amount of accounts receivable and retained earnings on the balance sheet. It also reduces the amount of revenue and the net income shown on the balance sheet. It does not affect the statement of cash flows. The effects on the financial statements follow.

	Assets			=	Liab.	+	Stockholders' Equity			Rev.	−	Exp.	=	Net Inc.	Cash Flow
Cash	+	Accts. Rec.	+	Inventory	=	Note Pay.	+	Com. Stk.	+	Retained Earnings					
NA	+	(75)	+	NA	=	NA	+	NA	+	(75)	(75)	−	NA	=	(75)	NA

The balance due on the account receivable is $7,425 ($8,500 original sales − $1,000 sales return − $75 discount). The collection increases the Cash account and decreases the Accounts Receivable account. The income statement is not affected. The cash inflow is shown in the operating activities section of the statement of cash flows. The effects on the financial statements follow.

	Assets			=	Liab.	+	Stockholders' Equity			Rev.	−	Exp.	=	Net Inc.	Cash Flow
Cash	+	Accts. Rec.	+	Inventory	=	Accts. Pay.	+	Com. Stk.	+	Retained Earnings					
7,425	+	(7,425)	+	NA	=	NA	+	NA	+	NA	NA	−	NA	=	NA	7,425 OA

Net Sales

The gross amount of sales minus **sales returns and allowance** and sales discounts is commonly called **net sales.** Companies are not required by GAAP to show sales returns and allowance and sales discount on their income statement. Indeed, most companies show only the amount of *net sales* on the income statement. In this case the net sales amount to $7,425 ($8,500 original sales − $1,000 sales return − $75 discount).

ALTERNATIVE 2   The collection occurs after the discount period has expired (after 10 days from the date of the sale).

Under these circumstances there is no sales discount. The amount collected is $7,500 ($8,500 original sale − $1,000 sales return). Net sales shown on the income statement would also be $7,500.

COMMON SIZE FINANCIAL STATEMENTS

How good is a $1,000,000 increase in net income? The answer is not clear because there is no indication as to the size of the company. A million dollar increase may be excellent for a small company but would be virtually meaningless for a company the size of Exxon. To enable meaningful comparisons analysts prepare **common size financial statements.** Common size statements display information in percentages as well as absolute dollar amounts.

To illustrate, we expand the income statements for JPS to include percentages. The results are shown in Exhibit 3.7. The percentage data are computed by defining net sales as the base figure, or 100 percent. The other amounts on the statements are then

LO 7

Use common sizes financial statements to evaluate managerial performance.

The income statement data show that compared to Zales, Blue Nile does save money by not operating bricks-and-mortar stores. This can be determined by comparing each company's net income to its sales. For Blue Nile this percentage is 4.2% ($12,800 ÷ $302,134), which means that while 4.2% of each dollar of revenue goes to profit, 95.8% goes to pay for expenses. For Zales this percentage is a *negative* 10.6% [($189,503) ÷ 1,779,744]. Clearly, Blue Nile did better than Zales. This result is despite the fact that compared to Blue Nile, Zales charges a higher price for the jewelry it sells. Compare each company's gross margin to its sales. Blue Nile's gross margin is 21.6% of its sales ($65,344 ÷ $302,134), which means that 78.4% of each dollar of revenue goes to pay for the product that was sold. For Zales these percentages are 46.7% for the gross margin [(1,779,744 − $948,572) ÷ 1,779,744] and 53.3% for cost of goods sold. This shows that while Blue Nile charges less for its products, it makes up for the lower gross margin with lower operating expenses.

shown as a percentage of net sales. For example, the *cost of goods sold percentage* is the dollar amount of *cost of goods sold* divided by the dollar amount of *net sales,* which produces a percentage of 66.7 percent ($8,000 ÷ $12,000) for 2012 and 46.5 percent ($11,500 ÷ $24,750) for 2013. Other income statement items are computed using the same approach.

These common size statements provide insight into the company's operating strategy. For example, assume JPS relocated its store in an upscale mall in early 2013.

EXHIBIT 3.7   Common Size Financial Statements

JUNE'S PLANT SHOP
Income Statement
For the Period Ended

	2012		2013	
Net sales*	$12,000	100.0%	$24,750	100.0%
Cost of goods sold	(8,000)	66.7	(11,500)	46.5
Gross margin	4,000	33.3	13,250	53.5
Less: Operating expenses				
Selling and administrative expense	(1,000)	8.3	(5,000)	20.2
Transportation-out			(450)	1.8
Operating income	3,000	25.0	7,800	31.5
Nonoperating items				
Interest expense			(360)	(1.5)
Gain on the sale of land			700	2.8
Net income	$ 3,000	25.0	$ 8,140	32.9

*Since JPS did not offer sales discounts or have sales returns and allowances during 2012 or 2013, the amount of sales revenue is equal to the amount of net sales. We use the term *net sales* here because it is more commonly used in business practice. Percentages do not add exactly because they have been rounded.

Management realized that the company would have to pay more for operating expenses but believed those expenses could be offset by charging significantly higher prices. The common size income statement confirms that the company's goals were accomplished. Note that the gross margin increased from 33.3 percent of sales to 53.5 percent, confirming that the company was able to increase prices. Also, note that operating expenses increased. Selling and administrative expense increased from 8.3 percent of sales to 20.2 percent. Also, the company experienced a new expense, transportation out, for delivering merchandise to its customers. These increases in expenses confirm the fact that JPS is paying more for rental space and providing additional services to its customers. The common size statements, therefore, support the conclusion that JPS's increase in net income from $3,000 to $8,140 was a result of management's new operating strategy. As a side note, the new operating strategy may also explain why JPS sold its land in late 2013. Considering the success the company experienced at the new location, there was no motive to build a store on the land.

A Look Back

Merchandising companies earn profits by selling inventory at prices that are higher than the cost paid for the goods. Merchandising companies include *retail companies* (companies that sell goods to the final consumer) and *wholesale companies* (companies that sell to other merchandising companies). The products sold by merchandising companies are called *inventory.* The costs to purchase inventory, to receive it, and to ready it for sale are *product costs,* which are first accumulated in an inventory account (balance sheet asset account) and then recognized as cost of goods sold (income statement expense account) in the period in which goods are sold. Purchases and sales of inventory can be recorded continually as goods are bought and sold (perpetual system) or at the end of the accounting period (periodic system, discussed in the chapter appendix).

Accounting for inventory includes the treatment of cash discounts, transportation costs, and returns and allowances. The cost of inventory is the list price less any purchase returns and allowances and purchase discounts, plus transportation-in costs. The cost of freight paid to acquire inventory (*transportation-in*) is considered a product cost. The cost of freight paid to deliver inventory to customers (*transportation-out*) is a selling expense. *Sales returns and allowances* and *sales discounts* are subtracted from sales revenue to determine the amount of *net sales* reported on the income statement. Purchase returns and allowances reduce product cost. Theoretically, the cost of lost, damaged, or stolen inventory is an operating expense. However, because these costs are usually immaterial in amount they are typically included as part of cost of goods sold on the income statement.

Some companies use a *multistep income statement* which reports product costs separately from selling and administrative costs. Cost of goods sold is subtracted from sales revenue to determine *gross margin.* Selling and administrative expenses are subtracted from gross margin to determine income from operations. Other companies report income using a *single-step format* in which the cost of goods sold is listed along with selling and administrative items in a single expense category that is subtracted in total from revenue to determine income from operations.

Managers of merchandising businesses operate in a highly competitive environment. They must manage company operations carefully to remain profitable. *Common size financial statements* (statements presented on a percentage basis) and ratio analysis are useful monitoring tools. Common size financial statements permit ready comparisons among different-size companies. Although a $1 million increase in sales may be good for a small company and bad for a large company, a 10 percent increase can apply to any size company.

>> A Look Forward

To this point, the text has explained the basic accounting cycle for service and merchandising businesses. Future chapters more closely address specific accounting issues. For example, in Chapter 5 you will learn how to deal with inventory items that are purchased at differing prices. Other chapters will discuss a variety of specific practices that are widely used by real-world companies.

APPENDIX

LO 8

Identify the primary features of the periodic inventory system.

Periodic Inventory System

Under certain conditions, it is impractical to record inventory sales transactions as they occur. Consider the operations of a fast-food restaurant. To maintain perpetual inventory records, the restaurant would have to transfer from the Inventory account to the Cost of Goods Sold account the *cost* of each hamburger, order of fries, soft drink, or other food items as they were sold. Obviously, recording the cost of each item at the point of sale would be impractical without using highly sophisticated computer equipment (recording the selling price the customer pays is captured by cash registers; the difficulty lies in capturing inventory cost).

The **periodic inventory system** offers a practical solution for recording inventory transactions in a low-technology, high-volume environment. Inventory costs are recorded in a Purchases account at the time of purchase. Purchase returns and allowances and transportation-in are recorded in separate accounts. No entries for the cost of merchandise purchases or sales are recorded in the Inventory account during the period. The cost of goods sold is determined at the end of the period as shown in Exhibit 3.8.

EXHIBIT 3.8

Schedule of Cost of Goods Sold for 2013	
Beginning inventory	$ 6,000
Purchases	11,000
Purchase returns and allowances	(1,000)
Purchase discounts	(200)
Transportation-in	300
Cost of goods available for sale	16,100
Ending inventory	4,600
Cost of goods sold	$11,500

The perpetual and periodic inventory systems represent alternative procedures for recording the same information. The amounts of cost of goods sold and ending inventory reported in the financial statements will be the same regardless of the method used.

The **schedule of cost of goods sold** presented in Exhibit 3.8 is used for internal reporting purposes. It is normally not shown in published financial statements. The amount of cost of goods sold is reported as a single line item on the income statement. The income statement in Exhibit 3.3 will be the same whether JPS maintains perpetual or periodic inventory records.

Advantages and Disadvantages of the Periodic System versus the Perpetual System

The chief advantage of the periodic method is recording efficiency. Recording inventory transactions occasionally (periodically) requires less effort than recording them continually (perpetually). Historically, practical limitations offered businesses like fast-food restaurants or grocery stores no alternative to using the periodic system. The sheer volume of transactions made recording individual decreases to the Inventory account balance as each item was sold impossible. Imagine the number of transactions a grocery store would have to record every business day to maintain perpetual records.

Although the periodic system provides a recordkeeping advantage over the perpetual system, perpetual inventory records provide significant control advantages over periodic records. With perpetual records, the book balance in the Inventory account should agree with the amount of inventory in stock at any given time. By comparing that book balance with the results of a physical inventory count, management can determine the amount of lost, damaged, destroyed, or stolen inventory. Perpetual records also permit more timely and accurate reorder decisions and profitability assessments.

When a company uses the *periodic* inventory system, lost, damaged, or stolen merchandise is automatically included in cost of goods sold. Because such goods are not included in the year-end physical count, they are treated as sold regardless of the reason for their absence. Since the periodic system does not separate the cost of lost, damaged, or stolen merchandise from the cost of goods sold, the amount of any inventory shrinkage is unknown. This feature is a major disadvantage of the periodic system. Without knowing the amount of inventory losses, management cannot weigh the costs of various security systems against the potential benefits.

Advances in such technology as electronic bar code scanning and increased computing power have eliminated most of the practical constraints that once prevented merchandisers with high-volume, low dollar-value inventories from recording inventory transactions on a continual basis. As a result, use of the perpetual inventory system has expanded rapidly in recent years and continued growth can be expected. This text, therefore, concentrates on the perpetual inventory system.

A step-by-step audio-narrated series of slides is provided on the text website at www.mhhe.com/edmondssurvey3e.

SELF-STUDY REVIEW PROBLEM

Academy Sales Company (ASC) started the 2012 accounting period with the balances given in the financial statements model shown below. During 2012 ASC experienced the following business events.

1. Purchased $16,000 of merchandise inventory on account, terms 2/10, n/30.
2. The goods that were purchased in Event 1 were delivered FOB shipping point. Freight costs of $600 were paid in cash by the responsible party.
3. Returned $500 of goods purchased in Event 1.
4a. Recorded the cash discount on the goods purchased in Event 1.
4b. Paid the balance due on the account payable within the discount period.
5a. Recognized $21,000 of cash revenue from the sale of merchandise.
5b. Recognized $15,000 of cost of goods sold.
6. The merchandise in Event 5a was sold to customers FOB destination. Freight costs of $950 were paid in cash by the responsible party.
7. Paid cash of $4,000 for selling and administrative expenses.
8. Sold the land for $5,600 cash.

Required

a. Record the above transactions in a financial statements model like the one shown below.

Event No.	Cash	+	Inventory	+	Land	=	Accts. Pay.	+	Com. Stk.	+	Ret. Earn.	Rev./ Gain	−	Exp.	=	Net Inc.	Cash Flow
Bal.	25,000	+	3,000	+	5,000	=	–0–	+	18,000	+	15,000	NA	−	NA	=	NA	NA

b. Prepare a schedule of cost of goods sold. (Appendix)
c. Prepare a multistep income statement. Include common size percentages on the income statement.
d. ASC's gross margin percentage in 2011 was 22%. Based on the common size data in the income statement, did ASC raise or lower its prices in 2012? (Appendix)
e. Assuming a 10 percent rate of growth, what is the amount of net income expected for 2013?

Solution

a.

Event No.	Cash	+	Inventory	+	Land	=	Accts. Pay.	+	Com. Stk.	+	Ret. Earn.	Rev./ Gain	−	Exp.	=	Net Inc.	Cash Flow
Bal.	25,000	+	3,000	+	5,000	=	−0−	+	18,000	+	15,000	NA	−	NA	=	NA	NA
1		+	16,000			=	16,000	+		+			−		=		
2	(600)	+	600			=		+		+			−		=		(600) OA
3		+	(500)			=	(500)	+		+			−		=		
4a		+	(310)			=	(310)	+		+			−		=		
4b	(15,190)	+				=	(15,190)	+		+			−		=		(15,190) OA
5a	21,000	+				=		+		+	21,000	21,000	−		=	21,000	21,000 OA
5b		+	(15,000)			=		+		+	(15,000)		−	15,000	=	(15,000)	
6	(950)	+				=		+		+	(950)		−	950	=	(950)	(950) OA
7	(4,000)	+				=		+		+	(4,000)		−	4,000	=	(4,000)	(4,000) OA
8	5,600	+			(5,000)	=		+		+	600	600	−		=	600	5,600 IA
Bal.	30,860	+	3,790		−0−	=	−0−	+	18,000	+	16,650	21,600	−	19,950	=	1,650	5,860 NC

b.

> ### ACADEMY SALES COMPANY
> #### Schedule of Cost of Goods Sold
> #### For the Period Ended December 31, 2012
>
> | | |
> |---|---|
> | Beginning inventory | $ 3,000 |
> | Plus purchases | 16,000 |
> | Less: Purchase returns and allowances | (500) |
> | Less: Purchases discounts | (310) |
> | Plus: Transportation-in | 600 |
> | Goods available for sale | 18,790 |
> | Less: Ending inventory | 3,790 |
> | Cost of goods sold | $(15,000) |

c.

> ### ACADEMY SALES COMPANY
> #### Income Statement*
> #### For the Period Ended December 31, 2012
>
> | | | |
> |---|---|---|
> | Net sales | $21,000 | 100.0% |
> | Cost of goods sold | (15,000) | 71.4 |
> | Gross margin | 6,000 | 28.6 |
> | Less: Operating expenses | | |
> | Selling and administrative expense | (4,000) | 19.0 |
> | Transportation-out | (950) | 4.5 |
> | Operating income | 1,050 | 5.0 |
> | Nonoperating items | | |
> | Gain on the sale of land | 600 | 2.9 |
> | Net income | $ 1,650 | 7.9 |
>
> *Percentages do not add exactly because they have been rounded.

d. All other things being equal, the higher the gross margin percentage, the higher the sales prices. Since the gross margin percentage increased from 22% to 28.6%, the data suggest that Academy raised its sales prices.

e. $1,155 [$1,050 + (.10 × $1,050)]. Note that the gain is not expected to recur.

KEY TERMS

Cash discount 94

Common size financial statements 103

Cost of goods available for sale 89

Cost of Goods Sold 89

FOB (free on board) destination 95

FOB (free on board) shipping point 95

Gain 98

Gross margin 89

Gross profit 89

Loss 98

Merchandise inventory 86

Merchandising businesses 86

Multistep income statement 99

Net sales 103

Operating income (or loss) 99

Period costs 89

Periodic inventory system 106

Perpetual inventory system 89

Product costs 89

Purchase discount 94

Purchase returns and allowances 93

Retail companies 86

Sales discounts 101

Sales returns and allowances 103

Schedule of cost of goods sold 106

Selling and administrative costs 89

Shrinkage 100

Single-step income statement 99

Transportation-in (freight-in) 95

Transportation-out (freight-out) 95

2/10, n/30 94

Wholesale companies 86

QUESTIONS

1. Define *merchandise inventory*. What types of costs are included in the Merchandise Inventory account?

2. What is the difference between a product cost and a selling and administrative cost?

3. How is the cost of goods available for sale determined?

4. What portion of cost of goods available for sale is shown on the balance sheet? What portion is shown on the income statement?

5. When are period costs expensed? When are product costs expensed?

6. If PetCo had net sales of $600,000, goods available for sale of $450,000, and cost of goods sold of $375,000, what is its gross margin? What amount of inventory will be shown on its balance sheet?

7. Describe how the perpetual inventory system works. What are some advantages of using the perpetual inventory system? Is it necessary to take a physical inventory when using the perpetual inventory system?

8. What are the effects of the following types of transactions on the accounting equation? Also identify the financial statements that are affected. (Assume that the perpetual inventory system is used.)
   a. Acquisition of cash from the issue of common stock.
   b. Contribution of inventory by an owner of a company.
   c. Purchase of inventory with cash by a company.
   d. Sale of inventory for cash.

9. Northern Merchandising Company sold inventory that cost $12,000 for $20,000 cash. How does this event affect the accounting equation? What financial statements and accounts are affected? (Assume that the perpetual inventory system is used.)

10. If goods are shipped FOB shipping point, which party (buyer or seller) is responsible for the shipping costs?

11. Define *transportation-in*. Is it a product or a period cost?

12. Quality Cellular Co. paid $80 for freight on merchandise that it had purchased for resale to customers (transportation-in) and paid $135 for freight on merchandise delivered to customers (transportation-out). The $80 payment is added to what account? The $135 payment is added to what account?

13. Why would a seller grant an allowance to a buyer of the his merchandise?

14. Dyer Department Store purchased goods with the terms 2/10, n/30. What do these terms mean?

15. Eastern Discount Stores incurred a $5,000 cash cost. How does the accounting for this cost differ if the cash were paid for inventory versus commissions to sales personnel?

16. What is the purpose of giving a cash discount to charge customers?

17. Define *transportation-out*. Is it a product cost or a period cost for the seller?

18. Ball Co. purchased inventory with a list price of $4,000 with the terms 2/10, n/30. What amount will be added to the Merchandise Inventory account?

19. Explain the difference between purchase returns and sales returns. How do purchase returns affect the financial statements of both buyer and seller? How do sales returns affect the financial statements of both buyer and seller?

20. Explain the difference between gross margin and a gain.

21. What is the difference between a multistep income statement and a single-step income statement?

22. What is the advantage of using common size income statements to present financial information for several accounting periods?

23. What is the purpose of preparing a schedule of cost of goods sold?

24. Explain how the periodic inventory system works. What are some advantages of using the periodic inventory system? What are some disadvantages of using the periodic inventory system? Is it necessary to take a physical inventory when using the periodic inventory system?

25. Why does the periodic inventory system impose a major disadvantage for management in accounting for lost, stolen, or damaged goods?

 MULTIPLE-CHOICE QUESTIONS

Multiple-choice questions are provided on the text website at www.mhhe.com/edmondssurvey3e.

EXERCISES

All applicable Exercises are available with McGraw-Hill's *Connect Accounting*.

When the instructions for *any* exercise or problem call for the preparation of an income statement, use the *multistep format* unless otherwise indicated.

LO 1, 2

Exercise 3-1 *Comparing a merchandising company with a service company*

The following information is available for two different types of businesses for the 2012 accounting period. Eady CPAs is a service business that provides accounting services to small businesses. Campus Clothing is a merchandising business that sells sports clothing to college students.

Data for Eady CPAs

1. Borrowed $40,000 from the bank to start the business.
2. Provided $30,000 of services to customers and collected $30,000 cash.
3. Paid salary expense of $20,000.

Data for Campus Clothing

1. Borrowed $40,000 from the bank to start the business.
2. Purchased $25,000 inventory for cash.
3. Inventory costing $16,400 was sold for $30,000 cash.
4. Paid $3,600 cash for operating expenses.

Required

a. Prepare an income statement, a balance sheet, and a statement of cash flows for each of the companies.
b. Which of the two businesses would have product costs? Why?
c. Why does Eady CPAs not compute gross margin on its income statement?
d. Compare the assets of both companies. What assets do they have in common? What assets are different? Why?

LO 2

Exercise 3-2 *Effect of inventory transactions on financial statements: perpetual system*

Mark Dixon started a small merchandising business in 2012. The business experienced the following events during its first year of operation. Assume that Dixon uses the perpetual inventory system.

1. Acquired $40,000 cash from the issue of common stock.
2. Purchased inventory for $30,000 cash.
3. Sold inventory costing $20,000 for $32,000 cash.

Required

a. Record the events in a statements model like the one shown below.

Assets			=	Equity			Rev.	−	Exp.	=	Net Inc.	Cash Flow
Cash	+	Inv.	=	Com. Stk.	+	Ret. Earn.						

b. Prepare an income statement for 2012 (use the multistep format).
c. What is the amount of total assets at the end of the period?

Exercise 3-3   *Effect of inventory transactions on the income statement and statement of cash flows: Perpetual system*   LO 2

During 2012, Knight Merchandising Company purchased $15,000 of inventory on account. Knight sold inventory on account that cost $12,500 for $17,500. Cash payments on accounts payable were $10,000. There was $11,000 cash collected from accounts receivable. Knight also paid $3,500 cash for operating expenses. Assume that Knight started the accounting period with $14,000 in both cash and common stock.

Required

a. Identify the events described in the preceding paragraph and record them in a horizontal statements model like the following one:

Assets						=	Liab.	+	Equity					Rev.	−	Exp.	=	Net inc.	Cash Flow
Cash	+	Accts. Rec.	+	Inv.		=	Accts. Pay.	+	Com. Stk.	+	Ret. Earn.								
14,000	+	NA	+	NA		=	NA	+	14,000	+	NA			NA	−	NA	=	NA	NA

b. What is the balance of accounts receivable at the end of 2012?
c. What is the balance of accounts payable at the end of 2012?
d. What are the amounts of gross margin and net income for 2012?
e. Determine the amount of net cash flow from operating activities.
f. Explain why net income and retained earnings are the same for Knight. Normally would these amounts be the same? Why or why not?

Exercise 3-4   *Recording inventory transactions in a financial statements model*   LO 2

Kona Clothing experienced the following events during 2012, its first year of operation:

1. Acquired $14,000 cash from the issue of common stock.
2. Purchased inventory for $8,000 cash.
3. Sold inventory costing $6,000 for $9,000 cash.
4. Paid $800 for advertising expense.

Required

Record the events in a statements model like the one shown below.

Assets			=	Equity			Rev.	−	Exp.	=	Net Inc.	Cash Flow
Cash	+	Inv.	=	Com. Stk.	+	Ret. Earn.						

Exercise 3-5   *Understanding the freight terms FOB shipping point and FOB destination*

Required

Determine which party, buyer or seller, is responsible for freight charges in each of the following situations:

a. Sold merchandise, freight terms, FOB destination.
b. Sold merchandise, freight terms, FOB shipping point.
c. Purchased merchandise, freight terms, FOB destination.
d. Purchased merchandise, freight terms, FOB shipping point.

LO 2, 3

Exercise 3-6   *Effect of purchase returns and allowances and freight costs on the financial statements: perpetual system*

The beginning account balances for Jerry's Auto Shop as of January 1, 2012 follows:

Account Titles	Beginning Balances
Cash	$28,000
Inventory	14,000
Common stock	36,000
Retained earnings	6,000
Total	$42,000

The following events affected the company during the 2012 accounting period:

1. Purchased merchandise on account that cost $18,000.
2. The goods in Event 1 were purchased FOB shipping point with freight cost of $1,000 cash.
3. Returned $3,600 of damaged merchandise for credit on account.
4. Agreed to keep other damaged merchandise for which the company received a $1,400 allowance.
5. Sold merchandise that cost $16,000 for $34,000 cash.
6. Delivered merchandise to customers in Event 5 under terms FOB destination with freight costs amounting to $800 cash.
7. Paid $12,000 on the merchandise purchased in Event 1.

Required

a. Organize appropriate ledger accounts under an accounting equation. Record the beginning balances and the transaction data in the accounts.
b. Prepare an income statement and a statement of cash flows for 2012.
c. Explain why a difference does or does not exist between net income and net cash flow from operating activities.

LO 2, 3

Exercise 3-7   *Accounting for product costs: Perpetual inventory system*

Which of the following would be *added* to the Inventory account for a merchandising business using the perpetual inventory system?

Required

a. Transportation-out.
b. Purchase discount.
c. Transportation-in.
d. Purchase of a new computer to be used by the business.
e. Purchase of inventory.
f. Allowance received for damaged inventory.

Exercise 3-8   *Effect of product cost and period cost: horizontal statements model*   LO 1, 2, 3

The Toy Store experienced the following events for the 2012 accounting period:

1. Acquired $20,000 cash from the issue of common stock.
2. Purchased $56,000 of inventory on account.
3. Received goods purchased in Event 2 FOB shipping point; freight cost of $600 paid in cash.
4. Sold inventory on account that cost $35,000 for $57,400.
5. Freight cost on the goods sold in Event 4 was $420. The goods were shipped FOB destination. Cash was paid for the freight cost.
6. Customer in Event 4 returned $4,000 worth of goods that had a cost of $2,400.
7. Collected $47,000 cash from accounts receivable.
8. Paid $44,000 cash on accounts payable.
9. Paid $1,100 for advertising expense.
10. Paid $1,000 cash for insurance expense.

Required

a. Which of these events affect period (selling and administrative) costs? Which result in product costs? If neither, label the transaction NA.
b. Record each event in a horizontal statements model like the following one. The first event is recorded as an example.

Assets				=	Liab.	+	Equity			Rev.	−	Exp.	=	Net Inc.	Cash Flow
Cash	+	Accts. Rec.	+ Inv.	=	Accts. Pay.	+	C. Stk.	+	Ret. Earn.						
20,000	+	NA	+ NA	=	NA	+	20,000	+	NA	NA	−	NA	=	NA	20,000 FA

Exercise 3-9   *Cash discounts and purchase returns*   LO 3

On April 6, 2012, Taylor Furnishings purchased $12,400 of merchandise from Bergin's Imports, terms 2/10 n/45. On April 8, Taylor returned $1,200 of the merchandise to Bergin's Imports for credit. Taylor paid cash for the merchandise on April 15, 2012.

Required

a. What is the amount that Taylor must pay Bergin's Imports on April 15?
b. Record the events in a horizontal statements model like the following one.

Assets			=	Liab.	+	Equity			Rev.	−	Exp.	=	Net Inc.	Cash Flow
Cash	+	Inv.	=	Accts. Pay.	+	C. Stock.	+	Ret. Earn.						

c. How much must Taylor pay for the merchandise purchased if the payment is not made until April 20, 2012?
d. Record the payment in event (c) in a horizontal statements model like the one above.
e. Why would Taylor want to pay for the merchandise by April 15?

Exercise 3-10   *Effect of sales returns and allowances and freight costs on the financial statements: perpetual system*   LO 2, 3

Stash Company began the 2012 accounting period with $10,000 cash, $38,000 inventory, $25,000 common stock, and $23,000 retained earnings. During the 2012 accounting period, Stash experienced the following events.

1. Sold merchandise costing $28,000 for $46,000 on account to Jack's Furniture Store.
2. Delivered the goods to Jack's under terms FOB destination. Freight costs were $500 cash.

3. Received returned goods from Jack's. The goods cost Stash $2,000 and were sold to Jack's for $3,000.
4. Granted Jack's $2,000 allowance for damaged goods that Jack's agreed to keep.
5. Collected partial payment of $25,000 cash from accounts receivable.

Required

a. Record the events in a statements model like the one shown below.

Assets				=	Equity			Rev.	−	Exp.	=	Net Inc.	Cash Flow
Cash	+	Accts. Rec.	+	Inv.	=	Com. Stk.	+	Ret. Earn.					

b. Prepare an income statement, a balance sheet, and a statement of cash flows.
c. Why would Stash grant the $2,000 allowance to Jack's? Who benefits more?

LO 2, 3

Exercise 3-11 *Effect of cash discounts on financial statements: perpetual system*

Campus Computers was started in 2012. The company experienced the following accounting events during its first year of operation.

1. Started business when it acquired $50,000 cash from the issue of common stock.
2. Purchased merchandise with a list price of $46,000 on account, terms 2/10, n/30.
3. Paid off one-half of the accounts payable balance within the discount period.
4. Sold merchandise on account that had a list price of $48,000. Credit terms were 1/20, n/30. The merchandise had cost Campus Computers $28,000.
5. Collected cash from the account receivable within the discount period.
6. Paid $7,200 cash for operating expenses.
7. Paid the balance due on accounts payable. The payment was not made within the discount period.

Required

a. Record the events in a horizontal statements model like the following one.

Assets				=	Liab.	+	Equity			Rev.	−	Exp.	=	Net Inc.	Cash Flow
Cash	+	Accts. Rec.	+	Inv.	=	Accts. Pay.	+	Com. Stk.	+	Ret. Earn.					

b. What is the amount of gross margin for the period? What is the net income for the period?
c. Why would Campus Computers sell merchandise with the terms 1/20, n/30?
d. What do the terms 2/10, n/30 in Event 2 mean to Campus Computers?

LO 2, 3

Exercise 3-12 *Comparing gross margin and gain on sale of land*

Usrey Sales Company had the following balances in its accounts on January 1, 2012.

Cash	$ 70,000
Merchandise Inventory	50,000
Land	120,000
Common Stock	100,000
Retained Earnings	140,000

Usrey experienced the following events during 2012.

1. Sold merchandise inventory that cost $40,000 for $75,000.
2. Sold land that cost $50,000 for $80,000.

Required

a. Determine the amount of gross margin recognized by Usrey.

b. Determine the amount of the gain on the sale of land recognized by Usrey.

c. Comment on how the gross margin versus the gain will be recognized on the income statement.

d. Comment on how the gross margin versus the gain will be recognized on the statement of cash flows.

Exercise 3-13   *Effect of inventory losses: perpetual system*

LO 2, 6

Reeves Design experienced the following events during 2012, its first year of operation.

1. Started the business when it acquired $40,000 cash from the issue of common stock.
2. Paid $28,000 cash to purchase inventory.
3. Sold inventory costing $21,500 for $34,200 cash.
4. Physically counted inventory showing $5,800 inventory was on hand at the end of the accounting period.

Required

a. Determine the amount of the difference between book balance and the actual amount of inventory as determined by the physical count.

b. Explain how differences between the book balance and the physical count of inventory could arise. Why is being able to determine whether differences exist useful to management?

Exercise 3-14   *Determining the effect of inventory transactions on the horizontal statements model: perpetual system*

LO 2

Causey Sales Company experienced the following events:

1. Purchased merchandise inventory for cash.
2. Purchased merchandise inventory on account.
3. Sold merchandise inventory for cash. Label the revenue recognition 3a and the expense recognition 3b.
4. Sold merchandise inventory on account. Label the revenue recognition 4a and the expense recognition 4b.
5. Returned merchandise purchased on account.
6. Paid cash for selling and administrative expenses.
7. Paid cash on accounts payable not within the discount period.
8. Paid cash for transportation-in.
9. Collected cash from accounts receivable.
10. Paid cash for transportation-out.

Required

Identify each event as asset source (AS), asset use (AU), asset exchange (AE), or claims exchange (CE). Also explain how each event affects the financial statements by placing a + for increase, − for decrease, or NA for not affected under each of the components in the following statements model. Assume the company uses the perpetual inventory system. The first event is recorded as an example.

Event No.	Event Type	Assets	=	Liab.	+	Equity	Rev.	−	Exp.	=	Net Inc.	Cash Flow
1	AE	+ −	=	NA	+	NA	NA	−	NA	=	NA	− OA

LO 4

Exercise 3-15   *Single-step and multistep income statements*

The following information was taken from the accounts of Healthy Foods Market, a small grocery store at December 31, 2012. The accounts are listed in alphabetical order, and all have normal balances.

Accounts payable	$ 300
Accounts receivable	1,040
Advertising expense	200
Cash	820
Common stock	600
Cost of goods sold	900
Interest expense	140
Merchandise inventory	500
Prepaid rent	280
Retained earnings	1,050
Sales revenue	2,400
Salaries expense	260
Supplies expense	210
Gain on sale of land	75

Required

First, prepare an income statement for the year using the single-step approach. Then prepare another income statement using the multistep approach.

LO 2

Exercise 3-16   *Determining the cost of financing inventory*

On January 1, 2012, Fran started a small flower merchandising business that she named Fran's Flowers. The company experienced the following events during the first year of operation.

1. Started the business by issuing common stock for $20,000 cash.
2. Paid $28,000 cash to purchase inventory.
3. Sold merchandise that cost $16,000 for $36,000 on account.
4. Collected $30,000 cash from accounts receivable.
5. Paid $7,500 for operating expenses.

Required

a. Organize ledger accounts under an accounting equation and record the events in the accounts.
b. Prepare an income statement, a balance sheet, and a statement of cash flows.
c. Since Fran sold inventory for $36,000, she will be able to recover more than half of the $40,000 she invested in the stock. Do you agree with this statement? Why or why not?

LO 3

Exercise 3-17   *Inventory financing costs*

Joan Sweatt comes to you for advice. She has just purchased a large amount of inventory with the terms 2/10, n/30. The amount of the invoice is $540,000. She is currently short of cash but has decent credit. She can borrow the money needed to settle the account payable at an annual interest rate of 7%. Joan is sure she will have the necessary cash by the due date of the invoice but not by the last day of the discount period.

Required

a. Convert the discount rate into an annual interest rate.
b. Make a recommendation regarding whether Sweatt should borrow the money and pay off the account payable within the discount period.

LO 8

Exercise 3-18   *Effect of inventory transactions on the income statement and balance sheet: periodic system (Appendix)*

Joe Dodd owns Joe's Sporting Goods. At the beginning of the year, Joe's had $8,400 in inventory. During the year, Joe's purchased inventory that cost $42,000. At the end of the year, inventory on hand amounted to $17,600.

Required

Calculate the following:

a. Cost of goods available for sale during the year.

b. Cost of goods sold for the year.

c. Amount of inventory Joe's would report on the year-end balance sheet.

Exercise 3-19   *Determining cost of goods sold: periodic system (Appendix)*   LO 8

Lane Antiques uses the periodic inventory system to account for its inventory transactions. The following account titles and balances were drawn from Lane's records: beginning balance in inventory, $24,000; purchases, $150,000; purchase returns and allowances, $10,000; sales, $400,000; sales returns and allowances, $2,500; freight-in, $750; and operating expenses, $26,000. A physical count indicated that $18,000 of merchandise was on hand at the end of the accounting period.

Required

a. Prepare a schedule of cost of goods sold.

b. Prepare a multistep income statement.

Exercise 3-20   *Using common size statements and ratios to make comparisons*   LO 7

At the end of 2012, the following information is available for Chicago and St. Louis companies:

	Chicago	St. Louis
Sales	$3,000,000	$3,000
Cost of goods sold	1,800,000	2,100
Selling and administrative expenses	960,000	780
Total assets	3,750,000	3,750
Stockholders' equity	1,000,000	1,200

Required

a. Prepare common size income statements for each company.

b. One company is a high-end retailer, and the other operates a discount store. Which is the discounter? Support your selection by referring to the common size statements.

PROBLEMS

All applicable Problems are available with McGraw-Hill's *Connect Accounting.*

Problem 3-21   *Basic transactions for three accounting cycles: perpetual system*   LO 2

Ginger's Flower Company was started in 2012 when it acquired $80,000 cash from the issue of common stock. The following data summarize the company's first three years' operating activities. Assume that all transactions were cash transactions.

CHECK FIGURES
2012 Net Income: $8,000
2014 Total Assets: $112,000

	2012	2013	2014
Purchases of inventory	$ 60,000	$ 90,000	$ 130,000
Sales	102,000	146,000	220,000
Cost of goods sold	54,000	78,000	140,000
Selling and administrative expenses	40,000	52,000	72,000

Required

Prepare an income statement (use multistep format) and balance sheet for each fiscal year. (*Hint:* Record the transaction data for each accounting period in the accounting equation before preparing the statements for that year.)

Problem 3-22 *Identifying product and period costs*

Required

Indicate whether each of the following costs is a product cost or a period (selling and administrative) cost.

a. Advertising expense.
b. Insurance on vans used to deliver goods to customers.
c. Salaries of sales supervisors.
d. Monthly maintenance expense for a copier.
e. Goods purchased for resale.
f. Cleaning supplies for the office.
g. Freight on goods purchased for resale.
h. Salary of the marketing director.
i. Freight on goods sold to customer with terms FOB destination.
j. Utilities expense incurred for office building.

Problem 3-23 *Identifying freight costs*

Required

For each of the following events, determine the amount of freight paid by The Dive Shop. Also indicate whether the freight cost would be classified as a product or period (selling and administrative) cost.

a. Purchased merchandise inventory with freight costs of $1,400. The merchandise was shipped FOB destination.
b. Shipped merchandise to customers, freight terms FOB destination. The freight costs were $300.
c. Purchased inventory with freight costs of $500. The goods were shipped FOB shipping point.
d. Sold merchandise to a customer. Freight costs were $800. The goods were shipped FOB shipping point.

Problem 3-24 *Effect of purchase returns and allowances and purchase discounts on the financial statements: perpetual system*

The following events were completed by Chan's Imports in September 2012.

Sept. 1 Acquired $60,000 cash from the issue of common stock.
       1 Purchased $36,000 of merchandise on account with terms 2/10, n/30.
       5 Paid $800 cash for freight to obtain merchandise purchased on September 1.
       8 Sold merchandise that cost $20,000 to customers for $38,000 on account, with terms 2/10, n/30.
       8 Returned $1,500 of defective merchandise from the September 1 purchase to the supplier.
      10 Paid cash for the balance due on the merchandise purchased on September 1.
      20 Received cash from customers of September 8 sale in settlement of the account balances, but not within the discount period.
      30 Paid $4,900 cash for selling expenses.

Required

a. Record each event in a statements model like the following one. The first event is recorded as an example.

Assets			=	Liab.	+	Equity			Rev.	−	Exp.	=	Net Inc.	Cash Flow
Cash	+ Accts. Rec.	+ Inv.	=	Accts. Pay.	+	Com. Stk.	+	Ret. Earn.						
60,000	+ NA	+ NA	=	NA	+	60,000	+	NA	NA	−	NA	=	NA	60,000 FA

b. Prepare an income statement for the month ending September 30.

c. Prepare a statement of cash flows for the month ending September 30.

d. Explain why there is a difference between net income and cash flow from operating activities.

Problem 3-25 *Comprehensive cycle problem: Perpetual system*

LO 2, 3, 5, 6

At the beginning of 2012, the Jeater Company had the following balances in its accounts:

Cash	$ 4,300
Inventory	9,000
Common stock	10,000
Retained earnings	3,300

During 2012, the company experienced the following events.

1. Purchased inventory that cost $2,200 on account from Blue Company under terms 1/10, n/30. The merchandise was delivered FOB shipping point. Freight costs of $110 were paid in cash.
2. Returned $200 of the inventory that it had purchased because the inventory was damaged in transit. The freight company agreed to pay the return freight cost.
3. Paid the amount due on its account payable to Blue Company within the cash discount period.
4. Sold inventory that had cost $3,000 for $5,500 on account, under terms 2/10, n/45.
5. Received merchandise returned from a customer. The merchandise originally cost $400 and was sold to the customer for $710 cash during the previous accounting period. The customer was paid $710 cash for the returned merchandise.
6. Delivered goods FOB destination in Event 4. Freight costs of $60 were paid in cash.
7. Collected the amount due on the account receivable within the discount period.
8. Took a physical count indicating that $7,970 of inventory was on hand at the end of the accounting period.

Required

a. Identify these events as asset source (AS), asset use (AU), asset exchange (AE), or claims exchange (CE).

b. Record each event in a statements model like the following one.

Event	Balance Sheet							Income Statement			Statement of Cash Flows
	Assets			=	Liab.	=	Equity	Rev. −	Exp. =	Net Inc.	
	Cash +	Accts. Rec. +	Mdse. Inv.	=	Accts. Pay. +		Ret. Earn.				

c. Prepare an income statement, a statement of changes in stockholders' equity, a balance sheet, and a statement of cash flows.

Problem 3-26 *Using common size income statements to make comparisons*

LO 7

The following income statements were drawn from the annual reports of Pierro Sales Company.

	2012*	2013*
Net sales	$520,600	$580,500
Cost of goods sold	(369,600)	(401,500)
Gross margin	151,000	179,000
Less: Operating expense		
Selling and administrative expenses	(64,800)	(81,300)
Net income	$ 86,200	$ 97,700

*All dollar amounts are reported in thousands.

The president's message in the company's annual report stated that the company had implemented a strategy to increase market share by spending more on advertising. The president indicated that prices held steady and sales grew as expected. Write a memo indicating whether you agree with the president's statements. How has the strategy affected profitability? Support your answer by measuring growth in sales and selling expenses. Also prepare common size income statements and make appropriate references to the differences between 2012 and 2013.

LO 5, 8

CHECK FIGURES
a. Cost of Goods Available for
   Sale: $48,675
b. Net Income: $55,000

Problem 3-27   *Preparing a schedule of cost of goods sold and multistep and single-step income statements: Periodic system (Appendix)*

The following account titles and balances were taken from the adjusted trial balance of Brisco Farm Co. for 2012. The company uses the periodic inventory system.

Account Title	Balance
Sales returns and allowances	$ 3,250
Miscellaneous expense	400
Transportation-out	700
Sales	69,750
Advertising expense	2,750
Salaries expense	8,500
Transportation-in	1,725
Purchases	42,000
Interest expense	360
Merchandise inventory, January 1	6,200
Rent expense	5,000
Merchandise inventory, December 31	4,050
Purchase returns and allowances	1,250
Loss on sale of land	3,400
Utilities expense	710

Required

a. Prepare a schedule to determine the amount of cost of goods sold.
b. Prepare a multistep income statement.
c. Prepare a single-step income statement.

LO 8

CHECK FIGURES
a. Ending Cash: $70,524
b. Cost of Goods Sold: $94,876

Problem 3-28   *Comprehensive cycle problem: Periodic system (Appendix)*

The following trial balance pertains to Nate's Grocery as of January 1, 2012:

Account Title	Beginning Balances
Cash	$26,000
Accounts receivable	4,000
Merchandise inventory	50,000
Accounts payable	4,000
Common stock	43,000
Retained earnings	33,000
Totals	$80,000

The following events occurred in 2012. Assume that Nate's uses the periodic inventory method.

1. Purchased land for $9,000 cash.
2. Purchased merchandise on account for $96,000, terms 1/10 n/45.
3. Paid freight of $1,000 cash on merchandise purchased FOB shipping point.
4. Returned $3,600 of defective merchandise purchased in Event 2.
5. Sold merchandise for $86,000 cash.
6. Sold merchandise on account for $90,000, terms 2/10 n/30.
7. Paid cash within the discount period on accounts payable due on merchandise purchased in Event 2.

8. Paid $11,600 cash for selling expenses.
9. Collected $50,000 of the accounts receivable from Event 6 within the discount period.
10. Collected $40,000 of the accounts receivable but not within the discount period.
11. Paid $6,400 of other operating expenses.
12. A physical count indicated that $47,600 of inventory was on hand at the end of the accounting period.

Required

a. Record the above transactions in a horizontal statements model like the following one.

	Balance Sheet										Income Statement				
Event	**Assets**				**=**	**Equity**					**Rev.**	**– Exp.**	**= Net Inc.**		**Statement of Cash Flows**
	Cash	+ Accts. Rec.	+ Mdse. Inv.	+ Land	=	Accts. Pay.	+ Com. Stock	+ Ret. Earn.							

b. Prepare a schedule of cost of goods sold and an income statement.

ANALYZE, THINK, COMMUNICATE

ATC 3-1   Business Application Case   *Understanding real world annual reports*

Use the Target Corporation's annual report in Appendix B to answer the following questions related to Target's 2009 fiscal year.

Required

a. What percentage of Target's *total revenues* end up as net earnings?
b. What percentage of Target's *sales* go to pay for the costs of the goods being sold?
c. What costs does Target include in its Cost of Sales account?
d. When does Target recognize revenue from the sale of gift cards?

ATC 3-2   Group Exercise   *Multistep income statement*

The following quarterly information is given for Raybon for the year ended 2012 (amounts shown are in millions).

	First Quarter	Second Quarter	Third Quarter	Fourth Quarter
Net Sales	$736.0	$717.4	$815.2	$620.1
Gross Margin	461.9	440.3	525.3	252.3
Net Income	37.1	24.6	38.6	31.4

Required

a. Divide the class into groups and organize the groups into four sections. Assign each section financial information for one of the quarters.
   (1) Each group should compute the cost of goods sold and operating expenses for the specific quarter assigned to its section and prepare a multistep income statement for the quarter.
   (2) Each group should compute the gross margin percentage and cost of goods sold percentage for its specific quarter.
   (3) Have a representative of each group put that quarter's sales, cost of goods sold percentage, and gross margin percentage on the board.

Class Discussion

b. Have the class discuss the change in each of these items from quarter to quarter and explain why the change might have occurred. Which was the best quarter and why?

ATC 3-3   Research Assignment   *Analyzing Amazon.com's income statement*

Complete the requirements below using the most recent financial statements available [20xx] on Amazon.com's corporate website. Obtain the statements on the internet by following the steps below. (Be aware that the formatting of the company's website may have changed since these instructions were written.)

- Go to www.amazon.com.
- At the bottom of the screen, under "Get to Know Us," click on "Investor Relations."
- Annual Reports and Proxies.
- Click on "20xx Annual Report" (the most recent year).

Read the following sections of the annual report:

- The income statement, which Amazon.com calls the "Consolidated Statement of Operations."
- In the footnotes section, "Note 1—Description of Business and Accounting Policies," read the subsections titled "*Revenues,*" "*Shipping Activities,*" and "*Cost of Sales.*"

Required

a. What percentage of Amazon's sales end up as net income?

b. What percentage of Amazon's sales go to pay for the costs of the goods being sold?

c. What specific criteria are necessary before Amazon will recognize a sale as having been completed and record the related revenue?

d. How does Amazon account for (report on its income statement) the shipping costs it incurs to ship goods to its customers?

ATC 3-4   Written Assignment, Critical Thinking   *Effect of sales returns on financial statements*

Bell Farm and Garden Equipment reported the following information for 2012:

Net Sales of Equipment	$2,450,567
Other Income	6,786
Cost of Goods Sold	1,425,990
Selling, General, and Administrative Expense	325,965
Net Operating Income	$ 705,398

Selected information from the balance sheet as of December 31, 2012, follows.

Cash and Marketable Securities	$113,545
Inventory	248,600
Accounts Receivable	82,462
Property, Plant, and Equipment—Net	335,890
Other Assets	5,410
Total Assets	$785,907

Assume that a major customer returned a large order to Bell on December 31, 2012. The amount of the sale had been $146,800 with a cost of sales of $94,623. The return was recorded in the books on January 1, 2013. The company president does not want to correct the books. He argues that it makes no difference as to whether the return is recorded in 2012 or 2013. Either way, the return has been duly recognized.

Required

a. Assume that you are the CFO for Bell Farm and Garden Equipment Co. Write a memo to the president explaining how omitting the entry on December 31, 2012, could cause the financial statements to be misleading to investors and creditors. Explain how omitting the return from the customer would affect net income and the balance sheet.

b. Why might the president want to record the return on January 1, 2013, instead of December 31, 2012?

CHAPTER 4

Internal Controls, Accounting for Cash, and Ethics

LEARNING OBJECTIVES

After you have mastered the material in this chapter, you will be able to:

1 Identify the key elements of a strong system of internal control.

2 Prepare a bank reconciliation.

3 Discuss the role of ethics in the accounting profession.

4 Describe the auditor's role in financial reporting.

CHAPTER OPENING

In the first three chapters, we covered the basics of the accounting system. By now you should understand how basic business events affect financial statements and how the accounting cycle works. Accounting is an elegant system that when implemented correctly provides meaningful information to investors and other stakeholders. However, without effective control, the accounting system can be manipulated in ways that may overstate business performance. This can lead investors to make bad decisions, which can result in huge losses when the true performance is revealed. This chapter discusses the importance of internal control systems. The chapter also discusses accounting for cash, an area where good internal controls are critical. The chapter concludes with a discussion on the importance of ethical conduct in the accounting profession.

The Curious Accountant

On December 11, 2008, Bernard Madoff was arrested on suspicion of having defrauded the clients of his investment company, Bernard L. Madoff Investments (BMI), of $50 billion. Later estimates would put the losses at over $60 billion. Although his clients believed the money they sent to BMI was being invested in the stock market, it was actually just being deposited into bank accounts.

Mr. Madoff was accused of operating the largest Ponzi scheme in history. Clients were sent monthly statements falsely showing that their investments were earning income and growing at a steady rate, even when the overall stock market was falling. When individual investors asked to withdraw their funds, they were simply given money that had been deposited by other investors.

This fraudulent system works as long as more new money is being deposited than is being withdrawn. Unfortunately for BMI, with the severe stock-market decline of 2008 too many clients got nervous and asked to withdraw their money, including the gains they believed they had earned over the years. At this point the Ponzi scheme failed.

How could such a pervasive fraud go undetected for so long? (Answer on page 136.)

KEY FEATURES OF INTERNAL CONTROL SYSTEMS

LO I

Identify the key elements of a strong system of internal control.

During the early 2000s a number of accounting related scandals cost investors billions. In 2001, Enron's share price went from $85 to $0.30 after it was revealed that the company had billions of dollars in losses that were not reported on the financial statements. Several months later, WorldCom reported an $11 billion accounting fraud, which included hundreds of millions in personal loans to then CEO, Bernie Ebbers.

The Enron and WorldCom accounting scandals had such devastating effects that they led congress to pass the Sarbanes-Oxley Act of 2002 (SOX). SOX requires public companies to evaluate their *internal control* and to publish those findings with their SEC filings. **Internal control** is the process designed to ensure reliable financial reporting, effective and efficient operations, and compliance with applicable laws and regulations. Safeguarding assets against theft and unauthorized use, acquisition, or disposal is also part of internal control.

Section 404 of Sarbanes-Oxley requires a statement of management's responsibility for establishing and maintaining adequate internal control over financial reporting by public companies. This section includes an assessment of the controls and the identification of the framework used for the assessment. The framework established by The Committee of Sponsoring Organizations of the Treadway Commission (COSO) in 1992 is the de facto standard by which SOX compliance is judged. COSO's framework titled *Internal Control—An Integrated Framework* recognizes five interrelated components including:

1. *Control Environment.* The integrity and ethical values of the company, including its code of conduct, involvement of the board of directors, and other actions that set the tone of the organization.

2. *Risk Assessment.* Management's process of identifying potential risks that could result in misstated financial statements and developing actions to address those risks.

3. *Control Activities.* These are the activities usually thought of as "the internal controls." They include such things as segregation of duties, account reconciliations, and information processing controls that are designed to safeguard assets and enable an organization to timely prepare reliable financial statements.

4. *Information and Communication.* The internal and external reporting process, and includes an assessment of the technology environment.

5. *Monitoring.* Assessing the quality of a company's internal control over time and taking actions as necessary to ensure it continues to address the risks of the organization.

In 2004 COSO updated the framework to help entities design and implement effective enterprise-wide approaches to risk management. The updated document is titled *Enterprise Risk Management (ERM)—An Integrated Framework.* The ERM framework introduces an enterprise-wide approach to risk management as well as concepts such as risk appetite, risk tolerance, and portfolio view. While SOX applies only to U.S. public companies, the ERM framework has been adopted by both public and private organizations around the world.

The ERM framework does not replace the internal control framework. Instead, it incorporates the internal control framework within it. Accordingly, companies may decide to look to the ERM framework both to satisfy their internal control needs and to move toward a fuller risk management process.

While a detailed discussion of the COSO documents is beyond the scope of this text, the following overview of the more common *control activities* of the internal control framework is insightful.

Separation of Duties

The likelihood of fraud or theft is reduced if collusion is required to accomplish it. Clear **separation of duties** is frequently used as a deterrent to corruption. When duties are separated, the work of one employee can act as a check on the work of another employee. For example, a person selling seats to a movie may be tempted to steal money received from customers who enter the theater. This temptation is reduced if the person staffing the box office is required to issue tickets that a second employee collects as people enter the theater. If ticket stubs collected by the second employee are compared with the cash receipts from ticket sales, any cash shortages would become apparent. Furthermore, friends and relatives of the ticket agent could not easily enter the theater without paying. Theft or unauthorized entry would require collusion between the ticket agent and the usher who collects the tickets. Both individuals would have to be dishonest enough to steal, yet trustworthy enough to convince each other they would keep the embezzlement secret. Whenever possible, the functions of *authorization, recording,* and *custody of assets* should be performed by separate individuals.

Quality of Employees

A business is only as good as the people it employs. Cheap labor is not a bargain if the employees are incompetent. Employees should be properly trained. In fact, they should be trained to perform a variety of tasks. The ability of employees to substitute for one another prevents disruptions when co-workers are absent because of illnesses, vacations, or other commitments. The capacity to rotate jobs also relieves boredom and increases respect for the contributions of other employees. Every business should strive to maximize the productivity of every employee. Ongoing training programs are essential to a strong system of internal control.

Bonded Employees

The best way to ensure employee honesty is to hire individuals with *high levels of personal integrity.* Employers should screen job applicants using interviews, background checks, and recommendations from prior employers or educators. Even so, screening programs may fail to identify character weaknesses. Further, unusual circumstances may cause honest employees to go astray. Therefore, employees in positions of trust should be bonded. A **fidelity bond** provides insurance that protects a company from losses caused by employee dishonesty.

Required Absences

Employees should be required to take regular vacations and their duties should be rotated periodically. Employees may be able to cover up fraudulent activities if they are always present at work. Consider the case of a parking meter collection agent who covered the same route for several years with no vacation. When the agent became sick, a substitute collected more money each day than the regular reader usually reported. Management checked past records and found that the ill meter reader had been understating the cash receipts and pocketing the difference. If management had required vacations or rotated the routes, the embezzlement would have been discovered much earlier.

Procedures Manual

Appropriate accounting procedures should be documented in a **procedures manual.** The manual should be routinely updated. Periodic reviews should be conducted to ensure that employees are following the procedures outlined in the manual.

Authority and Responsibility

Employees are motivated by clear lines of authority and responsibility. They work harder when they have the authority to use their own judgment and they exercise reasonable caution when they are held responsible for their actions. Businesses should prepare an **authority manual** that establishes a definitive *chain of command.* The authority manual should guide both specific and general authorizations. **Specific authorizations** apply to specific positions within the organization. For example, investment decisions are authorized at the division level while hiring decisions are authorized at the departmental level. In contrast, **general authority** applies across different levels of management. For example, employees at all levels may be required to fly coach or to make purchases from specific vendors.

Prenumbered Documents

How would you know if a check were stolen from your check book? If you keep a record of your check numbers, the missing number would tip you off immediately. Businesses also use prenumbered checks to avoid the unauthorized use of their bank accounts. In fact, prenumbered forms are used for all important documents such as purchase orders, receiving reports, invoices, and checks. To reduce errors, prenumbered forms should be as simple and easy to use as possible. Also, the documents should allow for authorized signatures. For example, credit sales slips should be signed by the customer to clearly establish who made the purchase, reducing the likelihood of unauthorized transactions.

Physical Control

Employees walk away with billions of dollars of business assets each year. To limit losses, companies should establish adequate physical control over valuable assets. For example, inventory should be kept in a storeroom and not released without proper authorization. Serial numbers on equipment should be recorded along with the name of the individual who is responsible for the equipment. Unannounced physical counts should be conducted randomly to verify the presence of company-owned equipment. Certificates of deposit and marketable securities should be kept in fireproof vaults. Access to these vaults should be limited to authorized personnel. These procedures protect the documents from fire and limit access to only those individuals who have the appropriate security clearance to handle the documents.

In addition to safeguarding assets, there should be physical control over the accounting records. The accounting journals, ledgers, and supporting documents should be kept in a fireproof safe. Only personnel responsible for recording transactions in the journals should have access to them. With limited access, there is less chance that someone will change the records to conceal fraud or embezzlement.

Performance Evaluations

Because few people can evaluate their own performance objectively, internal controls should include independent verification of employee performance. For example, someone other than the person who has control over inventory should take a physical count of inventory. Internal and external audits serve as independent verification of performance. Auditors should evaluate the effectiveness of the internal control system as well as verify the accuracy of the accounting records. In addition, the external auditors attest to the company's use of generally accepted accounting principles in the financial statements.

Limitations

A system of internal controls is designed to prevent or detect errors and fraud. However, no control system is foolproof. Internal controls can be circumvented by collusion among employees. Two or more employees working together can hide embezzlement by covering for each other. For example, if an embezzler goes on vacation, fraud will not be reported by a replacement who is in collusion with the embezzler. No system can prevent all fraud. However, a good system of internal controls minimizes illegal or unethical activities by reducing temptation and increasing the likelihood of early detection.

✓ CHECK YOURSELF 4.1

What are nine features of an internal control system?

Answer

The nine features follow.

1. Separating duties so that fraud or theft requires collusion.
2. Hiring and training competent employees.
3. Bonding employees to recover losses through insurance.

4. Requiring employees to be absent from their jobs so that their replacements can discover errors or fraudulent activity that might have occurred.
5. Establishing proper procedures for processing transactions.
6. Establishing clear lines of authority and responsibility.
7. Using prenumbered documents.
8. Implementing physical controls such as locking cash in a safe.
9. Conducting performance evaluations through independent internal and external audits.

ACCOUNTING FOR CASH

For financial reporting purposes, **cash** generally includes currency and other items that are payable *on demand,* such as checks, money orders, bank drafts, and certain savings accounts. Savings accounts that impose substantial penalties for early withdrawal should be classified as *investments* rather than cash. Postdated checks or IOUs represent *receivables* and should not be included in cash. As illustrated in Exhibit 4.1, most companies combine currency and other payable on demand items in a single balance sheet account with varying titles.

Companies must maintain a sufficient amount of cash to pay employees, suppliers, and other creditors. When a company fails to pay its legal obligations, its creditors can force the company into bankruptcy. Even so, management should avoid accumulating more cash than is needed. The failure to invest excess cash in earning assets reduces profitability. Cash inflows and outflows must be managed to prevent a shortage or surplus of cash.

Controlling Cash

Controlling cash, more than any other asset, requires strict adherence to internal control procedures. Cash has universal appeal. A relatively small suitcase filled with high-denomination currency can represent significant value. Furthermore, the rightful owner of currency is difficult to prove. In most cases, possession constitutes ownership. As a result, cash is highly susceptible to theft and must be carefully protected. Cash is most susceptible to embezzlement when it is received or disbursed. The following controls should be employed to reduce the likelihood of theft.

Cash Receipts

A record of all cash collections should be prepared immediately upon receipt. The amount of cash on hand should be counted regularly. Missing amounts of money can be detected by comparing the actual cash on hand with the book balance. Employees who receive cash should give customers a copy of a written receipt. Customers usually review their receipts to ensure they have gotten credit for the amount paid and call any errors to the receipts clerk's attention. This not only reduces errors but also provides a control on the clerk's honesty. Cash receipts should be deposited in a bank on a timely basis. Cash collected late in the day should be deposited in a night depository. Every effort should be made to minimize the amount of cash on hand. Keeping large amounts of cash on hand not only increases the risk of loss from theft but also places employees in danger of being harmed by criminals who may be tempted to rob the company.

Cash Payments

To effectively control cash, a company should make all disbursements using checks, thereby providing a record of cash payments. All checks should be prenumbered, and unused checks should be locked up. Using prenumbered checks allows companies to easily identify lost or stolen checks by comparing the numbers on unused and canceled checks with the numbers used for legitimate disbursements.

EXHIBIT 4.1

Balance Sheet Classifications That Include the Word Cash

- Cash
- Cash and cash equivalents
- Cash and equivalents
- Cash combined with marketable securities
- Other

Data Source: AICPA, *Accounting Trends and Techniques.*

REALITY BYTES

Could you afford to buy a safe like the one shown here? The vault is only one of many expensive security devices used by banks to safeguard cash. By using checking accounts, companies are able to avoid many of the costs associated with keeping cash safe. In addition to providing physical control, checking accounts enable companies to maintain a written audit trail of cash receipts and payments. Checking accounts represent the most widely used internal control device in modern society. It is difficult to imagine a business operating without the use of checking accounts.

The duties of approving disbursements, signing checks, and recording transactions should be separated. If one person is authorized to approve, sign, and record checks, he or she could falsify supporting documents, write an unauthorized check, and record a cover-up transaction in the accounting records. By separating these duties, the check signer reviews the documentation provided by the approving individual before signing the check. Likewise, the recording clerk reviews the work of both the approving person and the check signer when the disbursement is recorded in the accounting records. Thus writing unauthorized checks requires trilevel collusion.

Supporting documents with authorized approval signatures should be required when checks are presented to the check signer. For example, a warehouse receiving order should be matched with a purchase order before a check is approved to pay a bill from a supplier. Before payments are approved, invoice amounts should be checked and payees verified as valid vendors. Matching supporting documents with proper authorization discourages employees from creating phony documents for a disbursement to a friend or fictitious business. Also, the approval process serves as a check on the accuracy of the work of all employees involved.

Supporting documents should be marked *Paid* when the check is signed. If the documents are not indelibly marked, they could be retrieved from the files and resubmitted for a duplicate, unauthorized payment. A payables clerk could collude with the payee to split extra cash paid out by submitting the same supporting documents for a second payment.

All spoiled and voided checks should be defaced and retained. If defaced checks are not retained, an employee could steal a check and then claim that it was written incorrectly and thrown away. The clerk could then use the stolen check to make an unauthorized payment.

Checking Account Documents

The previous section explained the need for businesses to use checking accounts. A description of four main types of forms associated with a bank checking account follows.

Signature Card

A bank **signature card** shows the bank account number and the signatures of the people authorized to sign checks. The card is retained in the bank's files. If a bank employee is unfamiliar with the signature on a check, he or she can refer to the signature card to verify the signature before cashing the check.

Deposit Ticket

Each deposit of cash or checks is accompanied by a **deposit ticket,** which normally identifies the account number and the name of the account. The depositor lists the individual amounts of currency, coins, and checks, as well as the total deposited, on the deposit ticket.

Bank Check

A written check affects three parties: (1) the person or business writing the check (the *payer*); (2) the bank on which the check is drawn; and (3) the person or business to whom the check is payable (the *payee*). Companies often write **checks** using multicopy, prenumbered forms, with the name of the issuing business preprinted on the face of each check. A remittance notice is usually attached to the check forms. This portion of the form provides the issuer space to record what the check is for (e.g., what invoices are being paid), the amount being disbursed, and the date of payment. When signed by the person whose signature is on the signature card, the check authorizes the bank to transfer the face amount of the check from the payer's account to the payee.

Bank Statement

Periodically, the bank sends the depositor a **bank statement.** The bank statement is presented from the bank's point of view. Checking accounts are liabilities to a bank because the bank is obligated to pay back the money that customers have deposited in their accounts. Therefore, in the bank's accounting records a customer's checking account has a *credit* balance. As a result, **bank statement debit memos** describe transactions that reduce the customer's account balance (the bank's liability). **Bank statement credit memos** describe activities that increase the customer's account balance (the bank's liability). Since a checking account is an asset (cash) to the depositor, a *bank statement debit memo* requires a *credit entry* to the cash account on the depositor's books. Likewise, when a bank tells you that it has credited your account, you will debit your cash account in response.

Bank statements normally report (a) the balance of the account at the beginning of the period; (b) additions for customer deposits made during the period; (c) other additions described in credit memos (e.g., for interest earned); (d) subtractions for the payment of checks drawn on the account during the period; (e) other subtractions described in debit memos (e.g., for service charges); (f) a running balance of the account; and (g) the balance of the account at the end of the period. The sample bank statement in Exhibit 4.2 on the next page illustrates these items. Normally, the canceled checks or copies of them are enclosed with the bank statement.

RECONCILING THE BANK ACCOUNT

Usually the ending balance reported on the bank statement differs from the balance in the depositor's cash account as of the same date. The discrepancy is normally attributable to timing differences. For example, a depositor deducts the amount of a check from its cash account when it writes the check. However, the bank does not deduct the amount of the check from the depositor's account until the payee presents it for payment, which may be days, weeks, or even months after the check is written. As a result, the balance on the depositor's books is lower than the balance on the bank's books. Companies prepare a **bank reconciliation** to explain the differences between the cash balance reported on the bank statement and the cash balance recorded in the depositor's accounting records.

LO 2

Prepare a bank reconciliation.

Determining True Cash Balance

A bank reconciliation normally begins with the cash balance reported by the bank which is called the **unadjusted bank balance.** The adjustments necessary to determine the amount of cash that the depositor actually owns as of the date of the bank statement are then added to and subtracted from the unadjusted bank balance. The final total is the **true cash balance.** The true cash balance is independently reached a second time by making adjustments to the **unadjusted book balance.** The bank account is reconciled when the true cash balance determined from the perspective of the unadjusted

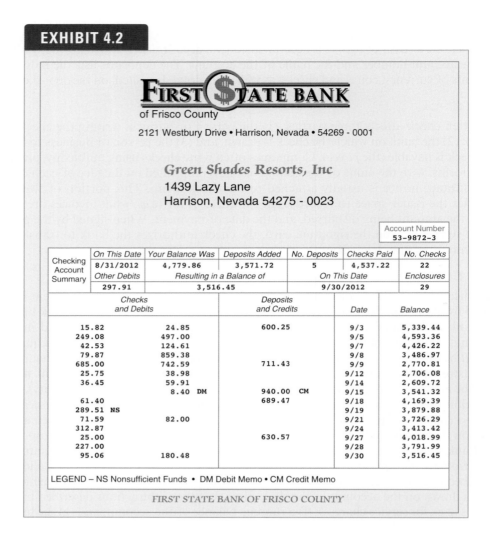

EXHIBIT 4.2

FIRST $ TATE BANK
of Frisco County

2121 Westbury Drive • Harrison, Nevada • 54269 - 0001

Green Shades Resorts, Inc
1439 Lazy Lane
Harrison, Nevada 54275 - 0023

Account Number
53-9872-3

Checking Account Summary	On This Date	Your Balance Was	Deposits Added	No. Deposits	Checks Paid	No. Checks
	8/31/2012	4,779.86	3,571.72	5	4,537.22	22
	Other Debits	Resulting in a Balance of			On This Date	Enclosures
	297.91	3,516.45			9/30/2012	29

Checks and Debits		Deposits and Credits	Date	Balance
15.82	24.85	600.25	9/3	5,339.44
249.08	497.00		9/5	4,593.36
42.53	124.61		9/7	4,426.22
79.87	859.38		9/8	3,486.97
685.00	742.59	711.43	9/9	2,770.81
25.75	38.98		9/12	2,706.08
36.45	59.91		9/14	2,609.72
	8.40 DM	940.00 CM	9/15	3,541.32
61.40		689.47	9/18	4,169.39
289.51 NS			9/19	3,879.88
71.59	82.00		9/21	3,726.29
312.87			9/24	3,413.42
25.00		630.57	9/27	4,018.99
227.00			9/28	3,791.99
95.06	180.48		9/30	3,516.45

LEGEND – NS Nonsufficient Funds • DM Debit Memo • CM Credit Memo

FIRST STATE BANK OF FRISCO COUNTY

bank balance agrees with the true cash balance determined from the perspective of the unadjusted *book* balance. The procedures a company uses to determine the *true cash balance* from the two different perspectives are outlined here.

Adjustments to the Bank Balance

A typical format for determining the true cash balance beginning with the unadjusted bank balance is

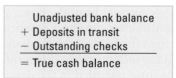

Unadjusted bank balance
+ Deposits in transit
− Outstanding checks
= True cash balance

Deposits in transit. Companies frequently leave deposits in the bank's night depository or make them on the day following the receipt of cash. Such deposits are called **deposits in transit.** Because these deposits have been recorded in the depositor's accounting records but have not yet been added to the depositor's account by the bank, they must be added to the unadjusted bank balance.

Outstanding checks. These are disbursements that have been properly recorded as cash deductions on the depositor's books. However, the bank has not deducted the amounts from the depositor's bank account because the checks have not yet been presented by the payee to the bank for payment; that is, the checks have not cleared the bank. **Outstanding checks** must be subtracted from the unadjusted bank balance to determine the true cash balance.

Adjustments to the Book Balance

A typical format for determining the true cash balance beginning with the unadjusted book balance is as follows.

> Unadjusted book balance
> + Accounts receivable collections
> + Interest earned
> − Bank service charges
> − Non-sufficient-funds (NSF) checks
> = True cash balance

Accounts receivable collections.   To collect cash as quickly as possible, many companies have their customers send payments directly to the bank. The bank adds the collection directly to the depositor's account and notifies the depositor about the collection through a credit memo that is included on the bank statement. The depositor adds the amount of the cash collections to the unadjusted book balance in the process of determining the true cash balance.

Interest earned.   Banks pay interest on certain checking accounts. The amount of the interest is added directly to the depositor's bank account. The bank notifies the depositor about the interest through a credit memo that is included on the bank statement. The depositor adds the amount of the interest revenue to the unadjusted book balance in the process of determining the true cash balance.

Service charges.   Banks frequently charge depositors fees for services performed. They may also charge a penalty if the depositor fails to maintain a specified minimum cash balance throughout the period. Banks deduct such fees and penalties directly from the depositor's account and advise the depositor of the deduction through a debit memo that is included on the bank statement. The depositor deducts such **service charges** from the unadjusted book balance to determine the true cash balance.

Non-sufficient-funds (NSF) checks.   **NSF checks** are checks that a company obtains from its customers and deposits in its checking account. However, when the checks are submitted to the customers' banks for payment, the banks refuse payment because there is insufficient money in the customers' accounts. When such checks are returned, the amounts of the checks are deducted from the company's bank account balance. The company is advised of NSF checks through debit memos that appear on the bank statement. The depositor deducts the amounts of the NSF checks from the unadjusted book balance in the process of determining the true cash balance.

Correction of Errors

In the course of reconciling the bank statement with the cash account, the depositor may discover errors in the bank's records, the depositor's records, or both. If an error is found on the bank statement, an adjustment for it is made to the unadjusted bank balance to determine the true cash balance, and the bank should be notified immediately to correct its records. Errors made by the depositor require adjustments to the book balance to arrive at the true cash balance.

Certified Checks

A **certified check** is guaranteed for payment by a bank. Whereas a regular check is deducted from the customer's account when it is presented for payment, a certified check is deducted from the customer's account when the bank certifies that the check is good.

Certified checks, therefore, *have* been deducted by the bank in determining the unadjusted bank balance, whether they have cleared the bank or remain outstanding as of the date of the bank statement. Since certified checks are deducted both from bank and depositor records immediately, they do not cause differences between the depositor and bank balances. As a result, certified checks are not included in a bank reconciliation.

Illustrating a Bank Reconciliation

The following example illustrates preparing the bank reconciliation for Green Shades Resorts, Inc. (GSRI). The bank statement for GSRI is displayed in Exhibit 4.2. Exhibit 4.3 illustrates the completed bank reconciliation. The items on the reconciliation are described below.

Adjustments to the Bank Balance

As of September 30, 2012, the bank statement showed an unadjusted balance of $3,516.45. A review of the bank statement disclosed three adjustments that had to be made to the unadjusted bank balance to determine GSRI's true cash balance.

1. Comparing the deposits on the bank statement with deposits recorded in GSRI's accounting records indicated there was $724.11 of deposits in transit.

2. An examination of the returned checks disclosed that the bank had erroneously deducted a $25 check written by Green Valley Resorts from GSRI's bank account. This amount must be added back to the unadjusted bank balance to determine the true cash balance.

3. The checks returned with the bank statement were sorted and compared to the cash records. Three checks with amounts totaling $235.25 were outstanding.

After these adjustment are made GSRI's true cash balance is determined to be $4,030.31.

EXHIBIT 4.3

GREEN SHADES RESORTS, INC.
Bank Reconciliation
September 30, 2012

Unadjusted bank balance, September 30, 2012	$3,516.45
Add: Deposits in transit	724.11
Bank error: Check drawn on Green Valley Resorts charged to GSRI	25.00
Less: Outstanding checks	

Check No.	Date	Amount
639	Sept. 18	$ 13.75
646	Sept. 20	29.00
672	Sept. 27	192.50

Total	(235.25)
True cash balance, September 30, 2012	$4,030.31
Unadjusted book balance, September 30, 2012	$3,361.22
Add: Receivable collected by bank	940.00
Error made by accountant (Check no. 633 recorded as $63.45 instead of $36.45)	27.00
Less: Bank service charges	(8.40)
NSF check	(289.51)
True cash balance, September 30, 2012	$4,030.31

Adjustments to the Book Balance

As indicated in Exhibit 4.3, GSRI's unadjusted book balance as of September 30, 2012, was $3,361.22. This balance differs from GSRI's true cash balance because of four unrecorded accounting events:

1. The bank collected a $940 account receivable for GSRI.
2. GSRI's accountant made a $27 recording error.
3. The bank charged GSRI an $8.40 service fee.
4. GSRI had deposited a $289.51 check from a customer who did not have sufficient funds to cover the check.

Two of these four adjustments increase the unadjusted cash balance. The other two decrease the unadjusted cash balance. After the adjustments have been recorded, the cash account reflects the true cash balance of $4,030.31 ($3,361.22 unadjusted cash balance + $940.00 receivable collection + $27.00 recording error − $8.40 service charge − $289.51 NSF check). Because the true balance determined from the perspective of the bank statement agrees with the true balance determined from the perspective of GSRI's books, the bank statement has been successfully reconciled with the accounting records.

Updating GSRI's Accounting Records

Each of the adjustments to the book balance must be recorded in GSRI's financial records. The effects of each adjustment on the financial statements are as follows.

ADJUSTMENT 1   *Recording the $940 receivable collection increases cash and reduces accounts receivable.*

The event is an asset exchange transaction. The effect of the collection on GSRI's financial statements is

Assets		=	Liab.	+	Equity	Rev.	−	Exp.	=	Net Inc.	Cash Flow
Cash +	Accts. Rec.										
940 +	(940)	=	NA	+	NA	NA	−	NA	=	NA	940 OA

ADJUSTMENT 2   *Assume the $27 recording error occurred because GSRI's accountant accidentally transposed two numbers when recording check no. 633 for utilities expense.*

The check was written to pay utilities expense of $36.45 but was recorded as a $63.45 disbursement. Since cash payments are overstated by $27.00 ($63.45 − $36.45), this amount must be added back to GSRI's cash balance and deducted from the utilities expense account, which increases net income. The effects on the financial statements are

Assets	=	Liab.	+	Equity	Rev.	−	Exp.	=	Net Inc.	Cash Flow
Cash	=			Ret. Earn.						
27	=	NA	+	27	NA	−	(27)	=	27	27 OA

ADJUSTMENT 3   *The $8.40 service charge is an expense that reduces assets, stockholders' equity, net income, and cash.*

The effects are

Assets	=	Liab.	+	Equity	Rev.	−	Exp.	=	Net Inc.	Cash Flow
Cash	=			Ret. Earn.						
(8.40)	=	NA	+	(8.40)	NA	−	8.40	=	(8.40)	(8.40) OA

ADJUSTMENT 4   *The $289.51 NSF check reduces GSRI's cash balance.*

When it originally accepted the customer's check, GSRI increased its cash account. Because there is not enough money in the customer's bank account to pay the check, GSRI didn't actually receive cash so GSRI must reduce its cash account. GSRI will still try to collect the money from the customer. In the meantime, it will show the amount of the NSF check as an account receivable. The adjusting entry to record the NSF check is an asset exchange transaction. Cash decreases and accounts receivable increases. The effect on GSRI's financial statements is

	Assets		=	Liab.	+	Equity	Rev.	−	Exp.	=	Net Inc.	Cash Flow
Cash	+	Accts. Rec.	=									
(289.51)	+	289.51	=	NA	+	NA	NA	−	NA	=	NA	(289.51) OA

Answers to The Curious Accountant

As this chapter explains, separation of duties is one of the primary features of a good system of internal controls. However, separation of duties is not designed to detect fraud at the very top level of management. Mr. Madoff ran BMI with almost complete control; he had no boss.

Even with a good system of internal controls, there is always some level of trust required in business. Mr. Madoff had an excellent reputation in the investment community. He had even been the president of the NASDAQ. His investors trusted him and assumed they could depend on his independent auditor to detect any major problems with the way BMI was investing, or not investing, their money.

Federal prosecutors believe that BMI's auditor, David Friehling, did very little in the way of properly auditing BMI's books. In fact, on March 18, 2009, he also was arrested and charged with falsely certifying BMI's financial statements. He faces up to 105 years in prison if convicted.

On March 12, 2009, the 70-year-old Mr. Madoff pled guilty to 11 felony charges. On June 29, 2009, he was sentenced to a term of 150 years in prison.

✓ CHECK YOURSELF 4.2

The following information was drawn from Reliance Company's October bank statement. The unadjusted bank balance on October 31 was $2,300. The statement showed that the bank had collected a $200 account receivable for Reliance. The statement also included $20 of bank service charges for October and a $100 check payable to Reliance that was returned NSF. A comparison of the bank statement with company accounting records indicates that there was a $500 deposit in transit and $1,800 of checks outstanding at the end of the month. Based on this information, determine the true cash balance on October 31.

Answer   Since the unadjusted book balance is not given, start with the unadjusted bank balance to determine the true cash balance. The collection of the receivable, the bank service charges, and the NSF check are already recognized in the unadjusted bank balance, so these items are not used to determine the true cash balance. Determine the true cash balance by adding the deposit in transit to and subtracting the outstanding checks from the unadjusted bank balance. The true cash balance is $1,000 ($2,300 unadjusted bank balance + $500 deposit in transit − $1,800 outstanding checks).

IMPORTANCE OF ETHICS

The chapter began with a discussion of the importance of internal control systems in preventing accounting scandals. After the Enron and WorldCom scandals and the passage of the Sarbanes-Oxley Act, much more attention has been paid to establishing effective internal control systems. However, despite this increase in legislation and awareness, accounting scandals continue to occur. In 2008, Lehman Brothers declared bankruptcy after it was discovered that the company had kept more than $50 billion in loans off the balance sheet by classifying them as sales. Several months later, Bernie Madoff used a Ponzi scheme to leave his investors with more than $21.2 billion in cash losses. These examples illustrate that legislation alone will not prevent accounting scandals. To prevent a scandal it is necessary to develop a culture that fosters and promotes ethical conduct.

The accountant's role in society requires trust and credibility. Accounting information is worthless if the accountant is not trustworthy. Similarly, tax and consulting advice is useless if it comes from an incompetent person. The high ethical standards required by the profession state "a certified public accountant assumes an obligation of self-discipline above and beyond requirements of laws and regulations." The **American Institute of Certified Public Accountants** requires its members to comply with the **Code of Professional Conduct.** Section I of the Code includes six articles that are summarized in Exhibit 4.4. The importance of ethical conduct is universally recognized across a broad spectrum of accounting organizations. The Institute of Management Accountants requires its members to follow a set of Standards of Ethical Conduct. The Institute of Internal Auditors also requires its members to subscribe to the organization's Code of Ethics.

Common Features of Criminal and Ethical Misconduct

Unfortunately, it takes more than a code of conduct to stop fraud. People frequently engage in activities that they know are unethical or even criminal. The auditing profession has identified three elements that are typically present when fraud occurs.

1. The availability of an opportunity.
2. The existence of some form of pressure leading to an incentive.
3. The capacity to rationalize.

LO 3

Discuss the role of ethics in the accounting profession.

EXHIBIT 4.4

Articles of AICPA Code of Professional Conduct

Article I Responsibilities
In carrying out their responsibilities as professionals, members should exercise sensitive professional and moral judgments in all their activities.

Article II The Public Interest
Members should accept the obligation to act in a way that will serve the public interest, honor the public trust, and demonstrate commitment to professionalism.

Article III Integrity
To maintain and broaden public confidence, members should perform all professional responsibilities with the highest sense of integrity.

Article IV Objectivity and Independence
A member should maintain objectivity and be free of conflicts of interest in discharging professional responsibilities. A member in public practice should be independent in fact and appearance when providing auditing and other attestation services.

Article V Due Care
A member should observe the profession's technical and ethical standards, strive continually to improve competence and the quality of services, and discharge professional responsibility to the best of the member's ability.

Article VI Scope and Nature of Services
A member in public practice should observe the principles of the Code of Professional Conduct in determining the scope and nature of services to be provided.

The three elements are frequently arranged in the shape of a triangle as shown in Exhibit 4.5.

Opportunity is shown at the head to the triangle because without opportunity fraud could not exist. The most effective way to reduce opportunities for ethical or criminal misconduct is to implement an effective set of internal controls. *Internal controls* are policies and procedures that a business implements to reduce opportunities

EXHIBIT 4.5

The Fraud Triangle

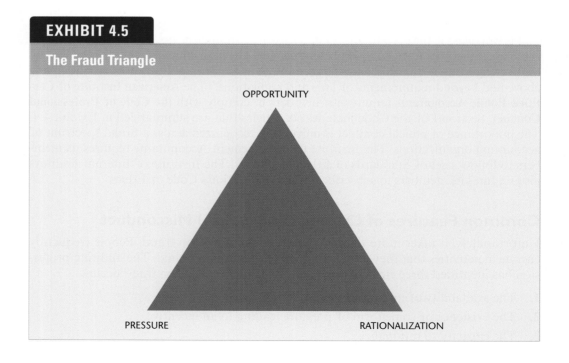

for fraud and to assure that its objectives will be accomplished. Specific controls are tailored to meet the individual needs of particular businesses. For example, banks use elaborate vaults to protect cash and safety deposit boxes, but universities have little use for this type of equipment. Even so, many of the same procedures are used by a wide variety of businesses. The internal control policies and procedures that have gained widespread acceptance are discussed in a subsequent chapter.

Only a few employees turn to the dark side even when internal control is weak and opportunities abound. So, what causes one person to commit fraud and another to remain honest? The second element of the fraud triangle recognizes **pressure** as a key ingredient of misconduct. A manager who is told "either make the numbers or you are fired" is more likely to cheat than one who is told to "tell it like it is." Pressure can come from a variety of sources.

- Personal vices such as drug addiction, gambling, and promiscuity.
- Intimidation from superiors.
- Personal debt from credit cards, consumer and mortgage loans, or poor investments.
- Family expectations to provide a standard of living that is beyond one's capabilities.
- Business failure caused by poor decision making or temporary factors such as a poor economy.
- Loyalty or trying to be agreeable.

The third and final element of the fraud triangle is **rationalization.** Few individuals think of themselves as evil. They develop rationalizations to justify their misconduct. Common rationalizations include the following.

- Everybody does it.
- They are not paying me enough. I'm only taking what I deserve.
- I'm only borrowing the money. I'll pay it back.
- The company can afford it. Look what they are paying the officers.
- I'm taking what my family needs to live like everyone else.

Most people are able to resist pressure and the tendency to rationalize ethical or legal misconduct. However, some people will yield to temptation. What can accountants do to protect themselves and their companies from unscrupulous characters? The answer lies in personal integrity. The best indicator of personal integrity is past performance. Accordingly, companies must exercise due care in performing appropriate background investigations before hiring people to fill positions of trust.

Ethical misconduct is a serious offense in the accounting profession. A single mistake can destroy an accounting career. If you commit a white-collar crime, you normally lose the opportunity to hold a white-collar job. Second chances are rarely granted; it is extremely important that you learn how to recognize and avoid the common features of ethical misconduct. To help you prepare for the real-world situations you are likely to encounter, we include ethical dilemmas in the end-of-chapter materials. When working with these dilemmas, try to identify the (1) opportunity, (2) pressure, and (3) rationalization associated with the particular ethical situation described. If you are not an ethical person, accounting is not the career for you.

ROLE OF THE INDEPENDENT AUDITOR

As previously explained, financial statements are prepared in accordance with certain rules called *generally accepted accounting principles (GAAP)*. Thus, when General Electric publishes its financial statements, it is saying, "here are our financial statements prepared according to GAAP." How can a financial analyst know that a company really did follow GAAP? Analysts and other statement users rely on **audits** conducted by **certified public accountants (CPAs).**

Describe the auditor's role in financial reporting.

The primary roles of an independent auditor (CPA) are summarized below:

1. Conducts a financial audit (a detailed examination of a company's financial statements and underlying accounting records).

2. Assumes both legal and professional responsibilities to the public as well as to the company paying the auditor.

3. Determines if financial statements are *materially* correct rather than *absolutely* correct.

4. Presents conclusions in an audit report that includes an opinion as to whether the statements are prepared in conformity with GAAP. In rare cases, the auditor issues a disclaimer.

5. Maintains professional confidentiality of client records. The auditor is not, however, exempt from legal obligations such as testifying in court.

The Financial Statement Audit

What is an audit? There are several types of audits. The type most relevant to this course is a **financial statement audit,** often referred to as simply a financial audit. The financial audit is a detailed examination of a company's financial statements and the documents that support those statements. It also tests the reliability of the accounting system used to produce the financial reports. A financial audit is conducted by an **independent auditor.**

The term *independent auditor* typically refers to a *firm* of certified public accountants. CPAs are licensed by state governments to provide services to the public. They are to be as independent of the companies they audit as is reasonably possible. To help assure independence, CPAs and members of their immediate families may not be employees of the companies they audit. Further, they cannot have investments in the companies they audit. Although CPAs are paid by the companies they audit, the audit fee may not be based on the outcome of the audit.

Although the independent auditors are chosen by, paid by, and can be fired by their client companies, the auditors are primarily responsible to *the public.* In fact, auditors have a legal responsibility to those members of the public who have a financial interest in the company being audited. If investors in a company lose money, they sometimes sue the independent auditors in an attempt to recover their losses, especially if the losses were related to financial failure. A lawsuit against auditors will succeed only if the auditors failed in their professional responsibilities when conducting the audit. Auditors are not responsible for the success or failure of a company. Instead, they are responsible for the appropriate reporting of that success or failure. While recent debacles such as Bernard Madoff Investments produce spectacular headlines, auditors are actually not sued very often, considering the number of audits they perform.

Materiality and Financial Audits

Auditors do not guarantee that financial statements are absolutely correct—only that they are free from *material* misstatements. This is where things get a little fuzzy. What is a *material misstatement?* The concept of materiality is very subjective. If ExxonMobil inadvertently overstated its sales by $1 million, would this be material? In 2009, ExxonMobil had approximately $311 billion of sales! A $1 million error in computing sales at ExxonMobil is like a $1 error in computing the pay of a person who makes $311,000 per year—not material at all! An error, or other reporting problem, is **material** if knowing about it would influence the decisions of an *average prudent investor.*

Financial audits are not directed toward the discovery of fraud. Auditors are, however, responsible for providing *reasonable assurance* that statements are free from material misstatements, whether caused by errors or fraud. Also, auditors are responsible for evaluating whether internal control procedures are in place to help prevent material misstatements due to fraud. If fraud is widespread in a company, normal audit procedures should detect it.

Accounting majors take at least one and often two or more courses in auditing to understand how to conduct an audit. An explanation of auditing techniques is beyond the scope of this course, but at least be aware that auditors do not review how the company accounted for every transaction. Along with other methods, auditors use statistics to choose representative samples of transactions to examine.

Types of Audit Opinions

Once an audit is complete, the auditors present their conclusions in a report that includes an *audit opinion.* There are three basic types of audit opinions.

An **unqualified opinion,** despite its negative-sounding name, is the most favorable opinion auditors can express. It means the auditor believes the financial statements are in compliance with GAAP without qualification, reservation, or exception. Most audits result in unqualified opinions because companies correct any reporting deficiencies the auditors find before the financial statements are released.

The most negative report an auditor can issue is an **adverse opinion.** An adverse opinion means that one or more departures from GAAP are so material that the financial statements do not present a fair picture of the company's status. The auditor's report explains the unacceptable accounting practice(s) that resulted in the adverse opinion being issued. Adverse opinions are very rare because public companies are required by law to follow GAAP.

A **qualified opinion** falls between an unqualified and an adverse opinion. A qualified opinion means that for the most part, the company's financial statements are in compliance with GAAP, but the auditors have reservations about something in the statements. The auditors' report explains why the opinion is qualified. A qualified opinion usually does not imply a serious accounting problem, but users should read the auditors' report and draw their own conclusions.

If an auditor is unable to perform the audit procedures necessary to determine whether the statements are prepared in accordance with GAAP, the auditor cannot issue an opinion on the financial statements. Instead, the auditor issues a **disclaimer of opinion.** A disclaimer means that the auditor is unable to obtain enough information to confirm compliance with GAAP.

Regardless of the type of report they issue, auditors are only expressing their judgment about whether the financial statements present a fair picture of a company. They do not provide opinions regarding the investment quality of a company.

The ultimate responsibility for financial statements rests with the executives of the reporting company. Just like auditors, managers can be sued by investors who believe they lost money due to improper financial reporting. This is one reason all business persons should understand accounting fundamentals.

Confidentiality

The **confidentiality** rules in the AICPA's code of ethics for CPAs prohibits auditors from *voluntarily disclosing* information they have acquired as a result of their accountant-client relationships. However, accountants may be required to testify in a court of law. In general, federal law does not recognize an accountant-client privilege as it does with attorneys and clergy. Some federal courts have taken exception to this position, especially as it applies to tax cases. State law varies with respect to accountant-client privilege. Furthermore, if auditors terminate a client relationship because of ethical or legal disagreements and they are subsequently contacted by a successor auditor, they are required to inform the successor of the reasons for the termination. In addition, auditors must consider the particular circumstances of a case when assessing the appropriateness of disclosing confidential information. Given the diverse legal positions governing accountant-client confidentiality, auditors should seek legal counsel prior to disclosing any information obtained in an accountant-client relationship.

To illustrate, assume that Joe Smith, CPA, discovers that his client Jane Doe is misrepresenting information reported in her financial statements. Smith tries to convince Doe to correct the misrepresentations, but she refuses to do so. Smith is required by the code of ethics to terminate his relationship with Doe. However, Smith is not permitted to disclose Doe's dishonest reporting practices unless he is called on to testify in a legal hearing or to respond to an inquiry by Doe's successor accountant.

With respect to the discovery of significant fraud, the auditor is required to inform management at least one level above the position of the employee who is engaged in the fraud and to notify the board of directors of the company. Suppose that Joe Smith, CPA, discovers that Jane Doe, employee of Western Company, is embezzling money from Western. Smith is required to inform Doe's supervisor and to notify Western's board of directors. However, Smith is prohibited from publicly disclosing the fraud.

<< A Look Back

The policies and procedures used to provide reasonable assurance that the objectives of an enterprise will be accomplished are called *internal controls*. While the mechanics of internal control systems vary from company to company, the more prevalent features include the following.

1. *Separation of duties.* Whenever possible, the functions of authorization, recording, and custody should be exercised by different individuals.

2. *Quality of employees.* Employees should be qualified to competently perform the duties that are assigned to them. Companies must establish hiring practices to screen out unqualified candidates. Furthermore, procedures should be established to ensure that employees receive appropriate training to maintain their competence.

3. *Bonded employees.* Employees in sensitive positions should be covered by a fidelity bond that provides insurance to reimburse losses due to illegal actions committed by employees.

4. *Required absences.* Employees should be required to take extended absences from their jobs so that they are not always present to hide unscrupulous or illegal activities.

5. *Procedures manual.* To promote compliance, the procedures for processing transactions should be clearly described in a manual.

6. *Authority and responsibility.* To motivate employees and promote effective control, clear lines of authority and responsibility should be established.

7. *Prenumbered documents.* Prenumbered documents minimize the likelihood of missing or duplicate documents. Prenumbered forms should be used for all important documents such as purchase orders, receiving reports, invoices, and checks.

8. *Physical control.* Locks, fences, security personnel, and other physical devices should be employed to safeguard assets.

9. *Performance evaluations.* Because few people can evaluate their own performance objectively, independent performance evaluations should be performed. Substandard performance will likely persist unless employees are encouraged to take corrective action.

Because cash is such an important business asset and because it is tempting to steal, much of the discussion of internal controls in this chapter focused on cash controls. Special procedures should be employed to control the receipts and payments of cash. One of the most common control policies is to use *checking accounts* for all payments except petty cash disbursements.

A *bank reconciliation* should be prepared each month to explain differences between the bank statement and a company's internal accounting records. A common reconciliation format determines the true cash balance based on both bank and book records. Items that typically appear on a bank reconciliation include the following:

Unadjusted bank balance	xxx	Unadjusted book balance	xxx
Add		Add	
Deposits in transit	xxx	Interest revenue	xxx
		Collection of receivables	xxx
Subtract		Subtract	
Outstanding checks	xxx	Bank service charges	xxx
		NSF checks	xxx
True cash balance	xxx	True cash balance	xxx

Agreement of the two true cash balances provides evidence that accounting for cash transactions has been accurate.

The chapter discussed the importance of ethics in the accounting profession. The *American Institute of Public Accountants* requires all of its members to comply with the *Code of Professional Conduct.* Situations where *opportunity, pressure,* and *rationalization* exist can lead employees to conduct unethical acts, which, in cases like Enron, have destroyed the organization. Finally, the chapter discussed the auditor's role in financial reporting, including the materiality concept and the types of audit opinions that may be issued.

A Look Forward

The next chapter focuses on more specific issues related to accounts receivables and inventory. Accounting for receivables and payable was introduced in Chapter 2, using relatively simple illustrations. For example, we assumed that customers who purchased services on account always paid their bills. In real business practice, some customers do not pay their bills. Among other topics, Chapter 5 examines how companies account for uncollectible accounts receivable.

Accounting for inventory was discussed in Chapter 3. However, we assumed that all inventory items were purchased at the same price. This is unrealistic given that the price of goods is constantly changing. Chapter 5 discusses how to account for inventory items that are purchased at different times and different prices.

A step-by-step audio-narrated series of slides is provided on the text website at www.mhhe.com/edmondssurvey3e.

 SELF-STUDY REVIEW PROBLEM

The following information pertains to Terry's Pest Control Company (TPCC) for July:

1. The unadjusted bank balance at July 31 was $870.
2. The bank statement included the following items:
    (a) A $60 credit memo for interest earned by TPCC.
    (b) A $200 NSF check made payable to TPCC.
    (c) A $110 debit memo for bank service charges.
3. The unadjusted book balance at July 31 was $1,400.

4. A comparison of the bank statement with company accounting records disclosed the following:

(a) A $400 deposit in transit at July 31.

(b) Outstanding checks totaling $120 at the end of the month.

Required

Prepare a bank reconciliation.

Solution

TERRY'S PEST CONTROL COMPANY
Bank Reconciliation
July 31

Unadjusted bank balance	$ 870
Add: Deposits in transit	400
Less: Outstanding checks	(120)
True cash balance	$1,150
Unadjusted book balance	$1,400
Add: Interest revenue	60
Less: NSF check	(200)
Less: Bank service charges	(110)
True cash balance	$1,150

KEY TERMS

Adverse opinion 141
American Institute of Certified Public Accountants 137
Audits 139
Authority manual 127
Bank reconciliation 131
Bank statement 131
Bank statement credit memo 131
Bank statement debit memo 131
Cash 129
Certified check 133
Certified public accountants (CPAs) 139

Checks 131
Code of Professional Conduct 137
Confidentiality 141
Deposit ticket 131
Deposits in transit 132
Disclaimer of opinion 141
Fidelity bond 127
Financial statement audit 140
General authority 127
Independent auditor 140
Internal controls 126
Material 140
Non-sufficient-funds (NSF) checks 133

Opportunity 138
Outstanding checks 133
Pressure 139
Procedures manual 127
Qualified opinion 141
Rationalization 139
Separation of duties 126
Service charges 133
Signature card 130
Specific authorizations 127
True cash balance 131
Unadjusted bank balance 131
Unadjusted book balance 131
Unqualified opinion 141

QUESTIONS

1. What motivated congress to pass the Sarbanes-Oxley Act (SOX) of 2002?

2. Define the term *internal control*.

3. Explain the relationship between SOX and COSO.

4. Name and briefly define the five components of COSO's internal control framework.

5. Explain how COSO's *Enterprise Risk Management—An Integrated Framework* project relates to COSO's *Internal Control—An Integrated Framework* project.

6. List several control activities of an effective internal control system.

7. What is meant by *separation of duties?* Give an illustration.

8. What are the attributes of a high-quality employee?

9. What is a fidelity bond? Explain its purpose.

10. Why is it important that every employee periodically take a leave of absence or vacation?

11. What are the purpose and importance of a procedures manual?

12. What is the difference between specific and general authorizations?

13. Why should documents (checks, invoices, receipts) be prenumbered?

14. What procedures are important in the physical control of assets and accounting records?

15. What is the purpose of independent verification of performance?

16. What items are considered cash?

17. Why is cash more susceptible to theft or embezzlement than other assets?

18. Giving written copies of receipts to customers can help prevent what type of illegal acts?

19. What procedures can help to protect cash receipts?

20. What procedures can help protect cash disbursements?

21. What effect does a debit memo in a bank statement have on the Cash account? What effect does a credit memo in a bank statement have on the Cash account?

22. What information is normally included in a bank statement?

23. Why might a bank statement reflect a balance that is larger than the balance recorded in the depositor's books? What could cause the bank balance to be smaller than the book balance?

24. What is the purpose of a bank reconciliation?

25. What is an outstanding check?

26. What is a deposit in transit?

27. What is a certified check?

28. How is an NSF check accounted for in the accounting records?

29. Name and comment on the three elements of the fraud triangle.

30. What are the six articles of ethical conduct set out under section I of the AICPA's Code of Professional Conduct?

MULTIPLE-CHOICE QUESTIONS

Multiple-choice questions are provided on the text website at www.mhhe.com/edmondssurvey3e.

EXERCISES

All applicable Exercises are available with McGraw-Hill's *Connect Accounting.*

Exercise 4-1   *SOX and COSO's Internal Control Frameworks*   **LO 1**

Required

a. Explain what the acronym SOX refers to.

b. Define the acronym COSO and explain how it relates to SOX.

c. Name and briefly define the five components of COSO's internal control framework.

d. Define the acronym ERM and explain how it relates to COSO's internal control framework.

Exercise 4-2   *Control activities of a strong internal control system*   **LO 1**

Required

List and describe nine control activities of a strong internal control system discussed in this chapter.

Exercise 4-3   *Internal controls for small businesses*   **LO 1**

Required

Assume you are the owner of a small business that has only two employees.

a. Which of the internal control procedures are most important to you?

b. How can you overcome the limited opportunity to use the separation-of-duties control procedure?

Exercise 4-4   *Internal control for cash*   **LO 1**

Required

a. Why are special controls needed for cash?

b. What is included in the definition of *cash*?

LO 1

Exercise 4-5   *Internal control procedures to prevent deception*

Emergency Care Medical Centers (ECMC) hired a new physician, Ken Major, who was an immediate success. Everyone loved his bedside manner; he could charm the most cantankerous patient. Indeed, he was a master salesman as well as an expert physician. Unfortunately, Major misdiagnosed a case that resulted in serious consequences to the patient. The patient filed suit against ECMC. In preparation for the defense, ECMC's attorneys discovered that Major was indeed an exceptional salesman. He had worked for several years as district marketing manager for a pharmaceutical company. In fact, he was not a physician at all! He had changed professions without going to medical school. He had lied on his application form. His knowledge of medical terminology had enabled him to fool everyone. ECMC was found negligent and lost a $3 million lawsuit.

Required

Identify the relevant internal control procedures that could have prevented the company's losses. Explain how these procedures would have prevented Major's deception.

LO 1

Exercise 4-6   *Internal control procedures to prevent embezzlement*

Bell Gates was in charge of the returns department at The Software Company. She was responsible for evaluating returned merchandise. She sent merchandise that was reusable back to the warehouse, where it was restocked in inventory. Gates was also responsible for taking the merchandise that she determined to be defective to the city dump for disposal. She had agreed to buy a tax planning program for one of her friends at a discount through her contacts at work. That is when the idea came to her. She could simply classify one of the reusable returns as defective and bring it home instead of taking it to the dump. She did so and made a quick $150. She was happy, and her friend was ecstatic; he was able to buy a $400 software package for only $150. He told his friends about the deal, and soon Gates had a regular set of customers. She was caught when a retail store owner complained to the marketing manager that his pricing strategy was being undercut by The Software Company's direct sales to the public. The marketing manager was suspicious because The Software Company had no direct marketing program. When the outside sales were ultimately traced back to Gates, the company discovered that it had lost over $10,000 in sales revenue because of her criminal activity.

Required

Identify an internal control procedure that could have prevented the company's losses. Explain how the procedure would have stopped the embezzlement.

LO 2

Exercise 4-7   *Treatment of NSF check*

Rankin Stationery's bank statement contained a $250 NSF check that one of its customers had written to pay for supplies purchased.

Required

a. Show the effects of recognizing the NSF check on the financial statements by recording the appropriate amounts in a horizontal statements model like the following one:

Assets		= Liab.	+ Equity	Rev.	− Exp.	= Net Inc.	Cash Flow
Cash +	Accts. Rec.						

b. Is the recognition of the NSF check on Rankin's books an asset source, use, or exchange transaction?

c. Suppose the customer redeems the check by giving Rankin $270 cash in exchange for the bad check. The additional $20 was a service fee charged by Rankin. Show the effects on the financial statements in the horizontal statements model in Requirement *a*.

d. Is the receipt of cash referenced in Requirement *c* an asset source, use, or exchange transaction?

Exercise 4-8   *Adjustments to the balance per books*

LO 2

Required

Identify which of the following items are added to or subtracted from the unadjusted *book balance* to arrive at the true cash balance. Distinguish the additions from the subtractions by placing a + beside the items that are added to the unadjusted book balance and a − beside those that are subtracted from it. The first item is recorded as an example.

Reconciling Items	Book Balance Adjusted?	Added or Subtracted?
Outstanding checks	No	N/A
Interest revenue earned on the account		
Deposits in transit		
Service charge		
Automatic debit for utility bill		
Charge for checks		
NSF check from customer		
ATM fee		

Exercise 4-9   *Adjustments to the balance per bank*

LO 2

Required

Identify which of the following items are added to or subtracted from the unadjusted *bank balance* to arrive at the true cash balance. Distinguish the additions from the subtractions by placing a + beside the items that are added to the unadjusted bank balance and a − beside those that are subtracted from it. The first item is recorded as an example.

Reconciling Items	Bank Balance Adjusted?	Added or Subtracted?
Bank service charge	No	N/A
Outstanding checks		
Deposits in transit		
Debit memo		
Credit memo		
ATM fee		
Petty cash voucher		
NSF check from customer		
Interest revenue		

Exercise 4-10   *Adjusting the cash account*

LO 2

As of June 30, 2012, the bank statement showed an ending balance of $13,879.85. The unadjusted Cash account balance was $13,483.75. The following information is available:

1. Deposit in transit, $1,476.30.
2. Credit memo in bank statement for interest earned in June, $35.
3. Outstanding check, $1,843.74.
4. Debit memo for service charge, $6.34.

Required

Determine the true cash balance by preparing a bank reconciliation as of June 30, 2012, using the preceding information.

LO 2

Exercise 4-11 *Determining the true cash balance, starting with the unadjusted bank balance*

The following information is available for Hamby Company for the month of June:

1. The unadjusted balance per the bank statement on June 30 was $68,714.35.
2. Deposits in transit on June 30 were $1,464.95.
3. A debit memo was included with the bank statement for a service charge of $25.38.
4. A $4,745.66 check written in June had not been paid by the bank.
5. The bank statement included a $944 credit memo for the collection of a note. The principal of the note was $859, and the interest collected amounted to $85.

Required

Determine the true cash balance as of June 30 (*Hint:* It is not necessary to use all of the preceding items to determine the true balance.)

LO 2

Exercise 4-12 *Determining the true cash balance, starting with the unadjusted book balance*

Crumbley Company had an unadjusted cash balance of $6,450 as of May 31. The company's bank statement, also dated May 31, included a $38 NSF check written by one of Crumbley's customers. There were $548.60 in outstanding checks and $143.74 in deposits in transit as of May 31. According to the bank statement, service charges were $30, and the bank collected a $450 note receivable for Crumbley. The bank statement also showed $18 of interest revenue earned by Crumbley.

Required

Determine the true cash balance as of May 31. (*Hint:* It is not necessary to use all of the preceding items to determine the true balance.)

LO 3

Exercise 4-13 *AICPA Code of Professional Conduct*

Walter Walker owns and operates Walker Enterprises. Walter's sister, Sarah, is the independent public accountant for Walker Enterprises. Sarah worked for the Walker Enterprises for five years before she started her independent CPA practice. Walter considered hiring a different accounting firm but ultimately decided that no one knew his business as well as his sister.

Required

Use the AICPA Code of Professional Conduct to evaluate the appropriateness of Sarah's client relationship with Walker Enterprises.

LO 3

Exercise 4-14 *AICPA Code of Professional Conduct*

Courtney Simmons owns the fastest growing CPA practice in her local community. She attributes her success to her marketing skills. She makes a special effort to get to know her clients personally. She attends their weddings, anniversary celebrations, and birthday parties on a regular basis. Courtney always brings lavish presents, and her clients reciprocate by showering her with expensive gifts on her special occasions. This social activity consumes a lot of time. Indeed, it has cut into the time she once spent on continuing education. Even so, her practice has grown at the rate of 25 percent per year for the last three years. Courtney could not be happier with her progress.

Required

Use the AICPA Code of Professional Conduct to evaluate the appropriateness of Courtney's marketing strategy.

LO 3

Exercise 4-15 *Fraud triangle*

Bill Perry is a CPA with a secret. His secret is that he gambles on sports. Bill knows that his profession disapproves of gambling, but considers the professional standards to be misguided in his case. Bill really doesn't consider his bets to be gambling because he spends a lot of time studying sports facts. He believes that he is simply making educated decisions based on facts. He argues that using sports, facts to place bets is no different than using accounting information to buy stock.

Required

Use the fraud triangle as a basis to comment on Bill Perry's gambling activities.

Exercise 4-16 *Confidentiality and the auditor*

West Aston discovered a significant fraud in the accounting records of a high profile client. The story has been broadcast on national airways. Aston was unable to resolve his remaining concerns with the company's management team and ultimately resigned from the audit engagement. Aston knows that he will be asked by several interested parties, including his friends and relatives, the successor auditor, and prosecuting attorneys in a court of law to tell what he knows. He has asked you for advice.

Required

Write a memo that explains Aston's disclosure responsibilities to each of the interested parties.

Exercise 4-17 *Auditor responsibilities*

You have probably heard it is unwise to bite the hand that feeds you. Independent auditors are chosen by, paid by, and can be fired by the companies they audit. What keeps the auditor independent? In other words, what stops an auditor from blindly following the orders of a client?

Required

Write a memo that explains the reporting responsibilities of an independent auditor.

PROBLEMS

All applicable Problems are available with McGraw-Hill's *Connect Accounting*.

Problem 4-18 *Using internal control to restrict illegal or unethical behavior*

Required

For each of the following fraudulent acts, describe one or more internal control procedures that could have prevented (or helped prevent) the problems.

a. Everyone in the office has noticed what a dedicated employee Jennifer Reidel is. She never misses work, not even for a vacation. Reidel is in charge of the petty cash fund. She transfers funds from the company's bank account to the petty cash account on an as-needed basis. During a surprise audit, the petty cash fund was found to contain fictitious receipts. Over a three-year period, Reidel had used more than $4,000 of petty cash to pay for personal expenses.

b. Bill Bruton was hired as the vice president of the manufacturing division of a corporation. His impressive resume listed a master's degree in business administration from a large state university and numerous collegiate awards and activities, when in fact Bruton had only a high school diploma. In a short time, the company was in poor financial condition because of his inadequate knowledge and bad decisions.

c. Havolene Manufacturing has good internal control over its manufacturing materials inventory. However, office supplies are kept on open shelves in the employee break room. The office supervisor has noticed that he is having to order paper, tape, staplers, and pens with increasing frequency.

Problem 4-19 *Preparing a bank reconciliation*

Bob Carson owns a card shop, Card Talk. The following cash information is available for the month of August, 2012.

As of August 31, the bank statement shows a balance of $17,000. The August 31 unadjusted balance in the Cash account of Card Talk is $16,000. A review of the bank statement revealed the following information:

1. A deposit of $2,260 on August 31, 2012, does not appear on the August bank statement.
2. It was discovered that a check to pay for baseball cards was correctly written and paid by the bank for $4,040 but was recorded on the books as $4,400.

3. When checks written during the month were compared with those paid by the bank, three checks amounting to $3,000 were found to be outstanding.

4. A debit memo for $100 was included in the bank statement for the purchase of a new supply of checks.

Required

Prepare a bank reconciliation at the end of August showing the true cash balance.

Problem 4-20   *Missing information in a bank reconciliation*

The following data apply to Superior Auto Supply Inc. for May 2012.

1. Balance per the bank on May 31, $8,000.
2. Deposits in transit not recorded by the bank, $975.
3. Bank error; check written by Allen Auto Supply was charged to Superior Auto Supply's account, $650.
4. The following checks written and recorded by Superior Auto Supply were not included in the bank statement:

3013	$ 385
3054	735
3056	1,900

5. Note collected by the bank, $500.
6. Service charge for collection of note, $10.
7. The bookkeeper recorded a check written for $188 to pay for the May utilities expense as $888 in the cash disbursements journal.
8. Bank service charge in addition to the note collection fee, $25.
9. Customer checks returned by the bank as NSF, $125.

Required

Determine the amount of the unadjusted cash balance per Superior Auto Supply's books.

Problem 4-21   *Adjustments to the cash account based on the bank reconciliation*

Required

Determine whether the following items included in Yang Company's bank reconciliation will require adjustments or corrections on Yang's books.

a. An $877 deposit was recorded by the bank as $778.
b. Four checks totaling $450 written during the month of January were not included with the January bank statement.
c. A $54 check written to Office Max for office supplies was recorded in the general journal as $45.
d. The bank statement indicated that the bank had collected a $330 note for Yang.
e. Yang recorded $500 of receipts on January 31, which were deposited in the night depository of the bank. These deposits were not included in the bank statement.
f. Service charges of $22 for the month of January were listed on the bank statement.
g. The bank charged a $297 check drawn on Cave Restaurant to Yang's account. The check was included in Yang's bank statement.
h. A check of $31 was returned by the bank because of insufficient funds and was noted on the bank statement. Yang received the check from a customer and thought that it was good when it was deposited into the account.

Problem 4-22   *Bank reconciliation and adjustments to the cash account*   **LO 2**

The following information is available for Cooters Garage for March 2012:

BANK STATEMENT
HAZARD STATE BANK
215 MAIN STREET
HAZARD, GA 30321

Cooters Garage	Account number
629 Main Street	62-00062
Hazard, GA 30321	March 31, 2012

Beginning balance 3/1/2012	$15,000.00
Total deposits and other credits	7,000.00
Total checks and other debits	6,000.00
Ending balance 3/31/2012	16,000.00

Checks and Debits		Deposits and Credits	
Check No.	Amount	Date	Amount
1462	$1,163.00	March 1	$1,000.00
1463	62.00	March 2	1,340.00
1464	1,235.00	March 6	210.00
1465	750.00	March 12	1,940.00
1466	1,111.00	March 17	855.00
1467	964.00	March 22	1,480.00
DM	15.00	CM	175.00
1468	700.00		

The following is a list of checks and deposits recorded on the books of Cooters Garage for March 2012:

Date	Check No.	Amount of Check	Date	Amount of Deposit
March 1	1463	$ 62.00	March 1	$1,340.00
March 5	1464	1,235.00	March 5	210.00
March 6	1465	750.00		
March 9	1466	1,111.00	March 10	1,940.00
March 10	1467	964.00		
March 14	1468	70.00	March 16	855.00
March 19	1469	1,500.00	March 19	1,480.00
March 28	1470	102.00	March 29	2,000.00

Other Information

1. Check no. 1462 was outstanding from February.
2. A credit memo for collection of accounts receivable was included in the bank statement.
3. All checks were paid at the correct amount.
4. The bank statement included a debit memo for service charges.
5. The February 28 bank reconciliation showed a deposit in transit of $1,000.
6. Check no. 1468 was for the purchase of equipment.
7. The unadjusted Cash account balance at March 31 was $16,868.

Required

a. Prepare the bank reconciliation for Cooters Garage at the end of March.
b. Explain how the adjustments described above affect the cash account.

LO 1, 2

CHECK FIGURE
a. True Cash Balance, Jun 30, 2012: $2,093

Problem 4-23   *Bank reconciliation and internal control*

Following is a bank reconciliation for Surf Shop for June 30, 2012:

	Cash Account	Bank Statement
Balance as of 6/30/2012	$ 1,618	$ 3,000
Deposit in transit		600
Outstanding checks		(1,507)
Note collected by bank	2,000	
Bank service charge	(25)	
NSF check	(1,500)	
Adjusted cash balance as of 6/30/2012	$ 2,093	$ 2,093

When reviewing the bank reconciliation, Surf's auditor was unable to locate any reference to the NSF check on the bank statement. Furthermore, the clerk who reconciles the bank account and records the adjusting entries could not find the actual NSF check that should have been included in the bank statement. Finally, there was no specific reference in the accounts receivable supporting records identifying a party who had written a bad check.

Required

a. Prepare a corrected bank reconciliation.
b. What is the total amount of cash missing, and how was the difference between the "true cash" per the bank and the "true cash" per the books hidden on the reconciliation prepared by the former employee?
c. What could Surf's Shop do to avoid cash theft in the future?

LO 3

Problem 4-24   *Fraud Triangle*

Pete Chalance is an accountant with a shady past. Suffice it to say that he owes some very unsavory characters a lot of money. Despite his past, Pete works hard at keeping up a strong professional image. He is a manager at Smith and Associates, a fast-growing CPA firm. Pete is highly regarded around the office because he is a strong producer of client revenue. Indeed, on several occasions he exceeded his authority in establishing prices with clients. This is typically a partner's job but who could criticize Pete, who is most certainly bringing in the business. Indeed, Pete is so good that he is able to pull off the following scheme. He bills clients at inflated rates and then reports the ordinary rate to his accounting firm. Say, for example, the normal charge for a job is $2,500. Pete will smooth talk the client, then charge him $3,000. He reports the normal charge of $2,500 to his firm and keeps the extra $500 for himself. He knows it isn't exactly right. Even so, his firm gets its regular charges and the client willingly pays for the services rendered. He thinks to himself, as he pockets his ill-gotten gains, who is getting hurt anyway?

Required

The text discusses three common features (conditions) that motivate ethical misconduct. Identify and explain each of the three features as they appear in the above scenario.

LO 4

Problem 4-25   *Materiality and the auditor*

Sharon Waters is an auditor. Her work at two companies disclosed inappropriate recognition of revenue. Both cases involved dollar amounts in the $100,000 range. In one case. Waters considered the item material and required her client to restate earnings. In the other case, Waters dismissed the misstatement as being immaterial.

Required

Write a memo that explains how a $100,000 misstatement of revenue is acceptable for one company but unacceptable for a different company.

Problem 4-26   *Types of audit reports*

Jim Morris is a partner of a regional accounting firm. Mr. Morris was hired by a client to audit the company's books. After extensive work, Mr. Morris determined that he was unable to perform the appropriate audit procedures.

Required

a. Name the type of audit report that Mr. Morris should issue with respect to the work that he did accomplish.

b. If Mr. Morris had been able to perform the necessary audit procedures, there are three types of audit reports that he could have issued depending on the outcome of the audit. Name and describe these three types of audit reports.

ANALYZE, THINK, COMMUNICATE

ATC 4-1   Business Application Case   *Understanding real-world annual reports*

Use the Target Corporation's annual report in Appendix B to answer the following questions.

Required

a. Instead of "Cash," the company's balance sheet uses the account name "Cash and cash equivalents." How does the company define cash equivalents?

b. The annual report has two reports in which management is clearly identified as having responsibility for the company's financial reporting and internal controls. What are the names of these reports and on what pages are they located?

ATC 4-2   Group Assignment   *Bank reconciliations*

The following cash and bank information is available for three companies at June 30, 2012.

Cash and Adjustment Information	Peach Co.	Apple Co.	Pear Co.
Unadjusted cash balance per books, 6/30	$45,620	$32,450	$23,467
Outstanding checks	1,345	2,478	2,540
Service charge	50	75	35
Balance per bank statement, 6/30	48,632	37,176	24,894
Credit memo for collection of notes receivable	4,500	5,600	3,800
NSF check	325	145	90
Deposits in transit	2,500	3,200	4,800
Credit memo for interest earned	42	68	12

Required

a. Organize the class into three sections and divide each section into groups of three to five students. Assign Peach Co. to section 1, Apple Co. to section 2, and Pear Co. to section 3.

Group Tasks

(1) Prepare a bank reconciliation for the company assigned to your group.

(2) Select a representative from a group in each section to put the bank reconciliation on the board.

Class Discussion:

b. Discuss the cause of the difference between the unadjusted cash balance and the ending balance for the bank statement. Also, discuss types of adjustment that are commonly made to the bank balance and types of adjustment that are commonly made to the unadjusted book balance.

ATC 4-3   Research Assignment   *Investigating Cash and Management Issues at Smucker's*

Using the most current Form 10-K available on EDGAR, or the company's website, answer the following questions about the **J. M. Smucker Company**. Instructions for using EDGAR are in Appendix A. *Note: In some years the financial statements, footnotes, etc., portion of Smucker's annual report have been located at the end of the Form 10-K, in or just after "Item 15."*

Required

a. Instead of "Cash," the company's balance sheet uses the account name "Cash and cash equivalents." How does the company define cash equivalents?

b. The annual report has two reports in which management clearly acknowledges its responsibility for the company's financial reporting and internal controls. What are the names of these reports and on what pages are they located?

ATC 4-4   Writing Assignment   *Internal control procedures*

Sarah Johnson was a trusted employee of Evergreen Trust Bank. She was involved in everything. She worked as a teller, she accounted for the cash at the other teller windows, and she recorded many of the transactions in the accounting records. She was so loyal that she never would take a day off, even when she was really too sick to work. She routinely worked late to see that all the day's work was posted into the accounting records. She would never take even a day's vacation because they might need her at the bank. Adam and Jammie, CPAs, were hired to perform an audit, the first complete audit that had been done in several years. Johnson seemed somewhat upset by the upcoming audit. She said that everything had been properly accounted for and that the audit was a needless expense. When Adam and Jammie examined some of the bank's internal control procedures, it discovered problems. In fact, as the audit progressed, it became apparent that a large amount of cash was missing. Numerous adjustments had been made to customer accounts with credit memorandums, and many of the transactions had been posted several days late. In addition, there were numerous cash payments for "office expenses." When the audit was complete, it was determined that more than $100,000 of funds was missing or improperly accounted for. All fingers pointed to Johnson. The bank's president, who was a close friend of Johnson, was bewildered. How could this type of thing happen at this bank?

Required

Prepare a written memo to the bank president, outlining the procedures that should be followed to prevent this type of problem in the future.

ATC 4-5   Ethical Dilemma   *I need just a little extra money*

John Riley, a certified public accountant, has worked for the past eight years as a payroll clerk for Southeast Industries, a small furniture manufacturing firm in the Northeast. John recently experienced unfortunate circumstances. His teenage son required major surgery and the medical bills not covered by John's insurance have financially strained John's family.

John works hard and is a model employee. Although he received regular performance raises during his first few years with Southeast. John's wages have not increased in three years. John asked his supervisor, Bill Jameson, for a raise. Bill agreed that John deserved a raise, but told him he could not currently approve one because of sluggish sales.

A disappointed John returned to his duties while the financial pressures in his life continued. Two weeks later, Larry Tyler, an assembly worker at Southwest, quit over a dispute with management. John conceived an idea. John's duties included not only processing employee terminations but also approving time cards before paychecks were issued and then distributing the paychecks to firm personnel. John decided to delay processing Mr. Tyler's termination, to forge timecards for Larry Tyler for the next few weeks, and to cash the checks himself. Since he distributed paychecks, no one would find out, and John reasoned that he was really entitled to the extra money anyway. In fact, no one did discover his maneuver and John stopped the practice after three weeks.

Required

a. Does John's scheme affect Southeast's balance sheet? Explain your answer.

b. Review the AICPA's Articles of Professional Conduct and comment on any of the standards that have been violated.

c. Identify the three elements of unethical and criminal conduct recognized in the fraud triangle.

CHAPTER 5

Accounting for Receivables and Inventory Cost Flow

LEARNING OBJECTIVES

After you have mastered the material in this chapter, you will be able to:

1 Explain how the allowance method of accounting for uncollectible accounts affects financial statements.

2 Determine uncollectible accounts expense using the percent of revenue method.

3 Determine uncollectible accounts expense using the percent of receivables method.

4 Explain how accounting for notes receivable affects financial statements.

5 Explain how accounting for credit card sales affects financial statements.

6 Explain how different inventory cost flow methods (specific identification, FIFO, LIFO, and weighted average) affect financial statements.

CHAPTER OPENING

Many people buy on impulse. If they must wait, the desire to buy wanes. To take advantage of impulse buyers, most merchandising companies offer customers credit because it increases their sales. A disadvantage of this strategy occurs when some customers are unable or unwilling to pay their bills. Nevertheless, the widespread availability of credit suggests that the advantages of increased sales outweigh the disadvantages of some uncollectible accounts.

When a company allows a customer to "buy now and pay later," the company's right to collect cash in the future is called an **account receivable.** Typically, amounts due from individual accounts receivable are relatively small and the collection period is short. Most accounts receivable are collected within 30 days. When a longer credit term is needed or when a receivable is large, the seller usually requires the buyer to issue a note reflecting a credit agreement between the parties. The note specifies the maturity date, interest rate, and other credit terms. Receivables evidenced by such notes are called **notes receivable.** Accounts and notes receivable are reported as assets on the balance sheet.

The Curious Accountant

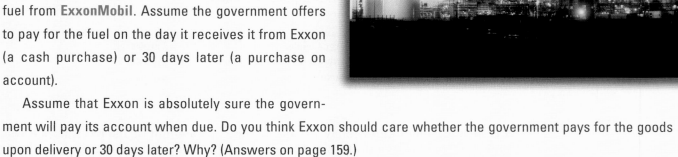

Suppose the U.S. government purchases $10 million of fuel from **ExxonMobil**. Assume the government offers to pay for the fuel on the day it receives it from Exxon (a cash purchase) or 30 days later (a purchase on account).

Assume that Exxon is absolutely sure the government will pay its account when due. Do you think Exxon should care whether the government pays for the goods upon delivery or 30 days later? Why? (Answers on page 159.)

ALLOWANCE METHOD OF ACCOUNTING FOR UNCOLLECTIBLE ACCOUNTS

Explain how the allowance method of accounting for uncollectible accounts affects financial statements.

Most companies do not expect to collect the full amount (face value) of their accounts receivable. Even carefully screened credit customers sometimes don't pay their bills. The **net realizable value** of accounts receivable represents the amount of receivables a company estimates it will actually collect. The net realizable value is the *face value* less an *allowance for doubtful accounts.*

The **allowance for doubtful accounts** represents a company's estimate of the amount of uncollectible receivables. To illustrate, assume a company with total accounts receivable of $50,000 estimates that $2,000 of its receivables will not be collected. The net realizable value of receivables is computed as follows.

Accounts receivable	$50,000
Less: Allowance for doubtful accounts	(2,000)
Net realizable value of receivables	$48,000

A company cannot know today, of course, the exact amount of the receivables it will not be able to collect in the future. The *allowance for doubtful accounts* and the *net realizable value* are necessarily *estimated amounts.* The net realizable value, however, more closely measures the cash that will ultimately be collected than does the face value. To avoid overstating assets, companies usually report receivables on their balance sheets at the net realizable value.

Reporting accounts receivable in the financial statements at net realizable value is commonly called the **allowance method of accounting for uncollectible accounts.** The following section illustrates using the allowance method for Allen's Tutoring Services (ATS).

Accounting Events Affecting the 2012 Period

Allen's Tutoring Services is a small company that provides tutoring services to college students. Allen's started operations on January 1, 2012. During 2012, Allen's experienced three types of accounting events. These events are discussed below.

EVENT 1   Revenue Recognition
Allen's Tutoring Services recognized $14,000 of service revenue earned on account during 2012.

This is an asset source transaction. Allen's Tutoring Services obtained assets (accounts receivable) by providing services to customers. Both assets and stockholders' equity (retained earnings) increase. The event increases revenue and net income. Cash flow is not affected. These effects follow.

Event No.	Assets	=	Liab.	+	Equity	Rev.	–	Exp.	=	Net Inc.	Cash Flow
	Accts. Rec.	=			Ret. Earn.						
1	14,000	=	NA	+	14,000	14,000	–	NA	=	14,000	NA

EVENT 2   Collection of Receivables
Allen's Tutoring Services collected $12,500 cash from accounts receivable in 2012.

This event is an asset exchange transaction. The asset cash increases; the asset accounts receivable decreases. Total assets remains unchanged. Net income is not affected

Exxon would definitely prefer to make the sale to the government in cash rather than on account. Even though it may be certain to collect its accounts receivable, the sooner Exxon gets its cash, the sooner the cash can be reinvested.

The interest cost related to a small account receivable of $50 that takes 30 days to collect may seem immaterial; at 4 percent, the lost interest amounts to less than $.20. However, when one considers that Exxon had approximately $27.6 billion of accounts receivable, the cost of financing receivables for a real-world company becomes apparent. At 4 percent, the cost of waiting 30 days to collect $27.6 billion of cash is $90.7 million ($27.6 billion $\times$ .04 $\times$ [30 $\div$ 365]). For one full year, the cost to Exxon would be more than $1.1 billion ($27.6 billion $\times$ 0.04). In 2009, it took Exxon approximately 32 days to collect its accounts receivable, and the weighted-average interest rate on its debt was approximately 4 percent.

because the revenue was recognized in the previous transaction. The cash inflow is reported in the operating activities section of the statement of cash flows.

Event No.	Assets			=	Liab.	+	Equity	Rev.	−	Exp.	=	Net Inc.	Cash Flow
	Cash	+	Accts. Rec.										
2	12,500	+	(12,500)	=	NA	+	NA	NA	−	NA	=	NA	12,500 OA

Accounting for Uncollectible Accounts Expense

EVENT 3   Recognizing Uncollectible Accounts Expense

Allen's Tutoring Services recognized uncollectible accounts expense for accounts expected to be uncollectible in the future.

The year-end balance in the accounts receivable account is $1,500 ($14,000 of revenue on account − $12,500 of collections). Although Allen's Tutoring Services has the legal right to receive this $1,500 in 2013, the company is not likely to collect the entire amount because some of its customers may not pay the amounts due. Allen's will not know the actual amount of uncollectible accounts until some future time when the customers default (fail to pay). However, the company can *estimate* the amount of receivables that will be uncollectible.

Suppose Allen's Tutoring Services estimates that $75 of the receivables is uncollectible. To improve financial reporting, the company can recognize the estimated expense in 2012. In this way, uncollectible accounts expense and the related revenue will be recognized in the same accounting period (2012). Recognizing an estimated expense is more useful than recognizing no expense. The *matching* of revenues and expenses is improved and the statements are, therefore, more accurate.

The estimated amount of **uncollectible accounts expense** is recognized in a year-end adjusting entry. The adjusting entry reduces the book value of total assets, reduces stockholders' equity (retained earnings), and reduces the amount of reported net income. The statement of cash flows is not affected. The effects of recognizing uncollectible accounts expense are shown here.

Event No.	Assets			=	Liab.	+	Equity	Rev.	–	Exp.	=	Net Inc.	Cash Flow
	Accts. Rec.	–	Allow.	=			Ret. Earn.						
3	NA	–	75	=	NA	+	(75)	NA	–	75	=	(75)	NA

Instead of decreasing the receivables account directly, the asset reduction is recorded in the **contra asset account,** Allowance for Doubtful Accounts. Recall that the contra account is subtracted from the accounts receivable balance to determine the net realizable value of receivables, as follows for ATS.

Accounts receivable	$1,500
Less: Allowance for doubtful accounts	(75)
Net realizable value of receivables	$1,425

Generally accepted accounting principles require disclosure of both the net realizable value and the amount of the allowance account. Many companies disclose these amounts directly in the balance sheet in a manner similar to that shown in the text box above. Other companies disclose this information in the footnotes to the financial statements.

Financial Statements

The financial statements for Allen's Tutoring Services' 2012 accounting period are shown in Exhibit 5.1. As previously indicated, estimating uncollectible accounts improves the usefulness of the 2012 financial statements in two ways. First, the balance sheet reports the amount of cash ($1,500 − $75 = $1,425) the company actually expects to collect (net realizable value of accounts receivable). Second, the income statement provides a clearer picture of managerial performance because it better *matches* the uncollectible accounts expense with the revenue it helped produce. The statements in Exhibit 5.1 show that the cash flow from operating activities ($12,500)

EXHIBIT 5.1

Financial Statements for 2012

Income Statement		Balance Sheet			Statement of Cash Flows	
Service revenue	$14,000	Assets			Operating Activities	
Uncollectible accts. exp.	(75)	Cash		$12,500	Inflow from customers	$12,500
Net income	$13,925	Accounts receivable	$1,500		Investing Activities	0
		Less: Allowance	(75)		Financing Activities	0
		Net realizable value		1,425	Net change in cash	12,500
		Total assets		$13,925	Plus: Beginning cash balance	0
		Stockholders' equity			Ending cash balance	$12,500
		Retained earnings		$13,925		

✓ **CHECK YOURSELF 5.1**

Pamlico Inc. began operations on January 1, 2013. During 2013, it earned $400,000 of revenue on account. The company collected $370,000 of accounts receivable. At the end of the year, Pamlico estimates uncollectible accounts expense will be 1 percent of sales. Based on this information alone, what is the net realizable value of accounts receivable as of December 31, 2013?

Answer Accounts receivable at year end are $30,000 ($400,000 sales on account − $370,000 collection of receivables). The amount in the allowance for doubtful accounts would be $4,000 ($400,000 credit sales × 0.01). The net realizable value of accounts receivable is therefore $26,000 ($30,000 − $4,000).

differs from net income ($13,925). The statement of cash flows reports only cash collections, whereas the income statement reports revenues earned on account less the estimated amount of uncollectible accounts expense.

Accounting Events Affecting the 2013 Period

To further illustrate accounting for uncollectible accounts, we discuss six accounting events affecting Allen's Tutoring Services during 2013.

Accounting for Write-Off of Uncollectible Accounts Receivable

EVENT 1   Write-Off of Uncollectible Accounts Receivable
Allen's Tutoring Services wrote off $70 of uncollectible accounts receivable.

This is an asset exchange transaction. The amount of the uncollectible accounts is removed from the Accounts Receivable account and from the Allowance for Doubtful Accounts account. Because the balances in both the Accounts Receivable and the Allowance accounts decrease, the net realizable value of receivables—and therefore total assets—remains unchanged. The write-off does not affect the income statement. Because the uncollectible accounts expense was recognized in the previous year, the expense would be double counted if it were recognized again at the time an uncollectible account is written off. Finally, the statement of cash flows is not affected by the write-off. These effects are shown in the following statements model.

Event No.	Assets			=	Liab.	+	Equity	Rev.	−	Exp.	=	Net Inc.	Cash Flow
	Accts. Rec.	−	Allow.										
1	(70)	−	(70)	=	NA	+	NA	NA	−	NA	=	NA	NA

The computation of the *net realizable value,* before and after the write-off, is shown below.

	Before Write-Off	After Write-Off
Accounts receivable	$1,500	$1,430
Less: Allowance for doubtful accounts	(75)	(5)
Net realizable value	$1,425	$1,425

EVENT 2   Revenue Recognition
Allen's Tutoring Services provided $10,000 of tutoring services on account during 2013.

Assets (accounts receivable) and stockholders' equity (retained earnings) increase. Recognizing revenue increases net income. Cash flow is not affected. These effects are illustrated below.

Event No.	Assets	=	Liab.	+	Equity	Rev.	−	Exp.	=	Net Inc.	Cash Flow
	Accts. Rec.	=			Ret. Earn.						
2	10,000	=	NA	+	10,000	10,000	−	NA	=	10,000	NA

EVENT 3   Collection of Accounts Receivable
Allen's Tutoring Services collected $8,430 cash from accounts receivable.

The balance in the Cash account increases, and the balance in the Accounts Receivable account decreases. Total assets are unaffected. Net income is not affected because revenue was recognized previously. The cash inflow is reported in the operating activities section of the statement of cash flows.

Event No.	Assets			=	Liab.	+	Equity	Rev.	−	Exp.	=	Net Inc.	Cash Flow
	Cash	+	Accts. Rec.										
3	8,430	+	(8,430)	=	NA	+	NA	NA	−	NA	=	NA	8,430 OA

Accounting for Recovery of an Uncollectible Account Receivable

EVENT 4   Recovery of an Uncollectible Account: Reinstate Receivable
Allen's Tutoring Services recovered a receivable that it had previously written off.

Occasionally, a company receives payment from a customer whose account was previously written off. In such cases, the customer's account should be reinstated and the cash received should be recorded the same way as any other collection on account. The account receivable is reinstated because a complete record of the customer's payment history may be useful if the customer requests credit again at some future date. To illustrate, assume that Allen's Tutoring Services received a $10 cash payment from a customer whose account had previously been written off. The first step is to **reinstate** the account receivable by reversing the previous write-off. The balances in the Accounts Receivable and the Allowance accounts increase. Since the Allowance is a contra asset account, the increase in it offsets the increase in the Accounts Receivable account, and total assets are unchanged. Net income and cash flow are unaffected. These effects are shown here.

Event No.	Assets			=	Liab.	+	Equity	Rev.	−	Exp.	=	Net Inc.	Cash Flow
	Accts. Rec.	−	Allow.										
4	10	−	10	=	NA	+	NA	NA	−	NA	=	NA	NA

EVENT 5   Recovery of an Uncollectible Account: Collection of Receivable
Allen's Tutoring Services recorded collection of the reinstated receivable.

The collection of $10 is recorded like any other collection of a receivable account. Cash increases, and accounts receivable decreases.

Event No.	Assets			=	Liab.	+	Equity	Rev.	−	Exp.	=	Net Inc.	Cash Flow
	Cash	+	Accts. Rec.										
5	10	+	(10)	=	NA	+	NA	NA	−	NA	=	NA	10 OA

ESTIMATING UNCOLLECTIBLE ACCOUNTS EXPENSE USING THE PERCENT OF REVENUE (SALES) METHOD

Companies recognize the estimated amount of uncollectible accounts expense in a period-end adjusting entry. Since Allen's Tutoring Service began operations in 2012, it had no previous credit history upon which to base its estimate. After consulting trade publications and experienced people in the same industry, ATS made an educated guess as to the amount of expense it should recognize for its first year. In its second year of operation, however, ATS can use its first-year experience as a starting point for estimating the second year (2013) uncollectible accounts expense.

LO 2

Determine uncollectible accounts expense using the percent of revenue method.

At the end of 2012 ATS estimated uncollectible accounts expense to be $75 on service revenue of $14,000. In 2013 ATS actually wrote off $70 of which $10 was later recovered. ATS therefore experienced actual uncollectible accounts of $60 on service revenue of $14,000 for an uncollectible accounts rate of approximately .43 percent of service revenue. ATS could apply this percentage to the 2013 service revenue to estimate the 2013 uncollectible accounts expense. In practice, many companies determine the percentage estimate of uncollectible accounts on a three- or five-year moving average.

Companies adjust the historical percentage for anticipated future circumstances. For example, they reduce it if they adopt more rigorous approval standards for new credit applicants. Alternatively, they may increase the percentage if economic forecasts signal an economic downturn that would make future defaults more likely. A company will also increase the percentage if it has specific knowledge one or more of its customers is financially distressed. Multiplying the service revenue by the percentage estimate of uncollectible accounts is commonly called the **percent of revenue method** of estimating uncollectible accounts expense.

EVENT 6   Adjustment for Recognition of Uncollectible Accounts Expense
Using the percent of revenue method, Allen's Tutoring Services recognized uncollectible accounts expense for 2013.

ATS must record this adjustment as of December 31, 2013, to update its accounting records before preparing the 2013 financial statements. After reviewing its credit history, economic forecasts, and correspondence with customers, management estimates uncollectible accounts expense to be 1.35 percent of service revenue, or $135 ($10,000 service revenue × .0135). Recognizing the $135 uncollectible accounts expense decreases both assets (net realizable of receivables) and stockholders' equity (retained earnings). The expense recognition decreases net income. The statement of cash flows is not affected. The financial statements are affected as shown here.

Event No.	Assets			=	Liab.	+	Equity	Rev.	−	Exp.	=	Net Inc.	Cash Flow
	Accts. Rec.	−	Allow.	=			Ret. Earn.						
6	NA	−	135	=	NA	+	(135)	NA	−	135	=	(135)	NA

Analysis of Financial Statements

Exhibit 5.2 displays the 2013 financial statements. The amount of uncollectible accounts expense ($135) differs from the ending balance of the Allowance account ($150). The balance in the Allowance account was $15 before the 2013 adjusting entry for

EXHIBIT 5.2

Financial Statements for 2013

Income Statement		Balance Sheet			Statement of Cash Flows	
Service revenue	$10,000	Assets			Operating Activities	
Uncollectible accts. exp.	(135)	Cash		$20,940	Inflow from customers	$ 8,440
Net income	$ 9,865	Accounts receivable	$3,000		Investing Activities	0
		Less: Allowance	(150)		Financing Activities	0
		Net realizable value		2,850	Net change in cash	8,440
		Total assets		$23,790	Plus: Beginning cash balance	12,500
		Stockholders' equity			Ending cash balance	$20,940
		Retained earnings		$23,790		

uncollectible accounts expense was recorded. At the end of 2012, Allen's Tutoring Services estimated there would be $75 of uncollectible accounts as a result of 2012 revenue earned on account. Actual write-offs, however, amounted to $70 and $10 of that amount was recovered, indicating the actual uncollectible accounts expense for 2012 was only $60. Hindsight shows the expense for 2012 was overstated by $15. However, if no estimate had been made, the amount of uncollectible accounts expense would have been understated by $60. In some accounting periods estimated uncollectible accounts expense will likely be overstated; in others it may be understated. The allowance method cannot produce perfect results, but it does improve the accuracy of the financial statements.

Because no dividends were paid, retained earnings at the end of 2013 equals the December 31, 2012, retained earnings plus 2013 net income (that is, $13,925 + $9,865 = $23,790). Again, the cash flow from operating activities ($8,440) differs from net income ($9,865) because the statement of cash flows does not include the effects of revenues earned on account and the recognition of uncollectible accounts expense.

✓ CHECK YOURSELF 5.2

Maher Company had beginning balances in Accounts Receivable and Allowance for Doubtful Accounts of $24,200 and $2,000, respectively. During the accounting period Maher earned $230,000 of revenue on account and collected $232,500 of cash from receivables. The company also wrote off $1,950 of uncollectible accounts during the period. Maher estimates uncollectible accounts expense will be 1 percent of credit sales. Based on this information, what is the net realizable value of receivables at the end of the period?

Answer   The balance in the Accounts Receivable account is $19,750 ($24,200 + $230,000 − $232,500 − $1,950). The amount of uncollectible accounts expense for the period is $2,300 ($230,000 × 0.01). The balance in the Allowance for Doubtful Accounts is $2,350 ($2,000 − $1,950 + $2,300). The net realizable value of receivables is therefore $17,400 ($19,750 − $2,350).

ESTIMATING UNCOLLECTIBLE ACCOUNTS EXPENSE USING THE PERCENT OF RECEIVABLES METHOD

LO 3

Determine uncollectible accounts expense using the percent of receivables method.

As an alternative to the percent of revenue method, which focuses on estimating the *expense* of uncollectible accounts, companies may estimate the amount of the adjusting entry to record uncollectible accounts expense using the **percent of receivables method.** The percent of receivables method focuses on estimating the most accurate amount for the balance sheet *Allowance for Doubtful Accounts* account.

EXHIBIT 5.3

PYRAMID CORPORATION
Accounts Receivable Aging Schedule
December 31, 2013

Customer Name	Total Balance	Current	Number of Days Past Due 0–30	31–60	61–90	Over 90
J. Davis	$ 6,700	$ 6,700				
B. Diamond	4,800	2,100	$ 2,700			
K. Eppy	9,400	9,400				
B. Gilman	2,200				$1,000	$1,200
A. Kelly	7,300	7,300				
L. Niel	8,600	1,000	6,000	$ 1,600		
L. Platt	4,600			4,600		
J. Turner	5,500			3,000	2,000	500
H. Zachry	6,900		3,000	3,900		
Total	$56,000	$26,500	$11,700	$13,100	$3,000	$1,700

The longer an account receivable remains outstanding, the less likely it is to be collected. Companies using the percent of receivables method typically determine the age of their individual accounts receivable accounts as part of estimating the allowance for doubtful accounts. An **aging of accounts receivable** schedule classifies all receivables by their due date. Exhibit 5.3 shows an aging schedule for Pyramid Corporation as of December 31, 2013.

A company estimates the required Allowance for Doubtful Accounts balance by applying different percentages to each category in the aging schedule. The percentage for each category is based on a company's previous collection experience for each of the categories. The percentages become progressively higher as the accounts become older. Exhibit 5.4 illustrates computing the allowance balance Pyramid Corporation requires.

The computations in Exhibit 5.4 mean the *ending balance* in the Allowance for Doubtful Accounts account should be $3,760. This balance represents the amount Pyramid will subtract from total accounts receivable to determine the net realizable value of receivables. To determine the amount of the adjusting entry to recognize uncollectible accounts expense, Pyramid must take into account any existing balance in the allowance account *before* recording the adjustment. For example, if Pyramid Corporation had a $500 balance in the Allowance account before the year-end adjustment,

EXHIBIT 5.4

Balance Required in the Allowance for Doubtful Accounts at December 31, 2013

Number of Days Past Due	Receivables Amount	Percentage Likely to Be Uncollectible	Required Allowance Account Balance
Current	$26,500	.01	$ 265
0–30	11,700	.05	585
31–60	13,100	.10	1,310
61–90	3,000	.25	750
Over 90	1,700	.50	850
Total	$56,000		$3,760

the adjusting entry would need to add $3,260 ($3,760 − $500) to the account. The effects on the financial statements are shown below.

Assets			= Liab.	+	Equity	Rev.	−	Exp.	=	Net Inc.	Cash Flow
Accts. Rec.	−	Allow. =			Ret. Earn.						
NA	−	3,260 =	NA	+	(3,260)	NA	−	3,260	=	3,260	NA

Matching Revenues and Expenses versus Asset Measurement

The *percent of revenue* method, with its focus on determining the uncollectible accounts expense, is often called the income statement approach. The *percent of receivables* method, focused on determining the best estimate of the allowance balance, is frequently called the balance sheet approach. Which estimating method is better? In any given year, the results will vary slightly between approaches. In the long run, however, the percentages used in either approach are based on a company's actual history of uncollectible accounts. Accountants routinely revise their estimates as more data become available, using hindsight to determine if the percentages should be increased or decreased. Either approach provides acceptable results.

ACCOUNTING FOR NOTES RECEIVABLE (PROMISSORY NOTES)

Explain how accounting for notes receivable affects financial statements.

Companies typically do not charge their customers interest on accounts receivable that are not past due. When a company extends credit for a long time or when the amount of credit it extends is large, however, the cost of granting free credit and the potential for disputes about payment terms both increase. To address these concerns, the parties frequently enter into a credit agreement, the terms of which are legally documented in a **promissory note.**

To illustrate, assume Allen's Tutoring Services (ATS) loans some of its idle cash to an individual, Stanford Cummings, so Cummings can buy a car. ATS and Cummings agree that Cummings will repay the money borrowed plus interest at the end of one year. They also agree that ATS will hold the title to the car to secure the debt. Exhibit 5.5 illustrates a promissory note that outlines this credit agreement. For ATS, the credit arrangement represents a *note receivable*.

EXHIBIT 5.5

Promissory Note

Promissory Note

<u>$15,000</u> (3)   <u>November 1, 2012</u>

Amount   **Date**

For consideration received, <u>Stanford Cummings</u> **hereby promises to pay to the order of:**

Allen's Tutoring Services (2)

Fifteen thousand and no/100   **Dollars**

payable on   October 31, 2013 (5)

plus interest thereon at the rate of <u>6</u> **percent per year.** (4)

Collateral Description   Automobile title (6)

Signature   *Stanford Cummings* (1)

Features of this note are discussed below. Each feature is cross referenced with a number that corresponds to an item on the promissory note in Exhibit 5.5. Locate each feature in Exhibit 5.5 and read the corresponding description of the feature below.

1. Maker—The person responsible for making payment on the due date is the **maker** of the note. The maker may also be called the *borrower* or *debtor.*

2. Payee—The person to whom the note is made payable is the **payee.** The payee may also be called the *creditor* or *lender.* The payee loans money to the maker and expects the return of the principal and the interest due.

3. Principal—The amount of money loaned by the payee to the maker of the note is the **principal.**

4. Interest—The economic benefit earned by the payee for loaning the principal to the maker is **interest,** which is normally expressed as an annual percentage of the principal amount. For example, a note with a 6 percent interest rate requires interest payments equal to 6 percent of the principal amount every year the loan is outstanding.

5. Maturity Date—The date on which the maker must repay the principal and make the final interest payment to the payee is the **maturity date.**

6. Collateral—Assets belonging to the maker that are assigned as security to ensure that the principal and interest will be paid when due are called **collateral.** In this example, if Cummings fails to pay ATS the amount due, ownership of the car Cummings purchased will be transferred to ATS.

How Accounting for Notes Receivable Affects Financial Statements

We illustrate accounting for notes receivable using the credit agreement evidenced by the promissory note in Exhibit 5.5. Allen's Tutoring Services engaged in many transactions during 2012; we discuss here only transactions directly related to the note receivable.

EVENT 1   Loan of Money

The note shows that ATS loaned $15,000 to Stanford Cummings on November 1, 2012. This event is an asset exchange. The asset account Cash decreases and the asset account Notes Receivable increases. The income statement is not affected. The statement of cash flows shows a cash outflow for investing activities. The effects on the financial statements are shown below.

	Assets					=	Liab.	+	Equity	Rev.	−	Exp.	=	Net Inc.	Cash Flow	
Date	Cash	+	Notes Rec.	+	Int. Rec.	=			Ret. Earn.							
11/01/12	(15,000)	+	15,000	+	NA	=	NA	+	NA	NA	−	NA	=	NA	(15,000)	IA

EVENT 2   Accrual of Interest

For ATS, loaning money to the maker of the note, Stanford Cummings, represents investing in the note receivable. Cummings will repay the principal ($15,000) plus interest of 6 percent of the principal amount ($0.06 \times \$15,000 = \$900$), or a total of $15,900, on October 31, 2013, one year from the date he borrowed the money from ATS.

Conceptually, lenders *earn* interest continually even though they do not *collect* cash payment for it every day. Each day, the amount of interest due, called **accrued interest,** is greater than the day before. Companies would find it highly impractical to attempt to record (recognize) accrued interest continually as the amount due increased.

Businesses typically solve the recordkeeping problem by only recording accrued interest when it is time to prepare financial statements or when it is due. At such times, the accounts are *adjusted* to reflect the amount of interest currently due. For example, ATS recorded the asset exchange immediately upon investing in the Note Receivable on November 1, 2012. ATS did not, however, recognize any interest earned on the note until the balance sheet date, December 31, 2012. At year-end ATS made an entry to recognize the interest it had earned during the previous two months (November 1 through December 31). This entry is an **adjusting entry** because it adjusts (updates) the account balances prior to preparing financial statements.

ATS computed the amount of accrued interest by multiplying the principal amount of the note by the annual interest rate and by the length of time for which the note has been outstanding.

Principal × Annual interest rate × Time outstanding = Interest revenue

$15,000 ×   0.06   ×   (2/12)   = $150

ATS recognized the $150 of interest revenue in 2012 although ATS will not collect the cash until 2013. This practice illustrates the **matching concept.** Interest revenue is recognized in (matched with) the period in which it is earned regardless of when the related cash is collected. The adjustment is an asset source transaction. The asset account Interest Receivable increases, and the stockholders' equity account Retained Earnings increases. The income statement reflects an increase in revenue and net income. The statement of cash flows is not affected because ATS will not collect cash until the maturity date (October 31, 2013). The effects on the financial statements are shown below.

	Assets				=	Liab.	+	Equity	Rev.	−	Exp.	=	Net Inc.	Cash Flow
Date	Cash	+	Notes Rec.	+	Int. Rec.	=			Ret. Earn.						
12/31/12	NA	+	NA	+	150	=	NA	+	150	150	−	NA	=	150	NA

EVENT 3   Collection of Principal and Interest on the Maturity Date

ATS collected $15,900 cash on the maturity date. The collection included $15,000 for the principal plus $900 for the interest. Recall that ATS previously accrued interest in the December 31, 2012, adjusting entry for the two months in 2012 that the note was outstanding. Since year-end, ATS has earned an additional 10 months of interest revenue. ATS must recognize this interest revenue before recording the cash collection. The amount of interest earned in 2013 is computed as follows.

Principal × Annual interest rate × Time outstanding = Interest revenue

$15,000 ×   0.06   ×   (10/12)   = $750

The effects on the financial statements are shown below.

	Assets				=	Liab.	+	Equity	Rev.	−	Exp.	=	Net Inc.	Cash Flow
Date	Cash	+	Notes Rec.	+	Int. Rec.	=			Ret. Earn.						
10/31/13	NA	+	NA	+	750	=	NA	+	750	750	−	NA	=	750	NA

The total amount of accrued interest is now $900 ($150 accrued in 2012 plus $750 accrued in 2013). The $15,900 cash collection is an asset exchange transaction. The asset account Cash increases and two asset accounts, Notes Receivable and Interest Receivable, decrease. The income statement is not affected. The statement of cash flows shows a $15,000 inflow from investing activities (recovery of principal) and a $900 inflow from operating activities (interest collection). The effects on the financial statements are shown below.

	Assets					=	Liab.	+	Equity	Rev.	−	Exp.	=	Net Inc.	Cash Flow
Date	Cash	+	Notes Rec.	+	Int. Rec.	=			Ret. Earn.						
10/31/13	15,900	+	(15,000)	+	(900)	=	NA	+	NA	NA	−	NA	=	NA	15,000 IA 900 OA

Financial Statements

The financial statements reveal key differences between the timing of revenue recognition and the exchange of cash. These differences are highlighted below.

	2012	2013	Total
Interest revenue recognized	$150	$750	$900
Cash inflow from operating activities	0	900	900

Accrual accounting calls for recognizing revenue in the period in which it is earned regardless of when cash is collected.

Income Statement

Although generally accepted accounting principles require reporting receipts of or payments for interest on the statement of cash flows as operating activities, they do not specify how to classify interest on the income statement. In fact, companies traditionally report interest on the income statement as a nonoperating item. Interest is therefore frequently reported in two different categories within the same set of financial statements.

Balance Sheet

As with other assets, companies report interest receivable and notes receivable on the balance sheet in order of their liquidity. **Liquidity** refers to how quickly assets are expected to be converted to cash during normal operations. In the preceding example, ATS expects to convert its accounts receivable to cash before it collects the interest receivable and note receivable. Companies commonly report interest and notes receivable after accounts receivable. Exhibit 5.6 shows a partial balance sheet for Southern Company to illustrate the presentation of receivables.

EXHIBIT 5.6

Typical Balance Sheet Presentation of Receivables

SOUTHERN COMPANY
Partial Balance Sheet
As of December 31, 2012

Cash		$xxxx
Accounts receivable	$xxxx	
Less: Allowance for doubtful accounts	(xxxx)	
Net realizable value of accounts receivable		xxxx
Interest receivable		xxxx
Notes receivable		xxxx

✓ CHECK YOURSELF 5.3

On October 1, 2012, Mei Company accepted a promissory note for a loan it made to the Asia Pacific Company. The note had a $24,000 principal amount, a four-month term, and an annual interest rate of 4 percent. Determine the amount of interest revenue and the cash inflow from operating activities Mei will report in its 2012 and 2013 financial statements.

Answer The computation of accrued interest revenue is shown below. The interest rate is stated in annual terms even though the term of the note is only four months. Interest rates are commonly expressed as an annual percentage regardless of the term of the note. The *time outstanding* in the following formulas is therefore expressed as a fraction of a year. Mei charged annual interest of 4 percent, but the note was outstanding for only 3/12 of a year in 2012 and 1/12 of a year in 2013.

2012
Principal × Annual interest rate × Time outstanding = Interest revenue
$24,000 × 0.04 × (3/12) = $240

2013
Principal × Annual interest rate × Time outstanding = Interest revenue
$24,000 × 0.04 × (1/12) = $80

In 2012, Mei's cash inflow from interest will be zero.
In 2013, Mei will report a $320 ($240 + $80) cash inflow from operating activities for interest.

ACCOUNTING FOR CREDIT CARD SALES

LO 5

Explain how accounting for credit card sales affects financial statements.

Maintaining accounts and notes receivable is expensive. In addition to uncollectible accounts expense, companies extending credit to their customers incur considerable costs for such clerical tasks as running background checks and maintaining customer records. Many businesses find it more efficient to accept third-party credit cards instead of offering credit directly to their customers. Credit card companies service the merchant's credit sales for a fee that typically ranges between 2 and 8 percent of gross sales.

The credit card company provides customers with plastic cards that permit cardholders to charge purchases at various retail outlets. When a sale takes place, the seller records the transaction on a receipt the customer signs. The receipt is forwarded to the credit card company, which immediately pays the merchant.

The credit card company deducts its service fee from the gross amount of the sale and pays the merchant the net balance (gross amount of sale less credit card fee) in cash. The credit card company collects the gross sale amount directly from the customer. The merchant avoids the risk of uncollectible accounts as well as the cost of maintaining customer credit records. To illustrate, assume that Allen's Tutoring Service experiences the following events.

EVENT 1 Recognition of Revenue and Expense on Credit Card Sales
ATS accepts a credit card payment for $1,000 of services rendered.

Assume the credit card company charges a 5 percent fee for handling the transaction ($1,000 × 0.05 = $50). ATS's income increases by the amount of revenue ($1,000) and decreases by the amount of the credit card expense ($50). Net income increases by $950. The event increases an asset, accounts receivable, due from the credit card company, and stockholders' equity (retained earnings) by $950 ($1,000 revenue − $50 credit card expense). Cash flow is not affected. These effects are shown here.

Event No.	Assets	=	Liab.	+	Equity	Rev.	−	Exp.	=	Net Inc.	Cash Flow
	Accts. Rec.	=			Ret. Earn.						
1	950	=	NA	+	950	1,000	−	50	=	950	NA

EVENT 2   Collection of Credit Card Receivable
The collection of the receivable due from the credit card company is recorded like any other receivable collection.

When ATS collects the net amount of $950 ($1,000 − $50) from the credit card company, one asset account (Cash) increases and another asset account (Accounts Receivable) decreases. Total assets are not affected. The income statement is not affected. A $950 cash inflow is reported in the operating activities section of the statement of cash flows. These effects are illustrated below.

Event No.	Assets			=	Liab.	+	Equity	Rev.	−	Exp.	=	Net Inc.	Cash Flow	
	Cash	+	Accts. Rec.											
2	950	+	(950)	=	NA	+	NA	NA	−	NA	=	NA	950	OA

As mentioned earlier, two costs of extending credit to customers are bad debts expense and record-keeping costs. These costs can be significant. Large companies spend literally millions of dollars to buy the equipment and pay the staff necessary to operate entire departments devoted to managing accounts receivable. Further, there is an implicit interest charge associated with extending credit. When a customer is permitted to delay payment, the creditor forgoes the opportunity to invest the amount the customer owes.

INVENTORY COST FLOW METHODS

In Chapter 3, we used the simplifying assumption that identical inventory items cost the same amount. In practice, businesses often pay different amounts for identical items. Suppose The Mountain Bike Company (TMBC) sells high-end Model 201 helmets. Even though all Model 201 helmets are identical, the price TMBC pays for each helmet frequently changes.

Assume TMBC purchases one Model 201 helmet at a cost of $100. Two weeks later, TMBC purchases a second Model 201 helmet. Because the supplier has raised prices, the second helmet costs $110. If TMBC sells one of its two helmets, should it record $100 or $110 as cost of goods sold? The following section of this chapter discusses several acceptable alternative methods for determining the amount of cost of goods sold under generally accepted accounting principles.

Recall that when goods are sold, product costs flow (are transferred) from the Inventory account to the Cost of Goods Sold account. Four acceptable methods for determining the amount of cost to transfer are (1) specific identification; (2) first-in, first-out (FIFO); (3) last-in, first-out (LIFO); and (4) weighted average.

LO 6

Explain how different inventory cost flow methods (specific identification, FIFO, LIFO, and weighted average) affect financial statements.

Specific Identification

Suppose TMBC tags inventory items so that it can identify which one is sold at the time of sale. TMBC could then charge the actual cost of the specific item sold to cost of goods sold. Recall that the first inventory item TMBC purchased cost $100 and the second item cost $110. Using **specific identification,** cost of goods sold would be $100 if the first item purchased were sold or $110 if the second item purchased were sold.

When a company's inventory consists of many low-priced, high-turnover goods, the record keeping necessary to use specific identification isn't practical. Imagine the difficulty of recording the cost of each specific food item in a grocery store. Another disadvantage of the specific identification method is the opportunity for managers to manipulate the income statement. For example, TMBC can report a lower cost of goods sold by selling the first instead of the second item. Specific identification is, however, frequently used for high-priced, low-turnover inventory items such as automobiles. For big ticket items like cars, customer demands for specific products limit management's ability to select which merchandise is sold and volume is low enough to manage the recordkeeping.

First-In, First-Out (FIFO)

The **first-in, first-out (FIFO) cost flow method** requires that the cost of the items purchased *first* be assigned to cost of goods sold. Using FIFO, TMBC's cost of goods sold is $100.

Last-In, First-Out (LIFO)

The **last-in, first-out (LIFO) cost flow method** requires that the cost of the items purchased *last* be charged to cost of goods sold. Using LIFO, TMBC's cost of goods sold is $110.

Weighted Average

To use the **weighted-average cost flow method,** first calculate the average cost per unit by dividing the *total cost* of the inventory available by the *total number* of units available. In the case of TMBC, the average cost per unit of the inventory is $105 ([$100 + $110] ÷ 2). Cost of goods sold is then calculated by multiplying the average cost per unit by the number of units sold. Using weighted average, TMBC's cost of goods sold is $105 ($105 × 1).

Physical Flow

The preceding discussion pertains to the flow of *costs* through the accounting records, *not* the actual **physical flow of goods.** Goods usually move physically on a FIFO basis, which means that the first items of merchandise acquired by a company (first-in) are the first items sold to its customers (first-out). The inventory items on hand at the end of the accounting period are typically the last items in (the most recently acquired goods). If companies did not sell their oldest inventory items first, inventories would include dated, less marketable merchandise. *Cost flow,* however, can differ from *physical flow.* For example, a company may use LIFO or weighted average for financial reporting even if its goods flow physically on a FIFO basis.

EFFECT OF COST FLOW ON FINANCIAL STATEMENTS

Effect on Income Statement

The cost flow method a company uses can significantly affect the gross margin reported in the income statement. To demonstrate, assume that TMBC sold the inventory item discussed previously for $120. The amounts of gross margin using the FIFO, LIFO, and weighted-average cost flow assumptions are shown in the following table.

	FIFO	LIFO	Weighted Average
Sales	$120	$120	$120
Cost of goods sold	(100)	(110)	(105)
Gross margin	$ 20	$ 10	$ 15

Even though the physical flow is assumed to be identical for each method, the gross margin reported under FIFO is double the amount reported under LIFO. Companies experiencing identical economic events (same units of inventory purchased and sold) can report significantly different results in their financial statements. Meaningful financial analysis requires an understanding of financial reporting practices.

Effect on Balance Sheet

Because total product costs are allocated between costs of goods sold and ending inventory, the cost flow method a company uses affects its balance sheet as well as its income statement. Because FIFO transfers the first cost to the income statement, it leaves the last cost on the balance sheet. Similarly, by transferring the last cost to the income statement, LIFO leaves the first cost in ending inventory. The weighted-average method bases both cost of goods sold and ending inventory on the average cost per unit. To illustrate, the ending inventory TMBC would report on the balance sheet using each of the three cost flow methods is shown in the following table.

	FIFO	LIFO	Weighted Average
Ending inventory	$110	$100	$105

EXHIBIT 5.7

Use of Inventory Cost Flow Methods

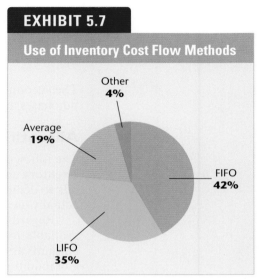

Data Source: AICPA, *Accounting Trends and Techniques.*

The FIFO, LIFO, and weighted-average methods are all used extensively in business practice. The same company may even use one cost flow method for some of its products and different cost flow methods for other products. Exhibit 5.7 illustrates the relative use of the different cost flow methods among U.S. companies.

✓ CHECK YOURSELF 5.4

Nash Office Supply (NOS) purchased two Model 303 copiers at different times. The first copier purchased cost $400 and the second copier purchased cost $450. NOS sold one of the copiers for $600. Determine the gross margin on the sale and the ending inventory balance assuming NOS accounts for inventory using (1) FIFO, (2) LIFO, and (3) weighted average.

Answer

	FIFO	LIFO	Weighted Average
Sales	$600	$600	$600
Cost of goods sold	(400)	(450)	(425)
Gross margin	$200	$150	$175
Ending inventory	$450	$400	$425

Multiple Layers with Multiple Quantities

The previous example illustrates different **inventory cost flow methods** using only two cost layers ($100 and $110) with only one unit of inventory in each layer. Actual business inventories are considerably more complex. Most real-world inventories are composed of multiple cost layers with different quantities of inventory in each layer. The underlying allocation concepts, however, remain unchanged.

For example, a different inventory item The Mountain Bike Company (TMBC) carries in its stores is a bike called the Eraser. TMBC's beginning inventory and two purchases of Eraser bikes are described below.

Jan. 1	Beginning inventory	10 units @ $200	=	$ 2,000
Mar. 18	First purchase	20 units @ $220	=	4,400
Aug. 21	Second purchase	25 units @ $250	=	6,250
Total cost of the 55 bikes available for sale				$12,650

The accounting records for the period show that TMBC paid cash for all Eraser bike purchases and that it sold 43 bikes at a cash price of $350 each.

Allocating Cost of Goods Available for Sale

The following discussion shows how to determine the cost of goods sold and ending inventory amounts under FIFO, LIFO, and weighted average. We show all three methods to demonstrate how they affect the financial statements differently; TMBC would actually use only one of the methods.

Regardless of the cost flow method chosen, TMBC must allocate the cost of goods available for sale ($12,650) between cost of goods sold and ending inventory. The amounts assigned to each category will differ depending on TMBC's cost flow method. Computations for each method are shown below.

FIFO Inventory Cost Flow

Recall that TMBC sold 43 Eraser bikes during the accounting period. The FIFO method transfers to the Cost of Goods Sold account the *cost of the first 43 bikes* TMBC had available to sell. The first 43 bikes acquired by TMBC were the 10 bikes in the beginning inventory (these were purchased in the prior period) plus the 20 bikes purchased in March and 13 of the bikes purchased in August. The expense recognized for the cost of these bikes ($9,650) is computed as follows.

Jan. 1	Beginning inventory	10 units @ $200	=	$2,000
Mar. 18	First purchase	20 units @ $220	=	4,400
Aug. 21	Second purchase	13 units @ $250	=	3,250
Total cost of the 43 bikes sold				$9,650

Because TMBC had 55 bikes available for sale it would have 12 bikes (55 available − 43 sold) in ending inventory. The cost assigned to these 12 bikes (the ending balance in the Inventory account) equals the cost of goods available for sale minus the cost of goods sold as shown below.

Cost of goods available for sale	$12,650
Cost of goods sold	(9,650)
Ending inventory balance	$ 3,000

We show the allocation of the cost of goods available for sale between cost of goods sold and ending inventory graphically below.

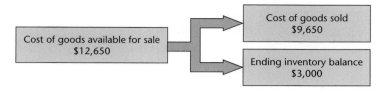

LIFO Inventory Cost Flow

Under LIFO, the cost of goods sold is the cost of the last 43 bikes acquired by TMBC, computed as follows.

Aug. 21	Second purchase	25 units @ $250 =	$ 6,250
Mar. 18	First purchase	18 units @ $220 =	3,960
Total cost of the 43 bikes sold			$10,210

The LIFO cost of the 12 bikes in ending inventory is computed as shown below.

Cost of goods available for sale	$12,650
Cost of goods sold	(10,210)
Ending inventory balance	$ 2,440

We show the allocation of the cost of goods available for sale between cost of goods sold and ending inventory graphically below.

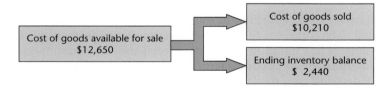

Weighted-Average Cost Flow

The weighted-average cost per unit is determined by dividing the *total cost of goods available for sale* by the *total number of units* available for sale. For TMBC, the weighted-average cost per unit is $230 ($12,650 ÷ 55). The weighted-average cost of goods sold is determined by multiplying the average cost per unit by the number of units sold ($230 × 43 = $9,890). The cost assigned to the 12 bikes in ending inventory is $2,760 (12 × $230).

We show the allocation of the cost of goods available for sale between cost of goods sold and ending inventory graphically below.

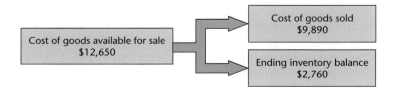

Effect of Cost Flow on Financial Statements

Exhibit 5.8 displays partial financial statements for The Mountain Bike Company (TMBC). This exhibit includes only information pertaining to the Eraser bikes inventory item described above. Other financial statement data are omitted.

EXHIBIT 5.8

TMBC COMPANY
Comparative Financial Statements

Partial Income Statements

	FIFO	LIFO	Weighted Average
Sales	$15,050	$15,050	$15,050
Cost of goods sold	(9,650)	(10,210)	(9,890)
Gross margin	5,400	4,840	5,160

Partial Balance Sheets

	FIFO	LIFO	Weighted Average
Assets			
Cash	$ xx	$ xx	$ xx
Accounts receivable	xx	xx	xx
Inventory	3,000	2,440	2,760

Partial Statements of Cash Flows

	FIFO	LIFO	Weighted Average
Operating Activities			
Cash inflow from customers	$15,050	$15,050	$15,050
Cash outflow for inventory	(10,650)	(10,650)	(10,650)

Recall that assets are reported on the balance sheet in order of liquidity (how quickly they are expected to be converted to cash). Because companies frequently sell inventory on account, inventory is less liquid than accounts receivable. As a result, companies commonly report inventory below accounts receivable on the balance sheet.

Exhibit 5.8 demonstrates that the amounts reported for gross margin on the income statement and inventory on the balance sheet differ significantly. The cash flow from operating activities on the statement of cash flows, however, is identical under all three methods. Regardless of cost flow reporting method, TMBC paid $10,650 cash ($4,400 first purchase + $6,250 second purchase) to purchase inventory and received $15,050 cash for inventory sold.

The Impact of Income Tax

Based on the financial statement information in Exhibit 5.8, which cost flow method should TMBC use? Most people initially suggest FIFO because FIFO reports the highest gross margin and the largest balance in ending inventory. However, other factors are relevant. FIFO produces the highest gross margin; it also produces the highest net income and the highest income tax expense. In contrast, LIFO results in recognizing the lowest gross margin, lowest net income, and the lowest income tax expense.

Will investors favor a company with more assets and higher net income or one with lower tax expense? Recognize that specific identification, FIFO, LIFO, and weighted average are *different methods of reporting the same information.* TMBC experienced only one set of events pertaining to Eraser bikes. Exhibit 5.8 reports those same events three different ways. However, if the FIFO reporting method causes TMBC to pay more taxes than the LIFO method, using FIFO will cause a real reduction in the value of the company. Paying more money in taxes leaves less money in the company. Knowledgeable investors would be more attracted to TMBC if it uses LIFO because the lower tax payments allow the company to keep more value in the business.

Research suggests that, as a group, investors are knowledgeable. They make investment decisions based on economic substance regardless of how information is reported in financial statements.

The Income Statement versus the Tax Return

In some instances companies may use one accounting method for financial reporting and a different method to compute income taxes (the tax return must explain any differences). With respect to LIFO, however, the Internal Revenue Service requires that companies using LIFO for income tax purposes must also use LIFO for financial reporting. A company could not, therefore, get both the lower tax benefit provided by LIFO and the financial reporting advantage offered under FIFO.

Inflation versus Deflation

Our illustration assumes an inflationary environment (rising inventory prices). In a deflationary environment, the impact of using LIFO versus FIFO is reversed. LIFO produces tax advantages in an inflationary environment, while FIFO produces tax advantages in a deflationary environment. Companies operating in the computer industry where prices are falling would obtain a tax advantage by using FIFO. In contrast, companies that sell medical supplies in an inflationary environment would obtain a tax advantage by using LIFO.

Full Disclosure and Consistency

Generally accepted accounting principles allow each company to choose the inventory cost flow method best suited to its reporting needs. Because results can vary considerably among methods, however, the GAAP principle of **full disclosure** requires that financial statements disclose the method chosen. In addition, so that a company's financial statements are comparable from year to year, the GAAP principle of **consistency** generally requires that companies use the same cost flow method each period. The limited exceptions to the consistency principle are described in more advanced accounting courses.

✓ CHECK YOURSELF 5.5

The following information was drawn from the inventory records of Fields, Inc.

Beginning inventory	200 units @ $20
First purchase	400 units @ $22
Second purchase	600 units @ $24

Assume that Fields sold 900 units of inventory.

1. Determine the amount of cost of goods sold using FIFO.

2. Would using LIFO produce a higher or lower amount of cost of goods sold? Why?

Answer

1. Cost of goods sold using FIFO

Beginning inventory	200 units @ $20	=	$ 4,000
First purchase	400 units @ $22	=	8,800
Second purchase	300 units @ $24	=	7,200
Total cost of goods sold			$20,000

2. The inventory records reflect an inflationary environment of steadily rising prices. Since LIFO charges the latest costs (in this case the highest costs) to the income statement, using LIFO would produce a higher amount of cost of goods sold than would using FIFO.

REALITY BYTES

To avoid spoilage or obsolescence, most companies use the first-in, first-out (FIFO) approach for the flow of physical goods. The older goods (first units purchased) are sold before the newer goods are sold. For example, Kroger's and other food stores stack older merchandise at the front of the shelf where customers are more likely to pick it up first. As a result, merchandise is sold before it becomes dated. However, when timing is not an issue, convenience may dictate the use of the last-in, first-out (LIFO) method. Examples of products that frequently move on a LIFO basis include rock, gravel, dirt, or other non-wasting assets. Indeed, rock, gravel, and dirt are normally stored in piles that are unprotected from weather. New inventory is simply piled on top of the old. Inventory that is sold is taken from the top of the pile because it is convenient to do so. Accordingly, the last inventory purchased is the first inventory sold. For example, Vulcan Materials Co., which claims to be the nation's largest producer of construction aggregates (stone and gravel), uses LIFO. Regardless of whether the flow of physical goods occurs on a LIFO or FIFO basis, costs can flow differently. The flow of inventory through the physical facility is a separate issue from the flow of costs through the accounting system.

FOCUS ON INTERNATIONAL ISSUES

LIFO IN OTHER COUNTRIES

This chapter introduced a rather strange inventory cost flow assumption called LIFO. As explained, the primary advantage of LIFO is to reduce a company's income taxes. Given the choice, companies that use LIFO to reduce their taxes would probably prefer to use another method when preparing their GAAP—based financial statements, but the IRS does not permit this. Thus, they are left with no choice but to use the seemingly counterintuitive LIFO assumption for GAAP as well tax reporting.

What happens in countries other than the United States? International Financial Reporting Standards (IFRS) do not allow the use of LIFO. Most industrialized nations are now using IFRS. You can see the impact of this disparity if you review the annual report of a U.S. company that uses LIFO *and* has significant operations in other countries. Very often it will explain that LIFO is used to calculate inventory (and cost of goods sold) for domestic operations, but another method is used for activities outside the United States.

For example, here is an excerpt from General Electric's 2009 Form 10-K, Note 1.

All inventories are stated at the lower of cost or realizable values. Cost for a significant portion of GE U.S. inventories is determined on a last-in, first-out (LIFO) basis. Cost of other GE inventories is determined on a first-in, first-out (FIFO) basis. LIFO was used for 39% and 40% of GE inventories at December 31, 2009 and 2008, respectively.

If the company has its headquarters in the United States, why not simply use LIFO in its foreign operations? In addition to having to prepare financial statements for the United States, the company probably has to prepare statements for its local operations using the reporting standards of the local country.

Prior to the establishment of IFRS each country was responsible for issuing its own, local GAAP. Even then, most countries did not allow for the use of LIFO.

A Look Back <<

We first introduced accounting for receivables in Chapter 2. This chapter presented additional complexities related to accounts receivable, such as the *allowance method of accounting for uncollectible accounts.* The allowance method improves matching of expenses with revenues. It also provides a more accurate measure of the value of accounts receivable on the balance sheet.

Under the allowance method, estimated uncollectible accounts expense is recorded in an adjusting entry at the end of the period in which a company has made credit sales. There are two methods commonly used to estimate the amount of uncollectible accounts expense: the percent of revenue method and the percent of receivables method. With the percent of revenue method, uncollectible accounts expense is measured as a percent of the period's sales. With the percent of receivables method, a company analyzes its accounts receivable at the end of the period, usually classifying them by age, to estimate the amount of the accounts receivable balance that is likely to be uncollectible. The balance in the Allowance for Doubtful Accounts account is then adjusted to equal the estimated amount of uncollectible accounts. Uncollectible accounts expense decreases the net realizable value of receivables (accounts receivable − allowance for doubtful accounts), stockholders' equity, and net income.

The allowance method of accounting for uncollectible accounts is conceptually superior to the *direct write-off method,* in which uncollectible accounts expense is recognized when an account is determined to be uncollectible. The direct write-off method fails to match revenues with expenses and overstates accounts receivable on the balance sheet. It is easier to use, however, and is permitted by generally accepted accounting principles if the amount of uncollectible accounts expense is immaterial.

The chapter also introduced notes receivable and accounting for *accrued interest.* When the term of a promissory note extends over more than one accounting period, companies must record adjusting entries to recognize interest in the appropriate accounting period, even if the cash exchange of interest occurs in a different accounting period.

We also discussed accounting for credit card sales, a vehicle that shifts uncollectible accounts expense to the credit card issuer. Many companies find the benefits of accepting major credit cards to be worth the credit card expense consequently incurred. Finally, we addressed the costs of making credit sales. In addition to uncollectible accounts expense, interest is a major cost of financing receivables.

This chapter also, discussed the inventory cost flow methods of first-in, first-out (FIFO); last-in, first-out (LIFO); weighted average; and specific identification. Under FIFO, the cost of the items purchased first is reported on the income statement, and the cost of the items purchased last is reported on the balance sheet. Under the weighted-average method, the average cost of inventory is reported on both the income statement and the balance sheet. Finally, under specific identification the actual cost of goods is reported on the income statement and the balance sheet.

A Look Forward

Chapter 6 discusses accounting for long-term assets such as buildings and equipment. As with inventory cost flow, GAAP allows companies to use different accounting methods to report on similar types of business events. Life would be easier for accounting students if all companies used the same accounting methods. However, the business world is complex. For the foreseeable future, people are likely to continue to have diverse views as to the best way to account for a variety of business transactions. To function effectively in today's business environment, it is important for you to be able to recognize differences in reporting practices.

A step-by-step audio-narrated series of slides is provided on the text website at www.mhhe.com/edmondssurvey3e.

SELF-STUDY REVIEW PROBLEM 1

During 2012 Calico Company experienced the following accounting events.

1. Provided $120,000 of services on account.
2. Collected $85,000 cash from accounts receivable.
3. Wrote off $1,800 of accounts receivable that were uncollectible.
4. Loaned $3,000 to an individual, Emma Gardner, in exchange for a note receivable.
5. Paid $90,500 cash for operating expenses.
6. Estimated that uncollectible accounts expense would be 2 percent of revenue earned on account. Recorded the year-end adjusting entry.
7. Recorded the year-end adjusting entry for accrued interest on the note receivable (see Event 4). Calico made the loan on August 1. It had a six-month term and a 6 percent rate of interest.

Calico's ledger balances on January 1, 2012, were as follows.

Event No.	Cash	+	Accts. Rec.	−	Allow.	+	Notes Rec.	+	Int. Rec.	=		Liab.	+	Com. Stk.	+	Ret. Earn.
							Assets								**Equity**	
Bal.	12,000		18,000		2,200	+	NA	+	NA	=	NA	+	20,000	+	7,800

Required

a. Record the 2012 events in ledger accounts using the horizontal format shown above.
b. Determine net income for 2012.
c. Determine net cash flow from operating activities for 2012.
d. Determine the net realizable value of accounts receivable at December 31, 2012.
e. What amount of interest revenue will Calico recognize on its note receivable in 2013?

Solution to Requirement a.

Event No.	Cash	+	Accts. Rec.	−	Allow.	+	Notes Rec.	+	Int. Rec.	=		Liab.	+	Com. Stk.	+	Ret. Earn.
						Assets									**Equity**	
Bal.	12,000	+	18,000	−	2,200	+	NA	+	NA	=	NA	+	20,000	+	7,800
1	NA	+	120,000	−	NA	+	NA	+	NA	=	NA	+	NA	+	120,000
2	85,000	+	(85,000)	−	NA	+	NA	+	NA	=	NA	+	NA	+	NA
3	NA	+	(1,800)	−	(1,800)	+	NA	+	NA	=	NA	+	NA	+	NA
4	(3,000)	+	NA	−	NA	+	3,000	+	NA	=	NA	+	NA	+	NA
5	(90,500)	+	NA	−	NA	+	NA	+	NA	=	NA	+	NA	+	(90,500)
6	NA	+	NA	−	2,400	+	NA	+	NA	=	NA	+	NA	+	(2,400)
7	NA	+	NA	−	NA	+	NA	+	75*	=	NA	+	NA	+	75
Totals	3,500	+	51,200	−	2,800	+	3,000	+	75	=	NA	+	20,000	+	34,975

*$3,000 × .06 × 5/12 = $75.

Solution to Requirements b–e.

b. Net income is $27,175 ($120,000 − $90,500 − $2,400 + $75).
c. Net cash flow from operating activities is an outflow of $5,500 ($85,000 − $90,500).
d. The net realizable value of accounts receivable is $48,400 ($51,200 − $2,800).
e. In 2013, Calico will recognize interest revenue for one month: $3,000 × .06 × 1/12 = $15.

A step-by-step audio-narrated series of slides is provided on the text website at www.mhhe.com/edmondssurvey3e

SELF-STUDY REVIEW PROBLEM 2

Erie Jewelers sells gold earrings. Its beginning inventory of Model 407 gold earrings consisted of 100 pairs of earrings at $50 per pair. Erie purchased two batches of Model 407 earrings during the year. The first batch purchased consisted of 150 pairs at $53 per pair; the second batch consisted of 200 pairs at $56 per pair. During the year, Erie sold 375 pairs of Model 407 earrings.

Required

Determine the amount of product cost Erie would allocate to cost of goods sold and ending inventory assuming that Erie uses (a) FIFO, (b) LIFO, and (c) weighted average.

Solution to Requirements *a–c*

Goods Available for Sale				
Beginning inventory	100	@	$50	=	$ 5,000
First purchase	150	@	53	=	7,950
Second purchase	200	@	56	=	11,200
Goods available for sale	450				$24,150

a. FIFO

Cost of Goods Sold	Pairs		Cost per Pair		Cost of Goods Sold
From beginning inventory	100	@	$50	=	$ 5,000
From first purchase	150	@	53	=	7,950
From second purchase	125	@	56	=	7,000
Total pairs sold	375				$19,950

Ending inventory = Goods available for sale − Cost of goods sold
Ending inventory = $24,150 − $19,950 = $4,200

b. LIFO

Cost of Goods Sold	Pairs		Cost per Pair		Cost of Goods Sold
From second purchase	200	@	$56	=	$11,200
From first purchase	150	@	53	=	7,950
From beginning inventory	25	@	50	=	1,250
Total pairs sold	375				$20,400

Ending inventory = Goods available for sale − Cost of goods sold
Ending inventory = $24,150 − $20,400 = $3,750

c. Weighted average

Goods available for sale ÷ Total pairs = Cost per pair
$24,150 ÷ 450 = $53.6667

Cost of goods sold   375 units @ $53.6667 = $20,125
Ending inventory   75 units @ $53.6667 = $4,025

KEY TERMS

Account receivable 156
Accrued interest 167
Adjusting entry 168
Aging of accounts
 receivable 165
Allowance for doubtful
 accounts 158
Allowance method of
 accounting for uncollectible
 accounts 158
Collateral 167
Consistency 177
Contra asset account 160
First-in, first-out (FIFO) cost
 flow method 172

Full disclosure 177
Interest 167
Inventory cost flow
 methods 174
Last-in, first-out (LIFO) cost
 flow method 172
Liquidity 169
Maker 167
Matching concept 168
Maturity date 167
Net realizable value 158
Notes receivable 156
Payee 167
Percent of receivables
 method 164

Percent of revenue
 method 163
Physical flow of goods 172
Principal 167
Promissory note 166
Reinstate 162
Specific identification 172
Uncollectible accounts
 expense 159
Weighted-average cost flow
 method 172

QUESTIONS

1. What is the difference between accounts receivable and notes receivable?
2. What is the *net realizable value* of receivables?
3. What type of account is the Allowance for Doubtful Accounts?
4. What are two ways in which estimating uncollectible accounts improves the accuracy of the financial statements?
5. When using the allowance method, why is uncollectible accounts expense an estimated amount?
6. What is the most common format for reporting accounts receivable on the balance sheet? What information does this method provide beyond showing only the net amount?
7. Why is it necessary to reinstate a previously written off account receivable before the collection is recorded?
8. What are some factors considered in estimating the amount of uncollectible accounts receivable?
9. What is the effect on the accounting equation of recognizing uncollectible accounts expense?
10. What is the effect on the accounting equation of writing off an uncollectible account receivable when the allowance method is used?
11. How does the recovery of a previously written-off account affect the income statement when the allowance method is used? How does the recovery of a previously written-off account affect the statement of cash flows when the allowance method is used?
12. What is the advantage of using the allowance method of accounting for uncollectible accounts?
13. How do companies determine the percentage estimate of uncollectible accounts when using the percent of revenue method?
14. What is an advantage of using the percent of receivables method of estimating uncollectible accounts expense?
15. What is "aging of accounts receivable"?
16. What is a promissory note?
17. Define the following terms:
    a. Maker
    b. Payee
    c. Principal
    d. Interest
    e. Maturity date
    f. Collateral
18. What is the formula for computing interest revenue?
19. What is accrued interest?
20. How does the accrual of interest revenue or expense illustrate the matching concept?
21. Assets are listed on the balance sheet in the order of their liquidity. Explain this statement.
22. When is an adjusting entry for accrued interest generally recorded?
23. Assume that on July 1, 2010, Big Corp. loaned Little Corp. $12,000 for a period of one year at 6 percent interest. What amount of interest revenue will Big report for 2010?

What amount of cash will Big receive upon maturity of the note?

24. In which section of the statement of cash flows will Big report the cash collected in question 23?

25. Why is it generally beneficial for a business to accept major credit cards as payment for goods and services even when the fee charged by the credit card company is substantial?

26. What types of costs do businesses avoid when they accept major credit cards as compared with handling credit sales themselves?

27. Name and describe the four cost flow methods discussed in this chapter.

28. What are some advantages and disadvantages of the specific identification method of accounting for inventory?

29. What are some advantages and disadvantages of using the FIFO method of inventory valuation?

30. What are some advantages and disadvantages of using the LIFO method of inventory valuation?

31. In an inflationary period, which inventory cost flow method will produce the highest net income? Explain.

32. In an inflationary period, which inventory cost flow method will produce the largest

amount of total assets on the balance sheet? Explain.

33. What is the difference between the flow of costs and the physical flow of goods?

34. Does the choice of cost flow method (FIFO, LIFO, or weighted average) affect the statement of cash flows? Explain.

35. Assume that Key Co. purchased 1,000 units of merchandise in its first year of operations for $25 per unit. The company sold 850 units for $40. What is the amount of cost of goods sold using FIFO? LIFO? Weighted average?

36. Assume that Key Co. purchased 1,500 units of merchandise in its second year of operation for $27 per unit. Its beginning inventory was determined in Question 35. Assuming that 1,500 units are sold, what is the amount of cost of goods sold using FIFO? LIFO? Weighted average?

37. Refer to Questions 35 and 36. Which method might be preferable for financial statements? For income tax reporting? Explain.

38. In an inflationary period, which cost flow method, FIFO or LIFO, produces the larger cash flow? Explain.

39. Which inventory cost flow method produces the highest net income in a deflationary period?

 ## MULTIPLE-CHOICE QUESTIONS

Multiple-choice questions are provided on the text website at www.mhhe.com/edmondssurvey3e

EXERCISES

All applicable Exercises are available with McGraw-Hill's *Connect Accounting*.

Exercise 5-1 *Accounting for bad debts: allowance method*   **LO 1**

Nina's Accounting Service began operation on January 1, 2012. The company experienced the following events for its first year of operations.

Events Affecting 2012:

1. Provided $120,000 of accounting services on account.
2. Collected $90,000 cash from accounts receivable.
3. Paid salaries of $24,000 for the year.
4. Adjusted the accounts to reflect management's expectations that uncollectible accounts expense would be $1,200.

Required

a. Organize the transaction data in accounts under on accounting equation.

b. Prepare an income statement, a balance sheet, and a statement of cash flows for 2012.

LO 1

Exercise 5-2 *Analysis of financial statement effects of accounting for uncollectible accounts under the allowance method*

Businesses using the allowance method for the recognition of uncollectible accounts expense commonly experience four accounting events.

1. Recognition of revenue on account.
2. Collection of cash from accounts receivable.
3. Write-off of uncollectible accounts.
4. Recognition of uncollectible accounts expense through a year-end adjusting entry.

Required

Show the effect of each event on the elements of the financial statements, using a horizontal statements model like the one shown here. Use the following coding scheme to record your answers: increase is +, decrease is −, not affected is NA. In the cash flow column, indicate whether the item is an operating activity (OA), investing activity (IA), or financing activity (FA). The first transaction is entered as an example.

Event No.	Assets	=	Liab.	+	Equity	Rev.	−	Exp.	=	Net Inc.	Cash Flow
1	+		NA		+	+		NA		+	NA

LO 2

Exercise 5-3 *Effect of recognizing uncollectible accounts expense on financial statements: percent of revenue allowance method*

Big A's Auto Service was started on January 1, 2012. The company experienced the following events during its first two years of operation.

Events Affecting 2012

1. Provided $30,000 of repair services on account.
2. Collected $25,000 cash from accounts receivable.
3. Adjusted the accounting records to reflect the estimate that uncollectible accounts expense would be 1 percent of the service revenue on account.

Events Affecting 2013

1. Wrote off a $280 account receivable that was determined to be uncollectible.
2. Provided $35,000 of repair services on account.
3. Collected $31,000 cash from accounts receivable.
4. Adjusted the accounting records to reflect the estimate that uncollectible accounts expense would be 1 percent of the service revenue on account.

Required

a. Organize the transaction data in accounts under an accounting equation.
b. Determine the following amounts:
   (1) Net income for 2012.
   (2) Net cash flow from operating activities for 2012.
   (3) Balance of accounts receivable at the end of 2012.
   (4) Net realizable value of accounts receivable at the end of 2012.
c. Repeat Requirement *b* for the 2013 accounting period.

LO 2

Exercise 5-4 *Analyzing financial statement effects of accounting for uncollectible accounts using the percent of revenue allowance method*

Gray Bros. uses the allowance method to account for bad debts expense. Gray experienced the following four events in 2012.

1. Recognition of $48,000 of service revenue on account.
2. Collection of $42,000 cash from accounts receivable.

3. Determination that $300 of its accounts were not collectible and wrote off these receivables.

4. Recognition of uncollectible accounts expense for the year. Gray estimates that bad debts expense will be 2 percent of its service revenue.

Required

Show the effect of each of these events on the elements of the financial statements, using a horizontal statements model like the following one. Use + for increase, − for decrease, and NA for not affected. In the cash flow column, indicate whether the item is an operating activity (OA), investing activity (IA), or financing activity (FA).

Event No.	Assets				=	Liab.	+	Equity	Rev.	−	Exp.	=	Net Inc.	Cash Flow
	Cash	+	Accts. Rec.	−	Allow.	=			Ret. Earn.						

Exercise 5-5   *Analyzing account balances for a company using the allowance method of accounting for uncollectible accounts*

LO 1

The following account balances come from the records of Teton Company.

	Beginning Balance	Ending Balance
Accounts Receivable	$3,000	$3,500
Allowance for Doubtful Accounts	120	200

During the accounting period, Teton recorded $12,000 of service revenue on account. The company also wrote off a $150 account receivable.

Required

a. Determine the amount of cash collected from receivables.

b. Determine the amount of uncollectible accounts expense recognized during the period.

Exercise 5-6   *Effect of recovering a receivable previously written off*

LO 1, 2

The accounts receivable balance for City Shoe Repair at December 31, 2012, was $84,000. Also on that date, the balance in the Allowance for Doubtful Accounts was $2,400. During 2013, $2,100 of accounts receivable were written off as uncollectible. In addition, City Shoe Repair unexpectedly collected $150 of receivables that had been written off in a previous accounting period. Sales on account during 2013 were $218,000, and cash collections from receivables were $220,000. Uncollectible accounts expense was estimated to be 1 percent of the sales on account for the period.

Required

a. Organize the information in accounts under an accounting equation.

b. Based on the preceding information, compute (after year-end adjustment):

(1) Balance of Allowance for Doubtful Accounts at December 31, 2013.

(2) Balance of Accounts Receivable at December 31, 2013.

(3) Net realizable value of Accounts Receivable at December 31, 2013.

c. What amount of uncollectible accounts expense will City Shoe Repair report for 2013?

d. Explain how the $150 recovery of receivables affected the accounting equation.

Exercise 5-7   *Accounting for uncollectible accounts: percent of revenue allowance method*

LO 2

Classic Auto Parts sells new and used auto parts. Although a majority of its sales are cash sales, it makes a significant amount of credit sales. During 2012, its first year of operations, Classic Auto Parts experienced the following:

Sales on account	$280,000
Cash sales	650,000
Collections of accounts receivable	265,000
Uncollectible accounts charged off during the year	1,200

Required

Assume that Classic Auto Parts uses the allowance method of accounting for uncollectible accounts and estimates that 1 percent of its sales on account will not be collected. Answer the following questions:

a. What is the Accounts Receivable balance at December 31, 2012?

b. What is the ending balance of the Allowance for Doubtful Accounts at December 31, 2012, after all entries and adjusting entries are posted?

c. What is the amount of uncollectible accounts expense for 2012?

d. What is the net realizable value of accounts receivable at December 31, 2012?

LO 2

Exercise 5-8 *Determining account balances: allowance method of accounting for uncollectible accounts*

During the first year of operation, 2012, Coggins Repair Co. recognized $400,000 of service revenue on account. At the end of 2012, the accounts receivable balance was $68,000. For this first year in business, the owner believes uncollectible accounts expense will be about 1 percent of sales on account.

Required

a. What amount of cash did Coggins collect from accounts receivable during 2012?

b. Assuming Coggins uses the allowance method to account for uncollectible accounts, what amount should Coggins record as uncollectible accounts expense for 2012?

c. What is the net realizable value of receivables at the end of 2012?

d. Show the effects of the above transactions on the financial statements by recording the appropriate amounts in a horizontal statements model like the one shown here. In the Cash Flow column, indicate whether the item is an operating activity (OA), investing activity (IA), or financing activity (FA). Use NA for not affected.

Assets			=	Liab.	+	Equity	Rev.	−	Exp.	=	Net Inc.	Cash Flow
Cash	+	Accts. Rec.	−	Allow.								

LO 3

Exercise 5-9 *Accounting for uncollectible accounts: percent of receivables allowance method*

King Service Co. experienced the following transactions for 2012, its first year of operations:

1. Provided $66,000 of services on account.
2. Collected $42,000 cash from accounts receivable.
3. Paid $26,000 of salaries expense for the year.
4. King adjusted the accounts using the following information from an accounts receivable aging schedule:

Number of Days Past Due	Amount	Percent Likely to Be Uncollectible	Allowance Balance
Current	$16,000	.01	
0–30	3,000	.05	
31–60	2,000	.10	
61–90	1,000	.30	
Over 90 days	2,000	.50	

Required

a. Organize the information in accounts under an accounting equation.

b. Prepare the income statement for King Service Co. for 2012.

c. What is the net realizable value of the accounts receivable at December 31, 2012?

Exercise 5-10 *Effect of recognizing uncollectible accounts on the financial statements: percent of receivables allowance method*

LO 3

Bourret Inc. experienced the following events for the first two years of its operations.

2012:

1. Provided $60,000 of services on account.
2. Provided $25,000 of services and received cash.
3. Collected $35,000 cash from accounts receivable.
4. Paid $12,000 of salaries expense for the year.
5. Adjusted the accounting records to reflect uncollectible accounts expense for the year. Bourret estimates that 5 percent of the ending accounts receivable balance will be uncollectible.

2013:

1. Wrote off an uncollectible account of $650.
2. Provided $80,000 of services on account.
3. Provided $15,000 of services and collected cash.
4. Collected $62,000 cash from accounts receivable.
5. Paid $20,000 of salaries expense for the year.
6. Adjusted the accounts to reflect uncollectible accounts expense for the year. Bourret estimates that 5 percent of the ending accounts receivable balance will be uncollectible.

Required

a. Organize the transaction data in accounts under an accounting equation.
b. Prepare the income statement, statement of changes in stockholders' equity, balance sheet, and statement of cash flows for 2012.
c. What is the net realizable value of the accounts receivable at December 31, 2012?
d. Repeat Requirements *a, b,* and *c* for 2013.

Exercise 5-11 *Accounting for notes receivable*

LO 4

Babb Enterprises loaned $25,000 to Sneathen Co. on September 1, 2012, for one year at 6 percent interest.

Required

Show the effects of the following transactions in a horizontal statements model like the one shown below.

(1) The loan to Sneathen Co.
(2) The adjusting entry at December 31, 2012.
(3) The adjusting entry and collection of the note on September 1, 2013.

Date			Assets				=	Liab.	+	Equity	Rev.	−	Exp.	=	Net Inc.	Cash Flow
	Cash	+	Notes Rec.	+	Int. Rec.	=				Ret. Earn.						

Exercise 5-12 *Notes receivable—accrued interest*

LO 4

On March 1, 2012, Jason's Deli loaned $12,000 to Mark Johnson for one year at 5 percent interest.

Required

Answer the following questions.

a. What is Jason's interest income for 2012?
b. What is Jason's total amount of receivables at December 31, 2012?
c. What amounts will be reported on Jason's 2012 statement of cash flows?
d. What is Jason's interest income for 2013?
e. What is the total amount of cash that Jason's will collect in 2013 from Mark Johnson?

   f. What amounts will be reported on Jason's 2013 statement of cash flows?

   g. What is the total amount of interest Jason's Deli earned from the loan to Mark Johnson?

LO 2, 4

Exercise 5-13   *Comprehensive single-cycle problem*

The following post-closing trial balance was drawn from the accounts of Spruce Timber Co. as of December 31, 2012.

	Debit	Credit
Cash	$ 6,000	
Accounts receivable	18,000	
Allowance for doubtful accounts		$ 2,000
Inventory	24,000	
Accounts payable		9,200
Common stock		20,000
Retained earnings		16,800
Totals	$48,000	$48,000

Transactions for 2013

   1. Acquired an additional $10,000 cash from the issue of common stock.

   2. Purchased $60,000 of inventory on account.

   3. Sold inventory that cost $62,000 for $95,000. Sales were made on account.

   4. Wrote off $1,100 of uncollectible accounts.

   5. On September 1, Spruce loaned $9,000 to Pine Co. The note had a 7 percent interest rate and a one-year term.

   6. Paid $15,800 cash for salaries expense.

   7. Collected $80,000 cash from accounts receivable.

   8. Paid $52,000 cash on accounts payable.

   9. Paid a $5,000 cash dividend to the stockholders.

   10. Estimated uncollectible accounts expense to be 1 percent of sales on account.

   11. Recorded the accrued interest at December 31, 2013.

Required

   a. Organize the transaction data in accounts under on accounting equation.

   b. Prepare an income statement, a statement of changes in stockholders' equity, a balance sheet, and a statement of cash flows for 2013.

LO 5

Exercise 5-14   *Effect of credit card sales on financial statements*

Royal Carpet Cleaning provided $90,000 of services during 2012, its first year of operations. All customers paid for the services with major credit cards. Royal submitted the credit card receipts to the credit card company immediately. The credit card company paid Royal cash in the amount of face value less a 3 percent service charge.

Required

   a. Record the credit card sales and the subsequent collection of accounts receivable in a horizontal statements model like the one shown below. In the Cash Flow column, indicate whether the item is an operating activity (OA), investing activity (IA), or financing activity (FA). Use NA to indicate that an element is not affected by the event.

Assets		=	Liab.	+	Equity	Rev.	−	Exp.	=	Net Inc.	Cash Flow
Cash	+ Accts. Rec.										

b. Answer the following questions:

(1) What is the amount of total assets at the end of the accounting period?

(2) What is the amount of revenue reported on the income statement?

(3) What is the amount of cash flow from operating activities reported on the statement of cash flows?

(4) Why would Royal Carpet Cleaning accept credit cards instead of providing credit directly to its customers? In other words, why would Royal be willing to pay 3 percent of sales to have the credit card company handle its sales on account?

Exercise 5-15   *Recording credit card sales*   LO 5

Baucom Company accepted credit cards in payment for $6,850 of merchandise sold during March 2012. The credit card company charged Baucom a 3 percent service fee. The credit card company paid Baucom as soon as it received the invoices. Cost of goods sold amounted to $3,800.

Required

Based on this information alone, what is the amount of net income earned during the month of March?

Exercise 5-16   *Effect of inventory cost flow assumption on financial statements*   LO 6

Required

For each of the following situations, indicate whether FIFO, LIFO, or weighted average applies.

a. In a period of rising prices, net income would be highest.

b. In a period of rising prices, cost of goods sold would be highest.

c. In a period of rising prices, ending inventory would be highest.

d. In a period of falling prices, net income would be highest.

e. In a period of falling prices, the unit cost of goods would be the same for ending inventory and cost of goods sold.

Exercise 5-17   *Allocating product cost between cost of goods sold and ending*   LO 6
                          inventory

Mix Co. started the year with no inventory. During the year, it purchased two identical inventory items. The inventory was purchased at different times. The first purchase cost $1,200 and the other, $1,500. One of the items was sold during the year.

Required

Based on this information, how much product cost would be allocated to cost of goods sold and ending inventory on the year-end financial statements, assuming use of

a. FIFO?

b. LIFO?

c. Weighted average?

Exercise 5-18   *Allocating product cost between cost of goods sold and ending*   LO 6
                          inventory: multiple purchases

Laird Company sells coffee makers used in business offices. Its beginning inventory of coffee makers was 200 units at $45 per unit. During the year, Laird made two batch purchases of coffee makers. The first was a 300-unit purchase at $50 per unit; the second was a 350-unit purchase at $52 per unit. During the period, Laird sold 800 coffee makers.

Required

Determine the amount of product costs that would be allocated to cost of goods sold and ending inventory, assuming that Laird uses

a. FIFO.

b. LIFO.

c. Weighted average.

Exercise 5-19   *Effect of inventory cost flow (FIFO, LIFO, and weighted average) on gross margin*

The following information pertains to Porter Company for 2012.

Beginning inventory	70 units @ $13
Units purchased	280 units @ $18

Ending inventory consisted of 30 units. Porter sold 320 units at $30 each. All purchases and sales were made with cash.

Required

a. Compute the gross margin for Porter Company using the following cost flow assumptions: (1) FIFO, (2) LIFO, and (3) weighted average.

b. What is the dollar amount of difference in net income between using FIFO versus LIFO? (Ignore income tax considerations.)

c. Determine the cash flow from operating activities, using each of the three cost flow assumptions listed in Requirement *a.* Ignore the effect of income taxes. Explain why these cash flows have no differences.

Exercise 5-20   *Effect of inventory cost flow on ending inventory balance and gross margin*

Bristol Sales had the following transactions for DVDs in 2012, its first year of operations.

Jan. 20	Purchased 75 units @ $17	=	$1,275
Apr. 21	Purchased 450 units @ $19	=	8,550
July 25	Purchased 200 units @ $23	=	4,600
Sept. 19	Purchased 100 units @ $29	=	2,900

During the year, Bristol Sales sold 775 DVDs for $60 each.

Required

a. Compute the amount of ending inventory Bristol would report on the balance sheet, assuming the following cost flow assumptions: (1) FIFO, (2) LIFO, and (3) weighted average.

b. Compute the difference in gross margin between the FIFO and LIFO cost flow assumptions.

Exercise 5-21   *Income tax effect of shifting from FIFO to LIFO*

The following information pertains to the inventory of the La Bonne Company:

Jan. 1	Beginning inventory	500 units @ $20
Apr. 1	Purchased	2,500 units @ $25
Oct. 1	Purchased	800 units @ $26

During the year, La Bonne sold 3,400 units of inventory at $40 per unit and incurred $17,000 of operating expenses. La Bonne currently uses the FIFO method but is considering a change to LIFO. All transactions are cash transactions. Assume a 30 percent income tax rate.

Required

a. Prepare income statements using FIFO and LIFO.

b. Determine the amount of income taxes La Bonne would save if it changed cost flow methods.

c. Determine the cash flow from operating activities under FIFO and LIFO.

d. Explain why cash flow from operating activities is lower under FIFO when that cost flow method produced the higher gross margin.

Exercise 5-22 *Effect of FIFO versus LIFO on income tax expense*   LO 6

Holly Hocks, Inc. had cash sales of $225,000 for 2012, its first year of operation. On April 2, the company purchased 200 units of inventory at $190 per unit. On September 1, an additional 150 units were purchased for $210 per unit. The company had 50 units on hand at the end of the year. The company's income tax rate is 40 percent. All transactions are cash transactions.

Required

a. The preceding paragraph describes five accounting events: (1) a sales transaction, (2) the first purchase of inventory, (3) the second purchase of inventory, (4) the recognition of cost of goods sold expense, and (5) the payment of income tax expense. Record the amounts of each event in horizontal statements models like the following ones, assuming first a FIFO and then a LIFO cost flow.

Effect of Events on Financial Statements											
Panel 1: FIFO Cost Flow											
Event No.	Balance Sheet						Income Statement				Statement of Cash Flows
	Cash	+	Inventory	=	C. Stk.	+	Ret. Earn.	Rev.	−	Exp.	=	Net Inc.	
Panel 2: LIFO Cost Flow											
Event No.	Balance Sheet						Income Statement				Statement of Cash Flows
	Cash	+	Inventory	=	C. Stk.	+	Ret. Earn.	Rev.	−	Exp.	=	Net Inc.	

b. Compute net income using FIFO.
c. Compute net income using LIFO.
d. Explain the difference, if any, in the amount of income tax expense incurred using the two cost flow assumptions.
e. How does the use of the FIFO versus the LIFO cost flow assumptions affect the statement of cash flows?

PROBLEMS

All applicable Problems are available with McGraw-Hill's Connect Accounting.

Problem 5-23 *Accounting for uncollectible accounts—two cycles using the percent of revenue allowance method*   LO 2

The following transactions apply to Sharp Consulting for 2012, the first year of operation:

1. Recognized $65,000 of service revenue earned on account.
2. Collected $58,000 from accounts receivable.
3. Adjusted accounts to recognize uncollectible accounts expense. Sharp uses the allowance method of accounting for uncollectible accounts and estimates that uncollectible accounts expense will be 2 percent of sales on account.

The following transactions apply to Sharp Consulting for 2013:

1. Recognized $72,500 of service revenue on account.
2. Collected $66,000 from accounts receivable.
3. Determined that $900 of the accounts receivable were uncollectible and wrote them off.
4. Collected $100 of an account that had been previously written off.

CHECK FIGURES
c. Ending Accounts Receivable, 2012: $7,000
d. Net Income, 2013: $23,275

5. Paid $48,500 cash for operating expenses.

6. Adjusted accounts to recognize uncollectible accounts expense for 2012. Sharp estimates that uncollectible accounts expense will be 1 percent of sales on account.

Required

Complete all the following requirements for 2012 and 2013. Complete all requirements for 2012 prior to beginning the requirements for 2013.

a. Identify the type of each transaction (asset source, asset use, asset exchange, or claims exchange).

b. Show the effect of each transaction on the elements of the financial statements, using a horizontal statements model like the one shown here. Use + for increase, − for decrease, and NA for not affected. Also, in the Cash Flow column, indicate whether the item is an operating activity (OA), investing activity (IA), or financing activity (FA). The first transaction is entered as an example.

Event No.	Assets	=	Liab.	+	Equity	Rev.	−	Exp.	=	Net Inc.	Cash Flow
1	+		NA		+	+		NA		+	NA

c. Organize the transaction data in accounts under an accounting equation.

d. Prepare the income statement, statement of changes in stockholders' equity, balance sheet, and statement of cash flows.

LO 2

CHECK FIGURE
a. Net Realizable Value: $133,150

Problem 5-24   *Determining account balances: percent of revenue allowance method of accounting for uncollectible accounts*

The following information pertains to Leslie's Floor Store sales on account and accounts receivable.

Accounts receivable balance, January 1, 2012	$ 52,500
Allowance for doubtful accounts, January 1, 2012	4,725
Sales on account, 2012	925,000
Cost of goods sold, 2012	615,000
Collections of accounts receivable, 2012	835,000

After several collection attempts, Leslie's wrote off $3,100 of accounts that could not be collected. Leslie's estimates that bad debts expense will be 0.5 percent of sales on account.

Required

a. Compute the following amounts.

   (1) Using the allowance method, the amount of uncollectible accounts expense for 2012.

   (2) Net realizable value of receivables at the end of 2012.

b. Explain why the uncollectible accounts expense amount is different from the amount that was written off as uncollectible.

LO 3

Problem 5-25   *Accounting for uncollectible accounts: percent of receivables allowance method*

CHECK FIGURES
b. Net Income: $62,520
   Total Assets: $157,520

Hammond Inc. experienced the following transactions for 2012, its first year of operations:

1. Issued common stock for $80,000 cash.

2. Purchased $225,000 of merchandise on account.

3. Sold merchandise that cost $148,000 for $294,000 on account.

4. Collected $242,000 cash from accounts receivable.

5. Paid $210,000 on accounts payable.

6. Paid $46,000 of salaries expense for the year.

7. Paid other operating expenses of $35,000.

8. Hammond adjusted the accounts using the following information from an accounts receivable aging schedule.

Number of Days Past Due	Amount	Percent Likely to Be Uncollectible	Allowance Balance
Current	$33,000	.01	
0–30	12,000	.05	
31–60	3,000	.10	
61–90	2,500	.20	
Over 90 days	1,500	.50	

Required

a. Organize the transaction data in accounts under an accounting equation.

b. Prepare the income statement, statement of changes in stockholders' equity, balance sheet, and statement of cash flows for Hammond Inc. for 2012.

c. What is the net realizable value of the accounts receivable at December 31, 2012?

Problem 5-26 *Determination of account balances—percent of receivables allowance method of accounting for uncollectible accounts*

LO 2

During the first year of operation, 2012, Martin's Appliance recognized $292,000 of service revenue on account. At the end of 2012, the accounts receivable balance was $57,400. Even though this is his first year in business, the owner believes he will collect all but about 4 percent of the ending balance.

CHECK FIGURE
c. Net Realizable Value $55,104

Required

a. What amount of cash was collected by Martin's during 2012?

b. Assuming the use of an allowance system to account for uncollectible accounts, what amount should Martin record as uncollectible accounts expense in 2012?

c. What is the net realizable value of receivables at the end of 2012?

d. Show the effect of the above transactions on the financial statements by recording the appropriate amounts in a horizontal statements model like the one shown here. When you record amounts in the Cash Flow column, indicate whether the item is an operating activity (OA), investing activity (IA), or financing activity (FA). The letters NA indicate that an element is not affected by the event.

Assets			=	Liab.	+	Equity	Rev.	−	Exp.	=	Net Inc.	Cash Flow
Cash	+	Accts. Rec.	−.	Allow.								

Problem 5-27 *Accounting for notes receivable and uncollectible accounts using the percent of sales allowance method*

LO 2, 4

The following transactions apply to Bialis Co. for 2012, its first year of operations.

CHECK FIGURE
b. Net Income $53,340

1. Issued $100,000 of common stock for cash.

2. Provided $86,000 of services on account.

3. Collected $75,000 cash from accounts receivable.

4. Loaned $10,000 to Horne Co. on October 1, 2012. The note had a one-year term to maturity and an 8 percent interest rate.

5. Paid $32,000 of salaries expense for the year.

6. Paid a $2,000 dividend to the stockholders.

7. Recorded the accrued interest on December 31, 2012 (see item 4).

8. Uncollectible accounts expense is estimated to be 1 percent of service revenue on account.

Required

a. Show the effects of the above transactions in a horizontal statements model like the one shown below.

Event	Assets					Equity		Rev. − Exp. = Net Inc.	Cash Flows
	Cash +	Accts. Rec. − Allow. for Doubtful Accts.	+ Notes Rec.	+ Int. Rec.	=	Com. Stk.	+ Ret. Earn.		

b. Prepare the income statement, balance sheet, and statement of cash flows for 2012.

LO 3, 5

Problem 5-28 *Accounting for credit card sales and uncollectible accounts: percent of receivables allowance method*

eXcel

CHECK FIGURES
b. Net Income: $39,760
Total Assets: $99,760

Bishop Supply Company had the following transactions in 2012:

1. Acquired $60,000 cash from the issue of common stock.
2. Purchased $180,000 of merchandise for cash in 2012.
3. Sold merchandise that cost $110,000 for $200,000 during the year under the following terms:

$ 50,000	Cash sales
140,000	Credit card sales (The credit card company charges a 3 percent service fee.)
10,000	Sales on account

4. Collected all of the accounts receivable from the credit card company.
5. Collected $9,200 of accounts receivable.
6. Paid selling and administrative expenses of $46,000.
7. Determined that 5 percent of the ending accounts receivable balance would be uncollectible.

Required

a. Record the above events in a horizontal statements model like the following one. When you record amounts in the Cash Flow column, indicate whether the item is an operating activity (OA), an investing activity (IA), or a financing activity (FA). The letters NA indicate that an element is not affected by the event.

Event	Balance Sheet							Income Statement				Statemt. of Cash Flows
	Assets				=	Equity		Rev.	− Exp.	=	Net Inc.	
	Cash +	Accts. Rec.	− Allow	+ Mdse. Inv.	=	Com. Stk.	+ Ret. Earn.					

b. Prepare an income statement, a statement of changes in stockholders' equity, a balance sheet, and a statement of cash flows for 2012.

LO 1, 4, 5

Problem 5-29 *Effect of transactions on the elements of financial statements*

Required

Identify each of the following independent transactions as asset source (AS), asset use (AU), asset exchange (AE), or claims exchange (CE). Also explain how each event affects assets, liabilities, stockholders' equity, net income, and cash flow by placing a + for increase, − for decrease, or NA for not affected under each of the categories. The first event is recorded as an example.

Event	Type of Event	Assets	Liabilities	Common Stock	Retained Earnings	Net Income	Cash Flow
a	AE	+/−	NA	NA	NA	NA	+

a. Collected cash from accounts receivable.

b. Recovered an uncollectible account that was previously written off.

c. Paid cash for land.

d. Paid cash for other operating expenses.

e. Sold merchandise at a price above cost. Accepted payment by credit card. The credit card company charges a service fee. The receipts have not yet been forwarded to the credit card company.

f. Sold land for cash at its cost.

g. Paid cash to satisfy salaries payable.

h. Submitted receipts to the credit card company (see *e* above) and collected cash.

i. Loaned Carl Maddox cash. The loan had a 5 percent interest rate and a one-year term to maturity.

j. Paid cash to creditors on accounts payable.

k. Accrued three months' interest on the note receivable (see *i* above).

l. Provided services for cash.

m. Paid cash for salaries expense.

n. Provided services on account.

o. Wrote off an uncollectible account (use allowance method).

Problem 5-30   *Multistep income statement and balance sheet*

LO 1, 4

eXcel

Required

Use the following information to prepare a multistep income statement and a classified balance sheet for Usrey Equipment Co. for 2012. (*Hint:* Some of the items will *not* appear on either statement, and ending retained earnings must be calculated.)

Salaries expense	$130,000	Interest receivable (short term)	$ 400
Common stock	68,000	Beginning retained earnings	41,200
Notes receivable (long term)	10,000	Operating expenses	34,000
Allowance for doubtful accounts	4,000	Cash flow from investing activities	80,000
Accumulated depreciation	10,000	Prepaid rent	8,000
Notes payable (long term)	26,900	Land	60,000
Salvage value of equipment	4,000	Cash	20,000
Interest payable (short term)	1,200	Inventory	16,000
Uncollectible accounts expense	20,000	Accounts payable	1,800
Supplies	900	Interest expense	5,000
Office equipment	42,000	Salaries payable	3,400
Interest revenue	10,800	Unearned revenue	16,000
Sales revenue	400,000	Cost of goods sold	175,000
Dividends	8,000	Accounts receivable	50,000
Rent expense	4,000		

CHECK FIGURES
Total Current Assets: $101,300
Total Current Liabilities: $22,400

Problem 5-31   *Missing information*

LO 2, 4

The following information comes from the accounts of Kemper Company:

CHECK FIGURES
a. Net Realizable Value: $33,600
b. Interest Revenue: $4,000

Account Title	Beginning Balance	Ending Balance
Accounts Receivable	$30,000	$36,000
Allowance for Doubtful Accounts	1,800	2,400
Notes Receivable	50,000	50,000
Interest Receivable	1,000	5,000

Required

a. There were $180,000 in sales on account during the accounting period. Write offs of uncollectible accounts were $2,100. What was the amount of cash collected from accounts receivable? What amount of uncollectible accounts expense was reported on the income statement? What was the net realizable value of receivables at the end of the accounting period?

b. The note has an 8 percent interest rate and 24 months to maturity. What amount of interest revenue was recognized during the period? How much cash was collected for interest?

LO 2, 4, 5

Problem 5-32   *Comprehensive accounting cycle problem (uses percent of revenue allowance method)*

CHECK FIGURES
Net Income: $113,150
Total Assets: $308,650

The following trial balance was prepared for Lakeview Sales and Service on December 31, 2012, after the closing entries were posted.

Account Title	Debit	Credit
Cash	$ 87,100	
Accounts Receivable	18,760	
Allowance for Doubtful Accounts		$ 960
Inventory	94,600	
Accounts Payable		44,000
Common Stock		90,000
Retained Earnings		65,500
Totals	$200,460	$200,460

Lakeview had the following transactions in 2013:

1. Purchased merchandise on account for $270,000.
2. Sold merchandise that cost $215,000 on account for $350,000.
3. Performed $80,000 of services for cash.
4. Sold merchandise for $76,000 to credit card customers. The merchandise cost $47,500. The credit card company charges a 5 percent fee.
5. Collected $360,000 cash from accounts receivable.
6. Paid $274,000 cash on accounts payable.
7. Paid $126,000 cash for selling and administrative expenses.
8. Collected cash for the full amount due from the credit card company (see item 4).
9. Loaned $60,000 to R. Shell. The note had an 8 percent interest rate and a one-year term to maturity.
10. Wrote off $650 of accounts as uncollectible.
11. Made the following adjusting entries:
    (a) Recorded three months' interest on the note at December 31, 2013 (see item 9).
    (b) Estimated uncollectible accounts expense to be .5 percent of sales on account.

Required

a. Organize the transaction data in accounts under an accounting equation.
b. Prepare an income statement, a statement of changes in stockholders' equity, a balance sheet, and a statement of cash flows for 2013.

LO 6
eXcel

Problem 5-33   *Effect of different inventory cost flow methods on financial statements*

CHECK FIGURES
a. Cost of Goods Sold—FIFO: $27,540
b. Net Income—LIFO: $6,780

The accounting records of Clear Photography, Inc., reflected the following balances as of January 1, 2012:

Cash	$18,000
Beginning inventory	13,500 (150 units @ $90)
Common stock	15,000
Retained earnings	16,500

The following five transactions occurred in 2012:

1. First purchase (cash)   120 units @ $92
2. Second purchase (cash)   200 units @ $100
3. Sales (all cash)   300 units @ $185
4. Paid $15,000 cash for operating expenses.
5. Paid cash for income tax at the rate of 40 percent of income before taxes.

Required

a. Compute the cost of goods sold and ending inventory, assuming (1) FIFO cost flow, (2) LIFO cost flow, and (3) weighted-average cost flow.

b. Use a vertical model to prepare the 2012 income statement, balance sheet, and statement of cash flows under FIFO, LIFO, and weighted average. (*Hint:* Record the events under an accounting equation before preparing the statements.)

ANALYZE, THINK, COMMUNICATE

ATC 5-1   Business Application Case   *Understanding real-world annual reports*

Use the Target Corporation's annual report in Appendix B to answer the following questions. related to Target's 2009 fiscal year.

Required

a. What percentage of Target's total assets was comprised of credit card receivables?
b. Approximately what percentage of credit card receivables did the company think will not be collected in 2009 and 2008?
c. What is Target's policy regarding when to write off credit card receivables?
d. What percentage of Target's total assets was comprised of inventory?
e. What cost flow method did Target use to account for its inventory?
f. Target had arrangements with some of its vendors such that it does not purchase or pay for merchandise inventory until the merchandise is sold to outside customers. Was the cost of these goods ever included in the Inventory account?

ATC 5-2   Group Assignment   *Inventory cost flow*

The accounting records of Robin Co. showed the following balances at January 1, 2012:

Cash	$30,000
Beginning inventory (100 units @ $50, 70 units @ $55)	8,850
Common stock	20,000
Retained earnings	18,850

Transactions for 2012 were as follows:

Purchased 100 units @ $54 per unit.
Purchased 250 units @ $58 per unit.
Sold 220 units @ $80 per unit.
Sold 200 units @ $90 per unit.
Paid operating expenses of $3,200.
Paid income tax expense. The income tax rate is 30%.

Required

a. Organize the class into three sections, and divide each section into groups of three to five students. Assign each section one of the cost flow methods, FIFO, LIFO, or weighted average. The company uses the perpetual inventory system.

Group Tasks

Determine the amount of ending inventory, cost of goods sold, gross margin, and net income after income tax for the cost flow method assigned to your section. Also prepare an income statement using that cost flow assumption.

Class Discussion

b. Have a representative of each section put its income statement on the board. Discuss the effect that each cost flow method has on assets (ending inventory), net income, and cash flows. Which method is preferred for tax reporting? For financial reporting? What restrictions are placed on the use of LIFO for tax reporting?

ATC 5-3   Research Assignment   *Analyzing two real-world companies' accounts receivable*

Using the most current annual reports or the Forms 10-K for Pfizer, one of the world's largest pharmaceutical manufacturers, and Walgreens, the drugstore chain, complete the requirements below. To obtain the Forms 10-K, use either the EDGAR system following the instructions in Appendix A or the companies' websites. The annual reports can be found on the companies' websites.

Required

a. For each company, compute accounts receivable as a percentage of revenue. Show your computations?

b. Which company appears to be making more of its sales on account? Explain your answer.

c. Try to provide a logical explanation as to why one of these companies is making more of its sales on account that the other.

ATC 5-4   Writing Assignment   *Cost of charge sales*

Paul Smith is opening a plumbing supply store in University City. He plans to sell plumbing parts and materials to both wholesale and retail customers. Since contractors (wholesale customers) prefer to buy parts and materials and pay at the end of the month, Paul expects he will have to offer charge accounts. He plans to offer charge sales to the wholesale customers only and to require retail customers to pay with either cash or credit cards. Paul wondered what expenses his business would incur relative to the charge sales and the credit cards.

Required

a. What issues will Paul need to consider if he allows wholesale customers to buy plumbing supplies on account?

b. Write a memo to Paul Smith outlining the potential cost of accepting charge customers. Discuss the difference between the allowance method for uncollectible accounts and the direct write-off method. Also discuss the cost of accepting credit cards.

ATC 5-5   Ethical Dilemma   *How bad can it be?*

Alonzo Saunders owns a small training services company that is experiencing growing pains. The company has grown rapidly by offering liberal credit terms to its customers. Although his competitors require payment for services within 30 days, Saunders permits his customers to delay payment for up to 90 days. Saunders' customers thereby have time to fully evaluate the training that employees receive before they must pay for that training. Saunders guarantees satisfaction. If a customer is unhappy, the customer does not have to pay. Saunders works with reputable companies, provides top-quality training, and rarely encounters dissatisfied customers.

The long collection period, however, has created a cash flow problem. Saunders has a $100,000 accounts receivable balance, but needs cash to pay current bills. He has recently negotiated a loan agreement with National Bank of Brighton County that should solve his cash flow problems. The loan agreement requires that Saunders pledge the accounts receivable as collateral for the loan. The bank agreed to loan Saunders 70 percent of the receivables balance, thereby giving him access to $70,000 cash. Saunders is satisfied with this arrangement because he estimates he needs approximately $60,000.

On the day Saunders was to execute the loan agreement, he heard a rumor that his biggest customer was experiencing financial problems and might declare bankruptcy. The customer owed Saunders $45,000. Saunders promptly called the customer's chief accountant and learned "off the record" that the rumor was true. The accountant told Saunders that the company's net worth was negative and most of its assets were pledged as collateral for bank loans. In his opinion, Saunders was unlikely to collect the balance due. Saunders' immediate concern was the impact the circumstances would have on his loan agreement with the bank.

Saunders uses the direct write-off method to recognize uncollectible accounts expense. Removing the $45,000 receivable from the collateral pool would leave only $55,000 of receivables, reducing the available credit to $38,500 ($55,000 × 0.70). Even worse, recognizing the uncollectible accounts expense would so adversely affect his income statement that the bank might further reduce the available credit by reducing the percentage of receivables allowed under the loan agreement. Saunders will have to attest to the quality of the receivables at the date of the loan but reasons that since the information he obtained about the possible bankruptcy was "off the record" he is under no obligation to recognize the uncollectible accounts expense until the receivable is officially uncollectible.

Required

a. How are income and assets affected by the decision not to act on the bankruptcy information?

b. Review the AICPA's Articles of Professional Conduct (see Chapter 4) and comment on any of the standards that would be violated by the actions Saunders is contemplating.

c. How do the elements of the fraud triangle (see Chapter 4) apply to this case?

CHAPTER 6

Accounting for Long-Term Operational Assets

LEARNING OBJECTIVES

After you have mastered the material in this chapter, you will be able to:

1 Identify different types of long-term operational assets.

2 Determine the cost of long-term operational assets.

3 Explain how different depreciation methods affect financial statements.

4 Determine how gains and losses on disposals of long-term operational assets affect financial statements.

5 Show how revising estimates affects financial statements.

6 Explain how continuing expenditures for operational assets affect financial statements.

7 Explain how expense recognition for natural resources (depletion) affects financial statements.

8 Explain how expense recognition for intangible assets (amortization) affects financial statements.

9 Explain how expense recognition choices and industry characteristics affect financial performance measures.

CHAPTER OPENING

Companies use assets to produce revenue. Some assets, like inventory or office supplies, are called **current assets** because they are used relatively quickly (within a single accounting period). Other assets, like equipment or buildings, are used for extended periods of time (two or more accounting periods). These assets are called **long-term operational assets.**[1] Accounting for long-term assets raises several questions. For example, what is the cost of the asset? Is it the list price only or should the cost of transportation, transit insurance,

---

[1] Classifying assets as current versus long term is explained in more detail in Chapter 7.

setup, and so on be added to the list price? Should the cost of a long-term asset be recognized as expense in the period the asset is purchased or should the cost be expensed over the useful life of the asset? What happens in the accounting records when a long-term asset is retired from use? This chapter answers these questions. It explains accounting for long-term operational assets from the date of purchase through the date of disposal.

The Curious Accountant

In the normal course of operations, most companies acquire long-term assets each year. The way in which a company hopes to make money with these assets varies according to the type of business and the asset acquired. During 2009, **Weyerhaeuser Company** made cash acquisitions of property and equipment of $187 million and cash acquisitions of timber and timberlands of $52 million.

Can you think of how Weyerhaeuser's use of trees to produce revenue differs from its use of trucks? Do you think the procedures used to account for timber should be similar to or different from those used to account for trucks, and if so, how? (Answers on page 205.)

TANGIBLE VERSUS INTANGIBLE ASSETS

Long-term assets may be tangible or intangible. **Tangible assets** have a physical presence; they can be seen and touched. Tangible assets include equipment, machinery, natural resources, and land. In contrast, intangible assets have no physical form. Although they may be represented by physical documents, **intangible assets** are, in fact, rights or privileges. They cannot be seen or touched. For example, a patent represents an exclusive legal *privilege* to produce and sell a particular product. It protects inventors by making it illegal for others to profit by copying their inventions. Although a patent may be represented by legal documents, the privilege is the actual asset. Because the privilege cannot be seen or touched, the patent is an intangible asset.

Tangible Long-Term Assets

Tangible long-term assets are classified as (1) property, plant, and equipment; (2) natural resources, or (3) land.

Property, Plant, and Equipment

Property, plant, and equipment is sometimes called *plant assets* or *fixed assets.* Examples of property, plant, and equipment include furniture, cash registers, machinery, delivery trucks, computers, mechanical robots, and buildings. The level of detail used to account for these assets varies. One company may include all office equipment in one account, whereas another company might divide office equipment into computers, desks, chairs, and so on. The term used to recognize expense for property, plant, and equipment is **depreciation.**

Natural Resources

Mineral deposits, oil and gas reserves, timber stands, coal mines, and stone quarries are examples of **natural resources.** Conceptually, natural resources are inventories. When sold, the cost of these assets is frequently expensed as *cost of goods sold.* Although inventories are usually classified as short-term assets, natural resources are normally classified as long term because the resource deposits generally have long lives. For example, it may take decades to extract all of the diamonds from a diamond mine. The term used to recognize expense for natural resources is **depletion.**

Land

Land is classified separately from other property because land is not subject to depreciation or depletion. Land has an infinite life. It is not worn out or consumed as it is used. When buildings or natural resources are purchased simultaneously with land, the amount paid must be divided between the land and the other assets because of the non-depreciable nature of the land.

Intangible Assets

Intangible assets fall into two categories, those with *identifiable useful lives* and those with *indefinite useful lives.*

Intangible Assets with Identifiable Useful Lives

Intangible assets with identifiable useful lives include patents and copyrights. These assets may become obsolete (a patent may become worthless if new technology provides a superior product) or may reach the end of their legal lives. The term used when recognizing expense for intangible assets with identifiable useful lives is called **amortization.**

Intangible Assets with Indefinite Useful Lives

The benefits of some intangible assets may extend so far into the future that their useful lives cannot be estimated. For how many years will the **Coca-Cola** trademark attract customers? When will the value of a McDonald's franchise end? There are no answers to these questions. Intangible assets such as renewable franchises, trademarks, and goodwill have indefinite useful lives. The costs of such assets are not expensed unless the value of the assets becomes impaired.

DETERMINING THE COST OF LONG-TERM ASSETS

The **historical cost concept** requires that an asset be recorded at the amount paid for it. This amount includes the purchase price plus any costs necessary to get the asset in the location and condition for its intended use. Common cost components are:

LO 2

Determine the cost of long-term operational assets.

■ *Buildings:* (1) purchase price, (2) sales taxes, (3) title search and transfer document costs, (4) realtor's and attorney's fees, and (5) remodeling costs.

■ *Land:* (1) purchase price, (2) sales taxes, (3) title search and transfer document costs, (4) realtor's and attorney's fees, (5) costs for removal of old buildings, and (6) grading costs.

■ *Equipment:* (1) purchase price (less discounts), (2) sales taxes, (3) delivery costs, (4) installation costs, and (5) costs to adapt for intended use.

The cost of an asset does not include payments for fines, damages, and so on that could have been avoided.

✓ CHECK YOURSELF 6.1

Sheridan Construction Company purchased a new bulldozer that had a $260,000 list price. The seller agreed to allow a 4 percent cash discount in exchange for immediate payment. The bulldozer was delivered FOB shipping point at a cost of $1,200. Sheridan hired a new employee to operate the dozer for an annual salary of $36,000. The employee was trained to operate the dozer for a one-time training fee of $800. The cost of the company's theft insurance policy increased by $300 per year as a result of adding the dozer to the policy. The dozer had a five-year useful life and an expected salvage value of $26,000. Determine the asset's cost.

Answer

List price	$260,000
Less: Cash discount ($260,000 × 0.04)	(10,400)
Shipping cost	1,200
Training cost	800
Total asset cost (amount capitalized)	$251,600

Basket Purchase Allocation

Acquiring a group of assets in a single transaction is known as a **basket purchase.** The total price of a basket purchase must be allocated among the assets acquired. Accountants commonly allocate the purchase price using the **relative fair market value method.** To illustrate, assume that Beatty Company purchased land and a building for $240,000 cash. A real estate appraiser determined the fair market value of each asset to be

Building	$270,000
Land	90,000
Total	$360,000

The appraisal indicates that the land is worth 25 percent ($90,000 ÷ $360,000) of the total value and the building is worth 75 percent ($270,000 ÷ $360,000). Using these percentages, the actual purchase price is allocated as follows.

Building	0.75 × $240,000 =	$180,000
Land	0.25 × $240,000 =	60,000
Total		$240,000

METHODS OF RECOGNIZING DEPRECIATION EXPENSE

LO 3

Explain how different depreciation methods affect financial statements.

The life cycle of an operational asset involves (1) acquiring the funds to buy the asset, (2) purchasing the asset, (3) using the asset, and (4) retiring (disposing of) the asset. These stages are illustrated in Exhibit 6.1. The stages involving (1) acquiring funds and (2) purchasing assets have been discussed previously. This section of the chapter describes how accountants recognize the *use* of assets (Stage 3). As they are used, assets suffer from wear and tear called *depreciation.* Ultimately, assets depreciate to the point that they are no longer useful in the process of earning revenue. This process usually takes several years. The amount of an asset's cost that is allocated to expense during an accounting period is called **depreciation expense.**

An asset that is fully depreciated by one company may still be useful to another company. For example, a rental car that is no longer useful to Hertz may still be useful to a local delivery company. As a result, companies are frequently able to sell their fully depreciated assets to other companies or individuals. The expected market value of a fully depreciated asset is called its **salvage value.** The total amount of depreciation a company recognizes for an asset, its **depreciable cost,** is the difference between its original cost and its salvage value.

For example, assume a company purchases an asset for $5,000. The company expects to use the asset for 5 years (the **estimated useful life**) and then to sell it for $1,000 (salvage value). The depreciable cost of the asset is $4,000 ($5,000 − $1,000). The portion of the depreciable cost ($4,000) that represents its annual usage is recognized as depreciation expense.

Accountants must exercise judgment to estimate the amount of depreciation expense to recognize each period. For example, suppose you own a personal computer. You know how much the computer cost, and you know you will eventually need to replace it. How would you determine the amount the computer depreciates each year you use it? Businesses may use any of several acceptable methods to estimate the amount of depreciation expense to recognize each year.

The method used to recognize depreciation expense should match the asset's usage pattern. More expense should be recognized in periods when the asset is used more and less in periods when the asset is used less. Because assets are used to produce revenue, matching expense recognition with asset usage also matches expense recognition with revenue recognition. Three alternative methods for recognizing depreciation expense are (1) straight-line, (2) double-declining-balance, and (3) units-of-production.

The *straight-line* method produces the same amount of depreciation expense each accounting period. *Double-declining-balance,* an accelerated method, produces more depreciation expense in the early years of an asset's life, with a declining amount of expense in later years. *Units-of-production* produces varying amounts of depreciation expense in different accounting periods (more in some accounting periods and less in others). Exhibit 6.2 shows the relative use of different depreciation methods by U.S. companies.

EXHIBIT 6.1

Life Cycle of an Operational Asset

EXHIBIT 6.2

Depreciation Methods Used by U.S. Companies

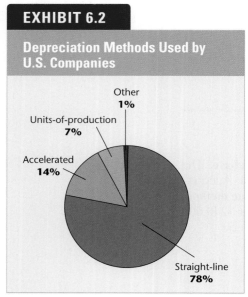

Data Source: AICPA Accounting Trends and Techniques.

Equipment is a long-term asset used for the purpose of producing revenue. A portion of the equipment's cost is recognized as depreciation expense each accounting period. The expense recognition for the cost of equipment is therefore spread over the useful life of the asset. Timber, however, is not used until the trees are grown. Conceptually, the costs of the trees should be treated as inventories and expensed as cost of goods sold at the time the products made from trees are sold. Even so, some timber companies recognize a periodic charge called *depletion* in a manner similar to that used for depreciation.

Accounting for unusual long-term assets such as timber requires an understanding of specialized "industry practice" accounting rules that are beyond the scope of this course. Many industries have unique accounting problems, and business managers in such industries must understand specialized accounting rules that relate to their companies.

Dryden Enterprises Illustration

To illustrate the different depreciation methods, consider a van purchased by Dryden Enterprises. Dryden plans to use the van as rental property. The van had a list price of $23,500. Dryden obtained a 10 percent cash discount from the dealer. The van was delivered FOB shipping point, and Dryden paid an additional $250 for transportation costs. Dryden also paid $2,600 for a custom accessory package to increase the van's appeal as a rental vehicle. The cost of the van is computed as follows.

List price	$23,500	
Less: Cash discount	(2,350)	$23,500 × 0.10
Plus: Transportation costs	250	
Plus: Cost of customization	2,600	
Total	$24,000	

The van has an estimated *salvage value* of $4,000 and an *estimated useful life* of four years. The following section examines three different patterns of expense recognition for this van.

Straight-Line Depreciation

The first scenario assumes the van is used evenly over its four-year life. The revenue from renting the van is assumed to be $8,000 per year. The matching concept calls for the expense recognition pattern to match the revenue stream. Because the same amount of revenue is recognized in each accounting period, Dryden should use **straight-line depreciation** because it produces equal amounts of depreciation expense each year.

Life Cycle Phase 1

The first phase of the asset life cycle is to acquire funds to purchase the asset. Assume Dryden acquired $25,000 cash on January 1, 2010, by issuing common stock. The effects on the financial statements follow.

Assets				=	Equity			Rev.	−	Exp.	=	Net Inc.	Cash Flow
Cash	+ Van	− Acc. Dep.		=	Com. Stk.	+	Ret. Earn.						
25,000	+ NA	− NA		=	25,000	+	NA	NA	−	NA	=	NA	25,000 FA

Life Cycle Phase 2

The second phase of the life cycle is to purchase the van. Assume Dryden bought the van on January 1, 2010, using funds from the stock issue. The cost of the van, previously computed, was $24,000 cash. The effects on the financial statements are:

Assets				=	Equity			Rev.	−	Exp.	=	Net Inc.	Cash Flow
Cash	+ Van	− Acc. Dep.		=	Com. Stk.	+	Ret. Earn.						
(24,000)	+ 24,000	− NA		=	NA	+	NA	NA	−	NA	=	NA	(24,000) IA

Life Cycle Phase 3

Dryden used the van by renting it to customers. The rent revenue each year is $8,000 cash. The effects on the financial statements are shown next.

Assets				=	Equity			Rev.	−	Exp.	=	Net Inc.	Cash Flow
Cash	+ Van	− Acc. Dep.		=	Com. Stk.	+	Ret. Earn.						
8,000	+ NA	− NA		=	NA	+	8,000	8,000	−	NA	=	8,000	8,000 OA

Although illustrated only once, these effects occur four times—once for each year Dryden earns revenue by renting the van.

At the end of each year, Dryden adjusts its accounts to recognize depreciation expense. The amount of depreciation recognized using the straight-line method is calculated as follows.

$$(\text{Asset cost} - \text{Salvage value}) \div \text{Useful life} = \text{Depreciation expense}$$

$$(\$24,000 - \$4,000) \div 4 \text{ years} = \$5,000 \text{ per year}$$

Recognizing depreciation expense is an asset use transaction that reduces assets and equity. The asset reduction is reported using a **contra asset account** called **Accumulated Depreciation.** Recognizing depreciation expense *does not affect cash flow.* The entire cash outflow for this asset occurred in January 2010 when Dryden purchased the van. Depreciation reflects *using* tangible assets, not spending cash to purchase them. The effects on the financial statements are as follows.

Assets				=	Equity			Rev.	−	Exp.	=	Net Inc.	Cash Flow
Cash	+ Van	− Acc. Dep.		=	Com. Stk.	+	Ret. Earn.						
NA	+ NA	− 5,000		=	NA	+	(5,000)	NA	−	5,000	=	(5,000)	NA

The Depreciation *Expense* account, like other expense accounts, is closed to the Retained Earnings account at the end of each year. The *Accumulated* Depreciation account, in contrast, increases each year, *accumulating* the total amount of depreciation recognized on the asset to date.

Life Cycle Phase 4

The final stage in the life cycle of a tangible asset is its disposal and removal from the company's records. Dryden retired the van from service on January 1, 2014, selling it for $4,500 cash. The van's **book value** (cost − accumulated depreciation) when it was sold was $4,000 ($24,000 cost − $20,000 accumulated depreciation), so Dryden recognized a $500 gain ($4,500 − $4,000) on the sale.

Determine how gains and losses on disposals of long-term operational assets affect financial statements.

Gains are *like* revenues in that they increase assets or decrease liabilities. Gains are *unlike* revenues in that gains result from peripheral (incidental) transactions rather than routine operating activities. Dryden is not in the business of selling vans. Dryden's normal business activity is renting vans. Because selling vans is incidental to Dryden's normal operations, gains are reported separately, after operating income, on the income statement.

If Dryden had sold the asset for less than book value, the company would have recognized a loss on the asset disposal. Losses are similar to expenses in that they decrease assets or increase liabilities. However, like gains, losses result from peripheral transactions. Losses are reported as nonoperating items on the income statement.

The effects of the asset disposal on the financial statements are shown next.

Assets			=	Equity			Rev. or Gain	−	Exp. or Loss	=	Net Inc.	Cash Flow
Cash	+	Van	−	Acc. Dep.	=	Com. Stk.	+	Ret. Earn.				
4,500	+	(24,000)	−	(20,000)	=	NA	+	500	500	−	NA	=	500	4,500 IA

Although the gain reported on the 2014 income statement is $500, the cash inflow from selling the van is $4,500. Gains and losses are not reported on the statement of cash flows. Instead they are included in the total amount of cash collected from the sale of the asset. In this case, the entire $4,500 is shown in the cash flow from investing activities section of the 2014 statement of cash flows.

Financial Statements

Exhibit 6.3 displays a vertical statements model that shows the financial results for the Dryden illustration from 2010 through 2014. Study the exhibit until you understand how all the figures were derived. The amount of depreciation expense ($5,000) reported on the income statement is constant each year from 2010 through 2013. The amount of accumulated depreciation reported on the balance sheet grows from $5,000 to $10,000, to $15,000, and finally to $20,000. The Accumulated Depreciation account is a *contra asset account* that is subtracted from the Van account in determining total assets.

Study the timing differences between cash flow and net income. Dryden spent $24,000 cash to acquire the van. Over the van's life cycle, Dryden collected $36,500 [($8,000 revenue × 4 years = $32,000) plus ($4,500 from the asset disposal) = $36,500]. The $12,500 difference between the cash collected and the cash paid ($36,500 − $24,000) equals the total net income earned during the van's life cycle.

Although the amounts are the same, the timing of the cash flows and the income recognition are different. For example, in 2010 there was a $24,000 cash outflow to purchase the van and an $8,000 cash inflow from customers. In contrast, the income statement reports net income of $3,000. In 2014, Dryden reported a $500 gain on the asset disposal, but the amount of operating income and the cash flow from operating

EXHIBIT 6.3	Financial Statements under Straight-Line Depreciation

DRYDEN ENTERPRISES
Financial Statements

	2010	2011	2012	2013	2014
Income Statements					
Rent revenue	$ 8,000	$ 8,000	$ 8,000	$ 8,000	$ 0
Depreciation expense	(5,000)	(5,000)	(5,000)	(5,000)	0
Operating income	3,000	3,000	3,000	3,000	0
Gain on sale of van	0	0	0	0	500
Net income	$ 3,000	$ 3,000	$ 3,000	$ 3,000	$ 500
Balance Sheets					
Assets					
Cash	$ 9,000	$17,000	$25,000	$33,000	$37,500
Van	24,000	24,000	24,000	24,000	0
Accumulated depreciation	(5,000)	(10,000)	(15,000)	(20,000)	0
Total assets	$28,000	$31,000	$34,000	$37,000	$37,500
Stockholders' equity					
Common stock	$25,000	$25,000	$25,000	$25,000	$25,000
Retained earnings	3,000	6,000	9,000	12,000	12,500
Total stockholders' equity	$28,000	$31,000	$34,000	$37,000	$37,500
Statements of Cash Flows					
Operating Activities					
Inflow from customers	$ 8,000	$ 8,000	$ 8,000	$ 8,000	$ 0
Investing Activities					
Outflow to purchase van	(24,000)				
Inflow from sale of van					4,500
Financing Activities					
Inflow from stock issue	25,000				
Net Change in Cash	9,000	8,000	8,000	8,000	4,500
Beginning cash balance	0	9,000	17,000	25,000	33,000
Ending cash balance	$ 9,000	$17,000	$25,000	$33,000	$37,500

activities is zero for that year. The gain is only indirectly related to cash flows. The $4,500 of cash received on disposal is reported as a cash inflow from investing activities. Because gains and losses result from peripheral transactions, they do not affect operating income or cash flow from operating activities.

Double-Declining-Balance Depreciation

For the second scenario, assume demand for the van is strong when it is new, but fewer people rent the van as it ages. As a result, the van produces smaller amounts of revenue as time goes by. To match expenses with revenues, it is reasonable to recognize more depreciation expense in the van's early years and less as it ages.

Double-declining-balance depreciation produces a large amount of depreciation in the first year of an asset's life and progressively smaller levels of expense in each succeeding year. Because the double-declining-balance method recognizes depreciation expense more rapidly than the straight-line method does, it is called an **accelerated**

depreciation method. Depreciation expense recognized using double-declining-balance is computed in three steps.

1. *Determine the straight-line rate.* Divide one by the asset's useful life. Because the estimated useful life of Dryden's van is four years, the straight-line rate is 25 percent (1 ÷ 4) per year.

2. *Determine the double-declining-balance rate.* Multiply the straight-line rate by 2 (*double* the rate). The double-declining-balance rate for the van is 50 percent (25 percent × 2).

3. *Determine the depreciation expense.* Multiply the double-declining-balance rate by the book value of the asset *at the beginning of the period* (recall that book value is historical cost minus *accumulated depreciation*). The following table shows the amount of depreciation expense Dryden will recognize over the van's useful life (2010–2013).

Year	Book Value at Beginning of Period	×	Double the Straight-Line Rate	=	Annual Depreciation Expense	
2010	($24,000 − $ 0) ×		0.50	=	$12,000	
2011	(24,000 − 12,000) ×		0.50	=	6,000	
2012	(24,000 − 18,000) ×		0.50	=	~~3,000~~	2,000
2013	(24,000 − 20,000) ×		0.50	=	~~2,000~~	0

Regardless of the depreciation method used, *an asset cannot be depreciated below its salvage value.* This restriction affects depreciation computations for the third and fourth years. Because the van had a cost of $24,000 and a salvage value of $4,000, the total amount of depreciable cost (historical cost − salvage value) is $20,000 ($24,000 − $4,000). Because $18,000 ($12,000 + $6,000) of the depreciable cost is recognized in the first two years, only $2,000 ($20,000 − $18,000) remains to be recognized after the second year. Depreciation expense recognized in the third year is therefore $2,000 even though double-declining-balance computations suggest that $3,000 should be recognized. Similarly, zero depreciation expense is recognized in the fourth year even though the computations indicate a $2,000 charge.

✓ CHECK YOURSELF 6.2

Olds Company purchased an asset that cost $36,000 on January 1, 2012. The asset had an expected useful life of five years and an estimated salvage value of $5,000. Assuming Olds uses the double-declining-balance method, determine the amount of depreciation expense and the amount of accumulated depreciation Olds would report on the 2014 financial statements.

Answer

Year	Book Value at Beginning of Period ×	Double the Straight-Line Rate* =	Annual Depreciation Expense
2012	($36,000 − $ 0) ×	0.40 =	$14,400
2013	(36,000 − 14,400) ×	0.40 =	8,640
2014	(36,000 − 23,040) ×	0.40 =	5,184
Total accumulated depreciation at December 31, 2014			$28,224

*Double-declining-balance rate = 2 × Straight-line rate = 2 × (1 ÷ 5 years) = 0.40

EXHIBIT 6.4   Financial Statements under Double-Declining-Balance Depreciation

DRYDEN ENTERPRISES
Financial Statements

	2010	2011	2012	2013	2014
Income Statements					
Rent revenue	$15,000	$ 9,000	$ 5,000	$ 3,000	$ 0
Depreciation expense	(12,000)	(6,000)	(2,000)	0	0
Operating income	3,000	3,000	3,000	3,000	0
Gain on sale of van	0	0	0	0	500
Net income	$ 3,000	$ 3,000	$ 3,000	$ 3,000	$ 500
Balance Sheets					
Assets					
Cash	$16,000	$25,000	$30,000	$33,000	$37,500
Van	24,000	24,000	24,000	24,000	0
Accumulated depreciation	(12,000)	(18,000)	(20,000)	(20,000)	0
Total assets	$28,000	$31,000	$34,000	$37,000	$37,500
Stockholders' equity					
Common stock	$25,000	$25,000	$25,000	$25,000	$25,000
Retained earnings	3,000	6,000	9,000	12,000	12,500
Total stockholders' equity	$28,000	$31,000	$34,000	$37,000	$37,500
Statements of Cash Flows					
Operating Activities					
Inflow from customers	$15,000	$ 9,000	$ 5,000	$ 3,000	$ 0
Investing Activities					
Outflow to purchase van	(24,000)				
Inflow from sale of van					4,500
Financing Activities					
Inflow from stock issue	25,000				
Net Change in Cash	16,000	9,000	5,000	3,000	4,500
Beginning cash balance	0	16,000	25,000	30,000	33,000
Ending cash balance	$16,000	$25,000	$30,000	$33,000	$37,500

Effects on the Financial Statements

Exhibit 6.4 displays financial statements for the life of the asset assuming Dryden uses double-declining-balance depreciation. The illustration assumes a cash revenue stream of $15,000, $9,000, $5,000, and $3,000 for the years 2010, 2011, 2012, and 2013, respectively. Trace the depreciation expense from the table above to the income statements. Reported depreciation expense is greater in the earlier years and smaller in the later years of the asset's life.

The double-declining-balance method smooths the amount of net income reported over the asset's useful life. In the early years, when heavy asset use produces higher revenue, depreciation expense is also higher. Similarly, in the later years, lower levels of revenue are matched with lower levels of depreciation expense. Net income is constant at $3,000 per year.

The depreciation method a company uses *does not* affect how it acquires the financing, invests the funds, and retires the asset. For Dryden's van, the accounting effects of these life cycle phases are the same as under the straight-line approach. Similarly, the *recording procedures* are not affected by the depreciation method. Different depreciation methods affect only the amount of depreciation expense recorded each year, not which accounts are used.

Units-of-Production Depreciation

Suppose rental demand for Dryden's van depends on general economic conditions. In a robust economy, travel increases, and demand for renting vans is high. In a stagnant economy, demand for van rentals declines. In such circumstances, revenues fluctuate from year to year. To accomplish the matching objective, depreciation should also fluctuate from year to year. A method of depreciation known as **units-of-production depreciation** accomplishes this goal by basing depreciation expense on actual asset usage.

Computing depreciation expense using units-of-production begins with identifying a measure of the asset's productive capacity. For example, the number of miles Dryden expects its van to be driven may be a reasonable measure of its productive capacity. If the depreciable asset were a saw, an appropriate measure of productive capacity could be the number of board feet the saw was expected to cut during its useful life. In other words, the basis for measuring production depends on the nature of the depreciable asset.

To illustrate computing depreciation using the units-of-production depreciation method, assume that Dryden measures productive capacity based on the total number of miles the van will be driven over its useful life. Assume Dryden estimates this productive capacity to be 100,000 miles. The first step in determining depreciation expense is to compute the cost per unit of production. For Dryden's van, this amount is total depreciable cost (historical cost − salvage value) divided by total units of expected productive capacity (100,000 miles). The depreciation cost per mile is therefore $0.20 ([$24,000 cost − $4,000 salvage] ÷ 100,000 miles). Annual depreciation expense is computed by multiplying the cost per mile by the number of miles driven. Odometer readings indicate the van was driven 40,000 miles, 20,000 miles, 30,000 miles, and 15,000 miles in 2010, 2011, 2012, and 2013, respectively. Dryden developed the following schedule of depreciation charges.

Year	Cost per Mile (a)	Miles Driven (b)	Depreciation Expense (a × b)
2010	$.20	40,000	$8,000
2011	.20	20,000	4,000
2012	.20	30,000	6,000
2013	.20	15,000	~~3,000~~ 2,000

As pointed out in the discussion of the double-declining-balance method, an asset cannot be depreciated below its salvage value. Because $18,000 of the $20,000 ($24,000 cost − $4,000 salvage) depreciable cost is recognized in the first three years of using the van, only $2,000 ($20,000 − $18,000) remains to be charged to depreciation in the fourth year, even though the depreciation computations suggest the charge should be $3,000. As the preceding table indicates, the general formula for computing units-of-production depreciation is

$$\frac{\text{Cost} - \text{Salvage value}}{\text{Total estimated units of production}} \times \begin{array}{c}\text{Units of production}\\ \text{in current}\\ \text{year}\end{array} = \begin{array}{c}\text{Annual}\\ \text{depreciation}\\ \text{expense}\end{array}$$

EXHIBIT 6.5	Financial Statements under Units-of-Production Depreciation

DRYDEN ENTERPRISES
Financial Statements

	2010	2011	2012	2013	2014
Income Statements					
Rent revenue	$11,000	$ 7,000	$ 9,000	$ 5,000	$ 0
Depreciation expense	(8,000)	(4,000)	(6,000)	(2,000)	0
Operating income	3,000	3,000	3,000	3,000	0
Gain on sale of van	0	0	0	0	500
Net income	$ 3,000	$ 3,000	$ 3,000	$ 3,000	$ 500
Balance Sheets					
Assets					
Cash	$12,000	$19,000	$28,000	$33,000	$37,500
Van	24,000	24,000	24,000	24,000	0
Accumulated depreciation	(8,000)	(12,000)	(18,000)	(20,000)	0
Total assets	$28,000	$31,000	$34,000	$37,000	$37,500
Stockholders' equity					
Common stock	$25,000	$25,000	$25,000	$25,000	$25,000
Retained earnings	3,000	6,000	9,000	12,000	12,500
Total stockholders' equity	$28,000	$31,000	$34,000	$37,000	$37,500
Statements of Cash Flows					
Operating Activities					
Inflow from customers	$11,000	$ 7,000	$ 9,000	$ 5,000	$ 0
Investing Activities					
Outflow to purchase van	(24,000)				
Inflow from sale of van					4,500
Financing Activities					
Inflow from stock issue	25,000				
Net Change in Cash	12,000	7,000	9,000	5,000	4,500
Beginning cash balance	0	12,000	19,000	28,000	33,000
Ending cash balance	$12,000	$19,000	$28,000	$33,000	$37,500

Exhibit 6.5 displays financial statements that assume Dryden uses units-of-production depreciation. The exhibit assumes a cash revenue stream of $11,000, $7,000, $9,000, and $5,000 for 2010, 2011, 2012, and 2013, respectively. Trace the depreciation expense from the schedule above to the income statements. Depreciation expense is greater in years the van is driven more and smaller in years the van is driven less, providing a reasonable matching of depreciation expense with revenue produced. Net income is again constant at $3,000 per year.

Comparing the Depreciation Methods

The total amount of depreciation expense Dryden recognized using each of the three methods was $20,000 ($24,000 cost − $4,000 salvage value). The different methods affect the *timing,* but not the *total amount,* of expense recognized. The different methods simply assign the $20,000 to different accounting periods. Exhibit 6.6 presents graphically the differences among the three depreciation methods discussed above. A company should use the method that most closely matches expenses with revenues.

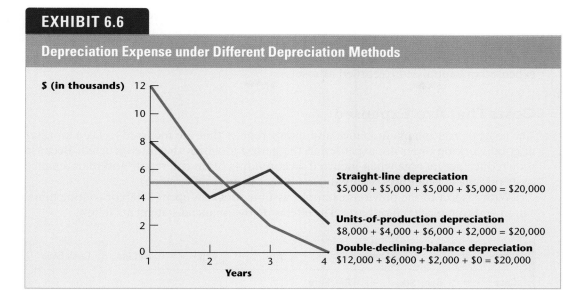

EXHIBIT 6.6

Depreciation Expense under Different Depreciation Methods

Straight-line depreciation
$5,000 + $5,000 + $5,000 + $5,000 = $20,000

Units-of-production depreciation
$8,000 + $4,000 + $6,000 + $2,000 = $20,000

Double-declining-balance depreciation
$12,000 + $6,000 + $2,000 + $0 = $20,000

REVISION OF ESTIMATES

In order to report useful financial information on a timely basis, accountants must make many estimates of future results, such as the salvage value and useful life of depreciable assets and uncollectible accounts expense. Estimates are frequently revised when new information surfaces. Because revisions of estimates are common, generally accepted accounting principles call for incorporating the revised information into present and future calculations. Prior reports are not corrected.

LO 5

Show how revising estimates affects financial statements.

To illustrate, assume that McGraw Company purchased a machine on January 1, 2012, for $50,000. McGraw estimated the machine would have a useful life of 8 years and a salvage value of $3,000. Using the straight-line method, McGraw determined the annual depreciation charge as follows:

$$(\$50,000 - \$3,000) \div 8 \text{ years} = \$5,875 \text{ per year}$$

At the beginning of the fifth year, accumulated depreciation on the machine is $23,500 ($5,875 × 4). The machine's book value is $26,500 ($50,000 − $23,500). At this point, what happens if McGraw changes its estimates of useful life or the salvage value? Consider the following revision examples independently of each other.

Revision of Life

Assume McGraw revises the expected life to 14, rather than 8, years. The machine's *remaining* life would then be 10 more years instead of 4 more years. Assume salvage value remains $3,000. Depreciation for each remaining year is:

$$(\$26,500 \text{ book value} - \$3,000 \text{ salvage}) \div 10\text{-year remaining life} = \$2,350$$

Revision of Salvage

Alternatively, assume the original expected life remained 8 years, but McGraw revised its estimate of salvage value to $6,000. Depreciation for each of the remaining four years would be

$$(\$26,500 \text{ book value} - \$6,000 \text{ salvage}) \div 4\text{-year remaining life} = \$5,125$$

The revised amounts are determined for the full year, regardless of when McGraw revised its estimates. For example, if McGraw decides to change the estimated useful life on October 1, 2017, the change would be effective as of January 1, 2017. The year-end adjusting entry for depreciation would include a full year's depreciation calculated on the basis of the revised estimated useful life.

CONTINUING EXPENDITURES FOR PLANT ASSETS

Explain how continuing expenditures for operational assets affect financial statements.

Most plant assets require additional expenditures for maintenance or improvement during their useful lives. Accountants must determine if these expenditures should be expensed or capitalized (recorded as assets).

Costs That Are Expensed

The costs of routine maintenance and minor repairs that are incurred to *keep* an asset in good working order are expensed in the period in which they are incurred. Because they reduce net income when incurred, accountants often call repair and maintenance costs **revenue expenditures** (companies subtract them from revenue).

With respect to the previous example, assume McGraw spent $500 for routine lubrication and to replace minor parts. The effects on the financial statements follow.

Assets	=	Equity			Rev.	−	Exp.	=	Net Inc.	Cash Flow
Cash	=	Com. Stk.	+	Ret. Earn.						
(500)	=	NA	+	(500)	NA	−	500	=	(500)	(500) OA

Costs That Are Capitalized

Substantial amounts spent to improve the quality or extend the life of an asset are described as **capital expenditures.** Capital expenditures are accounted for in one of two ways, depending on whether the cost incurred *improves the quality* or *extends the life* of the asset.

Improving Quality

Expenditures such as adding air conditioning to an existing building or installing a trailer hitch on a vehicle improve the quality of service these assets provide. If a capital expenditure improves an asset's quality, the amount is added to the historical cost of the asset. The additional cost is expensed through higher depreciation charges over the asset's remaining useful life.

To demonstrate, return to the McGraw Company example. Recall that the machine originally cost $50,000, had an estimated salvage of $3,000, and had a predicted life of 8 years. Recall further that accumulated depreciation at the beginning of the fifth year is $23,500 ($5,875 × 4) so the book value is $26,500 ($50,000 − $23,500). Assume McGraw makes a major expenditure of $4,000 in the machine's fifth year to improve its productive capacity. The effects on the financial statements follow.

Assets					=	Equity			Rev.	−	Exp.	=	Net Inc.	Cash Flow
Cash	+	Mach.	−	Acc. Dep.	=	Com. Stk.	+	Ret. Earn.						
(4,000)	+	4,000	−	NA	=	NA	+	NA	NA	−	NA	=	NA	(4,000) IA

After recording the expenditure, the machine account balance is $54,000 and the asset's book value is $30,500 ($54,000 − $23,500). The depreciation charges for each of the remaining four years are

($30,500 book value − $3,000 salvage) ÷ 4-year remaining life = $6,875

Extending Life

Expenditures such as replacing the roof of an existing building or putting a new engine in an old vehicle extend the useful life of these assets. If a capital expenditure extends the life of an asset rather than improving the asset's quality of service, accountants view the expenditure as canceling some of the depreciation previously charged to expense. The event is still an asset exchange; cash decreases, and the book value of the machine increases. However, the increase in the book value of the machine results from reducing the balance in the contra asset account, Accumulated Depreciation.

To illustrate, assume that instead of increasing productive capacity, McGraw's $4,000 expenditure had extended the useful life of the machine by two years. The effects of the expenditure on the financial statements follow.

Assets					=	Equity			Rev.	−	Exp.	=	Net Inc.	Cash Flow
Cash	+	Mach.	−	Acc. Dep.	=	Com. Stk.	+	Ret. Earn.						
(4,000)	+	NA	−	(4,000)	=	NA	+	NA	NA	−	NA	=	NA	(4,000) IA

After the expenditure is recognized, the book value is the same as if the $4,000 had been added to the Machine account ($50,000 cost − $19,500 adjusted balance in Accumulated Depreciation = $30,500). Depreciation expense for each of the remaining six years follows.

($30,500 book value − $3,000 salvage) ÷ 6-year remaining life = $4,583

✓ CHECK YOURSELF 6.3

On January 1, 2012, Dager Inc. purchased an asset that cost $18,000. It had a five-year useful life and a $3,000 salvage value. Dager uses straight-line depreciation. On January 1, 2014, it incurred a $1,200 cost related to the asset. With respect to this asset, determine the amount of expense and accumulated depreciation Dager would report in the 2014 financial statements under each of the following assumptions.

1. The $1,200 cost was incurred to repair damage resulting from an accident.

2. The $1,200 cost improved the operating capacity of the asset. The total useful life and salvage value remained unchanged.

3. The $1,200 cost extended the useful life of the asset by one year. The salvage value remained unchanged.

Answer

1. Dager would report the $1,200 repair cost as an expense. Dager would also report depreciation expense of $3,000 ([$18,000 − $3,000] ÷ 5). Total expenses related to this asset in 2014 would be $4,200 ($1,200 repair expense + $3,000 depreciation expense). Accumulated depreciation at the end of 2014 would be $9,000 ($3,000 depreciation expense × 3 years).

2. The $1,200 cost would be capitalized in the asset account, increasing both the book value of the asset and the annual depreciation expense.

	After Effects of Capital Improvement
Amount in asset account ($18,000 + $1,200)	$19,200
Less: Salvage value	(3,000)
Accumulated depreciation on January 1, 2014	(6,000)
Remaining depreciable cost before recording 2014 depreciation	$10,200
Depreciation for 2014 ($10,200 ÷ 3 years)	$ 3,400
Accumulated depreciation at December 31, 2014 ($6,000 + $3,400)	$ 9,400

(continued)

3. The $1,200 cost would be subtracted from the Accumulated Depreciation account, increasing the book value of the asset. The remaining useful life would increase to four years, which would decrease the depreciation expense.

	After Effects of Capital Improvement
Amount in asset account	$18,000
Less: Salvage value	(3,000)
Accumulated depreciation on January 1, 2014 ($6,000 − $1,200)	(4,800)
Remaining depreciable cost before recording 2014 depreciation	$10,200
Depreciation for 2014 ($10,200 ÷ 4 years)	$ 2,550
Accumulated depreciation at December 31, 2014 ($4,800 + $2,550)	$ 7,350

NATURAL RESOURCES

LO 7

Explain how expense recognition for natural resources (depletion) affects financial statements.

The cost of natural resources includes not only the purchase price but also related items such as the cost of exploration, geographic surveys, and estimates. The process of expensing natural resources is commonly called depletion.[2] The most common method used to calculate depletion is units-of-production.

To illustrate, assume Apex Coal Mining paid $4,000,000 cash to purchase a mine with an estimated 16,000,000 tons of coal. The unit depletion charge is

$$\$4,000,000 \div 16,000,000 \text{ tons} = \$0.25 \text{ per ton}$$

If Apex mines 360,000 tons of coal in the first year, the depletion charge is:

$$360,000 \text{ tons} \times \$0.25 \text{ per ton} = \$90,000$$

The depletion of a natural resource has the same effect on the accounting equation as other expense recognition events. Assets (in this case, a *coal mine*) and stockholders' equity decrease. The depletion expense reduces net income. The effects on the financial statements follow.

Assets			=	Equity			Rev.	−	Exp.	=	Net Inc.	Cash Flow	
Cash	+	Coal Mine	=	Com. Stk.	+	Ret. Earn.							
(4,000,000)	+	4,000,000	=	NA	+	NA	NA	−	NA	=	NA	(4,000,000)	IA
NA	+	(90,000)	=	NA	+	(90,000)	NA	−	90,000	=	(90,000)	NA	

INTANGIBLE ASSETS

LO 8

Explain how expense recognition for intangible assets (amortization) affects financial statements.

Intangible assets provide rights, privileges, and special opportunities to businesses. Common intangible assets include trademarks, patents, copyrights, franchises, and goodwill. Some of the unique characteristics of these intangible assets are described in the following sections.

Trademarks

A **trademark** is a name or symbol that identifies a company or a product. Familiar trademarks include the Polo emblem, the name *Coca-Cola*, and the Nike slogan, "Just

[2]In practice, the depletion charge is considered a product cost and allocated between inventory and cost of goods sold. This text uses the simplifying assumption that all resources are sold in the same accounting period in which they are extracted. The full depletion charge is therefore expensed in the period in which the resources are extracted.

FOCUS ON INTERNATIONAL ISSUES

RESEARCH *AND* DEVELOPMENT VS. RESEARCH *OR* DEVELOPMENT

For many years some thought the companies that followed U.S. GAAP were at a disadvantage when it came to research and development (R&D) costs, because these companies had to immediately expense such cost, while the accounting rules of some other countries allowed R&D cost to be capitalized. Remember, recording costs as an asset—capitalizing it—means that net income is not immediately reduced. The global movement toward using IFRS is reducing, but not eliminating, the different accounting treatments for R&D.

Like U.S. GAAP, IFRS require *research* costs to be expensed, but they allow *development* costs to be capitalized. This IFRS rule itself can present challenges, because sometimes it is not clear where research ends and development begins. Basically, once research has produced a product, patent, and so forth, that the company believes will result in a revenue generating outcome, any additional costs to get it ready for market are development costs.

do it." Trademarks are registered with the federal government and have an indefinite legal lifetime.

The costs incurred to design, purchase, or defend a trademark are capitalized in an asset account called Trademarks. Companies want their trademarks to become familiar but also face the risk of a trademark being used as the generic name for a product. To protect a trademark, companies in this predicament spend large sums on legal fees and extensive advertising programs to educate consumers. Well-known trademarks that have been subject to this problem include Coke, Xerox, Kleenex, and Vaseline.

Patents

A **patent** grants its owner an exclusive legal right to produce and sell a product that has one or more unique features. Patents issued by the U.S. Patent Office have a legal life of 20 years. Companies may obtain patents through purchase, lease, or internal development. The costs capitalized in the Patent account are usually limited to the purchase price and legal fees to obtain and defend the patent. The research and development costs that are incurred to develop patentable products are usually expensed in the period in which they are incurred.

Copyrights

A **copyright** protects writings, musical compositions, works of art, and other intellectual property for the exclusive benefit of the creator or persons assigned the right by the creator. The cost of a copyright includes the purchase price and any legal costs associated with obtaining and defending the copyright. Copyrights granted by the federal government extend for the life of the creator plus 70 years. A radio commercial could legally use a Bach composition as background music; it could not, however, use the theme song from the movie, *The Matrix,* without obtaining permission from the copyright owner. The cost of a copyright is often expensed early because future royalties may be uncertain.

Franchises

Franchises grant exclusive rights to sell products or perform services in certain geographic areas. Franchises may be granted by governments or private businesses. Franchises granted

REALITY BYTES

On March 9, 2009, Merck & Company (Merck), one of the world's largest pharmaceutical companies, agreed to pay $41.1 billion to acquire Schering-Plough Corporation (S-P), another pharmaceutical company. At the time, S-P's balance sheet showed net assets (assets minus liabilities) of approximately $10.5 billion. Why would Merck pay the owners of S-P almost four times the net value of the assets shown on the company's balance sheet?

Merck was willing to pay four times the book value of the assets for three reasons. First, the value of the assets on S-P's balance sheet represented the historical cost of the assets. The current market value of these assets was probably higher than their historical cost, especially for assets such as the S-P's drug patents. Second, Merck believed that the two companies combined could operate at a lower cost than the two could as separate companies, thus increasing the total earnings they could generate. Finally, Merck probably believed that S-P had *goodwill* that enables a company to use its assets in a manner that will generate above average earnings. In other words, Merck was paying for a hidden asset not shown on S-P's balance sheet.

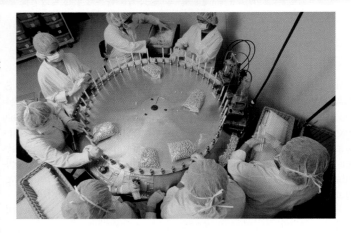

by governments include federal broadcasting licenses. Private business franchises include fast-food restaurant chains and brand labels such as Healthy Choice. The legal and useful lives of a franchise are frequently difficult to determine. Judgment is often crucial to establishing the estimated useful life for franchises.

Goodwill

Goodwill is the value attributable to favorable factors such as reputation, location, and superior products. Consider the most popular restaurant in your town. If the owner sells the restaurant, do you think the purchase price would be simply the total value of the chairs, tables, kitchen equipment, and building? Certainly not, because much of the restaurant's value lies in its popularity; in other words, its ability to generate a high return is based on the goodwill (reputation) of the business.

Calculating goodwill can be complex; here we present a simple example to illustrate how it is determined. Suppose the accounting records of a restaurant named Bendigo's show

$$\text{Assets} = \text{Liabilities} + \text{Stockholders' Equity}$$
$$\$200,000 = \$50,000 + \$150,000$$

Assume a buyer agrees to purchase the restaurant by paying the owner $300,000 cash and assuming the existing liabilities. In other words, the restaurant is purchased at a price of $350,000 ($300,000 cash + $50,000 assumed liabilities). Now assume that the assets of the business (tables, chairs, kitchen equipment, etc.) have a fair market value of only $280,000. Why would the buyer pay $350,000 to purchase assets with a market value of $280,000? Obviously, the buyer is purchasing more than just the assets. The buyer is purchasing the business's goodwill. The amount of the goodwill is the difference between the purchase price and the fair market value of the assets. In this case, the goodwill is $70,000 ($350,000 − $280,000). The effects of the purchase on the financial statements of the buyer follow.

Assets				=	Liab.	+	Equity	Rev.	−	Exp.	=	Net Inc.	Cash Flow
Cash	+	Rest. Assets	+	Goodwill									
(300,000)	+	280,000	+	70,000	=	50,000	+	NA	NA	−	NA	=	NA	(300,000) IA

The fair market value of the restaurant assets represents the historical cost to the new owner. It becomes the basis for future depreciation charges.

EXPENSE RECOGNITION FOR INTANGIBLE ASSETS

As mentioned earlier, intangible assets fall into two categories, those with *identifiable useful lives* and those with *indefinite useful lives.* Expense recognition for intangible assets depends on which classification applies.

Expensing Intangible Assets with Identifiable Useful Lives

The costs of intangible assets with identifiable useful lives are normally expensed on a straight-line basis using a process called *amortization.* An intangible asset should be amortized over the shorter of two possible time periods: (1) its legal life or (2) its useful life.

To illustrate, assume that Flowers Industries purchased a newly granted patent for $44,000 cash. Although the patent has a legal life of 20 years, Flowers estimates that it will be useful for only 11 years. The annual amortization charge is therefore $4,000 ($44,000 ÷ 11 years). The effects on the financial statements follow.

Assets			=	Equity			Rev.	−	Exp.	=	Net Inc.	Cash Flow
Cash	+	Patent	=	Com. Stk.	+	Ret. Earn.						
(44,000)	+	44,000	=	NA	+	NA	NA	−	NA	=	NA	(44,000) IA
NA	+	(4,000)	=	NA	+	(4,000)	NA	−	4,000	=	(4,000)	NA

Impairment Losses for Intangible Assets with Indefinite Useful Lives

Intangible assets with indefinite useful lives must be tested for impairment annually. The impairment test consists of comparing the fair value of the intangible asset to its carrying value (book value). If the fair value is less than the book value, an impairment loss must be recognized.

To illustrate, return to the example of the Bendigo's restaurant purchase. Recall that the buyer of Bendigo's paid $70,000 for goodwill. Assume the restaurant experiences a significant decline in revenue because many of its former regular customers are dissatisfied with the food prepared by the new chef. Suppose the decline in revenue is so substantial that the new owner believes the Bendigo's name is permanently impaired. The owner decides to hire a different chef and change the name of the restaurant. In this case, the business has suffered a permanent decline in value of goodwill. The company must recognize an impairment loss.

The restaurant's name has lost its value, but the owner believes the location continues to provide the opportunity to produce above-average earnings. Some, but not all, of the goodwill has been lost. Assume the fair value of the remaining goodwill is determined to be $40,000. The impairment loss to recognize is $30,000 ($70,000 − $40,000). The loss reduces the intangible asset (goodwill), stockholder's equity (retained earnings), and net income. The statement of cash flows would not be affected. The effects on the financial statements follow.

Assets	=	Liab.	+	Equity	Rev.	−	Exp./Loss	=	Net Inc.	Cash Flow
Goodwill	=			Ret. Earn.						
(30,000)	=	NA	+	(30,000)	NA	−	30,000	=	(30,000)	NA

BALANCE SHEET PRESENTATION

This chapter has explained accounting for the acquisition, expense recognition, and disposal of a wide range of long-term assets. Exhibit 6.7 illustrates typical balance sheet presentation of many of the assets discussed.

EXHIBIT 6.7

Balance Sheet Presentation of Operational Assets

Partial Balance Sheet

Long-Term Assets			
Plant and equipment			
Buildings	$4,000,000		
Less: Accumulated depreciation	(2,500,000)	$1,500,000	
Equipment	1,750,000		
Less: Accumulated depreciation	(1,200,000)	550,000	
Total plant and equipment			$2,050,000
Land			850,000
Natural resources			
Mineral deposits (Less: Depletion)		2,100,000	
Oil reserves (Less: Depletion)		890,000	
Total natural resources			2,990,000
Intangibles			
Patents (Less: Amortization)		38,000	
Goodwill		175,000	
Total intangible assets			213,000
Total long-term assets			$6,103,000

EFFECT OF JUDGMENT AND ESTIMATION

Explain how expense recognition choices and industry characteristics affect financial performance measures.

Managers may have differing opinions about which allocation method (straight-line, accelerated, or units-of-production) best matches expenses with revenues. As a result, one company may use straight-line depreciation while another company in similar circumstances uses double-declining-balance. Because the allocation method a company uses affects the amount of expense it recognizes, analysts reviewing financial statements must consider the accounting procedures companies use in preparing the statements.

Assume that two companies, Alpha and Zeta, experience identical economic events in 2011 and 2012. Both generate revenue of $50,000 and incur cost of goods sold of $30,000 during each year. In 2011, each company pays $20,000 for an asset with an expected useful life of five years and no salvage value. How will the companies' financial statements differ if one uses straight-line depreciation and the other uses the double-declining-balance method? To answer this question, first compute the depreciation expense for both companies for 2011 and 2012.

If Alpha Company uses the straight-line method, depreciation for 2011 and 2012 is

(Cost − Salvage) ÷ Useful life = Depreciation expense per year

($20,000 − $0) ÷   5 years   = $4,000

In contrast, if Zeta Company uses the double-declining-balance method, Zeta recognizes the following amounts of depreciation expense for 2011 and 2012.

	(Cost − Accumulated Depreciation)	×	2 × (Straight-Line Rate)	=	Depreciation Expense
2011	($20,000 − $ 0)	×	[2 × (1 ÷ 5)]	=	$8,000
2012	($20,000 − $8,000)	×	[2 × (1 ÷ 5)]	=	$4,800

Based on these computations, the income statements for the two companies are:

Income Statements				
	2011		**2012**	
	Alpha Co.	**Zeta Co.**	**Alpha Co.**	**Zeta Co.**
Sales	$50,000	$50,000	$50,000	$50,000
Cost of goods sold	(30,000)	(30,000)	(30,000)	(30,000)
Gross margin	20,000	20,000	20,000	20,000
Depreciation expense	(4,000)	(8,000)	(4,000)	(4,800)
Net income	$16,000	$12,000	$16,000	$15,200

The relevant sections of the balance sheets are

Plant Assets				
	2011		**2012**	
	Alpha Co.	**Zeta Co.**	**Alpha Co.**	**Zeta Co.**
Assets	$20,000	$20,000	$20,000	$20,000
Accumulated depreciation	(4,000)	(8,000)	(8,000)	(12,800)
Book value	$16,000	$12,000	$12,000	$ 7,200

The depreciation method is not the only aspect of expense recognition that can vary between companies. Companies may also make different assumptions about the useful lives and salvage values of long-term operational assets. Thus, even if the same depreciation method is used, depreciation expense may still differ.

Because the depreciation method and the underlying assumptions regarding useful life and salvage value affect the determination of depreciation expense, they also affect the amounts of net income, retained earnings, and total assets.

To promote meaningful analysis, public companies are required to disclose all significant accounting policies used to prepare their financial statements. This disclosure is usually provided in the footnotes that accompany the financial statements.

EFFECT OF INDUSTRY CHARACTERISTICS

As indicated in previous chapters, industry characteristics affect financial performance measures. For example, companies in manufacturing industries invest heavily in machinery while insurance companies rely more on human capital. Manufacturing companies therefore have relatively higher depreciation charges than insurance companies. To illustrate how the type of industry affects financial reporting, examine Exhibit 6.8. This exhibit compares the ratio of sales to property, plant, and equipment for two companies in each of three different industries.

EXHIBIT 6.8

Industry Data Reflecting the Use of Long-Term Tangible Assets

Industry	Company	Sales ÷ Property, Plant, and Equipment
Cable Companies	Charter Communications	0.90
	Cox Communications	0.73
Airlines	American	1.35
	United	1.31
Employment Agencies	Kelly Services	31.91
	Robert Half	30.20

The table indicates that for every $1.00 invested in property, plant, and equipment, **Kelly Services** produced $31.91 of sales. In contrast, **Cox Communications** and **United Airlines** produced only $0.73 and $1.31, respectively, for each $1.00 they invested in operational assets. Does this mean the management of Kelly is doing a better job than the management of Cox Communications or United Airlines? Not necessarily. It means that these companies operate in different economic environments. In other words, it takes significantly more equipment to operate a cable company or an airline than it takes to operate an employment agency.

 ## A Look Back

This chapter explains that the primary objective of recognizing depreciation is to match the cost of a long-term tangible asset with the revenues the asset is expected to generate. The matching concept also applies to natural resources (depletion) and intangible assets (amortization). The chapter explains how alternative methods can be used to account for the same event (e.g., straight-line versus double-declining-balance depreciation). Companies experiencing exactly the same business events could produce different financial statements. The alternative accounting methods for depreciating, depleting, or amortizing assets include the (1) straight-line, (2) double-declining-balance, and (3) units-of-production methods.

The *straight-line method* produces equal amounts of expense in each accounting period. The amount of the expense recognized is determined using the formula [(cost − salvage) ÷ number of years of useful life]. The *double-declining-balance method* produces proportionately larger amounts of expense in the early years of an asset's useful life and increasingly smaller amounts of expense in the later years of the asset's useful life. The formula for calculating double-declining-balance depreciation is [book value at beginning of period × (2 × the straight-line rate)]. The *units-of-production method* produces expense in direct proportion to the number of units produced during an accounting period. The formula for the amount of expense recognized each period is [(cost − salvage) ÷ total estimated units of production = allocation rate × units of production in current accounting period].

This chapter showed how to account for *changes in estimates* such as the useful life or the salvage value of a depreciable asset. Changes in estimates do not affect the amount of depreciation recognized previously. Instead, the remaining book value of the asset is expensed over its remaining useful life.

After an asset has been placed into service, companies typically incur further costs for maintenance, quality improvement, and extensions of useful life. *Maintenance costs* are expensed in the period in which they are incurred. *Costs that improve the quality* of an asset are added to the cost of the asset, increasing the book value and the amount of future depreciation charges. *Costs that extend the useful life* of an asset are subtracted from the asset's Accumulated Depreciation account thereby increasing the book value of the asset.

A Look Forward

In Chapter 7 we move from the assets section of the balance sheet to issues in accounting for liabilities.

A step-by-step audio-narrated series of slides is provided on the text website at www.mhhe.com/edmondssurvey3e

 ## SELF-STUDY REVIEW PROBLEM

The following information pertains to a machine purchased by Bakersfield Company on January 1, 2012.

Purchase price	$ 63,000
Delivery cost	$ 2,000
Installation charge	$ 3,000
Estimated useful life	8 years
Estimated units the machine will produce	130,000
Estimated salvage value	$ 3,000

The machine produced 14,400 units during 2012 and 17,000 units during 2013.

Required

Determine the depreciation expense Bakersfield would report for 2012 and 2013 using each of the following methods.

a. Straight-line.
b. Double-declining-balance.
c. Units-of-production.

Solution to Requirements a–c.

a. Straight-line

Purchase price	$63,000
Delivery cost	2,000
Installation charge	3,000
Total cost of machine	68,000
Less: Salvage value	(3,000)
	$65,000 ÷ 8 = $8,125 Depreciation per year
2012	$ 8,125
2013	$ 8,125

b. Double-declining-balance

Year	Cost	−	Accumulated Depreciation at Beginning of Year	×	2 × S-L Rate	=	Annual Depreciation
2012	$68,000	−	$ 0	×	(2 × 0.125)	=	$17,000
2013	68,000	−	17,000	×	(2 × 0.125)	=	12,750

c. Units-of-production

   (1) (Cost − Salvage value) ÷ Estimated units of production = Depreciation cost per unit produced

$$\frac{\$68,000 - \$3,000}{130,000} = \$0.50 \text{ per unit}$$

   (2) Cost per unit × Annual units produced = Annual depreciation expense

   2012 $0.50 × 14,400 = $7,200
   2013   0.50 × 17,000 = 8,500

KEY TERMS

Accelerated depreciation
   method 208
Accumulated Depreciation 206
Amortization 202
Basket purchase 203
Book value 207
Capital expenditures 214
Contra asset account 206
Copyright 217
Current assets 200
Depletion 202
Depreciable cost 204

Depreciation 202
Depreciation expense 204
Double-declining-balance
   depreciation 208
Estimated useful life 204
Franchise 217
Goodwill 218
Historical cost concept 203
Intangible assets 202
Long-term operational
   assets 200
Natural resources 202

Patent 217
Property, plant, and
   equipment 202
Relative fair market value
   method 203
Revenue expenditures 214
Salvage value 204
Straight-line depreciation 205
Tangible assets 202
Trademark 216
Units-of-production
   depreciation 211

QUESTIONS

1. What is the difference between the functions of long-term operational assets and investments?

2. What is the difference between tangible and intangible assets? Give an example of each.

3. What is the difference between goodwill and specifically identifiable intangible assets?

4. Define *depreciation*. What kind of asset depreciates?

5. Why are natural resources called *wasting assets?*

6. Is land a depreciable asset? Why or why not?

7. Define *amortization*. What kind of assets are *amortized?*

8. Explain the historical cost concept as it applies to long-term operational assets. Why is the book value of an asset likely to be different from the current market value of the asset?

9. What different kinds of expenditures might be included in the recorded cost of a building?

10. What is a basket purchase of assets? When a basket purchase is made, how is cost assigned to individual assets?

11. What are the stages in the life cycle of a long-term operational asset?

12. Explain straight-line, units-of-production, and double-declining-balance depreciation.

When is it appropriate to use each of these depreciation methods?

13. What effect does the recognition of depreciation expense have on total assets? On total equity?

14. Does the recognition of depreciation expense affect cash flows? Why or why not?

15. MalMax purchased a depreciable asset. What would be the difference in total assets at the end of the first year if MalMax chooses straight-line depreciation versus double-declining-balance depreciation?

16. John Smith mistakenly expensed the cost of a long-term tangible fixed asset. Specifically, he charged the cost of a truck to a delivery expense account. How will this error affect the income statement and the balance sheet in the year in which the mistake is made?

17. What is *salvage value?*

18. What type of account (classification) is Accumulated Depreciation?

19. How is the book value of an asset determined?

20. Why is depreciation that has been recognized over the life of an asset shown in a contra account? Why not just reduce the asset account?

21. Assume that a piece of equipment cost $5,000 and had accumulated depreciation of

$3,000. What is the book value of the equipment? Is the book value equal to the fair market value of the equipment? Explain.

22. Why would a company choose to depreciate one piece of equipment using the double-declining-balance method and another piece of equipment using straight-line depreciation?

23. Why may it be necessary to revise the estimated life of a plant asset? When the estimated life is revised, does it affect the amount of depreciation per year? Why or why not?

24. How are capital expenditures made to improve the quality of a capital asset accounted for? Would the answer change if the expenditure extended the life of the asset but did not improve quality? Explain.

25. When a long-term operational asset is sold at a gain, how is the balance sheet affected? Is the statement of cash flows affected? If so, how?

26. Define *depletion*. What is the most commonly used method of computing depletion?

27. List several common intangible assets. How is the life determined that is to be used to compute amortization?

28. List some differences between U.S. GAAP and GAAP of other countries with respect to amortization and accounting for intangibles.

29. How can judgment and estimation affect information reported in the financial statements?

MULTIPLE-CHOICE QUESTIONS

Multiple-choice questions are provided on the text website at www.mhhe.com/edmondssurvey3e

EXERCISES

All applicable Exercises are available with McGraw-Hill's *Connect Accounting*.

Unless specifically included, ignore income tax considerations in all exercises and problems.

Exercise 6-1   *Long-term operational assets used in a business*   LO 1

Required

Give some examples of long-term operational assets that each of the following companies is likely to own: *(a)* AT&T, *(b)* Caterpillar, *(c)* Amtrak, and *(d)* The Walt Disney Co.

Exercise 6-2   *Identifying long-term operational assets*   LO 1

Required

Which of the following items should be classified as long-term operational assets?

a. Cash	**g.** Inventory
b. Buildings	**h.** Patent
c. Production machinery	**i.** Tract of timber
d. Accounts receivable	**j.** Land
e. Prepaid rent	**k.** Computer
f. Franchise	**l.** Goodwill

Exercise 6-3   *Classifying tangible and intangible assets*   LO 1

Required

Identify each of the following long-term operational assets as either tangible (T) or intangible (I).

a. Retail store building	**g.** 18-wheel truck
b. Shelving for inventory	**h.** Timber
c. Trademark	**i.** Log loader
d. Gas well	**j.** Dental chair
e. Drilling rig	**k.** Goodwill
f. FCC license for TV station	**l.** Computer software

LO 2

Exercise 6-4   *Determining the cost of an asset*

Northeast Logging Co. purchased an electronic saw to cut various types and sizes of logs. The saw had a list price of $120,000. The seller agreed to allow a 5 percent discount because Northeast paid cash. Delivery terms were FOB shipping point. Freight cost amounted to $2,500. Northeast had to hire an individual to operate the saw. Northeast had to build a special platform to mount the saw. The cost of the platform was $1,000. The saw operator was paid an annual salary of $40,000. The cost of the company's theft insurance policy increased by $2,000 per year as a result of acquiring of the saw. The saw had a four-year useful life and an expected salvage value of $10,000.

Required

Determine the amount to be capitalized in the asset account for the purchase of the saw.

LO 2

Exercise 6-5   *Allocating costs on the basis of relative market values*

Midwest Company purchased a building and the land on which the building is situated for a total cost of $900,000 cash. The land was appraised at $200,000 and the building at $800,000.

Required

a. What is the accounting term for this type of acquisition?

b. Determine the amount of the purchase cost to allocate to the land and the amount to allocate to the building.

c. Would the company recognize a gain on the purchase? Why or why not?

d. Record the purchase in a statements model like the following one.

Assets	= Liab. + Equity	Rev. − Exp. = Net Inc.	Cash Flow
Cash + Land + Building			

LO 2

Exercise 6-6   *Allocating costs for a basket purchase*

Jourdan Company purchased a restaurant building, land, and equipment for $700,000 cash. The appraised value of the assets was as follows:

Land	$160,000
Building	400,000
Equipment	240,000
Total	$800,000

Required

a. Compute the amount to be recorded on the books for each of the assets.

b. Record the purchase in a horizontal statements model like the following one.

Assets			= Liab. + Equity	Rev. − Exp. = Net Inc.	Cash Flow
Cash + Land + Building + Equip.					

LO 3

Exercise 6-7   *Effect of depreciation on the accounting equation and financial statements*

The following events apply to The Pizza Factory for the 2012 fiscal year:

1. The company started when it acquired $18,000 cash from the issue of common stock.

2. Purchased a new pizza oven that cost $15,000 cash.

3. Earned $26,000 in cash revenue.
4. Paid $13,000 cash for salaries expense.
5. Paid $6,000 cash for operating expenses.
6. Adjusted the records to reflect the use of the pizza oven. The oven, purchased on January 1, 2012, has an expected useful life of five years and an estimated salvage value of $3,000. Use straight-line depreciation. The adjusting entry was made as of December 31, 2012.

Required

a. Record the above transactions in a horizontal statements model like the following one.

Event	Balance Sheet							Income Statement				Statemt. of Cash Flows
	Assets			=	Equity			Rev.	− Exp.	=	Net Inc.	
	Cash	+ Equip.	− A. Depr.	=	Com. Stock	+	Ret. Earn.					

b. What amount of depreciation expense would The Pizza Factory report on the 2012 income statement?
c. What amount of accumulated depreciation would The Pizza Factory report on the December 31, 2012, balance sheet?
d. Would the cash flow from operating activities be affected by depreciation in 2012?

Exercise 6-8 *Effect of double-declining-balance depreciation on financial statements*   LO 3

Smith Company started operations by acquiring $100,000 cash from the issue of common stock. On January 1, 2012, the company purchased equipment that cost $100,000 cash. The equipment had an expected useful life of five years and an estimated salvage value of $20,000. Smith Company earned $92,000 and $65,000 of cash revenue during 2012 and 2013, respectively. Smith Company uses double-declining-balance depreciation.

Required

a. Record the above transactions in a horizontal statements model like the following one.

Event	Balance Sheet							Income Statement				Statemt. of Cash Flows
	Assets			=	Equity			Rev.	− Exp.	=	Net Inc.	
	Cash	+ Equip.	− A. Depr.	=	Com. Stock	+	Ret. Earn.					

b. Prepare income statements, balance sheets, and statements of cash flows for 2012 and 2013. Use a vertical statements format.

Exercise 6-9 *Events related to the acquisition, use, and disposal of a tangible plant asset: straight-line depreciation*   LO 3, 4

CJ's Pizza purchased a delivery van on January 1, 2012, for $25,000. In addition, CJ's paid sales tax and title fees of $1,000 for the van. The van is expected to have a four-year life and a salvage value of $6,000.

Required

a. Using the straight-line method, compute the depreciation expense for 2012 and 2013.
b. Assume the truck was sold on January 1, 2015, for $12,000. Determine the amount of gain or loss that would be recognized on the asset disposal.

LO 3

Exercise 6-10 *Computing and recording straight-line versus double-declining-balance depreciation*

At the beginning of 2012, Precision Manufacturing purchased a new computerized drill press for $50,000. It is expected to have a five-year life and a $5,000 salvage value.

Required

a. Compute the depreciation for each of the five years, assuming that the company uses
   (1) Straight-line depreciation.
   (2) Double-declining-balance depreciation.
b. Record the purchase of the drill press and the depreciation expense for the first year under the straight-line and double-declining-balance methods in a financial statements model like the following one:

Assets					Equity	Rev.	–	Exp.	=	Net Inc.	Cash Flow
Cash	+	Drill Press	–	Acc. Dep.	=	Ret. Earn					

LO 4

Exercise 6-11 *Effect of the disposal of plant assets on the financial statements*

A plant asset with a cost of $40,000 and accumulated depreciation of $36,000 is sold for $6,000.

Required

a. What is the book value of the asset at the time of sale?
b. What is the amount of gain or loss on the disposal?
c. How would the sale affect net income (increase, decrease, no effect) and by how much?
d. How would the sale affect the amount of total assets shown on the balance sheet (increase, decrease, no effect) and by how much?
e. How would the event affect the statement of cash flows (inflow, outflow, no effect) and in what section?

LO 4

Exercise 6-12 *Effect of gains and losses on the accounting equation and financial statements*

On January 1, 2011, Gert Enterprises purchased a parcel of land for $12,000 cash. At the time of purchase, the company planned to use the land for future expansion. In 2012, Gert Enterprises changed its plans and sold the land.

Required

a. Assume that the land was sold for $11,200 in 2012.
   (1) Show the effect of the sale on the accounting equation.
   (2) What amount would Gert report on the income statement related to the sale of the land?
   (3) What amount would Gert report on the statement of cash flows related to the sale of the land?
b. Assume that the land was sold for $13,500 in 2012.
   (1) Show the effect of the sale on the accounting equation.
   (2) What amount would Gert report on the income statement related to the sale of the land?
   (3) What amount would Gert report on the statement of cash flows related to the sale of the land?

LO 3, 4

Exercise 6-13 *Double-declining-balance and units-of-production depreciation: gain or loss on disposal*

Print Service Co. purchased a new color copier at the beginning of 2011 for $35,000. The copier is expected to have a five-year useful life and a $5,000 salvage value. The expected copy production was estimated at 2,000,000 copies. Actual copy production for the five years was as follows:

2011	550,000
2012	480,000
2013	380,000
2014	390,000
2015	240,000
Total	2,040,000

The copier was sold at the end of 2015 for $5,200.

Required

a. Compute the depreciation expense for each of the five years, using double-declining-balance depreciation.
b. Compute the depreciation expense for each of the five years, using units-of-production depreciation. (Round cost per unit to three decimal places.)
c. Calculate the amount of gain or loss from the sale of the asset under each of the depreciation methods.

Exercise 6-14 *Revision of estimated useful life*   LO 5

On January 1, 2012, Harris Machining Co. purchased a compressor and related installation equipment for $64,000. The equipment had a three-year estimated life with a $4,000 salvage value. Straight-line depreciation was used. At the beginning of 2014, Harris revised the expected life of the asset to four years rather than three years. The salvage value was revised to $3,000.

Required

Compute the depreciation expense for each of the four years.

Exercise 6-15 *Distinguishing between revenue expenditures and capital*   LO 6
expenditures

Zell's Shredding Service has just completed a minor repair on a shredding machine. The repair cost was $900, and the book value prior to the repair was $5,000. In addition, the company spent $8,000 to replace the roof on a building. The new roof extended the life of the building by five years. Prior to the roof replacement, the general ledger reflected the Building account at $90,000 and related Accumulated Depreciation account at $40,000.

Required

After the work was completed, what book value should Zell's report on the balance sheet for the shredding machine and the building?

Exercise 6-16 *Effect of revenue expenditures versus capital expenditures on*   LO 6
financial statements

Sequoia Construction Company purchased a forklift for $110,000 cash. It had an estimated useful life of four years and a $10,000 salvage value. At the beginning of the third year of use, the company spent an additional $8,000 that was related to the forklift. The company's financial condition just prior to this expenditure is shown in the following statements model.

Assets			=	Equity			Rev.	−	Exp.	=	Net Inc.	Cash Flow
Cash	+	Forklift	Acc. Depr.	=	Com. Stk.	+	Ret. Earn.						
12,000	+	110,000	50,000	=	24,000	+	48,000	NA	−	NA	=	NA	NA

Required

Record the $8,000 expenditure in the statements model under each of the following *independent* assumptions:

a. The expenditure was for routine maintenance.
b. The expenditure extended the forklift's life.
c. The expenditure improved the forklift's operating capacity.

LO 6

Exercise 6-17 *Effect of revenue expenditures versus capital expenditures on financial statements*

On January 1, 2012, Valley Power Company overhauled four turbine engines that generate power for customers. The overhaul resulted in a slight increase in the capacity of the engines to produce power. Such overhauls occur regularly at two-year intervals and have been treated as maintenance expense in the past. Management is considering whether to capitalize this year's $25,000 cash cost in the engine asset account or to expense it as a maintenance expense. Assume that the engines have a remaining useful life of two years and no expected salvage value. Assume straight-line depreciation.

Required

a. Determine the amount of additional depreciation expense Valley would recognize in 2012 and 2013 if the cost were capitalized in the Engine account.
b. Determine the amount of expense Valley would recognize in 2012 and 2013 if the cost were recognized as maintenance expense.
c. Determine the effect of the overhaul on cash flow from operating activities for 2012 and 2013 if the cost were capitalized and expensed through depreciation charges.
d. Determine the effect of the overhaul on cash flow from operating activities for 2012 and 2013 if the cost were recognized as maintenance expense.

LO 7

Exercise 6-18 *Computing and recording depletion expense*

Ecru Sand and Gravel paid $600,000 to acquire 800,000 cubic yards of sand reserves. The following statements model reflects Ecru's financial condition just prior to purchasing the sand reserves. The company extracted 420,000 cubic yards of sand in year 1 and 360,000 cubic yards in year 2.

Assets			=	Equity			Rev.	−	Exp.	=	Net Inc.	Cash Flow
Cash	+	Sand Res.	=	Com. Stk.	+	Ret. Earn.						
700,000	+	NA	=	700,000	+	NA	NA	−	NA	=	NA	NA

Required

a. Compute the depletion charge per unit.
b. Record the acquisition of the sand reserves and the depletion expense for years 1 and 2 in a financial statements model like the preceding one.

LO 8

Exercise 6-19 *Computing and recording the amortization of intangibles*

Texas Manufacturing paid cash to purchase the assets of an existing company. Among the assets purchased were the following items.

| Patent with 5 remaining years of legal life | $36,000 |
| Goodwill | 40,000 |

Texas's financial condition just prior to the purchase of these assets is shown in the following statements model:

Assets					=	Liab.	+	Equity	Rev.	−	Exp.	=	Net Inc.	Cash Flow
Cash	+	Patent	+	Goodwill										
94,000	+	NA	+	NA	=	NA	+	94,000	NA	−	NA	=	NA	NA

Required

a. Compute the annual amortization expense for these items if applicable.

b. Record the purchase of the intangible assets and the related amortization expense for year 1 in a horizontal statements model like the preceding one.

Exercise 6-20   *Computing and recording goodwill*   LO 8

Mike Wallace purchased the business Magnum Supply Co. for $275,000 cash and assumed all liabilities at the date of purchase. Magnum's books showed assets of $280,000, liabilities of $40,000, and equity of $240,000. An appraiser assessed the fair market value of the tangible assets at $270,000 at the date of purchase. Wallace's financial condition just prior to the purchase is shown in the following statements model.

Assets					=	Liab.	+	Equity	Rev.	−	Exp.	=	Net Inc.	Cash Flow
Cash	+	Assets	+	Goodwill										
325,000	+	NA	+	NA	=	NA	+	325,000	NA	−	NA	=	NA	NA

Required

a. Compute the amount of goodwill purchased.

b. Record the purchase in a financial statements model like the preceding one.

Exercise 6-21   *Performing ratio analysis using real-world data*   LO 9

American Greetings Corporation manufactures and sells greeting cards and related items such as gift wrapping paper. CSX Corporation is one of the largest railway networks in the nation. The following data were taken from one of the companies' December 28, 2007, annual report and from the other's February 28, 2007, annual report. Revealing which data relate to which company was intentionally omitted. For one company, the dollar amounts are in thousands, while for the other they are in millions.

	Company 1	Company 2
Sales	$10,030	$1,744,603
Depreciation costs	883	46,975
Net earnings	1,336	42,378
Current assets	2,491	799,281
Property, plant, and equipment	21,780	285,072
Total assets	$25,534	$1,778,214

Required

a. Calculate depreciation costs as a percentage of sales for each company.

b. Calculate property, plant, and equipment as a percentage of total assets for each company.

c. Based on the information now available to you, decide which data relate to which company. Explain the rationale for your decision.

d. Which company appears to be using its assets most efficiently? Explain your answer.

PROBLEMS

All applicable Problems are available with McGraw-Hill's
Connect Accounting.

connect
ǀACCOUNTING

Problem 6-22   *Accounting for acquisition of assets including a basket purchase*   LO 2

Khan Company made several purchases of long-term assets in 2012. The details of each purchase are presented here.

New Office Equipment

1. List price: $40,000; terms: 1/10 n/30; paid within the discount period.
2. Transportation-in: $800.
3. Installation: $500.
4. Cost to repair damage during unloading: $500.
5. Routine maintenance cost after eight months: $120.

Basket Purchase of Office Furniture, Copier, Computers, and Laser Printers for $50,000 with Fair Market Values

1. Office furniture, $24,000.
2. Copier, $9,000.
3. Computers and printers, $27,000.

Land for New Headquarters with Old Barn Torn Down

1. Purchase price, $80,000.
2. Demolition of barn, $5,000.
3. Lumber sold from old barn, $2,000.
4. Grading in preparation for new building, $8,000.
5. Construction of new building, $250,000.

Required

In each of these cases, determine the amount of cost to be capitalized in the asset accounts.

Problem 6-23 *Accounting for depreciation over multiple accounting cycles: straight-line depreciation*

KC Company began operations when it acquired $30,000 cash from the issue of common stock on January 1, 2011. The cash acquired was immediately used to purchase equipment for $30,000 that had a $5,000 salvage value and an expected useful life of four years. The equipment was used to produce the following revenue stream (assume all revenue transactions are for cash). At the beginning of the fifth year, the equipment was sold for $4,500 cash. KC uses straight-line depreciation.

	2011	2012	2013	2014	2015
Revenue	$7,500	$8,000	$8,200	$7,000	$0

Required

Prepare income statements, statements of changes in stockholders' equity, balance sheets, and statements of cash flows for each of the five years.

Problem 6-24 *Purchase and use of tangible asset: three accounting cycles, double-declining-balance depreciation*

The following transactions pertain to Optimal Solutions Inc. Assume the transactions for the purchase of the computer and any capital improvements occur on January 1 each year.

2012

1. Acquired $60,000 cash from the issue of common stock.
2. Purchased a computer system for $25,000 cash. It has an estimated useful life of five years and a $3,000 salvage value.
3. Paid $1,500 sales tax on the computer system.
4. Collected $35,000 in data entry fees from clients.
5. Paid $1,200 in fees to service the computers.
6. Recorded double-declining-balance depreciation on the computer system for 2012.
7. Closed the revenue and expense accounts to Retained Earnings at the end of 2013.

2013

1. Paid $800 for repairs to the computer system.
2. Bought a case of toner cartridges for the printers that are part of the computer system, $1,200.
3. Collected $38,000 in data entry fees from clients.
4. Paid $900 in fees to service the computers.
5. Recorded double-declining-balance depreciation for 2013.
6. Closed the revenue and expense accounts to Retained Earnings at the end of 2013.

2014

1. Paid $3,000 to upgrade the computer system, which extended the total life of the system to six years.
2. Paid $900 in fees to service the computers.
3. Collected $35,000 in data entry fees from clients.
4. Recorded double-declining-balance depreciation for 2014.
5. Closed the revenue and expense accounts at the end of 2014.

Required

a. Record the above transactions in a horizontal statements model like the following one.

	Balance Sheet							Income Statement				Statemt. of Cash Flows
Event	**Assets**				**=**	**Equity**		**Rev.**	**– Exp.**	**=**	**Net Inc.**	
	Cash	+	Equip.	– A. Depr.	=	Com. Stock	+ Ret. Earn.					

b. Use a vertical model to present financial statements for 2012, 2013, and 2014.

Problem 6-25 *Calculating depreciation expense using four different methods*

O'Brian Service Company purchased a copier on January 1, 2012, for $17,000 and paid an additional $200 for delivery charges. The copier was estimated to have a life of four years or 800,000 copies. Salvage was estimated at $1,200. The copier produced 230,000 copies in 2012 and 250,000 copies in 2013.

Required

Compute the amount of depreciation expense for the copier for calendar years 2012 and 2012, using these methods:

a. Straight-line.
b. Units-of-production.
c. Double-declining-balance.

Problem 6-26 *Effect of straight-line versus double-declining-balance depreciation on the recognition of expense and gains or losses*

Same Day Laundry Services purchased a new steam press on January 1, for $35,000. It is expected to have a five-year useful life and a $3,000 salvage value. Same Day expects to use the steam press more extensively in the early years of its life.

Required

a. Calculate the depreciation expense for each of the five years, assuming the use of straight-line depreciation.
b. Calculate the depreciation expense for each of the five years, assuming the use of double-declining-balance depreciation.

c. Would the choice of one depreciation method over another produce a different amount of cash flow for any year? Why or why not?

d. Assume that Same Day Laundry Services sold the steam press at the end of the third year for $20,000. Compute the amount of gain or loss using each depreciation method.

LO 3, 4

Problem 6-27   *Computing and recording units-of-production depreciation*

McNabb Corporation purchased a delivery van for $25,500 in 2012. The firm's financial condition immediately prior to the purchase is shown in the following horizontal statements model:

Assets			=	Equity			Rev.	−	Exp.	=	Net Inc.	Cash Flow
Cash	+	Book Value of Van	=	Com. Stk.	+	Ret. Earn.						
50,000	+	NA	=	50,000	+	NA	NA	−	NA	=	NA	NA

CHECK FIGURES
a. Depreciation Expense, 2012:
$7,500
c. Gain on Sale: $1,000

The van was expected to have a useful life of 150,000 miles and a salvage value of $3,000. Actual mileage was as follows:

2012	50,000
2013	70,000
2014	58,000

Required

a. Compute the depreciation for each of the three years, assuming the use of units-of-production depreciation.

b. Assume that McNabb earns $21,000 of cash revenue during 2012. Record the purchase of the van and the recognition of the revenue and the depreciation expense for the first year in a financial statements model like the preceding one.

c. Assume that McNabb sold the van at the end of the third year for $4,000. Calculate the amount of gain or lose from the sale.

LO 3

Problem 6-28   *Determining the effect of depreciation expense on financial statements*

CHECK FIGURES
a. Company A, Net Income:
$20,000
c. Company A, Highest Book
Value: $17,750

Three different companies each purchased a machine on January 1, 2012, for $54,000. Each machine was expected to last five years or 200,000 hours. Salvage value was estimated to be $4,000. All three machines were operated for 50,000 hours in 2012, 55,000 hours in 2013, 40,000 hours in 2014, 44,000 hours in 2015, and 31,000 hours in 2016. Each of the three companies earned $30,000 of cash revenue during each of the five years. Company A uses straight-line depreciation, company B uses double-declining-balance depreciation, and company C uses units-of-production depreciation.

Required

Answer each of the following questions. Ignore the effects of income taxes.

a. Which company will report the highest amount of net income for 2012?

b. Which company will report the lowest amount of net income for 2014?

c. Which company will report the highest book value on the December 31, 2014, balance sheet?

d. Which company will report the highest amount of retained earnings on the December 31, 2015, balance sheet?

e. Which company will report the lowest amount of cash flow from operating activities on the 2014 statement of cash flows?

LO 7

Problem 6-29   *Accounting for depletion*

CHECK FIGURES
a. Coal Mine Depletion, 2012:
$280,000
b. Total Natural Resources:
$2,971,000

Favre Exploration Corporation engages in the exploration and development of many types of natural resources. In the last two years, the company has engaged in the following activities:

Jan. 1, 2012   Purchased a coal mine estimated to contain 200,000 tons of coal for $800,000.
July 1, 2012   Purchased for $1,950,000 a tract of timber estimated to yield 3,000,000 board feet of lumber and to have a residual land value of $150,000.

July 5, 2012   Purchased a silver mine estimated to contain 30,000 tons of silver for $750,000.
Aug. 1, 2012   Purchased for $736,000 oil reserves estimated to contain 250,000 barrels of oil, of which 20,000 would be unprofitable to pump.

Required

a. Determine the amount of depletion expense that would be recognized on the 2012 income statement for each of the four reserves, assuming 70,000 tons of coal, 1,000,000 board feet of lumber, 9,000 tons of silver, and 50,000 barrels of oil are extracted.

b. Prepare the portion of the December 31, 2012, balance sheet that reports natural resources.

Problem 6-30   *Recording continuing expenditures for plant assets*

LO 3, 4, 5, 6

CHECK FIGURES
b. 2013 Depreciation Expense: $7,000
d. Loss on Sale: $3,250

Big Sky Inc. recorded the following transactions over the life of a piece of equipment purchased in 2011:

Jan. 1, 2011   Purchased the equipment for $36,000 cash. The equipment is estimated to have a five-year life and $6,000 salvage value and was to be depreciated using the straight-line method.
Dec. 31, 2011   Recorded depreciation expense for 2011.
May 5, 2012   Undertook routine repairs costing $750.
Dec. 31, 2012   Recorded depreciation expense for 2012.
Jan. 1, 2013   Made an adjustment costing $3,000 to the equipment. It improved the quality of the output but did not affect the life estimate.
Dec. 31, 2013   Recorded depreciation expense for 2013.
Mar. 1, 2014   Incurred $320 cost to oil and clean the equipment.
Dec. 31, 2014   Recorded depreciation expense for 2014.
Jan. 1, 2015   Had the equipment completely overhauled at a cost of $7,500. The overhaul was estimated to extend the total life to seven years and revised the salvage value to $4,000.
Dec. 31, 2015   Recorded depreciation expense for 2015.
July 1, 2016   Sold the equipment for $9,000 cash.

Required

a. Use a horizontal statements model like the following one to show the effects of these transactions on the elements of the financial statements. Use + for increase, − for decrease, and NA for not affected. The first event is recorded as an example.

Date	Assets	=	Liabilities	+	Equity	Net Inc.	Cash Flow
Jan. 1, 2011	+ −		NA		NA	NA	− IA

b. Determine the amount of depreciation expense Big Sky will report on the income statements for the years 2011 through 2015.

c. Determine the book value (cost − accumulated depreciation) Big Sky will report on the balance sheets at the end of the years 2011 through 2015.

d. Determine the amount of the gain or loss Big Sky will report on the disposal of the equipment on July 1, 2016.

Problem 6-31   *Accounting for continuing expenditures*

LO 5, 6, 7

CHECK FIGURE
Depreciation Expense: $8,000

Vernon Manufacturing paid $58,000 to purchase a computerized assembly machine on January 1, 2012. The machine had an estimated life of eight years and a $2,000 salvage value. Vernon's financial condition as of January 1, 2015, is shown in the following financial statements model. Vernon uses the straight-line method for depreciation.

Assets					=	Equity			Rev.	−	Exp.	=	Net Inc.	Cash Flow
Cash	+	Mach.	−	Acc. Dep.	=	Com. Stk.	+	Ret. Earn.						
15,000	+	58,000	−	21,000	=	8,000	+	44,000	NA	−	NA	=	NA	NA

Vernon Manufacturing made the following expenditures on the computerized assembly machine in 2015.

Jan. 2   Added an overdrive mechanism for $6,000 that would improve the overall quality of the performance of the machine but would not extend its life. The salvage value was revised to $3,000.
Aug. 1   Performed routine maintenance, $1,150.
Oct. 2   Replaced some computer chips (considered routine), $950.
Dec. 31   Recognized 2015 depreciation expense.

Required

Record the 2015 transactions in a statements model like the preceding one.

LO 8

CHECK FIGURE
Goodwill Purchased: $130,000

Problem 6-32   *Accounting for intangible assets*

Mia-Tora Company purchased a fast-food restaurant for $1,400,000. The fair market values of the assets purchased were as follows. No liabilities were assumed.

Equipment	$320,000
Land	200,000
Building	650,000
Franchise (5-year life)	100,000

Required

Calculate the amount of goodwill purchased.

LO 8

CHECK FIGURE
Impairment Loss: $40,000

Problem 6-33   *Accounting for goodwill*

Springhill Co. purchased the assets of Canyon Co. for $1,000,000 in 2012. The estimated fair market value of the assets at the purchase date was $920,000. Goodwill of $80,000 was recorded at purchase. In 2013, because of negative publicity, one-half of the goodwill purchased from Canyon Co. was judged to be permanently impaired.

Required

Explain how the recognition of the impairment of the goodwill will affect the 2013 balance sheet, income statement, and statement of cash flows.

LO 9

Problem 6-34   *Performing ratio analysis using real-world data*

Cooper Tire Rubber Company claims to be the fourth largest tire manufacturer in North America. Goodyear Tire & Rubber Company is the largest tire manufacturer in North America. The following information was taken from these companies' December 31, 2007, annual reports. All dollar amounts are in thousands.

	Cooper Tire	Goodyear Tire
Sales	$2,932,575	$19,644,000
Depreciation costs	131,007	610,000
Buildings, machinery, and equipment		
(net of accumulated depreciation)	949,458	4,383,000
Total assets	2,296,868	17,028,000
Depreciation method	"Straight-line or accelerated"	Straight-line
Estimated life of assets:		
Buildings	10 to 40 years	8 to 45 years
Machinery and equipment	4 to 14 years	3 to 30 years

Required

a. Calculate depreciation costs as a percentage of sales for each company.

b. Calculate buildings, machinery, and equipment as a percentage of total assets for each company.

c. Which company appears to be using its assets most efficiently? Explain your answer.

d. Identify some of the problems a financial analyst encounters when trying to compare the use of long-term assets of Cooper versus Goodyear.

ANALYZE, THINK, COMMUNICATE

ATC 6-1   Business Applications Case   *Understanding real-world annual reports*

Required

Use the Target Corporation's annual report in Appendix B to answer the following questions.

a. What method of depreciation does Target use?

b. What types of intangible assets does Target have?

c. What are the estimated lives that Target uses for the various types of long-term assets?

d. As of January 30, 2010, what is the original cost of Target's: Land; Buildings and improvements; and Fixtures and equipment (see the footnotes)?

e. What was Target's depreciation expense and amortization expense for 2009 (see the footnotes)?

ATC 6-2   Group Assignment   *Different depreciation methods*

Sweet's Bakery makes cakes, pies, and other pastries that it sells to local grocery stores. The company experienced the following transactions during 2012.

1. Started business by acquiring $60,000 cash from the issue of common stock.
2. Purchased bakery equipment for $46,000 with a four year life and a $6,000 salvage value.
3. Had cash sales in 2012 amounting to $42,000.
4. Paid $8,200 of cash for supplies which were all used during the year to make baked goods.
5. Paid other operating expenses of $12,000 for 2012.

Required

a. Organize the class into two sections and divide each section into groups of three to five students. Assign each section a depreciation method: straight-line or double-declining-balance.

Group Task

Prepare an income statement and a balance sheet using the preceding information and the depreciation method assigned to your group.

Class Discussion

b. Have a representative of each section put its income statement on the board. Are there differences in net income? How will these differences in the amount of depreciation expense change over the life of the equipment?

ATC 6-3   Research Assignment   *Comparing Microsoft's and Intel's operational assets*

Companies in different industries often use different proportions of current versus long-term assets to accomplish their business objective. The technology revolution resulting from the silicon microchip has often been led by two well-known companies: Microsoft and Intel. Although often thought of together, these companies are really very different. Using either the most current Forms 10-K or annual reports for Microsoft Corporation and Intel Corporation, complete the requirements below. To obtain the Forms 10-K, use either the EDGAR system following the instructions in Appendix A or the company's website. Microsoft's annual report is available on its website; Intel's annual report is its Form 10-K.

Required

a. Fill in the missing data in the following table. The percentages must be computed; they are not included in the companies 10-Ks. (*Note:* The percentages for current assets and property, plant, and equipment will not sum to 100.)

	Current Assets	Property, Plant, and Equipment	Total Assets
Microsoft			
Dollar Amount	$	$	$
% of Total Assets	%	%	100%
Intel			
Dollar Amount	$	$	$
% of Total Assets	%	%	100%

b. Briefly explain why these two companies have different percentages of their assets in current assets versus property, plant, and equipment.

ATC 6-4   Writing Assignment   *Impact of historical cost on asset presentation on the balance sheet*

Assume that you are examining the balance sheets of two companies and note the following information.

	Company A	Company B
Equipment	$1,130,000	$900,000
Accumulated Depreciation	(730,000)	(500,000)
Book Value	$ 400,000	$400,000

Maxie Smith, a student who has had no accounting courses, remarks that Company A and Company B have the same amount of equipment.

Required

In a short paragraph, explain to Maxie that the two companies do not have equal amounts of equipment. You may want to include in your discussion comments regarding the possible age of each company's equipment, the impact of the historical cost concept on balance sheet information, and the impact of different depreciation methods on book value.

ATC 6-5   Ethical Dilemma   *What's an expense?*

Several years ago, Wilson Blowhard founded a communications company. The company became successful and grew by expanding its customer base and acquiring some of its competitors. In fact, most of its growth resulted from acquiring other companies. Mr. Blowhard is adamant about continuing the company's growth and increasing its net worth. To achieve these goals, the business's net income must continue to increase at a rapid pace.

If the company's net worth continues to rise, Mr. Blowhard plans to sell the company and retire. He is, therefore, focused on improving the company's profit any way he can.

In the communications business, companies often use the lines of other communications companies. This line usage is a significant operating expense for Mr. Blowhard's company. Generally accepted accounting principles require operating costs like line use to be expensed as they are incurred each year. Each dollar of line cost reduces net income by a dollar.

After reviewing the company's operations, Mr. Blowhard concluded that the company did not currently need all of the line use it was paying for. It was really paying the owner of the lines now so that the line use would be available in the future for all of Mr. Blowhard's expected new customers. Mr. Blowhard instructed his accountant to capitalize all of the line cost charges and depreciate them over 10 years. The accountant reluctantly followed Mr. Blowhard's instructions and the company's net income for the current year showed a significant increase over the prior year's net income. Mr. Blowhard had found a way to report continued growth in the company's net income and increase the value of the company.

Required

a. How does Mr. Blowhard's scheme affect the amount of income that the company would otherwise report in its financial statements and how does the scheme affect the company's balance sheet? Explain your answer.

b. Review the AICPA's Articles of Professional Conduct (see Chapter 4) and comment on any of the standards that were violated.

c. Review the fraud triangle discussed in Chapter 4 and comment on the features of the fraud triangle that are evident in this case.

CHAPTER 7

Accounting for Liabilities

LEARNING OBJECTIVES

After you have mastered the material in this chapter, you will be able to:

1 Show how notes payable and related interest expense affect financial statements.

2 Show how sales tax liabilities affect financial statements.

3 Define contingent liabilities and explain how they are reported in financial statements.

4 Explain how warranty obligations affect financial statements.

5 Show how installment notes affect financial statements.

6 Show how a line of credit affects financial statements.

7 Explain how to account for bonds issued at face value and their related interest costs.

8 Use the straight-line method to amortize bond discounts and premiums.

9 Distinguish between current and noncurrent assets and liabilities.

10 Prepare a classified balance sheet.

11 Use the effective interest rate method to amortize bond discounts and premiums. (Appendix)

CHAPTER OPENING

Chapter 2 discussed several types of liabilities with known amounts due, including accounts payable, salaries payable, and unearned revenue. This chapter introduces other liabilities with known amounts due: notes payable, sales taxes payable, lines of credit, and bond liabilities. We also discuss a contingent liability called warranties payable. We begin with a discussion of **current liabilities,** those that are payable within one year or the operating cycle, whichever is longer.

The Curious Accountant

For its 2008 fiscal year Ford Motor Company reported a net loss of $14.7 billion. The previous year it had reported a loss of $2.8 billion. The company had $9.7 billion of interest expense in 2008 and $10.9 billion in 2007.

With such huge losses on its income statement, do you think Ford was able to make the interest payments on its debt? If so, how? (Answer on page 249.)

ACCOUNTING FOR CURRENT LIABILITIES

Accounting for Notes Payable

Show how notes payable and related interest expense affect financial statements.

Our discussion of promissory notes in Chapter 5 focused on the payee, the company with a note receivable on its books. In this chapter we focus on the maker of the note, the company with a note payable on its books. Because the maker of the note issues (gives) the note to the payee, the maker is sometimes called the **issuer.**

To illustrate, assume that on September 1, 2012, Herrera Supply Company (HSC) borrowed $90,000 from the National Bank. As evidence of the debt, Herrera issued a **note payable** that had a one-year term and an annual interest rate of 9 percent.

Issuing the note is an asset source transaction. The asset account Cash increases and the liability account Notes Payable increases. The income statement is not affected. The statement of cash flows shows a $90,000 cash inflow from financing activities. The effects on the financial statements are as follows.

	Assets	=	Liabilities			+	Stockholders' Equity			Rev.	–	Exp.	=	Net Inc.	Cash Flow
Date	Cash	=	Notes Pay.	+	Int. Pay.	+	Com. Stk.	+	Ret. Earn.						
09/01/12	90,000	=	90,000	+	NA	+	NA	+	NA	NA	–	NA	=	NA	90,000 FA

On December 31, 2012, HSC would recognize four months (September 1 through December 31) of accrued interest expense. The accrued interest is $2,700 [$90,000 × 0.09 × (4 ÷ 12)]. Recognizing the accrued interest expense increases the liability account Interest Payable and decreases retained earnings. It is a claims exchange event. The income statement would report interest expense although HSC had not paid any cash for interest in 2012. The effects on the financial statements are as follows.

	Assets	=	Liabilities			+	Stockholders' Equity			Rev.	–	Exp.	=	Net Inc.	Cash Flow
Date	Cash	=	Notes Pay.	+	Int. Pay.	+	Com. Stk.	+	Ret. Earn.						
12/31/12	NA	=	NA	+	2,700	+	NA	+	(2,700)	NA	–	2,700	=	(2,700)	NA

HSC would record three events on August 31, 2013 (the maturity date). The first event recognizes $5,400 of interest expense that accrued in 2013 from January 1 through August 31 [$90,000 × 0.09 × (8 ÷ 12)]. The effects on the financial statements are as follows.

	Assets	=	Liabilities			+	Stockholders' Equity			Rev.	–	Exp.	=	Net Inc.	Cash Flow
Date	Cash	=	Notes Pay.	+	Int. Pay.	+	Com. Stk.	+	Ret. Earn.						
08/31/13	NA	=	NA	+	5,400	+	NA	+	(5,400)	NA	–	5,400	=	(5,400)	NA

The second event recognizes HSC's cash payment for interest on August 31, 2013. This event is an asset use transaction that reduces both the Cash and Interest Payable accounts for the total amount of interest due, $8,100 [$90,000 × 0.09 × (12 ÷ 12)]. The interest payment includes the four months' interest accrued in 2012 and the eight months accrued in 2013 ($2,700 + $5,400 = $8,100). There is no effect on the income statement because HSC recognized the interest expense in two previous journal entries.

The statement of cash flows would report an $8,100 cash outflow from operating activities. The effects on the financial statements follow.

	Assets	=		Liabilities			+	Stockholders' Equity			Rev.	–	Exp.	=	Net Inc.	Cash Flow
Date	Cash	=	Notes Pay.	+	Int. Pay.	+		Com. Stk.	+	Ret. Earn.						
08/31/13	(8,100)	=	NA	+	(8,100)	+		NA	+	NA	NA	–	NA	=	NA	(8,100) OA

The third event on August 31, 2013, reflects repaying the principal. This event is an asset use transaction. The Cash account and the Notes Payable account each decrease by $90,000. There is no effect on the income statement. The statement of cash flows would show a $90,000 cash outflow from financing activities. Recall that paying interest is classified as an operating activity even though repaying the principal is a financing activity. The effects on the financial statements are as follows.

	Assets	=		Liabilities			+	Stockholders' Equity			Rev.	–	Exp.	=	Net Inc.	Cash Flow
Date	Cash	=	Notes Pay.	+	Int. Pay.	+		Com. Stk.	+	Ret. Earn.						
08/31/13	(90,000)	=	(90,000)	+	NA	+		NA	+	NA	NA	–	NA	=	NA	(90,000) FA

✓ CHECK YOURSELF 7.1

On October 1, 2012, Mellon Company issued an interest-bearing note payable to Better Banks Inc. The note had a $24,000 principal amount, a four-month term, and an annual interest rate of 4 percent. Determine the amount of interest expense and the cash outflow from operating activities Mellon will report in its 2012 and 2013 financial statements.

Answer   The computation of accrued interest expense is shown below. Unless otherwise specified, the interest rate is stated in annual terms even though the term of the note is only four months. Interest rates are commonly expressed as an annual percentage regardless of the term of the note. The *time outstanding* in the following formulas is therefore expressed as a fraction of a year. Mellon paid interest at an annual rate of 4 percent, but the note was outstanding for only 3/12 of a year in 2012 and 1/12 of a year in 2013.

    2012
    Principal × Annual interest rate × Time outstanding = Interest expense
    $24,000 ×   0.04   ×   (3/12)   = $240

    2013
    Principal × Annual interest rate × Time outstanding = Interest expense
    $24,000 ×   0.04   ×   (1/12)   = $80

Mellon will report a $320 ($240 + $80) cash outflow from operating activities for interest in 2013.

Accounting for Sales Tax

Most states require retail companies to collect a sales tax on items sold to their customers. The retailer collects the tax from its customers and remits the tax to the state at regular intervals. The retailer has a current liability for the amount of sales tax collected but not yet paid to the state.

Show how sales tax liabilities affect financial statements.

To illustrate, assume Herrera Supply Company (HSC) sells merchandise to a customer for $2,000 cash plus tax in a state where the sales tax rate is 6 percent. The effects on the financial statements are shown below.[1]

Assets	=	Liab.	+		Equity		Rev.	−	Exp.	=	Net Inc.	Cash Flow	
Cash	=	Sales Tax Pay.	+	Com. Stk.	+	Ret. Earn.							
2,120	=	120	+	NA	+	2,000	2,000	−	NA	=	2,000	2,120	OA

Remitting the tax (paying cash to the tax authority) is an asset use transaction. Both the Cash account and the Sales Tax Payable account decrease. The effects on the financial statements are as follows.

Assets	=	Liab.	+		Equity		Rev.	−	Exp.	=	Net Inc.	Cash Flow	
Cash	=	Sales Tax Pay.	+	Com. Stk.	+	Ret. Earn.							
(120)	=	(120)	+	NA	+	NA	NA	−	NA	=	NA	(120)	OA

Contingent Liabilities

LO 3

Define contingent liabilities and explain how they are reported in financial statements.

A **contingent liability** is a potential obligation arising from a past event. The amount or existence of the obligation depends on some future event. A pending lawsuit, for example, is a contingent liability. Depending on the outcome, a defendant company could be required to pay a large monetary settlement or could be relieved of any obligation. Generally accepted accounting principles require that companies classify contingent liabilities into three different categories depending on the likelihood of their becoming actual liabilities. The categories and the accounting for each are described below.

1. If the likelihood of a future obligation arising is *probable* (likely) and its amount can be *reasonably estimated,* a liability is recognized in the financial statements. Contingent liabilities in this category include warranties, vacation pay, and sick leave.

2. If the likelihood of a future obligation arising is *reasonably possible* but not likely or if it is probable but *cannot be reasonably estimated,* no liability is reported on the balance sheet. The potential liability is, however, disclosed in the footnotes to the financial statements. Contingent liabilities in this category include legal challenges, environmental damages, and government investigations.

3. If the likelihood of a future obligation arising is *remote,* no liability need be recognized in the financial statements or disclosed in the footnotes to the statements.[2]

Determining whether a contingent liability is probable, reasonably possible, or remote requires professional judgment. Even seasoned accountants seek the advice of attorneys, engineers, insurance agents, and government regulators before classifying significant contingent liabilities. Professional judgment is also required to distinguish between contingent liabilities and **general uncertainties.** All businesses face uncertainties such as competition and damage from floods or storms. Such uncertainties are not contingent liabilities, however, because they do not arise from past events.

---

[1]The entry to record cost of goods sold for this sale is intentionally omitted.

[2]Companies may, if desired, voluntarily disclose contingent liabilities classified as remote.

EXHIBIT 7.1

Reporting Contingent Liabilities

Exhibit 7.1 summarizes the three categories of contingent liabilities and the accounting for each category.

Warranty Obligations

To attract customers, many companies guarantee their products or services. Such guarantees are called **warranties.** Warranties take many forms. Usually, they extend for a specified period of time. Within this period, the seller promises to replace or repair defective products without charge. Although the amount and timing of warranty obligations are uncertain, warranties usually represent liabilities that must be reported in the financial statements.

To illustrate accounting for warranty obligations, assume Herrera Supply Company (HSC) had cash of $2,000, inventory of $6,000, common stock of $5,000, and retained earnings of $3,000 on January 1, 2012. The 2012 accounting period is affected by three accounting events: (1) sale of merchandise under warranty; (2) recognition of warranty obligations to customers who purchased the merchandise; and (3) settlement of a customer's warranty claim.

LO 4

Explain how warranty obligations affect financial statements.

EVENT 1   Sale of Merchandise
HSC sold for $7,000 cash merchandise that had cost $4,000.

In the following statements model, revenue from the sale is referenced as 1a and the cost of the sale as 1b. The effects of the sales transaction on the financial statements are shown below.

Event No.	Assets			=	Liab.	+	Equity	Rev.	−	Exp.	=	Net Inc.	Cash Flow
	Cash	+	Inventory	=			Ret. Earn.						
1a	7,000	+	NA	=	NA	+	7,000	7,000	−	NA	=	7,000	7,000 OA
1b	NA	+	(4,000)	=	NA	+	(4,000)	NA	−	4,000	=	(4,000)	NA

EVENT 2   Recognition of Warranty Expense
HSC guaranteed the merchandise sold in Event 1 to be free from defects for one year following the date of sale.

Although the exact amount of future warranty claims is unknown, HSC must inform financial statement users of the company's obligation. HSC must estimate the amount of the warranty liability and report the estimate in the 2012 financial statements. Assume the warranty obligation is estimated to be $100. Recognizing this obligation increases liabilities (warranties payable) and reduces stockholders' equity (retained earnings). Recognizing the warranty expense reduces net income. The statement of cash flows is not affected when the obligation and the corresponding expense are recognized. The effects on the financial statements follow.

Event No.	Assets	=	Liab. Warr. Pay.	+	Equity Ret. Earn.	Rev.	−	Exp.	=	Net Inc.	Cash Flow
2	NA	=	100	+	(100)	NA	−	100	=	(100)	NA

EVENT 3   Settlement of Warranty Obligation
HSC paid $40 cash to repair defective merchandise returned by a customer.

The cash payment for the repair is not an expense. Warranty expense was recognized in the period in which the sale was made. The payment reduces an asset (cash) and a liability (warranties payable). The income statement is not affected by the repairs payment. However, there is a $40 cash outflow reported in the operating activities section of the statement of cash flows. The effects on the financial statements follow.

Event No.	Assets Cash	=	Liab. Warr. Pay.	+	Equity Ret. Earn.	Rev.	−	Exp.	=	Net Inc.	Cash Flow
3	(40)	=	(40)	+	NA	NA	−	NA	=	NA	(40) OA

Financial Statements

The financial statements for HSC's 2012 accounting period are shown in Exhibit 7.2.

EXHIBIT 7.2

Financial Statements for 2012

Income Statement		Balance Sheet		Statement of Cash Flows	
Sales revenue	$7,000	Assets		**Operating Activities**	
Cost of goods sold	(4,000)	Cash	$ 8,960	Inflow from customers	$7,000
Gross margin	3,000	Inventory	2,000	Outflow for warranty	(40)
Warranty expense	(100)	Total assets	$10,960	Net inflow from	
Net income	$2,900	Liabilities		operating activities	6,960
		Warranties payable	$ 60	**Investing Activities**	0
		Stockholders' equity		**Financing Activities**	0
		Common stock	5,000	Net change in cash	6,960
		Retained earnings	5,900	Plus: Beginning cash balance	2,000
		Total liab. and stockholders' equity	$10,960	Ending cash balance	$8,960

REALITY BYTES

Many of the items we purchase come with a manufacturer's warranty, but companies that sell electronics and electrical appliances often offer to sell you an extended warranty that provides protection after the manufacturer's warranty has expired. Why do they offer this option to customers, and how do these warranties differ from the standard manufactures' warranties?

Companies such as Best Buy offer to sell customers extended warranties because they make a significant profit on them. If you buy an extended warranty from Best Buy, the retailer is not actually the one who is promising to repair your product; that will be done by a third party. Best Buy simply receives a commission for selling the warranty. In 2010 such commissions accounted for 2.0 percent of the company's total revenues, and since it had to incur very little expense to earn these revenues, they are mostly profit.

The typical manufacturer's warranty, as you have learned in this chapter, is an expense recognized at the time of the sale. However, companies that provide extended warranties must recognize the warranty revenue over the life of the warranty, not immediately upon sale. Remember, this is referring to the third-party warranty provider, not Best Buy. Since Best Buy is simply earning a commission from selling the warranty, it gets to recognize all of the revenue at the time of the sale.

✓ CHECK YOURSELF 7.2

Flotation Systems, Inc. (FSI) began operations in 2012. Its sales were $360,000 in 2012 and $410,000 in 2013. FSI estimates the cost of its one-year product warranty will be 2 percent of sales. Actual cash payments for warranty claims amounted to $5,400 during 2012 and $8,500 during 2013. Determine the amount of warranty expense that FSI would report on its 2012 and 2013 year-end income statements. Also, determine the amount of warranties payable FSI would report on its 2012 and 2013 year-end balance sheet.

Answer FSI would report Warranty Expense on the December 31, 2012, income statement of $7,200 ($360,000 × .02). Warranty Expense on the December 31, 2013, income statement is $8,200 ($410,000 × .02).

FSI would report Warranties Payable on the December 31, 2012, balance sheet of $1,800 ($7,200 − $5,400). Warranties Payable on the December 31, 2013, balance sheet is $1,500 ($1,800 + $8,200 − $8,500).

ACCOUNTING FOR LONG-TERM DEBT

Most businesses finance their investing activities with long-term debt. Recall that current liabilities mature within one year or a company's operating cycle, whichever is longer. Other liabilities are **long-term liabilities.** Long-term debt agreements vary with respect to requirements for paying interest charges and repaying principal (the amount borrowed). Interest payments may be due monthly, annually, at some other interval, or at the maturity date. Interest charges may be based on a **fixed interest rate** that remains constant during the term of the loan or may be based on a **variable interest rate** that fluctuates up or down during the loan period.

Principal repayment is generally required either in one lump sum at the maturity date or in installments that are spread over the life of the loan. For example, each monthly payment on your car loan probably includes both paying interest and repaying some of the principal. Repaying a portion of the principal with regular payments that also include interest is often called loan **amortization**.[3] This section explains accounting for interest and principal with respect to the major forms of long-term debt financing.

Installment Notes Payable

LO 5

Show how installment notes affect financial statements.

Loans that require payments of principal and interest at regular intervals (amortizing loans) are typically represented by **installment notes.** The terms of installment notes usually range from two to five years. To illustrate accounting for installment notes, assume Blair Company was started on January 1, 2012, when it borrowed $100,000 cash from the National Bank. In exchange for the money, Blair issued the bank a five-year installment note with a 9 percent fixed interest rate. The effects on the financial statements are as follows.

	Assets	=	Liab.	+		Equity			Rev.	−	Exp.	=	Net Inc.	Cash Flow
Date	Cash	=	Note Pay.	+	Com. Stk.	+	Ret. Earn.							
2012 Jan. 1	100,000	=	100,000	+	NA	+	NA		NA	−	NA	=	NA	100,000 FA

The loan agreement required Blair to pay five equal installments of $25,709[4] on December 31 of each year from 2012 through 2016. Exhibit 7.3 shows the allocation of each payment between principal and interest. When Blair pays the final installment, both the principal and interest will be paid in full. The amounts shown in Exhibit 7.3 are computed as follows.

1. The Interest Expense (Column D) is computed by multiplying the Principal Balance on Jan. 1 (Column B) by the interest rate. For example, interest expense for 2012 is $100,000 × .09 = $9,000; for 2013 it is $83,291 × .09 = $7,496; and so on.

EXHIBIT 7.3

Amortization Schedule for Installment Note Payable

Accounting Period Column A	Principal Balance on Jan. 1 Column B	Cash Payment on Dec. 31 Column C	Interest Expense Column D	Principal Repayment Column E	Principal Balance on Dec. 31 Column F
2012	$100,000	$25,709	$9,000	$16,709	$83,291
2013	83,291	25,709	7,496	18,213	65,078
2014	65,078	25,709	5,857	19,852	45,226
2015	45,226	25,709	4,070	21,639	23,587
2016	23,587	25,710*	2,123	23,587	0

*All computations are rounded to the nearest dollar. To fully liquidate the liability, the final payment is one dollar more than the others because of rounding differences.

[3]In Chapter 6 the term *amortization* described the expense recognized when the *cost of an intangible asset* is systematically allocated to expense over the useful life of the asset. This chapter shows that the term amortization refers more broadly to a variety of allocation processes. Here it means the systematic process of allocating the *principal repayment* over the life of a loan.

[4]The amount of the annual payment is determined using the present value concepts presented in a later chapter. Usually the lender (bank or other financial institution) calculates the amount of the payment for the customer. In this chapter we provide the amount of the annual payment.

Answers to The Curious Accountant

Ford Motor Company was able to make its interest payments in 2008 for two reasons. (1) Interest is paid with cash, not accrued earnings. Many of the expenses on the company's income statement did not require the use of cash. The company's statement of cash flows shows that net cash flow from operating activities, *after making interest payments,* was a negative $179 million in 2008, which is much smaller than the $14.7 billion it reported as a net loss. Ford made up for the negative cash flow from operating activities by using some of the cash it had on hand at the beginning of 2008. (2) The net loss the company incurred was *after* interest expense had been deducted. The capacity of operations to support interest payments is measured by the amount of earnings before interest deductions. For example, look at the 2012 income statement for Blair Company in Exhibit 7.4. This statement shows only $3,000 of net income, but $12,000 of cash revenue was available for the payment of interest. Similarly, Ford's 2008 net loss is not an indication of the company's ability to pay interest in the short run. Fortunatly, in 2009 Ford had positive net income of $2.7 billion and positive cash flows from operating activities of $16.0 billion.

2. The Principal Repayment (Column E) is computed by subtracting the Interest Expense (Column D) from the Cash Payment on Dec. 31 (Column C). For example, the Principal Repayment for 2012 is $25,709 − $9,000 = $16,709; for 2013 it is $25,709 − $7,496 = $18,213; and so on.

3. The Principal Balance on Dec. 31 (Column F) is computed by subtracting the Principal Repayment (Column E) from the Principal Balance on Jan. 1 (Column B). For example, the Principal Balance on Dec. 31 for 2012 is $100,000 − $16,709 = $83,291; on December 31, 2013, the principal balance is $83,291 − $18,213 = $65,078; and so on. The Principal Balance on Dec. 31 (ending balance) for 2012 ($83,291) is also the Principal Balance on Jan. 1 (beginning balance) for 2013; the principal balance on December 31, 2013, is the principal balance on January 1, 2014; and so on.

Although the amounts for interest expense and principal repayment differ each year, the effects of the annual payment on the financial statements are the same. On the balance sheet, assets (cash) decrease by the total amount of the payment; liabilities (note payable) decrease by the amount of the principal repayment; and stockholders' equity (retained earnings) decreases by the amount of interest expense. Net income decreases from recognizing interest expense. On the statement of cash flows, the portion of the cash payment applied to interest is reported in the operating activities section and the portion applied to principal is reported in the financing activities section. The effects on the financial statements are as follows.

	Assets	=	Liab.	+		Equity		Rev.	−	Exp.	=	Net Inc.	Cash Flow	
Date	Cash	=	Note Pay.	+	Com. Stk.	+	Ret. Earn.							
2012 Dec. 31	(25,709)	=	(16,709)	+	NA	+	(9,000)	NA	−	9,000	=	(9,000)	(9,000) OA (16,709) FA	

EXHIBIT 7.4

BLAIR COMPANY
Financial Statements

	2012	2013	2014	2015	2016
Income Statements					
Rent revenue	$12,000	$12,000	$12,000	$12,000	$12,000
Interest expense	(9,000)	(7,496)	(5,857)	(4,070)	(2,123)
Net income	$ 3,000	$ 4,504	$ 6,143	$ 7,930	$ 9,877
Balance Sheets					
Assets					
Cash	$86,291	$72,582	$58,873	$45,164	$31,454
Liabilities					
Note payable	$83,291	$65,078	$45,226	$23,587	$ 0
Stockholders' equity					
Retained earnings	3,000	7,504	13,647	21,577	31,454
Total liabilities and stk. equity	$86,291	$72,582	$58,873	$45,164	$31,454
Statements of Cash Flows					
Operating Activities					
Inflow from customers	$ 12,000	$12,000	$12,000	$12,000	$12,000
Outflow for interest	(9,000)	(7,496)	(5,857)	(4,070)	(2,123)
Investing Activities	0	0	0	0	0
Financing Activities					
Inflow from note issue	100,000	0	0	0	0
Outflow to repay note	(16,709)	(18,213)	(19,852)	(21,639)	(23,587)
Net change in cash	86,291	(13,709)	(13,709)	(13,709)	(13,710)
Plus: Beginning cash balance	0	86,291	72,582	58,873	45,164
Ending cash balance	$ 86,291	$72,582	$58,873	$45,164	$31,454

Exhibit 7.4 displays income statements, balance sheets, and statements of cash flows for Blair Company for the accounting periods 2012 through 2016. The illustration assumes that Blair earned $12,000 of rent revenue each year. Because some of the principal

✓ CHECK YOURSELF 7.3

On January 1, 2011, Krueger Company issued a $50,000 installment note to State Bank. The note had a 10-year term and an 8 percent interest rate. Krueger agreed to repay the principal and interest in 10 annual payments of $7,451.47 at the end of each year. Determine the amount of principal and interest Krueger paid during the first and second year that the note was outstanding.

Answer

Accounting Period	Principal Balance January 1 A	Cash Payment December 31 B	Applied to Interest C = A × 0.08	Applied to Principal B − C
2011	$50,000.00	$7,451.47	$4,000.00	$3,451.47
2012	46,548.53	7,451.47	3,723.88	3,727.59

is repaid each year, the note payable amount reported on the balance sheet and the amount of the interest expense on the income statement both decline each year.

Line of Credit

A **line of credit** enables a company to borrow or repay funds as needed. For example, a business may borrow $50,000 one month and make a partial repayment of $10,000 the next month. Credit agreements usually specify a limit on the amount that can be borrowed. Exhibit 7.5 shows that credit agreements are widely used.

Show how a line of credit affects financial statements.

Interest rates on lines of credit normally vary with fluctuations in some designated interest rate benchmark such as the rate paid on U.S. Treasury bills. For example, a company may pay 4 percent interest one month and 4.5 percent the next month, even if the principal balance remains constant.

Lines of credit typically have one-year terms. Although they are classified on the balance sheet as short-term liabilities, lines of credit are frequently extended indefinitely by simply renewing the credit agreement.

To illustrate accounting for a line of credit, assume Lagoon Company owns a wholesale jet-ski distributorship. In the spring, Lagoon borrows money using a line of credit to finance building up its inventory. Lagoon repays the loan over the summer months using cash generated from jet-ski sales. Borrowing or repaying events occur on the first of the month. Interest payments occur at the end of each month. Exhibit 7.6 presents all 2013 line of credit events.

Each borrowing event (March 1, April 1, and May 1) is an asset source transaction. Both cash and the line of credit liability increase. Each repayment (June 1, July 1, and August 1) is an asset use transaction. Both cash and the line of credit liability decrease. Each month's interest expense recognition and payment is an asset use transaction. Assets (cash) and stockholders' equity (retained earnings) decrease, as does net income. The effects of the events on the financial statements are shown in Exhibit 7.7.

EXHIBIT 7.5

Percentage of U.S. Companies Disclosing Credit Agreements

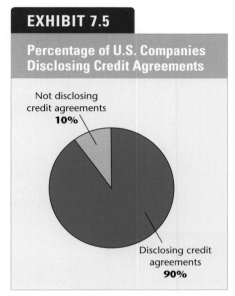

Data source: AICPA, *Accounting Trends and Techniques*, 2006.

EXHIBIT 7.6

Summary of 2013 Line of Credit Events

Date	Amount Borrowed (Repaid)	Loan Balance at End of Month	Effective Interest Rate per Month (%)	Interest Expense (rounded to nearest $1)
Mar. 1	$20,000	$ 20,000	0.09 ÷ 12	$150
Apr. 1	30,000	50,000	0.09 ÷ 12	375
May 1	50,000	100,000	0.105 ÷ 12	875
June 1	(10,000)	90,000	0.10 ÷ 12	750
July 1	(40,000)	50,000	0.09 ÷ 12	375
Aug. 1	(50,000)	0	0.09 ÷ 12	0

Bond Liabilities

Many companies borrow money directly from the public by selling **bond certificates,** otherwise called *issuing* bonds. Bond certificates describe a company's obligation to pay interest and to repay the principal. The seller, or **issuer,** of a bond is the borrower; the buyer of a bond, or **bondholder,** is the lender.

Explain how to account for bonds issued at face value and their related interest costs.

From the issuer's point of view, a bond represents an obligation to pay a sum of money to the bondholder on the bond's maturity date. The amount due at maturity is

EXHIBIT 7.7

Date		Assets	=	Liabilities	+	Equity	Rev.	−	Exp.	=	Net Inc.	Cash Flow	
Mar.	1	20,000	=	20,000	+	NA	NA	−	NA	=	NA	20,000	FA
	31	(150)	=	NA	+	(150)	NA	−	150	=	(150)	(150)	OA
Apr.	1	30,000	=	30,000	+	NA	NA	−	NA	=	NA	30,000	FA
	30	(375)	=	NA	+	(375)	NA	−	375	=	(375)	(375)	OA
May	1	50,000	=	50,000	+	NA	NA	−	NA	=	NA	50,000	FA
	31	(875)	=	NA	+	(875)	NA	−	875	=	(875)	(875)	OA
June	1	(10,000)	=	(10,000)	+	NA	NA	−	NA	=	NA	(10,000)	FA
	30	(750)	=	NA	+	(750)	NA	−	750	=	(750)	(750)	OA
July	1	(40,000)	=	(40,000)	+	NA	NA	−	NA	=	NA	(40,000)	FA
	31	(375)	=	NA	+	(375)	NA	−	375	=	(375)	(375)	OA
Aug.	1	(50,000)	=	(50,000)	+	NA	NA	−	NA	=	NA	(50,000)	FA
	31	NA	=	NA	+	NA	NA	−	NA	=	NA	NA	

the **face value** of the bond. Most bonds also require the issuer to make cash interest payments based on a **stated interest rate** at regular intervals over the life of the bond. Exhibit 7.8 shows a typical bond certificate.

EXHIBIT 7.8

Bond Certificate

Advantages of Issuing Bonds

Bond financing offers companies the following advantages.

1. Bonds usually have longer terms than notes issued to banks. While typical bank loan terms range from 2 to 5 years, bonds normally have 20-year terms to maturity. Longer terms to maturity allow companies to implement long-term strategic plans without having to worry about frequent refinancing arrangements.

2. Bond interest rates may be lower than bank interest rates. Banks earn profits by borrowing money from the public (depositors) at low interest rates, then loaning that money to companies at higher rates. By issuing bonds directly to the public, companies can pay lower interest costs by eliminating the middle man (banks).

Bonds Issued at Face Value

Assume Marsha Mason needs cash in order to seize a business opportunity. Mason knows of a company seeking a plot of land on which to store its inventory of crushed stone. Mason also knows of a suitable tract of land she could purchase for $100,000. The company has agreed to lease the land it needs from Mason for $12,000 per year. Mason lacks the funds to buy the land.

Some of Mason's friends recently complained about the low interest rates banks were paying on certificates of deposit. Mason suggested that her friends invest in bonds instead of CDs. She offered to sell them bonds with a 9 percent stated interest rate. The terms specified in the bond agreement Mason drafted included making interest payments in cash on December 31 of each year, a five-year term to maturity, and pledging the land as collateral for the bonds.[5] Her friends were favorably impressed, and Mason issued the bonds to them in exchange for cash on January 1, 2012.

Mason used the bond proceeds to purchase the land and immediately contracted to lease it for five years. On December 31, 2016, the maturity date of the bonds, Mason sold the land for its $100,000 book value and used the proceeds from the sale to repay the bond liability.

Mason's business venture involved six distinct accounting events.

1. Received $100,000 cash from issuing five-year bonds at face value.
2. Invested proceeds from the bond issue to purchase land for $100,000 cash.
3. Earned $12,000 cash revenue annually from leasing the land.
4. Paid $9,000 annual interest on December 31 of each year.
5. Sold the land for $100,000 cash.
6. Repaid the bond principal to bondholders.

Effect of Events on Financial Statements

EVENT 1   Issue Bonds for Cash
Issuing bonds is an asset source transaction.

Assets (cash) and liabilities (bonds payable) increase. Net income is not affected. The $100,000 cash inflow is reported in the financing activities section of the statement of cash flows. These effects are shown here.

Assets	=	Liab.	+	Equity	Rev.	–	Exp.	=	Net Inc.	Cash Flow
Cash	=	Bonds Pay.								
100,000	=	100,000	+	NA	NA	–	NA	=	NA	100,000 FA

EVENT 2   Investment in Land
Paying $100,000 cash to purchase land is an asset exchange transaction.

The asset cash decreases and the asset land increases. The income statement is not affected. The cash outflow is reported in the investing activities section of the statement of cash flows. These effects are illustrated below.

Assets			=	Liab.	+	Equity	Rev.	–	Exp.	=	Net Inc.	Cash Flow
Cash	+	Land										
(100,000)	+	100,000	=	NA	+	NA	NA	–	NA	=	NA	(100,000) IA

EVENT 3   Revenue Recognition
Recognizing $12,000 cash revenue from renting the property is an asset source transaction.

This event is repeated each year from 2012 through 2016. The event increases assets and stockholders' equity. Recognizing revenue increases net income. The cash inflow is reported in the operating activities section of the statement of cash flows. These effects follow.

Assets	=	Liab.	+	Equity	Rev.	–	Exp.	=	Net Inc.	Cash Flow
Cash	=			Ret. Earn.						
12,000	=	NA	+	12,000	12,000	–	NA	=	12,000	12,000 OA

[5]In practice, bonds are usually issued for much larger sums of money, often hundreds of millions of dollars. Also, terms to maturity are normally long, with 20 years being common. Using such large amounts for such long terms is unnecessarily cumbersome for instructional purposes. The effects of bond issues can be illustrated efficiently by using smaller amounts of debt with shorter maturities, as assumed in the case of Marsha Mason.

EVENT 4   Expense Recognition
Mason's $9,000 ($100,000 × 0.09) cash payment represents interest expense.

This event is also repeated each year from 2012 through 2016. The interest payment is an asset use transaction. Cash and stockholders' equity (retained earnings) decrease. The expense recognition decreases net income. The cash outflow is reported in the operating activities section of the statement of cash flows. These effects follow.

Assets	=	Liab.	+	Equity	Rev.	−	Exp.	=	Net Inc.	Cash Flow
Cash	=			Ret. Earn.						
(9,000)	=	NA	+	(9,000)	NA	−	9,000	=	(9,000)	(9,000) OA

EVENT 5   Sale of Investment in Land
Selling the land for cash equal to its $100,000 book value is an asset exchange transaction.

Cash increases and land decreases. Because there was no gain or loss on the sale, the income statement is not affected. The cash inflow is reported in the investing activities section of the statement of cash flows. These effects follow.

Assets			=	Liab.	+	Equity	Rev.	−	Exp.	=	Net Inc.	Cash Flow
Cash	+	Land										
100,000	+	(100,000)	=	NA	+	NA	NA	−	NA	=	NA	100,000 IA

EVENT 6   Payoff of Bond Liability
Repaying the face value of the bond liability is an asset use transaction.

Cash and bonds payable decrease. The income statement is not affected. The cash outflow is reported in the financing activities section of the statement of cash flows.

Assets	=	Liab.	+	Equity	Rev.	−	Exp.	=	Net Inc.	Cash Flow
Cash	=	Bonds Pay.								
(100,000)	=	(100,000)	+	NA	NA	−	NA	=	NA	(100,000) FA

Financial Statements

Exhibit 7.9 displays Mason Company's financial statements. For simplicity, the income statement does not distinguish between operating and nonoperating items. Rent revenue and interest expense are constant across all accounting periods, so Mason recognizes $3,000 of net income in each accounting period. On the balance sheet, cash increases by $3,000 each year because cash revenue exceeds cash paid for interest. Land remains constant each year at its $100,000 historical cost until it is sold in 2016. Similarly, the bonds payable liability is reported at $100,000 from the date the bonds were issued in 2012 until they are paid off on December 31, 2016.

Compare Blair Company's income statements in Exhibit 7.4 with Mason Company's income statements in Exhibit 7.9. Both Blair and Mason borrowed $100,000 cash at a 9 percent stated interest rate for five-year terms. Blair, however, repaid its liability

EXHIBIT 7.9

Mason Company Financial Statements

Bonds Issued at Face Value

	2012	2013	2014	2015	2016
Income Statements					
Rent revenue	$ 12,000	$ 12,000	$ 12,000	$ 12,000	$ 12,000
Interest expense	(9,000)	(9,000)	(9,000)	(9,000)	(9,000)
Net income	$ 3,000	$ 3,000	$ 3,000	$ 3,000	$ 3,000
Balance Sheets					
Assets					
Cash	$ 3,000	$ 6,000	$ 9,000	$ 12,000	$ 15,000
Land	100,000	100,000	100,000	100,000	0
Total assets	$103,000	$106,000	$109,000	$112,000	$ 15,000
Liabilities					
Bonds payable	$100,000	$100,000	$100,000	$100,000	$ 0
Stockholders' equity					
Retained earnings	3,000	6,000	9,000	12,000	15,000
Total liabilities and stockholders' equity	$103,000	$106,000	$109,000	$112,000	$ 15,000
Statements of Cash Flows					
Operating Activities					
Inflow from customers	$ 12,000	$ 12,000	$ 12,000	$ 12,000	$ 12,000
Outflow for interest	(9,000)	(9,000)	(9,000)	(9,000)	(9,000)
Investing Activities					
Outflow to purchase land	(100,000)				
Inflow from sale of land					100,000
Financing Activities					
Inflow from bond issue	100,000				
Outflow to repay bond liab.					(100,000)
Net change in cash	3,000	3,000	3,000	3,000	3,000
Plus: Beginning cash balance	0	3,000	6,000	9,000	12,000
Ending cash balance	$ 3,000	$ 6,000	$ 9,000	$ 12,000	$ 15,000

under the terms of an installment note while Mason did not repay any principal until the end of the five-year bond term. Because Blair repaid part of the principal balance on the installment loan each year, Blair's interest expense declined each year. The interest expense on Mason's bond liability, however, remained constant because the full principal amount was outstanding for the entire five-year bond term.

Effect of Semiannual Interest Payments

The previous examples assumed that interest payments were made annually. In practice, most bond agreements call for interest to be paid semiannually, which means that interest is paid in cash twice each year. If Marsha Mason's bond certificate had stipulated semiannual interest payments, her company would have paid $4,500 ($100,000 × 0.09 = $9,000 ÷ 2 = $4,500) cash to bondholders for interest on June 30 and December 31 of each year.

AMORTIZATION USING THE STRAIGHT-LINE METHOD

Bonds Issued at a Discount

Use the straight-line method to amortize bond discounts and premiums.

Return to the Mason Company illustration with one change. Assume Mason's bond certificates have a 9 percent stated rate of interest printed on them. Suppose Mason's friends find they can buy bonds from another entrepreneur willing to pay a higher rate of interest. They explain to Mason that business decisions cannot be made on the basis of friendship. Mason provides a counteroffer. There is no time to change the bond certificates, so Mason offers to accept $95,000 for the bonds today and still repay the full face value of $100,000 at the maturity date. The $5,000 difference is called a **bond discount.** Mason's friends agree to buy the bonds for $95,000.

Effective Interest Rate

The bond discount increases the interest Mason must pay. First, Mason must still make the annual cash payments described in the bond agreement. In other words, Mason must pay cash of $9,000 (.09 × $100,000) annually even though she actually borrowed only $95,000. Second, Mason will have to pay back $5,000 more than she received ($100,000 − $95,000). The extra $5,000 (bond discount) is additional interest. Although the $5,000 of additional interest is not paid until maturity, when spread over the life of the bond, it amounts to $1,000 of additional interest expense per year.

   The actual rate of interest that Mason must pay is called the **effective interest rate.** A rough estimate of the effective interest rate for the discounted Mason bonds is 10.5 percent [($9,000 annual stated interest + $1,000 annual amortization of the discount) ÷ $95,000 amount borrowed]. Selling the bonds at a $5,000 discount permits Mason to raise the 9 percent stated rate of interest to an effective rate of roughly 10.5 percent. Deeper discounts would raise the effective rate even higher. More shallow discounts would reduce the effective rate of interest. Mason can set the effective rate of interest to any level desired by adjusting the amount of the discount.

Bond Prices

It is common business practice to use discounts to raise the effective rate of interest above the stated rate. Bonds frequently sell for less than face value. Bond prices are normally expressed *as a percentage of the face value.* For example, Mason's discounted bonds sold for 95, meaning the bonds sold at 95 percent of face value ($100,000 × .95 = $95,000). Amounts of less than 1 percentage point are usually expressed as a fraction. Therefore, a bond priced at 98 3/4 sells for 98.75 percent of face value.

Financial Statement Effects

To illustrate accounting for bonds issued at a discount, return to the Mason Company example using the assumption the bonds are issued for 95 instead of face value. We examine the same six events using this revised assumption. This revision changes some amounts reported on the financial statements. For example, Event 1 in year 2012 reflects receiving only $95,000 cash from the bond issue. Because Mason had only $95,000 available to invest in land, the illustration assumes that Mason acquired a less desirable piece of property which generated only $11,400 of rent revenue per year.

EVENT 1   Bonds with a face value of $100,000 are issued at 95.

Because Mason must pay the face value at maturity, the $100,000 face value of the bonds is recorded in the Bonds Payable account. The $5,000 discount is recorded in a separate contra liability account called **Discount on Bonds Payable.** As shown below, the contra account is subtracted from the face value to determine the **carrying value** (book value) of the bond liability on January 1, 2012.

Bonds payable	$100,000
Less: Discount on bonds payable	(5,000)
Carrying value	$ 95,000

The bond issue is an asset source transaction. Both assets and total liabilities increase by $95,000. Net income is not affected. The cash inflow is reported in the financing activities section of the statement of cash flows. The effects on the financial statements are shown here.

Assets	=	Liabilities	+	Equity	Rev.	–	Exp.	=	Net Inc.	Cash Flow
Cash	=	Carrying Value of Bond Liability	+	Equity						
95,000	=	95,000	+	NA	NA	–	NA	=	NA	95,000 FA

EVENT 2 Paid $95,000 cash to purchase land.

The asset cash decreases and the asset land increases. The income statement is not affected. The cash outflow is reported in the investing activities section of the statement of cash flows. The effects on the financial statements are shown here.

	Assets		=	Liab.	+	Equity	Rev.	–	Exp.	=	Net Inc.	Cash Flow
Cash	+	Land										
(95,000)	+	95,000	=	NA	+	NA	NA	–	NA	=	NA	(95,000) IA

EVENT 3 Recognized $11,400 cash revenue from renting the land.

This event is repeated each year from 2012 through 2016. The event is an asset source transaction that increases assets and stockholders' equity. Recognizing revenue increases net income. The cash inflow is reported in the operating activities section of the statement of cash flows. The effects on the financial statements are shown here.

Assets	=	Liab.	+	Equity	Rev.	–	Exp.	=	Net Inc.	Cash Flow
Cash	=			Ret. Earn.						
11,400	=	NA	+	11,400	11,400	–	NA	=	11,400	11,400 OA

EVENT 4 Recognized interest expense. The interest cost of borrowing has two components: the $9,000 paid in cash each year and the $5,000 discount paid at maturity.

Using **straight-line amortization,** the amount of the discount recognized as expense in each accounting period is $1,000 ($5,000 discount ÷ 5 years). Mason will therefore recognize $10,000 of interest expense each year ($9,000 at the stated interest rate plus

$1,000 amortization of the bond discount). On the balance sheet, the asset cash decreases by $9,000, the carrying value of the bond liability increases by $1,000 (through a decrease in the bond discount), and retained earnings (interest expense) decreases by $10,000. The effects on the financial statements are shown here.

Assets	=	Liabilities	+	Equity	Rev.	−	Exp.	=	Net Inc.	Cash Flow	
Cash	=	Carrying Value of Bond Liability	+	Ret. Earn.							
(9,000)	=	1,000	+	(10,000)	NA	−	10,000	=	(10,000)	(9,000)	OA

EVENT 5   Sold the land for cash equal to its $95,000 book value.

Cash increases and land decreases. Because there was no gain or loss on the sale, the income statement is not affected. The cash inflow is reported in the investing activities section of the statement of cash flows. The effects on the financial statements are shown here.

Assets			=	Liab.	+	Equity	Rev.	−	Exp.	=	Net Inc.	Cash Flow	
Cash	+	Land											
95,000	+	(95,000)	=	NA	+	NA	NA	−	NA	=	NA	95,000	IA

EVENT 6   Paid the bond liability.

Cash and bonds payable decrease. The income statement is not affected. For reporting purposes, the cash outflow is separated into two parts on the statement of cash flows: $95,000 of the cash outflow is reported in the financing activities section because it represents repaying the principal amount borrowed; the remaining $5,000 cash outflow is reported in the operating activities section because it represents the interest arising from issuing the bonds at a discount. In practice, the amount of the discount is frequently immaterial and is combined in the financing activities section with the principal repayment. The effects on the financial statements are shown here.

Assets	=	Liab.	+	Equity	Rev.	−	Exp.	=	Net Inc.	Cash Flow	
Cash	=	Bonds Pay.									
(100,000)	=	(100,000)	+	NA	NA	−	NA	=	NA	(95,000) FA (5,000) OA	

Financial Statements

Exhibit 7.10 displays Mason Company's financial statements assuming the bonds were issued at a discount. Contrast the net income reported in Exhibit 7.10 (bonds issued at a discount) with the net income reported in Exhibit 7.9 (bonds sold at face value). Two factors cause the net income in Exhibit 7.10 to be lower. First, because the bonds were sold at a discount, Mason Company had less money to spend on its land investment. It bought less desirable land which generated less revenue. Second, the effective interest rate was higher than the stated rate, resulting in higher interest expense. Lower revenues coupled with higher expenses result in less profitability.

On the balance sheet, the carrying value of the bond liability increases each year until the maturity date, December 31, 2016, when it is equal to the $100,000 face value of the bonds (the amount Mason is obligated to pay). Because Mason did not pay any

EXHIBIT 7.10

Mason Company Financial Statements

Bonds Issued at a Discount

	2012	2013	2014	2015	2016
Income Statements					
Rent revenue	$ 11,400	$ 11,400	$ 11,400	$ 11,400	$ 11,400
Interest expense	(10,000)	(10,000)	(10,000)	(10,000)	(10,000)
Net income	$ 1,400	$ 1,400	$ 1,400	$ 1,400	$ 1,400
Balance Sheets					
Assets					
Cash	$ 2,400	$ 4,800	$ 7,200	$ 9,600	$ 7,000
Land	95,000	95,000	95,000	95,000	0
Total assets	$ 97,400	$ 99,800	$102,200	$104,600	$ 7,000
Liabilities					
Bonds payable	$100,000	$100,000	$100,000	$100,000	$ 0
Discount on bonds payable	(4,000)	(3,000)	(2,000)	(1,000)	0
Carrying value of bond liab.	96,000	97,000	98,000	99,000	0
Stockholders' equity					
Retained earnings	1,400	2,800	4,200	5,600	7,000
Total liabilities and					
stockholders' equity	$ 97,400	$ 99,800	$102,200	$104,600	$ 7,000
Statements of Cash Flows					
Operating Activities					
Inflow from customers	$ 11,400	$ 11,400	$ 11,400	$ 11,400	$ 11,400
Outflow for interest	(9,000)	(9,000)	(9,000)	(9,000)	(14,000)
Investing Activities					
Outflow to purchase land	(95,000)				
Inflow from sale of land					95,000
Financing Activities					
Inflow from bond issue	95,000				
Outflow to repay bond liab.					(95,000)
Net change in cash	2,400	2,400	2,400	2,400	(2,600)
Plus: Beginning cash balance	0	2,400	4,800	7,200	9,600
Ending cash balance	$ 2,400	$ 4,800	$ 7,200	$ 9,600	$ 7,000

dividends, the retained earnings of $7,000 on December 31, 2016, is equal to the total amount of net income reported over the five-year period ($1,400 × 5). All earnings were retained in the business.

Several factors account for the differences between net income and cash flow. First, although $10,000 of interest expense is reported on each income statement, only $9,000 of cash was paid for interest each year until 2016, when $14,000 was paid for interest ($9,000 based on the stated rate + $5,000 for discount). The $1,000 difference between interest expense and cash paid for interest in 2012, 2013, 2014, and 2015 results from amortizing the bond discount. The cash outflow for the interest related to the discount is included in the $100,000 payment made at maturity on December 31, 2016. Even though $14,000 of cash is paid for interest in 2016, only $10,000 is recognized as interest expense on the income statement that year. Although the total increase in cash over the five-year life of the business ($7,000) is equal to the total net income reported for the same period, there are significant timing differences between when the interest expense is recognized and when the cash outflows occur to pay for it.

CHECK YOURSELF 7.4

On January 1, 2012, Moffett Company issued bonds with a $600,000 face value at 98. The bonds had a 9 percent annual interest rate and a 10-year term. Interest is payable in cash on December 31 of each year. What amount of interest expense will Moffett report on the 2014 income statement? What carrying value for bonds payable will Moffett report on the December 31, 2014, balance sheet?

Answer The bonds were issued at a $12,000 ($600,000 × 0.02) discount. The discount will be amortized over the 10-year life at the rate of $1,200 ($12,000 ÷ 10 years) per year. The amount of interest expense for 2014 is $55,200 ($600,000 × .09 = $54,000 annual cash interest + $1,200 discount amortization).

The carrying value of the bond liability is equal to the face value less the unamortized discount. By the end of 2014, $3,600 of the discount will have been amortized ($1,200 × 3 years = $3,600). The unamortized discount as of December 31, 2014, will be $8,400 ($12,000 − $3,600). The carrying value of the bond liability as of December 31, 2014, will be $591,600 ($600,000 − $8,400).

Bonds Issued at a Premium

When bonds are sold for more than their face value, the difference between the amount received and the face value is called a **bond premium.** Bond premiums reduce the effective interest rate. For example, assume Mason Company issued its 9 percent bonds at 105, receiving $105,000 cash on the issue date. The company is still only required to repay the $100,000 face value of the bonds at the maturity date. The $5,000 difference between the amount received and the amount repaid at maturity reduces the total amount of interest expense. The premium is recorded in a separate liability account called **Premium on Bonds Payable.** This account is reported on the balance sheet as an addition to Bonds Payable, increasing the carrying value of the bond liability. On the issue date, the bond liability would be reported on the balance sheet as follows:

Bonds payable	$100,000
Plus: Premium on bonds payable	5,000
Carrying value	$105,000

The entire $105,000 cash inflow is reported in the financing activities section of the statement of cash flows even though the $5,000 premium is conceptually an operating activities cash flow because it pertains to interest. In practice, premiums are usually so small they are immaterial and the entire cash inflow is normally classified as a financing activity. The effects on the financial statements are shown here.

	Assets	=	Liabilities	+	Equity	Rev.	−	Exp.	=	Net Inc.	Cash Flow
Date	Cash	=	Carrying Value of Bond Liability								
Jan. 1	105,000	=	105,000	+	NA	NA	−	NA	=	NA	105,000 FA
Dec. 31	(9,000)		(1,000)		(8,000)			8,000		(8,000)	9,000 OA

The Market Rate of Interest

When a bond is issued, the effective interest rate is determined by current market conditions. Market conditions are influenced by many factors such as the state of the economy, government policy, and the law of supply and demand. These conditions are collectively reflected in the **market interest rate.** The *effective rate of interest* investors are willing to accept *for a particular bond* equals the *market rate of interest* for other investments with similar levels of risk at the time the bond is issued. When the market rate of interest is higher than the stated rate of interest, bonds will sell at a discount so as to increase the effective rate of interest to the market rate. When the market rate is lower than the stated rate, bonds will sell at a premium so as to reduce the effective rate to the market rate.

SECURITY FOR LOAN AGREEMENTS

In general, large loans with long terms to maturity pose more risk to lenders (creditors) than small loans with short terms. To reduce the risk that they won't get paid, lenders frequently require borrowers (debtors) to pledge designated assets as **collateral** for loans. For example, when a bank makes a car loan, it usually retains legal title to the car until the loan is fully repaid. If the borrower fails to make the monthly payments, the bank repossesses the car, sells it to someone else, and uses the proceeds to pay the original owner's debt. Similarly, assets like accounts receivable, inventory, equipment, buildings, and land may be pledged as collateral for business loans.

In addition to requiring collateral, creditors often obtain additional protection by including **restrictive covenants** in loan agreements. Such covenants may restrict additional borrowing, limit dividend payments, or restrict salary increases. If the loan restrictions are violated, the borrower is in default and the loan balance is due immediately.

Finally, creditors often ask key personnel to provide copies of their personal tax returns and financial statements. The financial condition of key executives is important because they may be asked to pledge personal property as collateral for business loans, particularly for small businesses.

CURRENT VERSUS NONCURRENT

Because meeting obligations on time is critical to business survival, financial analysts and creditors are interested in whether companies will have enough money available to pay bills when they are due. Most businesses provide information about their bill-paying ability by classifying their assets and liabilities according to liquidity. The more quickly an asset is converted to cash or consumed, the more *liquid* it is. Assets are usually divided into two major classifications: *current* and *noncurrent*. Current items are also referred to as *short term* and noncurrent items as *long term*.

A **current (short-term) asset** is expected to be converted to cash or consumed within one year or an operating cycle, whichever is longer. An **operating cycle** is defined as the average time it takes a business to convert cash to inventory, inventory to accounts receivable, and accounts receivable back to cash. For most businesses, the operating cycle is less than one year. As a result, the one-year rule normally prevails with respect to classifying assets as current. The current assets section of a balance sheet typically includes the following items.

> Current Assets
>   Cash
>   Marketable securities
>   Accounts receivable
>   Short-term notes receivable
>   Interest receivable
>   Inventory
>   Supplies
>   Prepaid items

LO 9

Distinguish between current and noncurrent assets and liabilities.

Given the definition of current assets, it seems reasonable to assume that **current (short-term) liabilities** would be those due within one year or an operating cycle, whichever is longer. This assumption is usually correct. However, an exception is made for long-term renewable debt. For example, consider a liability that was issued with a 20-year term to maturity. After 19 years, the liability becomes due within one year and is, therefore, a current liability. Even so, the liability will be classified as long term if the company plans to issue new long-term debt and to use the proceeds from that debt to repay the maturing liability. This situation is described as *refinancing short-term debt on a long-term basis.* In general, if a business does not plan to use any of its current assets to repay a debt, that debt is listed as long term even if it is due within one year. The current liabilities section of a balance sheet typically includes the following items.

LO 10

Prepare a classified balance sheet.

> Current Liabilities
>   Accounts payable
>   Short-term notes payable
>   Wages payable
>   Taxes payable
>   Interest payable

Balance sheets that distinguish between current and noncurrent items are called **classified balance sheets.** To enhance the usefulness of accounting information, most real-world balance sheets are classified. Exhibit 7.11 displays an example of a classified balance sheet.

EXHIBIT 7.11

LIMBAUGH COMPANY
Classified Balance Sheet
As of December 31, 2012

Assets

Current Assets			
Cash		$ 20,000	
Accounts receivable		35,000	
Inventory		230,000	
Prepaid rent		3,600	
Total current assets			$288,600
Property, Plant, and Equipment			
Office equipment	$ 80,000		
Less: Accumulated depreciation	(25,000)	55,000	
Building	340,000		
Less: Accumulated depreciation	(40,000)	300,000	
Land		120,000	
Total property, plant, and equipment			475,000
Total assets			$763,600

Liabilities and Stockholders' Equity

Current Liabilities			
Accounts payable		$ 32,000	
Notes payable		120,000	
Salaries payable		32,000	
Unearned revenue		9,800	
Total current liabilities			$193,800
Long-Term Liabilities			
Note payable			100,000
Total liabilities			293,800
Stockholders' Equity			
Common stock		200,000	
Retained earnings		269,800	469,800
Total liabilities and stockholders' equity			$763,600

FOCUS ON INTERNATIONAL ISSUES

As discussed in earlier chapters, most industrialized countries require companies to use international financial accounting standards (IFRS), which are similar to the GAAP used in the United States. The globalization of accounting standards should, therefore, make it easier to read a company's annual report regardless of its country or origin. However, there are still language differences between companies; German companies prepare their financial reports using IFRS, but in German, while the UK companies use English.

Suppose language is not an issue. For example companies in the United States, England, and even India, prepare their annual reports in English. Thus, one would expect to find few differences between financial reports prepared by companies in these countries. However, if a person who learned accounting in the United States looks at the balance sheet of a U.K. company he or she might think the statement is a bit "backwards," and if he or she reviews the balance sheet of an Indian company they may find it to be upside down.

Like U.S. companies, U.K. companies report assets at the top, or left, of the balance sheet, and liabilities and stockholders' equity on the bottom or right. However, unlike the United States, U.K. companies typically show long-term assets before current assets. Even more different are balance sheets of Indian companies, which begin with stockholders' equity and then liabilities at the top or left, and then show assets on the bottom or right. Like the U.K. statements, those in India show long-term assets before current assets. Realize that most of the accounting rules established by IFRS or U.S. GAAP deal with measurement issues. Assets can be measured using the same rules, but be disclosed in different manners. IFRS require companies to classify assets and liabilities as current versus noncurrent, but the order in which these categories are listed on the balance sheet is not specified.

For an example of financial statement for a U.K. company, go to www.itvplc.com. Click on "Investors" and then "Reports and accounts." For an example of an Indian company's annual report, go to www.tatamotors.com. Click on "Investors Centre," then "Reports & Filings," and then "Annual Reports."

A Look Back

Chapter 7 discussed accounting for current liabilities and long-term debt. Current liabilities are obligations due within one year or the company's operating cycle, whichever is longer. The chapter expanded the discussion of promissory notes begun in Chapter 5. Chapter 5 introduced accounting for the note payee, the lender; Chapter 7 discussed accounting for the note maker (issuer), the borrower. Notes payable and related interest payable are reported as liabilities on the balance sheet. Chapter 7 also discussed accounting for the contingent liability and warranty obligations.

Long-term notes payable mature in two to five years and usually require payments that include a return of principal plus interest. *Lines of credit* enable companies to borrow limited amounts on an as-needed basis. Although lines of credit normally have one-year terms, companies frequently renew them, extending the effective maturity date to the intermediate range of five or more years. Interest on a line of credit is normally paid monthly. Long-term debt financing for more than 10 years usually requires issuing *bonds*.

>> A Look Forward

A company seeking long-term financing might choose to use debt, such as the types of bonds or term loans that were discussed in this chapter. Owners' equity is another source of long-term financing. Several equity alternatives are available, depending on the type of business organization the owners choose to establish. For example, a company could be organized as a sole proprietorship, partnership, or corporation. Chapter 8 presents accounting issues related to equity transactions for each of these types of business structures.

APPENDIX

Amortization Using the Effective Interest Rate Method

Use the effective interest rate method to amortize bond discounts and premiums.

To this point we have demonstrated the straight-line method for amortizing bond discounts and premiums. While this method is easy to understand, it is inaccurate because it does not show the correct amount of interest expense incurred during each accounting period. To illustrate, return to the case of Mason Company demonstrated in Exhibit 7.10 (page 259). Recall that the exhibit shows the effects of accounting for a $100,000 face value bond with a 9 percent stated rate of interest that was issued at a price of 95. The carrying value of the bond liability on the January 1, 2012, issue date was $95,000. The bond discount was amortized using the straight-line method.

Recall that the straight-line method amortizes the discount equally over the life of the bond. Specifically, there is a $5,000 discount which is amortized over a 5-year life resulting in a $1,000 amortization per year. As the discount is amortized the bond liability (carrying value of the bond) increases. Specifically, the carrying value of the bond liability shown in Exhibit 7.10 increases as follows:

Accounting Period	2012	2013	2014	2015
Carrying value as of December 31	$96,000	$97,000	$98,000	$99,000

While the carrying value of the bond liability increases steadily, the straight-line method recognizes the same amount of interest expense ($9,000 stated rate of interest + $1,000 discount amortization = $10,000 interest expense) per year. This straight-line recognition pattern is irrational because the amount of interest expense recognized should increase as the carrying value of the bond liability increases. A more accurate recognition pattern can be accomplished by using an approach called the **effective interest rate method.**

Amortizing Bond Discounts

The effective interest rate is determined by the price that the buyer of a bond is willing to pay on the issue date. In the case of Mason Company the issue price of $95,000 for bonds with a $100,000 face value, a 9 percent stated rate of interest, and a 5-year term produces an effective interest rate of approximately 10.33 percent.[6] Since the effective interest rate is based on the market price of the bonds on the day of issue, it is sometimes called *the market rate of interest.*

Interest recognition under the effective interest method is accomplished as follows:

1. Determine the cash payment for interest by multiplying the stated rate of interest times the face value of the bonds.

---

[6]In practice the effective rate of interest is calculated using software programs, interest formulas, or interest tables.

EXHIBIT 7.12

Amortization Schedule for Bond Discount

	(A) Cash Payment	(B) Interest Expense	(C) Discount Amortization	(D) Carrying Value
January 1, 2012				$ 95,000
December 31, 2012	$ 9,000	$ 9,814	$ 814	95,814
December 31, 2013	9,000	9,898	898	96,712
December 31, 2014	9,000	9,990	990	97,702
December 31, 2015	9,000	10,093	1,093	98,795
December 31, 2016	9,000	10,205	1,205	100,000
Totals	$45,000	$50,000	$5,000	

(A) Stated rate of interest times the face value of the bonds ($100,000 × .09).
(B) Effective interest rate times the carrying value at the beginning of the period. For the 2012 accounting period the amount is $9,814 ($95,000 × .1033).
(C) Interest Expense − Cash Payment. For 2012 the discount amortization is $814 ($9,814 − $9,000 = $814).
(D) Carrying value at beginning of period plus portion of discount amortized. For the accounting period ending December 31, 2012, the amount is $95,814 ($95,000 + $814).

2. Determine the amount of interest expense by multiplying the effective rate of interest times the carrying value of the bond liability.

3. Determine the amount of the amortization of the bond discount by subtracting the cash payment from the interest expense.

4. Update the carrying value of the liability by adding the amount of the discount amortization to the amount of the carrying value at the beginning of the accounting period.

Applying these procedures to the Mason Company illustration produces the amortization schedule shown in Exhibit 7.12.

The recognition of interest expense at the end of each accounting period has the following effects on the financial statements. On the balance sheet, assets decrease, liabilities increase, and retained earnings decrease. On the income statement, expenses increase and net income decreases. There is a cash outflow in the operating activities of the statement of cash flows. The effects on the financial statements are shown here.

Assets	=	Liabilities	+	Equity	Rev.	−	Exp.	=	Net Inc.	Cash Flow
Cash	=	Carrying Value of Bond Liab.	+	Ret. Earn.						
(9,000)	=	814	+	(9,814)	NA	−	9,814	=	(9,814)	(9,000) OA

Exhibit 7.13 shows the financial statements for Mason Company for 2012 through 2016. The statements assume the same events as described as those used to construct Exhibit 7.10 (page 259). These events are summarized below:

1. Mason issues a $100,000 face value bond with a 9 percent stated rate of interest. The bond has a 5-year term and is issued at a price of 95. Annual interest is paid with cash on December 31 of each year.

2. Mason uses the proceeds from the bond issue to purchase land.

3. Leasing the land produces rent revenue of $11,400 cash per year.

4. On the maturity date of the bond, the land is sold and the proceeds from the sale are used to repay the bond liability.

EXHIBIT 7.13

Financial Statements

Under the Assumption that Bonds Are Issued at a Discount

	2012	2013	2014	2015	2016
Income Statements					
Rent revenue	$ 11,400	$ 11,400	$ 11,400	$ 11,400	$ 11,400
Interest expense	(9,814)	(9,898)	(9,990)	(10,093)	(10,205)
Net income	$ 1,586	$ 1,502	$ 1,410	$ 1,307	$ 1,195
Balance Sheets					
Assets:					
Cash	$ 2,400	$ 4,800	$ 7,200	$ 9,600	$ 7,000
Land	95,000	95,000	95,000	95,000	0
Total assets	$ 97,400	$ 99,800	$102,200	$104,600	$ 7,000
Liabilities					
Bond payable	$100,000	$100,000	$100,000	$100,000	$ 0
Discount on bonds payable	(4,186)	(3,288)	(2,298)	(1,205)	0
Carrying value of bond liab.	95,814	96,712	97,702	98,795	0
Equity					
Retained earnings	1,586	3,088	4,498	5,805	7,000
Total liabilities and equity	$ 97,400	$ 99,800	$102,200	$104,600	$ 7,000
Statements of Cash Flows					
Operating Activities					
Inflow from customers	$ 11,400	$ 11,400	$ 11,400	$ 11,400	$ 11,400
Outflow for interest	(9,000)	(9,000)	(9,000)	(9,000)	(14,000)
Investing Activities					
Outflow to purchase land	(95,000)				
Inflow from sale of land					95,000
Financing Activities					
Inflow from bond issue	95,000				
Outflow to repay bond liab.					(95,000)
Net change in cash	2,400	2,400	4,800	7,200	(2,600)
Beginning cash balance	0	2,400	2,400	2,400	9,600
Ending cash balance	$ 2,400	$ 4,800	$ 7,200	$ 9,600	$ 7,000

The only difference between the two exhibits is that Exhibit 7.10 was constructed assuming that the bond discount was amortized using the straight-line method while Exhibit 7.13 assumes that the discount was amortized using the effective interest rate method.

Notice that interest expense under the effective interest rate method (Exhibit 7.13) increases each year while interest expense under the straight-line method (Exhibit 7.10, page 259) remains constant for all years. This result occurs because the effective interest rate method amortizes increasingly larger amounts of the discount (see Column C of Exhibit 7.12) as the carrying value of the bond liability increases. In contrast, the straight-line method amortized the bond discount at a constant rate of $1,000 per year over the life of the bond. Even so, total amount of interest expense recognized over the life of the bond is the same ($50,000) under both methods. Since the effective interest rate method matches the interest expense with the carrying value of the bond liability,

EXHIBIT 7.14

Amortization Schedule for Bond Premium

	(A) Cash Payment	(B) Interest Expense	(C) Premium Amortization	(D) Carrying Value
January 1, 2012				$107,985
December 31, 2012	$10,000	$ 8,639	$1,361	106,624
December 31, 2013	10,000	8,530	1,470	105,154
December 31, 2014	10,000	8,413	1,587	103,567
December 31, 2015	10,000	8,285	1,715	101,852
December 31, 2016	10,000	8,148	1,852	100,000
Totals	$50,000	$42,015	$7,985	

(A) Stated rate of interest times the face value of the bonds ($100,000 × .10).
(B) Effective interest times the carrying value at the beginning of the period. For the 2012 accounting period the amount is $8,639 ($107,985 × .08).
(C) Cash Payment − Interest Expense. For 2012 the premium amortization is $1,361 ($10,000 − $8,639 = $1,361).
(D) Carrying value at beginning of period minus the portion of premium amortized. For the accounting period ending December 31, 2012, the amount is $106,624 ($107,985 − 1,361).

it is the theoretically preferred approach. Indeed, accounting standards require the use of the effective interest rate method when the differences between it and the straight-line method are material.

The amortization of the discount affects the carrying value of the bond as well as the amount of interest expense. Under the effective interest method the rate of growth of the carrying value of the bond increases as the maturity date approaches. In contrast, under the straight-line method the rate of growth of the carrying value of the bond remains constant at $1,000 per year throughout the life of the bond.

Finally, notice that cash flow is not affected by the method of amortization. The exact same cash flow consequences occur under both the straight-line (Exhibit 7.10) and the effective interest rate method (Exhibit 7.13).

Amortizing Bond Premiums

Bond premiums can also be amortized using the effective interest rate method. To illustrate, assume United Company issued a $100,000 face value bond with a 10 percent stated rate of interest. The bond had a 5-year term. The bond was issued at a price of $107,985. The effective rate of interest is 8 percent. United's accountant prepared the amortization schedule shown in Exhibit 7.14.

The recognition of interest expense at the end of each accounting period has the following effects on the financial statements. On the balance sheet assets decrease, liabilities decrease, and retained earnings decrease. On the income statement expenses increase and net income decreases. There is a cash outflow in the operating activities of the statement of cash flows. The effects on the financial statements are shown here.

Assets	=	Liabilities	+	Equity	Rev.	−	Exp.	=	Net Inc.	Cash Flow	
Cash	=	Carrying Value of Bond Liab.	+	Ret. Earn.							
(10,000)	=	(1,361)	+	(8,639)	NA	−	8,639	=	(8,639)	(8,639)	OA
										(1,361)	FA

A step-by-step audio-narrated series of slides is provided on the text website at www.mhhe.com/edmondssurvey3e.

SELF-STUDY REVIEW PROBLEM

Perfect Picture Inc. (PPI) experienced the following transactions during 2012. The transactions are summarized (transaction data pertain to the full year) and limited to those that affect the company's current liabilities.

1. PPI had cash sales of $820,000. The state requires that PPI charge customers an 8 percent sales tax (ignore cost of goods sold).
2. PPI paid the state sales tax authority $63,000.
3. On March 1, PPI issued a note payable to the County Bank. PPI received $50,000 cash (principal balance). The note had a one-year term and a 6 percent annual interest rate.
4. On December 31, PPI recognized accrued interest on the note issued in Event 3.
5. On December 31, PPI recognized warranty expense at the rate of 3 percent of sales.
6. PPI paid $22,000 cash to settle warranty claims.
7. On January 1, 2011, PPI issued a $100,000 installment note. The note had a 10-year term and an 8 percent interest rate. PPI agreed to repay the principal and interest in 10 annual interest payments of $14,902.94 at the end of each year.

Required

Prepare the liabilities section of the December 31, 2012, balance sheet.

Solution

PERFECT PICTURE INC.
Partial Balance Sheet
December 31, 2012

Current Liabilities	
Sales tax payable	$ 2,600
Notes payable	50,000
Interest payable	2,500
Warranties payable	2,600
Installment note payable	85,642
Total liabilities	$143,342

Explanations for amounts shown in the balance sheet:

1. Sales Tax Payable: $820,000 × 0.08 = $65,600 Amount Due − $63,000 Amount Paid = $2,600 Liability as of December 31, 2012.
2. Note Payable: $50,000 Borrowed with no repayment.
3. Interest Payable: $50,000 × 0.06 × 10/12 = $2,500.
4. Warranty Payable: $820,000 × 0.03 = $24,600 Estimated Warranty Liability − $22,000 Cash Paid to Settle Warranty Claims = $2,600 Remaining Liability.
5. Installment Note Payable:

Accounting Period	Principal Bal. January 1 A	Cash Payment December 31 B	Applied to Interest C = A × 0.08	Applied to Principal B − C
2011	$100,000.00	$14,902.94	$8,000.00	$6,902.94
2012	93,097.06	14,902.94	7,447.76	7,455.18
2013*	85,641.88			

*The amount due on December 31, 2012, is the same as the amount due on January 1, 2013. The amount shown on the balance sheet has been rounded to the nearest dollar.

KEY TERMS

Amortization 248
Bond certificates 251
Bond discount 256
Bond premium 260
Bondholder 251
Carrying value 257
Classified balance sheets 262
Collateral 261
Contingent liability 244
Current (short-term) asset 261
Current (short-term) liabilities 261

Discount on Bonds Payable 256
Effective interest rate 256
Effective interest rate method 264
Face value 252
Fixed interest rate 247
General uncertainties 244
Going concern assumption 240
Installment notes 248
Issuer 242, 251
Line of credit 251

Long-term liabilities 247
Market Interest rate 260
Note payable 242
Operating cycle 261
Premium on Bonds Payable 260
Restrictive covenants 261
Stated interest rate 252
Straight-line amortization 257
Variable interest rate 247
Warranties 245

QUESTIONS

1. What type of transaction is a cash payment to creditors? How does this type of transaction affect the accounting equation?

2. What is a current liability? Distinguish between a current liability and a long-term debt.

3. How does recording accrued interest affect the accounting equation?

4. Who is the maker of a note payable?

5. What is the going concern assumption? Does it affect the way liabilities are reported in the financial statements?

6. Why is it necessary to make an adjustment at the end of the accounting period for unpaid interest on a note payable?

7. Assume that on October 1, 2012, Big Company borrowed $10,000 from the local bank at 6 percent interest. The note is due on October 1, 2013. How much interest does Big pay in 2012? How much interest does Big pay in 2013? What amount of cash does Big pay back in 2013?

8. When a business collects sales tax from customers, is it revenue? Why or why not?

9. What is a contingent liability?

10. List the three categories of contingent liabilities.

11. Are contingent liabilities recorded on a company's books? Explain.

12. What is the difference in accounting procedures for a liability that is probable and estimable and one that is reasonably possible but not estimable?

13. What type of liabilities are not recorded on a company's books?

14. What does the term *warranty* mean?

15. What effect does recognizing future warranty obligations have on the balance sheet? On the income statement?

16. When is warranty cost reported on the statement of cash flows?

17. What is the difference between classification of a note as short term or long term?

18. At the beginning of year 1, B Co. has a note payable of $72,000 that calls for an annual payment of $16,246, which includes both principal and interest. If the interest rate is 8 percent, what is the amount of interest expense in year 1 and in year 2? What is the balance of the note at the end of year 2?

19. What is the purpose of a line of credit for a business? Why would a company choose to obtain a line of credit instead of issuing bonds?

20. What are the primary sources of debt financing for most large companies?

21. What are some advantages of issuing bonds versus borrowing from a bank?

22. What are some disadvantages of issuing bonds?

23. Why can a company usually issue bonds at a lower interest rate than the company would pay if the funds were borrowed from a bank?

24. If Roc Co. issued $100,000 of 5 percent, 10-year bonds at the face amount, what is the effect of the issuance of the bonds on the financial statements? What amount of interest expense will Roc Co. recognize each year?

25. What mechanism is used to adjust the stated interest rate to the market rate of interest?

26. When the effective interest rate is higher than the stated interest rate on a bond issue, will the bond sell at a discount or premium? Why?

27. What type of transaction is the issuance of bonds by a company?

28. What factors may cause the effective interest rate and the stated interest rate to be different?

29. If a bond is selling at 97 ½, how much cash will the company receive from the sale of a $1,000 bond?

30. How is the carrying value of a bond computed?

31. Gay Co. has a balance in the Bonds Payable account of $25,000 and a balance in the Discount on Bonds Payable account of $5,200. What is the carrying value of the bonds? What is the total amount of the liability?

32. When the effective interest rate is higher than the stated interest rate, will interest expense be higher or lower than the amount of interest paid?

33. What is a classified balance sheet?

MULTIPLE-CHOICE QUESTIONS

Multiple-choice questions are provided on the text website at www.mhhe.com/edmondssurvey3e

EXERCISES

All applicable Exercises are available with McGraw-Hill's *Connect Accounting*.

LO 1

Exercise 7-1   *Recognizing accrued interest expense*

Classic Corporation borrowed $90,000 from the bank on November 1, 2012. The note had an 8 percent annual rate of interest and matured on April 30, 2013. Interest and principal were paid in cash on the maturity date.

Required

a. What amount of interest expense was paid in cash in 2012?

b. What amount of interest expense was reported on the 2012 income statement?

c. What amount of total liabilities was reported on the December 31, 2012, balance sheet?

d. What total amount of cash was paid to the bank on April 30, 2013, for principal and interest?

e. What amount of interest expense was reported on the 2013 income statement?

LO 1

Exercise 7-2   *Effects of recognizing accrued interest on financial statements*

Scott Perkins started Perkins Company on January 1, 2012. The company experienced the following events during its first year of operation.

1. Earned $1,500 of cash revenue for performing services.

2. Borrowed $2,400 cash from the bank.

3. Adjusted the accounting records to recognize accrued interest expense on the bank note. The note, issued on August 1, 2012, had a one-year term and a 7 percent annual interest rate.

Required

a. What is the amount of interest expense in 2012?

b. What amount of cash was paid for interest in 2012?

c. Use a horizontal statements model to show how each event affects the balance sheet, income statement, and statement of cash flows. Indicate whether the event increases (I), decreases (D), or does not affect (NA) each element of the financial statements. In the Cash Flows column, designate the cash flows as operating activities (OA), investing activities (IA), or financing activities (FA). The first transaction has been recorded as an example.

Event No.	Balance Sheet										Income Statement					Statement of Cash Flows
	Cash	=	Notes Pay.	+	Int. Pay.	+	Com. Stk.	+	Ret. Earn.		Rev.	−	Exp.	=	Net Inc.	
1	I	=	NA	+	NA	+	NA	+	I		I	−	NA	=	I	I OA

Exercise 7-3 *Recording sales tax expense*   LO 2

The University Book Store sells books and other supplies to students in a state where the sales tax rate is 7 percent. The University Book Store engaged in the following transactions for 2012. Sales tax of 7 percent is collected on all sales.

1. Book sales, not including sales tax, for 2012 amounted to $275,000 cash.
2. Cash sales of miscellaneous items in 2012 were $150,000, not including tax.
3. Cost of goods sold amounted to $210,000 for the year.
4. Paid $130,000 in operating expenses for the year.
5. Paid the sales tax collected to the state agency.

Required

a. What is the total amount of sales tax the University Book Store collected and paid for the year?
b. What is the University Book Store's net income for the year?

Exercise 7-4 *Recognizing sales tax payable*   LO 2

The following selected transactions apply to Big Stop for November and December 2012. November was the first month of operations. Sales tax is collected at the time of sale but is not paid to the state sales tax agency until the following month.

1. Cash sales for November 2012 were $65,000 plus sales tax of 8 percent.
2. Big Stop paid the November sales tax to the state agency on December 10, 2012.
3. Cash sales for December 2012 were $80,000 plus sales tax of 8 percent.

Required

a. Show the effect of the above transactions on a statements model like the one shown below.

Assets	=	Liabilities	+	Equity		Income Statement		
Cash	=	Sales Tax Pay.	+	Com. Stk. + Ret. Earn.		Rev. − Exp. = Net Inc.		Cash Flow

b. What was the total amount of sales tax paid in 2012?
c. What was the total amount of sales tax collected in 2012?
d. What is the amount of the sales tax liability as of December 31, 2012?
e. On which financial statement will the sales tax liability appear?

Exercise 7-5 *Contingent liabilities*   LO 3

The following legal situations apply to Stringer Corp. for 2012:

1. A customer slipped and fell on a slick floor while shopping in the retail store. The customer has filed a $5 million lawsuit against the company. Stringer's attorney knows that the company will have to pay some damages but is reasonably certain that the suit can be settled for $500,000.
2. The EPA has assessed a fine against Stringer of $250,000 for hazardous emissions from one of its manufacturing plants. The EPA had previously issued a warning to Stringer and required Stringer to make repairs within six months. Stringer began to make the repairs, but was not able to complete them within the six-month period. Because Stringer has started the repairs, Stringer's attorney thinks the fine will be reduced to $100,000. He is approximately 80 percent certain that he can negotiate the fine reduction because of the repair work that has been completed.
3. One of Stringer's largest manufacturing facilities is located in "tornado alley." Property is routinely damaged by storms. Stringer estimates it may have property damage of as much as $300,000 this coming year.

Required

a. Discuss the various categories of contingent liabilities.
b. For each item above determine the correct accounting treatment.

LO 4

Exercise 7-6   *Effect of warranties on income and cash flow*

To support herself while attending school, Ellen Abba sold stereo systems to other students. During the first year of operation, she sold systems that had cost her $120,000 cash for $226,000 cash. She provided her customers with a one-year warranty against defects in parts. Based on industry standards, she estimated that warranty claims would amount to 5 percent of sales. During the year she paid $920 cash to replace a defective tuner.

Required

a. Prepare an income statement and a statement of cash flows for Abba's first year of operation.
b. Explain the difference between net income and the amount of cash flow from operating activities.

LO 4

Exercise 7-7   *Effect of warranty obligations and payments on financial statements*

The Ja-San Company provides a 120-day parts-and-labor warranty on all merchandise it sells. Ja-San estimates the warranty expense for the current period to be $1,250. During the period a customer returned a product that cost $920 to repair.

Required

a. Show the effects of these transactions on the financial statements using a horizontal statements model like the example shown here. Use a + to indicate increase, a − for decrease, and NA for not affected. In the Cash Flow column, indicate whether the item is an operating activity (OA), investing activity (IA), or financing activity (FA).

Assets	=	Liab.	+	Equity	Rev.	−	Exp.	=	Net Inc.	Cash Flow

b. Discuss the advantage of estimating the amount of warranty expense.

LO 2, 4, 9

Exercise 7-8   *Current liabilities*

The following transactions apply to Mabry Equipment Sales Corp. for 2012:

1. The business was started when Mabry Corp. received $50,000 from the issue of common stock.
2. Purchased $175,000 of merchandise on account.
3. Sold merchandise for $200,000 cash (not including sales tax). Sales tax of 8 percent is collected when the merchandise is sold. The merchandise had a cost of $125,000.
4. Provided a six-month warranty on the merchandise sold. Based on industry estimates, the warranty claims would amount to 4 percent of merchandise sales.
5. Paid the sales tax to the state agency on $150,000 of the sales.
6. On September 1, 2012, borrowed $20,000 from the local bank. The note had a 6 percent interest rate and matures on March 1, 2013.
7. Paid $5,600 for warranty repairs during the year.
8. Paid operating expenses of $54,000 for the year.
9. Paid $125,000 of accounts payable.
10. Recorded accrued interest at the end of the year.

Required

a. Record the above transactions in a horizontal statements model like the following one.

	Balance Sheet									Income Statement			Statemt. of Cash Flows
Event	Assets	=	Liabilities					+	Equity	Rev. − Exp. = Net Inc.			
	Cash + Mdse. Inv.		Acct. Pay. +	Sales Tax Pay. +	War. Pay. +	Int. Pay. +	Notes Pay. +		Com. Stock + Ret. Earn.				

b. Prepare the income statement, balance sheet, and statement of cash flows for 2012.

c. What is the total amount of current liabilities at December 31, 2012?

Exercise 7-9 *How credit terms affect financial statements*

LO 5

Miller Co. is planning to finance an expansion of its operations by borrowing $200,000. State Bank has agreed to loan Miller the funds. Miller has two repayment options: (1) to issue a note with the principal due in 10 years and with interest payable annually or (2) to issue a note to repay $20,000 of the principal each year along with the annual interest based on the unpaid principal balance. Assume the interest rate is 6 percent for each option.

Required

a. What amount of interest will Miller pay in year 1
  (1) Under option 1?
  (2) Under option 2?

b. What amount of interest will Miller pay in year 2
  (1) Under option 1?
  (2) Under option 2?

c. Explain the advantage of each option.

Exercise 7-10 *Amortization schedule for an installment note*

LO 5

On January 1, 2012, Rupp Co. borrowed $150,000 cash from Central Bank by issuing a five-year, 8 percent note. The principal and interest are to be paid by making annual payments in the amount of $37,568. Payments are to be made December 31 of each year, beginning December 31, 2012.

Required

Prepare an amortization schedule for the interest and principal payments for the five-year period.

Exercise 7-11 *Financial statement effects of an installment note*

LO 5

Fred Blan started a business by issuing a $70,000 face value note to First State Bank on January 1, 2012. The note had a 7 percent annual rate of interest and a five-year term. Payments of $17,072 are to be made each December 31 for five years.

Required

a. What portion of the December 31, 2012, payment is applied to
  (1) Interest expense?
  (2) Principal?

b. What is the principal balance on January 1, 2013?

c. What portion of the December 31, 2013, payment is applied to
  (1) Interest expense?
  (2) Principal?

Exercise 7-12 *Amortization of a long-term loan*

LO 5

A partial amortization schedule for a ten-year note payable that Muro Co. issued on January 1, 2012, is shown here:

Accounting Period	Principal Balance January 1	Cash Payment	Applied to Interest	Applied to Principal
2012	$200,000	$32,549	$20,000	$12,549
2013	187,451	32,549	18,745	13,804

Required

a. What rate of interest is Muro Co. paying on the note?
b. Using a financial statements model like the one shown below, record the appropriate amounts for the following two events.
   (1) January 1, 2012, issue of the note payable.
   (2) December 31, 2012, payment on the note payable.

Event No.	Assets	=	Liab.	+	Equity	Rev.	−	Exp.	=	Net Inc.	Cash Flow
1											

c. If the company earned $75,000 cash revenue and paid $35,000 in cash expenses in addition to the interest in 2012, what is the amount of each of the following?
   (1) Net income for 2012.
   (2) Cash flow from operating activities for 2012.
   (3) Cash flow from financing activities for 2012.
d. What is the amount of interest expense on this loan for 2014?

LO 6

Exercise 7-13 *Effect of a line of credit on financial statements*

Song Company has a line of credit with State Bank. Song can borrow up to $200,000 at any time over the course of the 2012 calendar year. The following table shows the prime rate expressed as an annual percentage along with the amounts borrowed and repaid during 2012. Song agreed to pay interest at an annual rate equal to 2 percent above the bank's prime rate. Funds are borrowed or repaid on the first day of each month. Interest is payable in cash on the last day of the month. The interest rate is applied to the outstanding monthly balance. For example, Song pays 7 percent (5 percent + 2 percent) annual interest on $100,000 for the month of January.

Month	Amount Borrowed or (Repaid)	Prime Rate for the Month, %
January	$100,000	5
February	50,000	6
March	(40,000)	7
April through October	No change	No change
November	(80,000)	6
December	(20,000)	5

Required

Show the effects of these transactions on the financial statements using a horizontal statements model like the one shown here. Use a + to indicate increase, a − for decrease, and NA for not affected. In the Cash Flow column, indicate whether the item is an operating activity (OA), investing activity (IA), or financing activity (FA).

Assets	=	Liabilities	+	Equity	Rev.	−	Exp.	=	Net Inc.	Cash Flow

What is the total amount of interest expense paid for 2012?

LO 7

Exercise 7-14 *Two complete accounting cycles: bonds issued at face value with annual interest*

Polledo Company issued $350,000 of 20-year, 6 percent bonds on January 1, 2012. The bonds were issued at face value. Interest is payable in cash on December 31 of each year. Polledo immediately invested the proceeds from the bond issue in land. The land was leased for an annual $56,000 of cash revenue, which was collected on December 31 of each year, beginning December 31, 2012.

Required

a. Organize the transaction data in accounts under the accounting equation.

b. Prepare the income statement, balance sheet, and statement of cash flows for 2012 and 2013.

Exercise 7-15   *Annual versus semiannual interest for bonds issued at face value*   LO 7

Nash Co. issued bonds with a face value of $120,000 on January 1, 2012. The bonds had a 6 percent stated rate of interest and a five-year term. The bonds were issued at face value.

Required

a. What total amount of interest will Nash pay in 2012 if bond interest is paid annually each December 31?

b. What total amount of interest will Nash pay in 2012 if bond interest is paid semiannually each June 30 and December 31?

c. Write a memo explaining which option Nash would prefer.

Exercise 7-16   *Determining cash receipts from bond issues*   LO 8

Required

Compute the cash proceeds from bond issues under the following terms. For each case, indicate whether the bonds sold at a premium or discount.

a. Pro, Inc., issued $300,000 of 8-year, 7 percent bonds at 101.

b. Sim Co. issued $150,000 of 4-year, 6 percent bonds at 98.

c. Chu Co. issued $200,000 of 10-year, 7 percent bonds at 102 ¼.

d. Sing, Inc., issued $100,000 of 5-year, 6 percent bonds at 97 ½.

Exercise 7-17   *Stated rate of interest versus the market rate of interest*   LO 8

Required

Indicate whether a bond will sell at a premium (P), discount (D), or face value (F) for each of the following conditions:

a. _____ The market rate of interest is equal to the stated rate.

b. _____ The market rate of interest is less than the stated rate.

c. _____ The market rate of interest is higher than the stated rate.

d. _____ The stated rate of interest is higher than the market rate.

e. _____ The stated rate of interest is less than the market rate.

Exercise 7-18   *Identifying bond premiums and discounts*   LO 8

Required

In each of the following situations, state whether the bonds will sell at a premium or discount.

a. Stokes issued $200,000 of bonds with a stated interest rate of 8 percent. At the time of issue, the market rate of interest for similar investments was 7 percent.

b. Shaw issued $100,000 of bonds with a stated interest rate of 8 percent. At the time of issue, the market rate of interest for similar investments was 9 percent.

c. Link, Inc., issued callable bonds with a stated interest rate of 8 percent. The bonds were callable at 101. At the date of issue, the market rate of interest was 9 percent for similar investments.

Exercise 7-19   *Determining the amount of bond premiums and discounts*   LO 8

Required

For each of the following situations, calculate the amount of bond discount or premium, if any.

a. Best Co. issued $110,000 of 6 percent bonds at 102.

b. Morris, Inc., issued $60,000 of 10-year, 8 percent bonds at 98.

c. Yang, Inc., issued $100,000 of 15-year, 9 percent bonds at 102 ¼.

d. Jones Co. issued $500,000 of 20-year, 8 percent bonds at 98 ¾.

LO 8

Exercise 7-20 *Straight-line amortization of a bond discount*

Sanders Company issued $200,000 face value of bonds on January 1, 2012. The bonds had a 6 percent stated rate of interest and a 10-year term. Interest is paid in cash annually, beginning December 31, 2012. The bonds were issued at 98.

Required

a. Use a financial statements model like the one shown below to demonstrate how (1) the January 1, 2012, bond issue and (2) the December 31, 2012, recognition of interest expense, including the amortization of the discount and the cash payment, affects the company's financial statements. Use + for increase, − for decrease, and NA for not affected.

Event No.	Assets	=	Liab.	+	Equity	Rev.	−	Exp.	=	Net Inc.	Cash Flow
1											

b. Determine the amount of interest expense reported on the 2012 income statement.

c. Determine the carrying value (face value less discount or plus premium) of the bond liability as of December 31, 2012.

d. Determine the amount of interest expense reported on the 2013 income statement.

e. Determine the carrying value (face value less discount or plus premium) of the bond liability as of December 31, 2013.

LO 8

Exercise 7-21 *Straight-line amortization of a bond premium*

High Company issued $100,000 face value of bonds on January 1, 2012. The bonds had a 5 percent stated rate of interest and a 10-year term. Interest is paid in cash annually, beginning December 31, 2012. The bonds were issued at 102.

Required

a. Use a financial statements model like the one shown below to demonstrate how (1) the January 1, 2012 bond issue and (2) the December 31, 2012 recognition of interest expense, including the amortization of the premium and the cash payment, affects the company's financial statements. Use + for increase, − for decrease, and NA for not affected.

Event No.	Assets	=	Liab.	+	Equity	Rev.	−	Exp.	=	Net Inc.	Cash Flow
1											

b. Determine the carrying value (face value less discount or plus premium) of the bond liability as of December 31, 2012.

c. Determine the amount of interest expense reported on the 2012 income statement.

d. Determine the carrying value of the bond liability as of December 31, 2013.

e. Determine the amount of interest expense reported on the 2013 income statement.

LO 10

Exercise 7-22 *Preparing a classified balance sheet*

Required

Use the following information to prepare a classified balance sheet for Steller Co. at the end of 2012.

Accounts receivable	$42,500
Accounts payable	8,000
Cash	15,260
Common stock	42,000
Long-term notes payable	23,000
Merchandise inventory	29,000
Office equipment	28,500
Retained earnings	45,460
Prepaid insurance	3,200

Exercise 7-23 *Effective interest amortization of a bond discount*

LO 11

On January 1, 2012, Sea View Condo Association issued bonds with a face value of $200,000, a stated rate of interest of 8 percent, and a 10-year term to maturity. Interest is payable in cash on December 31 of each year. The effective rate of interest was 10 percent at the time the bonds were issued. The bonds sold for $175,442. Sea View used the effective interest rate method to amortize bond discount.

Required

a. Determine the amount of the discount on the day of issue.
b. Determine the amount of interest expense recognized on December 31, 2012.
c. Determine the carrying value of the bond liability on December 31, 2012.

Exercise 7-24 *Effective interest amortization of a bond discount*

LO 11

On January 1, 2012, Woodland Enterprises issued bonds with a face value of $50,000, a stated rate of interest of 8 percent, and a five-year term to maturity. Interest is payable in cash on December 31 of each year. The effective rate of interest was 10 percent at the time the bonds were issued. The bonds sold for $46,209. Woodland used the effective interest rate method to amortize bond discount.

Required

a. Prepare an amortization table as shown below:

	Cash Payment	Interest Expense	Discount Amortization	Carrying Value
January 1, 2012				46,209
December 31, 2012	4,000	4,621	621	46,830
December 31, 2013	?	?	?	?
December 31, 2014	?	?	?	?
December 31, 2015	?	?	?	?
December 31, 2016	?	?	?	?
Totals	20,000	23,791	3,791	

b. What item(s) in the table would appear on the 2013 balance sheet?
c. What item(s) in the table would appear on the 2013 income statement?
d. What item(s) in the table would appear on the 2013 statement of cash flows?

Exercise 7-25 *Effective interest versus straight-line amortization*

LO 11

On January 1, 2012, Smith and Associates issued bonds with a face value of $1,000,000, a stated rate of interest of 9 percent, and a 20-year term to maturity. Interest is payable in cash on December 31 of each year. The effective rate of interest was 11 percent at the time the bonds were issued.

Required

Write a brief memo explaining whether the effective interest rate method or the straight-line method will produce the highest amount of interest expense recognized on the 2012 income statement.

PROBLEMS

All applicable Problems are available with McGraw-Hill's *Connect Accounting.*

Problem 7-26 *Accounting for short-term debt and sales tax—two accounting cycles*

LO 1, 2, 3, 4

The following transactions apply to Artesia Co. for 2012, its first year of operations.

CHECK FIGURE
Net Income 2012: $46,500

1. Received $40,000 cash from the issue of a short-term note with a 5 percent interest rate and a one-year maturity. The note was issued on April 1, 2012.

2. Received $120,000 cash plus applicable sales tax from performing services. The services are subject to a sales tax rate of 6 percent.

3. Paid $72,000 cash for other operating expenses during the year.

4. Paid the sales tax due on $100,000 of the service revenue for the year. Sales tax on the balance of the revenue is not due until 2013.

5. Recognized the accrued interest at December 31, 2012.

The following transactions apply to Artesia Co. for 2013.

1. Paid the balance of the sales tax due for 2012.

2. Received $145,000 cash plus applicable sales tax from performing services. The services are subject to a sales tax rate of 6 percent.

3. Repaid the principal of the note and applicable interest on April 1, 2013.

4. Paid $85,000 of other operating expenses during the year.

5. Paid the sales tax due on $120,000 of the service revenue. The sales tax on the balance of the revenue is not due until 2014.

Required

a. Organize the transaction data in accounts under an accounting equation.

b. Prepare an income statement, a statement of changes in stockholders' equity, a balance sheet, and a statement of cash flow for 2012 and 2013.

LO 1

CHECK FIGURES
b. $12,000
i. $38,800

Problem 7-27   *Effect of accrued interest on financial statements*

Norman Co. borrowed $15,000 from the local bank on April 1, 2012, when the company was started. The note had an 8 percent annual interest rate and a one-year term to maturity. Norman Co. recognized $42,000 of revenue on account in 2012 and $56,000 of revenue on account in 2013. Cash collections from accounts receivable were $38,000 in 2012 and $58,000 in 2013. Norman Co. paid $26,000 of salaries expense in 2012 and $32,000 of salaries expense in 2013. Norman Co. paid the loan and interest at the maturity date.

Required

a. Organize the information in accounts under an accounting equation.

b. What amount of net cash flow from operating activities would be reported on the 2012 cash flow statement?

c. What amount of interest expense would be reported on the 2012 income statement?

d. What amount of total liabilities would be reported on the December 31, 2012, balance sheet?

e. What amount of retained earnings would be reported on the December 31, 2012, balance sheet?

f. What amount of cash flow from financing activities would be reported on the 2012 statement of cash flows?

g. What amount of interest expense would be reported on the 2013 income statement?

h. What amount of cash flows from operating activities would be reported on the 2013 cash flow statement?

i. What amount of assets would be reported on the December 31, 2013, balance sheet?

LO 1, 2, 4

CHECK FIGURE
Total Current Liabilities: $44,050

Problem 7-28   *Current liabilities*

The following selected transactions were taken from the books of Caledonia Company for 2012.

1. On March 1, 2012, borrowed $50,000 cash from the local bank. The note had a 6 percent interest rate and was due on September 1, 2012.

2. Cash sales for the year amounted to $225,000 plus sales tax at the rate of 7 percent.

3. Caledonia provides a 90-day warranty on the merchandise sold. The warranty expense is estimated to be 2 percent of sales.

4. Paid the sales tax to the state sales tax agency on $190,000 of the sales.

5. Paid the note due on September 1 and the related interest.

6. On October 1, 2012, borrowed $40,000 cash from the local bank. The note had a 7 percent interest rate and a one-year term to maturity.

7. Paid $3,600 in warranty repairs.

8. A customer has filed a lawsuit against Caledonia for $100,000 for breach of contract. The company attorney does not believe the suit has merit.

Required

a. Answer the following questions:

   (1) What amount of cash did Caledonia pay for interest during the year?

   (2) What amount of interest expense is reported on Caledonia's income statement for the year?

   (3) What is the amount of warranty expense for the year?

b. Prepare the current liabilities section of the balance sheet at December 31, 2012.

c. Show the effect of these transactions on the financial statements using a horizontal statements model like the one shown here. Use a + to indicate increase, a − for decrease, and NA for not affected. In the Cash Flow column, indicate whether the item is an operating activity (OA), investing activity (IA), or financing activity (FA). The first transaction is recorded as an example.

Assets	=	Liabilities	+	Equity	Rev.	−	Exp.	=	Net Inc.	Cash Flow
+		+		NA	NA		NA		NA	+ FA

Problem 7-29 *Contingent liabilities*

LO 3

Required

a. Give an example of a contingent liability that is probable and reasonably estimable. How would this type of liability be shown in the accounting records?

b. Give an example of a contingent liability that is reasonably possible or probable but not reasonably estimable. How would this type of liability be shown in the accounting records?

c. Give an example of a contingent liability that is remote. How is this type of liability shown in the accounting records?

Problem 7-30 *Multistep income statement and classified balance sheet*

LO 10

e**X**cel

Required

Use the following information to prepare a multistep income statement and a classified balance sheet for Douglas Company for 2012. (*Hint:* Some of the items will *not* appear on either statement, and ending retained earnings must be calculated.)

Other operating expenses	$ 90,000	Cash	$ 23,000
Land	50,000	Interest receivable (short term)	800
Accumulated depreciation	38,000	Cash flow from investing activities	102,000
Accounts payable	60,000	Allowance for doubtful accounts	7,000
Unearned revenue	58,000	Interest payable (short term)	3,000
Warranties payable (short term)	2,000	Sales revenue	500,000
Equipment	77,000	Uncollectible accounts expense	14,000
Notes payable (long term)	129,000	Interest expense	32,000
Salvage value of equipment	7,000	Accounts receivable	113,000
Dividends	12,000	Salaries payable	12,000
Warranty expense	5,000	Supplies	3,000
Beginning retained earnings	28,800	Prepaid rent	14,000
Interest revenue	6,000	Common stock	52,000
Gain on sale of equipment	10,000	Cost of goods sold	179,000
Inventory	154,000	Salaries expense	122,000
Notes receivable (short term)	17,000		

CHECK FIGURES
Total Current Assets: $317,800
Total Current Liabilities: $135,000

LO 5

Problem 7-31   *Effect of an installment note on financial statements*

On January 1, 2012, Sneed Co. borrowed cash from Best Bank by issuing a $100,000 face value, four-year term note that had a 10 percent annual interest rate. The note is to be repaid by making annual cash payments of $31,547 that include both interest and principal on December 31 of each year. Sneed used the proceeds from the loan to purchase land that generated rental revenues of $40,000 cash per year.

Required

a. Prepare an amortization schedule for the four-year period.
b. Organize the information in accounts under an accounting equation.
c. Prepare an income statement, a balance sheet, and a statement of cash flows for each of the four years.
d. Does cash outflow from operating activities remain constant or change each year? Explain.

LO 5

Problem 7-32   *Accounting for an installment note payable*

The following transactions apply to Whitter Co. for 2012, its first year of operations.

1. Received $100,000 cash in exchange for issuance of common stock.
2. Secured a $200,000, 10-year installment loan from First Bank. The interest rate was 6 percent and annual payments are $27,174.
3. Purchased land for $60,000.
4. Provided services for $120,000 cash.
5. Paid other operating expenses of $85,000.
6. Paid the annual payment on the loan.

Required

a. Organize the transaction data in accounts under an accounting equation.
b. Prepare an income statement and balance sheet for 2012.
c. What is the interest expense for 2013? 2014?

LO 6

Problem 7-33   *Accounting for a line of credit*

Acqua Marine Co. uses a line of credit to help finance its inventory purchases. Acqua Marine sells boats and equipment and uses the line of credit to build inventory for its peak sales months, which tend to be clustered in the summer months. Account balances at the beginning of 2012 were as follows.

Cash	$100,000
Inventory	125,000
Common stock	150,000
Retained earnings	75,000

Acqua Marine experienced the following transactions for April, May, and June, 2012.

1. April 1, 2012, obtained approval for a line of credit of up to $500,000. Funds are to be obtained or repaid on the first day of each month. The interest rate is the bank prime rate plus 1 percent.
2. April 1, 2012, borrowed $160,000 on the line of credit. The bank's prime interest rate is 5 percent for January.
3. April 15, purchased inventory on account, $130,000.
4. April 31, paid other operating expenses of $46,000.
5. In April, sold inventory for $275,000 on account. The inventory had cost $150,000.
6. April 30, paid the interest due on the line of credit.
7. May 1, borrowed $120,000 on the line of credit. The bank's prime rate is 6 percent for May.
8. May 1, paid the accounts payable from transaction 3.

9. May 10, collected $262,000 of the sales on account.

10. May 20, purchased inventory on account, $215,000.

11. May sales on account were $375,000. The inventory had cost $180,000.

12. May 31, paid the interest due on the line of credit.

13. June 1, repaid $80,000 on the line of credit. The bank's prime rate is 6 percent for June.

14. June 5, paid $200,000 of the accounts payable.

15. June 10, collected $380,000 from accounts receivable.

16. June 20, purchased inventory on account, $195,000.

17. June sales on account were $415,000. The inventory had cost $170,000.

18. June 31, paid the interest due on the line of credit.

Required

a. What is the amount of interest expense for April? May? June?

b. What amount of cash was paid for interest in April? May? June?

Problem 7-34 *Effect of a line of credit on financial statements*

LO 6

Inman Company has a line of credit with Bay Bank. Inman can borrow up to $300,000 at any time over the course of the 2012 calendar year. The following table shows the prime rate expressed as an annual percentage along with the amounts borrowed and repaid during 2012. Inman agreed to pay interest at an annual rate equal to 1 percent above the bank's prime rate. Funds are borrowed or repaid on the first day of each month. Interest is payable in cash on the last day of the month. The interest rate is applied to the outstanding monthly balance. For example, Inman pays 6 percent (5 percent + 1 percent) annual interest on $90,000 for the month of January.

CHECK FIGURES
b. Interest Expense: $7,111
Total Assets: $98,889

Month	Amount Borrowed or (Repaid)	Prime Rate for the Month, %
January	$90,000	5
February	50,000	5
March	(30,000)	6
April through October	No change	No change
November	(20,000)	6
December	(30,000)	5

Inman earned $46,000 of cash revenue during 2012.

Required

a. Organize the information in accounts under an accounting equation.

b. Prepare an income statement, balance sheet, and statement of cash flows for 2012.

c. Write a memo discussing the advantages to a business of arranging a line of credit.

Problem 7-35 *Effect of debt transactions on financial statements*

LO 1, 6, 7

Required

Show the effect of each of the following independent accounting events on the financial statements using a horizontal statements model like the following one. Use + for increase, − for decrease, and NA for not affected. The first event is recorded as an example.

Event No.	Assets	=	Liab.	+	Equity	Rev.	−	Exp.	=	Net Inc.	Cash Flow
a	+		+		NA	NA		NA		NA	+ FA

a. Borrowed funds using a line of credit.

b. Made an interest payment for funds that had been borrowed against a line of credit.

c. Issued a bond at face value.

d. Made an interest payment on a bond that had been issued at face value.

e. Made a cash payment on a note payable for both interest and principal.

LO 8

Problem 7-36   *Straight-line amortization of a bond discount*

Hale Co. was formed when it acquired cash from the issue of common stock. The company then issued bonds at a discount on January 1, 2012. Interest is payable on December 31 with the first payment made December 31, 2012. On January 2, 2012, Hale Co. purchased a piece of land that produced rent revenue annually. The rent is collected on December 31 of each year, beginning December 31, 2012. At the end of the six-year period (January 1, 2018), the land was sold at a gain, and the bonds were paid off at face value. A summary of the transactions for each year follows:

2012

1. Acquired cash from the issue of common stock.
2. Issued six-year bonds.
3. Purchased land.
4. Received land rental income.
5. Recognized interest expense, including the amortization of the discount, and made the cash payment for interest on December 31.

2013–2017

6. Received land rental income.
7. Recognized interest expense, including the amortization of the discount, and made the cash payment for interest December 31.

2018

8. Sold the land at a gain.
9. Retired the bonds at face value.

Required

Identify each of these 9 transactions as asset source (AS), asset use (AU), asset exchange (AE), or claims exchange (CE). Explain how each event affects assets, liabilities, equity, net income, and cash flow by placing a + for increase, − for decrease, or NA for not affected under each of the categories. In the Cash Flow column, indicate whether the item is an operating activity (OA), investing activity (IA), or financing activity (FA). The first event is recorded as an example.

Event No.	Type of Event	Assets	=	Liabilities	+	Common Stock	+	Retained Earnings	Net Income	Cash Flow
1	AS	+		NA		+		NA	NA	+ FA

LO 8

CHECK FIGURES
c. 2012 Interest Expense: $6,250
d. 2012 Interest Paid: $3,500

Problem 7-37   *Straight-line amortization of a bond discount*

During 2012 and 2013, Gupta Co. completed the following transactions relating to its bond issue. The company's fiscal year ends on December 31.

2012

Mar. 1   Issued $100,000 of eight-year, 7 percent bonds for $96,000. The semiannual cash payment for interest is due on March 1 and September 1, beginning September 2012.

Sept. 1   Recognized interest expense including the amortization of the discount and made the semiannual cash payment for interest.

Dec. 31   Recognized accrued interest expense including the amortization of the discount.

2013

Mar. 1   Recognized interest expense including the amortization of the discount and made the semiannual cash payment for interest.

Sept. 1   Recognized interest expense including the amortization of the discount and made the semiannual cash payment for interest.

Dec. 31   Recognized accrued interest expense including the amortization of the discount.

Required

a. When the bonds were issued, was the market rate of interest more or less than the stated rate of interest? If the bonds had sold at face value, what amount of cash would Gupta Co. have received?

b. Prepare the liabilities section of the balance sheet at December 31, 2012 and 2013.

c. Determine the amount of interest expense Gupta would report on the income statements for 2012 and 2013.

d. Determine the amount of interest Gupta would pay to the bondholders in 2012 and 2013.

Exercise 7-38   *Effective interest amortization for a bond premium*   **LO 11**

On January 1, 2012, Crume Incorporated issued bonds with a face value of $100,000, a stated rate of interest of 9 percent, and a five-year term to maturity. Interest is payable in cash on December 31 of each year. The effective rate of interest was 8 percent at the time the bonds were issued. The bonds sold for $103,993. Crume used the effective interest rate method to amortize bond discount.

Required

a. Prepare an amortization table as shown below:

	Cash Payment	Interest Expense	Premium Amortization	Carrying Value
January 1, 2012				103,993
December 31, 2012	9,000	8,319	681	103,312
December 31, 2013	?	?	?	?
December 31, 2014	?	?	?	?
December 31, 2015	?	?	?	?
December 31, 2016	?	?	?	?
Totals	45,000	41,007	3,993	

b. What item(s) in the table would appear on the 2014 balance sheet?

c. What item(s) in the table would appear on the 2014 income statement?

d. What item(s) in the table would appear on the 2014 statement of cash flows?

ANALYZE, THINK, COMMUNICATE

ATC 7-1   Business Application Case   *Understanding real-world annual reports*

Use the Target Corporation's annual report in Appendix B to answer the following questions related to Target's 2009 fiscal year. You will need to read carefully the company's Consolidated Statements of Financial Position (balance sheets) as well as footnotes 16 through 19.

Target Corporation

Required

a. What percentage of Target's assets was being financed with liabilities (versus shareholders' equity)?

b. How does Target account for bank overdrafts, and how much overdrafts did it have as of January 30, 2010?

c. What was the average interest rate that Target paid on its borrowings?

d. Target reported Accrued and Other Liabilities of $3,120 as of January 30, 2010. What was the largest subcategory of liabilities included in this account?

ATC 7-2 Group Assignment *Missing information*

The following three companies issued the following bonds:

1. Lot, Inc., issued $100,000 of 8 percent, five-year bonds at 102 ¼ on January 1, 2012. Interest is payable annually on December 31.
2. Max, Inc., issued $100,000 of 8 percent, five-year bonds at 98 on January 1, 2012. Interest is payable annually on December 31.
3. Par, Inc., issued $100,000 of 8 percent, five-year bonds at 104 on January 1, 2012. Interest is payable annually on December 31.

Required

a. Organize the class into three sections and divide each section into groups of three to five students. Assign each of the sections one of the companies.

Group Tasks

(1) Compute the following amounts for your company (use straight-line amortization):
    (a) Cash proceeds from the bond issue.
    (b) Interest paid in 2012.
    (c) Interest expense for 2012.
(2) Prepare the liabilities section of the balance sheet as of December 31, 2012.

Class Discussion

b. Have a representative of each section put the liabilities section for its company on the board.
c. Is the amount of interest expense different for the three companies? Why or why not?
d. Is the amount of interest paid different for each of the companies? Why or why not?
e. Is the amount of total liabilities different for each of the companies? Why or why not?

ATC 7-3 Research Assignment *Analyzing two real-world companies' use of liabilities*

Complete the requirements below using the most current annual reports or the Forms 10-K for Lowe's, a company that sells home-building supplies, and Dominion Resources, one of the nation's leading generators of energy. To obtain the Forms 10-K, use either the EDGAR system following the instructions in Appendix A or the companies' websites. The annual reports can be found on the companies' websites.

Required

a. Which of these two companies is using debt to finance its assets the most? Show your computations.
b. Provide a logical explanation as to why one of these companies uses more debt to finance its assets than the other.
c. Lowe's has some lines of credit type arrangements? How much money is available to Lowe's under these credit arrangements?

ATC 7-4 Writing Assignment *Definition of elements of financial statements*

Putting "yum" on people's faces around the world is the mission of YUM Brands, Inc. Yum was spun off from PepsiCo in 1997. A spin-off occurs when a company separates its operations into two or more distinct companies. The company was originally composed of KFC, Pizza Hut, and Taco Bell and was operated as a part of PepsiCo prior to the spin-off. In 2002 YUM acquired A & W All American Foods and Long John Silver's units. YUM's long-term debt in 2007 was $2.9 billion. YUM's net income before interest and taxes in 2007 was $1.36 million.

Required

a. If YUM's debt remains constant at $2.9 billion for 2008, how much interest will YUM incur in 2008, assuming the average interest rate is 6 percent?
b. Does the debt seem excessive compared with the amount of 2007 net income before interest and taxes? Explain.

c. Assuming YUM pays tax at the rate of 25 percent, what amount of tax will YUM pay in 2007?

d. Assume you are the president of the company. Write a memo to the shareholders explaining how YUM is able to meet its obligations and increase stockholders' equity.

ATC 7-5   Ethical Dilemma   *Sometimes debt is not debt*

David Sheridan was a well-respected CPA in his mid-fifties. After spending 10 years at a national accounting firm, he was hired by Global, Inc., a multinational corporation headquartered in the United States. He patiently worked his way up to the top of Global's accounting department and in the early 1990s, took over as chief financial officer for the company. As the Internet began to explode, management at Global, Inc., decided to radically change the nature of its business to one of e-commerce. Two years after the transition, Internet commerce began to slow down, and Global was in dire need of cash in order to continue operations. Management turned to the accounting department.

Global, Inc., needed to borrow a substantial amount of money but couldn't afford to increase the amount of liabilities on the balance sheet for fear of the stock price dropping and banks becoming nervous and demanding repayment of existing loans. David discovered a way that would allow the company to raise the needed cash to continue operations without having to report the long-term notes payable on the balance sheet. Under an obscure rule, companies can set up separate legal organizations that do not have to be reported on the parent company's financial statements, if a third party contributes just 3 percent of the start-up capital. David called a friend, Brian Johnson, and asked him to participate in a business venture with Global. Brian agreed, and created a special purpose entity with Global named BrianCo. For his participation, Brian was awarded a substantial amount of valuable Global stock. Brian then went to a bank and used the stock as collateral to borrow a large sum of money for BrianCo. Then, Global sold some of its poor or underperforming assets to BrianCo for the cash that Brian borrowed. In the end, Global got rid of bad assets, received the proceeds of the long-term note payable, and did not have to show the liability on the balance sheet. Only the top executives and the accountants that worked closely with David knew of the scheme, and they planned to use this method only until the e-commerce portion of Global became profitable again.

Required

a. How did David's scheme affect the overall appearance of Global's financial statements? Why was this important to investors and creditors?

b. Review the AICPA's Articles of Professional Conduct (see Chapter 4) and comment on any of the standards that have been violated.

c. Name the features of the fraud triangle and explain how they materialize in this case.

CHAPTER 8

Proprietorships, Partnerships, and Corporations

LEARNING OBJECTIVES

After you have mastered the material in this chapter, you will be able to:

1 Identify the primary characteristics of sole proprietorships, partnerships, and corporations.

2 Analyze financial statements to identify the different types of business organizations.

3 Explain the characteristics of major types of stock issued by corporations.

4 Explain how to account for different types of stock issued by corporations.

5 Show how treasury stock transactions affect a company's financial statements.

6 Explain the effects of declaring and paying cash dividends on a company's financial statements.

7 Explain the effects of stock dividends and stock splits on a company's financial statements.

8 Show how the appropriation of retained earnings affects financial statements.

9 Explain some uses of accounting information in making stock investment decisions.

CHAPTER OPENING

You want to start a business. How should you structure it? Should it be a sole proprietorship, partnership, or corporation? Each form of business structure presents advantages and disadvantages. For example, a sole proprietorship allows maximum independence and control while partnerships and corporations allow individuals to pool resources and talents with other people. This chapter discusses these and other features of the three primary forms of business structure.

The Curious Accountant

Imagine your rich uncle rewarded you for doing well in your first accounting course by giving you $10,000 to invest in the stock of one company. After reviewing many recent annual reports, you narrowed your choice to two companies with the following characteristics:

Mystery Company A: This company began operations in 2003, but did not begin selling its stock to the public until April 16, 2009. In its first six years of operations it had total earnings of approximately $1.6 million. By the time it went public it was already a leader in its field. At its current price of $23 you could buy approximately 435 shares. A friend told you that a globally minded person like you would be crazy not to buy this stock.

Mystery Company B: This company has been in existence since 1837 and has made a profit most years. In the most recent five years, its net earnings totaled over $51.8 *billion*, and it paid dividends of over $21 *billion*. This stock is selling for about $62 per share, so you can buy 161 shares of it. Your friend said "you would have to be goofy to buy this stock."

The names of the real-world companies described above are disclosed later. Based on the information provided, which company's stock would you buy? (Answer on page 290.)

FORMS OF BUSINESS ORGANIZATIONS

Identify the primary characteristics of sole proprietorships, partnerships, and corporations.

Sole proprietorships are owned by a single individual who is responsible for making business and profit distribution decisions. If you want to be the absolute master of your destiny, you should organize your business as a proprietorship. Establishing a sole proprietorship is usually as simple as obtaining a business license from local government authorities. Usually no legal ownership agreement is required.

Partnerships allow persons to share their talents, capital, and the risks and rewards of business ownership. Because two or more individuals share ownership, partnerships require clear agreements about how authority, risks, and profits will be shared. Prudent partners minimize misunderstandings by hiring attorneys to prepare a **partnership agreement** which defines the responsibilities of each partner and describes how income or losses will be divided. Because the measurement of income affects the distribution of profits, partnerships frequently hire accountants to ensure that records are maintained in accordance with generally accepted accounting principles (GAAP). Partnerships (and sole proprietorships) also may need professional advice to deal with tax issues.

A **corporation** is a separate legal entity created by the authority of a state government. The paperwork to start a corporation is complex. For most laypersons, engaging professional attorneys and accountants to assist with the paperwork is well worth the fees charged.

Each state has separate laws governing establishing corporations. Many states follow the standard provisions of the Model Business Corporation Act. All states require the initial application to provide **articles of incorporation** which normally include the following information: (1) the corporation's name and proposed date of incorporation; (2) the purpose of the corporation; (3) the location of the business and its expected life (which can be *perpetuity,* meaning *endless*); (4) provisions for capital stock; and (5) the names and addresses of the members of the first board of directors, the individuals with the ultimate authority for operating the business. If the articles are in order, the state establishes the legal existence of the corporation by issuing a charter of incorporation. The charter and the articles are public documents.

ADVANTAGES AND DISADVANTAGES OF DIFFERENT FORMS OF BUSINESS ORGANIZATION

Each form of business organization presents a different combination of advantages and disadvantages. Persons wanting to start a business or invest in one should consider the characteristics of each type of business structure.

Regulation

Few laws specifically affect the operations of proprietorships and partnerships. Corporations, however, are usually heavily regulated. The extent of government regulation depends on the size and distribution of a company's ownership interests. Ownership interests in corporations are normally evidenced by **stock certificates.**

Ownership of corporations can be transferred from one individual to another through exchanging stock certificates. As long as the exchanges (buying and selling of shares of stock, often called *trading*) are limited to transactions between individuals, a company is defined as a **closely held corporation.** However, once a corporation reaches a certain size, it may list its stock on a stock exchange such as the New York Stock Exchange or the American Stock Exchange. Trading on a stock exchange is limited to the stockbrokers who are members of the exchange. These brokers represent buyers and sellers who are willing to pay the brokers commissions for exchanging stock certificates on their behalf. Although closely held corporations are relatively free from government regulation, companies whose stock is publicly traded on the exchanges by brokers are subject to extensive regulation.

The extensive regulation of trading on stock exchanges began in the 1930s. The stock market crash of 1929 and the subsequent Great Depression led Congress to pass the **Securities Act of 1933** and the **Securities Exchange Act of 1934** to regulate issuing stock and to govern the exchanges. The 1934 act also created the Securities and Exchange Commission (SEC) to enforce the securities laws. Congress gave the SEC legal authority to establish accounting principles for corporations that are registered on the exchanges. However, the SEC has generally deferred its rule-making authority to private sector accounting bodies such as the Financial Accounting Standards Board (FASB), effectively allowing the accounting profession to regulate itself.

A number of high-profile business failures around the turn of the last century raised questions about the effectiveness of self-regulation and the usefulness of audits to protect the public. The Sarbanes-Oxley Act of 2002 was adopted to address these concerns. The act creates a five-member Public Company Accounting Oversight Board (PCAOB) with the authority to set and enforce auditing, attestation, quality control, and ethics standards for auditors of public companies. The PCAOB is empowered to impose disciplinary and remedial sanctions for violations of its rules, securities laws, and professional auditing and accounting standards. Public corporations operate in a complex regulatory environment that requires the services of attorneys and professional accountants.

Double Taxation

Corporations pay income taxes on their earnings and then owners pay income taxes on distributions (dividends) received from corporations. As a result, distributed corporate profits are taxed twice—first when income is reported on the corporation's income tax return and a second time when distributions are reported on individual owners' tax returns. This phenomenon is commonly called **double taxation** and is a significant disadvantage of the corporate form of business organization.

To illustrate, assume Glide Corporation earns pretax income of $100,000. Glide is in a 30 percent tax bracket. The corporation itself will pay income tax of $30,000 ($100,000 × 0.30). If the corporation distributes the after-tax income of $70,000 ($100,000 − $30,000) to individual stockholders in 15 percent tax brackets,[1] the $70,000 dividend will be reported on the individual tax returns, requiring tax payments of $10,500 ($70,000 × .15). Total income tax of $40,500 ($30,000 + $10,500) is due on $100,000 of earned income. In contrast, consider a proprietorship that is owned by an individual in a 30 percent tax bracket. If the proprietorship earns and distributes $100,000 profit, the total tax would be only $30,000 ($100,000 × .30).

Double taxation can be a burden for small companies. To reduce that burden, tax laws permit small closely held corporations to elect "S Corporation" status. S Corporations are taxed as proprietorships or partnerships. Also, many states have recently enacted laws permitting the formation of **limited liability companies (LLCs)** which offer many of the benefits of corporate ownership yet are in general taxed as partnerships. Because proprietorships and partnerships are not separate legal entities, company earnings are taxable to the owners rather than the company itself.

Limited Liability

Given the disadvantages of increased regulation and double taxation, why would anyone choose the corporate form of business structure over a partnership or proprietorship? A major reason is that the corporate form limits an investor's potential liability as an owner of a business venture. Because a corporation is legally separate from its owners, creditors cannot claim owners' personal assets as payment for the company's debts. Also, plaintiffs

---

[1]As a result of the Jobs and Growth Tax Relief Reconciliation Act (JGTRRA) of 2003, dividends received in tax years after 2002 are taxed at a maximum rate of 15 percent for most taxpayers. Lower income individuals pay a 5 percent tax on dividends received on December 31, 2007, or earlier. This rate falls to zero in 2008. The provisions of JGTRRA are set to expire on December 31, 2008.

Answers *to* The Curious Accountant

Mystery Company A is Rosetta Stone, Inc., as of July 7, 2010. The company's main products provide computer-aided learning of over 30 languages. The company has developed a visually based learning system that does not require much translation from one language to another. Therefore, the same product used by an English speaker to learn Spanish can, with only minimal changes, be used by a French speaker to learn Spanish. Some analysts believe this gives the company opportunities for large growth without a correspondingly large increase in investment.

Mystery Company B is Procter & Gamble, Inc. (as of July 7, 2010). Of course, only the future will tell which company is the better investment.

must sue the corporation, not its owners. The most that owners of a corporation can lose is the amount they have invested in the company (the value of the company's stock).

Unlike corporate stockholders, the owners of proprietorships and partnerships are *personally liable* for actions they take in the name of their companies. In fact, partners are responsible not only for their own actions but also for those taken by any other partner on behalf of the partnership. The benefit of **limited liability** is one of the most significant reasons the corporate form of business organization is so popular.

Continuity

Unlike partnerships or proprietorships, which terminate with the departure of their owners, a corporation's life continues when a shareholder dies or sells his or her stock. Because of **continuity** of existence, many corporations formed in the 1800s still thrive today.

Transferability of Ownership

The **transferability** of corporate ownership is easy. An investor simply buys or sells stock to acquire or give up an ownership interest in a corporation. Hundreds of millions of shares of stock are bought and sold on the major stock exchanges each day.

Transferring the ownership of proprietorships is much more difficult. To sell an ownership interest in a proprietorship, the proprietor must find someone willing to purchase the entire business. Because most proprietors also run their businesses, transferring ownership also requires transferring management responsibilities. Consider the difference in selling $1 million of Exxon stock versus selling a locally owned gas station. The stock could be sold on the New York Stock Exchange within minutes. In contrast, it could take years to find a buyer who is financially capable of and interested in owning and operating a gas station.

Transferring ownership in partnerships can also be difficult. As with proprietorships, ownership transfers may require a new partner to make a significant investment and accept management responsibilities in the business. Further, a new partner must accept and be accepted by the other partners. Personality conflicts and differences in management style can cause problems in transferring ownership interests in partnerships.

Management Structure

Partnerships and proprietorships are usually managed by their owners. Corporations, in contrast, have three tiers of management authority. The *owners* (**stockholders**) represent the highest level of organizational authority. The stockholders *elect* a **board of directors** to oversee company operations. The directors then *hire* professional executives to manage the company on a daily basis. Because large corporations can offer high salaries and challenging career opportunities, they can often attract superior managerial talent.

While the management structure used by corporations is generally effective, it sometimes complicates dismissing incompetent managers. The chief executive officer (CEO) is usually a member of the board of directors and is frequently influential in choosing other board members. The CEO is also in a position to reward loyal board members. As a result, board members may be reluctant to fire the CEO or other top executives even if the individuals are performing poorly. Corporations operating under such conditions are said to be experiencing **entrenched management.**

Ability to Raise Capital

Because corporations can have millions of owners (shareholders), they have the opportunity to raise huge amounts of capital. Few individuals have the financial means to build and operate a telecommunications network such as AT&T or a marketing distribution system such as Walmart. However, by pooling the resources of millions of owners through public stock and bond offerings, corporations generate the billions of dollars of capital needed for such massive investments. In contrast, the capital resources of proprietorships and partnerships are limited to a relatively small number of private owners. Although proprietorships and partnerships can also obtain resources by borrowing, the amount creditors are willing to lend them is usually limited by the size of the owners' net worth.

APPEARANCE OF CAPITAL STRUCTURE IN FINANCIAL STATEMENTS

The ownership interest (equity) in a business is composed of two elements: (1) owner/investor contributions and (2) retained earnings. The way these two elements are reported in the financial statements differs for each type of business structure (proprietorship, partnership, or corporation).

Presentation of Equity in Proprietorships

Owner contributions and retained earnings are combined in a single Capital account on the balance sheets of proprietorships. To illustrate, assume that Worthington Sole Proprietorship was started on January 1, 2012, when it acquired a $5,000 capital contribution from its owner, Phil Worthington. During the first year of operation, the company generated $4,000 of cash revenues, incurred $2,500 of cash expenses, and distributed $1,000 cash to the owner. Exhibit 8.1 displays 2012 financial statements for Worthington's company. Note on the *capital statement* that distributions are called **withdrawals.** Verify that the $5,500 balance in the Capital account on the balance sheet includes the $5,000 owner contribution and the retained earnings of $500 ($1,500 net income − $1,000 withdrawal).

LO 2

Analyze financial statements to identify the different types of business organizations.

EXHIBIT 8.1

WORTHINGTON SOLE PROPRIETORSHIP
Financial Statements
As of December 31, 2012

Income Statement		Capital Statement		Balance Sheet	
Revenue	$4,000	Beginning capital balance	$ 0	Assets	
Expenses	2,500	Plus: Investment by owner	5,000	Cash	$5,500
Net income	$1,500	Plus: Net income	1,500	Equity	
		Less: Withdrawal by owner	(1,000)	Worthington, capital	$5,500
		Ending capital balance	$5,500		

✓ CHECK YOURSELF 8.1

Weiss Company was started on January 1, 2012, when it acquired $50,000 cash from its owner(s). During 2012 the company earned $72,000 of net income. Explain how the equity section of Weiss's December 31, 2012, balance sheet would differ if the company were a proprietorship versus a corporation.

Answer *Proprietorship* records combine capital acquisitions from the owner and earnings from operating the business in a single capital account. In contrast, *corporation* records separate capital acquisitions from the owners and earnings from operating the business. If Weiss were a proprietorship, the equity section of the year-end balance sheet would report a single capital component of $122,000. If Weiss were a corporation, the equity section would report two separate equity components, most likely common stock of $50,000 and retained earnings of $72,000.

Presentation of Equity in Partnerships

The financial statement format for reporting partnership equity is similar to that used for proprietorships. Contributed capital and retained earnings are combined. However, a separate capital account is maintained for each partner in the business to reflect each partner's ownership interest.

To illustrate, assume that Sara Slater and Jill Johnson formed a partnership on January 1, 2012. The partnership acquired $2,000 of capital from Slater and $4,000 from Johnson. The partnership agreement called for each partner to receive an annual distribution equal to 10 percent of her capital contribution. Any further earnings were to be retained in the business and divided equally between the partners. During 2012, the company earned $5,000 of cash revenue and incurred $3,000 of cash expenses, for net income of $2,000 ($5,000 − $3,000). As specified by the partnership agreement, Slater received a $200 ($2,000 × 0.10) cash withdrawal and Johnson received $400 ($4,000 × 0.10). The remaining $1,400 ($2,000 − $200 − $400) of income was retained in the business and divided equally, adding $700 to each partner's capital account.

Exhibit 8.2 displays financial statements for the Slater and Johnson partnership. Again, note that distributions are called *withdrawals.* Also find on the balance sheet a *separate capital account* for each partner. Each capital account includes the amount of the partner's contributed capital plus her proportionate share of the retained earnings.

EXHIBIT 8.2

SLATER AND JOHNSON PARTNERSHIP
Financial Statements
As of December 31, 2012

Income Statement		Capital Statement		Balance Sheet	
Revenue	$5,000	Beginning capital balance	$ 0	Assets	
Expenses	3,000	Plus: Investment by owners	6,000	Cash	$7,400
Net income	$2,000	Plus: Net income	2,000	Equity	
		Less: Withdrawal by owners	(600)	Slater, capital	$2,700
		Ending capital balance	$7,400	Johnson, capital	4,700
				Total capital	$7,400

Presentation of Equity in Corporations

Corporations have more complex capital structures than proprietorships and partnerships. Explanations of some of the more common features of corporate capital structures and transactions follow.

CHARACTERISTICS OF CAPITAL STOCK

Stock issued by corporations may have a variety of different characteristics. For example, a company may issue different classes of stock that grant owners different rights and privileges. Also, the number of shares a corporation can legally issue may differ from the number it actually has issued. Further, a corporation can even buy back its own stock. Finally, a corporation may assign different values to the stock it issues. Accounting for corporate equity transactions is discussed in the next section of the text.

Explain the characteristics of major types of stock issued by corporations.

Par Value

Many states require assigning a **par value** to stock. Historically, par value represented the maximum liability of the investors. Par value multiplied by the number of shares of stock issued represents the minimum amount of assets that must be retained in the company as protection for creditors. This amount is known as **legal capital.** To ensure that the amount of legal capital is maintained in a corporation, many states require that purchasers pay at least the par value for a share of stock initially purchased from a corporation. To minimize the amount of assets that owners must maintain in the business, many corporations issue stock with very low par values, often $1 or less. Therefore, *legal capital* as defined by par value has come to have very little relevance to investors or creditors. As a result, many states allow corporations to issue no-par stock.

Stated Value

No-par stock may have a stated value. Like par value, **stated value** is an arbitrary amount assigned by the board of directors to the stock. It also has little relevance to investors and creditors. Stock with a par value and stock with a stated value are accounted for exactly the same way. When stock has no par or stated value, accounting for it is slightly different. These accounting differences are illustrated later in this chapter.

Other Valuation Terminology

The price an investor must pay to purchase a share of stock is the **market value.** The sales price of a share of stock may be more or less than the par value. Another term analysts frequently associate with stock is *book value.* **Book value per share** is calculated by dividing total stockholders' equity (assets − liabilities) by the number of shares of stock owned by investors. Book value per share differs from market value per share because equity is measured in historical dollars and market value reflects investors' estimates of a company's current value.

Stock: Authorized, Issued, and Outstanding

As part of the regulatory function, states approve the maximum number of shares of stock corporations are legally permitted to issue. This maximum number is called **authorized stock.** Authorized stock that has been sold to the public is called **issued stock.** When a corporation buys back some of its issued stock from the public, the repurchased stock is called **treasury stock.** Treasury stock is still considered to be issued stock, but it is no longer outstanding. **Outstanding stock** (total issued stock minus treasury stock) is stock owned by investors outside the corporation. For example, assume a company that is authorized to issue 150 shares of stock issues 100 shares to investors, and then buys back 20 shares of treasury stock. There are 150 shares authorized, 100 shares issued, and 80 shares outstanding.

FOCUS ON **INTERNATIONAL ISSUES**

PICKY, PICKY, PICKY ...

Considering the almost countless number of differences that could exist between U.S. GAAP and IFRS, it is not surprising that some of those that do exist relate to very specific issues. Consider the case of the timing of stock splits.

Assume a company that ends its fiscal year on December 31, 2011, declares a 2-for-1 stock split on January 15, 2012, before it has issued its 2011 annual report. Should the company apply the effects of the stock split retroactively to is 2011 financial statements, or begin showing the effects of the split on its 2012 statements? Under U.S. GAAP the split must be applied retroactively to the 2011 statements since they had not been issued at the time of the split. Under IFRS the 2011 statements would not show the effects of the split, but the 2012 statements would. By the way, an event that occurs between a company's fiscal year-end and the date its annual report is released is called a *subsequent event* by accountants.

Obviously no one can know every GAAP rule, much less all of the differences between GAAP and IFRS. This is why it is important to learn how to find answers to specific accounting questions as well as to develop an understanding of the basic accounting rules. Most important, if you are not sure you know the answer, do not assume you do.

Classes of Stock

The corporate charter defines the number of shares of stock authorized, the par value or stated value (if any), and the classes of stock that a corporation can issue. Most stock issued is either *common* or *preferred*.

Common Stock

All corporations issue **common stock.** Common stockholders bear the highest risk of losing their investment if a company is forced to liquidate. On the other hand, they reap the greatest rewards when a corporation prospers. Common stockholders generally enjoy several rights, including: (1) the right to buy and sell stock, (2) the right to share in the distribution of profits, (3) the right to share in the distribution of corporate assets in the case of liquidation, (4) the right to vote on significant matters that affect the corporate charter, and (5) the right to participate in the election of directors.

Preferred Stock

Many corporations issue **preferred stock** in addition to common stock. Holders of preferred stock receive certain privileges relative to holders of common stock. In exchange for special privileges in some areas, preferred stockholders give up rights in other areas. Preferred stockholders usually have no voting rights and the amount of their dividends is usually limited. Preferences granted to preferred stockholders include the following.

1. *Preference as to assets.* Preferred stock often has a liquidation value. In case of bankruptcy, preferred stockholders must be paid the liquidation value before any assets are distributed to common stockholders. However, preferred stockholder claims still fall behind creditor claims.

2. *Preference as to dividends.* Preferred shareholders are frequently guaranteed the right to receive dividends before common stockholders. The amount of the preferred dividend is normally stated on the stock certificate. It may be stated as a

dollar value (say, $5) per share or as a percentage of the par value. Most preferred stock has **cumulative dividends,** meaning that if a corporation is unable to pay the preferred dividend in any year, the dividend is not lost but begins to accumulate. Cumulative dividends that have not been paid are called **dividends in arrears.** When a company pays dividends, any preferred stock arrearages must be paid before any other dividends are paid. Noncumulative preferred stock is not often issued because preferred stock is much less attractive if missed dividends do not accumulate.

To illustrate the effects of preferred dividends, consider Dillion, Incorporated, which has the following shares of stock outstanding.

> Preferred stock, 4%, $10 par, 10,000 shares
> Common stock, $10 par, 20,000 shares

Assume the preferred stock dividend has not been paid for two years. If Dillion pays $22,000 in dividends, how much will each class of stock receive? It depends on whether the preferred stock is cumulative.

Allocation of Distribution for Cumulative Preferred Stock

	To Preferred	To Common
Dividends in arrears	$ 8,000	$ 0
Current year's dividends	4,000	10,000
Total distribution	$12,000	$10,000

Allocation of Distribution for Noncumulative Preferred Stock

	To Preferred	To Common
Dividends in arrears	$ 0	$ 0
Current year's dividends	4,000	18,000
Total distribution	$4,000	$18,000

The total annual dividend on the preferred stock is $4,000 (0.04 × $10 par × 10,000 shares). If the preferred stock is cumulative, the $8,000 in arrears must be paid first. Then $4,000 for the current year's dividend is paid next. The remaining $10,000 goes to common stockholders. If the preferred stock is noncumulative, the $8,000 of dividends from past periods is ignored. This year's $4,000 preferred dividend is paid first, with the remaining $18,000 going to common.

Other features of preferred stock may include the right to participate in distributions beyond the established amount of the preferred dividend, the right to convert preferred stock to common stock or to bonds, and the potential for having the preferred stock called (repurchased) by the corporation. Detailed discussion of these topics is left to more advanced courses. Exhibit 8.3 indicates that roughly 25 percent of U.S. companies have preferred shares outstanding.

EXHIBIT 8.3

Presence of Preferred Stock in the Capital Structure of U.S. Companies

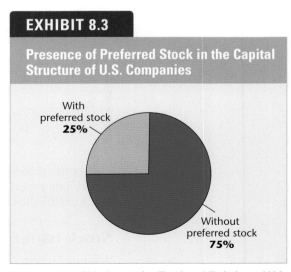

Data source: AICPA, Accounting Trends and Techniques, 2006.

ACCOUNTING FOR STOCK TRANSACTIONS ON THE DAY OF ISSUE

Explain how to account for different types of stock issued by corporations.

Issuing stock with a par or stated value is accounted for differently from issuing no-par stock. For stock with either a par or stated value, the total amount acquired from the owners is divided between two separate equity accounts. The amount of the par or stated value is recorded in the stock account. Any amount received above the par or stated value is recorded in an account called **Paid-in Capital in Excess of Par** (or **Stated) Value.**

Issuing Par Value Stock

To illustrate the issue of common stock with a par value, assume that Nelson Incorporated is authorized to issue 250 shares of common stock. During 2012, Nelson issued 100 shares of $10 par common stock for $22 per share. The event increases assets and stockholders' equity by $2,200 ($22 × 100 shares). The increase in stockholders' equity is divided into two parts, $1,000 of par value ($10 per share × 100 shares) and $1,200 ($2,200 − $1,000) received in excess of par value. The income statement is not affected. The $2,200 cash inflow is reported in the financing activities section of the statement of cash flows. The effects on the financial statements follow.

Assets	=	Liab.	+	Equity			Rev.	−	Exp.	=	Net Inc.	Cash Flow
Cash	=			Com. Stk.	+	PIC in Excess						
2,200	=	NA	+	1,000	+	1,200	NA	−	NA	=	NA	2,200 FA

The *legal capital* of the corporation is $1,000, the total par value of the issued common stock. The number of shares issued can be easily verified by dividing the total amount in the common stock account by the par value ($1,000 ÷ $10 = 100 shares).

Stock Classification

Assume Nelson Incorporated obtains authorization to issue 400 shares of Class B, $20 par value common stock. The company issues 150 shares of this stock at $25 per share. The event increases assets and stockholders' equity by $3,750 ($25 × 150 shares). The increase in stockholders' equity is divided into two parts, $3,000 of par value ($20 per share × 150 shares) and $750 ($3,750 − $3,000) received in excess of par value. The income statement is not affected. The $3,750 cash inflow is reported in the financing activities section of the statement of cash flows. The effects on the financial statements follow.

Assets	=	Liab.	+	Equity			Rev.	−	Exp.	=	Net Inc.	Cash Flow
Cash	=			Com. Stk.	+	PIC in Excess						
3,750	=	NA	+	3,000	+	750	NA	−	NA	=	NA	3,750 FA

As the preceding event suggests, companies can issue numerous classes of common stock. The specific rights and privileges for each class are described in the individual stock certificates.

Stock Issued at Stated Value

Assume Nelson is authorized to issue 300 shares of a third class of stock, 7 percent cumulative preferred stock with a stated value of $10 per share. Nelson issued 100 shares of the preferred stock at a price of $22 per share. The effects on the financial statements are identical to those described for the issue of the $10 par value common stock.

Assets	=	Liab.	+	Equity			Rev.	–	Exp.	=	Net Inc.	Cash Flow
Cash	=			Pfd. Stk.	+	PIC in Excess						
2,200	=	NA	+	1,000	+	1,200	NA	–	NA	=	NA	2,200 FA

Stock Issued with No Par Value

Assume that Nelson Incorporated is authorized to issue 150 shares of a fourth class of stock. This stock is no-par common stock. Nelson issues 100 shares of this no-par stock at $22 per share. The entire amount received ($22 × 100 = $2,200) is recorded in the stock account. The effects on the financial statements follow.

Assets	=	Liab.	+	Equity			Rev.	–	Exp.	=	Net Inc.	Cash Flow
Cash	=			Com. Stk.	+	PIC in Excess						
2,200	=	NA	+	2,200	+	NA	NA	–	NA	=	NA	2,200 FA

Financial Statement Presentation

Exhibit 8.4 displays Nelson Incorporated's balance sheet after the four stock issuances described above. The exhibit assumes that Nelson earned and retained $5,000 of cash income during 2012. The stock accounts are presented first, followed by the paid-in capital in excess of par (or stated) value accounts. A wide variety of reporting formats is used in practice. For example, another popular format is to group accounts by stock class, with the paid-in capital in excess accounts listed with their associated stock accounts. Alternatively, many companies combine the different classes of stock into a single amount and provide the detailed information in footnotes to the financial statements.

EXHIBIT 8.4

NELSON INCORPORATED
Balance Sheet
As of December 31, 2012

Assets	
Cash	$15,350
Stockholders' equity	
Preferred stock, $10 stated value, 7% cumulative, 300 shares authorized, 100 issued and outstanding	$ 1,000
Common stock, $10 par value, 250 shares authorized, 100 issued and outstanding	1,000
Common stock, class B, $20 par value, 400 shares authorized, 150 issued and outstanding	3,000
Common stock, no par, 150 shares authorized, 100 issued and outstanding	2,200
Paid-in capital in excess of stated value—preferred	1,200
Paid-in capital in excess of par value—common	1,200
Paid-in capital in excess of par value—class B common	750
Total paid-in capital	10,350
Retained earnings	5,000
Total stockholders' equity	$15,350

STOCKHOLDERS' EQUITY TRANSACTIONS AFTER THE DAY OF ISSUE

Treasury Stock

LO 5

Show how treasury stock transactions affect a company's financial statements.

When a company buys its own stock, the stock purchased is called *treasury stock*. Why would a company buy its own stock? Common reasons include (1) to have stock available to give employees pursuant to stock option plans, (2) to accumulate stock in preparation for a merger or business combination, (3) to reduce the number of shares outstanding in order to increase earnings per share, (4) to keep the price of the stock high when it appears to be falling, and (5) to avoid a hostile takeover (removing shares from the open market reduces the opportunity for outsiders to obtain enough voting shares to gain control of the company).

Conceptually, purchasing treasury stock is the reverse of issuing stock. When a business issues stock, the assets and equity of the business increase. When a business buys treasury stock, the assets and equity of the business decrease. To illustrate, return to the Nelson Incorporated example. Assume that in 2013 Nelson paid $20 per share to buy back 50 shares of the $10 par value common stock that it originally issued at $22 per share. The purchase of treasury stock is an asset use transaction. Assets and stockholders' equity decrease by the cost of the purchase ($20 × 50 shares = $1,000). The income statement is not affected. The cash outflow is reported in the financing activities section of the statement of cash flows. The effects on the financial statements follow.

Assets	=	Liab.	+	Equity			Rev.	−	Exp.	=	Net Inc.	Cash Flow
Cash	=			Other Equity Accts.	−	Treasury Stk.						
(1,000)	=	NA	+	NA	−	1,000	NA	−	NA	=	NA	(1,000) FA

The Treasury Stock account is a contra equity account. It is deducted from the other equity accounts in determining total stockholders' equity. In this example, the Treasury Stock account contains the full amount paid ($1,000). The original issue price and the par value of the stock have no effect on the Treasury Stock account. Recognizing the full amount paid in the treasury stock account is called the **cost method of accounting for treasury stock** transactions. Although other methods could be used, the cost method is the most common.

Assume Nelson reissues 30 shares of treasury stock at a price of $25 per share. As with any other stock issue, the sale of treasury stock is an asset source transaction. In this case, assets and stockholders' equity increase by $750 ($25 × 30 shares). The income statement is not affected. The cash inflow is reported in the financing activities section of the statement of cash flows. The effects on the financial statements follow.

Assets	=	Liab.	+	Equity					Rev.	−	Exp.	=	Net Inc.	Cash Flow
Cash	=			Other Equity Accounts	−	Treasury Stock	+	PIC from Treasury Stk.						
750	=	NA	+	NA	−	(600)	+	150	NA	−	NA	=	NA	750 FA

The decrease in the Treasury Stock account increases stockholders' equity. The $150 difference between the cost of the treasury stock ($20 per share × 30 shares = $600) and the sales price ($750) is *not* reported as a gain. The sale of treasury stock is a capital acquisition, not a revenue transaction. The $150 is additional paid-in capital. *Corporations do not recognize gains or losses on the sale of treasury stock.*

After selling 30 shares of treasury stock, 20 shares remain in Nelson's possession. These shares cost $20 each, so the balance in the Treasury Stock account is now $400 ($20 × 20 shares). Treasury stock is reported on the balance sheet directly below retained earnings. Although this placement suggests that treasury stock reduces retained earnings, the reduction actually applies to the entire stockholders' equity section. Exhibit 8.5 on page 302 shows the presentation of treasury stock in the balance sheet.

✓ CHECK YOURSELF 8.2

On January 1, 2012, Janell Company's Common Stock account balance was $20,000. On April 1, 2012, Janell paid $12,000 cash to purchase some of its own stock. Janell resold this stock on October 1, 2012, for $14,500. What is the effect on the company's cash and stockholders' equity from both the April 1 purchase and the October 1 resale of the stock?

Answer The April 1 purchase would reduce both cash and stockholders' equity by $12,000. The treasury stock transaction represents a return of invested capital to those owners who sold stock back to the company.

The sale of the treasury stock on October 1 would increase both cash and stockholders' equity by $14,500. The difference between the sales price of the treasury stock and its cost ($14,500 − $12,000) represents additional paid-in capital from treasury stock transactions. The stockholders' equity section of the balance sheet would include Common Stock, $20,000, and Additional Paid-in Capital from Treasury Stock Transactions, $2,500.

Cash Dividend

Cash dividends are affected by three significant dates: *the declaration date, the date of record,* and *the payment date.* Assume that on October 15, 2013, the board of Nelson Incorporated declared a 7% cash dividend on the 100 outstanding shares of its $10 stated value preferred stock. The dividend will be paid to stockholders of record as of November 15, 2013. The cash payment will be made on December 15, 2013.

LO 6

Explain the effects of declaring and paying cash dividends on a company's financial statements.

Declaration Date

Although corporations are not required to declare dividends, they are legally obligated to pay dividends once they have been declared. They must recognize a liability on the **declaration date** (in this case, October 15, 2013). The increase in liabilities is accompanied by a decrease in retained earnings. The income statement and statement of cash flows are not affected. The effects on the financial statements of *declaring* the $70 (0.07 × $10 × 100 shares) dividend follow.

Assets	=	Liab.	+	Equity			Rev.	−	Exp.	=	Net Inc.	Cash Flow
Cash	=	Div. Pay.	+	Com. Stk.	+	Ret. Earn.						
NA	=	70	+	NA	+	(70)	NA	−	NA	=	NA	NA

Date of Record

Cash dividends are paid to investors who owned the preferred stock on the **date of record** (in this case November 15, 2013). Any stock sold after the date of record but

REALITY BYTES

As you have learned, dividends, unlike interest on bonds, do not have to be paid. In fact, a company's board of directors must vote to pay dividends before they can be paid. Even so, once a company establishes a practice of paying a dividend of a given amount each period, usually quarterly, the company is reluctant to not pay the dividend. Furthermore, it is usually a significant news event when a company decides to increase the amount of its regular dividend.

When times are bad, however, dividends are often reduced, or eliminated entirely, as a quick way to conserve the company's cash. This occurred often as a result of the economic downturn of 2008. An article in the Feburary 28, 2009, edition of *The Wall Street Journal* listed ten large companies who had recently reduced or eliminated their common stock dividend. The companies named were: Blackstone Group, CBS, Citigroup, Dow Chemical, General Electric, JP Morgan Chase, Motorola, New York Times, Pfizer, and Textron. The article also noted that for the month of January 2009, dividends paid by companies in the S&P 500 Index were 24 percent lower than they had been in January 2008.

before the payment date (in this case December 15, 2013) is traded **ex-dividend,** meaning the buyer will not receive the upcoming dividend. The date of record is merely a cutoff date. It does not affect the financial statements.

Payment Date

Nelson actually paid the cash dividend on the **payment date.** This event has the same effect as paying any other liability. Assets (cash) and liabilities (dividends payable) both decrease. The income statement is not affected. The cash outflow is reported in the financing activities section of the statement of cash flows. The effects of the cash payment on the financial statements follow.

Assets	=	Liab.	+	Equity			Rev.	−	Exp.	=	Net Inc.	Cash Flow	
Cash	=	Div. Pay.	+	Com. Stk.	+	Ret. Earn.							
(70)	=	(70)	+	NA	+	NA	NA	−	NA	=	NA	(70)	FA

Stock Dividend

LO 7

Explain the effects of stock dividends and stock splits on a company's financial statements.

Dividends are not always paid in cash. Companies sometimes choose to issue **stock dividends,** wherein they distribute additional shares of stock to the stockholders. To illustrate, assume that Nelson Incorporated decided to issue a 10 percent stock dividend on its class B, $20 par value common stock. Because dividends apply to outstanding shares only, Nelson will issue 15 (150 outstanding shares × 0.10) additional shares of class B stock.

Assume the new shares are distributed when the market value of the stock is $30 per share. As a result of the stock dividend, Nelson will transfer $450 ($30 × 15 new shares) from retained earnings to paid-in capital.[2] The stock dividend is an equity exchange

---

[2]The accounting here applies to small stock dividends. Accounting for large stock dividends is explained in a more advanced course.

transaction. The income statement and statement of cash flows are not affected. The effects of the stock dividend on the financial statements follow.

Assets	=	Liab.	+	Equity						Rev.	−	Exp.	=	Net Inc.	Cash Flow
				Com. Stk.	+	PIC in Excess	+	Ret. Earn.							
NA	=	NA	+	300	+	150	+	(450)		NA	−	NA	=	NA	NA

Stock dividends have no effect on assets. They merely increase the number of shares of stock outstanding. Because a greater number of shares represents the same owner- ship interest in the same amount of assets, the market value per share of a company's stock normally declines when a stock dividend is distributed. A lower market price makes the stock more affordable and may increase demand for the stock, which benefits both the company and its stockholders.

Stock Split

A corporation may also reduce the market price of its stock through a **stock split.** A stock split replaces existing shares with a greater number of new shares. Any par or stated value of the stock is proportionately reduced to reflect the new number of shares outstanding. For example, assume Nelson Incorporated declared a 2-for-1 stock split on the 165 outstanding shares (150 originally issued + 15 shares distributed in a stock dividend) of its $20 par value, class B common stock. Nelson notes in the accounting records that the 165 old $20 par shares are replaced with 330 new $10 par shares. Inves- tors who owned the 165 shares of old common stock would now own 330 shares of the new common stock.

Stock splits have no effect on the dollar amounts of assets, liabilities, and stock- holders' equity. They only affect the number of shares of stock outstanding. In Nelson's case, the ownership interest that was previously represented by 165 shares of stock is now represented by 330 shares. Because twice as many shares now represent the same ownership interest, the market value per share should be one-half as much as it was prior to the split. However, as with a stock dividend, the lower market price will prob- ably stimulate demand for the stock. As a result, doubling the number of shares will likely reduce the market price to slightly more than one-half of the pre-split value. For example, if the stock were selling for $30 per share before the 2-for-1 split, it might sell for $15.50 after the split.

Appropriation of Retained Earnings

The board of directors may restrict the amount of retained earnings available to distrib- ute as dividends. The restriction may be required by credit agreements, or it may be discretionary. A retained earnings restriction, often called an *appropriation,* is an equity exchange event. It transfers a portion of existing retained earnings to **Appropriated Retained Earnings.** Total retained earnings remains unchanged. To illustrate, assume that Nelson appropriates $1,000 of retained earnings for future expansion. The income statement and the statement of cash flows are not affected. The effects on the financial statements of appropriating $1,000 of retained earnings follow.

Show how the appropriation of retained earnings affects financial statements.

Assets	=	Liab.	+	Equity						Rev.	−	Exp.	=	Net Inc.	Cash Flow
				Com. Stk.	+	Ret. Earn.	+	App. Ret. Earn.							
NA	=	NA	+	NA	+	(1,000)	+	1,000		NA	−	NA	=	NA	NA

FINANCIAL STATEMENT PRESENTATION

The 2012 and 2013 events for Nelson Incorporated are summarized below. Events 1 through 8 are cash transactions. The results of the 2012 transactions (nos. 1–5) are reflected in Exhibit 8.4. The results of the 2013 transactions (nos. 6–9) are shown in Exhibit 8.5.

1. Issued 100 shares of $10 par value common stock at a market price of $22 per share.
2. Issued 150 shares of class B, $20 par value common stock at a market price of $25 per share.
3. Issued 100 shares of $10 stated value, 7 percent cumulative preferred stock at a market price of $22 per share.
4. Issued 100 shares of no-par common stock at a market price of $22 per share.
5. Earned and retained $5,000 cash from operations.
6. Purchased 50 shares of $10 par value common stock as treasury stock at a market price of $20 per share.
7. Sold 30 shares of treasury stock at a market price of $25 per share.
8. Declared and paid a $70 cash dividend on the preferred stock.
9. Issued a 10 percent stock dividend on the 150 shares of outstanding class B, $20 par value common stock (15 additional shares). The additional shares were issued when the market price of the stock was $30 per share. There are 165 (150 + 15) class B common shares outstanding after the stock dividend.
10. Issued a 2-for-1 stock split on the 165 shares of class B, $20 par value common stock. After this transaction, there are 330 shares outstanding of the class B common stock with a $10 par value.
11. Appropriated $1,000 of retained earnings.

EXHIBIT 8.5

NELSON INCORPORATED
Balance Sheet
As of December 31, 2013

Assets		
Cash		$21,030
Stockholders' equity		
Preferred stock, $10 stated value, 7% cumulative,		
300 shares authorized, 100 issued and outstanding	$1,000	
Common stock, $10 par value, 250 shares authorized,		
100 issued, and 80 outstanding	1,000	
Common stock, class B, $10 par, 800 shares authorized,		
330 issued and outstanding	3,300	
Common stock, no par, 150 shares authorized,		
100 issued and outstanding	2,200	
Paid-in capital in excess of stated value—preferred	1,200	
Paid-in capital in excess of par value—common	1,200	
Paid-in capital in excess of par value—class B common	900	
Paid-in capital in excess of cost of treasury stock	150	
Total paid-in capital		$10,950
Retained earnings		
Appropriated	1,000	
Unappropriated	9,480	
Total retained earnings		10,480
Less: Treasury stock, 20 shares @ $20 per share		(400)
Total stockholders' equity		$21,030

The illustration assumes that Nelson earned net income of $6,000 in 2013. The ending retained earnings balance is determined as follows: Beginning Balance $5,000 − $70 Cash Dividend − $450 Stock Dividend + $6,000 Net Income = $10,480.

INVESTING IN CAPITAL STOCK

Stockholders may benefit in two ways when a company generates earnings. The company may distribute the earnings directly to the stockholders in the form of dividends. Alternatively, the company may retain some or all of the earnings to finance growth and increase its potential for future earnings. If the company retains earnings, the market value of its stock should increase to reflect its greater earnings prospects. How can analysts use financial reporting to help assess the potential for dividend payments or growth in market value?

Explain some uses of accounting information in making stock investment decisions.

Receiving Dividends

Is a company likely to pay dividends in the future? The financial statements can help answer this question. They show if dividends were paid in the past. Companies with a history of paying dividends usually continue to pay dividends. Also, to pay dividends in the future, a company must have sufficient cash and retained earnings. These amounts are reported on the balance sheet and the statement of cash flows.

Increasing the Price of Stock

Is the market value (price) of a company's stock likely to increase? Increases in a company's stock price occur when investors believe the company's earnings will grow. Financial statements provide information that is useful in predicting the prospects for earnings growth. Here also, a company's earnings history is an indicator of its growth potential. However, because published financial statements report historical information, investors must recognize their limitations. Investors want to know about the future. Stock prices are therefore influenced more by forecasts than by history.

For example:

■ On April 15, 2009, Abbott Laboratories, Inc., announced that profits for the first quarter of its 2009 fiscal year were 53 percent higher than profits in the same quarter of 2008. In reaction to this news, the price of Abbott's stock *fell* by almost 5 percent. Why did the stock market respond in this way? Because company's revenues for the quarter were less than had been expected by analysts who follow the company.

■ On May 18, 2009, Lowe's Companies, Inc., announced first quarter earnings were $0.32 per share, which was 22 percent lower than for the same period of the previous year. The stock market's reaction to the news was to *increase* the price of Lowe's stock by 8 percent. The market reacted this way because the analysts were expecting earnings per share for the first quarter to be only $0.25 per share.

In each case, investors reacted to the potential for earnings growth rather than the historical earnings reports. Because investors find forecasted statements more relevant to decision making than historical financial statements, most companies provide forecasts in addition to historical financial statements.

The value of a company's stock is also influenced by nonfinancial information that financial statements cannot provide. For example, suppose ExxonMobil announced in the middle of its fiscal year that it had just discovered substantial oil reserves on property to which it held drilling rights. Consider the following questions:

■ What would happen to the price of ExxonMobil's stock on the day of the announcement?

■ What would happen to ExxonMobil's financial statements on that day?

The price of ExxonMobil's stock would almost certainly increase as soon as the discovery was made public. However, nothing would happen to its financial statements on that day. There would probably be very little effect on its financial statements for that year. Only after the company begins to develop the oil field and sell the oil will its financial statements reflect the discovery. Changes in financial statements tend to lag behind the announcements companies make regarding their earnings potential.

Stock prices are also affected by general economic conditions and consumer confidence as well as the performance measures reported in financial statements. For example, the stock prices of virtually all companies declined sharply immediately after the September 11, 2001, terrorist attacks on the World Trade Center and the Pentagon. Historically based financial statements are of little benefit in predicting general economic conditions or changes in consumer confidence.

Exercising Control through Stock Ownership

The more influence an investor has over the operations of a company, the more the investor can benefit from owning stock in the company. For example, consider a power company that needs coal to produce electricity. The power company may purchase some common stock in a coal mining company to ensure a stable supply of coal. What percentage of the mining company's stock must the power company acquire to exercise significant influence over the mining company? The answer depends on how many investors own stock in the mining company and how the number of shares is distributed among the stockholders.

The greater its number of stockholders, the more *widely held* a company is. If stock ownership is concentrated in the hands of a few persons, a company is *closely held.* Widely held companies can generally be controlled with smaller percentages of ownership than closely held companies. Consider a company in which no existing investor owns more than 1 percent of the voting stock. A new investor who acquires a 5 percent interest would immediately become, by far, the largest shareholder and would likely be able to significantly influence board decisions. In contrast, consider a closely held company in which one current shareholder owns 51 percent of the company's stock. Even if another investor acquired the remaining 49 percent of the company, that investor could not control the company.

Financial statements contain some, but not all, of the information needed to help an investor determine ownership levels necessary to permit control. For example, the financial statements disclose the total number of shares of stock outstanding, but they normally contain little information about the number of shareholders and even less information about any relationships between shareholders. Relationships between shareholders are critically important because related shareholders, whether bound by family or business interests, might exercise control by voting as a block. For publicly traded companies, information about the number of shareholders and the identity of some large shareholders is disclosed in reports filed with the Securities and Exchange Commission.

 # A Look Back

Starting a business requires obtaining financing; it takes money to make money. Although some money may be borrowed, lenders are unlikely to make loans to businesses that lack some degree of owner financing. Equity financing is therefore critical to virtually all profit-oriented businesses. This chapter has examined some of the issues related to accounting for equity transactions.

The idea that a business must obtain financing from its owners was one of the first events presented in this textbook. This chapter discussed the advantages and disadvantages of organizing a business as a sole proprietorship versus a partnership versus a corporation. These advantages and disadvantages include the following.

1. *Double taxation*—Income of corporations is subject to double taxation, but that of proprietorships and partnerships is not.

2. *Regulation*—Corporations are subject to more regulation than are proprietorships and partnerships.

3. *Limited liability*—An investor's personal assets are not at risk as a result of owning corporate securities. The investor's liability is limited to the amount of the investment. In general proprietorships and partnerships do not offer limited liability. However, laws in some states permit the formation of limited liability companies which operate like proprietorships and partnerships yet place some limits on the personal liability of their owners.

4. *Continuity*—Proprietorships and partnerships dissolve when one of the owners leaves the business. Corporations are separate legal entities that continue to exist regardless of changes in ownership.

5. *Transferability*—Ownership interests in corporations are easier to transfer than those of proprietorships or partnerships.

6. *Management structure*—Corporations are more likely to have independent professional managers than are proprietorships or partnerships.

7. *Ability to raise capital*—Because they can be owned by millions of investors, corporations have the opportunity to raise more capital than proprietorships or partnerships.

Corporations issue different classes of common stock and preferred stock as evidence of ownership interests. In general, *common stock* provides the widest range of privileges including the right to vote and participate in earnings. *Preferred stockholders* usually give up the right to vote in exchange for preferences such as the right to receive dividends or assets upon liquidation before common stockholders. Stock may have a *par value* or *stated value,* which relates to legal requirements governing the amount of capital that must be maintained in the corporation. Corporations may also issue *no-par stock,* avoiding some of the legal requirements that pertain to par or stated value stock.

Stock that a company issues and then repurchases is called *treasury stock.* Purchasing treasury stock reduces total assets and stockholders' equity. Reselling treasury stock represents a capital acquisition. The difference between the reissue price and the cost of the treasury stock is recorded directly in the equity accounts. Treasury stock transactions do not result in gains or losses on the income statement.

Companies may issue *stock splits* or *stock dividends.* These transactions increase the number of shares of stock without changing the net assets of a company. The per share market value usually drops when a company issues stock splits or dividends.

A Look Forward

Financial statement analysis is so important that Chapter 9 is devoted solely to a detailed discussion of this subject. The chapter covers vertical analysis (analyzing relationships within a specific statement) and horizontal analysis (analyzing relationships across accounting periods). Finally, the chapter discusses limitations associated with financial statement analysis.

A step-by-step audio-narrated series of slides is provided on the text website at www.mhhe.com/edmondssurvey3e.

SELF-STUDY REVIEW PROBLEM

Edwards Inc. experienced the following events:

1. Issued common stock for cash.
2. Declared a cash dividend.
3. Issued noncumulative preferred stock for cash.
4. Appropriated retained earnings.
5. Distributed a stock dividend.
6. Paid cash to purchase treasury stock.
7. Distributed a 2-for-1 stock split.
8. Issued cumulative preferred stock for cash.
9. Paid a cash dividend that had previously been declared.
10. Sold treasury stock for cash at a higher amount than the cost of the treasury stock.

Required

Show the effect of each event on the elements of the financial statements using a horizontal statements model like the one shown here. Use + for increase, − for decrease, and NA for not affected. In the Cash Flow column, indicate whether the item is an operating activity (OA), investing activity (IA), or a financing activity (FA). The first transaction is entered as an example.

Event	Assets	=	Liab.	+	Equity	Rev.	−	Exp.	=	Net Inc.	Cash Flow
1	+		NA		+	NA		NA		NA	+ FA

Solution to Self-Study Review Problem

Event	Assets	=	Liab.	+	Equity	Rev.	−	Exp.	=	Net Inc.	Cash Flow
1	+		NA		+	NA		NA		NA	+ FA
2	NA		+		−	NA		NA		NA	NA
3	+		NA		+	NA		NA		NA	+ FA
4	NA		NA		− +	NA		NA		NA	NA
5	NA		NA		− +	NA		NA		NA	NA
6	−		NA		−	NA		NA		NA	− FA
7	NA		NA		NA	NA		NA		NA	NA
8	+		NA		+	NA		NA		NA	+ FA
9	−		−		NA	NA		NA		NA	− FA
10	+		NA		+	NA		NA		NA	+ FA

KEY TERMS

Ex-dividend 300
Issued stock 293
Legal capital 293
Limited liability 290
Limited liability companies (LLCs) 289
Market value 293
Outstanding stock 293
Paid-in Capital in Excess of Par Value 296

Par value 293
Partnerships 288
Partnership agreement 288
Payment date 300
Preferred stock 294
Securities Act of 1933 and Securities Exchange Act of 1934 289
Sole proprietorships 288

Stated value 293
Stock certificates 288
Stock dividends 300
Stockholders 290
Stock split 301
Transferability 290
Treasury stock 293
Withdrawals 291

QUESTIONS

1. What are the three major forms of business organizations? Describe each.

2. How are sole proprietorships formed?

3. Discuss the purpose of a partnership agreement. Is such an agreement necessary for partnership formation?

4. What is meant by the phrase *separate legal entity?* To which type of business organization does it apply?

5. What is the purpose of the articles of incorporation? What information do they provide?

6. What is the function of the stock certificate?

7. What prompted Congress to pass the Securities Act of 1933 and the Securities Exchange Act of 1934? What is the purpose of these laws?

8. What are the advantages and disadvantages of the corporate form of business organization?

9. What is a limited liability company? Discuss its advantages and disadvantages.

10. How does the term *double taxation* apply to corporations? Give an example of double taxation.

11. What is the difference between contributed capital and retained earnings for a corporation?

12. What are the similarities and differences in the equity structure of a sole proprietorship, a partnership, and a corporation?

13. Why is it easier for a corporation to raise large amounts of capital than it is for a partnership?

14. What is the meaning of each of the following terms with respect to the corporate form of organization?
    (a) Legal capital
    (b) Par value of stock
    (c) Stated value of stock
    (d) Market value of stock
    (e) Book value of stock
    (f) Authorized shares of stock
    (g) Issued stock
    (h) Outstanding stock
    (i) Treasury stock
    (j) Common stock
    (k) Preferred stock
    (l) Dividends

15. What is the difference between cumulative preferred stock and noncumulative preferred stock?

16. What is no-par stock? How is it recorded in the accounting records?

17. Assume that Best Co. has issued and outstanding 1,000 shares of $100 par value, 10 percent, cumulative preferred stock. What is the dividend per share? If the preferred dividend is two years in arrears, what total amount of dividends must be paid before the common shareholders can receive any dividends?

18. If Best Co. issued 10,000 shares of $20 par value common stock for $30 per share, what amount is added to the Common Stock account? What amount of cash is received?

19. What is the difference between par value stock and stated value stock?

20. Why might a company repurchase its own stock?

21. What effect does the purchase of treasury stock have on the equity of a company?

22. Assume that Day Company repurchased 1,000 of its own shares for $30 per share and sold the shares two weeks later for $35 per share. What is the amount of gain on the sale? How is it reported on the balance sheet? What type of account is treasury stock?

23. What is the importance of the declaration date, record date, and payment date in conjunction with corporate dividends?

24. What is the difference between a stock dividend and a stock split?

25. Why would a company choose to distribute a stock dividend instead of a cash dividend?

26. What is the primary reason that a company would declare a stock split?

27. If Best Co. had 10,000 shares of $20 par value common stock outstanding and declared a 5-for-1 stock split, how many shares would then be outstanding and what would be their par value after the split?

28. When a company appropriates retained earnings, does the company set aside cash for a specific use? Explain.

29. What is the largest source of financing for most U.S. businesses?

30. What is meant by *equity financing?* What is meant by *debt financing?*

31. What is a widely held corporation? What is a closely held corporation?

32. What are some reasons that a corporation might not pay dividends?

MULTIPLE-CHOICE QUESTIONS

Multiple-choice questions are provided on the text website at www.mhhe.com/edmondssurvey3e

EXERCISES

All applicable Exercises are available with McGraw-Hill's
Connect Accounting.

LO 1, 2

Exercise 8-1 *Effect of accounting events on the financial statements of a sole proprietorship*

A sole proprietorship was started on January 1, 2012, when it received $60,000 cash from Mark Pruitt, the owner. During 2012, the company earned $40,000 in cash revenues and paid $19,300 in cash expenses. Pruitt withdrew $5,000 cash from the business during 2012.

Required

Prepare the income statement, capital statement (statement of changes in equity), balance sheet, and statement of cash flows for Pruitt's 2012 fiscal year.

LO 1, 2

Exercise 8-2 *Effect of accounting events on the financial statements of a partnership*

Justin Harris and Paul Berryhill started the HB partnership on January 1, 2012. The business acquired $56,000 cash from Harris and $84,000 from Berryhill. During 2012, the partnership earned $65,000 in cash revenues and paid $32,000 for cash expenses. Harris withdrew $2,000 cash from the business, and Berryhill withdrew $3,000 cash. The net income was allocated to the capital accounts of the two partners in proportion to the amounts of their original investments in the business.

Required

Prepare the income statement, capital statement, balance sheet, and statement of cash flows for the HB partnership for the 2012 fiscal year.

LO 1, 2

Exercise 8-3 *Effect of accounting events on the financial statements of a corporation*

Morris Corporation was started with the issue of 5,000 shares of $10 par common stock for cash on January 1, 2012. The stock was issued at a market price of $18 per share. During 2012, the company earned $63,000 in cash revenues and paid $41,000 for cash expenses. Also, a $4,000 cash dividend was paid to the stockholders.

Required

Prepare the income statement, statement of changes in stockholders' equity, balance sheet, and statement of cash flows for Morris Corporation's 2012 fiscal year.

Exercise 8-4   *Effect of issuing common stock on the balance sheet*   LO 4

Newly formed Home Medical Corporation has 100,000 shares of $5 par common stock authorized. On March 1, 2012, Home Medical issued 10,000 shares of the stock for $12 per share. On May 2 the company issued an additional 20,000 shares for $20 per share. Home Medical was not affected by other events during 2012.

Required

a. Record the transactions in a horizontal statements model like the following one. In the Cash Flow column, indicate whether the item is an operating activity (OA), investing activity (IA), or financing activity (FA). Use NA to indicate that an element was not affected by the event.

Assets	=	Liab.	+		Equity		Rev.	−	Exp.	=	Net Inc.	Cash Flow
Cash	=		+	Com. Stk.	+	Paid-in Excess						

b. Determine the amount Home Medical would report for common stock on the December 31, 2012, balance sheet.
c. Determine the amount Home Medical would report for paid-in capital in excess of par.
d. What is the total amount of capital contributed by the owners?
e. What amount of total assets would Home Medical report on the December 31, 2012, balance sheet?

Exercise 8-5   *Recording and reporting common and preferred stock transactions*   LO 4

Rainoy, Inc., was organized on June 5, 2012. It was authorized to issue 400,000 shares of $10 par common stock and 50,000 shares of 4 percent cumulative class A preferred stock. The class A stock had a stated value of $25 per share. The following stock transactions pertain to Rainoy, Inc.

1. Issued 20,000 shares of common stock for $15 per share.
2. Issued 10,000 shares of the class A preferred stock for $30 per share.
3. Issued 50,000 shares of common stock for $18 per share.

Required

Prepare the stockholders' equity section of the balance sheet immediately after these transactions have been recognized.

Exercise 8-6   *Effect of no-par common and par preferred stock on the horizontal statements model*   LO 4

Eaton Corporation issued 5,000 shares of no-par common stock for $20 per share. Eaton also issued 2,000 shares of $50 par, 6 percent noncumulative preferred stock at $60 per share.

Required

Record these events in a horizontal statements model like the following one. In the cash flow column, indicate whether the item is an operating activity (OA), investing activity (IA), or financing activity (FA). Use NA to indicate that an element was not affected by the event.

Assets	=		Equity			Rev.	−	Exp.	=	Net Inc.	Cash Flow
Cash	=	Pfd. Stk.	+ Com. Stk.	+	PIC in Excess						

Exercise 8-7   *Issuing stock for assets other than cash*   LO 4

Kaylee Corporation was formed when it issued shares of common stock to two of its shareholders. Kaylee issued 5,000 shares of $10 par common stock to K. Breslin in exchange for $60,000 cash (the issue price was $12 per share). Kaylee also issued 2,500 shares of stock to T. Lindsay in exchange for a one-year-old delivery van on the same day. Lindsay had originally paid $35,000 for the van.

Required

a. What was the market value of the delivery van on the date of the stock issue?

b. Show the effect of the two stock issues on Kaylee's books in a horizontal statements model like the following one. In the Cash Flow column, indicate whether the item is an operating activity (OA), investing activity (IA), or financing activity (FA). Use NA to indicate that an element was not affected by the event.

Assets	=	Equity	Rev.	−	Exp.	=	Net Inc.	Cash Flow
Cash + Van =	Com. Stk.	+ PIC in Excess						

LO 5

Exercise 8-8 *Treasury stock transactions*

Graves Corporation repurchased 2,000 shares of its own stock for $40 per share. The stock has a par of $10 per share. A month later Graves resold 1,200 shares of the treasury stock for $48 per share.

Required

What is the balance of the treasury stock account after these transactions are recognized?

LO 5

Exercise 8-9 *Recording and reporting treasury stock transactions*

The following information pertains to Smoot Corp. at January 1, 2012.

Common stock, $10 par, 10,000 shares authorized, 2,000 shares issued and outstanding	$20,000
Paid-in capital in excess of par, common stock	15,000
Retained earnings	65,000

Smoot Corp. completed the following transactions during 2012:

1. Issued 1,000 shares of $10 par common stock for $28 per share.
2. Repurchased 200 shares of its own common stock for $25 per share.
3. Resold 50 shares of treasury stock for $26 per share.

Required

a. How many shares of common stock were outstanding at the end of the period?

b. How many shares of common stock had been issued at the end of the period?

c. Organize the transactions data in accounts under the accounting equation.

d. Prepare the stockholders' equity section of the balance sheet reflecting these transactions. Include the number of shares authorized, issued, and outstanding in the description of the common stock.

LO 6

Exercise 8-10 *Effect of cash dividends on financial statements*

On October 1, 2012, Smart Corporation declared a $60,000 cash dividend to be paid on December 30 to shareholders of record on November 20.

Required

Record the events occurring on October 1, November 20, and December 30 in a horizontal statements model like the following one. In the Cash Flow column, indicate whether the item is an operating activity (OA), investing activity (IA), or financing activity (FA).

Date	Assets = Liab. + Com. Stock + Ret. Earn.	Rev. − Exp. = Net Inc.	Cash Flow

Exercise 8-11   *Accounting for cumulative preferred dividends*   LO 6

When Polledo Corporation was organized in January 2012, it immediately issued 5,000 shares of $50 par, 5 percent, cumulative preferred stock and 10,000 shares of $10 par common stock. The company's earnings history is as follows: 2012, net loss of $15,000; 2013, net income of $60,000; 2014, net income of $95,000. The corporation did not pay a dividend in 2012.

Required

a. How much is the dividend arrearage as of January 1, 2013?
b. Assume that the board of directors declares a $40,000 cash dividend at the end of 2013 (remember that the 2012 and 2013 preferred dividends are due). How will the dividend be divided between the preferred and common stockholders?

Exercise 8-12   *Cash dividends for preferred and common shareholders*

B&S Corporation had the following stock issued and outstanding at January 1, 2012:

1. 100,000 shares of $5 par common stock.
2. 5,000 shares of $100 par, 5 percent, noncumulative preferred stock.

On May 10, B&S Corporation declared the annual cash dividend on its 5,000 shares of preferred stock and a $1 per share dividend for the common shareholders. The dividends will be paid on June 15 to the shareholders of record on May 30.

Required

Determine the total amount of dividends to be paid to the preferred shareholders and common shareholders.

Exercise 8-13   *Cash dividends: common and preferred stock*   LO 6

Varsity Corp. had the following stock issued and outstanding at January 1, 2012.

1. 200,000 shares of no-par common stock.
2. 10,000 shares of $100 par, 8 percent, cumulative preferred stock. (Dividends are in arrears for one year, 2011.)

On February 1, 2012, Varsity declared a $200,000 cash dividend to be paid March 31 to shareholders of record on March 10.

Required

What amount of dividends will be paid to the preferred shareholders versus the common shareholders?

Exercise 8-14   *Accounting for stock dividends*   LO 7

Rollins Corporation issued a 5 percent stock dividend on 10,000 shares of its $10 par common stock. At the time of the dividend, the market value of the stock was $14 per share.

Required

a. Compute the amount of the stock dividend.
b. Show the effects of the stock dividend on the financial statements using a horizontal statements model like the following one.

Assets	=	Liab.	+	Com. Stk.	+	PIC in Excess	+	Ret. Earn.	Rev.	−	Exp.	=	Net Inc.	Cash Flow

Exercise 8-15   *Determining the effects of stock splits on the accounting records*   LO 7

The market value of Coe Corporation's common stock had become excessively high. The stock was currently selling for $180 per share. To reduce the market price of the common stock, Coe declared a 2-for-1 stock split for the 300,000 outstanding shares of its $10 par common stock.

Required

a. How will Coe Corporation's books be affected by the stock split?

b. Determine the number of common shares outstanding and the par value after the split.

c. Explain how the market value of the stock will be affected by the stock split.

Exercise 8-16   *Corporate announcements*

Super Drugs (one of the three largest drug makers) just reported that its 2012 third-quarter profits had increased substantially over its 2011 third-quarter profits. In addition to this announcement, the same day, Super Drugs also announced that the Food and Drug Administration had just denied approval of a new drug used to treat high blood pressure that Super Drugs developed. The FDA was concerned about potential side effects of the drug.

Required

Using the above information, answer the following questions.

a. What do you think will happen to the stock price of Super Drugs on the day these two announcements are made? Explain your answer.

b. How will the balance sheet be affected on that day by the above announcements?

c. How will the income statement be affected on that day by the above announcements?

d. How will the statement of cash flows be affected on that day by the above announcements?

PROBLEMS

All applicable Problems are available with McGraw-Hill's
Connect Accounting.

Problem 8-17   *Effect of business structure on financial statements*

Calloway Company was started on January 1, 2012, when the owners invested $40,000 cash in the business. During 2012, the company earned cash revenues of $18,000 and incurred cash expenses of $12,500. The company also paid cash distributions of $3,000.

Required

Prepare the 2012 income statement, capital statement (statement of changes in equity), balance sheet, and statement of cash flows using each of the following assumptions. (Consider each assumption separately.)

a. Calloway is a sole proprietorship owned by Macy Calloway.

b. Calloway is a partnership with two partners, Macy Calloway and Artie Calloway. Macy Calloway invested $25,000 and Artie Calloway invested $15,000 of the $40,000 cash that was used to start the business. A. Calloway was expected to assume the vast majority of the responsibility for operating the business. The partnership agreement called for A. Calloway to receive 60 percent of the profits and M. Calloway to get the remaining 40 percent. With regard to the $3,000 distribution, A. Calloway withdrew $1,200 from the business and M. Calloway withdrew $1,800.

c. Calloway is a corporation. It issued 5,000 shares of $5 par common stock for $40,000 cash to start the business.

Problem 8-18   *Recording and reporting stock transactions and cash dividends across two accounting cycles*

Davis Corporation was authorized to issue 100,000 shares of $10 par common stock and 50,000 shares of $50 par, 6 percent, cumulative preferred stock. Davis Corporation completed the following transactions during its first two years of operation.

2012

Jan. 2 Issued 5,000 shares of $10 par common stock for $28 per share.

     15 Issued 1,000 shares of $50 par preferred stock for $70 per share.

Feb. 14   Issued 15,000 shares of $10 par common stock for $30 per share.

Dec. 31   During the year, earned $170,000 of cash service revenue and paid $110,000 of cash operating expenses.

    31   Declared the cash dividend on outstanding shares of preferred stock for 2012. The dividend will be paid on January 31 to stockholders of record on January 15, 2013.

2013

Jan. 31   Paid the cash dividend declared on December 31, 2012.

Mar. 1   Issued 2,000 shares of $50 par preferred stock for $58 per share.

June 1   Purchased 500 shares of common stock as treasury stock at $43 per share.

Dec. 31   During the year, earned $210,000 of cash service revenue and paid $175,000 of cash operating expenses.

    31   Declared the dividend on the preferred stock and a $0.60 per share dividend on the common stock.

Required

a.   Organize the transaction data in accounts under an accounting equation.

b.   Prepare the stockholders' equity section of the balance sheet at December 31, 2012.

c.   Prepare the balance sheet at December 31, 2013.

Problem 8-19   *Recording and reporting treasury stock transactions*

Midwest Corp. completed the following transactions in 2012, the first year of operation.

1.   Issued 20,000 shares of $10 par common stock at par.
2.   Issued 2,000 shares of $30 stated value preferred stock at $32 per share.
3.   Purchased 500 shares of common stock as treasury stock for $15 per share.
4.   Declared a 5 percent dividend on preferred stock.
5.   Sold 300 shares of treasury stock for $18 per share.
6.   Paid the cash dividend on preferred stock that was declared in Event 4.
7.   Earned cash service revenue of $75,000 and incurred cash operating expenses of $42,000.
8.   Appropriated $6,000 of retained earnings.

Required

a.   Organize the transaction in accounts under an accounting equation.

b.   Prepare the stockholders' equity section of the balance sheet as of December 31, 2012.

Problem 8-20   *Recording and reporting treasury stock transactions*

Boley Corporation reports the following information in its January 1, 2012, balance sheet:

Stockholders' equity	
Common stock, $10 par value,	
50,000 shares authorized, 30,000 shares issued and outstanding	$300,000
Paid-in capital in excess of par value	150,000
Retained earnings	100,000
Total stockholders' equity	$550,000

During 2012, Boley was affected by the following accounting events.

1.   Purchased 1,000 shares of treasury stock at $18 per share.
2.   Reissued 600 shares of treasury stock at $20 per share.
3.   Earned $64,000 of cash service revenues.
4.   Paid $38,000 of cash operating expenses.

Required

Prepare the stockholders' equity section of the year-end balance sheet.

LO 5, 6, 8

CHECK FIGURE
b. Total Paid-In Capital: $264,900

LO 5

CHECK FIGURES
Total Paid-In Capital: $451,200
Total Stockholders' Equity:
$570,000

Problem 8-21   *Recording and reporting stock dividends*

Chan Corp. completed the following transactions in 2012, the first year of operation.

1. Issued 20,000 shares of $20 par common stock for $30 per share.
2. Issued 5,000 shares of $50 par, 5 percent, preferred stock at $51 per share.
3. Paid the annual cash dividend to preferred shareholders.
4. Issued a 5 percent stock dividend on the common stock. The market value at the dividend declaration date was $40 per share.
5. Later that year, issued a 2-for-1 split on the 21,000 shares of outstanding common stock.
6. Earned $210,000 of cash service revenues and paid $140,000 of cash operating expenses.

Required

a. Record each of these events in a horizontal statements model like the following one. In the Cash Flow column, indicate whether the item is an operating activity (OA), investing activity (IA), or financing activity (FA). Use NA to indicate that an element is not affected by the event.

Assets = Liab. +	Equity					Rev. − Exp. = Net Inc.	Cash Flow
	Pfd. Stk. +	Com. Stk. +	PIC in Excess PS +	PIC in Excess CS +	Ret. Earn.		

b. Prepare the stockholders' equity section of the balance sheet at the end of 2012.

Problem 8-22   *Analyzing the stockholders' equity section of the balance sheet*

The stockholders' equity section of the balance sheet for Brawner Company at December 31, 2012, is as follows:

Stockholders' Equity

Paid-in capital		
Preferred stock, ? par value, 6% cumulative, 50,000 shares authorized, 30,000 shares issued and outstanding	$300,000	
Common stock, $10 stated value, 150,000 shares authorized, 50,000 shares issued and ? outstanding	500,000	
Paid-in capital in excess of par—Preferred	30,000	
Paid-in capital in excess of stated value—Common	200,000	
Total paid-in capital		$1,030,000
Retained earnings		250,000
Treasury stock, 1,000 shares		(100,000)
Total stockholders' equity		$1,180,000

Note: The market value per share of the common stock is $25, and the market value per share of the preferred stock is $12.

Required

a. What is the par value per share of the preferred stock?
b. What is the dividend per share on the preferred stock?
c. What is the number of common stock shares outstanding?
d. What was the average issue price per share (price for which the stock was issued) of the common stock?
e. Explain the difference between the average issue price and the market price of the common stock.
f. If Brawner declared a 2-for-1 stock split on the common stock, how many shares would be outstanding after the split? What amount would be transferred from the retained earnings account because of the stock split? Theoretically, what would be the market price of the common stock immediately after the stock split?

Problem 8-23   *Different forms of business organization*   LO 1

Shawn Bates was working to establish a business enterprise with four of his wealthy friends. Each of the five individuals would receive a 20 percent ownership interest in the company. A primary goal of establishing the enterprise was to minimize the amount of income taxes paid. Assume that the five investors are taxed at the rate of 15% on dividend income and 30% on all other income and that the corporate tax rate is 30 percent. Also assume that the new company is expected to earn $400,000 of cash income before taxes during its first year of operation. All earnings are expected to be immediately distributed to the owners.

Required

Calculate the amount of after-tax cash flow available to each investor if the business is established as a partnership versus a corporation. Write a memo explaining the advantages and disadvantages of these two forms of business organization. Explain why a limited liability company may be a better choice than either a partnership or a corporation.

Problem 8-24   *Effects of equity transactions on financial statements*   LO 4–8

The following events were experienced by Abbot Inc.:

1. Issued cumulative preferred stock for cash.
2. Issued common stock for cash.
3. Distributed a 2-for-1 stock split on the common stock.
4. Issued noncumulative preferred stock for cash.
5. Appropriated retained earnings.
6. Sold treasury stock for an amount of cash that was more than the cost of the treasury stock.
7. Distributed a stock dividend.
8. Paid cash to purchase treasury stock.
9. Declared a cash dividend.
10. Paid the cash dividend declared in Event 9.

Required

Show the effect of each event on the elements of the financial statements using a horizontal statements model like the following one. Use + for increase, − for decrease, and NA for not affected. In the Cash Flow column, indicate whether the item is an operating activity (OA), investing activity (IA), or financing activity (FA). The first transaction is entered as an example.

Event No.	Assets	=	Liab.	+	Equity	Rev.	−	Exp.	=	Net Inc.	Cash Flow
1	+		NA		+	NA		NA		NA	+ FA

ANALYZE, THINK, COMMUNICATE

ATC 8-1   Business Applications Case   *Understanding real-world annual reports*

Use the Target Corporation's annual report in Appendix B to answer the following questions.

Required

a. What is the par value per share of Target's stock?
b. How many shares of Target's common stock were *outstanding* as of January 31, 2010?
c. Target's annual report provides some details about the company's executive officers. How many are identified? What is their minimum, maximum, and average age? How many are females?
d. Target's balance sheet does not show a balance for treasury stock. Does this mean the company has not repurchased any of its own stock? Explain.

ATC 8-2   Group Assignment   *Missing information*

Listed here are the stockholders' equity sections of three public companies for years ending in 2008 and 2007:

	2008	2007
Wendy's (in thousands) (merger with Triare in 2008)		
Stockholders' equity		
Common stock, ?? stated value per share, authorized:		
1,500,000; 470,424 in 2008 and 93,576 in		
2007 shares issued, respectively	$ 47,042	$ 9,357
Capital in excess of stated value	2,752,987	291,122
Retained earnings	(357,541)	167,267
Acc. other comp. income (loss)	(43,253)	(2,098)
Treasury stock, at cost: 1,220 in 2008 and 841 in 2007	(15,944)	(16,774)
Coca-Cola (in millions)		
Stockholders' equity		
Common stock, ?? par value per share, authorized:		
5,600; issued: 3,519 shares in 2008 and 3,519 shares in 2007	880	880
Capital surplus	7,966	7,378
Reinvested earnings	38,513	36,235
Acc. other comp. inc. (loss)	(2,674)	(626)
Treasury stock, at cost: (1,207 shares in 2008; 1,201 shares in 2007)	(24,213)	(23,375)
Harley-Davidson (dollar amounts are presented in thousands)		
Stockholders' equity		
Common stock, ?? par value per share, authorized: 800,000,000, issued:		
335,653,577 in 2008 and 335,211,201 shares in 2007	3,357	3,352
Additional paid-in capital	846,796	812,224
Retained earnings	6,458,778	6,117,567
Acc. other comp. inc. (loss)	(522,526)	(137,258)
Treasury stock, at cost: 102,889,370 for 2008 and 96,725,399 for 2007	(4,670,802)	(4,420,394)

Required

a. Divide the class in three sections and divide each section into groups of three to five students. Assign each section one of the companies.

Group Tasks

Based on the company assigned to your group, answer the following questions.

b. What is the per share par or stated value of the common stock in 2008?
c. What was the average issue price of the common stock for each year?
d. How many shares of stock are outstanding at the end of each year?
e. What is the average cost per share of the treasury stock for 2008?
f. Do the data suggest that your company was profitable in 2008?
g. Can you determine the amount of net income from the information given? What is missing?
h. What is the total stockholders' equity of your company for each year?

Class Discussion

i. Have each group select a representative to present the information about its company. Compare the share issue price and the par or stated value of the companies.
j. Compare the average issue price to the current market price for each of the companies. Speculate about what might cause the difference.

ATC 8-3   Research Assignment   *Analyzing PepsiCo's equity structure*

Using either Big Lots, Inc. most current Form 10-K or the company's annual report, answer the questions below. To obtain the Form 10-K use either the EDGAR system following the instructions in Appendix A or the company's website. The company's annual report is available on its website.

Required

a. What is the *book value* of Big Lots' stockholders' equity that is shown on the company's balance sheet?

b. What is the par value of Big Lots' common stock?

c. Does Big Lots have any treasury stock? If so, how many shares of treasury stock does the company hold?

d. Why does the stock of a company such as a Big Lots have a market value that is higher than its book value?

ATC 8-4   Writing Assignment   *Comparison of organizational forms*

Jim Baku and Scott Hanson are thinking about opening a new restaurant. Baku has extensive marketing experience but does not know that much about food preparation. However, Hanson is an excellent chef. Both will work in the business, but Baku will provide most of the funds necessary to start the business. At this time, they cannot decide whether to operate the business as a partnership or a corporation.

Required

Prepare a written memo to Baku and Hanson describing the advantages and disadvantages of each organizational form. Also, from the limited information provided, recommend the organizational form you think they should use.

ATC 8-5   Ethical Dilemma   *Bad news versus very bad news*

Louise Stinson, the chief financial officer of Bostonian Corporation, was on her way to the president's office. She was carrying the latest round of bad news. There would be no executive bonuses this year. Corporate profits were down. Indeed, if the latest projections held true, the company would report a small loss on the year-end income statement. Executive bonuses were tied to corporate profits. The executive compensation plan provided for 10 percent of net earnings to be set aside for bonuses. No profits meant no bonuses. While things looked bleak, Stinson had a plan that might help soften the blow.

After informing the company president of the earnings forecast, Stinson made the following suggestion: Because the company was going to report a loss anyway, why not report a big loss? She reasoned that the directors and stockholders would not be much more angry if the company reported a large loss than if it reported a small one. There were several questionable assets that could be written down in the current year. This would increase the current year's loss but would reduce expenses in subsequent accounting periods. For example, the company was carrying damaged inventory that was estimated to have a value of $2,500,000. If this estimate were revised to $500,000, the company would have to recognize a $2,000,000 loss in the current year. However, next year when the goods were sold, the expense for cost of goods sold would be $2,000,000 less and profits would be higher by that amount. Although the directors would be angry this year, they would certainly be happy next year. The strategy would also have the benefit of adding $200,000 to next year's executive bonus pool ($2,000,000 × 0.10). Furthermore, it could not hurt this year's bonus pool because there would be no pool this year because the company is going to report a loss.

Some of the other items that Stinson is considering include (1) converting from straight-line to accelerated depreciation, (2) increasing the percentage of receivables estimated to be uncollectible in the current year and lowering the percentage in the following year, and (3) raising the percentage of estimated warranty claims in the current period and lowering it in the following period. Finally, Stinson notes that two of the company's department stores have been experiencing losses. The company could sell these stores this year and thereby improve earnings next year. Stinson admits that the sale would result in significant losses this year, but she smiles as she thinks of next year's bonus check.

Required

a. Explain how each of the three numbered strategies for increasing the amount of the current year's loss would affect the stockholders' equity section of the balance sheet in the current year. How would the other elements of the balance sheet be affected?

b. If Stinson's strategy were effectively implemented, how would it affect the stockholders' equity in subsequent accounting periods?

c. Comment on the ethical implications of running the company for the sake of management (maximization of bonuses) versus the maximization of return to stockholders.

d. Formulate a bonus plan that will motivate managers to maximize the value of the firm instead of motivating them to manipulate the reporting process.

e. How would Stinson's strategy of overstating the amount of the reported loss in the current year affect the company's current P/E ratio?

CHAPTER 9

Financial Statement Analysis

LEARNING OBJECTIVES

After you have mastered the material in this chapter, you will be able to:

1 Describe factors associated with communicating useful information.

2 Differentiate between horizontal and vertical analysis.

3 Explain ratio analysis.

4 Calculate ratios for assessing a company's liquidity.

5 Calculate ratios for assessing a company's solvency.

6 Calculate ratios for assessing company management's effectiveness.

7 Calculate ratios for assessing a company's position in the stock market.

8 Explain the limitations of financial statement analysis.

CHAPTER OPENING

Expressing financial statement information in the form of ratios enhances its usefulness. Ratios permit comparisons over time and among companies, highlighting similarities, differences, and trends. Proficiency with common financial statement analysis techniques benefits both internal and external users. Before beginning detailed explanations of numerous ratios and percentages, however, we consider factors relevant to communicating useful information.

The Curious Accountant

On September 7, 2009, **Kraft Foods, Inc.**, announced that it had made an offer to the board of directors of **Cadbury PLC** to purchase their company for $16.7 billion in cash and stock. The CEO of Cadbury promptly rejected the offer, and a four month war of words began. Among other things, Cadbury's CEO described Kraft as an "unfocused conglomerate," with "unappealing categories," and hav-ing "a management that underperforms." He said that Kraft's offer greatly undervalued Cadbury. Meanwhile, the CEO of Kraft said its offer for Cadbury was "full and fair." Upon making its offer to Cadbury's board, Kraft also stipulated that if the board did not accept the offer by January 20, 2010, Kraft would make its offer to buy the company's stock directly to Cadbury's shareholders.

When a company makes a bid for one of its competitors, it often causes other companies to enter the bidding process. Analysts predicted that **Hershey** and **Nestle** would soon make their own offers for Cadbury. These offers did not materialize, although there were rumors that Hershey was preparing to make an offer of $18.8 billion.

On the morning of January 19, 2010, the last day before Kraft planned to take its offer directly to Cadbury's share-holders, the two companies announced they had reached an agreement. Kraft would buy Cadbury for $19.4 billion.

If after four months of waiting for Cadbury to accept its offer no other company was willing to make a competing bid for Cadbury, why whould Kraft agree to buy it at a price that was 16 percent higher than its original offer? (Answer on page 323.)

FACTORS IN COMMUNICATING USEFUL INFORMATION

The primary objective of accounting is to provide information useful for decision making. To provide information that supports this objective, accountants must consider the intended users, the types of decisions users make with financial statement information, and available means of analyzing the information.

The Users

Users of financial statement information include managers, creditors, stockholders, potential investors, and regulatory agencies. These individuals and organizations use financial statements for different purposes and bring varying levels of sophistication to understanding business activities. For example, investors range from private individuals who know little about financial statements to large investment brokers and institutional investors capable of using complex statistical analysis techniques. At what level of user knowledge should financial statements be aimed? Condensing and reporting complex business transactions at a level easily understood by nonprofessional investors is increasingly difficult. Current reporting standards target users that have a reasonably informed knowledge of business, though that level of sophistication is difficult to define.

The Types of Decisions

Just as the knowledge level of potential users varies, the information needs of users vary, depending on the decision at hand. A supplier considering whether or not to sell goods on account to a particular company wants to evaluate the likelihood of getting paid; a potential investor in that company wants to predict the likelihood of increases in the market value of the company's common stock. Financial statements, however, are designed for general purposes; they are not aimed at any specific user group. Some disclosed information, therefore, may be irrelevant to some users but vital to others. Users must employ different forms of analysis to identify information most relevant to a particular decision.

Financial statements can provide only highly summarized economic information. The costs to a company of providing excessively detailed information would be prohibitive. In addition, too much detail leads to **information overload,** the problem of having so much data that important information becomes obscured by trivial information. Users faced with reams of data may become so frustrated attempting to use it that they lose the value of *key* information that is provided.

Information Analysis

Because of the diversity of users, their different levels of knowledge, the varying information needs for particular decisions, and the general nature of financial statements, a variety of analysis techniques has been developed. In the following sections, we explain several common methods of analysis. The choice of method depends on which technique appears to provide the most relevant information in a given situation.

METHODS OF ANALYSIS

Financial statement analysis should focus primarily on isolating information useful for making a particular decision. The information required can take many forms but usually involves comparisons, such as comparing changes in the same item for the same company over a number of years, comparing key relationships within the same year, or comparing the operations of several different companies in the same industry. This chapter discusses three categories of analysis methods: horizontal, vertical, and ratio. Exhibits 9.1 and 9.2 present comparative financial statements for Milavec Company. We refer to these statements in the examples of analysis techniques.

EXHIBIT 9.1

MILAVEC COMPANY
Income Statements and Statements of Retained Earnings
For the Years Ending December 31

	2012	2011
Sales	$900,000	$800,000
Cost of goods sold		
Beginning inventory	43,000	40,000
Purchases	637,000	483,000
Goods available for sale	680,000	523,000
Ending inventory	70,000	43,000
Cost of goods sold	610,000	480,000
Gross margin	290,000	320,000
Operating expenses	248,000	280,000
Income before taxes	42,000	40,000
Income taxes	17,000	18,000
Net income	25,000	22,000
Plus: Retained earnings, beginning balance	137,000	130,000
Less: Dividends	0	15,000
Retained earnings, ending balance	$162,000	$137,000

EXHIBIT 9.2

MILAVEC COMPANY
Balance Sheets
As of December 31

	2012	2011
Assets		
Cash	$ 20,000	$ 17,000
Marketable securities	20,000	22,000
Notes receivable	4,000	3,000
Accounts receivable	50,000	56,000
Merchandise inventory	70,000	43,000
Prepaid items	4,000	4,000
Property, plant, and equipment (net)	340,000	310,000
Total assets	$508,000	$455,000
Liabilities and Stockholders' Equity		
Accounts payable	$ 40,000	$ 38,000
Salaries payable	2,000	3,000
Taxes payable	4,000	2,000
Bonds payable, 8%	100,000	100,000
Preferred stock, 6%, $100 par, cumulative	50,000	50,000
Common stock, $10 par	150,000	125,000
Retained earnings	162,000	137,000
Total liabilities and stockholders' equity	$508,000	$455,000

Horizontal Analysis

Horizontal analysis, also called **trend analysis,** refers to studying the behavior of individual financial statement items over several accounting periods. These periods may be several quarters within the same fiscal year or they may be several different years. The analysis of a given item may focus on trends in the absolute dollar amount of the item or trends in percentages. For example, a user may observe that revenue increased from one period to the next by $42 million (an absolute dollar amount) or that it increased by a percentage such as 15 percent.

Absolute Amounts

The **absolute amounts** of particular financial statement items have many uses. Various national economic statistics, such as gross domestic product and the amount spent to replace productive capacity, are derived by combining absolute amounts reported by businesses. Financial statement users with expertise in particular industries might evaluate amounts reported for research and development costs to judge whether a company is spending excessively or conservatively. Users are particularly concerned with how amounts change over time. For example, a user might compare a pharmaceutical company's revenue before and after the patent expired on one of its drugs.

Comparing only absolute amounts has drawbacks, however, because *materiality* levels differ from company to company or even from year to year for a given company. The **materiality** of information refers to its relative importance. An item is considered material if knowledge of it would influence the decision of a reasonably informed user. Generally accepted accounting principles permit companies to account for *immaterial* items in the most convenient way, regardless of technical accounting rules. For example, companies may expense, rather than capitalize and depreciate, relatively inexpensive long-term assets like pencil sharpeners or waste baskets even if the assets have useful lives of many years. The concept of materiality, which has both quantitative and qualitative aspects, underlies all accounting principles.

It is difficult to judge the materiality of an absolute financial statement amount without considering the size of the company reporting it. For reporting purposes, Exxon Corporation's financial statements are rounded to the nearest million dollars. For Exxon, a $400,000 increase in sales is not material. For a small company, however, $400,000 could represent total sales, a highly material amount. Meaningful comparisons between the two companies' operating performance are impossible using only absolute amounts. Users can surmount these difficulties with percentage analysis.

Percentage Analysis

Percentage analysis involves computing the percentage relationship between two amounts. In horizontal percentage analysis, a financial statement item is expressed as a percentage of the previous balance for the same item. Percentage analysis sidesteps the materiality problems of comparing different size companies by measuring changes in percentages rather than absolute amounts. Each change is converted to a percentage of the base year. Exhibit 9.3 presents a condensed version of Milavec's income statement with horizontal percentages for each item.

The percentage changes disclose that, even though Milavec's net income increased slightly more than sales, products may be underpriced. Cost of goods sold increased much more than sales, resulting in a lower gross margin. Users would also want to investigate why operating expenses decreased substantially despite the increase in sales.

EXHIBIT 9.3

MILAVEC COMPANY
Comparative Income Statements
For the Years Ending December 31

	2012	2011	Percentage Difference
Sales	$900,000	$800,000	+12.5%*
Cost of goods sold	610,000	480,000	+27.1
Gross margin	290,000	320,000	−9.4
Operating expenses	248,000	280,000	−11.4
Income before taxes	42,000	40,000	+5.0
Income taxes	17,000	18,000	−5.6
Net income	$ 25,000	$ 22,000	+13.6

*($900,000 − $800,000) ÷ $800,000; all changes expressed as percentages of previous totals.

Whether basing their analyses on absolute amounts, percentages, or ratios, users must avoid drawing overly simplistic conclusions about the reasons for the results. Numerical relationships flag conditions requiring further study. A change that appears favorable on the surface may not necessarily be a good sign. Users must evaluate the underlying reasons for the change.

✓ CHECK YOURSELF 9.1

The following information was drawn from the annual reports of two retail companies (amounts are shown in millions). One company is an upscale department store; the other is a discount store. Based on this limited information, identify which company is the upscale department store.

	Jenkins Co.	Horn's Inc.
Sales	$325	$680
Cost of goods sold	130	408
Gross margin	$195	$272

Answer Jenkins' gross margin represents 60 percent ($195 ÷ $325) of sales. Horn's gross margin represents 40 percent ($272 ÷ $680) of sales. Because an upscale department store would have higher margins than a discount store, the data suggest that Jenkins is the upscale department store.

Answers to The Curious Accountant

Obviously Kraft agreed to acquire Cadbury because it believed it could make a profit on the investment. Two major reasons were discussed as to why Kraft would want Cadbury. First, Cadbury was a bigger player than Kraft in important markets outside of the United States. Owning Cadbury would make it easier for Kraft to expand globally, especially in several rapidly developing markets, including Egypt, India, Mexico, and Thailand. Second, in 2008, Mars, Inc. had acquired the giant chewing gum company, Wm. Wrigley Jr. Company, making it a much larger confectionary company. By purchasing Cadbury, Kraft felt it could better compete with Mars.

Kraft's optimism about its purchase of Cadbury does not guarantee that the investment will be successful. In the late 1980s and early 1990s Hershey's purchased several Dutch, German, and Italian confectionary companies that, a few years later, it sold at losses. How do companies decide what another company is worth, and how can such successful companies as Hershey, Nestlé, Kraft, and Cadbury have such different opinions about the value of an investment? Valuing a potential investment is the result of extensive financial analysis, as discussed in this chapter, and capital budgeting techniques, discussed in Chapter 16. As these references indicate, such decision making is based on estimates about future events. Predicting the future is imperfect, no matter how well trained the forecaster might be.

Does this mean that financial analysis is useless? No. Consider someone planning to drive across the United States. Would they prefer to take the trip with a map or without? Obviously they would prefer to have a map or GPS, even though they know neither device is perfect. Similarly, just as five different financial analysts may reach five different amounts they think a company is worth; five individuals planning a trip from Key West, Florida, to Anchorage Alaska, could look at the same map and decide on five different ways to get there. Only after the trips have been completed can we say which person made the best decision.

Sources: "Cadbury Sour on Kraft Bid," *The Wall Street Journal,* September 8, 2009, pp. A–1 and A–17; "Nestlé's Undercooked Deal Making," *The Wall Street Journal,* January 9 & 10, 2010, pp. B–10; "Kraft Near Deal for Cadbury," *The Wall Street Journal,* January 19, 2010, pp. A–1 and A–6; "Kraft Wins a Reluctant Cadbury with Help of Clock, Hedge Funds," *The Wall Street Journal,* January 20, 2010, pp. B–1 and B–6; and "Hershey, On Its Own, Has Limited Options," *The Wall Street Journal,* January 20, 2010, p. B–6.

When comparing more than two periods, analysts use either of two basic approaches: (1) choosing one base year from which to calculate all increases or decreases or (2) calculating each period's percentage change from the preceding figure. For example, assume Milavec's sales for 2009 and 2010 were $600,000 and $750,000, respectively.

	2012	2011	2010	2009
Sales	$900,000	$800,000	$750,000	$600,000
Increase over 2009 sales	50.0%	33.3%	25.0%	–
Increase over preceding year	12.5%	6.7%	25.0%	–

Analysis discloses that Milavec's 2012 sales represented a 50 percent increase over 2009 sales, and a large increase (25 percent) occurred in 2010. From 2010 to 2011, sales increased only 6.7 percent but in the following year increased much more (12.5 percent).

Vertical Analysis

Vertical analysis uses percentages to compare individual components of financial statements to a key statement figure. Horizontal analysis compares items over many time periods; vertical analysis compares many items within the same time period.

Vertical Analysis of the Income Statement

Vertical analysis of an income statement (also called a *common size* income statement) involves converting each income statement component to a percentage of sales. Although vertical analysis suggests examining only one period, it is useful to compare common size income statements for several years. Exhibit 9.4 presents Milavec's income statements, along with vertical percentages, for 2012 and 2011. This analysis discloses that cost of goods sold increased significantly as a percentage of sales. Operating expenses and income taxes, however, decreased in relation to sales. Each of these observations indicates a need for more analysis regarding possible trends for future profits.

EXHIBIT 9.4

MILAVEC COMPANY
Vertical Analysis of Comparative Income Statements

	2012		2011	
	Amount	Percentage* of Sales	Amount	Percentage* of Sales
Sales	$900,000	100.0%	$800,000	100.0%
Cost of goods sold	610,000	67.8	480,000	60.0
Gross margin	290,000	32.2	320,000	40.0
Operating expenses	248,000	27.6	280,000	35.0
Income before taxes	42,000	4.7	40,000	5.0
Income taxes	17,000	1.9	18,000	2.3
Net income	$ 25,000	2.8%	$ 22,000	2.8%

*Percentages may not add exactly due to rounding.

Vertical Analysis of the Balance Sheet

Vertical analysis of the balance sheet involves converting each balance sheet component to a percentage of total assets. The vertical analysis of Milavec's balance sheets in Exhibit 9.5 discloses few large percentage changes from the preceding year. Even small individual percentage changes, however, may represent substantial dollar increases. For example, inventory constituted 9.5% of total assets in 2011 and 13.8% in 2012. While this appears to be a small increase, it actually represents a 62.8% increase in the inventory account balance ([\$70,000 − \$43,000] ÷ \$43,000) from 2011 to 2012. Careful analysis requires considering changes in both percentages *and* absolute amounts.

Ratio Analysis

Explain ratio analysis.

Ratio analysis involves studying various relationships between different items reported in a set of financial statements. For example, net earnings (net income) reported on the income statement may be compared to total assets reported on the balance sheet. Analysts calculate many different ratios for a wide variety of purposes. The remainder of this chapter is devoted to discussing some of the more commonly used ratios.

EXHIBIT 9.5

MILAVEC COMPANY
Vertical Analysis of Comparative Balance Sheets

	2012	Percentage* of Total	2011	Percentage* of Total
Assets				
Cash	$ 20,000	3.9%	$ 17,000	3.7%
Marketable securities	20,000	3.9	22,000	4.8
Notes receivable	4,000	0.8	3,000	0.7
Accounts receivable	50,000	9.8	56,000	12.3
Merchandise inventory	70,000	13.8	43,000	9.5
Prepaid items	4,000	0.8	4,000	0.9
Total current assets	168,000	33.1	145,000	31.9
Property, plant, and equipment	340,000	66.9	310,000	68.1
Total assets	$508,000	100.0%	$455,000	100.0%
Liabilities and Stockholders' Equity				
Accounts payable	$ 40,000	7.9%	$ 38,000	8.4%
Salaries payable	2,000	0.4	3,000	0.7
Taxes payable	4,000	0.8	2,000	0.4
Total current liabilities	46,000	9.1	43,000	9.5
Bonds payable, 8%	100,000	19.7	100,000	22.0
Total liabilities	146,000	28.7	143,000	31.4
Preferred stock 6%, $100 par	50,000	9.8	50,000	11.0
Common stock, $10 par	150,000	29.5	125,000	27.5
Retained earnings	162,000	31.9	137,000	30.1
Total stockholders' equity	362,000	71.3	312,000	68.6
Total liabilities and stockholders' equity	$508,000	100.0%	$455,000	100.0%

*Percentages may not add exactly due to rounding.

Objectives of Ratio Analysis

As suggested earlier, various users approach financial statement analysis with many different objectives. Creditors are interested in whether a company will be able to pay its debts on time. Both creditors and stockholders are concerned with how the company is financed, whether through debt, equity, or earnings. Stockholders and potential investors analyze past earnings performance and dividend policy for clues to the future value of their investments. In addition to using internally generated data to analyze operations, company managers find much information prepared for external purposes useful for examining past operations and planning future policies. Although many of these objectives are interrelated, it is convenient to group ratios into categories such as measures of debt-paying ability and measures of profitability.

MEASURES OF DEBT-PAYING ABILITY

Liquidity Ratios

Liquidity ratios indicate a company's ability to pay short-term debts. They focus on current assets and current liabilities. The examples in the following section use the financial statement information reported by Milavec Company.

Calculate ratios for assessing a company's liquidity.

Working Capital

Working capital is current assets minus current liabilities. Current assets include assets most likely to be converted into cash or consumed in the current operating period.

Current liabilities represent debts that must be satisfied in the current period. Working capital therefore measures the excess funds the company will have available for operations, excluding any new funds it generates during the year. Think of working capital as the cushion against short-term debt-paying problems. Working capital at the end of 2012 and 2011 for Milavec Company was as follows.

	2012	2011
Current assets	$168,000	$145,000
− Current liabilities	46,000	43,000
Working capital	$122,000	$102,000

Milavec's working capital increased from 2011 to 2012, but the numbers themselves say little. Whether $122,000 is sufficient or not depends on such factors as the industry in which Milavec operates, its size, and the maturity dates of its current obligations. We can see, however, that the increase in working capital is primarily due to the increase in inventories.

Current Ratio

Working capital is an absolute amount. Its usefulness is limited by the materiality difficulties discussed earlier. It is hard to draw meaningful conclusions from comparing Milavec's working capital of $122,000 with another company that also has working capital of $122,000. By expressing the relationship between current assets and current liabilities as a ratio, however, we have a more useful measure of the company's debt-paying ability relative to other companies. The **current ratio,** also called the **working capital ratio,** is calculated as follows.

$$\text{Current ratio} = \frac{\text{Current assets}}{\text{Current liabilities}}$$

To illustrate using the current ratio for comparisons, consider Milavec's current position relative to Laroque's, a larger firm with current assets of $500,000 and current liabilities of $378,000.

	Milavec	Laroque
Current assets (a)	$168,000	$500,000
− Current liabilities (b)	46,000	378,000
Working capital	$122,000	$122,000
Current ratio (a ÷ b)	3.65:1	1.32:1

The current ratio is expressed as the number of dollars of current assets for each dollar of current liabilities. In the above example, both companies have the same amount of working capital. Milavec, however, appears to have a much stronger working capital position. Any conclusions from this analysis must take into account the circumstances of the particular companies; there is no single ideal current ratio that suits all companies. In recent years the average current ratio of the 30 companies that constitute the Dow Jones Industrial Average was around 1.21:1; the individual company ratios, however, ranged from .05:1 to 3.0:1. A current ratio can be too high. Money invested in factories and developing new products is usually more profitable than money held as large cash balances or invested in inventory.

Quick Ratio

The **quick ratio,** also known as the **acid-test ratio,** is a conservative variation of the current ratio. The quick ratio measures a company's *immediate* debt-paying ability. Only cash, receivables, and current marketable securities *(quick assets)* are included in the numerator. Less liquid current assets, such as inventories and prepaid items, are omitted. Inventories may take several months to sell; prepaid items reduce otherwise necessary expenditures but do not lead eventually to cash receipts. The quick ratio is computed as follows.

$$\text{Quick ratio} = \frac{\text{Quick assets}}{\text{Current liabilities}}$$

Milavec Company's current ratios and quick ratios for 2012 and 2011 follow.

	2012	2011
Current ratio	$168,000 ÷ $46,000	$145,000 ÷ $43,000
	3.65:1	3.37:1
Quick ratio	$94,000 ÷ $46,000	$98,000 ÷ $43,000
	2.04:1	2.28:1

The decrease in the quick ratio from 2011 to 2012 reflects both a decrease in quick assets and an increase in current liabilities. The result indicates that the company is less liquid (has less ability to pay its short-term debt) in 2012 than it was in 2011.

Accounts Receivable Ratios

Offering customers credit plays an enormous role in generating revenue, but it also increases expenses and delays cash receipts. To minimize uncollectible accounts expense and collect cash for use in current operations, companies want to collect receivables as quickly as possible without losing customers. Two relationships are often examined to assess a company's collection record: *accounts receivable turnover* and *average number of days to collect receivables (average collection period)*.

Accounts receivable turnover is calculated as follows.

$$\text{Accounts receivable turnover} = \frac{\text{Net credit sales}}{\text{Average accounts receivable}}$$

Net credit sales refers to total sales on account less sales discounts, allowances, and returns. When most sales are credit sales or when a breakdown of total sales between cash sales and credit sales is not available, the analyst must use total sales in the numerator. The denominator is based on *net accounts receivable* (receivables after subtracting the allowance for doubtful accounts). Because the numerator represents a whole period, it is preferable to use average receivables in the denominator if possible. When comparative statements are available, the average can be based on the beginning and ending balances. Milavec Company's accounts receivable turnover is computed as follows.

	2012	2011
Net sales (assume all on account) (a)	$900,000	$800,000
Beginning receivables (b)	$ 56,000	$ 55,000*
Ending receivables (c)	50,000	56,000
Average receivables (d) = (b + c) ÷ 2	$ 53,000	$ 55,500
Accounts receivable turnover (a ÷ d)	16.98	14.41

*The beginning receivables balance was drawn from the 2010 financial statements, which are not included in the illustration.

The 2012 accounts receivable turnover of 16.98 indicates Milavec collected its average receivables almost 17 times that year. The higher the turnover, the faster the collections. A company can have cash flow problems and lose substantial purchasing power if resources are tied up in receivables for long periods.

Average number of days to collect receivables is calculated as follows.

$$\text{Average number of days to collect receivables} = \frac{365 \text{ days}}{\text{Accounts receivable turnover}}$$

This ratio offers another way to look at turnover by showing the number of days, on average, it takes to collect a receivable. If receivables were collected 16.98 times in 2012, the average collection period was 21 days, 365 ÷ 16.98 (the number of days in the year divided by accounts receivable turnover). For 2011, it took an average of 25 days (365 ÷ 14.41) to collect a receivable.

Although the collection period improved, no other conclusions can be reached without considering the industry, Milavec's past performance, and the general economic environment. In recent years the average time to collect accounts receivable for the 25 nonfinancial companies that make up the Dow Jones Industrial Average was around 49 days. (Financial firms are excluded because, by the nature of their business, they have very long collection periods.)

Inventory Ratios

A fine line exists between having too much and too little inventory in stock. Too little inventory can result in lost sales and costly production delays. Too much inventory can use needed space, increase financing and insurance costs, and become obsolete. To help analyze how efficiently a company manages inventory, we use two ratios similar to those used in analyzing accounts receivable.

Inventory turnover indicates the number of times, on average, that inventory is totally replaced during the year. The relationship is computed as follows.

$$\text{Inventory turnover} = \frac{\text{Cost of goods sold}}{\text{Average inventory}}$$

The average inventory is usually based on the beginning and ending balances that are shown in the financial statements. Inventory turnover for Milavec was as follows.

	2012	2011
Cost of goods sold (a)	$610,000	$480,000
Beginning inventory (b)	$ 43,000	$ 40,000*
Ending inventory (c)	70,000	43,000
Average inventory (d) = (b + c) ÷ 2	$ 56,500	$ 41,500
Inventory turnover (a ÷ d)	10.80	11.57

*The beginning inventory balance was drawn from the company's 2010 financial statements, which are not included in the illustration.

Generally, a higher turnover indicates that merchandise is being handled more efficiently. Trying to compare firms in different industries, however, can be misleading. Inventory turnover for grocery stores and many retail outlets is high. Because of the nature of the goods being sold, inventory turnover is much lower for appliance and jewelry stores. We look at this issue in more detail when we discuss return on investment.

Average number of days to sell inventory is determined by dividing the number of days in the year by the inventory turnover as follows.

$$\text{Average number of days to sell inventory} = \frac{365 \text{ days}}{\text{Inventory turnover}}$$

The result approximates the number of days the firm could sell inventory without purchasing more. For Milavec, this figure was 34 days in 2012 (365 ÷ 10.80) and 32 days in 2011 (365 ÷ 11.57). In recent years it took around 72 days, on average, for the companies in the Dow Jones Industrial Average to sell their inventory. The time it took individual companies to sell their inventory varied by industry, ranging from 10 days to 292 days.

Solvency Ratios

Solvency ratios are used to analyze a company's long-term debt-paying ability and its financing structure. Creditors are concerned with a company's ability to satisfy outstanding obligations. The larger a company's liability percentage, the greater the risk that the company could fall behind or default on debt payments. Stockholders, too, are concerned about a company's solvency. If a company is unable to pay its debts, the owners could lose their investment. Each user group desires that company financing choices minimize its investment risk, whether their investment is in debt or stockholders' equity.

Calculate ratios for assessing a company's solvency.

Debt Ratios

The following ratios represent two different ways to express the same relationship. Both are frequently used.

Debt to assets ratio.   This ratio measures the percentage of a company's assets that are financed by debt.

Debt to equity ratio.   As used in this ratio, *equity* means stockholders' equity. The debt to equity ratio compares creditor financing to owner financing. It is expressed as the dollar amount of liabilities for each dollar of stockholders' equity.

These ratios are calculated as follows.

$$\text{Debt to assets} = \frac{\text{Total liabilities}}{\text{Total assets}}$$

$$\text{Debt to equity} = \frac{\text{Total liabilities}}{\text{Total stockholders' equity}}$$

Applying these formulas to Milavec Company's results produces the following.

	2012	2011
Total liabilities (a)	$146,000	$143,000
Total stockholders' equity (b)	362,000	312,000
Total assets (liabilities + stockholders' equity) (c)	$508,000	$455,000
Debt to assets (a ÷ c)	29%	31%
Debt to equity ratio (a ÷ b)	0.40:1	0.46:1

Each year less than one-third of the company's assets were financed with debt. The amount of liabilities per dollar of stockholders' equity declined by 0.06. It is difficult to judge whether the reduced percentage of liabilities is favorable. In general, a lower level of liabilities provides greater security because the likelihood of bankruptcy is reduced. Perhaps, however, the company is financially strong enough to incur more liabilities and benefit from financial leverage. The 25 nonfinancial companies that make up the Dow Jones Industrial Average report around 33 percent of their assets, on average, are financed through borrowing.

Number of Times Interest Is Earned

The **times interest earned** ratio measures the burden a company's interest payments represent. Users often consider times interest is earned along with the debt ratios when evaluating financial risk. The numerator of this ratio uses *earnings before interest and taxes (EBIT),* rather than net earnings, because the amount of earnings *before* interest and income taxes is available for paying interest.

$$\text{Times interest earned} = \frac{\text{Earnings before interest expense and taxes}}{\text{Interest expense}}$$

Dividing EBIT by interest expense indicates how many times the company could have made its interest payments. Obviously, interest is paid only once, but the more times it *could* be paid, the bigger the company's safety net. Although interest is paid from cash, not accrual earnings, it is standard practice to base this ratio on accrual-based EBIT, not a cash-based amount. For Milavec, this calculation is as follows.

	2012	2011
Income before taxes	$42,000	$40,000
Interest expense (b)	8,000	8,000*
Earnings before interest and taxes (a)	$50,000	$48,000
Times interest earned (a ÷ b)	6.25 times	6 times

*Interest on bonds: $100,000 × .08 = $8,000.

Any expense or dividend payment can be analyzed this way. Another frequently used calculation is the number of times the preferred dividend is earned. In that case, the numerator is net income (after taxes) and the denominator is the amount of the annual preferred dividend.

✓ CHECK YOURSELF 9.2

Selected data for Riverside Corporation and Academy Company follow (amounts are shown in millions).

	Riverside Corporation	Academy Company
Total liabilities (a)	$650	$450
Stockholders' equity (b)	300	400
Total liabilities + stockholders' equity (c)	$950	$850
Interest expense (d)	$ 65	$ 45
Income before taxes (e)	140	130
Earnings before interest and taxes (f)	$205	$175

Based on this information alone, which company would likely obtain the less favorable interest rate on additional debt financing?

Answer   Interest rates vary with risk levels. Companies with less solvency (long-term debt-paying ability) generally must pay higher interest rates to obtain financing. Two solvency measures for the two companies follow. Recall:

Total assets = Liabilities + Stockholders' equity

	Riverside Corporation	Academy Company
Debt to assets ratio (a ÷ c)	68.4%	52.9%
Times interest earned (f ÷ d)	3.15 times	3.89 times

Because Riverside has a higher percentage of debt and a lower times interest earned ratio, the data suggest that Riverside is less solvent than Academy. Riverside would therefore likely have to pay a higher interest rate to obtain additional financing.

Plant Assets to Long-Term Liabilities

Companies often pledge plant assets as collateral for long-term liabilities. Financial statement users may analyze a firm's ability to obtain long-term financing on the strength of its asset base. Effective financial management principles dictate that asset purchases should be financed over a time span about equal to the expected lives of the assets. Short-term assets should be financed with short-term liabilities; the current ratio, introduced earlier, indicates how well a company manages current debt. Long-lived assets should be financed with long-term liabilities, and the **plant assets to long-term liabilities** ratio suggests how well long-term debt is managed. It is calculated as follows.

$$\text{Plant assets to long-term liabilities} = \frac{\text{Net plant assets}}{\text{Long-term liabilities}}$$

For Milavec Company, these ratios follow.

	2012	2011
Net plant assets (a)	$340,000	$310,000
Bonds payable (b)	100,000	100,000
Plant assets to long-term liabilities (a ÷ b)	3.4:1	3.1:1

MEASURES OF PROFITABILITY

Profitability refers to a company's ability to generate earnings. Both management and external users desire information about a company's success in generating profits and how these profits are used to reward investors. Some of the many ratios available to measure different aspects of profitability are discussed in the following two sections.

Measures of Managerial Effectiveness

The most common ratios used to evaluate managerial effectiveness measure what percentage of sales results in earnings and how productive assets are in generating those sales. As mentioned earlier, the *absolute amount* of sales or earnings means little without also considering company size.

LO 6

Calculate ratios for assessing company management's effectiveness.

Net Margin (or Return on Sales)

Gross margin and *gross profit* are alternate terms for the amount remaining after subtracting the expense cost of goods sold from sales. **Net margin,** sometimes called *operating margin, profit margin,* or the *return on sales ratio,* describes the percent remaining of each sales dollar after subtracting other expenses as well as cost of goods sold. Net margin can be calculated in several ways; some of the more common methods only subtract normal operating expenses or all expenses other than income tax expense. For simplicity, our calculation uses net income (we subtract all expenses). Net income divided by net sales expresses net income (earnings) as a percentage of sales, as follows.

$$\text{Net margin} = \frac{\text{Net income}}{\text{Net sales}}$$

For Milavec Company, the net margins for 2012 and 2011 were as follows.

	2012	2011
Net income (a)	$ 25,000	$ 22,000
Net sales (b)	900,000	800,000
Net margin (a ÷ b)	2.78%	2.75%

Milavec has maintained approximately the same net margin. Obviously, the larger the percentage, the better; a meaningful interpretation, however, requires analyzing the company's history and comparing the net margin to other companies in the same industry. The average net margin for the 30 companies that make up the Dow Jones Industrial Average has been around 12 percent in recent years; some companies, such as **Pfizer** with 40 percent, have been much higher than the average. Of course, if a company has a net loss, its net margin for that year will be negative.

Asset Turnover Ratio

The **asset turnover ratio** (sometimes called *turnover of assets ratio*) measures how many sales dollars were generated for each dollar of assets invested. As with many ratios used in financial statement analysis, users may define the numerator and denominator of this ratio in different ways. For example, they may use total assets or only include operating assets. Because the numerator represents a whole period, it is preferable to use average assets in the denominator if possible, especially if the amount of assets changed significantly during the year. We use average total assets in our illustration.

$$\text{Asset turnover} = \frac{\text{Net sales}}{\text{Average total assets}}$$

For Milavec, the asset turnover ratios were as follows.

	2012	2011
Net sales (a)	$900,000	$800,000
Beginning assets (b)	$455,000	$420,000*
Ending assets (c)	508,000	455,000
Average assets (d) = (b + c) ÷ 2	$481,500	$437,500
Asset turnover (a ÷ d)	1.87	1.83

*The beginning asset balance was drawn from the 2010 financial statements, which are not included in the illustration.

As with most ratios, the implications of a given asset turnover ratio are affected by other considerations. Asset turnover will be high in an industry that requires only minimal investment to operate, such as real estate sales companies. On the other hand, industries that require large investments in plant and machinery, like the auto industry, are likely to have lower asset turnover ratios. The asset turnover ratios of the companies that make up the Dow Jones Industrial Average have averaged around 0.90 in recent years. This means that annual sales have averaged 90 percent of their assets.

Return on Investment

Return on investment (ROI), also called *return on assets* or *earning power,* is the ratio of wealth generated (net income) to the amount invested (average total assets) to generate the wealth. ROI can be calculated as follows.[1]

$$\text{ROI} = \frac{\text{Net income}}{\text{Average total assets}}$$

---

[1]Detailed coverage of the return on investment ratio is provided in Chapter 15. As discussed in that chapter, companies frequently manipulate the formula to improve managerial motivation and performance. For example, instead of using net income, companies frequently use operating income because net income may be affected by items that are not controllable by management such as loss on a plant closing, storm damage, and so on.

For Milavec, ROI was as follows.

2012

$25,000 ÷ $481,500* = 5.19%

2011

$22,000 ÷ $437,500* = 5.03%

*The computation of average assets is shown above.

In general, higher ROIs suggest better performance. The ROI of the large companies that make up the Dow Jones Industrial Average averaged around 9 percent. These data suggest that Milavec is performing below average, and therefore signals a need for further evaluation that would lead to improved performance.

Return on Equity

Return on equity (ROE) is often used to measure the profitability of the stockholders' investment. ROE is usually higher than ROI because of financial leverage. Financial leverage refers to using debt financing to increase the assets available to a business beyond the amount of assets financed by owners. As long as a company's ROI exceeds its cost of borrowing (interest expense), the owners will earn a higher return on their investment in the company by using borrowed money. For example, if a company borrows money at 8 percent and invests it at 10 percent, the owners will enjoy a return that is higher than 10 percent. ROE is computed as follows.

$$\text{ROE} = \frac{\text{Net income}}{\text{Average total stockholders' equity}}$$

If the amount of stockholders' equity changes significantly during the year, it is desirable to use average equity rather than year-end equity in the denominator. The ROE figures for Milavec Company were as follows.

	2012	2011
Net income (a)	$ 25,000	$ 22,000
Preferred stock, 6%, $100 par, cumulative	50,000	50,000
Common stock, $10 par	150,000	125,000
Retained earnings	162,000	137,000
Total stockholders' equity (b)	$362,000	$312,000
ROE (a ÷ b)	6.9%	7.1%

The slight decrease in ROE is due primarily to the increase in common stock. The effect of the increase in total stockholders' equity offsets the effect of the increase in earnings. This information does not disclose whether Milavec had the use of the additional stockholder investment for all or part of the year. If the data are available, calculating a weighted average amount of stockholders' equity provides more meaningful results.

We mentioned earlier the companies that make up the Dow Jones Industrial Average had an average ROI of 9 percent. The average ROE for the companies in the Dow was 25 percent, indicating effective use of financial leverage.

Stock Market Ratios

LO 7

Calculate ratios for assessing a company's position in the stock market.

Existing and potential investors in a company's stock use many common ratios to analyze and compare the earnings and dividends of different size companies in different industries. Purchasers of stock can profit in two ways: through receiving dividends and through increases in stock value. Investors consider both dividends and overall earnings performance as indicators of the value of the stock they own.

Earnings per Share

Perhaps the most frequently quoted measure of earnings performance is **earnings per share (EPS)**. EPS calculations are among the most complex in accounting, and more advanced textbooks devote entire chapters to the subject. At this level, we use the following basic formula.

$$\text{Earnings per share} = \frac{\text{Net earnings available for common stock}}{\text{Average number of outstanding common shares}}$$

EPS pertains to shares of *common stock*. Limiting the numerator to earnings available for common stock eliminates the annual preferred dividend ($0.06 \times \$50,000 = \$3,000$) from the calculation. Exhibit 9.1 shows that Milavec did not pay the preferred dividends in 2012. Because the preferred stock is cumulative, however, the preferred dividend is in arrears and not available to the common stockholders. The number of common shares outstanding is determined by dividing the book value of the common stock by its par value per share ($\$150,000 \div \$10 = 15,000$ for 2012 and $\$125,000 \div \$10 = 12,500$ for 2011). Using these data, Milavec's 2012 EPS is calculated as follows.

$$\frac{\$25,000 \text{ (net income)} - \$3,000 \text{ (preferred dividend)}}{(15,000 + 12,500)/2 \text{ (average outstanding common shares)}} = \$1.60 \text{ per share}$$

Investors attribute a great deal of importance to EPS figures. The amounts used in calculating EPS, however, have limitations. Many accounting choices, assumptions, and estimates underlie net income computations, including alternative depreciation methods, different inventory cost flow assumptions, and estimates of future uncollectible accounts or warranty expenses, to name only a few. The denominator is also inexact because various factors (discussed in advanced accounting courses) affect the number of shares to include. Numerous opportunities therefore exist to manipulate EPS figures. Prudent investors consider these variables in deciding how much weight to attach to earnings per share.

Book Value

Book value per share is another frequently quoted measure of a share of stock. It is calculated as follows.

$$\text{Book value per share} = \frac{\text{Stockholders' equity} - \text{Preferred rights}}{\text{Outstanding common shares}}$$

Instead of describing the numerator as stockholders' equity, we could have used assets minus liabilities, the algebraic computation of a company's "net worth." Net worth is a misnomer. A company's accounting records reflect book values, not worth. Because assets are recorded at historical costs and different methods are used to transfer asset costs to expense, the book value of assets after deducting liabilities means little if anything. Nevertheless, investors use the term *book value per share* frequently.

Preferred rights represents the amount of money required to satisfy the claims of preferred stockholders. If the preferred stock has a call premium, the call premium amount is subtracted. In our example, we assume the preferred stock can be retired at par. Book value per share for 2012 was therefore as follows.

$$\frac{\$362,000 - \$50,000}{15,000 \text{ shares}} = \$20.80 \text{ per share}$$

Price-Earnings Ratio

The **price-earnings ratio,** or *P/E ratio,* compares the earnings per share of a company to the market price for a share of the company's stock. Assume Avalanche Company and Brushfire Company each report earnings per share of $3.60. For the same year, Cyclone Company reports EPS of $4.10. Based on these data alone, Cyclone stock may seem to be the best investment. Suppose, however, that the price for one share of stock in each company is $43.20, $36.00, and $51.25, respectively. Which stock would you buy? Cyclone's stock price is the highest, but so is its EPS. The P/E ratio provides a common base of comparison.

$$\text{Price-earnings ratio} = \frac{\text{Market price per share}}{\text{Earnings per share}}$$

The P/E ratios for the three companies are

Avalanche	Brushfire	Cyclone
12.0	10.0	12.5

Brushfire might initially seem to be the best buy for your money. Yet there must be some reason that Cyclone's stock is selling at 12½ times earnings. In general, a higher P/E ratio indicates the market is more optimistic about a company's growth potential than it is about a company with a lower P/E ratio. The market price of a company's stock reflects judgments about both the company's current results and expectations about future results. Investors cannot make informed use of these ratios for investment decisions without examining the reasons behind the ratios. Recently the average P/E ratio for the companies in the Dow Jones Industrial Average was around 18.

Dividend Yield

There are two ways to profit from a stock investment. One, investors can sell the stock for more than they paid to purchase it (if the stock price rises). Two, the company that issued the stock can pay cash dividends to the shareholders. Most investors view rising stock prices as the primary reward for investing in stock. The importance of receiving dividends, however, should not be overlooked. Evaluating dividend payments is more complex than simply comparing the dividends per share paid by one company to the dividends per share paid by another company. Receiving a $1 dividend on a share purchased for $10 is a much better return than receiving a $1.50 dividend on stock bought for $100. Computing the **dividend yield** simplifies comparing dividend payments. Dividend yield measures dividends received as a percentage of a stock's market price.

$$\text{Dividend yield} = \frac{\text{Dividends per share}}{\text{Market price per share}}$$

To illustrate, consider Dragonfly Inc. and Elk Company. The information for calculating dividend yield follows.

	Dragonfly	Elk
Dividends per share (a)	$ 1.80	$ 3.00
Market price per share (b)	40.00	75.00
Dividend yield (a ÷ b)	4.5%	4.0%

Even though the dividend per share paid by Elk Company is higher, the yield is lower (4.0 percent versus 4.5 percent) because Elk's stock price is so high. The dividend yields for the companies included in the Dow Jones Industrial Average were averaging around 2.3 percent.

Other Ratios

Investors can also use a wide array of other ratios to analyze profitability. Most **profitability ratios** use the same reasoning. For example, you can calculate the *yield* of a variety of financial investments. Yield represents the percentage the amount received is of the amount invested. The dividend yield explained above could be calculated for either common or preferred stock. Investors could measure the earnings yield by calculating earnings per share as a percentage of market price. Yield on a bond can be calculated the same way: interest received divided by the price of the bond.

The specific ratios presented in this chapter are summarized in Exhibit 9.6.

EXHIBIT 9.6

Summary of Key Relationships

Liquidity Ratios	1. Working capital	Current assets − Current liabilities
	2. Current ratio	Current assets ÷ Current liabilities
	3. Quick (acid-test) ratio	(Current assets − Inventory − Prepaid Items) ÷ Current liabilities
	4. Accounts receivable turnover	Net credit sales ÷ Average receivables
	5. Average number of days to collect receivables	365 ÷ Accounts receivable turnover
	6. Inventory turnover	Cost of goods sold ÷ Average inventory
	7. Average number of days to sell inventory	365 ÷ Inventory turnover
Solvency Ratios	8. Debt to assets ratio	Total liabilities ÷ Total assets
	9. Debt to equity ratio	Total liabilities ÷ Total stockholders' equity
	10. Times interest earned	Earnings before interest expense and taxes ÷ Interest expense
	11. Plant assets to long-term liabilities	Net plant assets ÷ Long-term liabilities
Profitability Ratios	12. Net margin	Net income ÷ Net sales
	13. Asset turnover	Net sales ÷ Average total assets
	14. Return on investment (also: return on assets)	Net income ÷ Average total assets
	15. Return on equity	Net income ÷ Average total stockholders' equity
Stock Market Ratios	16. Earnings per share	Net earnings available for common stock ÷ Average outstanding common shares
	17. Book value per share	(Stockholders' equity − Preferred rights) ÷ Outstanding common shares
	18. Price-earnings ratio	Market price per share ÷ Earnings per share
	19. Dividend yield	Dividends per share ÷ Market price per share

PRESENTATION OF ANALYTICAL RELATIONSHIPS

To communicate with users, companies present analytical information in endless different ways in annual reports. Although providing diagrams and illustrations in annual reports is not usually required, companies often include various forms of graphs and charts along with the underlying numbers to help users interpret financial statement data more easily. Common types presented include bar charts, pie charts, and line graphs. Exhibits 9.7, 9.8, and 9.9 show examples of these forms.

EXHIBIT 9.7

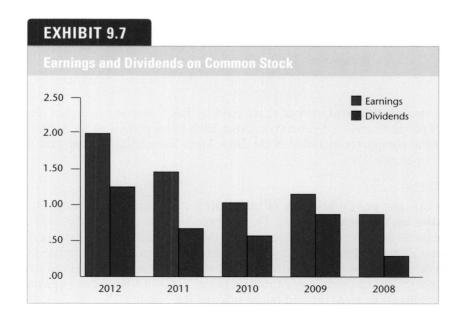

Earnings and Dividends on Common Stock

EXHIBIT 9.8

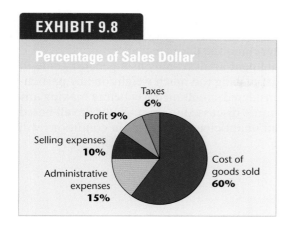

Percentage of Sales Dollar

- Taxes **6%**
- Profit **9%**
- Selling expenses **10%**
- Administrative expenses **15%**
- Cost of goods sold **60%**

EXHIBIT 9.9

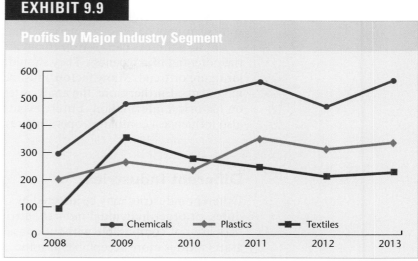

Profits by Major Industry Segment

Chemicals   Plastics   Textiles

2008   2009   2010   2011   2012   2013

LIMITATIONS OF FINANCIAL STATEMENT ANALYSIS

Analyzing financial statements is analogous to choosing a new car. Each car is different, and prospective buyers must evaluate and weigh a myriad of features: gas mileage, engine size, manufacturer's reputation, color, accessories, and price, to name a few. Just as it is difficult to compare a Toyota minivan to a Ferrari sports car, so it is difficult to compare a small textile firm to a giant oil company. To make a meaningful assessment, the potential car buyer must focus on key data that can be comparably expressed for

LO 8

Explain the limitations of financial statement analysis.

REALITY BYTES

The single most important source of financial information is a company's annual report, but decision makers should also consider other sources. Interested persons can access quarterly and annual reports through the SEC's EDGAR database, and often from company websites. Many companies will provide printed versions of these reports upon request. Companies also post information on their websites that is not included in their annual reports. For example, some automobile companies provide very detailed production data through their corporate websites.

Users can frequently obtain information useful in analyzing a particular company from independent sources as well as from the company itself. For example, the websites of popular news services, such as CNN (www.money.cnn.com) and CNBC (www.moneycentral.msn.com) provide archived news stories and independent financial information about many companies. The websites of brokerage houses like www.schwab.com offer free financial information about companies. Finally, libraries often subscribe to independent services that evaluate companies as potential investments. One example worth reviewing is *Value Line Investment Survey*.

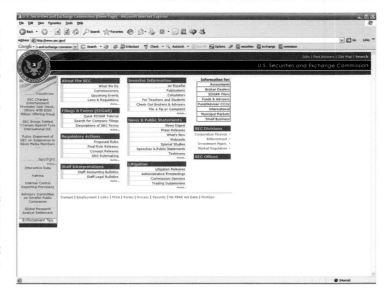

each car, such as gas mileage. The superior gas mileage of the minivan may pale in comparison to the thrill of driving the sports car, but the price of buying and operating the sports car may be the characteristic that determines the ultimate choice.

External users can rely on financial statement analysis only as a general guide to the potential of a business. They should resist placing too much weight on any particular figure or trend. Many factors must be considered simultaneously before making any judgments. Furthermore, the analysis techniques discussed in this chapter are all based on historical information. Future events and unanticipated changes in conditions will also influence a company's operating results.

Different Industries

Different industries may be affected by unique social policies, special accounting procedures, or other individual industry attributes. Ratios of companies in different industries are not comparable without considering industry characteristics. A high debt to assets ratio is more acceptable in some industries than others. Even within an industry, a particular business may require more or less working capital than the industry average. If so, the working capital and quick ratios would mean little compared to those of other firms, but may still be useful for trend analysis.

Because of industry-specific factors, most professional analysts specialize in one, or only a few, industries. Financial institutions such as brokerage houses, banks, and insurance companies typically employ financial analysts who specialize in areas such as mineral or oil extraction, chemicals, banking, retail, insurance, bond markets, or automobile manufacturing.

Changing Economic Environment

When comparing firms, analysts must be alert to changes in general economic trends from year to year. Significant changes in fuel costs and interest rates in recent years make old rule-of-thumb guidelines for evaluating these factors obsolete. In addition, the presence or absence of inflation affects business prospects.

Accounting Principles

Financial statement analysis is only as reliable as the data on which it is based. Although most companies follow generally accepted accounting principles, a wide variety of acceptable accounting methods is available from which to choose, including different inventory and depreciation methods, different schedules for recognizing revenue, and different ways to account for oil and gas exploration costs. Analyzing statements of companies that seem identical may produce noncomparable ratios if the companies used different accounting methods. Analysts may seek to improve comparability by trying to recast different companies' financial statements as if the same accounting methods had been applied.

Accrual accounting requires the use of many estimates; uncollectible accounts expense, warranty expense, asset lives, and salvage value are just a few. The reliability of the resulting financial reports depends on the expertise and integrity of the persons who make the estimates.

The quality and usefulness of accounting information are influenced by underlying accounting concepts. Two particular concepts, *conservatism* and *historical cost,* have a tremendous impact on financial reporting. Conservatism dictates recognizing estimated losses as soon as they occur, but gain recognition is almost always deferred until the gains are actually realized. Conservatism produces a negative bias in financial statements. There are persuasive arguments for the conservatism principle, but users should be alert to distortions it may cause in accounting information.

The pervasive use of the historical cost concept is probably the greatest single cause of distorted financial statement analysis results. The historical cost of an asset does not represent its current value. The asset purchased in 1982 for $10,000 is not comparable in value to the asset purchased in 2012 for $10,000 because of changes in the value of the dollar. Using historical cost produces financial statements that report dollars with differing purchasing power in the same statement. Combining these differing dollar values is akin to adding miles to kilometers. To get the most from analyzing financial statements, users should be cognizant of these limitations.

✓ CHECK YOURSELF 9.3

The return on equity for Gup Company is 23.4 percent and for Hunn Company is 17 percent. Does this mean Gup Company is better managed than Hunn Company?

Answer   No single ratio can adequately measure management performance. Even analyzing a wide range of ratios provides only limited insight. Any useful interpretation requires the analyst to recognize the limitations of ratio analysis. For example, ratio norms typically differ between industries and may be affected by changing economic factors. In addition, companies' use of different accounting practices and procedures produces different ratio results even when underlying circumstances are comparable.

A Look Back

Financial statement analysis involves many factors, among them user characteristics, information needs for particular types of decisions, and how financial information is analyzed. Analytical techniques include *horizontal, vertical,* and *ratio analysis.* Users commonly calculate ratios to measure a company's liquidity, solvency, and profitability. The specific ratios presented in this chapter are summarized in Exhibit 9.6. Although ratios are easy to calculate and provide useful insights into business operations, when interpreting analytical results, users should consider limitations resulting from differing industry characteristics, differing economic conditions, and the fundamental accounting principles used to produce reported financial information.

A Look Forward

This chapter concludes the *financial* accounting portion of the text. Beginning with Chapter 10, we introduce various tools from a branch of the field called *managerial* accounting. Managerial accounting focuses on meeting the accounting information needs of decision makers inside, rather than outside, a company. In addition to financial statement data, inside users require detailed, forward looking information that includes nonfinancial as well as financial components. We begin with a chapter that discusses the value management accounting adds to the decision making process.

www.mhhe.com/edmondssurvey3e

**A step-by-step audio-narrated series of slides is provided on the text
website at www.mhhe.com/edmondssurvey3e**

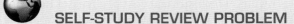

SELF-STUDY REVIEW PROBLEM

Financial statements for Stallings Company follow.

INCOME STATEMENTS		
For the Years Ended December 31		
	2013	2012
Revenues		
Net sales	$315,000	$259,000
Expenses		
Cost of goods sold	(189,000)	(154,000)
General, selling, and administrative expenses	(54,000)	(46,000)
Interest expense	(4,000)	(4,500)
Income before taxes	68,000	54,500
Income tax expense (40%)	(27,200)	(21,800)
Net income	$ 40,800	$ 32,700

Balance Sheets as of December 31		
	2013	2012
Assets		
Current assets		
Cash	$ 6,500	$ 11,500
Accounts receivable	51,000	49,000
Inventories	155,000	147,500
Total current assets	212,500	208,000
Plant and equipment (net)	187,500	177,000
Total assets	$400,000	$385,000
Liabilities and Stockholders' Equity		
Liabilities		
Current liabilities		
Accounts payable	$ 60,000	$ 81,500
Other	25,000	22,500
Total current liabilities	85,000	104,000
Bonds payable	100,000	100,000
Total liabilities	185,000	204,000
Stockholders' equity		
Common stock (50,000 shares, $3 par)	150,000	150,000
Paid-in capital in excess of par value	20,000	20,000
Retained earnings	45,000	11,000
Total stockholders' equity	215,000	181,000
Total liabilities and stockholders' equity	$400,000	$385,000

Required

a. Use horizontal analysis to determine which expense item increased by the highest percentage from 2012 to 2013.

b. Use vertical analysis to determine whether the inventory balance is a higher percentage of total assets at the end of 2012 or 2013.

c. Calculate the following ratios for 2012 and 2013. When data limitations prohibit computing averages, use year-end balances in your calculations.

   (1) Net margin
   (2) Return on investment

(3) Return on equity

(4) Earnings per share

(5) Price-earnings ratio (market price per share at the end of 2013 and 2012 was $12.04 and $8.86, respectively)

(6) Book value per share of common stock

(7) Times interest earned

(8) Working capital

(9) Current ratio

(10) Acid-test ratio

(11) Accounts receivable turnover

(12) Inventory turnover

(13) Debt to equity

Solution to Requirement *a*

Income tax expense increased by the greatest percentage. Computations follow.

Cost of goods sold ($189,000 − $154,000) ÷ $154,000 = 22.73%

General, selling, and administrative ($54,000 − $46,000) ÷ $46,000 = 17.39%

Interest expense decreased.

Income tax expense ($27,200 − $21,800) ÷ $21,800 = 24.77%

Solution to Requirement *b*

2012: $147,500 ÷ $385,000 = 38.31%

2013: $155,000 ÷ $400,000 = 38.75%

Inventory is slightly larger relative to total assets at the end of 2013.

Solution to Requirement *c*

		2013	2012
1.	$\dfrac{\text{Net income}}{\text{Net sales}}$	$\dfrac{\$40,800}{\$315,000} = 12.95\%$	$\dfrac{\$32,700}{\$259,000} = 12.63\%$
2.	$\dfrac{\text{Net income}}{\text{Average total assets}}$	$\dfrac{\$40,800}{\$392,500} = 10.39\%$	$\dfrac{\$32,700}{\$385,000} = 8.49\%$
3.	$\dfrac{\text{Net income}}{\text{Average total stockholders' equity}}$	$\dfrac{\$40,800}{\$198,000} = 20.61\%$	$\dfrac{\$32,700}{\$181,000} = 18.07\%$
4.	$\dfrac{\text{Net income}}{\text{Average common shares outstanding}}$	$\dfrac{\$40,800}{50,000 \text{ shares}} = \$0.816$	$\dfrac{\$32,700}{50,000 \text{ shares}} = \$0.654$
5.	$\dfrac{\text{Market price per share}}{\text{Earnings per share}}$	$\dfrac{\$12.04}{\$0.816} = 14.75 \text{ times}$	$\dfrac{\$8.86}{\$0.654} = 13.55 \text{ times}$
6.	$\dfrac{\text{Stockholders' equity} - \text{Preferred rights}}{\text{Outstanding common shares}}$	$\dfrac{\$215,000}{50,000 \text{ shares}} = \$4.30$	$\dfrac{\$181,000}{50,000 \text{ shares}} = \$3.62$
7.	$\dfrac{\text{Net income} + \text{Taxes} + \text{Interest expense}}{\text{Interest expense}}$	$\dfrac{\$40,800 + \$27,200 + \$4,000}{\$4,000} = 18 \text{ times}$	$\dfrac{\$32,700 + \$21,800 + \$4,500}{\$4,500} = 13.1 \text{ times}$
8.	Current assets − Current liabilities	$212,500 − 85,000 = 127,500$	$208,000 − 104,000 = 104,000$
9.	$\dfrac{\text{Current assets}}{\text{Current liabilities}}$	$\dfrac{\$212,500}{\$85,000} = 2.5:1$	$\dfrac{\$208,000}{\$104,000} = 2:1$
10.	$\dfrac{\text{Quick assets}}{\text{Current liabilities}}$	$\dfrac{\$57,500}{\$85,000} = 0.68:1$	$\dfrac{\$60,500}{\$104,000} = 0.58:1$
11.	$\dfrac{\text{Net credit sales}}{\text{Average accounts receivable}}$	$\dfrac{\$315,000}{\$50,000} = 6.3 \text{ times}$	$\dfrac{\$259,000}{\$49,000} = 5.29 \text{ times}$
12.	$\dfrac{\text{Cost of goods sold}}{\text{Average inventory}}$	$\dfrac{\$189,000}{\$151,250} = 1.25 \text{ times}$	$\dfrac{\$154,000}{\$147,500} = 1.04 \text{ times}$
13.	$\dfrac{\text{Total liabilities}}{\text{Total stockholders' equity}}$	$\dfrac{\$185,000}{\$215,000} = 86.05\%$	$\dfrac{\$204,000}{\$181,000} = 112.71\%$

KEY TERMS

QUESTIONS

1. Why are ratios and trends used in financial analysis?

2. What do the terms *liquidity* and *solvency* mean?

3. What is apparent from a horizontal presentation and a vertical presentation of financial statement information?

4. What is the significance of inventory turnover, and how is it calculated?

5. What is the difference between the current ratio and the quick ratio? What does each measure?

6. Why are absolute amounts of limited use when comparing companies?

7. What is the difference between return on investment and return on equity?

8. Which ratios are used to measure long-term debt-paying ability? How is each calculated?

9. What are some limitations of the earnings per share figure?

10. What is the formula for calculating return on investment (ROI)?

11. What is information overload?

12. What is the price-earnings ratio? Explain the difference between it and the dividend yield.

13. What environmental factors must be considered in analyzing companies?

14. How do accounting principles affect financial statement analysis?

 ## MULTIPLE-CHOICE QUESTIONS

 Multiple-choice questions are provided on the text website at www.mhhe.com/edmondssurvey3e.

EXERCISES

 All applicable Exercises are available with McGraw-Hill's *Connect Accounting*.

LO 4

Exercise 9-1   *Inventory turnover*

Selected financial information for Feemster Company for 2012 follows.

Sales	$2,000,000
Cost of goods sold	1,400,000
Merchandise inventory	
Beginning of year	155,000
End of year	195,000

Required

Assuming that the merchandise inventory buildup was relatively constant, how many times did the merchandise inventory turn over during 2012?

Exercise 9-2 *Times interest earned*

LO 5

The following data come from the financial records of Bynum Corporation for 2011.

Sales	$840,000
Interest expense	5,000
Income tax expense	27,000
Net income	28,000

Required

How many times was interest earned in 2011?

Exercise 9-3 *Current ratio*

LO 4

Meador Corporation wrote off a $1,000 uncollectible account receivable against the $12,000 balance in its allowance account.

Required

Explain the effect of the write-off on Meador's current ratio.

Exercise 9-4 *Working capital and current ratio*

LO 4

On June 30, 2011, Weslaco Company's total current assets were $500,000 and its total current liabilities were $275,000. On July 1, 2011, Weslaco issued a short-term note to a bank for $40,000 cash.

Required

a. Compute Weslaco's working capital before and after issuing the note.
b. Compute Weslaco's current ratio before and after issuing the note.

Exercise 9-5 *Working capital and current ratio*

LO 4

On June 30, 2011, Weslaco Company's total current assets were $500,000 and its total current liabilities were $275,000. On July 1, 2011, Weslaco issued a long-term note to a bank for $40,000 cash.

Required

a. Compute Weslaco's working capital before and after issuing the note.
b. Compute Weslaco's current ratio before and after issuing the note.

Exercise 9-6 *Horizontal analysis*

LO 2, 3

Pettit Corporation reported the following operating results for two consecutive years.

	2011	2010	Percentage Change
Sales	$1,300,000	$1,000,000	
Cost of goods sold	800,000	600,000	
Gross margin	500,000	400,000	
Operating expenses	300,000	200,000	
Income before taxes	200,000	200,000	
Income taxes	61,000	53,000	
Net income	$ 139,000	$ 147,000	

Required

a. Compute the percentage changes in Pettit Corporation's income statement components between the two years.

b. Comment on apparent trends disclosed by the percentage changes computed in Requirement *a*.

LO 2

Exercise 9-7   *Vertical analysis*

Conroe Company reported the following operating results for two consecutive years.

2011	Amount	Percent of Sales
Sales	$1,000,000	
Cost of goods sold	550,000	
Gross margin	450,000	
Operating expenses	130,000	
Income before taxes	320,000	
Income taxes	80,000	
Net income	$240,000	

2012	Amount	Percent of Sales
Sales	$1,080,000	
Cost of goods sold	600,000	
Gross margin	480,000	
Operating expenses	150,000	
Income before taxes	330,000	
Income taxes	82,000	
Net income	$248,000	

Required

Express each income statement component for each of the two years as a percent of sales.

LO 4, 5

Exercise 9-8   *Ratio analysis*

Balance sheet data for Kamel Corporation follow.

Current assets	$ 240,000
Long-term assets (net)	760,000
Total assets	$1,000,000
Current liabilities	$ 150,000
Long-term liabilities	450,000
Total liabilities	600,000
Total stockholders' equity	400,000
Total liabilities and stockholders' equity	$1,000,000

Required

Compute the following:

Working capital	_____
Current ratio	_____
Debt to assets ratio	_____
Debt to equity ratio	_____

Exercise 9-9   *Ratio analysis*

LO 7

For 2011, Stanton Corporation reported after-tax net income of $3,600,000. During the year, the number of shares of stock outstanding remained constant at 10,000 of $100 par, 9 percent preferred stock and 400,000 shares of common stock. The company's total stockholders' equity was $20,000,000 at December 31, 2011. Stanton Corporation's common stock was selling at $52 per share at the end of its fiscal year. All dividends for the year had been paid, including $4.80 per share to common stockholders.

Required

Compute the following:

a. Earnings per share
b. Book value per share of common stock
c. Price-earnings ratio
d. Dividend yield

Exercise 9-10   *Ratio analysis*

LO 4, 5, 6, 7

Required

Match each of the following ratios with the formula used to compute it.

_____ 1. Working capital	a. Net income ÷ Average total stockholders' equity
_____ 2. Current ratio	b. Cost of goods sold ÷ Average inventory
_____ 3. Quick ratio	c. Current assets − Current liabilities
_____ 4. Accounts receivable turnover	d. 365 ÷ Inventory turnover
_____ 5. Average number of days to collect receivables	e. Net income ÷ Average total assets
	f. (Net income − Preferred dividends) ÷ Average outstanding common shares
_____ 6. Inventory turnover	
_____ 7. Average number of days to sell inventory	g. (Current assets − Inventory − Prepaid items) ÷ Current liabilities
_____ 8. Debt to assets ratio	h. Total liabilities ÷ Total assets
_____ 9. Debt to equity ratio	i. 365 days ÷ Accounts receivable turnover
_____ 10. Return on investment	j. Total liabilities ÷ Total stockholders' equity
_____ 11. Return on equity	k. Net credit sales ÷ Average accounts receivables
_____ 12. Earnings per share	l. Current assets ÷ Current liabilities

Exercise 9-11   *Horizontal and vertical analysis*

LO 2

Income statements for Thompson Company for 2011 and 2012 follow.

	2012	2011
Sales	$200,000	$180,000
Cost of goods sold	142,000	120,000
Selling expenses	20,000	18,000
Administrative expenses	12,000	14,000
Interest expense	3,000	5,000
Total expenses	177,000	157,000
Income before taxes	23,000	23,000
Income taxes expense	5,000	3,000
Net income	$ 18,000	$ 20,000

Required

a. Perform a horizontal analysis, showing the percentage change in each income statement component between 2011 and 2012.

b. Perform a vertical analysis, showing each income statement component as a percent of sales for each year.

LO 4, 5, 6, 7

Exercise 9-12   *Ratio analysis*

Compute the specified ratios using Hilda Company's balance sheet at December 31, 2011.

Assets	
Cash	$ 15,000
Marketable securities	8,000
Accounts receivable	13,000
Inventory	11,000
Property and equipment	170,000
Accumulated depreciation	(12,500)
Total assets	$204,500
Equities	
Accounts payable	$ 8,500
Current notes payable	3,500
Mortgage payable	4,500
Bonds payable	21,500
Common stock	114,000
Retained earnings	52,500
Total liabilities and stockholders' equity	$204,500

The average number of common stock shares outstanding during 2011 was 880 shares. Net income for the year was $15,000.

Required

Compute each of the following:

a. Current ratio
b. Earnings per share
c. Quick (acid-test) ratio
d. Return on investment
e. Return on equity
f. Debt to equity ratio

LO 4, 5, 6, 7

Exercise 9-13   *Comprehensive analysis*

Required

Indicate the effect of each of the following transactions on (1) the current ratio, (2) working capital, (3) stockholders' equity, (4) book value per share of common stock, (5) retained earnings. Assume that the current ratio is greater than 1.0.

a. Collected account receivable.
b. Wrote off account receivable.
c. Converted a short-term note payable to a long-term note payable.
d. Purchased inventory on account.
e. Declared cash dividend.
f. Sold merchandise on account at a profit.
g. Issued stock dividend.
h. Paid account payable.
i. Sold building at a loss.

Exercise 9-14   *Accounts receivable turnover, inventory turnover, and net margin*   **LO 4, 6**

Selected data from Warren Company follow.

Balance Sheet Data As of December 31		
	2011	2010
Accounts receivable	$400,000	$376,000
Allowance for doubtful accounts	(20,000)	(16,000)
Net accounts receivable	$380,000	$360,000
Inventories, lower of cost or market	$480,000	$440,000

Income Statement Data For the Year Ended December 31		
	2011	2010
Net credit sales	$2,000,000	$1,760,000
Net cash sales	400,000	320,000
Net sales	2,400,000	2,080,000
Cost of goods sold	1,600,000	1,440,000
Selling, general, and administrative expenses	240,000	216,000
Other expenses	40,000	24,000
Total operating expenses	$1,880,000	$1,680,000

Required

Compute the following:

a. The accounts receivable turnover for 2011.
b. The inventory turnover for 2011.
c. The net margin for 2010.

Exercise 9-15   *Comprehensive analysis*   **LO 4, 5**

The December 31, 2012, balance sheet for Kessler Inc. is presented here. These are the only accounts on Kessler's balance sheet. Amounts indicated by question marks (?) can be calculated using the additional information following the balance sheet.

Assets	
Cash	$ 25,000
Accounts receivable (net)	?
Inventory	?
Property, plant, and equipment (net)	294,000
	$432,000
Liabilities and Stockholders' Equity	
Accounts payable (trade)	$?
Income taxes payable (current)	25,000
Long-term debt	?
Common stock	300,000
Retained earnings	?
	$?
continued	

Required

Determine the following.

a. The balance in trade accounts payable as of December 31, 2012.

b. The balance in retained earnings as of December 31, 2012.

c. The balance in the inventory account as of December 31, 2012.

PROBLEMS

All applicable Problems are available with McGraw-Hill's *Connect Accounting*.

LO 2

Problem 9-16   *Vertical analysis*

The following percentages apply to Lowther Company for 2011 and 2012.

	2012	2011
Sales	100.0%	100.0%
Cost of goods sold	61.0	64.0
Gross margin	39.0	36.0
Selling and administrative expenses	26.5	20.5
Interest expense	2.5	2.0
Total expenses	29.0	22.5
Income before taxes	10.0	13.5
Income tax expense	5.5	7.0
Net income	4.5%	6.5%

Required

Assuming that sales were $500,000 in 2011 and $600,000 in 2012, prepare income statements for the two years.

LO 5, 6, 7

Problem 9-17   *Ratio analysis*

Weimar Company's income statement information follows.

	2011	2010
Net sales	$420,000	$260,000
Income before interest and taxes	110,000	85,500
Net income after taxes	55,500	63,000
Interest expense	9,000	8,000
Stockholders' equity, December 31 (2009: $200,000)	305,000	235,000
Common stock, December 31	260,000	230,000

The average number of shares outstanding was 7,800 for 2011 and 6,900 for 2010.

Required

Compute the following ratios for Weimar for 2011 and 2010.

a. Times interest earned.

b. Earnings per share based on the average number of shares outstanding.

c. Price-earnings ratio (market prices: 2011, $64 per share; 2010, $78 per share).

d. Return on average equity.

e. Net margin.

Problem 9-18   *Effect of transactions on current ratio and working capital*   **LO 4**

Sherman Manufacturing has a current ratio of 3:1 on December 31, 2011. Indicate whether each of the following transactions would increase (+), decrease (−), or have no affect (NA) Sherman's current ratio and its working capital.

Required

a. Paid cash for a trademark.

b. Wrote off an uncollectible account receivable.

c. Sold equipment for cash.

d. Sold merchandise at a profit (cash).

e. Declared a cash dividend.

f. Purchased inventory on account.

g. Scrapped a fully depreciated machine (no gain or loss).

h. Issued a stock dividend.

i. Purchased a machine with a long-term note.

j. Paid a previously declared cash dividend.

k. Collected accounts receivable.

l. Invested in current marketable securities.

Problem 9-19   *Ratio analysis*   **LO 7**

Selected data for Richmond Company for 2011 and additional information on industry averages follow.

CHECK FIGURE
a. Earnings per share: $3.50

Earnings (net income)	$ 174,000
Preferred stock (13,200 shares at $50 par, 4%)	$ 660,000
Common stock (45,000 shares, market value $56)	510,000
Retained earnings	562,500
	$1,732,500
Less: Treasury stock	
Preferred (1,800 shares)	$54,000
Common (1,800 shares)	24,000 78,000
Total stockholders' equity	$1,654,500

Industry averages	
Earnings per share	$ 5.20
Price-earnings ratio	9.50
Return on equity	11.20%

Required

a. Calculate and compare Richmond Company's ratios with the industry averages.

b. Discuss factors you would consider in deciding whether to invest in the company.

LO 2

CHECK FIGURES
D. $337,500
F. $97,500

Problem 9-20   *Supply missing balance sheet numbers*

The bookkeeper for Lowell's Country Music Bar went insane and left this incomplete balance sheet. Lowell's working capital is $90,000 and its debt to assets ratio is 40 percent.

Assets

Current assets	
Cash	$ 21,000
Accounts receivable	42,000
Inventory	(A)
Prepaid items	9,000
Total current assets	(B)
Long-term assets	
Building	(C)
Less: Accumulated depreciation	(39,000)
Total long-term assets	210,000
Total assets	$ (D)

Liabilities and Stockholders' Equity

Liabilities	
Current liabilities	
Accounts payable	$ (E)
Notes payable	12,000
Income tax payable	10,500
Total current liabilities	37,500
Long-term liabilities	
Mortgage payable	(F)
Total liabilities	(G)
Stockholders' equity	
Common stock	105,000
Retained earnings	(H)
Total stockholders' equity	(I)
Total liabilities and stockholders' equity	$ (J)

Required

Complete the balance sheet by supplying the missing amounts.

LO 4, 5, 6, 7

eXcel

CHECK FIGURES
d. 2012: $0.72
k. 2011: 5.47 times

Problem 9-21   *Ratio analysis*

The following financial statements apply to Bassie Company.

	2012	2011
Revenues		
Net sales	$210,000	$175,000
Other revenues	4,000	5,000
Total revenues	214,000	180,000
Expenses		
Cost of goods sold	126,000	103,000
Selling expenses	21,000	19,000
General and administrative expenses	11,000	10,000
Interest expense	3,000	3,000
Income tax expense	21,000	18,000
Total expenses	182,000	153,000

continued

	2012	2011
Earnings from continuing operations		
before extraordinary items	32,000	27,000
Extraordinary gain (net of $3,000 tax)	4,000	0
Net earnings	$ 36,000	$ 27,000
Assets		
Current assets		
Cash	$ 4,000	$ 8,000
Marketable securities	1,000	1,000
Accounts receivable	35,000	32,000
Inventories	100,000	96,000
Prepaid items	3,000	2,000
Total current assets	143,000	139,000
Plant and equipment (net)	105,000	105,000
Intangibles	20,000	0
Total assets	$268,000	$244,000
Liabilities and Stockholders' Equity		
Liabilities		
Current liabilities		
Accounts payable	$ 40,000	$ 54,000
Other	17,000	15,000
Total current liabilities	57,000	69,000
Bonds payable	66,000	67,000
Total liabilities	123,000	136,000
Stockholders' equity		
Common stock (50,000 shares)	115,000	115,000
Retained earnings	30,000	(7,000)
Total stockholders' equity	145,000	108,000
Total liabilities and stockholders' equity	$268,000	$244,000

Required

Calculate the following ratios for 2011 and 2012. When data limitations prohibit computing averages, use year-end balances in your calculations.

a. Net margin

b. Return on investment

c. Return on equity

d. Earnings per share

e. Price-earnings ratio (market prices at the end of 2011 and 2012 were $5.94 and $4.77, respectively)

f. Book value per share of common stock

g. Times interest earned

h. Working capital

i. Current ratio

j. Quick (acid-test) ratio

k. Accounts receivable turnover

l. Inventory turnover

m. Debt to equity ratio

n. Debt to assets ratio

LO 2

Problem 9-22 *Horizontal analysis*

Financial statements for Bernard Company follow.

BERNARD COMPANY
Balance Sheets
As of December 31

	2012	2011
Assets		
Current assets		
Cash	$ 16,000	$ 12,000
Marketable securities	20,000	6,000
Accounts receivable (net)	54,000	46,000
Inventories	135,000	143,000
Prepaid items	25,000	10,000
Total current assets	250,000	217,000
Investments	27,000	20,000
Plant (net)	270,000	255,000
Land	29,000	24,000
Total assets	$576,000	$516,000
Liabilities and Stockholders' Equity		
Liabilities		
Current liabilities		
Notes payable	$ 17,000	$ 6,000
Accounts payable	113,800	100,000
Salaries payable	21,000	15,000
Total current liabilities	151,800	121,000
Noncurrent liabilities		
Bonds payable	100,000	100,000
Other	32,000	27,000
Total noncurrent liabilities	132,000	127,000
Total liabilities	283,800	248,000
Stockholders' equity		
Preferred stock, par value $10, 4% cumulative, non-participating; 8,000 shares authorized and issued	80,000	80,000
Common stock, no par; 50,000 shares authorized; 10,000 shares issued	80,000	80,000
Retained earnings	132,200	108,000
Total stockholders' equity	292,200	268,000
Total liabilities and stockholders' equity	$576,000	$516,000

BERNARD COMPANY
Statements of Income and Retained Earnings
For the Years Ended December 31

	2012	2011
Revenues		
Sales (net)	$230,000	$210,000
Other revenues	8,000	5,000
Total revenues	238,000	215,000

continued

	2012	2011
Expenses		
Cost of goods sold	120,000	103,000
Selling, general, and administrative expenses	55,000	50,000
Interest expense	8,000	7,200
Income tax expense	23,000	22,000
Total expenses	206,000	182,200
Net earnings (net income)	32,000	32,800
Retained earnings, January 1	108,000	83,000
Less: Preferred stock dividends	2,800	2,800
Common stock dividends	5,000	5,000
Retained earnings, December 31	$132,200	$108,000

Required

Prepare a horizontal analysis of both the balance sheet and income statement.

Problem 9-23   *Ratio analysis*

LO 2, 3, 4, 5, 6, 7

Required

Use the financial statements for Bernard Company from Problem 9-22 to calculate the following for 2012 and 2011.

CHECK FIGURES
k. 2012: 2.0:1
p. 2011: $2.96

a. Working capital
b. Current ratio
c. Quick ratio
d. Accounts receivable turnover (beginning receivables at January 1, 2011, were $47,000)
e. Average number of days to collect accounts receivable
f. Inventory turnover (beginning inventory at January 1, 2011, was $140,000)
g. Average number of days to sell inventory
h. Debt to assets ratio
i. Debt to equity ratio
j. Times interest earned
k. Plant assets to long-term debt
l. Net margin
m. Asset turnover
n. Return on investment
o. Return on equity
p. Earnings per share
q. Book value per share of common stock
r. Price-earnings ratio (market price per share: 2011, $11.75; 2012, $12.50)
s. Dividend yield on common stock

Problem 9-24   *Vertical analysis*

LO 2

Required

Use the financial statements for Bernard Company from Problem 9-22 to perform a vertical analysis of both the balance sheets and income statements for 2012 and 2011.

CHECK FIGURE
2012 Retained Earnings: 23%

ANALYZE, THINK, COMMUNICATE

ATC 9-1   Business Applications Case   *Analyzing the Kroger Company and Whole Foods Market*

The following information relates to The Kroger Company and Whole Foods Market, Inc. for their 2009 and 2008 fiscal years.

THE KROGER COMPANY
Selected Financial Information
(Amounts in millions, except per share amounts)

	January 31, 2009	February 2, 2008
Total current assets	$ 7,206	$ 7,114
Merchandise inventories	6,459	6,063
Property and equipment, net of depreciation	13,161	12,498
Total assets	23,211	22,299
Total current liabilities	7,629	8,689
Total long-term liabilities	10,311	8,696
Total liabilities	17,940	17,385
Total shareholders' equity	5,271	4,914
Revenue	76,000	70,235
Cost of goods sold	58,564	53,779
Gross profit	17,436	16,456
Operating income	2,451	2,301
Earnings from continuing operations before income tax expense	1,966	1,827
Income tax expense	717	646
Net earnings	1,249	1,181
Basic earnings per share	$ 1.92	$ 1.71

WHOLE FOODS MARKET, INC.
Selected Financial Information
(Amounts in millions except per share data)

	September 27, 2009	September 28, 2008
Total current assets	$1,055	$ 623
Merchandise inventory	311	327
Property and equipment, net of depreciation	1,898	1,900
Total assets	3,783	3,381
Total current liabilities	684	666
Total long-term liabilities	1,058	1,209
Total liabilities	1,742	1,875
Total stockholders' equity	2,041	1,506
Revenues	$8,032	$7,954
Cost of goods sold	5,277	5,247
Gross profit	2,754	2,707
Operating income	284	236
Earnings from continuing operations before income taxes	251	207
Income tax expense	104	92
Net earnings	147	115
Basic earnings per share	$ 0.85	$ 0.82

Required

a. Compute the following ratios for the companies' 2009 fiscal years:

(1) Current ratio.

(2) Average days to sell inventory. (Use average inventory.)

(3) Debt to assets ratio.

(4) Return on investment. (Use average assets and use "earnings from continuing operations" rather than "net earnings.")

(5) Gross margin percentage.

(6) Asset turnover. (Use average assets.)

(7) Return on sales. (Use "earnings from continuing operations" rather than "net earnings.")

(8) Plant assets to long-term debt ratio.

b. Which company appears to be more profitable? Explain your answer and identify which of the ratio(s) from Requirement *a* you used to reach your conclusion.

c. Which company appears to have the higher level of financial risk? Explain your answer and identify which of the ratio(s) from Requirement *a* you used to reach your conclusion.

d. Which company appears to be charging higher prices for its goods? Explain your answer and identify which of the ratio(s) from Requirement *a* you used to reach your conclusion.

e. Which company appears to be the more efficient at using its assets? Explain your answer and identify which of the ratio(s) from Requirement *a* you used to reach your conclusion.

ATC 9-2   Group Assignment   *Ratio analysis and logic*

Presented here are selected data from the 10-K reports of four companies. The four companies, in alphabetical order, are

BellSouth Corporation, a telephone company that operates in the southeastern United States.

Caterpillar, Inc., a manufacturer of heavy machinery.

Dollar General Corporation, a company that owns Dollar General Stores discount stores.

Tiffany & Company, a company that operates high-end jewelry stores.

The data, presented in the order of the amount of sales, are as follows. Dollar amounts are in millions.

	A	B	C	D
Sales	$20,561	$18,110	$2,627.3	$1,017.6
Cost of goods sold	6,254	13,374	1,885.2	453.4
Net earnings	3,261	1,665	144.6	72.8
Inventory or NA	2,603	632.0	386.4	NA
Materials and supplies	398	NA	NA	NA
Accounts receivable	4,750	3,331	0	99.5
Total assets	36,301	20,756	914.8	827.1

Required

a. Divide the class into groups of four or five students per group and then organize the groups into four sections. Assign Task 1 to the first section of groups, Task 2 to the second section, Task 3 to the third section, and Task 4 to the fourth section.

Group Tasks

(1) Assume that you represent BellSouth Corporation. Identify the set of financial data (Column A, B, C, or D) that relates to your company.

(2) Assume that you represent Caterpillar, Inc. Identify the set of financial data (Column A, B, C, or D) that relates to your company.

(3) Assume that you represent Dollar General Corporation. Identify the set of financial data (Column A, B, C, or D) that relates to your company.

(4) Assume that you represent Tiffany & Company. Identify the set of financial data (Column A, B, C, or D) that relates to your company.

Hint: Use a gross margin ratio (gross margin ÷ sales), a net margin ratio (net income ÷ sales), and return on assets (net income ÷ total assets) to facilitate identifying the financial data related to your particular company.

b. Select a representative from each section. Have the representatives explain the rationale for the group's selection. The explanation should include a set of ratios that support the group's conclusion.

ATC 9-3   Research Assignment   *Analyzing Whirlpool's Acquisition of Maytag*

To complete the requirements below you will need to obtain Whirlpool's income statements for 2005, 2007, and 2008, and its balance sheets for 2004 through 2008. The easiest way to obtain these income statements is to retrieve the company's 2005 and 2008 Form 10-Ks. To obtain the Form 10-Ks you can use either the EDGAR system following the instructions in Appendix A, or they can be found under the "Investors" link on the company's corporate website, www.whirlpoolcorp.com. On March 31, 2006, Whirlpool Corporation acquired Maytag, another manufacturer of home appliances. The company's 2006, 2007, and 2008 financial statements include the activities of Maytag; its 2005 and 2004 statements do not.

Required

a. Compute the following ratios for 2005, 2007, and 2008. Show your calculations.

Gross margin percentage	Net margin
Return on investment	Return on equity
Current ratio	Debt to assets ratio

b. Based on the ratios computed in Requirement *a*, comment on the apparent effects of Whirlpool's acquisition of Maytag. Assume any significant change in these ratios was the result of the acquisition.

c. Based on this limited analysis, does it appear that the short-term effects of the acquisition were good or bad for Whirlpool?

ATC 9-4   Writing Assignment   *Identifying companies based on financial statement information*

The following ratios are for four companies in different industries. Some of these ratios have been discussed in the textbook, others have not, but their names explain how the ratio was computed. These data are for the companies' 2008 fiscal years. The four sets of ratios, presented randomly are:

	Company 1	Company 2	Company 3	Company 4
Current assets ÷ Total assets	47%	11%	15%	20%
Average days to sell inventory	33	138	7	9
Average days to collect receivables	25	83	3	21
Return on assets	5%	4%	4%	18%
Gross profit ÷ Sales	20%	40%	20%	54%
Asset turnover	0.46	0.71	2.19	1.39
Sales ÷ Number of full-time employees	$453,407	$341,958	$49,865	$29,057

The four companies to which these ratios relate, listed in alphabetical order, are:

Caterpillar, Inc., a company that manufactures heavy construction equipment.

Denny's Corporation, which operated over 1,541 restaurants as of December 31, 2008.

Molson Coors Brewing, Inc., a company that produces beer and related products.

Weight Watchers International, Inc., a company that provides weight-loss services and products.

Required

Determine which company should be matched with each set of ratios. Write a memorandum explaining the rationale for your decisions.

ATC 9-5   Ethical Dilemma   *Making the ratios look good*

J. Talbot is the accounting manager for Kolla Waste Disposal Corporation. Kolla is having its worst financial year since its inception. The company is expected to report a net loss. In the midst of such bad news, Ms. Talbot surprised the company president, Mr. Winston, by suggesting that the company write off approximately 25 percent of its garbage trucks. Mr. Winston responded by noting that the trucks could still be operated for another two or three years. Ms. Talbot replied, "We may use them for two or three more years, but you couldn't sell them on the street if you had to. Who wants to buy a bunch of old garbage trucks and besides, it will make next year's financials so sweet. No one will care about the additional write-off this year. We are already showing a loss. Who will care if we lose a little bit more?"

Required

a. How will the write-off affect the following year's return on assets ratio?

b. How will the write-off affect the asset and income growth percentages?

c. Would writing off the garbage trucks for the reasons stated present any ethical concerns for Kolla? Explain.

CHAPTER 10

An Introduction to Managerial Accounting

LEARNING OBJECTIVES

After you have mastered the material in this chapter, you will be able to:

1 Distinguish between managerial and financial accounting.

2 Identify the cost components of a product made by a manufacturing company: the cost of materials, labor, and overhead.

3 Explain the effects on financial statements of product costs versus general, selling, and administrative costs.

4 Prepare a schedule of cost of goods manufactured and sold.

5 Distinguish product costs from upstream and downstream costs.

6 Explain how product costing differs in service, merchandising, and manufacturing companies.

7 Show how just-in-time inventory can increase profitability.

8 Identify and explain the standards contained in IMA's Statement of Ethical Professional Practice.

9 Identify emerging trends in accounting (Appendix A).

CHAPTER OPENING

Andy Grove, Senior Advisor to Executive Management of Intel Corporation, is credited with the motto "Only the paranoid survive." Mr. Grove describes a wide variety of concerns that make him paranoid. Specifically, he declares:

I worry about products getting screwed up, and I worry about products getting introduced prematurely. I worry about factories not performing well, and I worry about having too many factories. I worry about hiring the right people, and I worry about morale slacking off. And, of course, I worry about competitors. I worry about other people figuring out how to do what we do better or cheaper, and displacing us with our customers.

Do Intel's historically based financial statements contain the information Mr. Grove needs? No. **Financial accounting** is not designed to satisfy all the information needs of business managers. Its scope is limited to the needs of external users such as investors and creditors. The field of accounting designed to meet the needs of internal users is called **managerial accounting.**

The Curious Accountant

In the first course of accounting, you learned how retailers, such as Sears, account for the cost of equipment that lasts more than one year. Recall that the equipment was recorded as an asset when purchased, and then it was depreciated over its expected useful life. The depreciation charge reduced the company's assets and increased its expenses. This approach was justified under the matching principle, which seeks to recognize costs as expenses in the same period that the cost (resource) is used to generate revenue.

Is depreciation always shown as an expense on the income statement? The answer may surprise you. Consider the following scenario. Schwinn manufactures the bicycles that it sells to Sears. In order to produce the bicycles, Schwinn had to purchase a robotic machine that it expects can be used to produce 50,000 bicycles.

Do you think Schwinn should account for depreciation on its manufacturing equipment the same way Sears accounts for depreciation on its registers at the checkout counters? If not, how should Schwinn account for its depreciation? Remember the matching principle when thinking of your answer. (Answer on page 368.)

DIFFERENCES BETWEEN MANAGERIAL AND FINANCIAL ACCOUNTING

Distinguish between managerial and financial accounting.

While the information needs of internal and external users overlap, the needs of managers generally differ from those of investors or creditors. Some distinguishing characteristics are discussed in the following section.

Users and Types of Information

Financial accounting provides information used primarily by investors, creditors, and others *outside* a business. In contrast, managerial accounting focuses on information used by executives, managers, and employees who work *inside* the business. These two user groups need different types of information.

Internal users need information to *plan, direct,* and *control* business operations. The nature of information needed is related to an employee's job level. Lower level employees use nonfinancial information such as work schedules, store hours, and customer service policies. Moving up the organizational ladder, financial information becomes increasingly important. Middle managers use a blend of financial and nonfinancial information, while senior executives concentrate on financial data. To a lesser degree, senior executives also use general economic data and nonfinancial operating information. For example, an executive may consider the growth rate of the economy before deciding to expand the company's workforce.

External users (investors and creditors) have greater needs for general economic information than do internal users. For example, an investor debating whether to purchase stock versus bond securities might be more interested in government tax policy than financial statement data. Exhibit 10.1 summarizes the information needs of different user groups.

Level of Aggregation

External users generally desire *global information* that reflects the performance of a company as a whole. For example, an investor is not so much interested in the performance of a particular Sears store as she is in the performance of Sears Roebuck Company versus that of JC Penney Company. In contrast, internal users focus on detailed information about specific subunits of the company. To meet the needs of the different user groups, financial accounting data are more aggregated than managerial accounting data.

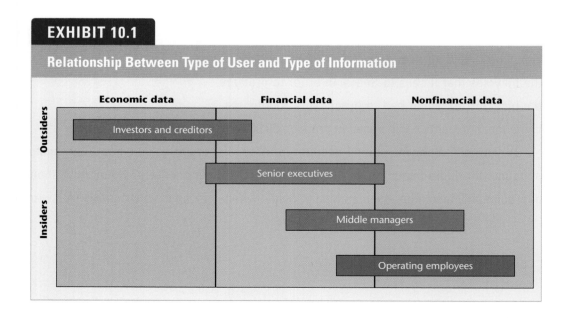

EXHIBIT 10.1

Relationship Between Type of User and Type of Information

Regulation

As previously discussed, the information in financial statements is highly regulated to protect the public interest.

Beyond financial statement data, much of the information generated by management accounting systems is proprietary information not available to the public. Because this information is not distributed to the public, it need not be regulated to protect the public interest. Management accounting is restricted only by the **value-added principle.** Management accountants are free to engage in any information gathering and reporting activity so long as the activity adds value in excess of its cost. For example, management accountants are free to provide forecasted information to internal users. In contrast, financial accounting as prescribed by GAAP does not permit forecasting.

Information Characteristics

While financial accounting is characterized by its objectivity, reliability, consistency, and historical nature, managerial accounting is more concerned with relevance and timeliness. Managerial accounting uses more estimates and fewer facts than financial accounting. Financial accounting reports what happened yesterday; managerial accounting reports what is expected to happen tomorrow.

Time Horizon and Reporting Frequency

Financial accounting information is reported periodically, normally at the end of a year. Management cannot wait until the end of the year to discover problems. Planning, controlling, and directing require immediate attention. Managerial accounting information is delivered on a continuous basis.

FOCUS ON INTERNATIONAL ISSUES

FINANCIAL ACCOUNTING VERSUS MANAGERIAL ACCOUNTING—AN INTERNATIONAL PERSPECTIVE

This chapter has already explained some of the conceptual differences between financial and managerial accounting, but these differences have implications for international businesses as well. With respect to financial accounting, publicly traded companies in most countries must follow the generally accepted accounting principles (GAAP) for their country, but these rules can vary from country to country. Generally, companies that are audited under the auditing standards of the United States follow the standards established by the Financial Accounting Standards Board. Most companies located outside of the United States follow the standards established by the International Accounting Standards Board. For example, the United States is one of very few countries whose GAAP allow the use of the LIFO inventory cost flow assumption.

Conversely, most of the managerial accounting concepts introduced in this course can be used by businesses in any country. For example, *activity-based management (ABM)* is a topic addressed in the appendix to this chapter and is used by many companies in the United States. Meanwhile, a study published in *Accountancy Ireland** found that approximately one-third of the companies surveyed in Ireland, the United Kingdom, and New Zealand were also either using ABM, or were considering adopting it.

*Bernard Pierce, "Activity-Based Costing; the Irish Experience: True Innovation or Passing Fad?" *Accountancy Ireland,* October 2004, pp. 28–31.

EXHIBIT 10.2

Comparative Features of Managerial versus Financial Accounting Information

Features	Managerial Accounting	Financial Accounting
Users	Insiders including executives, managers, and operators	Outsiders including investors, creditors, government agencies, analysts, and reporters
Information type	Economic and physical data as well as financial data	Financial data
Level of aggregation	Local information on subunits of the organization	Global information on the company as a whole
Regulation	No regulation, limited only by the value-added principle	Regulation by SEC, FASB, and other determiners of GAAP
Information characteristics	Estimates that promote relevance and enable timeliness	Factual information that is characterized by objectivity, reliability, consistency, and accuracy
Time horizon	Past, present, and future	Past only, historically based
Reporting frequency	Continuous reporting	Delayed with emphasis on annual reports

Exhibit 10.2 summarizes significant differences between financial and managerial accounting.

PRODUCT COSTING IN MANUFACTURING COMPANIES

LO 2

Identify the cost components of a product made by a manufacturing company: the cost of materials, labor, and overhead.

A major focus for managerial accountants is determining **product cost.**[1] Managers need to know the cost of their products for a variety of reasons. For example, **cost-plus pricing** is a common business practice.[2] **Product costing** is also used to control business operations. It is useful in answering questions such as: Are costs higher or lower than expected? Who is responsible for the variances between expected and actual costs? What actions can be taken to control the variances?

The cost of making products includes the cost of materials, labor, and other resources (usually called **overhead**). To understand how these costs affect financial statements, consider the example of Tabor Manufacturing Company.

Tabor Manufacturing Company

Tabor Manufacturing Company makes wooden tables. The company spent $1,000 cash to build four tables: $390 for materials, $470 for a carpenter's labor, and $140 for tools used in making the tables. How much is Tabor's expense? The answer is zero. The $1,000 cash has been converted into products (four tables). The cash payments for materials, labor, and tools (overhead) were *asset exchange* transactions. One asset (cash) decreased while another asset (tables) increased. Tabor will not recognize any expense until the tables are sold; in the meantime, the cost of the tables is held in an asset account called **Finished Goods Inventory.** Exhibit 10.3 illustrates how cash is transformed into inventory.

Average Cost per Unit

How much did each table made by Tabor cost? The *actual* cost of each of the four tables likely differs. The carpenter probably spent a little more time on some of the tables than

---

[1]This text uses the term *product* in a generic sense to mean both goods and services.
[2]Other pricing strategies will be introduced in subsequent chapters.

EXHIBIT 10.3

Transforming the Asset Cash Into the Asset Finished Goods Inventory

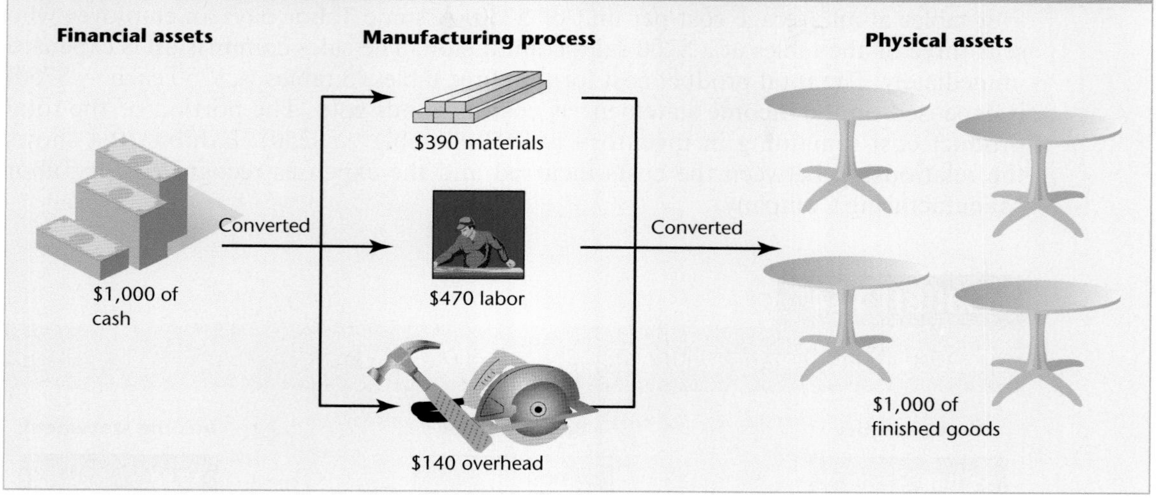

others. Material and tool usage probably varied from table to table. Determining the exact cost of each table is virtually impossible. Minute details such as a second of labor time cannot be effectively measured. Even if Tabor could determine the exact cost of each table, the information would be of little use. Minor differences in the cost per table would make no difference in pricing or other decisions management needs to make. Accountants therefore normally calculate cost per unit as an *average*. In the case of Tabor Manufacturing, the **average cost** per table is $250 ($1,000 ÷ 4 units). Unless otherwise stated, assume *cost per unit* means *average cost per unit*.

✓ CHECK YOURSELF 10.1

All boxes of General Mills' Total Raisin Bran cereal are priced at exactly the same amount in your local grocery store. Does this mean that the actual cost of making each box of cereal was exactly the same?

Answer   No, making each box would not cost exactly the same amount. For example, some boxes contain slightly more or less cereal than other boxes. Accordingly, some boxes cost slightly more or less to make than others do. General Mills uses average cost rather than actual cost to develop its pricing strategy.

Costs Can Be Assets or Expenses

It might seem odd that wages earned by production workers are recorded as inventory instead of being expensed. Remember, however, that expenses are assets used in the process of *earning revenue*. The cash paid to production workers is not used to produce revenue. Instead, the cash is used to produce inventory. Revenue will be earned when the inventory is used (sold). So long as the inventory remains on hand, all product costs (materials, labor, and overhead) remain in an inventory account.

When a table is sold, the average cost of the table is transferred from the Inventory account to the Cost of Goods Sold (expense) account. If some tables remain unsold at the end of the accounting period, part of the *product costs* is reported as an asset (inventory) on the balance sheet while the other part is reported as an expense (cost of goods sold) on the income statement.

Costs that are not classified as product costs are normally expensed in the period in which they are incurred. These costs include *general operating costs, selling and administrative costs, interest costs,* and the *cost of income taxes.*

To illustrate, return to the Tabor Manufacturing example. Recall that Tabor made four tables at an average cost per unit of $250. Assume Tabor pays an employee who sells three of the tables at a $200 sales commission. The sales commission is expensed immediately. The total product cost for the three tables (3 tables × $250 each = $750) is expensed on the income statement as cost of goods sold. The portion of the total product cost remaining in inventory is $250 (1 table × $250). Exhibit 10.4 shows the relationship between the costs incurred and the expenses recognized for Tabor Manufacturing Company.

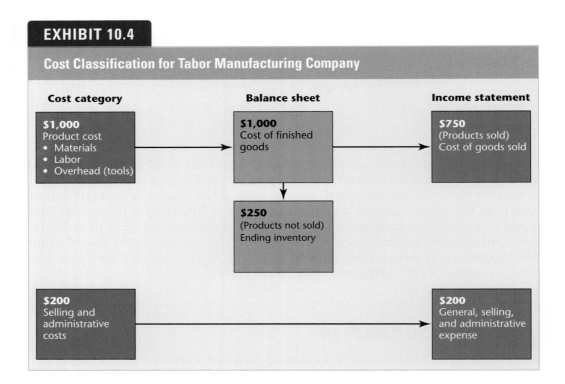

EXHIBIT 10.4

Cost Classification for Tabor Manufacturing Company

Cost category	Balance sheet	Income statement
$1,000 Product cost • Materials • Labor • Overhead (tools)	**$1,000** Cost of finished goods	**$750** (Products sold) Cost of goods sold
	$250 (Products not sold) Ending inventory	
$200 Selling and administrative costs		**$200** General, selling, and administrative expense

EFFECT OF PRODUCT COSTS ON FINANCIAL STATEMENTS

LO 3

Explain the effects on financial statements of product costs versus general, selling, and administrative costs.

We illustrate accounting for product costs in manufacturing companies with Patillo Manufacturing Company, a producer of ceramic pottery. Patillo, started on January 1, 2012, experienced the following accounting events during its first year of operations.[3] *Assume that all transactions except 6, 8, and 10 are cash transactions.*

1. Acquired $15,000 cash by issuing common stock.
2. Paid $2,000 for materials that were used to make products. All products started were completed during the period.
3. Paid $1,200 for salaries of selling and administrative employees.
4. Paid $3,000 for wages of production workers.
5. Paid $2,800 for furniture used in selling and administrative offices.

---

[3]This illustration assumes that all inventory started during the period was completed during the period. Patillo therefore uses only one inventory account, Finished Goods Inventory. Many manufacturing companies normally have three categories of inventory on hand at the end of an accounting period: Raw Materials Inventory, Work in Process Inventory (inventory of partially completed units), and Finished Goods Inventory.

6. Recognized depreciation on the office furniture purchased in Event 5. The furniture was acquired on January 1, had a $400 estimated salvage value, and a four-year useful life. The annual depreciation charge is $600 [($2,800 − $400) ÷ 4].

7. Paid $4,500 for manufacturing equipment.

8. Recognized depreciation on the equipment purchased in Event 7. The equipment was acquired on January 1, had a $1,500 estimated salvage value, and a three-year useful life. The annual depreciation charge is $1,000 [($4,500 − $1,500) ÷ 3].

9. Sold inventory to customers for $7,500 cash.

10. The inventory sold in Event 9 cost $4,000 to make.

The effects of these transactions on the balance sheet, income statement, and statement of cash flows are shown in Exhibit 10.5. Study each row in this exhibit, paying particular attention to how similar costs such as salaries for selling and administrative personnel and wages for production workers have radically different effects on the financial statements. The example illustrates the three elements of product costs, materials (Event 2), labor (Event 4), and overhead (Event 8). These events are discussed in more detail below.

EXHIBIT 10.5

Effect of Product versus Selling and Administrative Costs on Financial Statements

Event No.	Cash	+	Inventory	+	Office Furn.*	+	Manuf. Equip.*	=	Com. Stk.	+	Ret. Earn.	Rev.	−	Exp.	=	Net Inc.	Cash Flow	
					Assets						**Equity**							
1	15,000							=	15,000								15,000	FA
2	(2,000)	+	2,000														(2,000)	OA
3	(1,200)							=			(1,200)		−	1,200	=	(1,200)	(1,200)	OA
4	(3,000)	+	3,000														(3,000)	OA
5	(2,800)	+			2,800												(2,800)	IA
6					(600)			=			(600)		−	600	=	(600)		
7	(4,500)	+					4,500										(4,500)	IA
8			1,000	+			(1,000)											
9	7,500							=			7,500	7,500			=	7,500	7,500	OA
10			(4,000)					=			(4,000)		−	4,000	=	(4,000)		
Totals	9,000	+	2,000	+	2,200	+	3,500	=	15,000	+	1,700	7,500	−	5,800	=	1,700	9,000	NC

*Negative amounts in these columns represent accumulated depreciation.

Materials Costs (Event 2)

Materials used to make products are usually called **raw materials.** The cost of raw materials is first recorded in an asset account (Inventory). The cost is then transferred from the Inventory account to the Cost of Goods Sold account at the time the goods are sold. Remember that materials cost is only one component of total manufacturing costs. When inventory is sold, the combined cost of materials, labor, and overhead is expensed as *cost of goods sold.* The costs of materials that can be easily and conveniently traced to products are called **direct raw materials** costs.

Labor Costs (Event 4)

The salaries paid to selling and administrative employees (Event 3) and the wages paid to production workers (Event 4) are accounted for differently. Salaries paid to selling and administrative employees are expensed immediately, but the cost of production wages is added to inventory. Production wages are expensed as part of cost of goods sold at the time the inventory is sold. Labor costs that can be easily and conveniently traced to products are called **direct labor** costs. The cost flow of wages for production employees versus salaries for selling and administrative personnel is shown in Exhibit 10.6.

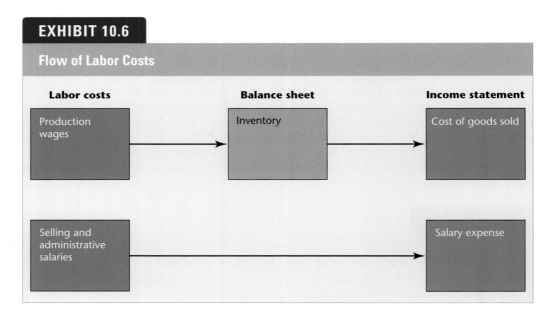

EXHIBIT 10.6

Flow of Labor Costs

Labor costs	Balance sheet	Income statement
Production wages	Inventory	Cost of goods sold
Selling and administrative salaries		Salary expense

Overhead Costs (Event 8)

Although depreciation cost totaled $1,600 ($600 on office furniture and $1,000 on manufacturing equipment), only the $600 of depreciation on the office furniture is expensed directly on the income statement. The depreciation on the manufacturing equipment is split between the income statement (cost of goods sold) and the balance sheet (inventory). The depreciation cost flow for the manufacturing equipment versus the office furniture is shown in Exhibit 10.7.

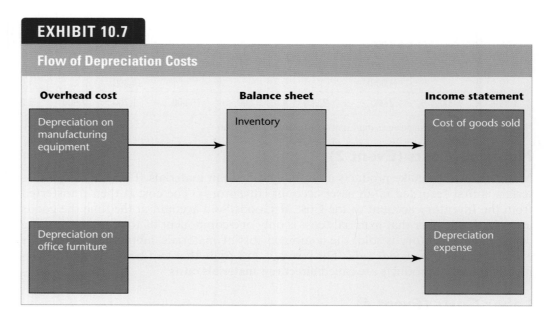

EXHIBIT 10.7

Flow of Depreciation Costs

Overhead cost	Balance sheet	Income statement
Depreciation on manufacturing equipment	Inventory	Cost of goods sold
Depreciation on office furniture		Depreciation expense

Total Product Cost

A summary of Patillo Manufacturing's total product cost is shown in Exhibit 10.8.

EXHIBIT 10.8

Schedule of Inventory Costs	
Materials	$2,000
Labor	3,000
Manufacturing overhead*	1,000
Total product costs	6,000
Less: Cost of goods sold	(4,000)
Ending inventory balance	$2,000

*Depreciation ([$4,500 − $1,500] ÷ 3)

EXHIBIT 10.9

PATILLO MANUFACTURING COMPANY
Financial Statements

Income Statement for 2012

Sales revenue	$ 7,500
Cost of goods sold	(4,000)
Gross margin	3,500
G, S, & A expenses	
Salaries expense	(1,200)
Depreciation expense—office furniture	(600)
Net income	$ 1,700

Balance Sheet as of December 31, 2012

Cash		$ 9,000
Finished goods inventory		2,000
Office furniture	$2,800	
Accumulated depreciation	(600)	
Book value		2,200
Manufacturing equipment	4,500	
Accumulated depreciation	(1,000)	
Book value		3,500
Total assets		$16,700
Stockholders' equity		
Common stock		$15,000
Retained earnings		1,700
Total stockholders' equity		$16,700

Statement of Cash Flows for 2012

Operating Activities	
Inflow from revenue	$ 7,500
Outflow for inventory	(5,000)
Outflow for S&A salaries	(1,200)
Net inflow from operating activities	1,300
Investing Activities	
Outflow for equipment and furniture	(7,300)
Financing Activities	
Inflow from stock issue	15,000
Net change in cash	9,000
Beginning cash balance	-0-
Ending cash balance	$ 9,000

General, Selling, and Administrative Costs

General, selling, and administrative costs (G,S,&A) are normally expensed *in the period* in which they are incurred. Because of this recognition pattern, nonproduct expenses are sometimes called **period costs.** In Patillo's case, the salaries expense for selling and administrative employees and the depreciation on office furniture are period costs reported directly on the income statement.

The income statement, balance sheet, and statement of cash flows for Patillo Manufacturing are displayed in Exhibit 10.9.

The $4,000 cost of goods sold reported on the income statement includes a portion of the materials, labor, and overhead costs incurred by Patillo during the year. Similarly, the $2,000 of finished goods inventory on the balance sheet includes materials, labor, and overhead costs. These product costs will be recognized as expense in the next accounting period when the goods are sold. Initially classifying a cost as a product cost delays, but does not eliminate, its recognition as an expense. All product costs are ultimately recognized as expense (cost of goods sold). Cost classification does not affect cash flow. Cash inflows and outflows are recognized in the period that cash is collected or paid regardless of whether the cost is recorded as an asset or expensed on the income statement.

Overhead Costs: A Closer Look

Costs such as depreciation on manufacturing equipment cannot be easily traced to products. Suppose that Patillo Manufacturing makes both tables and chairs. What part of the depreciation is caused by manufacturing tables versus manufacturing chairs? Similarly, suppose a production supervisor oversees employees who work on both tables and chairs. How much of the supervisor's salary relates to tables and how much to chairs? Likewise, the cost of glue used in the production department would be difficult to trace to tables versus chairs. You could count the drops of glue used on each product, but the information would not be useful enough to merit the time and money spent collecting the data.

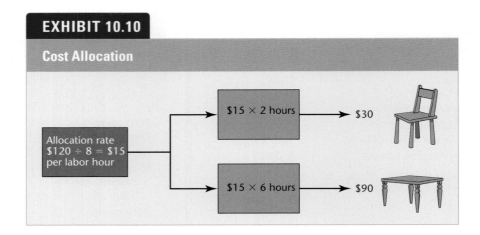

EXHIBIT 10.10

Cost Allocation

Allocation rate $120 ÷ 8 = $15 per labor hour

$15 × 2 hours → $30

$15 × 6 hours → $90

Costs that cannot be traced to products and services in a *cost-effective* manner are called **indirect costs.** The indirect costs incurred to make products are called **manufacturing overhead.** Some of the items commonly included in manufacturing overhead are indirect materials, indirect labor, factory utilities, rent of manufacturing facilities, and depreciation on manufacturing assets.

Because indirect costs cannot be effectively traced to products, they are normally assigned to products using **cost allocation,** a process of dividing a total cost into parts and assigning the parts to relevant cost objects. To illustrate, suppose that production workers spend an eight-hour day making a chair and a table. The chair requires two hours to complete and the table requires six hours. Now suppose that $120 of utilities cost is consumed during the day. How much of the $120 should be assigned to each piece of furniture? The utility cost cannot be directly traced to each specific piece of furniture, but the piece of furniture that required more labor also likely consumed more of the utility cost. Using this line of reasoning, it is rational to allocate the utility cost to the two pieces of furniture based on *direct labor hours* at a rate of $15 per hour ($120 ÷ 8 hours). The chair would be assigned $30 ($15 per hour × 2 hours) of the utility cost and the table would be assigned the remaining $90 ($15 × 6 hours) of utility cost. The allocation of the utility cost is shown in Exhibit 10.10.

We discuss the details of cost allocation in a later chapter. For now, recognize that overhead costs are normally allocated to products rather than traced directly to them.

Answers to **The Curious Accountant**

As you have seen, accounting for depreciation related to manufacturing assets is different from accounting for depreciation for nonmanufacturing assets. Depreciation on the checkout equipment at **Sears** is recorded as depreciation expense. Depreciation on manufacturing equipment at **Schwinn** is considered a product cost. It is included first as a part of the cost of inventory and eventually as a part of the expense, cost of goods sold. Recording depreciation on manufacturing equipment as an inventory cost is simply another example of the matching principle, because the cost does not become an expense until revenue from the product sale is recognized.

Manufacturing Product Cost Summary

As explained, the cost of a product made by a manufacturing company is normally composed of three categories: direct materials, direct labor, and manufacturing overhead. Relevant information about these three cost components is summarized in Exhibit 10.11.

EXHIBIT 10.11

Components of Manufacturing Product Cost

Component 1—Direct Materials
Sometimes called *raw materials*. In addition to basic resources such as wood or metals, it can include manufactured parts. For example, engines, glass, and car tires can be considered as raw materials for an automotive manufacturer. If the amount of a material in a product is known, it can usually be classified as a direct material. The cost of direct materials can be easily traced to specific products.

Component 2—Direct Labor
The cost of wages paid to factory workers involved in hands-on contact with the products being manufactured. If the amount of time employees worked on a product can be determined, this cost can usually be classified as direct labor. Like direct materials, labor costs must be easily traced to a specific product in order to be classified as a direct cost.

Component 3—Manufacturing Overhead
Costs that cannot be easily traced to specific products. Accordingly, these costs are called indirect costs. They can include but are not limited to the following:

1. Indirect materials such as glue, nails, paper, and oil. Indeed, note that indirect materials used in the production process may not appear in the finished product. An example is a chemical solvent used to clean products during the production process but not a component material found in the final product.

2. Indirect labor such as the cost of salaries paid to production supervisors, inspectors, and maintenance personnel.

3. Rental cost for manufacturing facilities and equipment.

4. Utility costs.

5. Depreciation.

6. Security.

7. The cost of preparing equipment for the manufacturing process (i.e., setup costs).

8. Maintenance cost for the manufacturing facility and equipment.

✓ CHECK YOURSELF 10.2

Lawson Manufacturing Company paid production workers wages of $100,000. It incurred materials costs of $120,000 and manufacturing overhead costs of $160,000. Selling and administrative salaries were $80,000. Lawson started and completed 1,000 units of product and sold 800 of these units. The company sets sales prices at $220 above the average per unit production cost. Based on this information alone, determine the amount of gross margin and net income. What is Lawson's pricing strategy called?

Answer   Total product cost is $380,000 ($100,000 labor + $120,000 materials + $160,000 overhead). Cost per unit is $380 ($380,000 ÷ 1,000 units). The sales price per unit is $600 ($380 + $220). Cost of goods sold is $304,000 ($380 × 800 units). Sales revenue is $480,000 ($600 × 800 units). Gross margin is $176,000 ($480,000 revenue − $304,000 cost of goods sold). Net income is $96,000 ($176,000 gross margin − $80,000 selling and administrative salaries). Lawson's pricing strategy is called *cost-plus* pricing.

SCHEDULE OF COST OF GOODS MANUFACTURED AND SOLD

LO 4

Prepare a schedule of cost of goods manufactured and sold.

To this point, we assumed all inventory started during an accounting period was also completed during that accounting period. All product costs (materials, labor, and manufacturing overhead) were either in inventory or expensed as cost of goods sold. At the end of an accounting period, however, most real-world companies have raw materials on hand, and manufacturing companies are likely to have in inventory items that have been started but are not completed. Most manufacturing companies accumulate product costs in three distinct inventory accounts: (1) **Raw Materials Inventory,** which includes lumber, metals, paints, and chemicals that will be used to make the company's products; (2) **Work in Process Inventory,** which includes partially completed products; and (3) **Finished Goods Inventory,** which includes completed products that are ready for sale.

The cost of materials is first recorded in the Raw Materials Inventory account. The cost of materials placed in production is then transferred from the Raw Materials Inventory account to the Work in Process Inventory account. The costs of labor and overhead are added to the Work in Process Inventory account. The cost of the goods completed during the period is transferred from the Work in Process Inventory account to the Finished Goods Inventory account. The cost of the goods that are sold during the accounting period is transferred from the Finished Goods Inventory account to the Cost of Goods Sold account. The balances that remain in the Raw Materials, Work in Process, and Finished Goods Inventory accounts are reported on the balance sheet. The amount of product cost transferred to the Cost of Goods Sold account is expensed on the income statement. Exhibit 10.12 shows the flow of manufacturing costs through the accounting records.

To help managers analyze manufacturing costs, companies frequently summarize product cost information is a report called a **schedule of cost of goods manufactured and sold.** To illustrate, assume that in 2013 Patillo Manufacturing Company purchased $37,950 of raw materials inventory. During 2013 Patillo used $37,000 of raw materials, incurred $34,600 of labor costs, and $26,700 of overhead costs in the process of making inventory. Also, during 2013 the company completed work on products that cost $94,600. Recall that Patillo had zero balances in its Raw Materials and Work in Process Inventory accounts at the end of 2012. It had a $2,000 balance in its Finished Goods Inventory account at the end of 2012. The 2012 ending balance becomes the

EXHIBIT 10.12

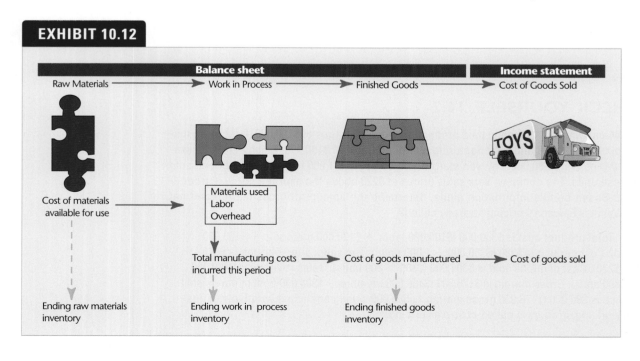

EXHIBIT 10.13

PATILLO MANUFACTURING COMPANY
Schedule of Cost of Goods Manufactured and Sold
For the Year Ended December 31, 2013

Beginning raw materials Inventory	$ 0
Plus: Raw materials purchases	37,950
Less: Ending raw materials inventory	(950)
Raw materials used	37,000
Labor	34,600
Overhead	26,700
Total manufacturing costs	98,300
Plus: Beginning work in process inventory	0
Total work in process inventory	98,300
Less: Ending work in process inventory	(3,700)
Cost of goods manufactured	94,600
Plus: Beginning finished goods inventory	2,000
Cost of goods available for sale	96,600
Less: Ending finished goods inventory	(3,200)
Cost of goods sold	$93,400

2013 beginning balance for finished goods. The 2013 ending balances for the inventory accounts were as follows: Raw Materials Inventory, $950; Work in Process Inventory, $3,700; Finished Goods Inventory, $3,200. Finally, during 2013 Patillo had sales revenue of $153,000. Patillo's schedule of cost of goods manufactured and sold for 2013 is shown in Exhibit 10.13

The $93,400 of cost of goods sold would appear on Patillo's 2013 income statement. A partial income statement for Patillo is shown in Exhibit 10.14

EXHIBIT 10.14

PATILLO MANUFACTURING COMPANY
Income Statement
For the Year Ended December 31, 2013

Sales revenue	$153,000
Cost of goods sold	(93,400)
Gross margin	$ 59,600

UPSTREAM AND DOWNSTREAM COSTS

Most companies incur product-related costs before and after, as well as during, the manufacturing process. For example, Ford Motor Company incurs significant research and development costs prior to mass producing a new car model. These **upstream costs** occur before the manufacturing process begins. Similarly, companies normally incur significant costs after the manufacturing process is complete. Examples of **downstream costs** include transportation, advertising, sales commissions, and bad debts. While upstream and downstream costs are not considered to be product costs for financial reporting purposes, profitability analysis requires that they be considered in cost-plus pricing decisions. To be profitable, a company must recover the total cost of developing, producing, and delivering its products to customers.

LO 5

Distinguish product costs from upstream and downstream costs.

PRODUCT COSTING IN SERVICE AND MERCHANDISING COMPANIES

Companies are frequently classified as being service, merchandising, or manufacturing businesses. As the name implies, service organizations provide services, rather than physical products, to consumers. For example, St. Jude Children's Hospital provides treatment programs aimed at healing patient diseases. Other common service providers include

LO 6

Explain how product costing differs in service, merchandising, and manufacturing companies.

public accountants, lawyers, restaurants, dry cleaning establishments, and lawn care companies. Merchandising businesses are sometimes called retail or wholesale companies; they sell goods other companies make. **The Home Depot, Inc., Costco Wholesale Corporation**, and **Best Buy Co., Inc.**, are merchandising companies. Manufacturing companies make the goods they sell to their customers. **Toyota Motor Corporation, Texaco, Inc.**, and **American Standard Companies, Inc.**, are manufacturing businesses.

How do manufacturing companies differ from service and merchandising businesses? Do service and merchandising companies incur materials, labor, and overhead costs? Yes. For example, **Ernst & Young**, a large accounting firm, must pay employees (labor costs), use office supplies (material costs), and incur utilities, depreciation, and so on (overhead costs) in the process of conducting audits. ***The primary difference between manufacturing entities and service companies is that the products provided by service companies are consumed immediately.*** In contrast, products made by manufacturing companies can be held in the form of inventory until they are sold to consumers. Similarly, most labor and overhead costs incurred by merchandising companies result from providing assistance to customers. These costs are normally treated as general, selling, and administrative expenses rather than accumulated in inventory accounts. Indeed, merchandising companies are often viewed as service companies rather than considered a separate business category.

The important point to remember is that all business managers are expected to control costs, improve quality, and increase productivity. Like managers of manufacturing companies, managers of service and merchandising businesses can benefit from the analysis of the cost of satisfying their customers. For example, **Wendy's**, a service company, can benefit from knowing how much a hamburger costs in the same manner that **Bayer Corporation**, a manufacturing company, benefits from knowing the cost of a bottle of aspirin.

✓ CHECK YOURSELF 10.3

The cost of making a **Burger King** hamburger includes the cost of materials, labor, and overhead. Does this mean that Burger King is a manufacturing company?

Answer   No, Burger King is not a manufacturing company. It is a service company because its products are consumed immediately. In contrast, there may be a considerable delay between the time the product of a manufacturing company is made and the time it is consumed. For example, it could be several months between the time **Ford Motor Company** makes an Explorer and the time the Explorer is ultimately sold to a customer. The primary difference between service and manufacturing companies is that manufacturing companies have inventories of products and service companies do not.

JUST-IN-TIME INVENTORY

Show how just-in-time inventory can increase profitability.

Companies attempt to minimize the amount of inventory they maintain because of the high cost of holding it. Many **inventory holding costs** are obvious: financing, warehouse space, supervision, theft, damage, and obsolescence. Other costs are hidden: diminished motivation, sloppy work, inattentive attitudes, and increased production time.

Many businesses have been able to simultaneously reduce their inventory holding costs and increase customer satisfaction by making products available **just in time (JIT)** for customer consumption. For example, hamburgers that are cooked to order are fresher and more individualized than those that are prepared in advance and stored until a customer orders one. Many fast-food restaurants have discovered that JIT systems lead not only to greater customer satisfaction but also to lower costs through reduced waste.

Just-in-Time Illustration

To illustrate the benefits of a JIT system, consider Paula Elliot, a student at a large urban university. She helps support herself by selling flowers. Three days each week, Paula drives to a florist, purchases 25 single-stem roses, returns to the school, and sells the flowers to individuals from a location on a local street corner. She pays $2 per rose and sells each one for $3. Some days she does not have enough flowers to meet customer demand. Other days, she must discard one or two unsold flowers; she believes quality is important and refuses to sell flowers that are not fresh. During May, she purchased 300 roses and sold 280. She calculated her driving cost to be $45. Exhibit 10.15 displays Paula's May income statement.

After studying just-in-time inventory systems in her managerial accounting class, Paula decided to apply the concepts to her small business. She *reengineered* her distribution system by purchasing her flowers from a florist within walking distance of her sales location. She had considered purchasing from this florist earlier but had rejected the idea because the florist's regular selling price of $2.25 per rose was too high. After learning about *most-favored customer status,* she developed a strategy to get a price reduction. By guaranteeing that she would buy at least 30 roses per week, she was able to convince the local florist to match her current cost of $2.00 per rose. The local florist agreed that she could make purchases in batches of any size so long as the total amounted to at least 30 per week. Under this arrangement, Paula was able to buy roses *just in time* to meet customer demand. Each day she purchased a small number of flowers. When she ran out, she simply returned to the florist for additional ones.

The JIT system also enabled Paula to eliminate the cost of the *nonvalue-added activity* of driving to her former florist. Customer satisfaction actually improved because no one was ever turned away because of the lack of inventory. In June, Paula was able to buy and sell 310 roses with no waste and no driving expense. The June income statement is shown in Exhibit 10.16.

Paula was ecstatic about her $115 increase in profitability ($310 in June − $195 in May = $115 increase), but she was puzzled about the exact reasons for the change. She had saved $40 (20 flowers × $2 each) by avoiding waste and eliminated $45 of driving expenses. These two factors explained only $85 ($40 waste + $45 driving expense) of the $115 increase. What had caused the remaining $30 ($115 − $85) increase in profitability? Paula asked her accounting professor to help her identify the remaining $30 difference.

The professor explained that May sales had suffered from *lost opportunities*. Recall that under the earlier inventory system, Paula had to turn away some prospective customers because she sold out of flowers before all customers were served. Sales increased from 280 roses in May to 310 roses in June. A likely explanation for the 30 unit difference (310 − 280) is that customers who would have purchased flowers in May were unable to do so because of a lack of availability. May's sales suffered from the lost opportunity to earn a gross margin of $1 per flower on 30 roses, a $30 **opportunity cost.** This opportunity cost is the missing link in explaining the profitability difference between May and June. The total $115 difference consists of (1) $40 savings from waste elimination, (2) $45 savings from eliminating driving expense, and (3) opportunity cost of $30. The subject of opportunity cost has widespread application and is discussed in more depth in subsequent chapters of the text.

EXHIBIT 10.15

Income Statement for May

Sales revenue (280 units × $3 per unit)	$840
Cost of goods sold (280 units × $2 per unit)	(560)
Gross margin	280
Driving expense	(45)
Waste (20 units × $2 per unit)	(40)
Net income	$195

EXHIBIT 10.16

Income Statement for June

Sales revenue (310 units × $3 per unit)	$930
Cost of goods sold (310 units × $2 per unit)	(620)
Gross margin	310
Driving expense	0
Net income	$310

✓ CHECK YOURSELF 10.4

A strike at a General Motors brake plant caused an almost immediate shutdown of many of the company's assembly plants. What could have caused such a rapid and widespread shutdown?

Answer A rapid and widespread shutdown could have occurred because General Motors uses a just-in-time inventory system. With a just-in-time inventory system, there is no stockpile of inventory to draw on when strikes or other forces disrupt inventory deliveries. This illustrates a potential negative effect of using a just-in-time inventory system.

STATEMENT OF ETHICAL PROFESSIONAL PRACTICE

Identify and explain the standards contained in IMA's Statement of Ethical Professional Practice.

Management accountants must be prepared not only to make difficult choices between legitimate alternatives but also to face conflicts of a more troubling nature, such as pressure to

1. Undertake duties they have not been trained to perform competently.
2. Disclose confidential information.
3. Compromise their integrity through falsification, embezzlement, bribery, and so on.
4. Issue biased, misleading, or incomplete reports.

In Chapter 4 we explained how the American Institute of Certified Public Accountants' Code of Professional Conduct provides guidance for CPAs to avoid unethical behavior. To provide Certified Management Accountants (CMAs) with guidance for ethical conduct the Institute of Management Accountants (IMA) issued a *Statement of Ethical Professional Practice,* which is shown in Exhibit 10.17. Management accountants are also frequently required to abide by organizational codes of ethics. Failure to adhere to professional and organizational ethical standards can lead to personal disgrace, loss of employment, or imprisonment.

EXHIBIT 10.17

Statement of Ethical Professional Practice

Members of IMA shall behave ethically. A commitment to ethical professional practice includes overarching principles that express our values, and standards that guide our conduct. IMA's overarching ethical principles include: Honesty, Fairness, Objectivity, and Responsibility. Members shall act in accordance with these principles and shall encourage others within their organizations to adhere to them. A member's failure to comply with the following standards may result in disciplinary action.

Competence Each member has a responsibility to
- Maintain an appropriate level of professional expertise by continually developing knowledge and skills.
- Perform professional duties in accordance with relevant laws, regulations, and technical standards.
- Provide decision support information and recommendations that are accurate, clear, concise, and timely.
- Recognize and communicate professional limitations or other constraints that would preclude responsible judgment or successful performance of an activity.

Confidentiality Each member has a responsibility to
- Keep information confidential except when disclosure is authorized or legally required.
- Inform all relevant parties regarding appropriate use of confidential information. Monitor subordinates' activities to ensure compliance.
- Refrain from using confidential information for unethical or illegal advantage.

Integrity Each member has a responsibility to
- Mitigate actual conflicts of interest and avoid apparent conflicts of interest. Advise all parties of any potential conflicts.
- Refrain from engaging in any conduct that would prejudice carrying out duties ethically.
- Abstain from engaging in or supporting any activity that might discredit the profession.

Credibility Each member has a responsibility to
- Communicate information fairly and objectively.
- Disclose all relevant information that could reasonably be expected to influence an intended user's understanding of the reports, analyses, or recommendations.
- Disclose delays or deficiencies in information, timeliness, processing, or internal controls in conformance with organization policy and/or applicable law.

Resolution of Ethical Conflict In applying these standards, you may encounter problems identifying unethical behavior or resolving an ethical conflict. When faced with ethical issues, follow your organization's established policies on the resolution of such conflict. If these policies do not resolve the ethical conflict, consider the following courses of action.
- Discuss the issue with your immediate supervisor except when it appears that the supervisor is involved. In that case, present the issue to the next level. If you cannot achieve a satisfactory resolution, submit the issue to the next management level. Communication of such problems to authorities or individuals not employed or engaged by the organization is not considered appropriate, unless you believe there is a clear violation of the law.
- Clarify relevant ethical issues by initiating a confidential discussion with an IMA Ethics Counselor or other impartial advisor to obtain a better understanding of possible courses of action.
- Consult your own attorney as to legal obligations and rights concerning the ethical conflict.

REALITY BYTES

Unethical behavior occurs in all types of organizations. In its *2007 National Government Ethics Survey,* the Ethics Resource Center reported its findings on the occurrences and reporting of unethical behavior in local, state, and federal governments.

Fifty-seven percent of those surveyed reported having observed unethical conduct during the past year. Unethical conduct was reported most often by those in local governments (63%) and least often at the federal level (52%). The definition of ethical misconduct used in the study was quite broad, ranging from behavior such as an individual putting his or her personal interest ahead of the interest of the organization, to sexual harassment, to taking bribes. The more egregious offences, such as discrimination or taking bribes, were reported much less often than activities such as lying to customers, vendors, or the public.

Once observed, unethical behavior often was not reported. For example, only 25 percent of observed incidents of the alteration of financial records were reported to supervisors or whistleblower hotlines, and only 54 percent of observed bribes were reported.

The survey also found that only 18 percent of government entities have ethics and compliance programs in place that could be considered well-implemented. However, where well-implemented programs do exist, observed unethical misconduct is less likely to occur and more likely to be reported. In these entities only 36 percent of respondents said they had observed misconduct (compared to 57 percent overall), and when they did observe misconduct, 75 percent said they reported it.

For the complete *2007 National Government Ethics Survey,* go to www.ethics.org.

A Look Back

Managerial accounting focuses on the information needs of *internal* users, while *financial accounting* focuses on the information needs of *external* users. Managerial accounting uses economic, operating, and nonfinancial, as well as financial, data. Managerial accounting information is local (pertains to the company's subunits), is limited by cost/benefit considerations, is more concerned with relevance and timeliness, and is future oriented. Financial accounting information, on the other hand, is more global than managerial accounting information. It supplies information that applies to the whole company. Financial accounting is regulated by numerous authorities, is characterized by objectivity, is focused on reliability and accuracy, and is historical in nature.

Both managerial and financial accounting are concerned with product costing. Financial accountants need product cost information to determine the amount of inventory reported on the balance sheet and the amount of cost of goods sold reported on the income statement. Managerial accountants need to know the cost of products for pricing decisions and for control and evaluation purposes. When determining unit product costs, managers use the average cost per unit. Determining the actual cost of each product requires an unreasonable amount of time and record keeping and it makes no difference in product pricing and product cost control decisions.

Product costs are the costs incurred to make products: the costs of direct materials, direct labor, and overhead. *Overhead costs* are product costs that cannot be cost effectively traced to a product; therefore, they are assigned to products using *cost allocation*. Overhead costs include indirect materials, indirect labor, depreciation, rent, and utilities for manufacturing facilities. Product costs are first accumulated in an asset account (Inventory). They are expensed as cost of goods sold in the period the inventory is sold. The difference between sales revenue and cost of goods sold is called *gross margin.*

General, selling, and administrative costs are classified separately from product costs. They are subtracted from gross margin to determine net income. General, selling, and administrative costs can be divided into two categories. Costs incurred before the manufacturing process begins (research and development costs) are *upstream costs.* Costs incurred after manufacturing is complete (transportation) are *downstream costs.* Service companies, like manufacturing companies, incur materials, labor, and overhead costs, but the products provided by service companies are consumed immediately. Therefore, service company product costs are not accumulated in an Inventory account.

A code of ethical conduct is needed in the accounting profession because accountants hold positions of trust and face conflicts of interest. In recognition of the temptations that accountants face, the IMA has issued a *Statement of Ethical Professional Practice,* which provides accountants guidance in resisting temptations and in making difficult decisions.

Emerging trends such as *just-in-time inventory* and *activity-based management* are methods that many companies have used to reengineer their production and delivery systems to eliminate waste, reduce errors, and minimize costs. Activity-based management seeks to eliminate or reduce *nonvalue-added activities* and to create new *value-added activities.* Just-in-time inventory seeks to reduce inventory holding costs and to lower prices for customers by making inventory available just in time for customer consumption.

>> A Look Forward

In addition to distinguishing costs by product versus G, S, & A classification, other classifications can be used to facilitate managerial decision making. In the next chapter, costs are classified according to the *behavior* they exhibit when the number of units of product increases or decreases (volume of activity changes). You will learn to distinguish between costs that vary with activity volume changes versus costs that remain fixed with activity volume changes. You will learn not only to recognize *cost behavior* but also how to use such recognition to evaluate business risk and opportunity.

APPENDIX A

Identify emerging trends in accounting.

Emerging Trends in Managerial Accounting

Global competition has forced many companies to reengineer their production and delivery systems to eliminate waste, reduce errors, and minimize costs. A key ingredient of successful **reengineering** is benchmarking. **Benchmarking** involves identifying the **best practices** used by world-class competitors. By studying and mimicking these practices, a company uses benchmarking to implement highly effective and efficient operating methods. Best practices employed by world-class companies include total quality management (TQM), activity-based management (ABM), and value-added assessment.

Total Quality Management

To promote effective and efficient operations, many companies practice **total quality management (TQM).** TQM is a two-dimensional management philosophy using (1) a systematic problem-solving philosophy that encourages frontline workers to achieve *zero defects* and (2) an organizational commitment to achieving *customer satisfaction.* A key component of TQM is **continuous improvement,** an ongoing process through which employees strive to eliminate waste, reduce response time, minimize defects, and simplify the design and delivery of products and services to customers.

Activity-Based Management

Simple changes in perspective can have dramatic results. For example, imagine how realizing the world is round instead of flat changed the nature of travel. A recent change in perspective developing in management accounting is the realization that an organization cannot manage *costs*. Instead, it manages the *activities* that cause costs to be incurred. **Activities** represent the measures an organization takes to accomplish its goals.

The primary goal of all organizations is to provide products (goods and services) their customers *value*. The sequence of activities used to provide products is called a **value chain. Activity-based management** assesses the value chain to create new or refine existing **value-added activities** and to eliminate or reduce *nonvalue-added activities*. A value-added activity is any unit of work that contributes to a product's ability to satisfy customer needs. For example, cooking is an activity that adds value to food served to a hungry customer. **Nonvalue-added activities** are tasks undertaken that do not contribute to a product's ability to satisfy customer needs. Waiting for the oven to preheat so that food can be cooked does not add value. Most customers value cooked food, but they do not value waiting for it.

To illustrate, consider the value-added activities undertaken by a pizza restaurant. Begin with a customer who is hungry for pizza; certain activities must occur to satisfy that hunger. These activities are pictured in Exhibit 10.18. At a minimum, the restaurant must conduct research and development (devise a recipe), obtain raw materials (acquire the ingredients), manufacture the product (combine and bake the ingredients), market the product (advertise its availability), and deliver the product (transfer the pizza to the customer).

EXHIBIT 10.18

Value Chain

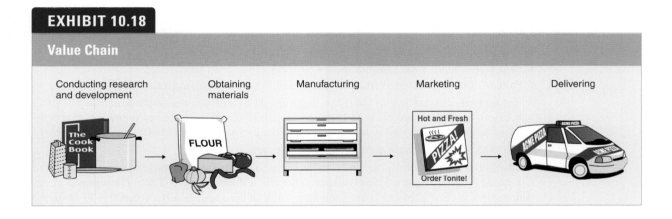

| Conducting research and development | Obtaining materials | Manufacturing | Marketing | Delivering |

Businesses gain competitive advantages by adding activities that satisfy customer needs. For example, **Domino's Pizza** grew briskly by recognizing the value customers placed on the convenience of home pizza delivery. Alternatively, **Little Caesar's** has been highly successful by satisfying customers who value low prices. Other restaurants capitalize on customer values pertaining to taste, ambience, or location. Businesses can also gain competitive advantages by identifying and eliminating nonvalue-added activities, providing products of comparable quality at lower cost than competitors.

Value Chain Analysis Across Companies

Comprehensive value chain analysis extends from obtaining raw materials to the ultimate disposition of finished products. It encompasses the activities performed not only by a particular organization but also by that organization's suppliers and those who service its finished products. For example, **PepsiCo** must be concerned with the activities of the company that supplies the containers for its soft drinks as well as the retail companies that sell its products. If cans of Pepsi fail to open properly, the customer is more likely to blame PepsiCo than the supplier of the cans. Comprehensive value chain analysis can lead to identifying and eliminating nonvalue-added activities that occur between companies. For example, container producers could be encouraged to build manufacturing facilities near Pepsi's bottling factories, eliminating the nonvalue-added activity of transporting empty containers from the manufacturer to the bottling facility. The resulting cost savings benefits customers by reducing costs without affecting quality.

A step-by-step audio-narrated series of slides is provided on the text website at www.mhhe.com/edmondssurvey3e.

SELF-STUDY REVIEW PROBLEM

Tuscan Manufacturing Company makes a unique headset for use with mobile phones. The company had the following amounts in its accounts at the beginning of 2012: Cash, $795,000; Raw Materials Inventory, $5,000; Work in process Inventory, $11,000; Finished Goods Inventory, $39,000; Common Stock, $650,000; and Retained Earnings, $200,000. Tuscan experienced the following accounting events during 2012. Other than the adjusting entries for depreciation, assume that all transactions are cash transactions.

1. Paid $50,000 of research and development costs to create the headset.
2. Paid $139,000 for raw materials will be used to make headsets.
3. Placed $141,000 of the raw materials cost into the process of manufacturing headsets.
4. Paid $82,200 for salaries of selling and administrative employees.
5. Paid $224,000 for wages of production workers.
6. Paid $48,000 to purchase furniture used in selling and administrative offices.
7. Recognized depreciation on the office furniture. The furniture was acquired January 1, 2012. It has an $8,000 salvage value and a four-year useful life. The amount of depreciation is computed as [(cost − salvage) ÷ useful life]. Specifically, ($48,000 − $8,000) ÷ 4 = $10,000.
8. Paid $65,000 to purchase manufacturing equipment.
9. Recognized depreciation on the manufacturing equipment. The equipment was acquired January 1, 2012. It has a $5,000 salvage value and a three-year useful life. The amount of depreciation is computed as [(cost − salvage) ÷ useful life]. Specifically, ($65,000 − $5,000) ÷ 3 = $20,000.
10. Paid $136,000 for rent and utility costs on the manufacturing facility.
11. Paid $41,000 for inventory holding expenses for completed headsets (rental of warehouse space, salaries of warehouse personnel, and other general storage costs.)
12. Completed and transferred headsets that had a total cost of $520,000 from work in process inventory to finished goods.
13. Sold headsets for $738,200.
14. It cost Tuscan $517,400 to make the headsets sold in Event 13.

Required

a. Show how these events affect the balance sheet, income statement, and statement of cash flows by recording them in a horizontal financial statement model.
b. Explain why Tuscan's recognition of cost of goods sold expense had no impact on cash flow.
c. Prepare a schedule of costs of goods manufactured and sold, an income statement, and a balance sheet.
d. Distinguish between the product costs and the upstream and downstream costs that Tuscan incurred.

Solution to Requirement a

Event No.	Cash +	Raw Mat. Inv. +	WIP Inv. +	Finished Goods Inv. +	Office Furn.* +	Manuf. Equip.* =	Com. Stk. +	Ret. Earn.	Rev. −	Exp. = Net Inc.	Cash Flow
	795,000	5,000	11,000	39,000		=	650,000	200,000		=	
1	(50,000)					=		(50,000)		− 50,000 = (50,000)	(50,000) OA
2	(139,000)	139,000				=				=	(139,000) OA
3		(141,000)	141,000			=				=	
4	(82,200)					=		(82,200)		− 82,200 = (82,200)	(82,200) OA
5	(224,000)		224,000			=				=	(224,000) OA
6	(48,000)				48,000	=				=	(48,000) IA
7					(10,000)	=		(10,000)		− 10,000 = (10,000)	
8	(65,000)					65,000 =				=	(65,000) IA
9			20,000			(20,000) =				=	
10	(136,000)		136,000			=				=	(136,000) OA
11	(41,000)					=		(41,000)		− 41,000 = (41,000)	(41,000) OA
12			(520,000)	520,000		=				=	
13	738,200					=		738,200	738,200	= 738,200	738,200 0A
14				(517,400)		=		(517,400)		− 517,400 = (517,400)	
Totals	748,000 +	3,000 +	12,000 +	41,600 +	38,000 +	45,000 =	650,000 +	237,600	738,200 −	700,600 = 37,600	(47,000) NC

*Negative amounts in these columns represent accumulated depreciation.

Solution to Requirement b

Tuscan does not recognize a cash outflow at the time the goods are sold because the cash is paid when the materials, labor, and overhead are acquired.

Solution to Requirement c

TUSCAN MANUFACTURING COMPANY
Schedule of Cost of Goods Manufactured and Sold
For the Year Ended December 31, 2012

Beginning raw materials Inventory	$ 5,000
Plus: Raw materials purchases	139,000
Less: Ending raw materials inventory	(3,000)
Raw materials used	141,000
Labor	224,000
Overhead	156,000
Total manufacturing costs	521,000
Plus: Beginning work in process inventory	11,000
Total work in process inventory	532,000
Less: Ending work in process inventory	(12,000)
Cost of goods manufactured	520,000
Plus: Beginning finished goods inventory	39,000
Cost of goods available for sale	559,000
Less: Ending finished goods inventory	(41,600)
Cost of goods sold	$517,400

TUSCAN MANUFACTURING COMPANY
Income Statement
For the Year Ended December 31, 2012

Sales revenue	$738,200
Cost of goods sold	(517,400)
Gross margin	220,800
Research and development expenses	(50,000)
Selling and administrative salary expense	(82,200)
Selling and administrative depreciation expense	(10,000)
Inventory holding expenses	(41,000)
Net Income	$ 37,600

TUSCAN MANUFACTURING COMPANY
Balance Sheet
As of December 31, 2012

Assets	
Cash	$748,000
Raw materials inventory	3,000
Work in process inventory	12,000
Finished goods inventory	41,600
Manufacturing equipment less accumulated depreciation	45,000
Office furniture less accumulated depreciation	38,000
Total assets	$887,600
Equity	
Common stock	$650,000
Retained earnings	237,600
Total stockholders' equity	$887,600

Solution to Requirement d

Inventory product costs for manufacturing companies focus on the costs necessary to make the product. The cost of research and development (Event 1) occurs before the inventory is made and is therefore an upstream cost, not an inventory (product) cost. The inventory holding costs (Event 11) are incurred after the inventory has been made and are therefore downstream costs, not product costs. Selling costs (included in Events 4 and 7) are normally incurred after products have been made and are therefore usually classified as downstream costs. Administrative costs (also included in Events 4 and 7) are not related to making products and are therefore not classified as product costs. Administrative costs may be incurred before, during, or after products are made, so they may be classified as either upstream or downstream costs. Only the costs of materials, labor, and overhead that are actually incurred for the purpose of making goods (Events 3, 5, 9, and 10) are classified as product costs.

KEY TERMS

Activities 377
Activity-based management (ABM) 377
Average cost 363
Benchmarking 376
Best practices 376
Continuous improvement 376

Cost allocation 368
Cost-plus pricing 362
Direct labor 366
Direct raw materials 365
Downstream costs 371
Financial accounting 359
Finished Goods Inventory 370

General, selling, and administrative costs 367
Indirect costs 368
Inventory holding costs 372
Just in time (JIT) 372
Managerial accounting 359
Manufacturing overhead 368

QUESTIONS

1. What are some differences between financial and managerial accounting?

2. What does the value-added principle mean as it applies to managerial accounting information? Give an example of value-added information that may be included in managerial accounting reports but is not shown in publicly reported financial statements.

3. How does product costing used in financial accounting differ from product costing used in managerial accounting?

4. What does the statement "costs can be assets or expenses" mean?

5. Why are the salaries of production workers accumulated in an inventory account instead of being directly expensed on the income statement?

6. How do product costs affect the financial statements? How does the classification of product cost (as an asset vs. an expense) affect net income?

7. What is an indirect cost? Provide examples of product costs that would be classified as indirect.

8. How does a product cost differ from a general, selling, and administrative cost? Give examples of each.

9. Why is cost classification important to managers?

10. What is cost allocation? Give an example of a cost that needs to be allocated.

11. What are some of the common ethical conflicts that accountants encounter?

12. What costs should be considered in determining the sales price of a product?

13. What is a just-in-time (JIT) inventory system? Name some inventory costs that can be eliminated or reduced by its use.

14. What are the two dimensions of a total quality management (TQM) program? Why is TQM being used in business practice? (Appendix)

15. What does the term *reengineering* mean? Name some reengineering practices. (Appendix)

16. How has the Institute of Management Accountants responded to the need for high standards of ethical conduct in the accounting profession? (Appendix)

17. What does the term *activity-based management* mean? (Appendix)

18. What is a value chain? (Appendix)

19. What do the terms *value-added activity* and *nonvalue-added activity* mean? Provide an example of each type of activity. (Appendix)

MULTIPLE-CHOICE QUESTIONS

Multiple-choice questions are provided on the text website at www.mhhe.com/edmondssurvey3e.

EXERCISES

All applicable Exercises are available with McGraw-Hill's Connect Accounting.

Exercise 10-1   *Identifying financial versus managerial accounting characteristics*   **LO 1**

Required

Indicate whether each of the following is representative of managerial or of financial accounting.

a. Information is factual and is characterized by objectivity, reliability, consistency, and accuracy.

b. Information is reported continuously and has a current or future orientation.

c. Information is provided to outsiders including investors, creditors, government agencies, analysts, and reporters.

d. Information is regulated by the SEC, FASB, and other sources of GAAP.

e. Information is based on estimates that are bounded by relevance and timeliness.

f. Information is historically based and usually reported annually.

g. Information is local and pertains to subunits of the organization.

h. Information includes economic and nonfinancial data as well as financial data.

i. Information is global and pertains to the company as a whole.

j. Information is provided to insiders including executives, managers, and operators.

LO 2

Exercise 10-2　*Identifying product versus general, selling, and administrative costs*

Required

Indicate whether each of the following costs should be classified as a product cost or as a general, selling, and administrative cost.

a. Direct materials used in a manufacturing company.

b. Indirect materials used in a manufacturing company.

c. Salaries of employees working in the accounting department.

d. Commissions paid to sales staff.

e. Interest on the mortgage for the company's corporate headquarters.

f. Indirect labor used to manufacture inventory.

g. Attorney's fees paid to protect the company from frivolous lawsuits.

h. Research and development costs incurred to create new drugs for a pharmaceutical company.

i. The cost of secretarial supplies used in a doctor's office.

j. Depreciation on the office furniture of the company president.

LO 2

Exercise 10-3　*Classifying costs: product or G, S, & A/asset or expense*

Required

Use the following format to classify each cost as a product cost or a general, selling, and administrative (G, S, & A) cost. Also indicate whether the cost would be recorded as an asset or an expense. The first item is shown as an example.

Cost Category	Product/ G, S, & A	Asset/ Expense
Research and development costs	G, S, & A	Expense
Cost to set up manufacturing facility		
Utilities used in factory		
Cars for sales staff		
Distributions to stockholders		
General office supplies		
Raw materials used in the manufacturing process		
Cost to rent office equipment		
Wages of production workers		
Advertising costs		
Promotion costs		
Production supplies		
Depreciation on administration building		
Depreciation on manufacturing equipment		

Exercise 10-4 *Identifying effect of product versus general, selling, and*   **LO 2, 3**
administrative costs on financial statements

Required

Nailry Industries recognized accrued compensation cost. Use the following model to show how this event would affect the company's financial statement under the following two assumptions: (1) the compensation is for office personnel and (2) the compensation is for production workers. Use pluses or minuses to show the effect on each element. If an element is not affected, indicate so by placing the letters NA under the appropriate heading.

	Assets	=	Liab.	+	Equity	Rev.	−	Exp.	=	Net Inc.	Cash Flow
1.											
2.											

Exercise 10-5 *Identify effect of product versus general, selling, and administrative*   **LO 2, 3**
costs on financial statements

Required

Milby Industries recognized the annual cost of depreciation on its December 31 financial statement. Using the following horizontal financial statements model, indicate how this event affected the company's financial statements under the following two assumptions: (1) the depreciation was on office furniture and (2) the depreciation was on manufacturing equipment. Indicate whether the event increases (I), decreases (D), or has no affect (NA) on each element of the financial statements. Also, in the Cash Flow column, indicate whether the cash flow is for operating activities (OA), investing activities (IA), or financing activities (FA). (Note: Show accumulated depreciation as a decrease in the book value of the appropriate asset account.)

Event No.	Assets					Equity							
	Cash	+	Inventory	+	Manuf. Equip.	+	Office Furn.	=	Com. Stk.	+	Ret. Earn.	Rev. − Exp. = Net Inc.	Cash Flow
1.													
2.													

Exercise 10-6 *Identifying product costs in a manufacturing company*   **LO 2**

Tiffany Crissler was talking to another accounting student, Bill Tyrone. Upon discovering that the accounting department offered an upper-level course in cost measurement, Tiffany remarked to Bill, "How difficult can it be? My parents own a toy store. All you have to do to figure out how much something costs is look at the invoice. Surely you don't need an entire course to teach you how to read an invoice."

Required

a. Identify the three main components of product cost for a manufacturing entity.

b. Explain why measuring product cost for a manufacturing entity is more complex than measuring product cost for a retail toy store.

c. Assume that Tiffany's parents rent a store for $7,500 per month. Different types of toys use different amounts of store space. For example, displaying a bicycle requires more store space than displaying a deck of cards. Also, some toys remain on the shelf longer than others. Fad toys sell quickly, but traditional toys sell more slowly. Under these circumstances, how would you determine the amount of rental cost required to display each type of toy? Identify two other costs incurred by a toy store that may be difficult to allocate to individual toys.

LO 2, 3

Exercise 10-7 *Identifying product versus general, selling, and administrative costs*

A review of the accounting records of Rayford Manufacturing indicated that the company incurred the following payroll costs during the month of August.

1. Salary of the company president—$32,000.
2. Salary of the vice president of manufacturing—$16,000.
3. Salary of the chief financial officer—$18,800.
4. Salary of the vice president of marketing—$15,600.
5. Salaries of middle managers (department heads, production supervisors) in manufacturing plant—$196,000.
6. Wages of production workers—$938,000.
7. Salaries of administrative secretaries—$112,000.
8. Salaries of engineers and other personnel responsible for maintaining production equipment—$178,000.
9. Commissions paid to sales staff—$252,000.

Required

a. What amount of payroll cost would be classified as general, selling, and administrative expense?
b. Assuming that Rayford made 4,000 units of product and sold 3,600 of them during the month of August, determine the amount of payroll cost that would be included in cost of goods sold.

LO 2, 3

Exercise 10-8 *Recording product versus general, selling, and administrative costs in a financial statements model*

Pappas Manufacturing experienced the following events during its first accounting period.

1. Recognized depreciation on manufacturing equipment.
2. Recognized depreciation on office furniture.
3. Recognized revenue from cash sale of products.
4. Recognized cost of goods sold from sale referenced in Event 3.
5. Acquired cash by issuing common stock.
6. Paid cash to purchase raw materials that were used to make products.
7. Paid wages to production workers.
8. Paid salaries to administrative staff.

Required

Use the following horizontal financial statements model to show how each event affects the balance sheet, income statement, and statement of cash flows. Indicate whether the event increases (I), decreases (D), or has no effect (NA) on each element of the financial statements. In the Cash Flow column, indicate whether the cash flow is for operating activities (OA), investing activities (IA), or financing activities (FA). The first transaction has been recorded as an example. (*Note:* Show accumulated depreciation as decrease in the book value of the appropriate asset account.)

Event No.			Assets				Equity					
	Cash	+	Inventory	+	Manuf. Equip.	+	Office Furn.	=	Com. Stk.	+	Ret. Earn.	Rev. − Exp. = Net Inc.	Cash Flow
1.	NA		I		D		NA		NA		NA	NA NA NA	NA

LO 2, 3

Exercise 10-9 *Allocating product costs between ending inventory and cost of goods sold*

Howle Manufacturing Company began operations on January 1. During the year, it started and completed 1,700 units of product. The company incurred the following costs.

1. Raw materials purchased and used—$3,150.
2. Wages of production workers—$3,530.

3. Salaries of administrative and sales personnel—$1,995.
4. Depreciation on manufacturing equipment—$4,370.
5. Depreciation on administrative equipment—$1,835.

Howle sold 1,020 units of product.

Required

a. Determine the total product cost for the year.
b. Determine the total cost of the ending inventory.
c. Determine the total of cost of goods sold.

Exercise 10-10   *Financial statement effects for manufacturing versus service organizations*   LO 6

The following financial statements model shows the effects of recognizing depreciation in two different circumstances. One circumstance represents recognizing depreciation on a machine used in a factory. The other circumstance recognizes depreciation on computers used in a consulting firm. The effects of each event have been recorded using the letter (I) to represent increase, (D) for decrease, and (NA) for no effect.

Event No.		Assets				Equity						
	Cash	+	Inventory	+	Equip.	=	Com. Stk.	+	Ret. Earn.	Rev.	−	Exp.	=	Net Inc.	Cash Flow

Event No.	Cash	+	Inventory	+	Equip.	=	Com. Stk.	+	Ret. Earn.	Rev.	−	Exp.	=	Net Inc.	Cash Flow
1.	NA		NA		D		NA		D	NA		I		D	NA
2.	NA		I		D		NA		NA	NA		NA		NA	NA

Required

a. Identify the event that represents depreciation on the computers.
b. Explain why recognizing depreciation on equipment used in a manufacturing company affects financial statements differently from recognizing depreciation on equipment used in a service organization.

Exercise 10-11   *Identifying the effect of product versus general, selling, and administrative cost on the income statement and statement of cash flows*   LO 3

Each of the following events describes acquiring an asset that requires a year-end adjusting entry. December 31st is the end of year.

1. Paid $14,000 cash on January 1 to purchase printers to be used for administrative purposes. The printers had an estimated useful life of four years and a $2,000 salvage value.
2. Paid $14,000 cash on January 1 to purchase manufacturing equipment. The equipment had an estimated useful life of four years and a $2,000 salvage value.
3. Paid $12,000 cash in advance on May 1 for a one-year rental contract on administrative offices.
4. Paid $12,000 cash in advance on May 1 for a one-year rental contract on manufacturing facilities.
5. Paid $2,000 cash to purchase supplies to be used by the marketing department. At the end of the year, $400 of supplies were still on hand.
6. Paid $2,000 cash to purchase supplies to be used in the manufacturing process. At the end of the year, $400 of supplies were still on hand.

Required

Explain how acquiring the asset and making the adjusting entry affect the amount of net income and the cash flow reported on the year-end financial statements. Also, in the Cash Flow column, indicate whether the cash flow is for operating activities (OA), investing activities (IA), or financing activities (FA). Use (NA) for no effect. Assume a December 31 annual closing date.

The first event has been recorded as an example. Assume that any products that have been made have not been sold.

	Net Income	Cash Flow
Event No.	Amount of Change	Amount of Change
1. Purchase of printers	NA	(14,000) IA
1. Make adjusting entry	(3,000)	NA

LO 4

Exercise 10-12   *Missing information in a schedule of cost of goods manufactured*

Required

Supply the missing information on the following schedule of cost of goods manufactured.

DEWBERRY CORPORATION
Schedule of Cost of Goods Manufactured
For the Year Ended December 31, 2011

Raw materials		
Beginning inventory	$?	
Plus: Purchases	120,000	
Raw materials available for use	$148,000	
Minus: Ending raw materials inventory	?	
Cost of direct raw materials used		$124,000
Direct labor		?
Manufacturing overhead		24,000
Total manufacturing costs		310,000
Plus: Beginning work in process inventory		?
Total work in process		?
Minus: Ending work in process inventory		46,000
Cost of goods manufactured		$306,000

LO 4

Exercise 10-13   *Cost of goods manufactured and sold*

The following information pertains to Pandey Manufacturing Company for March 2012. Assume actual overhead equaled applied overhead.

March 1	
Inventory balances	
Raw materials	$125,000
Work in process	120,000
Finished goods	78,000
March 31	
Inventory balances	
Raw materials	$ 85,000
Work in process	145,000
Finished goods	80,000
During March	
Costs of raw materials purchased	$120,000
Costs of direct labor	100,000
Costs of manufacturing overhead	63,000
Sales revenues	350,000

Required

a. Prepare a schedule of cost of goods manufactured and sold.

b. Calculate the amount of gross margin on the income statement.

Exercise 10-14   *Upstream and downstream costs*

During 2011, Gallo Manufacturing Company incurred $90,000,000 of research and development (R&D) costs to create a long-life battery to use in computers. In accordance with FASB standards, the entire R&D cost was recognized as an expense in 2011. Manufacturing costs (direct materials, direct labor, and overhead) were expected to be $260 per unit. Packaging, shipping, and sales commissions were expected to be $50 per unit. Gallo expected to sell 2,000,000 batteries before new research renders the battery design technologically obsolete. During 2011, Gallo made 440,000 batteries and sold 400,000 of them.

Required

a. Identify the upstream and downstream costs.

b. Determine the 2011 amount of cost of goods sold and the ending inventory balance.

c. Determine the sales price assuming that Gallo desired to earn a profit margin equal to 25 percent of the *total cost* of developing, making, and distributing the batteries.

d. Prepare an income statement for 2011. Use the sales price determined in Requirement *c.*

e. Why would Gallo price the batteries at a level that would generate a loss for the 2011 accounting period?

Exercise 10-15   *Statement of Ethical Professional Practice*

In February 2006 former senator Warren Rudman of New Hampshire completed a 17-month investigation of an $11 billion accounting scandal at Fannie Mae (a major enterprise involved in home mortgage financing). The Rudman investigation concluded that Fannie Mae's CFO and controller used an accounting gimmick to manipulate financial statements in order to meet earnings-per-share (EPS) targets. Meeting the EPS targets triggered bonus payments for the executives. Fannie Mae's problems continued after 2006, and on September 8, 2008, it went into conservatorship under the control of the Federal Housing Financing Agency. The primary executives at the time of the Rudman investigation were replaced, and the enterprise reported a $59.8 billion loss in 2008.

Required

Review the principles of ethical professional practice shown in Exhibit 10.17. Identify and comment on which of the ethical principles the CFO and controller violated.

Exercise 10-16   *Using JIT to minimize waste and lost opportunity*

Ann Kyser, a teacher at Hewitt Middle School, is in charge of ordering the T-shirts to be sold for the school's annual fund-raising project. The T-shirts are printed with a special Hewitt School logo. In some years, the supply of T-shirts has been insufficient to satisfy the number of sales orders. In other years, T-shirts have been left over. Excess T-shirts are normally donated to some charitable organization. T-shirts cost the school $8 each and are normally sold for $14 each. Ms. Kyser has decided to order 800 shirts.

Required

a. If the school receives actual sales orders for 725 shirts, what amount of profit will the school earn? What is the cost of waste due to excess inventory?

b. If the school receives actual sales orders for 825 shirts, what amount of profit will the school earn? What amount of opportunity cost will the school incur?

c. Explain how a JIT inventory system could maximize profitability by eliminating waste and opportunity cost.

Exercise 10-17   *Using JIT to minimize holding costs*

Lee Pet Supplies purchases its inventory from a variety of suppliers, some of which require a six-week lead time before delivery. To ensure that she has a sufficient supply of goods on hand, Ms. Polk, the owner, must maintain a large supply of inventory. The cost of this inventory averages $21,000. She usually finances the purchase of inventory and pays a 9 percent annual finance charge. Ms. Polk's accountant has suggested that she should establish a relationship with a single large distributor who can satisfy all of her orders within a two-week time period. Given this quick turnaround time, she will be able to reduce her average inventory balance to $4,000.

Ms. Polk also believes that she could save $2,500 per year by reducing phone bills, insurance, and warehouse rental space costs associated with ordering and maintaining the larger level of inventory.

Required

a. Is the new inventory system available to Ms. Polk a pure or approximate just-in-time system?

b. Based on the information provided, how much of Ms. Polk's inventory holding cost could be eliminated by taking the accountant's advice?

LO 9

Exercise 10-18   *Value chain analysis (Appendix)*

Sonic Company manufactures and sells high-quality audio speakers. The speakers are encased in solid walnut cabinets supplied by Moore Cabinet Inc. Moore packages the speakers in durable moisture-proof boxes and ships them by truck to Sonic's manufacturing facility, which is located 50 miles from the cabinet factory.

Required

Identify the nonvalue-added activities that occur between the companies described in the above scenario. Explain how these nonvalue-added activities could be eliminated.

PROBLEMS

All applicable Problems are available with McGraw-Hill's *Connect Accounting*.

LO 2, 3

CHECK FIGURES
a. Average Cost per Unit: $8.40
f. $90,400

Problem 10-19   *Product versus general, selling, and administrative costs*

Jolly Manufacturing Company was started on January 1, 2011, when it acquired $90,000 cash by issuing common stock. Jolly immediately purchased office furniture and manufacturing equipment costing $10,000 and $28,000, respectively. The office furniture had a five-year useful life and a zero salvage value. The manufacturing equipment had a $4,000 salvage value and an expected useful life of three years. The company paid $12,000 for salaries of administrative personnel and $16,000 for wages to production personnel. Finally, the company paid $18,000 for raw materials that were used to make inventory. All inventory was started and completed during the year. Jolly completed production on 5,000 units of product and sold 4,000 units at a price of $12 each in 2011. (Assume all transactions are cash transactions.)

Required

a. Determine the total product cost and the average cost per unit of the inventory produced in 2011.

b. Determine the amount of cost of goods sold that would appear on the 2011 income statement.

c. Determine the amount of the ending inventory balance that would appear on the December 31, 2011, balance sheet.

d. Determine the amount of net income that would appear on the 2011 income statement.

e. Determine the amount of retained earnings that would appear on the December 31, 2011, balance sheet.

f. Determine the amount of total assets that would appear on the December 31, 2011, balance sheet.

g. Determine the amount of net cash flow from operating activities that would appear on the 2011 statement of cash flows.

h. Determine the amount of net cash flow from investing activities that would appear on the 2011 statement of cash flows.

LO 3

eXcel

CHECK FIGURES
Cash balance: $33,000
Net income: $4,600

Problem 10-20   *Effect of product versus period costs on financial statements*

Hoen Manufacturing Company experienced the following accounting events during its first year of operation. With the exception of the adjusting entries for depreciation, all transactions are cash transactions.

1. Acquired $50,000 cash by issuing common stock.

2. Paid $8,000 for the materials used to make products, all of which were started and completed during the year.

3. Paid salaries of $4,400 to selling and administrative employees.
4. Paid wages of $7,000 to production workers.
5. Paid $9,600 for furniture used in selling and administrative offices. The furniture was acquired on January 1. It had a $1,600 estimated salvage value and a four-year useful life.
6. Paid $13,000 for manufacturing equipment. The equipment was acquired on January 1. It had a $1,000 estimated salvage value and a three-year useful life.
7. Sold inventory to customers for $25,000 that had cost $14,000 to make.

Required

Explain how these events would affect the balance sheet, income statement, and statement of cash flows by recording them in a horizontal financial statements model as indicated here. The first event is recorded as an example. In the Cash Flow column, indicate whether the amounts represent financing activities (FA), investing activities (IA), or operating activities (OA).

Event No.	Assets				Equity							
	Cash	+ Inventory	+ Manuf. Equip.*	+ Office Furn.*	= Com. Stk.	+ Ret. Earn.	Rev.	− Exp.	= Net Inc.	Cash Flow	
1	50,000				50,000					50,000	FA

*Record accumulated depreciation as negative amounts in these columns.

Problem 10-21 *Product versus general, selling, and administrative costs*

LO 3

The following transactions pertain to 2012, the first year operations of Hall Company. All inventory was started and completed during 2012. Assume that all transactions are cash transactions.

CHECK FIGURES
Net income: $36
Total assets: $4,036

1. Acquired $4,000 cash by issuing common stock.
2. Paid $720 for materials used to produce inventory.
3. Paid $1,800 to production workers.
4. Paid $540 rental fee for production equipment.
5. Paid $180 to administrative employees.
6. Paid $144 rental fee for administrative office equipment.
7. Produced 300 units of inventory of which 200 units were sold at a price of $12 each.

Required

Prepare an income statement, balance sheet, and statement of cash flows.

Problem 10-22 *Schedule of cost of goods manufactured and sold*

LO 4

Kirsoff Company makes eBook readers. The company had the following amounts at the beginning of 2011: Cash, $660,000; Raw Materials Inventory, $51,000; Work in Process Inventory, $18,000; Finished Goods Inventory, $43,000; Common Stock, $583,000; and Retained Earnings, $189,000. Kirsoff experienced the following accounting events during 2011. Other than the adjusting entries for depreciation, assume that all transactions are cash transactions.

1. Paid $23,000 of research and development costs.
2. Paid $47,000 for raw materials that will be used to make eBook readers.
3. Placed $83,000 of the raw materials cost into the process of manufacturing eBook readers.
4. Paid $60,000 for salaries of selling and administrative employees.
5. Paid $91,000 for wages of production workers.
6. Paid $90,000 to purchase equipment used in selling and administrative offices.
7. Recognized depreciation on the office equipment. The equipment was acquired on January, 1, 2011. It has a $10,000 salvage value and a five-year life. The amount of depreciation is computed as [(Cost − salvage) ÷ useful life]. Specifically, ($90,000 − $10,000) ÷ 5 = $16,000.

8. Paid $165,000 to purchase manufacturing equipment.

9. Recognized depreciation on the manufacturing equipment. The equipment was acquired on January 1, 2011. It has a $25,000 salvage value and a seven-year life. The amount of depreciation is computed as [(Cost − salvage) ÷ useful life]. Specifically, ($165,000 − $25,000) ÷ 7 = $20,000.

10. Paid $45,000 for rent and utility costs on the manufacturing facility.

11. Paid $70,000 for inventory holding expenses for completed eBook readers (rental of warehouse space, salaries of warehouse personnel, and other general storage cost).

12. Completed and transferred eBook readers that had total cost of $240,000 from work in process inventory to finished goods.

13. Sold 1,000 eBook readers for $420,000.

14. It cost Kirsoff $220,000 to make the eBook readers sold in Event 13.

Required

a. Show how these events affect the balance sheet, income statement, and statement of cash flows by recording them in a horizontal financial statements model.

b. Explain why Kirsoff's recognition of cost of goods sold had no impact on cash flow.

c. Prepare a schedule of cost of goods manufactured and sold, a formal income statement, and a balance sheet for the year.

d. Distinguish between the product costs and the upstream costs that Kirsoff incurred.

e. The company president believes that Kirsoff could save money by buying the inventory that it currently makes. The warehouse manager said that would not be a good idea because the purchase price of $230 per unit was above the $220 average cost per unit of making the product. Assuming the purchased inventory would be available on demand, explain how the company could be correct and why the production manager could be biased in his assessment of the option to buy the inventory.

LO 3, 6

CHECK FIGURES
a. Net loss: $20,000
b. Total assets: $55,000
c. Net income: $11,000

Problem 10-23   *Service versus manufacturing companies*

Goree Company began operations on January 1, 2011, by issuing common stock for $30,000 cash. During 2011, Goree received $40,000 cash from revenue and incurred costs that required $60,000 of cash payments.

Required

Prepare an income statement, balance sheet, and statement of cash flows for Goree Company for 2011, under each of the following independent scenarios.

a. Goree is a promoter of rock concerts. The $60,000 was paid to provide a rock concert that produced the revenue.

b. Goree is in the car rental business. The $60,000 was paid to purchase automobiles. The automobiles were purchased on January 1, 2011, had four-year useful lives and no expected salvage value. Goree uses straight-line depreciation. The revenue was generated by leasing the automobiles.

c. Goree is a manufacturing company. The $60,000 was paid to purchase the following items.

   (1) Paid $8,000 cash to purchase materials that were used to make products during the year.

   (2) Paid $20,000 cash for wages of factory workers who made products during the year.

   (3) Paid $2,000 cash for salaries of sales and administrative employees.

   (4) Paid $30,000 cash to purchase manufacturing equipment. The equipment was used solely to make products. It had a three-year life and a $6,000 salvage value. The company uses straight-line depreciation.

   (5) During 2011, Goree started and completed 2,000 units of product. The revenue was earned when Goree sold 1,500 units of product to its customers.

d. Refer to Requirement *c*. Could Goree determine the actual cost of making the 90th unit of product? How likely is it that the actual cost of the 90th unit of product was exactly the same as the cost of producing the 408th unit of product? Explain why management may be more interested in average cost than in actual cost.

Problem 10-24 *Importance of cost classification and ethics*

Cooke Manufacturing Company (CMC) was started when it acquired $40,000 by issuing common stock. During the first year of operations, the company incurred specifically identifiable product costs (materials, labor, and overhead) amounting to $24,000. CMC also incurred $16,000 of engineering design and planning costs. There was a debate regarding how the design and planning costs should be classified. Advocates of Option 1 believe that the costs should be classified as upstream general, selling, and administrative costs. Advocates of Option 2 believe it is more appropriate to classify the design and planning costs as product costs. During the year, CMC made 4,000 units of product and sold 3,000 units at a price of $24 each. All transactions were cash transactions.

CHECK FIGURES
a. Option 1: NI = $38,000
   Option 2: Total Assets = $82,000

Required

a. Prepare an income statement, balance sheet, and statement of cash flows under each of the two options.

b. Identify the option that results in financial statements that are more likely to leave a favorable impression on investors and creditors.

c. Assume that CMC provides an incentive bonus to the CFO who is a CMA. The bonus is equal to 13 percent of net income. Compute the amount of the bonus under each of the two options. Identify the option that provides the CFO with the higher bonus.

d. Assume the CFO knows that the design and planning costs are upstream costs that must be recognized as general, selling, and administrative expenses (Option 1). Even so, the CFO convinces management to classify the upstream costs as product cost in order to increase his bonus. Identify two principles in the Statement of Ethical Professional Practice that are violated by the CFO's behavior.

e. Comment on the conflict of interest between the company president as determined in Requirement *c* and owners of the company as indicated in Requirement *d*. Describe an incentive compensation plan that would avoid a conflict of interest between the president and the owners.

Problem 10-25 *Using JIT to reduce inventory holding costs*

Burt Manufacturing Company obtains its raw materials from a variety of suppliers. Burt's strategy is to obtain the best price by letting the suppliers know that it buys from the lowest bidder. Approximately four years ago, unexpected increase in demand resulted in materials shortages. Burt was unable to find the materials it needed even though it was willing to pay premium prices. Because of the lack of raw materials, Burt was forced to close its manufacturing facility for two weeks. Its president vowed that her company would never again be at the mercy of its suppliers. She immediately ordered her purchasing agent to perpetually maintain a one-month supply of raw materials. Compliance with the president's orders resulted in a raw materials inventory amounting to approximately $1,600,000. Warehouse rental and personnel costs to maintain the inventory amounted to $8,000 per month. Burt has a line of credit with a local bank that calls for a 12 percent annual rate of interest. Assume that Burt finances the raw materials inventory with the line of credit.

CHECK FIGURE
a. $288,000

Required

a. Based on the information provided, determine the annual holding cost of the raw materials inventory.

b. Explain how a JIT system could reduce Burt's inventory holding cost.

c. Explain how most-favored customer status could enable Burt to establish a JIT inventory system without risking the raw materials shortages experienced in the past.

Problem 10-26 *Using JIT to minimize waste and lost opportunity*

CMA Review Inc. provides review courses for students studying to take the CMA exam. The cost of textbooks is included in the registration fee. Text material requires constant updating and is useful for only one course. To minimize printing costs and ensure availability of books on the first day of class, CMA Review has books printed and delivered to its offices two weeks in advance of the first class. To ensure that enough books are available, CMA Review normally orders 10 percent more than expected enrollment. Usually there is an oversupply of books that is thrown away. However, demand occasionally exceeds expectations by more than 10 percent and there are too few books available for student use. CMA Review had been forced to turn away students because of lack of textbooks. CMA Review expects to enroll approximately 100 students per course. The tuition fee is $800 per student. The cost of teachers is $25,000 per course, textbooks cost $60 each, and other operating expenses are estimated to be $35,000 per course.

Required

a. Prepare an income statement, assuming that 95 students enroll in a course. Determine the cost of waste associated with unused books.

b. Prepare an income statement, assuming that 115 students attempt to enroll in the course. Note that five students are turned away because of too few textbooks. Determine the amount of lost profit resulting from the inability to serve the five additional students.

c. Suppose that textbooks can be produced through a high-speed copying process that permits delivery *just in time* for class to start. The cost of books made using this process, however, is $65 each. Assume that all books must be made using the same production process. In other words, CMA Review cannot order some of the books using the regular copy process and the rest using the high-speed process. Prepare an income statement under the JIT system assuming that 95 students enroll in a course. Compare the income statement under JIT with the income statement prepared in Requirement *a*. Comment on how the JIT system would affect profitability.

d. Assume the same facts as in Requirement *c* with respect to a JIT system that enables immediate delivery of books at a cost of $65 each. Prepare an income statement under the JIT system, assuming that 115 students enroll in a course. Compare the income statement under JIT with the income statement prepared in Requirement *b*. Comment on how the JIT system would affect profitability.

e. Discuss the possible effect of the JIT system on the level of customer satisfaction.

LO 9

Problem 10-27 *Value chain analysis (Appendix)*

Jensen Company invented a new process for manufacturing ice cream. The ingredients are mixed in high-tech machinery that forms the product into small round beads. Like a bag of balls, the ice cream beads are surrounded by air pockets in packages. This design has numerous advantages. First, each bite of ice cream melts quickly in a person's mouth, creating a more flavorful sensation when compared to ordinary ice cream. Also, the air pockets mean that a typical serving includes a smaller amount of ice cream. This not only reduces materials cost but also provides the consumer with a low-calorie snack. A cup appears full of ice cream, but it is really half full of air. The consumer eats only half the ingredients that are contained in a typical cup of blended ice cream. Finally, the texture of the ice cream makes scooping it out of a large container easy. The frustration of trying to get a spoon into a rock-solid package of blended ice cream has been eliminated. Jensen Company named the new product Sonic Cream.

Like many other ice cream producers, Jensen Company purchases its raw materials from a food wholesaler. The ingredients are mixed in Jensen's manufacturing plant. The packages of finished product are distributed to privately owned franchise ice cream shops that sell Sonic Cream directly to the public.

Jensen provides national advertising and is responsible for all research and development costs associated with making new flavors of Sonic Cream.

Required

a. Based on the information provided, draw a comprehensive value chain for Jensen Company that includes its suppliers and customers.

b. Identify the place in the chain where Jensen Company is exercising its opportunity to create added value beyond that currently being provided by its competitors.

ANALYZE, THINK, COMMUNICATE

ATC 10-1   Business Applications Case   *Financial versus managerial accounting*

The following information was taken from the 2008 and 2009 Form 10-Ks for Dell, Inc.

	Fiscal Year Ended	
	January 30, 2009	**February 1, 2008**
Number of regular employees	76,500	82,700
Number of temporary employees	2,400	5,500
Revenues (in millions)	$61,101	$61,133
Properties owned or leased in the U.S.	7.4 million square feet	8.2 million square feet
Properties owned or leased outside the U.S.	9.4 million square feet	9.7 million square feet
Total assets (in millions)	$26,500	$27,561
Gross margin (in millions)	$10,957	$11,671

Required

a. Explain whether each line of information in the table above would best be described as being primarily financial accounting or managerial accounting in nature.

b. Provide some additional examples of managerial and financial accounting information that could apply to Dell.

c. If you analyze only the data you identified as financial in nature, does it appear that Dell's 2009 fiscal year was better or worse than its 2008 fiscal year? Explain.

d. If you analyze only the data you identified as managerial in nature, does it appear that Dell's 2009 fiscal year was better or worse than its 2008 fiscal year? Explain.

ATC 10-2   Group Assignment   *Product versus upstream and downstream costs*

Victor Holt, the accounting manager of Sexton Inc., gathered the following information for 2011. Some of it can be used to construct an income statement for 2011. Ignore items that do not appear on an income statement. Some computations may be required. For example, the cost of manufacturing equipment would not appear on the income statement. However, the cost of manufacturing equipment is needed to compute the amount of depreciation. All units of product were started and completed in 2011.

1. Issued $864,000 of common stock.
2. Paid engineers in the product design department $10,000 for salaries that were accrued at the end of the previous year.
3. Incurred advertising expenses of $70,000.
4. Paid $720,000 for materials used to manufacture the company's product.
5. Incurred utility costs of $160,000. These costs were allocated to different departments on the basis of square footage of floor space. Mr. Holt identified three departments and determined the square footage of floor space for each department to be as shown in the table below.

Department	Square Footage
Research and development	10,000
Manufacturing	60,000
Selling and administrative	30,000
Total	100,000

6. Paid $880,000 for wages of production workers.
7. Paid cash of $658,000 for salaries of administrative personnel. There was $16,000 of accrued salaries owed to administrative personnel at the end of 2011. There was no beginning balance in the Salaries Payable account for administrative personnel.
8. Purchased manufacturing equipment two years ago at a cost of $10,000,000. The equipment had an eight-year useful life and a $2,000,000 salvage value.

9. Paid $390,000 cash to engineers in the product design department.

10. Paid a $258,000 cash dividend to owners.

11. Paid $80,000 to set up manufacturing equipment for production.

12. Paid a one-time $186,000 restructuring cost to redesign the production process to implement a just-in-time inventory system.

13. Prepaid the premium on a new insurance policy covering nonmanufacturing employees. The policy cost $72,000 and had a one-year term with an effective starting date of May 1. Four employees work in the research and development department and eight employees in the selling and administrative department. Assume a December 31 closing date.

14. Made 69,400 units of product and sold 60,000 units at a price of $70 each.

Required

a. Divide the class into groups of four or five students per group, and then organize the groups into three sections. Assign Task 1 to the first section of groups, Task 2 to the second section of groups, and Task 3 to the third section of groups.

Group Tasks

(1) Identify the items that are classified as product costs and determine the amount of cost of goods sold reported on the 2011 income statement.

(2) Identify the items that are classified as upstream costs and determine the amount of upstream cost expensed on the 2011 income statement.

(3) Identify the items that are classified as downstream costs and determine the amount of downstream cost expensed on the 2011 income statement.

b. Have the class construct an income statement in the following manner. Select a member of one of the groups assigned the first group task identifying the product costs. Have that person go to the board and list the costs included in the determination of cost of goods sold. Anyone in the other groups who disagrees with one of the classifications provided by the person at the board should voice an objection and explain why the item should be classified differently. The instructor should lead the class to a consensus on the disputed items. After the amount of cost of goods sold is determined, the student at the board constructs the part of the income statement showing the determination of gross margin. The exercise continues in a similar fashion with representatives from the other sections explaining the composition of the upstream and downstream costs. These items are added to the income statement started by the first group representative. The final result is a completed income statement.

ATC 10-3　Research Assignment　*Identifying product costs at Snap-on, Inc.*

Use the 2008 Form 10-K for Snap-on, Inc., to complete the requirements below. To obtain the Form 10-K you can use the EDGAR system following the instructions in Appendix A, or it can be found under "Corporate Information" on the company's corporate website: www.snapon.com. Read carefully the following portions of the document.

■　"Products and Services" on page 5.

■　"Consolidated Statement of Earnings" on page 55.

■　The following parts of Note 1 on page 60:

- "Shipping and handling"
- "Advertising and promotion"

■　"Note 4: Inventories" on page 66.

Required

a. Does the level of detail that Snap-on provides regarding costs incurred to manufacture its products suggest the company's financial statements are designed primarily to meet the needs of external or internal users?

b. Does Snap-on treat shipping and handling costs as product or nonproduct costs?

c. Does Snap-on treat advertising and promotion costs as product or nonproduct costs?

d. In Chapter 3 you learned about a class of inventory called merchandise inventory. What categories of inventory does Snap-on report in its annual report?

ATC 10-4   Writing Assignment   *Emerging practices in managerial accounting*

An annual report of the Maytag Corporation contained the following excerpt:

> *The Company announced the restructuring of its major appliance operations in an effort to strengthen its position in the industry and to deliver improved performance to both customers and shareowners. This included the consolidation of two separate organizational units into a single operation responsible for all activities associated with the manufacture and distribution of the Company's brands of major appliances and the closing of a cooking products plant in Indianapolis, Indiana, with transfer of that production to an existing plant in Cleveland, Tennessee.*

The restructuring cost Maytag $40 million and disrupted the lives of many of the company's employees.

Required

Assume that you are Maytag's vice president of human relations. Write a letter to the employees who are affected by the restructuring. The letter should explain why it was necessary for the company to undertake the restructuring. Your explanation should refer to the ideas discussed in the section "Emerging Trends in Managerial Accounting" of this chapter (see Appendix A).

ATC 10-5   Ethical Dilemma   *Product cost versus selling and administrative expense*

Emma Emerson is a proud woman with a problem. Her daughter has been accepted into a prestigious law school. While Ms. Emerson beams with pride, she is worried sick about how to pay for the school; she is a single parent who has to support herself and her three children. She had to go heavily into debt to finance her own education. Even though she now has a good job, family needs have continued to outpace her income and her debt burden is staggering. She knows she will be unable to borrow the money needed for her daughter's law school.

Ms. Emerson is the chief financial officer (CFO) of a small manufacturing company. She has just accepted a new job offer. She has not yet told her employer that she will be leaving in a month. She is concerned that her year-end incentive bonus may be affected if her boss learns of her plans to leave. She plans to inform the company immediately after receiving the bonus. She knows her behavior is less than honorable, but she believes that she has been underpaid for a long time. Her boss, a relative of the company's owner, makes twice what she makes and does half the work. Why should she care about leaving with a little extra cash? Indeed, she is considering an opportunity to boost the bonus.

Ms. Emerson's bonus is based on a percentage of net income. Her company recently introduced a new product line that required substantial production start-up costs. Ms. Emerson is fully aware that GAAP requires these costs to be expensed in the current accounting period, but no one else in the company has the technical expertise to know exactly how the costs should be treated. She is considering misclassifying the start-up costs as product costs. If the costs are misclassified, net income will be significantly higher, resulting in a nice boost in her incentive bonus. By the time the auditors discover the misclassification, Ms. Emerson will have moved on to her new job. If the matter is brought to the attention of her new employer, she will simply plead ignorance. Considering her daughter's needs, Ms. Emerson decides to classify the start-up costs as product costs.

Required

a. Based on this information, indicate whether Ms. Emerson believes the number of units of product sold will be equal to, less than, or greater than the number of units made. Write a brief paragraph explaining the logic that supports your answer.

b. Explain how the misclassification could mislead an investor or creditor regarding the company's financial condition.

c. Explain how the misclassification could affect income taxes.

d. Identify the specific components of the fraud triangle the were present in this case.

e. Review the Statement of Ethical Professional Practice shown in Exhibit 10.14 and identify at least two principles that Ms. Emerson's misclassification of the start-up costs violated.

f. Describe the maximum penalty that could be imposed under the Sarbanes-Oxley Act for the actions Ms. Emerson has taken.

CHAPTER 11

Cost Behavior, Operating Leverage, and Profitability Analysis

LEARNING OBJECTIVES

After you have mastered the material in this chapter, you will be able to:

1 Identify and describe fixed, variable, and mixed cost behavior.

2 Demonstrate the effects of operating leverage on profitability.

3 Prepare an income statement using the contribution margin approach.

4 Calculate the magnitude of operating leverage.

5 Demonstrate how the relevant range and decision context affect cost behavior.

6 Calculate the break-even point.

7 Calculate the sales volume required to attain a target profit.

8 Calculate the margin of safety in units, dollars, and percentage.

CHAPTER OPENING

Three college students are planning a vacation. One of them suggests inviting a fourth person along, remarking that four can travel for the same cost as three. Certainly, some costs will be the same whether three or four people go on the trip. For example, the hotel room costs $800 per week, regardless of whether three or four people stay in the room. In accounting terms the cost of the hotel room is a fixed cost. The total amount of a fixed cost does not change when volume changes. The total hotel room cost is $800 whether 1, 2, 3, or 4 people use the room. In contrast, some costs vary in direct proportion with changes in volume. When volume increases, total variable cost increases; when volume decreases, total variable cost decreases. For example, the cost of tickets to a theme park is a **variable cost**. The total cost of tickets increases proportionately with each vacationer who goes to the theme park. Cost behavior (fixed versus variable) can significantly impact profitability. This chapter explains cost behavior and ways it can be used to increase profitability.

The Curious Accountant

News flash! On April 29, 2009, Eastman Kodak, Inc., announced that its first quarter's revenues decreased 29 percent compared to the same quarter in 2008, yet its earnings had decreased by 213 percent. On May 4, 2009, Walt Disney announced that a decrease in revenue of 7 percent for the just-ended quarter would cause its earnings to decrease 46 percent compared to the same quarter in 2008. On April 12, 2009, Apple computer reported that its revenue for the quarter had increased by 9 percent compared to the previous year, but its earnings increased by 15 percent.

Can you explain why such relatively small changes in these companies' revenues resulted in such relatively large changes in their earnings or losses? In other words, if a company's sales increase 10 percent, why do its earnings not also increase 10 percent? (Answer on page 402.)

FIXED COST BEHAVIOR

LO 1

Identify and describe fixed, variable, and mixed cost behavior.

How much more will it cost to send one additional employee to a sales meeting? If more people buy our products, can we charge less? If sales increase by 10 percent, how will profits be affected? Managers seeking answers to such questions must consider **cost behavior.** Knowing how costs behave relative to the level of business activity enables managers to more effectively plan and control costs. To illustrate, consider the entertainment company Star Productions, Inc. (SPI).

SPI specializes in promoting rock concerts. It is considering paying a band $48,000 to play a concert. Obviously, SPI must sell enough tickets to cover this cost. In this example, the relevant activity base is the number of tickets sold. The cost of the band is a **fixed cost** because it does not change regardless of the number of tickets sold. Exhibit 11.1 illustrates the fixed cost behavior pattern, showing the *total cost* and the *cost per unit* at three different levels of activity.

Total versus *per-unit* fixed costs behave differently. The total cost for the band remains constant (fixed) at $48,000. In contrast, fixed cost per unit decreases as volume (number of tickets sold) increases. The term *fixed cost* is consistent with the behavior of *total cost.* Total fixed cost remains constant (fixed) when activity changes. However, there is a contradiction between the term *fixed cost per unit* and the *per-unit behavior pattern of a fixed cost.* Fixed cost per unit is *not* fixed. It changes with the number of tickets sold. This contradiction in terminology can cause untold confusion. Study carefully the fixed cost behavior patterns in Exhibit 11.2.

EXHIBIT 11.1

Fixed Cost Behavior

Number of tickets sold (a)	2,700	3,000	3,300
Total cost of band (b)	$48,000	$48,000	$48,000
Cost per ticket sold (b ÷ a)	$17.78	$16.00	$14.55

EXHIBIT 11.2

Fixed Cost Behavior

	When Activity Increases	When Activity Decreases
Total fixed cost	Remains constant	Remains constant
Fixed cost **per unit**	Decreases	Increases

The fixed cost data in Exhibit 11.1 help SPI's management decide whether to sponsor the concert. For example, the information influences potential pricing choices. The per-unit costs represent the minimum ticket prices required to cover the fixed cost at various levels of activity. SPI could compare these per-unit costs to the prices of competing entertainment events (such as the prices of movies, sporting events, or theater tickets). If the price is not competitive, tickets will not sell and the concert will lose money. Management must also consider the number of tickets to be sold. The volume data in Exhibit 11.1 can be compared to the band's track record of ticket sales at previous concerts. A proper analysis of these data can reduce the risk of undertaking an unprofitable venture.

OPERATING LEVERAGE

LO 2

Demonstrate the effects of operating leverage on profitability.

Heavy objects can be moved with little effort using *physical* leverage. Business managers apply **operating leverage** to magnify small changes in revenue into dramatic changes in profitability. The *lever* managers use to achieve disproportionate changes between revenue and profitability is fixed costs. The leverage relationships between revenue, fixed costs, and profitability are displayed in Exhibit 11.3.

When all costs are fixed, every sales dollar contributes one dollar toward the potential profitability of a project. Once sales dollars cover fixed costs, each

EXHIBIT 11.3

Operating Leverage

Small percentage change in revenue

Dramatic percentage change in profitability

Fixed costs

FOCUS ON INTERNATIONAL ISSUES

COST-VOLUME-PROFIT ANALYSIS AT A GERMAN CHEMICAL COMPANY

The greater the percentage of a company's total costs that are fixed, the more sensitive the company's earnings are to changes in revenue or volume. Operating leverage, the relationship between the changes in revenue and changes in earnings, introduced earlier, applies to companies throughout the world, large or small.

Large chemical manufacturers have significant fixed costs. It takes a lot of buildings and equipment to produce chemicals. BASF claims to be the largest chemical company in the world. It has its headquarters in Ludwigshafen, Germany. From 2004 through 2006 BASF's revenues increased 40.2 percent, but its earnings increased 60.4 percent. In other words, its earnings grew one and one-half times faster than its revenues.

Studying BASF offers insight into a true global enterprise. Though headquartered in Germany, it has manufacturing facilities at 150 locations throughout the world. Only 21 percent of its 2006 revenue came from sales within Germany, which was 1 percent less than the revenue it earned in the United States. Although its financial statements are presented in euros and prepared in accordance with international financial accounting standards, its stock is traded on the New York Stock Exchange as well as on the Frankfurt Stock Exchange.

additional sales dollar represents pure profit. As a result, a small change in sales volume can significantly affect profitability. To illustrate, assume SPI estimates it will sell 3,000 tickets for $18 each. A 10 percent difference in actual sales volume will produce a 90 percent difference in profitability. Examine the data in Exhibit 11.4 to verify this result.[1]

EXHIBIT 11.4

Effect of Operating Leverage on Profitability

Number of tickets sold	2,700	⇐ −10% ⇐	3,000	⇒ +10% ⇒	3,300
Sales revenue ($18 per ticket)	$48,600		$54,000		$59,400
Cost of band (fixed cost)	(48,000)		(48,000)		(48,000)
Gross margin	$ 600	⇐ −90% ⇐	$ 6,000	⇒ +90% ⇒	$11,400

Calculating Percentage Change

The percentages in Exhibit 11.4 are computed as follows.

(Alternative measure − Base measure) ÷ Base measure = % change

The base measure is the starting point. To illustrate, compute the percentage change in gross margin when moving from 3,000 units (base measure) to 3,300 units (the alternative measure).

(Alternative measure − Base measure) ÷ Base measure = % change

($11,400 − $6,000) ÷ $6,000 = 90%

---

[1]Do not confuse operating leverage with financial leverage. Companies employ *financial leverage* when they use debt to profit from investing money at a higher rate of return than the rate they pay on borrowed money. Companies employ *operating leverage* when they use proportionately more fixed costs than variable costs to magnify the effect on earnings of changes in revenues.

The percentage *decline* in profitability is similarly computed:

(**Alternative measure** − **Base measure**) ÷ **Base measure** = **% change**

($600 − $6,000) ÷ $6,000 = (90%)

Risk and Reward Assessment

Risk refers to the possibility that sacrifices may exceed benefits. A fixed cost represents a commitment to an economic sacrifice. It represents the ultimate risk of undertaking a particular business project. If SPI pays the band but nobody buys a ticket, the company will lose $48,000. SPI can avoid this risk by substituting *variable costs* for the *fixed cost.*

REALITY BYTES

The relationship among the costs to produce goods, the volume of goods produced, the price charged for those goods, and the profit earned is relevant to all industries, but perhaps no industry demonstrates the effects of these relationships more dramatically than automobile manufacturing. First, the automobile industry is characterized by having a lot of fixed production-costs for things such as buildings, equipment, research, and development, but also financing costs associated with borrowed funds, such as the interest expense on bonds. Second, the industry is globally competitive, and companies in the United States are often at a cost disadvantage. Some of this cost disadvantage comes from obvious sources, such as having to pay higher wages than do companies in countries such as South Korea. Finally, for many customers, price and quality are more important than brand loyalty.

Over the past decades, domestic auto makers, and in particular General Motors (GM), have used different strategies to try to deal with the issues mentioned above. Early on, it had a dominant market share. As long as it produced more cars than its competitors, its fixed cost per car was lower, resulting in better profits. In the 1980s, however, foreign manufactures began increasing their market share and decreasing GM's. As its relative levels of production fell, its fixed cost per unit increased. In response, GM and others tried to regain market share by lowering prices, largely through rebates. Unfortunately this did not work, so the lower prices, combined with the higher relative fixed costs, seriously eroded profits.

These problems reached a crisis in 2008 and 2009 when GM and Chrysler sought financial help from the government and entered expedited bankruptcy proceedings.

What did GM and Chrysler hope to achieve? Primarily they needed to lower their costs, especially their fixed costs. As a result of bankruptcy proceedings, they were able to greatly reduce interest and principal payments on their outstanding bonds (fixed costs), reduce the number of brands (fixed costs), shut down some plants (fixed costs), reduce health care costs to retirees (fixed costs), and reduce the number of dealers. While reducing the number of dealers did reduce some cost to the companies, it also reduced price competition among the dealers, which had the potential of allowing the companies to charge more for their cars. All of these changes, it was hoped, would allow the companies to return to profitability.

However, before a company can be profitable, it must break even. At one time GM's break-even point was estimated at around 16 million vehicles per year. GM's CEO until 2000, Rick Wagoner, had implemented changes that reduced the company's break-even point to 12 million units. On March 29, 2009, as a condition of receiving government support, the administration of President Barack Obama asked Mr. Wagoner to resign as GM's CEO. Perhaps lost by many in the news coverage of Mr. Wagoner's resignation were reports by several news organizations that officials at the U.S. Treasury Department would ask the new leadership at GM to take steps to reduce the company's break-even point to 10 million units.

It would be a major achievement if GM can reduce its break even from 16 million units to 10 million units in the span of a few years. This may not be enough, however. In 2008 GM sold only 8.8 million units, and its sales in the first quarter of 2009 were even lower than the same quarter of 2008. Furthermore, it should be remembered that the objective of businesses is not simply to break even, but to make a profit.

VARIABLE COST BEHAVIOR

To illustrate variable cost behavior, assume SPI arranges to pay the band $16 per ticket sold instead of a fixed $48,000. Exhibit 11.5 shows the total cost of the band and the cost per ticket sold at three different levels of activity.

LO 1

Identify and describe fixed, variable, and mixed cost behavior.

EXHIBIT 11.5

Variable Cost Behavior

Number of tickets sold (a)	2,700	3,000	3,300
Total cost of band (b)	$43,200	$48,000	$52,800
Cost per ticket sold (b ÷ a)	$16	$16	$16

Because SPI will pay the band $16 for each ticket sold, the *total* variable cost increases in direct proportion to the number of tickets sold. If SPI sells one ticket, total band cost will be $16 (1 × $16); if SPI sells two tickets, total band cost will be $32 (2 × $16); and so on. The total cost of the band increases proportionately as ticket sales move from 2,700 to 3,000 to 3,300. The variable cost *per ticket* remains $16, however, regardless of whether the number of tickets sold is 1, 2, 3, or 3,000. The behavior of variable cost *per unit* is contradictory to the word *variable*. Variable cost per unit remains *constant* regardless of how many tickets are sold. Study carefully the variable cost behavior patterns in Exhibit 11.6.

EXHIBIT 11.6

Variable Cost Behavior

	When Activity Increases	When Activity Decreases
Total variable cost	Increases proportionately	Decreases proportionately
Variable cost **per unit**	Remains constant	Remains constant

Risk and Reward Assessment

Shifting the cost structure from fixed to variable enables SPI to avoid the fixed cost risk. If no one buys a ticket, SPI loses nothing because it incurs no cost. If only one person buys a ticket at an $18 ticket price, SPI earns a $2 profit ($18 sales revenue − $16 cost of band). Should managers therefore avoid fixed costs whenever possible? Not necessarily.

Shifting the cost structure from fixed to variable reduces not only the level of risk but also the potential for profits. Managers cannot avoid the risk of fixed costs without also sacrificing the benefits. Variable costs do not offer operating leverage. Exhibit 11.7 shows that a variable cost structure produces a proportional relationship between sales and profitability. A 10 percent increase or decrease in sales results in a corresponding 10 percent increase or decrease in profitability.

LO 2

Demonstrate the effects of operating leverage on profitability.

EXHIBIT 11.7

Variable Cost Eliminates Operating Leverage

Number of tickets sold	2,700	⇐ −10% ⇐	3,000	⇒ +10% ⇒	3,300
Sales revenue ($18 per ticket)	$48,600		$54,000		$59,400
Cost of band ($16 variable cost)	(43,200)		(48,000)		(52,800)
Gross margin	$ 5,400	⇐ −10% ⇐	$ 6,000	⇒ +10% ⇒	$ 6,600

✓ **CHECK YOURSELF 11.1**

Suppose that you are sponsoring a political rally at which Ralph Nader will speak. You estimate that approximately 2,000 people will buy tickets to hear Mr. Nader's speech. The tickets are expected to be priced at $12 each. Would you prefer a contract that agrees to pay Mr. Nader $10,000 or one that agrees to pay him $5 per ticket purchased?

Answer   Your answer would depend on how certain you are that 2,000 people will purchase tickets. If it were likely that many more than 2,000 tickets would be sold, you would be better off with a fixed cost structure, agreeing to pay Mr. Nader a flat fee of $10,000. If attendance numbers are highly uncertain, you would be better off with a variable cost structure thereby guaranteeing a lower cost if fewer people buy tickets.

Answers to The Curious Accountant

The explanation for how a company's earnings can rise faster, as a percentage, than its revenue rises is operating leverage, and operating leverage is due entirely to fixed costs. As the chapter explains, when a company's output goes up, its fixed cost per unit goes down. As long as it can keep prices about the same, this lower unit cost will result in higher profit per unit sold. In real-world companies, the relationship between changing sales levels and changing earnings levels can be very complex, but the existence of fixed costs helps to explain why a 9 percent rise in revenue can cause a 15 percent rise in net earnings.

✓ **CHECK YOURSELF 11.2**

If both **Kroger Food Stores** and **Delta Airlines** were to experience a 5 percent increase in revenues, which company would be more likely to experience a higher percentage increase in net income?

Answer   Delta would be more likely to experience a higher percentage increase in net income because a large portion of its cost (e.g., employee salaries and depreciation) is fixed, while a large portion of Kroger's cost is variable (e.g., cost of goods sold).

AN INCOME STATEMENT UNDER THE CONTRIBUTION MARGIN APPROACH

LO 3

Prepare an income statement using the contribution margin approach.

The impact of cost structure on profitability is so significant that managerial accountants frequently construct income statements that classify costs according to their behavior patterns. Such income statements first subtract variable costs from revenue; the resulting subtotal is called the **contribution margin.** The contribution margin represents the amount available to cover fixed expenses and thereafter to provide company profits. Net income is computed by subtracting the fixed costs from the contribution margin. A contribution margin style income statement cannot be used for public reporting (GAAP prohibits its use in external financial reports), but it is widely used for internal reporting purposes. Exhibit 11.8 illustrates income statements prepared using the contribution margin approach.

EXHIBIT 11.8

Income Statements

	Company Name	
	Bragg	**Biltmore**
Variable cost per unit (a)	$ 6	$ 12
Sales revenue (10 units × $20)	$200	$200
Variable cost (10 units × a)	(60)	(120)
Contribution margin	140	80
Fixed cost	(120)	(60)
Net income	$ 20	$ 20

MEASURING OPERATING LEVERAGE USING CONTRIBUTION MARGIN

A contribution margin income statement allows managers to easily measure operating leverage. The magnitude of operating leverage can be determined as follows.

$$\text{Magnitude of operating leverage} = \frac{\text{Contribution margin}}{\text{Net income}}$$

LO 4

Calculate the magnitude of operating leverage.

Applying this formula to the income statement data reported for Bragg Company and Biltmore Company in Exhibit 11.8 produces the following measures.

Bragg Company:

$$\text{Magnitude of operating leverage} = \frac{140}{20} = 7$$

Biltmore Company:

$$\text{Magnitude of operating leverage} = \frac{80}{20} = 4$$

The computations show that Bragg is more highly leveraged than Biltmore. Bragg's change in profitability will be seven times greater than a given percentage change in revenue. In contrast, Biltmore's profits change by only four times the percentage change in revenue. For example, a 10 percent increase in revenue produces a 70 percent increase (10 percent × 7) in profitability for Bragg Company and a 40 percent increase (10 percent × 4) in profitability for Biltmore Company. The income statements in Exhibits 11.9 and 11.10 confirm these expectations.

EXHIBIT 11.9

Comparative Income Statements for Bragg Company

Units (a)	10		11
Sales revenue ($20 × a)	$200	⇒ +10% ⇒	$220
Variable cost ($6 × a)	(60)		(66)
Contribution margin	140		154
Fixed cost	(120)		(120)
Net income	$ 20	⇒ +70% ⇒	$ 34

EXHIBIT 11.10

Comparative Income Statements for Biltmore Company

Units (a)	10		11
Sales revenue ($20 × a)	$200	⇒ +10% ⇒	$220
Variable cost ($12 × a)	(120)		(132)
Contribution margin	80		88
Fixed cost	(60)		(60)
Net income	$ 20	⇒ +40% ⇒	$ 28

Operating leverage itself is neither good nor bad; it represents a strategy that can work to a company's advantage or disadvantage, depending on how it is used. The next section explains how managers can use operating leverage to create a competitive business advantage.

✓ **CHECK YOURSELF 11.3**

Boeing Company's 2001 10K annual report filed with the Securities and Exchange Commission refers to "higher commercial airlines segment margins." Is Boeing referring to gross margins or contribution margins?

Answer Because the data come from the company's external annual report, the reference must be to gross margins (revenue − cost of goods sold), a product cost measure. The contribution margin (revenue − variable cost) is a measure used in internal reporting.

COST BEHAVIOR SUMMARIZED

Identify and describe fixed, variable, and mixed cost behavior.

The term *fixed* refers to the behavior of *total* fixed cost. The cost *per unit* of a fixed cost *varies inversely* with changes in the level of activity. As activity increases, fixed cost per unit decreases. As activity decreases, fixed cost per unit increases. These relationships are graphed in Exhibit 11.11.

The term *variable* refers to the behavior of *total* variable cost. Total variable cost increases or decreases proportionately with changes in the volume of activity. In contrast, variable cost *per unit* remains *fixed* at all levels of activity. These relationships are graphed in Exhibit 11.12.

The relationships between fixed and variable costs are summarized in the chart in Exhibit 11.13. Study these relationships thoroughly.

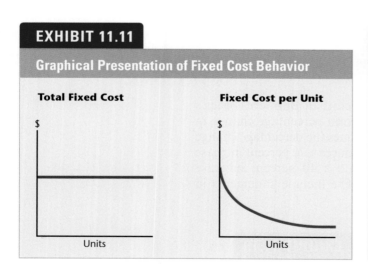

EXHIBIT 11.11 Graphical Presentation of Fixed Cost Behavior

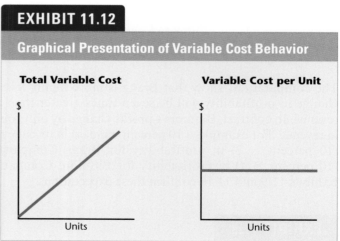

EXHIBIT 11.12 Graphical Presentation of Variable Cost Behavior

EXHIBIT 11.13

Fixed and Variable Cost Behavior

When Activity Level Changes	Total Cost	Cost per Unit
Fixed costs	Remains constant	Changes *inversely*
Variable costs	Changes in direct proportion	Remains constant

Mixed Costs (Semivariable Costs)

Mixed costs (semivariable costs) include both fixed and variable components. For example, Star Productions, Inc., frequently arranges backstage parties at which VIP guests meet members of the band. Party costs typically include a room rental fee and the costs of refreshments. The room rental fee is fixed; it remains unchanged regardless of the number of party guests. In contrast, the refreshments costs are variable; they depend on the number of people attending the party. The total party cost is a mixed cost.

Assuming a room rental fee of $1,000 and refreshments costs of $20 per person, the total mixed cost at any volume of activity can be computed as follows.

$$\text{Total cost} = \text{Fixed cost} + (\text{Variable cost per party guest} \times \text{Number of guests})$$

If 60 people attend the backstage party the total mixed cost is

$$\text{Total cost} = \$1,000 + (\$20 \times 60) = \$2,200$$

If 90 people attend the backstage party the total mixed cost is

$$\text{Total cost} = \$1,000 + (\$20 \times 90) = \$2,800$$

Exhibit 11.14 illustrates a variety of mixed costs businesses commonly encounter.

EXHIBIT 11.14

Examples of Mixed Costs

Type of Cost	Fixed Cost Component(s)	Variable Cost Component(s)
Cost of sales staff	Monthly salary	Bonus based on sales volume
Truck rental	Monthly rental fee	Cost of gas, tires, and maintenance
Legal fees	Monthly retainer	Reimbursements to attorney for out-of-pocket costs (copying, postage, travel, filing fees)
Outpatient service cost	Salaries of doctors and nurses, depreciation of facility, utilities	Medical supplies such as bandages, sterilization solution, and paper products
Phone services	Monthly connection fee	Per-minute usage fee
LP gas utility cost	Container rental fee	Cost of gas consumed
Cable TV services	Monthly fee	Pay-per-view charges
Training cost	Instructor salary, facility cost	Textbooks, supplies
Shipping and handling	Salaries of employees who process packages	Boxes, packing supplies, tape, and other shipping supplies, postage
Inventory holding cost	Depreciation on inventory warehouse, salaries of employees managing inventory	Delivery costs, interest on funds borrowed to finance inventory, cost of supplies

The Relevant Range

Suppose SPI, the rock concert promoter mentioned earlier, must pay $5,000 to rent a concert hall with a seating capacity of 4,000 people. Is the cost of the concert hall fixed or variable? Because total cost remains unchanged regardless of whether one ticket, 4,000 tickets, or any number in between is sold, the cost is fixed relative to ticket sales. However, what if demand for tickets is significantly more than 4,000? In that case, SPI might rent a larger concert hall at a higher cost. In other words, *the cost is fixed only for a designated range of activity (1 to 4,000).*

A similar circumstance affects many variable costs. For example, a supplier may offer a volume discount to buyers who purchase more than a specified number of products. The point is that descriptions of cost behavior pertain to a specified range of activity. The range of activity over which the definitions of fixed and variable costs are valid is commonly called the **relevant range.**

LO 5

Demonstrate how the relevant range and decision context affect cost behavior.

Context-Sensitive Definitions of Fixed and Variable

The behavior pattern of a particular cost may be either fixed or variable, depending on the context. For example, the cost of the band was fixed at $48,000 when SPI was considering hiring it to play a single concert. Regardless of how many tickets SPI sold, the total band cost was $48,000. However, the band cost becomes variable if SPI decides to hire it to perform at a series of concerts. The total cost and the cost per concert for one, two, three, four, or five concerts are shown in Exhibit 11.15.

In this context, the total cost of hiring the band increases proportionately with the number of concerts while cost per concert remains constant. The band cost is therefore variable. The same cost can behave as either a fixed cost or a variable cost, depending on the **activity base.** When identifying a cost as fixed or variable, first ask, fixed or variable *relative to what activity base?* The cost of the band is fixed relative to *the number of tickets sold for a specific concert;* it is variable relative to *the number of concerts produced.*

EXHIBIT 11.15

Cost Behavior Relative to Number of Concerts

	1	2	3	4	5
Number of concerts (a)	1	2	3	4	5
Cost per concert (b)	$48,000	$48,000	$ 48,000	$ 48,000	$ 48,000
Total cost (a × b)	$48,000	$96,000	$144,000	$192,000	$240,000

✓ CHECK YOURSELF 11.4

Is the compensation cost for managers of Pizza Hut Restaurants a fixed cost or a variable cost?

Answer The answer depends on the context. For example, because a store manager's salary remains unchanged regardless of how many customers enter a particular restaurant, it can be classified as a fixed cost relative to the number of customers at a particular restaurant. However, the more restaurants that Pizza Hut operates, the higher the total managers' compensation cost will be. Accordingly, managers' salary cost would be classified as a variable cost relative to the number of restaurants opened.

DETERMINING THE BREAK-EVEN POINT

Calculate the break-even point.

Bright Day Distributors sells nonprescription health food supplements including vitamins, herbs, and natural hormones in the northwestern United States. Bright Day recently obtained the rights to distribute the new herb mixture Delatine. Recent scientific research found that Delatine delayed aging in laboratory animals. The researchers hypothesized that the substance would have a similar effect on humans. Their theory could not be confirmed because of the relatively long human life span. The news media reported the research findings; as stories turned up on television and radio news, talk shows, and in magazines, demand for Delatine increased.

Bright Day plans to sell the Delatine at a price of $36 per bottle. Delatine costs $24 per bottle. Bright Day's management team suspects that enthusiasm for Delatine will abate quickly as the news media shift to other subjects. To attract customers immediately, the product managers consider television advertising. The marketing manager suggests running a campaign of several hundred cable channel ads at an estimated cost of $60,000.

Bright Day's first concern is whether it can sell enough units to cover its costs. The president made this position clear when he said, "We don't want to lose money on this product. We have to sell at least enough units to break even." In accounting terms, the **break-even point** is where profit (income) equals zero. So how many bottles of Delatine must be sold to produce a profit of zero? The break-even point is commonly computed using either the *equation method,* or the *contribution margin per unit method.* Both of these approaches produce the same result. They are merely different ways to arrive at the same conclusion.

Equation Method

The **equation method** begins by expressing the income statement as follows.

$$\text{Sales} - \text{Variable costs} - \text{Fixed costs} = \text{Profit (Net income)}$$

As previously stated, profit at the break-even point is zero. Therefore, the break-even point for Delatine is computed as follows.

$$\text{Sales} - \text{Variable costs} - \text{Fixed costs} = \text{Profit}$$

$$\$36N - \$24N - \$60,000 = \$0$$

$$\$12N = \$60,000$$

$$N = \$60,000 \div \$12$$

$$N = 5,000 \text{ Units}$$

Where:

N = Number of units

$\$36$ = Sales price per unit

$\$24$ = Variable cost per unit

$\$60,000$ = Fixed costs

✓ CHECK YOURSELF 11.5

B-Shoc is an independent musician who is considering whether to independently produce and sell a CD. B-Shoc estimates fixed costs of $5,400 and variable costs of $2.00 per unit. The expected selling price is $8.00 per CD. Use the equation method to determine B-Shoc's break-even point.

Answer

$$\text{Sales} - \text{Variable costs} - \text{Fixed costs} = \text{Profit}$$

$$\$8N - \$2N - \$5,400 = \$0$$

$$\$6N = \$5,400$$

$$N = \$5,400 \div \$6$$

$$N = 900 \text{ Units (CDs)}$$

Where:

N = Number of units

$\$8$ = Sales price per unit

$\$2$ = Variable cost per unit

$\$5,400$ = Fixed costs

Contribution Margin Per Unit Method

Recall that the *total contribution margin* is the amount of sales minus total variable cost. The **contribution margin per unit** is the sales price per unit minus the variable cost per unit. Therefore, the contribution margin per unit for Delatine is

Sales price per unit	$36
Less: Variable cost per unit	(24)
Contribution margin per unit	$12

For every bottle of Delatine it sells, Bright Day earns a $12 contribution margin. In other words, every time Bright Day sells a bottle of Delatine, it receives enough money to pay $24 to cover the variable cost of the bottle of Delatine and still has $12 left to go toward paying the fixed cost. Bright Day will reach the break-even point when it sells enough bottles of Delatine to cover its fixed costs. Therefore the break-even point can be determined as follows.

$$\text{Break-even point in units} = \frac{\text{Fixed costs}}{\text{Contribution margin per unit}}$$

$$\text{Break-even point in units} = \frac{\$60,000}{\$12}$$

$$\text{Break-even point in units} = 5,000 \text{ Units}$$

This result is the same as that determined under the equation method. Indeed, the contribution margin per unit method formula is an abbreviated version of the income statement formula used in the equation method. The proof is provided in the footnote below.[2]

Both the *equation method* and the *contribution margin per unit method* yield the amount of break-even sales measured *in units.* To determine the amount of break-even sales measured *in dollars,* multiply the number of units times the sales price per unit. For Delatine the break-even point measured in dollars is $180,000 (5,000 units × $36 per unit). The following income statement confirms this result.

Sales revenue (5,000 units × $36)	$180,000
Total variable expenses (5,000 units × $24)	(120,000)
Total contribution margin (5,000 units × $12)	60,000
Fixed expenses	(60,000)
Net income	$ 0

[2]The formula for the *contribution margin per unit method* is (where N is the number of units at the break-even point).

N = Fixed costs ÷ Contribution margin per unit

The income statement formula for the *equation method* produces the same result as shown below (where N is the number of units at the break-even point).

Sales − Variable costs − Fixed costs = Profit

Sales price per unit (N) − Variable cost per unit (N) − Fixed costs = Profit

Contribution margin per unit (N) − Fixed costs = Profit

Contribution margin per unit (N) − Fixed costs = 0

Contribution margin per unit (N) = Fixed costs

N = Fixed costs ÷ Contribution margin per unit

DETERMINING THE SALES VOLUME NECESSARY TO REACH A DESIRED PROFIT

Bright Day's president decides the ad campaign should produce a $40,000 profit. He asks the accountant to determine the sales volume that is required to achieve this level of profitability. Using the *equation method*, the sales volume in units required to attain the desired profit is computed as follows.

$$\text{Sales} - \text{Variable costs} - \text{Fixed costs} = \text{Profit}$$

$$\$36N - \$24N - \$60,000 = \$40,000$$

$$\$12N = \$60,000 + \$40,000$$

$$N = \$100,000 \div \$12$$

$$N = 8,333 \text{ Units}$$

Where:

N = Number of units

$36 = Sales price per unit

$24 = Variable cost per unit

$60,000 = Fixed costs

$40,000 = Desired profit

The accountant used the *contribution margin per unit method* to confirm these computations as follows.

$$\text{Sales volume in units} = \frac{\text{Fixed costs} + \text{Desired profit}}{\text{Contribution margin per unit}}$$

$$= \frac{\$60,000 + \$40,000}{\$12} = 8,333.33 \text{ units}$$

The required volume in sales dollars is this number of units multiplied by the sales price per unit (8,333.33 units × $36 = $300,000). The following income statement confirms this result; all amounts are rounded to the nearest whole dollar.

Sales revenue (8,333.33 units × $36)	$300,000
Total variable expenses (8,333.33 units × $24)	(200,000)
Total contribution margin (8,333.33 units × $12)	100,000
Fixed expenses	(60,000)
Net income	$ 40,000

In practice, the company will not sell partial bottles of Delatine. The accountant rounds 8,333.33 bottles to whole units. For planning and decision making, managers frequently make decisions using approximate data. Accuracy is desirable, but it is not as important as relevance. Do not be concerned when computations do not produce whole numbers. Rounding and approximation are common characteristics of managerial accounting data.

LO 7

Calculate the sales volume required to attain a target profit.

✓ CHECK YOURSELF 11.6

VolTech Company manufactures small engines that it sells for $130 each. Variable costs are $70 per unit. Fixed costs are expected to be $100,000. The management team has established a target profit of $188,000. Use the contribution margin per unit method to determine how many engines VolTech must sell to attain the target profit.

Answer

$$\text{Sales volume in units} = \frac{\text{Fixed costs} + \text{Desired profit}}{\text{Contribution margin per unit}} = \frac{100,000 + 188,000}{\$130 - \$70} = 4,800 \text{ Units}$$

CALCULATING THE MARGIN OF SAFETY

LO 8

Calculate the margin of safety in units, dollars, and percentage.

Based on the sales records of other products, Bright Day's marketing department believes that budgeted sales of 8,333 units is an attainable goal. Even so, the company president is concerned because Delatine is a new product and no one can be certain about how the public will react to it. He is willing to take the risk of introducing a new product that fails to produce a profit, but he does not want to take a loss on the product. He therefore focuses on the gap between the budgeted sales and the sales required to break even. The amount of this gap, called the *margin of safety,* can be measured in units or in sales dollars as shown here.

	In Units	In Dollars
Budgeted sales	8,333	$300,000
Break-even sales	(5,000)	(180,000)
Margin of safety	3,333	$120,000

The **margin of safety** measures the cushion between budgeted sales and the break-even point. It quantifies the amount by which actual sales can fall short of expectations before the company will begin to incur losses.

To help compare diverse products or companies of different sizes, the margin of safety can be expressed as a percentage. Divide the margin of safety by the budgeted sales volume[3] as shown here.

$$\text{Margin of safety} = \frac{\text{Budgeted sales} - \text{Break-even sales}}{\text{Budgeted sales}}$$

$$\text{Margin of safety} = \frac{\$300,000 - \$180,000}{\$300,000} \times 100 = 40\%$$

This analysis suggests actual sales would have to fall short of expected sales by 40 percent before Bright Day would experience a loss on Delatine. The large margin of safety suggests the proposed advertising program to market Delatine has minimal risk.

✓ CHECK YOURSELF 11.7

Suppose that Bright Day is considering the possibility of selling a protein supplement that will cost Bright Day $5 per bottle. Bright Day believes that it can sell 4,000 bottles of the supplement for $25 per bottle. Fixed costs associated with selling the supplement are expected to be $42,000. Does the supplement have a wider margin of safety than Delatine?

Answer   Calculate the break-even point for the protein supplement.

$$\text{Break-even volume in units} = \frac{\text{Fixed costs}}{\text{Contribution margin per unit}} = \frac{\$42,000}{\$25 - \$5} = 2,100 \text{ Units}$$

Calculate the margin of safety. Note that the margin of safety expressed as a percentage can be calculated using the number of units or sales dollars. Using either units or dollars yields the same percentage.

$$\text{Margin of safety} = \frac{\text{Budgeted sales} - \text{Break-even sales}}{\text{Budgeted sales}} = \frac{4,000 - 2,100}{4,000} = 47.5\%$$

The margin of safety for Delatine (40.0 percent) is below that for the protein supplement (47.5 percent). This suggests that Bright Day is more likely to incur losses selling Delatine than selling the supplement.

---

[3]The margin of safety percentage can be based on actual as well as budgeted sales. For example, an analyst could compare the margins of safety of two companies under current operating conditions by substituting actual sales for budgeted sales in the computation, as follows: ([Actual sales − Break-even sales] ÷ Actual sales).

A Look Back

To plan and control business operations effectively, managers need to understand how different costs behave in relation to changes in the volume of activity. Total *fixed cost* remains constant when activity changes. Fixed cost per unit decreases with increases in activity and increases with decreases in activity. In contrast, total *variable cost* increases proportionately with increases in activity and decreases proportionately with decreases in activity. Variable cost per unit remains constant regardless of activity levels. The definitions of fixed and variable costs have meaning only within the context of a specified range of activity (the relevant range) for a defined period of time. In addition, cost behavior depends on the relevant volume measure (a store manager's salary is fixed relative to the number of customers visiting a particular store but is variable relative to the number of stores operated). A mixed cost has both fixed and variable cost components.

Fixed costs allow companies to take advantage of *operating leverage.* With operating leverage, each additional sale decreases the cost per unit. This principle allows a small percentage change in volume of revenue to cause a significantly larger percentage change in profits. The *magnitude of operating leverage* can be determined by dividing the contribution margin by net income. When all costs are fixed and revenues have covered fixed costs, each additional dollar of revenue represents pure profit. Having a fixed cost structure (employing operating leverage) offers a company both risks and rewards. If sales volume increases, fixed costs do not increase, allowing profits to soar. Alternatively, if sales volume decreases, fixed costs do not decrease and profits decline significantly more than revenues. Companies with high variable costs in relation to fixed costs do not experience as great a level of operating leverage. Their costs increase or decrease in proportion to changes in revenue. These companies face less risk but fail to reap disproportionately higher profits when volume soars.

Under the contribution margin approach, variable costs are subtracted from revenue to determine the *contribution margin.* Fixed costs are then subtracted from the contribution margin to determine net income. The contribution margin represents the amount available to pay fixed costs and provide a profit. Although not permitted by GAAP for external reporting, many companies use the contribution margin format for internal reporting purposes.

The *break-even point* (the point where total revenue equals total cost) in units can be determined by dividing fixed costs by the contribution margin per unit. The break-even point in sales dollars can be determined by multiplying the number of break-even units by the sales price per unit. To determine sales in units to obtain a designated profit, the sum of fixed costs and desired profit is divided by the contribution margin per unit.

The *margin of safety* is the number of units or the amount of sales dollars by which actual sales can fall below expected sales before a loss is incurred. The margin of safety can also be expressed as a percentage to permit comparing different size companies. The margin of safety can be computed as a percentage by dividing the difference between budgeted sales and break-even sales by the amount of budgeted sales.

A Look Forward

The next chapter begins investigating cost measurement. Accountants seek to determine the cost of certain objects. A cost object may be a product, a service, a department, a customer, or any other thing for which the cost is being determined. Some costs can be directly traced to a cost object, while others are difficult to trace. Costs that are difficult to trace to cost objects are called *indirect costs,* or *overhead.* Indirect costs are assigned to cost objects through *cost allocation.* The next chapter introduces the basic concepts and procedures of cost allocation.

A step-by-step audio-narrated series of slides is provided on the text website at www.mhhe.com/edmondssurvey3e.

SELF-STUDY REVIEW PROBLEM 1

Mensa Mountaineering Company (MMC) provides guided mountain climbing expeditions in the Rocky Mountains. Its only major expense is guide salaries; it pays each guide $4,800 per climbing expedition. MMC charges its customers $1,500 per expedition and expects to take five climbers on each expedition.

Part 1

Base your answers on the preceding information.

Required

a. Determine the total cost of guide salaries and the cost of guide salaries per climber assuming that four, five, or six climbers are included in a trip. Relative to the number of climbers in a single expedition, is the cost of guides a fixed or a variable cost?

b. Relative to the number of expeditions, is the cost of guides a fixed or a variable cost?

c. Determine the profit of an expedition assuming that five climbers are included in the trip.

d. Determine the profit assuming a 20 percent increase (six climbers total) in expedition revenue. What is the percentage change in profitability?

e. Determine the profit assuming a 20 percent decrease (four climbers total) in expedition revenue. What is the percentage change in profitability?

f. Explain why a 20 percent shift in revenue produces more than a 20 percent shift in profitability. What term describes this phenomenon?

Part 2

Assume that the guides offer to make the climbs for a percentage of expedition fees. Specifically, MMC will pay guides $960 per climber on the expedition. Assume also that the expedition fee charged to climbers remains at $1,500 per climber.

Required

g. Determine the total cost of guide salaries and the cost of guide salaries per climber assuming that four, five, or six climbers are included in a trip. Relative to the number of climbers in a single expedition, is the cost of guides a fixed or a variable cost?

h. Relative to the number of expeditions, is the cost of guides a fixed or a variable cost?

i. Determine the profit of an expedition assuming that five climbers are included in the trip.

j. Determine the profit assuming a 20 percent increase (six climbers total) in expedition revenue. What is the percentage change in profitability?

k. Determine the profit assuming a 20 percent decrease (four climbers total) in expedition revenue. What is the percentage change in profitability?

l. Explain why a 20 percent shift in revenue does not produce more than a 20 percent shift in profitability.

Solution to Part 1, Requirement *a*

Number of climbers (a)	4	5	6
Total cost of guide salaries (b)	$4,800	$4,800	$4,800
Cost per climber (b ÷ a)	1,200	960	800

Because the total cost remains constant (fixed) regardless of the number of climbers on a particular expedition, the cost is classified as fixed. Note that the cost per climber decreases as the number of climbers increases. This is the *per unit* behavior pattern of a fixed cost.

Solution to Part 1, Requirement *b*

Because the total cost of guide salaries changes proportionately each time the number of expeditions increases or decreases, the cost of salaries is variable relative to the number of expeditions.

Solution to Part 1, Requirements *c, d,* and *e*

Number of Climbers	4	Percentage Change	5	Percentage Change	6
Revenue ($1,500 per climber)	$6,000	⟸(20%)⟸	$7,500	⟹+20%⟹	$9,000
Cost of guide salaries (fixed)	4,800		4,800		4,800
Profit	$1,200	⟸(55.6%)⟸	$2,700	⟹+55.6%⟹	$4,200

Percentage change in revenue: ±$1,500 ÷ $7,500 = ±20%
Percentage change in profit: ±$1,500 ÷ $2,700 = ±55.6%

Solution to Part 1, Requirement *f*

Because the cost of guide salaries remains fixed while volume (number of climbers) changes, the change in profit, measured in absolute dollars, exactly matches the change in revenue. More specifically, each time MMC increases the number of climbers by one, revenue and profit increase by $1,500. Because the base figure for profit ($2,700) is lower than the base figure for revenue ($7,500), the percentage change in profit ($1,500 ÷ $2,700 = 55.6%) is higher than percentage change in revenue ($1,500 ÷ $7,500). This phenomenon is called *operating leverage.*

Solution for Part 2, Requirement *g*

Number of climbers (a)	4	5	6
Per climber cost of guide salaries (b)	$ 960	$ 960	$ 960
Cost per climber (b × a)	3,840	4,800	5,760

Because the total cost changes in proportion to changes in the number of climbers, the cost is classified as variable. Note that the cost per climber remains constant (stays the same) as the number of climbers increases or decreases. This is the *per unit* behavior pattern of a variable cost.

Solution for Part 2, Requirement *h*

Because the total cost of guide salaries changes proportionately with changes in the number of expeditions, the cost of salaries is also variable relative to the number of expeditions.

Solution for Part 2, Requirements *i, j,* and *k*

Number of Climbers	4	Percentage Change	5	Percentage Change	6
Revenue ($1,500 per climber)	$6,000	⟸(20%)⟸	$7,500	⟹+20%⟹	$9,000
Cost of guide salaries (variable)	3,840		4,800		5,760
Profit	$2,160	⟸(20%)⟸	$2,700	⟹+20%⟹	$3,240

Percentage change in revenue: ±$1,500 ÷ $7,500 = ±20%
Percentage change in profit: ±$540 ÷ $2,700 = ±20%

Solution for Part 2, Requirement *l*

Because the cost of guide salaries changes when volume (number of climbers) changes, the change in net income is proportionate to the change in revenue. More specifically, each time the number of climbers increases by one, revenue increases by $1,500 and net income increases by $540 ($1,500 − $960). Accordingly, the percentage change in net income will always equal the percentage change in revenue. This means that there is no operating leverage when all costs are variable.

A step-by-step audio-narrated series of slides is provided on the text website at www.mhhe.com/edmondssurvey3e.

SELF-STUDY REVIEW PROBLEM 2

Sharp Company makes and sells pencil sharpeners. The variable cost of each sharpener is $20. The sharpeners are sold for $30 each. Fixed operating expenses amount to $40,000.

Required

a. Determine the break-even point in units and sales dollars.

b. Determine the sales volume in units and dollars that is required to attain a profit of $12,000. Verify your answer by preparing an income statement using the contribution margin format.

c. Determine the margin of safety between sales required to attain a profit of $12,000 and break-even sales.

Solution to Requirement *a*

Formula for Computing Break-even Point in Units

Sales − Variable costs − Fixed costs = Profit
Sales price per unit (N) − Variable cost per unit (N) − Fixed costs = Profit
Contribution margin per unit (N) − Fixed costs = Profit
N = (Fixed costs + Profit) ÷ Contribution Margin per unit
N = ($40,000 + 0) ÷ ($30 − $20) = 4,000 Units

Break-even Point in Sales Dollars

Sales price	$ 30
× Number of units	4,000
Sales volume in dollars	$120,000

Solution to Requirement *b*

Formula for Computing Unit Sales Required to Attain Desired Profit

Sales − Variable costs − Fixed costs = Profit
Sales price per unit (N) − Variable cost per unit (N) − Fixed costs = Profit
Contribution margin per unit (N) − Fixed costs = Profit
N = (Fixed costs + Profit) ÷ Contribution margin per unit
N = ($40,000 + 12,000) ÷ ($30 − $20) = 5,200 Units

Sales Dollars Required to Attain Desired Profit

Sales price	$ 30
× Number of units	5,200
Sales volume in dollars	$156,000

Income Statement

Sales volume in units (a)	5,200
Sales revenue (a × $30)	$156,000
Variable costs (a × $20)	(104,000)
Contribution margin	52,000
Fixed costs	(40,000)
Net income	$ 12,000

Solution to Requirement *c*

Margin of Safety Computations	Units	Dollars
Budgeted sales	5,200	$156,000
Break-even sales	(4,000)	(120,000)
Margin of safety	1,200	$ 36,000

Percentage Computation

$$\frac{\text{Margin of safety in \$}}{\text{Budgeted sales}} = \frac{\$36,000}{\$156,000} = 23.08\%$$

KEY TERMS

Activity base 406	Cost behavior 398	Mixed costs (semivariable
Break-even point 407	Equation method 407	costs) 405
Contribution margin 402	Fixed cost 398	Operating leverage 398
Contribution margin per	Margin of	Relevant range 405
unit 408	safety 410	Variable cost 397

QUESTIONS

1. Define *fixed cost* and *variable cost* and give an example of each.

2. How can knowing cost behavior relative to volume fluctuations affect decision making?

3. Define the term *operating leverage* and explain how it affects profits.

4. How is operating leverage calculated?

5. Explain the limitations of using operating leverage to predict profitability.

6. If volume is increasing, would a company benefit more from a pure variable or a pure fixed cost structure? Which cost structure would be advantageous if volume is decreasing?

7. Explain the risk and rewards to a company that result from having fixed costs.

8. Are companies with predominately fixed cost structures likely to be most profitable?

9. How is the relevant range of activity related to fixed and variable cost? Give an example of how the definitions of these costs become invalid when volume is outside the relevant range.

10. Which cost structure has the greater risk? Explain.

11. The president of Bright Corporation tells you that he sees a dim future for his company. He feels that his hands are tied because fixed costs are too high. He says that fixed costs do not change and therefore the situation is hopeless. Do you agree? Explain.

12. All costs are variable because if a business ceases operations, its costs fall to zero. Do you agree with the statement? Explain.

13. Verna Salsbury tells you that she thinks the terms fixed cost and variable cost are confusing. She notes that fixed cost per unit changes when the number of units changes. Furthermore, variable cost per unit remains fixed regardless of how many units are produced. She concludes that the terminology seems to be backward. Explain why the terminology appears to be contradictory.

14. What does the term *break-even point* mean? Name the two ways it can be measured.

15. How does a contribution margin income statement differ from the income statement used in financial reporting?

16. If Company A has a projected margin of safety of 22 percent while Company B has a margin of safety of 52 percent, which company is at greater risk when actual sales are less than budgeted?

17. Mary Hartwell and Jane Jamail, college roommates, are considering the joint purchase of a computer that they can share to prepare class assignments. Ms. Hartwell wants a particular model that costs $2,000; Ms. Jamail prefers a more economical model that costs $1,500. In fact, Ms. Jamail is adamant about her position, refusing to contribute more than $750 toward the purchase. If Ms. Hartwell is also adamant about her position, should she accept Ms. Jamail's $750 offer and apply that amount toward the purchase of the more expensive computer?

MULTIPLE-CHOICE QUESTIONS

Multiple-choice questions are provided on the text website at www.mhhe.com/edmondssurvey3e.

EXERCISES

All applicable Exercises are available with McGraw-Hill's *Connect Accounting*.

LO 1, 5

Exercise 11-1   *Identifying cost behavior*

Deer Valley Kitchen, a fast-food restaurant company, operates a chain of restaurants across the nation. Each restaurant employs eight people; one is a manager who is paid a salary plus a bonus equal to 3 percent of sales. Other employees, two cooks, one dishwasher, and four waitresses, are paid salaries. Each manager is budgeted $3,000 per month for advertising cost.

Required

Classify each of the following costs incurred by Deer Valley Kitchen as fixed, variable, or mixed.

a. Cooks' salaries at a particular location relative to the number of customers.
b. Cost of supplies (cups, plates, spoons, etc.) relative to the number of customers.
c. Manager's compensation relative to the number of customers.
d. Waitresses' salaries relative to the number of restaurants.
e. Advertising costs relative to the number of customers for a particular restaurant.
f. Rental costs relative to the number of restaurants.

LO 1

Exercise 11-2   *Identifying cost behavior*

At the various activity levels shown, Amborse Company incurred the following costs.

	Units Sold	20	40	60	80	100
a.	Depreciation cost per unit	240.00	120.00	80.00	60.00	48.00
b.	Total rent cost	3,200.00	3,200.00	3,200.00	3,200.00	3,200.00
c.	Total cost of shopping bags	2.00	4.00	6.00	8.00	10.00
d.	Cost per unit of merchandise sold	90.00	90.00	90.00	90.00	90.00
e.	Rental cost per unit of merchandise sold	36.00	18.00	12.00	9.00	7.20
f.	Total phone expense	80.00	100.00	120.00	140.00	160.00
g.	Cost per unit of supplies	1.00	1.00	1.00	1.00	1.00
h.	Total insurance cost	480.00	480.00	480.00	480.00	480.00
i.	Total salary cost	$1,200.00	$1,600.00	$2,000.00	$2,400.00	$2,800.00
j.	Total cost of goods sold	1,800.00	3,600.00	5,400.00	7,200.00	9,000.00

Required

Identify each of these costs as fixed, variable, or mixed.

LO 1

Exercise 11-3   *Determining fixed cost per unit*

Henke Corporation incurs the following annual fixed costs.

Item	Cost
Depreciation	$ 50,000
Officers' salaries	120,000
Long-term lease	51,000
Property taxes	9,000

Required

Determine the total fixed cost per unit of production, assuming that Henke produces 4,000, 4,500, or 5,000 units.

Exercise 11-4   *Determining total variable cost*

LO 1

The following variable production costs apply to goods made by Watson Manufacturing Corporation.

Item	Cost per Unit
Materials	$5.00
Labor	2.50
Variable overhead	0.25
Total	$7.75

Required

Determine the total variable production cost, assuming that Watson makes 5,000, 15,000, or 25,000 units.

Exercise 11-5   *Fixed versus variable cost behavior*

LO 1, 2

Robbins Company's cost and production data for two recent months included the following.

	January	February
Production (units)	100	250
Rent	$1,500	$1,500
Utilities	$ 450	$1,125

Required

a. Separately calculate the rental cost per unit and the utilities cost per unit for both January and February.

b. Identify which cost is variable and which is fixed. Explain your answer.

Exercise 11-6   *Fixed versus variable cost behavior*

LO 1

Lovvern Trophies makes and sells trophies it distributes to little league ballplayers. The company normally produces and sells between 8,000 and 14,000 trophies per year. The following cost data apply to various activity levels.

Number of Trophies	8,000	10,000	12,000	14,000
Total costs incurred				
Fixed	$42,000			
Variable	42,000			
Total costs	$84,000			
Cost per unit				
Fixed	$ 5.25			
Variable	5.25			
Total cost per trophy	$10.50			

Required

a. Complete the preceding table by filling in the missing amounts for the levels of activity shown in the first row of the table. Round all cost per unit figures to the nearest whole penny.

b. Explain why the total cost per trophy decreases as the number of trophies increases.

LO 1, 5

Exercise 11-7   *Fixed versus variable cost behavior*

Harrel Entertainment sponsors rock concerts. The company is considering a contract to hire a band at a cost of $75,000 per concert.

Required

a. What are the total band cost and the cost per person if concert attendance is 2,000, 2,500, 3,000, 3,500, or 4,000?

b. Is the cost of hiring the band a fixed or a variable cost?

c. Draw a graph and plot total cost and cost per unit if attendance is 2,000, 2,500, 3,000, 3,500, or 4,000.

d. Identify Harrel's major business risks and explain how they can be minimized.

LO 1

Exercise 11-8   *Fixed versus variable cost behavior*

Harrel Entertainment sells souvenir T-shirts at each rock concert that it sponsors. The shirts cost $9 each. Any excess shirts can be returned to the manufacturer for a full refund of the purchase price. The sales price is $15 per shirt.

Required

a. What are the total cost of shirts and cost per shirt if sales amount to 2,000, 2,500, 3,000, 3,500, or 4,000?

b. Is the cost of T-shirts a fixed or a variable cost?

c. Draw a graph and plot total cost and cost per shirt if sales amount to 2,000, 2,500, 3,000, 3,500, or 4,000.

d. Comment on Harrel's likelihood of incurring a loss due to its operating activities.

LO 1

Exercise 11-9   *Graphing fixed cost behavior*

The following graphs depict the dollar amount of fixed cost on the vertical axes and the level of activity on the horizontal axes.

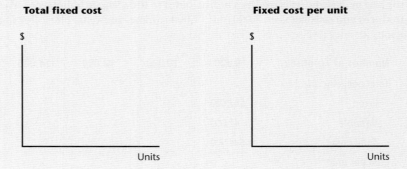

Total fixed cost   Fixed cost per unit

Required

a. Draw a line that depicts the relationship between total fixed cost and the level of activity.

b. Draw a line that depicts the relationship between fixed cost per unit and the level of activity.

Exercise 11-10 *Graphing variable cost behavior*

LO 1

The following graphs depict the dollar amount of variable cost on the vertical axes and the level of activity on the horizontal axes.

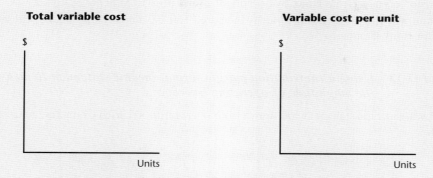

Total variable cost

$

Units

Variable cost per unit

$

Units

Required

a. Draw a line that depicts the relationship between total variable cost and the level of activity.

b. Draw a line that depicts the relationship between variable cost per unit and the level of activity.

Exercise 11-11 *Mixed cost at different levels of activity*

LO 1

Omar Corporation paid one of its sales representatives $4,300 during the month of March. The rep is paid a base salary plus $15 per unit of product sold. During March, the rep sold 200 units.

Required

Calculate the total monthly cost of the sales representative's salary for each of the following months.

Month	April	May	June	July
Number of units sold	240	150	250	160
Total variable cost				
Total fixed cost				
Total salary cost				

Exercise 11-12 *Using fixed cost as a competitive business strategy*

LO 1, 2

The following income statements illustrate different cost structures for two competing companies.

Income Statements		
	Company Name	
	Hank	**Rank**
Number of customers (a)	80	80
Sales revenue (a × $250)	$20,000	$20,000
Variable cost (a × $175)	N/A	(14,000)
Variable cost (a × $0)	0	N/A
Contribution margin	20,000	6,000
Fixed cost	(14,000)	0
Net income	$ 6,000	$ 6,000

Required

a. Reconstruct Hank's income statement, assuming that it serves 160 customers when it lures 80 customers away from Rank by lowering the sales price to $150 per customer.

b. Reconstruct Rank's income statement, assuming that it serves 160 customers when it lures 80 customers away from Hank by lowering the sales price to $150 per customer.

c. Explain why the price-cutting strategy increased Hank Company's profits but caused a net loss for Rank Company.

LO 3, 4

Exercise 11-13   *Using a contribution margin format income statement to measure the magnitude of operating leverage*

The following income statement was drawn from the records of Ulrich Company, a merchandising firm.

ULRICH COMPANY Income Statement For the Year Ended December 31, 2011	
Sales revenue (4,000 units × $150)	$600,000
Cost of goods sold (4,000 units × $80)	(320,000)
Gross margin	280,000
Sales commissions (10% of sales)	(60,000)
Administrative salaries expense	(90,000)
Advertising expense	(40,000)
Depreciation expense	(50,000)
Shipping and handling expenses (4,000 units × $1)	(4,000)
Net income	$ 36,000

Required

a. Reconstruct the income statement using the contribution margin format.

b. Calculate the magnitude of operating leverage.

c. Use the measure of operating leverage to determine the amount of net income Ulrich will earn if sales increase by 10 percent.

LO 4

Exercise 11-14   *Assessing the magnitude of operating leverage*

The following income statement applies to Stuart Company for the current year.

Income Statement	
Sales revenue (400 units × $25)	$10,000
Variable cost (400 units × $10)	(4,000)
Contribution margin	6,000
Fixed costs	(3,500)
Net income	$2,500

Required

a. Use the contribution margin approach to calculate the magnitude of operating leverage.

b. Use the operating leverage measure computed in Requirement *a* to determine the amount of net income that Stuart Company will earn if it experiences a 10 percent increase in revenue. The sales price per unit is not affected.

c. Verify your answer to Requirement *b* by constructing an income statement based on a 10 percent increase in sales revenue. The sales price is not affected. Calculate the percentage change in net income for the two income statements.

Exercise 11-15   *Break-even point*   LO 6

Connor Corporation sells products for $25 each that have variable costs of $13 per unit. Connor's annual fixed cost is $264,000.

Required

Determine the break-even point in units and dollars.

Exercise 11-16   *Desired profit*   LO 7

Garcia Company incurs annual fixed costs of $60,000. Variable costs for Garcia's product are $22.75 per unit, and the sales price is $35.00 per unit. Garcia desires to earn an annual profit of $45,000.

Required

Determine the sales volume in dollars and units required to earn the desired profit.

Exercise 11-17   *Determining fixed and variable cost per unit*   LO 1

Landry Corporation produced and sold 12,000 units of product during October. It earned a contribution margin of $96,000 on sales of $336,000 and determined that cost per unit of product was $25.

Required

Based on this information, determine the variable and fixed cost per unit of product.

Exercise 11-18   *Determining variable cost from incomplete cost data*   LO 1

Laya Corporation produced 200,000 watches that it sold for $16 each during 2012. The company determined that fixed manufacturing cost per unit was $7 per watch. The company reported a $800,000 gross margin on its 2011 financial statements.

Required

Determine the total variable cost, the variable cost per unit, and the total contribution margin.

Exercise 11-19   *Margin of safety*   LO 6, 7, 8

Information concerning a product produced by Askew Company appears here.

Sales price per unit	$145
Variable cost per unit	$55
Total annual fixed manufacturing and operating costs	$810,000

Required

Determine the following.

a. Contribution margin per unit.
b. Number of units that Askew must sell to break even.
c. Sales level in units that Askew must reach to earn a profit of $360,000.
d. Determine the margin of safety in units, sales dollars, and as a percentage.

Exercise 11-20   *Margin of safety*   LO 8

Jensen Company makes a product that sells for $38 per unit. The company pays $16 per unit for the variable costs of the product and incurs annual fixed costs of $176,000. Jensen expects to sell 21,000 units of product.

Required

Determine Jensen's margin of safety in units, sales dollars, and as a percentage.

PROBLEMS

All applicable Problems are available with McGraw-Hill's
Connect Accounting.

LO 1, 5

Problem 11-21   *Identifying cost behavior*

Required

Identify the following costs as fixed or variable.
Costs related to plane trips between Seattle, Washington, and Orlando, Florida, follow. Pilots are paid on a per trip basis.

a. Pilots' salaries relative to the number of trips flown.
b. Depreciation relative to the number of planes in service.
c. Cost of refreshments relative to the number of passengers.
d. Pilots' salaries relative to the number of passengers on a particular trip.
e. Cost of a maintenance check relative to the number of passengers on a particular trip.
f. Fuel costs relative to the number of trips.

First Federal Bank operates several branch offices in grocery stores. Each branch employs a supervisor and two tellers.

g. Tellers' salaries relative to the number of tellers in a particular district.
h. Supplies cost relative to the number of transactions processed in a particular branch.
i. Tellers' salaries relative to the number of customers served at a particular branch.
j. Supervisors' salaries relative to the number of branches operated.
k. Supervisors' salaries relative to the number of customers served in a particular branch.
l. Facility rental costs relative to the size of customer deposits.

Costs related to operating a fast-food restaurant follow.

m. Depreciation of equipment relative to the number of restaurants.
n. Building rental cost relative to the number of customers served in a particular restaurant.
o. Manager's salary of a particular restaurant relative to the number of employees.
p. Food cost relative to the number of customers.
q. Utility cost relative to the number of restaurants in operation.
r. Company president's salary relative to the number of restaurants in operation.
s. Land costs relative to the number of hamburgers sold at a particular restaurant.
t. Depreciation of equipment relative to the number of customers served at a particular restaurant.

LO 1, 6

Problem 11-22   *Cost behavior and averaging*

Carlia Weaver has decided to start Carlia Cleaning, a residential house cleaning service company. She is able to rent cleaning equipment at a cost of $750 per month. Labor costs are expected to be $75 per house cleaned and supplies are expected to cost $6 per house.

Required

a. Determine the total expected cost of equipment rental and the expected cost of equipment rental per house cleaned, assuming that Carlia Cleaning cleans 10, 20, or 30 houses during one month. Is the cost of equipment a fixed or a variable cost?
b. Determine the total expected cost of labor and the expected cost of labor per house cleaned, assuming that Carlia Cleaning cleans 10, 20, or 30 houses during one month. Is the cost of labor a fixed or a variable cost?
c. Determine the total expected cost of supplies and the expected cost of supplies per house cleaned, assuming that Carlia Cleaning cleans 10, 20, or 30 houses during one month. Is the cost of supplies a fixed or a variable cost?
d. Determine the total expected cost of cleaning houses, assuming that Carlia Cleaning cleans 10, 20, or 30 houses during one month.

e. Determine the expected cost per house, assuming that Carlia Cleaning cleans 10, 20, or 30 houses during one month. Why does the cost per unit decrease as the number of houses increases?

f. If Ms. Weaver tells you that she prices her services at 25% above cost, would you assume that she means average or actual cost? Why?

Problem 11-23   *Context-sensitive nature of cost behavior classifications*

LO 5

CHECK FIGURE
b. Average teller cost for 60,000
transactions: $1.50

Pacific Bank's start-up division establishes new branch banks. Each branch opens with three tellers. Total teller cost per branch is $90,000 per year. The three tellers combined can process up to 90,000 customer transactions per year. If a branch does not attain a volume of at least 60,000 transactions during its first year of operations, it is closed. If the demand for services exceeds 90,000 transactions, an additional teller is hired, and the branch is transferred from the start-up division to regular operations.

Required

a. What is the relevant range of activity for new branch banks?

b. Determine the amount of teller cost in total and the teller cost per transaction for a branch that processes 60,000, 70,000, 80,000, or 90,000 transactions. In this case (the activity base is the number of transactions for a specific branch), is the teller cost a fixed or a variable cost?

c. Determine the amount of teller cost in total and the teller cost per branch for Pacific Bank, assuming that the start-up division operates 10, 15, 20, or 25 branches. In this case (the activity base is the number of branches), is the teller cost a fixed or a variable cost?

Problem 11-24   *Context-sensitive nature of cost behavior classifications*

LO 5

CHECK FIGURES
a. Average cost at
400 units: $200
b. Average price at
250 units: $265

Susan Hicks operates a sales booth in computer software trade shows, selling an accounting software package, *Dollar System*. She purchases the package from a software manufacturer for $175 each. Booth space at the convention hall costs $10,000 per show.

Required

a. Sales at past trade shows have ranged between 200 and 400 software packages per show. Determine the average cost of sales per unit if Ms. Hicks sells 200, 250, 300, 350, or 400 units of *Dollar System* at a trade show. Use the following chart to organize your answer. Is the cost of booth space fixed or variable?

	Sales Volume in Units (a)				
	200	**250**	**300**	**350**	**400**
Total cost of software (a × $175)	$35,000				
Total cost of booth rental	10,000				
Total cost of sales (b)	$45,000				
Average cost per unit (b ÷ a)	$ 225				

b. If Ms. Hicks wants to earn a $50 profit on each package of software she sells at a trade show, what price must she charge at sales volumes of 200, 250, 300, 350, or 400 units?

c. Record the total cost of booth space if Ms. Hicks attends one, two, three, four, or five trade shows. Record your answers in the following chart. Is the cost of booth space fixed or variable relative to the number of shows attended?

	Number of Trade Shows Attended				
	1	**2**	**3**	**4**	**5**
Total cost of booth rental	$10,000				

d. Ms. Hicks provides decorative shopping bags to customers who purchase software packages. Some customers take the bags; others do not. Some customers stuff more than one software package into a single bag. The number of bags varies in relation to the number of units sold, but the relationship is not proportional. Assume that Ms. Hicks uses $30 of bags for every 50 software packages sold. What is the additional cost per unit sold? Is the cost fixed or variable?

LO 1, 2

CHECK FIGURES
Part 1, b: $2,200
Part 2, h: $3,000 & 10%
Part 3, k: cost per student for
22 students: $25

Problem 11-25   *Effects of operating leverage on profitability*

Webster Training Services (WTS) provides instruction on the use of computer software for the employees of its corporate clients. It offers courses in the clients' offices on the clients' equipment. The only major expense WTS incurs is instructor salaries; it pays instructors $5,000 per course taught. WTS recently agreed to offer a course of instruction to the employees of Chambers Incorporated at a price of $400 per student. Chambers estimated that 20 students would attend the course.

Base your answer on the preceding information.

Part 1:

Required

a. Relative to the number of students in a single course, is the cost of instruction a fixed or a variable cost?

b. Determine the profit, assuming that 20 students attend the course.

c. Determine the profit, assuming a 10 percent increase in enrollment (i.e., enrollment increases to 22 students). What is the percentage change in profitability?

d. Determine the profit, assuming a 10 percent decrease in enrollment (i.e., enrollment decreases to 18 students). What is the percentage change in profitability?

e. Explain why a 10 percent shift in enrollment produces more than a 10 percent shift in profitability. Use the term that identifies this phenomenon.

Part 2:

The instructor has offered to teach the course for a percentage of tuition fees. Specifically, she wants $250 per person attending the class. Assume that the tuition fee remains at $400 per student.

Required

f. Is the cost of instruction a fixed or a variable cost?

g. Determine the profit, assuming that 20 students take the course.

h. Determine the profit, assuming a 10 percent increase in enrollment (i.e., enrollment increases to 22 students). What is the percentage change in profitability?

i. Determine the profit, assuming a 10 percent decrease in enrollment (i.e., enrollment decreases to 18 students). What is the percentage change in profitability?

j. Explain why a 10 percent shift in enrollment produces a proportional 10 percent shift in profitability.

Part 3:

WTS sells a workbook with printed material unique to each course to each student who attends the course. Any workbooks that are not sold must be destroyed. Prior to the first class, WTS printed 20 copies of the books based on the client's estimate of the number of people who would attend the course. Each workbook costs $25 and is sold to course participants for $40. This cost includes a royalty fee paid to the author and the cost of duplication.

Required

k. Calculate the workbook cost in total and per student, assuming that 18, 20, or 22 students attempt to attend the course.

l. Classify the cost of workbooks as fixed or variable relative to the number of students attending the course.

m. Discuss the risk of holding inventory as it applies to the workbooks.

n. Explain how a just-in-time inventory system can reduce the cost and risk of holding inventory.

Problem 11-26 *Effects of fixed and variable cost behavior on the risk and rewards of business opportunities*

LO 1, 2

Eastern and Western Universities offer executive training courses to corporate clients. Eastern pays its instructors $5,310 per course taught. Western pays its instructors $295 per student enrolled in the class. Both universities charge executives a $340 tuition fee per course attended.

CHECK FIGURES
a. Western NI: $810
b. NI: $2,610

Required

a. Prepare income statements for Eastern and Western, assuming that 18 students attend a course.

b. Eastern University embarks on a strategy to entice students from Western University by lowering its tuition to $220 per course. Prepare an income statement for Eastern, assuming that the university is successful and enrolls 36 students in its course.

c. Western University embarks on a strategy to entice students from Eastern University by lowering its tuition to $220 per course. Prepare an income statement for Western, assuming that the university is successful and enrolls 36 students in its course.

d. Explain why the strategy described in Requirement *b* produced a profit but the same strategy described in Requirement *c* produced a loss.

e. Prepare income statements for Eastern and Western Universities, assuming that 15 students attend a course, assuming that both universities charge executives a $340 tuition fee per course attended.

f. It is always better to have fixed than variable cost. Explain why this statement is false.

g. It is always better to have variable than fixed cost. Explain why this statement is false.

Problem 11-27 *Analyzing operating leverage*

LO 3, 4

e**X**cel

Justin Zinder is a venture capitalist facing two alternative investment opportunities. He intends to invest $1 million in a start-up firm. He is nervous, however, about future economic volatility. He asks you to analyze the following financial data for the past year's operations of the two firms he is considering and give him some business advice.

	Company Name	
	Ensley	**Kelley**
Variable cost per unit (a)	$21.00	$10.50
Sales revenue (8,000 units × $28)	$224,000	$224,000
Variable cost (8,000 units × a)	(168,000)	(84,000)
Contribution margin	56,000	140,000
Fixed cost	(25,000)	(109,000)
Net income	$ 31,000	$ 31,000

CHECK FIGURES
b. % of change for Kelley: 45.16
c. % of change for Ensley: (18.06)

Required

a. Use the contribution margin approach to compute the operating leverage for each firm.

b. If the economy expands in coming years, Ensley and Kelley will both enjoy a 10 percent per year increase in sales, assuming that the selling price remains unchanged. Compute the change in net income for each firm in dollar amount and in percentage. (*Note:* Because the number of units increases, both revenue and variable cost will increase.)

c. If the economy contracts in coming years, Ensley and Kelley will both suffer a 10 percent decrease in sales volume, assuming that the selling price remains unchanged. Compute the change in net income for each firm in dollar amount and in percentage. (*Note:* Because the number of units decreases, both total revenue and total variable cost will decrease.)

d. Write a memo to Justin Zinder with your analyses and advice.

Problem 11-28 *Determining the break-even point and preparing a contribution margin income statement*

LO 3, 6

e**X**cel

Inman Manufacturing Company makes a product that it sells for $60 per unit. The company incurs variable manufacturing costs of $24 per unit. Variable selling expenses are $12 per unit, annual fixed manufacturing costs are $189,000, and fixed selling and administrative costs are $141,000 per year.

CHECK FIGURE
a. 13,750 units

Required

Determine the break-even point in units and dollars using the following approaches.

a. Equation method.

b. Contribution margin per unit.

c. Contribution margin ratio.

d. Confirm your results by preparing a contribution margin income statement for the break-even sales volume.

Problem 11-29   *Margin of safety and operating leverage*

Santiago Company is considering the addition of a new product to its cosmetics line. The company has three distinctly different options: a skin cream, a bath oil, or a hair coloring gel. Relevant information and budgeted annual income statements for each of the products follow.

Relevant Information			
	Skin Cream	**Bath Oil**	**Color Gel**
Budgeted sales in units (a)	50,000	90,000	30,000
Expected sales price (b)	$7.00	$4.00	$13.00
Variable costs per unit (c)	$4.00	$1.50	$ 9.00
Income Statements			
Sales revenue (a × b)	$350,000	$360,000	$390,000
Variable costs (a × c)	(200,000)	(135,000)	(270,000)
Contribution margin	150,000	225,000	120,000
Fixed costs	(120,000)	(210,000)	(104,000)
Net income	$ 30,000	$ 15,000	$ 16,000

Required

a. Determine the margin of safety as a percentage for each product.

b. Prepare revised income statements for each product, assuming a 20 percent increase in the budgeted sales volume.

c. For each product, determine the percentage change in net income that results from the 20 percent increase in sales. Which product has the highest operating leverage?

d. Assuming that management is pessimistic and risk averse, which product should the company add to its cosmetic line? Explain your answer.

e. Assuming that management is optimistic and risk aggressive, which product should the company add to its cosmetics line? Explain your answer.

ANALYZE, THINK, COMMUNICATE

ATC 11-1   Business Applications   *Operating leverage*

Description of Business for Amazon.com, Inc.

Amazon.com opened its virtual doors on the World Wide Web in July 1995 and we offer Earth's Biggest Selection. We seek to be Earth's most customer-centric company for three primary customer sets: consumer customers, seller customers and developer customers. In addition, we generate revenue through co-branded credit card agreements and other marketing and promotional services, such as online advertising.

Amazon.com	2008	2007
Operating revenue	$19,166	$14,835
Operating earnings	842	655

Description of Business for CSX, Inc.

CSX Corporations ("CSX") together with its subsidiaries (the "Company"), based in Jacksonville, Florida, is one of the nation's leading transportation suppliers. The Company's rail and inter-modal businesses provide rail-based transportation services including traditional rail service and the transport of intermodal containers and trailers.

CSX, Inc.	2008	2007
Operating revenue	$11,255	$10,030
Operating earnings	2,768	2,260

Required

a. Determine which company appears to have the higher operating leverage.

b. Write a paragraph or two explaining why the company you identified in Requirement *a* might be expected to have the higher operating leverage.

c. If revenues for both companies declined, which company do you think would likely experience the greater decline in operating earnings? Explain your answer.

ATC 11-2   Group Assignment   *Operating leverage*

The Parent Teacher Association (PTA) of Meadow High School is planning a fund-raising campaign. The PTA is considering the possibility of hiring Eric Logan, a world-renowned investment counselor, to address the public. Tickets would sell for $28 each. The school has agreed to let the PTA use Harville Auditorium at no cost. Mr. Logan is willing to accept one of two compensation arrangements. He will sign an agreement to receive a fixed fee of $10,000 regardless of the number of tickets sold. Alternatively, he will accept payment of $20 per ticket sold. In communities similar to that in which Meadow is located, Mr. Logan has drawn an audience of approximately 500 people.

Required

a. In front of the class, present a statement showing the expected net income assuming 500 people buy tickets.

b. Divide the class into groups and then organize the groups into four sections. Assign one of the following tasks to each section of groups.

Group Tasks

(1) Assume the PTA pays Mr. Logan a fixed fee of $10,000. Determine the amount of net income that the PTA will earn if ticket sales are 10 percent higher than expected. Calculate the percentage change in net income.

(2) Assume that the PTA pays Mr. Logan a fixed fee of $10,000. Determine the amount of net income that the PTA will earn if ticket sales are 10 percent lower than expected. Calculate the percentage change in net income.

(3) Assume that the PTA pays Mr. Logan $20 per ticket sold. Determine the amount of net income that the PTA will earn if ticket sales are 10 percent higher than expected. Calculate the percentage change in net income.

(4) Assume that the PTA pays Mr. Logan $20 per ticket sold. Determine the amount of net income that the PTA will earn if ticket sales are 10 percent lower than expected. Calculate the percentage change in net income.

c. Have each group select a spokesperson. Have one of the spokespersons in each section of groups go to the board and present the results of the analysis conducted in Requirement *b*. Resolve any discrepancies in the computations presented at the board and those developed by the other groups.

d. Draw conclusions regarding the risks and rewards associated with operating leverage. At a minimum, answer the following questions.

(1) Which type of cost structure (fixed or variable) produces the higher growth potential in profitability for a company?

(2) Which type of cost structure (fixed or variable) produces the higher risk of declining profitability for a company?

(3) Under what circumstances should a company seek to establish a fixed cost structure?

(4) Under what circumstances should a company seek to establish a variable cost structure?

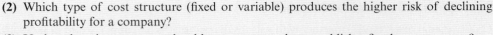

ATC 11-3   Research Assignment   *Fixed versus variable cost*

Use the 2008 Form 10-K for Black & Decker Corp. (B&D) to complete the requirements below. To obtain the Form 10-K you can use the EDGAR system following the instructions in Appendix A, or it can be found under "Investor Relations" on the company's corporate website: www.bdk.com. Be sure to read carefully the following portions of the document.

■ "General Development of the Business" on page 1.

■ "Consolidated Statement of Earnings" on page 36.

Required

a. Calculate the percentage decrease in B&D's sales and its "operating income" from 2007 to 2008.

b. Would fixed costs or variable costs be more likely to explain why B&D's operating earnings decreased by a bigger percentage than its sales?

c. On page 42 B&D reported that it incurred product development costs of $146 million in 2008. If this cost is thought of in the context of the number of units of products sold, should it be considered as primarily fixed or variable in nature?

d. If the product development costs are thought of in the context of the number of new products developed, should it be considered as primarily fixed or variable in nature?

ATC 11-4   Writing Assignment   *Operating leverage, margin of safety, and cost behavior*

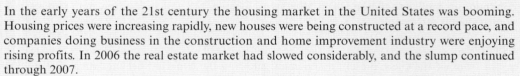

In the early years of the 21st century the housing market in the United States was booming. Housing prices were increasing rapidly, new houses were being constructed at a record pace, and companies doing business in the construction and home improvement industry were enjoying rising profits. In 2006 the real estate market had slowed considerably, and the slump continued through 2007.

Home Depot was one major company in the building supplies industry that was adversely affected by the slowdown in the housing market. On August 14, 2007, it announced that its revenues for the first half of the year were 3 percent lower than revenues were for the first six months of 2006. Of even greater concern was the fact that its earnings for the first half of 2007 were 21 percent lower than for the same period in the prior year.

Required

Write a memorandum that explains how a 3 percent decline in sales could cause a 21 percent decline in profits. Your memo should address the following:

a. An identification of the accounting concept involved.

b. A discussion of how various major types of costs incurred by Home Depot were likely affected by the decline in its sales.

c. The effect of the decline in sales on Home Depot's margin of safety.

ATC 11-5   Ethical Dilemma   *Profitability versus social conscience (effects of cost behavior)*

Advances in biological technology have enabled two research companies, Bio Labs Inc. and Scientific Associates, to develop an insect-resistant corn seed. Neither company is financially strong enough to develop the distribution channels necessary to bring the product to world markets. World Agra Distributors Inc. has negotiated contracts with both companies for the exclusive right to market their seed. Bio Labs signed an agreement to receive an annual royalty of $1,000,000. In contrast, Scientific Associates chose an agreement that provides for a royalty of $0.50 per pound of seed sold. Both agreements have a 10-year term. During 2010, World Agra sold approximately 1,600,000 pounds of the Bio Labs Inc. seed and 2,400,000 pounds of the Scientific Associates seed. Both types of seed were sold for $1.25 per pound. By the end of 2010, it was apparent that the seed developed by Scientific Associates was superior. Although insect infestation was virtually nonexistent for both types of seed, the seed developed by Scientific Associates produced corn that was sweeter and had consistently higher yields.

World Agra Distributors' chief financial officer, Roger Weatherstone, recently retired. To the astonishment of the annual planning committee, Mr. Weatherstone's replacement, Ray Borrough, adamantly recommended that the marketing department develop a major advertising campaign to promote the seed developed by Bio Labs Inc. The planning committee reluctantly approved the recommendation. A $100,000 ad campaign was launched; the ads emphasized the ability of the Bio Labs seed to avoid insect infestation. The campaign was silent with respect to taste or crop yield. It did not mention the seed developed by Scientific Associates. World Agra's sales staff was instructed to push the Bio Labs seed and to sell the Scientific Associates seed only on customer demand. Although total sales remained relatively constant during 2011, sales of the Scientific Associates seed fell to approximately 1,300,000 pounds while sales of the Bio Labs Inc. seed rose to 2,700,000 pounds.

Required

a. Determine the amount of increase or decrease in profitability experienced by World Agra in 2011 as a result of promoting Bio Labs seed. Support your answer with appropriate commentary.

b. Did World Agra's customers in particular and society in general benefit or suffer from the decision to promote the Bio Labs seed?

c. Review the standards of ethical conduct in Exhibit 10.17 of Chapter 10 and comment on whether Mr. Borrough's recommendation violated any of the principles in the Statement of Ethical Professional Practice.

d. Comment on your belief regarding the adequacy of the Statement of Ethical Professional Practice for Managerial Accountants to direct the conduct of management accountants.

CHAPTER 12

Cost Accumulation, Tracing, and Allocation

LEARNING OBJECTIVES

After you have mastered the material in this chapter, you will be able to:

1 Identify cost objects and cost drivers.

2 Distinguish direct costs from indirect costs.

3 Allocate indirect costs to cost objects.

4 Select appropriate cost drivers for allocating indirect costs.

5 Allocate costs to solve timing problems.

6 Explain the benefits and detriments of allocating pooled costs.

7 Recognize the effects of cost allocation on employee motivation.

CHAPTER OPENING

What does it cost? This is one of the questions most frequently asked by business managers. Managers must have reliable cost estimates to price products, evaluate performance, control operations, and prepare financial statements. As this discussion implies, managers need to know the cost of many different things. The things we are trying to determine the cost of are commonly called **cost objects.** For example, if we are trying to determine the cost of operating a department, that department is the cost object. Cost objects may be products, processes, departments, services, activities, and so on. This chapter explains techniques managerial accountants use to determine the cost of a variety of cost objects.

The Curious Accountant

A former patient of a California hospital complained about being charged $7 for a single aspirin tablet. After all, an entire bottle of 100 aspirins can be purchased at the local pharmacy store for around $2.

Can you think of any reasons, other than shameless profiteering, that a hospital would need to charge $7 for an aspirin? Remember that the hospital is not just selling the aspirin; it is also delivering it to the patient. (Answer on page 438.)

DETERMINE THE COST OF COST OBJECTS

Identify cost objects and cost drivers.

Accountants use **cost accumulation** to determine the cost of a particular object. Suppose the Atlanta Braves advertising manager wants to promote a Tuesday night ball game by offering free baseball caps to all children who attend. What would be the promotion cost? The team's accountant must *accumulate* many individual costs and add them together. For simplicity consider only three cost components: (1) the cost of the caps, (2) the cost of advertising the promotion, and (3) the cost of an employee to work on the promotion.

Cost accumulation begins with identifying the **cost objects.** The primary cost object is the cost of the promotion. Three secondary cost objects are (1) the cost of caps, (2) the cost of advertising, and (3) the cost of labor. The costs of the secondary cost objects are combined to determine the cost of the primary cost object.

Determining the costs of the secondary cost objects requires identifying what *drives* those costs. A **cost driver** has a *cause-and-effect* relationship with a cost object. For example, the *number of caps* (cost driver) has an effect on the *cost of caps* (cost object). The *number of advertisements* is a cost driver for the *advertising cost* (cost object); the *number of labor hours* worked is a cost driver for the *labor cost* (cost object). Using the following assumptions about unit costs and cost drivers, the accumulated cost of the primary cost object (cost of the cap promotion) is

Cost Object	Cost Per Unit	×	Cost Driver	=	Total Cost of Object
Cost of caps	$2.50	×	4,000 Caps	=	$10,000
Cost of advertising	$100.00	×	50 Advertisements	=	5,000
Cost of labor	$8.00	×	100 Hours	=	800
Cost of cap promotion					$15,800

The Atlanta Braves should run the promotion if management expects it to produce additional revenues exceeding $15,800.

Estimated versus Actual Cost

The accumulated cost of the promotion—$15,800—is an *estimate*. Management cannot know *actual* costs and revenues until after running the promotion. While actual information is more accurate, it is not relevant for deciding whether to run the promotion because the decision must be made before the actual cost is known. Managers must accept a degree of inaccuracy in exchange for the relevance of timely information. Many business decisions are based on estimated rather than actual costs.

Managers use cost estimates to set prices, bid on contracts, evaluate proposals, distribute resources, plan production, and set goals. Certain circumstances, however, require actual cost data. For example, published financial reports and managerial performance evaluations use actual cost data. Managers frequently accumulate both estimated and actual cost data for the same cost object. For example, companies use cost estimates to establish goals and use actual costs to evaluate management performance in meeting those goals. The following discussion provides a number of business examples that use estimated data, actual data, or a combination of both.

ASSIGNMENT OF COSTS TO OBJECTS IN A RETAIL BUSINESS

Exhibit 12.1 displays the January income statement for In Style, Inc. (ISI), a retail clothing store. ISI subdivides its operations into women's, men's, and children's departments. To encourage the departmental managers to maximize sales, ISI began paying the manager of each department a bonus based on a percentage of departmental sales revenue.

Although the bonus incentive increased sales revenue, it also provoked negative consequences. The departmental managers began to argue over floor space; each manager wanted more space to display merchandise. The managers reduced prices; they increased sales commissions. In the drive to maximize sales, the managers ignored the need to control costs. To improve the situation, the store manager decided to base future bonuses on each department's contribution to profitability rather than its sales revenue.

IDENTIFYING DIRECT AND INDIRECT COSTS

The new bonus strategy requires determining the cost of operating each department. Each department is a separate *cost object.* Assigning costs to the departments (cost objects) requires **cost tracing** and **cost allocation.** *Direct costs* can be easily traced to a cost object. *Indirect costs* cannot be easily traced to a cost object. Whether or not a cost is easily traceable requires *cost/benefit analysis.*

LO 2

Distinguish direct costs from indirect costs.

Some of ISI's costs can be easily traced to the cost objects (specific departments). The cost of goods sold is an example of an easily traced cost. Price tags on merchandise can be coded so cash register scanners capture the departmental code for each sale. The cost of goods sold is not only easily traceable but also very useful information. Companies need cost of goods sold information for financial reporting (income statement and balance sheet) and for management decisions (determining inventory reorder points, pricing strategies, and cost control). Because the cost of tracing *cost of goods sold* is small relative to the benefits obtained, cost of goods sold is a *direct cost.*

In contrast, the cost of supplies (shopping bags, sales slips, pens, staples, price tags) used by each department is much more difficult to trace. How could the number of staples used to seal shopping bags be traced to any particular department? The sales staff could count the number of staples used, but doing so would be silly for the benefits obtained. Although tracing the cost of supplies to each department may be possible, it is not worth the effort of doing so. The cost of supplies is therefore an *indirect cost.* Indirect costs are also called **overhead costs.**

Direct and indirect costs can be described as follows.

EXHIBIT 12.1	
Income Statement	
IN STYLE, INC. Income Statement For the Month Ended January 31	
Sales	$360,000
Cost of goods sold	(216,000)
Gross margin	144,000
Sales commissions	(18,000)
Dept. managers' salaries	(12,000)
Store manager's salary	(9,360)
Depreciation	(16,000)
Rental fee for store	(18,400)
Utilities	(2,300)
Advertising	(7,200)
Supplies	(900)
Net income	$ 59,840

> **Direct costs** can be traced to cost objects in a *cost-effective* manner.
> **Indirect costs** cannot be traced to objects in a *cost-effective* manner.

By analyzing the accounting records, ISI's accountant classified the costs from the income statement in Exhibit 12.1 as direct or indirect, as shown in Exhibit 12.2. The next paragraph explains the classifications.

All figures represent January costs. Items 1 through 4 are direct costs, traceable to the cost objects in a cost-effective manner. Cost of goods sold is traced to departments at the point of sale using cash register scanners. Sales commissions are based on a percentage of departmental sales and are therefore easy to trace to the departments. Departmental managers' salaries are also easily traceable to the departments. Equipment, furniture, and fixtures are tagged with department codes that permit tracing depreciation charges directly to specific departments. Items 5 through 8 are incurred on behalf of the company as a whole and are therefore not directly traceable to a specific department. Although Item 9 could be traced to specific departments, the cost of doing so would exceed the benefits. The cost of supplies is therefore also classified as indirect.

EXHIBIT 12.2

Income Statement Classification of Costs

Cost Item	Direct Costs			Indirect Costs
	Women's	Men's	Children's	
1. Cost of goods sold—$216,000	$120,000	$58,000	$38,000	
2. Sales commissions—$18,000	9,500	5,500	3,000	
3. Dept. managers' salaries—$12,000	5,000	4,200	2,800	
4. Depreciation—$16,000	7,000	5,000	4,000	
5. Store manager's salary				$ 9,360
6. Rental fee for store				18,400
7. Utilities				2,300
8. Advertising				7,200
9. Supplies				900
Totals	$141,500	$72,700	$47,800	$38,160

Cost Classifications—Independent and Context Sensitive

Whether a cost is direct or indirect is independent of whether it is fixed or variable. In the ISI example, both cost of goods sold and the cost of supplies vary relative to sales volume (both are variable costs), but cost of goods sold is direct and the cost of supplies is indirect. Furthermore, the cost of rent and the cost of depreciation are both fixed relative to sales volume, but the cost of rent is indirect and the cost of depreciation is direct. In fact, the very same cost can be classified as direct or indirect, depending on the cost object. The store manager's salary is not directly traceable to a specific department, but it is traceable to a particular store.

Similarly, identifying costs as direct or indirect is independent of whether the costs are relevant to a given decision. ISI could avoid both cost of goods sold and the cost of supplies for a particular department if that department were eliminated. Both costs are relevant to a segment elimination decision, yet one is direct, and the other is indirect. You cannot memorize costs as direct or indirect, fixed or variable, relevant or not relevant. When trying to identify costs as to type or behavior, you must consider the context in which the costs occur.

ALLOCATING INDIRECT COSTS TO OBJECTS

Allocate indirect costs to cost objects.

Common costs support multiple cost objects, but cannot be directly traced to any specific object. In the case of In Style, Inc., the cost of renting the store (common cost) supports the women's, men's, and children's departments (cost objects). The departmental managers may shirk responsibility for the rental cost by claiming that others higher up the chain of command are responsible. Responsibility can be motivated at the departmental level by assigning (*allocating*) a portion of the total rental cost to each department.

To accomplish appropriate motivation, authority must accompany responsibility. In other words, the departmental managers should be held responsible for a portion of rental cost only if they are able to exercise some degree of control over that cost. For example, if managers are assigned a certain amount of the rental cost for each square foot of space they use, they should have the authority to establish the size of the space used by their departments. **Controllable costs** are costs that can be influenced by a manager's decisions and actions. The controllability concept is discussed in more detail in a later chapter.

Cost **allocation** involves dividing a total cost into parts and assigning the parts to designated cost objects. How should ISI allocate the $38,160 of indirect costs to each of the three departments? First, identify a cost driver for each cost to be allocated.

REALITY BYTES

How does Southwest Airlines know the cost of flying a passenger from Houston, Texas, to Los Angeles, California? The fact is that Southwest does not know the actual cost of flying particular passengers anywhere. There are many indirect costs associated with flying passengers. Some of these include the cost of planes, fuel, pilots, office buildings, and ground personnel. Indeed, besides insignificant food and beverage costs, there are few costs that could be traced directly to customers. Southwest and other airlines are forced to use allocation and averaging to determine the estimated cost of providing transportation services to customers. Estimated rather than actual cost is used for decision-making purposes.

Consider that in its 2008 annual report Southwest reported the average operating expenses of flying one passenger one mile (called a *passenger mile*) were 10.2¢. However, this number was based on 103.3 billion "available passenger miles." In 2008 Southwest operated at 71.2 percent of capacity, not 100 percent, so it was only able to charge passengers for 73.5 billion passenger miles. Thus, its average operating expenses were closer to 14.4¢ for each mile for which they were able to charge. Had they operated at a higher capacity, their average costs would have been lower.

For example, there is a cause-and-effect relationship between store size and rent cost; the larger the building, the higher the rent cost. This relationship suggests that the more floor space a department occupies, the more rent cost that department should bear. To illustrate, assume ISI's store capacity is 23,000 square feet and the women's, men's, and children's departments occupy 12,000, 7,000, and 4,000 square feet, respectively. ISI can achieve a rational allocation of the rent cost using the following two-step process.[1]

Step 1. Compute the *allocation rate* by dividing the *total cost to be allocated* ($18,400 rental fee) by the *cost driver* (23,000 square feet of store space). *The cost driver is also called the* **allocation base.** This computation produces the **allocation rate,** as follows:

Total cost to be allocated   ÷   Cost driver (allocation base)   =   Allocation rate

$18,400 rental fee   ÷   23,000 square feet   = $0.80 per square foot

Step 2. Multiply the *allocation rate* by the *weight of the cost driver* (weight of the base) to determine the allocation *per cost object,* as follows.

Cost Object	Allocation Rate	×	Number of Square Feet	=	Allocation per Cost Object
Women's department	$0.80	×	12,000	=	$ 9,600
Men's department	0.80	×	7,000	=	5,600
Children's department	0.80	×	4,000	=	3,200
Total			23,000		$18,400

---

[1]Other mathematical approaches achieve the same result. This text consistently uses the two-step method described here. Specifically, the text determines allocations by (1) computing a *rate* and (2) multiplying the *rate* by the *weight of the base* (cost driver).

It is also plausible to presume utilities cost is related to the amount of floor space a department occupies. Larger departments will consume more heating, lighting, air conditioning, and so on than smaller departments. Floor space is a reasonable cost driver for utility cost. Based on square footage, ISI can allocate utility cost to each department as follows.

Step 1. Compute the allocation rate by dividing the total cost to be allocated ($2,300 utility cost) by the cost driver (23,000 square feet of store space):

Total cost to be allocated	÷	Cost driver	= Allocation rate
$2,300 utility cost	÷ 23,000 square feet	=	$0.10 per square foot

Step 2. Multiply the *allocation rate* by the *weight of the cost driver* to determine the allocation *per cost object.*

Cost Object	Allocation Rate	×	Number of Square Feet	=	Allocation per Cost Object
Women's department	$0.10	×	12,000	=	$1,200
Men's department	0.10	×	7,000	=	700
Children's department	0.10	×	4,000	=	400
Total			23,000		$2,300

✓ CHECK YOURSELF 12.1

HealthCare, Inc., wants to estimate the cost of operating the three departments (Dermatology, Gynecology, and Pediatrics) that serve patients in its Health Center. Each department performed the following number of patient treatments during the most recent year of operation: Dermatology, 2,600; Gynecology, 3,500; and Pediatrics, 6,200. The annual salary of the Health Center's program administrator is $172,200. How much of the salary cost should HealthCare allocate to the Pediatrics Department?

Answer

Step 1 Compute the *allocation rate.*

Total cost to be allocated	÷	Cost Driver (patient treatments)	=	Allocation rate
$172,200 salary cost	÷	(2,600 + 3,500 + 6,200)	=	$14 per patient treatment

Step 2 Multiply the *allocation rate* by the *weight of the cost driver* (weight of the base) to determine the allocation per *cost object.*

Cost Object	Allocation Rate	×	No. of Treatments	=	Allocation per Cost Object
Pediatrics department	$14	×	6,200	=	$86,800

SELECTING A COST DRIVER

LO 4

Select appropriate cost drivers for allocating indirect costs.

Companies can frequently identify more than one cost driver for a particular indirect cost. For example, ISI's shopping bag cost is related to both the *number of sales transactions* and the *volume of sales dollars.* As either of these potential cost drivers increases, shopping bag usage also increases. The most useful cost driver is the one with the strongest cause-and-effect relationship.

Consider shopping bag usage for T-shirts sold in the children's department versus T-shirts sold in the men's department. Assume ISI studied T-shirt sales during the first week of June and found the following.

Department	Children's	Men's
Number of sales transactions	120	92
Volume of sales dollars	$1,440	$1,612

Given that every sales transaction uses a shopping bag, the children's department uses far more shopping bags than the men's department even though it has a lower volume of sales dollars. A reasonable explanation for this circumstance is that children's T-shirts sell for less than men's T-shirts. The number of sales transactions is the better cost driver because it has a stronger cause-and-effect relationship with shopping bag usage than does the volume of sales dollars. Should ISI therefore use the number of sales transactions to allocate supply cost to the departments? Not necessarily.

The *availability of information* also influences cost driver selection. While the number of sales transactions is the more accurate cost driver, ISI could not use this allocation base unless it maintains records of the number of sales transactions per department. If the store tracks the volume of sales dollars but not the number of transactions, it must use dollar volume even if the number of transactions is the better cost driver. For ISI, sales volume in dollars appears to be the best *available* cost driver for allocating supply cost.

Assuming that sales volume for the women's, men's, and children's departments was $190,000, $110,000, and $60,000, respectively, ISI can allocate the supplies cost as follows.

Step 1. Compute the allocation rate by dividing the total cost to be allocated ($900 supplies cost) by the cost driver ($360,000 total sales volume).

Total cost to be allocated	÷	Cost driver	=	Allocation rate
$900 supplies cost	÷	$360,000 sales volume	=	$0.0025 per sales dollar

Step 2. Multiply the allocation rate by the weight of the cost driver to determine the allocation per cost object.

Cost Object	Allocation Rate	×	Sales Volume	=	Allocation per Cost Object
Women's department	$0.0025	×	$190,000	=	$475
Men's department	0.0025	×	110,000	=	275
Children's department	0.0025	×	60,000	=	150
Total			$360,000		$900

ISI believes sales volume is also the appropriate allocation base for advertising cost. The sales generated in each department were likely influenced by the general advertising campaign. ISI can allocate advertising cost as follows.

Step 1. Compute the allocation rate by dividing the total cost to be allocated ($7,200 advertising cost) by the cost driver ($360,000 total sales volume).

Total cost to be allocated	÷	Cost driver	=	Allocation rate
$7,200 advertising cost	÷	$360,000 sales volume	=	$0.02 per sales dollar

Answers to The Curious Accountant

When we compare the cost that a hospital charges for an aspirin to the price we pay for an aspirin, we are probably not considering the full cost that we incur to purchase aspirin. If someone asks you what you pay for an aspirin, you would probably take the price of a bottle, say $2, and divide it by the number of pills in the bottle, say 100. This would suggest their cost is $0.02 each. Now, consider what it cost to buy the aspirins when all costs are considered. First, there is your time to drive to the store; what do you get paid per hour? Then, there is the cost of operating your automobile. You get the idea; in reality, the cost of an aspirin, from a business perspective, is much more than just the cost of the pills alone.

Exhibit 12.3 shows the income statement of Hospital Corporation of America (HCA) for three recent years. HCA claims to be " . . . one of the leading health care services companies in the United States." In 2008 it operated 271 facilities in 20 states and England. As you can see, while it generated over $28 billion in revenue, it also incurred a lot of expenses. Look at its first two expense categories. Although it incurred $4.6 billion in supplies expenses, it incurred almost two and a half times this amount in compensation expense. In other words, it cost a lot more to have someone deliver the aspirin to your bed than the aspirin itself costs.

In 2008 HCA earned $673 million from its $28.4 billion in revenues. This is a return on sales percentage of 2.4 percent ($.673 ÷ $28.4). Therefore, on a $7 aspirin, HCA would earn 17 cents of profit, which is still not a bad profit for selling one aspirin. As a comparison, in 2008, Walgreens return on sales was 3.7 percent.

EXHIBIT 12.3

HCA, INC.
Consolidated Income Statements
for the Years Ended December 31, 2008, 2007, and 2006
(Dollars in millions, except per share amounts)

	2008	2007	2006
Revenues	$28,374	$26,858	$25,477
Salaries and benefits	11,440	10,714	10,409
Supplies	4,620	4,395	4,322
Other operating expenses	4,554	4,241	4,056
Provision for doubtful accounts	3,409	3,130	2,660
Gains on investments		(8)	(243)
Equity in earnings of affiliates	(223)	(206)	(197)
Depreciation and amortization	1,416	1,426	1,391
Interest expense	2,021	2,215	955
Gains on sales of facilities	(97)	(471)	(205)
Transaction costs			442
Impairment of long-lived assets	64	24	24
Total expenses	27,204	25,460	23,614
Income before minority interests and income taxes	1,170	1,398	1,863
Minority interests in earnings of consolidated entities	229	208	201
Income before income taxes	941	1,190	1,662
Provision for income taxes	268	316	626
Net income	$ 673	$ 874	$ 1,036

Step 2. Multiply the allocation rate by the weight of the cost driver to determine the allocation per cost object.

Cost Object	Allocation Rate	×	Sales Volume	=	Allocation per Cost Object
Women's department	$0.02	×	$190,000	=	$3,800
Men's department	0.02	×	110,000	=	2,200
Children's department	0.02	×	60,000	=	1,200
Total			$360,000		$7,200

There is no strong cause-and-effect relationship between the store manager's salary and the departments. ISI pays the store manager the same salary regardless of sales level, square footage of store space, number of labor hours, or any other identifiable variable. Because no plausible cost driver exists, ISI must allocate the store manager's salary arbitrarily. Here the manager's salary is simply divided equally among the departments as follows.

Step 1. Compute the allocation rate by dividing the total cost to be allocated ($9,360 manager's monthly salary) by the allocation base (number of departments).

Total cost to be allocated ÷ Cost driver = Allocation rate

$9,360 store manager's salary ÷ 3 departments = $3,120 per department

Step 2. Multiply the allocation rate by the weight of the cost driver to determine the allocation per cost object.

Cost Object	Allocation Rate	×	Number of Departments	=	Allocation per Cost Object
Women's department	$3,120	×	1	=	$3,120
Men's department	3,120	×	1	=	3,120
Children's department	3,120	×	1	=	3,120
Total			3		$9,360

As the allocation of the store manager's salary demonstrates, many allocations are arbitrary or based on a weak relationship between the allocated cost and the allocation base (cost driver). Managers must use care when making decisions using allocated costs.

Behavioral Implications

Using the indirect cost allocations just discussed, Exhibit 12.4 shows the profit each department generated in January. ISI paid the three departmental managers bonuses based on each department's contribution to profitability. The store manager noticed an immediate change in the behavior of the departmental managers. For example, the manager of the women's department offered to give up 1,000 square feet of floor space because she believed reducing the selection of available products would not reduce sales significantly. Customers would simply buy different brands. Although sales would not decline dramatically, rent and utility cost allocations to the women's department would decline, increasing the profitability of the department.

EXHIBIT 12.4

Profit Analysis by Department

	Department			
	Women's	Men's	Children's	Total
Sales	$190,000	$110,000	$60,000	$360,000
Cost of goods sold	(120,000)	(58,000)	(38,000)	(216,000)
Sales commissions	(9,500)	(5,500)	(3,000)	(18,000)
Dept. managers' salary	(5,000)	(4,200)	(2,800)	(12,000)
Depreciation	(7,000)	(5,000)	(4,000)	(16,000)
Store manager's salary	(3,120)	(3,120)	(3,120)	(9,360)
Rental fee for store	(9,600)	(5,600)	(3,200)	(18,400)
Utilities	(1,200)	(700)	(400)	(2,300)
Advertising	(3,800)	(2,200)	(1,200)	(7,200)
Supplies	(475)	(275)	(150)	(900)
Departmental profit	$ 30,305	$ 25,405	$ 4,130	$ 59,840

In contrast, the manager of the children's department wanted the extra space. He believed the children's department was losing sales because it did not have enough floor space to display a competitive variety of merchandise. Customers came to the store to shop at the women's department, but they did not come specifically for children's wear. With additional space, the children's department could carry items that would draw customers to the store specifically to buy children's clothing. He believed the extra space would increase sales enough to cover the additional rent and utility cost allocations.

The store manager was pleased with the emphasis on profitability that resulted from tracing and assigning costs to specific departments.

EFFECTS OF COST BEHAVIOR ON SELECTING THE MOST APPROPRIATE COST DRIVER

Select appropriate cost drivers for allocating indirect costs.

As previously mentioned, indirect costs may exhibit variable or fixed cost behavior patterns. Failing to consider the effects of cost behavior when allocating indirect costs can lead to significant distortions in product cost measurement. We examine the critical relationships between cost behavior and cost allocation in the next section of the text.

Using Volume Measures to Allocate Variable Overhead Costs

A *causal relationship* exists between variable overhead product costs (indirect materials, indirect labor, inspection costs, utilities, etc.) and the volume of production. For example, the cost of indirect materials such as glue, staples, screws, nails, and varnish will increase or decrease in proportion to the number of desks a furniture manufacturing company makes. *Volume measures are good cost drivers* for allocating variable overhead costs.

Volume can be expressed by such measures as the number of units produced, the number of labor hours worked, or the amount of *direct* materials used in production. Given the variety of possible volume measures, how does management identify the most appropriate cost driver (allocation base) for assigning particular overhead costs? Consider the case of Filmier Furniture Company.

Using Units as the Cost Driver

During the most recent year, Filmier Furniture Company produced 4,000 chairs and 1,000 desks. It incurred $60,000 of *indirect materials* cost during the period. How much of this cost should Filmier allocate to chairs versus desks? Using number of units as the cost driver produces the following allocation.

Step 1. Compute the allocation rate.

Total cost to be allocated ÷ Cost driver = Allocation rate

$60,000 indirect materials cost ÷ 5,000 units = $12 per unit

Step 2. Multiply the allocation rate by the weight of the cost driver to determine the allocation per cost object.

Product	Allocation Rate	×	Number of Units Produced	=	Allocated Cost
Desks	$12	×	1,000	=	$12,000
Chairs	12	×	4,000	=	48,000
Total			5,000	=	$60,000

Using Direct Labor Hours as the Cost Driver

Using the number of units as the cost driver assigns an *equal amount* ($12) of indirect materials cost to each piece of furniture. However, if Filmier uses more indirect materials to make a desk than to make a chair, assigning the same amount of indirect materials cost to each is inaccurate. Assume Filmier incurs the following direct costs to make chairs and desks.

	Desks	Chairs	Total
Direct labor hours	3,500 hrs.	2,500 hrs.	6,000 hrs.
Direct materials cost	$1,000,000	$500,000	$1,500,000

Both direct labor hours and direct materials cost are volume measures that indicate Filmier uses more indirect materials to make a desk than a chair. It makes sense that the amount of direct labor used is related to the amount of indirect materials used. Because production workers use materials to make furniture, it is plausible to assume that the more hours they work, the more materials they use. Using this reasoning, Filmier could assign the indirect materials cost to the chairs and desks as follows.

Step 1. Compute the allocation rate.

Total cost to be allocated ÷ Cost driver = Allocation rate

$60,000 indirect materials cost ÷ 6,000 hours = $10 per hour

Step 2. Multiply the allocation rate by the weight of the cost driver.

Product	Allocation Rate	×	Number of Labor Hours	=	Allocated Cost
Desks	$10.00	×	3,500	=	$35,000
Chairs	10.00	×	2,500	=	25,000
Total			6,000	=	$60,000

Basing the allocation on labor hours rather than number of units assigns a significantly larger portion of the indirect materials cost to desks ($35,000 versus $12,000). Is this allocation more accurate? Suppose the desks, but not the chairs, require elaborate, labor-intensive carvings. A significant portion of the labor is then not related to consuming indirect materials (glue, staples, screws, nails, and varnish). It would therefore be inappropriate to allocate the indirect materials cost based on direct labor hours.

Using Direct Material Dollars as the Cost Driver

If labor hours is an inappropriate allocation base, Filmier can consider direct material usage, measured in material dollars, as the allocation base. It is likely that the more lumber (direct material) Filmier uses, the more glue, nails, and so forth (indirect materials) it uses. It is reasonable to presume direct materials usage drives indirect materials usage. Using direct materials dollars as the cost driver for indirect materials produces the following allocation.

Step 1. Compute the allocation rate.

$$\text{Total cost to be allocated} \div \text{Cost driver} = \text{Allocation rate}$$

$$\text{\$60,000 indirect materials cost} \div \text{\$1,500,000 direct material dollars} = \text{\$0.04 per direct material dollars}$$

Step 2. Multiply the allocation rate by the weight of the cost driver.

Product	Allocation Rate	×	Number of Direct Material Dollars	=	Allocated Cost
Desks	$0.04	×	$1,000,000	=	$40,000
Chairs	0.04	×	500,000	=	20,000
Total			$1,500,000	=	$60,000

Selecting the Best Cost Driver

Which of the three volume-based cost drivers (units, labor hours, or direct material dollars) results in the most accurate allocation of the overhead cost? Management must use judgment to decide. In this case, direct material dollars appears to have the most convincing relationship to indirect materials usage. If the cost Filmier was allocating were fringe benefits, however, direct labor hours would be a more appropriate cost driver. If the cost Filmier was allocating were machine maintenance cost, a different volume-based cost driver, machine hours, would be an appropriate base. The most accurate allocations of indirect costs may actually require using multiple cost drivers.

✓ CHECK YOURSELF 12.2

Boston Boat Company builds custom sailboats for customers. During the current accounting period, the company built five different-sized boats that ranged in cost from $35,000 to $185,000. The company's manufacturing overhead cost for the period was $118,000. Would you recommend using the number of units (boats) or direct labor hours as the base for allocating the overhead cost to the five boats? Why?

Answer   Using the number of units as the allocation base would assign the same amount of overhead cost to each boat. Because larger boats require more overhead cost (supplies, utilities, equipment, etc.) than smaller boats, there is no logical link between the number of boats and the amount of overhead cost required to build a particular boat. In contrast, there is a logical link between direct labor hours used and overhead cost incurred. The more labor used, the more supplies, utilities, equipment, and so on used. Because larger boats require more direct labor than smaller boats, using direct labor hours as the allocation base would allocate more overhead cost to larger boats and less overhead cost to smaller boats, producing a logical overhead allocation. Therefore, Boston should use direct labor hours as the allocation base.

Allocating Fixed Overhead Costs

Fixed costs present a different cost allocation problem. By definition, the volume of production does not drive fixed costs. Suppose Lednicky Bottling Company rents its manufacturing facility for $28,000 per year. The rental cost is fixed regardless of how much product Lednicky bottles. However, Lednicky may still use a volume-based cost driver as the allocation base. The object of allocating fixed costs to products is to distribute a *rational share* of the overhead cost to each product. Selecting an allocation base that spreads total overhead cost equally over total production often produces a rational distribution. For example, assume Lednicky produced 2,000,000 bottles of apple juice during 2011. If it sold 1,800,000 bottles of the juice during 2011, how much of the $28,000 of rental cost should Lednicky allocate to ending inventory and how much to cost of goods sold? A rational allocation follows.

Step 1.   Compute the allocation rate.

Total cost to be allocated   ÷   Allocation base (cost driver)   =   Allocation rate

$28,000 rental cost   ÷   2,000,000 units   = $0.014 per bottle of juice

Because the base (number of units) used to allocate the cost does not drive the cost, it is sometimes called an *allocation base* instead of a *cost driver*. However, many managers use the term cost driver in conjunction with fixed cost even though that usage is technically inaccurate. The terms allocation base and cost driver are frequently used interchangeably.

Step 2.   Multiply the allocation rate by the weight of the cost driver.

Financial Statement Item	Allocation Rate	×	Number of Bottles	=	Allocated Cost
Inventory	$0.014	×	200,000	=	$ 2,800
Cost of goods sold	0.014	×	1,800,000	=	25,200

Using number of units as the allocation base assigns equal amounts of the rental cost to each unit of product. Equal allocation is appropriate so long as the units are homogeneous. If the units are not identical, however, Lednicky may need to choose a different allocation base to rationally distribute the rental cost. For example, if some of the bottles are significantly larger than others, Lednicky may find using some physical measure, like liters of direct material used, to be a more appropriate allocation base. Whether an indirect cost is fixed or variable, selecting the most appropriate allocation base requires sound reasoning and judgment.

ALLOCATING COSTS TO SOLVE TIMING PROBLEMS

Allocate costs to solve timing problems.

Under certain circumstances products may be made before or after the costs associated with making them have been incurred. Suppose, for example, premiums for an annual insurance policy are paid in March. The insurance cost benefits the products made in the months before and after March as well as those produced in March. Allocation can be used to spread the insurance cost over products made during the entire accounting period rather than charging the total cost only to products made in March.

Monthly fluctuations in production volume complicate fixed cost allocations. To illustrate, assume Grave Manufacturing pays its production supervisor a monthly salary of $3,000. Furthermore, assume Grave makes 800 units of product in January and 1,875 in February. How much salary cost should Grave assign to the products made in January and February, respectively? The allocation seems simple. Just divide the $3,000 monthly salary cost by the number of units of product made each month as follows.

January $3,000 ÷   800 units = $3.75 cost per unit

February $3,000 ÷ 1,875 units = $1.60 cost per unit

If Grave Manufacturing based a cost-plus pricing decision on these results, it would price products made in January significantly higher than products made in February. It is likely such price fluctuations would puzzle and drive away customers. Grave needs an allocation base that will spread the annual salary cost evenly over annual production. A timing problem exists, however, because Grave must allocate the salary cost before the end of the year. In order to price its products, Grave needs to know the allocated amount before the actual cost information is available. Grave can manage the timing problem by using estimated rather than actual costs.

Grave Manufacturing can *estimate* the annual cost of the supervisor's salary (indirect labor) as $36,000 ($3,000 × 12 months). The *actual* cost of indirect labor may differ because the supervisor might receive a pay raise or be replaced with a person who earns less. Based on current information, however, $36,000 is a reasonable estimate of the annual indirect labor cost. Grave must also estimate total annual production volume. Suppose Grave produced 18,000 units last year and expects no significant change in the current year. It can allocate indirect labor cost for January and February as follows.

Step 1. Compute the allocation rate.

Total cost to be allocated ÷ Allocation base = Allocation rate
(cost driver)

$36,000   ÷   18,000 units = $2.00 per unit

Step 2. Multiply the rate by the weight of the base (number of units per month) to determine how much of the salary cost to allocate to each month's production.

Month	Allocation Rate	×	Number of Units Produced	=	Allocation per Month
January	$2.00	×	800	=	$1,600
February	2.00	×	1,875	=	3,750

Grave Manufacturing will add these indirect cost allocations to other product costs to determine the total estimated product cost to use in cost-plus pricing or other managerial decisions.

Because the overhead allocation rate is determined *before* actual cost and volume data are available, it is called the **predetermined overhead rate.** Companies use predetermined overhead rates for product costing estimates and pricing decisions during a year, but they must use actual costs in published year-end financial statements. If necessary, companies adjust their accounting records at year-end when they have used estimated data on an interim basis. The procedures for making such adjustments are discussed in a later chapter.

AGGREGATING AND DISAGGREGATING INDIVIDUAL COSTS INTO COST POOLS

Allocating *individually* every single indirect cost a company incurs would be tedious and not particularly useful relative to the benefit obtained. Instead, companies frequently accumulate many individual costs into a single **cost pool.** The total of the pooled cost is then allocated to the cost objects. For example, a company may accumulate costs for gas, water, electricity, and telephone service into a single utilities cost pool. It would then allocate the total cost in the utilities cost pool to the cost objects rather than individually allocating each of the four types of utility costs.

How far should pooling costs go? Why not pool utility costs with indirect labor costs? If the forces driving the utility costs are different from the forces driving the labor costs, pooling the costs will likely reduce the reliability of any associated cost allocations. To promote accuracy, pooling should be limited to costs with common cost drivers.

Costs that have been pooled for one purpose may require disaggregation for a different purpose. Suppose all overhead costs are pooled for the purpose of determining the cost of making a product. Further, suppose that making the product requires two processes that are performed in different departments. A cutting department makes heavy use of machinery to cut raw materials into product parts. An assembly department uses human labor to assemble the parts into a finished product. Now suppose the objective changes from determining the cost of making the product to determining the cost of operating each department. Under these circumstances, it may be necessary to disaggregate the total overhead cost into smaller pools such as a utility cost pool, an indirect labor cost pool, and so on so that different drivers can be used to allocate these costs to the two departments.

LO 6

Explain the benefits and detriments of allocating pooled costs.

COST ALLOCATION: THE HUMAN FACTOR

Cost allocations significantly affect individuals. They may influence managers' performance evaluations and compensation. They may dictate the amount of resources various departments, divisions, and other organizational subunits receive. Control over resources usually offers managers prestige and influence over organization operations. The following scenario illustrates the emotional impact and perceptions of fairness of cost allocation decisions.

LO 7

Recognize the effects of cost allocation on employee motivation.

Using Cost Allocations in a Budgeting Decision

Sharon Southport, dean of the School of Business at a major state university, is in dire need of a budgeting plan. Because of cuts in state funding, the money available to the School of Business for copying costs next year will be reduced substantially. Dean Southport supervises four departments: management, marketing, finance, and accounting. The Dean knows the individual department chairpersons will be unhappy and frustrated with the deep cuts they face.

Using Cost Drivers to Make Allocations

To address the allocation of copying resources, Dean Southport decided to meet with the department chairs. She explained that the total budgeted for copying costs will be $36,000. Based on past usage, department allocations would be as follows: $12,000 for management, $10,000 for accounting, $8,000 for finance, and $6,000 for marketing.

Dr. Bill Thompson, the management department chair, immediately protested that his department could not operate on a $12,000 budget for copy costs. Management has more faculty members than any other department. Dr. Thompson argued that copy costs are directly related to the number of faculty members, so copy funds should be allocated based on the number of faculty members. Dr. Thompson suggested that number of faculty members rather than past usage should be used as the allocation base.

Because the School of Business has 72 faculty members (29 in management, 16 in accounting, 12 in finance, and 15 in marketing), the allocation should be as follows.

Step 1. Compute the allocation rate.

Total cost to be allocated ÷ Cost driver = Allocation rate

$36,000 ÷ 72 = $500 per faculty member

Step 2. Multiply the rate by the weight of the driver (the number of faculty per department) to determine the allocation per object (department).

Department	Allocation Rate	×	Number of Faculty	=	Allocation per Department	Allocation Based on Past Usage
Management	$500	×	29		$14,500	$12,000
Accounting	500	×	16		8,000	10,000
Finance	500	×	12		6,000	8,000
Marketing	500	×	15		7,500	6,000
Total					$36,000	$36,000

Seeing these figures, Dr. Bob Smethers, chair of the accounting department, questioned the accuracy of using the number of faculty members as the cost driver. Dr. Smethers suggested the number of *students* rather than the number of *faculty members* drives the cost of copying. He argued that most copying results from duplicating syllabi, exams, and handouts. The accounting department teaches mass sections of introductory accounting that have extremely high student/teacher ratios. Because his department teaches more students, it spends more on copying costs even though it has fewer faculty members. Dr. Smethers recomputed the copy cost allocation as follows.

Step 1. Compute the allocation rate based on number of students. University records indicate that the School of Business taught 1,200 students during the most recent academic year. The allocation rate (copy cost per student) follows.

Total cost to be allocated ÷ Cost driver = Allocation rate

$36,000 ÷ 1,200 = $30 per student

Step 2. Multiply the rate by the weight of the driver (number of students taught by each department) to determine the allocation per object (department).

Department	Allocation Rate	×	Number of Students	=	Allocation per Department	Allocation Based on Past Usage
Management	$30	×	330		$ 9,900	$12,000
Accounting	30	×	360		10,800	10,000
Finance	30	×	290		8,700	8,000
Marketing	30	×	220		6,600	6,000
Total					$36,000	$36,000

Choosing the Best Cost Driver

Dr. Thompson objected vigorously to using the number of students as the cost driver. He continued to argue that the size of the faculty is a more appropriate allocation base. The chair of the finance department sided with Dr. Smethers, the chair of the marketing department kept quiet, and the dean had to settle the dispute.

Dean Southport recognized that the views of the chairpersons were influenced by self-interest. The allocation base affects the amount of resources available to each department. Furthermore, the dean recognized that the size of the faculty does drive some of the copying costs. For example, the cost of copying manuscripts that faculty submit for publication relates to faculty size. The more articles faculty submit, the higher the copying cost. Nevertheless, the dean decided the number of students has the most significant impact on copying costs. She also wanted to encourage faculty members to minimize the impact of funding cuts on student services. Dean Southport therefore decided to allocate copying costs based on the number of students taught by each department. Dr. Thompson stormed angrily out of the meeting. The dean developed a budget by assigning the available funds to each department using the number of students as the allocation base.

Controlling Emotions

Dr. Thompson's behavior may relieve his frustration but it doesn't indicate clear thinking. Dean Southport recognized that Dr. Thompson's contention that copy costs were related to faculty size had some merit. Had Dr. Thompson offered a compromise rather than an emotional outburst, he might have increased his department's share of the funds. Perhaps a portion of the allocation could have been based on the number of faculty members with the balance allocated based on the number of students. Had Dr. Thompson controlled his anger, the others might have agreed to compromise. Technical expertise in computing numbers is of little use without the interpersonal skills to persuade others. Accountants may provide numerical measurements, but they should never forget the impact of their reports on the people in the organization.

A Look Back

Managers need to know the costs of products, processes, departments, activities, and so on. The target for which accountants attempt to determine cost is a *cost object*. Knowing the cost of specific objects enables management to control costs, evaluate performance, and price products. *Direct costs* can be cost-effectively traced to a cost object. *Indirect costs* cannot be easily traced to designated cost objects.

The same cost can be direct or indirect, depending on the cost object to which it is traced. For example, the salary of a Burger King restaurant manager can be directly traced to a particular store but cannot be traced to particular food items made and sold in the store. Classifying a cost as direct or indirect is independent of whether the cost behaves as fixed or variable; it is also independent of whether the cost is relevant to a given decision. A direct cost could be either fixed or variable or either relevant or irrelevant, depending on the context and the designated cost object.

Indirect costs are assigned to cost objects using *cost allocation*. Allocation divides an indirect cost into parts and distributes the parts among the relevant cost objects. Companies frequently allocate costs to cost objects in proportion to the *cost drivers* that cause the cost to be incurred. The first step in allocating an indirect cost is to determine the allocation rate by dividing the total cost to be allocated by the chosen cost driver. The next step is to multiply the allocation rate by the amount of the cost driver for a particular object. The result is the amount of indirect cost to assign to the cost object.

A particular indirect cost may be related to more than one driver. The best cost driver is the one that most accurately reflects the amount of the resource used by the cost object. Objects that consume the most resources should be allocated a proportionately greater share of the costs. If no suitable cost driver exists, companies may use arbitrary allocations such as dividing a total cost equally among cost objects.

Cost allocations have behavioral implications. Using inappropriate cost drivers can distort allocations and lead managers to make choices that are detrimental to the company's profitability.

A Look Forward

The next chapter introduces the concept of *cost relevance*. Applying the concepts you have learned to real-world business problems can be challenging. Frequently, so much data is available that it is difficult to distinguish important from useless information. The next chapter will help you learn to identify information that is relevant in a variety of short-term decision-making scenarios including special offers, outsourcing, segment elimination, and asset replacement.

A step-by-step audio-narrated series of slides is provided on the text website at www.mhhe.com/edmondssurvey3e.

SELF-STUDY REVIEW PROBLEM

New budget constraints have pressured Body Perfect Gym to control costs. The owner of the gym, Mr. Ripple, has notified division managers that their job performance evaluations will be highly influenced by their ability to minimize costs. The gym has three divisions: weight lifting, aerobics, and spinning. The owner has formulated a report showing how much it cost to operate each of the three divisions last year. In preparing the report, Mr. Ripple identified several indirect costs that must be allocated among the divisions. These indirect costs are $4,200 of laundry expense, $48,000 of supplies, $350,000 of office rent, $50,000 of janitorial services, and $120,000 for administrative salaries. To provide a reasonably accurate cost allocation, Mr. Ripple has identified several potential cost drivers. These drivers and their association with each division follow.

Cost Driver	Weight Lifting	Aerobics	Spinning	Total
Number of participants	26	16	14	56
Number of instructors	10	8	6	24
Square feet of gym space	12,000	6,000	7,000	25,000
Number of staff	2	2	1	5

Required

a. Identify the appropriate cost objects.

b. Identify the most appropriate cost driver for each indirect cost, and compute the allocation rate for assigning each indirect cost to the cost objects.

c. Determine the amount of supplies expense that should be allocated to each of the three divisions.

d. The spinning manager wants to use the number of staff rather than the number of instructors as the allocation base for the supplies expense. Explain why the spinning manager would take this position.

e. Identify two cost drivers other than your choice for Requirement b that could be used to allocate the cost of the administrative salaries to the three divisions.

Solution to Requirement a

The objective is to determine the cost of operating each division. Therefore, the cost objects are the three divisions (weight lifting, aerobics, and spinning).

Solution to Requirement b

The costs, appropriate cost drivers, and allocation rates for assigning the costs to the departments follow.

Cost	Base	Computation	Allocation Rate
Laundry expense	Number of participants	$ 4,200 ÷ 56	$75 per participant
Supplies	Number of instructors	48,000 ÷ 24	$2,000 per instructor
Office rent	Square feet	350,000 ÷ 25,000	$14 per square foot
Janitorial service	Square feet	50,000 ÷ 25,000	$2 per square foot
Administrative salaries	Number of divisions	120,000 ÷ 3	$40,000 per division

There are other logical cost drivers. For example, the cost of supplies could be allocated based on the number of staff. It is also logical to use a combination of cost drivers. For example, the allocation for the cost of supplies could be based on the combined number of instructors and staff. For this problem, we assumed that Mr. Ripple chose the number of instructors as the base for allocating supplies expense.

Solution to Requirement c

Department	Cost to Be Allocated	Allocation Rate	×	Weight of Base	=	Amount Allocated
Weight lifting	Supplies	$2,000	×	10	=	$20,000
Aerobics	Supplies	2,000	×	8	=	16,000
Spinning	Supplies	2,000	×	6	=	12,000
Total						$48,000

Solution to Requirement d

If the number of staff were used as the allocation base, the allocation rate for supplies would be as follows.

$$\$48,000 \div 5 \text{ staff} = \$9,600 \text{ per staff member}$$

Using this rate, the total cost of supplies would be allocated among the three divisions as follows.

Department	Cost to Be Allocated	Allocation Rate	×	Weight of Base	=	Amount Allocated
Weight lifting	Supplies	$9,600	×	2	=	$19,200
Aerobics	Supplies	9,600	×	2	=	19,200
Spinning	Supplies	9,600	×	1	=	9,600
Total						$48,000

By using the number of staff as the allocation base instead of the number of instructors, the amount of overhead cost allocated to the spinning division falls from $12,000 to $9,600. Because managers are evaluated based on minimizing costs, it is clearly in the spinning manager's self-interest to use the number of staff as the allocation base.

Solution to Requirement e

Among other possibilities, bases for allocating the administrative salaries include the number of participants, the number of lessons, or the number of instructors.

KEY TERMS

Allocation 434
Allocation base 435
Allocation rate 435
Common costs 434
Controllable costs 434
Cost accumulation 432

Cost allocation 433
Cost driver 432
Cost objects 432
Cost pool 445
Cost tracing 433
Direct cost 433

Indirect cost 433
Overhead costs 433
Predetermined overhead
rate 445

QUESTIONS

1. What is a cost object? Identify four different cost objects in which an accountant would be interested.

2. Why is cost accumulation imprecise?

3. If the cost object is a manufactured product, what are the three major cost categories to accumulate?

4. What is a direct cost? What criteria are used to determine whether a cost is a direct cost?

5. Why are the terms *direct cost* and *indirect cost* independent of the terms *fixed cost* and *variable cost?* Give an example to illustrate.

6. Give an example of why the statement, "All direct costs are avoidable," is incorrect.

7. What are the important factors in determining the appropriate cost driver to use in allocating a cost?

8. How is an allocation rate determined? How is an allocation made?

9. In a manufacturing environment, which costs are direct and which are indirect in product costing?

10. Why are some manufacturing costs not directly traceable to products?

11. What is the objective of allocating indirect manufacturing overhead costs to the product?

12. On January 31, the managers of Integra Inc. seek to determine the cost of producing their product during January for product pricing and control purposes. The company can easily determine the costs of direct materials and direct labor used in January production, but many fixed indirect costs are not affected by the level of production activity and have not yet been incurred. The managers can reasonably estimate the overhead costs for the year based on the fixed indirect costs incurred in past periods. Assume the managers decide to allocate an equal amount of these estimated costs to the products produced each month. Explain why this practice may not provide a reasonable estimate of product costs in January.

13. Respond to the following statement: "The allocation base chosen is unimportant. What is important in product costing is that overhead costs be assigned to production in a specific period by an allocation process."

14. Larry Kwang insists that the costs of his school's fund-raising project should be determined after the project is complete. He argues that only after the project is complete can its costs be determined accurately and that it is a waste of time to try to estimate future costs. Georgia Sundum counters that waiting until the project is complete

will not provide timely information for planning expenditures. How would you arbitrate this discussion? Explain the trade-offs between accuracy and timeliness.

15. Define the term *cost pool*. How are cost pools important in allocating costs?

MULTIPLE-CHOICE QUESTIONS

Multiple-choice questions are provided on the text website at www.mhhe.com/edmondssurvey3e.

EXERCISES

All applicable Exercises are available with McGraw-Hill's *Connect Accounting*.

Exercise 12-1   *Allocating costs between divisions*   LO 3

Sims Services Company (SSC) has 50 employees, 38 of whom are assigned to Division A and 12 to Division B. SSC incurred $296,000 of fringe benefits cost during 2011.

Required

Determine the amount of the fringe benefits cost to be allocated to Division A and to Division B.

Exercise 12-2   *Direct versus indirect costs*   LO 2

Jeelani Construction Company is composed of two divisions: (1) Home Construction and (2) Commercial Construction. The Home Construction Division is in the process of building 12 houses and the Commercial Construction Division is working on 3 projects. Cost items of the company follow.

Company president's salary
Depreciation on crane used in commercial construction
Depreciation on home office building
Salary of corporate office manager
Wages of workers assigned to a specific construction project
Supplies used by the Commercial Construction Division
Labor on a particular house
Salary of the supervisor of commercial construction projects
Supplies, such as glue and nails, used by the Home Construction Division
Cost of building permits
Materials used in commercial construction projects
Depreciation on home building equipment (small tools such as hammers or saws)

Required

a. Identify each cost as being a direct or indirect cost assuming the cost objects are the individual products (houses or projects).

b. Identify each cost as being a direct or indirect cost, assuming the cost objects are the two divisions.

c. Identify each cost as being a direct or indirect cost assuming the cost object is Jeelani Construction Company as a whole.

Exercise 12-3   *Allocating overhead cost among products*   LO 3, 4

Dew Hats Inc. manufactures three different styles of hats: Vogue, Beauty, and Glamour. Dew expects to incur $576,000 of overhead cost during the next fiscal year. Other budget information follows:

	Vogue	Beauty	Glamour	Total
Direct labor hours	2,000	4,000	6,000	12,000
Machine hours	1,200	1,400	1,400	4,000

Required

a. Use direct labor hours as the cost driver to compute the allocation rate and the budgeted overhead cost for each product.

b. Use machine hours as the cost driver to compute the allocation rate and the budgeted overhead cost for each product.

c. Describe a set of circumstances where it would be more appropriate to use direct labor hours as the allocation base.

d. Describe a set of circumstances where it would be more appropriate to use machine hours as the allocation base.

LO 3, 4

Exercise 12-4   *Allocating overhead costs among products*

Nevin Company makes three products in its factory: plastic cups, plastic tablecloths, and plastic bottles. The expected overhead costs for the next fiscal year include the following.

Factory manager's salary	$260,000
Factory utility cost	121,000
Factory supplies	56,000
Total overhead costs	$437,000

Nevin uses machine hours as the cost driver to allocate overhead costs. Budgeted machine hours for the products are as follows.

Cups	420 hours
Tablecloths	740
Bottles	1,140
Total machine hours	2,300

Required

a. Allocate the budgeted overhead costs to the products.

b. Provide a possible explanation as to why Nevin chose machine hours, instead of labor hours, as the allocation base.

LO 3, 4

Exercise 12-5   *Allocating costs among products*

Deka Construction Company expects to build three new homes during a specific accounting period. The estimated direct materials and labor costs are as follows.

Expected Costs	Home 1	Home 2	Home 3
Direct labor	$60,000	$ 90,000	$170,000
Direct materials	90,000	130,000	180,000

Assume Deka needs to allocate two major overhead costs ($40,000 of employee fringe benefits and $20,000 of indirect materials costs) among the three jobs.

Required

Choose an appropriate cost driver for each of the overhead costs and determine the total cost of each home.

LO 3, 5

Exercise 12-6   *Allocating to smooth cost over varying levels of production*

Production workers for Nabors Manufacturing Company provided 280 hours of labor in January and 500 hours in February. Nabors expects to use 4,000 hours of labor during the year. The rental fee for the manufacturing facility is $8,000 per month.

Required

Explain why allocation is needed. Based on this information, how much of the rental cost should be allocated to the products made in January and to those made in February?

Exercise 12-7   *Allocating to solve a timing problem*

Production workers for Bianco Manufacturing Company provided 3,600 hours of labor in January and 1,900 hours in February. The company, whose operation is labor intensive, expects to use 32,000 hours of labor during the year. Bianco paid a $8,000 annual premium on July 1 of the prior year for an insurance policy that covers the manufacturing facility for the following 12 months.

Required

Explain why allocation is needed. Based on this information, how much of the insurance cost should be allocated to the products made in January and to those made in February?

Exercise 12-8   *Allocating a fixed cost*

Stevens Air is a large airline company that pays a customer relations representative $4,000 per month. The representative, who processed 1,000 customer complaints in January and 1,300 complaints in February, is expected to process 12,000 customer complaints during 2012.

Required

a. Determine the total cost of processing customer complaints in January and in February.

b. Explain why allocating the cost of the customer relations representative would or would not be relevant to decision making.

Exercise 12-9   *Allocating overhead cost to accomplish smoothing*

Woods Corporation expects to incur indirect overhead costs of $60,000 per month and direct manufacturing costs of $11 per unit. The expected production activity for the first four months of 2012 is as follows.

	January	February	March	April
Estimated production in units	4,000	7,000	3,000	6,000

Required

a. Calculate a predetermined overhead rate based on the number of units of product expected to be made during the first four months of the year.

b. Allocate overhead costs to each month using the overhead rate computed in Requirement *a*.

c. Calculate the total cost per unit for each month using the overhead allocated in Requirement *b*.

Exercise 12-10   *Pooling overhead costs*

Jasti Manufacturing Company produced 1,200 units of inventory in January 2011. It expects to produce an additional 8,400 units during the remaining 11 months of the year. In other words, total production for 2011 is estimated to be 9,600 units. Direct materials and direct labor costs are $64 and $52 per unit, respectively. Jasti Company expects to incur the following manufacturing overhead costs during 2011.

Production supplies	$ 4,800
Supervisor salary	192,000
Depreciation on equipment	144,000
Utilities	36,000
Rental fee on manufacturing facilities	96,000

Required

a. Combine the individual overhead costs into a cost pool and calculate a predetermined overhead rate assuming the cost driver is number of units.

b. Determine the cost of the 1,200 units of product made in January.

c. Is the cost computed in Requirement *b* actual or estimated? Could Jasti improve accuracy by waiting until December to determine the cost of products?

LO 3, 5

Exercise 12-11 *How fixed cost allocation affects a pricing decision*

Mallett Manufacturing Co. expects to make 30,000 chairs during 2011. The company made 3,200 chairs in January. Materials and labor costs for January were $16,000 and $24,000, respectively. Mallett produced 2,500 chairs in February. Materials and labor costs for February were $8,000 and $12,000, respectively. The company paid the $240,000 annual rental fee on its manufacturing facility on January 1, 2011. Ignore other manufacturing overhead costs.

Required

Assuming that Mallett desires to sell its chairs for cost plus 40 percent of cost, what price should be charged for the chairs produced in January and February?

LO 6

Exercise 12-12 *Cost pools*

Richter Department Stores Inc. has three departments: women's, men's, and children's. The following are the indirect costs related to its operations.

Medical insurance
Salaries of secretaries
Water bill
Vacation pay
Sewer bill
Staples
Natural gas bill
Pens
Ink cartridges
Payroll taxes
Paper rolls for cash registers

Required

a. Organize the costs in the following three pools: indirect materials, indirect labor, and indirect utilities, assuming that each department is a cost object.
b. Identify an appropriate cost driver for each pool.
c. Explain why accountants use cost pools.

LO 7

Exercise 12-13 *Human factor*

Dearman Clinics provides medical care in three departments: internal medicine (IM), pediatrics (PD), and obstetrics gynecology (OB). The estimated costs to run each department follow.

	IM	PD	OB
Physicians	$400,000	$300,000	$200,000
Nurses	80,000	120,000	160,000

Dearman expects to incur $450,000 of indirect (overhead) costs in the next fiscal year.

Required

a. Based on the information provided, name four allocation bases that could be used to assign the overhead cost to each department.
b. Assume the manager of each department is permitted to recommend how the overhead cost should be allocated to the departments. Which of the allocation bases named in Requirement *a* is the manager of OB most likely to recommend? Explain why. What argument may the manager of OB use to justify his choice of the allocation base?
c. Which of the allocation bases would result in the fairest allocation of the overhead cost from the perspective of the company president?
d. Explain how classifying overhead costs into separate pools could improve the fairness of the allocation of the overhead costs.

PROBLEMS

All applicable Problems are available with McGraw-Hill's
Connect Accounting.

Problem 12-14 *Cost accumulation and allocation*

Singh Manufacturing Company makes two different products, M and N. The company's two departments are named after the products; for example, Product M is made in Department M. Singh's accountant has identified the following annual costs associated with these two products.

LO 1, 2, 3, 4, 5

e**X**cel

CHECK FIGURE
c. Price for N: $493.68

Financial data	
Salary of vice president of production division	$180,000
Salary of supervisor Department M	76,000
Salary of supervisor Department N	56,000
Direct materials cost Department M	300,000
Direct materials cost Department N	420,000
Direct labor cost Department M	240,000
Direct labor cost Department N	680,000
Direct utilities cost Department M	120,000
Direct utilities cost Department N	24,000
General factorywide utilities	36,000
Production supplies	36,000
Fringe benefits	138,000
Depreciation	720,000
Nonfinancial data	
Machine hours Department M	5,000
Machine hours Department N	1,000

Required

a. Identify the costs that are (1) direct costs of Department M, (2) direct costs of Department N, and (3) indirect costs.

b. Select the appropriate cost drivers for the indirect costs and allocate these costs to Departments M and N.

c. Determine the total estimated cost of the products made in Departments M and N. Assume that Singh produced 2,000 units of Product M and 4,000 units of Product N during the year. If Singh prices its products at cost plus 40 percent of cost, what price per unit must it charge for Product M and for Product N?

Problem 12-15 *Selecting an appropriate cost driver (What is the base?)*

LO 1, 3, 4

The Vest School of Vocational Technology has organized the school training programs into three departments. Each department provides training in a different area as follows: nursing assistant, dental hygiene, and office technology. The school's owner, Wilma Vest, wants to know how much it costs to operate each of the three departments. To accumulate the total cost for each department, the accountant has identified several indirect costs that must be allocated to each. These costs are $10,080 of telephone expense, $2,016 of supplies expense, $720,000 of office rent, $144,000 of janitorial services, and $150,000 of salary paid to the dean of students. To provide a reasonably accurate allocation of costs, the accountant has identified several possible cost drivers. These drivers and their association with each department follow.

Cost Driver	Department 1	Department 2	Department 3
Number of telephones	28	32	52
Number of faculty members	20	16	12
Square footage of office space	28,800	16,800	12,000
Number of secretaries	2	2	2

Required

a. Identify the appropriate cost objects.

b. Identify the appropriate cost driver for each indirect cost and compute the allocation rate for assigning each indirect cost to the cost objects.

c. Determine the amount of telephone expense that should be allocated to each of the three departments.

d. Determine the amount of supplies expense that should be allocated to Department 3.

e. Determine the amount of office rent that should be allocated to Department 2.

f. Determine the amount of janitorial services cost that should be allocated to Department 1.

g. Identify two cost drivers not listed here that could be used to allocate the cost of the dean's salary to the three departments.

LO 1, 2, 3, 4

Problem 12-16   *Cost allocation in a service industry*

Kirby Airlines is a small airline that occasionally carries overload shipments for the overnight delivery company Never-Fail Inc. Never-Fail is a multimillion-dollar company started by Jack Never immediately after he failed to finish his first accounting course. The company's motto is "We Never-Fail to Deliver Your Package on Time." When Never-Fail has more freight than it can deliver, it pays Kirby to carry the excess. Kirby contracts with independent pilots to fly its planes on a per trip basis. Kirby recently purchased an airplane that cost the company $5,500,000. The plane has an estimated useful life of 25,000,000 miles and a zero salvage value. During the first week in January, Kirby flew two trips. The first trip was a round trip flight from Chicago to San Francisco, for which Kirby paid $350 for the pilot and $300 for fuel. The second flight was a round trip from Chicago to New York. For this trip, it paid $300 for the pilot and $150 for fuel. The round trip between Chicago and San Francisco is approximately 4,400 miles and the round trip between Chicago and New York is 1,600 miles.

Required

a. Identify the direct and indirect costs that Kirby incurs for each trip.

b. Determine the total cost of each trip.

c. In addition to depreciation, identify three other indirect costs that may need to be allocated to determine the cost of each trip.

LO 1, 3, 4

Problem 12-17   *Cost allocation in a manufacturing company*

Hunt Manufacturing Company makes tents that it sells directly to camping enthusiasts through a mail-order marketing program. The company pays a quality control expert $72,000 per year to inspect completed tents before they are shipped to customers. Assume that the company completed 1,600 tents in January and 1,200 tents in February. For the entire year, the company expects to produce 15,000 tents.

Required

a. Explain how changes in the cost driver (number of tents inspected) affect the total amount of fixed inspection cost.

b. Explain how changes in the cost driver (number of tents inspected) affect the amount of fixed inspection cost per unit.

c. If the cost objective is to determine the cost per tent, is the expert's salary a direct or an indirect cost?

d. How much of the expert's salary should be allocated to tents produced in January and February?

LO 1, 4, 7

Problem 12-18   *Fairness and cost pool allocation*

Daniel Manufacturing Company uses two departments to make its products. Department I is a cutting department that is machine intensive and uses very few employees. Machines cut and form parts and then place the finished parts on a conveyor belt that carries them to Department II where they are assembled into finished goods. The assembly department is labor intensive and requires many workers to assemble parts into finished goods. The company's manufacturing facility incurs two significant overhead costs, employee fringe benefits and utility costs. The annual costs of fringe benefits are $252,000 and utility costs are $180,000. The typical consumption patterns for the two departments are as follows.

	Department I	Department II	Total
Machine hours used	16,000	4,000	20,000
Direct labor hours used	5,000	13,000	18,000

The supervisor of each department receives a bonus based on how well the department controls costs. The company's current policy requires using a single activity base (machine hours or labor hours) to allocate the total overhead cost of $432,000.

Required

a. Assume that you are the supervisor of Department I. Choose the allocation base that would minimize your department's share of the total overhead cost. Calculate the amount of overhead that would be allocated to both departments using the base that you selected.

b. Assume that you are the supervisor of Department II. Choose the allocation base that would minimize your department's share of the total overhead cost. Calculate the amount of overhead that would be allocated to both departments using the base that you selected.

c. Assume that you are the plant manager and have the authority to change the company's overhead allocation policy. Formulate an overhead allocation policy that would be fair to the supervisors of both Department I and Department II. Compute the overhead allocations for each department using your policy.

d. Explain why it is necessary to disaggregate the overhead cost pool in order to accomplish fairness.

Problem 12-19   *Allocation to accomplish smoothing*

LO 1, 3, 5

CHECK FIGURES
a. $4
d. March cost: $62

O'Hara Corporation estimated its overhead costs would be $24,000 per month except for January when it pays the $72,000 annual insurance premium on the manufacturing facility. Accordingly, the January overhead costs were expected to be $96,000 ($72,000 + $24,000). The company expected to use 7,000 direct labor hours per month except during July, August, and September when the company expected 9,000 hours of direct labor each month to build inventories for high demand that normally occurs during the holiday season. The company's actual direct labor hours were the same as the estimated hours. The company made 3,500 units of product in each month except July, August, and September in which it produced 4,500 units each month. Direct labor costs were $24 per unit, and direct materials costs were $10 per unit.

Required

a. Calculate a predetermined overhead rate based on direct labor hours.

b. Determine the total allocated overhead cost for January, March, and August.

c. Determine the cost per unit of product for January, March, and August.

d. Determine the selling price for the product, assuming that the company desires to earn a gross margin of $20 per unit.

Problem 12-20   *Allocating indirect costs between products*

LO 1, 3, 5

CHECK FIGURES
a. Cost/unit for EZRecords: $200
b. Cost/unit for ProOffice: $220

Erin Tarver is considering expanding her business. She plans to hire a salesperson to cover trade shows. Because of compensation, travel expenses, and booth rental, fixed costs for a trade show are expected to be $12,000. The booth will be open 30 hours during the trade show. Ms. Tarver also plans to add a new product line, ProOffice, which will cost $180 per package. She will continue to sell the existing product, EZRecords, which costs $100 per package. Ms. Tarver believes that the salesperson will spend approximately 20 hours selling EZRecords and 10 hours marketing ProOffice.

Required

a. Determine the estimated total cost and cost per unit of each product, assuming that the salesperson is able to sell 80 units of EZRecords and 50 units of ProOffice.

b. Determine the estimated total cost and cost per unit of each product, assuming that the salesperson is able to sell 200 units of EZRecords and 100 units of ProOffice.

c. Explain why the cost per unit figures calculated in Requirement *a* are different from the amounts calculated in Requirement *b*. Also explain how the differences in estimated cost per unit will affect pricing decisions.

ANALYZE, THINK, COMMUNICATE

ATC 12-1   Business Applications Case   *Allocating fixed costs at Porsche*

During its fiscal year ending on July 31, 2008, the Dr. Ing. h.c. F. Porsche AG, commonly known as "Porsche," manufactured 105,162 vehicles. During that same year Porsche recorded depreciation on property, plant, and equipment of €281,813,000. (Porsche's financial information is reported in euros, and € is the symbol for the euro.) For the purposes of this problem assume that all of the depreciation related to manufacturing activities.

Required

a. Indicate whether the depreciation charge is a

   (1) Product cost, or a general, selling, and administrative cost.

   (2) Relevant cost with respect to a special order decision.

   (3) Fixed or variable cost relative to the volume of production.

   (4) Direct or indirect if the cost object is the cost of vehicles made in the 2008 fiscal year.

b. Assume that Porsche incurred depreciation of €23,500,000 during each month of the 2008 fiscal year, but that it produced 10,000 vehicles during February and 7,000 during March. Based on monthly costs and production levels, what was the average amount of depreciation cost per vehicle produced during each of these two months, assuming each vehicle was charged the same amount of depreciation?

c. If Porsche had expected to produce 108,000 vehicles during 2008, and had estimated its annual depreciation costs to be €285,000,000, what would have been its predetermined overhead charge per vehicle for depreciation? Explain the advantage of using this amount to determine the cost of manufacturing a car in February and March versus the amounts you computed in Requirement *b*.

d. If Porsche's management had estimated the profit per vehicle based on its budgeted production of 108,000 units, would you expect its actual profit per vehicle to be higher or lower than expected? Explain.

ATC 12-2   Group Assignment   *Selection of the cost driver*

Vulcan College School of Business is divided into three departments, accounting, marketing, and management. Relevant information for each of the departments follows.

Cost Driver	Accounting	Marketing	Management
Number of students	1,400	800	400
Number of classes per semester	64	36	28
Number of professors	20	24	10

Vulcan is a private school that expects each department to generate a profit. It rewards departments for profitability by assigning 20 percent of each department's profits back to that department. Departments have free rein as to how to use these funds. Some departments have used them to supply professors with computer technology. Others have expanded their travel budgets.

The practice has been highly successful in motivating the faculty to control costs. The revenues and direct costs for the year 2011 follow.

	Accounting	Marketing	Management
Revenue	$29,600,000	$16,600,000	$8,300,000
Direct costs	24,600,000	13,800,000	6,600,000

Vulcan allocates to the School of Business $4,492,800 of indirect overhead costs such as administrative salaries and costs of operating the registrar's office and the bookstore.

Required

a. Divide the class into groups and organize the groups into three sections. Assign each section a department. Assume that the dean of the school is planning to assign an equal amount of the college overhead to each department. Have the students in each group prepare a response to the dean's plan. Each group should select a spokesperson who is prepared to answer the following questions.

   (1) Is your group in favor of or opposed to the allocation plan suggested by the dean?

   (2) Does the plan suggested by the dean provide a fair allocation? Why?

   The instructor should lead a discussion designed to assess the appropriateness of the dean's proposed allocation plan.

b. Have each group select the cost driver (allocation base) that best serves the self-interest of the department it represents.

c. Consensus on Requirement *c* should be achieved before completing Requirement *d*. Each group should determine the amount of the indirect cost to be allocated to each department using the cost driver that best serves the self-interest of the department it represents. Have a spokesperson from each section go to the board and show the income statement that would result for each department.

d. Discuss the development of a cost driver(s) that would promote fairness rather than self-interest in allocating the indirect costs.

ATC 12-3   Research Assignment   *Using real-world data from Pepsi Bottling Group*

Use the 2008 Form 10-K for Pepsi Bottling Group to complete the requirements below. Pepsi Bottling Group (PBG) is a separate company from PepsiCo, so do not confuse them. To obtain the Form 10-K you can use the EDGAR system following the instructions in Appendix A, or it can be found under "Investor Relations" link on the company's corporate website: www.pbg.com. The company includes its Form 10-K as a part of its 2008 Annual Report, or it can be found separately under "SEC Filings." Be sure to read carefully the following sections of the document.

Under "Item 1. Business" read subsections titled "Introduction," "Principal Products," "Raw Materials and Other Supplies," and "Seasonality."

In the footnotes section of the report, under "Note 2—Summary of Significant Accounting Policies," read the subsections titled "Advertising and Marketing Costs" and "Shipping and Handling Costs."

"Note 5—Balance Sheet Details" in the footnotes section of the report.

Required

a. Does PBG consider *shipping and handling costs* and *advertising and marketing costs* to be direct or indirect costs in relation to the manufacturing of its products? Explain.

b. Assume that when PBG ships orders of bottled drinks, each shipment includes several different products such as Pepsi, Lipton tea, and Starbucks Frappuccino. If PBG wanted to allocate the shipping costs among the various products, what would be an appropriate cost driver? Explain the rationale for your choice.

c. Assume that PBG incurs some advertising cost that cannot be directly traced to a single product such as Pepsi or Diet Pepsi. If PBG wanted to allocate the advertising costs among the various products being advertised jointly, what would be an appropriate way of making this allocation? Explain the rationale for your choice.

d. As *Note 4* indicates, PBG computes depreciation expense on three separate classes of assets. For which of these classes of assets could its depreciation expense be directly traced to the production of soft drinks? Which class would least likely be traceable to the production of soft drinks? Explain.

e. Based on PBG's discussion of the seasonality of its business, should the depreciation of production equipment recorded in a given month be based on the volume of drinks produced that month, or should the depreciation be one-twelfth of the estimated annual depreciation PBG expects to incur? Explain your answer.

ATC 12-4   Writing Assignment   *Selection of the appropriate cost driver*

Bullions Enterprises, Inc. (BEI), makes gold, silver, and bronze medals used to recognize outstanding athletic performance in regional and national sporting events. The per unit direct costs of producing the medals follow.

	Gold	Silver	Bronze
Direct materials	$300	$130	$ 35
Labor	120	120	120

During 2011, BEI made 1,200 units of each type of medal for a total of 3,600 (1,200 × 3) medals. All medals are created through the same production process, and they are packaged and shipped in identical containers. Indirect overhead costs amounted to $324,000. BEI currently uses the number of units as the cost driver for the allocation of overhead cost. As a result, BEI allocated $90 ($324,000 ÷ 3,600 units) of overhead cost to each medal produced.

Required

The president of the company has questioned the wisdom of assigning the same amount of overhead to each type of medal. He believes that overhead should be assigned on the basis of the cost to produce the medals. In other words, more overhead should be charged to expensive gold medals, less to silver, and even less to bronze. Assume that you are BEI's chief financial officer. Write a memo responding to the president's suggestion.

ATC 12-5   Ethical Dilemma   *Allocation to achieve fairness*

The American Acupuncture Association offers continuing professional education courses for its members at its annual meeting. Instructors are paid a fee for each student attending their courses but are charged a fee for overhead costs that is deducted from their compensation. Overhead costs include fees paid to rent instructional equipment such as overhead projectors, provide supplies to participants, and offer refreshments during coffee breaks. The number of courses offered is used as the allocation base for determining the overhead charge. For example, if overhead costs amount to $5,000 and 25 courses are offered, each course is allocated an overhead charge of $200 ($5,000 ÷ 25 courses). Heidi McCarl, who taught one of the courses, received the following statement with her check in payment for her instructional services.

Instructional fees (20 students × $50 per student)	$1,000
Less: Overhead charge	(200)
Less: Charge for sign language assistant	(240)
Amount due instructor	$ 560

Although Ms. McCarl was well aware that one of her students was deaf and required a sign language assistant, she was surprised to find that she was required to absorb the cost of this service.

Required

a. Given that the Americans with Disabilities Act stipulates that the deaf student cannot be charged for the cost of providing sign language, who should be required to pay the cost of sign language services?

b. Explain how allocation can be used to promote fairness in distributing service costs to the disabled. Describe two ways to treat the $240 cost of providing sign language services that improve fairness.

CHAPTER 13

Relevant Information for Special Decisions

LEARNING OBJECTIVES

After you have mastered the material in this chapter, you will be able to:

1 Identify the characteristics of relevant information.

2 Distinguish between unit-level, batch-level, product-level, and facility-level costs and understand how these costs affect decision making.

3 Make appropriate special order decisions.

4 Make appropriate outsourcing decisions.

5 Make appropriate segment elimination decisions.

6 Make appropriate asset replacement decisions.

CHAPTER OPENING

Mary Daniels paid $25,000 cash to purchase a car that she rents to a relative. The car has a five-year useful life and a $5,000 salvage value. After renting the car for one year, the relative offered to buy the car from Ms. Daniels at a price of $18,000. While talking to her neighbor about the offer, the neighbor said the price was too low. Indeed, the neighbor showed her research data that proved the market value of the car was $19,000 and offered to pay her that amount for the car. Ms. Daniels really wanted to get rid of the car but ultimately decided not to sell it because she did not want to take a loss on the car.[1] Did Ms. Daniels make the right decision?

---

[1]Depreciation is $4,000 [($25,000 − $5,000) ÷ 5] per year. The book value of the car after one year is $21,000 ($25,000 cost − $4,000 accumulated depreciation). If Ms. Daniels accepts the neighbor's $19,000 offer, she will have to recognize a $2,000 loss ($21,000 book value − $19,000 selling price).

Whether Ms. Daniels will be better off selling the car or keeping it is unknown. However, it is certain that she based her decision on irrelevant data. Ms. Daniels incurred a loss when the value of the car dropped. She cannot avoid a loss that already exists. Past mistakes should not affect current decisions. The current value of the car is $19,000. Ms. Daniels's decision is whether to take the money or keep the car. The book value of the car is not relevant.

The Curious Accountant

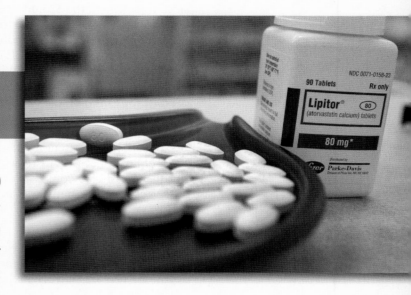

In July 2009, the authors compared the prices of 10 of the top selling prescription drugs at two large on-line pharmacies, one in the United States and one in Canada. The analysis showed the Canadian prices for these 10 popular prescription drugs, such as **Lipitor** and **Zocor**, were only 51 percent of prices charged in the United States.

Major pharmaceutical companies have earnings before tax that average around 25 percent of sales, indicating that their costs average around 75 percent of the prices they charge. In other words, it costs approximately $75 to generate $100 of revenue. Given that drugs are sold in Canada for 51 percent of the U.S. sales price, a drug that is sold in the U.S. for $100 would be sold in Canada for only $51.

How can drugs be sold in Canada for less ($51) than cost ($75)? (Answer on page 470.)

RELEVANT INFORMATION

How can you avoid irrelevant information when making decisions? Two primary characteristics distinguish relevant from useless information. Specifically, **relevant information** (1) differs among the alternatives and (2) is future oriented.

The first characteristic recognizes that relevant information differs for one or more of the alternatives being considered. For example, in the Daniels case the offers to buy the car are relevant because the amounts of the offers are different. Ms. Daniels will receive $18,000 if she accepts the relative's offer or, alternatively, $19,000 if she accepts the neighbor's offer. In other words, the offering price makes a difference to the decision. In contrast, the $25,000 original cost is not relevant because it is the same regardless of whether the car is sold to the relative or the neighbor.

The second characteristic of relevant information is that it impacts the future. "Don't cry over spilt milk." "It's water over the dam." These aphorisms remind people they cannot change the past. With regard to business decisions, the principle means you cannot avoid a cost that has already been incurred. In the Daniels example, the historical cost ($25,000) of the car is not relevant to a decision regarding whether to sell the car today. The current market value of $19,000 is relevant to the decision regarding whether to sell the car today.

It is interesting to note that the two characteristics are merely different views of the same concept because historical information does not differ between the alternatives. In other words, we could say that historical costs are not relevant because they do not differ between alternatives associated with current decisions.

Sunk Cost

Historical costs are frequently called *sunk costs.* Because **sunk costs** have been incurred in past transactions, they cannot be changed and are not relevant for making current decisions. The $25,000 original cost of the car in the Daniels example is a sunk cost.

Why even bother to collect historical information if it is not relevant? Historical information may be useful in predicting the future. A company that earned $5 million last year is more likely to earn $5 million this year than a company that earned $5,000 last year. The predictive capacity is relevant because it provides insight into the future.

Opportunity Costs

An **opportunity cost** is the sacrifice that is incurred in order to obtain an alternative opportunity. For example, in the above case, Ms. Daniels must give up the opportunity to obtain $19,000 in order to keep the car. So, the opportunity cost of owning the car is $19,000. Because this cost differs between the alternatives of owning the car versus selling it and because it affects the present or future, it is relevant to the decision regarding whether to keep or sell the car.

Notice that Ms. Daniels has two offers to sell the car, the relative's $18,000 offer and the neighbor's $19,000. Does this mean that the opportunity cost of keeping the car is $37,000 ($18,000 + $19,000)? No. Opportunity costs are not cumulative. Ms. Daniels really has only one opportunity. If she accepts the neighbor's offer, she must reject the relative's offer or vice versa. Accountants normally measure opportunity cost as the highest value of the available alternatives. In this case, the opportunity cost of keeping the car is $19,000.

✓ CHECK YOURSELF 13.1

Aqua, Inc., makes statues for use in fountains. On January 1, 2010, the company paid $13,500 for a mold to make a particular type of statue. The mold had an expected useful life of four years and a salvage value of $1,500. On January 1, 2012, the mold had a market value of $3,000 and a salvage value of $1,200. The expected useful life did not change. What is the relevant cost of using the mold during 2012?

Answer The relevant cost of using the mold in 2012 is the opportunity cost [(market value − salvage value) ÷ remaining useful life], in this case, ($3,000 − $1,200) ÷ 2 = $900. The book value of the asset and associated depreciation is based on a sunk cost that cannot be avoided because it has already been incurred and therefore is not relevant to current decisions. In contrast, Aqua could avoid the opportunity cost (market value) by selling the mold.

Relevance Is an Independent Concept

The concept of relevance is independent from the concept of cost behavior. In a given circumstance, **relevant costs** could be either fixed or variable. Consider the following illustration. Executives of Better Bakery Products are debating whether to add a new product, either cakes or pies, to the company's line. Projected costs for the two options follow.

Cost of Cakes		Cost of Pies	
Materials (per unit)	$ 1.50	Materials (per unit)	$ 2.00
Direct labor (per unit)	1.00	Direct labor (per unit)	1.00
Supervisor's salary*	25,000.00	Supervisor's salary*	25,000.00
Franchise fee†	50,000.00	Advertising‡	40,000.00

*It will be necessary to hire a new production supervisor at a cost of $25,000 per year.

†Cakes will be distributed under a nationally advertised label. Better Bakery pays an annual franchise fee for the right to use the product label. Because of the established brand name, Better Bakery will not be required to advertise the product.

‡Better Bakery will market the pies under its own name and will advertise the product in the local market in which the product sells.

Which costs are relevant? Fifty cents per unit of the materials can be avoided by choosing cakes instead of pies. A portion of the materials cost is therefore relevant. Labor costs will be one dollar per unit whether Better Bakery makes cakes or pies. Labor cost is therefore not relevant. Although both materials and direct labor are variable costs, one is relevant but the other is not.

REALITY BYTES

Determining what price to charge for their company's goods or services is one of the most difficult decisions that business managers make. Charge too much and customers will go elsewhere. Charge less than customers are willing to pay and they lose the opportunity to earn profits. This problem is especially difficult when managers are deciding if they should reduce (mark down) the price of aging inventory—for example, flowers that are beginning to wilt, fruit that is beginning to overripen, or clothing that is going out of season.

At first managers may be reluctant to mark down the inventory below its cost because this would cause the company to take a loss on the aging inventory. However, the concept of sunk cost applies here. Because the existing inventory has already been purchased, its cost is sunk. Because the cost is sunk it is not relevant to the decision. Does this mean the merchandise should be sold for any price? Not necessarily. The concept of opportunity cost must also be considered.

If the goods are marked down too far, too quickly, they may be sold for less than is possible. The lost potential revenue is an opportunity cost. To minimize the opportunity cost, the amount of a markdown must be the smallest amount necessary to sell the merchandise. The decision is further complicated by qualitative considerations. If a business develops a reputation for repeated markdowns, customers may hesitate to buy goods, thinking that the price will fall further if they only wait a while. The result is a dilemma as to when and how much to mark down aging inventories.

How do managers address this dilemma? Part of the answer has been the use of technology. For years airlines have used computerized mathematical models to help them decide how many seats on a particular flight should be sold at a discount. More recently, retailers began using this same type of modeling software. Such software allows retailers to take fewer markdowns at more appropriate times, thereby resulting in higher overall gross profit margins.

Because Better Bakery must hire a supervisor under either alternative, the supervisor's salary is not relevant. The franchise fee can be avoided if Better Bakery makes pies and advertising costs can be avoided if it makes cakes. All three of these costs are fixed, but only two are relevant. Finally, all the costs (whether fixed or variable) could be avoided if Better Bakery rejects both products. Whether a cost is fixed or variable has no bearing on its relevance.

Relevance Is Context Sensitive

A particular cost that is relevant in one context may be irrelevant in another. Consider a store that carries men's, women's, and children's clothing. The store manager's salary could not be avoided by eliminating the children's department, but it could be avoided if the entire store were closed. The salary is not relevant to deciding whether to eliminate the children's department but is relevant with respect to deciding to close the store. In one context, the salary is not relevant. In the other context, it is relevant.

Relationship Between Relevance and Accuracy

Information need not be exact to be relevant. You may decide to delay purchasing a laptop computer you want if you know its price is going to drop even if you don't know exactly how much the price decrease will be. You know part of the cost can be avoided by waiting; you are just not sure of the amount.

The most useful information is both relevant and precise. Totally inaccurate information is useless. Likewise, irrelevant information is useless regardless of its accuracy.

Quantitative versus Qualitative Characteristics of Decision Making

Relevant information can have both **quantitative** and **qualitative characteristics.** The previous examples focused on quantitative data. Now consider qualitative issues. Suppose you are deciding which of two laptop computers to purchase. Computer A costs

$300 more than Computer B. Both computers satisfy your technical requirements; however, Computer A has a more attractive appearance. From a quantitative standpoint, you would select Computer B because you could avoid $300 of cost. However, if the laptop will be used in circumstances where clients need to be impressed, appearance—a qualitative characteristic—may be more important than minimizing cost. You might purchase Computer A even though quantitative factors favor Computer B. Both qualitative and quantitative data are relevant to decision making.

As with quantitative data, qualitative features must *differ* between the alternatives to be relevant. If the two computers were identical in appearance, attractiveness would not be relevant to making the decision.

Differential Revenue and Avoidable Cost

Because relevant revenue *differs* among the alternatives, it is sometimes called **differential revenue.** To illustrate, assume Pecks Department Stores sells men's, women's, and children's clothing and is considering eliminating the children's line. The revenue generated by the children's department is differential (relevant) revenue because Pecks' total revenue would be different if the children's department were eliminated.

Why would Pecks consider eliminating the children's department and thereby lose the differential (relevant) revenue? Pecks may be able to save more by eliminating the cost of operating the department than it loses in differential revenue. Some but not all of the costs associated with operating the children's department can be saved. For example, if Pecks Department Stores eliminates the children's department, the company can eliminate the cost of the department manager's salary but cannot get rid of the salary of the company president. The costs that stay the same are not relevant. The costs that can be *avoided* by closing the department are relevant. Indeed, relevant costs are frequently called *avoidable costs.*

Avoidable costs are the costs managers can eliminate by making specific choices. In the Pecks example, the cost of the department manager's salary is an avoidable (relevant) cost. The cost of the president's salary is not avoidable and is not relevant to the elimination decision.

RELATIONSHIP OF COST AVOIDANCE TO A COST HIERARCHY

Classifying costs into one of four hierarchical levels helps identify avoidable costs.[2]

1. *Unit-level costs.* Costs incurred each time a company generates one unit of product are **unit-level costs.**[3] Examples include the cost of direct materials, direct labor, inspections, packaging, shipping, and handling. Incremental (additional) unit-level costs increase *with each additional unit of product generated. Unit-level costs can be avoided by eliminating the production of a single unit of product.*

2. *Batch-level costs.* Many products are generated in batches rather than individual units. For example, a heating and air conditioning technician may service a batch of air conditioners in an apartment complex. Some of the job costs apply only to individual units, and other costs relate to the entire batch. For instance, the labor to service each air conditioner is a unit-level cost, but the cost of driving to the site is a **batch-level cost.**

    Classifying costs as unit- versus batch-level frequently depends on the context rather than the type of cost. For example, shipping and handling costs to send

LO 2

Distinguish between unit-level, batch-level, product-level, and facility-level costs and understand how these costs affect decision making.

[2]R. Cooper and R. S. Kaplan, *The Design of Cost Management Systems* (Englewood Cliffs, NJ: Prentice-Hall, 1991). Our classifications are broader than those typically presented. They encompass service and merchandising companies as well as manufacturing businesses. The original cost hierarchy was developed as a platform for activity-based costing, a topic introduced later. These classifications are equally useful as a tool for identifying avoidable costs.

[3]Recall that we use the term *product* in a generic sense to represent producing goods or services.

200 computers to a university are batch-level costs. In contrast, the shipping and handling cost to deliver a single computer to each of a number of individual customers is a unit-level cost. Eliminating a batch of work avoids both batch-level and unit-level costs. Similarly, adding a batch of work increases batch-level and unit-level costs. Increasing the number of units in a particular batch increases unit-level but not batch-level costs. Decreasing the number of units in a batch reduces unit-level costs but not batch-level costs.

3. *Product-level costs.* Costs incurred to support specific products or services are called **product-level costs.** Product-level costs include quality inspection costs, engineering design costs, the costs of obtaining and defending patents, the costs of regulatory compliance, and inventory holding costs such as interest, insurance, maintenance, and storage. *Product-level costs can be avoided by discontinuing a product line.* For example, suppose the Snapper Company makes the engines used in its lawn mowers. Buying engines from an outside supplier instead of making them would allow Snapper to avoid the product-level costs such as legal fees for patents, manufacturing supervisory costs of producing the engines, and the maintenance and inventory costs of holding engine parts.

4. *Facility-level costs.* **Facility-level costs** are incurred to support the entire company. They are not related to any specific product, batch, or unit of product. Because these costs maintain the facility as a whole, they are frequently called *facility-sustaining costs.* Facility-level costs include building rent or depreciation, personnel administration and training, property and real estate taxes, insurance, maintenance, administrative salaries, general selling costs, landscaping, utilities, and security. Total facility-level costs cannot be avoided unless the entire company is dissolved. However, eliminating a business segment (such as a division, department, or office) may enable a company to avoid some facility-level costs. For example, if a bank eliminates one of its branches, it can avoid the costs of renting, maintaining, and insuring that particular branch building. In general, *segment-level* facility costs can be avoided when a segment is eliminated. In contrast, *corporate-level* facility costs cannot be avoided unless the corporation is eliminated.

Precise distinctions between the various categories are often difficult to draw. One company may incur sales staff salaries as a facility-level cost while another company may pay sales commissions traceable to product lines or even specific units of a product line. Cost classifications cannot be memorized. Classifying specific cost items into the appropriate categories requires thoughtful judgment.

RELEVANT INFORMATION AND SPECIAL DECISIONS

Make appropriate special order decisions.

Four types of special decisions are frequently encountered in business practice: (1) special order, (2) outsourcing, (3) segment elimination, and (4) asset replacement. These four types of decisions are discussed in the following sections of this chapter.

Special Order Decisions

Occasionally, a company receives an offer to sell its goods at a price significantly below its normal selling price. The company must make a **special order decision** to accept or reject the offer.

Quantitative Analysis

Assume Premier Office Products manufactures printers. Premier expects to make and sell 2,000 printers in 10 batches of 200 units per batch during the coming year. Expected production costs are summarized in Exhibit 13.1.

Adding its normal markup to the total cost per unit, Premier set the selling price at $360 per printer.

Suppose Premier receives a *special order* from a new customer for 200 printers. If Premier accepts the order, its expected sales would increase from 2,000 units to 2,200 units. But the special order customer is willing to pay only $250 per printer. This price is well below not only Premier's normal selling price of $360 but also the company's expected per unit cost of $329.25. Should Premier accept or reject the special order? At first glance, it seems Premier should reject the special order because the customer's offer is below the expected cost per unit. Analyzing relevant costs and revenue leads, however, to a different conclusion.

The quantitative analysis follows in three steps.

EXHIBIT 13.1

Budgeted Cost for Expected Production of 2,000 Printers

Unit-level costs		
Materials costs (2,000 units × $90)	$180,000	
Labor costs (2,000 units × $82.50)	165,000	
Overhead (2,000 units × $7.50)	15,000	
Total unit-level costs (2,000 × $180)		$360,000
Batch-level costs		
Assembly setup (10 batches × $1,700)	17,000	
Materials handling (10 batches × $500)	5,000	
Total batch-level costs (10 batches × $2,200)		22,000
Product-level costs		
Engineering design	14,000	
Production manager salary	63,300	
Total-product-level costs		77,300
Facility-level costs		
Segment-level costs:		
Division manager's salary	85,000	
Administrative costs	12,700	
Allocated—corporate-level costs:		
Company president's salary	43,200	
Building rental	27,300	
General expenses	31,000	
Total facility-level costs		199,200
Total expected cost		$658,500

Cost per unit: $658,500 ÷ 2,000 = $329.25

Step 1. **Determine the amount of the relevant (differential) revenue Premier will earn by accepting the special order.** Premier's alternatives are (1) to accept or (2) to reject the special order. If Premier accepts the special order, additional revenue will be $50,000 ($250 × 200 units). If Premier rejects the special order, additional revenue will be zero. Because the amount of revenue differs between the alternatives, the $50,000 is relevant.

Step 2. **Determine the amount of the relevant (differential) cost Premier will incur by accepting the special order.** Examine the costs in Exhibit 13.1. If Premier accepts the special order, it will incur additional unit-level costs (materials, labor, and overhead). It will also incur the cost of one additional 200-unit batch. The unit- and batch-level costs are relevant because Premier could avoid them by rejecting the special order. The other costs in Exhibit 13.1 are not relevant because Premier will incur them whether it accepts or rejects the special order.

Step 3. **Accept the special order if the relevant revenue exceeds the relevant (avoidable) cost. Reject the order if relevant cost exceeds relevant revenue.** Exhibit 13.2 summarizes the relevant figures. Because the relevant revenue exceeds the relevant cost, Premier should accept the special order because profitability will increase by $11,800.

EXHIBIT 13.2

Relevant Information for Special Order of 200 Printers

Differential revenue ($250 × 200 units)	$50,000
Avoidable unit-level costs ($180 × 200 units)	(36,000)
Avoidable batch-level costs ($2,200 × 1 batch)	(2,200)
Contribution to income	$11,800

Answers to The Curious Accountant

There are several factors that enable drug companies to reduce their prices to certain customers. One significant factor is the issue of relevant cost. Pharmaceutical manufacturers have a substantial amount of fixed cost, such as research and development. For example, in 2009 **Pfizer Inc.** had research and development expenses that were 15.7 percent of sales, while its cost of goods sold expense was at 17.8 percent of sales. With respect to a special order decision, the research and development costs would not change and therefore would not be relevant. In contrast, the unit-level cost of goods sold would increase and therefore would be relevant. Clearly, relevant costs are significantly less than the total cost. If Canadian prices are based on relevant costs, that is, if drug companies view Canadian sales as a special order opportunity, the lower prices may provide a contribution to profitability even though they are significantly less than the prices charged in the United States.

Opportunity Costs

Premier can consider the special order because it has enough excess productive capacity to make the additional units. Suppose Premier has the opportunity to lease its excess capacity (currently unused building and equipment) for $15,000. If Premier uses the excess capacity to make the additional printers, it must forgo the opportunity to lease the excess capacity to a third party. Sacrificing the potential leasing income represents an opportunity cost of accepting the special order. Adding this opportunity cost to the other relevant costs increases the cost of accepting the special order to $53,200 ($38,200 unit-level and batch-level costs + $15,000 opportunity cost). The avoidable costs would then exceed the differential revenue, resulting in a projected loss of $3,200 ($50,000 differential revenue − $53,200 avoidable costs). Under these circumstances Premier would be better off rejecting the special order and leasing the excess capacity.

Relevance and the Decision Context

Assume Premier does not have the opportunity to lease its excess capacity. Recall the original analysis indicated the company could earn an $11,800 contribution to profit by accepting a special order to sell 200 printers at $250 per unit (see Exhibit 13.2). Because Premier can earn a contribution to profit by selling printers for $250 each, can the company reduce its normal selling price (price charged to existing customers) to $250? The answer is no, as illustrated in Exhibit 13.3.

EXHIBIT 13.3

Projections Based on 2,200 Printers at a Sales Price of $250 per Unit

Revenue ($250 × 2,200 units)		$ 550,000
Unit-level supplies and inspection ($180 × 2,200 units)	$396,000	
Batch-level costs ($2,200 × 11 batches)	24,200	
Product-level costs	77,300	
Facility-level costs	199,200	
Total cost		(696,700)
Projected loss		$(146,700)

If a company is to be profitable, it must ultimately generate revenue in excess of total costs. Although the facility-level and product-level costs are not relevant to the special order decision, they are relevant to the operation of the business as a whole.

Qualitative Characteristics

Should a company ever reject a special order if the relevant revenues exceed the relevant costs? Qualitative characteristics may be even more important than quantitative ones. If Premier's regular customers learn the company sold printers to another buyer at $250 per unit, they may demand reduced prices on future purchases. Exhibit 13.3 shows Premier cannot reduce the price for all customers. Special order customers should therefore come from outside Premier's normal sales territory. In addition, special order customers should be advised that the special price does not apply to repeat business. Cutting off a special order customer who has been permitted to establish a continuing relationship is likely to lead to ill-feelings and harsh words. A business's reputation can depend on how management handles such relationships. Finally, at full capacity, Premier should reject any special orders at reduced prices because filling those orders reduces its ability to satisfy customers who pay full price.

Outsourcing Decisions

Make appropriate outsourcing decisions.

Companies can sometimes purchase products they need for less than it would cost to make them. This circumstance explains why automobile manufacturers purchase rather than make many of the parts in their cars or why a caterer might buy gourmet desserts from a specialty company. Buying goods and services from other companies rather than producing them internally is commonly called **outsourcing.**

Quantitative Analysis

Assume Premier Office Products is considering whether to outsource production of the printers it currently makes. A supplier has offered to sell an unlimited supply of printers to Premier for $240 each. The estimated cost of making the printers is $329.25 per unit (see Exhibit 13.1). The data suggest that Premier could save money by outsourcing. Analyzing relevant costs proves this presumption wrong.

A two-step quantitative analysis for the outsourcing decision follows:

Step 1. **Determine the production costs Premier can avoid if it outsources printer production.** A review of Exhibit 13.1 discloses the costs Premier could avoid by outsourcing. If Premier purchases the printers, it can avoid the unit-level costs (materials, labor, overhead), and the batch-level costs (assembly setup, and materials handling). It can also avoid the product-level costs (engineering design costs and production manager salary). Deciding to outsource will not, however, affect the facility-level costs. Because Premier will incur them whether or not it outsources printer production, the facility-level costs are not relevant to the outsourcing decision. Exhibit 13.4 shows the avoidable (relevant) costs of outsourcing.

Step 2. **Compare the avoidable (relevant) production costs with the cost of buying the product and select the lower-cost option.** Because the relevant production cost is less than the purchase price of the printers ($229.65 per unit versus $240.00), the quantitative analysis suggests that Premier should continue to make the printers. Profitability would decline by $20,700 [$459,300 − ($240 × 2,000)] if printer production were outsourced.

That test was so easy. Why is your score so bad?

I outsourced my homework.

EXHIBIT 13.4

Relevant Cost for Expected Production for Outsourcing 2,000 Printers

Unit-level costs ($180 × 2,000 units)	$360,000
Batch-level costs ($2,200 × 10 batches)	22,000
Product-level costs	77,300
Total relevant cost	$459,300
Cost per unit: $459,300 ÷ 2,000 = $229.65	

EXHIBIT 13.5

Relevant Cost for Expected Production for Outsourcing 3,000 Printers

Unit-level costs ($180 × 3,000 units)	$540,000
Batch-level costs ($2,200 × 15 batches)	33,000
Product-level costs	77,300
Opportunity cost	40,000
Total relevant cost	$690,300

Cost per unit: $690,300 ÷ 3,000 units = $230.10

Opportunity Costs

Suppose Premier's accountant determines that the space Premier currently uses to manufacture printers could be leased to a third party for $40,000 per year. By using the space to manufacture printers, Premier is *forgoing the opportunity* to earn $40,000. Because this *opportunity cost* can be avoided by purchasing the printers, it is relevant to the outsourcing decision. After adding the opportunity cost to the other relevant costs, the total relevant cost increases to $499,300 ($459,300 + $40,000) and the relevant cost per unit becomes $249.65 ($499,300 ÷ 2,000). Because Premier can purchase printers for $240, it should outsource printer production. It would be better off buying the printers and leasing the manufacturing space.

Evaluating the Effect of Growth on the Level of Production

The decision to outsource would change if expected production increased from 2,000 to 3,000 units. Because some of the avoidable costs are fixed relative to the level of production, cost per unit decreases as volume increases. For example, the product-level costs (engineering design, production manager's salary, and opportunity cost) are fixed relative to the level of production. Exhibit 13.5 shows the relevant cost per unit if Premier expects to produce 3,000 printers.

At 3,000 units of production, the relevant cost of making printers is less than the cost of outsourcing ($230.10 versus $240.00). If management believes the company is likely to experience growth in the near future, it should reject the outsourcing option. Managers must consider potential growth when making outsourcing decisions.

Qualitative Features

A company that uses **vertical integration** controls the full range of activities from acquiring raw materials to distributing goods and services. Outsourcing reduces the level of vertical integration, passing some of a company's control over its products to outside suppliers. The reliability of the supplier is critical to an outsourcing decision. An unscrupulous supplier may lure an unsuspecting manufacturer into an outsourcing decision using **low-ball pricing.** Once the manufacturer is dependent on the supplier, the supplier raises prices. If a price sounds too good to be true, it probably is too good to be true. Other potential problems include product quality and delivery commitments. If the printers do not work properly or are not delivered on time, Premier's customers will be dissatisfied with Premier, not the supplier. Outsourcing requires that Premier depend on the supplier to deliver quality products at designated prices according to a specified schedule. Any supplier failures will become Premier's failures.

To protect themselves from unscrupulous or incompetent suppliers, many companies establish a select list of reliable **certified suppliers.** These companies seek to become the preferred customers of the suppliers by offering incentives such as guaranteed volume purchases with prompt payments. These incentives motivate the suppliers to ship high-quality products on a timely basis. The purchasing companies recognize that prices ultimately depend on the suppliers' ability to control costs, so the buyers and suppliers work together to minimize costs. For example, buyers may share confidential information about their production plans with suppliers if such information would enable the suppliers to more effectively control costs.

Companies must approach outsourcing decisions cautiously even when relationships with reliable suppliers are ensured. Outsourcing has both internal and external effects. It usually displaces employees. If the supplier experiences difficulties, reestablishing internal production capacity is expensive once a trained workforce has been released. Loyalty and trust are difficult to build but easy to destroy. In fact, companies must consider not only the employees who will be discharged but also the morale of

FOCUS ON **INTERNATIONAL ISSUES**

In recent years there has been much discussion about American companies outsourcing work to workers in other countries. However, some activities that are seldom outsourced by American companies are routinely outsourced by companies in other countries. In fact, sometimes the "foreign country" that provides the outsourcing is the United States.

Consider an example from the automotive industry. While American automobile companies may use parts that were manufactured in another country, the final assembly of cars they sell in the United States is usually performed in their own plants in the United States or Canada. Japanese auto companies also tend to perform the final assembly of their cars in their own plants, which may be located in another country. In contrast, European car makers are more willing to outsource the final assembly, as well as engineering and parts production, to independent companies. For example, most, if not all, BMW X3s are not assembled at a BMW plant, but by the employees of Magna Steyr in Graz, Austria. This company, by the way, is a subsidiary of Magna International, which is a Canadian company. And that Porsche Boxster or Cayman you are hoping to receive as a graduation gift—it almost certainly will be built by Valmet Automotive in Finland. In fact, Valmet assembled 22,356 of the 105,162 vehicles that Porsche produced in 2008.

Source: Companies' annual reports.

---

those who remain. Cost reductions achieved through outsourcing are of little benefit if they are acquired at the expense of low morale and reduced productivity.

In spite of the potential pitfalls outsourcing entails, the vast majority of U.S. businesses engage in some form of it. Such widespread acceptance suggests that most companies believe the benefits achieved through outsourcing exceed the potential shortcomings.

✓ CHECK YOURSELF 13.2

Addison Manufacturing Company pays a production supervisor a salary of $48,000 per year. The supervisor manages the production of sprinkler heads that are used in water irrigation systems. Should the production supervisor's salary be considered a relevant cost to a special order decision? Should the production supervisor's salary be considered a relevant cost to an outsourcing decision?

Answer   The production supervisor's salary is not a relevant cost to a special order decision because Addison would pay the salary regardless of whether it accepts or rejects a special order. Because the cost does not differ for the alternatives, it is not relevant. In contrast, the supervisor's salary would be relevant to an outsourcing decision. Addison could dismiss the supervisor if it purchased the sprinkler heads instead of making them. Because the salary could be avoided by purchasing heads instead of making them, the salary is relevant to an outsourcing decision.

Segment Elimination Decisions

Businesses frequently organize their operations into subcomponents called **segments.** Segment data are used to make comparisons among different products, departments, or divisions. For example, in addition to the companywide income statement provided for external users, JCPenney may prepare separate income statements for each retail store

LO 5

Make appropriate segment elimination decisions.

EXHIBIT 13.6

Projected Revenues and Costs by Segment

	Copiers	Computers	Printers	Total
Projected revenue	$550,000	$850,000	$720,000	$2,120,000
Projected costs				
Unit-level costs				
Materials costs	(120,000)	(178,000)	(180,000)	(478,000)
Labor costs	(160,000)	(202,000)	(165,000)	(527,000)
Overhead	(30,800)	(20,000)	(15,000)	(65,800)
Batch-level costs				
Assembly setup	(15,000)	(26,000)	(17,000)	(58,000)
Materials handling	(6,000)	(8,000)	(5,000)	(19,000)
Product-level costs				
Engineering design	(10,000)	(12,000)	(14,000)	(36,000)
Production manager salary	(52,000)	(55,800)	(63,300)	(171,100)
Facility-level costs				
Segment level				
Division manager salary	(82,000)	(92,000)	(85,000)	(259,000)
Administrative costs	(12,200)	(13,200)	(12,700)	(38,100)
Allocated—corporate-level				
Company president salary	(34,000)	(46,000)	(43,200)	(123,200)
Building rental	(19,250)	(29,750)	(27,300)	(76,300)
General facility expenses	(31,000)	(31,000)	(31,000)	(93,000)
Projected income (loss)	$(22,250)	$136,250	$ 61,500	$ 175,500

for internal users. Executives can then evaluate managerial performance by comparing profitability measures among stores. *Segment reports* can be prepared for products, services, departments, branches, centers, offices, or divisions. These reports normally show segment revenues and costs. The primary objective of segment analysis is to determine whether relevant revenues exceed relevant costs.

Quantitative Analysis

Assume Premier Office Products makes copy equipment and computers as well as printers. Each product line is made in a separate division of the company. Division (segment) operating results for the most recent year are shown in Exhibit 13.6. Initial review of the results suggests the copier division should be eliminated because it is operating at a loss. However, analyzing the relevant revenues and expenses leads to a different conclusion.

A three-step quantitative analysis for the segment elimination decision follows.

Step 1.　**Determine the amount of relevant (differential) revenue that pertains to eliminating the copier division.** The alternatives are (1) to eliminate or (2) to continue to operate the copier division. If Premier eliminates the copier line it will lose the $550,000 of revenue the copier division currently produces. If the division continues to operate, Premier will earn the revenue. Because the revenue differs between the alternatives, it is relevant.

Step 2.　**Determine the amount of cost Premier can avoid if it eliminates the copier division.** If it eliminates copiers, Premier can avoid the unit-level, batch-level, product-level, and segment-level facility-sustaining costs. The relevant revenue and the avoidable costs are shown in Exhibit 13.7.

　　　Premier will incur the corporate-level facility-sustaining costs whether it eliminates the copier segment or continues to operate it. Because these costs do not differ between the alternatives, they are not relevant to the elimination decision.

Step 3. **If the relevant revenue is less than the avoidable cost, eliminate the segment (division). If not, continue to operate it.** Because operating the segment is contributing $62,000 per year to company profitability (see Exhibit 13.7), Premier should not eliminate the copier division. Exhibit 13.8 shows Premier's estimated revenues and costs if the computers and printers divisions were operated without the copier division. Projected company profit declines by $62,000 ($175,500 − $113,500) without the copier segment, confirming that eliminating it would be detrimental to Premier's profitability.

Qualitative Considerations in Decisions to Eliminate Segments

As with other special decisions, management should consider qualitative factors when determining whether to eliminate segments. Employee lives will be disrupted; some employees may be reassigned elsewhere in the company, but others will be discharged. As with outsourcing decisions, reestablishing internal production capacity is difficult once a trained workforce has been released. Furthermore, employees in other segments, suppliers, customers, and investors may believe that the elimination of a segment implies the company as a whole is experiencing financial difficulty. These individuals may lose confidence in the company and seek business contacts with other companies they perceive to be more stable.

Management must also consider the fact that sales of different product lines are frequently interdependent. Some customers prefer one-stop shopping; they want to buy

EXHIBIT 13.7	
Relevant Revenue and Cost Data for Copier Segment	
Projected revenue	$550,000
Projected costs	
Unit-level costs	
Materials costs	(120,000)
Labor costs	(160,000)
Overhead	(30,800)
Batch-level costs	
Assembly setup	(15,000)
Materials handling	(6,000)
Product-level costs	
Engineering design	(10,000)
Production manager salary	(52,000)
Facility-level costs	
Segment level	
Division manager salary	(82,000)
Administrative costs	(12,200)
Projected income (loss)	$ 62,000

EXHIBIT 13.8			
Projected Revenues and Costs Without Copier Division			
	Computers	**Printers**	**Total**
Projected revenue	$850,000	$720,000	$1,570,000
Projected costs			
Unit-level costs			
Materials costs	(178,000)	(180,000)	(358,000)
Labor costs	(202,000)	(165,000)	(367,000)
Overhead	(20,000)	(15,000)	(35,000)
Batch-level costs			
Assembly setup	(26,000)	(17,000)	(43,000)
Materials handling	(8,000)	(5,000)	(13,000)
Product-level costs			
Engineering design	(12,000)	(14,000)	(26,000)
Production manager salary	(55,800)	(63,300)	(119,100)
Facility-level costs			
Segment level			
Division manager salary	(92,000)	(85,000)	(177,000)
Administrative costs	(13,200)	(12,700)	(25,900)
Allocated—corporate-level*			
Company president salary	(63,000)	(60,200)	(123,200)
Building rental	(39,375)	(36,925)	(76,300)
General facility expenses	(46,500)	(46,500)	(93,000)
Projected income (loss)	$ 94,125	$ 19,375	$ 113,500

*The corporate-level facility costs that were previously *allocated* to the copier division have been reassigned on the basis of one-half to the computer division and one-half to the printer division.

all their office equipment from one supplier. If Premier no longer sells copiers, customers may stop buying its computers and printers. Eliminating one segment may reduce sales of other segments.

What will happen to the space Premier used to make the copiers? Suppose Premier decides to make telephone systems in the space it previously used for copiers. The contribution to profit of the telephone business would be an *opportunity cost* of operating the copier segment. As demonstrated in previous examples, adding the opportunity cost to the avoidable costs of operating the copier segment could change the decision.

As with outsourcing, volume changes can affect elimination decisions. Because many costs of operating a segment are fixed, the cost per unit decreases as production increases. Growth can transform a segment that is currently producing real losses into a segment that produces real profits. Managers must consider growth potential when making elimination decisions.

✓ CHECK YOURSELF 13.3

Capital Corporation is considering eliminating one of its operating segments. Capital employed a real estate broker to determine the marketability of the building that houses the segment. The broker obtained three bids for the building: $250,000, $262,000, and $264,000. The book value of the building is $275,000. Based on this information alone, what is the relevant cost of the building?

Answer   The book value of the building is a sunk cost that is not relevant. There are three bids for the building, but only one is relevant because Capital could sell the building only once. The relevant cost of the building is the highest opportunity cost, which in this case is $264,000.

Summary of Relationships Between Avoidable Costs and the Hierarchy of Business Activity

A relationship exists between the cost hierarchy and the different types of special decisions just discussed. A special order involves making additional units of an existing product. Deciding to accept a special order affects unit-level and possibly batch-level costs. In contrast, outsourcing a product stops the production of that product. Outsourcing can avoid many product-level as well as unit- and batch-level costs. Finally, if a company eliminates an entire business segment, it can avoid some of the facility-level costs. The more complex the decision level, the more opportunities there are to avoid costs. Moving to a higher category does not mean, however, that all costs at the higher level of activity are avoidable. For example, all product-level costs may not be avoidable if a company chooses to outsource a product. The company may still incur inventory holding costs or advertising costs whether it makes or buys the product. Understanding the relationship between decision type and level of cost hierarchy helps when identifying avoidable costs. The relationships are summarized in Exhibit 13.9. For each type of decision, look for avoidable costs in the categories marked with an X. Remember also that sunk costs cannot be avoided.

EXHIBIT 13.9

Relationship Between Decision Type and Level of Cost Hierarchy

Decision Type	Unit level	Batch level	Product level	Facility level
Special order	X	X		
Outsourcing	X	X	X	
Elimination	X	X	X	X

Equipment Replacement Decisions

Equipment may become technologically obsolete long before it fails physically. Managers should base **equipment replacement decisions** on profitability analysis rather than physical deterioration. Assume Premier Office Products is considering replacing an existing machine with a new one. The following table summarizes pertinent information about the two machines.

LO 6

Make appropriate asset replacement decisions.

Old Machine		New Machine	
Original cost	$ 90,000	Cost of the new machine	$29,000
Accumulated depreciation	(33,000)	Salvage value (in 5 years)	4,000
Book value	$ 57,000	Operating expenses	
		($4,500 × 5 years)	22,500
Market value (now)	$ 14,000		
Salvage value (in 5 years)	2,000		
Annual depreciation expense	11,000		
Operating expenses			
($9,000 × 5 years)	45,000		

Quantitative Analysis

First determine what relevant costs Premier will incur if it keeps the *old machine.*

1. The *original cost* ($90,000), *current book value* ($57,000), *accumulated depreciation* ($33,000), and *annual depreciation expense* ($11,000) are different measures of a cost that was incurred in a prior period. They represent irrelevant sunk costs.

2. The $14,000 market value represents the current sacrifice Premier must make if it keeps using the existing machine. In other words, if Premier does not keep the machine, it can sell it for $14,000. In economic terms, *forgoing the opportunity* to sell the machine costs as much as buying it. The *opportunity cost* is therefore relevant to the replacement decision.

3. The salvage value of the old machine reduces the opportunity cost. Premier can sell the old machine now for $14,000 or use it for five more years and then sell it for $2,000. The opportunity cost of using the old machine for five more years is therefore $12,000 ($14,000 − $2,000).

4. Because the $45,000 ($9,000 × 5) of operating expenses will be incurred if the old machine is used but can be avoided if it is replaced, the operating expenses are relevant costs.

Next, determine what relevant costs will be incurred if Premier purchases and uses the *new machine.*

1. The cost of the new machine represents a future economic sacrifice Premier must incur if it buys the new machine. It is a relevant cost.

2. The salvage value reduces the cost of purchasing the new machine. Part ($4,000) of the $29,000 cost of the new machine will be recovered at the end of five years. The relevant cost of purchasing the new machine is $25,000 ($29,000 − $4,000).

3. The $22,500 ($4,500 × 5) of operating expenses will be incurred if the new machine is purchased; it can be avoided if the new machine is not purchased. The operating expenses are relevant costs.

The relevant costs for the two machines are summarized here.

Old Machine		New Machine	
Opportunity cost	$14,000	Cost of the new machine	$29,000
Salvage value	(2,000)	Salvage value	(4,000)
Operating expenses	45,000	Operating expenses	22,500
Total	$57,000	Total	$47,500

The analysis suggests that Premier should acquire the new machine because buying it produces the lower relevant cost. The $57,000 cost of using the old machine can be *avoided* by incurring the $47,500 cost of acquiring and using the new machine. Over the five-year period, Premier would save $9,500 ($57,000 − $47,500) by purchasing the new machine. One caution: this analysis ignores income tax effects and the time value of money, which are explained later. The discussion in this chapter focuses on identifying and using relevant costs in decision making.

« A Look Back

Decision making requires managers to choose from alternative courses of action. Successful decision making depends on a manager's ability to identify *relevant information.* Information that is relevant for decision making differs among the alternatives and is future oriented. Relevant revenues are sometimes called *differential revenues* because they differ among the alternatives. Relevant costs are sometimes called *avoidable costs* because they can be eliminated or avoided by choosing a specific course of action.

Costs that do not differ among the alternatives are not avoidable and therefore not relevant. *Sunk costs* are not relevant in decision making because they have been incurred in past transactions and therefore cannot be avoided. *Opportunity costs* are relevant because they represent potential benefits that may or may not be realized, depending on the decision maker's choice. In other words, future benefits that differ among the alternatives are relevant. Opportunity costs are not recorded in the financial accounting records.

Cost behavior (fixed or variable) is independent from the concept of relevance. Furthermore, a cost that is relevant in one decision context may be irrelevant in another context. Decision making depends on qualitative as well as quantitative information. *Quantitative information refers to information that can be measured using numbers. Qualitative information* is nonquantitative information such as personal preferences or opportunities.

Classifying costs into one of four hierarchical levels facilitates identifying relevant costs. *Unit-level costs* such as materials and labor are incurred each time a single unit of product is made. These costs can be avoided by eliminating the production of a single unit of product. *Batch-level costs* are associated with producing a group of products. Examples include setup costs and inspection costs related to a batch (group) of work rather than a single unit. Eliminating a batch would avoid both batch-level costs and unit-level costs. *Product-level costs* are incurred to support specific products or services (design and regulatory compliance costs). Product-level costs can be avoided by discontinuing a product line. *Facility-level costs,* like the president's salary, are incurred on behalf of the whole company or a segment of the company. In segment elimination decisions, the facility-level costs related to a particular segment being considered for elimination are relevant and avoidable. Those applying to the company as a whole are not avoidable.

Four types of special decisions that are frequently encountered in business are (1) *special orders,* (2) *outsourcing,* (3) *elimination decisions,* and (4) *asset replacement.* The relevant costs in a special order decision are the unit-level and batch-level costs that will be incurred if the special order is accepted. If the differential revenues from the special order exceed the relevant costs, the order should be accepted. Outsourcing decisions determine whether goods and services should be purchased from other companies. The relevant costs are the unit-level, batch-level, and product-level costs that could be avoided if the company outsources the product or service. If these costs are more than the cost to buy and the qualitative characteristics are satisfactory, the company should outsource. Segment-related unit-level, batch-level, product-level, and facility-level costs that can be avoided when a segment is eliminated are relevant. If the segment's avoidable costs exceed its differential revenues, it should be eliminated, assuming favorable qualitative factors. Asset replacement decisions compare the relevant costs of existing equipment with the relevant costs of new equipment to determine whether replacing the old equipment would be profitable.

A Look Forward

The next chapter introduces key concepts associated with planning and cost control. It shows you how to develop a master budget including the preparation of four operating budgets: (1) a sales budget, (2) an inventory purchases budget, (3) a selling and administrative expense budget and (4) a cash budget. The chapter explains how data from the operating budgets are used to prepare pro forma (budgeted) financial statements. In addition to the quantitative aspects, the chapter discusses the effect of the budgeting process on human behavior.

A step-by-step audio-narrated series of slides is provided on the text website at www.mhhe.com/edmondssurvey3e

 ## SELF-STUDY REVIEW PROBLEM

Flying High Inc. (FHI) is a division of The Master Toy Company. FHI makes remote-controlled airplanes. During 2011, FHI incurred the following costs in the process of making 5,000 planes.

Unit-level materials costs (5,000 units @ $80)	$ 400,000
Unit-level labor costs (5,000 units @ $90)	450,000
Unit-level overhead costs (5,000 @ $70)	350,000
Depreciation cost on manufacturing equipment*	50,000
Other manufacturing overhead†	140,000
Inventory holding costs	240,000
Allocated portion of The Master Toy Company's facility-level costs	600,000
Total costs	$2,230,000

*The manufacturing equipment, which originally cost $250,000, has a book value of $200,000, a remaining useful life of four years, and a zero salvage value. If the equipment is not used in the production process, it can be leased for $30,000 per year.

†Includes supervisors' salaries and rent for the manufacturing building.

Required

a. FHI uses a cost-plus pricing strategy. FHI sets its price at product cost plus $100. Determine the price that FHI should charge for its remote-controlled airplanes.

b. Assume that a potential customer that operates a chain of high-end toy stores has approached FHI. A buyer for this chain has offered to purchase 1,000 planes from FHI at a price of $275 each. Ignoring qualitative considerations, should FHI accept or reject the order?

c. FHI has the opportunity to purchase the planes from Arland Manufacturing Company for $325 each. Arland maintains adequate inventories so that it can supply its customers with planes on demand. Should FHI accept the opportunity to outsource the making of its planes?

d. Use the contribution margin format to prepare an income statement based on historical cost data. Prepare a second income statement that reflects the relevant cost data that Master Toy should consider in a segment elimination decision. Based on a comparison of these two statements, indicate whether Master Toy should eliminate the FHI division.

e. FHI is considering replacing the equipment it currently uses to manufacture its planes. It could purchase replacement equipment for $480,000 that has an expected useful life of four years and a salvage value of $40,000. The new equipment would increase productivity substantially, reducing unit-level labor costs by 20 percent. Assume that FHI would maintain its production and sales at 5,000 planes per year. Prepare a schedule that shows the relevant costs of operating the old equipment versus the costs of operating the new equipment. Should FHI replace the equipment?

Solution to Requirement a

Product Cost for Remote-Controlled Airplanes

Unit-level materials costs (5,000 units × $80)	$ 400,000
Unit-level labor costs (5,000 units × $90)	450,000
Unit-level overhead costs (5,000 units × $70)	350,000
Depreciation cost on manufacturing equipment	50,000
Other manufacturing overhead	140,000
Total product cost	$1,390,000

The cost per unit is $278 ($1,390,000 ÷ 5,000 units). The sales price per unit is $378 ($278 + $100). Depreciation expense is included because cost-plus pricing is usually based on historical cost rather than relevant cost. To be profitable in the long run, a company must ultimately recover the amount it paid for the equipment (the historical cost of the equipment). The inventory holding costs and the allocated facility-level costs are not included because they are not product costs.

Solution to Requirement b

The incremental (relevant) cost of making 1,000 additional airplanes follows. The depreciation expense is not relevant because it represents a sunk cost. The other manufacturing overhead costs are not relevant because they will be incurred regardless of whether FHI makes the additional planes.

Per Unit Relevant Product Cost for Airplanes

Unit-level materials costs	$ 80
Unit-level labor costs	90
Unit-level overhead costs	70
Total relevant product cost	$240

Because the relevant (incremental) cost of making the planes is less than the incremental revenue, FHI should accept the special order. Accepting the order will increase profits by $35,000 [($275 incremental revenue − $240 incremental cost) × 1,000 units].

Solution to Requirement c

Distinguish this decision from the special order opportunity discussed in Requirement *b*. That special order (Requirement *b*) decision hinged on the cost of making additional units with the existing production process. In contrast, a make-or-buy decision compares current production with the possibility of making zero units (closing down the entire manufacturing process). If the manufacturing process were shut down, FHI could avoid the unit-level costs, the cost of the lost opportunity to lease the equipment, the other manufacturing overhead costs, and the inventory holding costs. Because the planes can be purchased on demand, there is no need to maintain any inventory. The allocated portion of the facility-level costs is not relevant because it would be incurred regardless of whether FHI manufactured the planes. The relevant cost of making the planes follows.

Relevant Manufacturing Cost for Airplanes

Unit-level materials costs (5,000 units × $80)	$ 400,000
Unit-level labor costs (5,000 units × $90)	450,000
Unit-level overhead costs (5,000 units × $70)	350,000
Opportunity cost of leasing the equipment	30,000
Other manufacturing overhead costs	140,000
Inventory holding cost	240,000
Total product cost	$1,610,000

The relevant cost per unit is $322 ($1,610,000 ÷ 5,000 units). Because the relevant cost of making the planes ($322) is less than the cost of purchasing them ($325), FHI should continue to make the planes.

Solution to Requirement d

Income Statements		
	Historical Cost Data	**Relevant Cost Data**
Revenue (5,000 units × $378)	$1,890,000	$1,890,000
Less variable costs:		
Unit-level materials costs (5,000 units × $80)	(400,000)	(400,000)
Unit-level labor costs (5,000 units × $90)	(450,000)	(450,000)
Unit-level overhead costs (5,000 units × $70)	(350,000)	(350,000)
Contribution margin	690,000	690,000
Depreciation cost on manufacturing equipment	(50,000)	
Opportunity cost of leasing manufacturing equipment		(30,000)
Other manufacturing overhead costs	(140,000)	(140,000)
Inventory holding costs	(240,000)	(240,000)
Allocated facility-level administrative costs	(600,000)	
Net Loss	$ (340,000)	
Contribution to Master Toy's Profitability		$ 280,000

Master Toy should not eliminate the segment (FHI). Although it appears to be incurring a loss, the allocated facility-level administrative costs are not relevant because Master Toy would incur these costs regardless of whether it eliminated FHI. Also, the depreciation cost on the manufacturing equipment is not relevant because it is a sunk cost. However, because the company could lease the equipment if the segment were eliminated, the $30,000 potential rental fee represents a relevant opportunity cost. The relevant revenue and cost data show that FHI is contributing $280,000 to the profitability of The Master Toy Company.

Solution to Requirement e

The relevant costs of using the old equipment versus the new equipment are the costs that differ for the two alternatives. In this case relevant costs include the purchase price of the new equipment, the opportunity cost of the old equipment, and the labor costs. These items are summarized in the following table. The data show the total cost over the four-year useful life of the replacement equipment.

Relevant Cost Comparison		
	Old Equipment	**New Equipment**
Opportunity to lease the old equipment ($30,000 × 4 years)	$ 120,000	
Cost of new equipment ($480,000 − $40,000)		$ 440,000
Unit-level labor costs (5,000 units × $90 × 4 years)	1,800,000	
Unit-level labor costs (5,000 units × $90 × 4 years × .80)		1,440,000
Total relevant costs	$1,920,000	$1,880,000

Because the relevant cost of operating the new equipment is less than the cost of operating the old equipment, FHI should replace the equipment.

KEY TERMS

QUESTIONS

1. Identify the primary qualities of revenues and costs that are relevant for decision making.

2. Are variable costs always relevant? Explain.

3. Identify the four hierarchical levels used to classify costs. When can each of these levels of costs be avoided?

4. Describe the relationship between relevance and accuracy.

5. "It all comes down to the bottom line. The numbers never lie." Do you agree with this conclusion? Explain your position.

6. Carmon Company invested $300,000 in the equity securities of Mann Corporation. The current market value of Carmon's investment in Mann is $250,000. Carmon currently needs funds for operating purposes. Although interest rates are high, Carmon's president has decided to borrow the needed funds instead of selling the investment in Mann. He explains that his company cannot afford to take a $50,000 loss on the Mann stock. Evaluate the president's decision based on this information.

7. What is an opportunity cost? How does it differ from a sunk cost?

8. A local bank advertises that it offers a free noninterest-bearing checking account if the depositor maintains a $500 minimum balance in the account. Is the checking account truly free?

9. A manager is faced with deciding whether to replace machine A or machine B. The original cost of machine A was $20,000 and that of machine B was $30,000. Because the two cost figures differ, they are relevant to the manager's decision. Do you agree? Explain your position.

10. Are all fixed costs unavoidable?

11. Identify two qualitative considerations that could be associated with special order decisions.

12. Which of the following would not be relevant to a make-or-buy decision?

  (a) Allocated portion of depreciation expense on existing facilities.

  (b) Variable cost of labor used to produce products currently purchased from suppliers.

  (c) Warehousing costs for inventory of completed products (inventory levels will be constant regardless of whether products are purchased or produced).

  (d) Cost of materials used to produce the items currently purchased from suppliers.

  (e) Property taxes on the factory building.

13. What two factors should be considered in deciding how to allocate shelf space in a retail establishment?

14. What level(s) of costs is (are) relevant in special order decisions?

15. Why would a company consider outsourcing products or services?

16. Chris Sutter, the production manager of Satellite Computers, insists that the DVD drives used in the company's upper-end computers be outsourced because they can be purchased from a supplier at a lower cost per unit than the company is presently incurring to produce the drives. Jane Meyers, his assistant, insists that if sales growth continues at the current levels, the company will be able to produce the drives in the near future at a lower cost because of the company's predominately fixed cost structure. Does Ms. Meyers have a legitimate argument? Explain.

17. Identify some qualitative factors that should be considered in addition to quantitative costs in deciding whether to outsource.

18. The managers of Wilcox Inc. are suggesting that the company president eliminate one of the company's segments that is operating at a loss. Why may this be a hasty decision?

19. Why would a supervisor choose to continue using a more costly old machine instead of replacing it with a less costly new machine?

MULTIPLE-CHOICE QUESTIONS

Multiple-choice questions are provided on the text website at www.mhhe.com/edmondssurvey3e.

EXERCISES

All applicable Exercises are available with McGraw-Hill's *Connect Accounting.*

Exercise 13-1   *Distinction between relevance and cost behavior*

LO 1

Leah Friend is trying to decide which of two different kinds of candy to sell in her retail candy store. One type is a name-brand candy that will practically sell itself. The other candy is cheaper to purchase but does not carry an identifiable brand name. Ms. Friend believes that she will have to incur significant advertising costs to sell this candy. Several cost items for the two types of candy are as follows.

Brandless Candy		Name-Brand Candy	
Cost per box	$ 6.00	Cost per box	$ 7.00
Sales commissions per box	1.00	Sales commissions per box	1.00
Rent of display space	1,500.00	Rent of display space	1,500.00
Advertising	3,000.00	Advertising	2,000.00

Required

Identify each cost as being relevant or irrelevant to Ms. Friend's decision and indicate whether it is fixed or variable relative to the number of boxes sold.

Exercise 13-2   *Distinction between relevance and cost behavior*

LO 1, 2

Stanley Company makes and sells a single product. Stanley incurred the following costs in its most recent fiscal year.

Cost Items Appearing on the Income Statement	
Materials cost ($10 per unit)	Sales commissions (2% of sales)
Company president's salary	Salaries of administrative personnel
Depreciation on manufacturing equipment	Shipping and handling ($0.50 per unit)
Customer billing costs (1% of sales)	Depreciation on office furniture
Rental cost of manufacturing facility	Manufacturing supplies ($0.25 per unit)
Advertising costs ($200,000 per year)	Production supervisor's salary
Labor cost ($8 per unit)	

Stanley could purchase the products that it currently makes. If it purchased the items, the company would continue to sell them using its own logo, advertising program, and sales staff.

Required

Identify each cost as relevant or irrelevant to the outsourcing decision and indicate whether the cost is fixed or variable relative to the number of products manufactured and sold.

Exercise 13-3   *Distinction between avoidable costs and cost behavior*

LO 1

Medallion Company makes fine jewelry that it sells to department stores throughout the United States. Medallion is trying to decide which of two bracelets to manufacture. Medallion has a labor contract that prohibits the company from laying off workers freely. Cost data pertaining to the two choices follow.

	Bracelet A	Bracelet B
Cost of materials per unit	$ 25	$ 32
Cost of labor per unit	32	32
Advertising cost per year	8,000	6,000
Annual depreciation on existing equip.	5,000	4,000

Required

a. Identify the fixed costs and determine the amount of fixed cost for each product.

b. Identify the variable costs and determine the amount of variable cost per unit for each product.

c. Identify the avoidable costs and determine the amount of avoidable cost for each product.

LO 1, 2, 3

Exercise 13-4   *Special order decision*

Norman Concrete Company pours concrete slabs for single-family dwellings. Wayne Construction Company, which operates outside Norman's normal sales territory, asks Norman to pour 40 slabs for Wayne's new development of homes. Norman has the capacity to build 300 slabs and is presently working on 250 of them. Wayne is willing to pay only $2,500 per slab. Norman estimates the cost of a typical job to include unit-level materials, $1,000; unit-level labor, $600; and an allocated portion of facility-level overhead, $700.

Required

Should Norman accept or reject the special order to pour 40 slabs for $2,500 each? Support your answer with appropriate computations.

LO 1, 2, 3

Exercise 13-5   *Special order decision*

Issa Company manufactures a personal computer designed for use in schools and markets it under its own label. Issa has the capacity to produce 25,000 units a year but is currently producing and selling only 15,000 units a year. The computer's normal selling price is $1,600 per unit with no volume discounts. The unit-level costs of the computer's production are $600 for direct materials, $300 for direct labor, and $120 for indirect unit-level manufacturing costs. The total product- and facility-level costs incurred by Issa during the year are expected to be $2,100,000 and $800,000, respectively. Assume that Issa receives a special order to produce and sell 3,000 computers at $1,200 each.

Required

Should Issa accept or reject the special order? Support your answer with appropriate computations.

LO 3

Exercise 13-6   *Identifying qualitative factors for a special order decision*

Required

Describe the qualitative factors that Issa should consider before accepting the special order described in Exercise 13-5.

LO 3

Exercise 13-7   *Using the contribution margin approach for a special order decision*

Shenyang Company, which produces and sells a small digital clock, bases its pricing strategy on a 35 percent markup on total cost. Based on annual production costs for 10,000 units of product, computations for the sales price per clock follow.

Unit-level costs	$150,000
Fixed costs	50,000
Total cost (a)	200,000
Markup (a × 0.35)	70,000
Total sales (b)	$270,000
Sales price per unit (b ÷ 10,000)	$27

Required

a. Shenyang has excess capacity and receives a special order for 4,000 clocks for $17 each. Calculate the contribution margin per unit; based on it, should Shenyang accept the special order?

b. Support your answer by preparing a contribution margin income statement for the special order.

Exercise 13-8   *Outsourcing decision*

LO 4

Roaming Bicycle Manufacturing Company currently produces the handlebars used in manufacturing its bicycles, which are high-quality racing bikes with limited sales. Roaming produces and sells only 6,000 bikes each year. Due to the low volume of activity, Roaming is unable to obtain the economies of scale that larger producers achieve. For example, Roaming could buy the handlebars for $35 each; they cost $38 each to make. The following is a detailed breakdown of current production costs.

Item	Unit Cost	Total
Unit-level costs		
Materials	$18	$108,000
Labor	12	72,000
Overhead	3	18,000
Allocated facility-level costs	5	30,000
Total	$38	$228,000

After seeing these figures, Roaming's president remarked that it would be foolish for the company to continue to produce the handlebars at $38 each when it can buy them for $35 each.

Required

Do you agree with the president's conclusion? Support your answer with appropriate computations.

Exercise 13-9   *Establishing price for an outsourcing decision*

LO 4

Lunn Inc. makes and sells lawn mowers for which it currently makes the engines. It has an opportunity to purchase the engines from a reliable manufacturer. The annual costs of making the engines are shown here.

Cost of materials (15,000 units × $24)	$360,000
Labor (15,000 units × $26)	390,000
Depreciation on manufacturing equipment*	42,000
Salary of supervisor of engine production	85,000
Rental cost of equipment used to make engines	23,000
Allocated portion of corporate-level facility-sustaining costs	80,000
Total cost to make 15,000 engines	$980,000

*The equipment has a book value of $90,000 but its market value is zero.

Required

a. Determine the maximum price per unit that Lunn would be willing to pay for the engines.

b. Would the price computed in Requirement *a* change if production increased to 18,750 units? Support your answer with appropriate computations.

Exercise 13-10   *Outsourcing decision with qualitative factors*

LO 4

Nadir Corporation, which makes and sells 79,400 radios annually, currently purchases the radio speakers it uses for $12 each. Each radio uses one speaker. The company has idle capacity and is considering the possibility of making the speakers that it needs. Nadir estimates that the cost of materials and labor needed to make speakers would be a total of $10 for each speaker. In addition, the costs of supervisory salaries, rent, and other manufacturing costs would be $168,000. Allocated facility-level costs would be $99,600.

Required

a. Determine the change in net income Nadir would experience if it decides to make the speakers.

b. Discuss the qualitative factors that Nadir should consider.

LO 4

Exercise 13-11   *Outsourcing decision affected by opportunity costs*

Pace Electronics currently produces the shipping containers it uses to deliver the electronics products it sells. The monthly cost of producing 9,000 containers follows.

Unit-level materials	$ 6,000
Unit-level labor	6,600
Unit-level overhead	4,200
Product-level costs*	10,800
Allocated facility-level costs	26,400

*One-third of these costs can be avoided by purchasing the containers.

Ace Container Company has offered to sell comparable containers to Pace for $2.70 each.

Required

a. Should Pace continue to make the containers? Support your answer with appropriate computations.

b. Pace could lease the space it currently uses in the manufacturing process. If leasing would produce $10,800 per month, would your answer to Requirement *a* be different? Explain.

LO 6

Exercise 13-12   *Opportunity cost*

Lynch Freight owns a truck that cost $30,000. Currently, the truck's book value is $18,000, and its expected remaining useful life is four years. Lynch has the opportunity to purchase for $26,000 a replacement truck that is extremely fuel efficient. Fuel cost for the old truck is expected to be $5,000 per year more than fuel cost for the new truck. The old truck is paid for but, in spite of being in good condition, can be sold for only $12,000.

Required

Should Lynch replace the old truck with the new fuel-efficient model, or should it continue to use the old truck until it wears out? Explain.

LO 1

Exercise 13-13   *Opportunity costs*

Steve Denmark owns his own taxi, for which he bought an $18,000 permit to operate two years ago. Mr. Denmark earns $36,000 a year operating as an independent but has the opportunity to sell the taxi and permit for $73,000 and take a position as dispatcher for Sartino Taxi Co. The dispatcher position pays $31,000 a year for a 40-hour week. Driving his own taxi, Mr. Denmark works approximately 55 hours per week. If he sells his business, he will invest the $73,000 and can earn a 10 percent return.

Required

a. Determine the opportunity cost of owning and operating the independent business.

b. Based solely on financial considerations, should Mr. Denmark sell the taxi and accept the position as dispatcher?

c. Discuss the qualitative as well as quantitative factors that Mr. Denmark should consider.

LO 5

Exercise 13-14   *Segment elimination decision*

Chamberline Company operates three segments. Income statements for the segments imply that profitability could be improved if Segment A were eliminated.

CHAMBERLINE COMPANY
Income Statements for the Year 2012

Segment	A	B	C
Sales	$162,000	$235,000	$245,000
Cost of goods sold	(121,000)	(92,000)	(95,000)
Sales commissions	(15,000)	(22,000)	(22,000)
Contribution margin	26,000	121,000	128,000
General fixed oper. exp. (allocation of president's salary)	(44,000)	(52,000)	(44,000)
Advertising expense (specific to individual divisions)	(3,000)	(10,000)	0
Net income	$(21,000)	$ 59,000	$ 84,000

Required

a. Explain the effect on profitability if Segment A is eliminated.

b. Prepare comparative income statements for the company as a whole under two alternatives: (1) the retention of Segment A and (2) the elimination of Segment A.

Exercise 13-15   *Segment elimination decision*   LO 5

Baich Transport Company divides its operations into four divisions. A recent income statement for Koslov Division follows.

BAICH TRANSPORT COMPANY
Koslov Division
Income Statement for the Year 2012

Revenue	$ 500,000
Salaries for drivers	(350,000)
Fuel expenses	(50,000)
Insurance	(70,000)
Division-level facility-sustaining costs	(40,000)
Companywide facility-sustaining costs	(130,000)
Net loss	$(140,000)

Required

a. Should Koslov Division be eliminated? Support your answer by explaining how the division's elimination would affect the net income of the company as a whole. By how much would companywide income increase or decrease?

b. Assume that Koslov Division is able to increase its revenue to $540,000 by raising its prices. Would this change the decision you made in Requirement *a*? Determine the amount of the increase or decrease that would occur in companywide net income if the segment were eliminated if revenue were $540,000.

c. What is the minimum amount of revenue required to justify continuing the operation of Koslov Division?

Exercise 13-16   *Identifying avoidable cost of a segment*   LO 5

Safar Corporation is considering the elimination of one of its segments. The segment incurs the following fixed costs. If the segment is eliminated, the building it uses will be sold.

Advertising expense	$ 80,000
Supervisory salaries	160,000
Allocation of companywide facility-level costs	49,000
Original cost of building	110,000
Book value of building	50,000
Market value of building	80,000
Maintenance costs on equipment	70,000
Real estate taxes on building	6,000

Required

Based on this information, determine the amount of avoidable cost associated with the segment.

LO 1, 6

Exercise 13-17   *Asset replacement decision*

A machine purchased three years ago for $300,000 has a current book value using straight-line depreciation of $175,000; its operating expenses are $30,000 per year. A replacement machine would cost $240,000, have a useful life of nine years, and would require $13,000 per year in operating expenses. It has an expected salvage value of $57,000 after nine years. The current disposal value of the old machine is $70,000; if it is kept nine more years, its residual value would be $10,000.

Required

Based on this information, should the old machine be replaced? Support your answer.

LO 6

Exercise 13-18   *Asset replacement decision*

Rainger Company is considering replacement of some of its manufacturing equipment. Information regarding the existing equipment and the potential replacement equipment follows.

Existing Equipment		Replacement Equipment	
Cost	$120,000	Cost	$105,000
Operating expenses*	120,000	Operating expenses*	95,000
Salvage value	30,000	Salvage value	20,000
Market value	60,000	Useful life	8 years
Book value	33,000		
Remaining useful life	8 years		

*The amounts shown for operating expenses are the cumulative total of all such expected expenses to be incurred over the useful life of the equipment.

Required

Based on this information, recommend whether to replace the equipment. Support your recommendation with appropriate computations.

LO 6

Exercise 13-19   *Asset replacement decision*

Hardin Company paid $90,000 to purchase a machine on January 1, 2009. During 2011, a technological breakthrough resulted in the development of a new machine that costs $120,000. The old machine costs $45,000 per year to operate, but the new machine could be operated for only $15,000 per year. The new machine, which will be available for delivery on January 1, 2012, has an expected useful life of four years. The old machine is more durable and is expected to have a remaining useful life of four years. The current market value of the old machine is $30,000. The expected salvage value of both machines is zero.

Required

Based on this information, recommend whether to replace the machine. Support your recommendation with appropriate computations.

LO 1, 5

Exercise 13-20   *Annual versus cumulative data for replacement decision*

Because of rapidly advancing technology, Andersen Publications Inc. is considering replacing its existing typesetting machine with leased equipment. The old machine, purchased two years ago, has an expected useful life of six years and is in good condition. Apparently, it will continue to perform as expected for the remaining four years of its expected useful life. A four-year lease for equipment with comparable productivity can be obtained for $14,000 per year. The following data apply to the old machine.

Original cost	$160,000
Accumulated depreciation	55,000
Current market value	74,000
Estimated salvage value	10,000

Required

a. Determine the annual opportunity cost of using the old machine. Based on your computations, recommend whether to replace it.

b. Determine the total cost of the lease over the four-year contract. Based on your computations, recommend whether to replace the old machine.

PROBLEMS

All applicable Problems are available with McGraw-Hill's *Connect Accounting.*

Problem 13-21 *Context-sensitive relevance*

LO 1

Required

Respond to each requirement independently.

a. Describe two decision-making contexts, one in which unit-level materials costs are avoidable, and the other in which they are unavoidable.

b. Describe two decision-making contexts, one in which batch-level setup costs are avoidable, and the other in which they are unavoidable.

c. Describe two decision-making contexts, one in which advertising costs are avoidable, and the other in which they are unavoidable.

d. Describe two decision-making contexts, one in which rent paid for a building is avoidable, and the other in which it is unavoidable.

e. Describe two decision-making contexts, one in which depreciation on manufacturing equipment is avoidable, and the other in which it is unavoidable.

Problem 13-22 *Context-sensitive relevance*

LO 1

Chapman Construction Company is a building contractor specializing in small commercial buildings. The company has the opportunity to accept one of two jobs; it cannot accept both because they must be performed at the same time and Chapman does not have the necessary labor force for both jobs. Indeed, it will be necessary to hire a new supervisor if either job is accepted. Furthermore, additional insurance will be required if either job is accepted. The revenue and costs associated with each job follow.

CHECK FIGURES
a. Contribution to profit for Job A: $264,250
b. Contribution to profit: $(3,220)

Cost Category	Job A	Job B
Contract price	$800,000	$700,000
Unit-level materials	243,700	223,450
Unit-level labor	249,150	305,000
Unit-level overhead	18,000	12,600
Supervisor's salary	116,670	116,670
Rental equipment costs	24,900	27,300
Depreciation on tools (zero market value)	19,900	19,900
Allocated portion of companywide facility-sustaining costs	10,400	8,600
Insurance cost for job	18,200	18,200

Required

a. Assume that Chapman has decided to accept one of the two jobs. Identify the information relevant to selecting one job versus the other. Recommend which job to accept and support your answer with appropriate computations.

b. Assume that Job A is no longer available. Chapman's choice is to accept or reject Job B alone. Identify the information relevant to this decision. Recommend whether to accept or reject Job B. Support your answer with appropriate computations.

Problem 13-23   *Effect of order quantity on special order decision*

Ellis Quilting Company makes blankets that it markets through a variety of department stores. It makes the blankets in batches of 1,000 units. Ellis made 20,000 blankets during the prior accounting period. The cost of producing the blankets is summarized here.

Materials cost ($25 per unit × 20,000)	$ 500,000
Labor cost ($22 per unit × 20,000)	440,000
Manufacturing supplies ($2 × 20,000)	40,000
Batch-level costs (20 batches at $4,000 per batch)	80,000
Product-level costs	160,000
Facility-level costs	290,000
Total costs	$1,510,000
Cost per unit = $1,510,000 ÷ 20,000 = $75.50	

Required

a. Kent Motels has offered to buy a batch of 500 blankets for $56 each. Ellis's normal selling price is $90 per unit. Based on the preceding quantitative data, should Ellis accept the special order? Support your answer with appropriate computations.

b. Would your answer to Requirement *a* change if Kent offered to buy a batch of 1,000 blankets for $56 per unit? Support your answer with appropriate computations.

c. Describe the qualitative factors that Ellis Quilting Company should consider before accepting a special order to sell blankets to Kent Motels.

Problem 13-24   *Effects of the level of production on an outsourcing decision*

Seymour Chemical Company makes a variety of cosmetic products, one of which is a skin cream designed to reduce the signs of aging. Seymour produces a relatively small amount (15,000 units) of the cream and is considering the purchase of the product from an outside supplier for $4.50 each. If Seymour purchases from the outside supplier, it would continue to sell and distribute the cream under its own brand name. Seymour's accountant constructed the following profitability analysis.

Revenue (15,000 units × $10)	$150,000
Unit-level materials costs (15,000 units × $1.40)	(21,000)
Unit-level labor costs (15,000 units × $0.50)	(7,500)
Unit-level overhead costs (15,000 × $0.10)	(1,500)
Unit-level selling expenses (15,000 × $0.20)	(3,000)
Contribution margin	117,000
Skin cream production supervisor's salary	(44,000)
Allocated portion of facility-level costs	(11,300)
Product-level advertising cost	(34,000)
Contribution to companywide income	$ 27,700

Required

a. Identify the cost items relevant to the make-or-outsource decision.

b. Should Seymour continue to make the product or buy it from the supplier? Support your answer by determining the change in net income if Seymour buys the cream instead of making it.

c. Suppose that Seymour is able to increase sales by 10,000 units (sales will increase to 25,000 units). At this level of production, should Seymour make or buy the cream? Support your answer by explaining how the increase in production affects the cost per unit.

d. Discuss the qualitative factors that Seymour should consider before deciding to outsource the skin cream. How can Seymour minimize the risk of establishing a relationship with an unreliable supplier?

Problem 13-25   *Outsourcing decision affected by equipment replacement*

Jenkins Bike Company (JBC) makes the frames used to build its bicycles. During 2011, JBC made 20,000 frames; the costs incurred follow.

Unit-level materials costs (20,000 units × $45)	$ 900,000
Unit-level labor costs (20,000 units × $51)	1,020,000
Unit-level overhead costs (20,000 × $9)	180,000
Depreciation on manufacturing equipment	90,000
Bike frame production supervisor's salary	70,000
Inventory holding costs	290,000
Allocated portion of facility-level costs	500,000
Total costs	$3,050,000

CHECK FIGURES
a. Avoidable cost per
   unit: $123.60
b. Avoidable cost per unit with
   new equipment: $30.90

JBC has an opportunity to purchase frames for $110 each.

Additional Information

1. The manufacturing equipment, which originally cost $450,000, has a book value of $360,000, a remaining useful life of four years, and a zero salvage value. If the equipment is not used to produce bicycle frames, it can be leased for $70,000 per year.

2. JBC has the opportunity to purchase for $910,000 new manufacturing equipment that will have an expected useful life of four years and a salvage value of $70,000. This equipment will increase productivity substantially, reducing unit-level labor costs by 60 percent. Assume that JBC will continue to produce and sell 20,000 frames per year in the future.

3. If JBC outsources the frames, the company can eliminate 80 percent of the inventory holding costs.

Required

a. Determine the avoidable cost per unit of making the bike frames, assuming that JBC is considering the alternatives between making the product using the existing equipment and outsourcing the product to the independent contractor. Based on the quantitative data, should JBC outsource the bike frames? Support your answer with appropriate computations.

b. Assuming that JBC is considering whether to replace the old equipment with the new equipment, determine the avoidable cost per unit to produce the bike frames using the new equipment and the avoidable cost per unit to produce the bike frames using the old equipment. Calculate the impact on profitability if the bike frames were made using the old equipment versus the new equipment.

c. Assuming that JBC is considering to either purchase the new equipment or outsource the bike frame, calculate the impact on profitability between the two alternatives.

d. Discuss the qualitative factors that JBC should consider before making a decision to outsource the bike frame. How can JBC minimize the risk of establishing a relationship with an unreliable supplier?

Problem 13-26   *Eliminating a segment*

Levene Boot Co. sells men's, women's, and children's boots. For each type of boot sold, it operates a separate department that has its own manager. The manager of the men's department has a sales staff of nine employees, the manager of the women's department has six employees, and the manager of the children's department has three employees. All departments are housed in a single store. In recent years, the children's department has operated at a net loss and is expected to continue doing so. Last year's income statements follow.

LO 5

CHECK FIGURE
a. Contribution to profit: $14,225

	Men's Department	Women's Department	Children's Department
Sales	$600,000	$420,000	$160,000
Cost of goods sold	(265,500)	(176,400)	(96,875)
Gross margin	334,500	243,600	63,125
Department manager's salary	(52,000)	(41,000)	(21,000)
Sales commissions	(106,200)	(75,600)	(27,900)
Rent on store lease	(21,000)	(21,000)	(21,000)
Store utilities	(4,000)	(4,000)	(4,000)
Net income (loss)	$151,300	$102,000	$(10,775)

Required

a. Determine whether to eliminate the children's department.

b. Confirm the conclusion you reached in Requirement *a* by preparing income statements for the company as a whole with and without the children's department.

c. Eliminating the children's department would increase space available to display men's and women's boots. Suppose management estimates that a wider selection of adult boots would increase the store's net earnings by $32,000. Would this information affect the decision that you made in Requirement *a*? Explain your answer.

Problem 13-27   *Effect of activity level and opportunity cost on segment elimination decision*

Levert Manufacturing Co. produces and sells specialized equipment used in the petroleum industry. The company is organized into three separate operating branches: Division A, which manufactures and sells heavy equipment; Division B, which manufactures and sells hand tools; and Division C, which makes and sells electric motors. Each division is housed in a separate manufacturing facility. Company headquarters is located in a separate building. In recent years, Division B has been operating at a loss and is expected to continue doing so. Income statements for the three divisions for 2010 follow.

	Division A	Division B	Division C
Sales	$3,000,000	$ 900,000	$3,800,000
Less: Cost of goods sold			
Unit-level manufacturing costs	(1,800,000)	(600,000)	(2,280,000)
Rent on manufacturing facility	(410,000)	(225,000)	(300,000)
Gross margin	790,000	75,000	1,220,000
Less: Operating expenses			
Unit-level selling and admin. expenses	(187,500)	(42,500)	(237,500)
Division-level fixed selling and			
admin. expenses	(250,000)	(65,000)	(310,000)
Headquarters facility-level costs	(150,000)	(150,000)	(150,000)
Net income (loss)	$ 202,500	$(182,500)	$ 522,500

Required

a. Based on the preceding information, recommend whether to eliminate Division B. Support your answer by preparing companywide income statements before and after eliminating Division B.

b. During 2010, Division B produced and sold 20,000 units of hand tools. Would your recommendation in response to Requirement *a* change if sales and production increase to 30,000 units in 2011? Support your answer by comparing differential revenue and avoidable costs for Division B, assuming that it sells 30,000 units.

c. Suppose that Levert could sublease Division B's manufacturing facility for $475,000. Would you operate the division at a production and sales volume of 30,000 units, or would you close it? Support your answer with appropriate computations.

Problem 13-28   *Comprehensive problem including special order, outsourcing, and segment elimination decisions*

Huffman Inc. makes and sells state-of-the-art electronics products. One of its segments produces The Math Machine, an inexpensive calculator. The company's chief accountant recently prepared the following income statement showing annual revenues and expenses associated with the segment's operating activities. The relevant range for the production and sale of the calculators is between 30,000 and 60,000 units per year.

|---|---|
Revenue (40,000 units × $8)	$ 320,000
Unit-level variable costs	
Materials cost (40,000 × $2)	(80,000)
Labor cost (40,000 × $1)	(40,000)
Manufacturing overhead (40,000 × $0.50)	(20,000)
Shipping and handling (40,000 × $0.25)	(10,000)
Sales commissions (40,000 × $1)	(40,000)
Contribution margin	130,000
Fixed expenses	
Advertising costs	(20,000)
Salary of production supervisor	(60,000)
Allocated companywide facility-level expenses	(80,000)
Net loss	$ (30,000)

Required (Consider each of the requirements independently.)

a. A large discount store has approached the owner of Huffman about buying 5,000 calculators. It would replace The Math Machine's label with its own logo to avoid affecting Huffman's existing customers. Because the offer was made directly to the owner, no sales commissions on the transaction would be involved, but the discount store is willing to pay only $4.50 per calculator. Based on quantitative factors alone, should Huffman accept the special order? Support your answer with appropriate computations. Specifically, by what amount would the special order increase or decrease profitability?

b. Huffman has an opportunity to buy the 40,000 calculators it currently makes from a reliable competing manufacturer for $4.90 each. The product meets Huffman's quality standards. Huffman could continue to use its own logo, advertising program, and sales force to distribute the products. Should Huffman buy the calculators or continue to make them? Support your answer with appropriate computations. Specifically, how much more or less would it cost to buy the calculators than to make them? Would your answer change if the volume of sales were increased to 60,000 units?

c. Because the calculator division is currently operating at a loss, should it be eliminated from the company's operations? Support your answer with appropriate computations. Specifically, by what amount would the segment's elimination increase or decrease profitability?

ANALYZE, THINK, COMMUNICATE

f3-1 Business Application Case *Analyzing inventory reductions at Supervalu*

On January 12, 2010, Supervalu, Inc., announced it was planning to reduce the number of different items it carries in its inventory by as much as 25 percent. Supervalu is one of the largest grocery store companies in the United States. It operates more than 2,400 stores under 14 different brand names, including Albertsons, Farm Fresh, Jewel-Osco, and Save-A-Lot. The company also has a segment that provides third-party supply-chain services.

The planned reduction in inventory items was going to be accomplished more by reducing the number of different package sizes than by reducing entire product brands. The new approach was also intended to allow the company to get better prices from its vendors and to put more emphasis on its own store brands.

Required

a. Identify some costs savings Supervalu might realize by reducing the number of items it carries in inventory by 25 percent. Be as specific as possible and use your imagination.

b. Consider the additional information presented below, which is hypothetical. All dollar amounts are in thousands; unit amounts are not. Assume that Supervalu decides to eliminate one product line, Sugar-Bits, for one of its segments that currently produces three products. As a result, the following are expected to occur:

(1) The number of units sold for the segment is expected to drop by only 40,000 because of the elimination of Sugar-Bits, since most customers are expected to purchase a Fiber-Treats or Carbo-Crunch product instead. The shift of sales from Sugar-Bits to Fiber-Treats and Carbo-Crunch is expected to be evenly split. In other words, the sales of Fiber-Treats and Carbo-Crunch will each increase by 100,000 units.

(2) Rent is paid for the entire production facility, and the space used by Sugar-Bits cannot be sublet.

(3) Utilities costs are expected to be reduced by $24,000.

(4) The supervisors for Sugar-Bits were all terminated. No new supervisor will be hired for Fiber-Treats or Carbo-Crunch.

(5) Half of the equipment being used to produce Sugar-Bits is also used to produce the other two products, and its depreciation must be absorbed by those products. The remaining equipment has a book value of $200,000 and can be sold for $150,000.

(6) Facility-level costs will continue to be allocated between the product lines based on the number of units produced.

Product-line Earnings Statements
(Dollar amounts are in thousands)

Annual Costs of Operating Each Product Line	Fiber-Treats	Carbo-Crunch	Sugar-Bits	Total
Sales in units	480,000	480,000	240,000	1,200,000
Sales in dollars	$ 480,000	$ 480,000	$ 240,000	$1,200,000
Unit-level costs:				
Cost of production	48,000	48,000	26,400	122,400
Sales commissions	6,000	6,000	2,400	14,400
Shipping and handling	10,800	9,600	4,800	25,200
Miscellaneous	3,600	2,400	2,400	8,400
Total unit-level costs	68,400	66,000	36,000	170,400
Product-level costs:				
Supervisors salaries	4,800	3,600	1,200	9,600
Facility-level costs:				
Rent	48,000	48,000	24,000	120,000
Utilities	60,000	60,000	30,000	150,000
Depreciation on equipment	192,000	192,000	96,000	480,000
Allocated company-wide expenses	12,000	12,000	6,000	30,000
Total facility-level costs	312,000	312,000	156,000	780,000
Total product cost	385,200	381,600	193,200	960,000
Profit on products	$ 94,800	$ 98,400	$ 46,800	$ 240,000

Prepare revised product-line earnings statements based on the elimination of Sugar-Bits. It will be necessary to calculate some per-unit data to accomplish this.

ATC 13-2 Group Assignment *Relevance and cost behavior*

Maccoa Soft, a division of Zayer Software Company, produces and distributes an automated payroll software system. A contribution margin format income statement for Maccoa Soft for the past year follows.

Revenue (12,000 units × $1,200)	$14,400,000
Unit-level variable costs	
Product materials cost (12,000 × $60)	(720,000)
Installation labor cost (12,000 × $200)	(2,400,000)
Manufacturing overhead (12,000 × $2)	(24,000)
Shipping and handling (12,000 × $25)	(300,000)
Sales commissions (12,000 × $300)	(3,600,000)
Nonmanufacturing miscellaneous costs (12,000 × $5)	(60,000)
Contribution margin (12,000 × $608)	7,296,000
Fixed costs	
Research and development	(2,700,000)
Legal fees to ensure product protection	(780,000)
Advertising costs	(1,200,000)
Rental cost of manufacturing facility	(600,000)
Depreciation on production equipment (zero market value)	(300,000)
Other manufacturing costs (salaries, utilities, etc.)	(744,000)
Division-level facility sustaining costs	(1,730,000)
Allocated companywide facility-level costs	(1,650,000)
Net loss	$(2,408,000)

Required

a. Divide the class into groups and then organize the groups into three sections. Assign Task 1 to the first section, Task 2 to the second section, and Task 3 to the third section. Each task should be considered independently of the others.

Group Tasks

(1) Assume that Maccoa has excess capacity. The sales staff has identified a large franchise company with 200 outlets that is interested in Maccoa's software system but is willing to pay only $800 for each system. Ignoring qualitative considerations, should Maccoa accept the special order?

(2) Maccoa has the opportunity to purchase a comparable payroll system from a competing vendor for $600 per system. Ignoring qualitative considerations, should Maccoa outsource producing the software? Maccoa would continue to sell and install the software if the manufacturing activities were outsourced.

(3) Given that Maccoa is generating a loss, should Zayer eliminate it? Would your answer change if Maccoa could increase sales by 1,000 units?

b. Have a representative from each section explain its respective conclusions. Discuss the following.

(1) Representatives from Section 1 should respond to the following: The analysis related to the special order (Task 1) suggests that all variable costs are always relevant. Is this conclusion valid? Explain your answer.

(2) Representatives from Section 2 should respond to the following: With respect to the outsourcing decision, identify a relevant fixed cost and a nonrelevant fixed cost. Discuss the criteria for determining whether a cost is or is not relevant.

(3) Representatives from Section 3 should respond to the following: Why did the segment elimination decision change when the volume of production and sales increased?

ATC 13-3   Research Assignment   *Using real world data from Pfizer*

On September 20, 2008, *The Wall Street Journal* (WSJ) reported that Pfizer was going to discontinue efforts to develop drugs related to the treatment of heart disease, obesity, and bone health. Pfizer wanted to focus its resources on areas it thought would be more profitable (p. B-1). On January 17, 2009, the WSJ reported that Pfizer planned to lay off as many as 2,400 salespersons, which would be one-third of its sales force. As a part of its efforts to reduce costs, Pfizer had reduced its workforce by 35,000 employees from January 2007 to January 2009 (p. B-5). On July 7, 2009, the WSJ reported that Pfizer, along with other pharmaceutical companies, was increasing its efforts to sell patented durgs (versus generic drugs) to customers in poorer nations. To accomplish this they were offering these customers lower prices. For example, Pfizer sells drugs in Venezuela for 30 percent less than the price at which it sells the same drugs in the United States (p. A-1).

Required

a. By stopping the development of drugs related to the treatment of heart disease, obesity, and bone health Pfizer hoped to reduce the amount spend on research and development. Relative to the level of sales, should R&D costs be considered:
  ■ Fixed costs or variable costs
  ■ Marginal costs or not

b. Were the R&D costs that Pfizer had spent in past years to develop drugs related to heart disease relevant to its decision to discontinue their future development? If they were not relevant costs, what kind of cost were they?

c. Explain how Pfizer can afford to sell drugs in Venezuela for 30 percent lower prices than it sells them for in the United States.

d. Obtain Pfizer's annual report for 2008. Pfizer's annual reports can be found at its website: www.pfizer.com. Calculate its operating costs as a percentage of revenue for 2006, 2007, and 2008. (The easiest way to do this is to calculate its "income from continuing operations" as a percentage of revenue, and subtract that amount from 1.0.) Does it appear that Pfizer is accomplishing its goal of reducing its cost? Show supporting computations.

ATC 13-4   Writing Assignment   *Relevant versus full cost*

State law permits the State Department of Revenue to collect taxes for municipal governments that operate within the state's jurisdiction and allows private companies to collect taxes for municipalities. To promote fairness and to ensure the financial well-being of the state, the law dictates that the Department of Revenue must charge municipalities a fee for collection services that is above the cost of providing such services but does not define the term *cost*. Until recently, Department of Revenue officials have included a proportionate share of all departmental costs such as depreciation on buildings and equipment, supervisory salaries, and other facility-level overhead costs when determining the cost of providing collection services, a measurement approach known as full costing. The full costing approach has led to a pricing structure that places the Department of Revenue at a competitive disadvantage relative to private collection companies. Indeed, highly efficient private companies have been able to consistently underbid the Revenue Department for municipal customers. As a result, it has lost 30 percent of its municipal collection business over the last two years. The inability to be price competitive led the revenue commissioner to hire a consulting firm to evaluate the current practice of determining the cost to provide collection services.

The consulting firm concluded that the cost to provide collection services should be limited to the relevant costs associated with providing those services, defined as the difference between the costs that would be incurred if the services were provided and the costs that would be incurred if the services were not provided. According to this definition, the costs of depreciation, supervisory salaries, and other facility-level overhead costs are not included because they are the same regardless of whether the Department of Revenue provides collection services to municipalities. The Revenue Department adopted the relevant cost approach and immediately reduced the price it charges municipalities to collect their taxes and rapidly recovered the collection business it had lost. Indeed, several of the private collection companies were forced into bankruptcy. The private companies joined together and filed suit against the Revenue Department, charging that the new definition of cost violates the intent of the law.

Required

a. Assume that you are an accountant hired as a consultant for the private companies. Write a brief memo explaining why it is inappropriate to limit the definition of the costs of providing collection services to relevant costs.

b. Assume that you are an accountant hired as a consultant for the Department of Revenue. Write a brief memo explaining why it is appropriate to limit the definition of the costs of providing collection services to relevant costs.

c. Speculate on how the matter will be resolved.

ATC 13-5 Ethical Dilemma *Asset replacement clouded by self-interest*

John Dillworth is in charge of buying property used as building sites for branch offices of the National Bank of Commerce. Mr. Dillworth recently paid $110,000 for a site located in a growing section of the city. Shortly after purchasing this lot, Mr. Dillworth had the opportunity to purchase a more desirable lot at a significantly lower price. The traffic count at the new site is virtually twice that of the old site, but the price of the lot is only $80,000. It was immediately apparent that he had overpaid for the previous purchase. The current market value of the purchased property is only $75,000. Mr. Dillworth believes that it would be in the bank's best interest to buy the new lot, but he does not want to report a loss to his boss, Kelly Fullerton. He knows that Ms. Fullerton will severely reprimand him, even though she has made her share of mistakes. In fact, he is aware of a significant bad loan that Ms. Fullerton recently approved. When confronted with the bad debt by the senior vice president in charge of commercial lending, Ms. Fullerton blamed the decision on one of her former subordinates, Ira Sacks. Ms. Fullerton implied that Mr. Sacks had been dismissed for reckless lending decisions when, in fact, he had been an excellent loan officer with an uncanny ability to assess the creditworthiness of his customers. Indeed, Mr. Sacks had voluntarily resigned to accept a better position.

Required

a. Determine the amount of the loss that would be recognized on the sale of the existing branch site.

b. Identify the type of cost represented by the $110,000 original purchase price of the land. Also identify the type of cost represented by its current market value of $75,000. Indicate which cost is relevant to a decision as to whether the original site should be replaced with the new site.

c. Is Mr. Dillworth's conclusion that the old site should be replaced supported by quantitative analysis? If not, what facts do justify his conclusion?

d. Assuming that Mr. Dillworth is a certified management accountant (CMA), do you believe the failure to replace the land violates any of the standards of ethical conduct in Exhibit 10.17 in Chapter 10? If so, which standards would be violated?

e. Discuss the ethical dilemma that Mr. Dillworth faces within the context of Donald Cressey's common features of ethical misconduct that were outlined in Chapter 1.

f. Would Mr. Dillworth be subject to criminal penalties under the Sarbanes-Oxley Act? Explain your answer.

CHAPTER 14

Planning for Profit and Cost Control

LEARNING OBJECTIVES

After you have mastered the material in this chapter, you will be able to:

1 Describe the budgeting process and the benefits it provides.

2 Explain the relationship between budgeting and human behavior.

3 Prepare a sales budget and related schedule of cash receipts.

4 Prepare an inventory purchases budget and related schedule of cash payments.

5 Prepare a selling and administrative expense budget and related schedule of cash payments.

6 Prepare a cash budget.

7 Prepare a pro forma income statement, balance sheet, and statement of cash flows.

CHAPTER OPENING

Planning is crucial to operating a profitable business. Expressing business plans in financial terms is commonly called **budgeting.** The budgeting process involves coordinating the financial plans of all areas of the business. For example, the production department cannot prepare a manufacturing plan until it knows how many units of product to produce. The number of units to produce depends on the marketing department's sales projection. The marketing department cannot project sales volume until it knows what products the company will sell. Product information comes from the research and development department. The point should be clear: a company's master budget results from combining numerous specific plans prepared by different departments.

Master budget preparation is normally supervised by a committee. The budget committee is responsible for settling disputes among various departments over budget matters. The committee also monitors reports on how various segments are progressing toward achieving their budget goals. The budget committee is not an accounting committee. It is a high-level committee that normally includes the company president, vice presidents of marketing, purchasing, production, and finance, and the controller.

The Curious Accountant

People in television commercials often say they shop at a particular store because, "my family is on a budget." The truth is, most families do not have a formal budget. What these people mean is that they need to be sure their spending does not exceed their available cash.

When a family expects to spend more money in a given year than it will earn, it must plan on borrowing the funds needed to make up the difference. However, even if a family's income for a year will exceed its spending, it may still need to borrow money because the timing of its cash inflows may not match the timing of its cash outflows. Whether a budget is being prepared for a family or a business, those preparing the budget must understand the specific issues that entity is facing if potential financial problems are to be anticipated. There is no such thing as a "one size fits all" budget.

The **United States Olympic Committee (USOC)**, like all large organizations, devotes considerable effort to budget planning. Think about the Olympic Games, and how the USOC generates revenues and incurs expenditures. Can you identify any unusual circumstances the USOC is facing that complicate its budgeting efforts? (Answer on page 513.)

THE PLANNING PROCESS

Planning normally addresses short, intermediate, and long-range time horizons. Short-term plans are more specific than long-term plans. Consider, for example, your decision to attend college. Long-term planning requires considering general questions such as

- Do I want to go to college?
- How do I expect to benefit from the experience?
- Do I want a broad knowledge base, or am I seeking to learn specific job skills?
- In what field do I want to concentrate my studies?

Many students go to college before answering these questions. They discover the disadvantages of poor planning the hard way. While their friends are graduating, they are starting over in a new major.

Intermediate-range planning usually covers three to five years. In this stage, you consider which college to attend, how to support yourself while in school, and whether to live on or off campus.

Short-term planning focuses on the coming year. In this phase you plan specific courses to take, decide which instructors to choose, schedule part-time work, and join a study group. Short-term plans are specific and detailed. Their preparation may seem tedious, but careful planning generally leads to efficient resource use and high levels of productivity.

THREE LEVELS OF PLANNING FOR BUSINESS ACTIVITY

Businesses describe the three levels of planning as *strategic planning, capital budgeting,* and *operations budgeting.* **Strategic planning** involves making long-term decisions such as defining the scope of the business, determining which products to develop or discontinue, and identifying the most profitable market niche. Upper-level management is responsible for these decisions. Strategic plans are descriptive rather than quantitative. Objectives such as "to have the largest share of the market" or "to be the best-quality producer" result from strategic planning. Although strategic planning is an integral component of managing a business, an in-depth discussion of it is beyond the scope of this text.

Capital budgeting focuses on intermediate range planning. It involves such decisions as whether to buy or lease equipment, whether to stimulate sales, or whether to increase the company's asset base. Capital budgeting is discussed in detail in a later chapter.

Operations budgeting concentrates on short-term plans. A key component of operations budgeting is the *master budget* which describes short-term objectives in specific amounts of sales targets, production goals, and financing plans. The master budget describes how management intends to achieve its objectives and directs the company's short-term activities.

The master budget normally covers one year. It is frequently divided into quarterly projections and often subdivides quarterly data by month. Effective managers cannot wait until year-end to know whether operations conform to budget targets. Monthly data provide feedback to permit making necessary corrections promptly.

Many companies use **perpetual,** or **continuous, budgeting** covering a 12-month reporting period. As the current month draws to a close, an additional month is added at the end of the budget period, resulting in a continuous 12-month budget. A perpetual budget offers the advantage of keeping management constantly focused on thinking ahead to the next 12 months. The more traditional annual approach to budgeting invites a frenzied stop-and-go mentality, with managers preparing the budget in a year-end rush that is soon forgotten. Changing conditions may not be discussed until the next year-end budget is due. A perpetual budget overcomes these disadvantages.

ADVANTAGES OF BUDGETING

Budgeting is costly and time-consuming. The sacrifices, however, are more than offset by the benefits. Budgeting promotes planning and coordination; it enhances performance measurement and corrective action.

Planning

Almost everyone makes plans. Each morning, most people think about what they will do during the day. Thinking ahead is planning. Most business managers think ahead about how they will direct operations. Unfortunately, planning is frequently as informal as making a few mental notes. Informal planning cannot be effectively communicated. The business manager might know what her objectives are, but neither her superiors nor her subordinates know. Because it serves as a communication tool, budgeting can solve these problems. The budget formalizes and documents managerial plans, clearly communicating objectives to both superiors and subordinates.

Coordination

Sometimes a choice benefits one department at the expense of another. For example, a purchasing agent may order large quantities of raw materials to obtain discounts from suppliers. But excessive quantities of materials pose a storage problem for the inventory supervisor who must manage warehouse costs. The budgeting process forces coordination among departments to promote decisions in the best interests of the company as a whole.

Performance Measurement

Budgets are specific, quantitative representations of management's objectives. Comparing actual results to budget expectations provides a way to evaluate performance. For example, if a company budgets sales of $10 million, it can judge the performance of the sales department against that level. If actual sales exceed $10 million, the company should reward the sales department; if actual sales fall below $10 million, the company should seek an explanation for the shortfall from the sales manager.

Corrective Action

Budgeting provides advance notice of potential shortages, bottlenecks, or other weaknesses in operating plans. For example, a cash budget alerts management to when the company can expect cash shortages during the coming year. The company can make borrowing arrangements well before it needs the money. Without knowing ahead of time, management might be unable to secure necessary financing on short notice, or it may have to pay excessively high interest rates to obtain funds. Budgeting advises managers of potential problems in time for them to carefully devise effective solutions.

BUDGETING AND HUMAN BEHAVIOR

Effective budgeting requires genuine sensitivity on the part of upper management to the effect on employees of budget expectations. People are often uncomfortable with budgets. Budgets are constraining. They limit individual freedom in favor of an established plan. Many people find evaluation based on budget expectations stressful. Most students experience a similar fear about testing. Like examinations, budgets represent

LO 2

Explain the relationship between budgeting and human behavior.

standards by which performance is evaluated. Employees worry about whether their performance will meet expectations.

The attitudes of high-level managers significantly impact budget effectiveness. Subordinates are keenly aware of management's expectations. If upper-level managers degrade, make fun of, or ignore the budget, subordinates will follow suit. If management uses budgets to humiliate, embarrass, or punish subordinates, employees will resent the treatment and the budgeting process. Upper-level managers must demonstrate that they view the budget as a sincere effort to express realistic goals employees are expected to meet. An honest, open, respectful atmosphere is essential to budgeting success.

Participative budgeting has frequently proved successful in creating a healthy atmosphere. This technique invites participation in the budget process by personnel at all levels of the organization, not just upper-level managers. Information flows from the bottom up as well as from the top down during budget preparation. Because they are directly responsible for meeting budget goals, subordinates can offer more realistic targets. Including them in budget preparation fosters development of a team effort. Participation fosters more cooperation and motivation, and less fear. With participative budgeting, subordinates cannot complain that the budget is management's plan. The budget is instead a self-imposed constraint. Employees can hold no one responsible but themselves if they fail to accomplish the budget objectives they established.

Upper management participates in the process to ensure that employee-generated objectives are consistent with company objectives. Furthermore, if subordinates were granted complete freedom to establish budget standards, they might be tempted to adopt lax standards to ensure they will meet them. Both managers and subordinates must cooperate if the participatory process is to produce an effective budget. If developed carefully, budgets can motivate employees to achieve superior performance. Normal human fears must be overcome, and management must create an honest budget atmosphere.

THE MASTER BUDGET

LO 1

Describe the budgeting process and the benefits it provides.

The **master budget** is a group of detailed budgets and schedules representing the company's operating and financial plans for a future accounting period. The master budget usually includes (1) *operating budgets,* (2) *capital budgets,* and (3) *pro forma financial statements.* The budgeting process normally begins with preparing the **operating budgets,** which focus on detailed operating activities. This chapter illustrates operating budgets for Hampton Hams, a retail sales company that uses (1) a sales budget, (2) an inventory purchases budget, (3) a selling and administrative (S&A) expense budget, and (4) a cash budget.

The sales budget includes a schedule of cash receipts from customers. The inventory purchases and S&A expense budgets include schedules of cash payments for inventory and expenses. Preparing the master budget begins with the sales forecast. Based on the sales forecast, the detailed budgets for inventory purchases and operating expenses are developed. The schedules of cash receipts and cash payments provide the foundation for preparing the cash budget.

The **capital budget** describes the company's intermediate-range plans for investments in facilities, equipment, new products, store outlets, and lines of business. The capital budget affects several operating budgets. For example, equipment acquisitions result in additional depreciation expense on the S&A expense budget. The cash flow effects of capital investments influence the cash budget.

The operating budgets are used to prepare *pro forma statements.* **Pro forma financial statements** are based on projected (budgeted) rather than historical information. Hampton Hams prepares a pro forma income statement, balance sheet, and statement of cash flows.

Exhibit 14.1 shows how information flows in a master budget.

EXHIBIT 14.1

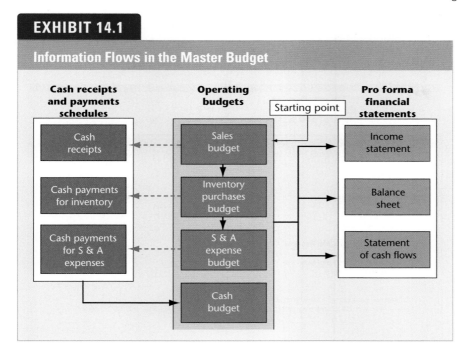

Information Flows in the Master Budget

HAMPTON HAMS BUDGETING ILLUSTRATION

Hampton Hams (HH), a major corporation, sells cured hams nationwide through retail outlets in shopping malls. By focusing on a single product and standardized operations, the company controls costs stringently. As a result, it offers high-quality hams at competitive prices.

Hampton Hams has experienced phenomenal growth during the past five years. It opened two new stores in Indianapolis, Indiana, last month and plans to open a third new store in October. Hampton Hams finances new stores by borrowing on a line of credit arranged with National Bank. National's loan officer has requested monthly budgets for each of the first three months of the new store's operations. The accounting department is preparing the new store's master budget for October, November, and December. The first step is developing a sales budget.

Sales Budget

Preparing the master budget begins with the sales forecast. The accuracy of the sales forecast is critical because all the other budgets are derived from the sales budget. Normally, the marketing department coordinates the development of the sales forecast. Sales estimates frequently flow from the bottom up to the higher management levels. Sales personnel prepare sales projections for their products and territories and pass them up the line where they are combined with the estimates of other sales personnel to develop regional and national estimates. Using various information sources, upper-level sales managers adjust the estimates generated by sales personnel. Adjustment information comes from industry periodicals and trade journals, economic analysis, marketing surveys, historical sales figures, and changes in competition. Companies assimilate this data using sophisticated computer programs, statistical techniques, and quantitative methods, or, simply, professional judgment. Regardless of the technique, the senior vice president of sales ultimately develops a sales forecast for which she is held responsible.

To develop the sales forecast for HH's new store, the sales manager studied the sales history of existing stores operating in similar locations. He then adjusted for start-up conditions. October is an opportune time to open a new store because customers will learn the store's location before the holiday season. The sales manager expects significant sales growth in November and December as customers choose the company's hams as the centerpiece for many Thanksgiving and winter holiday dinner tables.

LO 3

Prepare a sales budget and related schedule of cash receipts.

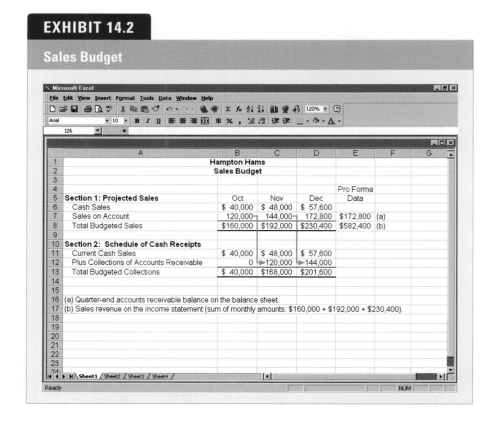

EXHIBIT 14.2

Sales Budget

The new store's sales are expected to be $160,000 in October ($40,000 in cash and $120,000 on account). Sales are expected to increase 20 percent per month during November and December. Based on these estimates, the sales manager prepared the sales budget in Exhibit 14.2.

Projected Sales

The sales budget has two sections. Section 1 shows the projected sales for each month. The November sales forecast reflects a 20 percent increase over October sales. For example, November *cash sales* are calculated as $48,000 [$40,000 + ($40,000 × 0.20)] and December *cash sales* as $57,600 [$48,000 + ($48,000 × 0.20)]. *Sales on account* are similarly computed.

Schedule of Cash Receipts

Section 2 is a schedule of the cash receipts for the projected sales. This schedule is used later to prepare the cash budget. The accountant has assumed in this schedule that Hampton Hams will collect accounts receivable from credit sales *in full* in the month following the sale. In practice, collections may be spread over several months, and some receivables may become bad debts that are never collected. Regardless of additional complexities, the objective is to estimate the amount and timing of expected cash receipts.

In the HH case, *total cash receipts* are determined by adding the current month's *cash sales* to the cash collected from the previous month's *credit sales* (accounts receivable balance). Cash receipts for each month are determined as follows.

■ October receipts are projected to be $40,000. Because the store opens in October, no accounts receivable from September exist to be collected in October. Cash receipts for October equal the amount of October's cash sales.

■ November receipts are projected to be $168,000 ($48,000 November cash sales + $120,000 cash collected from October sales on account).

■ December receipts are projected to be $201,600 ($57,600 December cash sales + $144,000 cash collected from November sales on account).

FOCUS ON INTERNATIONAL ISSUES

CASH FLOW PLANNING IN BORDEAUX

The year 2009 was considered a great year for wine in the Bordeaux region of France, and the winemakers could look forward to selling their wines for high prices, but there was one catch; these wines would not be released to consumers until late in 2012. The winemakers had incurred most of their costs in 2009 when the vines were being tended and the grapes were being processed into wine. In many industries this would mean the companies would have to finance their inventory for almost four years—not an insignificant cost. The company must finance the inventory by either borrowing the money, which results in out-of-pocket interest expense, or using its own funds. The second option generates an opportunity cost resulting from the interest revenue that could have been earned if these funds were not being used to finance the inventory.

To address this potential cash flow problem, many of the winemakers in Bordeaux offer some of their wines for sale as "futures." That means the wines are purchased and paid for while they are still aging in barrels in France. Selling wine as futures reduces the time inventory must be financed from four years to only one to two years. Of course there are other types of costs in such deals. For one, the wines must be offered at lower prices than they are expected to sell for upon release. The winemakers have obviously decided this cost is less than the cost of financing inventory through borrowed money, or they would not do it.

Companies in other industries use similar techniques to speed up cash flow, such as factoring of accounts receivable. A major reason entities prepare cash budgets is to be sure they will have enough cash on hand to pay bills as they come due. If the budget indicates a temporary cash flow deficit, action must be taken to avoid the problem, and new budgets must be prepared based on these options. Budgeting is not a static process.

Pro Forma Financial Statement Data

The Pro Forma Data column in the sales budget displays two figures HH will report on the quarter-end (December 31) budgeted financial statements. Because HH expects to collect December credit sales in January, the *accounts receivable balance* will be $172,800 on the December 31, 2012, pro forma balance sheet (shown later in Exhibit 14.7).

The $582,400 of *sales revenue* in the Pro Forma Data column will be reported on the budgeted income statement for the quarter (shown later in Exhibit 14.6). The sales revenue represents the sum of October, November, and December sales ($160,000 + $192,000 + $230,400 = $582,400).

Inventory Purchases Budget

The inventory purchases budget shows the amount of inventory HH must purchase each month to satisfy the demand projected in the sales budget. The *total inventory needed* each month equals the amount of inventory HH plans to sell that month plus the amount of inventory HH wants on hand at month-end. To the extent that total inventory needed exceeds the inventory on hand at the beginning of the month, HH will need to purchase additional inventory. The amount of inventory to purchase is computed as follows.

Prepare an inventory purchases budget and related schedule of cash payments.

Cost of budgeted sales	XXX
Plus: Desired ending inventory	XXX
Total inventory needed	XXX
Less: Beginning inventory	(XXX)
Required purchases	XXX

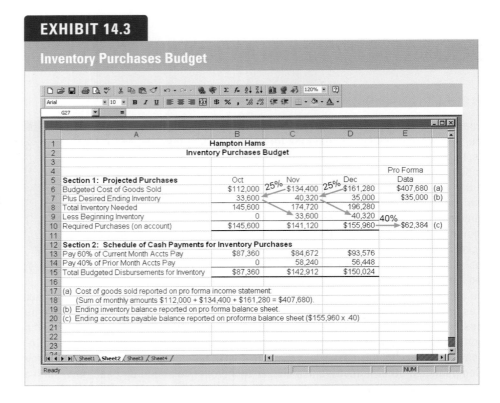

EXHIBIT 14.3

Inventory Purchases Budget

	A	B	C	D	E	
1		Hampton Hams				
2		Inventory Purchases Budget				
3						
4					Pro Forma	
5	**Section 1: Projected Purchases**	Oct	Nov	Dec	Data	
6	Budgeted Cost of Goods Sold	$112,000	25% $134,400	25% $161,280	$407,680	(a)
7	Plus Desired Ending Inventory	33,600	40,320	35,000	$35,000	(b)
8	Total Inventory Needed	145,600	174,720	196,280		
9	Less Beginning Inventory	0	33,600	40,320	40%	
10	Required Purchases (on account)	$145,600	$141,120	$155,960	$62,384	(c)
11						
12	**Section 2: Schedule of Cash Payments for Inventory Purchases**					
13	Pay 60% of Current Month Accts Pay	$87,360	$84,672	$93,576		
14	Pay 40% of Prior Month Accts Pay	0	58,240	56,448		
15	Total Budgeted Disbursements for Inventory	$87,360	$142,912	$150,024		
16						
17	(a) Cost of goods sold reported on pro forma income statement:					
18	(Sum of monthly amounts $112,000 + $134,400 + $161,280 = $407,680).					
19	(b) Ending inventory balance reported on pro forma balance sheet.					
20	(c) Ending accounts payable balance reported on proforma balance sheet ($155,960 x .40)					
21						
22						
23						

It is HH's policy to maintain an ending inventory equal to 25 percent of the next month's *projected cost of goods sold.* HH's cost of goods sold normally equals 70 percent of *sales.* Using this information and the sales budget, the accounting department prepared the inventory purchases budget shown in Exhibit 14.3.

Section 1 of the inventory purchases budget shows required purchases for each month. HH determined *budgeted cost of goods sold* for October by multiplying October *budgeted sales* by 70 percent ($160,000 × 0.70 = $112,000). Budgeted cost of goods sold for November and December were similarly computed. The October *desired ending inventory* was computed by multiplying November *budgeted cost of goods sold* by 25 percent ($134,400 × 0.25 = $33,600). Desired ending inventory for November is $40,320 ($161,280 × .25). Desired ending inventory for December is based on January projected cost of goods sold (not shown in the exhibit). HH expects ham sales to decline after the winter holidays. Because January projected cost of goods sold is only $140,000, the December desired ending inventory falls to $35,000 ($140,000 × .25).

Schedule of Cash Payments for Inventory Purchases

Section 2 is the schedule of cash payments for inventory purchases. HH makes all inventory purchases on account. The supplier requires that HH pay for 60 percent of inventory purchases in the month goods are purchased. HH pays the remaining 40 percent the month after purchase.

Cash payments are projected as follows (amounts are rounded to the nearest whole dollar).

- October cash payments for inventory are $87,360. Because the new store opens in October, no accounts payable balance from September remains to be paid in October. Cash payments for October equal 60 percent of October inventory purchases.

- November cash payments for inventory are $142,912 (40 percent of October purchases + 60 percent of November purchases).

- December cash payments for inventory are $150,024 (40 percent of November purchases + 60 percent of December purchases).

Pro Forma Financial Statement Data

The Pro Forma Data column in the inventory purchases budget displays three figures HH will report on the quarter-end budgeted financial statements. The $407,680 *cost of goods sold* reported on the pro forma income statement (shown later in Exhibit 14.6) is the sum of the monthly cost of goods sold amounts ($112,000 + $134,400 + $161,280 = $407,680).

The $35,000 *ending inventory* as of December 31, 2012, is reported on the pro forma balance sheet (shown later in Exhibit 14.7). December 31 is the last day of both the month of December and the three-month quarter represented by October, November, and December.

The $62,384 of *accounts payable* reported on the pro forma balance sheet (shown later in Exhibit 14.7) represents the 40 percent of December inventory purchases HH will pay for in January ($155,960 × .40).

✓ CHECK YOURSELF 14.1

Main Street Sales Company purchased $80,000 of inventory during June. Purchases are expected to increase by 2 percent per month in each of the next three months. Main Street makes all purchases on account. It normally pays cash to settle 70 percent of its accounts payable during the month of purchase and settles the remaining 30 percent in the month following purchase. Based on this information, determine the accounts payable balance Main Street would report on its July 31 balance sheet.

Answer   Purchases for the month of July are expected to be $81,600 ($80,000 × 1.02). Main Street will pay 70 percent of the resulting accounts payable in cash during July. The remaining 30 percent represents the expected balance in accounts payable as of July 31. Therefore, the balance would be $24,480 ($81,600 × 0.3).

Selling and Administrative Expense Budget

Section 1 of Exhibit 14.4 shows the selling and administrative (S&A) expense budget for Hampton Hams' new store. Most of the projected expenses are self-explanatory; depreciation and interest, however, merit comment. The depreciation expense is based on projections in the *capital expenditures budget.* Although not presented in this chapter, the capital budget calls for the cash purchase of $130,000 of store fixtures. The fixtures were purchased on October 1. The supplier allows a thirty-day inspection period. As a result, payment for the fixtures was made at the end of October. The fixtures are expected to have a useful life of 10 years and a $10,000 salvage value. Using the straight-line method, HH estimates annual depreciation expense at $12,000 ([$130,000 − $10,000] ÷ 10). Monthly depreciation expense is $1,000 ($12,000 annual charge ÷ 12 months).

Interest expense is missing from the S&A expense budget. HH cannot estimate interest expense until it completes its borrowing projections. Expected borrowing (financing activities) and related interest expense are shown in the *cash budget.*

Schedule of Cash Payments for Selling and Administrative Expenses

Section 2 of the S&A expense budget shows the schedule of cash payments. There are several differences between the S&A expenses recognized on the pro forma income statement and the cash payments for S&A expenses. First, Hampton Hams pays sales commissions and utilities expense the month following their incurrence. Because the store opens in October there are no payments due from September. Cash payments for sales commissions and utilities in October are zero. In November, HH will pay the October expenses for these items and in December it will pay the November sales commissions and utilities expenses. Depreciation expense does not affect the cash payments

LO 5

Prepare a selling and administrative expense budget and related schedule of cash payments.

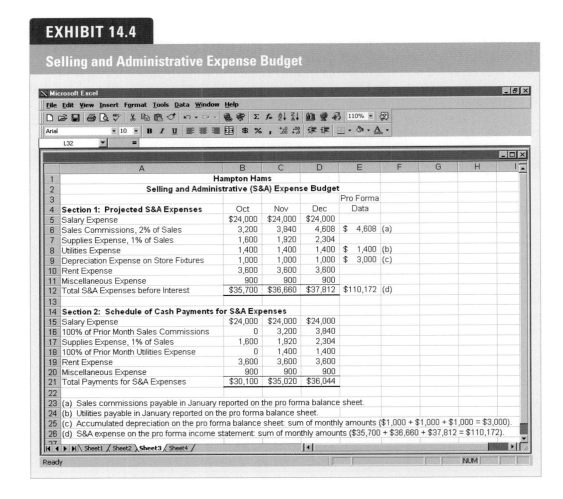

EXHIBIT 14.4

Selling and Administrative Expense Budget

	Oct	Nov	Dec	Pro Forma Data	
Hampton Hams					
Selling and Administrative (S&A) Expense Budget					
Section 1: Projected S&A Expenses					
Salary Expense	$24,000	$24,000	$24,000		
Sales Commissions, 2% of Sales	3,200	3,840	4,608	$ 4,608	(a)
Supplies Expense, 1% of Sales	1,600	1,920	2,304		
Utilities Expense	1,400	1,400	1,400	$ 1,400	(b)
Depreciation Expense on Store Fixtures	1,000	1,000	1,000	$ 3,000	(c)
Rent Expense	3,600	3,600	3,600		
Miscellaneous Expense	900	900	900		
Total S&A Expenses before Interest	$35,700	$36,660	$37,812	$110,172	(d)
Section 2: Schedule of Cash Payments for S&A Expenses					
Salary Expense	$24,000	$24,000	$24,000		
100% of Prior Month Sales Commissions	0	3,200	3,840		
Supplies Expense, 1% of Sales	1,600	1,920	2,304		
100% of Prior Month Utilities Expense	0	1,400	1,400		
Rent Expense	3,600	3,600	3,600		
Miscellaneous Expense	900	900	900		
Total Payments for S&A Expenses	$30,100	$35,020	$36,044		

(a) Sales commissions payable in January reported on the pro forma balance sheet.
(b) Utilities payable in January reported on the pro forma balance sheet.
(c) Accumulated depreciation on the pro forma balance sheet: sum of monthly amounts ($1,000 + $1,000 + $1,000 = $3,000).
(d) S&A expense on the pro forma income statement: sum of monthly amounts ($35,700 + $36,660 + $37,812 = $110,172).

schedule. The cash outflow for the store fixtures occurs when the assets are purchased, not when they are depreciated. The cost of the investment in store fixtures is in the cash budget, not in the cash outflow for S&A expenses.

Pro Forma Financial Statement Data

The Pro Forma Data column of the S&A expense budget displays four figures HH will report on the quarter-end budgeted financial statements. The first and second figures are the sales commissions payable ($4,608) and utilities payable ($1,400) on the pro forma balance sheet in Exhibit 14.7. Because December sales commissions and utilities expense are not paid until January, these amounts represent liabilities as of December 31. The third figure in the column ($3,000) is the amount of accumulated depreciation on the pro forma balance sheet in Exhibit 14.7. Because depreciation accumulates, the $3,000 balance is the sum of the monthly depreciation amounts ($1,000 + $1,000 + $1,000 = $3,000). The final figure in the Pro Forma Data column ($110,172) is the total S&A expenses reported on the pro forma income statement in Exhibit 14.6. The total S&A expense is the sum of the monthly amounts ($35,700 + $36,660 + 37,812 = $110,172).

Cash Budget

Prepare a cash budget.

Little is more important to business success than effective cash management. If a company experiences cash shortages, it will be unable to pay its debts and may be forced into bankruptcy. If excess cash accumulates, a business loses the opportunity to earn investment income or reduce interest costs by repaying debt. Preparing a **cash budget** alerts management to anticipated cash shortages or excess cash balances. Management

EXHIBIT 14.5

Cash Budget

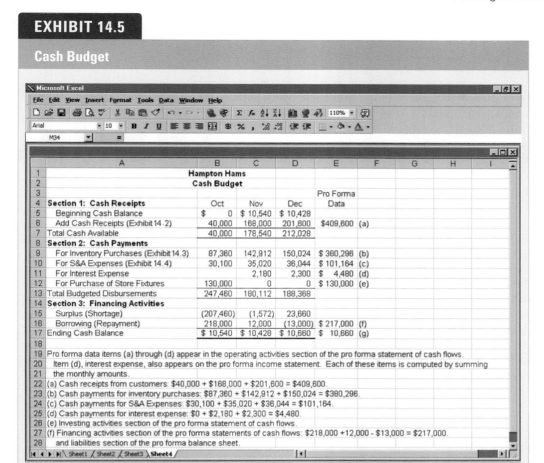

	Oct	Nov	Dec	Pro Forma Data	
Hampton Hams					
Cash Budget					
Section 1: Cash Receipts	Oct	Nov	Dec	Pro Forma Data	
Beginning Cash Balance	$ 0	$ 10,540	$ 10,428		
Add Cash Receipts (Exhibit 14.2)	40,000	168,000	201,600	$409,600	(a)
Total Cash Available	40,000	178,540	212,028		
Section 2: Cash Payments					
For Inventory Purchases (Exhibit 14.3)	87,360	142,912	150,024	$ 380,296	(b)
For S&A Expenses (Exhibit 14.4)	30,100	35,020	36,044	$ 101,164	(c)
For Interest Expense		2,180	2,300	$ 4,480	(d)
For Purchase of Store Fixtures	130,000	0	0	$ 130,000	(e)
Total Budgeted Disbursements	247,460	180,112	188,368		
Section 3: Financing Activities					
Surplus (Shortage)	(207,460)	(1,572)	23,660		
Borrowing (Repayment)	218,000	12,000	(13,000)	$ 217,000	(f)
Ending Cash Balance	$ 10,540	$ 10,428	$ 10,660	$ 10,660	(g)

Pro forma data items (a) through (d) appear in the operating activities section of the pro forma statement of cash flows. Item (d), interest expense, also appears on the pro forma income statement. Each of these items is computed by summing the monthly amounts.
(a) Cash receipts from customers: $40,000 + $168,000 + $201,600 = $409,600.
(b) Cash payments for inventory purchases: $87,360 + $142,912 + $150,024 = $380,296.
(c) Cash payments for S&A Expenses: $30,100 + $35,020 + $36,044 = $101,164.
(d) Cash payments for interest expense: $0 + $2,180 + $2,300 = $4,480.
(e) Investing activities section of the pro forma statement of cash flows.
(f) Financing activities section of the pro forma statements of cash flows: $218,000 +12,000 - $13,000 = $217,000.
  and liabilities section of the pro forma balance sheet.

can plan financing activities, making advance arrangements to cover anticipated shortages by borrowing and planning to repay past borrowings and make appropriate investments when excess cash is expected.

The cash budget is divided into three major sections: (1) a cash receipts section, (2) a cash payments section, and (3) a financing section. Much of the data needed to prepare the cash budget are included in the cash receipts and payments schedules previously discussed; however, further refinements to project financing needs and interest costs are sometimes necessary. The completed cash budget is shown in Exhibit 14.5.

Cash Receipts Section

The total cash available (Exhibit 14.5, row 7) is determined by adding the beginning cash balance to the cash receipts from customers. There is no beginning cash balance in October because the new store is opening that month. The November beginning cash balance is the October ending cash balance. The December beginning cash balance is the November ending cash balance. Cash receipts from customers comes from the *schedule of cash receipts* in the sales budget (Exhibit 14.2, section 2, row 13).

Cash Payments Section

Cash payments include expected cash outflows for inventory purchases, S&A expenses, interest expense, and investments. The cash payments for inventory purchases comes from the *schedule of cash payments for inventory purchases* (Exhibit 14.3, section 2, row 15). The cash payments for S&A expenses comes from the *schedule of cash payments for S&A expenses* (Exhibit 14.4, section 2, row 21).

REALITY BYTES

BUDGETING IN GOVERNMENTAL ENTITIES

This chapter has presented several reasons organizations should prepare budgets, but for governmental entities, budgets are not simply good planning tools—law requires them. If a manager at a commercial enterprise does not accomplish the budget objectives established for his or her part of the business, the manager may receive a poor performance evaluation. At worst, the manager may be fired. If managers of governmental agencies spend more than their budgets allow, they may have broken the law. In some cases the managers could be required to personally repay the amount by which the budget was exceeded. Because governmental budgets are enacted by the relevant elected bodies, to violate the budget is to break the law.

   Because budgets are so important for governments and are not to be exceeded, government accounting practices require that budgeted amounts be formally entered into the bookkeeping system. As you learned in your first course of accounting, companies do not alter their records when they order goods; they only make an entry when the goods are received. Governmental accounting systems are different. Each time goods or services are ordered by a government, an "encumbrance" is recorded against the budgeted amount so that agencies do not commit to spend more money than their budgets allow.

HH borrows or repays principal and pays interest on the last day of each month. The cash payments for interest are determined by multiplying the loan balance for the month by the monthly interest rate. Because there is no outstanding debt during October, there is no interest payment at the end of October. HH expects outstanding debt of $218,000 during the month of November. The bank charges interest at the rate of 12% per year, or 1% per month. The November interest expense and cash payment for interest is $2,180 ($218,000 × .01). The outstanding loan balance during December is $230,000. The December interest expense and cash payment for interest is $2,300 ($230,000 × .01). Determining the amount to borrow or repay at the end of each month is discussed in more detail in the next section of the text.

   Finally, the cash payment for the store fixtures comes from the *capital expenditures budget* (not shown in this chapter).

Financing Section

HH has a line of credit under which it can borrow or repay principal in increments of $1,000 at the end of each month as needed. HH desires to maintain an ending cash balance of at least $10,000 each month. With the $207,460 projected cash shortage in row 15 of the cash budget ($40,000 cash balance in row 7 less $247,460 budgeted cash payments in row 13), HH must borrow $218,000 on October 31 to maintain an ending cash balance of at least $10,000. This $218,000 balance is outstanding during November. On November 30, HH must borrow an additional $12,000 to cover the November projected cash shortage of $1,572 plus the $10,000 desired ending cash balance. HH projects a surplus of $23,660 for the month of December. This surplus will allow HH to repay $13,000 of debt and still maintain the desired $10,000 cash balance.

Pro Forma Financial Statement Data

Figures in the Pro Forma Data column of the cash budget (Exhibit 14.5) are alphabetically referenced. The cash receipts from customers, item (a), and the cash payment items (b), (c), and (d) are reported in the operating activities section of the pro forma statement of cash flows (Exhibit 14.8). The interest expense, item (d), is also reported on the pro forma income statement (Exhibit 14.6). The figures are determined by summing the monthly amounts. The $130,000 purchase of store fixtures, item (e), is reported in the investing activities section of the pro forma statement of cash flows. The $217,000 net borrowings, item (f), is reported in the financing activities section of the pro forma statement of cash flows (Exhibit 14.8) and also as a liability on the pro forma balance sheet (Exhibit 14.7). The $10,660 ending cash balance, item (g), is reported as the ending balance on the pro forma statement of cash flows and as an asset on the pro forma balance sheet.

✓ CHECK YOURSELF 14.2

Astor Company expects to incur the following operating expenses during September: Salary Expense, $25,000; Utility Expense, $1,200; Depreciation Expense, $5,400; and Selling Expense, $14,000. In general, it pays operating expenses in cash in the month in which it incurs them. Based on this information alone, determine the total amount of cash outflow Astor would report in the Operating Activities section of the pro forma statement of cash flows.

Answer Depreciation is not included in cash outflows because companies do not pay cash when they recognize depreciation expense. The total cash outflow is $40,200 ($25,000 + $1,200 + $14,000).

Pro Forma Income Statement

Exhibit 14.6 shows the budgeted income statement for Hampton Hams' new store. The figures for this statement come from Exhibits 14.2, 14.3, 14.4, and 14.5. The budgeted income statement provides an advance estimate of the new store's expected profitability. If expected profitability is unsatisfactory, management could decide to abandon the project or modify planned activity. Perhaps HH could lease less costly store space, pay employees a lower rate, or reduce the number of employees hired. The pricing strategy could also be examined for possible changes.

LO 7

Prepare a pro forma income statement, balance sheet, and statement of cash flows.

Budgets are usually prepared using spreadsheets or computerized mathematical models that allow managers to easily undertake "what-if" analysis. What if the growth rate differs from expectations? What if interest rates increase or decrease? Exhibits 14.2 through 14.5 in this chapter were prepared using Microsoft Excel. When variables such as growth rate, collection assumptions, or interest rates are changed, the spreadsheet software instantly recalculates the budgets. Although managers remain responsible for data analysis and decision making, computer technology offers powerful tools to assist in those tasks.

EXHIBIT 14.6

HAMPTON HAMS
Pro Forma Income Statement
For the Quarter Ended December 31, 2012

		Data Source
Sales revenue	$ 582,400	Exhibit 14.2
Cost of goods sold	(407,680)	Exhibit 14.3
Gross margin	174,720	
Selling and administrative expenses	(110,172)	Exhibit 14.4
Operating income	64,548	
Interest expense	(4,480)	Exhibit 14.5
Net income	$ 60,068	

Pro Forma Balance Sheet

Most of the figures on the pro forma balance sheet in Exhibit 14.7 have been explained. The new store has no contributed capital because its operations will be financed through debt and retained earnings. The amount of retained earnings equals the amount of net income because no earnings from prior periods exist and no distributions are planned.

EXHIBIT 14.7

HAMPTON HAMS
Pro Forma Balance Sheet
As of the Quarter Ended December 31, 2012

			Data Source
Assets			
Cash		$ 10,660	Exhibit 14.5
Accounts receivable		172,800	Exhibit 14.2
Inventory		35,000	Exhibit 14.3
Store fixtures	$130,000		Exhibit 14.4 Discussion
Accumulated depreciation	(3,000)		Exhibit 14.4 Discussion
Book value of store fixtures		127,000	
Total assets		$345,460	
Liabilities			
Accounts payable		$ 62,384	Exhibit 14.3
Sales commissions payable		4,608	Exhibit 14.4
Utilities payable		1,400	Exhibit 14.4
Line of credit borrowings		217,000	Exhibit 14.5
Equity			
Retained earnings		60,068	
Total liabilities and equity		$345,460	

Pro Forma Statement of Cash Flows

Exhibit 14.8 shows the pro forma statement of cash flows. All information for this statement comes from the cash budget in Exhibit 14.5.

EXHIBIT 14.8

HAMPTON HAMS
Pro Forma Statement of Cash Flows
For the Quarter Ended December 31, 2012

Cash flow from operating activities		
Cash receipts from customers	$409,600	
Cash payments for inventory	(380,296)	
Cash payments for S&A expenses	(101,164)	
Cash payments for interest expense	(4,480)	
Net cash flow for operating activities		$ (76,340)
Cash flow from investing activities		
Cash outflow to purchase fixtures		(130,000)
Cash flow from financing activities		
Inflow from borrowing on line of credit		217,000
Net change in cash		10,660
Plus beginning cash balance		0
Ending cash balance		$ 10,660

Answers to The Curious Accountant

Budget preparation at the USOC is complicated by the fact that the timing of its revenues does not match the timing of its expenditures. The USOC spends a lot of money helping to train athletes for the United States Olympic team. Training takes place year-round, every year, for many athletes. The USOC's training facilities in Colorado must also be maintained continuously.

Conversely, much of the USOC's revenues are earned in big batches, received every two years. This money comes from fees the USOC receives for the rights to broadcast the Olympic games on television in the United States. Most companies have a one-year budget cycle during which they attempt to anticipate the coming year's revenues and expenses. This model would not work well for the USOC. For example, in 2008, a year of summer Olympics, the USOC reported revenues of $201.7 million and a deficit of $30.6 million. In 2007, a year with no Olympic games, the USOC reported revenues of $146.1 million and a deficit of $35.0 million. In 2006, a year of winter games, the USOC had revenues of $239.7 million and a surplus of $74.9 million.

Every business, like every family, faces its own set of circumstances. Those individuals responsible for preparing an entity's budget must have a thorough understanding of the environment in which the entity operates. This is the reason the budget process must be participatory if it is to be successful. No one person, or small group, can anticipate all the issues that a large organization will face in the coming budget period; they need input from employees at all levels.

Source: Form 990s filed by the USOC with the IRS.

✓ CHECK YOURSELF 14.3

How do pro forma financial statements differ from the financial statements presented in a company's annual report to stockholders?

Answer   Pro forma financial statements are based on estimates and projections about business events that a company expects to occur in the future. The financial statements presented in a company's annual report to stockholders are based on historical events that occurred prior to the preparation of the statements.

A Look Back

The planning of financial matters is called *budgeting.* The degree of detail in a company's budget depends on the budget period. Generally, the shorter the time period, the more specific the plans. *Strategic planning* involves long-term plans, such as the overall objectives of the business. Examples of strategic planning include which products to manufacture and sell and which market niches to pursue. Strategic plans are stated in broad, descriptive terms. Capital budgeting deals with intermediate investment planning. *Operations budgeting* focuses on short-term plans and is used to create the master budget.

A budget committee is responsible for consolidating numerous departmental budgets into a master budget for the whole company. The *master budget* has detailed objectives stated in specific amounts; it describes how management intends to achieve its objectives. The master budget usually covers one year. Budgeting supports planning, coordination, performance measurement, and corrective action.

Employees may be uncomfortable with budgets, which can be constraining. Budgets set standards by which performance is evaluated. To establish an effective budget system, management should recognize the effect on human behavior of budgeting. Upper-level management must set a positive atmosphere by taking budgets seriously and avoiding using them to humiliate subordinates. One way to create the proper atmosphere is to encourage subordinates' participation in the budgeting process; *participative budgeting* can lead to goals that are more realistic about what can be accomplished and to establish a team effort in trying to reach those goals.

The primary components of the master budget are the *operating budgets,* the *capital budgets,* and the *pro forma financial statements.* The budgeting process begins with preparing the operating budgets, which consist of detailed schedules and budgets prepared by various company departments. The first operating budget to be prepared is the sales budget. The detailed operating budgets for inventory purchases and S&A expenses are based on the projected sales from the sales budget. The information in the schedules of cash receipts (prepared in conjunction with the sales budget) and cash payments (prepared in conjunction with the inventory purchases and S&A expense budgets) is used in preparing the cash budget. The cash budget subtracts cash payments from cash receipts; the resulting cash surplus or shortage determines the company's financing activities.

The capital budget describes the company's long-term plans regarding investments in facilities, equipment, new products, or other lines of business. The information from the capital budget is used as input to several of the operating budgets.

The pro forma financial statements are prepared from information in the operating budgets. The operating budgets for sales, inventory purchases, and S&A expenses contain information that is used to prepare the income statement and balance sheet. The cash budget includes the amount of interest expense reported on the income statement, the ending cash balance, the capital acquisitions reported on the balance sheet, and most of the information included in the statement of cash flows.

>> A Look Forward

Once a company has completed its budget, it has defined its plans. Then the plans must be followed. The next chapter investigates the techniques used to evaluate performance. You will learn to compare actual results to budgets, to calculate variances, and to identify the parties who are normally accountable for deviations from expectations. Finally, you will learn about the human impact management must consider in taking corrective action when employees fail to accomplish budget goals.

A step-by-step audio-narrated series of slides is provided on the text website at www.mhhe.com/edmondssurvey3e.

SELF-STUDY REVIEW PROBLEM

The Getaway Gift Company operates a chain of small gift shops that are located in prime vacation towns. Getaway is considering opening a new store on January 1, 2012. Getaway's president recently attended a business seminar that explained how formal budgets could be useful in judging the new store's likelihood of succeeding. Assume you are the company's accountant. The president has asked you to explain the budgeting process and to provide sample reports that show the new store's operating expectations for the first three months (January, February, and March). Respond to the following specific requirements.

Required

a. List the operating budgets and schedules included in a master budget.

b. Explain the difference between pro forma financial statements and the financial statements presented in a company's annual reports to shareholders.

c. Prepare a sample sales budget and a schedule of expected cash receipts using the following assumptions. Getaway estimates January sales will be $400,000 of which $100,000 will be cash and $300,000 will be credit. The ratio of cash sales to sales on account is expected to remain constant over the three-month period. The company expects sales to increase 10 percent per month. The company expects to collect 100 percent of the accounts receivable generated by credit sales in the month following the sale. Use this information to determine the amount of accounts receivable that Getaway would report on the March 31 pro forma balance sheet and the amount of sales it would report on the first quarter pro forma income statement.

d. Prepare a sample inventory purchases budget using the following assumptions. Cost of goods sold is 60 percent of sales. The company desires to maintain a minimum ending inventory equal to 25 percent of the following month's cost of goods sold. Getaway makes all inventory purchases on account. The company pays 70 percent of accounts payable in the month of purchase. It pays the remaining 30 percent in the following month. Prepare a schedule of expected cash payments for inventory purchases. Use this information to determine the amount of cost of goods sold Getaway would report on the first quarter pro forma income statement and the amounts of ending inventory and accounts payable it would report on the March 31 pro forma balance sheet.

Solution to Requirement a

A master budget would include (1) a sales budget and schedule of cash receipts, (2) an inventory purchases budget and schedule of cash payments for inventory, (3) a general, selling, and administrative expenses budget and a schedule of cash payments related to these expenses, and (4) a cash budget.

Solution to Requirement b

Pro forma statements result from the operating budgets listed in the response to Requirement *a*. Pro forma statements describe the results of expected future events. In contrast, the financial statements presented in a company's annual report reflect the results of events that have actually occurred in the past.

Solution to Requirement c

General Information				
Sales growth rate 10%				Pro Forma Statement Data
Sales Budget	**January**	**February**	**March**	
Sales				
Cash sales	$100,000	$110,000	$121,000	
Sales on account	300,000	330,000	363,000	$ 363,000*
Total sales	$400,000	$440,000	$484,000	$1,324,000†
Schedule of Cash Receipts				
Current cash sales	$100,000	$110,000	$121,000	
Plus 100% of previous month's credit sales	0	300,000	330,000	
Total budgeted collections	$100,000	$410,000	$451,000	

*Ending accounts receivable balance reported on March 31 pro forma balance sheet.

†Sales revenue reported on first quarter pro forma income statement (sum of monthly sales).

Solution to Requirement d

General Information

Cost of goods sold percentage 60%
Desired ending inventory percentage of COGS 25%

Pro Forma
Statement Data

Inventory Purchases Budget	January	February	March	
Budgeted cost of goods sold	$240,000	$264,000	$290,400	$794,400*
Plus: Desired ending inventory	66,000	72,600	79,860	79,860†
Inventory needed	306,000	336,600	370,260	
Less: Beginning inventory	0	(66,000)	(72,600)	
Required purchases	$306,000	$270,600	$297,660	89,298‡
Schedule of Cash Payments for Inventory Purchases				
70% of current purchases	$214,200	$189,420	$208,362	
30% of prior month's purchases	0	91,800	81,180	
Total budgeted payments for inventory	$214,200	$281,220	$289,542	

*Cost of goods sold reported on first quarter pro forma income statement (sum of monthly amounts).

†Ending inventory balance reported on March 31 pro forma balance sheet.

‡Ending accounts payable balance reported on pro forma balance sheet ($297,660 × 0.3).

KEY TERMS

Budgeting 498
Capital budget 502
Capital budgeting 500
Cash budget 508
Master budget 502

Operating budgets 502
Operations budgeting 500
Participative budgeting 502
Perpetual (continuous)
  budgeting 500

Pro forma financial
  statements 502
Srategic planning 500

QUESTIONS

1. Budgets are useful only for small companies that can estimate sales with accuracy. Do you agree with this statement?
2. Why does preparing the master budget require a committee?
3. What are the three levels of planning? Explain each briefly.
4. What is the primary factor that distinguishes the three different levels of planning from each other?
5. What is the advantage of using a perpetual budget instead of the traditional annual budget?
6. What are the advantages of budgeting?
7. How may budgets be used as a measure of performance?
8. Ken Shilov, manager of the marketing department, tells you that "budgeting simply does not work." He says that he made budgets for his employees and when he reprimanded them for failing to accomplish

budget goals, he got unfounded excuses. Suggest how Mr. Shilov could encourage employee cooperation.
9. What is a master budget?
10. What is the normal starting point in developing the master budget?
11. How does the level of inventory affect the production budget? Why is it important to manage the level of inventory?
12. What are the components of the cash budget? Describe each.
13. The primary reason for preparing a cash budget is to determine the amount of cash to include on the budgeted balance sheet. Do you agree or disagree with this statement? Explain.
14. What information does the pro forma income statement provide? How does its preparation depend on the operating budgets?
15. How does the pro forma statement of cash flows differ from the cash budget?

MULTIPLE-CHOICE QUESTIONS

Multiple-choice questions are provided on the text website at
www.mhhe.com/edmondssurvey3e.

EXERCISES

All applicable Exercises are available with McGraw-Hill's
Connect Accounting.

Exercise 14-1   *Budget responsibility*

LO 1, 2

Sonya Huffman, the accountant, is a perfectionist. No one can do the job as well as she can. Indeed, she has found budget information provided by the various departments to be worthless. She must change everything they give her. She has to admit that her estimates have not always been accurate, but she shudders to think of what would happen if she used the information supplied by the marketing and operating departments. No one seems to care about accuracy. Indeed, some of the marketing staff have even become insulting. When Ms. Huffman confronted one of the salesmen with the fact that he was behind in meeting his budgeted sales forecast, he responded by saying, "They're your numbers. Why don't you go out and make the sales? It's a heck of a lot easier to sit there in your office and make up numbers than it is to get out and get the real work done." Ms. Huffman reported the incident, but, of course, nothing was done about it.

Required

Write a short report suggesting how the budgeting process could be improved.

Exercise 14-2   *Preparing a sales budget*

LO 3, 7

Welch Company, which expects to start operations on January 1, 2011, will sell digital cameras in shopping malls. Welch has budgeted sales as indicated in the following table. The company expects a 10 percent increase in sales per month for February and March. The ratio of cash sales to sales on account will remain stable from January through March.

Sales	January	February	March
Cash sales	$ 40,000	?	?
Sales on account	100,000	?	?
Total budgeted sales	$140,000	?	?

Required

a. Complete the sales budget by filling in the missing amounts.

b. Determine the amount of sales revenue Welch will report on its first quarter pro forma income statement.

Exercise 14-3   *Preparing a schedule of cash receipts*

LO 3, 7

The budget director of Ginger's Florist has prepared the following sales budget. The company had $300,000 in accounts receivable on July 1. Ginger's Florist normally collects 100 percent of accounts receivable in the month following the month of sale.

Sales	July	August	September
Sales Budget			
Cash sales	$ 70,000	$ 75,000	$ 80,000
Sales on account	90,000	108,000	129,600
Total budgeted sales	$160,000	$183,000	$209,600
Schedule of Cash Receipts			
Current cash sales	?	?	?
Plus collections from accounts receivable	?	?	?
Total budgeted collections	$370,000	$165,000	$188,000

Required

a. Complete the schedule of cash receipts by filling in the missing amounts.

b. Determine the amount of accounts receivable the company will report on its third quarter pro forma balance sheet.

LO 3

Exercise 14-4   *Preparing sales budgets with different assumptions*

Applebaum Corporation, which has three divisions, is preparing its sales budget. Each division expects a different growth rate because economic conditions vary in different regions of the country. The growth expectations per quarter are 4 percent for East Division, 2 percent for West Division, and 6 percent for South Division.

Division	First Quarter	Second Quarter	Third Quarter	Fourth Quarter
East Division	$100,000	?	?	?
West Division	300,000	?	?	?
South Division	200,000	?	?	?

Required

a. Complete the sales budget by filling in the missing amounts. (Round figures to the nearest dollar.)

b. Determine the amount of sales revenue that the company will report on its quarterly pro forma income statements.

LO 3

Exercise 14-5   *Determining cash receipts from accounts receivable*

Janice's Dress Delivery operates a mail-order business that sells clothes designed for frequent travelers. It had sales of $560,000 in December. Because Janice's Dress Delivery is in the mail-order business, all sales are made on account. The company expects a 30 percent drop in sales for January. The balance in the Accounts Receivable account on December 31 was $96,400 and is budgeted to be $73,600 as of January 31. Janice's Dress Delivery normally collects accounts receivable in the month following the month of sale.

Required

a. Determine the amount of cash Janice's Dress Delivery expects to collect from accounts receivable during January.

b. Is it reasonable to assume that sales will decline in January for this type of business? Why or why not?

LO 3

Exercise 14-6   *Using judgment in making a sales forecast*

Contrell Inc. is a candy store located in a large shopping mall.

Required

Write a brief memo describing the sales pattern that you would expect Contrell to experience during the year. In which months will sales likely be high? In which months will sales likely be low? Explain why.

LO 4

Exercise 14-7   *Preparing an inventory purchases budget*

Naftel Company sells lamps and other lighting fixtures. The purchasing department manager prepared the following inventory purchases budget. Naftel's policy is to maintain an ending inventory balance equal to 10 percent of the following month's cost of goods sold. April's budgeted cost of goods sold is $75,000.

	January	February	March
Budgeted cost of goods sold	$50,000	$54,000	$60,000
Plus: Desired ending inventory	5,400	?	?
Inventory needed	55,400	?	?
Less: Beginning inventory	5,000	?	?
Required purchases (on account)	$50,400	?	?

Required

a. Complete the inventory purchases budget by filling in the missing amounts.

b. Determine the amount of cost of goods sold the company will report on its first quarter pro forma income statement.

c. Determine the amount of ending inventory the company will report on its pro forma balance sheet at the end of the first quarter.

Exercise 14-8 *Preparing a schedule of cash payments for inventory purchases*

LO 4

Sciara Books buys books and magazines directly from publishers and distributes them to grocery stores. The wholesaler expects to purchase the following inventory.

	April	May	June
Required purchases (on account)	$100,000	$120,000	$132,000

Sciara Books' accountant prepared the following schedule of cash payments for inventory purchases. Sciara Books' suppliers require that 90 percent of purchases on account be paid in the month of purchase; the remaining 10 percent are paid in the month following the month of purchase.

Schedule of Cash Payments for Inventory Purchases

	April	May	June
Payment for current accounts payable	$90,000	?	?
Payment for previous accounts payable	8,000	?	?
Total budgeted payments for inventory	$98,000	?	?

Required

a. Complete the schedule of cash payments for inventory purchases by filling in the missing amounts.

b. Determine the amount of accounts payable the company will report on its pro forma balance sheet at the end of the second quarter.

Exercise 14-9 *Determining the amount of expected inventory purchases and cash payments*

LO 4

Tobert Company, which sells electric razors, had $300,000 of cost of goods sold during the month of June. The company projects a 5 percent increase in cost of goods sold during July. The inventory balance as of June 30 is $28,000, and the desired ending inventory balance for July is $29,000. Tobert pays cash to settle 80 percent of its purchases on account during the month of purchase and pays the remaining 20 percent in the month following the purchase. The accounts payable balance as of June 30 was $35,000.

Required

a. Determine the amount of purchases budgeted for July.

b. Determine the amount of cash payments budgeted for inventory purchases in July.

Exercise 14-10 *Preparing a schedule of cash payments for selling and administrative expenses*

LO 5

The budget director for Metro Cleaning Services prepared the following list of expected operating expenses. All expenses requiring cash payments are paid for in the month incurred except salary expense and insurance. Salary is paid in the month following the month in which it is incurred. The insurance premium for six months is paid on October 1. October is the first month of operations; accordingly, there are no beginning account balances.

	October	November	December
Budgeted S&A Expenses			
Equipment lease expense	$ 6,000	$ 6,000	$ 6,000
Salary expense	6,100	6,600	7,000
Cleaning supplies	2,800	2,730	3,066
Insurance expense	1,200	1,200	1,200
Depreciation on computer	1,800	1,800	1,800
Rent	1,700	1,700	1,700
Miscellaneous expenses	700	700	700
Total S&A expenses	$20,300	$20,730	$21,466
Schedule of Cash Payments for S&A Expenses			
Equipment lease expense	?	?	?
Prior month's salary expense, 100%	?	?	?
Cleaning supplies	?	?	?
Insurance premium	?	?	?
Depreciation on computer	?	?	?
Rent	?	?	?
Miscellaneous expenses	?	?	?
Total disbursements for S&A expenses	$18,400	$17,230	$18,066

Required

a. Complete the schedule of cash payments for S&A expenses by filling in the missing amounts.

b. Determine the amount of salaries payable that the company will report on its pro forma balance sheet at the end of the fourth quarter.

c. Determine the amount of prepaid insurance the company will report on its pro forma balance sheet at the end of the fourth quarter.

LO 4

Exercise 14-11 *Preparing inventory purchases budgets with different assumptions*

Executive officers of Dominick Company are wrestling with their budget for the next year. The following are two different sales estimates provided by two different sources.

Source of Estimate	First Quarter	Second Quarter	Third Quarter	Fourth Quarter
Sales manager	$380,000	$310,000	$280,000	$480,000
Marketing consultant	520,000	460,000	410,000	650,000

Dominick's past experience indicates that cost of goods sold is about 60 percent of sales revenue. The company tries to maintain 10 percent of the next quarter's expected cost of goods sold as the current quarter's ending inventory. This year's ending inventory is $29,000. Next year's ending inventory is budgeted to be $30,000.

Required

a. Prepare an inventory purchases budget using the sales manager's estimate.

b. Prepare an inventory purchases budget using the marketing consultant's estimate.

LO 5, 7

Exercise 14-12 *Determining the amount of cash payments and pro forma statement data for selling and administrative expenses*

January budgeted selling and administrative expenses for the retail shoe store that Kathy Sibley plans to open on January 1, 2011, are as follows: sales commissions, $25,000; rent, $16,000; utilities, $5,000; depreciation, $4,000; and miscellaneous, $2,000. Utilities are paid in the month after incurrence. Other expenses are expected to be paid in cash in the month in which they are incurred.

Required

a. Determine the amount of budgeted cash payments for January selling and administrative expenses.

b. Determine the amount of utilities payable that the store will report on the January 31st pro forma balance sheet.

c. Determine the amount of depreciation expense the store will report on the income statement for the year 2011, assuming that monthly depreciation remains the same for the entire year.

Exercise 14-13 *Preparing a cash budget*

LO 6, 7

The accountant for Teresa's Dress Shop prepared the following cash budget. Teresa's desires to maintain a cash cushion of $14,000 at the end of each month. Funds are assumed to be borrowed and repaid on the last day of each month. Interest is charged at the rate of 2 percent per month.

Cash Budget	July	August	September
Section 1: Cash receipts			
Beginning cash balance	$ 42,500	$?	$?
Add cash receipts	180,000	200,000	240,600
Total cash available (a)	222,500	?	?
Section 2: Cash payments			
For inventory purchases	165,526	140,230	174,152
For S&A expenses	54,500	60,560	61,432
For interest expense	0	?	?
Total budgeted disbursements (b)	220,026	?	?
Section 3: Financing activities			
Surplus (shortage)	2,474	?	?
Borrowing (repayments) (c)	11,526	?	?
Ending cash balance (a − b + c)	$ 14,000	$ 14,000	$ 14,000

Required

a. Complete the cash budget by filling in the missing amounts. Round all computations to the nearest whole dollar.

b. Determine the amount of net cash flows from operating activities Teresa's will report on the third quarter pro forma statement of cash flows.

c. Determine the amount of net cash flows from financing activities Teresa's will report on the third quarter pro forma statement of cash flows.

Exercise 14-14 *Determining amount to borrow and pro forma financial statement balances*

LO 6, 7

Athena Sudsberry owns a small restaurant in New York City. Ms. Sudsberry provided her accountant with the following summary information regarding expectations for the month of June. The balance in accounts receivable as of May 31 is $60,000. Budgeted cash and credit sales for June are $150,000 and $600,000, respectively. Credit sales are made through Visa and Master-Card and are collected rapidly. Eighty percent of credit sales is collected in the month of sale, and the remainder is collected in the following month. Ms. Sudsberry's suppliers do not extend credit. Consequently, she pays suppliers on the last day of the month. Cash payments for June are expected to be $700,000. Ms. Sudsberry has a line of credit that enables the restaurant to borrow funds on demand; however, they must be borrowed on the last day of the month. Interest is paid in cash also on the last day of the month. Ms. Sudsberry desires to maintain a $30,000 cash balance before the interest payment. Her annual interest rate is 9 percent. Disregard any credit card fees.

Required

a. Compute the amount of funds Ms. Sudsberry needs to borrow for June, assuming that the beginning cash balance is zero.

b. Determine the amount of interest expense the restaurant will report on the June pro forma income statement.

c. What amount will the restaurant report as interest expense on the July pro forma income statement?

Exercise 14-15 *Preparing pro forma income statements with different assumptions*

Norman Jelen, the controller of Wing Corporation, is trying to prepare a sales budget for the coming year. The income statements for the last four quarters follow.

	First Quarter	Second Quarter	Third Quarter	Fourth Quarter	Total
Sales revenue	$170,000	$200,000	$210,000	$260,000	$840,000
Cost of goods sold	102,000	120,000	126,000	156,000	504,000
Gross profit	68,000	80,000	84,000	104,000	336,000
Selling & admin. expense	17,000	20,000	21,000	26,000	84,000
Net income	$ 51,000	$ 60,000	$ 63,000	$ 78,000	$252,000

Historically, cost of goods sold is about 60 percent of sales revenue. Selling and administrative expenses are about 10 percent of sales revenue.

Sam Wing, the chief executive officer, told Mr. Jelen that he expected sales next year to be 10 percent for each respective quarter above last year's level. However, Glenda Sullivan, the vice president of sales, told Mr. Jelen that she believed sales growth would be only 5 percent.

Required

a. Prepare a pro forma income statement including quarterly budgets for the coming year using Mr. Wing's estimate.

b. Prepare a pro forma income statement including quarterly budgets for the coming year using Ms. Sullivan's estimate.

c. Explain why two executive officers in the same company could have different estimates of future growth.

PROBLEMS

All applicable Problems are available with McGraw-Hill's *Connect Accounting.*

Problem 14-16 *Preparing a sales budget and schedule of cash receipts*

McCarty Pointers Inc. expects to begin operations on January 1, 2012; it will operate as a specialty sales company that sells laser pointers over the Internet. McCarty expects sales in January 2012 to total $200,000 and to increase 10 percent per month in February and March. All sales are on account. McCarty expects to collect 70 percent of accounts receivable in the month of sale, 20 percent in the month following the sale, and 10 percent in the second month following the sale.

Required

a. Prepare a sales budget for the first quarter of 2012.

b. Determine the amount of sales revenue McCarty will report on the first 2012 quarterly pro forma income statement.

c. Prepare a cash receipts schedule for the first quarter of 2012.

d. Determine the amount of accounts receivable as of March 31, 2012.

Problem 14-17 *Preparing an inventory purchases budget and schedule of cash payments*

Spratt Inc. sells fireworks. The company's marketing director developed the following cost of goods sold budget for April, May, June, and July.

	April	May	June	July
Budgeted cost of goods sold	$60,000	$70,000	$80,000	$86,000

Spratt had a beginning inventory balance of $3,600 on April 1 and a beginning balance in accounts payable of $14,800. The company desires to maintain an ending inventory balance equal to 10 percent of the next period's cost of goods sold. Spratt makes all purchases on account. The company pays 60 percent of accounts payable in the month of purchase and the remaining 40 percent in the month following purchase.

Required

a. Prepare an inventory purchases budget for April, May, and June.

b. Determine the amount of ending inventory Spratt will report on the end-of-quarter pro forma balance sheet.

c. Prepare a schedule of cash payments for inventory for April, May, and June.

d. Determine the balance in accounts payable Spratt will report on the end-of-quarter pro forma balance sheet.

Problem 14-18 *Preparing pro forma income statements with different assumptions*

LO 7

CHECK FIGURE
a. 12.75%

Top executive officers of Zottoli Company, a merchandising firm, are preparing the next year's budget. The controller has provided everyone with the current year's projected income statement.

	Current Year
Sales revenue	$2,000,000
Cost of goods sold	1,400,000
Gross profit	600,000
Selling & admin. expenses	260,000
Net income	$ 340,000

Cost of goods sold is usually 70 percent of sales revenue, and selling and administrative expenses are usually 10 percent of sales plus a fixed cost of $60,000. The president has announced that the company's goal is to increase net income by 15 percent.

Required

The following items are independent of each other.

a. What percentage increase in sales would enable the company to reach its goal? Support your answer with a pro forma income statement.

b. The market may become stagnant next year, and the company does not expect an increase in sales revenue. The production manager believes that an improved production procedure can cut cost of goods sold by 2 percent. What else can the company do to reach its goal? Prepare a pro forma income statement illustrating your proposal.

c. The company decides to escalate its advertising campaign to boost consumer recognition, which will increase selling and administrative expenses to $340,000. With the increased advertising, the company expects sales revenue to increase by 15 percent. Assume that cost of goods sold remains a constant proportion of sales. Can the company reach its goal?

Problem 14-19 *Preparing a schedule of cash payments for selling and administrative expenses*

LO 5, 6

CHECK FIGURE
a. Sept.: $28,510

Prestia is a retail company specializing in men's hats. Its budget director prepared the list of expected operating expenses that follows. All items are paid when the expenses are incurred except sales commissions and utilities, which are paid in the month after they are incurred. July is the first month of operations, so there are no beginning account balances.

	July	August	September
Salary expense	$18,000	$18,000	$18,000
Sales commissions (4 percent of sales)	1,700	1,700	1,700
Supplies expense	360	390	420
Utilities	1,100	1,100	1,100
Depreciation on store equipment	3,000	3,000	3,000
Rent	6,600	6,600	6,600
Miscellaneous	690	690	690
Total S&A expenses before interest	$31,450	$31,480	$31,510

Required

a. Prepare a schedule of cash payments for selling and administrative expenses.

b. Determine the amount of utilities payable as of September 30.

c. Determine the amount of sales commissions payable as of September 30.

LO 6

CHECK FIGURE

Feb. cash surplus before financing activities: $7,010

Problem 14-20   *Preparing a cash budget*

Kinnion Medical Clinic has budgeted the following cash flows.

	January	February	March
Cash receipts	$100,000	$106,000	$126,000
Cash payments			
For inventory purchases	90,000	72,000	85,000
For S&A expenses	31,000	32,000	27,000

Kinnion Medical had a cash balance of $8,000 on January 1. The company desires to maintain a cash cushion of $5,000. Funds are assumed to be borrowed, in increments of $1,000, and repaid on the last day of each month; the interest rate is 1 percent per month. Kinnion pays its vendor on the last day of the month also. The company had a monthly $40,000 beginning balance in its line of credit liability account from this year's quarterly results.

Required

Prepare a cash budget. (Round all computations to the nearest whole dollar.)

LO 3, 4, 5

CHECK FIGURES

c. 1st QTR purchases for peaches: $141,120
2nd QTR purchases for oranges: $312,840

Problem 14-21   *Preparing budgets with multiple products*

Fresh Fruits Corporation wholesales peaches and oranges. Lashanda King is working with the company's accountant to prepare next year's budget. Ms. King estimates that sales will increase 5 percent for peaches and 10 percent for oranges. The current year's sales revenue data follow.

	First Quarter	Second Quarter	Third Quarter	Fourth Quarter	Total
Peaches	$220,000	$240,000	$300,000	$240,000	$1,000,000
Oranges	400,000	450,000	570,000	380,000	1,800,000
Total	$620,000	$690,000	$870,000	$620,000	$2,800,000

Based on the company's past experience, cost of goods sold is usually 60 percent of sales revenue. Company policy is to keep 20 percent of the next period's estimated cost of goods sold as the current period's ending inventory. (*Hint:* Use the cost of goods sold for the first quarter to determine the beginning inventory for the first quarter.)

Required

a. Prepare the company's sales budget for the next year for each quarter by individual product.

b. If the selling and administrative expenses are estimated to be $700,000, prepare the company's budgeted annual income statement.

c. Ms. King estimates next year's ending inventory will be $34,000 for peaches and $56,000 for oranges. Prepare the company's inventory purchases budgets for the next year showing quarterly figures by product.

LO 3, 4, 5, 6, 7

Problem 14-22   *Preparing a master budget for a retail company with no beginning account balances*

Patel Company is a retail company that specializes in selling outdoor camping equipment. The company is considering opening a new store on October 1, 2012. The company president formed a planning committee to prepare a master budget for the first three months of operation. He assigned you, the budget coordinator, the following tasks.

Required

a. October sales are estimated to be $120,000 of which 40 percent will be cash and 60 percent will be credit. The company expects sales to increase at the rate of 25 percent per month. Prepare a sales budget.

b. The company expects to collect 100 percent of the accounts receivable generated by credit sales in the month following the sale. Prepare a schedule of cash receipts.

c. The cost of goods sold is 60 percent of sales. The company desires to maintain a minimum ending inventory equal to 10 percent of the next month's cost of goods sold. However, ending inventory at December 31 is expected to be $12,000. Assume that all purchases are made on account. Prepare an inventory purchases budget.

d. The company pays 70 percent of accounts payable in the month of purchase and the remaining 30 percent in the following month. Prepare a cash payments budget for inventory purchases.

e. Budgeted selling and administrative expenses per month follow.

Salary expense (fixed)	$18,000
Sales commissions	5 percent of Sales
Supplies expense	2 percent of Sales
Utilities (fixed)	$1,400
Depreciation on store fixtures (fixed)*	$4,000
Rent (fixed)	$4,800
Miscellaneous (fixed)	$1,200

*The capital expenditures budget indicates that Patel will spend $164,000 on October 1 for store fixtures, which are expected to have a $20,000 salvage value and a three-year (36-month) useful life.

Use this information to prepare a selling and administrative expenses budget.

f. Utilities and sales commissions are paid the month after they are incurred; all other expenses are paid in the month in which they are incurred. Prepare a cash payments budget for selling and administrative expenses.

g. Patel borrows funds, in increments of $1,000, and repays them on the last day of the month. The company also pays its vendors on the last day of the month. It pays interest of 1 percent per month in cash on the last day of the month. To be prudent, the company desires to maintain a $12,000 cash cushion. Prepare a cash budget.

h. Prepare a pro forma income statement for the quarter.

i. Prepare a pro forma balance sheet at the end of the quarter.

j. Prepare a pro forma statement of cash flows for the quarter.

Problem 14-23   *Behavioral impact of budgeting*

Shahid Corporation has three divisions, each operating as a responsibility center. To provide an incentive for divisional executive officers, the company gives divisional management a bonus equal to 20 percent of the excess of actual net income over budgeted net income. The following is Chaudhry Division's current year's performance.

	Current Year
Sales revenue	$4,000,000
Cost of goods sold	2,500,000
Gross profit	1,500,000
Selling & admin. expenses	900,000
Net income	$ 600,000

The president has just received next year's budget proposal from the vice president in charge of Chaudhry Division. The proposal budgets a 5 percent increase in sales revenue with an extensive explanation about stiff market competition. The president is puzzled. Chaudhry has enjoyed revenue growth of around 10 percent for each of the past five years. The president had consistently approved the division's budget proposals based on 5 percent growth in the past. This time, the president wants to show that he is not a fool. "I will impose a 15 percent revenue increase to teach them a lesson!" the president says to himself smugly.

Assume that cost of goods sold and selling and administrative expenses remain stable in proportion to sales.

Required

a. Prepare the budgeted income statement based on Chaudhry Division's proposal of a 5 percent increase.

b. If growth is actually 10 percent as usual, how much bonus would Chaudhry Division's executive officers receive if the president had approved the division's proposal?

c. Prepare the budgeted income statement based on 15 percent increase that the president imposed.

d. If the actual results turn out to be a 10 percent increase as usual, how much bonus would Chaudhry Division's executive officers receive since the president imposed a 15 percent increase?

e. Propose a better budgeting procedure for Shahid.

ANALYZE, THINK, COMMUNICATE

ATC 14-1   Business Applications Case   *Preparing and using pro forma statements*

Nancy Pinedo and Justin Johnson recently graduated from the same university. After graduation they decided not to seek jobs at established organizations but, rather, to start their own small business hoping they could have more flexibility in their personal lives for a few years. Nancy's family has operated Mexican restaurants and taco-trucks for the past two generations, and Nancy noticed there were no taco-truck services in the town where their university was located. To reduce the amount they would need for an initial investment, they decided to start a business operating a taco-cart rather than a taco-truck, from which they would cook and serve traditional Mexican styled street food.

They bought a used taco-cart for $15,000. This cost, along with the cost for supplies to get started, a business license, and street vendor license brought their initial expenditures to $20,000. Five-thousand dollars came from personal savings they had accumulated by working part time during college, and they borrowed $15,000 from Nancy's parents. They agreed to pay interest on the outstanding loan balance each month based on an annual rate of 6 percent. They will repay the principal over the next few years as cash becomes available. They were able to rent space in a parking lot near the campus they had attended, believing that the students would welcome their food as an alternative to the typical fast food that was currently available.

After two months in business, September and October, they had average monthly revenues of $20,000 and out of pocket costs of $16,000 for rent, ingredients, paper supplies, and so on, but not interest. Justin thinks they should repay some of the money they borrowed, but Nancy thinks they should prepare a set of forecasted financial statements for their first year in business before deciding whether or not to repay any principal on the loan. She remembers a bit about budgeting from a survey of accounting course she took and thinks the results from their first two months in business can be extended over the next 10 months to prepare the budget they need. They estimate the cart will last at least five years, after which they expect to sell it for $5,000 and move on to something else in their lives. Nancy agrees to prepare a forecasted (pro forma) income statement, balance sheet, and statement of cash flows for their first year in business, which includes the two months already passed.

Required

a. Prepare the annual pro forma financial statements that you would expect Nancy to prepare based on her comments about her expectations for the business. Assume no principal will be repaid on the loan.

b. Review the statements you prepared for the first requirement and prepare a list of reasons why actual results for Justin and Nancy's business probably will not match their budgeted statements.

ATC 14-2   Group Assignment   *Master budget and pro forma statements*

The following trial balance was drawn from the records of Havel Company as of October 1, 2011.

Cash	$ 16,000	
Accounts receivable	60,000	
Inventory	40,000	
Store equipment	200,000	
Accumulated depreciation		$ 76,800
Accounts payable		72,000
Line of credit loan		100,000
Common stock		50,000
Retained earnings		17,200
Totals	$316,000	$316,000

Required

a. Divide the class into groups, each with four or five students. Organize the groups into three sections. Assign Task 1 to the first section, Task 2 to the second section, and Task 3 to the third section.

Group Tasks

(1) Based on the following information, prepare a sales budget and a schedule of cash receipts for October, November, and December. Sales for October are expected to be $180,000, consisting of $40,000 in cash and $140,000 on credit. The company expects sales to increase at the rate of 10 percent per month. All of accounts receivable is collected in the month following the sale.

(2) Based on the following information, prepare a purchases budget and a schedule of cash payments for inventory purchases for October, November, and December. Cost of goods sold for October is expected to be $72,000. Cost of goods sold is expected to increase by 10 percent per month in November and December. Havel expects January cost of goods sold to be $89,000. The company expects to maintain a minimum ending inventory equal to 20 percent of the next month's cost of goods sold. Seventy-five percent of accounts payable is paid in the month that the purchase occurs; the remaining 25 percent is paid in the following month.

(3) Based on the following selling and administrative expenses budgeted for October, prepare a selling and administrative expenses budget for October, November, and December.

     Cash payments for sales commissions and utilities are made in the month following the one in which the expense is incurred. Supplies and other operating expenses are paid in cash in the month in which they are incurred. As of October 1, no amounts were payable for either commissions or utilities from the previous month.

Sales commissions (10% increase per month)	$ 7,200
Supplies expense (10% increase per month)	1,800
Utilities (fixed)	2,200
Depreciation on store equipment (fixed)	1,600
Salary expense (fixed)	34,000
Rent (fixed)	6,000
Miscellaneous (fixed)	1,000

b. Select a representative from each section. Have the representatives supply the missing information in the following pro forma income statement and balance sheet for the fourth quarter of 2011. The statements are prepared as of December 31, 2011.

Income Statement	
Sales Revenue	$?
Cost of Goods Sold	?
Gross Margin	357,480
Operating Expenses	?
Operating Income	193,290
Interest Expense	(2,530)
Net Income	$190,760

Balance Sheet		
Assets		
Cash		$ 9,082
Accounts Receivable		?
Inventory		?
Store Equipment	$200,000	
Accumulated Depreciation Store Equipment	?	
Book Value of Equipment		118,400
Total Assets		$314,682
Liabilities		
Accounts Payable		?
Utilities Payable		?
Sales Commissions Payable		?
Line of Credit		23,936
Equity		
Common Stock		50,000
Retained Earnings		?
Total Liabilities and Equity		$314,682

c. Indicate whether Havel will need to borrow money during October.

ATC 14-3   Research Assignment   *Analyzing budget data for the United States government*

The annual budget of the United States is very complex, but this case requires that you analyze only a small portion of the historical tables that are presented as a part of each year's budget. The fiscal year of the federal government ends on September 30. Obtain the budget documents needed at www.gpoaccess.gov/usbudget by following these steps:

■ Under the "Previous Budgets" heading, click on "Browse"

■ Under the Barack H. Obama heading, click on "Fiscal Year 2010"

■ There are two options that can be used on the page that appears next:

   • Under the "Budget Documents" heading, you can select the PDF link beside the "Historical Table" subheading.

   • Scroll down to the "Spreadsheets" heading and click on the "Historical Tables" subheading. This option provides the data in an Excel compatible format.

■ Under whichever option you choose above, you will need to review Table 1.1, Table 1.2, and Table 4.2 to complete the requirements below.

Required

a. Table 1.2 shows the budget as a *percentage of gross domestic product* (GDP). Using the data in the third column, "Surplus or Deficit," determine how many years since 1960 the budget has shown a surplus and how many times it has shown a deficit. Ignore the "TQ" data between 1976 and 1977. This was a year that the government changed the ending date of its fiscal year.

b. Based on the data in Table 1.2, identify the three years with the highest deficits as a percentage of GDP. What were the deficit percentages for these years? Which year had the largest surplus and by what percentage?

c. Using your findings for Requirement *b*, regarding the year with the highest deficit as a percentage of GDP, go to Table 1.1 and calculate the deficit for that year as a *percentage of receipts*.

d. The president of the United States from 1993 through 2000 was Bill Clinton, a Democrat. The president from 2001 through 2009 was George Bush, a Republican. These men had significant input into the federal budget for the fiscal years 1994–2001 and 2002–2009, respectively. Table 4.2 shows what percentage of the total federal budget was directed toward each department within the government. Compare the data on Table 4.2 for 1994–2001, the Clinton years, to the data for 2002–2009, the Bush years. Identify the five departments that appear to have changed the most from the Clinton years to the Bush years. Ignore "Allowances" and "Undistributed offsetting receipts." Note, if you wish to approach this assignment more accurately, you can compute the average percentage for each department for the eight years each president served, and compare the two averages. The gpoaccess website includes a spreadsheet version of the historical data tables, allowing for a reasonably easy Excel analysis.

ATC 14-4   Writing Assignment   *Continuous budgeting*

Toll Brothers, Inc., is a large builder of luxury homes across the United States. From 2000 through 2006 it experienced continuous growth in revenues that averaged over 24 percent annually. Not only did it experience growth from year to year, but its revenue grew in each quarter of 2005 and 2006. Then things started to slow down. In 2007 its revenue dropped by 24 percent compared to 2006. Additionally, its revenue declined in two of the four quarters of 2007. Management of the company commented as follows in the company's 2007 annual report.

> *In the late summer and fall of 2005, there was a modest deceleration in the growth rate of demand. Additionally, in the aftermath of Hurricane Katrina, gas prices rose to $3.00/gallon and consumer confidence dropped precipitously. When the music stopped, many territories were overwhelmed with excess home inventories. . . . We believed that a national geographic presence would provide some diversification of risk to insulate us from the type of local market crashes or regional declines that had characterized previous industry downswings. . . . However, the national scope of this downturn and the rapidity with which it swept across the nation suggest that there was greater correlation among regional housing markets than we had previously believed.*

*   *   *

> *In January 2006, it appeared that consumer confidence was starting to firm until a wave of subprime fears in late February 2007 took the momentum away. The financial markets began to develop jitters as word spread that subprime loan foreclosures might soon bring hundreds of thousands of additional homes onto the market. . . .*

Required

Assume you are Toll Brothers' budget director. Write a memo to the management team explaining how the practice of continuous budgeting could overcome the shortcomings of an annual budget process in an uncertain market situation.

ATC 14-5   Ethical Dilemma   *Bad budget system or unethical behavior?*

Clarence Cleaver is the budget director for the Harris County School District. Mr. Cleaver recently sent an urgent e-mail message to Sally Simmons, principal of West Harris County High. The message severely reprimanded Ms. Simmons for failing to spend the funds allocated to her to purchase computer equipment. Ms. Simmons responded that her school already has a sufficient supply of computers; the computer lab is never filled to capacity and usually is less than half filled. Ms. Simmons suggested that she would rather use the funds for teacher training. She argued that the reason the existing computers are not fully utilized is that the teachers lack sufficient computer literacy necessary to make assignments for their students.

Mr. Cleaver responded that it is not Ms. Simmons's job to decide how the money is to be spent; that is the school board's job. It is the principal's job to spend the money as the board directed. He informed Ms. Simmons that if the money is not spent by the fiscal closing date, the school board would likely reduce next year's budget allotment. To avoid a potential budget cut, Mr. Cleaver reallocated Ms. Simmons's computer funds to Jules Carrington, principal of East Harris County High. Mr. Carrington knows how to buy computers regardless of whether they are needed. Mr. Cleaver's final words were, "Don't blame me if parents of West High students complain that East High has more equipment. If anybody comes to me, I'm telling them that you turned down the money."

Required

a. Do Mr. Cleaver's actions violate the standards of ethical conduct shown in Exhibit 10.17 of Chapter 10?

b. Explain how participative budgeting could improve the allocation of resources for the Harris County School District.

CHAPTER 15

Performance Evaluation

LEARNING OBJECTIVES

After you have mastered the material in this chapter, you will be able to:

1 Describe the concept of decentralization.

2 Distinguish between flexible and static budgets.

3 Classify variances as being favorable or unfavorable.

4 Compute and interpret sales and variable cost volume variances.

5 Compute and interpret flexible budget variances.

6 Evaluate investment opportunities using the return on investment technique.

7 Evaluate investment opportunities using the residual income technique.

CHAPTER OPENING

Walter Keller, a production manager, complained to the accountant, Kelly Oberson, that the budget system failed to control his department's labor cost. Ms. Oberson responded, "People, not budgets, control costs." Budgeting is one of many tools management uses to control business operations. Managers are responsible for using control tools effectively. **Responsibility accounting** focuses on evaluating the performance of individual managers. For example, expenses controlled by a production department manager are presented in one report and expenses controlled by a marketing department manager are presented in a different report. This chapter discusses the development and use of a responsibility accounting system.

The Curious Accountant

Gourmet Pizzas is located in an affluent section of a major metropolitan area. Its owner worked at a national-chain pizza restaurant while in college. He knew that even though the national pizza chains had a lot of stores, (in 2010 **Domino's**, **Pizza Hut**, and **Papa John's** had approximately 14,000 stores in the United States), more than half of the country's pizzas were sold by other, mostly independently owned, restaurants. Knowing he could not beat the big guys on price, Gourmet Pizzas focuses on quality. Its pizza dough is made from scratch on the premises from organically grown flour, and it offers a wide variety of unusual toppings, such as pancetta.

In order to determine a proper selling price for his pizzas, the owner estimated the cost of making the crusts, among other things. Knowing how much flour, yeast, and so on was needed to make the dough for one pizza and estimating the cost of these ingredients, he determined that the materials for the dough for each pizza should cost him 25 cents. However, after six months in business, he had spent $10,150 on materials for making his dough and had sold 32,750 pizzas. This resulted in an actual cost per pizza of 31 cents.

What are two general reasons that may explain why the materials cost for pizza dough was higher than Gourmet Pizzas' owner estimated? (Answer on page 533.)

Sources: Companies' SEC filings and **PMQ.com**.

DECENTRALIZATION CONCEPT

Describe the concept of decentralization.

Effective responsibility accounting requires clear lines of authority and responsibility. Divisions of authority and responsibility normally occur as a natural consequence of managing business operations. In a small business, one person can control everything: marketing, production, management, accounting. In contrast, large companies are so complex that authority and control must be divided among many people.

Consider the hiring of employees. A small business usually operates in a limited geographic area. The owner works directly with employees. She knows the job requirements, local wage rates, and the available labor pool. She is in a position to make informed hiring decisions. In contrast, a major corporation may employ thousands of employees throughout the world. The employees may speak different languages and have different social customs. Their jobs may require many different skills and pay a vast array of wage rates. The president of the corporation cannot make informed hiring decisions for the entire company. Instead, he delegates *authority* to a professional personnel manager and holds that manager *responsible* for hiring practices.

Decision-making authority is similarly delegated to individuals responsible for managing specific organization functions such as production, marketing, and accounting. Delegating authority and responsibility is referred to as **decentralization.**

Responsibility Centers

Decentralized businesses are usually subdivided into distinct reporting units called responsibility centers. A **responsibility center** is an organizational unit that controls identifiable revenue or expense items. The unit may be a division, a department, a subdepartment, or even a single machine. For example, a transportation company may identify a semitrailer truck as a responsibility center. The company holds the truck driver responsible for the revenues and expenses associated with operating the truck. Responsibility centers may be divided into three categories: cost, profit, and investment.

A **cost center** is an organizational unit that incurs expenses but does not generate revenue. Cost centers normally fall on the lower levels of an organization chart. The manager of a cost center is judged on his ability to keep costs within budget parameters.

A **profit center** differs from a cost center in that it not only incurs costs but also generates revenue. The manager of a profit center is judged on his ability to produce revenue in excess of expenses.

Investment center managers are responsible for revenues, expenses, and the investment of capital. Investment centers normally appear at the upper levels of an organization chart. Managers of investment centers are accountable for assets and liabilities as well as earnings.

Controllability Concept

The **controllability concept** is crucial to an effective responsibility accounting system. Managers should only be evaluated based on revenues or costs they control. Holding individuals responsible for things they cannot control is demotivating. Isolating control, however, may be difficult, as illustrated in the following case.

Dorothy Pasewark, a buyer for a large department store chain, was criticized when stores could not resell the merchandise she bought at the expected price. Ms. Pasewark countered that the sales staff caused the sluggish sales by not displaying the merchandise properly. The sales staff charged that the merchandise had too little sales potential to justify setting up more enticing displays. The division of influence between the buyer and the sales staff clouds the assignment of responsibility.

Because the exercise of control may be clouded, managers are usually held responsible for items over which they have *predominant* rather than *absolute* control. At times responsibility accounting may be imperfect. Management must strive to ensure that praise or criticism is administered as fairly as possible.

Answers to The Curious Accountant

As this chapter demonstrates, there are two primary reasons a company spends more or less to produce a product than it estimated it would.

First, the company may have paid more or less to purchase the inputs needed to produce the product than it estimated. Second, the company used a greater or lesser quantity of these inputs than expected. In the case of Gourmet Pizzas, it may have had to pay more for flour, yeast, cheese, and so on than the owner estimated. Or, it may have used more of these ingredients than expected. For example, if pizza dough sits around too long before being used, it may have to be thrown out. This waste was not anticipated when computing the cost to make only one pizza. Of course, the higher than expected cost could have been a combination of price and quantity factors.

Gourmet Pizza needs to determine if the difference between its expected costs and actual costs was because the estimates were faulty, or because the production process was inefficient. If the estimates were to blame, the owner would need to revise them so he can charge the proper price to his customers. If the production process is inefficient, he needs to correct it if he is to earn an acceptable level of profit.

PREPARING FLEXIBLE BUDGETS

A **flexible budget** is an extension of the *master budget* discussed previously. The master budget is based solely on the planned volume of activity. The master budget is frequently called a **static budget** because it remains unchanged even if the actual volume of activity differs from the planned volume. Flexible budgets differ from static budgets in that they show expected revenues and costs at a *variety* of volume levels.

To illustrate the differences between static and flexible budgets, consider Melrose Manufacturing Company, a producer of small, high-quality trophies used in award ceremonies. Melrose plans to make and sell 18,000 trophies during 2011. Management's best estimates of the expected sales price and per unit costs for the trophies are called *standard* prices and costs. The standard price and costs for the 18,000 trophies follow.

LO 2

Distinguish between flexible and static budgets.

Per unit sales price and variable costs	
Expected sales price	$80.00
Standard materials cost	12.00
Standard labor cost	16.80
Standard overhead cost	5.60
Standard general, selling, and administrative cost	15.00
Fixed costs	
Manufacturing overhead cost	$201,600
General, selling, and administrative cost	90,000

The static budget is highlighted with orange shading in Exhibit 15.1. Sales revenue is determined by multiplying the expected sales price per unit times the planned volume of activity ($80 × 18,000 = $1,440,000). Similarly, the variable costs are calculated by multiplying the standard cost per unit times the planned volume of activity. For example, the manufacturing materials cost is $216,000 ($12 × 18,000). The same computational procedures apply to the other variable costs. The variable costs are subtracted from the sales revenue to produce a contribution margin of $550,800. The fixed costs are subtracted from the contribution margin to produce a budgeted net income of $259,200.

EXHIBIT 15.1

Static and Flexible Budgets in Excel Spreadsheet

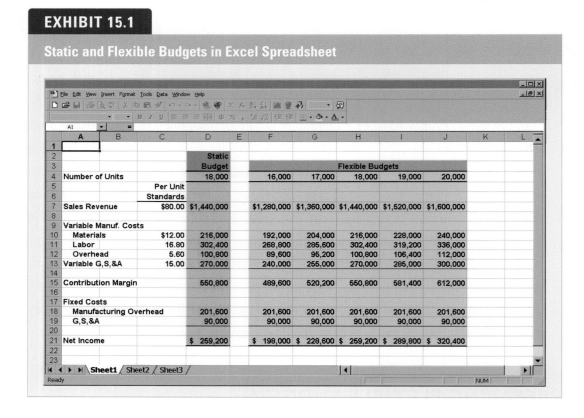

	Per Unit Standards	Static Budget (18,000)	Flexible Budgets				
			16,000	17,000	18,000	19,000	20,000
Number of Units		18,000	16,000	17,000	18,000	19,000	20,000
Sales Revenue	$80.00	$1,440,000	$1,280,000	$1,360,000	$1,440,000	$1,520,000	$1,600,000
Variable Manuf. Costs							
Materials	$12.00	216,000	192,000	204,000	216,000	228,000	240,000
Labor	16.80	302,400	268,800	285,600	302,400	319,200	336,000
Overhead	5.60	100,800	89,600	95,200	100,800	106,400	112,000
Variable G,S,&A	15.00	270,000	240,000	255,000	270,000	285,000	300,000
Contribution Margin		550,800	489,600	520,200	550,800	581,400	612,000
Fixed Costs							
Manufacturing Overhead		201,600	201,600	201,600	201,600	201,600	201,600
G,S,&A		90,000	90,000	90,000	90,000	90,000	90,000
Net Income		$ 259,200	$ 198,000	$ 228,600	$ 259,200	$ 289,800	$ 320,400

What happens if the number of units sold is different from the planned volume? In other words, *what* happens to net income *if* Melrose sells more or less than 18,000 units? Managers frequently use flexible budgets to examine such *what if* scenarios. Flexible budget income statements for Melrose at sales volumes of 16,000, 17,000, 18,000, 19,000, and 20,000 are highlighted with blue shading in Exhibit 15.1.

The flexible budgets are prepared with the same per-unit standard amounts and fixed cost data used to produce the static budget. The only difference is the expected number of units sold. For example, the sales revenue at 16,000 units is $1,280,000 ($80 × 16,000), at 17,000 units it is $1,360,000 ($80 × 17,000), and so on. The variable materials cost at 16,000 units is $192,000 ($12 × 16,000), at 17,000 units it is $204,000 ($12 × 17,000), and so on. The other variable costs are computed in the same manner. Note that the fixed costs are the same at all levels of activity because, by definition, they are not affected by changes in volume.

Other flexible budgets are possible. Indeed, a flexible budget can be prepared for any number of units sold. You have probably noticed that Exhibit 15.1 was prepared using an Excel spreadsheet. Excel offers the opportunity to prepare an unlimited number of flexible budgets with minimal effort. For example, formulas can be created with cell references so that new budgets can be created simply by changing the number of units entered in a single cell.

Managers use flexible budgets for both planning and performance evaluation. For example, managers may assess whether the company's cash position is adequate by assuming different levels of volume. They may judge if the number of employees, amounts of materials, and equipment and storage facilities are appropriate for a variety of different potential levels of volume. In addition to helping plan, flexible budgets are critical to implementing an effective performance evaluation system.

The static (master) budget of Parcel, Inc., called for a production and sales volume of 25,000 units. At that volume, total budgeted fixed costs were $150,000 and total budgeted variable costs were $200,000. Prepare a flexible budget for an expected volume of 26,000 units.

Answer Budgeted fixed costs would remain unchanged at $150,000 because changes in the volume of activity do not affect budgeted fixed costs. Budgeted variable costs would increase to $208,000, computed as follows: Calculate the budgeted variable cost per unit ($200,000 ÷ 25,000 units = $8) and then multiply that variable cost per unit by the expected volume ($8 × 26,000 units = $208,000).

DETERMINING VARIANCES FOR PERFORMANCE EVALUATION

One means of evaluating managerial performance is to compare *standard* amounts with *actual* results. The differences between the standard and actual amounts are called **variances;** variances can be either **favorable** or **unfavorable.** When actual sales revenue is greater than expected (planned) revenue, a company has a favorable sales variance because higher sales increase net income. When actual sales are less than expected, an unfavorable sales variance exists. When actual costs are *less* than standard costs, cost variances are favorable because lower costs increase net income. Unfavorable cost variances exist when actual costs are *more* than standard costs. These relationships are summarized below.

Classify variances as being favorable or unfavorable.

- When actual sales exceed expected sales, variances are favorable.
- When actual sales are less than expected sales, variances are unfavorable.
- When actual costs exceed standard costs, variances are unfavorable.
- When actual costs are less than standard costs, variances are favorable.

SALES AND VARIABLE COST VOLUME VARIANCES

The amount of a **sales volume variance** is the difference between the static budget (which is based on planned volume) and a flexible budget based on actual volume. Likewise, the **variable cost volume variances** are determined by calculating the differences between the static and flexible budget amounts. These variances measure management effectiveness in attaining the planned volume of activity. To illustrate, assume Melrose Manufacturing Company actually makes and sells 19,000 trophies during 2011. The planned volume of activity was 18,000 trophies. Exhibit 15.2 shows Melrose's static budget, flexible budget, and volume variances.

Compute and interpret sales and variable cost volume variances.

Interpreting the Sales and Variable Cost Volume Variances

Because the static and flexible budgets are based on the same standard sales price and per-unit variable costs, the variances are solely attributable to the difference between the planned and actual volume of activity. Marketing managers are usually responsible for the volume variances. Because the sales volume drives production levels, production managers have little control over volume. Exceptions occur; for example, if poor production quality control leads to inferior goods that are difficult to sell, the production

EXHIBIT 15.2

Melrose Manufacturing Company's Volume Variances

	Static Budget	Flexible Budget	Volume Variances	
Number of units	18,000	19,000	1,000	Favorable
Sales revenue	$1,440,000	$1,520,000	$80,000	Favorable
Variable manufacturing costs				
Materials	216,000	228,000	12,000	Unfavorable
Labor	302,400	319,200	16,800	Unfavorable
Overhead	100,800	106,400	5,600	Unfavorable
Variable G, S, & A	270,000	285,000	15,000	Unfavorable
Contribution margin	550,800	581,400	30,600	Favorable
Fixed costs				
Manufacturing overhead	201,600	201,600	0	
G, S, & A	90,000	90,000	0	
Net income	$ 259,200	$ 289,800	$30,600	Favorable

manager is responsible. The production manager is responsible for production delays that affect product availability, which may restrict sales volume. Under normal circumstances, however, the marketing campaign determines the volume of sales. Upper-level marketing managers develop the promotional program and create the sales plan; they are in the best position to explain why sales goals are or are not met. When marketing managers refer to **making the numbers,** they usually mean reaching the sales volume in the static (master) budget.

In the case of Melrose Manufacturing Company, the marketing manager not only achieved but also exceeded by 1,000 units the planned volume of sales. Exhibit 15.2 shows the activity variances resulting from the extra volume. At the standard price, the additional volume produces a favorable revenue variance of $80,000 (1,000 units × $80 per unit). The increase in volume also produces unfavorable variable cost variances. The net effect of producing and selling the additional 1,000 units is an increase of $30,600 in the contribution margin, a positive result. These preliminary results suggest that the marketing manager is to be commended. The analysis, however, is incomplete. For example, examining market share could reveal whether the manager won customers from competitors or whether the manager simply reaped the benefit of an unexpected industrywide increase in demand. The increase in sales volume could have been attained by reducing the sales price; the success of that strategy will be analyzed further in a later section of this chapter.

Because the variable costs in the flexible budget are higher than the variable costs in the static budget, the variable cost volume variances are *unfavorable.* The unfavorable classification may be misleading because it focuses solely on the cost component of the income statement. While costs are higher than expected, so too may be revenue. Indeed, as shown in Exhibit 15.2, the total of the unfavorable variable cost variances is more than offset by the favorable revenue variance, resulting in a higher contribution margin. Frequently, the assessment of variances requires a holistic perspective.

Fixed Cost Considerations

The fixed costs are the same in both the static and flexible budgets. By definition, the budgeted amount of fixed costs remains unchanged regardless of the volume of activity. However, this does not mean that there will be no fixed cost variances. Companies may certainly pay more or less than expected for a fixed cost. For example, a supervisor may receive an unplanned raise, causing actual salary costs to be more than the costs shown in the static budget. The difference between the *budgeted* fixed costs and the *actual* fixed costs is called a **spending variance.** Spending variances will be discussed in more detail later in the chapter. At this point, it is important to note that the reason the fixed cost variances shown in Exhibit 15.2 are zero is because we are comparing two budgets (static versus flexible). Because total fixed cost is not affected by the level of activity, there will be no fixed cost variances associated with static versus flexible budgets.

While total fixed cost does not change in response to changes in the volume of activity, fixed cost per unit does change. Changes in the fixed cost per unit have important implications for decision making. For example, consider the impact on cost-plus pricing decisions. Because actual volume is unknown until the end of the year, selling prices must be based on planned volume. At the *planned volume* of activity of 18,000 units, Melrose's fixed cost per unit is expected to be as follows.

Fixed manufacturing cost	$201,600	
Fixed G, S, & A cost	90,000	
Total fixed cost	$291,600 ÷ 18,000 units = $16.20 per trophy	

Based on the *actual volume* of 19,000 units, the fixed cost per unit is actually $15.35 per trophy ($291,600 ÷ 19,000 units). Because Melrose's prices were established using the $16.20 budgeted cost at planned volume rather than the $15.35 budgeted cost at actual volume, the trophies were overpriced, giving competitors a price advantage. Although Melrose sold more trophies than expected, sales volume might have been even greater if the trophies had been competitively priced.

Underpricing (not encountered by Melrose in this example) can also be detrimental. If planned volume is overstated, the estimated fixed cost per unit will be understated and prices will be set too low. When the higher amount of actual costs is subtracted from revenues, actual profits will be lower than expected. To monitor the effects of volume on fixed cost per unit, companies frequently calculate a **fixed cost volume variance.**

The fixed cost volume variance is *unfavorable* if actual volume is less than planned because cost per unit is higher than expected. Conversely, if actual volume is greater than planned, cost per unit is less than expected, resulting in a *favorable* variance. Both favorable and unfavorable variances can have negative consequences. Managers should strive for the greatest possible degree of accuracy.

FLEXIBLE BUDGET VARIANCES

For performance evaluation, management compares actual results to a flexible budget based on the *actual* volume of activity. Because the actual results and the flexible budget reflect the same volume of activity, any variances in revenues and variable costs result from differences between standard and actual per unit amounts. To illustrate computing and analyzing flexible budget variances, we assume that Melrose's *actual* per unit amounts during 2011 were those shown in the following table. The 2011 per unit *standard* amounts are repeated here for your convenience.

Compute and interpret flexible budget variances.

	Standard	Actual
Sales price	$80.00	$78.00
Variable materials cost	12.00	11.78
Variable labor cost	16.80	17.25
Variable overhead cost	5.60	5.75
Variable G, S, & A	15.00	14.90

Actual and budgeted fixed costs are shown in Exhibit 15.3.

Exhibit 15.3 shows Melrose's 2011 flexible budget, actual results, and flexible budget variances. The flexible budget is the same one compared to the static budget in Exhibit 15.2. Recall the flexible budget amounts come from multiplying the standard per-unit amounts by the actual volume of production. For example, the sales revenue in the flexible budget comes from multiplying the standard sales price by the actual volume ($80 × 19,000). The variable costs are similarly computed. The *actual results* are calculated by multiplying the actual per-unit sales price and cost figures from the preceding table by the actual volume of activity. For example, the sales revenue in the Actual Results column comes from multiplying the actual sales price by the actual volume ($78 × 19,000 = $1,482,000). The actual cost figures are similarly computed. The differences between the flexible budget figures and the actual results are the **flexible budget variances.**

EXHIBIT 15.3

Flexible Budget Variances for Melrose Manufacturing Company

	Flexible Budget	Actual Results	Flexible Budget Variances	
Number of units	19,000	19,000	0	
Sales revenue	$1,520,000	$1,482,000	$38,000	Unfavorable
Variable manufacturing costs				
Materials	228,000	223,820	4,180	Favorable
Labor	319,200	327,750	8,550	Unfavorable
Overhead	106,400	109,250	2,850	Unfavorable
Variable G, S, & A	285,000	283,100	1,900	Favorable
Contribution margin	581,400	538,080	43,320	Unfavorable
Fixed costs				
Manufacturing overhead	201,600	210,000	8,400*	Unfavorable
G, S, & A	90,000	85,000	5,000*	Favorable
Net income	$ 289,800	$ 243,080	$46,720	Unfavorable

*Since fixed costs are the same in the static and flexible budgets, the fixed cost flexible budget variances are the same as the spending variances.

Calculating the Sales Price Variance

Because both the flexible budget and actual results are based on the actual volume of activity, the flexible budget variance is attributable to sales price, not sales volume. In this case, the actual sales price of $78 per unit is less than the standard price of $80 per unit. Because Melrose sold its product for less than the standard sales price, the **sales price variance** is *unfavorable*. Even though the price variance is unfavorable, however, sales volume was 1,000 units more than expected. It is possible the marketing manager generated the additional volume by reducing the sales price. Whether the combination of lower sales price and higher sales volume is favorable or unfavorable depends on the amount of the unfavorable sales price variance versus the amount of the favorable sales volume variance. The *total* sales variance (price and volume) follows.

Actual sales (19,000 units × $78 per unit)	$1,482,000
Expected sales (18,000 units × $80 per unit)	1,440,000
Total sales variance	$ 42,000 Favorable

Alternatively,

Activity variance (sales volume)	$ 80,000	Favorable
Sales price variance	(38,000)	Unfavorable
Total sales variance	$ 42,000	Favorable

This analysis indicates that reducing the sales price had a favorable impact on *total* contribution margin. Use caution when interpreting variances as good or bad; in this instance, the unfavorable sales price variance was more than offset by the favorable sales volume variance. All unfavorable variances are not bad; all favorable variances are not good. Variances signal the need to investigate.

✓ CHECK YOURSELF 15.2

Scott Company's master budget called for a planned sales volume of 30,000 units. Budgeted direct materials cost was $4 per unit. Scott actually produced and sold 32,000 units with an actual materials cost of $3.90 per unit. Determine the volume variance for materials cost and identify the organizational unit most likely responsible for this variance. Determine the flexible budget variance for materials cost and identify the organizational unit most likely responsible for this variance.

Answer

Planned Volume	30,000	Actual Volume	32,000	Actual Volume	32,000
×		×		×	
Standard Cost	$4.00	Standard Cost	$4.00	Actual Cost	$3.90
	$120,000		$128,000		$124,800

Volume Variance for Materials Cost: **$8,000 Unfavorable**

Flexible Budget Variance for Materials Cost: **$3,200 Favorable**

The materials volume variance is unfavorable because the materials cost ($128,000) is higher than was expected ($120,000). However, this could actually be positive because higher volume was probably caused by increasing sales. Further analysis would be necessary to determine whether the overall effect on the company's profitability was positive or negative. The marketing department is most likely to be responsible for the volume variance.

The flexible budget materials cost variance is favorable because the cost of materials was less than expected at the actual volume of activity. Either the production department (used less than the expected amount of materials) or the purchasing department (obtained materials at a favorable price) is most likely to be responsible for this variance.

The Human Element Associated with Flexible Budget Variances

The flexible budget cost variances offer insight into management efficiency. For example, Melrose Manufacturing Company's favorable materials variance could mean purchasing agents were shrewd in negotiating price concessions, discounts, or delivery terms and therefore reduced the price the company paid for materials. Similarly, production employees may have used materials efficiently, using less than expected. The unfavorable labor variance could mean managers failed to control employee wages or motivate employees to work hard. As with sales variances, cost variances require careful analysis. A favorable variance may, in fact, mask unfavorable conditions. For example, the favorable materials variance might have been caused by paying low prices for inferior goods. Using substandard materials could have required additional labor in the production process, which would explain the unfavorable labor variance. Again, we caution that variances, whether favorable or unfavorable, alert management to investigate further.

Need for Standards

As the previous discussion suggests, standards are the building blocks for preparing the static and flexible budgets. Standard costs help managers plan and also establish benchmarks against which actual performance can be judged. Highlighting differences between standard (expected) and actual performance focuses management attention on the areas of greatest need. Because management talent is a valuable and expensive resource, businesses cannot afford to have managers spend large amounts of time on operations that are functioning normally. Instead, managers should concentrate on areas not performing as expected. In other words, management should attend to the exceptions; this management philosophy is known as **management by exception.**

Standard setting fosters using the management by exception principle. By reviewing performance reports that show differences between actual and standard costs, management can focus its attention on the items that show significant variances. Areas with only minor variances need little or no review.

MANAGERIAL PERFORMANCE MEASUREMENT

As previously discussed, managers are assigned responsibility for certain cost, profit, or investment centers. They are then evaluated based on how their centers perform relative to specific goals and objectives. The measurement techniques (variance analysis and contribution margin format income reporting) used for cost and profit centers have been discussed in this and previous chapters. The remainder of this chapter discusses performance measures for investment centers.

RETURN ON INVESTMENT

LO 6

Evaluate investment opportunities using the return on investment technique.

Society confers wealth, prestige, and power upon those who have control of assets. Unsurprisingly, managers are motivated to increase the amount of assets employed by the investment centers they control. When companies have additional assets available to invest, how do upper-level managers decide which centers should get them? The additional assets are frequently allotted to the managers who demonstrate the greatest potential for increasing the company's wealth. Companies often assess managerial potential by comparing the return on investment ratios of various investment centers. The **return on investment (ROI)** is the ratio of wealth generated (operating income) to the amount invested (operating assets) to generate the wealth. ROI is commonly expressed with the following equation.

$$\text{ROI} = \frac{\text{Operating income}}{\text{Operating assets}}$$

To illustrate using ROI for comparative evaluations, assume Panther Holding Company's corporate (first level) chief financial officer (CFO) determined the ROIs for the company's three divisions (second level investment centers). The CFO used the following accounting data from the records of each division.

	Lumber Manufacturing Division	Home Building Division	Furniture Manufacturing Division
Operating income	$ 60,000	$ 46,080	$ 81,940
Operating assets	300,000	256,000	482,000

The ROI for each division is:

Lumber manufacturing: $\dfrac{\text{Operating income}}{\text{Operating assets}} = \$60{,}000 \div \$300{,}000 = 20\%$

Home building: $\dfrac{\text{Operating income}}{\text{Operating assets}} = \$46{,}080 \div \$256{,}000 = 18\%$

Furniture manufacturing: $\dfrac{\text{Operating income}}{\text{Operating assets}} = \$81{,}940 \div \$482{,}000 = 17\%$

All other things being equal, higher ROIs indicate better performance. In this case the Lumber Manufacturing Division manager is the best performer. Assume Panther obtains additional funding for expanding the company's operations. Which investment center is most likely to receive the additional funds?

If the manager of the Lumber Manufacturing Division convinces the upper-level management team that his division would continue to outperform the other two divisions, the Lumber Manufacturing Division would most likely get the additional funding. The manager of the lumber division would then invest the funds in additional operating assets, which would in turn increase the division's operating income. As the division prospers, Panther would reward the manager for exceptional performance. Rewarding the manager of the lumber division would likely motivate the other managers to improve their divisional ROIs. Internal competition would improve the performance of the company as a whole.

Qualitative Considerations

Why do companies compute ROI using operating income and operating assets instead of using net income and total assets? Suppose Panther's corporate headquarters closes a furniture manufacturing plant because an economic downturn temporarily reduces the demand for furniture. It would be inappropriate to include these nonoperating plant assets in the denominator of the ROI computation. Similarly, if Panther sells the furniture plant and realizes a large gain on the sale, including the gain in the numerator of the ROI formula would distort the result. Because the manager of the Furniture Manufacturing Division does not control closing the plant or selling it, it is unreasonable to include the effects of these decisions in computing the ROI. These items would, however, be included in computing net income and total assets. Most companies use operating income and operating assets to compute ROI because those variables measure performance more accurately.

✓ CHECK YOURSELF 15.3

Green View is a lawn services company whose operations are divided into two districts. The District 1 manager controls $12,600,000 of operating assets. District 1 produced $1,512,000 of operating income during the year. The District 2 manager controls $14,200,000 of operating assets. District 2 reported $1,988,000 of operating income for the same period. Use return on investment to determine which manager is performing better.

Answer

District 1

ROI = Operating income ÷ Operating assets = $1,512,000 ÷ $12,600,000 = 12%

District 2

ROI = Operating income ÷ Operating assets = $1,988,000 ÷ $14,200,000 = 14%

Because the higher ROI indicates the better performance, the District 2 manager is the superior performer. This conclusion is based solely on quantitative results. In real-world practice, companies also consider qualitative factors.

Factors Affecting Return on Investment

Management can gain insight into performance by dividing the ROI formula into two separate ratios as follows.

$$ROI = \frac{\text{Operating income}}{\text{Sales}} \times \frac{\text{Sales}}{\text{Operating assets}}$$

The first ratio on the right side of the equation is called the margin. The **margin** is a measure of management's ability to control operating expenses relative to the level of sales. In general, high margins indicate superior performance. Management can increase the margin by reducing the level of operating expenses necessary to generate sales. Decreasing operating expenses increases profitability.

The second ratio in the expanded ROI formula is called turnover. **Turnover** is a measure of the amount of operating assets employed to support the achieved level of sales. Operating assets are scarce resources. To maximize profitability, they must be used wisely. Just as excessive expenses decrease profitability, excessive investments in operating assets also limit profitability.

Both the short and expanded versions of the ROI formula produce the same end result. To illustrate, we will use the ROI for the Lumber Manufacturing Division of Panther Holding Company. Recall that the division employed $300,000 of operating assets to produce $60,000 of operating income, resulting in the following ROI.

$$ROI = \frac{\text{Operating income}}{\text{Operating assets}} = \frac{\$60,000}{\$300,000} = 20\%$$

Further analysis of the accounting records indicates the Lumber Manufacturing Division had sales of $600,000. The following computation demonstrates that the expanded ROI formula produces the same result as the short formula.

$$ROI = \text{Margin} \times \text{Turnover}$$
$$= \frac{\text{Operating income}}{\text{Sales}} \times \frac{\text{Sales}}{\text{Operating assets}}$$
$$= \frac{\$60,000}{\$600,000} \times \frac{\$600,000}{\$300,000}$$
$$= .10 \times 2$$
$$= 20\%$$

Dividing the ROI formula into a margin and a turnover computation encourages managers to examine the benefits of controlling assets as well as expenses.

Because ROI blends many aspects of managerial performance into a single ratio that enables comparisons between companies, comparisons between investment centers within companies, and comparisons between different investment opportunities within an investment center, ROI has gained widespread acceptance as a performance measure.

✓ CHECK YOURSELF 15.4

What three actions can a manager take to improve ROI?

Answer
1. Increase sales
2. Reduce expenses
3. Reduce the investment base

RESIDUAL INCOME

Suppose Panther Holding Company evaluates the manager of the Lumber Manufacturing Division (LMD) based on his ability to maximize ROI. The corporation's overall ROI is approximately 18 percent. LMD, however, has consistently outperformed the other investment centers. Its ROI is currently 20 percent. Now suppose the manager has an opportunity to invest additional funds in a project likely to earn a 19 percent ROI. Would the manager accept the investment opportunity?

These circumstances place the manager in an awkward position. The corporation would benefit from the project because the expected ROI of 19 percent is higher than the corporate average ROI of 18 percent. Personally, however, the manager would suffer from accepting the project because it would reduce the division ROI to less than the current 20 percent. The manager is forced to choose between his personal best interests and the best interests of the corporation. When faced with decisions such as these, many managers choose to benefit themselves at the expense of their corporations, a condition described as **suboptimization.**

To avoid *suboptimization,* many businesses base managerial evaluation on **residual income.** This approach measures a manager's ability to maximize earnings above some targeted level. The targeted level of earnings is based on a minimum desired ROI. Residual income is calculated as follows.

$$\text{Residual income} = \text{Operating income} - (\text{Operating assets} \times \text{Desired ROI})$$

To illustrate, recall that LMD currently earns $60,000 of operating income with the $300,000 of operating assets it controls. ROI is 20 percent ($60,000 ÷ $300,000). Assume Panther's desired ROI is 18 percent. LMD's residual income is therefore

$$\text{Residual income} = \text{Operating income} - (\text{Operating assets} \times \text{Desired ROI})$$

$$= \$60,000 - (\$300,000 \times .18)$$

$$= \$60,000 - \$54,000$$

$$= \$6,000$$

Now assume that Panther Holding Company has $50,000 of additional funds available to invest. Because LMD consistently performs at a high level, Panther's corporate

LO 7

Evaluate investment opportunities using the residual income technique.

FOCUS ON INTERNATIONAL ISSUES

DO MANAGERS IN DIFFERENT COMPANIES STRESS THE SAME PERFORMANCE MEASURES?

About the only ratio companies are required to disclose in their annual reports to stockholders is the earnings per share ratio. Nevertheless, many companies choose to show their performance as measured by other ratios, as well as providing nonratio data not required by GAAP. The types of ratio data companies choose to include in their annual reports provides a sense of what performance measure they consider most important.

A review of several publicly traded companies from the United Kingdom, Japan, and the United States will show that the most common ratios presented are variations of the return on sales percentage and the return on investment percentage, although they may be called by different names. The country in which the company is located does not seem to determine which ratio it will emphasize.

One nonratio performance measure that is popular with companies in all three countries is free cash flow, and it is usually reported in total pounds, yen, or dollars. Be sure to exercise caution before comparing one company's free cash flow, return on sales, or return on investment to those of other companies. There are no official rules governing how these data are calculated, and different companies make different interpretations about how to compute these measurements.

management team offers the funds to the LMD manager. The manager believes he could invest the additional $50,000 at a 19 percent rate of return.

If the LMD manager's evaluation is based solely on ROI, he is likely to reject the additional funding because investing the funds at 19 percent would lower his overall ROI. If the LMD manager's evaluation is based on residual income, however, he is likely to accept the funds because an additional investment at 19 percent would increase his residual income as follows.

$$\text{Operating income} = \$50,000 \times .19$$
$$= \$9,500$$

$$\text{Residual income} = \text{Operating income} - (\text{Operating assets} \times \text{Desired ROI})$$
$$= \$9,500 - (\$50,000 \times .18)$$
$$= \$9,500 - \$9,000$$
$$= \$500$$

Accepting the new project would add $500 to LMD's residual income. If the manager of LMD is evaluated based on his ability to maximize residual income, he would benefit by investing in any project that returns an ROI in excess of the desired 18 percent. The reduction in LMD's overall ROI does not enter into the decision. The residual income approach solves the problem of suboptimization.

The primary disadvantage of the residual income approach is that it measures performance in absolute dollars. As a result, a manager's residual income may be larger simply because her investment base is larger rather than because her performance is superior.

To illustrate, return to the example where Panther Holding Company has $50,000 of additional funds to invest. Assume the manager of the Lumber Manufacturing Division (LMD) and the manager of the Furniture Manufacturing Division (FMD) each have investment opportunities expected to earn a 19 percent return. Recall that Panther's desired ROI is 18 percent. If corporate headquarters allots $40,000 of the

REALITY BYTES

Thinking about the *investment* in return on investment usually conjures up images of buildings and equipment, but investments typically include a much broader range of expenditures. For example, if **Walmart** plans to open a new store it has to make an investment in inventory to stock the store that is as permanent as the building. But investment expenditures can be for items much less tangible than inventory. Consider the making of a movie.

While it is true that making a movie can require expenditures for items such as cameras and sets, the single highest cost can often be for actors' salaries. Although movie fans may focus on how much a movie grosses at the box office, from a business perspective it is the movie's ROI that matters.

From an ROI perspective the question is, "which actors are worth the money they are paid?" To this end, BusinessWeek.com created the ROI Award for actors. Calculating ROI for an actor in a movie, rather than for the entire investment in the movie, can be tricky and requires several estimates. For example, should the credit for the spectacular success of the Harry Potter movies go to its main actor, Daniel Radcliffe, or the special effects, or the author, J. K. Rowling? Nevertheless, BusinessWeek.com reviewed the financial performance of movies starring various actors and actresses over the period of a few years and calculated an ROI for the leading stars.

And the winner is . . . ? In 2006 the ROI Award went to Tyler Perry who starred in *Diary of a Mad Black Woman* and *Madea's Family Reunion.* Mr. Perry's ROI was calculated at 120 percent, suggesting that for every dollar he was paid, the movie earned $2.20 for the movie's producers. As a comparison, Tom Cruise and Will Smith had ROIs of 53 percent. Mr. Perry's movies did not sell the most tickets, but they had the highest ROIs.

Source: *BusinessWeek.com* on MSN Money, July 19, 2006.

funds to the manager of LMD and $10,000 to the manager of FMD, the increase in residual income earned by each division is as follows.

LMD's Residual income = ($40,000 × .19) − ($40,000 × .18) = $400

FMD's Residual income = ($10,000 × .19) − ($10,000 × .18) = $100

Does LMD's higher residual income mean LMD's manager is outperforming FMD's manager? No. It means LMD's manager received more operating assets than FMD's manager received.

Calculating Multiple ROIs and/or RIs for the Same Company

You may be asked to calculate different ROI and RI measures for the same company. For example, ROI and/or RI may be calculated for the company as a whole, for segments of the company, for specific investment opportunities, and for individual managers. An example is shown in Check Yourself 15.5.

✓ CHECK YOURSELF 15.5

Tambor Incorporated (TI) earned operating income of $4,730,400 on operating assets of $26,280,000 during 2011. The Western Division earned $748,000 on operating assets of $3,400,000. TI has offered the Western Division $1,100,000 of additional operating assets. The manager of the Western Division believes he could use the additional assets to generate operating income amounting to $220,000. TI has a desired return on investment (ROI) of 17 percent. Determine the ROI and RI for TI, the Western Division, and the additional investment opportunity.

Answer

Return on investment (ROI) = Operating income ÷ Operating assets
ROI for TI = $4,730,400 ÷ $26,280,000 = 18%
ROI for Western Division = $748,000 ÷ $3,400,000 = 22%
ROI for Investment Opportunity = $220,000 ÷ $1,100,000 = 20%

Residual income (RI) = Operating income − (Operating assets × Desired ROI)
RI for TI = $4,730,400 − ($26,280,000 × .17) = $262,800
RI for Western Division = $748,000 − ($3,400,000 × .17) = $170,000
RI for Investment Opportunity = $220,000 − ($1,100,000 × .17) = $33,000

Responsibility Accounting and the Balanced Scorecard

Throughout the text we have discussed many financial measures companies use to evaluate managerial performance. Examples include standard cost systems to evaluate cost center managers; the contribution margin income statement to evaluate profit center managers; and ROI or residual income to evaluate the performance of investment center managers. Many companies may have goals and objectives such as "satisfaction guaranteed" or "we try harder" that are more suitably evaluated using nonfinancial measures. To assess how well they accomplish the full range of their missions, many companies use a *balanced scorecard.*

A **balanced scorecard** includes financial and nonfinancial performance measures. Standard costs, income measures, ROI, and residual income are common financial measures used in a balanced scorecard. Nonfinancial measures include defect rates, cycle time, on-time deliveries, number of new products or innovations, safety measures, and customer satisfaction surveys. Many companies compose their scorecards to highlight leading versus lagging measures. For example, customer satisfaction survey data is a leading indicator of the sales growth which is a lagging measure. The balanced scorecard is a holistic approach to evaluating managerial performance. It is gaining widespread acceptance among world-class companies.

‹‹ A Look Back

The practice of delegating authority and responsibility is referred to as *decentralization*. Clear lines of authority and responsibility are essential in establishing a responsibility accounting system. In a responsibility accounting system, segment managers are held accountable for profits based on the amount of control they have over the profits in their segment.

Responsibility reports are used to compare actual results with budgets. The reports should be simple with variances highlighted to promote the *management by exception* doctrine. Individual managers should be held responsible only for those revenues or costs they control. Each manager should receive only summary information about the performance of the responsibility centers under her supervision.

A *responsibility center* is the point in an organization where control over revenue or expense is located. *Cost centers* are segments that incur costs but do not generate revenues. *Profit centers* incur costs and also generate revenues, producing a measurable profit. *Investment centers* incur costs, generate revenues, and use identifiable capital investments.

One of the primary purposes of responsibility accounting is to evaluate managerial performance. Comparing actual results with standards and budgets and calculating *return on investment* are used for this purpose. Because return on investment uses revenues, expenses, and investment, problems with measuring these parameters must be considered. The return on investment can be analyzed in terms of the margin earned on sales as well as the turnover (asset utilization) during the period. The *residual income approach* is sometimes used to avoid *suboptimization,* which occurs when managers choose to reject investment projects that would benefit their company's ROI but would reduce their investment center's ROI. The residual income approach evaluates managers based on their ability to generate earnings above some targeted level of earnings.

›› A Look Forward

The next chapter expands on the concepts in this chapter. You will see how managers select investment opportunities that will affect their future ROIs. You will learn to apply present value techniques to compute the net present value and the internal rate of return for potential investment opportunities. You will also learn to use less sophisticated analytical techniques such as payback and the unadjusted rate of return.

A step-by-step audio-narrated series of slides is provided on the text website at www.mhhe.com/edmondssurvey3e.

SELF-STUDY REVIEW PROBLEM 1

Bugout Pesticides Inc. established the following standard price and costs for a termite control product that it sells to exterminators.

Variable price and cost data (per unit)	Standard	Actual
Sales price	$52.00	$49.00
Materials cost	10.00	10.66
Labor cost	12.00	11.90
Overhead cost	7.00	7.05
General, selling, and administrative (G, S, & A) cost	8.00	7.92
Expected fixed costs (in total)		
Manufacturing	$150,000	$140,000
General, selling, and administrative	60,000	64,000

Item to Classify	Standard	Actual	Type of Variance
Labor cost	$10.00 per hour	$9.60 per hour	Favorable
Labor usage	61,000 hours	61,800 hours	
Fixed cost spending	$400,000	$390,000	
Fixed cost per unit (volume)	$3.20 per unit	$3.16 per unit	
Sales volume	40,000 units	42,000 units	
Sales price	$3.60 per unit	$3.63 per unit	
Materials cost	$2.90 per pound	$3.00 per pound	
Materials usage	91,000 pounds	90,000 pounds	

Exercise 15-2   *Determining amount and type (favorable vs. unfavorable) of variance*   LO 3

Required

Compute variances for the following items and indicate whether each variance is favorable (F) or unfavorable (U).

Item	Budget	Actual	Variance	F or U
Sales price	$650	$525		
Sales revenue	$580,000	$600,000		
Cost of goods sold	$385,000	$360,000		
Material purchases at 5,000 pounds	$275,000	$280,000		
Materials usage	$180,000	$178,000		
Production volume	950 units	900 units		
Wages at 4,000 hours	$60,000	$58,700		
Labor usage at $16 per hour	$96,000	$97,000		
Research and development expense	$22,000	$25,000		
Selling and administrative expenses	$49,000	$40,000		

Exercise 15-3   *Preparing master and flexible budgets*   LO 2

Sexton Manufacturing Company established the following standard price and cost data.

Sales price	$8.00 per unit
Variable manufacturing cost	4.00 per unit
Fixed manufacturing costs	3,000 total
Fixed selling and administrative costs	1,000 total

Sexton planned to produce and sell 2,000 units. Actual production and sales amounted to 2,200 units.

Required

a. Prepare the pro forma income statement in contribution format that would appear in a master budget.

b. Prepare the pro forma income statement in contribution format that would appear in a flexible budget.

Exercise 15-4   *Determining sales and variable cost volume variances*   LO 4

Required

Use the information provided in Exercise 15-3.

a. Determine the sales and variable cost volume variances.

b. Classify the variances as favorable (F) or unfavorable (U).

c. Comment on the usefulness of the variances with respect to performance evaluation and identify the member of the management team most likely to be responsible for these variances.

d. Determine the amount of fixed cost that will appear in the flexible budget.

e. Determine the fixed cost per unit based on planned activity and the fixed cost per unit based on actual activity. Assuming Sexton uses information in the master budget to price the company's product, comment on how the volume variance could affect the company's profitability.

LO 5

Exercise 15-5   *Determining flexible budget variances*

Use the standard price and cost data provided in Exercise 15-3. Assume that the actual sales price is $7.65 per unit and that the actual variable cost is $4.25 per unit. The actual fixed manufacturing cost is $2,850, and the actual selling and administrative expenses are $1,025.

Required

a. Determine the flexible budget variances.

b. Classify the variances as favorable (F) or unfavorable (U).

c. Provide another name for the fixed cost flexible budget variance.

d. Comment on the usefulness of the variances with respect to performance evaluation and identify the member(s) of the management team who is (are) most likely to be responsible for these variances.

LO 2

Exercise 15-6   *Using a flexible budget to accommodate market uncertainty*

According to its original plan, Darey Consulting Services Company would charge its customers for service at $125 per hour in 2011. The company president expects consulting services provided to customers to reach 45,000 hours at that rate. The marketing manager, however, argues that actual results may range from 40,000 hours to 50,000 hours because of market uncertainty. Darey's standard variable cost is $48 per hour, and its standard fixed costs are $1,500,000.

Required

Develop flexible budgets based on the assumptions of service levels at 40,000 hours, 45,000 hours, and 50,000 hours.

LO 2

Exercise 15-7   *Evaluating a decision to increase sales volume by lowering sales price*

Ender Educational Services had budgeted its training service charge at $75 per hour. The company planned to provide 30,000 hours of training services during 2012. By reducing the service charge to $60 per hour, the company was able to increase the actual number of hours to 31,500.

Required

a. Determine the sales volume variance, and indicate whether it is favorable (F) or unfavorable (U).

b. Determine the flexible budget variance, and indicate whether it is favorable (F) or unfavorable (U).

c. Did reducing the price of training services increase profitability? Explain.

LO 3

Exercise 15-8   *Responsibility for the fixed cost volume variance*

Ragan Company expected to sell 400,000 of its pagers during 2011. It set the standard sales price for the pager at $30 each. During June, it became obvious that the company would be unable to attain the expected volume of sales. Ragan's chief competitor, Selma, Inc., had lowered prices and was pulling market share from Ragan. To be competitive, Ragan matched Selma's price, lowering its sales price to $28 per pager. Selma responded by lowering its price even further to $24 per pager. In an emergency meeting of key personnel, Ragan's accountant, Suzy Kennedy, stated, "Our cost structure simply won't support a sales price in the $24 range." The production manager, Larry Jones, said, "I don't understand why I'm here. The only unfavorable variance on my report is a fixed cost volume variance and that one is not my fault. We can't be making the product if the marketing department isn't selling it."

Required

a. Describe a scenario in which the production manager is responsible for the fixed cost volume variance.

b. Describe a scenario in which the marketing manager is responsible for the fixed cost volume variance.

c. Explain how a decline in sales volume would affect Ragan's ability to lower its sales price.

Exercise 15-9   *Income statement for internal use*   LO 2

Ladmilla Company has provided the following 2011 data.

Budget	
Sales	$500,000
Variable product costs	204,000
Variable selling expenses	50,000
Other variable expenses	3,600
Fixed product costs	16,600
Fixed selling expenses	24,300
Other fixed expenses	2,200
Interest expense	800
Variances	
Sales	8,600 U
Variable product costs	4,000 F
Variable selling expenses	2,500 U
Other variable expenses	1,200 U
Fixed product costs	220 F
Fixed selling expenses	390 F
Other fixed expenses	150 U
Interest expense	80 F

Required

a. Prepare in good form a budgeted and actual income statement for internal use. Separate operating income from net income in the statements.

b. Calculate variances and identify these as favorable (F) or unfavorable (U).

Exercise 15-10   *Evaluating a cost center including flexible budgeting concepts*   LO 5

Smiley Medical Equipment Company makes a blood pressure measuring kit. Elbert Jackson is the production manager. The production department's static budget and actual results for 2012 follow.

	Static Budget	Actual Results
	30,000 kits	*32,000 kits*
Direct materials	$210,000	$262,000
Direct labor	180,000	185,600
Variable manufacturing overhead	48,000	54,000
Total variable costs	438,000	501,600
Fixed manufacturing overhead	210,000	205,000
Total manufacturing cost	$648,000	$706,600

Required

a. Convert the static budget into a flexible budget.

b. Use the flexible budget to evaluate Mr. Jackson's performance.

c. Explain why Mr. Jackson's performance evaluation does not include sales revenue and net income.

Exercise 15-11   *Evaluating a profit center*   LO 6, 7

Pamila Smith, the president of Smith Toys Corporation, is trying to determine this year's pay raises for the store managers. Smith Toys has seven stores in the southwestern United States. Corporate headquarters purchases all toys from different manufacturers globally and distributes them to individual stores. Additionally, headquarters makes decisions regarding location and size of stores. These practices allow Smith Toys to receive volume discounts from vendors and to implement coherent marketing strategies. Within a set of general guidelines, store managers have the flexibility to adjust product prices and hire local employees. Ms. Smith is considering three possible performance measures for evaluating the individual stores: cost of goods sold, return on sales (net income divided by sales), and return on investment.

Required

a. Using the concept of controllability, advise Ms. Smith about the best performance measure.

b. Explain how a balanced scorecard can be used to help Ms. Smith.

LO 6

Exercise 15-12   *Return on investment*

An investment center of Aquilar Corporation shows an operating income of $7,500 on total operating assets of $60,000.

Required

Compute the return on investment.

LO 6

Exercise 15-13   *Return on investment*

Mitchell Company calculated its return on investment as 13 percent. Sales are now $270,000, and the amount of total operating assets is $450,000.

Required

a. If expenses are reduced by $27,000 and sales remain unchanged, what return on investment will result?

b. If both sales and expenses cannot be changed, what change in the amount of operating assets is required to achieve the same result?

LO 7

Exercise 15-14   *Residual income*

Schiavo Corporation has a desired rate of return of 8 percent. Frank Rodomil is in charge of one of Schiavo's three investment centers. His center controlled operating assets of $2,500,000 that were used to earn $260,000 of operating income.

Required

Compute Mr. Rodomil's residual income.

LO 7

Exercise 15-15   *Residual income*

Claire's Cough Drops operates two divisions. The following information pertains to each division for 2012.

	Division A	Division B
Sales	$200,000	$72,000
Operating income	$ 15,040	$ 8,100
Average operating assets	$ 63,000	$45,000
Company's desired rate of return	18%	18%

Required

a. Compute each division's residual income.

b. Which division increased the company's profitability more?

LO 6, 7

Exercise 15-16   *Return on investment and residual income*

Required

Supply the missing information in the following table for Ren Company.

Sales	$396,000
ROI	?
Operating assets	?
Operating income	?
Turnover	2.2
Residual income	?
Margin	0.13
Desired rate of return	18%

Exercise 15-17   *Comparing return on investment with residual income*   LO 6, 7

The Wade Division of Geisler Corporation has a current ROI of 20 percent. The company target ROI is 15 percent. The Wade Division has an opportunity to invest $5,000,000 at 18 percent but is reluctant to do so because its ROI will fall to 19.2 percent. The present investment base for the division is $7,500,000.

Required

Demonstrate how Geisler can motivate the Wade Division to make the investment by using the residual income method.

PROBLEMS

All applicable Problems are available with McGraw-Hill's
Connect Accounting.

connect
|ACCOUNTING

Problem 15-18   *Determining sales and variable cost volume variances*

LO 4

Todhunter Publications established the following standard price and costs for a hardcover picture book that the company produces.

CHECK FIGURES
a. NI = $81,000
b. NI at 29,000 units: $72,000

Standard price and variable costs:	
Sales price	$36.00
Materials	9.00
Labor	4.50
Overhead	6.30
General, selling, and administrative	7.20
Planned fixed costs:	
Manufacturing	$135,000
General, selling, and administrative	54,000

Todhunter planned to make and sell 30,000 copies of the book.

Required

a. Prepare the pro forma income statement that would appear in the master budget.
b. Prepare flexible budget income statements, assuming volumes of 29,000 and 31,000 units.
c. Determine the sales and variable cost volume variances, assuming volume is actually 31,000 units.
d. Indicate whether the variances are favorable (F) or unfavorable (U).
e. Comment on how Todhunter could use the variances to evaluate performance.

Problem 15-19   *Determining and interpreting flexible budget variances*

LO 5

Use the standard price and cost data supplied in Problem 15-18. Assume that Todhunter actually produced and sold 31,000 books. The actual sales price and costs incurred follow.

Actual price and variable costs:	
Sales price	$35.00
Materials	9.20
Labor	4.40
Overhead	6.35
General, selling, and administrative	7.00
Actual fixed costs:	
Manufacturing	$120,000
General, selling, and administrative	60,000

CHECK FIGURE
Flexible budget variance of NI:
$20,450 U

Required

a. Determine the flexible budget variances.

b. Indicate whether each variance is favorable (F) or unfavorable (U).

c. Identify the management position responsible for each variance. Explain what could have caused the variance.

Problem 15-20   *Flexible budget planning*

Luke Chou, the president of Digitech Computer Services, needs your help. He wonders about the potential effects on the firm's net income if he changes the service rate that the firm charges its customers. The following basic data pertain to fiscal year 2012.

Standard rate and variable costs:	
Service rate per hour	$80.00
Labor	40.00
Overhead	7.20
General, selling, and administrative	4.30
Expected fixed costs:	
Facility repair	$525,000.00
General, selling, and administrative	150,000.00

Required

a. Prepare the pro forma income statement that would appear in the master budget if the firm expects to provide 30,000 hours of services in 2012.

b. A marketing consultant suggests to Mr. Chou that the service rate may affect the number of service hours that the firm can achieve. According to the consultant's analysis, if Digitech charges customers $75 per hour, the firm can achieve 38,000 hours of services. Prepare a flexible budget using the consultant's assumption.

c. The same consultant also suggests that if the firm raises its rate to $85 per hour, the number of service hours will decline to 25,000. Prepare a flexible budget using the new assumption.

d. Evaluate the three possible outcomes you determined in Requirements *a*, *b*, and *c* and recommend a pricing strategy.

Problem 15-21   *Different types of responsibility centers*

Liberty National Bank is a large municipal bank with several branch offices. The bank's computer department handles all data processing for bank operations. In addition, the bank sells the computer department's expertise in systems development and excess machine time to several small business firms, serving them as a service bureau.

The bank currently treats the computer department as a cost center. The manager of the computer department prepares a cost budget annually for senior bank officials to approve. Monthly operating reports compare actual and budgeted expenses. Revenues from the department's service bureau activities are treated as other income by the bank and are not reflected on the computer department's operating reports. The costs of servicing these clients are included in the computer department reports, however.

The manager of the computer department has proposed that bank management convert the computer department to a profit or investment center.

Required

a. Describe the characteristics that differentiate a cost center, a profit center, and an investment center from each other.

b. Would the manager of the computer department be likely to conduct the operations of the department differently if the department were classified as a profit center or an investment center rather than as a cost center? Explain.

Problem 15-22   *Comparing return on investment and residual income*   LO 6, 7

Wells Corporation operates three investment centers. The following financial statements apply to the investment center named Huber Division.

CHECK FIGURE
c. 21.32%

HUBER DIVISION
Income Statement
For the Year Ended December 31, 2011

Sales revenue	$105,480
Cost of goods sold	(60,275)
Gross margin	45,205
Operating expenses	
Selling expenses	(2,840)
Depreciation expense	(4,205)
Operating income	38,160
Nonoperating income	
Gain on sale of land	(5,000)
Net income	$ 33,160

HUBER DIVISION
Balance Sheet
As of December 31, 2011

Assets	
Cash	$ 12,472
Accounts receivable	40,266
Merchandise inventory	36,000
Equipment less accum. dep.	90,258
Non-operating assets	9,000
Total assets	$187,996
Liabilities	
Accounts payable	$ 9,637
Notes payable	72,000
Stockholders' equity	
Common stock	80,000
Retained earnings	26,359
Total liab. and stk. equity	$187,996

Required

a. Should operating income or net income be used to determine the rate of return (ROI) for the Huber investment center? Explain your answer.

b. Should operating assets or total assets be used to determine the ROI for the Huber investment center? Explain your answer.

c. Calculate the ROI for Huber.

d. Wells has a desired ROI of 15 percent. Headquarters has $96,000 of funds to assign its investment centers. The manager of the Huber division has an opportunity to invest the funds at an ROI of 17 percent. The other two divisions have investment opportunities that yield only 16 percent. Even so, the manager of Huber rejects the additional funding. Explain why the manager of Huber would reject the funds under these circumstances.

e. Explain how residual income could be used to encourage the manager to accept the additional funds.

LO 6

CHECK FIGURES
c. 15%
d. (3) 18.75%

Problem 15-23   *Return on investment*

Soto Corporation's balance sheet indicates that the company has $300,000 invested in operating assets. During 2011, Soto earned operating income of $45,000 on $600,000 of sales.

Required

a. Compute Soto's profit margin for 2011.

b. Compute Soto's turnover for 2011.

c. Compute Soto's return on investment for 2011.

d. Recompute Soto's ROI under each of the following independent assumptions.

   (1) Sales increase from $600,000 to $750,000, thereby resulting in an increase in operating income from $45,000 to $60,000.

   (2) Sales remain constant, but Soto reduces expenses resulting in an increase in operating income from $45,000 to $48,000.

   (3) Soto is able to reduce its invested capital from $300,000 to $240,000 without affecting operating income.

LO 6, 7

CHECK FIGURES
b. The ROI would decline to 19.60%.
c. RI would increase by $60,000.

Problem 15-24   *Comparing return on investment and residual income*

The manager of the Cohen Division of Leland Manufacturing Corporation is currently producing a 20 percent return on invested capital. Leland's desired rate of return is 16 percent. The Cohen Division has $12,000,000 of capital invested in operating assets and access to additional funds as needed. The manager is considering a new investment in operating assets that will require a $3,000,000 capital commitment and promises an 18 percent return.

Required

a. Would it be advantageous for Leland Manufacturing Corporation if the Cohen Division makes the investment under consideration?

b. What effect would the proposed investment have on the Cohen Division's return on investment? Show computations.

c. What effect would the proposed investment have on the Cohen Division's residual income? Show computations.

d. Would return on investment or residual income be the better performance measure for the Cohen Division's manager? Explain.

ANALYZE, THINK, COMMUNICATE

ATC 15-1   Business Applications Case   *Static versus flexible budget variances*

Dan Ludwig is the manufacturing production supervisor for Atlantic Lighting Systems. Trying to explain why he did not get the year-end bonus that he had expected, he told his wife, "This is the dumbest place I ever worked. Last year the company set up this budget assuming it would sell 150,000 units. Well, it sold only 140,000. The company lost money and gave me a bonus for not using as much materials and labor as was called for in the budget. This year, the company has the same 150,000 units goal and it sells 160,000. The company's making all kinds of money. You'd think I'd get this big fat bonus. Instead, management tells me I used more materials and labor than was budgeted. They said the company would have made a lot more money if I'd stayed within my budget. I guess I gotta wait for another bad year before I get a bonus. Like I said, this is the dumbest place I ever worked."

Atlantic Lighting Systems's master budget and the actual results for the most recent year of operating activity follow.

	Master Budget	Actual Results	Variances	F or U
Number of units	150,000	160,000	10,000	
Sales revenue	$33,000,000	$35,520,000	$2,520,000	F
Variable manufacturing costs				
Materials	(4,800,000)	(5,300,000)	(500,000)	U
Labor	(4,200,000)	(4,400,000)	(200,000)	U
Overhead	(2,100,000)	(2,290,000)	(190,000)	U
Variable selling, general,				
and admin. costs	(5,250,000)	(5,450,000)	(200,000)	U
Contribution margin	16,650,000	18,080,000	1,430,000	F
Fixed costs				
Manufacturing overhead	(7,830,000)	(7,751,000)	79,000	F
Sellings, general, and admin. costs	(6,980,000)	(7,015,000)	(35,000)	U
Net income	$ 1,840,000	$ 3,314,000	$1,474,000	F

Required

a. Did Atlantic increase unit sales by cutting prices or by using some other strategy?

b. Is Mr. Ludwig correct in his conclusion that something is wrong with the company's performance evaluation process? If so, what do you suggest be done to improve the system?

c. Prepare a flexible budget and recompute the budget variances.

d. Explain what might have caused the fixed costs to be different from the amount budgeted.

e. Assume that the company's material price variance was favorable and its material usage variance was unfavorable. Explain why Mr. Ludwig may not be responsible for these variances. Now, explain why he may have been responsible for the material usage variance.

f. Assume the labor price variance is unfavorable. Was the labor usage variance favorable or unfavorable?

g. Is the fixed cost volume variance favorable or unfavorable? Explain the effect of this variance on the cost of each unit produced.

ATC 15-2   Group Assignment   *Return on investment versus residual income*

Bellco, a division of Becker International Corporation, is operated under the direction of Antoin Sedatt. Bellco is an independent investment center with approximately $72,000,000 of assets that generate approximately $8,640,000 in annual net income. Becker International has additional investment capital of $12,000,000 that is available for the division managers to invest. Mr. Sedatt is aware of an investment opportunity that will provide an 11 percent annual net return. Becker International's desired rate of return is 10 percent.

Required

Divide the class into groups of four or five students and then organize the groups into two sections. Assign Task 1 to the first section and Task 2 to the second section.

Group Tasks

1. Assume that Mr. Sedatt's performance is evaluated based on his ability to maximize return on investment (ROI). Compute ROI using the following two assumptions: Bellco retains its current asset size and Bellco accepts and invests the additional $12,000,000 of assets. Determine whether Mr. Sedatt should accept the opportunity to invest additional funds. Select a spokesperson to present the decision made by the group.

2. Assume that Mr. Sedatt's performance is evaluated based on his ability to maximize residual income. Compute residual income using the following two assumptions: Bellco retains its current asset base and Bellco accepts and invests the additional $12,000,000 of assets. Determine whether Mr. Sedatt should accept the opportunity to invest additional funds. Select a spokesperson to present the decision made by the group.

3. Have a spokesperson from one of the groups in the first section report the two ROIs and the group's recommendation for Mr. Sedatt. Have the groups in this section reach consensus on the ROI and the recommendation.

4. Have a spokesperson from the second section report the two amounts of residual income and disclose the group's recommendation for Mr. Sedatt. Have this section reach consensus on amounts of residual income.

5. Which technique (ROI or residual income) is more likely to result in suboptimization?

ATC 15-3   Research Assignment   *Using real world data from Papa John's*

Obtain the 2004, 2005, 2006, 2007, and 2008 income statements for Papa John's International, Inc. The 2006–2008 statements are included in Papa John's 2008 annual report and Form 10-Ks. The 2004 and 2005 statements are in its 2005 annual report.

To obtain the Form 10-Ks you can use either the EDGAR system following the instructions in Appendix A, or they can be found under "Investors" link on the company's corporate website; www.papajohns.com. The company's annual reports are also available on its website.

Required

a. Compute the percentage change for each of the following categories of revenues and expenses for 2004 to 2005, 2005 to 2006, and 2006 to 2007:

> **Domestic revenues:**
>   Company-owned restaurant sales
> **Domestic company-owned restaurant expenses:**
>   Cost of sales
>   Salaries and benefits
>   Advertising and related costs
>   Occupancy costs
>   Other operating expenses

Using an Excel spreadsheet will make this task much easier. Once these averages are obtained, (you should have three averages for each of the six revenue and expense items), calculate an average of the changes for each item. The answer for the "Occupancy coats" item is show as an example:

	Percentage Change
2004–2005	1.7%
2005–2006	3.2
2006–2007	17.0
Average of the changes	7.3%

b. Prepare a budgeted income statement for 2008 and compare the budgeted data to the actual results for 2008. To calculate budgeted amounts, multiply the average change in each revenue and expense item, from Requirement *b*, by the dollar amount of the corresponding revenue or expense from 2007. This will represent the budgeted amount for that item for 2008. Don't forget to use decimal data and not percentage data. Subtract the actual 2008 results from the budgeted results. Finally, divide the actual versus budgeted difference by the budgeted amount to determine a percentage variance from the budget. Calculate total for "Total domestic company-owned restaurant expenses" by adding the appropriate items. The answer for the "Occupancy costs" item is show as an example: (Dollar amounts are in thousands.)

	(1) 2007 Actual	(2) Average 3-year Change	(3) (1 × 2) 2008 Budget	(4) 2008 Actual	(5) (3 − 4) Variance	(5 ÷ 3) Percentage Variance from Budget
Occupancy costs	$31,866	1.073	$34,192	$34,973	$(781)	.028 [2.8%]

ATC 15-4   Writing Assignment   *Analyzing Segments at Coca-Cola*

The following excerpt is from Coca-Cola Company's 2009 annual report filed with the SEC.

Management evaluates the performance of our operating segments separately to individually monitor the different factors affecting financial performance. Our Company manages income taxes and financial costs, such as interest income and expense, on a global basis within the Corporate operating segment. We evaluate segment performance based on income or loss before income taxes.

Below are selected segment data for Coca-Cola Company for the 2009 and 2008 fiscal years. Dollar amounts are in millions.

	Eurasia & Africa	Europe	Latin America	North America	Pacific
2009 Fiscal Year					
Net operating revenues	$2,197	$3,203	$3,882	$ 8,271	$4,875
Income before taxes	810	2,976	2,039	1,701	1,866
Identifiable operating assets	1,155	3,047	2,480	10,941	1,929
2008 Fiscal Year					
Net operating revenues	$2,327	$5,801	$3,835	$ 8,280	$4,695
Income before taxes	823	3,182	2,098	1,579	1,841
Identifiable operating assets	956	3,012	1,849	10,845	1,444

Required

a. Compute the ROI for each of Coke's geographical segments for each fiscal year.

b. Assuming Coke's management expects a minimum return of 30%, calculate the residual income for each segment for each fiscal year.

c. Assume the management of Coke is considering a major expansion effort for the next five years. Write a brief memo that (1) explains which geographic segment you would recommend that Coke focus its expansion efforts, and (2) why the segment with the highest ROI is not the segment with the highest residual income.

ATC 15-5   Ethics Dilemma   *Fudging the standards*

Eric Dawson is a department manager at Lemhi, Inc., a manufacturing company. His department is responsible for assembling various products. Lemhi uses a standard costing system to help manage operations and evaluate its managers. In addition to his salary, Mr. Dawson has the potential to earn a bonus based on how well his department performs, and he, in turn, evaluates the workers in his department based on how well they perform their duties, based on the standard costing system.

Lemhi, Inc., has just received a contract to manufacture a new toy, called LogicBlock, for the Toys for the Imagination Company, and Mr. Dawson's department will be responsible for its assembly. The product designers and engineers at Lemhi believe it should take the workers in Mr. Dawson's department 23 minutes to assemble each toy. However, Mr. Dawson told his workers the standard time allowed to assemble each unit of LogicBlock is 21 minutes.

Required

a. Explain what Mr. Dawson is hoping to achieve by telling workers the time expected to assemble a toy is 21 minutes versus 23 minutes.

b. What do you think the short-term and long-term implications of this strategy are likely to be? Explain.

CHAPTER 16

Planning for Capital Investments

LEARNING OBJECTIVES

After you have mastered the material in this chapter, you will be able to:

1 Explain the time value of money concept and apply it to capital investment decisions.

2 Determine the present value of future cash flows.

3 Determine and interpret the net present value of an investment opportunity.

4 Determine and interpret the internal rate of return of an investment opportunity.

5 Identify cash flows associated with an investment opportunity.

6 Compare capital investment alternatives.

7 Determine the payback period for an investment opportunity.

8 Determine the unadjusted rate of return for an investment opportunity.

9 Conduct a postaudit of a completed investment.

CHAPTER OPENING

The president of EZ Rentals (EZ) is considering expanding the company's rental service business to include LCD projectors that can be used with notebook computers. A marketing study forecasts that renting projectors could generate revenue of $200,000 per year. The possibility of increasing revenue is alluring, but EZ's president has a number of unanswered questions. How much do the projectors cost? What is their expected useful life? Will they have a salvage value? Does EZ have the money to buy them? Does EZ have the technical expertise to support the product? How much will training cost? How long will customer demand last? What if EZ buys the projectors and they become technologically obsolete? How quickly will EZ be able to recover the investment? Are there more profitable ways to invest EZ's funds?

Spending large sums of money that will have long-term effects on company profits makes most managers anxious. What if a cell phone manufacturer spends millions of dollars to build a factory in the United States and its competitors locate their manufacturing facilities in countries that provide cheap labor? The manufacturer's cell phones will be overpriced, but it cannot move overseas because it cannot find a buyer for the factory. What if a pharmaceutical company spends millions of dollars to develop a drug which then fails to receive FDA approval? What if a communications company installs underground cable but satellite transmission steals its market? What if a company buys computer equipment that rapidly becomes technologically obsolete? Although these possibilities may be remote, they can be expensive when they do occur. For example, a recent annual report from Wachovia Bank discloses a $70 million dollar write-off of computer equipment. This chapter discusses some of the analytical techniques companies use to evaluate major investment opportunities.

The Curious Accountant

The August 28, 2009, drawing for the Mega millions multistate lottery produced two winning tickets. The tickets, which were purchased in California and New York, had an advertised value of $368 million. This amount, however, was based on the assumption that the winners would take their prize as 26 equal annual payments of $14,153,384. If the winnings were taken in this manner, the first payment would be made immediately, and the others would be paid annually over the next 25 years. The winner also had the option of taking an immediate, lump-sum payment of $231 million. With two winning tickets, each winner would receive one-half of these amounts.

Assume that you work as a personal financial planner and that one of your clients held one of the winning lottery tickets. If you think you could invest your client's winnings and earn an annual return of 7 percent, would you advise your client to take the lump-sum payment or the annual payments? Why? (The answer is on page 577.)

CAPITAL INVESTMENT DECISIONS

Explain the time value of money concept and apply it to capital investment decisions.

Purchases of long-term operational assets are **capital investments.** Capital investments differ from stock and bond investments in an important respect. Investments in stocks and bonds can be sold in organized markets such as the New York Stock Exchange. In contrast, investments in capital assets normally can be recovered only by using those assets. Once a company purchases a capital asset, it is committed to that investment for an extended period of time. If the market turns sour, the company is stuck with the consequences. It may also be unable to seize new opportunities because its capital is committed. Business profitability ultimately hinges, to a large extent, on the quality of a few key capital investment decisions.

A capital investment decision is essentially a decision to exchange current cash outflows for the expectation of receiving future cash inflows. For EZ Rentals, purchasing LCD projectors, cash outflows today, provides the opportunity to collect $200,000 per year in rental revenue, cash inflows in the future. Assuming the projectors have useful lives of four years and no salvage value, how much should EZ be willing to pay for the future cash inflows? If you were EZ's president, would you spend $700,000 today to receive $200,000 each year for the next four years? You would give up $700,000 today for the opportunity to receive $800,000 (4 × $200,000) in the future. What if you collect less than $200,000 per year? If revenue is only $160,000 per year, you would lose $60,000 [$700,000 − (4 × $160,000)]. Is $700,000 too much to pay for the opportunity to receive $200,000 per year for four years? If $700,000 is too much, would you spend $600,000? If not, how about $500,000? There is no one right answer to these questions. However, understanding the *time value of money* concept can help you develop a rational response.

Time Value of Money

The **time value of money** concept recognizes that *the present value of a dollar received in the future is less than a dollar.* For example, you may be willing to pay only $0.90 today for a promise to receive $1.00 one year from today. The further into the future the receipt is expected to occur, the smaller is its present value. In other words, one dollar to be received two years from today is worth less than one dollar to be received one year from today. Likewise, one dollar to be received three years from today is less valuable than one dollar to be received two years from today, and so on.

The present value of cash inflows decreases as the time until expected receipt increases for several reasons. First, you could deposit today's dollar in a savings account to earn *interest* that increases its total value. If you wait for your money, you lose the opportunity to earn interest. Second, the expectation of receiving a future dollar carries an element of *risk*. Changed conditions may result in the failure to collect. Finally, *inflation* diminishes the buying power of the dollar. In other words, the longer you must wait to receive a dollar, the less you will be able to buy with it.

When a company invests in capital assets, it sacrifices present dollars in exchange for the opportunity to receive future dollars. Because trading current dollars for future dollars is risky, companies expect compensation before they invest in capital assets. The compensation a company expects is called *return on investment (ROI)*. As discussed in Chapter 15, ROI is expressed as a percentage of the investment. For example, the ROI for a $1,000 investment that earns annual income of $100 is 10 percent ($100 ÷ $1,000 = 10%).

Determining the Minimum Rate of Return

To establish the minimum expected *return on investment* before accepting an investment opportunity, most companies consider their cost of capital. To attract capital, companies must provide benefits to their creditors and owners. Creditors expect interest payments; owners expect dividends and increased stock value. Companies that earn lower returns than their cost of capital eventually go bankrupt; they cannot continually pay out more than they collect. *The* **cost of capital** *represents the* **minimum rate of return** *on investments.* Calculating the cost of capital is a complex exercise which is beyond the scope of this text. It is addressed in finance courses. We discuss how management accountants *use* the cost of capital to evaluate investment opportunities. Companies describe the cost of capital in a variety of ways: the *minimum rate of return,* the *desired rate of return,* the *required rate of return,* the *hurdle rate,* the *cutoff rate,* or the *discount rate.* These terms are used interchangeably throughout this chapter.

✓ CHECK YOURSELF 16.1

Study the following cash inflow streams expected from two different potential investments.

	Year 1	Year 2	Year 3	Total
Alternative 1	$2,000	$3,000	$4,000	$9,000
Alternative 2	4,000	3,000	2,000	9,000

Based on visual observation alone, which alternative has the higher present value? Why?

Answer   Alternative 2 has the higher present value. The size of the discount increases as the length of the time period increases. In other words, a dollar received in year 3 has a lower present value than a dollar received in year 1. Because most of the expected cash inflows from Alternative 2 are received earlier than those from Alternative 1, Alternative 2 has a higher present value even though the total expected cash inflows are the same.

CONVERTING FUTURE CASH INFLOWS TO THEIR EQUIVALENT PRESENT VALUES

Given a desired rate of return and the amount of a future cash flow, present value can be determined using algebra. To illustrate, refer to the $200,000 EZ expects to earn the first year it leases LCD projectors.[1] Assuming EZ desires a 12 percent rate of return, what amount of cash would EZ be willing to invest today (present value outflow) to obtain a $200,000 cash inflow at the end of the year (future value)? The answer follows.[2]

$$\text{Investment} + (0.12 \times \text{Investment}) = \text{Future cash inflow}$$

$$1.12 \text{ Investment} = \$200,000$$

$$\text{Investment} = \$200,000 \div 1.12$$

$$\text{Investment} = \$178,571$$

If EZ invests $178,571 cash on January 1 and earns a 12 percent return on the investment, EZ will have $200,000 on December 31. An investor who is able to earn a 12 percent return on investment is indifferent between having $178,571 now or receiving

LO 2

Determine the present value of future cash flows.

---

[1]The following computations assume the $200,000 cash inflow is received on the last day of each year. In actual practice the timing of cash inflows is less precise and present value computations are recognized to be approximate, not exact.

[2]All computations in this chapter are rounded to the nearest whole dollar.

$200,000 one year from now. The two options are equal, as shown in the following mathematical proof:

$$\text{Investment} + (0.12 \times \text{Investment}) = \$200,000$$
$$\$178,571 + (0.12 \times \$178,571) = \$200,000$$
$$\$178,571 + 21,429 = \$200,000$$
$$\$200,000 = \$200,000$$

Present Value Table for Single-Amount Cash Inflows

The algebra illustrated above is used to convert a one-time future receipt of cash to its present value. One-time receipts of cash are frequently called **single-payment,** or **lump-sum,** cash flows. Because EZ desires a 12 percent rate of return, the present value of the first cash inflow is $178,571. We can also determine the present value of a $200,000 single amount (lump sum) at the end of the second, third, and fourth years. Instead of using cumbersome algebraic computations to convert these future values to their present value equivalents, financial analysts frequently use a table of conversion factors to convert future values to their present value equivalents. The table of conversion factors used to convert future values into present values is commonly called a **present value table.**[3] A typical present value table presents columns with different return rates and rows with different periods of time, like Table 1 in the Appendix located at the end of this chapter.

To illustrate using the present value table, locate the conversion factor in Table 1 at the intersection of the 12% column and the one-period row. The conversion factor is 0.892857. Multiplying this factor by the $200,000 expected cash inflow yields $178,571 ($200,000 × 0.892857). This is the same value determined algebraically in the previous section of this chapter. The conversion factors in the present value tables simplify converting future values to present values.

The conversion factors for the second, third, and fourth periods are 0.797194, 0.711780, and 0.635518, respectively. These factors are in the 12% column at rows 2, 3, and 4, respectively. Locate these factors in Table 1 of the Appendix. Multiplying the conversion factors by the future cash inflow for each period produces their present value equivalents, shown in Exhibit 16.1. Exhibit 16.1 indicates that investing $607,470 today at a 12 percent rate of return is equivalent to receiving $200,000 per year for four years. Because EZ Rentals desires to earn (at least) a 12 percent rate of return, the company should be willing to pay up to $607,470 to purchase the LCD projectors.

Present Value Table for Annuities

The algebra described previously for converting equal lump-sum cash inflows to present value equivalents can be further simplified by adding the present value table factors

EXHIBIT 16.1

Present Value of a $200,000 Cash Inflow to be Received for Four Years

PV	=	FV	×	Present Value Table Factor	=	Present Value Equivalent
Period 1 PV	=	$200,000	×	0.892857	=	$178,571
Period 2 PV	=	200,000	×	0.797194	=	159,439
Period 3 PV	=	200,000	×	0.711780	=	142,356
Period 4 PV	=	200,000	×	0.635518	=	127,104
Total						$607,470

[3]The present value table is based on the formula $[1 \div (1 + r)^n]$ where r equals the rate of return and n equals the number of periods.

together before multiplying them by the cash inflows. The total of the present value table factors in Exhibit 16.1 is 3.037349 (0.892857 + 0.797194 + 0.711780 + 0.635518). Multiplying this **accumulated conversion factor** by the expected annual cash inflow results in the same present value equivalent of $607,470 ($200,000 × 3.037349). As with lump-sum conversion factors, accumulated conversion factors can be calculated and organized in a table with *columns* for different rates of return and *rows* for different periods of time. Table 2 in the Appendix is a present value table of accumulated conversion factors. Locate the conversion factor at the intersection of the 12% column and the fourth time-period row. The factor at this intersection is 3.037349, confirming that the accumulated conversion factors represent the sum of the single-payment conversion factors.

The conversion factors in Table 2 apply to annuities. An **annuity** is a series of cash flows that meets three criteria: (1) equal payment amounts; (2) equal time intervals between payments; and (3) a constant rate of return. For EZ Rentals, the expected cash inflows from renting LCD projectors are all for equivalent amounts ($200,000); the expected intervals between cash inflows are equal lengths of time (one year); and the rate of return for each inflow is constant at 12 percent. The series of expected cash inflows from renting the projectors is therefore an annuity. The present value of an annuity table can be used only if all of these conditions are satisfied.

The present value of an annuity table (Table 2) simplifies converting future cash inflows to their present value equivalents. EZ Rentals can convert the cash inflows as shown in Exhibit 16.1, using four conversion factors, multiplying each conversion factor by the annual cash inflow (four multiplications), and adding the resulting products. In contrast, EZ can recognize that the series of payments is an annuity, which requires multiplying a single conversion factor from Table 2 by the amount of the annuity payment. Regardless of the conversion method, the result is the same (a present value of $607,470). Recall that EZ can also make the conversion using algebra. The table values are derived from algebraic formulas. The present value tables reduce the computations needed to convert future values to present values.

Software Programs That Calculate Present Values

Software programs offer an even more efficient means of converting future values into present value equivalents. These programs are frequently built into handheld financial calculators and computer spreadsheet programs. As an example, we demonstrate the procedures used in a Microsoft Excel spreadsheet.

An Excel spreadsheet offers a variety of financial functions, one of which converts a future value annuity into its present value equivalent. This present value function uses the syntax *PV(rate,nper,pmt)* in which *rate* is the desired rate of return, *nper* is the number of periods, and *pmt* is the amount of the payment (periodic cash inflow). To convert a future value annuity into its present value equivalent, provide the function with the appropriate amounts for the rate, number of periods, and amount of the annuity (cash inflows) into a spreadsheet cell. Press the Enter key and the present value equivalent appears in the spreadsheet cell.

The power of the spreadsheet to perform computations instantly is extremely useful for answering what-if questions. Exhibit 16.2 demonstrates this power by providing spreadsheet conversions for three different scenarios. The first scenario demonstrates the annuity assumptions for EZ Rentals, providing the present value equivalent ($607,470) of a four-year cash inflow of $200,000 per year at a 12 percent rate of interest. The present value is a *negative* number. This format indicates that an initial $607,470 *cash outflow* is required to obtain the four-year series of cash inflows. The present value equivalent in Scenario 2 shows the present value if the annuity assumptions reflect a 14 percent, rather than 12 percent, desired rate of return. The present value equivalent in Scenario 3 shows the present value if the annuity assumptions under Scenario 1 are changed to reflect annual cash inflows of $300,000, rather than $200,000. A wide range of scenarios could be readily considered by changing any or all the variables in the spreadsheet function. In each case, the computer does the calculations, giving the manager more time to analyze the data rather than compute it.

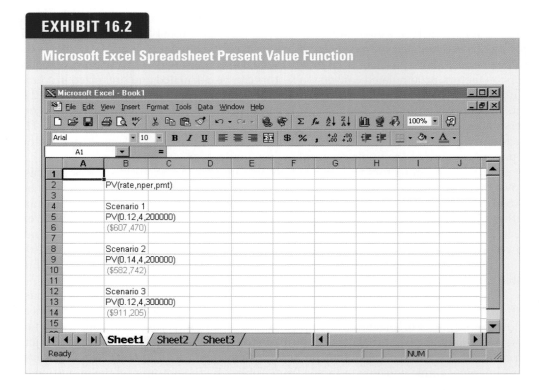

EXHIBIT 16.2

Microsoft Excel Spreadsheet Present Value Function

Although software is widely used in business practice, the diversity of interfaces used by different calculators and spreadsheet programs makes it unsuitable for textbook presentations. This text uses the present value tables in the Appendix in the text illustrations and the end-of-chapter exercises and problems. If you use software to solve these problems, your answers will be the same. All these tools—formulas, conversion tables, software—are based on the same mathematical principles and will produce the same results.

Ordinary Annuity Assumption

All the conversion methods described above assume the cash inflows occur at the *end* of each accounting period. This distribution pattern is called an **ordinary annuity.**[4] In practice, cash inflows are likely to be received throughout the period, not just at the end. For example, EZ Rentals is likely to collect cash revenue from renting projectors each month rather than in a single lump-sum receipt at the end of each of the four years. Companies frequently use the ordinary annuity assumption in practice because it simplifies time value of money computations. Because capital investment decisions are necessarily based on uncertain projections about future cash inflows, the lives of investment opportunities, and the appropriate rates of return, achieving pinpoint accuracy is impossible. Sacrificing precision for simplicity by using the ordinary annuity assumption is a reasonable trade-off in the decision-making process.

Reinvestment Assumption

The present value computations in the previous sections show that investing $607,470 today at a 12 percent rate of return is equivalent to receiving four individual $200,000 payments at the end of four successive years. Exhibit 16.3 illustrates that a cash inflow of $200,000 per year is equivalent to earning a 12 percent rate of return on a $607,470 investment.[5]

---

[4]When equal cash inflows occur at the *beginning* of each accounting period, the distribution is called an *annuity due.* Although some business transactions are structured as annuities due, they are less common than ordinary annuities. This text focuses on the ordinary annuity assumption.

[5]Exhibit 16.3 is analogous to an amortization table for a long-term note with equal payments of principal and interest.

EXHIBIT 16.3

Cash Flow Classifications for EZ's Investment in Projectors

Time Period	(a) Investment Balance During the Year	(b) Annual Cash Inflow	(c) Return on Investment (a × 0.12)	(d) Recovered Investment (b − c)	(e) Year-End Investment Balance (a − d)
1	$607,470	$200,000	$ 72,896	$127,104	$480,366
2	480,366	200,000	57,644	142,356	338,010
3	338,010	200,000	40,561	159,439	178,571
4	178,571	200,000	21,429	178,571	0
Totals		$800,000	$192,530	$607,470	

It is customary to assume that the desired rate of return includes the effects of *compounding.*[6] Saying an investment is "earning the desired rate of return" assumes the cash inflows generated by the investment are reinvested at the desired rate of return. In this case, we are assuming that EZ will reinvest the $200,000 annual cash inflows in other investments that will earn a 12 percent return.

TECHNIQUES FOR ANALYZING CAPITAL INVESTMENT PROPOSALS

Managers can choose from among numerous analytical techniques to help them make capital investment decisions. Each technique has advantages and disadvantages. A manager may apply more than one technique to a particular proposal to take advantage of more information. Because most companies have computer capabilities that include a variety of standard capital budgeting programs, applying different techniques to the same proposal normally requires little extra effort. Limiting analysis to only one tool could produce biased results. Obtaining more than one perspective offers substantial benefit.

Net Present Value

By using the present value conversion techniques described earlier, EZ Rentals' management determined it would be willing to invest $607,470 today (present value) to obtain a four-year, $200,000 future value annuity cash inflow. The $607,470 investment is *not* the cost of the LCD projectors, it is the amount EZ is willing to pay for them. The projectors may cost EZ Rentals more or less than their present value. To determine whether EZ should invest in the projectors, management must compare the present value of the future cash inflows ($607,470) to the cost of the projectors (the current cash outflow required to purchase them). Subtracting the cost of the investment from the present value of the future cash inflows determines the **net present value** of the investment opportunity. A positive net present value indicates the investment will yield a rate of return higher than 12 percent. A negative net present value means the return is less than 12 percent.

LO 3

Determine and interpret the net present value of an investment opportunity.

[6]*Compounding* refers to reinvesting investment proceeds so the total amount of invested capital increases, resulting in even higher returns. For example, assume $100 is invested at a 10 percent compounded annual rate of return. At the end of the first year, the investment yields a $10 return ($100 × 0.10). The $10 return plus any recovered investment is reinvested so that the total amount of invested capital at the beginning of the second year is $110. The return for the second year is $11 ($110 × 0.10). All funds are reinvested so that the return for the third year is $12.10 [($110 + $11) × 0.10].

To illustrate, assume EZ can purchase the projectors for $582,742. Assuming the desired rate of return is 12 percent, EZ should buy them. The net present value of the investment opportunity is computed as follows.

Present value of future cash inflows	$607,470
Cost of investment (required cash outflow)	(582,742)
Net present value	$ 24,728

The positive net present value suggests the investment will earn a rate of return in excess of 12 percent (if cash flows are indeed $200,000 each year). Because the projected rate of return is higher than the desired rate of return, this analysis suggests EZ should accept the investment opportunity. Based on the above analysis we are able to establish the following decision rule.

Net present value decision rule: If the net present value is equal to or greater than zero, accept the investment opportunity.

✓ CHECK YOURSELF 16.2

To increase productivity, Wald Corporation is considering the purchase of a new machine that costs $50,000. Wald expects using the machine to increase annual net cash inflows by $12,500 for each of the next five years. Wald desires a minimum annual rate of return of 10 percent on the investment. Determine the net present value of the investment opportunity and recommend whether Wald should acquire the machine.

Answer

Present value of future cash flows = Future cash flow × Table 2 factor ($n = 5, r = 10\%$)

Present value of future cash flows = $12,500 × 3.790787 = $47,385

Net present value = PV of future cash flows − Cost of machine

Net present value = $47,385 − $50,000 = ($2,615)

The negative net present value indicates the investment will yield a rate of return below the desired rate of return. Wald should not acquire the new machine.

Internal Rate of Return

LO 4

Determine and interpret the internal rate of return of an investment opportunity.

The net present value method indicates EZ's investment in the projectors will provide a return in excess of the desired rate, but it does not provide the actual rate of return to expect from the investment. If EZ's management team wants to know the rate of return to expect from investing in the projectors, it must use the *internal rate of return method*. The **internal rate of return** is the rate at which the present value of cash inflows equals the cash outflows. It is the rate that will produce a zero net present value. For EZ Rentals, the internal rate of return can be determined as follows. First, compute the *present value table factor* for a $200,000 annuity that would yield a $582,742 present value cash outflow (cost of investment).

Present value table factor × $200,000 = $582,742

Present value table factor = $582,742 ÷ $200,000

Present value table factor = 2.91371

Second, because the expected annual cash inflows represent a four-year annuity, scan Table 2 in the Appendix at period $n = 4$. Try to locate the table factor 2.91371. The rate listed at the top of the column in which the factor is located is the internal rate of return. Turn to Table 2 and determine the internal rate of return for EZ Rentals before you read further. The above factor is in the 14 percent column. The difference in the table value (2.913712) and the value computed here (2.91371) is not significant. If EZ invests $582,742 in the projectors and they produce a $200,000 annual cash flow for four years, EZ will earn a 14 percent rate of return on the investment.

The *internal rate of return* may be compared with a *desired rate of return* to determine whether to accept or reject a particular investment project. Assuming EZ desires to earn a minimum rate of return of 12 percent, the preceding analysis suggests it should accept the investment opportunity because the internal rate of return (14 percent) is higher than the desired rate of return (12 percent). An internal rate of return below the desired rate suggests management should reject a particular proposal. The desired rate of return is sometimes called the *cutoff rate* or the *hurdle rate.* To be accepted, an investment proposal must provide an internal rate of return higher than the hurdle rate, cutoff rate, or desired rate of return. These terms are merely alternatives for the *cost of capital.* Ultimately, to be accepted, an investment must provide an internal rate of return higher than a company's cost of capital. Based on the above analysis we are able to establish the following decision rule.

> **Internal rate of return decision rule:** If the internal rate of return is equal to or greater than the desired rate of return, accept the investment opportunity.

TECHNIQUES FOR MEASURING INVESTMENT CASH FLOWS

The EZ Rentals example represents a simple capital investment analysis. The investment option involved only one cash outflow and a single annuity inflow. Investment opportunities often involve a greater variety of cash outflows and inflows. The following section of this chapter discusses different types of cash flows encountered in business practice.

LO 5

Identify cash flows associated with an investment opportunity.

Cash Inflows

Cash inflows generated from capital investments come from *four basic sources.* As in the case of EZ Rentals, the most common source of cash inflows is incremental revenue. **Incremental revenue** refers to the *additional* cash inflows from operating activities generated by using additional capital assets. For example, a taxi company expects revenues from taxi fares to increase if it purchases additional taxicabs. Similarly, investing in new apartments should increase rent revenue; opening a new store should result in additional sales revenue.

A second type of cash inflow results from *cost savings.* Decreases in cash outflows have the same beneficial effect as increases in cash inflows. Either way, a firm's cash position improves. For example, purchasing an automated computer system may enable a company to reduce cash outflows for salaries. Similarly, relocating a manufacturing facility closer to its raw materials source can reduce cash outflows for transportation costs.

An investment's *salvage value* provides a third source of cash inflows. Even when one company has finished using an asset, the asset may still be useful to another company. Many assets are sold after a company no longer wishes to use them. The salvage value represents a one-time cash inflow obtained when a company terminates an investment.

Companies can also experience a cash inflow through a *reduction in the amount of* **working capital** needed to support an investment. A certain level of working capital is required to support most business investments. For example, a new retail store outlet requires cash, receivables, and inventory to operate. When an investment is terminated, the decrease in the working capital commitment associated with the investment normally results in a cash inflow.

Cash Outflows

Cash outflows fall into *three primary categories.* One category consists of outflows for the *initial investment.* Managers must be alert to all the cash outflows connected with purchasing a capital asset. The purchase price, transportation costs, installation costs, and training costs are examples of typical cash outflows related to an initial investment.

A second category of cash outflows may result from *increases in operating expenses.* If a company increases output capacity by investing in additional equipment, it may experience higher utility bills, labor costs, and maintenance expenses when it places the equipment into service. These expenditures increase cash outflows.

Third, *increases in working capital* commitments result in cash outflows. Frequently, investments in new assets must be supported by a certain level of working capital. For example, investing in a copy machine requires spending cash to maintain a supply of paper and toner. Managers should treat an increased working capital commitment as a cash outflow in the period the commitment occurs.

Exhibit 16.4 lists the cash inflows and outflows discussed above. The list is not exhaustive but does summarize the most common cash flows businesses experience.

EXHIBIT 16.4

Typical Cash Flows Associated With Capital Investments

Inflows	Outflows
1. Incremental revenue	1. Initial investment
2. Cost savings	2. Incremental expenses
3. Salvage values	3. Working capital commitments
4. Recovery of working capital	

TECHNIQUES FOR COMPARING ALTERNATIVE CAPITAL INVESTMENT OPPORTUNITIES

Compare capital investment alternatives.

The management of Torres Transfer Company is considering two investment opportunities. One alternative, involving the purchase of new equipment for $80,000, would enable Torres to modernize its maintenance facility. The equipment has an expected useful life of five years and a $4,000 salvage value. It would replace existing equipment that had originally cost $45,000. The existing equipment has a current book value of $15,000 and a trade-in value of $5,000. The old equipment is technologically obsolete but can operate for an additional five years. On the day Torres purchases the new equipment, it would also pay the equipment manufacturer $3,000 for training costs to teach employees to operate the new equipment. The modernization has two primary advantages. One, it will improve management of the small parts inventory. The company's accountant believes that by the end of the first year, the carrying value of the small parts inventory could be reduced by $12,000. Second, the modernization is expected to increase efficiency, resulting in a $21,500 reduction in annual operating expenses.

The other investment alternative available to Torres is purchasing a truck. Adding another truck would enable Torres to expand its delivery area and increase revenue. The truck costs $115,000. It has a useful life of five years and a $30,000 salvage value. Operating the truck will require the company to increase its inventory of supplies, its petty cash account, and its accounts receivable and payable balances. These changes would add $5,000 to the company's working capital base immediately upon buying the truck. The working capital cash outflow is expected to be recovered at the end of the truck's useful life. The truck is expected to produce $69,000 per year in additional revenues. The driver's salary and other operating expenses are expected to be $32,000 per year. A major overhaul costing $20,000 is expected to be required at the end of the third year of operation. Assuming Torres desires to earn a rate of return of 14 percent, which of the two investment alternatives should it choose?

Net Present Value

Begin the analysis by calculating the net present value of the two investment alternatives. Exhibit 16.5 shows the computations. Study this exhibit. Each alternative is analyzed using three steps. Step 1 requires identifying all cash inflows; some may be annuities, and others may be lump-sum receipts. In the case of Alternative 1, the cost

EXHIBIT 16.5

Net Present Value Analysis

	Amount	×	Conversion Factor	=	Present Value
Alternative 1: Modernize Maintenance Facility					
Step 1: Cash inflows					
1. Cost savings	$21,500	×	3.433081*	=	$ 73,811
2. Salvage value	4,000	×	0.519369†	=	2,077
3. Working capital recovery	12,000	×	0.877193‡	=	10,526
Total					$ 86,414
Step 2: Cash outflows					
1. Cost of equipment					
($80,000 cost—$5,000 trade-in)	$75,000	×	1.000000§	=	$ 75,000
2. Training costs	3,000	×	1.000000§	=	3,000
Total					$ 78,000
Step 3: Net present value					
Total present value of cash inflows					$ 86,414
Total present value of cash outflows					(78,000)
Net present value					$ 8,414
Alternative 2: Purchase Delivery Truck					
Step 1: Cash inflows					
1. Incremental revenue	$69,000	×	3.433081*	=	$236,883
2. Salvage value	30,000	×	0.519369†	=	15,581
2. Working capital recovery	5,000	×	0.519369†	=	2,597
Total					$255,061
Step 2: Cash outflows					
1. Cost of truck	$115,000	×	1.000000§	=	$115,000
2. Working capital increase	5,000	×	1.000000§	=	5,000
3. Increased operating expense	32,000	×	3.433081*	=	109,859
4. Major overhaul	20,000	×	0.674972§§	=	13,499
Total					$243,358
Step 3: Net present value					
Total present value of cash inflows					$255,061
Total present value of cash outflows					(243,358)
Net present value					$ 11,703

*Present value of annuity table 2, $n = 5$, $r = 14\%$.

†Present value of single payment table 1, $n = 5$, $r = 14\%$.

‡Present value of single payment table 1, $n = 1$, $r = 14\%$.

§Present value at beginning of period 1.

§§Present value of single payment table 1, $n = 3$, $r = 14\%$.

saving is an annuity, and the inflow from the salvage value is a lump-sum receipt. Once the cash inflows have been identified, the appropriate conversion factors are identified and the cash inflows are converted to their equivalent present values. Step 2 follows the same process to determine the present value of the cash outflows. Step 3 subtracts the present value of the outflows from the present value of the inflows to determine the net present value. The same three-step approach is used to determine the net present value of Alternative 2.

With respect to Alternative 1, the original cost and the book value of the existing equipment are ignored. As indicated in a previous chapter, these measures represent *sunk costs;* they are not relevant to the decision. The concept of relevance applies to long-term capital investment decisions just as it applies to short-term special decisions. To be relevant to a capital investment decision, costs or revenues must involve different present and future cash flows for each alternative. Because the historical cost of the old equipment does not differ between the alternatives, it is not relevant.

Because the *net present value* of each investment alternative is *positive,* either investment will generate a return in excess of 14 percent. Which investment is the more favorable? The data could mislead a careless manager. Alternative 2 might seem the better choice because it has a greater present value than Alternative 1 ($11,703 vs. $8,414). Net present value, however, is expressed in *absolute dollars.* The net present value of a more costly capital investment can be greater than the net present value of a smaller investment even though the smaller investment earns a higher rate of return.

To compare different size investment alternatives, management can compute a **present value index** by dividing the present value of cash inflows by the present value of cash outflows. *The higher the ratio, the higher the rate of return per dollar invested in the proposed project.* The present value indices for the two alternatives Torres Transfer Company is considering are as follows.

$$\text{Present value index for Alternative 1} = \frac{\text{Present value of cash inflows}}{\text{Present value of cash outflows}} = \frac{\$86,414}{\$78,000} = 1.108$$

$$\text{Present value index for Alternative 2} = \frac{\text{Present value of cash inflows}}{\text{Present value of cash outflows}} = \frac{\$255,061}{\$243,358} = 1.048$$

Management can use the present value indices to rank the investment alternatives. In this case, Alternative 1 yields a higher return than Alternative 2.

Internal Rate of Return

Management can also rank investment alternatives using the internal rate of return for each investment. Generally, *the higher the internal rate of return, the more profitable the investment.* We previously demonstrated how to calculate the internal rate of return for an investment that generates a simple cash inflow annuity. The computations are significantly more complex for investments with uneven cash flows. Recall that the internal rate of return is the rate that produces a zero net present value. Manually computing the rate that produces a zero net present value is a tedious trial-and-error process. You must first estimate the rate of return for a particular investment, then calculate the net present value. If the calculation produces a negative net present value, you try a lower estimated rate of return and recalculate. If this calculation produces a positive net present value, the actual internal rate of return lies between the first and second estimates. Make a third estimate and once again recalculate the net present value, and so on. Eventually you will determine the rate of return that produces a net present value of zero.

Many calculators and spreadsheet programs are designed to make these computations. We illustrate the process with a Microsoft Excel spreadsheet. Excel uses the syntax *IRR (values, guess)* in which *values* refers to cells that specify the cash flows for which you want to calculate the internal rate of return and *guess* is a number you estimate is close to the actual internal rate of return (IRR). The IRRs for the two investment alternatives available to Torres Transfer Company are shown in Exhibit 16.6. Study this exhibit. Excel requires netting cash outflows against cash inflows for each period in which both outflows and inflows are expected. For your convenience, we have labeled the net cash flows in the spreadsheet. Labeling is not necessary to execute the IRR function. The entire function, including values and guess, can be entered into a single cell of the spreadsheet. Persons familiar with spreadsheet programs learn to significantly simplify the input required.

The IRR results in Exhibit 16.6 confirm the ranking determined using the present value index. Alternative 1 (modernize maintenance facility), with an internal rate of return of 18.69 percent, ranks above Alternative 2 (purchase a truck) with an internal rate of return of 17.61 percent, even though Alternative 2 has a higher net present value (see Exhibit 16.5). Alternative 2, however, still may be the better investment option, depending on the amount available to invest. Suppose Torres has $120,000 of available funds to invest. Because Alternative 1 requires an initial investment of only $78,000, $42,000 ($120,000 − $78,000) of capital will not be invested. If Torres has no other investment

REALITY BYTES

Developing proficiency with present value mathematics is usually the most difficult aspect of capital budgeting for students taking their first managerial accounting course. In real-world companies, the most difficult aspect of capital budgeting is forecasting cash flows for several years into the future. Consider the following capital budgeting project.

In 1965 representatives from the Georgia Power Company visited Ms. Taylor's fifth grade class to tell her students about the Edwin I. Hatch Nuclear Plant that was going to be built nearby. One of the authors of this text was a student in that class.

In 1966 construction began on the first unit of the plant, and the plant started producing electricity in 1975. The next year, 10 years after hearing the presentation in his fifth grade class, the author worked on construction of the second unit of the plant during the summer before his senior year of college. This second unit began operations in 1978.

In its 2009 annual report, the Southern Company, which is now the major owner of the plant, stated that the Hatch plant is expected to operate until 2038, and that decommissioning of the plant will continue until 2061. The cost to construct both units of the plant was $934 million. The estimated cost to dismantle and decommission the plant is over $1 billion.

It seems safe to assume that the students in Ms. Taylor's fifth grade class were not among the first to hear about the power company's plans for the Hatch plant. Thus, we can reasonably conclude that the life of this capital project will be over 100 years, from around 1960 until 2061.

Try to imagine that you were assigned the task of predicting the cash inflows and outflows for a project that was expected to last 100 years. Clearly, mastering present value mathematics would not be your biggest worry.

EXHIBIT 16.6

Microsoft Excel Spreadsheet Internal Rate of Return Function

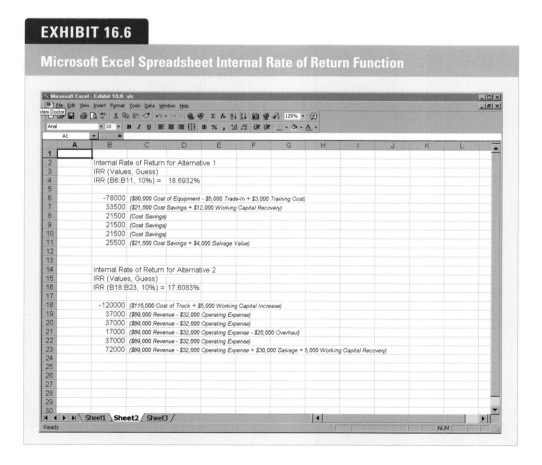

opportunities for this $42,000, the company would be better off investing the entire $120,000 in Alternative 2 ($115,000 cost of truck + $5,000 working capital increase). Earning 17.61 percent on a $120,000 investment is better than earning 18.69 percent on a $78,000 investment with no return on the remaining $42,000. Management accounting requires exercising judgment when making decisions.

Relevance and the Time Value of Money

Suppose you have the opportunity to invest in one of two capital projects. Both projects require an immediate cash outflow of $6,000 and will produce future cash inflows of $8,000. The only difference between the two projects is the timing of the inflows. The receipt schedule for both projects follows.

Year	Project 1	Project 2
1	$3,500	$2,000
2	3,000	2,000
3	1,000	2,000
4	500	2,000
Total	$8,000	$8,000

Because both projects cost the same and produce the same total cash inflows, they may appear to be equal. Whether you select Project 1 or Project 2, you pay $6,000 and receive $8,000. Because of the time value of money, however, Project 1 is preferable to Project 2. To see why, determine the net present value of both projects, assuming a 10 percent desired rate of return.

Computation of Net Present Value for Project 1 and Project 2

Net Present Value for Project 1

Period	Cash Inflow	×	Conversion Factor Table 1, $r = 10\%$	=	Present Value
1	$3,500	×	0.909091	=	$ 3,182
2	3,000	×	0.826446	=	2,479
3	1,000	×	0.751315	=	751
4	500	×	0.683013	=	342
Present value of future cash inflows					6,754
Present value of cash outflow					(6,000)
Net present value Project 1					$ 754

Net Present Value for Project 2

	Cash Inflow Annuity	×	Conversion Factor Table 2, $r = 10\%$, $n = 4$		
Present value of cash inflow	$2,000	×	3.169865		$ 6,340
Present value of cash outflow					(6,000)
Net present value Project 2					$ 340

The net present value of Project 1 ($754) exceeds the net present value of Project 2 ($340). The timing as well as the amount of cash flows has a significant impact on capital investment returns. Recall that to be relevant, costs or revenues must differ between alternatives. Differences in the timing of cash flow payments or receipts are also relevant for decision-making purposes.

One way to answer your client's question is to determine which option has the highest net present value. The present value of the lump-sum payment option is simple; it is the $115.5 [$231 ÷ 2] million the lottery is prepared to pay each of the winners now. The present value of the annuity option must be calculated, and it consists of two parts. The first of the 26 payments of $7,076,692 will be paid immediately, so it is worth $7,076,692 today. The remaining 25 payments will occur at one-year intervals, so their present value is computed as:

$$\$7,076,692 \times 11.653583^* = \$82,468,818$$

Adding $7,076,692 to $82,468,818 yields a present value of $89,545,510, which is a lot less than $115.5 million. This suggests your client should take the lump-sum payment. Of course, the risk of the lottery not making its annual payments is very low. There is a greater risk that a financial planner may not find investments to earn a 7% annual return, so the winner would have to consider his or her tolerance for risk before making a final decision.

In the case of these particular lottery winners, one chose the lump-sum payment and the other chose the annuity.

*This factor is not included in the tables at the end of the chapter, so it is provided here for the purposes of this illustration.

Tax Considerations

The previous examples have ignored the effect of income taxes on capital investment decisions. Taxes affect the amount of cash flows generated by investments. To illustrate, assume Wu Company purchases an asset that costs $240,000. The asset has a four-year useful life, no salvage value, and is depreciated on a straight-line basis. The asset generates cash revenue of $90,000 per year. Assume Wu's income tax rate is 40 percent. What is the net present value of the asset, assuming Wu's management desires to earn a 10 percent rate of return after taxes? The first step in answering this question is to calculate the annual cash flow generated by the asset, as shown in Exhibit 16.7.

EXHIBIT 16.7

Determining Cash Flow from Investment

	Period 1	Period 2	Period 3	Period 4
Cash revenue	$ 90,000	$ 90,000	$ 90,000	$ 90,000
Depreciation expense (noncash)	(60,000)	(60,000)	(60,000)	(60,000)
Income before taxes	30,000	30,000	30,000	30,000
Income tax at 40%	(12,000)	(12,000)	(12,000)	(12,000)
Income after tax	18,000	18,000	18,000	18,000
Depreciation add back	60,000	60,000	60,000	60,000
Annual cash inflow	$ 78,000	$ 78,000	$ 78,000	$ 78,000

Because recognizing depreciation expense does not require a cash payment (cash is paid when assets are purchased, not when depreciation is recognized), depreciation expense must be added back to after-tax income to determine the annual cash inflow. Once the cash flow is determined, the net present value is computed as shown here.

$$\begin{array}{c} \text{Cash flow} \\ \text{annuity} \end{array} \times \begin{array}{c} \text{Conversion factor} \\ \text{Table 2, } r = 10\%, n = 4 \end{array} = \begin{array}{c} \text{Present value} \\ \text{cash inflows} \end{array} - \begin{array}{c} \text{Present value} \\ \text{cash outflows} \end{array} = \begin{array}{c} \text{Net present} \\ \text{value} \end{array}$$

$$\$78,000 \times 3.169865 = \$247,249 - \$240,000 = \$7,249$$

The depreciation sheltered some of the income from taxation. Income taxes apply to income after deducting depreciation expense. Without depreciation expense, income taxes each year would have been $36,000 ($90,000 × 0.40) instead of $12,000 ($30,000 × 0.40). The $24,000 difference ($36,000 − $12,000) is known as a *depreciation tax shield.* The amount of the depreciation tax shield can also be computed by multiplying the depreciation expense by the tax rate ($60,000 × 0.40 = $24,000).

Because of the time value of money, companies benefit by maximizing the depreciation tax shield early in the life of an asset. For this reason, most companies calculate depreciation expense for tax purposes using the *modified accelerated cost recovery system (MACRS)* permitted by tax law rather than using straight-line depreciation. MACRS recognizes depreciation on an accelerated basis, assigning larger amounts of depreciation in the early years of an asset's useful life. The higher depreciation charges result in lower amounts of taxable income and lower income taxes. In the later years of an asset's useful life, the reverse is true, and lower depreciation charges result in higher taxes. Accelerated depreciation does not allow companies to avoid paying taxes but to delay them. The longer companies can delay paying taxes, the more cash they have available to invest.

TECHNIQUES THAT IGNORE THE TIME VALUE OF MONEY

LO 7

Determine the payback period for an investment opportunity.

Several techniques for evaluating capital investment proposals ignore the time value of money. Although these techniques are less accurate, they are quick and simple. When investments are small or the returns are expected within a short time, these techniques are likely to result in the same decisions that more sophisticated techniques produce.

Payback Method

The **payback method** is simple to apply and easy to understand. It shows how long it will take to recover the initial cash outflow (the cost) of an investment. The formula for computing the payback period, measured in years, is as follows.

Payback period = Net cost of investment ÷ Annual net cash inflow

To illustrate, assume Winston Cleaners can purchase a new ironing machine that will press shirts in half the time of the one currently used. The new machine costs $100,000 and will reduce labor cost by $40,000 per year over a four-year useful life. The payback period is computed as follows.

Payback period = $100,000 ÷ $40,000 = 2.5 years

Interpreting Payback

Generally, investments with shorter payback periods are considered better. Because the payback method measures only investment recovery, not profitability, however, this conclusion can be invalid when considering investment alternatives. To illustrate, assume Winston Cleaners also has the opportunity to purchase a different machine that costs $100,000 and provides an annual labor savings of $40,000. However, the second machine will last for five instead of four years. The payback period is still 2.5 years ($100,000 ÷ $40,000), but the second machine is a better investment because it improves profitability by providing an additional year of cost savings. The payback analysis does not measure this difference between the alternatives.

Unequal Cash Flows

The preceding illustration assumed Winston's labor cost reduction saved the same amount of cash each year for the life of the new machine. The payback method requires adjustment when cash flow benefits are unequal. Suppose a company purchases a machine for $6,000. The machine will be used erratically and is expected to provide incremental revenue over the next five years as follows.

2009	2010	2011	2012	2013
$3,000	$1,000	$2,000	$1,000	$500

Based on this cash inflow pattern, what is the payback period? There are two acceptable solutions. One accumulates the incremental revenue until the sum equals the amount of the original investment.

Year	Annual Amount	Cumulative Total
2009	$3,000	$3,000
2010	1,000	4,000
2011	2,000	6,000

This approach indicates the payback period is three years.

A second solution uses an averaging concept. The average annual cash inflow is determined. This figure is then used in the denominator of the payback equation. Using the preceding data, the payback period is computed as follows.

1. Compute the average annual cash inflow.

$$2009 + 2010 + 2011 + 2012 + 2013 = \text{Total} \div 5 = \text{Average}$$

$$\$3,000 + \$1,000 + \$2,000 + \$1,000 + \$500 = \$7,500 \div 5 = \$1,500$$

2. Compute the payback period.

$$\frac{\text{Net cost of investment}} {} \div \frac{\text{Average annual net cash inflow}} {} = 6,000 \div 1,500 = 4 \text{ years}$$

The average method is useful when a company purchases a number of similar assets with differing cash return patterns.

Unadjusted Rate of Return

The **unadjusted rate of return** method is another common evaluation technique. Investment cash flows are not adjusted to reflect the time value of money. The unadjusted rate of return is sometimes called the *simple rate of return.* It is computed as follows.

$$\frac{\text{Unadjusted}}{\text{rate of return}} = \frac{\text{Average incremental increase in annual net income}}{\text{Net cost of original investment}}$$

To illustrate computing the unadjusted rate of return, assume The Dining Table, Inc., is considering establishing a new restaurant that will require a $2,000,000 original investment. Management anticipates operating the restaurant for 10 years before significant

LO 8

Determine the unadjusted rate of return for an investment opportunity.

renovations will be required. The restaurant is expected to provide an average after-tax return of $280,000 per year. The unadjusted rate of return is computed as follows.

$$\text{Unadjusted rate of return} = \$280,000 \div \$2,000,000 = 14\% \text{ per year}$$

The accuracy of the unadjusted rate of return suffers from the failure to recognize the recovery of invested capital. With respect to a depreciable asset, the capital investment is normally recovered through revenue over the life of the asset. To illustrate, assume we purchase a $1,000 asset with a two-year life and a zero salvage value. For simplicity, ignore income taxes. Assume the asset produces $600 of cash revenue per year. The income statement for the first year of operation appears as follows.

Revenue	$ 600
Depreciation expense	(500)
Net income	$ 100

What is the amount of invested capital during the first year? First, a $1,000 cash outflow was used to purchase the asset (the original investment). Next, we collected $600 of cash revenue of which $100 was a *return on investment* (net income) and $500 was a **recovery of investment.** As a result, $1,000 was invested in the asset at the beginning of the year and $500 was invested at the end of the year. Similarly, we will recover an additional $500 of capital during the second year of operation, leaving zero invested capital at the end of the second year. Given that the cash inflows from revenue are collected somewhat evenly over the life of the investment, the amount of invested capital will range from a beginning balance of $1,000 to an ending balance of zero. On average, we will have $500 invested in the asset (the midpoint between $1,000 and zero). The average investment can be determined by dividing the total original investment by 2 ($1,000 ÷ 2 = $500). The unadjusted rate of return based on average invested capital can be calculated as follows.

$$\frac{\text{Unadjusted rate of return}}{\text{(Based on average investment)}} = \frac{\text{Average incremental increase in annual net income}}{\text{Net cost of original investment} \div 2}$$

$$= \frac{\$100}{\$1,000 \div 2} = 20\%$$

To avoid distortions caused by the failure to recognize the recovery of invested capital, the unadjusted rate of return should be based on the *average investment* when working with investments in depreciable assets.

✓ CHECK YOURSELF 16.3

EZ Rentals can purchase a van that costs $24,000. The van has an expected useful life of three years and no salvage value. EZ expects rental revenue from the van to be $12,000 per year. Determine the payback period and the unadjusted rate of return.

Answer

> **Payback = Cost of the investment ÷ Annual cash inflow**
>
> **Payback = $24,000 ÷ $12,000 = 2 years**
>
> **Unadjusted rate of return = Net income ÷ Average cost of the investment**

Revenue	$12,000	
Depreciation expense	(8,000)	[$24,000 ÷ 3 years]
Net income	$ 4,000	

> **Unadjusted rate of return = $4,000 ÷ ($24,000 ÷ 2) = 33.33%**

Real-World Reporting Practices

In a recent study, researchers found that companies in the forest products industry use discounted cash flow techniques more frequently when the capital project being considered is a long-term timber investment. The use of techniques that ignore the time value of money increased when other shorter-term capital investment projects were being considered. Exhibit 16.8 shows the researchers' findings.

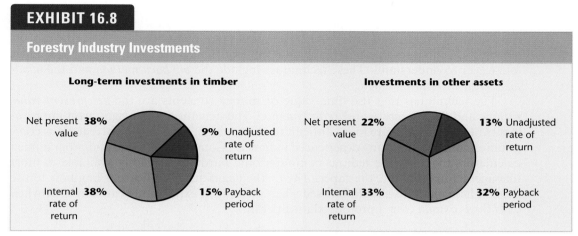

EXHIBIT 16.8

Forestry Industry Investments

Long-term investments in timber

Net present value **38%** | **9%** Unadjusted rate of return
Internal rate of return **38%** | **15%** Payback period

Investments in other assets

Net present value **22%** | **13%** Unadjusted rate of return
Internal rate of return **33%** | **32%** Payback period

Data Source: J. Bailes, J. Nielsen, and S. Lawton, "How Forest Product Companies Analyze Capital Budgets," *Management Accounting,* October 1998, pp. 24–30.

POSTAUDITS

LO 9

Conduct a postaudit of a completed investment.

The analytical techniques for evaluating capital investment proposals depend highly on estimates of future cash flows. Although predictions cannot be perfectly accurate, gross miscalculations can threaten the existence of an organization. For example, optimistic projections of future cash inflows that do not materialize will lead to investments that do not return the cost of capital. Managers must take their projections seriously. A postaudit policy can encourage managers to carefully consider their capital investment decisions. A **postaudit** is conducted at the completion of a capital investment project, using the same analytical technique that was used to justify the original investment. For example, if an internal rate of return was used to justify approving an investment project, the internal rate of return should be computed in the postaudit. In the postaudit computation, *actual* rather than estimated cash flows are used. Postaudits determine whether the expected results were achieved.

Postaudits should focus on continuous improvement rather than punishment. Managers who are chastised for failing to achieve expected results might become overly cautious when asked to provide estimates for future projects. Being too conservative can create problems as serious as those caused by being too optimistic. Managers can err two ways with respect to capital investment decisions. First, a manager might accept a project that should have been rejected. This mistake usually stems from excessively optimistic future cash flow projections. Second, a manager might reject a project that should have been accepted. These missed opportunities are usually the result of underestimating future cash flows. A too cautious manager can become unable to locate enough projects to fully invest the firm's funds.

Idle cash earns no return. If projects continue to outperform expectations, managers are probably estimating future cash flows too conservatively. If projects consistently fail to live up to expectations, managers are probably being too optimistic in their projections of future cash flows. Either way, the company suffers. The goal of a postaudit is to provide feedback that will help managers improve the accuracy of future cash flow projections, maximizing the quality of the firm's capital investments.

A Look Back <<

Capital expenditures have a significant, long-term effect on profitability. They usually involve major cash outflows that are recovered through future cash inflows. The most common cash inflows include incremental revenue, operating cost savings, salvage value, and working capital releases. The most common outflows are the initial investment, increases in operating expenses, and working capital commitments.

Several techniques for analyzing the cash flows associated with capital investments are available. The techniques can be divided into two categories: (1) techniques that use time value of money concepts and (2) techniques that ignore the time value of money. Generally, techniques that ignore the time value of money are less accurate but simpler and easier to understand. These techniques include the *payback method* and the *unadjusted rate of return method.*

The techniques that use time value of money concepts are the *net present value method* and the *internal rate of return method.* These methods offer significant improvements in accuracy but are more difficult to understand. They may involve tedious computations and require using experienced judgment. Computer software and programmed calculators that ease the tedious computational burden are readily available to most managers. Furthermore, the superiority of the techniques justifies learning how to use them. These methods should be used when investment expenditures are larger or when cash flows extend over a prolonged time period.

APPENDIX

TABLE 1   Present Value of $1

n	4%	5%	6%	7%	8%	9%	10%	12%	14%	16%	20%
1	0.961538	0.952381	0.943396	0.934579	0.925926	0.917431	0.909091	0.892857	0.877193	0.862069	0.833333
2	0.924556	0.907029	0.889996	0.873439	0.857339	0.841680	0.826446	0.797194	0.769468	0.743163	0.694444
3	0.888996	0.863838	0.839619	0.816298	0.793832	0.772183	0.751315	0.711780	0.674972	0.640658	0.578704
4	0.854804	0.822702	0.792094	0.762895	0.735030	0.708425	0.683013	0.635518	0.592080	0.552291	0.482253
5	0.821927	0.783526	0.747258	0.712986	0.680583	0.649931	0.620921	0.567427	0.519369	0.476113	0.401878
6	0.790315	0.746215	0.704961	0.666342	0.630170	0.596267	0.564474	0.506631	0.455587	0.410442	0.334898
7	0.759918	0.710681	0.665057	0.622750	0.583490	0.547034	0.513158	0.452349	0.399637	0.353830	0.279082
8	0.730690	0.676839	0.627412	0.582009	0.540269	0.501866	0.466507	0.403883	0.350559	0.305025	0.232568
9	0.702587	0.644609	0.591898	0.543934	0.500249	0.460428	0.424098	0.360610	0.307508	0.262953	0.193807
10	0.675564	0.613913	0.558395	0.508349	0.463193	0.422411	0.385543	0.321973	0.269744	0.226684	0.161506
11	0.649581	0.584679	0.526788	0.475093	0.428883	0.387533	0.350494	0.287476	0.236617	0.195417	0.134588
12	0.624597	0.556837	0.496969	0.444012	0.397114	0.355535	0.318631	0.256675	0.207559	0.168463	0.112157
13	0.600574	0.530321	0.468839	0.414964	0.367698	0.326179	0.289664	0.229174	0.182069	0.145227	0.093464
14	0.577475	0.505068	0.442301	0.387817	0.340461	0.299246	0.263331	0.204620	0.159710	0.125195	0.077887
15	0.555265	0.481017	0.417265	0.362446	0.315242	0.274538	0.239392	0.182696	0.140096	0.107927	0.064905
16	0.533908	0.458112	0.393646	0.338735	0.291890	0.251870	0.217629	0.163122	0.122892	0.093041	0.054088
17	0.513373	0.436297	0.371364	0.316574	0.270269	0.231073	0.197845	0.145644	0.107800	0.080207	0.045073
18	0.493628	0.415521	0.350344	0.295864	0.250249	0.211994	0.179859	0.130040	0.094561	0.069144	0.037561
19	0.474642	0.395734	0.330513	0.276508	0.231712	0.194490	0.163508	0.116107	0.082948	0.059607	0.031301
20	0.456387	0.376889	0.311805	0.258419	0.214548	0.178431	0.148644	0.103667	0.072762	0.051385	0.026084

TABLE 2   Present Value of an Annuity of $1

n	4%	5%	6%	7%	8%	9%	10%	12%	14%	16%	20%
1	0.961538	0.952381	0.943396	0.934579	0.925926	0.917431	0.909091	0.892857	0.877193	0.862069	0.833333
2	1.886095	1.859410	1.833393	1.808018	1.783265	1.759111	1.735537	1.690051	1.646661	1.605232	1.527778
3	2.775091	2.723248	2.673012	2.624316	2.577097	2.531295	2.486852	2.401831	2.321632	2.245890	2.106481
4	3.629895	3.545951	3.465106	3.387211	3.312127	3.239720	3.169865	3.037349	2.913712	2.798181	2.588735
5	4.451822	4.329477	4.212364	4.100197	3.992710	3.889651	3.790787	3.604776	3.433081	3.274294	2.990612
6	5.242137	5.075692	4.917324	4.766540	4.622880	4.485919	4.355261	4.111407	3.888668	3.684736	3.325510
7	6.002055	5.786373	5.582381	5.389289	5.206370	5.032953	4.868419	4.563757	4.288305	4.038565	3.604592
8	6.732745	6.463213	6.209794	5.971299	5.746639	5.534819	5.334926	4.967640	4.638864	4.343591	3.837160
9	7.435332	7.107822	6.801692	6.515232	6.246888	5.995247	5.759024	5.328250	4.946372	4.606544	4.030967
10	8.110896	7.721735	7.360087	7.023582	6.710081	6.417658	6.144567	5.650223	5.216116	4.833227	4.192472
11	8.760477	8.306414	7.886875	7.498674	7.138964	6.805191	6.495061	5.937699	5.452733	5.028644	4.327060
12	9.385074	8.863252	8.383844	7.942686	7.536078	7.160725	6.813692	6.194374	5.660292	5.197107	4.439217
13	9.985648	9.393573	8.852683	8.357651	7.903776	7.486904	7.103356	6.423548	5.842362	5.342334	4.532681
14	10.563123	9.898641	9.294984	8.745468	8.244237	7.786150	7.366687	6.628168	6.002072	5.467529	4.610567
15	11.118387	10.379658	9.712249	9.107914	8.559479	8.060688	7.606080	6.810864	6.142168	5.575456	4.675473
16	11.652296	10.837770	10.105895	9.446649	8.851369	8.312558	7.823709	6.973986	6.265060	5.668497	4.729561
17	12.165669	11.274066	10.477260	9.763223	9.121638	8.543631	8.021553	7.119630	6.372859	5.748704	4.774634
18	12.659297	11.689587	10.827603	10.059087	9.371887	8.755625	8.201412	7.249670	6.467420	5.817848	4.812195
19	13.133939	12.085321	11.158116	10.335595	9.603599	8.905115	8.364920	7.365777	6.550369	5.877455	4.843496
20	13.590326	12.462210	11.469921	10.594014	9.818147	9.128546	8.513564	7.469444	6.623131	5.928841	4.869580

A step-by-step audio-narrated series of slides is provided on the text website at www.mhhe.com/edmondssurvey3e.

SELF-STUDY REVIEW PROBLEM

The CFO of Advo Corporation is considering two investment opportunities. The expected future cash inflows for each opportunity follow.

	Year 1	Year 2	Year 3	Year 4
Project 1	$144,000	$147,000	$160,000	$178,000
Project 2	204,000	199,000	114,000	112,000

Both investments require an initial payment of $400,000. Advo's desired rate of return is 16 percent.

Required

a. Compute the net present value of each project. Which project should Advo adopt based on the net present value approach?

b. Based on the payback approach (incremental revenue summation method) which project should Advo adopt?

Solution to Requirement a

Project 1					
	Cash Inflows		Table Factor*		Present Value
Year 1	$144,000	×	0.862069	=	$124,138
Year 2	147,000	×	0.743163	=	109,245
Year 3	160,000	×	0.640658	=	102,505
Year 4	178,000	×	0.552291	=	98,308
PV of cash inflows					434,196
Cost of investment					(400,000)
Net present value					$ 34,196

*Table 1, $n = 1$ through 4, $r = 16\%$

Project 2					
	Cash Inflows		Table Factor*		Present Value
Year 1	$204,000	×	0.862069	=	$175,862
Year 2	199,000	×	0.743163	=	147,889
Year 3	114,000	×	0.640658	=	73,035
Year 4	112,000	×	0.552291	=	61,857
PV of cash inflows					458,643
Cost of investment					(400,000)
Net present value					$ 58,643

*Table 1, $n = 1$ through 4, $r = 16\%$

Advo should adopt Project 2 because it has a greater net present value.

Solution to Requirement b

Cash Inflows	Project 1	Project 2
Year 1	$144,000	$204,000
Year 2	147,000	199,000
Total	$291,000	$403,000

By the end of the second year, Project 2's cash inflows have more than paid for the cost of the investment. In contrast, Project 1 still falls short of investment recovery by $109,000 ($400,000 − $291,000). Advo should adopt Project 2 because it has a shorter payback period.

KEY TERMS

Accumulated conversion factor 567
Annuity 567
Capital investments 564
Cost of capital 565
Incremental revenue 571
Internal rate of return 571

Minimum rate of return 565
Net present value 569
Ordinary annuity 568
Payback method 578
Postaudit 581
Present value index 574
Present value table 566

Recovery of investment 580
Single-payment (lump-sum) 566
Time value of money 564
Unadjusted rate of return 579
Working capital 571

QUESTIONS

1. What is a capital investment? How does it differ from an investment in stocks or bonds?

2. What are three reasons that cash is worth more today than cash to be received in the future?

3. "A dollar today is worth more than a dollar in the future." "The present value of a future dollar is worth less than one dollar." Are these two statements synonymous? Explain.

4. Define the term *return on investment.* How is the return normally expressed? Give an example of a capital investment return.

5. How does a company establish its minimum acceptable rate of return on investments?

6. If you wanted to have $500,000 one year from today and desired to earn a 10 percent return, what amount would you need to invest today? Which amount has more value, the amount today or the $500,000 a year from today?

7. Why are present value tables frequently used to convert future values to present values?

8. Define the term *annuity.* What is one example of an annuity receipt?

9. How can present value "what-if" analysis be enhanced by using software programs?

10. Receiving $100,000 per year for five years is equivalent to investing what amount today at 14 percent? Provide a mathematical formula to solve this problem, assuming use of a present value annuity table to convert the future cash flows to their present value equivalents. Provide the expression for the Excel spreadsheet function that would perform the present value conversion.

11. Maria Espinosa borrowed $15,000 from the bank and agreed to repay the loan at 8 percent annual interest over four years, making payments of $4,529 per year. Because part of the bank's payment from Ms. Espinosa is a recovery of the original investment, what assumption must the bank make to earn its desired 8 percent compounded annual return?

12. Two investment opportunities have positive net present values. Investment A's net present value amounts to $40,000 while B's is only $30,000. Does this mean that A is the better investment opportunity? Explain.

13. What criteria determine whether a project is acceptable under the net present value method?

14. Does the net present value method provide a measure of the rate of return on capital investments?

15. Which is the best capital investment evaluation technique for ranking investment opportunities?

16. Paul Henderson is a manager for Spark Company. He tells you that his company always maximizes profitability by accepting the investment opportunity with the highest internal rate of return. Explain to Mr. Henderson how his company may improve profitability by sometimes selecting investment opportunities with lower internal rates of return.

17. What is the relationship between desired rate of return and internal rate of return?

18. What typical cash inflow and outflow items are associated with capital investments?

19. "I always go for the investment with the shortest payback period." Is this a sound strategy? Why or why not?

20. "The payback method cannot be used if the cash inflows occur in unequal patterns." Do you agree or disagree? Explain.

21. What are the advantages and disadvantages associated with the unadjusted rate of return method for evaluating capital investments?

22. How do capital investments affect profitability?

23. What is a postaudit? How is it useful in capital budgeting?

MULTIPLE-CHOICE QUESTIONS

Multiple-choice questions are provided on the text website at www.mhhe.com/edmondssurvey3e

EXERCISES

All applicable Exercises are available with McGraw-Hill's *Connect Accounting.*

Exercise 16-1   *Identifying cash inflows and outflows*   LO 5

Required

Indicate which of the following items will result in cash inflows and which will result in cash outflows. The first one is shown as an example.

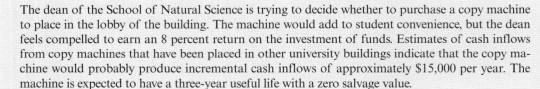

Item	Type of Cash Flow
a. Initial investment	Outflow
b. Salvage values	
c. Recovery of working capital	
d. Incremental expenses	
e. Working capital commitments	
f. Cost savings	
g. Incremental revenue	

LO 1, 2

Exercise 16-2 *Determining the present value of a lump-sum future cash receipt*

Stan Sweeney turned 20 years old today. His grandfather established a trust fund that will pay Mr. Sweeney $80,000 on his next birthday. However, Stan needs money today to start his college education. His father is willing to help and has agreed to give Stan the present value of the future cash inflow, assuming a 10 percent rate of return.

Required

a. Use a present value table to determine the amount of cash that Stan Sweeney's father should give him.

b. Use an algebraic formula to prove that the present value of the trust fund (the amount of cash computed in Requirement *a*) is equal to its $80,000 future value.

LO 1, 2

Exercise 16-3 *Determining the present value of a lump-sum future cash receipt*

Marsha Bittner expects to receive a $600,000 cash benefit when she retires five years from today. Ms. Bittner's employer has offered an early retirement incentive by agreeing to pay her $360,000 today if she agrees to retire immediately. Ms. Bittner desires to earn a rate of return of 12 percent.

Required

a. Assuming that the retirement benefit is the only consideration in making the retirement decision, should Ms. Bittner accept her employer's offer?

b. Identify the factors that cause the present value of the retirement benefit to be less than $600,000.

LO 1, 2

Exercise 16-4 *Determining the present value of an annuity*

The dean of the School of Natural Science is trying to decide whether to purchase a copy machine to place in the lobby of the building. The machine would add to student convenience, but the dean feels compelled to earn an 8 percent return on the investment of funds. Estimates of cash inflows from copy machines that have been placed in other university buildings indicate that the copy machine would probably produce incremental cash inflows of approximately $15,000 per year. The machine is expected to have a three-year useful life with a zero salvage value.

Required

a. Use Present Value Table 1 in the chapter's Appendix to determine the maximum amount of cash the dean should be willing to pay for a copy machine.

b. Use Present Value Table 2 in the chapter's Appendix to determine the maximum amount of cash the dean should be willing to pay for a copy machine.

c. Explain the consistency or lack of consistency in the answers to Requirements *a* and *b*.

LO 3

Exercise 16-5 *Determining net present value*

Metro Shuttle Inc. is considering investing in two new vans that are expected to generate combined cash inflows of $28,000 per year. The vans' combined purchase price is $91,000. The expected life and salvage value of each are four years and $21,000, respectively. Metro Shuttle has an average cost of capital of 14 percent.

Required

a. Calculate the net present value of the investment opportunity.

b. Indicate whether the investment opportunity is expected to earn a return that is above or below the cost of capital and whether it should be accepted.

Exercise 16-6   *Determining net present value*

LO 3

Dimitry Chernitsky is seeking part-time employment while he attends school. He is considering purchasing technical equipment that will enable him to start a small training services company that will offer tutorial services over the Internet. Dimitry expects demand for the service to grow rapidly in the first two years of operation as customers learn about the availability of the Internet assistance. Thereafter, he expects demand to stabilize. The following table presents the expected cash flows.

Year of Operation	Cash Inflow	Cash Outflow
2012	$13,500	$ 9,000
2013	19,500	12,000
2014	21,000	12,600
2015	21,000	12,600

In addition to these cash flows, Mr. Chernitsky expects to pay $21,000 for the equipment. He also expects to pay $3,600 for a major overhaul and updating of the equipment at the end of the second year of operation. The equipment is expected to have a $1,500 salvage value and a four-year useful life. Mr. Chernitsky desires to earn a rate of return of 8 percent.

Required

(Round computations to the nearest whole penny.)

a. Calculate the net present value of the investment opportunity.
b. Indicate whether the investment opportunity is expected to earn a return that is above or below the desired rate of return and whether it should be accepted.

Exercise 16-7   *Using present value index*

LO 3, 6

Alonso Company has a choice of two investment alternatives. The present value of cash inflows and outflows for the first alternative is $90,000 and $84,000, respectively. The present value of cash inflows and outflows for the second alternative is $220,000 and $213,000, respectively.

Required

a. Calculate the net present value of each investment opportunity.
b. Calculate the present value index for each investment opportunity.
c. Indicate which investment will produce the higher rate of return.

Exercise 16-8   *Determining the internal rate of return*

LO 4

Irving Manufacturing Company has an opportunity to purchase some technologically advanced equipment that will reduce the company's cash outflow for operating expenses by $1,280,000 per year. The cost of the equipment is $6,186,530.56. Irving expects it to have a 10-year useful life and a zero salvage value. The company has established an investment opportunity hurdle rate of 15 percent and uses the straight-line method for depreciation.

Required

a. Calculate the internal rate of return of the investment opportunity.
b. Indicate whether the investment opportunity should be accepted.

Exercise 16-9   *Using the internal rate of return to compare investment opportunities*

LO 4, 6

Hulsey and Wright (H&W) is a partnership that owns a small company. It is considering two alternative investment opportunities. The first investment opportunity will have a five-year useful life, will cost $9,335.16, and will generate expected cash inflows of $2,400 per year. The second investment is expected to have a useful life of three years, will cost $6,217.13, and will generate expected cash inflows of $2,500 per year. Assume that H&W has the funds available to accept only one of the opportunities.

Required

a. Calculate the internal rate of return of each investment opportunity.
b. Based on the internal rates of return, which opportunity should H&W select?
c. Discuss other factors that H&W should consider in the investment decision.

LO 1, 2, 5, 6

Exercise 16-10   *Determining the cash flow annuity with income tax considerations*

To open a new store, Alpha Tire Company plans to invest $240,000 in equipment expected to have a four-year useful life and no salvage value. Alpha expects the new store to generate annual cash revenues of $315,000 and to incur annual cash operating expenses of $195,000. Alpha's average income tax rate is 30 percent. The company uses straight-line depreciation.

Required

Determine the expected annual net cash inflow from operations for each of the first four years after Alpha opens the new store.

LO 5

Exercise 16-11   *Evaluating discounted cash flow techniques*

Rita Hendrix is angry with Bill Shaw. He is behind schedule developing supporting material for tomorrow's capital budget committee meeting. When she approached him about his apparent lackadaisical attitude in general and his tardiness in particular, he responded, "I don't see why we do this stuff in the first place. It's all a bunch of estimates. Who knows what future cash flows will really be? I certainly don't. I've been doing this job for five years, and no one has ever checked to see if I even came close at these guesses. I've been waiting for marketing to provide the estimated cash inflows on the projects being considered tomorrow. But, if you want my report now, I'll have it in a couple of hours. I can make up the marketing data as well as they can."

Required

Does Mr. Shaw have a point? Is there something wrong with the company's capital budgeting system? Write a brief response explaining how to improve the investment evaluation system.

LO 7

Exercise 16-12   *Determining the payback period*

Sky Airline Company is considering expanding its territory. The company has the opportunity to purchase one of two different used airplanes. The first airplane is expected to cost $18,000,000; it will enable the company to increase its annual cash inflow by $6,000,000 per year. The plane is expected to have a useful life of five years and no salvage value. The second plane costs $36,000,000; it will enable the company to increase annual cash flow by $9,000,000 per year. This plane has an eight-year useful life and a zero salvage value.

Required

a. Determine the payback period for each investment alternative and identify the alternative Sky should accept if the decision is based on the payback approach.

b. Discuss the shortcomings of using the payback method to evaluate investment opportunities.

LO 7

Exercise 16-13   *Determining the payback period with uneven cash flows*

Melton Company has an opportunity to purchase a forklift to use in its heavy equipment rental business. The forklift would be leased on an annual basis during its first two years of operation. Thereafter, it would be leased to the general public on demand. Melton would sell it at the end of the fifth year of its useful life. The expected cash inflows and outflows follow.

Year	Nature of Item	Cash Inflow	Cash Outflow
2012	Purchase price		$72,000
2012	Revenue	$30,000	
2013	Revenue	30,000	
2014	Revenue	21,000	
2014	Major overhaul		9,000
2015	Revenue	18,000	
2016	Revenue	14,400	
2016	Salvage value	9,600	

Required

a. Determine the payback period using the accumulated cash flows approach.

b. Determine the payback period using the average cash flows approach.

Exercise 16-14 *Determining the unadjusted rate of return*

LO 8

Lilly Painting Company is considering whether to purchase a new spray paint machine that costs $4,000. The machine is expected to save labor, increasing net income by $600 per year. The effective life of the machine is 15 years according to the manufacturer's estimate.

Required

a. Determine the unadjusted rate of return based on the average cost of the investment.

b. What is the predominant shortcoming of using the unadjusted rate of return to evaluate investment opportunities?

Exercise 16-15 *Computing the payback period and unadjusted rate of return for one investment opportunity*

LO 7, 8

Foy Rentals can purchase a van that costs $60,000; it has an expected useful life of three years and no salvage value. Foy uses straight-line depreciation. Expected revenue is $30,000 per year.

Required

a. Determine the payback period.

b. Determine the unadjusted rate of return based on the average cost of the investment.

PROBLEMS

All applicable Problems are available with McGraw-Hill's Connect Accounting.

|ACCOUNTING

Problem 16-16 *Using present value techniques to evaluate alternative investment opportunities*

LO 3, 5, 6

eXcel

Fast Delivery is a small company that transports business packages between New York and Chicago. It operates a fleet of small vans that moves packages to and from a central depot within each city and uses a common carrier to deliver the packages between the depots in the two cities. Fast recently acquired approximately $6 million of cash capital from its owners, and its president, Don Keenon, is trying to identify the most profitable way to invest these funds.

CHECK FIGURES
a. NPV of the vans investment: $100,811.42
b. NPV index of the trucks investment: 1.126

Clarence Roy, the company's operations manager, believes that the money should be used to expand the fleet of city vans at a cost of $720,000. He argues that more vans would enable the company to expand its services into new markets, thereby increasing the revenue base. More specifically, he expects cash inflows to increase by $280,000 per year. The additional vans are expected to have an average useful life of four years and a combined salvage value of $100,000. Operating the vans will require additional working capital of $40,000, which will be recovered at the end of the fourth year.

In contrast, Patricia Lipa, the company's chief accountant, believes that the funds should be used to purchase large trucks to deliver the packages between the depots in the two cities. The conversion process would produce continuing improvement in operating savings with reductions in cash outflows as the following.

Year 1	Year 2	Year 3	Year 4
$160,000	$320,000	$400,000	$440,000

The large trucks are expected to cost $800,000 and to have a four-year useful life and a $80,000 salvage value. In addition to the purchase price of the trucks, up-front training costs are expected to amount to $16,000. Fast Delivery's management has established a 16 percent desired rate of return.

Required

a. Determine the net present value of the two investment alternatives.

b. Calculate the present value index for each alternative.

c. Indicate which investment alternative you would recommend. Explain your choice.

Problem 16-17   *Using the payback period and unadjusted rate of return to evaluate alternative investment opportunities*

Louis Gallo owns a small retail ice cream parlor. He is considering expanding the business and has identified two attractive alternatives. One involves purchasing a machine that would enable Mr. Gallo to offer frozen yogurt to customers. The machine would cost $8,100 and has an expected useful life of three years with no salvage value. Additional annual cash revenues and cash operating expenses associated with selling yogurt are expected to be $5,940 and $900, respectively.

Alternatively, Mr. Gallo could purchase for $10,080 the equipment necessary to serve cappuccino. That equipment has an expected useful life of four years and no salvage value. Additional annual cash revenues and cash operating expenses associated with selling cappuccino are expected to be $8,280 and $2,430, respectively.

Income before taxes earned by the ice cream parlor is taxed at an effective rate of 20 percent.

Required

a. Determine the payback period and unadjusted rate of return (use average investment) for each alternative.

b. Indicate which investment alternative you would recommend. Explain your choice.

Problem 16-18   *Using net present value and internal rate of return to evaluate investment opportunities*

Veronica Tanner, the president of Tanner Enterprises, is considering two investment opportunities. Because of limited resources, she will be able to invest in only one of them. Project A is to purchase a machine that will enable factory automation; the machine is expected to have a useful life of four years and no salvage value. Project B supports a training program that will improve the skills of employees operating the current equipment. Initial cash expenditures for Project A are $100,000 and for Project B are $40,000. The annual expected cash inflows are $31,487 for Project A and $13,169 for Project B. Both investments are expected to provide cash flow benefits for the next four years. Tanner Enterprise's cost of capital is 8 percent.

Required

a. Compute the net present value of each project. Which project should be adopted based on the net present value approach?

b. Compute the approximate internal rate of return of each project. Which one should be adopted based on the internal rate of return approach?

c. Compare the net present value approach with the internal rate of return approach. Which method is better in the given circumstances? Why?

Problem 16-19   *Using net present value and payback period to evaluate investment opportunities*

Bruce Graham saved $250,000 during the 25 years that he worked for a major corporation. Now he has retired at the age of 50 and has begun to draw a comfortable pension check every month. He wants to ensure the financial security of his retirement by investing his savings wisely and is currently considering two investment opportunities. Both investments require an initial payment of $187,500. The following table presents the estimated cash inflows for the two alternatives.

	Year 1	Year 2	Year 3	Year 4
Opportunity #1	$ 55,625	$ 58,750	$78,750	$101,250
Opportunity #2	102,500	108,750	17,500	15,000

Mr. Graham decides to use his past average return on mutual fund investments as the discount rate; it is 8 percent.

Required

a. Compute the net present value of each opportunity. Which should Mr. Graham adopt based on the net present value approach?

b. Compute the payback period for each project. Which should Mr. Graham adopt based on the payback approach?

c. Compare the net present value approach with the payback approach. Which method is better in the given circumstances?

Problem 16-20 *Effects of straight-line versus accelerated depreciation on an investment decision*

LO 3, 6, 7, 8

eXcel

CHECK FIGURES
a. NPV = $71,810
d. Payback period: 2.32 years

Zito Electronics is considering investing in manufacturing equipment expected to cost $184,000. The equipment has an estimated useful life of four years and a salvage value of $24,000. It is expected to produce incremental cash revenues of $96,000 per year. Zito has an effective income tax rate of 30 percent and a desired rate of return of 12 percent.

Required

a. Determine the net present value and the present value index of the investment, assuming that Zito uses straight-line depreciation for financial and income tax reporting.

b. Determine the net present value and the present value index of the investment, assuming that Zito uses double-declining-balance depreciation for financial and income tax reporting.

c. Why do the net present values computed in Requirements *a* and *b* differ?

d. Determine the payback period and unadjusted rate of return (use average investment), assuming that Zito uses straight-line depreciation.

e. Determine the payback period and unadjusted rate of return (use average investment), assuming that Zito uses double-declining-balance depreciation. (Note: Use average annual cash flow when computing the payback period and average annual income when determining the unadjusted rate of return.)

f. Why are there no differences in the payback periods or unadjusted rates of return computed in Requirements *d* and *e*?

Problem 16-21 *Applying the net present value approach with and without tax considerations*

LO 3, 5, 6

eXcel

CHECK FIGURE
a. $(46,120.48)

Paxton Kingsley, the chief executive officer of Kingsley Corporation, has assembled his top advisers to evaluate an investment opportunity. The advisers expect the company to pay $400,000 cash at the beginning of the investment and the cash inflow for each of the following four years to be the following.

Year 1	Year 2	Year 3	Year 4
$84,000	$96,000	$120,000	$184,000

Mr. Kingsley agrees with his advisers that the company should use the discount rate (required rate of return) of 12 percent to compute net present value to evaluate the viability of the proposed project.

Required

a. Compute the net present value of the proposed project. Should Mr. Kingsley approve the project?

b. Wilma Pate, one of the advisers, is wary of the cash flow forecast and she points out that the advisers failed to consider that the depreciation on equipment used in this project will be tax deductible. The depreciation is expected to be $80,000 per year for the four-year period. The company's income tax rate is 30 percent per year. Use this information to revise the company's expected cash flow from this project.

c. Compute the net present value of the project based on the revised cash flow forecast. Should Mr. Kingsley approve the project?

Problem 16-22 *Comparing internal rate of return with unadjusted rate of return*

LO 4, 8

CHECK FIGURE
b. Internal rate of return: 12%

Walker Auto Repair Inc. is evaluating a project to purchase equipment that will not only expand the company's capacity but also improve the quality of its repair services. The board of directors requires all capital investments to meet or exceed the minimum requirement of a 10 percent rate of return. However, the board has not clearly defined the rate of return. The president and controller are pondering two different rates of return: unadjusted rate of return and internal rate of return. The equipment, which costs $100,000, has a life expectancy of five years. The increased net profit per year will be approximately $7,000, and the increased cash inflow per year will be approximately $27,700.

Required

a. If it uses the unadjusted rate of return (use average investment) to evaluate this project, should the company invest in the equipment?

b. If it uses the internal rate of return to evaluate this project, should the company invest in the equipment?

c. Which method is better for this capital investment decision?

LO 9

CHECK FIGURE
b. NPV: $(654,174)

Problem 16-23   *Postaudit evaluation*

Ernest Jones is reviewing his company's investment in a cement plant. The company paid $15,000,000 five years ago to acquire the plant. Now top management is considering an opportunity to sell it. The president wants to know whether the plant has met original expectations before he decides its fate. The company's discount rate for present value computations is 8 percent. Expected and actual cash flows follow.

	Year 1	Year 2	Year 3	Year 4	Year 5
Expected	$3,300,000	$4,920,000	$4,560,000	$4,980,000	$4,200,000
Actual	2,700,000	3,060,000	4,920,000	3,900,000	3,600,000

Required

a. Compute the net present value of the expected cash flows as of the beginning of the investment.

b. Compute the net present value of the actual cash flows as of the beginning of the investment.

c. What do you conclude from this postaudit?

ANALYZE, THINK, COMMUNICATE

ATC 16-1   Business Application Case   *Home remodeling decision*

Karen and Steve Catrow want to replace the windows in the older house they purchased recently. The company they have talked to about doing the work claims that new windows will reduce the couple's heating and cooling costs by around 30 percent. The Catrows have heard from real estate agents that they will get back 70 percent of the cost of the new windows when they sell their house. The new windows will cost $30,000.

The heating and cooling costs for the Catrow's house average around $5,000 per year, and they expect to stay in this house for 10 years. To pay for the windows they would have to withdraw the money from a mutual fund that has earned an average annual return of 4 percent over the past few years.

Required

a. From a financial planning perspective alone, determine whether or not the Catrows should purchase the replacement windows. Show supporting computations.

b. (Requirement *b* can be solved only with Excel, or similar software, or with a financial calculator.) Karen and Steve are not sure their mutual fund will continue to earn 4 percent annually over the next 10 years; therefore, they want to know the minimum return their fund would need to earn to make the new windows financially acceptable. Compute the internal rate of return for the replacement windows.

c. Identify some of the nonfinancial factors the couple may wish to consider in addition to the financial aspects of the decision above.

ATC 16-2   Group Assignment   *Net present value*

Espada Real Estate Investment Company (EREIC) purchases new apartment complexes, establishes a stable group of residents, and then sells the complexes to apartment management companies. The average holding time is three years. EREIC is currently investigating two alternatives.

1. EREIC can purchase Harding Properties for $4,500,000. The complex is expected to produce net cash inflows of $360,000, $502,500, and $865,000 for the first, second, and third years of operation, respectively. The market value of the complex at the end of the third year is expected to be $5,175,000.

2. EREIC can purchase Summit Apartments for $3,450,000. The complex is expected to produce net cash inflows of $290,000, $435,000, and $600,000 for the first, second, and third years of operation, respectively. The market value of the complex at the end of the third year is expected to be $4,050,000.

EREIC has a desired rate of return of 12 percent.

Required

a. Divide the class into groups of four or five students per group and then divide the groups into two sections. Assign Task 1 to the first section and Task 2 to the second section.

Group Tasks

(1) Calculate the net present value and the present value index for Harding Properties.

(2) Calculate the net present value and the present value index for Summit Apartments.

b. Have a spokesperson from one group in the first section report the amounts calculated by the group. Make sure that all groups in the section have the same result. Repeat the process for the second section. Have the class as a whole select the investment opportunity that EREIC should accept given that the objective is to produce the higher rate of return.

c. Assume that EREIC has $4,500,000 to invest and that any funds not invested in real estate properties must be invested in a certificate of deposit earning a 5 percent return. Would this information alter the decision made in Requirement *b*?

d. This requirement is independent of Requirement *c*. Assume there is a 10 percent chance that the Harding project will be annexed by the city of Hoover, which has an outstanding school district. The annexation would likely increase net cash flows by $37,500 per year and would increase the market value at the end of year 3 by $300,000. Would this information change the decision reached in Requirement *b*?

ATC 16-3   Research Assignment   *Capital Expenditures at the Archer Daniels Midland Company*

Obtain Archer Daniels Midland Company's (ADM) Form 10-K for the fiscal year ending on June 30, 2006 and 2009. To obtain the Form 10-K you can use the EDGAR system following the instructions in Appendix A, or it can be found under the "Investor Relations" link on the company's website at www.admworld.com/naen. Read the "General Development of Business" under the "Item I. Business" section of the 2006 10-K, and the Statement of Cash Flows and Note 15 of the 2009 10-K.

Required

a. What major plant expansions did ADM announce during 2006? How much does ADM estimate these expansions will cost?

b. How much did ADM spend on investing activities in its 2009 and 2008 fiscal years?

c. Where did ADM get the cash used to make these investments?

d. How much of ADM's investments in new property, plant, and equipment was related to its "corn processing" segment in 2009 and 2008?

ATC 16-4   Writing Assignment   *Limitations of capital investment techniques*

Webb Publishing Company is evaluating two investment opportunities. One is to purchase an Internet company with the capacity to open new marketing channels through which Webb can sell its books. This opportunity offers a high potential for growth but involves significant risk.

Indeed, losses are projected for the first three years of operation. The second opportunity is to purchase a printing company that would enable Webb to better control costs by printing its own books. The potential savings are clearly predictable but would make a significant change in the company's long-term profitability.

Required

Write a response discussing the usefulness of capital investment techniques (net present value, internal rate of return, payback, and unadjusted rate of return) in making a choice between these two alternative investment opportunities. Your response should discuss the strengths and weaknesses of capital budgeting techniques in general. Furthermore, it should include a comparison between techniques based on the time value of money versus those that are not.

ATC 16-5   Ethical Dilemma   *Postaudit*

Gaines Company recently initiated a postaudit program. To motivate employees to take the program seriously, Gaines established a bonus program. Managers receive a bonus equal to 10 percent of the amount by which actual net present value exceeds the projected net present value. Victor Holt, manager of the North Western Division, had an investment proposal on his desk when the new system was implemented. The investment opportunity required a $250,000 initial cash outflow and was expected to return cash inflows of $90,000 per year for the next five years. Gaines' desired rate of return is 10 percent. Mr. Holt immediately reduced the estimated cash inflows to $70,000 per year and recommended accepting the project.

Required

a. Assume that actual cash inflows turn out to be $91,000 per year. Determine the amount of Mr. Holt's bonus if the original computation of net present value were based on $90,000 versus $70,000.

b. Is Mr. Holt's behavior in violation of any of the standards of ethical conduct in Exhibit 10.17 of Chapter 10?

c. Speculate about the long-term effect the bonus plan is likely to have on the company.

d. Recommend how to compensate managers in a way that discourages gamesmanship.

Accessing the EDGAR Database through the Internet

Successful business managers need many different skills, including communication, interpersonal, computer, and analytical. Most business students become very aware of the data analysis skills used in accounting, but they may not be as aware of the importance of "data-finding" skills. There are many sources of accounting and financial data. The more sources you are able to use, the better.

One very important source of accounting information is the EDGAR database. Others are probably available at your school through the library or business school network. Your accounting instructor will be able to identify these for you and make suggestions regarding their use. By making the effort to learn to use electronic databases, you will enhance your abilities as a future manager and your marketability as a business graduate.

These instructions assume that you know how to access and use an Internet browser. Follow the instructions to retrieve data from the Securities and Exchange Commission's EDGAR database. Be aware that the SEC may have changed its interface since this appendix was written. Accordingly, be prepared for slight differences between the following instructions and what appears on your computer screen. Take comfort in the fact that changes are normally designed to simplify user access. If you encounter a conflict between the following instructions and the instructions provided in the SEC interface, remember that the SEC interface is more current and should take precedence over the following instructions.

Most companies provide links to their SEC filings from their corporate website. These links are often simpler to use and provide more choices regarding file formats than SEC's EDGAR site. On company websites, links to their SEC filings are usually found under one of the following links: "Investor Relations," "Company Info," or "About Us."

1. Connect to the EDGAR database through the following address: **http://www.sec.gov/.**

2. After the SEC homepage appears, under the heading **Filings and Forms,** click on **Search for Company Filings.**

3. On the screen that appears, click on **Company or Fund Name. . . .**

4. On the screen that appears, enter the name of the company whose file you wish to retrieve and click on the **Find Companies** button.

5. The following screen will present a list of companies that have the same, or similar, names to the one you entered. Identify the company you want and click on the CIK number beside it.

6. Enter the SEC form number that you want to retrieve in the window titled **Filling Type** that appears in the upper left portion of the screen. For example, if you want Form 10-K, which will usually be the case, enter **10-K** and click on the **Search** button.

7. A list of the forms you requested will be presented, along with the date they were filed. Click on the **Document** button next to the file you wish to retrieve.

8. You will be presented with a list of documents from which to select; usually you will want to choose the file **form10k.htm.**

9. Once the 10-K has been retrieved, you can search it online or save it on your computer.

10. Often the 10-K will have a table of contents that can help locate the part of the report you need. The financial statements are seldom located at the beginning of the Form 10-K. They are usually in either Section 8 or Section 15.

APPENDIX B

Portion of the Form 10-K for Target Corporation

This appendix contains a portion of the Form 10-K for the Target Corporation that was filed with the Securities and Exchange Commission on March 18, 2010. The document included in this appendix is Target's annual report, which was included *as a part* of its complete Form 10-K for the company's fiscal year ended January 31, 2010. Throughout this text this is referred to as the company's 2009 fiscal year.

This document is included for illustrative purposes, and it is intended to be used for educational purposes only. It should not be used for making investment decisions. Target Corporation's complete Form 10-K may be obtained from the SEC's EDGAR website, using the procedures explained in Appendix A. The Form 10-K may also be found on the company's website at www.target.com.

UNITED STATES
SECURITIES AND EXCHANGE COMMISSION
Washington, D.C. 20549

FORM 10–K/A
Amendment No. 1

(Mark One)

☒   **ANNUAL REPORT PURSUANT TO SECTION 13 OR 15(d) OF THE SECURITIES EXCHANGE ACT OF 1934**

For the fiscal year ended January 30, 2010

OR

☐   **TRANSITION REPORT PURSUANT TO SECTION 13 OR 15(d) OF THE SECURITIES EXCHANGE ACT OF 1934**

For the transition period from   to
Commission file number **1–6049**

TARGET CORPORATION
(Exact name of registrant as specified in its charter)

Minnesota	**41–0215170**
(State or other jurisdiction of incorporation or organization)	(I.R.S. Employer Identification No.)

1000 Nicollet Mall, Minneapolis, Minnesota	**55403**
(Address of principal executive offices)	(Zip Code)

Registrant's telephone number, including area code: 612/304–6073

Securities Registered Pursuant To Section 12(B) Of The Act:

Title of Each Class	Name of Each Exchange on Which Registered
Common Stock, par value $0.0833 per share	New York Stock Exchange

Securities registered pursuant to Section 12(g) of the Act: **None**

Indicate by check mark if the registrant is a well–known seasoned issuer, as defined in Rule 405 of the Securities Act. Yes ☒ No ☐

Indicate by check mark if the registrant is not required to file reports pursuant to Section 13 or Section 15(d) of the Act. Yes ☐ No ☒

Note – Checking the box above will not relieve any registrant required to file reports pursuant to Section 13 or 15(d) of the Exchange Act from their obligations under those Sections.

Indicate by check mark whether the registrant (1) has filed all reports required to be filed by Section 13 or 15(d) of the Securities Exchange Act of 1934 during the preceding 12 months (or for such shorter period that the registrant was required to file such reports), and (2) has been subject to such filing requirements for the past 90 days. Yes ☒ No ☐

Indicate by checkmark whether the registrant has submitted electronically and posted on its corporate Web site, if any, every Interactive Data File required to be submitted and posted pursuant to Rule 405 of Regulation S–T (§232.405 of this chapter) during the preceding 12 months (or for such shorter period that the registrant was required to submit and post such files. Yes ☒ No ☐

Indicate by check mark if disclosure of delinquent filers pursuant to Item 405 of Regulation S–K (§229.405 of this chapter) is not contained herein, and will not be contained, to the best of registrant's knowledge, in definitive proxy or information statements incorporated by reference in Part III of this Form 10–K or any amendment to this Form 10–K. ☒

Indicate by check mark whether the registrant is a large accelerated filer, an accelerated filer, a non–accelerated filer or a smaller reporting company (as defined in Rule 12b–2 of the Act).

Large accelerated filer ☒   Accelerated filer ☐   Non–accelerated filer ☐   Smaller reporting company ☐
                                                                  (Do not check if a
                                                             smaller reporting company)

Indicate by check mark whether the registrant is a shell company (as defined in Rule 12b–2 of the Act). Yes ☐ No ☒

Aggregate market value of the voting stock held by non–affiliates of the registrant on August 1, 2009 was $32,739,208,053, based on the closing price of $43.62 per share of Common Stock as reported on the New York Stock Exchange– Composite Index.

Indicate the number of shares outstanding of each of registrant's classes of Common Stock, as of the latest practicable date. Total shares of Common Stock, par value $0.0833, outstanding at March 10, 2010 were 739,316,518.

DOCUMENTS INCORPORATED BY REFERENCE

1.   Portions of Target's Proxy Statement to be filed on or about April 29, 2010 are incorporated into Part III.

EXPLANATORY NOTE

   The sole purpose of this Amendment No. 1 to the Annual Report on Form 10–K for the fiscal year ended January 30, 2010, as originally filed with the Securities and Exchange Commission on March 12, 2010, is to correct the number of shares of Common Stock outstanding at March 10, 2010 reported on the cover page.

   No other changes have been made to the Form 10–K other than the correction described above. This Amendment No. 1 does not reflect subsequent events occurring after the original filing date of the Form 10–K or modify or update in any way disclosures made in the Form 10–K.

TABLE OF CONTENTS

PART I

Item 1.   Business

General

Target Corporation (the Corporation or Target) was incorporated in Minnesota in 1902. We operate as two reportable segments: Retail and Credit Card.

Our Retail Segment includes all of our merchandising operations, including our large-format general merchandise and food discount stores in the United States and our fully integrated online business. We offer both everyday essentials and fashionable, differentiated merchandise at discounted prices. Our ability to deliver a shopping experience that is preferred by our customers, referred to as "guests," is supported by our strong supply chain and technology infrastructure, a devotion to innovation that is ingrained in our organization and culture, and our disciplined approach to managing our current business and investing in future growth. As a component of the Retail Segment, our online business strategy is designed to enable guests to purchase products seamlessly either online or by locating them in one of our stores with the aid of online research and location tools. Our online shopping site offers similar merchandise categories to those found in our stores, excluding food items and household essentials.

Our Credit Card Segment offers credit to qualified guests through our branded proprietary credit cards, the Target Visa and the Target Card (collectively, REDcards). Our Credit Card Segment strengthens the bond with our guests, drives incremental sales and contributes to our results of operations.

Financial Highlights

Our fiscal year ends on the Saturday nearest January 31. Unless otherwise stated, references to years in this report relate to fiscal years, rather than to calendar years. Fiscal year 2009 (2009) ended January 30, 2010, and consisted of 52 weeks. Fiscal year 2008 (2008) ended January 31, 2009 and consisted of 52 weeks. Fiscal year 2007 (2007) ended February 2, 2008 and consisted of 52 weeks.

For information on key financial highlights, see the items referenced in Item 6, Selected Financial Data, and Item 7, Management's Discussion and Analysis of Financial Condition and Results of Operations, of this Annual Report on Form 10-K.

Seasonality

Due to the seasonal nature of our business, a larger share of annual revenues and earnings traditionally occurs in the fourth quarter because it includes the peak sales period from Thanksgiving to the end of December.

Merchandise

We operate Target general merchandise stores, the majority of which offer a wide assortment of general merchandise and a limited assortment of food items. During 2009 we increased the offering within some of our general merchandise stores to include a deeper food assortment, including perishables and an expanded offering of dry, dairy and frozen items. In addition, we operate SuperTarget stores with a full line of food and general merchandise items. Target.com offers a wide assortment of general merchandise including many items found in our stores and a complementary assortment, such as extended sizes and colors, sold only online. A significant portion of our sales is from national brand merchandise. In addition, we sell merchandise under private-label brands including, but not limited to, Archer Farms®, Archer Farms® Simply Balanced™, Boots & Barkley®, Choxie®, Circo®, Durabuilt®, Embark®, Gilligan & O'Malley®, itso™, Kaori®, Market Pantry®, Merona®, Play Wonder®, Room Essentials®, Smith & Hawken®, Sutton and Dodge®, Target Home, Vroom®, up & up™, Wine Cube®, and Xhilaration®. We also sell merchandise through unique programs such as ClearRx ^{SM}, GO International®, Great Save ^{SM} and Home Design Event. In addition, we sell merchandise under exclusive licensed and designer brands including, but not limited to, C9 by Champion®, Chefmate®, Cherokee®, Converse® One Star®, Eddie Bauer®, Fieldcrest®, Genuine Kids by Osh Kosh®, Kitchen Essentials® by Calphalon®, Liz Lange® for Target®, Michael Graves Design™, Mossimo®, Nick & Nora®, Sean Conway™, Simply Shabby Chic®, Sonia Kashuk®, Thomas O'Brien®. We also generate revenue from in-store amenities such as Target Café^{SM}, Target Clinic®, Target Pharmacy®, and Target Photo^{SM}, and from leased or licensed departments such as Optical, Pizza Hut, Portrait Studio and Starbucks.

Effective inventory management is key to our future success. We utilize various techniques including demand forecasting and planning and various forms of replenishment management. We achieve effective inventory management by being in-stock in core product offerings, maintaining positive vendor relationships, and carefully planning inventory levels for seasonal and apparel items to minimize markdowns.

Sales by Product Category	Percentage of Sales		
	2009	**2008**	**2007**
Household essentials	**23%**	22%	21%
Hardlines	**22**	22	22
Apparel and accessories	**20**	20	22
Home furnishings and décor	**19**	21	22
Food and pet supplies	**16**	15	13
Total	**100%**	100%	100%

Household essentials includes pharmacy, beauty, personal care, baby care, cleaning and paper products. Hardlines includes electronics (including video game hardware and software), music, movies, books, computer software, sporting goods and toys. Apparel and accessories includes apparel for women, men, boys, girls, toddlers, infants, and newborns. It also includes intimate apparel, jewelry, accessories and shoes. Home furnishings and décor includes furniture, lighting, kitchenware, small appliances, home décor, bed and bath, home improvement, automotive and seasonal merchandise such as patio furniture and holiday décor. Food and pet supplies includes dry grocery, dairy, frozen food, beverages, candy, snacks, deli, bakery, meat, produce and pet supplies.

Distribution

The vast majority of our merchandise is distributed through our network of distribution centers. We operated 38 distribution centers, including 4 food distribution centers, at January 30, 2010. General merchandise is shipped to and from our distribution centers by common carriers. In addition, certain food items are distributed by third parties. Merchandise sold through Target.com is distributed through our own distribution network, through third parties, or shipped directly from vendors.

Employees

At January 30, 2010, we employed approximately 351,000 full-time, part-time and seasonal employees, referred to as "team members." During our peak sales period from Thanksgiving to the end of December, our employment levels peaked at approximately 390,000 team members. We consider our team member relations to be good. We offer a broad range of company-paid benefits to our team members. Eligibility for, and the level of, these benefits varies, depending on team members' full-time or part-time status, compensation level, date of hire and/or length of service. These company-paid benefits include a pension plan, 401(k) plan, medical and dental plans, a retiree medical plan, short-term and long-term disability insurance, paid vacation, tuition reimbursement, various team member assistance programs, life insurance and merchandise discounts.

Working Capital

Because of the seasonal nature of our business, our working capital needs are greater in the months leading up to our peak sales period from Thanksgiving to the end of December. The increase in working capital during this time is typically financed with cash flow provided by operations and short-term borrowings.

Additional details are provided in the Liquidity and Capital Resources section in Item 7, Management's Discussion and Analysis of Financial Condition and Results of Operations.

Competition

In our Retail Segment, we compete with traditional and off-price general merchandise retailers, apparel retailers, Internet retailers, wholesale clubs, category specific retailers, drug stores, supermarkets and other forms of retail commerce. Our ability to positively differentiate ourselves from other retailers largely determines our competitive position within the retail industry.

In our Credit Card Segment, our primary mission is to deliver financial products and services that drive sales and deepen guest relationships at Target. Our financial products compete with those of other issuers for market share of sales volume. Our ability to differentiate the value of our financial products primarily through our rewards programs, terms, credit line management, and guest service determines our competitive position among credit card issuers.

Intellectual Property

Our brand image is a critical element of our business strategy. Our principal trademarks, including Target, SuperTarget and our "Bullseye Design," have been registered with the U.S. Patent and Trademark Office. We also seek to obtain intellectual property protection for our private–label brands.

Geographic Information

Substantially all of our revenues are generated in, and long–lived assets are located in, the United States.

Available Information

Our Annual Report on Form 10–K, quarterly reports on Form 10–Q, current reports on Form 8–K and amendments to those reports filed or furnished pursuant to Section 13(a) or 15(d) of the Exchange Act are available free of charge at www.Target.com (click on "Investors" and "SEC Filings") as soon as reasonably practicable after we file such material with, or furnish it to, the Securities and Exchange Commission (SEC). Our Corporate Governance Guidelines, Business Conduct Guide, Corporate Responsibility Report and the position descriptions for our Board of Directors and Board committees are also available free of charge in print upon request or at www.Target.com (click on "Investors" and "Corporate Governance").

Item 1A. Risk Factors

Our business is subject to a variety of risks. The most important of these is our ability to remain relevant to our guests with a brand they trust. Meeting our guests' expectations requires us to manage various strategic, operational, compliance, and financial risks. Set forth below are the most significant risks that we face.

If we are unable to positively differentiate ourselves from other retailers, our results of operations could be adversely affected.

The retail business is highly competitive. In the past we have been able to compete successfully by differentiating our shopping experience by creating an attractive value proposition through a careful combination of price, merchandise assortment, convenience, guest service and marketing efforts. Guest perceptions regarding the cleanliness and safety of our stores, our in–stock levels and other factors also affect our ability to compete. No single competitive factor is dominant, and actions by our competitors on any of these factors could have an adverse effect on our sales, gross margin and expenses.

If we fail to anticipate and respond quickly to changing consumer preferences, our sales, gross margin and profitability could suffer.

A substantial part of our business is dependent on our ability to make trend–right decisions in apparel, home décor, seasonal offerings, food and other merchandise. Failure to accurately predict constantly changing consumer tastes, preferences, spending patterns and other lifestyle decisions may result in lost sales, spoilage and increased inventory markdowns, which would lead to a deterioration in our results of operations.

Our continued success is substantially dependent on positive perceptions of the Target brand.

We believe that one of the reasons our guests prefer to shop at Target and our team members choose Target as a place of employment is the reputation we have built over many years of serving our four primary constituencies: guests, team members, the communities in which we operate, and shareholders. To be successful in the future, we must continue to preserve, grow and leverage the value of our brand. Brand value is based in large part on perceptions of subjective qualities, and even isolated incidents that erode trust and confidence, particularly if they result in adverse publicity, governmental investigations or litigation, can have an adverse impact on these perceptions and lead to tangible adverse affects on our business, including consumer boycotts, loss of new store development opportunities, or team member recruiting difficulties.

We are highly susceptible to the state of macroeconomic conditions and consumer confidence in the United States.

All of our stores are located within the United States, making our results highly dependent on U.S. consumer confidence and the health of the U.S. economy. In addition, a significant portion of our total sales is derived from stores located in five states: California, Texas, Florida, Minnesota and Illinois, resulting in further dependence on local economic conditions in these states. Deterioration in macroeconomic conditions and consumer confidence could negatively affect our business in many ways, including slowing sales growth or reduction in overall sales, and reducing gross margins.

In addition to the impact of macroeconomic conditions on our retail sales, these same considerations impact the success of our Credit Card Segment, as any deterioration can adversely affect cardholders' ability to pay their balances and we may not be able to anticipate and respond to changes in the risk profile of our cardholders when extending credit, resulting in higher bad debt expense. The recent Credit Card Accountability, Responsibility and Disclosure Act of 2009 has significantly restricted our ability to make changes to cardholder terms that are commensurate with changes in the risk profile of our credit card receivables portfolio. Demand for consumer credit is also impacted by macroeconomic conditions and other factors, and our performance can also be adversely affected by consumer decisions to use debit cards or other forms of payment.

If we do not effectively manage our large and growing workforce, our results of operations could be adversely affected.

With over 350,000 team members, our workforce costs represent our largest operating expense, and our business is dependent on our ability to attract, train and retain a growing number of qualified team members. Many of those team members are in entry-level or part-time positions with historically high turnover rates. Our ability to meet our labor needs while controlling our costs is subject to external factors such as unemployment levels, prevailing wage rates, health care and other benefit costs and changing demographics. If we are unable to attract and retain adequate numbers of qualified team members, our operations, guest service levels and support functions could suffer. Those factors, together with increasing wage and benefit costs, could adversely affect our results of operations.

Lack of availability of suitable locations in which to build new stores could slow our growth, and difficulty in executing plans for new stores, expansions and remodels could increase our costs and capital requirements.

Our future growth is dependent, in part, on our ability to build new stores and expand and remodel existing stores in a manner that achieves appropriate returns on our capital investment. We compete with other retailers and businesses for suitable locations for our stores. In addition, for many sites we are dependent on a third party developer's ability to acquire land, obtain financing and secure the necessary zoning changes and permits for a larger project, of which our store may be one component. Turmoil in the financial markets has made it difficult for third party developers to obtain financing for new projects. Local land use and other regulations applicable to the types of stores we desire to construct may affect our ability to find suitable locations and also influence the cost of constructing, expanding and remodeling our stores. A significant portion of our expected new store development activity is planned to occur within fully developed markets, which is generally a more time-consuming and expensive undertaking than developments in undeveloped suburban and ex-urban markets.

Interruptions with our vendors and within our supply chain could adversely affect our results.

We are dependent on our vendors to supply merchandise in a timely and efficient manner. If a vendor fails to deliver on its commitments, whether due to financial difficulties or other reasons, we could experience merchandise out–of–stocks that could lead to lost sales. In addition, a large portion of our merchandise is sourced, directly or indirectly, from outside the United States, with China as our single largest source. Political or financial instability, trade restrictions, increased tariffs, currency exchange rates, the outbreak of pandemics, labor unrest, transport capacity and costs, port security or other events that could slow port activities and affect foreign trade are beyond our control and could disrupt our supply of merchandise and/or adversely affect our results of operations.

Failure to address product safety concerns could adversely affect our sales and results of operations.

If our merchandise offerings, including food, drug and children's products, do not meet applicable safety standards or our guests' expectations regarding safety, we could experience lost sales, experience increased costs and be exposed to legal and reputational risk. All of our vendors must comply with applicable product safety laws, and we are dependent on them to ensure that the products we buy comply with all safety standards. Events that give rise to actual, potential or perceived product safety concerns, including food or drug contamination, could expose us to government enforcement action or private litigation and result in costly product recalls and other liabilities. In addition, negative guest perceptions regarding the safety of the products we sell could cause our guests to seek alternative sources for their needs, resulting in lost sales. In those circumstances, it may be difficult and costly for us to regain the confidence of our guests.

If we fail to protect the security of personal information about our guests, we could be subject to costly government enforcement actions or private litigation and our reputation could suffer.

The nature of our business involves the receipt and storage of personal information about our guests. If we experience a data security breach, we could be exposed to government enforcement actions and private litigation. In addition, our guests could lose confidence in our ability to protect their personal information, which could cause them to discontinue usage of our credit card products, decline to use our pharmacy services, or stop shopping at our stores altogether. Such events could lead to lost future sales and adversely affect our results of operations.

Our failure to comply with federal, state or local laws, or changes in these laws could increase our expenses.

Our business is subject to a wide array of laws and regulations. Significant legislative changes that affect our relationship with our workforce (which is not represented by unions as of the end of 2009) could increase our expenses and adversely affect our operations. Examples of possible legislative changes affecting our relationship with our workforce include changes to an employer's obligation to recognize collective bargaining units, the process by which collective bargaining agreements are negotiated or imposed, minimum wage requirements, and health care mandates. In addition, changes in the regulatory environment regarding topics such as banking and consumer credit, Medicare reimbursements, privacy and information security, product safety or environmental protection, among others, could cause our expenses to increase without an ability to pass through any increased expenses through higher prices. In addition, if we fail to comply with applicable laws and regulations, particularly wage and hour laws, we could be subject to legal risk, including government enforcement action and class action civil litigation, which could adversely affect our results of operations.

Given the geographic concentration of our stores, natural disasters could adversely affect our results of operations.

Our three largest states, by total sales, are California, Texas and Florida, areas where hurricanes and earthquakes are prevalent. Such events could result in significant physical damage to or closure of one or more of our stores or distribution centers, and cause delays in the distribution of merchandise from our vendors to our distribution centers and stores, which could adversely affect our results of operations.

Changes in our effective income tax rate could affect our results of operations.

Our effective income tax rate is influenced by a number of factors. Changes in the tax laws, the interpretation of existing laws, or our failure to sustain our reporting positions on examination could adversely affect our effective tax rate. In addition, our effective income tax rate generally bears an inverse relationship to capital market returns due to the tax–free nature of investment vehicles used to economically hedge our deferred compensation liabilities.

If we are unable to access the capital markets or obtain bank credit, our growth plans, liquidity and results of operations could suffer.

We are dependent on a stable, liquid and well–functioning financial system to fund our operations and growth plans. In particular, we have historically relied on the public debt markets to raise capital for new store development and other capital expenditures, the commercial paper market and bank credit facilities to fund seasonal needs for working capital, and the asset–backed securities markets to partially fund our accounts receivable portfolio. In addition, we use a variety of derivative products to manage our exposure to market risk, principally interest rate and equity price fluctuations. Disruptions or turmoil in the financial markets could adversely affect our ability to meet our capital requirements, fund our working capital needs or lead to losses on derivative positions resulting from counterparty failures.

A significant disruption in our computer systems could adversely affect our results of operations.

We rely extensively on our computer systems to manage inventory, process transactions and summarize results. Our systems are subject to damage or interruption from power outages, telecommunications failures, computer viruses, security breaches and catastrophic events. If our systems are damaged or fail to function properly, we may incur substantial costs to repair or replace them, and may experience loss of critical data and interruptions or delays in our ability to manage inventories or process transactions, which could adversely affect our results of operations.

Item 1B.   Unresolved Staff Comments

Not applicable

Item 2.   Properties

At January 30, 2010, we had 1,740 stores in 49 states and the District of Columbia:

	Number of Stores	Retail Sq. Ft. (in thousands)		Number of Stores	Retail Sq. Ft. (in thousands)
Alabama	20	2,867	Montana	7	780
Alaska	3	504	Nebraska	14	2,006
Arizona	48	6,363	Nevada	19	2,461
Arkansas	8	1,028	New Hampshire	9	1,148
California	244	32,184	New Jersey	43	5,671
Colorado	42	6,275	New Mexico	9	1,024
Connecticut	20	2,672	New York	64	8,663
Delaware	2	268	North Carolina	47	6,167
District of Columbia	1	179	North Dakota	4	554
Florida	126	17,644	Ohio	63	7,868
Georgia	55	7,517	Oklahoma	14	2,022
Hawaii	3	542	Oregon	19	2,317
Idaho	6	664	Pennsylvania	59	7,713
Illinois	86	11,697	Rhode Island	4	517
Indiana	33	4,377	South Carolina	18	2,224
Iowa	22	3,015	South Dakota	5	580
Kansas	19	2,577	Tennessee	32	4,087
Kentucky	13	1,525	Texas	148	20,838
Louisiana	15	2,108	Utah	11	1,679
Maine	5	630	Vermont	—	—
Maryland	36	4,663	Virginia	56	7,448
Massachusetts	33	4,279	Washington	35	4,097
Michigan	60	7,141	West Virginia	6	755
Minnesota	73	10,456	Wisconsin	37	4,482
Mississippi	6	743	Wyoming	2	187
Missouri	36	4,735			
			Total	**1,740**	**231,941**

The following table summarizes the number of owned or leased stores and distribution centers at January 30, 2010:

	Stores	Distribution Centers (b)
Owned	1,492	29
Leased	81	8
Combined (a)	167	1
Total	**1,740**	**38**

(a) *Properties within the "combined" category are primarily owned buildings on leased land.*

(b) *The 38 distribution centers have a total of 48,588 thousand square feet.*

We own our corporate headquarters buildings located in Minneapolis, Minnesota, and we lease and own additional office space in the United States. Our international sourcing operations have 27 office locations in 18 countries, all of which are leased. We also lease office space in Bangalore, India, where we operate various support functions. Our properties are in good condition, well maintained and suitable to carry on our business.

For additional information on our properties, see also Capital Expenditures section in Item 7, Management's Discussion and Analysis of Financial Condition and Results of Operations and Notes 13 and 21 of the Notes to Consolidated Financial Statements included in Item 8, Financial Statements and Supplementary Data.

Item 3. Legal Proceedings

SEC Rule S–K Item 103 requires that companies disclose environmental legal proceedings involving a governmental authority when such proceedings involve potential monetary sanctions of $100,000 or more.

We are one of many defendants in a lawsuit filed on February 13, 2008, by the State of California involving environmental matters that may involve potential monetary sanctions in excess of $100,000. The allegation, initially made by the California Air Resources Board in April 2006, involves a nonfood product (hairspray) that allegedly contained levels of a volatile organic compound in excess of permissible levels. We anticipate that the settlement, to be fully indemnified by the vendor, is likely to exceed $100,000 but will not be material to our financial position, results of operations or cash flows. In addition, we are a defendant in a civil lawsuit filed by the California Attorney General in June 2009 alleging that we did not handle and dispose of certain unsold products as a hazardous waste. The case is in its early stages. We anticipate that this lawsuit may involve potential monetary sanctions in excess of $100,000, but will not be material to our financial position, results of operations or cash flows.

We are the subject of an ongoing Environmental Protection Agency (EPA) investigation for alleged violations of the Clean Air Act (CAA). In March 2009, the EPA issued a Finding of Violation (FOV) related to alleged violations of the CAA, specifically the National Emission Standards for Hazardous Air Pollutants (NESHAP) promulgated by the EPA for asbestos. The FOV pertains to the remodeling of 36 Target stores that occurred between January 1, 2003 and October 28, 2007. The EPA FOV process is ongoing and no specific relief has been sought to date by the EPA. We anticipate that any resolution of this matter will be in the form of monetary penalties that are likely to exceed $100,000 but will not be material to our financial position, results of operations or cash flows.

The American Jobs Creation Act of 2004 requires SEC registrants to disclose if they have been required to pay certain penalties for failing to disclose to the Internal Revenue Service their participation in listed transactions. We have not been required to pay any of the penalties set forth in Section 6707A(e)(2) of the Internal Revenue Code.

For a description of other legal proceedings, see Note 18 of the Notes to Consolidated Financial Statements included in Item 8, Financial Statements and Supplementary Data.

Item 4. Reserved

Item 4A. Executive Officers

The executive officers of Target as of March 10, 2010 and their positions and ages are as follows:

Name	Title	Age
Timothy R. Baer	Executive Vice President, General Counsel and Corporate Secretary	49
Michael R. Francis	Executive Vice President and Chief Marketing Officer	47
John D. Griffith	Executive Vice President, Property Development	48
Beth M. Jacob	Executive Vice President, Technology Services and Chief Information Officer	48
Jodeen A. Kozlak	Executive Vice President, Human Resources	46
Troy H. Risch	Executive Vice President, Stores	42
Douglas A. Scovanner	Executive Vice President and Chief Financial Officer	54
Terrence J. Scully	President, Target Financial Services	57
Gregg W. Steinhafel	Chairman of the Board, President and Chief Executive Officer	55
Kathryn A. Tesija	Executive Vice President, Merchandising	47

Each officer is elected by and serves at the pleasure of the Board of Directors. There is neither a family relationship between any of the officers named and any other executive officer or member of the Board of Directors nor any arrangement or understanding pursuant to which any person was selected as an officer. The service period of each officer in the positions listed and other business experience for the past five years is listed below.

Timothy R. Baer	Executive Vice President, General Counsel and Corporate Secretary since March 2007. Senior Vice President, General Counsel and Corporate Secretary from June 2004 to March 2007.
Michael R. Francis	Executive Vice President and Chief Marketing Officer since August 2008. Executive Vice President, Marketing from January 2003 to August 2008.
John D. Griffith	Executive Vice President, Property Development since January 2005.
Beth M. Jacob	Executive Vice President and Chief Information Officer since January 2010. Senior Vice President and Chief Information Officer from July 2008 to January 2010. Vice President, Guest Operations, Target Financial Services from August 2006 to July 2008. Vice President, Guest Contact Centers, Target Financial Services from September 2003 to August 2006.
Jodeen A. Kozlak	Executive Vice President, Human Resources since March 2007. Senior Vice President, Human Resources from February 2006 to March 2007. Vice President, Human Resources and Employee Relations General Counsel from November 2005 to February 2006. From June 2001 to November 2005 Ms. Kozlak held several positions in Employee Relations at Target.
Troy H. Risch	Executive Vice President, Stores since September 2006. Group Vice President from September 2005 to September 2006. Group Director from February 2002 to September 2005.
Douglas A. Scovanner	Executive Vice President and Chief Financial Officer since February 2000.
Terrence J. Scully	President, Target Financial Services since March 2003.
Gregg W. Steinhafel	Chief Executive Officer since May 2008. President since August 1999. Director since January 2007. Chairman of the Board since February 2009.
Kathryn A. Tesija	Executive Vice President, Merchandising since May 2008. Senior Vice President, Merchandising, from July 2001 to May 2008.

PART II

Item 5.   Market for the Registrant's Common Equity, Related Stockholder Matters and Issuer Purchases of Equity Securities

Our common stock is listed on the New York Stock Exchange under the symbol "TGT." We are authorized to issue up to 6,000,000,000 shares of common stock, par value $0.0833, and up to 5,000,000 shares of preferred stock, par value $0.01. At March 10, 2010, there were 17,562 shareholders of record. Dividends declared per share and the high and low closing common stock price for each fiscal quarter during 2009 and 2008 are disclosed in Note 29 of the Notes to Consolidated Financial Statements, included in Item 8, Financial Statements and Supplementary Data.

In November 2007, our Board of Directors authorized the repurchase of $10 billion of our common stock. In November 2008 we announced a temporary suspension of our open-market share repurchase program. In January 2010, we resumed open-market purchases of shares under this program. Since the inception of this share repurchase program, we have repurchased 103.6 million common shares for a total cash investment of $5,320 million ($51.36 per share).

The table below presents information with respect to Target common stock purchases made during the three months ended January 30, 2010, by Target or any "affiliated purchaser" of Target, as defined in Rule 10b-18(a)(3) under the Exchange Act.

Period	Total Number of Shares Purchased	Average Price Paid per Share	Total Number of Shares Purchased as Part of Publicly Announced Program	Approximate Dollar Value of Shares that May Yet Be Purchased Under the Program
November 1, 2009 through November 28, 2009	—	$ —	95,235,594	$ 5,103,322,945
November 29, 2009 through January 2, 2010	—	—	95,235,594	5,103,322,945
January 3, 2010 through January 30, 2010	8,335,800	50.74	103,571,394	4,680,327,198
	8,335,800	$ 50.74	103,571,394	$ 4,680,327,198

The table above includes shares of common stock reacquired from team members who wish to tender owned shares to satisfy the tax withholding on equity awards as part of our long-term incentive plans or to satisfy the exercise price on stock option exercises. For the three months ended January 30, 2010, 11,960 shares were acquired at an average per share price of $50.17 pursuant to our long-term incentive plans.

The table above includes shares reacquired upon settlement of prepaid forward contracts. For the three months ended January 30, 2010, no shares were reacquired through these contracts. At January 30, 2010, we held asset positions in prepaid forward contracts for 1.5 million shares of our common stock, for a total cash investment of $66 million, or an average per share price of $42.77. Refer to Notes 24 and 26 of the Notes to Consolidated Financial Statements for further details of these contracts.

Comparison of Cumulative Five Year Total Return

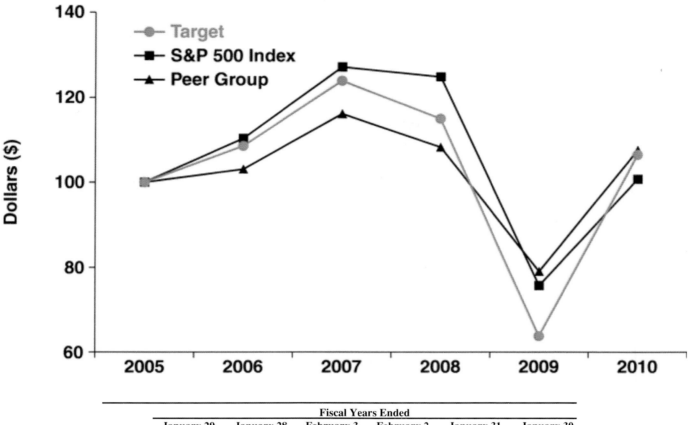

		Fiscal Years Ended				
	January 29, 2005	January 28, 2006	February 3, 2007	February 2, 2008	January 31, 2009	January 30, 2010
Target	$ 100.00	$ 108.57	$ 124.04	$ 115.10	$ 63.82	$ 106.62
S&P 500 Index	100.00	110.38	127.29	125.00	75.79	100.90
Peer Group	100.00	103.10	116.21	108.34	79.13	107.73

The graph above compares the cumulative total shareholder return on our common stock for the last five fiscal years with the cumulative total return on the S&P 500 Index and a peer group consisting of the companies comprising the S&P 500 Retailing Index and the S&P 500 Food and Staples Retailing Index (Peer Group) over the same period. The Peer Group index consists of 39 general merchandise, food and drug retailers and is weighted by the market capitalization of each component company. The graph assumes the investment of $100 in Target common stock, the S&P 500 Index and the Peer Group on January 29, 2005 and reinvestment of all dividends.

Item 6.   Selected Financial Data

	As of or for the Year Ended					
	2009	2008	2007	2006 (a)	2005	2004
Financial Results: (millions)						
Total revenues	$ 65,357	$ 64,948	$ 63,367	$ 59,490	$ 52,620	$ 46,839
Earnings from continuing operations	2,488	2,214	2,849	2,787	2,408	1,885
Net Earnings	2,488	2,214	2,849	2,787	2,408	3,198
Per Share:						
Basic earnings per share	3.31	2.87	3.37	3.23	2.73	2.09

Diluted earnings per share	**3.30**	2.86	3.33	3.21	2.71	2.07
Cash dividends declared per share	**0.67**	0.62	0.54	0.46	0.38	0.31
Financial Position: (millions)						
Total assets	**44,533**	44,106	44,560	37,349	34,995	32,293
Long–term debt, including current portion	**16,814**	18,752	16,590	10,037	9,872	9,538

(a)

Consisted of 53 weeks.

Item 7.   Management's Discussion and Analysis of Financial Condition and Results of Operations

Executive Summary

Our 2009 financial results in both of our business segments were affected by the challenging economy in which we operated. In light of that environment, performance in our Retail Segment was remarkable, as the segment generated the highest EBIT in the Corporation's history, in a year when comparable–store sales declined 2.5 percent. In the Credit Card Segment, disciplined management led to a 29.4 percent increase in segment profit in a year when Target's average investment in the portfolio declined about 32 percent, representing a near–doubling of segment pretax return on invested capital.

Cash flow provided by operations was $5,881 million, $4,430 million, and $4,125 million for 2009, 2008, and 2007, respectively. In 2009, we opened 76 new stores representing 58 stores net of 13 relocations and 5 closings. In 2008, we opened 114 new stores representing 91 stores net of 21 relocations and two closings.

Management's Discussion and Analysis is based on our Consolidated Financial Statements in Item 8, Financial Statements and Supplementary Data.

Analysis of Results of Operations

Retail Segment

Retail Segment Results (millions)	2009	2008	2007	Percent Change 2009/2008	2008/2007
Sales	$ 63,435	$ 62,884	$ 61,471	0.9%	2.3%
Cost of sales	44,062	44,157	42,929	(0.2)	2.9
Gross margin	19,373	18,727	18,542	3.5	1.0
SG&A expenses (a)	12,989	12,838	12,557	1.2	2.2
EBITDA	6,384	5,889	5,985	8.4	(1.6)
Depreciation and amortization	2,008	1,808	1,643	11.0	10.1
EBIT	$ 4,376	$ 4,081	$ 4,342	7.3%	(6.0)%

EBITDA is earnings before interest expense, income taxes, depreciation and amortization.

EBIT is earnings before interest expense and income taxes.

(a)

New account and loyalty rewards redeemed by our guests reduce reported sales. Our Retail Segment charges these discounts to our Credit Card Segment, and the reimbursements of $89 million in 2009, $117 million in 2008, and $114 million in 2007, are recorded as a reduction to SG&A expenses within the Retail Segment.

Retail Segment Rate Analysis	2009	2008	2007
Gross margin rate	30.5%	29.8%	30.2%
SG&A expense rate	20.5	20.4	20.4
EBITDA margin rate	10.1	9.4	9.7
Depreciation and amortization expense rate	3.2	2.9	2.7
EBIT margin rate	6.9	6.5	7.1

Retail Segment rate analysis metrics are computed by dividing the applicable amount by sales.

Sales

Sales include merchandise sales, net of expected returns, from our stores and our online business, as well as gift card breakage. Refer to Note 2 of the Notes to Consolidated Financial Statements for a definition of gift card breakage. Total sales for the Retail Segment for 2009 were $63,435 million, compared with $62,884 million in 2008 and $61,471 million in 2007. All periods were 52–week years. Growth in total sales between 2009 and 2008 as well as between 2008 and 2007 resulted from sales from additional stores opened, offset by lower comparable–store sales. In 2009, deflation affected sales growth by approximately

4 percentage points, compared with an inflationary impact of approximately 2 percentage points in 2008 and a deflationary impact of 2 percentage points in 2007.

Sales by Product Category	Percentage of Sales		
	2009	**2008**	**2007**
Household essentials	23%	22%	21%
Hardlines	22	22	22
Apparel and accessories	20	20	22
Home furnishings and décor	19	21	22
Food and pet supplies	16	15	13
Total	100%	100%	100%

Refer to the Merchandise section in Item 1, Business, for a description of our product categories.

Comparable–store sales is a measure that indicates the performance of our existing stores by measuring the growth in sales for such stores for a period over the comparable, prior–year period of equivalent length. The method of calculating comparable–store sales varies across the retail industry. As a result, our comparable–store sales calculation is not necessarily comparable to similarly titled measures reported by other companies.

Comparable–store sales are sales from our online business and sales from general merchandise and SuperTarget stores open longer than one year, including:

- sales from stores that have been remodeled or expanded while remaining open

- sales from stores that have been relocated to new buildings of the same format within the same trade area, in which the new store opens at about the same time as the old store closes

Comparable–store sales do not include:

- sales from general merchandise stores that have been converted, or relocated within the same trade area, to a SuperTarget store format

- sales from stores that were intentionally closed to be remodeled, expanded or reconstructed

Comparable–Store Sales	2009	2008	2007
Comparable–store sales	(2.5)%	(2.9)%	3.0%
Drivers of changes in comparable–store sales:			
Number of transactions	(0.2)%	(3.1)%	0.3%
Average transaction amount	(2.3)%	0.2%	2.6%
Units per transaction	(1.5)%	(2.1)%	1.1%
Selling price per unit	(0.8)%	2.3%	1.5%

The comparable–store sales increases or decreases above are calculated by comparing sales in fiscal year periods with comparable prior fiscal year periods of equivalent length.

In fiscal 2009, the change in comparable–store sales was driven by a decline in the average transaction amount, primarily due to a decrease in the number of units per transaction. In 2008, the change in comparable–store sales was driven by a decline in the number of transactions, slightly offset by an increase in average transaction amount, which reflects the effect of a higher selling price per unit sold partially offset by a decrease in number of units per transaction. Transaction–level metrics are influenced by a broad array of macroeconomic, competitive and consumer behavioral factors, as well as sales mix, and comparable–store sales rates are negatively impacted by transfer of sales to new stores.

Gross Margin Rate

Gross margin rate represents gross margin (sales less cost of sales) as a percentage of sales. See Note 3 of the Notes to Consolidated Financial Statements for a description of expenses included in cost of sales. Markup is the difference between an item's cost and its retail price (expressed as a percentage of its retail price). Factors that affect markup include vendor offerings and negotiations, vendor income, sourcing strategies, market forces like raw material and freight costs, and competitive influences. Markdowns are the reduction in the original or previous price of retail merchandise. Factors that affect markdowns include inventory management, competitive influences and economic conditions.

In 2009, our gross margin rate was 30.5 percent compared with 29.8 percent in 2008. Our 2009 gross margin rate benefitted from rate improvements within categories, partially offset by the mix impact of faster sales growth in lower margin rate categories (generally product categories of household essentials and food). The impact of rate performance within merchandise categories on gross margin rate was an approximate 1.1 percentage point increase for 2009. This increase is the result of improved markups and reduced markdowns. The impact of sales mix on gross margin rate was an approximate 0.4 percentage point reduction.

In 2008 our gross margin rate was 29.8 percent compared with 30.2 percent in 2007. Our 2008 gross margin rate was adversely affected by sales mix, which resulted in a 0.6 percentage point reduction in the gross margin rate. Sales in merchandise categories that yield lower gross margin rates outpaced sales in our higher margin apparel and home merchandise categories. This mix impact was partially offset by favorable supply chain expense rates, as well as higher gross margin rates within merchandise categories across our assortment, which had a combined impact on gross margin rate of an approximate 0.2 percentage point increase.

Selling, General and Administrative Expense Rate

Our selling, general and administrative (SG&A) expense rate represents SG&A expenses as a percentage of sales. See Note 3 of the Notes to Consolidated Financial Statements for a description of expenses included in SG&A expenses. SG&A expenses exclude depreciation and amortization, as well as expenses associated with our credit card operations, which are reflected separately in our Consolidated Statements of Operations.

SG&A expense rate was 20.5 percent in 2009 compared with 20.4 percent in both 2008 and 2007. The change in the rate was primarily driven by an approximate 0.4 percentage point impact from an increase in incentive compensation due to better than expected 2009 performance compared with 2008 results. The rate increase was partially offset by an approximate 0.2 percentage point impact from sustained productivity gains in our stores. Within SG&A expenses in 2008 and 2007, there were no expense categories that experienced a significant fluctuation as a percentage of sales, when compared with prior periods.

Depreciation and Amortization Expense Rate

Our depreciation and amortization expense rate represents depreciation and amortization expense as a percentage of sales. In 2009, our depreciation and amortization expense rate was 3.2 percent compared with 2.9 percent in 2008 and 2.7 percent in 2007. The increase in the rate was primarily due to accelerated depreciation on assets that will be replaced as part of our 340–store 2010 remodel program. The comparative increase in 2008 was due to increased capital expenditures, specifically related to investments in new stores.

Store Data

Number of Stores	Target general merchandise stores	SuperTarget stores	Total
January 31, 2009	1,443	239	1,682
Opened	63	13	76
Closed *(a)*	(17)	(1)	(18)
January 30, 2010	**1,489**	**251**	**1,740**
Retail Square Feet *(b)* (thousands)			
January 31, 2009	180,321	42,267	222,588
Opened	9,039	2,404	11,443
Closed *(a)*	(1,911)	(179)	(2,090)
January 30, 2010	**187,449**	**44,492**	**231,941**

(a) Includes 13 store relocations in the same trade area and 5 stores closed without replacement.

(b) Reflects total square feet less office, distribution center and vacant space.

Credit Card Segment

Credit card revenues are comprised of finance charges, late fees and other revenue, and third party merchant fees, or the amounts received from merchants who accept the Target Visa credit card.

Credit Card Segment Results	2009 Amount (in millions)	2009 Rate (d)	2008 Amount (in millions)	2008 Rate (d)	2007 Amount (in millions)	2007 Rate (d)
Finance charge revenue	$ 1,450	17.4%	$ 1,451	16.7%	$ 1,308	18.0%
Late fees and other revenue	349	4.2	461	5.3	422	5.8
Third party merchant fees	123	1.5	152	1.7	166	2.3
Total revenues	1,922	23.0	2,064	23.7	1,896	26.1
Bad debt expense	1,185	14.2	1,251	14.4	481	6.6
Operations and marketing expenses (a)	425	5.1	474	5.4	469	6.4
Depreciation and amortization	14	0.2	17	0.2	16	0.2
Total expenses	1,624	19.4	1,742	20.0	966	13.3
EBIT	298	3.5	322	3.7	930	12.8
Interest expense on nonrecourse debt collateralized by credit card receivables	97		167		133	
Segment profit	$ 201		$ 155		$ 797	
Average receivables funded by Target (b)	$ 2,866		$ 4,192		$ 4,888	
Segment pretax ROIC (c)	7.0%		3.7%		16.3%	

(a)

New account and loyalty rewards redeemed by our guests reduce reported sales. Our Retail Segment charges the cost of these discounts to our Credit Card Segment, and the reimbursements of $89 million in 2009, $117 million in 2008, and $114 million in 2007, are recorded as an increase to Operations and Marketing expenses within the Credit Card Segment.

(b)

Amounts represent the portion of average gross credit card receivables funded by Target. For 2009, 2008, and 2007, these amounts exclude $5,484 million, $4,503 million, and $2,387 million, respectively, of receivables funded by nonrecourse debt collateralized by credit card receivables.

(c)

ROIC is return on invested capital, and this rate equals our segment profit divided by average gross credit card receivables funded by Target, expressed as an annualized rate.

(d)

As an annualized percentage of average gross credit card receivables.

Spread Analysis – Total Portfolio	2009			2008			2007		
	Amount (in millions)	Rate		Amount (in millions)	Rate		Amount (in millions)	Rate	
EBIT	$ 298	3.5% *(b)*	$	322	3.7% *(b)*	$	930	12.8% *(b)*	
LIBOR *(a)*		0.3%			2.3%			5.1%	
Spread to LIBOR *(c)*	$ 270	3.2% *(b)*	$	118	1.4% *(b)*	$	558	7.7% *(b)*	

(a)

Balance–weighted one–month LIBOR.

(b)

As a percentage of average gross credit card receivables.

(c)

Spread to LIBOR is a metric used to analyze the performance of our total credit card portfolio because the majority of our portfolio earned finance charge revenue at rates tied to the Prime Rate, and the interest rate on all nonrecourse debt securitized by credit card receivables is tied to LIBOR.

Our primary measure of segment profit in our Credit Card Segment is the EBIT generated by our total credit card receivables portfolio less the interest expense on nonrecourse debt collateralized by credit card receivables. We analyze this measure of profit in light of the amount of capital we have invested in our credit card receivables. In addition, we measure the performance of our overall credit card receivables portfolio by calculating the dollar Spread to LIBOR at the portfolio level. This metric approximates overall financial performance of the entire credit card portfolio we manage by measuring the difference between EBIT earned on the portfolio and a hypothetical benchmark rate financing cost applied to the entire portfolio. The interest rate on all nonrecourse debt securitized by credit card receivables is tied to LIBOR. For the first quarter of 2009, the vast majority of our portfolio accrued finance charge revenue at rates tied to the Prime Rate. Effective April 2009, we implemented a terms change to our portfolio that established a minimum annual percentage rate (APR) applied to cardholder account balances. Under these terms, finance charges accrue at a fixed APR if the benchmark Prime Rate is less than 6%; if the Prime Rate is greater than 6%, finance charges accrue at the benchmark Prime Rate, plus a spread. Because the Prime Rate was less than 6% during 2009, the majority of our portfolio accrued finance charges at a fixed APR subsequent to this terms change. As a result of regulatory actions that impact our portfolio, effective January 2010, we implemented a second terms change that converted the minimum APR for the majority of our accounts to a variable rate, and we eliminated penalty pricing for all current, or nondelinquent accounts. Penalty pricing is the charging of a higher interest rate for a period of time, generally 12 months, and is triggered when a cardholder repeatedly fails to make timely payments.

In 2009, Credit Card Segment profit increased to $201 million from $155 million as a result of improved portfolio performance (Spread to LIBOR) and significantly lower funding costs. The reduction in our investment in the portfolio combined with these results produced a strong improvement in segment ROIC. Segment revenues were $1,922 million, a decrease of $143 million, or 6.9 percent, from the prior year. The decrease in revenue was driven by a lower Prime Rate, lower average receivables, higher finance charge and late–fee write–offs and lower late fees due to fewer delinquent accounts offset by the positive impacts of the terms changes implemented in late 2008 and April 2009. Segment expenses were $1,624 million, a decrease of $118 million, or 6.8 percent, from prior year driven by lower bad debt and operations and marketing expenses, on both a dollar and rate basis. Segment interest expense benefited from a significantly lower LIBOR rate compared to the prior year.

Segment profit and dollar Spread to LIBOR measures in 2008 were significantly impacted on both a rate and dollar basis by bad debt expense. Segment revenues were $2,064 million, an increase of $168 million, or 8.9 percent, from the prior year, driven by a 19.5 percent increase in average receivables. On a rate basis, revenue yield decreased 2.4 percentage points primarily due to a reduction in the Prime Rate index used to determine finance charge rates in the portfolio and lower external sales volume contributing to the decline in third party merchant fees. This negative pressure on revenue yield was offset modestly by the positive impact of terms changes implemented in 2008 that increased our effective yield. Segment expenses were $1,742 million, an increase of $776 million, or 80.3 percent, from the prior year driven by an increase in bad debt expense of $770 million. The increase in bad debt expense resulted from the increase in our incurred net write–off rate from 5.9 percent in 2007 to 9.3 percent in 2008 and the increase in the allowance for doubtful accounts of $440 million for anticipated future write–offs of current receivables. Segment profit decreased from 16.3 percent in 2007 to 3.7 percent in 2008 primarily due to the effect of bad debt expense, the reduction in receivables owned and funded by Target, and the impact of a lower Prime Rate during 2008.

Receivables Rollforward Analysis (millions)	Fiscal Year			Percent Change	
	2009	2008	2007	2009/2008	2008/2007
Beginning gross credit card receivables	$ 9,094	$ 8,624	$ 6,711	5.4%	28.5%
Charges at Target	3,553	4,207	4,491	(15.5)	(6.3)
Charges at third parties	6,763	8,542	9,398	(20.8)	(9.1)
Payments	(12,065)	(13,482)	(13,388)	(10.5)	0.7
Other	637	1,203	1,412	(47.1)	(14.8)
Period–end gross credit card receivables	$ 7,982	$ 9,094	$ 8,624	(12.2)%	5.4%
Average gross credit card receivables	$ 8,351	$ 8,695	$ 7,275	(4.0)%	19.5%
Accounts with three or more payments (60+ days) past due as a percentage of period–end credit card receivables	6.3%	6.1%	4.0%		
Accounts with four or more payments (90+ days) past due as a percentage of period–end gross credit card receivables	4.7%	4.3%	2.7%		
Credit card penetration (a)	5.6%	6.7%	7.3%		

(a)

Represents charges at Target (including sales taxes and gift cards) divided by sales (which excludes sales taxes and gift cards).

Allowance for Doubtful Accounts	Fiscal Year			Percent Change	
(millions)	2009	2008	2007	2009/2008	2008/2007
Allowance at beginning of period	$ 1,010	$ 570	$ 517	77.1%	10.4%
Bad debt expense	1,185	1,251	481	(5.3)	160.1
Net write–offs (a)	(1,179)	(811)	(428)	45.2	89.8
Allowance at end of period	$ 1,016	$ 1,010	$ 570	0.6%	77.1%
As a percentage of period–end gross credit card receivables	12.7%	11.1%	6.6%		
Net write–offs as a percentage of average gross credit card receivables (annualized)	14.1%	9.3%	5.9%		

(a)

Net write–offs include the principal amount of losses (excluding accrued and unpaid finance charges) less current period principal recoveries.

Our 2009 period–end gross credit card receivables were $7,982 million compared with $9,094 million in 2008, a decrease of 12.2 percent. Average gross credit card receivables in 2009 decreased 4.0 percent compared with 2008 levels. This change was driven by tighter risk management and underwriting initiatives that have significantly reduced available credit lines for higher–risk cardholders, fewer new accounts being opened, and a decrease in charge activity resulting from reductions in card usage by our guests, partially offset by the impact of a decline in payment rates.

Our 2008 period–end gross credit card receivables were $9,094 million compared with $8,624 million in 2007, an increase of 5.4 percent. Average gross credit card receivables in 2008 increased 19.5 percent compared with 2007 levels. This growth was driven by the annualization of the prior year's product change from proprietary Target Cards to higher–limit Target Visa cards and the impact of industry–wide declines in payment rates, offset in part by a reduction in charge activity resulting from reductions in card usage by our guests, and from risk management and underwriting initiatives that significantly reduced credit lines for higher risk cardholders.

Other Performance Factors

Net Interest Expense

Net interest expense was $801 million at the end of 2009, decreasing 7.5 percent, or $65 million from 2008. This decline was due to a decrease in the annualized average portfolio interest rate from 5.3 percent to 4.8 percent partially offset by a $16 million charge related to the early retirement of long–term debt. In 2008, net interest expense was $866 million compared with $647 million in 2007, an increase of 33.8 percent. This increase was due primarily to higher average debt balances supporting capital investment, share repurchase and the receivables portfolio, partially offset by a lower average portfolio net interest rate.

Provision for Income Taxes

Our effective income tax rate was 35.7 percent in 2009 and 37.4 percent in 2008. The decrease in the effective rate between periods is primarily due to nontaxable capital market returns on investments used to economically hedge the market risk in deferred compensation plans in 2009 compared with nondeductible losses in 2008. The 2009 effective income tax rate is also lower due to federal and state discrete items.

Our effective income tax rate for 2008 was 37.4 percent compared with 38.4 percent in 2007. The decrease in 2008 was primarily due to tax reserve reductions resulting from audit settlements and the effective resolution of other issues. The 2008 effective income tax rate was also lower due to a comparatively greater proportion of earnings subject to rate differences between taxing jurisdictions. These rate declines were partially offset by lower capital market returns on investments used to economically hedge the market risk in deferred compensation plans. Gains and losses from these investments are not taxable.

Analysis of Financial Condition

Liquidity and Capital Resources

Our 2009 operations were entirely funded by internally generated funds. Cash flow provided by operations was $5,881 in 2009 compared with $4,430 million in 2008. This strong cash flow allowed us to fund capital expenditures of $1,729 million and pay off $1.3 billion of maturing debt with internally generated funds. In addition we accelerated the payoff of a $550 million 2010 debt maturity, restarted our share repurchase program earlier than expected and experienced a $1.3 billion increase in marketable securities at January 30, 2010.

Our 2009 period–end gross credit card receivables were $7,982 million compared with $9,094 million in 2008, a decrease of 12.2 percent. Average gross credit card receivables in 2009 decreased 4.0 percent compared with 2008 levels. This change was driven by the factors indicated in the Credit Card Segment above. This trend and the factors influencing it are likely to continue into 2010. Due to the decrease in gross credit card receivables, Target Receivables Corporation (TRC), using cash flows from the receivables, repaid an affiliate of JPMorgan Chase (JPMC) $163 million during 2009 under the terms of our agreement with them as described in Note 10 of the Notes to Consolidated Financial Statements. To the extent the receivables balance continues to decline, TRC expects to continue to pay JPMC a prorata portion of principal collections such that the portion owned by JPMC would not exceed 47 percent.

Year-end inventory levels increased $474 million, or 7.1 percent from 2008, primarily due to unusually low inventory levels at the end of 2008 in response to the challenging economic environment. Inventory levels were also higher to support traffic-driving strategic initiatives, such as food and pharmacy, in addition to comparatively higher retail square footage. Accounts payable increased by $174 million, or 2.7 percent over the same period.

During 2009, we repurchased 9.9 million shares of our common stock for a total cash investment of $479 million ($48.54 per share) under a $10 billion share repurchase plan authorized by our Board of Directors in November 2007. In 2008, we repurchased 67.2 million shares of our common stock for a total cash investment of $3,395 million ($50.49 per share).

We paid dividends totaling $496 million in 2009 and $465 million in 2008, an increase of 6.7 percent. We declared dividends totaling $503 million ($0.67 per share) in 2009, an increase of 6.8 percent over 2008. In 2008, we declared dividends totaling $471 million ($0.62 per share), an increase of 3.8 percent over 2007. We have paid dividends every quarter since our first dividend was declared following our 1967 initial public offering, and it is our intent to continue to do so in the future.

Our financing strategy is to ensure liquidity and access to capital markets, to manage our net exposure to floating interest rate volatility, and to maintain a balanced spectrum of debt maturities. Within these parameters, we seek to minimize our borrowing costs.

Maintaining strong investment-grade debt ratings is a key part of our financing strategy. Our current debt ratings are as follows:

Debt Ratings	Moody's	Standard and Poor's	Fitch
Long-term debt	A2	A+	A
Commercial paper	P-1	A-1	F1
Securitized receivables *(a)*	Aa2	A+	n/a

(a)
These rated securitized receivables exclude the interest in our credit card receivables sold to JPMC.

At January 30, 2010 and January 31, 2009, there were no amounts outstanding under our commercial paper program. In past years, we funded our peak sales season working capital needs through our commercial paper program and then used the cash generated from that sales season to repay the commercial paper issued. In 2009 we funded our working capital needs through internally generated funds. Additionally and as described in Note 10 of the Notes to Consolidated Financial Statements, during 2008 we sold to JPMC an interest in our credit card receivables for approximately $3.8 billion. We received proceeds of approximately $3.6 billion, reflecting a 7 percent discount.

An additional source of liquidity is available to us through a committed $2 billion unsecured revolving credit facility obtained through a group of banks in April 2007, which will expire in April 2012. No balances were outstanding at any time during 2009 or 2008 under this facility.

Most of our long-term debt obligations contain covenants related to secured debt levels. In addition to a secured debt level covenant, our credit facility also contains a debt leverage covenant. We are, and expect to remain, in compliance with these covenants. Additionally, at January 30, 2010, no notes or debentures contained provisions requiring acceleration of payment upon a debt rating downgrade, except that certain outstanding notes allow the note holders to put the notes to us if within a matter of months of each other we experience both (i) a change in control; and (ii) our long-term debt ratings are either reduced and the resulting rating is non-investment grade, or our long-term debt ratings are placed on watch for possible reduction and those ratings are subsequently reduced and the resulting rating is non-investment grade.

Our interest coverage ratio represents the ratio of pretax earnings before fixed charges to fixed charges. Fixed charges include interest expense and the interest portion of rent expense. Our interest coverage ratio as calculated by the SEC's applicable rules was 5.1x in 2009, 4.3x in 2008, and 6.4x in 2007.

Capital Expenditures

Capital expenditures were $1,729 million in 2009 compared with $3,547 million in 2008 and $4,369 million in 2007. This decrease was driven by lower capital expenditures for new stores, remodels and technology-related assets. Our 2009 capital expenditures include $232 million related to stores that will open in 2010 and later years. Net property and equipment decreased $475 million in 2009 following an increase of $1,661 million in 2008.

Capital Expenditures	Percentage of Capital Expenditures		
	2009	2008	2007
New stores	52%	66%	71%
Remodels and expansions	17	8	7
Information technology, distribution and other	31	26	22
Total	100%	100%	100%

Commitments and Contingencies

At January 30, 2010, our contractual obligations were as follows:

Contractual Obligations	Payments Due by Period				
(millions)	Total	Less than 1 Year	1–3 Years	3–5 Years	After 5 Years
Long–term debt (a)					
Unsecured	$ 11,071	$ 786	$ 1,607	$ 502	$ 8,176
Nonrecourse	5,553	900	750	3,903	—
Interest payments – long–term debt					
Unsecured	10,405	693	1,240	1,061	7,411
Nonrecourse (b)	159	39	74	46	—
Capital lease obligations (c)	472	19	44	45	364
Operating leases (c)	4,000	264	324	265	3,147
Deferred compensation	394	41	87	96	170
Real estate obligations	222	222	—	—	—
Purchase obligations	2,016	597	685	627	107
Tax contingencies (d)	—	—	—	—	—
Contractual obligations	$ 34,292	$ 3,561	$ 4,811	$ 6,545	$ 19,375

(a)
> Required principal payments only. Excludes fair market value adjustments recorded in long–term debt, as required by derivative and hedging accounting rules. Principal amounts include the 47 percent interest in credit card receivables sold to JPMC at the principal amount. In the event of a decrease in the receivables principal balance, accelerated repayment of this obligation may occur.

(b)
> These payments vary with LIBOR and are calculated assuming LIBOR of 0.25 percent plus a spread, for each year outstanding.

(c)
> Total contractual lease payments include $2,016 million of operating lease payments related to options to extend the lease term that are reasonably assured of being exercised. These payments also include $196 million and $88 million of legally binding minimum lease payments for stores opening in 2010 or later for capital and operating leases, respectively. Capital lease obligations include interest. Refer to Note 21 of the Notes to Consolidated Financial Statements for a further description of leases.

(d)
> Estimated tax contingencies of $579 million, including interest and penalties, are not included in the table above because we are not able to make reasonably reliable estimates of the period of cash settlement.

Real estate obligations include commitments for the purchase, construction or remodeling of real estate and facilities. Purchase obligations include all legally binding contracts such as firm minimum commitments for inventory purchases, merchandise royalties, equipment purchases, marketing–related contracts, software acquisition/license commitments and service contracts.

We issue inventory purchase orders in the normal course of business, which represent authorizations to purchase that are cancelable by their terms. We do not consider purchase orders to be firm inventory commitments; therefore, they are excluded from the table above. We also issue trade letters of credit in the ordinary course of business, which are excluded from this table as these obligations are conditional on the purchase order not being cancelled. If we choose to cancel a purchase order, we may be obligated to reimburse the vendor for unrecoverable outlays incurred prior to cancellation.

We have not included obligations under our pension and postretirement health care benefit plans in the contractual obligations table above. Our historical practice regarding these plans has been to contribute amounts necessary to satisfy minimum pension funding requirements, plus periodic discretionary amounts determined to be appropriate. Further information on these plans, including our expected contributions for 2010, is included in Note 27 of the Notes to Consolidated Financial Statements.

We do not have any arrangements or relationships with entities that are not consolidated into the financial statements that are reasonably likely to materially affect our liquidity or the availability of capital resources.

Critical Accounting Estimates

Our analysis of operations and financial condition is based on our consolidated financial statements, prepared in accordance with U.S. generally accepted accounting principles (GAAP). Preparation of these consolidated financial statements requires us to make estimates and assumptions affecting the reported amounts of assets and liabilities at the date of the consolidated financial statements, reported amounts of revenues and expenses during the reporting period and related disclosures of contingent assets and liabilities. In the Notes to Consolidated Financial Statements, we describe the significant accounting policies used in preparing the consolidated financial statements. Our estimates are evaluated on an ongoing basis and are drawn from historical experience and other assumptions that we believe to be reasonable under the circumstances. Actual results could differ under different assumptions or conditions. However we do not believe there is a reasonable likelihood that there will be a material change in future estimates or assumptions. Our senior management has discussed the development and selection of our critical accounting estimates with the Audit Committee of our Board of Directors. The following items in our consolidated financial statements require significant estimation or judgment:

Inventory and cost of sales   We use the retail inventory method to account for substantially our entire inventory and the related cost of sales. Under this method, inventory is stated at cost using the last–in, first–out (LIFO) method as determined by applying a cost–to–retail ratio to each merchandise grouping's ending retail value. Cost includes the purchase price as adjusted for vendor income. Since inventory value is adjusted regularly to reflect market conditions, our inventory methodology reflects the lower of cost or market. We reduce inventory for estimated losses related to shrink and markdowns. Our shrink estimate is based on historical losses verified by ongoing physical inventory counts. Historically our actual physical inventory count results have shown our estimates to be reliable. Markdowns designated for clearance activity are recorded when the salability of the merchandise has diminished. Inventory is at risk of obsolescence if economic conditions change. Relevant economic conditions include changing consumer demand, customer preferences, changing consumer credit markets or increasing competition. We believe these risks are largely mitigated because our inventory typically turns in less than three months. Inventory is further described in Note 11 of the Notes to Consolidated Financial Statements.

Vendor income receivable   Cost of sales and SG&A expenses are partially offset by various forms of consideration received from our vendors. This "vendor income" is earned for a variety of vendor–sponsored programs, such as volume rebates, markdown allowances, promotions and advertising allowances, as well as for our compliance programs. We establish a receivable for the vendor income that is earned but not yet received. Based on the agreements in place, this receivable is computed by estimating when we have completed our performance and when the amount is earned. The majority of all year–end vendor income receivables are collected within the following fiscal quarter. Vendor income is described further in Note 4 of the Notes to Consolidated Financial Statements.

Allowance for doubtful accounts   When receivables are recorded, we recognize an allowance for doubtful accounts in an amount equal to anticipated future write–offs. This allowance includes provisions for uncollectible finance charges and other credit–related fees. We estimate future write–offs based on historical experience of delinquencies, risk scores, aging trends and industry risk trends. Substantially all accounts continue to accrue finance charges until they are written off. Accounts are automatically written off when they become 180 days past due. Management believes the allowance for doubtful accounts is adequate to cover anticipated losses in our credit card accounts receivable under current conditions; however, unexpected, significant deterioration in any of the factors mentioned above or in general economic conditions could materially change these expectations. Credit card receivables are described in Note 10 of the Notes to Consolidated Financial Statements.

Analysis of long–lived and intangible assets for impairment   We review assets at the lowest level for which there are identifiable cash flows, usually at the store level, on an annual basis or whenever an event or change in circumstances indicates the carrying value of the asset may not be recoverable. An impairment loss on a long–lived and identifiable intangible asset would be recognized when estimated undiscounted future cash flows from the operation and disposition of the asset are less than the asset carrying amount. Goodwill is tested for impairment by comparing its carrying value to a fair value estimated by discounting future cash flows. This test is performed at least annually or whenever an event or change in circumstances indicates the carrying value of the asset may not be recoverable. Impairment on long–lived assets of $49 million in 2009, $2 million in 2008 and $7 million in 2007 were recorded as a result of the tests performed.

Our estimates of future cash flows require us to make assumptions and to apply judgment, including forecasting future sales and expenses and estimating useful lives of the assets. These estimates can be affected by factors such as future store results, real estate values, and economic conditions that can be difficult to predict.

Insurance/self–insurance   We retain a substantial portion of the risk related to certain general liability, workers' compensation, property loss and team member medical and dental claims. However, we maintain stop–loss coverage to limit the exposure related to certain risks. Liabilities associated with these losses include estimates of both claims filed and losses incurred but not yet reported. We estimate our ultimate cost based on an analysis of historical data and actuarial estimates. General liability and workers' compensation liabilities are recorded at our estimate of their net present value; other liabilities referred to above are not discounted. We believe that the amounts accrued are adequate, although actual losses may differ from the amounts provided. Refer to Item 7A for further disclosure of the market risks associated with these exposures.

Income taxes   We pay income taxes based on the tax statutes, regulations and case law of the various jurisdictions in which we operate. Significant judgment is required in determining income tax provisions and in evaluating the ultimate resolution of tax matters in dispute with tax authorities. Historically, our assessments of the ultimate resolution of tax issues have been materially accurate. The current open tax issues are not dissimilar in size or substance from historical items. We believe the resolution of these matters will not have a material impact on our consolidated financial statements. Income taxes are described further in Note 22 of the Notes to Consolidated Financial Statements.

Pension and postretirement health care accounting   We fund and maintain a qualified defined benefit pension plan. We also maintain several smaller nonqualified plans and a postretirement health care plan for certain current and retired team members. The costs for these plans are determined based on actuarial calculations using the assumptions described in the following paragraphs. Eligibility for, and the level of, these benefits varies depending on team members' full–time or part–time status, date of hire and/or length of service.

Our expected long–term rate of return on plan assets is determined by the portfolio composition, historical long–term investment performance and current market conditions. Benefits expense recorded during the year is partially dependent upon the long–term rate of return used, and a 0.1 percent decrease in the expected long–term rate of return used to determine net pension and postretirement health care benefits expense would increase annual expense by approximately $2 million.

The discount rate used to determine benefit obligations is adjusted annually based on the interest rate for long–term high–quality corporate bonds as of the measurement date using yields for maturities that are in line with the duration of our pension liabilities. Historically, this same discount rate has also been used to determine net pension and postretirement health care benefits expense for the following plan year. The discount rates used to determine benefit obligations and benefits expense are included in Note 27 of the Notes to Consolidated Financial Statements. Benefits expense recorded during the year is partially dependent upon the discount rates used, and a 0.1 percent decrease to the weighted average discount rate used to determine net pension and postretirement health care benefits expense would increase annual expense by approximately $4 million.

Based on our experience, we use a graduated compensation growth schedule that assumes higher compensation growth for younger, shorter–service pension–eligible team members than it does for older, longer–service pension–eligible team members.

Pension and postretirement health care benefits are further described in Note 27 of the Notes to Consolidated Financial Statements.

New Accounting Pronouncements

Future Adoptions

In June 2009, the FASB issued SFAS No. 166, "Accounting for Transfers of Financial Assets an amendment of FASB Statement No. 140" (SFAS 166), codified in the Transfers and Servicing accounting principles, which amends the derecognition guidance in former FASB Statement No. 140 and eliminates the exemption from consolidation for qualifying special–purpose entities. This guidance will be effective for the

Corporation beginning in fiscal 2010 and adoption is not anticipated to affect our consolidated net earnings, cash flows or financial position.

In June 2009, the FASB issued SFAS No. 167, "Amendments to FASB Interpretation No. 46(R)" (SFAS 167), codified in the Consolidation accounting principles, which amends the consolidation guidance applicable to variable interest entities. The amendments will significantly affect the overall consolidation analysis under former FASB Interpretation No. 46(R). This guidance will be effective for the Corporation beginning in fiscal 2010 and adoption is not anticipated to affect our consolidated net earnings, cash flows or financial position.

Outlook

In the Retail Segment, we expect to generate increases in comparable–store sales, likely in the range of 2 to 4 percent for the year, including an expected 1 percentage point lift from our remodel program. While our comparable–store sales comparisons are easier in the spring than the fall, the expected incremental sales resulting from remodels will grow as the year progresses. Additionally, we expect total sales to increase by a mid–single digit percentage.

In 2010 we expect to generally preserve our 2009 EBIT margin rate in our Retail Segment, which if achieved would result in our Retail Segment EBIT increasing in line with total sales growth.

In our Credit Card Segment, we expect the lower consumer usage of credit and our risk management strategies to continue throughout 2010, resulting in a low double–digit percentage decline in gross credit card receivables by the end of the year. We also expect to maintain segment profit on a dollar basis at generally the level earned in 2009, generating a higher pretax segment ROIC in 2010 than in 2009.

We expect our 2010 book effective tax rate to approximate our long–term structural rate, likely in the range of 37.0 to 37.5 percent.

We also expect to continue to execute against our share repurchase authorization.

We expect our 2010 capital expenditures to be in the range of $2 to $2.5 billion, reflective of projects we will complete in 2010 as well as initial spending for our 2011 and 2012 new store programs. Our expectation is that our 2010 new store program will result in approximately 13 new stores and that our 2011 new store program will be in the range of 20 to 30 stores.

Due to the early repayment of an August 2010 debt maturity, the only significant remaining 2010 maturity, prior to our seasonal working capital peak (which typically occurs in October or November), is the $900 million public series borrowing collateralized by our credit card receivables due in October.

Forward–Looking Statements

This report contains forward–looking statements, which are based on our current assumptions and expectations. These statements are typically accompanied by the words "expect," "may," "could," "believe," "would," "might," "anticipates," or words of similar import. The principal forward looking statements in this report include: For our Retail Segment, our outlook for sales, expected merchandise returns, comparable–store sales trends and EBIT margin rates; for our Credit Card Segment, our outlook for year–end gross credit card receivables, portfolio size, future write–offs of current receivables, profit, ROIC, and the allowance for doubtful accounts; on a consolidated basis, the expected effective income tax rate, the continued execution of our share repurchase program, our expected capital expenditures and the number of stores to be opened in 2010 and 2011, the expected compliance with debt covenants, our intentions regarding future dividends, the anticipated impact of new accounting pronouncements, our expected future share–based compensation expense, our expected contributions and benefit payments related to our pension and postretirement health care plans, and the adequacy of our reserves for general liability, workers' compensation, property loss, and team member medical and dental, the expected outcome of claims and litigation, and the resolution of tax uncertainties.

All such forward–looking statements are intended to enjoy the protection of the safe harbor for forward–looking statements contained in the Private Securities Litigation Reform Act of 1995, as amended. Although we believe there is a reasonable basis for the forward–looking statements, our actual results could be materially different. The most important factors which could cause our actual results to differ from our forward–looking statements are set forth on our description of risk factors in Item 1A to this Form 10–K, which should be read in conjunction with the forward–looking statements in this report. Forward–looking statements speak only as of the date they are made, and we do not undertake any obligation to update any forward–looking statement.

Item 7A. Quantitative and Qualitative Disclosures About Market Risk

Our exposure to market risk results primarily from interest rate changes on our debt obligations, some of which are at a LIBOR–plus floating rate, and on our credit card receivables, the majority of which are assessed finance charges at a Prime–based floating rate. To manage our net interest margin, we generally maintain levels of floating–rate debt to generate similar changes in net interest expense as finance charge revenues fluctuate. The degree of floating asset and liability matching may vary over time and in different interest rate environments. At January 30, 2010, the amount of floating–rate credit card assets exceeded the amount of net floating–rate debt obligations by approximately $1 billion. As a result, based on our balance sheet position at January 30, 2010, the annualized effect of a 0.1 percentage point decrease in floating interest rates on our floating rate debt obligations, net of our floating rate credit card assets and marketable securities, would be to decrease earnings before income taxes by approximately $1 million. See further description in Note 20 of the Notes to Consolidated Financial Statements.

We record our general liability and workers' compensation liabilities at net present value; therefore, these liabilities fluctuate with changes in interest rates. Periodically, in certain interest rate environments, we economically hedge a portion of our exposure to these interest rate changes by entering into interest rate forward contracts that partially mitigate the effects of interest rate changes. Based on our balance sheet position at January 30, 2010, the annualized effect of a 0.5 percentage point decrease in interest rates would be to decrease earnings before income taxes by approximately $9 million.

In addition, we are exposed to market return fluctuations on our qualified defined benefit pension plans. The annualized effect of a one percentage point decrease in the return on pension plan assets would decrease plan assets by $22 million at January 30, 2010. The value of our pension liabilities is inversely related to changes in interest rates. To protect against declines in interest rates we hold high–quality, long–duration bonds and interest rate swaps in our pension plan trust. At year end, we had hedged approximately 50 percent of the interest rate exposure of our funded status.

As more fully described in Note 14 and Note 26 of the Notes to Consolidated Financial Statements, we are exposed to market returns on accumulated team member balances in our nonqualified, unfunded deferred compensation plans. We control the risk of offering the nonqualified plans by making investments in life insurance contracts and prepaid forward contracts on our own common stock that offset a substantial portion of our economic exposure to the returns on these plans. The annualized effect of a one percentage point change in market returns on our nonqualified defined contribution plans (inclusive of the effect of the investment vehicles used to manage our economic exposure) would not be significant.

We do not have significant direct exposure to foreign currency rates as all of our stores are located in the United States, and the vast majority of imported merchandise is purchased in U.S. dollars.

Overall, there have been no material changes in our primary risk exposures or management of market risks since the prior year.

Item 8. Financial Statements and Supplementary Data

Report of Management on the Consolidated Financial Statements

Management is responsible for the consistency, integrity and presentation of the information in the Annual Report. The consolidated financial statements and other information presented in this Annual Report have been prepared in accordance with accounting principles generally accepted in the United States and include necessary judgments and estimates by management.

To fulfill our responsibility, we maintain comprehensive systems of internal control designed to provide reasonable assurance that assets are safeguarded and transactions are executed in accordance with established procedures. The concept of reasonable assurance is based upon recognition that the cost of the controls should not exceed the benefit derived. We believe our systems of internal control provide this reasonable assurance.

The Board of Directors exercised its oversight role with respect to the Corporation's systems of internal control primarily through its Audit Committee, which is comprised of independent directors. The Committee oversees the Corporation's systems of internal control, accounting practices, financial reporting and audits to assess whether their quality, integrity and objectivity are sufficient to protect shareholders' investments.

In addition, our consolidated financial statements have been audited by Ernst & Young LLP, independent registered public accounting firm, whose report also appears on this page.

Gregg W. Steinhafel
Chief Executive Officer and President
March 12, 2010

Douglas A. Scovanner
Executive Vice President and
Chief Financial Officer

Report of Independent Registered Public Accounting Firm on Consolidated Financial Statements

The Board of Directors and Shareholders
Target Corporation

We have audited the accompanying consolidated statements of financial position of Target Corporation and subsidiaries (the Corporation) as of January 30, 2010 and January 31, 2009, and the related consolidated statements of operations, cash flows, and shareholders' investment for each of the three years in the period ended January 30, 2010. Our audits also included the financial statement schedule listed in Item 15(a). These financial statements and schedule are the responsibility of the Corporation's management. Our responsibility is to express an opinion on these financial statements and schedule based on our audits.

We conducted our audits in accordance with the standards of the Public Company Accounting Oversight Board (United States). Those standards require that we plan and perform the audit to obtain reasonable assurance about whether the financial statements are free of material misstatement. An audit includes examining, on a test basis, evidence supporting the amounts and disclosures in the financial statements. An audit also includes assessing the accounting principles used and significant estimates made by management, as well as evaluating the overall financial statement presentation. We believe that our audits provide a reasonable basis for our opinion.

In our opinion, the financial statements referred to above present fairly, in all material respects, the consolidated financial position of Target Corporation and subsidiaries at January 30, 2010 and January 31, 2009, and the consolidated results of their operations and their cash flows for each of the three years in the period ended January 30, 2010, in conformity with U.S. generally accepted accounting principles. Also, in our opinion, the related financial statement schedule, when considered in relation to the basic financial statements taken as a whole, presents fairly in all material respects the information set forth therein.

We also have audited, in accordance with the standards of the Public Company Accounting Oversight Board (United States), the Corporation's internal control over financial reporting as of January 30, 2010, based on criteria established in *Internal Control—Integrated Framework*, issued by the Committee of Sponsoring Organizations of the Treadway Commission and our report dated March 12, 2010, expressed an unqualified opinion thereon.

Ernst & Young LLP

Minneapolis, Minnesota
March 12, 2010

Report of Management on Internal Control

Our management is responsible for establishing and maintaining adequate internal control over financial reporting, as such term is defined in Exchange Act Rules 13a–15(f). Under the supervision and with the participation of our management, including our chief executive officer and chief financial officer, we assessed the effectiveness of our internal control over financial reporting as of January 30, 2010, based on the framework in *Internal Control—Integrated Framework*, issued by the Committee of Sponsoring Organizations of the Treadway Commission. Based on our assessment, we conclude that the Corporation's internal control over financial reporting is effective based on those criteria.

Our internal control over financial reporting as of January 30, 2010, has been audited by Ernst & Young LLP, the independent registered accounting firm who has also audited our consolidated financial statements, as stated in their report which appears on this page.

Gregg W. Steinhafel
Chief Executive Officer and President
March 12, 2010

Douglas A. Scovanner
Executive Vice President and
Chief Financial Officer

Report of Independent Registered Public Accounting Firm on Internal Control over Financial Reporting

The Board of Directors and Shareholders
Target Corporation

We have audited Target Corporation and subsidiaries' (the Corporation) internal control over financial reporting as of January 30, 2010, based on criteria established in *Internal Control—Integrated Framework*, issued by the Committee of Sponsoring Organizations of the Treadway Commission (the COSO criteria). The Corporation's management is responsible for maintaining effective internal control over financial reporting, and for its assessment of the effectiveness of internal control over financial reporting included in the accompanying Report of Management on Internal Control over Financial Reporting. Our responsibility is to express an opinion on the Corporation's internal control over financial reporting based on our audit.

We conducted our audit in accordance with the standards of the Public Company Accounting Oversight Board (United States). Those standards require that we plan and perform the audit to obtain reasonable assurance about whether effective internal control over financial reporting was maintained in all material respects. Our audit included obtaining an understanding of internal control over financial reporting, assessing the risk that a material weakness exists, testing and evaluating the design and operating effectiveness of internal control based on the assessed risk, and performing such other procedures as we considered necessary in the circumstances. We believe that our audit provides a reasonable basis for our opinion.

A company's internal control over financial reporting is a process designed to provide reasonable assurance regarding the reliability of financial reporting and the preparation of financial statements for external purposes in accordance with generally accepted accounting principles. A company's internal control over financial reporting includes those policies and procedures that (1) pertain to the maintenance of records that, in reasonable detail, accurately and fairly reflect the transactions and dispositions of the assets of the company, (2) provide reasonable assurance that transactions are recorded as necessary to permit preparation of financial statements in accordance with generally accepted accounting principles and that receipts and expenditures of the company are being made only in accordance with authorizations of management and directors of the company, and (3) provide reasonable assurance regarding prevention or timely detection of unauthorized acquisition, use or disposition of the company's assets that could have a material effect on the financial statements.

Because of its inherent limitations, internal control over financial reporting may not prevent or detect misstatements. Also, projections of any evaluation of effectiveness to future periods are subject to the risk that controls may become inadequate because of changes in conditions or that the degree of compliance with the policies or procedures may deteriorate.

In our opinion, the Corporation maintained, in all material respects, effective internal control over financial reporting as of January 30, 2010, based on the COSO criteria.

We also have audited, in accordance with the standards of the Public Company Accounting Oversight Board (United States), the consolidated statements of financial position of Target Corporation and subsidiaries as of January 30, 2010 and January 31, 2009, and the related consolidated statements of operations, cash flows and shareholders' investment for each of the three years in the period ended January 30, 2010, and our report dated March 12, 2010, expressed an unqualified opinion thereon.

Ernst + Young LLP

Minneapolis, Minnesota
March 12, 2010

Consolidated Statements of Operations

(millions, except per share data)		2009		2008		2007
Sales	$	**63,435**	$	62,884	$	61,471
Credit card revenues		**1,922**		2,064		1,896
Total revenues		**65,357**		64,948		63,367
Cost of sales		**44,062**		44,157		42,929
Selling, general and administrative expenses		**13,078**		12,954		12,670
Credit card expenses		**1,521**		1,609		837
Depreciation and amortization		**2,023**		1,826		1,659
Earnings before interest expense and income taxes		**4,673**		4,402		5,272
Net interest expense						
Nonrecourse debt collateralized by credit card receivables		**97**		167		133
Other interest expense		**707**		727		535
Interest income		**(3)**		(28)		(21)
Net interest expense		**801**		866		647
Earnings before income taxes		**3,872**		3,536		4,625
Provision for income taxes		**1,384**		1,322		1,776
Net earnings	$	**2,488**	$	2,214	$	2,849
Basic earnings per share	$	**3.31**	$	2.87	$	3.37
Diluted earnings per share	$	**3.30**	$	2.86	$	3.33
Weighted average common shares outstanding						
Basic		**752.0**		770.4		845.4
Diluted		**754.8**		773.6		850.8

See accompanying Notes to Consolidated Financial Statements.

Consolidated Statements of Financial Position

(millions, except footnotes)		January 30, 2010		January 31, 2009
Assets				
Cash and cash equivalents, including marketable securities of **$1,617** and $302	$	2,200	$	864
Credit card receivables, net of allowance of **$1,016** and $1,010		6,966		8,084
Inventory		7,179		6,705
Other current assets		2,079		1,835
Total current assets		18,424		17,488
Property and equipment				
Land		5,793		5,767
Buildings and improvements		22,152		20,430
Fixtures and equipment		4,743		4,270
Computer hardware and software		2,575		2,586
Construction–in–progress		502		1,763
Accumulated depreciation		(10,485)		(9,060)
Property and equipment, net		25,280		25,756
Other noncurrent assets		829		862
Total assets	$	44,533	$	44,106
Liabilities and shareholders' investment				
Accounts payable	$	6,511	$	6,337
Accrued and other current liabilities		3,120		2,913
Unsecured debt and other borrowings		796		1,262
Nonrecourse debt collateralized by credit card receivables		900		—
Total current liabilities		11,327		10,512
Unsecured debt and other borrowings		10,643		12,000
Nonrecourse debt collateralized by credit card receivables		4,475		5,490
Deferred income taxes		835		455
Other noncurrent liabilities		1,906		1,937
Total noncurrent liabilities		17,859		19,882
Shareholders' investment				
Common stock		62		63
Additional paid–in–capital		2,919		2,762
Retained earnings		12,947		11,443
Accumulated other comprehensive loss		(581)		(556)
Total shareholders' investment		15,347		13,712
Total liabilities and shareholders' investment	$	44,533	$	44,106

Common Stock Authorized 6,000,000,000 shares, $0.0833 par value; **744,644,454** shares issued and outstanding at January 30, 2010; 752,712,464 shares issued and outstanding at January 31, 2009.

Preferred Stock Authorized 5,000,000 shares, $0.01 par value; no shares were issued or outstanding at January 30, 2010 or January 31, 2009.

See accompanying Notes to Consolidated Financial Statements.

Consolidated Statements of Cash Flows

(millions)	2009	2008	2007
Operating activities			
Net earnings	$ 2,488	$ 2,214	$ 2,849
Reconciliation to cash flow			
Depreciation and amortization	2,023	1,826	1,659
Share–based compensation expense	103	72	73
Deferred income taxes	364	91	(70)
Bad debt expense	1,185	1,251	481
Loss / impairment of property and equipment, net	97	33	28
Other non–cash items affecting earnings	103	222	52
Changes in operating accounts providing / (requiring) cash:			
Accounts receivable originated at Target	(57)	(458)	(602)
Inventory	(474)	77	(525)
Other current assets	(280)	(224)	(139)
Other noncurrent assets	(127)	(76)	101
Accounts payable	174	(389)	111
Accrued and other current liabilities	257	(230)	62
Other noncurrent liabilities	25	(139)	124
Other	—	160	(79)
Cash flow provided by operations	5,881	4,430	4,125
Investing activities			
Expenditures for property and equipment	(1,729)	(3,547)	(4,369)
Proceeds from disposal of property and equipment	33	39	95
Change in accounts receivable originated at third parties	(10)	(823)	(1,739)
Other investments	3	(42)	(182)
Cash flow required for investing activities	(1,703)	(4,373)	(6,195)
Financing activities			
Additions to short–term notes payable	—	—	1,000
Reductions of short–term notes payable	—	(500)	(500)
Additions to long–term debt	—	3,557	7,617
Reductions of long–term debt	(1,970)	(1,455)	(1,326)
Dividends paid	(496)	(465)	(442)
Repurchase of stock	(423)	(2,815)	(2,477)
Premiums on call options	—	—	(331)
Stock option exercises and related tax benefit	47	43	210
Other	—	(8)	(44)
Cash flow provided by / (required for) financing activities	(2,842)	(1,643)	3,707
Net increase / (decrease) in cash and cash equivalents	1,336	(1,586)	1,637
Cash and cash equivalents at beginning of year	864	2,450	813
Cash and cash equivalents at end of year	$ 2,200	$ 864	$ 2,450

Cash paid for income taxes was **$1,040,** $1,399, and $1,734 during 2009, 2008, and 2007, respectively. Cash paid for interest (net of interest capitalized) was **$805,** $873, and $633 during 2009, 2008, and 2007, respectively.

See accompanying Notes to Consolidated Financial Statements.

Consolidated Statements of Shareholders' Investment

(millions, except footnotes)	Common Stock Shares	Stock Par Value	Additional Paid–in Capital	Retained Earnings	Accumulated Other Comprehensive Income/(Loss)		Total
					Pension and Other Benefit Liability Adjustments	Derivative Instruments, Foreign Currency and Other	
February 3, 2007	859.8	$ 72	$ 2,387	$ 13,417	$ (247)	$ 4	$ 15,633
Net earnings	—	—	—	2,849	—	—	2,849
Other comprehensive income							
Pension and other benefit liability adjustments, net of taxes of $38	—	—	—	—	59	—	59
Unrealized losses on cash flow hedges, net of taxes of $31	—	—	—	—	—	(48)	(48)
Total comprehensive income							2,860
Cumulative effect of adopting new accounting pronouncements	—	—	—	(31)	54	—	23
Dividends declared	—	—	—	(454)	—	—	(454)
Repurchase of stock	(46.2)	(4)	—	(2,689)	—	—	(2,693)
Premiums on call options	—	—	—	(331)	—	—	(331)
Stock options and awards	5.1	—	269	—	—	—	269
February 2, 2008	818.7	$ 68	$ 2,656	$ 12,761	$ (134)	$ (44)	$ 15,307
Net earnings	—	—	—	2,214	—	—	2,214
Other comprehensive income							
Pension and other benefit liability adjustments, net of taxes of $242	—	—	—	—	(376)	—	(376)
Unrealized losses on cash flow hedges, net of taxes of $2	—	—	—	—	—	(2)	(2)
Total comprehensive income							1,836
Dividends declared	—	—	—	(471)	—	—	(471)
Repurchase of stock	(67.2)	(5)	—	(3,061)	—	—	(3,066)
Stock options and awards	1.2	—	106	—	—	—	106

January 31, 2009	752.7	$ 63	$ 2,762	$ 11,443	$	(510)	$		(46)	$ 13,712
Net earnings	—	—	—	2,488		—			—	2,488
Other comprehensive income										
Pension and other benefit liability adjustments, net of taxes of $17	—	—	—	—		(27)			—	(27)
Unrealized gains on cash flow hedges, net of taxes of $2	—	—	—	—		—			4	4
Currency translation adjustment, net of taxes of $0	—	—	—	—		—			(2)	(2)
Total comprehensive income										2,463
Dividends declared	—	—	—	(503)		—			—	(503)
Repurchase of stock	(9.9)	(1)	—	(481)		—			—	(482)
Stock options and awards	1.8	—	157	—		—			—	157
January 30, 2010	**744.6**	**$ 62**	**$ 2,919**	**$ 12,947**	$	**(537)**	$		**(44)**	**$ 15,347**

Dividends declared per share were $0.67, $0.62, and $0.54 in 2009, 2008, and 2007, respectively.

See accompanying Notes to Consolidated Financial Statements.

Notes to Consolidated Financial Statements

1. Summary of Accounting Policies

Organization Target Corporation (Target or the Corporation) operates two reportable segments: Retail and Credit Card. Our Retail Segment includes all of our merchandising operations, including our large–format general merchandise and food discount stores in the United States and our fully integrated online business. Our Credit Card Segment offers credit to qualified guests through our branded proprietary credit cards, the Target Visa and the Target Card (collectively, REDcards). Our Credit Card Segment strengthens the bond with our guests, drives incremental sales and contributes to our results of operations.

Consolidation The consolidated financial statements include the balances of the Corporation and its subsidiaries after elimination of intercompany balances and transactions. All material subsidiaries are wholly owned. We consolidate variable interest entities where it has been determined that the Corporation is the primary beneficiary of those entities' operations. The variable interest entity consolidated is a bankruptcy–remote subsidiary through which we sell certain accounts receivable as a method of providing funding for our accounts receivable.

Use of estimates The preparation of our consolidated financial statements in conformity with U.S. generally accepted accounting principles (GAAP) requires management to make estimates and assumptions affecting reported amounts in the consolidated financial statements and accompanying notes. Actual results may differ significantly from those estimates.

Fiscal year Our fiscal year ends on the Saturday nearest January 31. Unless otherwise stated, references to years in this report relate to fiscal years, rather than to calendar years. Fiscal year 2009 (2009) ended January 30, 2010 and consisted of 52 weeks. Fiscal year 2008 (2008) ended January 31, 2009 and consisted of 52 weeks. Fiscal year 2007 (2007) ended February 2, 2008 and consisted of 52 weeks.

Reclassifications Certain prior year amounts have been reclassified to conform to the current year presentation.

Accounting policies applicable to the items discussed in the Notes to the Consolidated Financial Statement are described in the respective notes.

2. Revenues

Our retail stores generally record revenue at the point of sale. Sales from our online business include shipping revenue and are recorded upon delivery to the guest. Total revenues do not include sales tax as we consider ourselves a pass through conduit for collecting and remitting sales taxes. Generally, guests may return merchandise within 90 days of purchase. Revenues are recognized net of expected returns, which we estimate using historical return patterns as a percentage of sales. Commissions earned on sales generated by leased departments are included within sales and were $18 million in 2009, $19 million in 2008, and $17 million in 2007.

Revenue from gift card sales is recognized upon gift card redemption. Our gift cards do not have expiration dates. Based on historical redemption rates, a small and relatively stable percentage of gift cards will never be redeemed, referred to as "breakage." Estimated breakage revenue is recognized over time in proportion to actual gift card redemptions and was immaterial in 2009, 2008, and 2007.

Credit card revenues are recognized according to the contractual provisions of each credit card agreement. When accounts are written off, uncollected finance charges and late fees are recorded as a reduction of credit card revenues. Target retail sales charged to our credit cards totaled $3,277 million, $3,883 million, and $4,139 million in 2009, 2008, and 2007, respectively. We offer new account discounts and rewards programs on our REDcard products. These discounts are redeemable only on purchases made at Target. The discounts associated with our REDcard products are included as reductions in sales in our Consolidated Statements of Operations and were $94 million in 2009, $114 million in 2008, and $110 million in 2007.

3. Cost of Sales and Selling, General and Administrative Expenses

The following table illustrates the primary costs classified in each major expense category:

Cost of Sales	**Selling, General and Administrative Expenses**
Total cost of products sold including • Freight expenses associated with moving merchandise from our vendors to our distribution centers and our retail stores, and among our distribution and retail facilities • Vendor income that is not reimbursement of specific, incremental and identifiable costs Inventory shrink Markdowns Outbound shipping and handling expenses associated with sales to our guests Terms cash discount Distribution center costs, including compensation and benefits costs	Compensation and benefit costs including • Stores • Headquarters Occupancy and operating costs of retail and headquarters facilities Advertising, offset by vendor income that is a reimbursement of specific, incremental and identifiable costs Preopening costs of stores and other facilities Other administrative costs

The classification of these expenses varies across the retail industry.

4. Consideration Received from Vendors

We receive consideration for a variety of vendor–sponsored programs, such as volume rebates, markdown allowances, promotions and advertising allowances and for our compliance programs, referred to as "vendor income." Vendor income reduces either our inventory costs or SG&A expenses based on the provisions of the arrangement. Promotional and advertising allowances are intended to offset our costs of promoting and selling merchandise in our stores. Under our compliance programs, vendors are charged for merchandise shipments that do not meet our requirements (violations), such as late or incomplete shipments. These allowances are recorded when violations occur. Substantially all consideration received is recorded as a reduction of cost of sales.

We establish a receivable for vendor income that is earned but not yet received. Based on provisions of the agreements in place, this receivable is computed by estimating the amount earned when we have completed our performance. We perform detailed analyses to determine the appropriate level of the receivable in the aggregate. The majority of year–end receivables associated with these activities are collected within the following fiscal quarter.

5. Advertising Costs

Advertising costs are expensed at first showing or distribution of the advertisement and were $1,167 million in 2009, $1,233 million in 2008, and $1,195 million in 2007. Advertising vendor income that offset advertising expenses was approximately $130 million, $143 million, and $123 million 2009, 2008, and 2007, respectively. Newspaper circulars and media broadcast made up the majority of our advertising costs in all three years.

6. Earnings per Share

Basic earnings per share (EPS) is net earnings divided by the weighted average number of common shares outstanding during the period. Diluted EPS includes the incremental shares assumed to be issued upon the exercise of stock options and the incremental shares assumed to be issued under performance share and restricted stock unit arrangements.

Earnings Per Share (millions, except per share data)	Basic EPS			Diluted EPS		
	2009	2008	2007	2009	2008	2007
Net earnings	$ 2,488	$ 2,214	$ 2,849	$ 2,488	$ 2,214	$ 2,849
Adjustment for prepaid forward contracts	—	—	—	—	—	(11)
Net earnings for EPS calculation	$ 2,488	$ 2,214	$ 2,849	$ 2,488	$ 2,214	$ 2,838
Basic weighted average common shares outstanding	752.0	770.4	845.4	752.0	770.4	845.4
Incremental stock options, performance share units and restricted stock units	—	—	—	2.8	3.2	6.0
Adjustment for prepaid forward contracts	—	—	—	—	—	(0.6)
Weighted average common shares outstanding	752.0	770.4	845.4	754.8	773.6	850.8
Earnings per share	$ 3.31	$ 2.87	$ 3.37	$ 3.30	$ 2.86	$ 3.33

For the 2009, 2008, and 2007 EPS computations, 16.8 million, 10.5 million, and 6.3 million stock options, respectively, were excluded from the calculation of weighted average shares for diluted EPS because their effects were antidilutive. Refer to Note 26 for a description of the prepaid forward contracts referred to in the table above.

7. Other Comprehensive Income/(Loss)

Other comprehensive income/(loss) includes revenues, expenses, gains and losses that are excluded from net earnings under GAAP and are recorded directly to shareholders' investment. In 2009, 2008, and 2007, other comprehensive income/(loss) included gains and losses on certain hedge transactions, foreign currency translation adjustments and amortization of pension and postretirement plan amounts, net of related taxes. Significant items affecting other comprehensive income/(loss) are shown in the Consolidated Statements of Shareholders' Investment.

8. Fair Value Measurements

Fair value is the price at which an asset could be exchanged in a current transaction between knowledgeable, willing parties. A liability's fair value is defined as the amount that would be paid to transfer the liability to a new obligor, not the amount that would be paid to settle the liability with the creditor. Fair value measurements are categorized into one of three levels based on the lowest level of significant input used: Level 1 (unadjusted quoted prices in active markets); Level 2 (observable market inputs available at the measurement date, other than quoted prices included in Level 1); and Level 3 (unobservable inputs that cannot be corroborated by observable market data).

The following table presents financial assets and liabilities measured at fair value on a recurring basis:

Fair Value Measurements – Recurring Basis	**Fair Value at January 30, 2010**			**Fair Value at January 31, 2009**		
(millions)	Level 1	Level 2	Level 3	Level 1	Level 2	Level 3
Assets						
Cash and cash equivalents						
Marketable securities	$ 1,617	$ —	$ —	$ 302	$ —	$ —
Other current assets						
Prepaid forward contracts	79	—	—	68	—	—
Equity swaps	—	—	—	1	—	—
Other noncurrent assets						
Interest rate swaps *(a)*	—	131	—	—	163	—
Company–owned life insurance investments *(b)*	—	305	—	—	296	—
Total	$ 1,696	$ 436	$ —	$ 371	$ 459	$ —
Liabilities						
Other noncurrent liabilities						
Interest rate swaps	$ —	$ 23	$ —	$ —	$ 30	$ —
Total	$ —	$ 23	$ —	$ —	$ 30	$ —

(a)

    There were no interest rate swaps designated as accounting hedges at January 30, 2010 or January 31, 2009.

(b)

    Company–owned life insurance investments consist of equity index funds and fixed income assets. Amounts are presented net of loans that are secured by some of these policies of $244 million at January 30, 2010 and $197 million at January 31, 2009.

Position	**Valuation Technique**
Marketable securities	Initially valued at transaction price. Carrying value of cash equivalents (including money market funds) approximates fair value because maturities are less than three months.
Prepaid forward contracts	Initially valued at transaction price. Subsequently valued by reference to the market price of Target common stock.
Interest rate swaps/forward and equity swaps	Valuation models are calibrated to initial trade price. Subsequent valuations are based on observable inputs to the valuation model (*e.g.*, interest rates and credit spreads). Model inputs are changed only when corroborated by market data. A credit risk adjustment is made on each swap using observable market credit spreads.
Company–owned life insurance investments	Includes investments in separate accounts that are valued based on market rates credited by the insurer.

Certain assets are measured at fair value on a nonrecurring basis; that is, the instruments are not measured at fair value on an ongoing basis but are subject to fair value adjustments only in certain circumstances (for example, when there is evidence of impairment). The fair value measurements related to long–lived assets held for sale and held and used in the following table were determined using available market prices at the measurement date based on recent investments or pending transactions of similar assets, third–party independent appraisals, valuation multiples or public comparables. We classify these measurements as Level 2. The fair value measurement of an intangible asset was determined using unobservable inputs that reflect our own assumptions regarding how market participants price the intangible assets at the measurement date. We classify these measurements as Level 3.

Fair Value Measurements – Nonrecurring Basis (millions)	Other current assets Long–lived assets held for sale *(a)*	Property and equipment Long–lived assets held and used *(b)*	Other noncurrent assets Intangible asset
For the year ended January 30, 2010:			
Carrying amount	74	98	6
Fair value measurement	57	66	—
Gain/(loss)	(17)	(32)	(6)

(a)

Reported measurement is fair value less cost to sell. Costs to sell were approximately $3 million at January 30, 2010.

(b)

Primarily relates to real estate and buildings intended for sale in the future but not currently meeting the held for sale criteria. Reported measurement is fair value less cost to sell. Costs to sell were approximately $3 million at January 30, 2010.

The following table presents the carrying amounts and estimated fair values of financial instruments not measured at fair value in the Consolidated Statements of Financial Position. The fair value of marketable securities is determined using available market prices at the reporting date. The fair value of debt is generally measured using a discounted cash flow analysis based on our current market interest rates for similar types of financial instruments.

Financial Instruments Not Measured at Fair Value

	January 30, 2010	
(millions)	Carrying Amount	Fair Value
Financial assets		
Other current assets		
Marketable securities *(a)*	$ 27	$ 27
Other noncurrent assets		
Marketable securities *(a)*	5	5
Total	$ 32	$ 32
Financial liabilities		
Total debt *(b)*	$ 16,447	$ 17,487
Total	$ 16,447	$ 17,487

(a)

Amounts include held–to–maturity government and money market investments that are held to satisfy the capital requirements of Target Bank and Target National Bank.

(b)

Represents the sum of nonrecourse debt collateralized by credit card receivables and unsecured debt and other borrowings excluding unamortized swap valuation adjustments and capital lease obligations.

The carrying amounts of credit card receivables, net of allowance, accounts payable, and certain accrued and other current liabilities approximate fair value at January 30, 2010.

9. Cash Equivalents

Cash equivalents include highly liquid investments with an original maturity of three months or less from the time of purchase. Cash equivalents also include amounts due from credit card transactions with settlement terms of less than five days. Receivables resulting from third–party credit card sales within our Retail Segment are included within cash equivalents and were $313 million and $323 million at January 30, 2010 and January 31, 2009, respectively. Payables resulting from the use of the Target Visa at third–party merchants are included within cash equivalents and were $40 million and $53 million at January 30, 2010 and January 31, 2009, respectively.

10. Credit Card Receivables

Credit card receivables are recorded net of an allowance for doubtful accounts. The allowance, recognized in an amount equal to the anticipated future write–offs of existing receivables, was $1,016 million at January 30, 2010 and $1,010 million at January 31, 2009. This allowance includes provisions for uncollectible finance charges and other credit–related fees. We estimate future write–offs based on historical experience of delinquencies, risk scores, aging trends, and industry risk trends. Substantially all accounts continue to accrue finance charges until they are written off. Total receivables past due ninety days or more and still accruing finance charges were $371 million at January 30, 2010 and $393 million at January 31, 2009. Accounts are written off when they become 180 days past due.

Under certain circumstances, we offer cardholder payment plans that modify finance charges and minimum payments, which meet the accounting definition of a troubled debt restructuring (TDRs). These concessions are made on an individual cardholder basis for economic or legal reasons specific to each individual cardholder's circumstances. As a percentage of period–end gross receivables, receivables classified as TDRs were 6.7 percent at January 30, 2010 and 4.9 percent at January 31, 2009. Receivables classified as TDRs are treated consistently with other aged receivables in determining our allowance for doubtful accounts.

As a method of providing funding for our credit card receivables, we sell on an ongoing basis all of our consumer credit card receivables to Target Receivables Corporation (TRC), a wholly owned, bankruptcy remote subsidiary. TRC then transfers the receivables to the Target Credit Card Master Trust (the Trust), which from time to time will sell debt securities to third parties either directly or through a related trust. These debt securities represent undivided interests in the Trust assets. TRC uses the proceeds from the sale of debt securities and its share of collections on the receivables to pay the purchase price of the receivables to the Corporation.

We consolidate the receivables within the Trust and any debt securities issued by the Trust, or a related trust, in our Consolidated Statements of Financial Position based upon the applicable accounting guidance. The receivables transferred to the Trust are not available to general creditors of the Corporation. The payments to the holders of the debt securities issued by the Trust or the related trust are made solely from the assets transferred to the Trust or the related trust and are nonrecourse to the general assets of the Corporation. Upon termination of the securitization program and repayment of all debt securities, any remaining assets could be distributed to the Corporation in a liquidation of TRC.

In the second quarter of 2008, we sold an interest in our credit card receivables to JPMC. The interest sold represented 47 percent of the receivables portfolio at the time of the transaction. This transaction was accounted for as a secured borrowing, and accordingly, the credit card receivables within the Trust and the note payable issued are reflected in our Consolidated Statements of Financial Position. Notwithstanding this accounting treatment, the accounts receivable assets that collateralize the note payable supply the cash flow to pay principal and interest to the note holder; the receivables are not available to general creditors of the Corporation; and the payments to JPMC are made solely from the Trust and are nonrecourse to the general assets of the Corporation. Interest and principal payments due on the note are satisfied provided the cash flows from the Trust assets are sufficient. If the cash flows are less than the periodic interest, the available amount, if any, is paid with respect to interest. Interest shortfalls will be paid to the extent subsequent cash flows from the assets in the Trust are sufficient. Future principal payments will be made from JPMC's prorata share of cash flows from the Trust assets.

In the event of a decrease in the receivables principal amount such that JPMC's interest in the entire portfolio would exceed 47 percent for three consecutive months, TRC (using the cash flows from the assets in the Trust) would be required to pay JPMC a prorata amount of principal collections such that the portion owned by JPMC would not exceed 47 percent, unless JPMC provides a waiver. Conversely, at the option of the Corporation, JPMC may be required to fund an increase in the portfolio to maintain their 47 percent interest up to a maximum JPMC principal balance of $4.2 billion. If a three–month average of monthly finance charge excess (JPMC's prorata share of finance charge collections less write–offs and specified expenses) is less than 2 percent of the outstanding principal balance of JPMC's interest, the Corporation must implement mutually agreed upon underwriting strategies. If the three–month average finance charge excess falls below 1 percent of the outstanding principal balance of JPMC's interest, JPMC may compel the Corporation to implement underwriting and collections activities, provided those activities are compatible with the Corporation's systems, as well as consistent with similar credit card receivable portfolios managed by JPMC. If the Corporation fails to implement the activities, JPMC would cause the accelerated repayment of the note payable issued in the transaction. As noted in the preceding paragraph, payments would be made solely from the Trust assets.

11. Inventory

Substantially all of our inventory and the related cost of sales are accounted for under the retail inventory accounting method (RIM) using the last–in, first–out (LIFO) method. Inventory is stated at the lower of LIFO cost or market. Cost includes purchase price as reduced by vendor income. Inventory is also reduced for estimated losses related to shrink and markdowns. The LIFO provision is calculated based on inventory levels, markup rates and internally measured retail price indices.

Under RIM, inventory cost and the resulting gross margins are calculated by applying a cost–to–retail ratio to the retail value inventory. RIM is an averaging method that has been widely used in the retail industry due to its practicality. The use of RIM will result in inventory being valued at the lower of cost or market because permanent markdowns are currently taken as a reduction of the retail value of inventory.

We routinely enter into arrangements with vendors whereby we do not purchase or pay for merchandise until the merchandise is ultimately sold to a guest. Revenues under this program are included in sales in the Consolidated Statements of Operations, but the merchandise received under the program is not included in inventory in our Consolidated Statements of Financial Position because of the virtually simultaneous purchase and sale of this inventory. Sales made under these arrangements totaled $1,820 million in 2009, $1,524 million in 2008, and $1,643 million in 2007.

12. Other Current Assets

Other Current Assets (millions)		January 30, 2010		January 31, 2009
Deferred taxes	$	724	$	693
Other receivables *(a)*		526		433
Vendor income receivable		390		236
Other		439		473
Total	$	2,079	$	1,835

(a)

    Includes pharmacy receivables and income taxes receivable.

13. Property and Equipment

Property and equipment are recorded at cost, less accumulated depreciation. Depreciation is computed using the straight–line method over estimated useful lives or lease term if shorter. We amortize leasehold improvements purchased after the beginning of the initial lease term over the shorter of the assets' useful lives or a term that includes the original lease term, plus any renewals that are reasonably assured at the date the leasehold improvements are acquired. Depreciation expense for 2009, 2008, and 2007 was $1,999 million, $1,804 million, and $1,644 million, respectively. For income tax purposes, accelerated depreciation methods are generally used. Repair and maintenance costs are expensed as incurred and were $632 million in 2009, $609 million in 2008, and $592 million in 2007. Facility preopening costs, including supplies and payroll, are expensed as incurred.

Estimated Useful Lives	Life (in years)
Buildings and improvements	8–39
Fixtures and equipment	3–15
Computer hardware and software	4–7

Long–lived assets are reviewed for impairment annually and also when events or changes in circumstances indicate that the asset's carrying value may not be recoverable. Impairments of $49 million in 2009, $2 million in 2008 and $7 million in 2007 were recorded as a result of the tests performed. Additionally, we wrote off $37 million in 2009, $26 million in 2008 and $4 million in 2007 of capitalized construction in progress costs due to project scope changes.

14. Other Noncurrent Assets

Other Noncurrent Assets (millions)		January 30, 2010		January 31, 2009
Cash surrender value of life insurance *(a)*	$	319	$	305
Goodwill and intangible assets		239		231
Interest rate swaps *(b)*		131		163
Other		140		163
Total	$	829	$	862

(a)

    Company–owned life insurance policies on approximately 4,000 team members who are designated highly compensated under the Internal Revenue Code and have given their consent to be insured.

(b)

    See Notes 8 and 20 for additional information relating to our interest rate swaps.

15. Goodwill and Intangible Assets

Goodwill and intangible assets are recorded within other noncurrent assets at cost less accumulated amortization. Goodwill totaled $59 million at January 30, 2010 and $60 million at January 31, 2009. Goodwill is not amortized; instead, it is tested at least annually or whenever an event or change in circumstances indicates the carrying value of the asset may not be recoverable. Discounted cash flow models are used in determining fair value for the purposes of the required annual impairment analysis. An impairment loss on a long–lived and identifiable intangible asset would be recognized when estimated undiscounted future cash flows from the operation and disposition of the asset are less than the asset carrying amount.

No material impairments related to goodwill and intangible assets were recorded in 2009, 2008, or 2007 as a result of the tests performed. Intangible assets by major classes were as follows:

Intangible Assets	Leasehold Acquisition Costs		Other (a)		Total	
(millions)	Jan. 30, 2010	Jan. 31, 2009	Jan. 30, 2010	Jan. 31, 2009	Jan. 30, 2010	Jan. 31, 2009
Gross asset	$ 197	$ 196	$ 150	$ 129	$ 347	$ 325
Accumulated amortization	(62)	(54)	(105)	(100)	(167)	(154)
Net intangible assets	$ 135	$ 142	$ 45	$ 29	$ 180	$ 171

(a)
Other intangible assets relate primarily to acquired trademarks and customer lists.

Amortization is computed on intangible assets with definite useful lives using the straight–line method over estimated useful lives that typically range from 9 to 39 years for leasehold acquisition costs and from 3 to 15 years for other intangible assets. Amortization expense for 2009, 2008, and 2007 was $24 million, $21 million, and $15 million, respectively.

Estimated Amortization Expense (millions)	2010	2011	2012	2013	2014
Amortization expense	$23	$18	$13	$11	$10

16. Accounts Payable

We reclassify book overdrafts to accounts payable at period end. Overdrafts reclassified to accounts payable were $539 million at January 30, 2010 and $606 million at January 31, 2009.

17. Accrued and Other Current Liabilities

Accrued and Other Current Liabilities (millions)	January 30, 2010	January 31, 2009
Wages and benefits	$ 959	$ 727
Taxes payable (a)	490	430
Gift card liability (b)	387	381
Straight–line rent accrual	185	167
Workers' compensation and general liability	163	176
Dividends payable	127	120
Interest payable	105	130
Construction in progress	72	182
Other	632	600
Total	$ 3,120	$ 2,913

(a)
Taxes payable consist of real estate, team member withholdings and sales tax liabilities.

(b)
Gift card liability represents the amount of gift cards that have been issued but have not been redeemed, net of estimated breakage.

18. Commitments and Contingencies

Purchase obligations, which include all legally binding contracts, such as firm commitments for inventory purchases, merchandise royalties, equipment purchases, marketing–related contracts, software acquisition/license commitments and service contracts, were approximately $2,016 million and $570 million at January 30, 2010 and January 31, 2009, respectively. We issue inventory purchase orders, which represent authorizations to purchase that are cancelable by their terms. We do not consider purchase orders to be firm inventory commitments. We also issue trade letters of credit in the ordinary course of business, which are not firm commitments as they are conditional on the purchase order not being cancelled. If we choose to cancel a purchase order, we may be obligated to reimburse the vendor for unrecoverable outlays incurred prior to cancellation under certain circumstances.

Trade letters of credit totaled $1,484 million and $1,359 million at January 30, 2010 and January 31, 2009, respectively, a portion of which are reflected in accounts payable. Standby letters of credit, relating primarily to

24. Share Repurchase

In November 2007, our Board of Directors approved a share repurchase program totaling $10 billion that replaced a prior program. In November 2008, we announced that, in light of our business outlook, we were temporarily suspending our open-market share repurchase program. In January 2010, we resumed open-market purchases of shares under this program.

Share repurchases for the last three years, repurchased primarily through open market transactions, were as follows:

Share Repurchases (millions, except per share data)	Total Number of Shares Purchased		Average Price Paid per Share		Total Investment
2007 – Under a prior program	19.7	$	60.72	$	1,197
2007 – Under the 2007 program	26.5		54.64		1,445
2008	67.2		50.49		3,395
2009	**9.9**		**48.54**		**479**
Total	**123.3**	$	**52.85**	$	**6,516**

Of the shares reacquired and included above, a portion was delivered upon settlement of prepaid forward contracts. The prepaid forward contracts settled in 2009 had a total cash investment of $56 million and an aggregate market value of $60 million at their respective settlement dates. The prepaid forward contracts settled in 2008 had a total cash investment of $249 million and an aggregate market value of $251 million at their respective settlement dates. The prepaid forward contracts settled in 2007 had a total cash investment of $165 million and an aggregate market value of $215 million at their respective settlement dates. These contracts are among the investment vehicles used to reduce our economic exposure related to our nonqualified deferred compensation plans. The details of our positions in prepaid forward contracts have been provided in Note 26.

Our share repurchases during 2008 included 30 million shares that were acquired through the exercise of call options.

Call Option Repurchase Details

Series	Number of Options Exercised	Exercise Date	(amounts per share)								Total Cost (millions)
			Premium (a)		Strike Price		Total				
Series I	10,000,000	April 2008	$	11.04	$	40.32	$	51.36	$		514
Series II	10,000,000	May 2008		10.87		39.31		50.18			502
Series III	10,000,000	June 2008		11.20		39.40		50.60			506
Total	**30,000,000**		$	**11.04**	$	**39.68**	$	**50.71**	$		**1,522**

(a)

Paid in January 2008.

25. Share-Based Compensation

We maintain a long-term incentive plan for key team members and nonemployee members of our Board of Directors. Our long-term incentive plan allows us to grant equity-based compensation awards, including stock options, stock appreciation rights, performance share unit awards, restricted stock unit awards, restricted stock awards or a combination of awards.

A majority of granted awards are nonqualified stock options that vest annually in equal amounts over a four-year period and expire no later than 10 years after the grant date. Options granted to the nonemployee members of our Board of Directors become exercisable after one year and have a 10-year term.

We have issued performance share unit awards annually since January 2003. These awards represent shares potentially issuable in the future; historically, awards have been issued based upon the attainment of compound annual growth rates in revenue and EPS over a three year performance period. Beginning with the March 2009 grant, issuance is based upon the attainment of compound annual EPS growth rate and domestic market share change relative to a retail peer group over a three-year performance period.

We regularly issue restricted stock units with three-year cliff vesting to select team members. We also regularly issue restricted stock units to our Board of Directors. The number of unissued common shares reserved for future grants under the share–based compensation plans was 21,450,009 at January 30, 2010 and 25,755,800 at January 31, 2009.

Share–Based Compensation Award Activity

(number of options and units in thousands)	Stock Options (a)							
	Total Outstanding			Exercisable			Performance Share Units (d)	Restricted Stock Units
	No. of Options	Exercise Price (b)	Intrinsic Value (c)	No. of Options	Exercise Price (b)	Intrinsic Value (c)		
February 3, 2007	27,910	$ 41.95	$ 558	17,659	$ 35.32	$ 470	1,895	221
Granted	5,725	49.54					650	21
Expired/forfeited	(434)	52.67					—	—
Exercised/issued	(5,061)	28.00					(370)	(4)
February 2, 2008	28,140	$ 45.84	$ 298	16,226	$ 41.07	$ 245	2,175	238
Granted	9,914	34.64					764	315
Expired/forfeited	(756)	51.28					(176)	(2)
Exercised/issued	(937)	33.36					(740)	(2)
January 31, 2009	36,361	$ 43.00	$ 4	19,292	$ 43.80	$ 4	2,023	549
Granted	5,127	49.08					826	224
Expired/forfeited	(1,507)	46.14					(662)	—
Exercised/issued	(1,767)	35.34					(14)	(203)
January 30, 2010	38,214	$ 44.05	$ 331	22,446	$ 44.59	$ 189	2,173 (e)	570

(a)
Includes Stock Appreciation Rights granted to certain non–U.S. team members.

(b)
Weighted average per share.

(c)
Represents stock price appreciation subsequent to the grant date, in millions.

(d)
Assumes attainment of maximum payout rates as set forth in the performance criteria.

(e)
Because the performance criteria were not met, approximately 644 thousand of these performance share units outstanding at January 30, 2010 were not earned and will be forfeited in the first quarter of 2010.

We used a Black–Scholes valuation model to estimate the fair value of the options at grant date based on the assumptions noted in the following table. Volatility represents an average of market estimates for implied volatility of 5.5–year options on Target common stock. The expected life is estimated based on an analysis of options already exercised and any foreseeable trends or changes in recipients' behavior. The risk–free interest rate is an interpolation of the relevant U.S. Treasury security maturities as of each applicable grant date. The assumptions disclosed below represent a weighted average of the assumptions used for all of our stock option grants throughout the years.

Valuation of Share–Based Compensation	2009	2008	2007
Stock options weighted average valuation assumptions:			
Dividend yield	1.4%	1.9%	1.1%
Volatility	31%	47%	39%
Risk–free interest rate	2.7%	1.5%	3.2%
Expected life in years	5.5	5.5	5.5
Stock options grant date weighted average fair value	$ 14.18	$ 12.87	$ 18.08
Performance share units grant date weighted average fair value	$ 27.18	$ 51.68	$ 59.45
Restricted stock units grant date weighted average fair value	$ 48.94	$ 34.78	$ 57.70

Total share–based compensation expense recognized in the Consolidated Statements of Operations was $103 million, $72 million, and $73 million in 2009, 2008, and 2007, respectively. The related income tax benefit was $40 million, $28 million, and $28 million in 2009, 2008, and 2007, respectively.

Stock Options Exercises (millions)	2009	2008	2007
Compensation expense realized	$ 21	$ 14	$ 187
Related income tax benefit	8	5	73
Net cash proceeds	62	31	142

At January 30, 2010, there was $147 million of total unrecognized compensation expense related to nonvested stock options, which is expected to be recognized over a weighted average period of 1.4 years.

The weighted average remaining life of currently exercisable options is 4.9 years, and the weighted average remaining life of all outstanding options is 8.8 years. The total fair value of options vested was $85 million, $69 million, and $55 million, in 2009, 2008, and 2007, respectively.

Compensation expense associated with outstanding performance share units is recorded over the life of the awards. The expense recorded each period is dependent upon our estimate of the number of shares that will ultimately be issued. Future compensation expense for currently outstanding awards could reach a maximum of $51 million assuming payout of all outstanding awards. There were no share based liabilities paid during 2009. The total share based liabilities paid were $15 million in 2008 and $18 million in 2007.

Total unrecognized compensation expense related to restricted stock unit awards was $16 million as of January 30, 2010.

26. Defined Contribution Plans

Team members who meet certain eligibility requirements can participate in a defined contribution 401(k) plan by investing up to 80 percent of their compensation, as limited by statute or regulation. Generally, we match 100 percent of each team member's contribution up to 5 percent of total compensation. Company match contributions are made to the fund designated by the participant.

In addition, we maintain nonqualified, unfunded deferred compensation plans for approximately 3,500 current and retired team members. These team members choose from a menu of crediting rate alternatives that are the same as the investment choices in our 401(k) plan, including Target common stock. We credit an additional 2 percent per year to the accounts of all active participants, excluding executive officer participants, in part to recognize the risks inherent to their participation in a plan of this nature. We also maintain a nonqualified, unfunded deferred compensation plan that was frozen during 1996, covering 11 active and 50 retired participants. In this plan deferred compensation earns returns tied to market levels of interest rates, plus an additional 6 percent return, with a minimum of 12 percent and a maximum of 20 percent, as determined by the plan's terms.

The American Jobs Creation Act of 2004 added Section 409A to the Internal Revenue Code, changing the federal income tax treatment of nonqualified deferred compensation arrangements. Failure to comply with the new requirements would result in early taxation of nonqualified deferred compensation arrangements, as well as a 20 percent penalty tax and additional interest payable to the IRS. In response to these new requirements, we allowed participants to elect to accelerate the distribution dates for their account balances. Participant elections resulted in payments of $29 million in 2009 and $86 million in 2008.

We control some of our risk of offering the nonqualified plans through investing in vehicles, including company–owned life insurance and prepaid forward contracts in our own common stock that offset a substantial portion of our economic exposure to the returns of these plans. These investment vehicles are general corporate assets and are marked to market with the related gains and losses recognized in the Consolidated Statements of Operations in the period they occur. The total change in fair value for contracts indexed to our own common stock recorded in earnings was pretax income/(loss) of $36 million in 2009, $(19) million in 2008, and $6 million in 2007. During 2009 and 2008, we invested approximately $34 million and $215 million, respectively, in such investment instruments, and these investments are included in the Consolidated Statements of Cash Flows within other investing activities. Adjusting our position in these investment vehicles may involve repurchasing shares of Target common stock when settling the forward contracts. In 2009, 2008, and 2007, these repurchases totaled 1.5 million, 4.7 million, and 3.4 million shares, respectively, and are included in the total share repurchases described in Note 24.

Prepaid Forward Contracts on Target Common Stock				
(millions, except per share data)	Number of Shares	Contractual Price Paid per Share	Fair Value	Total Cash Investment
January 31, 2009	2.2	$ 39.98	$ 68	$ 88
January 30, 2010	**1.5**	**$ 42.77**	**$ 79**	**$ 66**

The settlement dates of these instruments are regularly renegotiated with the counterparty.

Defined Contribution Plan Expenses (millions)	2009	2008	2007
401(k) Defined Contribution Plan			
Matching contributions expense	$ 178	$ 178	$ 172
Nonqualified Deferred Compensation Plans			
Benefits expense/(income)	$ 83	$ (80)	$ 46
Related investment loss/(income) (a)	(77)	83	(26)
Nonqualified plan net expense	$ 6	$ 3	$ 20

(a)

Investment loss/(income) includes changes in unrealized gains and losses on prepaid forward contracts and unrealized and realized gains and losses on company–owned life insurance policies.

27. Pension and Postretirement Health Care Plans

We have qualified defined benefit pension plans covering all U.S. team members who meet age and service requirements, including in certain circumstances, date of hire. We also have unfunded nonqualified pension plans for team members with qualified plan compensation restrictions. Eligibility for, and the level of, these benefits varies depending on team members' date of hire, length of service and/or team member compensation. Upon retirement, team members also become eligible for certain health care benefits if they meet minimum age and service requirements and agree to contribute a portion of the cost. Effective January 1, 2009, our qualified defined benefit pension plan was closed to new participants, with limited exceptions.

We recognize that our obligations to plan participants can only be met over time through a combination of company contributions to these plans and earnings on plan assets. In light of this concept and as a result of declines in the market value of plan assets in 2008 (which were only partially offset by increases in 2009), we elected to contribute $252 million to our qualified plans during 2009. This restored the qualified plans to a fully–funded status at year–end on an ABO (Accumulated Benefit Obligation) basis.

During 2009 we amended our postretirement health care plan, resulting in a $46 million reduction to our recorded liability, with a corresponding increase to shareholders' equity of $28 million, net of taxes of $18 million. The financial benefits of this amendment will be recognized though a reduction of benefit plan expense over the next 6 years.

The following tables provide a summary of the changes in the benefit obligations, fair value of plan assets, and funded status and amounts recognized in our Consolidated Statement of Financial Position for our postretirement benefit plans:

Change in Projected Benefit Obligation	Pension Benefits				Postretirement Health Care Benefits	
	Qualified Plans		Nonqualified Plans			
(millions)	2009	2008	2009	2008	2009	2008
Benefit obligation at beginning of measurement period	$1,948	$1,811	$36	$33	$117	$108
Service cost	99	93	1	1	7	5
Interest cost	123	114	2	2	6	7
Actuarial (gain)/loss	155	21	(3)	4	33	10
Participant contributions	1	—	—	—	6	6
Benefits paid	(99)	(94)	(3)	(4)	(18)	(19)
Plan amendments	—	3	—	—	(64)	—
Benefit obligation at end of measurement period	$2,227	$1,948	$33	$36	$87	$117

Change in Plan Assets	Pension Benefits				Postretirement Health Care Benefits	
	Qualified Plans		Nonqualified Plans			
(millions)	2009	2008	2009	2008	2009	2008
Fair value of plan assets at beginning of measurement period	$ 1,771	$ 2,192	$ —	$ —	$ —	$ —
Actual return on plan assets	232	(430)	—	—	—	—
Employer contributions	252	103	3	4	12	13
Participant contributions	1	—	—	—	6	6
Benefits paid	(99)	(94)	(3)	(4)	(18)	(19)
Fair value of plan assets at end of measurement period	2,157	1,771	—	—	—	—
Benefit obligation at end of measurement period	2,227	1,948	33	36	87	117
Funded status	$ (70)	$ (177)	$ (33)	$ (36)	$ (87)	$ (117)

Amounts recognized in the Consolidated Statements of Financial Position consist of the following:

Recognition of Funded/(Underfunded) Status	Qualified Plans		Nonqualified Plans (a)	
(millions)	2009	2008	2009	2008
Other noncurrent assets	$ 2	$ 1	$ —	$ —
Accrued and other current liabilities	(1)	(1)	(13)	(13)
Other noncurrent liabilities	(71)	(177)	(107)	(140)
Net amounts recognized	$ (70)	$ (177)	$ (120)	$ (153)

(a)
    Includes postretirement health care benefits.

The following table summarizes the amounts recorded in accumulated other comprehensive income, which have not yet been recognized as a component of net periodic benefit expense:

Amounts in Accumulated Other Comprehensive Income	Pension Plans		Postretirement Health Care Plans	
(millions)	2009	2008	2009	2008
Net actuarial loss	$ 900	$ 828	$ 50	$ 19
Prior service credits	(5)	(7)	(62)	—
Amounts in accumulated other comprehensive income	$ 895	$ 821	$ (12)	$ 19

The following table summarizes the changes in accumulated other comprehensive income for the years ended January 30, 2010 and January 31, 2009, related to our pension and postretirement health care plans:

Change in Accumulated Other Comprehensive Income	Pension Benefits		Postretirement Health Care Benefits	
(millions)	Pretax	Net of tax	Pretax	Net of tax
February 2, 2008	$ 212	$ 129	$ 9	$ 5
Net actuarial loss	618	376	10	6
Amortization of net actuarial losses	(16)	(10)	—	—
Amortization of prior service costs and transition	7	4	—	—
January 31, 2009	$ 821	$ 499	$ 19	$ 11
Net actuarial loss	96	58	33	20
Amortization of net actuarial losses	(24)	(14)	(2)	(1)
Amortization of prior service costs and transition	2	1	2	1
Plan amendments	—	—	(64)	(38)
January 30, 2010	$ **895**	$ **544**	$ **(12)**	**(7)**

The following table summarizes the amounts in accumulated other comprehensive income expected to be amortized and recognized as a component of net periodic benefit expense in 2010:

Expected Amortization of Amounts in Accumulated Other Comprehensive Income (millions)	Pretax	Net of tax
Net actuarial loss	$ 49	$ 30
Prior service credits	(13)	(8)
Total amortization expense	$ **36**	$ **22**

The following table summarizes our net pension and postretirement health care benefits expense for the years 2009, 2008, and 2007:

Net Pension and Postretirement Health Care Benefits Expense (millions)	Pension Benefits			Postretirement Health Care Benefits		
	2009	2008	2007	2009	2008	2007
Service cost benefits earned during the period	$ 100	$ 94	$ 97	$ 7	$ 5	$ 4
Interest cost on projected benefit obligation	125	116	105	6	7	7
Expected return on assets	(177)	(162)	(152)	—	—	—
Amortization of losses	24	16	38	2	—	1
Amortization of prior service cost	(2)	(4)	(4)	(2)	—	—
Total	$ **70**	$ 60	$ 84	$ **13**	$ 12	$ 12

Prior service cost amortization is determined using the straight–line method over the average remaining service period of team members expected to receive benefits under the plan.

Defined Benefit Pension Plan Information (millions)	2009	2008
Accumulated benefit obligation (ABO) for all plans *(a)*	$ 2,118	$ 1,812
Projected benefit obligation for pension plans with an ABO in excess of plan assets *(b)*	48	1,979
Total ABO for pension plans with an ABO in excess of plan assets	42	1,808
Fair value of plan assets for pension plans with an ABO in excess of plan assets	—	1,765

(a)

The present value of benefits earned to date assuming no future salary growth.

(b)

The present value of benefits earned to date by plan participants, including the effect of assumed future salary increases.

Assumptions

Weighted average assumptions used to determine benefit obligations as of the measurement date were as follows:

Weighted Average Assumptions	Pension Benefits		Postretirement Health Care Benefits	
	2009	2008	2009	2008
Discount rate	5.85%	6.50%	4.85%	6.50%
Average assumed rate of compensation increase	4.00%	4.25%	n/a	n/a

Weighted average assumptions used to determine net periodic benefit expense for each fiscal year were as follows:

Weighted Average Assumptions	Pension Benefits			Postretirement Health Care Benefits		
	2009	**2008**	**2007**	**2009**	**2008**	**2007**
Discount rate	**6.50%**	6.45%	5.95%	**6.50%** *(a)*	6.45%	5.95%
Expected long–term rate of return on plan assets	**8.00%**	8.00%	8.00%	**n/a**	n/a	n/a
Average assumed rate of compensation increase	**4.25%**	4.25%	4.25%	**n/a**	n/a	n/a

(a)

Due to the remeasurement from the plan amendment in the third quarter of 2009, the discount rate was decreased from 6.50 percent to 4.85 percent.

The discount rate used to measure net periodic benefit expense each year is the rate as of the beginning of the year (*i.e.*, the prior measurement date). With an essentially stable asset allocation over the following time periods, our annualized rate of return on qualified plans' assets has averaged 4.6 percent, 4.5 percent and 8.9 percent for the 5–year, 10–year and 15–year periods, respectively, ended January 30, 2010.

The expected Market–Related Value of Assets ("MRV") is determined each year by adjusting the previous year's value by expected return, benefit payments, and cash contributions. The expected MRV is adjusted for asset gains and losses in equal 20 percent adjustments over a 5–year period.

Our expected annualized long–term rate of return assumptions as of January 30, 2010 were 8.5 percent for domestic and international equity securities, 5.5 percent for long–duration debt securities, 8.5 percent for balanced funds, and 10.0 percent for other investments. Balanced funds primarily invest in equities, nominal and inflation–linked fixed income securities, commodities, and public real estate. They seek to generate capital market returns while reducing market risk by investing globally in highly diversified portfolios of public securities. These estimates are a judgmental matter in which we consider the composition of our asset portfolio, our historical long–term investment performance and current market conditions. We review the expected long–term rate of return on an annual basis, and revise it accordingly. Additionally, we monitor the mix of investments in our portfolio to ensure alignment with our long–term strategy to manage pension cost and reduce volatility in our assets.

An increase in the cost of covered health care benefits of 7.5 percent for non–Medicare eligible individuals and 8.5 percent for Medicare eligible individuals was assumed for 2009. In 2010, the rate is assumed to be 7.5 percent for non–Medicare eligible individuals and 7.5 percent for Medicare eligible individuals. Both rates will be reduced to 5.0 percent in 2019 and thereafter.

A one percent change in assumed health care cost trend rates would have the following effects at January 30, 2010:

Health Care Cost Trend Rates – 1% Change (millions)	1% Increase	1% Decrease
Effect on total of service and interest cost components of net periodic postretirement health care benefit expense	$ 1	$ (1)
Effect on the health care component of the accumulated postretirement benefit obligation	$ 5	$ (5)

Plan Assets

The plan's asset allocation policy is designed to reduce the long–term cost of funding our pension obligations. The plan invests with both passive and active investment managers depending on the investment's asset class. The plan also seeks to reduce the risk associated with adverse movements in interest rates by employing an interest rate hedging program, which may include the use of interest rate swaps, total return swaps, and other instruments.

Our pension plan weighted average asset allocations at the measurement date by asset category were as follows:

Asset Category	Current targeted allocation	Actual allocation 2009	2008
Domestic equity securities *(a)*	20%	19%	25%
International equity securities	11	10	13
Debt securities	25	28	27
Balanced funds	30	19	5
Other *(b)*	14	24	30
Total	100%	100%	100%

(a)

Equity securities include our common stock in amounts substantially less than 1 percent of total plan assets as of January 30, 2010 and January 31, 2009.

(b)

Other assets include private equity, mezzanine and distressed debt, timber−related assets, and a 4 percent allocation to real estate.

The fair values of our pension plan assets as of the measurement date, by asset category are as follows:

Fair Value at January 30, 2010 (millions)	Total	Level 1	Level 2	Level 3
Cash and cash equivalents	$ 206	$ 206	$ —	$ —
Equity securities *(a)*	490	26	464	—
Fixed income *(b)*	588	—	588	—
Balanced funds	404	—	404	—
Other *(c)*	469	—	14	455
Total	$ 2,157	$ 232	$ 1,470	$ 455

(a)

This category includes investments in US small, mid, and large cap companies as well as common collective funds that represent passively managed index funds with holdings in domestic and international equities.

(b)

This category primarily consists of investments in government securities, corporate bonds, mortgage−backed securities and passively managed index funds with holdings in long−term government and corporate bonds.

(c)

This category invests primarily in private equity funds (including venture capital, mezzanine and high yield debt, natural resources, and timberland), multi−strategy hedge funds (including domestic and international equity securities, convertible bonds and other alternative investments), and real estate.

Level 3 Reconciliation		Actual return on plan assets *(a)*				
(millions)	Balance at February 1, 2009	Relating to assets still held at the reporting date	Relating to assets sold during the period	Purchases, sales and settlements	Transfers in and/or out of Level 3	Balance at January 30, 2010
Other	$ 448	$ (1)	$ 1	$ 7	$ —	$ 455

(a)

Represents realized and unrealized gains (losses) from changes in values of those financial instruments only for the period in which the instruments were classified as Level 3.

Position	Valuation Technique
Cash and cash equivalents	Initially valued at transaction price. Carrying value of cash equivalents (including money market funds) approximates fair value because maturities are generally less than three months.
Equity securities	Valued at the closing price reported on the major market on which the individual securities are traded.
Common collective funds/balanced funds/certain multi–strategy hedge funds	Valued using the net asset value ("NAV") provided by the administrator of the fund. The NAV is a quoted transactional price for participants in the fund, which do not represent an active market.
Fixed income securities	Valued using matrix pricing models and quoted prices of securities with similar characteristics.
Private equity/real estate/certain multi–strategy hedge funds	Valued by deriving Target's proportionate share of equity investment from audited financial statements. Private equity and real estate investments require significant judgment on the part of the fund manager due to the absence of quoted market prices, inherent lack of liquidity, and the long–term nature of such investments. Certain multi–strategy hedge funds represent funds of funds that include liquidity restrictions and for which timely valuation information is not available.

Contributions

In 2009, we made discretionary contributions of $252 million to our qualified defined benefit pension plans. We are not required to make any contributions in 2010, although we may choose to make discretionary contributions of up to $100 million. We expect to make contributions in the range of $10 million to $15 million to our postretirement health care benefit plan in 2010.

Estimated Future Benefit Payments

Benefit payments by the plans, which reflect expected future service as appropriate, are expected to be paid as follows:

Estimated Future Benefit Payments (millions)		Pension Benefits		Postretirement Health Care Benefits
2010	$	122	$	10
2011		131		9
2012		138		7
2013		145		8
2014		155		8
2015–2019		895		60

28. Segment Reporting

Our measure of profit for each segment is a measure that management considers analytically useful in measuring the return we are achieving on our investment.

Business Segment Results (millions)	2009			2008			2007		
	Retail	Credit Card	Total	Retail	Credit Card	Total	Retail	Credit Card	Total
Sales/Credit card revenues	$ 63,435 $	1,922 $	65,357 $	62,884 $	2,064 $	64,948 $	61,471 $	1,896 $	63,367
Cost of sales	44,062	—	44,062	44,157	—	44,157	42,929	—	42,929
Bad debt expense (a)	—	1,185	1,185	—	1,251	1,251	—	481	481
Selling, general and administrative/ Operations and marketing expenses (a) (b)	12,989	425	13,414	12,838	474	13,312	12,557	469	13,026
Depreciation and amortization	2,008	14	2,023	1,808	17	1,826	1,643	16	1,659
Earnings before interest expense and income taxes	4,376	298	4,673	4,081	322	4,402	4,342	930	5,272
Interest expense on nonrecourse debt collateralized by credit card receivables	—	97	97	—	167	167	—	133	133
Segment profit	$ 4,376 $	201 $	4,576 $	4,081 $	155 $	4,236 $	4,342 $	797 $	5,139
Unallocated (income)/expense:									
Other interest expense			707			727			535
Interest income			(3)			(28)			(21)
Earnings before income taxes			$ 3,872			$ 3,536			$ 4,625

(a)

The combination of bad debt expense and operations and marketing expenses within the Credit Card Segment represent credit card expenses on the Consolidated Statements of Operations.

(b)

New account and loyalty rewards redeemed by our guests reduce reported sales. Our Retail Segment charges the cost of these discounts to our Credit Card Segment, and the reimbursements of $89 million in 2009, $117 million in 2008, and $114 million in 2007 are recorded as a reduction to SG&A expenses within the Retail Segment and an increase to operations and marketing expenses within the Credit Card Segment.

Note: The sum of the segment amounts may not equal the total amounts due to rounding.

Total Assets by Business Segment (millions)	2009			2008		
	Retail	Credit Card	Total	Retail	Credit Card	Total
Total assets	$ 37,200 $	7,333 $	44,533 $	35,651 $	8,455 $	44,106

Substantially all of our revenues are generated in, and long–lived assets are located in, the United States.

29. Quarterly Results (Unaudited)

Due to the seasonal nature of our business, fourth quarter operating results typically represent a substantially larger share of total year revenues and earnings because they include our peak sales period from Thanksgiving through the end of December. We follow the same accounting policies for preparing quarterly and annual financial data. The table below summarizes quarterly results for 2009 and 2008:

Quarterly Results	First Quarter		Second Quarter		Third Quarter		Fourth Quarter		Total Year	
(millions, except per share data)	2009	2008	2009	2008	2009	2008	2009	2008	2009	2008
Total revenues	$ 14,833 $	14,802 $	15,067 $	15,472 $	15,276 $	15,114 $	20,181 $	19,560 $	65,357 $	64,948
Earnings before income taxes	824	957	957	1,003	683	633	1,409	943	3,872	3,536
Net earnings	522	602	594	634	436	369	936	609	2,488	2,214
Basic earnings per share	0.69	0.75	0.79	0.82	0.58	0.49	1.25	0.81	3.31	2.87
Diluted earnings per share	0.69	0.74	0.79	0.82	0.58	0.49	1.24	0.81	3.30	2.86
Dividends declared per share	0.16	0.14	0.17	0.16	0.17	0.16	0.17	0.16	0.67	0.62
Closing common stock price										
High	41.26	54.89	43.79	55.10	51.35	57.89	52.02	41.35	52.02	57.89
Low	25.37	48.50	36.75	43.68	41.38	32.69	45.30	26.96	25.37	26.96

Note: Per share amounts are computed independently for each of the quarters presented. The sum of the quarters may not equal the total year amount due to the impact of changes in average quarterly shares outstanding and all other quarterly amounts may not equal the total year due to rounding.

The Double-Entry Accounting System

INTRODUCTION

*To prepare financial statements, a company must have a system that captures the vast numbers of business transactions in which it engages each year. The most widely used system, **double-entry accounting**, is so effective it has been in use for hundreds of years! This Appendix explains the rules for recording transactions using double-entry accounting.*

DEBIT/CREDIT TERMINOLOGY

An account form known as a **T-account** is a good starting point for learning double-entry recording procedures. A T-account looks like the letter "T" drawn on a piece of paper. The account title is written across the top of the horizontal bar of the T. The left side of the vertical bar is the **debit** side, and the right side is the **credit** side. An account has been *debited* when an amount is written on the left side and *credited* when an amount is written on the right side. For any given account, the difference between the total debit and credit amounts is the **account balance.**

The rules for using debits and credits to record transactions in T-accounts are as follows.

				Claims				
Assets		=	**Liabilities**		+	**Equity**		
Debit	Credit		Debit	Credit		Debit	Credit	
+	−		−	+		−	+	

Notice that a debit can represent an increase or a decrease. Likewise, a credit can represent an increase or a decrease. Whether a debit or credit is an increase or a decrease depends on the type of account (asset, liability, or stockholders' equity) in question. The rules of debits and credits are summarized as follows.

1. Debits increase asset accounts; credits decrease asset accounts.
2. Debits decrease liability and stockholders' equity accounts; credits increase liability and stockholders' equity accounts.

We now demonstrate the use of debits and credits in the double-entry accounting system.

The General Journal

Businesses find it impractical to record every individual transaction directly into accounts. Imagine the number of cash transactions a grocery store has each day. To simplify recordkeeping, businesses rely on **source documents** such as cash register tapes as the basis for entering transaction data into the accounting system. Other source documents include invoices, time cards, check stubs, and deposit tickets.

Accountants further simplify recordkeeping by initially recording data from source documents into **journals.** Journals provide a chronological record of business transactions. *Transactions are recorded in journals before they are entered into ledger accounts.* Journals are therefore **books of original entry.** Companies may use different **special journals** to record specific types of recurring transactions. For example, a company may use one special journal to record sales on account, another to record purchases on account, a third to record cash receipts, and a fourth to record cash payments. Transactions that do not fall into any of these categories are recorded in the **general journal.** Although special journals can be useful, companies can keep records without them by recording all transactions in the general journal. For simplicity, this appendix illustrates a general journal only.

At a minimum, the general journal shows the dates, the account titles, and the amounts of each transaction. The date is recorded in the first column, followed by the title of the account to be debited. The title of the account to be credited is indented and written on the line directly below the account to be debited. The dollar amount of the transaction is recorded in the Debit and Credit columns. For example, providing services for $1,000 cash on August 1 would be recorded in general journal format as follows:

Date	Account Title	Debit	Credit
Aug. 1	Cash	1,000	
	Service Revenue		1,000

THE GENERAL LEDGER

The collection of all the accounts used by a particular business is called the **general ledger.** In a manual system, the ledger could be a book with pages for each account where entries are recorded by hand. In more sophisticated systems, the general ledger is maintained in electronic form. Data is entered into electronic ledgers using computer keyboards or scanners. Companies typically assign each ledger account a name and a number. A list of all ledger accounts and their account numbers is called the **chart of accounts.** As previously stated, accounting data are first recorded in journals. The data are then transferred to the ledger accounts through a process called **posting.** The posting process for the August 1, $1,000 revenue transaction is shown below.

Date	Account Title	Debit	Credit
Aug. 1	Cash	1,000	
	Service Revenue		1,000

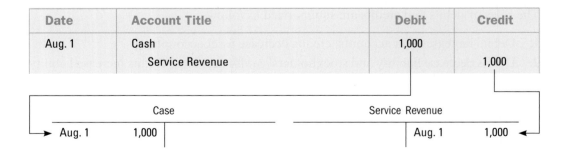

Case		Service Revenue	
Aug. 1	1,000	Aug. 1	1,000

ILLUSTRATION OF RECORDING PROCEDURES

We use the following transactions data to illustrate the process of recording transactions into a general journal and then posting them into a general ledger. The transactions data

EXHIBIT A.1

Event No.	Account Title	Debit	Credit
1	Cash	28,000	
	Common Stock		28,000
2	Supplies	1,100	
	Accounts Payable		1,100
3	Prepaid Rent	12,000	
	Cash		12,000
4	Accounts Receivable	23,000	
	Consulting Revenue		23,000
5	General Operating Expenses	16,000	
	Accounts Payable		16,000
6	Cash	20,000	
	Accounts Receivable		20,000
7	Accounts Payable	13,000	
	Cash		13,000
8	Dividends	1,000	
	Cash		1,000
9	Rent Expense	900	
	Supplies		900
10	Rent Expense	3,000	
	Prepaid Rent		3,000
11	Salaries Expense	1,200	
	Salaries Payable		1,200

applies to the Mestro Financial Services Company. The journal entries are shown in Exhibit A.1. The general ledger after posting is shown in Exhibit A.2.

1. Acquired $28,000 cash by issuing common stock on January 1, 2009.
2. Purchased $1,100 of supplies on account.
3. Paid $12,000 cash in advance for a one-year lease on office space.
4. Earned $23,000 of consulting revenue on account.
5. Incurred $16,000 of general operating expenses on account.
6. Collected $20,000 cash from receivables.
7. Paid $13,000 cash on accounts payable.
8. Paid a $1,000 cash dividend to stockholders.

Information for Adjusting Entries

9. There was $200 of supplies on hand at the end of the accounting period.
10. The one-year lease on the office space was effective beginning on October 1, 2009.
11. There was $1,200 of accrued salaries at the end of 2009.

EXHIBIT A.2

MESTRO FINANCIAL SERVICES COMPANY
T-Accounts, 2009

| Assets | | = | Liabilities | | + | Equity | |

Cash

1.	28,000	3.	12,000		
6.	20,000	7.	13,000		
		8.	1,000		
Bal.	22,000				

Accounts Receivable

4.	23,000	6.	20,000
Bal.	3,000		

Supplies

2.	1,100	9.	900
Bal.	200		

Prepaid Rent

3.	12,000	10.	3,000
Bal.	9,000		

Accounts Payable

7.	13,000	2.	1,100
		5.	16,000
		Bal.	4,100

Salaries Payable

	11.	1,200
	Bal.	1,200

Common Stock

	1.	28,000
	Bal.	28,000

Dividends

8.	1,000

Consulting Revenue

	4.	23,000

General Operating Expenses

5.	16,000

Salaries Expense

11.	1,200

Supplies Expense

9.	900

Rent Expense

10.	3,000

Trial Balance

To test accuracy, accountants regularly prepare an internal accounting schedule called a **trial balance.** A trial balance lists every ledger account and its balance. Debit balances are listed in one column and credit balances are listed in an adjacent column. The columns are totaled and the totals are compared. Exhibit A.3 displays the trial balance for Mestro Financial Services Company after the adjusting entries have been posted to the ledger.

If the debit total does not equal the credit total, the accountant knows to search for an error. Even if the totals are equal, however, there may be errors in the accounting records. For example, equal trial balance totals would not disclose errors like the following: failure to record transactions; misclassifications, such as debiting the wrong account; or incorrectly recording the amount of a transaction, such as recording a $200 transaction as $2,000. Equal debits and credits in a trial balance provide evidence rather than proof of accuracy.

Financial Statements

Supplemented with details from the Cash and Common Stock ledger accounts, the trial balance (Exhibit A.3) provides the information to prepare the financial statements shown in Exhibit A.4.

EXHIBIT A.3

MESTRO FINANCIAL SERVICES COMPANY
Trial Balance
December 31, 2009

Account Titles	Debit	Credit
Cash	$22,000	
Accounts receivable	3,000	
Supplies	200	
Prepaid rent	9,000	
Accounts payable		$ 4,100
Salaries payable		1,200
Common stock		28,000
Dividends	1,000	
Consulting revenue		23,000
General operating expenses	16,000	
Salaries expense	1,200	
Supplies expense	900	
Rent expense	3,000	
Totals	$56,300	$56,300

EXHIBIT A.4

MESTRO FINANCIAL SERVICES COMPANY
Financial Statements
For 2009

Income Statement
For the Year Ended December 31, 2009

Consulting revenue		$23,000
Expenses		
General operating expenses	$16,000	
Salaries expense	1,200	
Supplies expense	900	
Rent expense	3,000	
Total expenses		(21,100)
Net income		$ 1,900

Statement of Changes in Stockholders' Equity
For the Year Ended December 31, 2009

Beginning common stock	$ 0	
Plus: Common stock issued	28,000	
Ending common stock		$28,000
Beginning retained earnings	0	
Plus: Net income	1,900	
Less: Dividends	(1,000)	
Ending retained earnings		900
Total stockholders' equity		$28,900

continued

Balance Sheet As of December 31, 2009		
Assets		
Cash	$22,000	
Accounts receivable	3,000	
Supplies	200	
Prepaid rent	9,000	
Total assets		$34,200
Liabilities		
Accounts payable	$ 4,100	
Salaries payable	1,200	
Total liabilities		$ 5,300
Stockholders' equity		
Common stock	28,000	
Retained earnings	900	
Total stockholders' equity		28,900
Total liabilities and stockholders' equity		$34,200

Statement of Cash Flows For the Year Ended December 31, 2009		
Cash flows from operating activities		
Inflow from customers	$20,000	
Outflow for expenses	(25,000)	
Net cash flow for operating activities		$(5,000)
Cash flows from investing activities		0
Cash flows from financing activities		
Inflow from issue of common stock	28,000	
Outflow for dividends	(1,000)	
Net cash flow from financing activities		27,000
Net change in cash		22,000
Plus: Beginning cash balance		0
Ending cash balance		$22,000

KEY TERMS

Account balance 661	Double-entry	Posting 662
Books of original entry 662	accounting 661	Source documents 661
Chart of accounts 662	General journal 662	Special journals 662
Credit 661	General ledger 662	T-account 661
Debit 661	Journals 662	Trial balance 664

EXERCISES

Appendix 1-1 *Debit/credit terminology*

Required

For each of the following independent events, identify the account that would be debited and the account that would be credited. The accounts for the first event are identified as an example.

Event	Account Debited	Account Credited
a	Cash	Common Stock

a. Received cash by issuing common stock.

b. Received cash for services to be performed in the future.

c. Provided services on account.

d. Paid accounts payable.

e. Paid cash in advance for one year's rent.

f. Paid cash for operating expenses.

g. Paid salaries payable.

h. Purchased supplies on account.

i. Paid cash dividends to the stockholders.

j. Recognized revenue for services completed; previously collected the cash in Event *b*.

k. Received cash in payment of accounts receivable.

l. Paid salaries expense.

m. Recognized expense for prepaid rent that had been used up by the end of the accounting period.

Appendix 1-2   *Recording transactions in general journal and T-accounts*

The following events apply to Pearson Service Co. for 2009, its first year of operation.

1. Received cash of $50,000 from the issue of common stock.

2. Performed $90,000 worth of services on account.

3. Paid $64,000 cash for salaries expense.

4. Purchased supplies for $12,000 on account.

5. Collected $78,000 of accounts receivable.

6. Paid $8,500 of the accounts payable.

7. Paid a $5,000 dividend to the stockholders.

8. Had $1,500 of supplies on hand at the end of the period.

Required

a. Record these events in general journal form.

b. Post the entries to T-accounts and determine the ending balance in each account.

c. Determine the amount of total assets at the end of 2009.

d. Determine the amount of net income for 2009.

Appendix 1-3   *Recording events in the general journal, posting to T-accounts, and preparing a trial balance*

The following events apply to Complete Business Service in 2010, its first year of operations.

1. Received $30,000 cash from the issue of common stock.

2. Earned $25,000 of service revenue on account.

3. Incurred $10,000 of operating expenses on account.

4. Received $20,000 cash for performing services.

5. Paid $8,000 cash to purchase land.

6. Collected $22,000 of cash from accounts receivable.

7. Received a $6,000 cash advance for services to be provided in the future.

8. Purchased $900 of supplies on account.

9. Made a $7,500 payment on accounts payable.

10. Paid a $5,000 cash dividend to the stockholders.

11. Recognized $500 of supplies expense.

12. Recognized $5,000 of revenue for services provided to the customer in Event 7.

Required

a. Record the events in the general journal.

b. Post the events to T-accounts and determine the ending account balances.

c. Test the equality of the debit and credit balances of the T-accounts by preparing a trial balance.

Appendix 1-4   *One complete accounting cycle*

The following events apply to Paradise Vacations' first year of operations.

1. Acquired $20,000 cash from the issue of common stock on January 1, 2009.
2. Purchased $800 of supplies on account.
3. Paid $4,200 cash in advance for a one-year lease on office space.
4. Earned $28,000 of revenue on account.
5. Incurred $12,500 of other operating expenses on account.
6. Collected $24,000 cash from accounts receivable.
7. Paid $9,000 cash on accounts payable.
8. Paid a $3,000 cash dividend to the stockholders.

Information for Adjusting Entries

9. There was $150 of supplies on hand at the end of the accounting period.
10. The lease on the office space covered a one-year period beginning November 1.
11. There was $3,600 of accrued salaries at the end of the period.

Required

a. Record these transactions in general journal form.

b. Post the transaction data from the journal to ledger T-accounts.

c. Prepare a trial balance.

d. Prepare an income statement, statement of changes in stockholders' equity, a balance sheet, and a statement of cash flows.

absolute amounts   Dollar totals reported in accounts on financial reports that can be misleading because they make no reference to the relative size of the company being analyzed. *p. 321*

accelerated depreciation methods   Depreciation methods that recognize depreciation expense more rapidly in the early stages of an asset's life than in the later stages of its life. *p. 208*

account balance   Difference between total debits and total credits in an account. *p. 661*

accounting   Service-based profession that provides reliable and relevant financial information useful in making decisions. *p. 2*

accounting controls   Procedures designed to safeguard assets and to ensure accuracy and reliability of the accounting records and reports.

accounting equation   Expression of the relationship between the assets and the claims on those assets. *p. 12*

accounting event   Economic occurrence that causes changes in an enterprise's assets, liabilities, or equity. *p. 13*

accounting period   Span of time covered by the financial statements, normally one year, but may be a quarter, a month or some other time span. *p. 15*

account receivable   Expected future cash receipt arising from permitting a customer to *buy now and pay later;* typically a relatively small balance due within a short time period. *p. 46*

accounts   Records used for classifying and summarizing transaction data; subclassifications of financial statement elements. *p. 11*

accounts receivable turnover ratio   Financial ratio that measures how fast accounts receivable are turned into cash; computed by dividing sales by accounts receivable.

accrual   Recognition of events before exchanging cash. *p. 45*

accrual accounting   Accounting system that recognizes expenses or revenues when they occur regardless of when cash is exchanged. *p. 45*

accrued expenses   Expenses that are recognized before cash is paid. An example is accrued salaries expense. *p. 48*

accrued interest   Interest revenue or expense that is recognized before cash has been exchanged. *p. 167*

accumulated conversion factors   Factors used to convert a series of future cash inflows into their present value equivalent and that are applicable to cash inflows of equal amounts spread over equal interval time periods and that can be determined by computing the sum of the individual single factors used for each period. *p. 567*

accumulated depreciation   Contra asset account that indicates the sum of all depreciation expense recognized for an asset since the date of acquisition. *p. 206*

acid-test ratio   (quick ratio) Measure of immediate debt-paying ability; calculated by dividing very liquid assets (cash, receivables, and marketable securities) by current liabilities. *p. 326*

activities   The actions taken by an organization to accomplish its mission. *p. 377*

activity base   Factor that causes changes in variable cost; is usually some measure of volume when used to define cost behavior. *p. 406*

activity-based management (ABM)   Management of the activities of an organization to add the greatest value by developing products that satisfy the needs of that organization's customers. *p. 377*

adjusting entry   Entry that updates account balances prior to preparing financial statements. *p. 48*

administrative controls   Procedures designed to evaluate performance and the degree of compliance with a firm's policies and public laws.

adverse opinion   Opinion issued by a certified public accountant that means one or more departures from GAAP in a company's financial statements are so very material the auditors believe the financial statements do not fairly represent the company's status; contrast with *unqualified opinion. p. 141*

aging of accounts receivable   Classifying each account receivable by the number of days it has been outstanding. The aging schedule is used to develop an estimate of the amount of the allowance for doubtful accounts. *p. 165*

AICPA (American Institute of Certified Public Accountants)   National association that serves the educational and professional interests of members of the public accounting profession; membership is voluntary. *p. 137*

allocation   Process of dividing a total cost into parts and apportioning the parts among the relevant cost objects. *p. 434*

allocation base   Cost driver used as the basis for the allocation process. *p. 435*

allocation rate   Factor used to allocate or assign costs to a cost object; determined by taking the total cost to be allocated and dividing it by the appropriate cost driver. *p. 435*

allowance for doubtful accounts   Contra asset account that contains an amount equal to the accounts receivable that are expected to be uncollectible. *p. 158*

allowance method of accounting for uncollectible accounts   Method of accounting for bad debts in which bad debts are estimated and expensed in the same period in which the corresponding sales are recognized. The receivables are reported in the financial statements at net realizable value (the amount expected to be collected in cash). *p. 158*

amortization   Method of systematically allocating the costs of intangible assets to expense over their

useful lives; also term for converting the discount on a note or a bond to interest expense over a designated period. *pp. 202, 248*

amortizing   See *amortization.*

annual report   Document in which an organization provides information to stockholders, usually on an annual basis. *p. 25*

annuity   Series of equal payments made over a specified number of periods. *p. 567*

appropriated retained earnings   Retained earnings restricted by the board of directors for a specific purpose (e.g., to repay debt or for future expansion); although a part of total retained earnings, not available for distribution as dividends. *p. 301*

articles of incorporation   Items on an application filed with a state agency for the formation of a corporation; contains such information as the corporation's name, its purpose, its location, its expected life, provisions for its capital stock, and a list of the members of its board of directors. *p. 288*

articulation   Characteristic of financial statements that means they are interrelated. For example, the amount of net income reported on the income statement is added to beginning retained earnings as a component in calculating the ending retained earnings balance reported on the statement of changes in stockholders' equity. *p. 18*

asset exchange transaction   A transaction that decreases one asset while increasing another asset so that total assets do not change; for example, the purchase of land with cash. *pp. 14, 46*

assets   Economic resources used by a business to produce revenue. *p. 4*

asset source transaction   Transaction that increases an asset and a claim on assets; three types of asset source transactions are acquisitions from owners (equity), borrowings from creditors (liabilities), or earnings from operations (revenues). *p. 13*

asset turnover ratio   The amount of net income divided by average total assets. *p. 332*

asset use transaction   Transaction that decreases an asset and a claim on assets; the three types are distributions (transfers to owners), liability payments (to creditors), or expenses (used to operate the business). *pp. 25, 47*

audits   Detailed examination of some aspect of a company's accounting records or operating procedures in order to report the results to interested parties. *p. 139*

authority manual   A document that outlines the chain of command for authority and responsibility. The authority manual provides guidelines for specific positions such as personnel officer as well as general authority such as all vice presidents are authorized to spend up to a designated limit. *p. 127*

authorized stock   Number of shares that the corporation is approved by the state to issue. *p. 293*

average cost   The total cost of making products divided by the total number of products made. *p. 363*

average number of days to collect accounts receivable   Length of the average collection period for accounts receivable; computed by dividing 365 by the accounts receivable turnover ratio. *p. 328*

average number of days to sell inventory   Financial ratio that measures the average number of days that inventory stays in stock before being sold. *p. 328*

avoidable costs   Future costs that can be avoided by taking a specified course of action. To be avoidable in a decision-making context, costs must differ among the alternatives. For example, if the cost of material used to make two different products is the same for both products, that cost could not be avoided by choosing to produce one product over the other. Therefore, the material's cost would not be an avoidable cost. *p. 467*

balanced score card   A management evaluation tool that includes financial and nonfinancial measures. *p. 545*

balance sheet   Statement that lists the assets of a business and the corresponding claims (liabilities and equity) on those assets. *p. 9*

bank reconciliation   Schedule that identifies and explains differences between the cash balance reported by the bank and the cash balance in the firm's accounting records. *p. 131*

bank statement   Statement issued by a bank (usually monthly) that denotes all activity in the bank account for that period. *p. 131*

bank statement credit memo   Memorandum that describes an increase in the account balance. *p. 131*

bank statement debit memo   Memorandum that describes a decrease in the account balance. *p. 131*

basket purchase   Acquisition of several assets in a single transaction with no specific cost attributed to each asset. *p. 203*

batch-level costs   The costs associated with producing a batch of products. For example, the cost of setting up machinery to produce 1,000 products is a batch-level cost. The classification of batch-level costs is context sensitive. Postage for one product would be classified as a unit-level cost. In contrast, postage for a large number of products delivered in a single shipment would be classified as a batch-level cost. *p. 467*

benchmarking   Identifying the best practices used by world-class competitors. *p. 376*

best practices   Practices used by world-class companies. *p. 376*

board of directors   Group of individuals elected by the stockholders of a corporation to oversee its operations. *p. 290*

bond certificates   Debt securities used to obtain long-term financing in which a company borrows funds from a number of lenders, called *bondholders;* usually issued in denominations of $1,000. *p. 251*

bond discount   Difference between the selling price and the face amount of a bond sold for less than the face amount. *p. 256*

bond premium   Difference between the selling price and the face amount of a bond that is sold for more than the face amount. *p. 260*

bondholder   The party buying a bond (the lender or creditor). *p. 251*

book of original entry   A journal in which transactions are first recorded. *p. 662*

book value   Historical (original) cost of an asset minus the accumulated depreciation; alternatively, undepreciated amount to date. *p. 207*

book value per share   Value of stock determined by dividing the total stockholders' equity by the number of shares of stock. *pp. 293, 334*

break-even point   Point where total revenue equals total cost; can be expressed in units or sales dollars. *p. 407*

budgeting   Form of planning that formalizes a company's goals and objectives in financial terms. *p. 498*

capital budget   Budget that describes the company's plans regarding investments, new products, or lines of business for the coming year; is used as input to prepare many of the operating budgets and becomes a formal part of the master budget. *p. 502*

capital budgeting   Financial planning activities that cover the intermediate range of time such as whether to buy or lease equipment, whether to purchase a particular investment, or whether to increase operating expenses to stimulate sales. *p. 500*

capital expenditures   (on an existing asset) Substantial amounts of funds spent to improve an asset's quality or to extend its life. *p. 214*

capital investments   Expenditures for the purchase of operational assets that involve a long-term commitment of funds that can be critically important to the company's ultimate success; normally recovered through the use of the assets. *p. 564*

carrying value   Face amount of a bond liability less any unamortized bond discount or plus any unamortized bond premium. *p. 257*

cash   Coins, currency, checks, balances in checking and certain savings accounts, money orders, bank drafts, certificates of deposit, and other items that are payable on demand. *p. 129*

cash budget   A budget that focuses on cash receipts and payments that are expected to occur in the future. *p. 508*

cash discount   Discount offered on merchandise sold to encourage prompt payment; offered by sellers of merchandise and represent sales discounts to the seller when they are used and purchase discounts to the purchaser of the merchandise. *p. 94*

certified check   Check guaranteed by a bank to be drawn on an account having funds sufficient to pay the check. *p. 133*

certified suppliers   Suppliers who have gained the confidence of the buyer by providing quality goods and services at desirable prices and usually in accordance with strict delivery specifications; frequently provide the buyer with preferred customer status in exchange for guaranteed purchase quantities and prompt payment schedules. *p. 472*

chart of accounts   List of all ledger accounts and their corresponding account numbers. *p. 662*

checks   Prenumbered forms, sometimes multicopy, with the name of the business issuing them

preprinted on the face, indicating to whom they are paid, the amount of the payment, and the transaction date. *p. 131*

claims   Owners' and creditors' interests in a business's assets. *p. 4*

claims exchange transaction   Transaction that decreases one claim and increases another so that total claims do not change. For example, the accrual of interest expense is a claims exchange transaction; liabilities increase, and the recognition of the expense causes retained earnings to decrease. *p. 48*

classified balance sheet   Balance sheet that distinguishes between current and noncurrent items. *p. 262*

closely held corporation   Corporation whose stock is exchanged between a limited number of individuals. *p. 288*

closing   See *closing the books.*

closing the books   Process of transferring balances from temporary accounts (Revenue, Expense, and Dividends) to the permanent account (Retained Earnings). *p. 22*

Code of Professional Conduct   A set of guidelines established by the American Institute of Certified Public Accountants (AICPA) to promote high ethical conduct among its membership. *p. 137*

collateral   Assets pledged as security for a loan. *pp. 167, 261*

common costs   Costs that are incurred to support more than one cost object but cannot be traced to any specific object. *p. 434*

common size financial statements   Financial statements in which amounts are converted to percentages to allow a better comparison of period-to-period and company-to-company financial data since all information is placed on a common basis. *p. 103*

common stock   Basic class of corporate stock that carries no preferences as to claims on assets or dividends; certificates that evidence ownership in a company. *pp. 12, 294*

conservatism   A principle that guides accountants in uncertain circumstances to select the alternative that produces the lowest amount of net income. *p. 53*

consistency   The generally accepted accounting principle that a company should, in most circumstances, continually use the same accounting method(s) so that its financial statements are comparable across time. *p. 177*

contingent liability   A potential obligation, the amount of which depends on the outcome of future events. *p. 244*

continuity   Concept that describes the fact that a corporation's life may extend well beyond the time at which any particular shareholder decides to retire or to sell his or her stock. *p. 290*

continuous improvement   Total quality management (TQM) feature that refers to an ongoing process through which employees learn to eliminate waste, reduce response time, minimize defects, and simplify the design and delivery of products and services to customers. *p. 376*

contra asset account Account subtracted from another account with which it is associated; has the effect of reducing the asset account with which it is associated. pp. 160, 206

contribution margin Difference between a company's sales revenue and total variable cost; represents the amount available to cover fixed cost and thereafter to provide a profit. p. 402

contribution margin per unit The contribution margin per unit is equal to the sales price per unit minus the variable cost per unit. p. 408

controllability concept Evaluating managerial performance based only on revenue and costs under the manager's direct control. p. 532

controllable costs Costs that can be influenced by a particular manager's decisions and actions. p. 434

copyright Legal protection of writings, musical compositions, and other intellectual property for the exclusive use of the creator or persons assigned the right by the creator. p. 217

corporation Legal entity separate from its owners; formed when a group of individuals with a common purpose join together in an organization according to state laws. p. 288

cost Measure of resources used to acquire an asset or to produce revenue. p. 54

cost accumulation Process of determining the cost of a particular object by accumulating many individual costs into a single total cost. p. 432

cost allocation Process of dividing a total cost into parts and assigning the parts to relevant objects. pp. 368, 433

cost behavior How a cost reacts (goes up, down, or remains the same) relative to changes in some measure of activity (e.g., the behavior pattern of the cost of raw materials is to increase as the number of units of product made increases). p. 398

cost center Type of responsibility center which incurs costs but does not generate revenue. p. 532

cost driver Any factor, usually some measure of activity, that causes cost to be incurred, sometimes referred to as *activity base* or *allocation base.* Examples are labor hours, machine hours, or some other measure of activity whose change causes corresponding changes in the cost object. p. 432

cost method of accounting for treasury stock Method of accounting for treasury stock in which the purchase of treasury stock is recorded at its cost to the firm but does not consider the original issue price or par value. p. 298

cost objects Objects for which managers need to know the cost; can be products, processes, departments, services, activities, and so on. p. 432

cost of capital Return paid to investors and creditors for the use of their assets (capital); usually represents a company's minimum rate of return. p. 565

cost of goods available for sale Total costs paid to obtain goods and to make them ready for sale, including the cost of beginning inventory plus purchases and transportation-in costs, less purchase returns and allowances and purchase discounts. p. 89

cost of goods sold Total cost incurred for the goods sold during a specific accounting period. p. 89

cost-plus pricing Pricing strategy that sets the price at cost plus a markup equal to a percentage of the cost. p. 362

cost pool A collection of costs organized around a common cost driver. The cost pool as opposed to individual costs is allocated to cost objects using the common cost driver thereby promoting efficiency in the allocation process. p. 445

cost tracing Relating specific costs to the objects that cause their incurrence. p. 433

credit Entry that increases liability and equity accounts or decreases asset accounts. p. 661

creditors Individuals or institutions that have loaned goods or services to a business. p. 4

cumulative dividends Preferred dividends that accumulate from year to year until paid. p. 295

current (short-term) assets Assets that will be converted to cash or consumed within one year or an operating cycle, whichever is longer. p. 261

current (short-term) liability Obligation due within one year or an operating cycle, whichever is longer. p. 261

current ratio Measure of liquidity (short-term debt-paying ability); calculated by dividing current assets by current liabilities. p. 326

date of record Date that establishes who will receive the dividend payment: shareholders who actually own the stock on the record date will be paid the dividend even if the stock is sold before the dividend is paid. p. 299

debit Entry that increases asset accounts or decreases liability and equity accounts. p. 661

debt to assets ratio Financial ratio that measures a company's level of risk. p. 329

debt to equity ratio Financial ratio that compares creditor financing to owner financing, expressed as the dollar amount of liabilities for each dollar of stockholder's equity. p. 329

decentralization Practice of delegating authority and responsibility for the operation of business segments. p. 512

declaration date Date on which the board of directors actually declares a dividend. p. 299

deferral Recognition of revenue or expense in a period after the cash is exchanged. p. 45

depletion Method of systematically allocating the costs of natural resources to expense as the resources are removed from the land. p. 202

deposits in transit Deposits recorded in a depositor's books but not received and recorded by the bank. p. 132

deposit ticket Bank form that accompanies checks and cash deposited into a bank account; normally specifies the account number, name of the account, and a record of the checks and cash being deposited. p. 131

depreciable cost Original cost minus salvage value (of a long-term depreciable asset). p. 204

depreciation Decline in value of long-term tangible assets such as buildings, furniture, or equipment. It is systematically recognized by accountants as depreciation expense over the useful lives of the affected assets. p. 202

depreciation expense Portion of the original cost of a long-term tangible asset systematically allocated to an expense account in a given period. p. 204

differential revenues Future-oriented revenues that differ among the alternatives under consideration. p. 467

direct cost Cost that is easily traceable to a cost object and for which the sacrifice to trace is small in relation to the information benefits attained. p. 433

direct labor Wages paid to production workers whose efforts can be easily and conveniently traced to products. p. 366

direct raw materials Costs of raw materials used to make products that can be easily and conveniently traced to those products. p. 365

disclaimer of opinion Report on financial statements issued when the auditor is unable to obtain enough information to determine if the statements conform to GAAP; is neither positive nor negative. p. 141

discount on bonds payable Contra liability account used to record the amount of discount on a bond issue. p. 256

dividend Transfer of wealth from a business to its owners. p. 16

dividends in arrears Cumulative dividends on preferred stock that have not been paid; must be paid prior to paying dividends to common stockholders. p. 295

dividend yield Ratio for comparing stock dividends paid in relation to the market price; calculated as dividends per share divided by market price per share. p. 335

double-declining-balance depreciation Depreciation method that recognizes larger amounts of depreciation in the early stages of an asset's life and progressively smaller amounts as the asset ages. p. 208

double-entry accounting (bookkeeping) Method of keeping records that provides a system of checks and balances by recording transactions in a dual format. pp. 14, 661

double taxation Policy to tax corporate profits distributed to owners twice, once when the income is reported on the corporation's income tax return and again when the dividends are reported on the individual's return. p. 289

downstream costs Costs, such as delivery costs and sales commissions, incurred after the manufacturing process is complete. p. 371

earnings The difference between revenues and expenses. Same as net income or profit. p. 4

earnings per share Measure of the value of a share of common stock in terms of company earnings; calculated as net income available to common stockholders divided by the average number of outstanding common shares. p. 334

effective interest rate Yield rate of bonds, equal to the market rate of interest on the day the bonds are sold. p. 256

effective interest rate method   Method of amortizing bond discounts and premiums that bases interest computations on the carrying value of liability. As the liability increases or decreases, the amount of interest expense also increases or decreases. *p. 264*

elements   Primary components of financial statements including assets, liabilities, equity, contributions, revenue, expenses, distributions, and net income. *p. 10*

entity   See *reporting entities.*

entrenched management   Management that may have become ineffective but because of political implications may be difficult to remove. *p. 291*

equation method   Cost-volume-profit analysis technique that uses the algebraic relationship among sales, variable costs, fixed costs, and desired net income before taxes to solve for required sales volume. *p. 407*

equipment replacement decisions   Decisions regarding whether existing equipment should be replaced with newer equipment based on identification and comparison of the avoidable costs of the old and new equipment to determine which equipment is more profitable to operate. *p. 477*

equity   Portion of assets remaining after the creditors' claims have been satisfied (i.e., Assets Liabilities Equity); also called *residual interest* or *net assets. p. 12*

estimated useful life   Time for which an asset is expected to be used by a business. *p. 204*

ex-dividend   Stock traded after the date of record but before the payment date; does not receive the benefit of the upcoming dividend. *p. 300*

expenses   Economic sacrifices (decreases in assets or increase in liabilities) that are incurred in the process of generating revenue. *p. 15*

face value   Amount of the bond to be paid back (to the bondholders) at maturity. *p. 252*

facility-level costs   Costs incurred on behalf of the whole company or a segment of the company; not related to any specific product, batch, or unit of production or service and unavoidable unless the entire company or segment is eliminated. *p. 468*

favorable variance   Variance that occurs when actual costs are less than standard costs or when actual sales are higher than standard sales. *p. 535*

fidelity bond   Insurance policy that a company buys to insure itself against loss due to employee dishonesty. *p. 127*

financial accounting   Field of accounting designed to meet the information needs of external users of business information (creditors, investors, governmental agencies, financial analysts, etc.); its objective is to classify and record business events and transactions to facilitate the production of external financial reports (income statement, balance sheet, statement of cash flows, and statement of changes in equity). *p. 359*

Financial Accounting Standards Board (FASB)   Privately funded organization with the primary authority for the establishment of accounting standards in the United States. *p. 8*

financial audit   Detailed examination of a company's accounting records and the documents that support the information reported in the financial statements; includes testing the reliability of the underlying accounting system used to produce the financial reports. *p. 139*

financial statements   Primary means of communicating the financial information of an organization to the external users. The four general-purpose financial statements are the income statement, statement of changes in equity, balance sheet, and statement of cash flows. *p. 10*

financing activities   Cash inflows and outflows from transactions with investors and creditors (except interest). These cash flows include cash receipts from the issue of stock, borrowing activities, and cash disbursements associated with dividends. *p. 21*

finished goods inventory   Asset account used to accumulate the product costs (direct materials, direct labor, and overhead) associated with completed products that have not yet been sold. *p. 370*

first-in, first-out (FIFO) cost flow method   Inventory cost flow method that treats the first items purchased as the first items sold for the purpose of computing cost of goods sold. *p. 172*

fixed cost   Cost that in total remains constant when activity volume changes; varies per unit inversely with changes in the volume of activity. *p. 398*

fixed cost volume variance   The difference between the budgeted fixed cost and the applied fixed cost. *p. 537*

fixed interest rate   Interest rate (charge for the use of money) that does not change over the life of the loan. *p. 247*

flexible budgets   Budgets that show expected revenues and costs at a variety of different activity levels. *p. 533*

flexible budget variances   Differences between budgets based on standard amounts at the actual level of activity and actual results; caused by differences in standard and actual unit cost since the volume of activity is the same. *p. 538*

FOB (free on board) destination   Term that designates the seller as the responsible party for freight costs (transportation-in costs). *p. 95*

FOB (free on board) shipping point   Term that designates the buyer as the responsible party for freight costs (transportation-in costs). *p. 95*

franchise   Exclusive right to sell products or perform services in certain geographic areas. *p. 217*

full disclosure   The accounting principle that financial statements should include all information relevant to an entity's operations and financial condition. Full disclosure frequently requires adding footnotes to the financial statements. *p. 177*

gains   Increases in assets or decreases in liabilities that result from peripheral or incidental transactions. *p. 98*

general authority   Policies and procedures that apply across different levels of a company's management, such as everyone flies coach class. *p. 127*

general journal   Journal in which all types of accounting transactions can be entered but which is commonly used to record adjusting and closing entries and unusual types of transactions. *p. 661*

general ledger   Complete set of accounts used in accounting systems. *pp. 17, 662*

generally accepted accounting principles (GAAP)   Rules and regulations that accountants agree to follow when preparing financial reports for public distribution. *p. 8*

general, selling, and administrative costs   All costs not associated with obtaining or manufacturing a product; in practice are sometimes referred to as *period costs* because they are normally expensed in the period in which the economic sacrifice is incurred. *p. 367*

general uncertainties   Uncertainties inherent in operating a business, such as competition and damage from storms. Unlike contingent liabilities, these uncertainties arise from future rather than past events. *p. 244*

going concern assumption   Assumption that a company will continue to operate indefinitely, will pay its obligations and should therefore report those obligations at their full face value in the financial statements. *p. 240*

goodwill   Added value of a successful business that is attributable to factors—reputation, location, and superior products—that enable the business to earn above-average profits; stated differently, the excess paid for an existing business over the appraised value of the net assets. *p. 218*

gross margin (gross profit)   Difference between sales revenue and cost of goods sold; the amount a company makes from selling goods before subtracting operating expenses. *p. 89*

gross margin percentage   Expression of gross margin as a percentage of sales computed by dividing gross margin by net sales; the amount of each dollar of sales that is profit before deducting any operating expenses. *p. 107*

gross profit   See *gross margin.*

historical cost concept   Actual price paid for an asset when it was purchased. *pp. 16, 203*

horizontal analysis   Analysis technique that compares amounts of the same item over several time periods. *p. 321*

horizontal statements model   Arrangement of a set of financial statements horizontally across a sheet of paper. *p. 23*

income   Added value created in transforming resources into more desirable states. *p. 4*

income statement   Statement that measures the difference between the asset increases and the asset decreases associated with running a business. This definition is expanded in subsequent chapters as additional relationships among the elements of the financial statements are introduced. *p. 18*

incremental revenue   Additional cash inflows from operations generated by using an additional capital asset. *p. 571*

independent auditor   Licensed certified public accountant engaged to audit a company's financial statements; not an employee of the audited company. *p. 140*

indirect cost   Cost that cannot be easily traced to a cost object and for which the economic sacrifice to trace is not worth the informational benefits. *pp. 368, 433*

information overload Situation in which presentation of too much information confuses the user of the information. *p. 320*

installment notes Obligations that require regular payments of principal and interest over the life of the loan. *p. 248*

intangible assets Assets that may be represented by pieces of paper or contracts that appear tangible; however, the true value of an intangible asset lies in the rights and privileges extended to its owners. *p. 202*

interest Fee paid for the use of borrowed funds; also refers to revenue from debt securities. *pp. 5, 167*

internal controls A company's policies and procedures designed to reduce the opportunity for fraud and to provide reasonable assurance that its objectives will be accomplished. *p. 126*

internal rate of return Rate that will produce a present value of an investment's future cash inflows that equals cash outflows required to acquire the investment; alternatively, the rate that produces in a net present value of zero. *p. 571*

inventory cost flow methods Methods used to allocate the cost of goods available for sale between cost of goods sold and inventory. *p. 174*

inventory holding costs Costs associated with acquiring and retaining inventory including cost of storage space; lost, stolen, or damaged merchandise; insurance; personnel and management costs; and interest. *p. 372*

inventory turnover Ratio of cost of goods sold to inventory that indicates how many times a year the average inventory is sold (turned over). *p. 328*

investing activities One of the three categories of cash inflows and outflows shown on the statement of cash flows; includes cash received and spent by the business on productive assets and investments in the debt and equity of other companies. *p. 21*

investment center Type of responsibility center for which revenue, expense and capital investments can be measured. *p. 532*

investors Company or individual who gives assets or services in exchange for security certificates representing ownership interests. *p. 4*

issued stock Stock sold to the public. *p. 293*

issuer Individual or business that issues a note payable, bonds payable, or stock (the party receiving cash). See also *maker*. *pp. 242, 251*

journals Books of original entry in which accounting data are entered chronologically before posting to the ledger accounts. *p. 662*

just in time (JIT) Inventory flow system that minimizes the amount of inventory on hand by making inventory available for customer consumption on demand, therefore eliminating the need to store inventory. The system reduces explicit holding costs including financing, warehouse storage, supervision, theft, damage, and obsolescence. It also eliminates hidden opportunity costs such as lost revenue due to the lack of availability of inventory. *p. 372*

last-in, first-out (LIFO) cost flow method Inventory cost flow method that treats the last items purchased as the first items sold for the purpose of computing cost of goods sold. *p. 172*

legal capital Amount of assets that should be maintained as protection for creditors; the number of shares multiplied by the par value. *p. 293*

liabilities Obligations of a business to relinquish assets, provide services, or accept other obligations. *pp. 10, 241, 261*

limited liability Concept that investors in a corporation may not be held personally liable for the actions of the corporation (the creditors cannot lay claim to the owners' personal assets as payment for the corporation's debts). *p. 290*

limited liability companies (LLC) Organizations offering many of the best features of corporations and partnerships and with many legal benefits of corporations (e.g., limited liability and centralized management) but permitted by the Internal Revenue Service to be taxed as a partnership, thereby avoiding double taxation of profits. *p. 289*

line of credit Preapproved credit arrangement with a lending institution in which a business can borrow money by simply writing a check up to the approved limit. *p. 251*

liquidation Process of dividing up the assets and returning them to the resource providers. Creditors normally receive first priority in business liquidations; in other words, assets are distributed to creditors first. After creditor claims have been satisfied, the remaining assets are distributed to the investors (owners) of the business. *p. 4*

liquidity Ability to convert assets to cash quickly and meet short-term obligations. *pp. 20, 169*

liquidity ratios Measures of short-term debt-paying ability. *p. 325*

long-term liabilities Liabilities with maturity dates beyond one year or the company's operating cycle, whichever is longer; noncurrent liabilities. *p. 247*

long-term operational assets Assets used by a business to generate revenue; condition of being used distinguishes them from assets that are sold (inventory) and assets that are held (investments). *p. 200*

losses Decreases in assets or increases in liabilities that result from peripheral or incidental transactions. *p. 98*

low-ball pricing Pricing a product below competitors' price to lure customers away and then raising the price once customers depend on the supplier for the product. *p. 472*

maker The party issuing a note (the borrower). *p. 167*

making the numbers Expression that indicates marketing managers attained the planned master budget sales volume. *p. 536*

management by exception The philosophy of focusing management attention and resources only on those operations where performance deviates significantly from expectations. *p. 540*

managerial accounting Branch of accounting that provides information useful to internal decision makers and managers in operating an organization. *p. 6*

manufacturing business Companies that make the goods they sell to customers. *p. 24*

manufacturing overhead Production costs that cannot be traced directly to products. *p. 368*

margin Component in the determination of the return on investment. Computed by dividing operating income by sales. *p. 542*

margin of safety Difference between break-even sales and budgeted sales expressed in units, dollars, or as a percentage; the amount by which actual sales can fall below budgeted sales before a loss is incurred. *p. 410*

market rate of interest Interest rate currently available on a wide range of alternative investments with similar levels of risk. *p. 260*

market value The price at which securities sell in the secondary market: also called fair value. *p. 293*

master budget Composition of the numerous separate but interdependent departmental budgets that cover a wide range of operating and financial factors such as sales, production, manufacturing expenses, and administrative expenses. *p. 502*

matching concept Process of matching expenses with the revenues they produce; three ways to match expenses with revenues include matching expenses directly to revenues, matching expenses to the period in which they are incurred, and matching expenses systematically with revenues. *pp. 53, 18, 168*

materiality Concept that recognizes practical limits in financial reporting by allowing flexible handling of matters not considered material; information is considered material if the decisions of a reasonable person would be influenced by its omission or misstatement; can be measured in absolute, percentage, quantitative, or qualitative terms. *p. 321*

maturity date The date a liability is due to be settled (the date the borrower is expected to repay a debt). *p. 167*

merchandise business Companies that buy and resell merchandise inventory. *p. 86*

merchandise inventory Supply of finished goods held for resale to customers. *p. 86*

minimum rate of return Minimum amount of profitability required to persuade a company to accept an investment opportunity; also known as *desired rate of return, required rate of return, hurdle rate, cutoff rate,* and *discount rate. p. 565*

mixed costs (semivariable costs) Costs composed of a mixture of fixed and variable components. *p. 405*

multistep income statement Income statement format that matches particular revenue items with related expense items and distinguishes between recurring operating activities and nonoperating items such as gains and losses. *p. 98*

natural resources Mineral deposits, oil and gas reserves, and reserves of timber, mines, and quarries are examples; sometimes called *wasting assets* because their value wastes away as the resources are removed. *p. 202*

net income Increase in net assets resulting from operating the business. *p. 18*

net loss   Decrease in net assets resulting from operating the business. *p. 18*

net margin   Profitability measurement that indicates the percentage of each sales dollar resulting in profit; calculated as net income divided by net sales. *p. 331*

net present value   Evaluation technique that uses a desired rate of return to discount future cash flows back to their present value equivalents and then subtracts the cost of the investment from the present value equivalents to determine the net present value. A zero or positive net present value (present value of cash inflows equals or exceeds the present value of cash outflows) implies that the investment opportunity provides an acceptable rate of return. *p. 569*

net realizable value   Face amount of receivables less an allowance for accounts whose collection is doubtful (amount actually expected to be collected). *p. 158*

net sales   Sales less returns from customers and allowances or cash discounts given to customers. *p. 103*

non-sufficient-funds (NSF) check   Customer's check deposited but returned by the bank on which it was drawn because the customer did not have enough funds in its account to pay the check. *p. 133*

nonvalue-added activities   Tasks undertaken that do not contribute to a product's ability to satisfy customer needs. *p. 377*

note payable   A liability that results from executing a legal document called a *promissory note* which describes the interest rate, maturity date, collateral, and so on. *p. 242*

notes receivable   Notes that evidence rights to receive cash in the future from the maker of a *promissory note;* usually specify the maturity date, interest rate, and other credit terms. *p. 156*

operating activities   Cash inflows and outflows associated with operating the business. These cash flows normally result from revenue and expense transactions including interest. *p. 21*

operating budgets   Budgets prepared by different departments within a company that will become a part of the company's master budget; typically include a sales budget, an inventory purchases budget, a selling and administrative budget, and a cash budget. *p. 502*

operating cycle   Time required to turn cash into inventory, inventory into receivables, and receivables back to cash. *p. 261*

operating income (or loss)   Income statement subtotal representing the difference between operating revenues and operating expenses, but before recognizing gains and losses from peripheral activities which are added to or subtracted from operating income to determine net income or loss. *p. 99*

operating leverage   Operating condition in which a percentage change in revenue produces a proportionately larger percentage change in net income; measured by dividing the contribution margin by net income. The higher the proportion of fixed cost to total costs, the greater the operating leverage. *p. 398*

operations budgeting   Short-range planning activities such as the development and implementation of the master budget. *p. 502*

opportunity   An element of the fraud triangle that recognizes weaknesses in internal controls that enable the occurrence of fraudulent or unethical behavior. *p. 138*

opportunity cost   Cost of lost opportunities such as the failure to make sales due to an insufficient supply of inventory or the wage a working student forgoes to attend class. *pp. 373, 464*

ordinary annuity   Annuity whose cash inflows occur at the end of each accounting period. *p. 568*

outsourcing   The practice of buying goods and services from another company rather than producing them internally. *p. 471*

outstanding checks   Checks deducted from the depositor's cash account balance but not yet presented to the bank for payment. *p. 133*

outstanding stock   Stock owned by outside parties; normally the amount of stock issued less the amount of treasury stock. *p. 293*

overhead   Costs associated with producing products that cannot be cost effectively traced to products including indirect costs such as indirect materials, indirect labor, utilities, rent, and depreciation. *p. 362*

overhead costs   Indirect costs of doing business that cannot be directly traced to a product, department, or process, such as depreciation. *p. 433*

paid-in capital in excess of par (or stated) value   Any amount received above the par or stated value of stock when stock is issued. *p. 296*

participative budgeting   Budget technique that allows subordinates to participate with upper-level managers in setting budget objectives, thereby encouraging cooperation and support in the attainment of the company's goals. *p. 502*

partnership agreement   Legal document that defines the responsibilities of each partner and describes the division of income and losses. *p. 288*

partnerships   Business entities owned by at least two people who share talents, capital, and the risks of the business. *p. 288*

par value   Arbitrary value assigned to stock by the board of directors. *p. 293*

patent   Legal right granted by the U.S. Patent Office ensuring a company or an individual the exclusive right to a product or process. *p. 217*

payback method   Technique that evaluates investment opportunities by determining the length of time necessary to recover the initial net investment through incremental revenue or cost savings; the shorter the period, the better the investment opportunity. *p. 578*

payee   The party collecting cash. *p. 167*

payment date   Date on which a dividend is actually paid. *p. 300*

percentage analysis   Analysis of relationships between two different items to draw conclusions or make decisions. *p. 322*

percent of receivables method   Estimating the amount of the allowance for doubtful accounts as a percentage of the outstanding receivables balance. The percentage is typically based on a combination of factors such as historical experience, economic conditions, and the company's credit policies. *p. 164*

percent of revenue method   Estimating the amount of uncollectible accounts expense as a percentage of the revenue earned on account during the accounting period. The percentage is typically based on a combination of factors such as historical experience, economic conditions, and the company's credit policies. *p. 163*

period costs   General, selling, and administrative costs that are expensed in the period in which the economic sacrifice is made. *pp. 53, 89*

periodic inventory system   Method of accounting for changes in the Inventory account only at the end of the accounting period. *p. 106*

permanent accounts   Accounts that contain information transferred from one accounting period to the next. *p. 22*

perpetual (continuous) budgeting   Continuous budgeting activity normally covering a 12-month time span by replacing the current month's budget at the end of each month with a new budget; keeps management constantly involved in the budget process so that changing conditions are incorporated on a timely bases. *p. 500*

perpetual inventory system   Method of accounting for inventories that increases the Inventory account each time merchandise is purchased and decreases it each time merchandise is sold. *p. 106*

physical flow of goods   Physical movement of goods through the business; normally a FIFO flow so that the first goods purchased are the first goods delivered to customers, thereby reducing the likelihood of obsolete inventory. *p. 172*

plant assets to long-term liabilities   Financial ratio that suggests how well a company manages its long-term debt. *p. 321*

postaudit   Repeat calculation using the techniques originally employed to analyze an investment project; accomplished with the use of actual data available at the completion of the investment project so that the actual results can be compared with expected results based on estimated data at the beginning of the project. Its purpose is to provide feedback as to whether the expected results were actually accomplished in improving the accuracy of future analysis. *p. 581*

posting   Process of copying information from journals to ledgers. *p. 662*

predetermined overhead rate   Allocation rate calculated before actual costs or activity are known; determined by dividing the estimated overhead costs for the coming period by some measure of estimated total production activity for the period, such as the number of labor-hours or machine-hours. The base should relate rationally to overhead use. The rate is used throughout the accounting period to allocate overhead costs to work in process inventory based on actual production activity. *p. 445*

preferred stock   Stock that receives some form of preferential treatment (usually as to dividends) over common stock; normally has no voting rights. *p. 294*

premium on bonds payable   Difference between the selling price and the face amount of a bond that is sold for more than the face amount. *p. 260*

prepaid items   Deferred expenses. An example is prepaid insurance. *p. 54*

present value index   Present value of cash inflows divided by the present value of cash outflows. Higher index numbers indicate higher rates of return. *p. 574*

present value table   Table that consists of a list of factors to use in converting future values into their present value equivalents; composed of columns that represent different return rates and rows that depict different periods of time. *p. 566*

pressure   An element of the fraud triangle that recognizes conditions that motivate fraudulent or unethical behavior. *p. 139*

price-earnings (P/E) ratio   Measurement used to compare the values of different stocks in terms of earnings; calculated as market price per share divided by earnings per share. *p. 334*

principal   Amount of cash actually borrowed. *p. 167*

procedures manual   Manual that sets forth the accounting procedures to be followed. *p. 127*

product costing   Classification and accumulation of individual inputs (materials, labor, and overhead) for determining the cost of making a good or providing a service. *p. 362*

product costs   All costs related to obtaining or manufacturing a product intended for sale to customers; are accumulated in inventory accounts and expensed as cost of goods sold at the point of sale. For a manufacturing company, product costs include direct materials, direct labor, and manufacturing overhead. *pp. 89, 362*

productive assets   Assets used to operate the business; frequently called *long-term assets. p. 21*

product-level costs   Costs incurred to support different kinds of products or services; can be avoided by the elimination of a product line or a type of service. *p. 468*

profitability ratios   Measurements of a firm's ability to generate earnings. *p. 355*

profit center   Type of responsibility center for which both revenues and costs can be indentified. *p. 532*

pro forma financial statements   Budgeted financial statements prepared from the information in the master budget. *p. 502*

promissory note   A legal document representing a credit agreement between a lender and a borrower. The note specifies technical details such as the maker, payee, interest rate, maturity date, payment terms, and any collateral. *p. 166*

property, plant, and equipment   Category of assets, sometimes called *plant assets,* used to produce products or to carry on the administrative and selling functions of a business; includes machinery and equipment, buildings, and land. *p. 202*

purchase discount   Reduction in the gross price of merchandise extended under the condition that the purchaser pay cash for the merchandise within a stated time (usually within 10 days of the date of the sale). *p. 94*

purchase returns and allowances   A reduction in the cost of purchases resulting from dissatisfaction with merchandise purchased. *p. 93*

qualified opinion   Opinion issued by a certified public accountant that means the company's financial statements are, for the most part, in compliance with GAAP, but there is some circumstance (explained in the auditor's report) about which the auditor has reservations; contrast with *unqualified opinion. p. 141*

qualitative characteristics   Nonquantifiable features such as company reputation, welfare of employees, and customer satisfaction that can be affected by certain decisions. *p. 466*

quantitative characteristics   Numbers in decision making subject to mathematical manipulation, such as the dollar amounts of revenues and expenses. *p. 466*

quick ratio   See *acid-test ratio. p. 326*

ratio analysis   See *percentage analysis. p. 324*

rationalization   An element of the fraud triangle that recognizes a human tendency to justify fraudulent or unethical behavior. *p. 139*

raw materials   Physical commodities (e.g., wood, metal, paint) used in the manufacturing process. *p. 365*

raw materials inventory   Asset account used to accumulate the costs of materials (such as lumber, metals, paints, chemicals) that will be used to make a company's products. *p. 370*

realization   A term that usually refers to actually collecting cash. *p. 44*

recognition   Reporting an accounting event in the financial statements. *p. 44*

recovery of investment   Recovery of the funds used to acquire the original investment. *p. 580*

reengineering   Business practices designed by companies to make production and delivery systems more competitive in world markets by eliminating or minimizing waste, errors, and costs. *p. 376*

reinstate   Recording an account receivable previously written off back into the accounting records, generally when cash is collected long after the original due date. *p. 162*

relative fair market value method   Method of assigning value to individual assets acquired in a basket purchase in which each asset is assigned a percentage of the total price paid for all assets. The percentage assigned equals the market value of a particular asset divided by the total of the market values of all assets acquired in the basket purchase. *p. 203*

relevant costs   Future-oriented costs that differ between business alternatives; also known as *avoidable costs. p. 465*

relevant information   Decision-making information about costs, costs savings, or revenues that have these features: (1) future-oriented information and (2) the information differs between the alternatives; decision-specific (information that is relevant in one decision may not be relevant in another decision). *p. 464*

relevant range   Range of activity over which the definitions of fixed and variable costs are valid. *p. 405*

reliability concept   Information is reliable if it can be independently verified. Reliable information is factual rather than subjective. *p. 17*

reporting entities   Particular businesses or other organizations for which financial statements are prepared. *p. 9*

residual income   Approach that evaluates managers on their ability to maximize the dollar value of earnings above some targeted level of earnings. *p. 543*

responsibility accounting   Performance measure that evaluates managers based on how well they maximize the dollar value of earning above some target level of earnings. *p. 530*

responsibility center   Point in an organization where the control over revenue or expense items is located. *p. 532*

restrictive covenants   Special provisions specified in the loan contract that are designed to prohibit management from taking certain actions that place creditors at risk. *p. 261*

retail companies   Companies that sell goods to consumers. *p. 86*

retained earnings   Portion of stockholders' equity that includes all earnings retained in the business since inception (revenues minus expenses and distributions for all accounting periods). *p. 12*

return on equity   Measure of the profitability of a firm based on earnings generated in relation to stockholders' equity; calculated as net income divided by stockholders' equity. *p. 333*

return on investment   Measure of profitability based on the asset base of the firm. It is calculated as net income divided by average total assets. ROI is a product of net margin and asset turnover. *pp. 332, 540*

return on sales   Percent of net income generated by each $1 of sales; computed by dividing net income by net sales. *p. 103*

revenue   The economic benefit (increase in assets or decrease in liabilities) gained by providing goods or services to customers. *p. 10*

revenue expenditures   Costs incurred for repair or maintenance of long-term operational assets; recorded as expenses and subtracted from revenue in the accounting period in which incurred. *p. 214*

salaries payable   Amounts of future cash payments owed to employees for services that have already been performed. *p. 46*

sales discount   Cash discount extended by the seller of goods to encourage prompt payment. When the buyer of the goods takes advantage of the discount to pay less than the original selling price, the difference between the selling price and the cash collected is the sales discount. *p. 101*

sales price variance   Difference between actual sales and expected sales based on the standard sales price per unit times the actual level of activity. *p. 538*

sales return and allowances   A reduction in sales revenue resulting from dissatisfaction with merchandise sold. *p. 103*

sales volume variance Difference between sales based on a static budget (standard sales price times standard level of activity) and sales based on a flexible budget (standard sales price times actual level of activity). *p. 535*

salvage value Expected selling price of an asset at the end of its useful life. *p. 204*

Sarbanes-Oxley Act of 2002 Federal law established to promote ethical behavior in corporate governance and fairness in financial reporting. Key provisions of the act include a requirement that a company's chief executive officer (CEO) and chief financial officer (CFO) must certify in writing that they have reviewed the financial reports being issued, and that the reports present fairly the company's financial status. An executive who falsely certifies the company's financial reports is subject to significant fines and imprisonment. The act also establishes the Public Company Accounting Oversight Board (PCAOB). This Board assumes the primary responsibility for developing and enforcing auditing standards for CPAs who audit SEC companies. The Sarbanes-Oxley Act also prohibits auditors from providing most types of nonaudit services to companies they audit.

schedule of cost of goods sold Schedule that reflects the computation of the amount of the cost of goods sold under the periodic inventory system; an internal report not shown in the formal financial statements. *p. 106*

Securities Act of 1933 and Securities Exchange Act of 1934 Acts passed after the stock market crash of 1929 designed to regulate the issuance of stock and govern the stock exchanges; created the Securities and Exchange Commission (SEC), which has the authority to establish accounting policies for companies registered on the stock exchanges. *p. 289*

Securities and Exchange Commission (SEC) Government agency responsible for overseeing the accounting rules to be followed by companies required to be registered with it. *p. 289*

segment Component part of an organization that is designated as a reporting entity. *p. 473*

selling and administrative costs Costs that cannot be directly traced to products that are recognized as expenses in the period in which they are incurred. Examples include advertising expense and rent expense. *p. 89*

separation of duties Internal control feature of, whenever possible, assigning the functions of authorization, recording, and custody to different individuals. *p. 126*

service business Organizations such as accounting and legal firms, dry cleaners, and insurance companies that provide services to consumers. *p. 24*

service charges Fees charged by a bank for services performed or a penalty for the depositor's failing to maintain a specified minimum cash balance throughout the period. *p. 133*

shrinkage A term that reflects decreases in inventory for reasons other than sales to customers. *p. 100*

signature card Bank form that records the bank account number and the signatures of the people authorized to write checks on an account. *p. 130*

single-payment (lump-sum) A one-time receipt of cash which can be converted to its present value using a conversion factor. *p. 566*

single-step income statement Single comparison between total revenues and total expenses. *p. 99*

sole proprietorships Businesses (usually small) owned by one person. *p. 288*

solvency Ability of a business to pay liabilities in the long run.

solvency ratios Measures of a firm's long-term debt-paying ability. *p. 329*

source documents Documents such as a cash register tape, invoice, time card, or check stub that provide accounting information to be recorded in the accounting journals and ledgers. *p. 661*

special journals Journals designed to improve the efficiency of recording specific types of repetitive transactions. *p. 662*

special order decisions Decisions of whether to accept orders from nonregular customers who want to buy goods or services significantly below the normal selling price. If the order's relevant revenues exceed its avoidable costs, the order should be accepted. Qualitative features such as the order's effect on the existing customer base if accepted must also be considered. *p. 468*

specific authorizations Policies and procedures that apply to designated levels of management, such as the policy that the right to approve overtime pay may apply only to the plant manager. *p. 127*

specific identification Inventory method that allocates costs between cost of goods sold and ending inventory using the cost of the specific goods sold or retained in the business. *p. 172*

spending variance The difference between the actual fixed overhead costs and the budgeted fixed overhead costs. *p. 537*

stakeholders Parties interested in the operations of a business, including owners, lenders, employees, suppliers, customers, and government agencies. *p. 6*

stated interest rate Rate of interest specified in the bond contract that will be paid at specified intervals over the life of the bond. *p. 252*

stated value Arbitrary value assigned to stock by the board of directors. *p. 293*

statement of cash flows Statement that explains how a business obtained and used cash during an accounting period. *p. 10*

statement of changes in stockholders' equity Statement that summarizes the transactions occurring during the accounting period that affected the owners' equity. *p. 23*

static budgets Budgets such as the master budget based solely on the level of planned activity; remain constant even when volume of activity changes. *p. 533*

stock certificate Evidence of ownership interest issued when an investor contributes assets to a corporation; describes the rights and privileges that accompany ownership. *p. 298*

stock dividend Proportionate distribution of additional shares of the declaring corporation's stock. *p. 300*

stockholders Owners of a corporation. *p. 12*

stockholders' equity Stockholders' equity represents the portion of the assets that is owned by the stockholders. *pp. 10, 12*

stock split Proportionate increase in the number of outstanding shares; designed to reduce the market value of the stock and its par value. *p. 301*

straight-line amortization Method of amortization in which equal amounts of the account being reduced (e.g., Bond Discount, Bond Premium, Patent) are transferred to the appropriate expense account over the relevant time period. *p. 257*

straight-line depreciation Method of computing depreciation that allocates the cost of an asset to expense in equal amounts over its life. The formula for calculating straight line depreciation is [(Cost − Salvage)/Useful Life]. *p. 205*

strategic planning Planning activities associated with long-range decisions such as defining the scope of the business, determining which products to develop, deciding whether to discontinue a business segment, and determining which market niche would be most profitable. *p. 500*

suboptimization Situation in which managers act in their own self-interests even though the organization as a whole suffers. *p. 643*

sunk costs Costs that have been incurred in past transactions and therefore are not relevant for decision making. *p. 464*

T-account Simplified account form, named for its shape, with the account title placed at the top of a horizontal bar, debit entries listed on the left side of the vertical bar, and credit entries shown on the right side. *p. 661*

tangible assets Assets that can be touched, such as equipment, machinery, natural resources, and land. *p. 202*

temporary accounts Accounts used to collect information for a single accounting period (usually revenue, expense, and distribution accounts). *p. 22*

times interest earned ratio Ratio that computes how many times a company would be able to pay its interest by using the amount of earnings available to make interest payments; amount of earnings is net income before interest and income taxes. *p. 329*

time value of money Recognition that the present value of a promise to receive a dollar some time in the future is worth less than a dollar because of interest, risk, and inflation factors. For example, a person may be willing to pay $0.90 today for the right to receive $1.00 one year from today. *p. 564*

total quality management (TQM) Management philosophy that includes: (1) a continuous systematic problem-solving philosophy that engages personnel at all levels of the organization to eliminate waste, defects, and nonvalue-added activities; and (2) the effort to manage quality costs in a manner that leads to the highest level of customer satisfaction. *p. 19*

trademark Name or symbol that identifies a company or an individual product. *p. 376*

transaction Particular event that involves the transfer of something of value between two entities. *pp. 12, 46*

transferability Concept referring to the practice of dividing the ownership of corporations into small units that are represented by shares of stock, which permits the easy exchange of ownership interests. *p. 290*

transportation-in (freight-in) Cost of freight on goods purchased under terms FOB shipping point that is usually added to the cost of inventory and is a product cost. *p. 95*

transportation-out (freight-out) Freight cost for goods delivered to customers under terms FOB destination; a period cost expensed when it is incurred. *p. 95*

treasury stock Stock first issued to the public and then bought back by the corporation. *p. 293*

trend analysis Study of the performance of a business over a period of time. *p. 321*

trial balance List of ledger accounts and their balances that provides a check on the mathematical accuracy of the recording process. *p. 664*

true cash balance Actual balance of cash owned by a company at the close of business on the date of the bank statement. *p. 131*

turnover Component in the determination of the return on investment. Computed by dividing sales by operating assets. *p. 542*

2/10, n/30 Expression meaning the seller will allow the purchaser a 2 percent discount off the gross invoice price if the purchaser pays cash for the merchandise within 10 days from the date of purchase. *p. 94*

unadjusted bank balance Ending cash balance reported by the bank as of the date of the bank statement. *p. 131*

unadjusted book balance Balance of the Cash account as of the date of the reconciliation before making any adjustments. *p. 131*

unadjusted rate of return Measure of profitability computed by dividing the average incremental increase in annual net income by the average cost of the original investment (original cost ÷ 2). *p. 579*

uncollectible accounts expense Expense associated with uncollectible accounts receivable; the amount recognized may be estimated using the percent of revenue or the percent of receivables method, or actual losses may be recorded using the direct write-off method. *p. 159*

unearned revenue Revenue for which cash has been collected but the service has not yet been performed. *p. 55*

unfavorable variance Variance that occurs when actual costs exceed standard costs or when actual sales are less than standard sales. *p. 535*

unit-level costs Costs incurred each time a company makes a single product or performs a single service and that can be avoided by eliminating a unit of product or service. Likewise, unit-level costs increase with each additional product produced or service provided. *p. 467*

units-of-production depreciation Depreciation method based on a measure of production rather than a measure of time; for example, an automobile may be depreciated based on the expected miles to be driven rather than on a specific number of years. *p. 211*

unqualified opinion Opinion issued by a certified public accountant that means the company's financial statements are, in all material respects, in compliance with GAAP; the auditor has no reservations. Contrast with qualified opinion. *p. 141*

upstream costs Costs incurred before the manufacturing process begins, for example, research and development costs. *p. 371*

value-added activity Any unit of work that contributes to a product's ability to satisfy customer needs. *p. 377*

value-added principle The benefits attained (value added) from the process should exceed the cost of the process. *p. 361*

value chain Linked sequence of activities that create value for the customer. *p. 377*

variable cost Cost that in total changes in direct proportion to changes in volume of activity; remains constant per unit when volume of activity changes. *p. 387*

variable cost volume variance The difference between a variable cost calculated at the planned volume of activity and the same variable cost calculated at the actual volume of activity. *p. 535*

variable interest rate Interest rate that fluctuates (may change) from period to period over the life of the loan. *p. 247*

variances Differences between standard and actual amounts. *p. 535*

vertical analysis Analysis technique that compares items on financial statements to significant totals. *p. 324*

vertical integration Attainment of control over the entire spectrum of business activity from production to sales; as an example a grocery store that owns farms. *p. 472*

vertical statements model Arrangement of a full set of financial statements on a single page with account titles arranged from the top to the bottom of the page. *p. 62*

warranties Promises to correct deficiencies or dissatisfactions in quality, quantity, or performance of products or services sold. *p. 245*

weighted-average cost flow method Inventory cost flow method in which the cost allocated between inventory and cost of goods sold is based on the average cost per unit, which is determined by dividing total costs of goods available for sale during the accounting period by total units available for sale during the period. If the average is recomputed each time a purchase is made, the result is called a *moving average. p. 172*

wholesale companies Companies that sell goods to other businesses. *p. 86*

withdrawals Distributions to the owners of proprietorships and partnerships. *p. 291*

work in process inventory Asset account used to accumulate the product costs (direct materials, direct labor, and overhead) associated with incomplete products that have been started but are not yet completed. *p. 370*

working capital Current assets minus current liabilities. *p. 571*

working capital ratio Another term for the current ratio; calculated by dividing current assets by current liabilities. *p. 326*

PHOTO CREDITS

Chapter 1

p. 3 © Tim Boyle/Getty Images, p. 4 © David Buffington/Getty Images/ DAL, p. 8 © Paul Burns/Getty Images, p. 9 © Chip Somodevilla/Getty Images, p. 12 © James Colburn/ZUMA Press/Newscom, p. 24 left © Digital Vision/Punchstock/DAL, p. 24 middle © The McGraw-Hill Companies, Inc., Andrew Resek, photographer/DAL, p. 24 right © Getty Images/DAL, p. 25 © USCG/DAL

Chapter 2

p. 45 © Stockbyte/Picture Quest/DAL, p. 53 © Getty Images/ Stockbyte/DAL

Chapter 3

p. 87 © Steve Cole/Getty Images/DAL, p. 101 © Digital Vision/Getty Images/DAL

Chapter 4

p. 125 © Mario Tama/Getty Images, p. 130 © Royalty-Free/Corbis/DAL

Chapter 5

p. 157 © Royalty-Free/Corbis/DAL, p. 178 top © Martial Colomb/Getty Images/DAL, p. 178 bottom © Stan Honda/Getty Images

Chapter 6

p. 201 © Royalty-Free/Corbis/DAL, p. 217 © Photodisc/Getty Images/ DAL, p. 218 © Royalty-Free/Corbis/DAL

Chapter 7

p. 241 © Bill Pugliano/Getty Images, p. 247 © Digital Vision/Super-Stock/DAL, p. 263 © Royalty-Free/Corbis/DAL

Chapter 8

p. 287 © Royalty-Free/Corbis, p. 294 © Brand X Pictures/DAL, p. 300 © Roslan Rahman/AFP/Getty Images

Chapter 9

p. 319 © AP Photo/Paul Sakuma

Chapter 10

p. 359 © Schwinn via Getty Images, p. 361 © Adam Rountree/Bloomberg via Getty Images, p. 375 © Alex L. Fradkin/Getty Images/DAL

Chapter 11

p. 397 © AP Photo/Phil Coale, p. 399 © Peter Morgan/Corbis, p. 400 © Bill Pugliano/Getty Images

Chapter 12

p. 431 © Stockbyte/Punch Stock/DAL, p. 435 © Courtesy of Southwest Airlines

Chapter 13

p. 463 © Scott Olsen/Getty Images, p. 466 © Blend Images/Getty Images/DAL, p. 473 © AP Photo/Markus Leodolter

Chapter 14

p. 499 © Kyodo via AP Images, p. 505 © F. Schussler/PhotoLink/Getty Images/DAL, p. 510 © PhotoLink/Getty Images/DAL

Chapter 15

p. 531 © Brand X Pictures/Punch Stock/DAL, p. 543 © Brand X Pictures/ DAL, p. 544 © AP Photo/Kevork Djansezian

Chapter 16

p. 563 © AP Photo/Mike Derer, p. 575 © Creatas/Punch Stock/DAL

Page numbers followed by "n" indicate footnotes and source notes.